Take Pride in Your Success... with Business, 11

Study Tools for Success

Available at **www.cengagebrain.com**, there are a wealth of resources available FREE to help you be successful in your Introduction to Business course. At the student companion Web site, you will find a variety of study tools including:

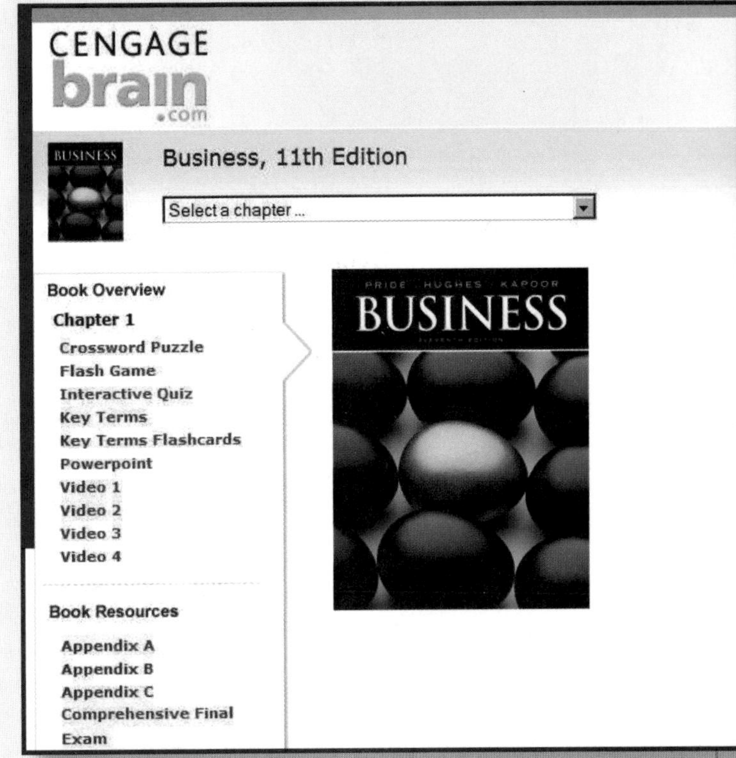

- Student PowerPoint® Slides
- Two Interactive Quizzes Per Chapter
- Key Terms
- Crossword Puzzles
- Chapter Videos
- And More!

Visit **WWW.CENGAGEBRAIN.COM** to access these free study tools today!

www.cengagebrain.com

BUSINESS

ELEVENTH EDITION

William M. Pride
Texas A&M University

Robert J. Hughes
Dallas County Community Colleges

Jack R. Kapoor
College of DuPage

Australia • Brazil • Japan • Korea • Mexico • Singapore • Spain • United Kingdom • United States

Business, 11e

William M. Pride, Robert J. Hughes, Jack R. Kapoor

Vice President of Editorial, Business: Jack W. Calhoun

Editor-in-Chief: Melissa Acuña

Senior Acquisitions Editor: Erin Joyner

Managing Developmental Editor: Joanne Dauksewicz

Editorial Assistant: Kayti Purkiss

Marketing Manager: Michelle Lockard

Senior Marketing Communications Manager: Sarah Greber

Marketing Coordinator: Leigh Smith

Senior Content Project Manager: Kim Kusnerak

Senior Media Editor: Kristen Meere

Frontlist Buyer, Manufacturing: Miranda Klapper

Production Service: S4 Carlisle Publishing Services

Senior Art Director: Stacy Jenkins Shirley

Cover/Internal Designer: Beckmeyer Design

Cover Image: © Getty Images/Nicholas Rigg

Rights Acquisitions Specialist/Text: Mardell Glinski Schultz

Text Permissions Researcher: Karyn Morrison

Rights Acquisitions Specialist/Images: Deanna Ettinger

Image Permissions Researcher: Terri Miller

Library of Congress Control Number: 2010939932

ISBN-13: 978-0-538-47808-3
ISBN-10: 0-538-47808-X
Loose Leaf Version ISBN 13: 978-1-111-52620-7
Loose Leaf Version ISBN 10: 1-111-52620-6

South-Western
5191 Natorp Boulevard
Mason, OH 45040
USA

Cengage Learning products are represented in Canada by Nelson Education, Ltd.

For your course and learning solutions, visit **www.cengage.com**
Purchase any of our products at your local college store or at our preferred online store **www.cengagebrain.com**

Printed in the United States of America
1 2 3 4 5 6 7 14 13 12 11 10

To Nancy, Allen, Michael, and Ashley

To my wife Peggy and to my mother Barbara Hughes

To my wife Theresa; my children Karen, Kathryn, and Dave; and in memory of my parents Ram and Sheela Kapoor

Brief Contents

Contents

About the Authors

> William M. Pride

Texas A&M University

William M. Pride is professor of marketing, Mays Business School at Texas A&M University. He received his PhD from Louisiana State University. He is the author of Cengage Learning's *Marketing,* 15th edition, and a market leader. Dr. Pride's research interests are in advertising, promotion, and distribution channels. Dr. Pride's research articles have appeared in major journals in the fields of advertising and marketing, such as *Journal of Marketing, Journal of Marketing Research, Journal of the Academy of Marketing Science,* and the *Journal of Advertising.* Dr. Pride is a member of the American Marketing Association, Academy of Marketing Science, Association of Collegiate Marketing Educators, Society for Marketing Advances, and the Marketing Management Association. Dr. Pride has taught principles of marketing and other marketing courses for more than 30 years at both the undergraduate and graduate levels.

> Robert J. Hughes

Richland College, Dallas County Community Colleges

Robert J. Hughes (PhD, University of North Texas) specializes in business administration and college instruction. He has taught Introduction to Business for more than 35 years both on campus and online for Richland College—one of seven campuses that are part of the Dallas County Community College District. In addition to *Business* and *Foundations of Business*, published by Cengage Learning, he has authored college textbooks in personal finance and business mathematics; served as a content consultant for two popular national television series, *It's Strictly Business* and *Dollars & Sense: Personal Finance for the 21st Century;* and is the lead author for a business math project utilizing computer-assisted instruction funded by the ALEKS Corporation. He is also active in many academic and professional organizations and has served as a consultant and investment advisor to individuals, businesses, and charitable organizations. Dr. Hughes is the recipient of three different Teaching in Excellence Awards at Richland College. According to Dr. Hughes, after 35 years of teaching Introduction to Business, the course is still exciting: "There's nothing quite like the thrill of seeing students succeed, especially in a course like Introduction to Business, which provides the foundation for not only academic courses, but also life in the real world."

> Jack R. Kapoor

College of DuPage

Jack R. Kapoor (EdD, Northern Illinois University) is professor of business and economics in the Business and Technology Division at the College of DuPage, where he has taught Introduction to Business, Marketing, Management, Economics, and Personal Finance since 1969. He previously taught at Illinois Institute of Technology's Stuart School of Management, San Francisco State University's School of World Business, and other colleges. Professor Kapoor was awarded the Business and Services Division's Outstanding Professor Award for 1999–2000. He served as an Assistant National Bank Examiner for the U.S. Treasury Department and as an international trade consultant to Bolting Manufacturing Co., Ltd., Mumbai, India.

Dr. Kapoor is known internationally as a coauthor of several textbooks, including *Foundations of Business*, 2nd edition (Cengage Learning), has served as a content consultant for the popular national television series *The Business File: An Introduction to Business,* and developed two full-length audio courses in business and personal finance. He has been quoted in many national newspapers and magazines, including *USA Today, U.S. News & World Report,* the *Chicago Sun-Times, Crain's Small Business*, the *Chicago Tribune*, and other publications.

Dr. Kapoor has traveled around the world and has studied business practices in capitalist, socialist, and communist countries.

Dear Business Students

Welcome to the new, eleventh edition of Business! This is where you can find out what it takes to be successful in today's competitive business world. Based on our many years of teaching and working with students, we know how hard it can be to start your career, get the promotion you really want, start your own business, or become the person you want to be. That's why we chose "SUCCESS" as the theme for this new edition. Just seven letters, but this one word says a lot about the new content and features in this book.

Beginning in Chapter 1, we discuss what it takes to be successful in the workplace. The theme of success is reinforced when we discuss the functional areas of business—management, marketing, information, accounting, and finance in the rest of the text. In addition, important topics like ethics and social responsibility, forms of business ownership, and small business receive special attention and are highlighted throughout the eleventh edition. As authors, we worked hard to make sure there's something in every chapter to help you understand the world of business and to become a better employee, a more informed consumer, and—if it's your dream—a successful small business owner.

This edition is packed with cutting-edge content that helps you make sense of the current economy and its impact on many areas of business as well as your world. Concise, completely new, eye-catching boxed features also reinforce the success theme, including Career Success, Ethical Challenges and Successful Solutions, Entrepreneurial Success, and Going for Success. A special Sustaining the Planet insert as well as a Spotlight feature presenting information in an illustrated, easy-to-understand format make the text even more relevant to real-world business.

It's important to begin reading this text with one thing in mind: This business course doesn't have to be difficult. In fact, learning about business and how you can become successful and be involved as an employee, business owner, consumer, or investor can be fun. As authors, we have done everything possible to eliminate the problems that students encounter in a typical class. All the content and features in the text along with powerful online learning tools on the student companion Web site (www.cengagebrain.com) are designed not only to improve your grade in this course, but to also make you successful in the workplace and as a consumer.

We invite you to examine the visual guide that follows to see how this new edition of Pride/Hughes/Kapoor can help you learn about business. We want you to be successful—in this course, in your career, and in your life!

Sincerely,

WMP, RJH, JRK

SUCCESS

Take Pride in Your Success

Let the story of our success become ***yours*** with the latest improvements in this best-selling introductory business text. Pride's ***Business, 11e*** equips you for career and business success with cutting-edge coverage of the functional areas of business–management, marketing, accounting, finance, and information technology. You'll also learn how today's economic crisis and the current political climate impact green and socially responsible business and global sustainability.

Ethical Challenges & SUCCESSful Solutions

Ethical Challenges &
SUCCESSFUL SOLUTIONS

Through Social Media, Do Workers Create Problems for Their Employers?

How should managers handle employee's use of social media such as Twitter, blogs, and Facebook? Despite the growing popularity of tweeting, blogging, and connecting with others on Facebook, LinkedIn, and other sites, some companies are concerned that employees will inadvertently disclose proprietary information or become involved in controversial conversations that could harm the company's image. Another reason for discouraging social media use is to keep employees focused on business activities during the workday.

Employers in a few industries—such as financial services—are required to monitor business-related messages that employees post on social-media sites to ensure that communications comply with government regulations. In most

facebook

Facebook helps you connect and share with the people in your life.

© E.D. Torial / Alamy

companies are free to set their own policies regarding the u social media.

A growing number of firms are encouraging employees to act with each other and with customers and suppliers using s media, as long as they follow specific guidelines. For example, policy requires employees to use respectful language, obey copy laws, and indicate that their views are personal rather than co rate. Kodak's employees must disclose their affiliation when dis ing anything related to the comp business and are not allowed to r any confidential information. The s media policy of online retailer Zapp short and to the point: "Be real an your best judgment."

Sources: Tamara Schweitzer, "Do You Need a Soci Media Policy?" *Inc.*, January 25, 2010, http://www com/articles/2010/01/need-a-social-media-polic David Scheer, "Brokers' Facebook, Twitter Posts M Tracked by Employers," *BusinessWeek*, January 25 http://www.businessweek.com

Building Skills for Career Success

1 JOURNALING FOR SUCCESS
Much of the information in this chapter was designed to get you to think about what it takes to be a successful employee in the competitive business world.

Assignment
Assume that you are now 25 years old and are interviewing for a position as a management trainee in a large corporation. Also assume that this position pays $45,000 a year.

1. Describe what steps you would take to prepare for this interview.
2. Assuming that you get the management trainee position, describe the personal traits or skills that you have that will help you to become successful.
3. Describe the one pe feel needs improve improving your wea

2 EXPLORING THE
The Internet is a global n accessed by anyone in th firm is most likely conne access through a comme Yahoo!, or a host of othe

To familiarize yourself able through the Interne

Building Skills for Career SUCCESS

Career SUCCESS

Clicking Your Career into High Gear

In today's competitive business world, you should be networking online if you want to click your career into high gear. You can use Facebook, Twitter, LinkedIn, and other networking Web sites to locate job openings, help prospective employers to find you, and make a good impression on current and future bosses.

For example, David Gallant posted his résumé on job-search Web sites and followed up on leads from tech industry sources even before he graduated from the University of New Hampshire. He also set up his own blog to showcase his skills and hobbies and started conversing with other tech enthusiasts via Twitter posts. When he noticed a tweet about a job opening in his field, he applied immediately. Before interviewing Gallant, company managers checked his blog page and Twitter posts—and they liked what they saw. Gallant's successfully: He was hired within two weeks of gra

How can you make the most of online network and join sites where you can connect with potential classmates, and others who may have, or may hea Second, be sure your online profiles, photographs, ar cate your abilities and interests without being offensi ing. Finally, be ready to click quickly when you spot a

© Stuwdamdorp / Alamy

Sources: James Limbach, "Soci Explodes as Job-Search Tool," November 23, 2009, http://ww .com/news04/2009/11/social_ .html; Sarah E. Needleman, "A Away," *Wall Street Journal*, Sept online.wsj.com/article/SB1000 4404574393102737256542.htr "Using Twitter and Facebook t June 8, 2009, http://www.time article/0,8599,1903083,00.htm "Twitter: The New Way to Find *Herald*, March 27, 2009, http:// articles/2009/03/27/12376571 Finds a Job Using Twitter," *Univ Information Technology Pipelin* http://pipeline.unh.edu/tag/tw

Career SUCCESS

Whether it's the latest business developments or traditional strengths, **everywhere you look in Pride's *Business, 11e,* you'll find success,** with features such as:

- Building Skills for Career Success
- Entrepreneurial Success
- Career Success
- Ethical Challenges and Successful Solutions
- *Going for Success*

Take Pride in Your Success

... with Relevant Examples from Apple & Amazon

Inside Business vignettes open each chapter with examples from REAL, LEADING organizations like Amazon, Apple, and Panera.

inside business

How Amazon Kindles Business Success

At the dawn of the Internet age, entrepreneur Jeff Bezos founded a Web-based bookstore he named Amazon.com to suggest the immense selection of titles on his virtual shelves. His plan was to create a customer-centered company using cutting-edge technology to keep prices low and provide good service. In the course of building his business, Bezos pioneered many features that have become staples of online retailing, including personalized product recommendations, customer reviews, and free shipping with a minimum order.

Today, the once-tiny enterprise with the quirky name has become a giant corporation that rings up more than $24 billion in annual sales worldwide. Amazon owns Zappos, the online shoe retailer known for outstanding service, and now sells everything from televisions, toys, and tools to computers, cameras, and clothing. It has also used its retailing expertise to become a virtual storefront for thousands of companies and individuals who sign up to sell goods and services on the Amazon Web site. In addition, it has used its tech expertise to offer on-demand services such as data storage and extra computing power to businesses of all sizes.

As CEO, Bezos continues to move Amazon in new directions. A few years ago, the company introduced the Kindle, an electronic handheld device that allows users to instantly download and read books and magazines when and where they please. The Kindle was innovative because it was the first e-book reader to connect wirelessly for content download without additional subscription or network fees. The initial response was so strong that Amazon struggled to meet the unexpectedly high demand.

Over time, Amazon has refined the Kindle by streamli the product more eco-friendly, cutting the price, and exp for instant download. Despite competition from bookst ics giant Sony, which have both launched wireless e-bo

Did You Know?

Amazon—the once-tiny enterprise with the quirky name—has become a giant corporation that rings up more than $24 billion in annual sales worldwide.

return to inside business

Amazon

When Amazon opened its virtual doors in 1995, founder Jeff Bezos had ambitious plans for building the world's biggest, best, and most customer-friendly online bookstore. The Web was still new and uncharted territory for businesses, and Amazon was breaking new ground by inviting customers to post their own book reviews and allowing them to buy with one click.

Within two years of its founding, Amazon had served millions of customers and raised millions of dollars for expansion by going public and selling corporate stock. Yet the company did not achieve profitability for several more years because Bezos was continually reinvesting in upgraded technology to enhance the customer experience and build the business. Moving into innov ucts such as the Kindle helped Amaz new chapter in its success story. Can th maintain its sales and profit momen coming years?

Questions

1. Of the environments that affect th world, which have had the most effect on Amazon?
2. During a recent year, Amazon' topped $900 million. Why do you online retailer is profitable? What a management take to continue to profits?

The text is **RELEVANT** and **EXCITING** as it focuses on Amazon's Kindle marketing and Apple's iPhone and iPad promotions.

Take Pride in Your Success... with Business, 11e

Keep up to date on the latest news **with BUSINESS EXAMPLES** from BP's oil spill and Toyota's quality crisis.

Up-to-the-minute coverage addresses:

- Most recent economic crisis and political developments
- Impact of high unemployment
- Continuing growth of the service sector
- Merger activity and productivity concerns
- Latest technology, including the explosive growth of computer apps for cell phones and iPods, social networking, and computer backup issues

ctor grew in the number of employees and economic importance, its productivy levels did not grow as fast. Today, many economic experts agree that improvg service-sector productivity can lead to higher overall productivity growth for e nation.

Finally, increased government regulation is frequently cited as a factor affectg productivity. Federal agencies such as the Occupational Safety and Health dministration, the Environmental Protection Agency, and the Food and Drug dministration are increasingly regulating business practices. Often, the time nployees spend complying with government reporting requirements can reduce oductivity growth rates. Even though executives, managers, and business owners ten cite increased regulation from all levels of government as a reason for low oductivity, the general public believes there is need for effective government gulations that improve working conditions, product safety, and the environent. For example, the recent British Petroleum oil spill in the Gulf of Mexico d the effect on nearby beaches and wetlands may have been prevented or at ast reduced if there had been more government regulation of offshore drilling. lthough there are two sides to the regulatory argument, what may be needed a new look at existing and proposed regulations that ensures regulations are eded and compliance is no more time consuming and expensive than absolutely cessary.

Describe how research and development lead to new products and services.

Where Do New Products and Services Come From?

No firm can produce a product or service until it has an idea. In other words, someone first must come up with a new way to satisfy a need—a new product or an improvement in an existing product. Both Apple's iPad and Amazon's Kindle began as an idea. Although no one can predict with 100 percent accuracy what types of products will be available in the next five years, it is safe to say that companies will continue to introduce new products that will change our everyday lives.

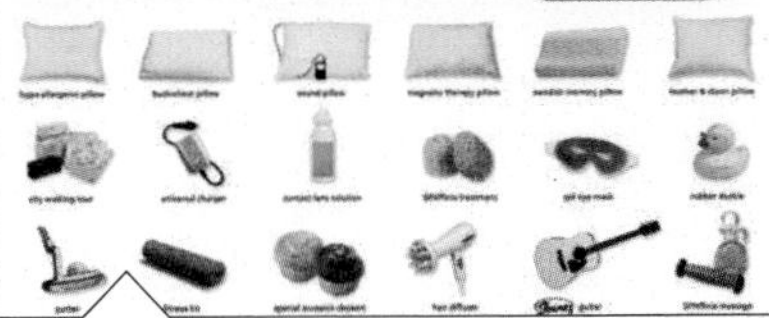

Home away from home. To make their guests feel at home, Affinia Hotels has developed a revolutionary new customer service program that allows guests to customize every aspect of their stay. Using the new online service, guests can pre-select "just the right features" that help make their stay perfect and at the same time build repeat business for this upscale hotel chain.

Research and Development

How did we get the iPad and the Kindle? We got them as a result of people working with new ideas that developed into useful products. In the same way, scientists and researchers working in businesses, colleges, and universities have produced many of the newer products we already take for granted.

These activities generally are referred to as *research and development*. For our purposes, **research and development (R&D)** are a set of activities intended to identify new ideas that have the potential to result in new goods and services.

Today, business firms use three general types of R&D activities. *Basic research* consists of activi...

Take Pride in Your Success

... with Videos and Cases Highlighting E*Trade and Frito-Lay

All-new Videos, new Video Cases and fresh Chapter Cases feature memorable organizations impacting business today, such as E*Trade, L.L. Bean, Whirlpool, and Chase Bank.

New dynamic videos for each chapter highlight **SUCCESSFUL BUSINESSES**, such as Nederlander Concerts, Burton Snowboards, Annie's Homegrown, BlueDot Furniture, Numi Organic Tea, and the Writer's Guild, illustrating memorable concepts from each chapter.

New ongoing Video Case featuring Cincinnati specialty ice cream retailer, Graeter's.

Get an insider's perspective as these engaging Video Cases at the end of each part look into **DAY-TO-DAY BUSINESS OPERATIONS.** You'll gain a better understanding of real challenges today's business owners face as they analyze problems and solutions and take action.

Take Pride in Your Success... with Business, 11e

SUCCESS

Sustaining the Planet

How the Sun and Earth Help Frito-Lay

Frito-Lay is one of many businesses moving toward sustainability by putting the sun and Earth to work. Every day, it produces 145,000 bags of SunChips in its solar-powered Modesto, California, plant and packages the chips in eco-friendly bags that can be composted into soil instead of taking up space in landfills. Take a look: http://sunchips.com/healthier_planet.shtml.

Learn about today's most **CURRENT BUSINESS CHALLENGES** with new examples and end-of-chapter cases in each chapter.

CHAPTER REVIEW

Questions

1. About 40 people will lose their jobs when Burton closes its Burlington factory, and the company is working with the state of Vermont to provide them with help in finding new employment. How do you think the factory closing might affect the productivity of the remaining headquarters staff? What impact could it have on product quality?
2. Do you think there will be an impact on quality when the design and development staff are separated from the factory floor by so many miles? Why or why not?
3. Can you reconcile the company's focus on product quality with its decision to concentrate manufacturing in a place where it's less expensive to operate? If so, how, and if not, why not?

Case 8.2 **Toyota's Quality Crisis**

Toyota Motor Corp., once the role model for world-class manufacturing, is facing a quality crisis. With $200 billion in annual sales and 320,000 employees worldwide, the Japan-based automaker has been driving hard for higher market share. However, after a string of recalls involving millions of vehicles, Toyota is now playing catch-up in the very area in which it has long prided itself—product quality. It also faces serious questions about its slow response to reports of defects.

Production efficiency has long been central to Toyota's culture and its financial strength. Its just-in-time inventory system, which minimizes holding costs, has been copied by manufacturers all over the world. Still, during the past decade alone, the company has boosted its bottom line by building new factories and wringing billions of dollars in savings from its production process. It has reduced the number of parts in its cars, redesigned ...

or regulators. That September, the U.S. National Highway Traffic Safety Administration put pressure on Toyota to recall cars because of "unintended acceleration" problems, some reportedly linked to fatal accidents. However, the company didn't announce its gas-pedal fix until November and didn't actually issue the recall until January 2010.

With U.S. regulators and the car-buying public expressing outrage at the slow speed of Toyota's response, Congress held hearings on the matter in March 2010. Toyota's president testified and offered a public apology. Toyota's top U.S. official, asked about the gas-pedal problem, told legislators: "We did not hide it. But it was not properly shared."

The crisis deepened in April, when U.S. regulators reviewing documents turned over by Toyota said they would slap the automaker with a multimillion ...

www.cengagebrain.com

Take Pride in Technology

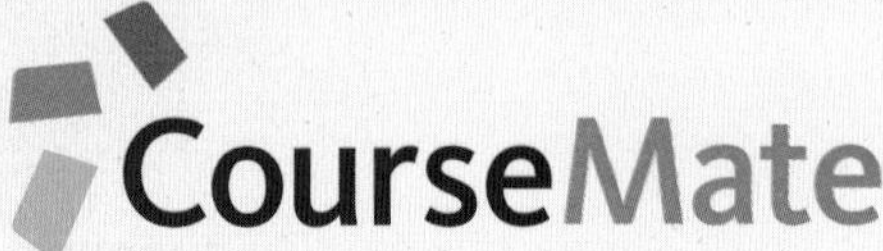

Reach a new level of interactive learning with Introduction to Business CourseMate. This unique online Web site makes course concepts come alive with interactive learning, study, and exam preparation tools supporting the printed text. CourseMate delivers what you need, including an interactive eBook, an interactive glossary, online quizzes and videos, NewsNow and more!

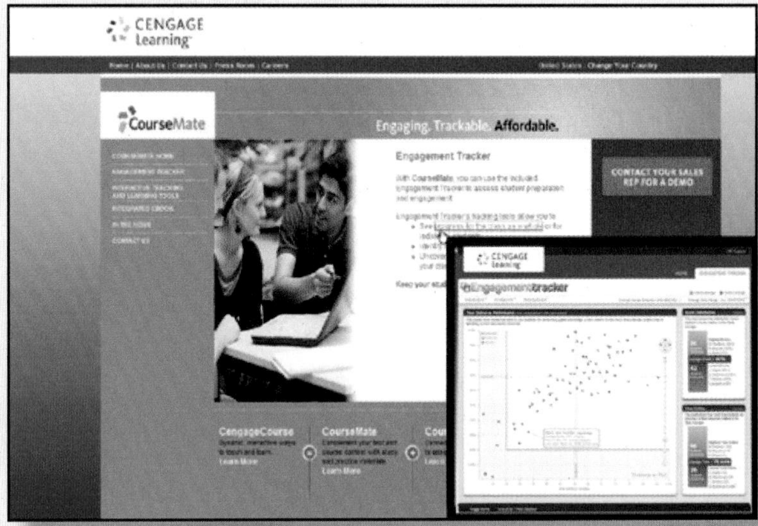

- **Interactive video exercises** allow you to relate the real-world events and issues shown in the chapter videos to specific in-text concepts.
- **Interactive decision-making scenarios** reinforce the text with memorable business scenarios and concise decision-making simulations that encourage you to see how business decisions lead to actionable business outcomes.

www.cengage.com/coursemate

CengageNOW™ Puts the Power of Learning in Your Hands

CengageNOW™ is an integrated, online learning system that delivers the success you need in your business course—NOW.

When you purchase CengageNOW with a new text, you also automatically receive access to the Business and Company Resource Center (BCRC) database.

- **A diagnostic Personalized Study Plan** identifies concepts most troublesome for you and creates an individualized study plan to focus your class preparation and study time.
- **Interactive Decision-Making Scenarios** reinforce the text with concise business scenarios that demonstrate real business decisions.
- **The integrated Business and Company Resource Center** keeps you abreast of the latest breaking business developments.

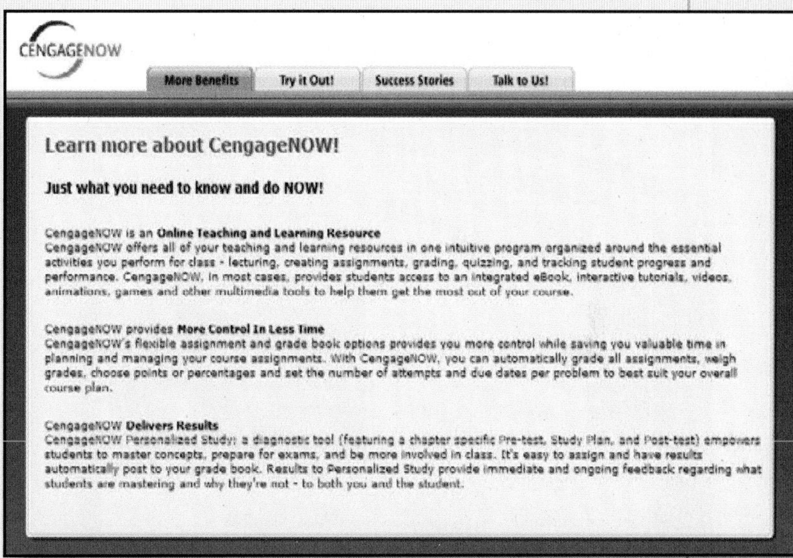

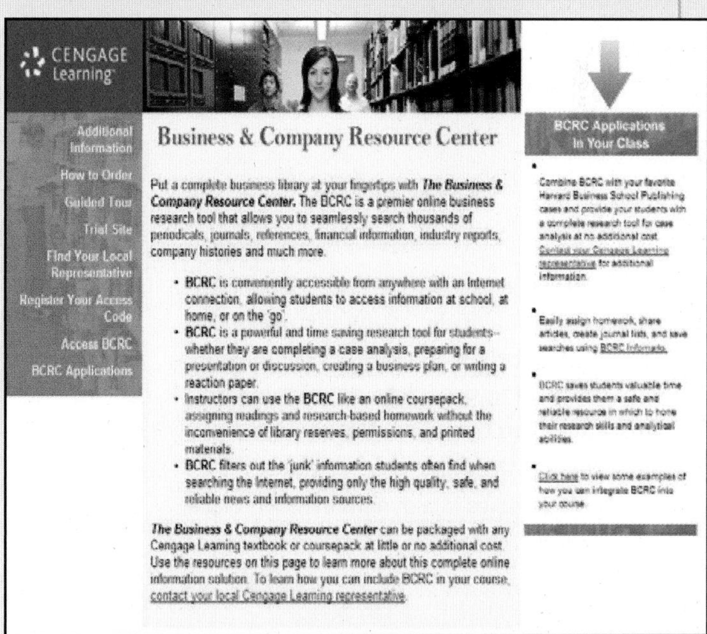

Take Pride in Technology

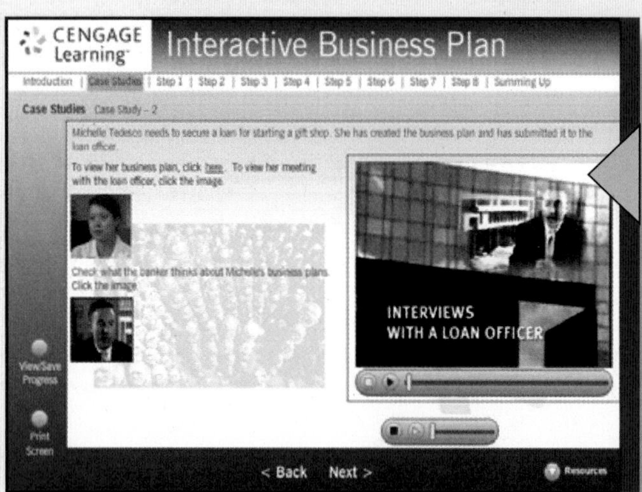

Build a Successful Business Plan

Interactive Business Plan

This powerful, interactive online tool walks you step-by-step through **building a successful business plan,** reinforcing skills that will benefit you throughout your career! Helpful informational modules detail each part of the business plan with templates and useful prompts that guide you in completing your own successful plan from the ground up.

Put Business Concepts into Practice

MikesBikes Simulation

Put key business concepts into practice as you run your own company and compete with other classmates in this engaging business simulation. This **hands-on approach to developing and implementing business strategies** lets you actually practice the cross-functional disciplines of business strategies in a dynamic marketplace while you analyze the changing needs of customers.

Acknowledgments

We thank Jack and Carmen Powers of Monroe Community College for their help with the Instructor Manual and Julie Boyles of Portland State University for her help with the Test Bank. We also thank Larry Flick, Three Rivers Community College, for developing our PowerPoints and e-Lectures and Kenneth Jones, Ivy Tech Community College—Central Indiana, for contributing classroom activities for our Instructor Manual. For their help developing our CNow quiz materials and homework problems, Course Mate decision scenarios and online quizzing, Business & Company Resource Center (BCRC) exercises, video guide and interactive video exercises, we thank LuAnn Bean, Florida Institute of Technology; Ashli Lane, Texas State University; Amit Shah, Frostburg State University; Christy Shell, Houston Community College; and Julie Boyles, Portland State University. We thank the R. Jan LeCroy Center for Educational Telecommunications of the Dallas County Community College District for the Telecourse partnership and for providing the related student and instructor materials. Finally, we thank the following people for their professional and technical assistance: Marian Wood, Elisa Adams, Barbara Paley, Ruth Beasley, Courtney Bohannon, Laurie Marshall, Tyler Sorensen, Saleha Amin, Brenda Lake, Clarissa Means, Theresa Kapoor, David Pierce, Kathryn Thumme, Margaret Hill, Nathan Heller, Karen Tucker, and Dave Kapoor.

For the generous gift of their time, and for their thoughtful and useful comments and suggestions, we are indebted to the following reviewers of the new eleventh edition or previous editions. Their suggestions have helped us improve and refine the text as well as the whole instructional package.

David V. Aiken
Hocking College
Phyllis C. Alderdice
Jefferson Community College
Marilyn Amaker
Orangeburg-Calhoun Technical College
Harold Amsbaugh
North Central Technical College
Carole Anderson
Clarion University
Lydia E. Anderson
Fresno City College
Maria Aria
Camden County College
James O. Armstrong, II
John Tyler Community College
Ed Atzenhoefer
Clark State Community College
Harold C. Babson
Columbus State Community College
Xenia P. Balabkins
Middlesex County College
Gloria Bemben
Finger Lakes Community College
Charles Bennett
Tyler Junior College
Patricia Bernson
County College of Morris
Robert W. Bitter
Southwest Missouri State University
Angela Blackwood
Belmont Abbey College
Wayne Blue
Allegany College of Maryland
Mary Jo Boehms
Jackson State Community College
Stewart Bonem
Cincinnati Technical College
James Boyle
Glendale Community College
Steve Bradley
Austin Community College
Lyle V. Brenna
Pikes Peak Community College
Tom Brinkman
Cincinnati Technical College
Robert Brinkmeyer
University of Cincinnati
Harvey S. Bronstein
Oakland Community College
Edward Brown
Franklin University
Joseph Brum
Fayetteville Technical Institute
Janice Bryan
Jacksonville College
Howard R. Budner
Manhattan Community College
Clara Buitenbos
Pan American University
C. Alan Burns
Lee College
Frank Busch
Louisiana Technical University
Paul Callahan
Cincinnati State University
Joseph E. Cantrell
De Anza College
Brahm Canzer
John Abbott College
Don Cappa
Chabot College
Robert Carrel
Vincennes University
Richard M. Chamberlain
Lorain County Community College

Bruce H. Charnov
Hofstra University
Lawrence Chase
Tompkins Cortland Community College
Felipe Chia
Harrisburg Area Community College
Michael Cicero
Highline Community College
William Clarey
Bradley University
Robert Coiro
LaGuardia Community College
Robert J. Cox
Salt Lake Community College
Susan Cremins
Westchester Community College
Bruce Cudney
Middlesex Community College
Andrew Curran
Antonelli Institute of Art and Photography
Gary Cutler
Dyersburg State Community College
Rex R. Cutshall
Vincennes University
John Daly
St. Edward's University
Brian Davis
Weber State University
Gregory Davis
Georgia Southwestern State University
Helen M. Davis
Jefferson Community College
Peter Dawson
Collin County Community College
Harris D. Dean
Lansing Community College
Wayne H. Decker
Memphis State University
Sharon Dexter
Southeast Community College
William M. Dickson
Green River Community College
M. Dougherty
Madison Area Technical College
Michael Drafke
College of DuPage
Richard Dugger
Kilgore College
Sam Dunbar
Delgado Community College
Robert Elk
Seminole Community College

Pat Ellebracht
Northeastern Missouri State University
Pat Ellsberg
Lower Columbia College
John H. Espey
Cecil Community College
Carleton S. Everett
Des Moines Area Community College
Frank M. Falcetta
Middlesex County College
Thomas Falcone
Indiana University of Pennsylvania
Janice Feldbauer
Austin Community College
Coe Fields
Tarrant County Junior College
Carol Fischer
University of Wisconsin—Waukesha
Larry A. Flick
Three Rivers Community College
Gregory F. Fox
Erie Community College
Michael Fritz
Portland Community College at Rock Creek
Fred Fry
Bradley University
Eduardo F. Garcia
Laredo Junior College
Arlen Gastineau
Valencia Community College
Richard Ghidella
Citrus College
Carmine Paul Gibaldi
St. John's University
Edwin Giermak
College of DuPage
Debbie Gilliard
Metropolitan State College
R. Gillingham
Vincennes University
Rick Giudicessi
Des Moines Area Community College
Robert Googins
Shasta College
Karen Gore
Ivy Technical State College
W. Michael Gough
De Anza College
Cheryl Davisson Gracie
Washtenaw Community College
Joseph Gray
Nassau Community College

Michael Griffin
University of Massachusetts—Dartmouth
Ricky W. Griffin
Texas A&M University
Stephen W. Griffin
Tarrant County Junior College
Roy Grundy
College of DuPage
John Gubbay
Moraine Valley Community College
Ronald Hadley
St. Petersburg Junior College
Carnella Hardin
Glendale Community College
Aristotle Haretos
Flagler College
Keith Harman
National-Louis University
Richard Hartley
Solano Community College
Richard Haskey
University of Wisconsin
Carolyn Hatton
Cincinnati State University
Linda Hefferin
Elgin Community College
Sanford Helman
Middlesex County College
Victor B. Heltzer
Middlesex County College
Ronald L. Hensell
Mendocino College
Leonard Herzstein
Skyline College
Donald Hiebert
Northern Oklahoma College
Nathan Himelstein
Essex County College
L. Duke Hobbs
Texas A&M University
Charles Hobson
Indiana University Northwest
Marie R. Hodge
Bowling Green State University
Gerald Hollier
University of Texas—Brownsville
Jay S. Hollowell
Commonwealth College
Townsend Hopper
Community College of Allegheny County—Allegheny
Joseph Hrebenak
Community College of Allegheny County—Allegheny
John Humphreys
Eastern New Mexico University

James L. Hyek
Los Angeles Valley College
James V. Isherwood
Community College of Rhode Island
Charleen S. Jaeb
Cuyahoga Community College
Sally Jefferson
Western Illinois University
Jenna Johannpeter
Belleville Area College
Gene E. A. Johnson
Clark College
Carol A. Jones
Cuyahoga Community College
Pat Jones
Eastern New Mexico University
Robert Kegel
Cypress College
Isaac W. J. Keim, III
Delta College
George Kelley
Erie Community College
Marshall Keyser
Moorpark College
Betty Ann Kirk
Tallahassee Community College
Edward Kirk
Vincennes University
Judith Kizzie
Clinton Community College
Karl Kleiner
Ocean County College
Clyde Kobberdahl
Cincinnati Technical College
Connie Koehler
McHenry County College
Robert Kreitner
Arizona State University
David Kroeker
Tabor College
Patrick Kroll
University of Minnesota, General College
Bruce Kusch
Brigham Young University
Kenneth Lacho
University of New Orleans
John Lathrop
New Mexico Junior College
R. Michael Lebda
DeVry Institute of Technology
Martin Lecker
SUNY Rockland Community College
George Leonard
St. Petersburg Junior College
Marvin Levine
Orange County Community College
Chad Lewis
Everett Community College
Jianwen Liao
Robert Morris College
Ronnie Liggett
University of Texas at Arlington
William M. Lindsay
Northern Kentucky University
Carl H. Lippold
Embry-Riddle Aeronautical University
Thomas Lloyd
Westmoreland County Community College
J. B. Locke
University of Mobile
Paul James Londrigan
Mott Community College
Kathleen Lorencz
Oakland Community College
Fritz Lotz
Southwestern College
Robert C. Lowery
Brookdale Community College
Anthony Lucas
Community College of Allegheny County—Allegheny
Monty Lynn
Abilene Christian University
Sheldon A. Mador
Los Angeles Trade and Technical College
Joan Mansfield
Central Missouri State University
Gayle J. Marco
Robert Morris College
John Martin
Mt. San Antonio Community College
Irving Mason
Herkimer County Community College
Douglas McCabe
Georgetown University
Barry McCarthy
Irvine Valley College
John F. McDonough
Menlo College
Catherine McElroy
Bucks County Community College
L. J. McGlamory
North Harris County College
Charles Meiser
Lake Superior State University
Ina Midkiff-Kennedy
Austin Community College—Northridge
Tony Mifsud
Rowan Cabarrus Community College
Edwin Miner
Phoenix College
Nancy Ray-Mitchell
McLennan Community College
Jim Moes
Johnson County Community College
Dominic Montileone
Delaware Valley College
Linda Morable
Dallas County Community Colleges
Charles Morrow
Cuyahoga Community College
T. Mouzopoulos
American College of Greece
Gary Mrozinski
Broome Community College
W. Gale Mueller
Spokane Community College
C. Mullery
Humboldt State University
Robert J. Mullin
Orange County Community College
Patricia Murray
Virginia Union University
Robert Nay
Stark Technical College
James Nead
Vincennes University
Jerry Novak
Alaska Pacific University
Grantley Nurse
Raritan Valley Community College
Gerald O'Bryan
Danville Area Community College
Larry Olanrewaju
Virginia Union University
David G. Oliver
Edison Community College
John R. Pappalardo
Keene State College
Dennis Pappas
Columbus Technical Institute
Roberta F. Passenant
Berkshire Community College
Clarissa M. H. Patterson
Bryant College

Kenneth Peissig
College of Menominee Nation
Jeffrey D. Penley
Catawba Valley Community College
Constantine Petrides
Manhattan Community College
Donald Pettit
Suffolk County Community College
Norman Petty
Central Piedmont Community College
Joseph Platts
Miami-Dade Community College
Gloria D. Poplawsky
University of Toledo
Greg Powell
Southern Utah University
Fred D. Pragasam
SUNY at Cobleskill
Peter Quinn
Commonwealth College
Kimberly Ray
North Carolina A & T State University
Robert Reinke
University of South Dakota
William Ritchie
Florida Gulf Coast University
Kenneth Robinson
Wesley College
John Roisch
Clark County Community College
Rick Rowray
Ball State University
Jill Russell
Camden County College
Karl C. Rutkowski
Pierce Junior College
Martin S. St. John
Westmoreland County Community College
Ben Sackmary
Buffalo State College
Eddie Sanders, Jr.
Chicago State University
P. L. Sandlin
East Los Angeles College
Nicholas Sarantakes
Austin Community College
Wallace Satchell
St. Philip's College
Warren Schlesinger
Ithaca College
Marilyn Schwartz
College of Marin
Jon E. Seely
Tulsa Junior College
John E. Seitz
Oakton Community College
J. Gregory Service
Broward Community College—North Campus
Lynne M. Severance
Eastern Washington University
Dennis Shannon
Southwestern Illinois College
Richard Shapiro
Cuyahoga Community College
Raymond Shea
Monroe Community College
Lynette Shishido
Santa Monica College
Cindy Simerly
Lakeland Community College
Anthony Slone
Elizabeth Community & Technical College
Anne Smevog
Cleveland Technical College
James Smith
Rocky Mountain College
David Sollars
Auburn University Montgomery
Carl Sonntag
Pikes Peak Community College
Russell W. Southhall
Laney College
Raymond Sparks
Pima College
John Spence
University of Southwestern Louisiana
Rieann Spence-Gale
Northern Virginia Community College
Nancy Z. Spillman
Economic Education Enterprises
Richard J. Stanish
Tulsa Junior College
Jeffrey Stauffer
Ventura College
Jim Steele
Chattanooga State Technical Community College
William A. Steiden
Jefferson Community College
E. George Stook
Anne Arundel Community College
W. Sidney Sugg
Lakeland Community College
Lynn Suksdorf
Salt Lake Community College
Richard L. Sutton
University of Nevada—Las Vegas
Robert E. Swindle
Glendale Community College
William A. Syvertsen
Fresno City College
Lynette Teal
Ivy Technical State College
Raymond D. Tewell
American River College
George Thomas
Johnston Technical College
Karen Thomas
St. Cloud University
Judy Thompson
Briar Cliff College
Paula Thompson
Fashion Institute of Technology
William C. Thompson
Foothill Community College
James B. Thurman
George Washington University
Patrick S. Tillman
Grayson County College
Frank Titlow
St. Petersburg College
Charles E. Tychsen
Northern Virginia Community College—Annandale
Ted Valvoda
Lakeland Community College
Robert H. Vaughn
Lakeland Community College
Frederick A. Viohl
Troy State University
C. Thomas Vogt
Allan Hancock College
Loren K. Waldman
Franklin University
Stephen R. Walsh
Providence College
Elizabeth Wark
Springfield College
John Warner
The University of New Mexico—Albuquerque
Randy Waterman
Dallas County Community Colleges
W. J. Waters, Jr.
Central Piedmont Community College
Philip A. Weatherford
Embry-Riddle Aeronautical University
Martin Welc
Saddleback College

Kenneth Wendeln
Indiana University
Jerry E. Wheat
Indiana University, Southeast Campus
Elizabeth White
Orange County Community College
Benjamin Wieder
Queensborough Community College

Ralph Wilcox
Kirkwood Community College
Charlotte Williams
Jones County Junior College
Larry Williams
Palomar College
Paul Williams
Mott Community College
Steven Winter
Orange County Community College

Wallace Wirth
South Suburban College
Amy Wojciechowski
West Shore Community College
Nathaniel Woods
Columbus State Community College
Gregory J. Worosz
Schoolcraft College
Marilyn Young
Tulsa Junior College

Many talented professionals at Cengage Learning have contributed to the development of *Business,* Eleventh Edition. We are especially grateful to Jack Calhoun, Melissa Acuña, Erin Joyner, Michelle Lockard, Stacy Shirley, Joanne Dauksewicz, Kim Kusnerak, Vanavan Jayaraman, Sarah Greber, Kristen Meere, Renee Yocum, Jana Lewis, and Kayti Purkiss. Their inspiration, patience, support, and friendship are invaluable.

PART 1

The Environment of Business

In Part 1 of *Business*, we begin with an examination of the world of business and how the economy affects our life. Next, we discuss ethical and social responsibility issues that affect business firms and our society. Then we explore the increasing importance of international business.

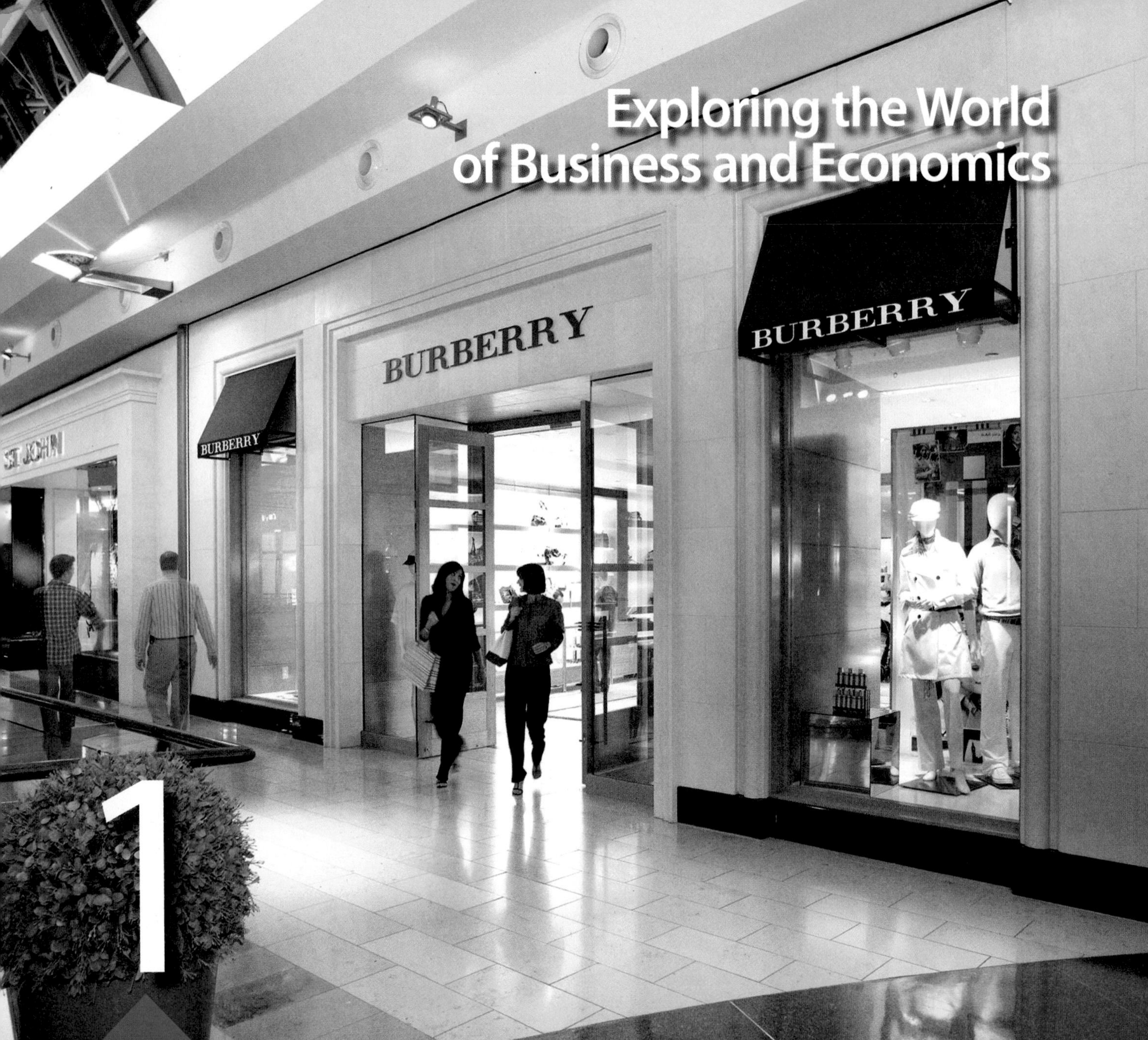

1 Exploring the World of Business and Economics

© AP Images/PRNewsFoto/The Mall at Millenia

Learning Objectives

What you will be able to do once you complete this chapter:

1. Discuss what you must do to be successful in the world of business.
2. Define *business* and identify potential risks and rewards.
3. Define *economics* and describe the two types of economic systems: capitalism and command economy.
4. Identify the ways to measure economic performance.
5. Outline the four types of competition.
6. Summarize the factors that affect the business environment and the challenges that American businesses will encounter in the future.

inside business

How Amazon Kindles Business Success

At the dawn of the Internet age, entrepreneur Jeff Bezos founded a Web-based bookstore he named Amazon.com to suggest the immense selection of titles on his virtual shelves. His plan was to create a customer-centered company using cutting-edge technology to keep prices low and provide good service. In the course of building his business, Bezos pioneered many features that have become staples of online retailing, including personalized product recommendations, customer reviews, and free shipping with a minimum order.

Today, the once-tiny enterprise with the quirky name has become a giant corporation that rings up more than $24 billion in annual sales worldwide. Amazon owns Zappos, the online shoe retailer known for outstanding service, and now sells everything from televisions, toys, and tools to computers, cameras, and clothing. It has also used its retailing expertise to become a virtual storefront for thousands of companies and individuals who sign up to sell goods and services on the Amazon Web site. In addition, it has used its tech expertise to offer on-demand services such as data storage and extra computing power to businesses of all sizes.

As CEO, Bezos continues to move Amazon in new directions. A few years ago, the company introduced the Kindle, an electronic handheld device that allows users to instantly download and read books and magazines when and where they please. The Kindle was innovative because it was the first e-book reader to connect wirelessly for content download without additional subscription or network fees. The initial response was so strong that Amazon struggled to meet the unexpectedly high demand.

Over time, Amazon has refined the Kindle by streamlining its design, adding features, making the product more eco-friendly, cutting the price, and expanding the catalog of content available for instant download. Despite competition from bookstore rival Barnes & Noble and electronics giant Sony, which have both launched wireless e-book readers, the Kindle remains popular with buyers in North America and beyond. Thanks to this and other entrepreneurial innovations, Amazon has kept sales growing for more than 15 years, even during the toughest of economic times. Now the challenge for Jeff Bezos is to extend that remarkable record of success and find new ways to kindle future profits.[1]

FYI

Did You Know?

Amazon—the once-tiny enterprise with the quirky name—has become a giant corporation that rings up more than $24 billion in annual sales worldwide.

Wow! What a challenging world we live in. Just for a moment, think about the economic problems listed here and how they affect not only businesses but also individuals.

- Unemployment rates hovering around 10 percent
- Reduced consumer spending
- A slowdown in the home-building industry and record home foreclosures
- A large number of troubled banks and financial institutions
- An increasing number of business failures
- Depressed stock values that reduced the value of investment and retirement accounts for most individuals

In fact, just about every person around the globe was affected in some way by the economic crisis that began in late 2007. Despite the efforts of the U.S. government and other world governments to provide the economic stimulus needed to stabilize the economy, it took nearly two years before the economy began to improve. Hopefully, by the time you read this material, the nation's economy will be much stronger. Still, it is important to remember the old adage, "History is a great teacher." Both the nation and individuals should take a look at what went wrong to avoid making the same mistakes in the future. In addition, it helps to keep one factor in mind: Despite all the problems just described, make no mistake about it, our economic system will survive. In fact, our economy continues to adapt and change to meet the challenges of an ever-changing world and to provide opportunities for those who want to achieve success.

Our economic system provides an amazing amount of freedom that allows businesses that range in size from the small corner grocer to Amazon.com—the company profiled in the Inside Business opening case for this chapter—to adapt to changing business environments. Within certain limits, imposed mainly to ensure public safety, the owners of a business can produce any legal good or service they choose and attempt to sell it at the price they set. This system of business, in which individuals decide what to produce, how to produce it, and at what price to sell it, is called **free enterprise**. Our free-enterprise system ensures, for example, that Amazon.com can sell everything from televisions, toys, and tools to computers, cameras, and clothing. Our system gives Amazon's owners and stockholders the right to make a profit from the company's success. It gives Amazon's management the right to compete with bookstore rival Barnes & Noble and electronics giant Sony. It also gives consumers the right to choose.

In this chapter, we look briefly at what business is and how it became that way. First, we discuss what you must do to be successful in the world of business and explore some important reasons for studying business. Then we define *business*, noting how business organizations satisfy their customers' needs and earn profits. Next, we examine how capitalism and command economies answer four basic economic questions. Then our focus shifts to how the nations of the world measure economic performance and to the four types of competitive situations. Next, we look at the events that helped shape today's business system, the current business environment, and the challenges that businesses face.

1

Discuss what you must do to be successful in the world of business.

Your Future in the Changing World of Business

The key word in this heading is *changing*. When faced with both economic problems and increasing competition not only from firms in the United States but also from international firms located in other parts of the world, employees and managers began to ask the question: What do we do now? Although this is a fair question, it is difficult to answer. Certainly, for a college student taking business courses or an employee just starting a career, the question is even more difficult to answer. Yet there are still opportunities out there for people who are willing to work hard, continue to learn, and possess the ability to adapt to change. Let's begin our discussion in this section with three basic concepts.

- What do you want?
- Why do you want it?
- Write it down!

During a segment on *The Oprah Winfrey Show*, Joe Dudley, one of the world's most successful black business owners, gave the preceding advice to anyone who wanted to succeed in business. His advice can help you achieve success. What is so amazing about Dudley's success is that he started a manufacturing business in his own kitchen, with his wife and children serving as the new firm's only employees. He went on to develop his own line of more than 400 hair-care and cosmetic products sold directly to cosmetologists, barbers, and beauty schools. Today, Mr. Dudley has built a multimillion-dollar empire—one of the most successful minority-owned companies in the nation. He is not only a successful business owner but also a winner of the Horatio Alger Award—an award given to outstanding individuals who have succeeded in the face of adversity.[2] Although many people would say that Joe Dudley was just lucky or happened to be in the right place at the right time, the truth is that

free enterprise the system of business in which individuals are free to decide what to produce, how to produce it, and at what price to sell it

he became a success because he had a dream and worked hard to turn his dream into a reality. Today, Dudley's vision is to see people succeed—to realize "The American Dream." He would be the first to tell you that you have the same opportunities that he had. According to Mr. Dudley, "Success is a journey, not just a destination."[3]

Whether you want to obtain part-time employment to pay college and living expenses, begin your career as a full-time employee, or start a business, you must *bring* something to the table that makes you different from the next person. Employers and our economic system are more demanding than ever before. Ask yourself: What can I do that will make employers want to pay me a salary? What skills do I have that employers need? With these two questions in mind, we begin the next section with another basic question: Why study business?

Why Study Business?

The potential benefits of higher education are enormous. To begin with, there are economic benefits. Over their lifetimes, college graduates on average earn much more than high school graduates. Although lifetime earnings are substantially higher for college graduates, so are annual income amounts (see Figure 1.1).

The nice feature of education and knowledge is that once you have it, no one can take it away. It is yours to use for a lifetime. In this section, we explore what you may expect to get out of this business course and text. You will find at least five compelling reasons for studying business.

For Help in Choosing a Career What do you want to do with the rest of your life? At some place and some time in your life, someone probably has asked you this same question. Like many people, you may find it a difficult question to answer. This business course will introduce you to a wide array of employment opportunities. In private enterprise, these range from small, local businesses owned by one individual to large companies such as American Express and Marriott International that are owned by thousands of stockholders. There are also employment opportunities with federal, state, county, and local governments and with not-for-profit organizations such as the Red Cross and Save the Children. For help in deciding which career might be right for you, read Appendix A: Careers in Business, which appears on the text Web site. To view this information:

1. Make an Internet connection and go to www.cengagebrain.com.
2. At the CengageBrain.com home page, search for the ISBN of your title (from the back cover of your book) using the search box at the top of the page. This will take you to the product page where free companion resources can be found.

In addition to career information in Appendix A, a number of additional Web sites provide information about career development. For more information, visit the following sites:

- Career Builder at http://www.careerbuilder.com
- Career One Stop at http://www.careeronestop.org

Figure 1.1 Who Makes the Most Money

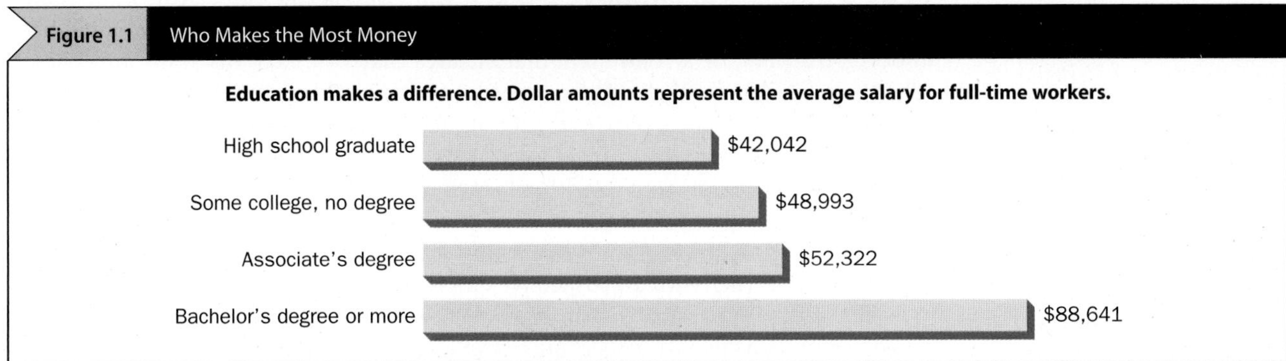

Source: The 2010 Statistical Abstract of the U. S. Web site at http://www.census.gov (accessed March 26, 2010). Salary amounts were obtained from Table 687.

Career
SUCCESS

Clicking Your Career into High Gear

In today's competitive business world, you should be networking online if you want to click your career into high gear. You can use Facebook, Twitter, LinkedIn, and other networking Web sites to locate job openings, help prospective employers to find you, and make a good impression on current and future bosses.

For example, David Gallant posted his résumé on job-search Web sites and followed up on leads from tech industry sources even before he graduated from the University of New Hampshire. He also set up his own blog to showcase his skills and hobbies and started conversing with other tech enthusiasts via Twitter posts. When he noticed a tweet about a job opening in his field, he applied immediately. Before interviewing Gallant, company managers checked his blog page and Twitter posts—and they liked what they saw. Gallant's job search ended successfully: He was hired within two weeks of graduation.

© Stuwdamdorp / Alamy

How can you make the most of online networking? First, identify and join sites where you can connect with potential employers, former classmates, and others who may have, or may hear of, job openings. Second, be sure your online profiles, photographs, and posts communicate your abilities and interests without being offensive or overly revealing. Finally, be ready to click quickly when you spot a job opening.

Sources: James Limbach, "Social Networking Explodes as Job-Search Tool," *ConsumerAffairs.com*, November 23, 2009, http://www.consumeraffairs.com/news04/2009/11/social_networking_jobs.html; Sarah E. Needleman, "A New Job Just a Tweet Away," *Wall Street Journal*, September 8, 2009, http://online.wsj.com/article/SB10001424052970204584404574393102737256542.html; Barbara Kiviat, "Using Twitter and Facebook to Find a Job," *Time*, June 8, 2009, http://www.time.com/time/business/article/0,8599,1903083,00.html; Glenda Kwek, "Twitter: The New Way to Find a Job," *Sydney Morning Herald*, March 27, 2009, http://www.smh.com.au/articles/2009/03/27/1237657117773.html; "UNH Grad Finds a Job Using Twitter," *University of New Hampshire Information Technology Pipeline*, March 27, 2009, http://pipeline.unh.edu/tag/twitter/.

- Monster at http://www.monster.com
- Yahoo! Hot Jobs at http://hotjobs.yahoo.com

One thing to remember as you think about what your ideal career might be is that a person's choice of a career ultimately is just a reflection of what he or she values and holds most important. What will give one individual personal satisfaction may not satisfy another. For example, one person may dream of a career as a corporate executive and becoming a millionaire before the age of 30. Another may choose a career that has more modest monetary rewards but that provides the opportunity to help others. One person may be willing to work long hours and seek additional responsibility to get promotions and pay raises. Someone else may prefer a less demanding job with little stress and more free time. What you choose to do with your life will be based on what you feel is most important. And *you* are a very important part of that decision.

To Be a Successful Employee Deciding on the type of career you want is only the first step. To get a job in your chosen field and to be successful at it, you will have to develop a plan, or a road map, that ensures that you have the skills and knowledge the job requires. You will be expected to have both the technical skills needed to accomplish a specific task and the ability to work well with many types of people in a culturally diverse workforce. **Cultural (or workplace) diversity** refers to the differences among people in a workforce owing to race, ethnicity, and gender. These skills, together with a working knowledge of the American business system and an appreciation for a culturally diverse workplace, can give you an inside edge when you are interviewing with a prospective employer.

cultural (or workplace) diversity differences among people in a workforce owing to race, ethnicity, and gender

This course, your instructor, and all the resources available at your college or university can help you to acquire the skills and knowledge you will need for a successful career. But do not underestimate your part in making your dream a reality. In addition to job-related skills and knowledge you need to be successful in a specific job, employers will also look for the following characteristics when hiring a new employee or promoting an existing employee:

- Honesty and integrity
- Willingness to work hard
- Dependability
- Time management skills
- Self-confidence
- Motivation
- Willingness to learn
- Communication skills
- Professionalism

The above skills and values are traits you will need to succeed in the workplace—and with work on your part you can learn and develop these traits to improve your chances of getting just the right job.

Employers will also be interested in any work experience you may have had in cooperative work/school programs, during summer vacations, or in part-time jobs during the school year. These things can make a difference when it is time to apply for the job you really want.

To Improve Your Management Skills Often, employees become managers or supervisors. In fact, many employees want to become managers because managers often receive higher salaries. Although management obviously can be a rewarding career, what is not so obvious is the amount of time and hard work needed to achieve the higher salaries. Today, managers have demanding jobs. For starters, employers expect more from managers and supervisors than ever before. Typically, the heavy workload requires that managers work long hours, and most do not get paid overtime. They also experience enormous demands on their time and face increased problems created by the economic crisis, increased competition, employee downsizing, the quest for improved quality, and the need for efficient use of the firm's resources.

To be an effective manager, managers must be able to perform four basic management functions: planning, organizing, leading and motivating, and controlling—all topics discussed in Chapter 6, Understanding the Management Process. To successfully perform these management functions, managers must possess three very important skills.

- *Interpersonal skills*—The ability to deal effectively with individual employees, other managers within the firm, and people outside the firm.
- *Technical skills*—The skill required to accomplish a specific kind of work being done in an organization. Although managers may not actually perform the technical tasks, they should be able to train employees and answer technical questions.
- *Conceptual skills*—The ability to think in abstract terms in order to see the "big picture." Conceptual skills help managers understand how the various parts of an organization or idea can fit together.

In addition to the three skills just described, a successful manager will need many of the same skills that an employee needs to be successful. For example, oral and written communication skills, willingness to work hard, and time-management skills are important for both employees and managers.

Putting moms to work. Dixie McDaniel de Andrade used her interpersonal, technical, and conceptual skills to build a successful (and profitable) business. Her business, Mom Corps of Miami, matches moms that want to work with employers who need employees that appreciate a flexible work schedule.

To Start Your Own Business Some people prefer to work for themselves, and they open their own businesses. To be successful, business owners must possess many of the same skills that successful employees have, and they must be willing to work hard and put in long hours.

It also helps if your small business can provide a product or service that customers want. For example, Mark Cuban started a small Internet company called Broadcast.com that provided hundreds of live and on-demand audio and video programs ranging from rap music to sporting events to business events over the Internet. Because Cuban's company met the needs of his customers, Broadcast.com was very successful. When Cuban sold Broadcast.com to Yahoo! Inc., he became a billionaire.[4]

Unfortunately, many small-business firms fail; approximately 70 percent of them fail within the first seven years. Typical reasons for business failures include undercapitalization (not enough money), poor business location, poor customer service, unqualified or untrained employees, fraud, lack of a proper business plan, and failure to seek outside professional help. The material in Chapter 5 and selected topics and examples throughout this text will help you to decide whether you want to open your own business. This material will also help you to overcome many of these problems.

To Become a Better Informed Consumer and Investor The world of business surrounds us. You cannot buy a home, a new Ford Fusion Hybrid from the local Ford dealer, a Black & Decker sander at an ACE Hardware store, a pair of jeans at Gap Inc., or a hot dog from a street vendor without entering a business transaction. Because you no doubt will engage in business transactions almost every day of your life, one very good reason for studying business is to become a more fully informed consumer. Many people also rely on a basic understanding of business to help them to invest for the future. According to Julie Stav, Hispanic stockbroker-turned-author/radio personality, "Take $25, add to it drive plus determination and then watch it multiply into an empire."[5] The author of *Get Your Share*, a *New York Times* best seller, believes that it is important to learn the basics about the economy and business, stocks, mutual funds, and other alternatives before investing your money. She also believes that it is never too early to start investing. Although this is an obvious conclusion, just dreaming of being rich does not make it happen. In fact, like many facets of life, it takes planning and determination to establish the type of investment program that will help you to accomplish your financial goals.

Special Note to Students

It is important to begin reading this text with one thing in mind: *This business course does not have to be difficult*. We have done everything possible to eliminate the problems that students encounter in a typical class. All the features in each chapter have been evaluated and recommended by instructors with years of teaching experience. In addition, business students were asked to critique each chapter component. Based on this feedback, the text includes the following features:

- *Learning objectives* appear at the beginning of each chapter.
- *Inside Business* is a chapter-opening case that highlights how successful companies do business on a day-to-day basis.
- *Margin notes* are used throughout the text to reinforce both learning objectives and key terms.
- *Boxed features* highlight how both employees and entrepreneurs can be successful.
- *Spotlight* features highlight interesting facts about business and society and often provide a real-world example of an important concept within a chapter.
- *Sustaining the Planet* features provide information about companies working to protect the environment.

- *End-of-chapter materials* provide questions about the opening case, a chapter summary, a list of key terms, review and discussion questions, and two cases. The last section of every chapter is entitled Building Skills for Career Success and includes exercises devoted to building communication skills with a journal exercise, exploring the Internet, developing critical-thinking skills, building team skills, and researching different careers.
- *End-of-part materials* provide a continuing video case about Graeter's Ice Cream, a company that operates a chain of retail outlets in the Cincinnati, Ohio, area and sells to more than 760 Kroger Stores throughout the country. Also, at the end of each major part is an exercise designed to help you to develop the components that are included in a typical business plan.

In addition to the text, a number of student supplements will help you to explore the world of business. We are especially proud of the Web site that accompanies this edition. There, you will find online study aids, such as key terms and definitions, crossword puzzles, interactive quizzes, student PowerPoint slides, and links to the videos for each chapter. If you want to take a look at the Internet support materials available for this edition of *Business*,

1. Make an Internet connection and go to www.cengagebrain.com.
2. At the CengageBrain.com home page, search for the ISBN of your title (from the back cover of your book) using the search box at the top of the page. This will take you to the product page where free companion resources can be found.

As authors, we want you to be successful. We know that your time is valuable and that your schedule is crowded with many different activities. We also appreciate the fact that textbooks are expensive. Therefore, we want you to use this text and get the most out of your investment. To help you get off to a good start, a number of suggestions for developing effective study skills and using this text are provided in Table 1.1. Why not take a look at these suggestions and use them to help you succeed in this course and earn a higher grade. Remember what Joe Dudley said, "Success is a journey, not just a destination."

Because a text should always be evaluated by the students and instructors who use it, we would welcome and sincerely appreciate your comments and suggestions. Please feel free to contact us by using one of the following e-mail addresses:

Bill Pride: **w-pride@tamu.edu**
Bob Hughes: **bhughes@dcccd.edu**
Jack Kapoor: **kapoorj@cdnet.cod.edu**

Table 1.1	Seven Ways to Use this Text and Its Resources
1. Prepare before you go to class.	Early preparation is the key to success in many of life's activities. Certainly, early preparation can help you to participate in class, ask questions, and improve your performance on examinations.
2. Read the chapter.	Although it may seem like an obvious suggestion, many students never take the time to really read the material. Find a quiet space where there are no distractions, and invest enough time to become a "content expert."
3. Underline or highlight important concepts.	Make this text yours. Do not be afraid to write on the pages of your text or highlight important material. It is much easier to review material if you have identified important concepts.
4. Take notes.	While reading, take the time to jot down important points and summarize concepts in your own words. Also, take notes in class.
5. Apply the concepts.	Learning is always easier if you can apply the content to your real-life situation. Think about how you could use the material either now or in the future.
6. Practice critical thinking.	Test the material in the text. Do the concepts make sense? To build critical-thinking skills, answer the questions that accompany the cases at the end of each chapter. Also, many of the exercises in the Building Skills for Career Success require critical thinking.
7. Prepare for the examinations.	Allow enough time to review the material before the examinations. Check out the summary and review questions at the end of the chapter. Then use the resources on the text Web site.

2

Define *business* and identify potential risks and rewards.

Business: A Definition

Business is the organized effort of individuals to produce and sell, for a profit, the goods and services that satisfy society's needs. The general term *business* refers to all such efforts within a society (as in "American business"). However, *a business* is a particular organization, such as Kraft Foods, Inc., or Cracker Barrel Old Country Stores. To be successful, a business must perform three activities. It must be organized, it must satisfy needs, and it must earn a profit.

The Organized Effort of Individuals

For a business to be organized, it must combine four kinds of resources: material, human, financial, and informational. *Material* resources include the raw materials used in manufacturing processes as well as buildings and machinery. For example, Sara Lee Corporation needs flour, sugar, butter, eggs, and other raw materials to produce the food products it sells worldwide. In addition, this Illinois-based company needs human, financial, and informational resources. *Human* resources are the people who furnish their labor to the business in return for wages. The *financial* resource is the money required to pay employees, purchase materials, and generally keep the business operating. *Information* is the resource that tells the managers of the business how effectively the other three resources are being combined and used (see Figure 1.2).

Today, businesses are usually organized as one of three specific types. *Manufacturing businesses* process various materials into tangible goods, such as delivery trucks, towels, or computers. Intel, for example, produces computer chips that, in turn, are sold to companies that manufacture computers. *Service businesses* produce services, such as haircuts, legal advice, or tax preparation. Some firms called *marketing intermediaries* buy products from manufacturers and then resell them. Sony Corporation is a manufacturer that produces stereo equipment, among other things. These products may be sold to a marketing intermediary such as Best Buy, which then resells the manufactured goods to consumers in their retail stores.

Satisfying Needs

business the organized effort of individuals to produce and sell, for a profit, the products and services that satisfy society's needs

The ultimate objective of every firm must be to satisfy the needs of its customers. People generally do not buy goods and services simply to own them; they buy products and services to satisfy particular needs. Some of us may feel that the need for transportation is best satisfied by an air-conditioned BMW with stereo compact-disc player, automatic transmission, power seats and windows, and remote-control side mirrors. Others may believe that a Chevrolet Aveo with a stick shift will do just fine. Both products are available to those who want them, along with a wide variety of other products that satisfy the need for transportation.

When firms lose sight of their customers' needs, they are likely to find the going rough. However, when businesses understand their customers' needs and work to satisfy those needs, they are usually successful. Back in 1962, Sam Walton opened his first discount store in Rogers, Arkansas. Although the original store was quite different from the Walmart Superstores you see today, the basic ideas of providing customer service and offering goods that satisfied needs at low prices are part of the reason why this firm has grown to become the largest retailer in the world. Although Walmart has over 8,400 retail stores in the United States and 14 other countries, this highly successful discount-store organization continues to open new stores to meet the needs of its customers around the globe.[6]

Organization at its best! While all businesses need to be organized, imagine what would happen on this construction site if this construction business weren't organized. To be successful, this business must use material, human, financial, and information resources to construct a new office building.

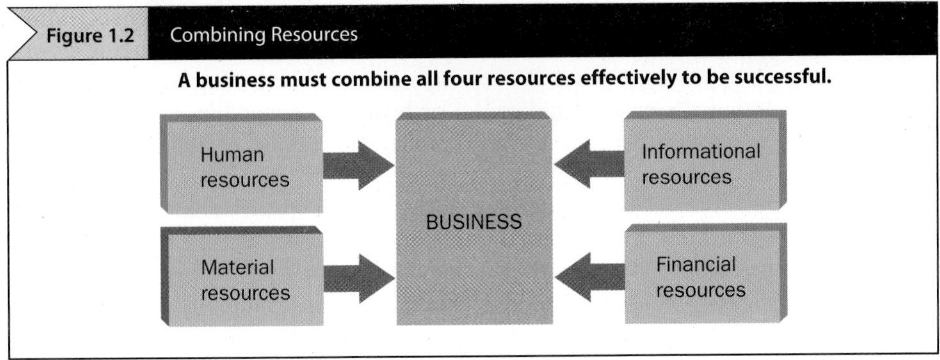

Business Profit

A business receives money (sales revenue) from its customers in exchange for goods or services. It must also pay out money to cover the expenses involved in doing business. If the firm's sales revenues are greater than its expenses, it has earned a profit. More specifically, as shown in Figure 1.3, **profit** is what remains after all business expenses have been deducted from sales revenue.

A negative profit, which results when a firm's expenses are greater than its sales revenue, is called a *loss*. A business cannot continue to operate at a loss for an indefinite period of time. Management and employees must find some way to increase sales revenues and reduce expenses to return to profitability. If some specific actions are not taken to eliminate losses, a firm may be forced to file for bankruptcy protection. In some cases, the pursuit of profits is so important that some corporate executives, including those from such corporations as Lehman Brothers, AIG, and mortgage lenders Freddie Mac and Fannie Mae, have fudged their profit figures to avoid disappointing shareholders, directors, Wall Street analysts, lenders, and other stakeholders. The term **stakeholders** is used to describe all the different people or groups of people who are affected by the policies, decisions, and activities made by an organization.

Although many people—especially stockholders and business owners—believe that profit is literally the bottom line or most important goal for a business, many stakeholders may be just as concerned about a firm's social responsibility record. Many corporations, for example, are careful to point out their efforts to sustain the planet, participate in the green ecological movement, and help people to live better lives in an annual social responsibility report. In its 57-page social responsibility report, General Mills describes how it has contributed approximately 5 percent of its pretax profits each year since 2000 to a wide variety of causes, including support for programs that feed the hungry and non-profit organizations in the United States and around the globe.[7] Although stockholders and business owners sometimes argue that the money that a business contributes to charitable causes could have been used to pay larger dividends to stockholders or increase the return on the owners' investment, the fact is that most socially responsible business firms feel social responsibility is the right thing to do and is good for business.

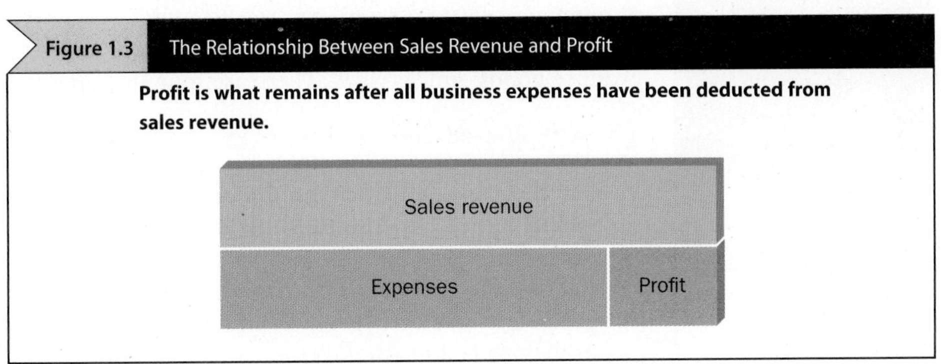

profit what remains after all business expenses have been deducted from sales revenue

stakeholders all the different people or groups of people who are affected by the policies and decisions made by an organization

The profit earned by a business becomes the property of its owners. Thus, in one sense, profit is the reward business owners receive for producing goods and services that consumers want. Profit is also the payment that business owners receive for assuming the considerable risks of business ownership. One of these is the risk of not being paid. Everyone else—employees, suppliers, and lenders—must be paid before the owners.

A second risk that owners undertake is the risk of losing whatever they have invested into the business. A business that cannot earn a profit is very likely to fail, in which case the owners lose whatever money, effort, and time they have invested.

To satisfy society's needs and make a profit, a business must operate within the parameters of a nation's economic system. In the next section, we define economics and describe two different types of economic systems.

3

Define *economics* and describe the two types of economic systems: capitalism and command economy.

Types of Economic Systems

economics the study of how wealth is created and distributed

microeconomics the study of the decisions made by individuals and businesses

macroeconomics the study of the national economy and the global economy

economy the way in which people deal with the creation and distribution of wealth

factors of production resources used to produce goods and services

Economics is the study of how wealth is created and distributed. By *wealth,* we mean "anything of value," including the products produced and sold by business. *How wealth is distributed* simply means "who gets what." Experts often use economics to explain the choices we make and how these choices change as we cope with the demands of everyday life. In simple terms, individuals, businesses, governments, and society must make decisions that reflect what is important to each group at a particular time. For example, suppose you want to take a weekend trip to some exotic vacation spot, and you also want to begin an investment program. Because of your financial resources, though, you cannot do both, so you must decide what is most important. Business firms, governments, and to some extent society face the same types of decisions. Each group must deal with scarcity when making important decisions. In this case, *scarcity* means "lack of resources"—money, time, natural resources, and so on—that are needed to satisfy a want or need.

Today, experts often study economic problems from two different perspectives: microeconomics and macroeconomics. **Microeconomics** is the study of the decisions made by individuals and businesses. Microeconomics, for example, examines how the prices of homes affect the number of homes individuals will buy. On the other hand, **macroeconomics** is the study of the national economy and the global economy. Macroeconomics examines the economic effect of national income, unemployment, inflation, taxes, government spending, interest rates, and similar factors on a nation and society.

New energy from an old source: the wind. To protect the environment, as well as to reduce our dependence on oil from foreign nations, many utility companies are developing alternative energy sources such as wind power. Once developed, wind energy may actually be cheaper than using foreign oil.

The decisions that individuals, business firms, government, and society make, and the way in which people deal with the creation and distribution of wealth determine the kind of economic system, or **economy**, that a nation has.

Over the years, the economic systems of the world have differed in essentially two ways: (1) the ownership of the factors of production and (2) how they answer four basic economic questions that direct a nation's economic activity.

Factors of production are the resources used to produce goods and services. There are four such factors:

- *Land and natural resources*—elements that can be used in the production process to make appliances, automobiles, and other products. Typical examples include crude oil, forests, minerals, land, water, and even air.
- *Labor*—the time and effort that we use to produce goods and services. It includes human resources such as managers and employees.

Entrepreneurial SUCCESS

Rob Kalin was trying to build a small business based on his handcrafted furniture when a lengthy Web search sent him down a different path to entrepreneurial success. The 25-year-old New York University graduate had spent several frustrating hours clicking around the Internet to locate an online outlet for his furniture. When he found nothing suitable, he decided to create a new online marketplace, Etsy.com, where artisans, customers, and vendors could connect with each other to buy and sell handmade products such as jewelry or art, vintage items, and craft supplies.

© Elena Elisseeva/Shutterstock.com

Kalin knew enough about the Web to design the basic site, and he recruited friends and former classmates to handle technical operations. A $50,000 investment from one of his furniture customers helped fund the fledgling firm, which opened its virtual doors in June 2005. That first year, Etsy sold $166,000 worth of crafts. During the second year, Kalin and his colleagues sought advice and investments from the co-founders of the photograph-sharing site Flickr. By the end of the second year, the company's merchandise sales topped $3.8 million. Etsy was on its way.

Today, Etsy employs 70 people and rings up $200 million in merchandise sales. Kalin sold a small percentage of the company in 2008 and, after hiring a new CEO, stepped back from day-to-day management. Two years later in 2010, Kalin took over again as CEO. He now devotes most of his time to planning for Etsy's future success.

Sources: Donna Fenn, "Meet Rob Kalin, the Man Behind Etsy.com," *Reader's Digest*, December 2009, http://www.rd.com/your-america-inspiring-people-and-stories/meet-rob-kalin-the-man-behind-etsycom/article169446.html; Cara S. Trager, "Crain's 2009 Top Entrepreneurs: Designer Crafts Artisan Community," *Crain's New York Business*, May 31, 2009, http://mycrains.crainsnewyork.com/small_business_awards/profiles/2009/210; Linda Tischler, "Fast Company 50 #44: Etsy," *Fast Company*, February 11, 2009, http://www.fastcompany.com/fast50_09/profile/list/etsy; http://www.etsy.com.

- *Capital*—the money, facilities, equipment, and machines used in the operation of organizations. Although most people think of capital as just money, it can also be the manufacturing equipment in a Pepperidge Farm production facility or a computer used in the corporate offices of McDonald's.
- *Entrepreneurship*—the activity that organizes land, labor, and capital. It is the willingness to take risks and the knowledge and ability to use the other factors of production efficiently. An **entrepreneur** is a person who risks his or her time, effort, and money to start and operate a business.

A nation's economic system significantly affects all the economic activities of its citizens and organizations. This far-reaching impact becomes more apparent when we consider that a country's economic system determines how the factors of production are used to meet the needs of society. Today, two different economic systems exist: capitalism and command economies. The way each system answers the four basic economic questions listed here determines a nation's economy.

1. What goods and services—and how much of each—will be produced?
2. How will these goods and services be produced?
3. For whom will these goods and services be produced?
4. Who owns and who controls the major factors of production?

Capitalism

Capitalism is an economic system in which individuals own and operate the majority of businesses that provide goods and services. Capitalism stems from the theories of the 18th-century Scottish economist Adam Smith. In his book *Wealth of Nations*, published in 1776, Smith argued that a society's interests are best served when the individuals within that society are allowed to pursue their own self-interest. In other words, people will work hard and invest long hours to produce goods and services only if they can reap the rewards of their labor—more pay or profits in the case

entrepreneur a person who risks time, effort, and money to start and operate a business

capitalism an economic system in which individuals own and operate the majority of businesses that provide goods and services

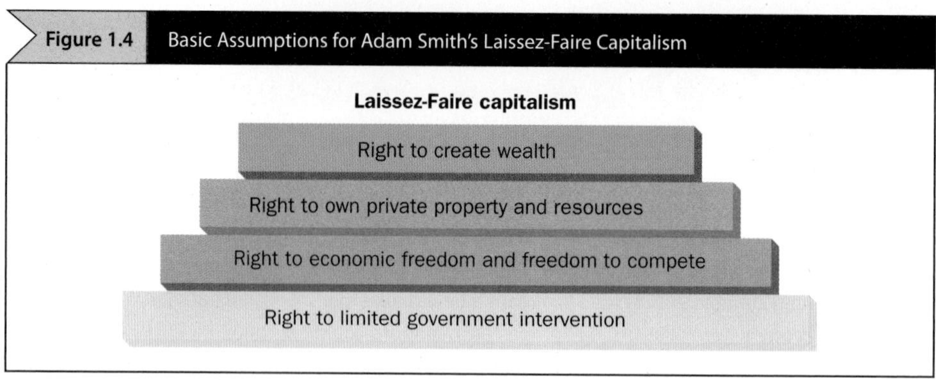

of a business owner. According to Smith, when individuals act to improve their own fortunes, they indirectly promote the good of their community and the people in that community. Smith went on to call this concept the "invisible hand." The **invisible hand** is a term created by Adam Smith to describe how an individual's own personal gain benefits others and a nation's economy. For example, the only way a small-business owner who produces shoes can increase personal wealth is to sell shoes to customers. To become even more prosperous, the small-business owner must hire workers to produce even more shoes. According to the invisible hand, people in the small-business owner's community not only would have shoes but also would have jobs working for the shoemaker. Thus, the success of people in the community and, to some extent, the nation's economy is tied indirectly to the success of the small-business owner.

Adam Smith's capitalism is based on the four fundamental issues illustrated in Figure 1.4.

invisible hand a term created by Adam Smith to describe how an individual's personal gain benefits others and a nation's economy

market economy an economic system in which businesses and individuals decide what to produce and buy, and the market determines quantities sold and prices

1. The creation of wealth is properly the concern of private individuals, not the government.
2. Private individuals must own private property and the resources used to create wealth.
3. Economic freedom ensures the existence of competitive markets that allow both sellers and buyers to enter and exit the market as they choose.
4. The role of government should be limited to providing defense against foreign enemies, ensuring internal order, and furnishing public works and education.

One factor that Smith felt was extremely important was the role of government. He believed that government should act only as rule maker and umpire. The French term *laissez faire* describes Smith's capitalistic system and implies that there should be no government interference in the economy. Loosely translated, this term means "let them do" (as they see fit).

Adam Smith's Laissez-Faire capitalism is also based on the concept of a market economy. A **market economy** (sometimes referred to as a *free-market economy*) is an economic system in which businesses and individuals decide what to produce and buy, and the market determines prices and quantities sold. The owners of resources should be free to determine how these resources are used and also to enjoy the income, profits, and other benefits derived from ownership of these resources.

Consumers—the biggest customer of American business. Consumers are a very important part of our capitalistic system because families like the one pictured here purchase approximately 70 percent of the goods and services produced by American business.

Capitalism in the United States

Our economic system is rooted in the Laissez-Faire capitalism of Adam Smith. However, our real-world economy is not as Laissez-Faire as Smith would have liked because

Figure 1.5 The Circular Flow in Our Mixed Economy

Our economic system is guided by the interaction of buyers and sellers, with the role of government being taken into account.

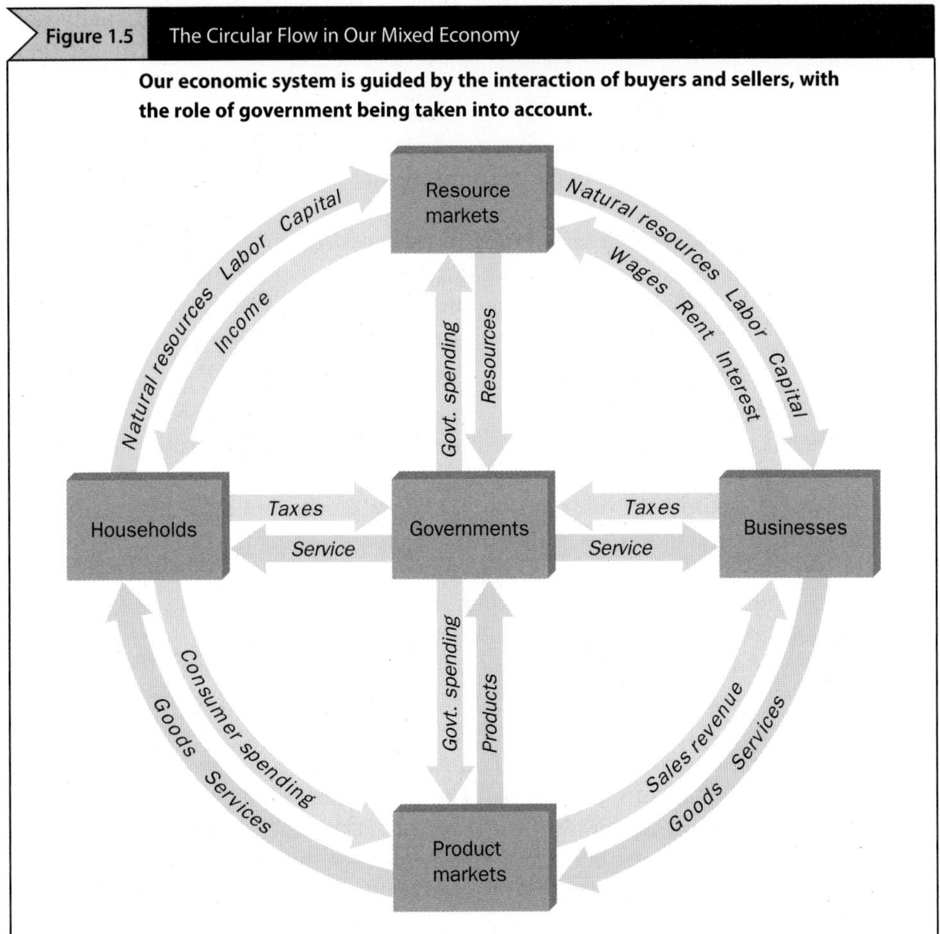

government participates as more than umpire and rule maker. Our economy is, in fact, a **mixed economy**, one that exhibits elements of both capitalism and socialism.

In a mixed economy, the four basic economic questions discussed at the beginning of this section (what, how, for whom, and who) are answered through the interaction of households, businesses, and governments. The interactions among these three groups are shown in Figure 1.5.

Households Households, made up of individuals, are the consumers of goods and services as well as owners of some of the factors of production. As *resource owners*, the members of households provide businesses with labor, capital, and other resources. In return, businesses pay wages, rent, and dividends and interest, which households receive as income.

As *consumers*, household members use their income to purchase the goods and services produced by business. Today, approximately 70 percent of our nation's total production consists of **consumer products**—goods and services purchased by individuals for personal consumption.[8] This means that consumers, as a group, are the biggest customers of American business.

Businesses Like households, businesses are engaged in two different exchanges. They exchange money for natural resources, labor, and capital and use these resources to produce goods and services. Then they exchange their goods and services for sales revenue. This sales revenue, in turn, is exchanged for additional resources, which are used to produce and sell more goods and services. Thus, the circular flow of Figure 1.5 is continuous.

Along the way, of course, business owners would like to remove something from the circular flow in the form of profits. Households try to retain some income

mixed economy an economy that exhibits elements of both capitalism and socialism

consumer products goods and services purchased by individuals for personal consumption

as savings. But are profits and savings really removed from the flow? Usually not! When the economy is running smoothly, households are willing to invest their savings in businesses. They can do so directly by buying stocks in businesses, by purchasing shares in mutual funds that purchase stocks in businesses, or by lending money to businesses. They can also invest indirectly by placing their savings in bank accounts. Banks and other financial institutions then invest these savings as part of their normal business operations.

When business profits are distributed to business owners, these profits become household income. (Business owners are, after all, members of households.) Thus, business profits, too, are retained in the business system, and the circular flow is complete. How, then, does government fit in?

Governments The Preamble to the Constitution sets forth the responsibility of the government to protect and promote public welfare. The numerous government services are important but they (1) would either not be produced by private business firms or (2) would be produced only for those who could afford them. Typical services include national defense, police, fire protection, education, and construction of roads and highways. To pay for all these services, governments collect a variety of taxes from households (such as personal income taxes and sales taxes) and from businesses (corporate income taxes).

Figure 1.5 shows this exchange of taxes for government services. It also shows government spending of tax dollars for resources and products required to provide these services.

Actually, with government included, our circular flow looks more like a combination of several flows. In reality, it is. The important point is that together the various flows make up a single unit—a complete economic system that effectively provides answers to the basic economic questions. Simply put, the system works.

Command Economies

Before we discuss how to measure a nation's economic performance, we look quickly at another economic system called a *command economy*. A **command economy** is an economic system in which the government decides what goods and services will be produced, how they will be produced, for whom available goods and services will be produced, and who owns and controls the major factors of production. The answers to all four basic economic questions are determined, at least to some degree, through centralized government planning. Today, two types of economic systems—*socialism* and *communism*—serve as examples of command economies.

Socialism In a socialist economy, the key industries are owned and controlled by the government. Such industries usually include transportation, utilities, communications, banking, and industries producing important materials such as steel. Land, buildings, and raw materials may also be the property of the state in a socialist economy. Depending on the country, private ownership of smaller businesses is permitted to varying degrees. Usually, people may choose their own occupations, although many work in state-owned industries.

What to produce and how to produce it are determined in accordance with national goals, which are based on projected needs and the availability of resources. The distribution of goods and services—who gets what—is also controlled by the state to the extent that it controls taxes, rents, and wages. Among the professed aims of socialist countries are the equitable distribution of income, the elimination of poverty, and the distribution of social services (such as medical care) to all who need them. The disadvantages of socialism include increased taxation and loss of incentive and motivation for both individuals and business owners.

Today, many of the nations that have been labeled as socialist nations traditionally, including France, Sweden, and India, are transitioning to a free-market economy. Currently, many countries that were once thought of as communist countries are

command economy an economic system in which the government decides what goods and services will be produced, how they will be produced, for whom available goods and services will be produced, and who owns and controls the major factors of production

now often referred to as socialist countries. Examples of former communist countries often referred to as socialists (or even capitalists) include most of the nations that were formerly part of the Union of Soviet Socialist Republics, China, and Vietnam.

Communism If Adam Smith was the father of capitalism, Karl Marx was the father of communism. In his writings during the mid-19th century, Marx advocated a classless society whose citizens together owned all economic resources. All workers would then contribute to this *communist* society according to their ability and would receive benefits according to their need.

Since the breakup of the Soviet Union and economic reforms in China and most of the Eastern European countries, the best remaining examples of communism are North Korea and Cuba. Today these so-called communist economies seem to practice a strictly controlled kind of socialism. Emphasis is placed on the production of goods the government needs rather than on the products that consumers might want, so there are frequent shortages of consumer goods. Workers have little choice of jobs, but special skills or talents seem to be rewarded with special privileges.

4

Identify the ways to measure economic performance.

Measuring Economic Performance

Today, it is hard to turn on the radio, watch the news on television, use the Internet, or read the newspaper without hearing or seeing something about the economy. Consider for just a moment the following questions:

- Are U.S. workers as productive as workers in other countries?
- Is the gross domestic product for the United States increasing or decreasing?
- What is the current balance of trade for our country?
- Why is the unemployment rate important?

The information needed to answer these questions, along with the answers to other similar questions, is easily obtainable from many sources. More important, the answers to these and other questions can be used to gauge the economic health of a nation. For individuals, the health of our nation's economy often affects the amount of interest you pay for homes, automobiles, credit card purchases, and other credit transactions. Finally, the health of the economy can also affect your ability to get a job or the financing you need to continue your education.

productivity the average level of output per worker per hour

The Importance of Productivity in the Global Marketplace

One way to measure a nation's economic performance is to assess its productivity. **Productivity** is the average level of output per worker per hour. An increase in productivity results in economic growth because a larger number of goods and services are produced by a given labor force. To see how productivity affects you and the economy, consider the following three questions:

Question: *How does productivity growth affect the economy?*

Answer: Because of productivity growth, it now takes just 90 workers to produce what 100 workers produced in 2001.[9] As a result, employers have reduced costs, earned more profits, and sold their products for less. Finally, productivity growth helps American business to compete more effectively with other nations in a competitive world.

Productivity can make a company more competitive in the global marketplace. The Shanghai Automotive Industry Corporation, often referred to as SAIC, is known for efficient production of some of China's best automobiles. Because increased productivity can reduce costs and increase profits, these SAIC workers used the latest technology to produce a new-entry-level car that debuted at the 2010 Beijing auto show.

Question: *How does a nation improve productivity?*

Answer: Reducing costs and enabling employees to work more efficiently are at the core of all attempts to improve productivity. For example, productivity in the United States is expected to improve dramatically as more economic activity is transferred onto the Internet, reducing costs for servicing customers and handling routine ordering functions between businesses. Other methods that can be used to increase productivity are discussed in detail in Chapter 8.

Question: *Is productivity growth always good?*

Answer: Although economists always point to increased efficiency and the ability to produce goods and services for lower costs as a positive factor, fewer workers producing more goods and services can lead to higher unemployment rates. In this case, increased productivity is good for employers but not good for unemployed workers seeking jobs in a very competitive work environment. For example, employers were reluctant to hire new employees in the midst of the recent economic crisis. Because they had been able to produce more goods and services with fewer employees, these same employers did not want to increase the firm's salary expense by hiring new employees. As a result, unemployment rates hovered at around 10 percent for much of 2009 and 2010 despite the federal government's efforts to create new jobs and reduce the number of unemployed workers.

Important Economic Indicators that Measure a Nation's Economy

In addition to productivity, a measure called *gross domestic product* can be used to measure the economic well-being of a nation. **Gross domestic product (GDP)** is the total dollar value of all goods and services produced by all people within the boundaries of a country during a one-year period. For example, the values of automobiles produced by employees in an American-owned General Motors plant and a Japanese-owned Toyota plant in the United States are both included in the GDP for the United States. The U.S. GDP was $14.3 trillion in 2009.[10] (*Note:* At the time of publication, 2009 was the last year for which complete statistics were available.)

The GDP figure facilitates comparisons between the United States and other countries because it is the standard used in international guidelines for economic accounting. It is also possible to compare the GDP for one nation over several different time periods. This comparison allows observers to determine the extent to which a nation is experiencing economic growth. For example, government experts project that GDP will grow to $21.8 trillion by the year 2018.[11]

To make accurate comparisons of the GDP for different years, we must adjust the dollar amounts for inflation. **Inflation** is a general rise in the level of prices. (The opposite of inflation is deflation.) **Deflation** is a general decrease in the level of prices. By using inflation-adjusted figures, we are able to measure the real GDP for a nation. In effect, it is now possible to compare the products and services produced by a nation in constant dollars—dollars that will purchase the same amount of goods and services. Figure 1.6 depicts the GDP of the United States in current dollars and the real GDP in inflation-adjusted dollars. Note that between 1990 and 2009, America's real GDP grew from $8 trillion to $13 trillion.[12]

In addition to GDP and real GDP, other economic measures exist that can be used to evaluate a nation's economy. Because of the recent economic crisis, one very important statistic that is in the news on a regular basis is the unemployment rate. The **unemployment rate** is the percentage of a nation's labor force unemployed at any time. According to the Bureau of Labor Statistics, when workers are unemployed, they, their families, and the country as a whole lose. Workers and their families lose wages, and the country loses the goods or services that could have been

gross domestic product (GDP) the total dollar value of all goods and services produced by all people within the boundaries of a country during a one-year period

inflation a general rise in the level of prices

deflation a general decrease in the level of prices

unemployment rate the percentage of a nation's labor force unemployed at any time

Figure 1.6 GDP in Current Dollars and in Inflation-Adjusted Dollars

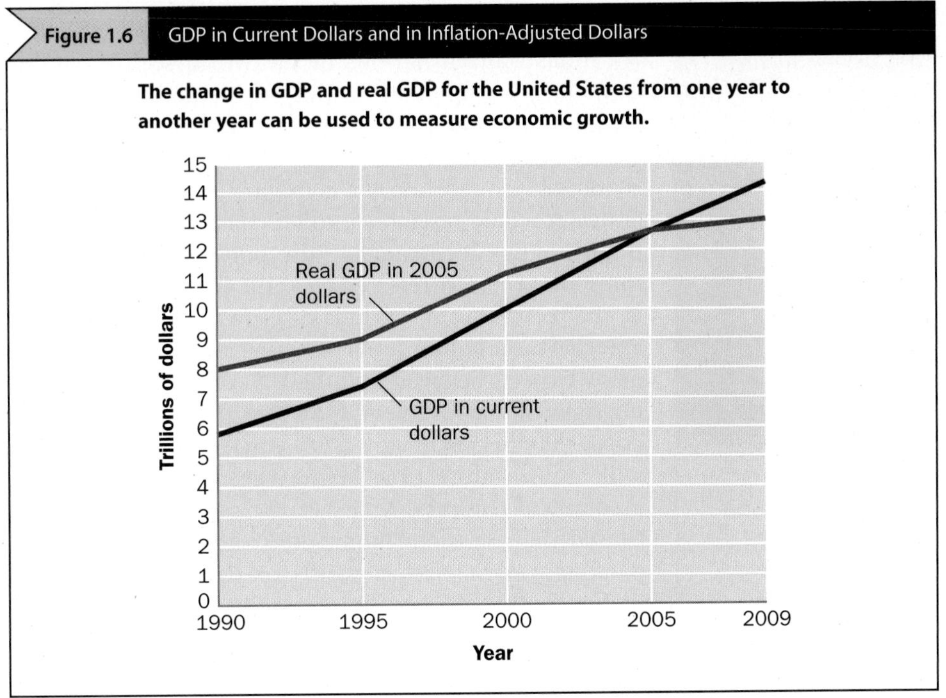

Source: U.S. Bureau of Economic Analysis Web site at http://www.bea.gov (accessed March 29, 2010).

produced. In addition, the purchasing power of these workers is lost, which can lead to unemployment for yet other workers.[13] Despite both federal and state programs to reduce the unemployment rate for the United States, it was hovering around 10 percent at the time of publication. This is an especially important statistic—especially if you are unemployed. The **consumer price index (CPI)** is a monthly index that measures the changes in prices of a fixed basket of goods purchased by a typical consumer in an urban area. Goods listed in the CPI include food and beverages, transportation, housing, clothing, medical care, recreation, education, communication, and other goods and services. Economists often use the CPI to determine the effect of inflation on not only the nation's economy but also individual consumers. Another monthly index is the producer price index. The **producer price index (PPI)** measures prices that producers receive for their finished goods. Because changes in the PPI reflect price increases or decreases at the wholesale level, the PPI is an accurate predictor of both changes in the CPI and prices that consumers will pay for many everyday necessities. Some additional economic measures are described in Table 1.2. Like the measures for GDP, these measures can be used to compare one economic statistic over different periods of time.

consumer price index (CPI) a monthly index that measures the changes in prices of a fixed basket of goods purchased by a typical consumer in an urban area

producer price index (PPI) an index that measures prices that producers receive for their finished goods

Table 1.2 Common Measures Used to Evaluate a Nation's Economic Health

Economic Measure	Description
1. Balance of trade	The total value of a nation's exports minus the total value of its imports over a specific period of time.
2. Bank credit	A statistic that measures the lending activity of commercial financial institutions.
3. Corporate profits	The total amount of profits made by corporations over selected time periods.
4. Inflation rate	An economic statistic that tracks the increase in prices of goods and services over a period of time. This measure is usually calculated on a monthly or an annual basis.
5. National income	The total income earned by various segments of the population, including employees, self-employed individuals, corporations, and other types of income.
6. New housing starts	The total number of new homes started during a specific time period.
7. Prime interest rate	The lowest interest rate that banks charge their most credit-worthy customers.

A sign of the times! Very few consumers will spend money on clothing and nonessential items if they are worried about losing their paycheck. To attract more customers during the recent economic crisis, this retailer offered a money-back guarantee—if customers lose their jobs.

The Business Cycle

All industrialized nations of the world seek economic growth, full employment, and price stability. However, a nation's economy fluctuates rather than grows at a steady pace every year. In fact, if you were to graph the economic growth rate for a country such as the United States, it would resemble a roller coaster ride with peaks (high points) and troughs (low points). These fluctuations are generally referred to as the **business cycle**, that is, the recurrence of periods of growth and recession in a nation's economic activity. At the time of publication, many experts believed that the U.S. economy was showing signs of improvement. However, the recent economic crisis that began in fall 2007 caused a recession that will require more time before the nation experiences a complete recovery. Many of the same industries that caused the recession—home construction, automobiles, banking, and finance—are still experiencing slow growth or financial problems. The nation's unemployment rate is still high. People are still frightened by the prospects of a troubled economy and are reluctant to spend money on consumer goods. Stock values, although improving, are still below the record values experienced a few years ago. Although the federal government has enacted a number of stimulus plans designed to help unemployed workers, to shore up the nation's banks and Wall Street firms, to reduce the number of home foreclosures, and to free up credit for both individuals and businesses, many experts still believe that we have serious financial problems. For one, the size of the national debt—a topic described later in this section—is a concern. To make matters worse, the recent economic crisis did not affect just the U.S. economy but also the economies of countries around the world. Unfortunately, many of the problems that caused the recent economic crisis are still there, and they will take years to correct and resolve.

The changes that result from either economic growth or economic downturn affect the amount of products and services that consumers are willing to purchase and, as a result, the amount of products and services produced by business firms. Generally, the business cycle consists of four states: the peak (sometimes called prosperity), recession, the trough, and recovery (sometimes called expansion).

During the *peak period*, the economy is at its highest point and unemployment is low. Total income is relatively high. As long as the economic outlook remains prosperous, consumers are willing to buy products and services. In fact, businesses often expand and offer new products and services during the peak period to take advantage of consumers' increased buying power.

Generally, economists define a **recession** as two or more consecutive three-month periods of decline in a country's GDP. Because unemployment rises during a recession, total buying power declines. The pessimism that accompanies a recession often stifles both consumer and business spending. As buying power decreases, consumers tend to become more value conscious and reluctant to purchase frivolous items. In response to a recession, many businesses focus on the products and services that provide the most value to their customers. Economists define a **depression** as a severe recession that lasts longer than a typical recession. A depression is characterized by extremely high unemployment rates, low wages, reduced purchasing power, lack of confidence in the economy, lower stock values, and a general decrease in business activity.

Economists refer to the third phase of the business cycle as the *trough*. The trough of a recession or depression is the turning point when a nation's

business cycle the recurrence of periods of growth and recession in a nation's economic activity

recession two or more consecutive three-month periods of decline in a country's GDP

depression a severe recession that lasts longer than a typical recession

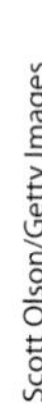

output and employment bottom out and reach their lowest levels. To offset the effects of recession and depression, the federal government uses both monetary and fiscal policies. **Monetary policies** are the Federal Reserve's decisions that determine the size of the supply of money in the nation and the level of interest rates. Through **fiscal policy**, the government can influence the amount of savings and expenditures by altering the tax structure and changing the levels of government spending.

Although the federal government collects approximately $3.0 trillion in annual revenues, the government often spends more than it receives, resulting in a **federal deficit**. For example, the government had a federal deficit for each year between 2002 and 2010. The total of all federal deficits is called the **national debt**. Today, the U.S. national debt is $12.7 trillion or approximately $41,000 for every man, woman, and child in the United States.[14]

Since World War II, business cycles have lasted from three to five years from one peak period to the next peak period. During the same time period, the average length of recessions has been 11 months.[15] Some experts believe that effective use of monetary and fiscal policies can speed up recovery and reduce the amount of time the economy is in recession. *Recovery* (or *expansion*) is movement of the economy from recession or depression to prosperity. High unemployment rates decline, income increases, and both the ability and the willingness to buy rise.

At the time of publication, many business leaders and politicians were debating whether the U.S. economy is still in recession, in the trough, or beginning recovery.

SPOTLIGHT

How Many People Are Really Unemployed?

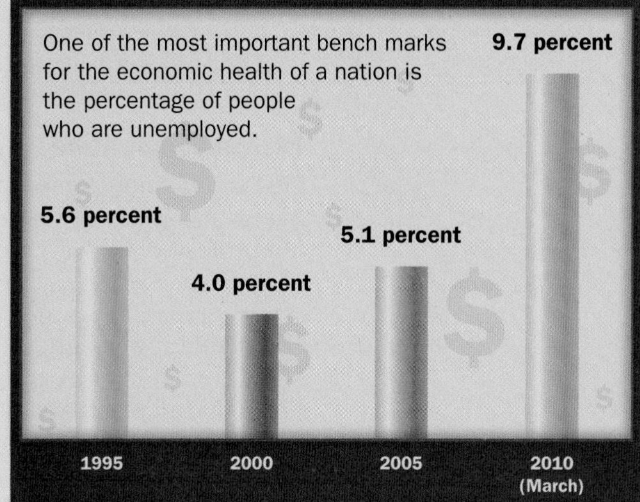

Source: The Bureau of Labor Statistics Web site at http://www.bls.gov (accessed April 5, 2010).

monetary policies Federal Reserve decisions that determine the size of the supply of money in the nation and the level of interest rates

Outline the four types of competition.

Types of Competition

Our capitalist system ensures that individuals and businesses make the decisions about what to produce, how to produce it, and what price to charge for the product. Mattel, Inc., for example, can introduce new versions of its famous Barbie doll, license the Barbie name, change the doll's price and method of distribution, and attempt to produce and market Barbie in other countries or over the Internet at http://www.mattel.com. Our system also allows customers the right to choose between Mattel's products and those produced by competitors.

Competition like that between Mattel and other toy manufacturers is a necessary and extremely important by-product of capitalism. Business **competition** is essentially a rivalry among businesses for sales to potential customers. In a capitalistic economy, competition also ensures that a firm will survive only if it serves its customers well by providing products and services that meet needs. Economists recognize four different degrees of competition ranging from ideal, complete competition to no competition at all. These are perfect competition, monopolistic competition, oligopoly, and monopoly. For a quick overview of the different types of competition, including numbers of firms and examples for each type, look at Table 1.3.

fiscal policy government influence on the amount of savings and expenditures; accomplished by altering the tax structure and by changing the levels of government spending

federal deficit a shortfall created when the federal government spends more in a fiscal year than it receives

national debt the total of all federal deficits

competition rivalry among businesses for sales to potential customers

Table 1.3	Four Different Types of Competition	
The number of firms determines the degree of competition within an industry.		
Type of Competition	**Number of Business Firms or Suppliers**	**Real-World Examples**
1. Perfect	Many	Corn, wheat, peanuts
2. Monopolistic	Many	Clothing, shoes
3. Oligopoly	Few	Automobiles, cereals
4. Monopoly	One	Software protected by copyright, many local public utilities

Perfect Competition

Perfect (or pure) competition is the market situation in which there are many buyers and sellers of a product, and no single buyer or seller is powerful enough to affect the price of that product. Note that this definition includes several important ideas. First, we are discussing the market for a single product, such as bushels of wheat. Second, there are no restrictions on firms entering the industry. Third, all sellers offer essentially the same product for sale. Fourth, all buyers and sellers know everything there is to know about the market (including, in our example, the prices that all sellers are asking for their wheat). And fifth, the overall market is not affected by the actions of any one buyer or seller.

When perfect competition exists, every seller should ask the same price that every other seller is asking. Why? Because if one seller wanted 50 cents more per bushel of wheat than all the others, that seller would not be able to sell a single bushel. Buyers could—and would—do better by purchasing wheat from the competition. On the other hand, a firm willing to sell below the going price would sell all its wheat quickly. However, that seller would lose sales revenue (and profit) because buyers are actually willing to pay more.

In perfect competition, then, sellers—and buyers as well—must accept the going price. The price of each product is determined by the actions of all buyers and all sellers together through the forces of supply and demand.

perfect (or pure) competition the market situation in which there are many buyers and sellers of a product, and no single buyer or seller is powerful enough to affect the price of that product

supply the quantity of a product that producers are willing to sell at each of various prices

demand the quantity of a product that buyers are willing to purchase at each of various prices

market price the price at which the quantity demanded is exactly equal to the quantity supplied

The Basics of Supply and Demand The **supply** of a particular product is the quantity of the product that producers are willing to sell at each of various prices. Producers are rational people, so we would expect them to offer more of a product for sale at higher prices and to offer less of the product at lower prices, as illustrated by the supply curve in Figure 1.7.

The **demand** for a particular product is the quantity that buyers are willing to purchase at each of various prices. Buyers, too, are usually rational, so we would expect them—as a group—to buy more of a product when its price is low and to buy less of the product when its price is high, as depicted by the demand curve in Figure 1.7.

Competition often equals lower prices. In the very competitive grocery industry, retailers know that nice stores, a wide selection of grocery items, *and* lower prices are all factors that determine where American consumers shop for grocery items.

The Equilibrium, or Market, Price There is always one certain price at which the demanded quantity of a product is exactly equal to the quantity of that product produced. Suppose that producers are willing to *supply* two million bushels of wheat at a price of $6 per bushel and that buyers are willing to *purchase* two million bushels at a price of $6 per bushel. In other words, supply and demand are in balance, or in equilibrium, at the price of $6. Economists call this price the *market price*. The **market price** of any product is the price at which the quantity demanded is exactly equal to the quantity supplied. If suppliers produce two million bushels, then no one who is willing to pay $6 per bushel will have to go without

Figure 1.7 Supply Curve and Demand Curve

The intersection of a supply curve and a demand curve is called the *equilibrium*, or *market, price*. This intersection indicates a single price and quantity at which suppliers will sell products and buyers will purchase them.

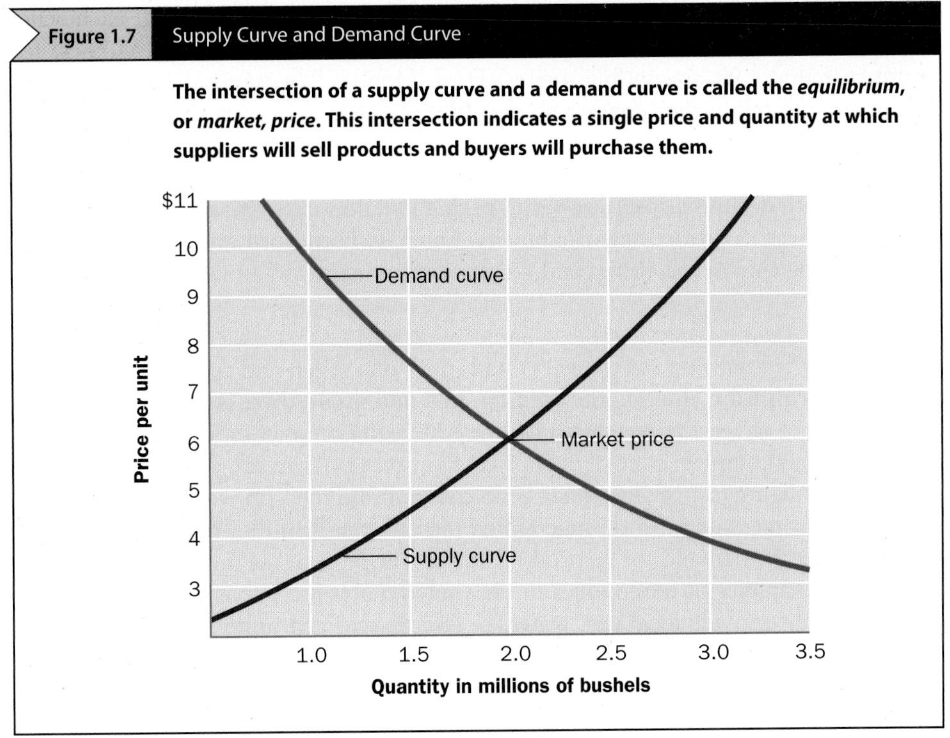

wheat, and no producer who is willing to sell at $6 per bushel will be stuck with unsold wheat.

In theory and in the real world, market prices are affected by anything that affects supply and demand. The *demand* for wheat, for example, might change if researchers suddenly discovered that it offered a previously unknown health benefit. Then buyers would demand more wheat at every price. Or the *supply* of wheat might change if new technology permitted the production of greater quantities of wheat from the same amount of acreage. Other changes that can affect competitive prices are shifts in buyer tastes, the development of new products, fluctuations in income owing to inflation or recession, or even changes in the weather that affect the production of wheat.

Perfect competition is quite rare in today's world. Many real markets, however, are examples of monopolistic competition.

Monopolistic Competition

Monopolistic competition is a market situation in which there are many buyers along with a relatively large number of sellers. The various products available in a monopolistically competitive market are very similar in nature, and they are all intended to satisfy the same need. However, each seller attempts to make its product different from the others by providing unique product features, an attention-getting brand name, unique packaging, or services such as free delivery or a lifetime warranty.

Product differentiation is the process of developing and promoting differences between one's products and all similar products. It is a fact of life for the producers of many consumer goods, from soaps to clothing to furniture to shoes. A furniture manufacturer such as Thomasville sees what looks like a mob of competitors, all trying to chip away at its share of the market. By differentiating each of its products from all similar products produced by competitors, Thomasville obtains some limited control over the market price of its product.

monopolistic competition a market situation in which there are many buyers along with a relatively large number of sellers who differentiate their products from the products of competitors

product differentiation the process of developing and promoting differences between one's products and all similar products

Oligopoly

An **oligopoly** is a market (or industry) situation in which there are few sellers. Generally, these sellers are quite large, and sizable investments are required to enter into their market. Examples of oligopolies are the automobile, airline, car rental, cereal, and farm implement industries.

oligopoly a market (or industry) in which there are few sellers

Because there are few sellers in an oligopoly, the market actions of each seller can have a strong effect on competitors' sales and prices. If General Motors, for example, reduces its automobile prices, Ford, Honda, Toyota, and Nissan usually do the same to retain their market shares. In the absence of much price competition, product differentiation becomes the major competitive weapon; this is very evident in the advertising of the major automobile manufacturers. For instance, when Toyota was faced with declining sales as a result of quality and safety issues, it began offering buyer incentives to attract new-car buyers. Quickly, both Ford and General Motors began offering similar incentives and for the same reason—to attract new-car buyers.

Monopoly

A **monopoly** is a market (or industry) with only one seller, and there are barriers to keep other firms from entering the industry. In a monopoly, there is no close substitute for the product or service. Because only one firm is the supplier of a product, it would seem that it has complete control over price. However, no firm can set its price at some astronomical figure just because there is no competition; the firm would soon find that it has no customers or sales revenue either. Instead, the firm in a monopoly position must consider the demand for its product and set the price at the most profitable level.

Classic examples of monopolies in the United States are public utilities, including companies that provide local gas, water, or electricity. Each utility firm operates in a **natural monopoly**, an industry that requires a huge investment in capital and within which any duplication of facilities would be wasteful. Natural monopolies are permitted to exist because the public interest is best served by their existence, but they operate under the scrutiny and control of various state and federal agencies. Although many public utilities are still classified as natural monopolies, there is increased competition in many industries. For example, there have been increased demands for consumer choice when selecting a company that provides electrical service to both homes and businesses.

A legal monopoly—sometimes referred to as a *limited monopoly*—is created when a government entity issues a franchise, license, copyright, patent, or trademark. For example, a copyright exists for a specific period of time and can be used to protect the owners of written materials from unauthorized use by competitors that have not shared in the time, effort, and expense required for their development. Because Microsoft owns the copyright on its popular Windows software, it enjoys a legal-monopoly position. Except for natural monopolies and legal monopolies, federal antitrust laws prohibit both monopolies and attempts to form monopolies.

6

Summarize the factors that affect the business environment and the challenges that American businesses will encounter in the future.

American Business Today

Although our economic system is far from perfect, it provides Americans with a high standard of living compared with people in other countries throughout the world. **Standard of living** is a loose, subjective measure of how well off an individual or a society is, mainly in terms of want satisfaction through goods and services. Also, our economic system offers solutions to many of the problems that plague society and provides opportunities for people who are willing to work and to continue learning.

To understand the current business environment and the challenges ahead, it helps to understand how business developed.

Early Business Development

Our American business system has its roots in the knowledge, skills, and values that the earliest settlers brought to this country. Refer to Figure 1.8 for an overall view of our nation's history, the development of our business system, and some major inventions that influenced the nation and our business system.

The first settlers in the New World were concerned mainly with providing themselves with basic necessities—food, clothing, and shelter. Almost all families lived on farms, and the entire family worked at the business of surviving. They used their surplus for trading, mainly by barter, among themselves and with the English trading

monopoly a market (or industry) with only one seller, and there are barriers to keep other firms from entering the industry

natural monopoly an industry requiring huge investments in capital and within which any duplication of facilities would be wasteful and thus not in the public interest

standard of living a loose, subjective measure of how well off an individual or a society is, mainly in terms of want satisfaction through goods and services

Figure 1.8 Time Line of American Business

Throughout the history of the United States, invention and innovation have led naturally to change and a more industrialized economy.

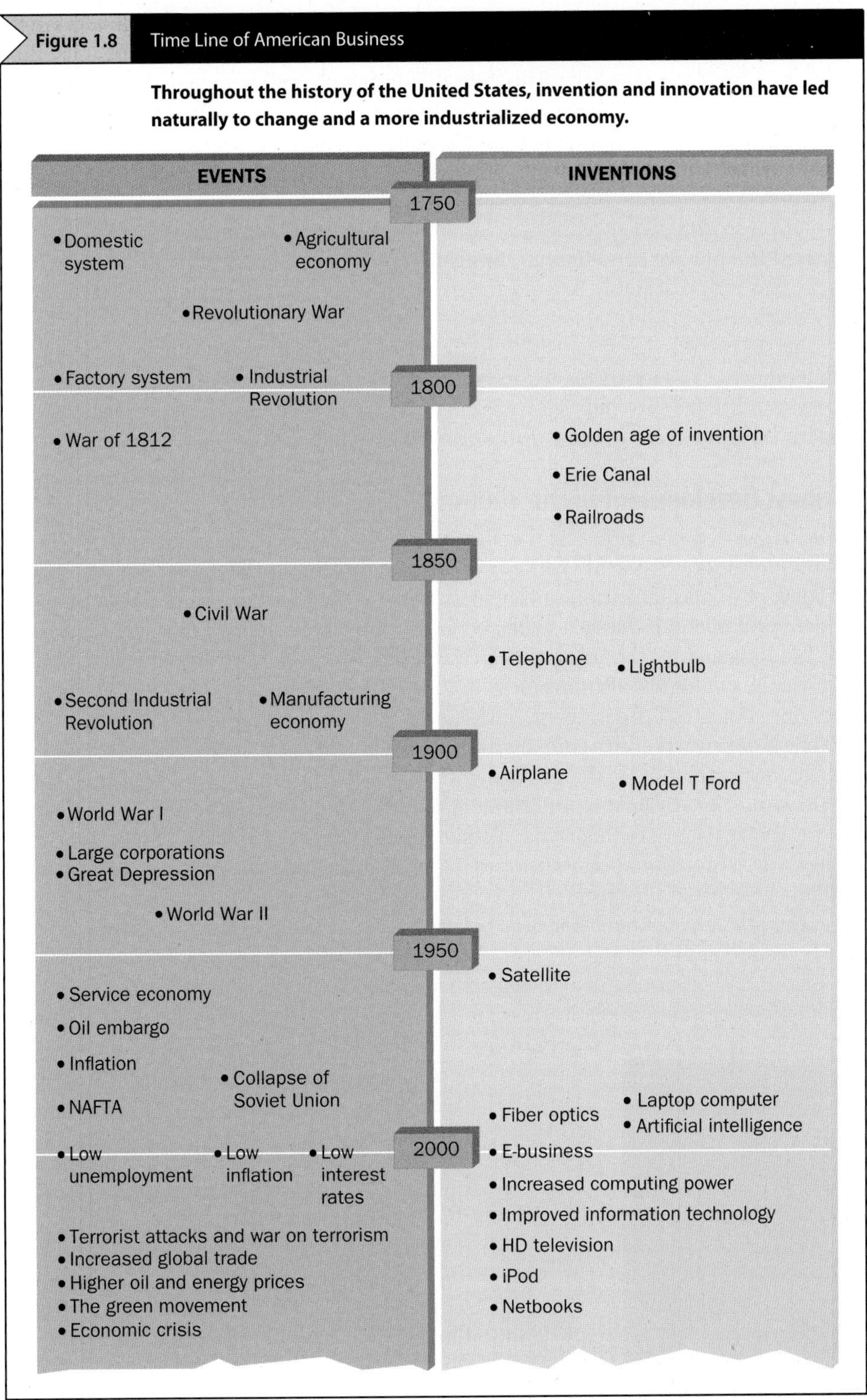

ships that called at the colonies. **Barter** is a system of exchange in which goods or services are traded directly for other goods or services without using money. As this trade increased, small-scale business enterprises began to appear. Some settlers were able to use their skills and their excess time to work under the domestic system of production. The **domestic system** was a method of manufacturing in which an entrepreneur distributed raw materials to various homes, where families would process them into finished goods. The merchant entrepreneur then offered the goods for sale.

Then, in 1789, a young English apprentice mechanic named Samuel Slater decided to sail to America. At this time, British law forbade the export of machinery,

barter a system of exchange in which goods or services are traded directly for other goods or services without using money

domestic system a method of manufacturing in which an entrepreneur distributes raw materials to various homes, where families process them into finished goods to be offered for sale by the merchant entrepreneur

technology, and skilled workers. To get around the law, Slater painstakingly memorized the plans for Richard Arkwright's water-powered spinning machine, which had revolutionized the British textile industry, and left England disguised as a farmer. A year later, he set up a textile factory in Pawtucket, Rhode Island, to spin raw cotton into thread. Slater's ingenuity resulted in America's first use of the **factory system** of manufacturing, in which all the materials, machinery, and workers required to manufacture a product are assembled in one place. The Industrial Revolution in America was born. A manufacturing technique called *specialization* was used to improve productivity. **Specialization** is the separation of a manufacturing process into distinct tasks and the assignment of the different tasks to different individuals.

The years from 1820 to 1900 were the golden age of invention and innovation in machinery. At the same time, new means of transportation greatly expanded the domestic markets for American products. Certainly, many characteristics of our modern business system took form during this time period.

Business Development in the 1900s

Industrial growth and prosperity continued well into the 20th century. Henry Ford's moving automotive assembly line, which brought the work to the worker, refined the concept of specialization and helped spur on the mass production of consumer goods. Fundamental changes occurred in business ownership and management as well. No longer were the largest businesses owned by one individual; instead, ownership was in the hands of thousands of corporate shareholders who were willing to invest in—but not to operate—a business.

The Roaring Twenties ended with the sudden crash of the stock market in 1929 and the near collapse of the economy. The Great Depression that followed in the 1930s was a time of misery and human suffering. People lost their faith in business and its ability to satisfy the needs of society without government involvement. After Franklin D. Roosevelt became president in 1933, the federal government devised a number of programs to get the economy moving again. In implementing these programs, the government got deeply involved in business for the first time.

To understand the major events that shaped the United States during the remainder of the 20th century, it helps to remember that the economy was compared to a roller coaster ride earlier in this chapter—periods of economic growth followed by periods of economic slowdown. Major events that shaped the nation's economy occurred during the period from 1940 to 2000:

- World War II, the Korean War, and the Vietnam War
- Rapid economic growth and higher standard of living during the 1950s and 1960s
- The social responsibility movement during the 1960s
- A shortage of crude oil and higher prices for most goods in the mid-1970s
- High inflation, high interest rates, and reduced business profits during the early 1980s
- Sustained economic growth in the 1990s

During the last part of the 20th century, the Internet became a major force in the economy, with computer hardware, software, and Internet service providers taking advantage of the increased need for information. e-Business—a topic we will continue to explore throughout this text—became an accepted method of conducting business. **e-Business** is the organized effort of individuals to produce and sell *through the Internet,* for a profit, the products and services that satisfy society's needs.

factory system a system of manufacturing in which all the materials, machinery, and workers required to manufacture a product are assembled in one place

specialization the separation of a manufacturing process into distinct tasks and the assignment of the different tasks to different individuals

e-business the organized effort of individuals to produce and sell *through the Internet*, for a profit, the products and services that satisfy society's needs

No one likes to wait in line. For an industrialized economy like the United States economy, crude oil is an essential natural resource. When the nation experienced a shortage of crude oil during the mid-1970s, people were forced to wait in line to buy gasoline for their cars. In addition to higher prices for gasoline and goods produced from petroleum, there was also an increase in transportation costs for finished goods.

Unfortunately, by the last part of the 20th century, a larger number of business failures and declining stock values were initial signs that larger economic problems were on the way.

A New Century: 2000 and Beyond

According to many economic experts, the time period from 2000 to 2010 might be characterized as the best of times and the worst of times rolled into one package. On the plus side, technology became available at an affordable price. Both individuals and businesses could now access information with the click of a button. They also could buy and sell merchandise online.

In addition to information technology, the growth of service businesses also changed the way American firms do business in the 21st century. Because service businesses employ approximately 85 percent of the nation's workforce, we now have a service economy.[16] A **service economy** is an economy in which more effort is devoted to the production of services than to the production of goods. Typical service businesses include restaurants, laundries and dry cleaners, real estate, movie theaters, repair companies, and other services that we often take for granted. In fact, when you look at where you spend your money, there is a good chance that a great deal of cash goes to the service sector of the economy. Because of the importance of this type of business, service businesses must find ways to improve productivity and cut costs while providing jobs for an even larger portion of the workforce. More information about how service businesses affect the economy is provided in Chapter 8, Producing Quality Goods and Services.

On the negative side, it is hard to watch television, surf the Web, listen to the radio, or read the newspaper without hearing some news about the economy. Because many of the economic indicators described in Table 1.2 on page 19 indicate troubling economic problems, there is still a certain amount of pessimism surrounding the economy.

The Current Business Environment

Before reading on, answer the following question:

In today's competitive business world, which of the following environments affects business?

a. The competitive environment
b. The global environment
c. The technological environment
d. The economic environment
e. All of the above

The correct answer is "e." All the environments listed affect business today. For example, businesses operate in a *competitive environment.* As noted earlier in this chapter, competition is a basic component of capitalism. Every day, business owners must figure out what makes their businesses successful and how their businesses are different from the competition. Often, the answer is contained in the basic definition of business provided on page 10. Just for a moment, review the definition:

Business is the organized effort of individuals to produce and sell, for a profit, the goods and services that satisfy society's needs.

Note the phrase *satisfy society's needs.* These three words say a lot about how well a successful firm competes with competitors. If you meet customer needs, then you have a better chance at success.

Related to the competitive environment is the *global environment.* Not only do American businesses have to compete with other American businesses, but they also must compete with businesses from all over the globe. According to global experts, China is the fastest-growing economy in the world. And China is not alone. Other countries around the world also compete with U.S. firms. There was once a time when the label "Made in the United States" gave U.S. businesses

service economy an economy in which more effort is devoted to the production of services than to the production of goods

Sustaining the Planet

How the Sun and Earth Help Frito-Lay

Frito-Lay is one of many businesses moving toward sustainability by putting the sun and Earth to work. Every day, it produces 145,000 bags of SunChips in its solar-powered Modesto, California, plant and packages the chips in eco-friendly bags that can be composted into soil instead of taking up space in landfills. Take a look: http://sunchips.com/healthier_planet.shtml.

an inside edge both at home and in the global marketplace. Now, other countries manufacture and sell goods. According to Richard Haass, president of the Council on Foreign Relations, "There will be winners and losers from globalization. We win every time we go shopping because prices are lower. Choice is greater because of globalization. But there are losers. There are people who will lose their jobs either to foreign competition or [to] technological innovation."[17]

Although both increased competition and technological innovation have changed the way we do business, the *technology environment* for U.S. businesses has never been more challenging. Although many of us take technological change for granted, it does change the way we do business. Changes in manufacturing equipment, communication with customers, and distribution of products are all examples of how technology has changed everyday business practices. Technology will continue to change. New technology will require businesses to spend additional money to keep abreast of an ever-changing technology environment and even more money to train employees to use the new technology.

In addition to the competitive, global, and technology environments, the *economic environment* must always be considered when making business decisions. Although many people believe that business has unlimited resources, the truth is that managers and business owners realize that there is never enough money to fund all the activities a business might want to fund. This fact is especially important when the nation's economy takes a nosedive or an individual firm's sales revenue and profits are declining. For example, both small and large business firms reduced both spending and hiring new employees over the last two years because of economic concerns related to the depressed housing, automotive, banking, and financial industries.

In addition to economic pressures, today's socially responsible managers and business owners must be concerned about the concept of sustainability. According to the U.S. Environmental Protection Agency, **sustainability** means meeting the needs of the present without compromising the ability of future generations to meet their own needs.[18] Although the word *green* used to mean a simple color in a box of crayons, today green means a new way of doing business. As a result, a combination of forces, including economic factors, growth in population, increased energy use, and concerns for the environment, is changing the way individuals live and businesses operate.

sustainability meeting the needs of the present without compromising the ability of future generations to meet their own needs

When you look back at the original question we asked at the beginning of this section, clearly, each different type of environment—competitive, global, technological, and economic—affects the way a business does *business*. As a result, there are always opportunities for improvement and challenges that must be considered.

The Challenges Ahead

There it is—the American business system in brief.

When it works well, it provides jobs for those who are willing to work, a standard of living that few countries can match, and many opportunities for personal advancement. However, like every other system devised by humans, it is not perfect. Our business system may give us prosperity, but it also gave us the Great Depression of the 1930s, the economic problems of the 1970s and the early 1980s, and the economic crisis that began in the fall of 2007.

Obviously, the system can be improved. Certainly, there are plenty of people who are willing to tell us exactly what they think the American economy needs. However, these people provide us only with conflicting opinions. Who is right and who is wrong? Even the experts cannot agree.

The experts do agree, however, that several key issues will challenge our economic system (and our nation) over the next decade. Some of the questions to be resolved include:

- How can we create a more stable economy and create new jobs for the unemployed?
- How can we regulate banks, savings and loan associations, credit unions, and other financial institutions to prevent the type of abuses that led to the banking crisis?
- How do we reduce the national debt and still maintain a healthy economy and stimulate business growth?
- How can we make American workers more productive and American firms more competitive in the global marketplace?
- How can we preserve the benefits of competition and small business in our American economic system?
- How can we encourage economic growth and at the same time continue to conserve natural resources and sustain our environment?
- How can we meet the needs of two-income families, single parents, older Americans, and the less fortunate who need health care and social programs to exist?
- How can we meet the challenges of managing culturally diverse workforces to address the needs of a culturally diverse marketplace?
- How can we defeat terrorism and resolve conflict with Iran, North Korea, and other countries throughout the world?

The answers to these questions are anything but simple. In the past, Americans have always been able to solve their economic problems through ingenuity and creativity. Now, as we continue the journey through the 21st century, we need that same ingenuity and creativity not only to solve our current problems but also to compete in the global marketplace and build a nation and economy for future generations.

According to economic experts, if we as a nation can become more competitive, we may solve many of our current economic problems. As an added bonus, increased competitiveness will also enable us to meet the social challenges we are currently facing. The way we solve these problems will affect our own future, our children's future, and that of our nation. Within the American economic and political system, the answers are ours to provide.

The American business system is not perfect by any means, but it does work reasonably well. We discuss some of its problems in Chapter 2 as we examine the topics of social responsibility and business ethics.

return to inside business

Amazon

When Amazon opened its virtual doors in 1995, founder Jeff Bezos had ambitious plans for building the world's biggest, best, and most customer-friendly online bookstore. The Web was still new and uncharted territory for businesses, and Amazon was breaking new ground by inviting customers to post their own book reviews and allowing them to buy with one click.

Within two years of its founding, Amazon had served millions of customers and raised millions of dollars for expansion by going public and selling corporate stock. Yet the company did not achieve profitability for several more years because Bezos was continually reinvesting in upgraded technology to enhance the customer experience and build the business. Moving into innovative products such as the Kindle helped Amazon write a new chapter in its success story. Can the company maintain its sales and profit momentum in the coming years?

Questions

1. Of the environments that affect the business world, which have had the most significant effect on Amazon?
2. During a recent year, Amazon's earnings topped $900 million. Why do you think this online retailer is profitable? What actions must management take to continue to earn record profits?

CHAPTER REVIEW

SUMMARY

Summary

1 Discuss what you must do to be successful in the world of business.

For many years, people in business—both employees and managers—assumed that prosperity would continue. When faced with both economic problems and increased competition, a large number of these people began to ask the question: What do we do now? Although this is a fair question, it is difficult to answer. Certainly, for a college student taking business courses or an employee just starting a career, the question is even more difficult to answer. And yet there are still opportunities out there for people who are willing to work hard, continue to learn, and possess the ability to adapt to change. To be sure, employers and our capitalistic economic system are more demanding than ever before. As you begin this course, ask yourself: What can I do that will make employers want to pay me a salary? What skills do I have that employers need? The kind of career you choose ultimately will depend on your own values and what you feel is most important in life. But deciding on the kind of career you want is only a first step. To get a job in your chosen field and to be successful at it, you will have to develop a plan, or a road map, that ensures that you have the necessary skills and the knowledge the job requires to become a better employee or manager. By studying business, you may also decide to start your own business and become a better consumer and investor.

2 Define *business* and identify potential risks and rewards.

Business is the organized effort of individuals to produce and sell, for a profit, the goods and services that satisfy society's needs. Four kinds of resources—material, human, financial, and informational—must be combined to start and operate a business. The three general types of businesses are manufacturers, service businesses, and marketing intermediaries. Profit is what remains after all business expenses are deducted from sales revenue. It is the payment that owners receive for assuming the risks of business—primarily the risks of not receiving payment and of losing whatever has been invested in the firm. Although many people believe that profit is literally the bottom line or most important goal for a business, many corporations are careful to point out their efforts to sustain the planet, participate in the green ecological movement, and help people to live better lives. The fact is that most business firms that are socially responsible feel that it is the right thing to do and is good for business.

3 Define *economics* and describe the two types of economic systems: capitalism and command economy.

Economics is the study of how wealth is created and distributed. An economic system must answer four questions: What goods and services will be produced?

How will they be produced? For whom will they be produced? Who owns and who controls the major factors of production? Capitalism (on which our economic system is based) is an economic system in which individuals own and operate the majority of businesses that provide goods and services. Capitalism stems from the theories of Adam Smith. Smith's pure Laissez-Faire capitalism is an economic system in which the factors of production are owned by private entities and all individuals are free to use their resources as they see fit; prices are determined by the workings of supply and demand in competitive markets; and the economic role of government is limited to rule maker and umpire. In his book *Wealth of Nations,* Smith argued that a society's interests are best served when the individuals within that society are allowed to pursue their own self-interest. Smith used the term *invisible hand* to describe how an individual's own personal gain benefits others and a nation's economy.

Our economic system today is a mixed economy. In the circular flow that characterizes our business system (see Figure 1.5), households and businesses exchange resources for goods and services, using money as the medium of exchange. In a similar manner, the government collects taxes from businesses and households and purchases products and resources with which to provide services.

In a command economy, government, rather than individuals, owns many of the factors of production and provides the answers to the three other economic questions. Socialist and communist economies are—at least in theory—command economies.

4 Identify the ways to measure economic performance.

One way to evaluate the performance of an economic system is to assess changes in productivity, which is the average level of output per worker per hour. Gross domestic product (GDP) can also be used to measure a nation's economic well-being and is the total dollar value of all goods and services produced by all people within the boundaries of a country during a one-year period. This figure facilitates comparisons between the United States and other countries because it is the standard used in international guidelines for economic accounting. It is also possible to adjust GDP for inflation and thus to measure real GDP. In addition to GDP, other economic indicators include a nation's balance of trade, bank credit, corporate profits, consumer price index (CPI), inflation rate, national income, new housing starts, prime interest rate, producer price index (PPI), and unemployment rate.

A nation's economy fluctuates rather than grows at a steady pace every year. These fluctuations are generally referred to as the business cycle. Generally, the business cycle consists of four states: the peak, recession, the trough, and recovery. Some experts believe that effective use of monetary policy (the Federal Reserve's decisions that determine the size of the supply of money and the level of interest rates) and fiscal policy (the government's influence on the amount of savings and expenditures) can speed up recovery.

5 Outline the four types of competition.

Competition is essentially a rivalry among businesses for sales to potential customers. In a capitalist economy, competition works to ensure the efficient and effective operation of business. Competition also ensures that a firm will survive only if it serves its customers well by providing products and services that meet their needs. Economists recognize four degrees of competition. Ranging from most to least competitive, the four degrees are perfect competition, monopolistic competition, oligopoly, and monopoly. The factors of supply and demand generally influence the price that customers pay producers for goods and services.

6 Summarize the factors that affect the business environment and the challenges that American businesses will encounter in the future.

From the beginning, through the Industrial Revolution of the early 19th century, and to the phenomenal expansion of American industry in the 19th and early 20th centuries, our government maintained an essentially Laissez-Faire attitude toward business. However, during the Great Depression of the 1930s, the federal government began to provide a number of social services to its citizens. The government's role in business has expanded considerably since then.

To understand the major events that shaped the United States during the remainder of the 20th century, it helps to remember that the economy was compared to a roller coaster ride earlier in this chapter—periods of economic growth followed by periods of economic slowdown. Events including wars, rapid economic growth, the social responsibility movement, a shortage of crude oil, high inflation, high interest rates, and reduced business profits all have affected business and the economy.

Now more than ever before, the way a business operates is affected by the competitive environment, global environment, technological environment, and economic environment. As a result, business has a number of opportunities for improvement and challenges for the future.

Key Terms

You should now be able to define and give an example relevant to each of the following terms:

free enterprise (4)
cultural (or workplace) diversity (6)
business (10)
profit (11)
stakeholders (11)
economics (12)
microeconomics (12)
macroeconomics (12)
economy (12)
factors of production (12)
entrepreneur (13)
capitalism (13)
invisible hand (14)
market economy (14)
mixed economy (15)
consumer products (15)
command economy (16)
productivity (17)
gross domestic product (GDP) (18)
inflation (18)
deflation (18)
unemployment rate (18)
consumer price index (CPI) (19)
producer price index (PPI) (19)
business cycle (20)
recession (20)
depression (20)
monetary policies (21)
fiscal policy (21)
federal deficit (21)
national debt (21)
competition (21)
perfect (or pure) competition (22)
supply (22)
demand (22)
market price (22)
monopolistic competition (23)
product differentiation (23)
oligopoly (23)
monopoly (24)
natural monopoly (24)
standard of living (24)
barter (25)
domestic system (25)
factory system (26)
specialization (26)
e-business (26)
service economy (27)
sustainability (28)

Review Questions

1. What reasons would you give if you were advising someone to study business?
2. What factors affect a person's choice of careers?
3. Describe the four resources that must be combined to organize and operate a business. How do they differ from the economist's factors of production?
4. Describe the relationship among profit, business risk, and the satisfaction of customers' needs.
5. What are the four basic economic questions? How are they answered in a capitalist economy?
6. Explain the invisible hand of capitalism.
7. Describe the four basic assumptions required for a Laissez-Faire capitalist economy.
8. Why is the American economy called a mixed economy?
9. Based on Figure 1.5, outline the economic interactions between business and households in our business system.
10. How does capitalism differ from socialism and communism?
11. How is productivity related to the unemployment rate?
12. Define gross domestic product. Why is this economic measure significant?
13. How is the producer price index related to the consumer price index?
14. What are the four steps in a typical business cycle? How are monetary and fiscal policies related to the business cycle?
15. Choose three of the economic measures described in Table 1.2 and describe why these indicators are important when measuring a nation's economy.
16. Identify and compare the four forms of competition.
17. Explain how the equilibrium, or market, price of a product is determined.
18. Four different environments that affect business were described in this chapter. Choose one of the environments and explain how it affects a small electronics manufacturer located in Oregon. Why?

Discussion Questions

1. In what ways have the economic problems caused by the recent crisis in the banking and financial industries affected business firms? In what ways have these problems affected employees and individuals?
2. What factors caused American business to develop into a mixed economic system rather than some other type of economic system?
3. Does an individual consumer really have a voice in answering the basic economic questions?
4. Is gross domestic product a reliable indicator of a nation's economic health? What might be a better indicator?
5. Discuss this statement: "Business competition encourages efficiency of production and leads to improved product quality."
6. In our business system, how is government involved in answering the four basic economic questions? Does government participate in the system or interfere with it?
7. Choose one of the challenges listed on page 29 and describe possible ways in which business and society could help to solve or eliminate the problem in the future.

Video Case 1.1

Entertainment Means Profits for Nederlander Concerts

Nederlander Concerts is based in Los Angeles, one of the two biggest markets in the U.S. concert industry (New York is the other). The company specializes in booking and promoting musical artists like the Goo Goo Dolls, Maroon 5, and Cyndi Lauper in small- to mid-sized venues across the western United States. It owns some of the theaters, amphitheaters, and arenas, including the Greek Theatre in Los Angeles, the Santa Barbara Bowl, the San Jose Civic Theater, and the Grove in Anaheim, and it rents space for concerts and events in other third-party venues along the West Coast. Nederlander Concerts also partners with some of California's major cities such as Santa Monica and San Jose to manage or operate their civic theaters and present events there.

Since Nederlander Concerts deliberately focuses on small- to mid-sized venues, it can offer a unique concert experience that brings audiences and performers closer together. It can therefore sell that high-quality experience at a higher price than seats in a bigger theater yield, and it can more often count on selling out the house, which helps the company and the artists to profit. The concert company's chief operating officer says, "The key areas or departments of the company include talent-buying and marketing, operations, finance, and business development. . . I have a talent-buying team, I have a marketing team, we have a general manager of the building, we have a substantial team of people who take care of the fans, take care of the artist, and look after the shows that we buy. We're in a competitive market, and it's pretty interesting what we do."

Although it might seem odd that the concert business is a competitive one, in fact Nederlander Concerts competes with other promoters (like Live Nation) not just for audiences at its events but for bookings by popular artists. Therefore, it counts as its clients or customers musicians as well as music lovers, and the performers need to be happy with the financial deal they are getting. As Nederlander's chief operating officer explains, "It's not always easy to get the show; there is competition. . . . We have a great reputation with the artist. But also there's one other factor, and that's making the deal. That's making your best offer. That's trying to think about whether the agent is . . . telling you that your competition is paying more, willing to go more. You have to get your own 'I won't go above' number and stop bidding (for the act), or you have to say, 'Okay, I'll pay a little bit more and try to get the show.' So there's a real gamesmanship between agent and buyer . . . the art of the deal is something we live with every day."

Given the talent, how does Nederlander find the audience? Says its vice president of marketing, "It's learning about the market, and picking up every newspaper you can find, listening to every radio station you can find, watching all of the TV, all the news programming . . . it still comes back to, who is the artist, and who is their audience? And how do you find them? . . . The number one reason why people don't go to a show, so they say, is that they don't know about it. Which is infuriating. But we just try to make that percentage of people . . . smaller, and smaller, and smaller."

When everything is going well, the company profits. "Where we like to do most of our business, and in fact is where we probably do 90 percent of our business, is in the venues that we own or operate, so that the risk profile of those shows goes down . . . we have more revenues coming in to ensure that we're able to cover the cost, including the cost of talent, and then walk away with a greater profit."[19]

Questions

1. Nederlander Concerts competes for audiences and with other concert arenas and promoters. Do you think it also competes for those audiences with TV, movies, CDs, DVDs, streaming video, and sports events? Why or why not? If yes, what implications does this type of competition have for Nederlander's business?
2. How many different groups can you think of whose needs Nederlander Concerts must satisfy to remain a successful business?
3. Give an example showing how Nederlander Concerts uses each of the four factors of production.

Case 1.2

Caterpillar Helps the World Build

From tractors to turbines, marine engines to mining equipment, Caterpillar makes the heavy equipment that powers progress and helps the world build. Formed in 1925 from the merger of two tractor manufacturers, Caterpillar has grown from its headquarters in Peoria, Illinois, into a successful $32 billion corporation with 110 factories and business operations in 23 countries. It also offers financing, insurance, and other services for dealers and business customers that buy its industrial products.

Caterpillar's sales contribute to the global economy by creating jobs for 94,000 in the company (including 44,000 employees located in North America) as well as for tens of thousands of workers employed by its network of suppliers and dealers. At the same time, Caterpillar's sales are affected, in large part, by local, regional, and international economic conditions. When the economy is expanding, customers such as construction firms need earthmoving equipment to tackle major projects, such as new housing, highways, pipelines, and mass transit systems. They also need demolition equipment, which Caterpillar makes, to clear the way for new projects.

During recessions, however, companies and governments often postpone or go slow on these types of projects, which in turn dampens demand for earthmovers and similar machinery. Still, Caterpillar has profited from the ongoing building boom in developing nations, where many infrastructure improvements move ahead regardless of what's happening in the rest of the world. These days, 69 percent of its sales come from outside the United States, up from 53 percent of sales just five years ago. Not surprisingly, Caterpillar's main competition in the global marketplace comes from multinational giants, such as Komatsu (based in Japan), CNH Global (based in the Netherlands), and Volvo (based in Sweden).

Before Caterpillar builds a new factory, it carefully researches the market. Recently, for example, it undertook a study of regional and global demand for excavating equipment. Although Caterpillar already operates excavator factories in the United States, Japan, and six other countries, it may open a new U.S. plant to serve all of North America if demand is strong enough. Instead of importing some models from its factory in Japan, as it does now, Caterpillar would make those products in the U.S. plant and have the Japanese facility make models that sell well in Asia.

Stepping up to sustainability, Caterpillar is going green on a global scale. It is constantly improving the efficiency of its products, reducing its use of power, doing more to recycle materials and cut waste, and finding new uses for old products. The company also offers training to help customers cut the amount of fuel they need to power their Caterpillar equipment, which saves users money as well as helps conserve scarce resources.

As a good corporate citizen, Caterpillar makes donations to non-profit organizations that support educational, health, and human services projects. It also contributes to environmental conservation organizations that protect natural resources and enhance sustainability around the world. Through the Caterpillar Employees United Way Appeal, the company and its employees make yearly donations to United Way groups in their local communities.

Caterpillar's managers and employees are required to follow the company's worldwide code of conduct in all their business dealings with suppliers, dealers, customers, and competitors. The code sets high standards for honest, ethical behavior; outlines how Caterpillar deals with potential conflicts of interest; and strictly forbids the use of "improper payments" such as bribes and kickbacks. Here's how the company sums up its commitment to being a responsible business: "We are global citizens and responsible members of our communities who are dedicated to safety, care for our environment, and manage our business ethically."[20]

Questions

1. How is Caterpillar using the factors of production to fuel global growth?
2. How would you characterize Caterpillar's competitive situation? What are the implications for how it does business?
3. What factors in the business environment appear to have the most influence on Caterpillar's ability to continue its business success? Explain.

Building Skills for Career Success

❶ JOURNALING FOR SUCCESS

Much of the information in this chapter was designed to get you to think about what it takes to be a successful employee in the competitive business world.

Assignment

Assume that you are now 25 years old and are interviewing for a position as a management trainee in a large corporation. Also assume that this position pays $45,000 a year.

1. Describe what steps you would take to prepare for this interview.
2. Assuming that you get the management trainee position, describe the personal traits or skills that you have that will help you to become successful.
3. Describe the one personal skill or trait that you feel needs improvement. How would you go about improving your weakness?

❷ EXPLORING THE INTERNET

The Internet is a global network of computers that can be accessed by anyone in the world. For example, your school or firm is most likely connected to the Web. You probably have access through a commercial service provider such as AT&T, Yahoo!, or a host of other smaller Internet service providers.

To familiarize yourself with the wealth of information available through the Internet and its usefulness to business students, this exercise focuses on information services available from a few popular search engines used to explore the Web.

To use one of these search engines, enter its Internet address in your Web browser. The addresses of some popular search engines are

http://www.ask.com
http://www.google.com
http://www.msn.com
http://www.yahoo.com

Visit the text Web site for updates to this exercise.

Assignment

1. Examine the ways in which two search engines present categories of information on their opening screens. Which search engine was better to use in your opinion? Why?
2. Think of a business topic that you would like to know more about; for example, careers, gross domestic product, or another concept introduced in this chapter. Using your preferred search engine, explore a few articles and reports provided on your topic. Briefly summarize your findings.

❸ DEVELOPING CRITICAL-THINKING SKILLS

Under capitalism, competition is a driving force that allows the market economy to work, affecting the supply of goods and services in the marketplace and the prices consumers pay for those goods and services. Let's see how competition works by pretending that you want to buy a new car.

Assignment

1. Brainstorm the following questions:
   a. Where would you go to get information about new cars?
   b. How will you decide on the make and model of car you want to buy, where to buy the car, and how to finance it?
   c. How is competition at work in this scenario?
   d. What are the pros and cons of competition as it affects the buyer?
2. Record your ideas.
3. Write a summary of the key points you learned about how competition works in the marketplace.

❹ BUILDING TEAM SKILLS

Over the past few years, employees have been expected to function as productive team members instead of working alone. People often believe that they can work effectively in teams, but many people find working with a group of people to be a challenge. Being an effective team member requires skills that encourage other members to participate in the team endeavor.

College classes that function as teams are more interesting and more fun to attend, and students generally learn more about the topics in the course. If your class is to function as a team, it is important to begin building the team early in the semester. One way to begin creating a team is to learn something about each student in the class. This helps team members to feel comfortable with each other and fosters a sense of trust.

Assignment

1. Find a partner, preferably someone you do not know.
2. Each partner has two to three minutes to answer the following questions:
   a. What is your name, and where do you work?
   b. What interesting or unusual thing have you done in your life? (Do not talk about work or college; rather, focus on such things as hobbies, travel, family, and sports.)
   c. Why are you taking this course, and what do you expect to learn? (Satisfying a degree requirement is not an acceptable answer.)
3. Introduce your partner to the class. Use one to two minutes, depending on the size of the class.

❺ RESEARCHING DIFFERENT CAREERS

In this chapter, *entrepreneurship* is defined as the willingness to take risks and the knowledge and ability to use the other factors of production efficiently. An *entrepreneur* is a person who risks his or her time, effort, and money to start and operate a business. Often, people believe that these terms apply only to small business. However, employees with entrepreneurial attitudes have recently advanced more rapidly in large companies as well.

Assignment

1. Go to the local library or use the Internet to research how large firms, especially corporations, are rewarding employees who have entrepreneurial skills.
2. Find answers to the following questions:
   a. Why is an entrepreneurial attitude important in corporations today?
   b. What makes an entrepreneurial employee different from other employees?
   c. How are these employees being rewarded, and are the rewards worth the effort?
3. Write a two-page report that summarizes your findings.

2 Being Ethical and Socially Responsible

© AP Images/PRNewsFoto/Marshall & Ilsley Corporation

Learning Objectives

What you will be able to do once you complete this chapter:

1. Understand what is meant by *business ethics*.
2. Identify the types of ethical concerns that arise in the business world.
3. Discuss the factors that affect the level of ethical behavior in organizations.
4. Explain how ethical decision making can be encouraged.
5. Describe how our current views on the social responsibility of business have evolved.
6. Explain the two views on the social responsibility of business and understand the arguments for and against increased social responsibility.
7. Discuss the factors that led to the consumer movement and list some of its results.
8. Analyze how present employment practices are being used to counteract past abuses.
9. Describe the major types of pollution, their causes, and their cures.
10. Identify the steps a business must take to implement a program of social responsibility.

FYI

inside business

Did You Know?

Divine Chocolate, which makes premium chocolate bars, is partly owned by 45,000 Fairtrade cocoa growers in Ghana.

Divine Chocolate's Recipe for Sales and Social Responsibility

Divine Chocolate has cooked up an unusual yet highly effective recipe for sales success and social responsibility. Competing against global giants such as Nestlé and Mars, Divine Chocolate has not only made a name for itself in the world of premium chocolate but has also improved the lives of thousands of cocoa farmers throughout Ghana.

The company's roots go back to the mid-1990s, when Ghana's government began allowing local companies to buy locally produced cocoa for resale in world markets. Seeing this as an opportunity to improve profits by banding together, several hundred small producers united in a cooperative association they named Kuapa Kokoo (good cocoa growers). Soon Kuapa Kokoo was certified to supply Fairtrade cocoa, meaning the growers were meeting high standards for cocoa quality, using earth-friendly production methods, and complying with requirements for safe and healthy working conditions.

Once Kuapa Kokoo's growers had achieved Fairtrade certification, they were guaranteed above-market prices for their cocoa beans. Members voted to use the extra money for digging new wells, opening day-care facilities, and funding other projects in their villages. The group also reinvested to build the business by expanding warehousing and conducting agricultural education programs for members. As word of Kuapa Kokoo's accomplishments spread, thousands of new members joined, which in turn brought the financial and social benefits to additional villages.

By 1998, Kuapa Kokoo was ready to embark on an even more ambitious business venture. With investments from several sources—including a trading company and the socially responsible Body Shop retail chain—the group formed Day Chocolate, based in London, to manufacture and market premium Divine Chocolate bars using the growers' finest Fairtrade cocoa. Because Kuapa Kokoo was part-owner, its members received a share of the profits from each Divine Chocolate bar sold.

In 2007, the U.K. company changed its name to Divine Chocolate and secured investments to start a new business in the United States. Like its U.K. counterpart, the U.S. Divine Chocolate began selling its Fairtrade chocolate bars through specialty food stores and upscale supermarkets. Today Kuapa Kokoo's 45,000 members produce 10 percent of Ghana's cocoa exports, and the profits from sales of Divine Chocolate are making a real difference to members in more than 1,200 villages.[1]

Obviously, organizations like Divine Chocolate want to be recognized as responsible corporate citizens. Such companies recognize the need to harmonize their operations with environmental demands and other vital social concerns. Not all firms, however, have taken steps to encourage a consideration of social responsibility and ethics in their decisions and day-to-day activities. Some managers still regard such business practices as a poor investment, in which the cost is not worth the return. Other managers—indeed, most managers—view the cost of these practices as a necessary business expense, similar to wages or rent.

Most managers today, like those at Divine Chocolate, are finding ways to balance a growing agenda of socially responsible activities with the drive to generate profits. This also happens to be a good way for a company to demonstrate its values and to attract like-minded employees, customers, and stockholders. In a highly competitive business environment, an increasing number of companies are, like Divine Chocolate, seeking to set themselves apart by developing a reputation for ethical and socially responsible behavior.

We begin this chapter by defining *business ethics* and examining ethical issues. Next, we look at the standards of behavior in organizations and how ethical behavior can be encouraged. We then turn to the topic of social responsibility. We compare and contrast two present-day models of social responsibility and present arguments for and against increasing the social responsibility of business. We then examine the major elements of the consumer movement. We discuss how social responsibility in business has affected employment practices and environmental concerns. Finally, we consider the commitment, planning, and funding that go into a firm's program of social responsibility.

Business Ethics Defined

1

Understand what is meant by *business ethics.*

Ethics is the study of right and wrong and of the morality of the choices individuals make. An ethical decision or action is one that is "right" according to some standard of behavior. **Business ethics** is the application of moral standards to business situations. Recent court cases involving unethical behavior have helped to make business ethics a matter of public concern. In one such case, Copley Pharmaceutical, Inc., pled guilty to federal criminal charges (and paid a $10.65 million fine) for falsifying drug manufacturers' reports to the Food and Drug Administration. In another much-publicized case, lawsuits against tobacco companies have led to $246 billion in settlements, although there has been only one class-action lawsuit filed on behalf of all smokers. The case, *Engle v. R. J. Reynolds*, could cost tobacco companies an estimated $500 billion. In yet another case, Adelphia Communications Corp., the nation's fifth-largest cable television company, agreed to pay $715 million to settle federal investigations stemming from rampant earnings manipulation by its founder John J. Rigas, and his son, Timothy J. Rigas. Prosecutors and government regulators charged that both father and son had misappropriated Adelphia funds for their own use and had failed to pay the corporation for securities they controlled. John Rigas and Timothy Rigas are serving 12 years and 17 years in prison, respectively. John Rigas applied for a presidential pardon in January 2009, but George W. Bush left office without making a decision on Rigas' request.[2]

Ethical Issues

2

Identify the types of ethical concerns that arise in the business world.

Ethical issues often arise out of a business's relationship with investors, customers, employees, creditors, or competitors. Each of these groups has specific concerns and usually exerts pressure on the organization's managers. For example, investors want management to make sensible financial decisions that will boost sales, profits, and returns on their investments. Customers expect a firm's products to be safe, reliable, and reasonably priced. Employees demand to be treated fairly in hiring, promotion, and compensation decisions. Creditors require accounts to be paid on time and the accounting information furnished by the firm to be accurate. Competitors expect the firm's competitive practices to be fair and honest. Consider TAP Pharmaceutical Products, Inc., whose sales representatives offered every urologist in the United States a big-screen TV, computers, fax machines, and golf vacations if the doctors prescribed TAP's new prostate cancer drug Lupron. Moreover, the sales representatives sold Lupron at cut-rate prices or gratis while defrauding Medicare. Recently, the federal government won an $875 million judgment against TAP when a former TAP vice president of sales, Douglas Durand, and Dr. Joseph Gerstein blew the whistle.[3]

In late 2006, Hewlett-Packard Co.'s chairman, Patricia Dunn, and general counsel, Ann Baskins, resigned amid allegations that the company used intrusive tactics in observing the personal lives of journalists and the company's directors, thus tarnishing Hewlett-Packard's reputation for integrity. According to Congressman

ethics the study of right and wrong and of the morality of the choices individuals make

business ethics the application of moral standards to business situations

John Dingell of Michigan, "We have before us witnesses from Hewlett-Packard to discuss a plunderers' operation that would make (former president) Richard Nixon blush were he still alive." Alternatively, consider Bernard Madoff, former stockbroker, financial advisor, and chairman of the NASDAQ stock exchange. In 2009, he was convicted of securities and other frauds including a Ponzi scheme that defrauded clients of $65 billion.

Businesspeople face ethical issues every day, and some of these issues can be difficult to assess. Although some types of issues arise infrequently, others occur regularly. Let's take a closer look at several ethical issues.

Fairness and Honesty

Fairness and honesty in business are two important ethical concerns. Besides obeying all laws and regulations, businesspeople are expected to refrain from knowingly deceiving, misrepresenting, or intimidating others. The consequences of failing to do so can be expensive. Recently, for example, Keith E. Anderson and Wayne Anderson, the leaders of an international tax shelter scheme known as Anderson's Ark and Associates, were sentenced to as many as 20 years in prison. The Andersons; Richard Marks, their chief accounting officer; and Karolyn Grosnickle, the chief administrative officer, were ordered to pay more than $200 million in fines and restitution.[4] In yet another case, the accounting firm PricewaterhouseCoopers LLP agreed to pay the U.S. government $42 million to resolve allegations that it made false claims in connection with travel reimbursements it collected for several federal agencies.[5]

Deere & Company requires each employee to deal fairly with its customers, suppliers, competitors, and employees. "No employee should take unfair advantage of anyone through manipulation, concealment, abuse of privileged information, misrepresentation of material facts or any other unfair dealing practice." Employees are encouraged to report possible violations of company ethics policies using a 24-hour hotline or anonymous e-mails.[6]

Personal data security breaches have become a major threat to personal privacy in the new millennium. Can businesses keep your personal data secure?

Organizational Relationships

A businessperson may be tempted to place his or her personal welfare above the welfare of others or the welfare of the organization. For example, in late 2002, former CEO of Tyco International, Ltd, Leo Dennis Kozlowski, was indicted for misappropriating $43 million in corporate funds to make philanthropic contributions in his own name, including $5 million to Seton Hall University, which named its new business-school building Kozlowski Hall. Furthermore, according to Tyco, the former CEO took $61.7 million in interest-free relocation loans without the board's permission. He allegedly used the money to finance many personal luxuries, including a $15 million yacht and a $3.9 million Renoir painting, and to throw a $2 million party for his wife's birthday. Mr. Kozlowski, currently serving up to 25 years in prison, paid $134 million in restitution to Tyco and criminal fines of $70 million. In 2009, the U.S. Supreme Court denied his petition for a judicial review.[7]

Meet New York Governor, David Paterson, arriving at his office on March 5, 2010. A state ethics panel accused him of seeking and accepting World Series tickets from the New York Yankees in 2009 despite a gift ban, then lying to the panel about it.

Relationships with customers and co-workers often create ethical problems. Unethical behavior in these areas includes taking credit for others' ideas or work, not meeting one's commitments in a mutual agreement, and pressuring others to behave unethically.

Conflict of Interest

Conflict of interest results when a businessperson takes advantage of a situation for his or her own personal interest rather than for the employer's interest. Such conflict may occur when payments and gifts make their way into business deals. A wise rule to remember is that anything given to a person that might unfairly influence that person's business decision is a bribe, and all bribes are unethical.

For example, Nortel Networks Corporation does not permit its employees, officers, and directors to accept any gifts or to serve as directors or officers of any organization that might supply goods or services to Nortel Networks. However, Nortel employees may work part-time with firms that are not competitors, suppliers, or customers. At AT&T, employees are instructed to discuss with their supervisors any investments that may seem improper. Verizon Communications forbids its employees and executives from holding a "significant" financial stake in vendors, suppliers, or customers.

At Procter & Gamble Company (P&G), all employees are obligated to act at all times solely in the best interests of the company. A conflict of interest arises when an employee has a personal relationship or financial or other interest that could interfere with this obligation, or when an employee uses his or her position with the company for personal gain. P&G requires employees to disclose all potential conflicts of interest and to take prompt actions to eliminate a conflict when the company asks them to do so. Generally, it is not acceptable to receive gifts, entertainment, or other gratuities from people with whom P&G does business because doing so could imply an obligation on the part of the company and potentially pose a conflict of interest.

Communications

Business communications, especially advertising, can present ethical questions. False and misleading advertising is illegal and unethical, and it can infuriate customers. Sponsors of advertisements aimed at children must be especially careful to avoid misleading messages. Advertisers of health-related products also must take precautions to guard against deception when using such descriptive terms as *low fat*, *fat free*, and *light*. In fact, the Federal Trade Commission has issued guidelines on the use of these labels.

Factors Affecting Ethical Behavior

3 Discuss the factors that affect the level of ethical behavior in organizations.

Is it possible for an individual with strong moral values to make ethically questionable decisions in a business setting? What factors affect a person's inclination to make either ethical or unethical decisions in a business organization? Although the answers to these questions are not entirely clear, three general sets of factors do appear to influence the standards of behavior in an organization. As shown in Figure 2.1, the sets consist of individual factors, social factors, and opportunities.

Figure 2.1 Factors that Affect the Level of Ethical Behavior in an Organization

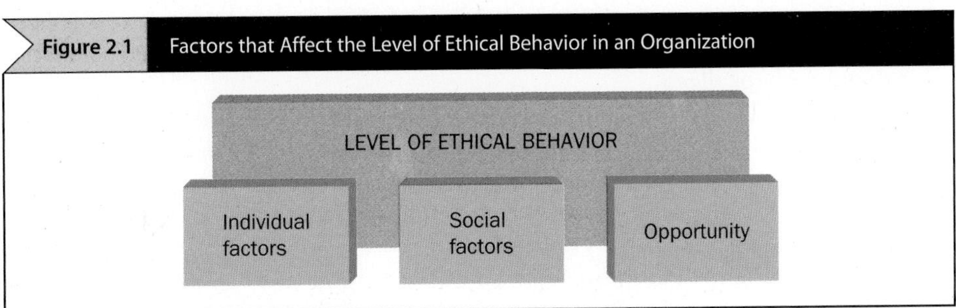

Source: Based on O. C. Ferrell and Larry Gresham, "A Contingency Framework for Understanding Ethical Decision Making in Marketing," *Journal of Marketing* (Summer 1985), 89.

Ethical Challenges & SUCCESSFUL SOLUTIONS

Green or Greenwashing?

Is it ethical for a company to say its product is "green" if even the tiniest aspect is not eco-friendly? Many customers seek out goods and services that are considered green because they are made in sustainable ways, for example, or are recyclable. But is a product truly green if it is delivered by a jet that burns fossil fuel? What if one or more parts are not biodegradable or the manufacturing operation consumes lots of energy?

The Federal Trade Commission enforces advertising guidelines to ensure that firms do not make misleading environmental claims. Yet, consumers may believe a company is not doing enough to make its products green or, at the other extreme, is in some way exaggerating—*greenwashing*—its environmental claims.

To earn and retain the trust of their customers, companies must therefore be as transparent as possible about how green their products and processes really are. The outdoor clothing company Patagonia is a leader here, disclosing the carbon footprint of many of its products and labeling items that contain non-ecofriendly materials. Apple, once a Greenpeace target because some products contained environmentally questionable chemicals, is forcing suppliers to replace those materials. The company is polishing its green credentials by publicly reporting its total annual company-wide carbon footprint.

Sources: "Facts Should Match 'Green' Image," *MMR*, November 16, 2009, 8; Weston Kosova, "It Ain't Easy Being Green," *Newsweek*, September 21, 2009, http://www.newsweek.com/id/215886; "FTC Cites Kmart, Tender, Dyna-E for False Green Claims," *Environmental Leader*, June 10, 2009, http://www.environmentalleader.com; Peter Burrows, "Finally, a Big Green Apple?" *BusinessWeek*, October 5, 2009, 68–69.

Individual Factors Affecting Ethics

Several individual factors influence the level of ethical behavior in an organization.

- *Individual knowledge of an issue*. How much an individual knows about an issue is one factor. A decision maker with a greater amount of knowledge regarding a situation may take steps to avoid ethical problems, whereas a less-informed person may take action unknowingly that leads to an ethical quagmire.
- *Personal values*. An individual's moral values and central, value-related attitudes also clearly influence his or her business behavior. Most people join organizations to accomplish personal goals.
- *Personal goals*. The types of personal goals an individual aspires to and the manner in which these goals are pursued have a significant impact on that individual's behavior in an organization. The actions of specific individuals in scandal-plagued companies, such as Adelphia, Arthur Anderson, Enron, Halliburton, Qwest, and WorldCom, often raise questions about individuals' personal character and integrity.

Social Factors Affecting Ethics

- *Cultural norms*. A person's behavior in the workplace, to some degree, is determined by cultural norms, and these social factors vary from one culture to another. For example, in some countries it is acceptable and ethical for customs agents to receive gratuities for performing ordinary, legal tasks that are a part of their jobs, whereas in other countries these practices would be viewed as unethical and perhaps illegal.
- *Co-workers*. The actions and decisions of co-workers constitute another social factor believed to shape a person's sense of business ethics. For example, if your co-workers make long-distance telephone calls on company time and at company expense, you might view that behavior as acceptable and ethical because everyone does it.
- *Significant others*. The moral values and attitudes of "significant others"—spouses, friends, and relatives, for instance—also can affect an employee's perception of what is ethical and unethical behavior in the workplace.

- *Use of the Internet.* Even the Internet presents new challenges for firms whose employees enjoy easy access to sites through convenient high-speed connections at work. An employee's behavior online can be viewed as offensive to co-workers and possibly lead to lawsuits against the firm if employees engage in unethical behavior on controversial Web sites not related to their job. Interestingly, one recent survey of employees found that most workers assume that their use of technology at work will be monitored. A large majority of employees approved of most monitoring methods such as monitoring faxes and e-mail, tracking Web use, and even recording telephone calls.

"Opportunity" as a Factor Affecting Ethics

- *Presence of opportunity. Opportunity* refers to the amount of freedom an organization gives an employee to behave unethically if he or she makes that choice. In some organizations, certain company policies and procedures reduce the opportunity to be unethical. For example, at some fast-food restaurants, one employee takes your order and receives your payment, and another fills the order. This procedure reduces the opportunity to be unethical because the person handling the money is not dispensing the product, and the person giving out the product is not handling the money.
- *Ethical codes.* The existence of an ethical code and the importance management places on this code are other determinants of opportunity (codes of ethics are discussed in more detail in the next section).
- *Enforcement.* The degree of enforcement of company policies, procedures, and ethical codes is a major force affecting opportunity. When violations are dealt with consistently and firmly, the opportunity to be unethical is reduced.

Do you make personal telephone calls on company time? Many individuals do. Although most employees limit personal calls to a few minutes, some make personal calls in excess of 30 minutes. Whether you use company time and equipment to make personal calls is an example of a personal ethical decision.

Now that we have considered some of the factors believed to influence the level of ethical behavior in the workplace, let us explore what can be done to encourage ethical behavior and to discourage unethical behavior.

Encouraging Ethical Behavior

4

Explain how ethical decision making can be encouraged.

Most authorities agree that there is room for improvement in business ethics. A more problematic question is: Can business be made more ethical in the real world? The majority opinion on this issue suggests that government, trade associations, and individual firms indeed can establish acceptable levels of ethical behavior.

Government's Role in Encouraging Ethics

The government can encourage ethical behavior by legislating more stringent regulations. For example, the landmark **Sarbanes-Oxley Act of 2002** provides sweeping new legal protection for those who report corporate misconduct. At the signing ceremony, President George W. Bush stated, "The act adopts tough new provisions to deter and punish corporate and accounting fraud and corruption, ensure justice for wrongdoers, and protect the interests of workers and shareholders." Among other things, the law deals with corporate responsibility, conflicts of interest, and corporate accountability. However, rules require enforcement, and the unethical businessperson frequently seems to "slip something by" without getting caught. Increased regulation may help, but it surely cannot solve the entire ethics problem.

Trade Associations' Role in Encouraging Ethics

Trade associations can and often do provide ethical guidelines for their members. These organizations, which operate within particular industries, are in an excellent position to exert pressure on members who stoop to questionable business

Sarbanes-Oxley Act of 2002 provides sweeping new legal protection for employees who report corporate misconduct

Meet Senators Sarbanes and Oxley. The Sarbanes-Oxley Act of 2002 adopted tough new provisions to deter and punish corporate and accounting fraud and corruption. Here, Senator Paul S. Sarbanes and John LaFalce congratulate each other as Senator Michael J. Oxley (middle) looks on. The legislation passed with near unanimous support.

practices. For example, recently, a pharmaceutical trade group adopted a new set of guidelines to halt the extravagant dinners and other gifts sales representatives often give to physicians. However, enforcement and authority vary from association to association. Because trade associations exist for the benefit of their members, harsh measures may be self-defeating.

Individual Companies' Role in Encouraging Ethics

Codes of ethics that companies provide to their employees are perhaps the most effective way to encourage ethical behavior. A **code of ethics** is a written guide to acceptable and ethical behavior as defined by an organization; it outlines uniform policies, standards, and punishments for violations. Because employees know what is expected of them and what will happen if they violate the rules, a code of ethics goes a long way toward encouraging ethical behavior. However, codes cannot possibly cover every situation. Companies also must create an environment in which employees recognize the importance of complying with the written code. Managers must provide direction by fostering communication, actively modeling and encouraging ethical decision making, and training employees to make ethical decisions.

During the 1980s, an increasing number of organizations created and implemented ethics codes. In a recent survey of *Fortune* 1,000 firms, 93 percent of the companies that responded reported having a formal code of ethics. Some companies are now even taking steps to strengthen their codes. For example, to strengthen its accountability, the Healthcare Financial Management Association recently revised its code to designate contact persons who handle reports of ethics violations, to clarify how its board of directors should deal with violations of business ethics, and to guarantee a fair hearing process. S. C. Johnson & Son, makers of Pledge, Drano, Windex, and many other household products, is another firm that recognizes that it must behave in ways the public perceives as ethical; its code includes expectations for employees and its commitment to consumers, the community, and society in general. As shown in Figure 2.2, the ethics code of electronics giant Texas Instruments (TI) includes issues relating to policies and procedures; laws and regulations; relationships with customers, suppliers, and competitors; conflicts of interest; handling of proprietary information; and code enforcement.

Assigning an ethics officer who coordinates ethical conduct gives employees someone to consult if they are not sure of the right thing to do. An ethics officer meets with employees and top management to provide ethical advice, establishes and maintains an anonymous confidential service to answer questions about ethical issues, and takes action on ethics code violations.

Sometimes even employees who want to act ethically may find it difficult to do so. Unethical practices can become ingrained in an organization. Employees with high personal ethics may then take a controversial step called *whistle-blowing*. **Whistle-blowing** is informing the press or government officials about unethical practices within one's organization.

The year 2002 was labeled as the "Year of the Whistle-blower." Consider Joe Speaker, a 40-year-old acting chief financial officer (CFO) at Rite Aid Corp. in 1999. He discovered that inventories at Rite Aid had been overvalued and that millions in expenses had not been reported properly. Further digging into Rite Aid's books revealed that $541 million in earnings over the previous two years was really $1.6 billion in losses. Mr. Speaker was a main government witness

code of ethics a guide to acceptable and ethical behavior as defined by the organization

whistle-blowing informing the press or government officials about unethical practices within one's organization

Figure 2.2 Defining Acceptable Behavior: Texas Instruments' Code of Ethics

Texas Instruments encourages ethical behavior through an extensive training program and a written code of ethics and shared values.

TEXAS INSTRUMENTS CODE OF ETHICS

"Integrity is the foundation on which TI is built. There is no other characteristic more essential to a TIer's makeup. It has to be present at all levels. Integrity is expected of managers and individuals when they make commitments. They are expected to stand by their commitments to the best of their ability.

One of TI's greatest strengths is its values and ethics. We had some early leaders who set those values as the standard for how they lived their lives. And it is important that TI grew that way. It's something that we don't want to lose. At the same time, we must move more rapidly. But we don't want to confuse that with the fact that we're ethical and we're moral. We're very responsible, and we live up to what we say."

Tom Engibous, President and CEO
Texas Instruments, 1997

We Respect and Value People By:

Treating others as we want to be treated.

- Exercising the basic virtues of respect, dignity, kindness, courtesy and manners in all work relationships.
- Recognizing and avoiding behaviors that others may find offensive, including the manner in which we speak and relate to one another and the materials we bring into the workplace, both printed and electronically.
- Respecting the right and obligation of every TIer to resolve concerns relating to ethics questions in the course of our duties without retribution and retaliation.
- Giving all TIers the same opportunity to have their questions, issues and situations fairly considered while understanding that being treated fairly does not always mean that we will all be treated the same.
- Trusting one another to use sound judgment in our use of TI business and information systems.
- Understanding that even though TI has the obligation to monitor its business information systems activity, we will respect privacy by prohibiting random searches of individual TIers' communications.
- Recognizing that conduct socially and professionally acceptable in one culture and country may be viewed differently in another.

We Are Honest By:

Representing ourselves and our intentions truthfully.

- Offering full disclosure and withdrawing ourselves from discussions and decisions when our business judgment appears to be in conflict with a personal interest.
- Respecting the rights and property of others, including their intellectual property. Accepting confidential or trade secret information only after we clearly understand our obligations as defined in a nondisclosure agreement.
- Competing fairly without collusion or collaboration with competitors to divide markets, set prices, restrict production, allocate customers or otherwise restrain competition.
- Assuring that no payments or favors are offered to influence others to do something wrong.
- Keeping records that are accurate and include all payments and receipts.
- Exercising good judgment in the exchange of business courtesies, meals and entertainment by avoiding activities that could create even the appearance that our decisions could be compromised.
- Refusing to speculate in TI stock through frequent buying and selling or through other forms of speculative trading.

Source: Courtesy of Texas Instruments, http://www.ti.com/corp/docs/csr/corpgov/conduct.shtml (accessed April 5, 2010).

when former Rite Aid Corp. Chairman and CEO Martin L. Grass went on trial. Mr. Speaker is among dozens of corporate managers who have blown the whistle. Enron's Sherron S. Watkins and WorldCom's Cynthia Cooper are now well-known whistle-blowers and *Time* magazine's persons of the year 2002. According to Linda Chatman Thomsen, deputy director for enforcement at the Securities and Exchange

Commission, "Whistle-blowers give us an insider's perspective and have advanced our investigation immeasurably."

Whistle-blowing could have averted disaster and prevented needless deaths in the *Challenger* space shuttle disaster, for example. How could employees have known about life-threatening problems and let them pass? Whistle-blowing, however, can have serious repercussions for employees: Those who "blow whistles" sometimes lose their jobs. However, the Sarbanes-Oxley Act of 2002 protects whistle-blowers who report corporate misconduct. Any executive who retaliates against a whistle-blower can be held criminally liable and imprisoned for up to ten years.

Retaliations do occur, however. For example, in 2005, the U.S. Court of Appeals for the 8th Circuit unanimously upheld the right of Jane Turner, a 25-year veteran FBI agent, to obtain monetary damages and a jury trial against the FBI. The court held that Ms. Turner presented sufficient facts to justify a trial by jury based on the FBI's retaliatory transfer of Ms. Turner from her investigatory position in Minot, North Dakota, to a demeaning desk job in Minneapolis. Kris Kolesnik, executive director of the National Whistle Blower Center, said, "Jane Turner is an American hero. She refused to be silent when her co-agents committed misconduct in a child rape case. She refused to be silent when her co-agents stole property from Ground Zero. She paid the price and lost her job. The 8th Circuit Court did the right thing and insured that justice will take place in her case." In 2008, the U.S. government was ordered to pay $1 million in legal fees to Turner's lawyers. In 2010, the Obama administration was attempting to pass a law that would further protect the government whistle-blowers.[8]

When firms set up anonymous hotlines to handle ethically questionable situations, employees actually may be more likely to engage in whistle-blowing. When firms instead create an environment that educates employees and nurtures ethical behavior, fewer ethical problems arise. Ultimately, the need for whistle-blowing is greatly reduced.

It is difficult for an organization to develop ethics codes, policies, and procedures to deal with all relationships and every situation. When no company policies or procedures exist or apply, a quick test to determine if a behavior is ethical is to see if others—co-workers, customers, and suppliers—approve of it. Ethical decisions will always withstand scrutiny. Openness and communication about choices will often build trust and strengthen business relationships. Table 2.1 provides some general guidelines for making ethical decisions.

Table 2.1 Guidelines for Making Ethical Decisions

1. Listen and learn.	Recognize the problem or decision-making opportunity that confronts your company, team, or unit. Don't argue, criticize, or defend yourself—keep listening and reviewing until you are sure that you understand others.
2. Identify the ethical issues.	Examine how co-workers and consumers are affected by the situation or decision at hand. Examine how you feel about the situation, and attempt to understand the viewpoint of those involved in the decision or in the consequences of the decision.
3. Create and analyze options.	Try to put aside strong feelings such as anger or a desire for power and prestige and come up with as many alternatives as possible before developing an analysis. Ask everyone involved for ideas about which options offer the best long-term results for you and the company. Then decide which option will increase your self-respect even if, in the long run, things don't work out the way you hope.
4. Identify the best option from your point of view.	Consider it and test it against some established criteria, such as respect, understanding, caring, fairness, honesty, and openness.
5. Explain your decision and resolve any differences that arise.	This may require neutral arbitration from a trusted manager or taking "time out" to reconsider, consult, or exchange written proposals before a decision is reached.

Source: Tom Rusk with D. Patrick Miller, "Doing the Right Thing," *Sky* (Delta Airlines), August 1993, 18–22.

Social Responsibility

Social responsibility is the recognition that business activities have an impact on society and the consideration of that impact in business decision making. In the first few days after Hurricane Katrina hit New Orleans, Walmart delivered $20 million in cash (including $4 million to employees displaced by the storm), 100 truckloads of free merchandise, and food for 100,000 meals. The company also promised a job elsewhere for every one of its workers affected by the catastrophe. Obviously, social responsibility costs money. It is perhaps not so obvious—except in isolated cases—that social responsibility is also good business. Customers eventually find out which firms act responsibly and which do not. Just as easily as they can purchase a product made by a company that is socially responsible, they can choose against buying from the firm that is not.

Consider the following examples of organizations that are attempting to be socially responsible:

- Social responsibility can take many forms—including flying lessons. Through Young Eagles, underwritten by S. C. Johnson, Phillips Petroleum, Lockheed Martin, Jaguar, and other corporations, 22,000 volunteer pilots have taken a half million youngsters on free flights designed to teach flying basics and inspire excitement about flying careers. Young Eagles is just one of the growing number of education projects undertaken by businesses building solid records as good corporate citizens.
- The General Mills Foundation, created in 1954, is one of the nation's largest company-sponsored foundations. Since the General Mills Foundation was created, it has awarded more than $420 million to its communities.

  In the Twin Cities, the General Mills Foundation provides grants for youth nutrition and fitness, education, arts and culture, social services, and the United Way. Beyond financial resources, the General Mills Foundation also supports organizations with volunteers and mentors who share their expertise and talents. For example, General Mills plays a leadership role in supporting education, arts, and cultural organizations by matching employee and retiree contributions dollar for dollar. General Mills Foundation institutions matched contributions of nearly $1.9 million to eligible accredited educational and employee-supported arts and cultural organizations in 2009. In 2009, the General Mills Foundation contributed nearly $21 million in grants in its communities.[9]
- As part of Dell's commitment to the community, the Dell Foundation contributes significantly to the quality of life in communities where Dell employees live and work. The Dell Foundation supports innovative and effective programs that provide fundamental prerequisites to equip youth to learn and excel in a world driven by the digital economy. The Dell Foundation supports a wide range of programs that benefit children from newborn to 17 years of age in Dell's principal U.S. locations and welcomes proposals from non-profit organizations that address health and human services, education, and technology access for youth.

  Dell's global outreach programs include projects that bring technology to underserved communities around the world. For example, Dell Brazil launched the Digital Citizen Project in 2002 in conjunction with the State Government of Rio Grande do Sul to provide

social responsibility the recognition that business activities have an impact on society and the consideration of that impact in business decision making

Triple Canopy helping the victims of the earthquake in Haiti. These waterproof tents were donated by Triple Canopy to the GHESKIO Center in Port-au-Prince, Haiti. Here, homeless victims replace hundreds of makeshift shelters with waterproof tents.

technical education to youth from low-income brackets through the creation of technology computing schools. In 2004, Dell partnered with Weyerhaeuser to deliver computers, keyboards, monitors, printers, and mouse pads to more than 100 schools in Uruguay, where the technology is estimated to benefit more than 32,700 students. In addition, employees in Dell's Asia–Pacific Customer Center volunteered to create The Smart Village Project, a program to educate students in villages located near Penang, Malaysia. Dell is currently working with the Malaysian government to expand the program to more villages. Globally, the Michael and Susan Dell Foundation has contributed more than $250 million to improve student performance and increase access to education so that all children have the opportunity to achieve their dreams.[10]

- Improving public schools around the world continues to be IBM's top social priority. Its efforts are focused on preparing the next generation of leaders and workers. Through Reinventing Education and other strategic efforts, IBM is solving education's toughest problems with solutions that draw on advanced information technologies and the best minds IBM can apply. Its programs are paving the way for reforms in school systems around the world.

  IBM launched the World Community Grid in November 2004. It combines excess processing power from thousands of computers into a virtual supercomputer. This grid enables researchers to gather and analyze unprecedented quantities of data aimed at advancing research on genomics, diseases, and natural disasters. The first project, the Human Proteome Folding Project, assists in identifying cures for diseases such as malaria and tuberculosis and has registered 85,000 devices around the world to date.

  In 2009, IBM hosted the first-ever Smarter Planet University Jam. More than 150 IBMers and approximately 2,000 faculty, students, and administrators—from more than 200 universities and research centers worldwide—brainstormed ideas on how technology and business can build a smarter planet. The 72-hour online dialogue centered on five themes: Smart Cities, Smarter Healthcare, Smart Grid, Smart Water Management & Green Planet, and Smarter Planet Skills and Education.[11]

- General Electric Company (GE) has a long history of supporting the communities where its employees work and live through GE's unique combination of resources, equipment, and employees' and retirees' hearts and souls. Today GE's responsibility extends to communities around the world.

  GE applies its long-standing spirit of innovation and unique set of capabilities to take on tough challenges in its communities. The company devotes its efforts in philanthropy to making communities around the world stronger. For example, the GE Foundation reallocated more than $20 million in 2009 to give greater support for organizations providing basic needs, such as food, clothing, and shelter. GE's Developing Health Globally™ program is working with local communities, health workers, and government ministries in Africa, Latin America, and Asia. It does not just provide usable equipment in rural hospitals and clinics—it also backs this up with capacity building for the equipment's long-term use, maintenance, and management. Through these efforts, GE can be confident that its donations are not only making a difference, but also that they as a company can learn more about how to develop technologies that meet the demand for health care in challenging environments.[12]

- With the help of dedicated Schwab volunteers, the Charles Schwab Foundation provides programs and funding to help individuals fill the information gap. For example, Schwab MoneyWise helps adults teach—and children learn—the basics of financial literacy. Interactive tools are available at http://schwabmoneywise.com, and local workshops cover topics such as getting kids started on a budget. In addition to these efforts, widely distributed publications and news columns by foundation President Carrie Schwab Pomerantz promote financial literacy on a wide range of topics—from saving for a child's education to bridging the health insurance gap for retirees.

The Charles Schwab Foundation matches employee gifts of $25 or more, up to $1,000 per employee during the calendar year. Recently, more than a one-third of Schwab employees participated in this program. In 2009, the Charles Schwab Foundation matched employee donations to 1,838 charitable organizations, for a combined total of $1.87 million.

More than half the employee gifts and matching funds go to education-related and health and human service charities. Over one-third of total contributions are given to community-service organizations.[13]

- Improving basic literacy skills in the United States is among the Verizon Foundation's major priorities because of its enormous impact on education, health, and economic development. Here in the United States, more than 30 million American adults have basic or below average literacy skills. Thinkfinity.org is designed to improve education and literacy achievement. This comprehensive free Web site delivers online resources to advance student achievement. Thinkfinity delivers top-quality K-12 lesson plans, student materials, interactive tools, and connections to educational Web sites. It gives teachers, instructors, and parents the tools they need to increase student performance.

  Recently, Verizon employees and retirees donated more than 608,000 hours of service and, with the Verizon Foundation, contributed more than $25 million in combined matching gift funds, making Verizon Volunteers one of the largest corporate volunteer incentive programs in the United States.
- ExxonMobil's commitment to education spans all levels of achievement. One of its corporate primary goals is to support basic education and literacy programs in the developing world. In areas of the world where basic education levels have been met, ExxonMobil supports education programs in science, technology, engineering, and mathematics.

  ExxonMobil recognizes the essential role that proficiency in math and science plays not only in the energy business but also in fostering innovation and facilitating human progress. The company encourages new generations to pursue studies and careers in fields involving mathematics and science. Toward this goal, it supports programs focused on laying the foundation for long-term educational improvements, such as the National Math and Science Initiative and the Mickelson ExxonMobil Teachers Academy.

  Recently, more than 24,900 ExxonMobil employees, retirees, and their families worldwide donated more than 690,000 volunteer hours to 5,350 charitable organizations in 30 countries through company-sponsored volunteer programs. Of the total volunteers, 14,300 participants donated more than 87,200 hours to more than 1,000 organizations in countries outside the United States. ExxonMobil employees and retirees donated $36 million through ExxonMobil's matching gift, disaster relief, and employee-giving programs. When combined with corporate donations, ExxonMobil—together with its employees and retirees—contributed $225 million to community investments around the world.[14]
- AT&T has built a tradition of supporting education, health and human services, the environment, public policy, and the arts in the communities it serves since Alexander Graham Bell founded the company over a century ago. Since 1984, AT&T has invested more than $600 million in support of education. Currently, more than half the company's contribution dollars, employee volunteer time, and community-service activities are directed toward education. Since 1911, AT&T has been a sponsor to the Telephone Pioneers of America, the world's largest industry-based volunteer organization consisting of nearly 750,000 employees and retirees from the telecommunications industry. Each year, the Pioneers volunteer millions of hours and raise millions of dollars for health and human services and the environment. In schools and neighborhoods, the Pioneers strengthen connections and build communities.

In 2009, responding to President Barack Obama's call to action for all Americans to participate in the annual national day of service, Share Our Strength, AT&T Inc., the Communications Workers of America, and the AT&T Pioneers announced two new programs in the fight against childhood hunger. The text-donation program encourages wireless phone users, including AT&T customers, to donate to Share Our Strength via their mobile phones. In addition, the groups sponsored a nationwide AT&T employee food drive. Share Our Strength, a national organization dedicated to ending childhood hunger, provides support for hundreds of hunger-relief organizations. Donations are used to help provide food for 12.4 million children at risk of hunger in America.[15]

- At Merck & Co., Inc., the Patient Assistance Program makes the company's medicines available to low-income Americans and their families at no cost. When patients do not have health insurance or a prescription drug plan and are unable to afford the Merck medicines their doctors prescribe, they can work with their physicians to contact the Merck Patient Assistance Program. For more than 50 years, Merck has provided its medicines completely free of charge to people in need through this program. Patients can get information through http://www.merck.com; by calling a toll-free number, 1-800-727-5400; or from their physician's office. For eligible patients, the medicines are shipped directly to their home or the prescribing physician's office. Each applicant may receive up to one year of medicines, and patients may reapply to the program if their need continues.

  Established in 1957, the Merck Company Foundation has contributed more than $560 million to develop and initiate programs that help improve the health and well-being of people around the world. According to Richard T. Clark, chairman, president, and CEO, "Merck established the Foundation more than 50 years ago because we knew that along with corporate success comes social responsibility."

  Education programs often link social responsibility with corporate self-interest. For example, Bayer and Merck, two major pharmaceuticals firms, promote science education as a way to enlarge the pool of future employees. Students who visit the Bayer Science Forum in Elkhart, Indiana, work alongside scientists conducting a variety of experiments. Workshops created by the Merck Institute for Science Education show teachers how to put scientific principles into action through hands-on experiments.

These are just a few illustrations from the long list of companies, big and small, that attempt to behave in socially responsible ways. In general, people are more likely to want to work for and buy from such organizations.

5

Describe how our current views on the social responsibility of business have evolved.

The Evolution of Social Responsibility in Business

Business is far from perfect in many respects, but its record of social responsibility today is much better than that in past decades. In fact, present demands for social responsibility have their roots in outraged reactions to the abusive business practices of the early 1900s.

Historical Evolution of Business Social Responsibility

During the first quarter of the 20th century, businesses were free to operate pretty much as they chose. Government protection of workers and consumers was minimal. As a result, people either accepted what business had to offer or they did without. Working conditions often were deplorable by today's standards. The average workweek in most industries exceeded 60 hours, no minimum-wage law existed, and employee benefits were almost nonexistent. Work areas were crowded and unsafe, and industrial accidents were the rule rather than the exception. To improve working conditions, employees organized and joined labor unions. During the early 1900s, however, businesses—with the help of government—were able to use court orders, brute force, and even the few existing antitrust laws to defeat union attempts to improve working conditions.

During this period, consumers generally were subject to the doctrine of **caveat emptor**, a Latin phrase meaning "let the buyer beware." In other words, "what you see is what you get," and if it is not what you expected, too bad. Although victims of unscrupulous business practices could take legal action, going to court was very expensive, and consumers rarely won their cases. Moreover, no consumer groups or government agencies existed to publicize their consumers' grievances or to hold sellers accountable for their actions.

Breaking away from fossil fuels. Today's consumers are more open to transportation alternatives, such as the electric car, because they are concerned about the negative impact of gasoline-run vehicles.

Before the 1930s, most people believed that competition and the action of the marketplace would, in time, correct abuses. Government, therefore, became involved in day-to-day business activities only in cases of obvious abuse of the free-market system. Six of the more important business-related federal laws passed between 1887 and 1914 are described in Table 2.2. As you can see, these laws were aimed more at encouraging competition than at correcting abuses, although two of them did deal with the purity of food and drug products.

The collapse of the stock market on October 29, 1929, triggered the Great Depression and years of dire economic problems for the United States. Factory production fell by almost half, and up to 25 percent of the nation's workforce was unemployed. Before long, public pressure mounted for the government to "do something" about the economy and about worsening social conditions.

Soon after Franklin D. Roosevelt became president in 1933, he instituted programs to restore the economy and improve social conditions. The government passed laws to correct what many viewed as the monopolistic abuses of big business, and provided various social services for individuals. These massive federal programs became the foundation for increased government involvement in the dealings between business and society.

As government involvement has increased, so has everyone's awareness of the social responsibility of business. Today's business owners are concerned about the return on their investment, but at the same time most of them demand ethical behavior from employees. In addition, employees demand better working conditions, and consumers want safe, reliable products. Various advocacy groups echo

Table 2.2 Early Government Regulations that Affected American Business

Six of the important business-related federal laws passed between 1887 and 1914 were aimed more at encouraging competition than at correcting abuses.

Government Regulation	Major Provisions
Interstate Commerce Act (1887)	First federal act to regulate business practices; provided regulation of railroads and shipping rates
Sherman Antitrust Act (1890)	Prevented monopolies or mergers where competition was endangered
Pure Food and Drug Act (1906)	Established limited supervision of interstate sales of food and drugs
Meat Inspection Act (1906)	Provided for limited supervision of interstate sales of meat and meat products
Federal Trade Commission Act (1914)	Created the Federal Trade Commission to investigate illegal trade practices
Clayton Antitrust Act (1914)	Eliminated many forms of price discrimination that gave large businesses a competitive advantage over smaller firms

caveat emptor a Latin phrase meaning "let the buyer beware"

these concerns and also call for careful consideration of Earth's delicate ecological balance. Therefore, managers must operate in a complex business environment—one in which they are just as responsible for their managerial actions as for their actions as individual citizens. Interestingly, today's high-tech and Internet-based firms fare relatively well when it comes to environmental issues, worker conditions, the representation of minorities and women in upper management, animal testing, and charitable donations.

6

Explain the two views on the social responsibility of business and understand the arguments for and against increased social responsibility.

Two Views of Social Responsibility

Government regulation and public awareness are *external* forces that have increased the social responsibility of business. However, business decisions are made within the firm—there, social responsibility begins with the attitude of management. Two contrasting philosophies, or models, define the range of management attitudes toward social responsibility.

The Economic Model

According to the traditional concept of business, a firm exists to produce quality goods and services, earn a reasonable profit, and provide jobs. In line with this concept, the **economic model of social responsibility** holds that society will benefit most when business is left alone to produce and market profitable products that society needs. The economic model has its origins in the 18th century, when businesses were owned primarily by entrepreneurs or owner-managers. Competition was vigorous among small firms, and short-run profits and survival were the primary concerns.

To the manager who adopts this traditional attitude, social responsibility is someone else's job. After all, stockholders invest in a corporation to earn a return on their investment, not because the firm is socially responsible, and the firm is legally obligated to act in the economic interest of its stockholders. Moreover, profitable firms pay federal, state, and local taxes that are used to meet the needs of society. Thus, managers who concentrate on profit believe that they fulfill their social responsibility indirectly through the taxes paid by their firms. As a result, social responsibility becomes the problem of the government, various environmental groups, charitable foundations, and similar organizations.

The Socioeconomic Model

In contrast, some managers believe that they have a responsibility not only to stockholders but also to customers, employees, suppliers, and the general public. This broader view is referred to as the **socioeconomic model of social responsibility**, which places emphasis not only on profits but also on the impact of business decisions on society.

Recently, increasing numbers of managers and firms have adopted the socioeconomic model, and they have done so for at least three reasons. First, business is dominated by the corporate form of ownership, and the corporation is a creation of society. If a corporation does not perform as a good citizen, society can and will demand changes. Second, many firms have begun to take pride in their social responsibility records, among them Starbucks Coffee, Hewlett-Packard, Colgate-Palmolive, and Coca-Cola. Each of these companies is a winner of a Corporate Conscience Award in the areas of environmental concern, responsiveness to employees, equal opportunity, and community involvement. Of course, many other corporations are much more socially responsible today than they were ten years ago. Third, many businesspeople believe that it is in their best interest to take the initiative in this area. The alternative may be legal action brought against the firm by some special-interest group; in such a situation, the firm may lose control of its activities.

economic model of social responsibility the view that society will benefit most when business is left alone to produce and market profitable products that society needs

socioeconomic model of social responsibility the concept that business should emphasize not only profits but also the impact of its decisions on society

The Pros and Cons of Social Responsibility

Business owners, managers, customers, and government officials have debated the pros and cons of the economic and socioeconomic models for years. Each side seems to have four major arguments to reinforce its viewpoint.

Arguments for Increased Social Responsibility Proponents of the socioeconomic model maintain that a business must do more than simply seek profits. To support their position, they offer the following arguments:

1. Because business is a part of our society, it cannot ignore social issues.
2. Business has the technical, financial, and managerial resources needed to tackle today's complex social issues.
3. By helping resolve social issues, business can create a more stable environment for long-term profitability.
4. Socially responsible decision making by firms can prevent increased government intervention, which would force businesses to do what they fail to do voluntarily.

These arguments are based on the assumption that a business has a responsibility not only to its stockholders but also to its customers, employees, suppliers, and the general public.

Sustaining the Planet

Sustainability

What are major companies and non-profit groups doing to preserve the environment? Hundreds of organizations, including AT&T, Burt's Bees, General Mills, Hitachi America, Microsoft, PepsiCo, Union Bank, Vivendi, and Yahoo!, post the latest news about their sustainability initiatives and accomplishments on Corporate Social Responsibility Newswire. Take a look: http://www.csrwire.com/.

Arguments Against Increased Social Responsibility Opponents of the socioeconomic model argue that business should do what it does best: earn a profit by manufacturing and marketing products that people want. Those who support this position argue as follows:

1. Business managers are responsible primarily to stockholders, so management must be concerned with providing a return on owners' investments.
2. Corporate time, money, and talent should be used to maximize profits, not to solve society's problems.
3. Social problems affect society in general, so individual businesses should not be expected to solve these problems.
4. Social issues are the responsibility of government officials who are elected for that purpose and who are accountable to the voters for their decisions.

These arguments obviously are based on the assumption that the primary objective of business is to earn profits and that government and social institutions should deal with social problems.

Table 2.3 compares the economic and socioeconomic viewpoints in terms of business emphasis. Today, few firms are either purely economic or purely socioeconomic in outlook; most have chosen some middle ground between the two extremes. However, our society generally seems to want—and even to expect—some degree of social responsibility from business. Thus, within this middle ground, businesses are leaning toward the socioeconomic view. In the next several sections, we look at some results of this movement in four specific areas: consumerism, employment practices, concern for the environment, and implementation of social responsibility programs.

Table 2.3 A Comparison of the Economic and Socioeconomic Models of Social Responsibility as Implemented in Business

Economic Model Primary Emphasis		Socioeconomic Model Primary Emphasis
1. Production	Middle ground	1. Quality of life
2. Exploitation of natural resources		2. Conservation of natural resources
3. Internal, market-based decisions		3. Market-based decisions, with some community controls
4. Economic return (profit)		4. Balance of economic return and social return
5. Firm's or manager's interest		5. Firm's and community's interests
6. Minor role for government		6. Active government

Source: Adapted from Keith Davis, William C. Frederick, and Robert L. Blomstron, *Business and Society: Concepts and Policy Issues* (New York: McGraw-Hill, 1980), 9. Used by permission of McGraw-Hill Book Company.

7

Discuss the factors that led to the consumer movement and list some of its results.

consumerism all activities undertaken to protect the rights of consumers

Consumerism

Consumerism consists of all activities undertaken to protect the rights of consumers. The fundamental issues pursued by the consumer movement fall into three categories: environmental protection, product performance and safety, and information disclosure. Although consumerism has been with us to some extent since the early 19th century, the consumer movement became stronger in the 1960s. It was then that President John F. Kennedy declared that the consumer was entitled to a new "Bill of Rights."

The right to be informed. The Consumer Bill of Rights asserts consumers' basic rights. The right to be informed and the right to choose means that consumers must have complete information about a product and a choice of products.

The Six Basic Rights of Consumers

President Kennedy's Consumer Bill of Rights asserted that consumers have a right to safety, to be informed, to choose, and to be heard. Two additional rights added since 1975 are the right to consumer education and the right to courteous service. These six rights are the basis of much of the consumer-oriented legislation passed during the last 45 years. These rights also provide an effective outline of the objectives and accomplishments of the consumer movement.

The Right to Safety The consumers' right to safety means that the products they purchase must be safe for their intended use, must include thorough and explicit directions for proper use, and must be tested by the manufacturer to ensure product quality and reliability. There are several reasons why American business firms must be concerned about product safety.

Corrective Actions Can Be Expensive. Federal agencies, such as the Food and Drug Administration and the Consumer Product Safety Commission, have the power to force businesses that make or sell defective products to take corrective actions. Such actions include offering refunds, recalling defective products, issuing public warnings, and reimbursing consumers—all of which can be expensive.

Increasing Number of Lawsuits. Business firms also should be aware that consumers and the government have been winning an increasing number of product-liability lawsuits against sellers of defective products. Moreover, the amount of the awards in these suits has been increasing steadily. Fearing the outcome of numerous lawsuits filed around the nation, tobacco giants Philip Morris and R. J. Reynolds, which for decades had denied that cigarettes cause illness, began negotiating in 1997 with state attorneys general, plaintiffs' lawyers, and antismoking activists. The tobacco giants proposed sweeping curbs on their sales and advertising practices and the payment of hundreds of billions of dollars in compensation.

Consumer Demand. Yet another major reason for improving product safety is consumers' demand for safe products. People simply will stop buying a product they believe is unsafe or unreliable.

The Right to Be Informed The right to be informed means that consumers must have access to complete information about a product before they buy it. Detailed information about ingredients and nutrition must be provided on food containers, information about fabrics and laundering methods must be attached to clothing, and lenders must disclose the true cost of borrowing the money they make available to customers who purchase merchandise on credit.

In addition, manufacturers must inform consumers about the potential dangers of using their products. Manufacturers that fail to provide such information can be held responsible for personal injuries suffered because of their products. For example, Maytag provides customers with a lengthy booklet that describes how they should use an automatic clothes washer. Sometimes such warnings seem excessive, but they are necessary if user injuries (and resulting lawsuits) are to be avoided.

The Right to Choose The right to choose means that consumers must have a choice of products, offered by different manufacturers and sellers, to satisfy a particular need. The government has done its part by encouraging competition through antitrust legislation. The greater the competition, the greater is the choice available to consumers.

Competition and the resulting freedom of choice provide additional benefits for customers by reducing prices. For example, when personal computers were introduced, they cost more than $5,000. Thanks to intense competition and technological advancements, personal computers today can be purchased for less than $500.

The Right to Be Heard This fourth right means that someone will listen and take appropriate action when customers complain. Actually, management began to listen to consumers after World War II, when competition between businesses that manufactured and sold consumer goods increased. One way that firms got a competitive edge was to listen to consumers and provide the products they said they wanted and needed. Today, businesses are listening even more attentively, and many larger firms have consumer relations departments that can be contacted easily via toll-free telephone numbers. Other groups listen, too. Most large cities and some states have consumer affairs offices to act on citizens' complaints.

Additional Consumer Rights In 1975, President Gerald Ford added to the Consumer Bill of Rights the right to consumer education, which entitles people to be fully informed about their rights as consumers. In 1994, President Bill Clinton added a sixth right, the right to service, which entitles consumers to convenience, courtesy, and responsiveness from manufacturers and sellers of consumer products.

Major Consumerism Forces

The major forces in consumerism are individual consumer advocates and organizations, consumer education programs, and consumer laws. Consumer advocates, such as Ralph Nader, take it on themselves to protect the rights of consumers.

They band together into consumer organizations, either independently or under government sponsorship. Some organizations, such as the National Consumers' League and the Consumer Federation of America, operate nationally, whereas others are active at state and local levels. They inform and organize other consumers, raise issues, help businesses to develop consumer-oriented programs, and pressure lawmakers to enact consumer protection laws. Some consumer advocates and organizations encourage consumers to boycott products and businesses to which they have objections. Today, the consumer movement has adopted corporate-style marketing and addresses a broad range of issues. Current campaigns include efforts (1) to curtail the use of animals for testing purposes, (2) to reduce liquor and cigarette billboard advertising in low-income, inner-city neighborhoods, and (3) to encourage recycling.

Educating consumers to make wiser purchasing decisions is perhaps one of the most far-reaching aspects of consumerism. Increasingly, consumer education is becoming a part of high school and college curricula and adult-education programs. These programs cover many topics—for instance, what major factors should be considered when buying specific products, such as insurance, real estate, automobiles, appliances and furniture, clothes, and food; the provisions of certain consumer-protection laws; and the sources of information that can help individuals become knowledgeable consumers.

Major advances in consumerism have come through federal legislation. Some laws enacted in the last 50 years to protect your rights as a consumer are listed and described in Table 2.4.

Here is the 2009 list of proposed legislation to protect consumers and investors:[16]

- Accountability and Transparency in Rating Agencies Act of 2009
- Consumer Financial Protection Agency Act of 2009
- Corporate and Financial Institution Compensation Fairness Act of 2009
- Credit Risk Retention Act of 2009
- Dissolution Authority for Large, Interconnected Financial Companies Act of 2009
- Federal Insurance Office Act of 2009
- Financial Stability Improvement Act of 2009
- Investor Protection Act of 2009
- Over-the-Counter Derivatives Markets Act of 2009
- Private Fund Investment Advisers Registration Act of 2009

Most businesspeople now realize that they ignore consumer issues only at their own peril. Managers know that improper handling of consumer complaints can result in lost sales, bad publicity, and lawsuits.

8

Analyze how present employment practices are being used to counteract past abuses.

Employment Practices

Managers who subscribe to the socioeconomic view of a business's social responsibility, together with significant government legislation enacted to protect the buying public, have broadened the rights of consumers. The last five decades have seen similar progress in affirming the rights of employees to equal treatment in the workplace.

Everyone should have the opportunity to land a job for which he or she is qualified and to be rewarded on the basis of ability and performance. This is an important issue for society, and it also makes good business sense. Yet, over the years, this opportunity has been denied to members of various minority groups. A **minority** is a racial, religious, political, national, or other group regarded as different from the larger group of which it is a part and that is often singled out for unfavorable treatment.

minority a racial, religious, political, national, or other group regarded as different from the larger group of which it is a part and that is often singled out for unfavorable treatment

The federal government responded to the outcry of minority groups during the 1960s and 1970s by passing a number of laws forbidding discrimination in

Table 2.4 Major Federal Legislation Protecting Consumers Since 1960

Legislation	Major Provisions
Federal Hazardous Substances Labeling Act (1960)	Required warning labels on household chemicals if they were highly toxic
Kefauver-Harris Drug Amendments (1962)	Established testing practices for drugs and required manufacturers to label drugs with generic names in addition to trade names
Cigarette Labeling Act (1965)	Required manufacturers to place standard warning labels on all cigarette packages and advertising
Fair Packaging and Labeling Act (1966)	Called for all products sold across state lines to be labeled with net weight, ingredients, and manufacturer's name and address
Motor Vehicle Safety Act (1966)	Established standards for safer cars
Truth in Lending Act (1968)	Required lenders and credit merchants to disclose the full cost of finance charges in both dollars and annual percentage rates
Credit Card Liability Act (1970)	Limited credit-card holder's liability to $50 per card and stopped credit-card companies from issuing unsolicited cards
Fair Credit Reporting Act (1971)	Required credit bureaus to provide credit reports to consumers regarding their own credit files; also provided for correction of incorrect information
Consumer Product Safety Commission Act (1972)	Established an abbreviated procedure for registering certain generic drugs
Fair Credit Billing Act (1974)	Amended the Truth in Lending Act to enable consumers to challenge billing errors
Equal Credit Opportunity Act (1974)	Provided equal credit opportunities for males and females and for married and single individuals
Magnuson-Moss Warranty-Federal Trade Commission Act (1975)	Provided for minimum disclosure standards for written consumer-product warranties for products that cost more than $15
Amendments to the Equal Credit Opportunity Act (1976, 1994)	Prevented discrimination based on race, creed, color, religion, age, and income when granting credit
Fair Debt Collection Practices Act (1977)	Outlawed abusive collection practices by third parties
Nutrition Labeling and Education Act (1990)	Required the Food and Drug Administration to review current food labeling and packaging focusing on nutrition label content, label format, ingredient labeling, food descriptors and standards, and health messages
Telephone Consumer Protection Act (1991)	Prohibited the use of automated dialing and prerecorded-voice calling equipment to make calls or deliver messages
Consumer Credit Reporting Reform Act (1997)	Placed more responsibility for accurate credit data on credit issuers; required creditors to verify that disputed data are accurate and to notify a consumer before reinstating the data
Children's Online Privacy Protection Act (2000)	Placed parents in control over what information is collected online from their children younger than 13 years; required commercial Web site operators to maintain the confidentiality, security, and integrity of personal information collected from children
Do Not Call Implementation Act (2003)	Directed the FCC and the FTC to coordinate so that their rules are consistent regarding telemarketing call practices including the Do Not Call Registry and other lists, as well as call abandonment
Credit Card Accountability, Responsibility, and Disclosure Act (2009)	Provided the most sweeping changes in credit card protections since the Truth in Lending Act of 1968
Wall Street Reform and Consumer Protection Act of 2010	Promoted the financial stability of the United States by improving accountability and responsibility in the financial system; established a new Consumer Financial Protection Agency to regulate home mortgages, car loans, and credit cards; became Public Law on July 21, 2010

the workplace. (These laws are discussed in Chapter 9 in the context of human resources management.) Now, 46 years after passage of the first of these (the Civil Rights Act of 1964), abuses still exist. An example is the disparity in income levels for whites, blacks, Hispanics, and Asians, as illustrated in Figure 2.3. Lower incomes and higher unemployment rates also characterize Native Americans, handicapped persons, and women. Responsible managers have instituted a number of programs to counteract the results of discrimination.

Figure 2.3 Comparative Income Levels

This chart shows the median household incomes of Asian, white, Hispanic, and African-American workers in 2008.

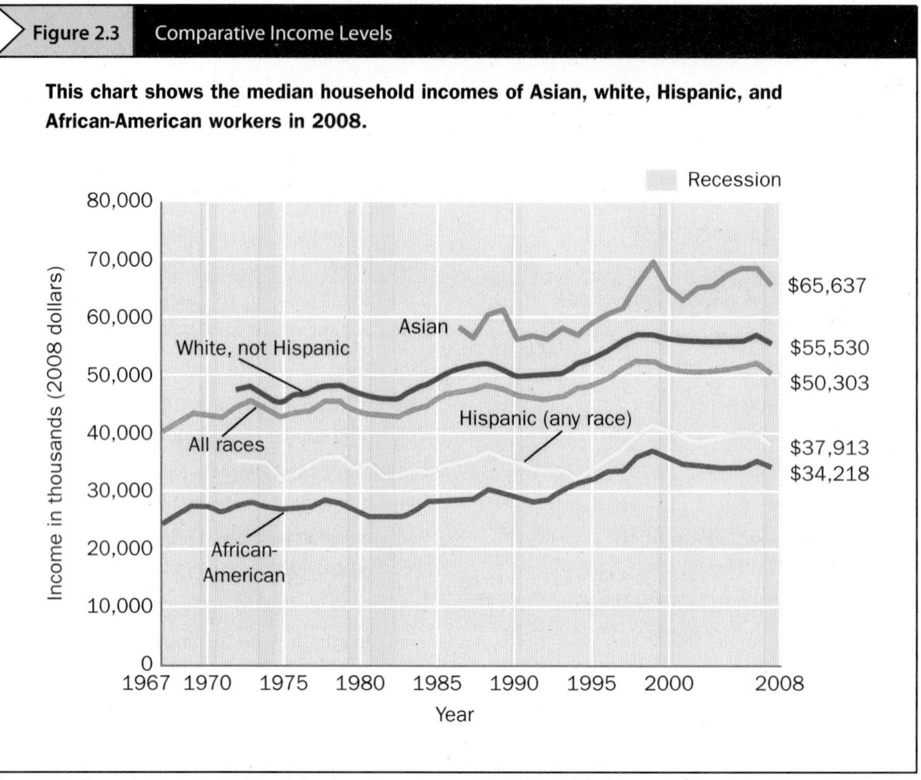

Source: U.S. Census Bureau, Current Population Survey, 1968 to 2008 Annual Social and Economic Supplements, *Income, Poverty, and Health Insurance Coverage in the United States: 2008*, issued August 2009, U.S. Census Bureau, U.S. Department of Commerce, 7, http://www.census.gov/prod/2009pubs/p60-236.pdf (accessed April 18, 2010).

Affirmative Action Programs

affirmative action program a plan designed to increase the number of minority employees at all levels within an organization

An **affirmative action program** is a plan designed to increase the number of minority employees at all levels within an organization. Employers with federal contracts of more than $50,000 per year must have written affirmative action plans. The objective of such programs is to ensure that minorities are represented within the organization in approximately the same proportion as in the surrounding community. If 25 percent of the electricians in a geographic area in which a company is located are African-Americans, then approximately 25 percent of the electricians it employs also should be African-Americans. Affirmative action plans encompass all areas of human resources management: recruiting, hiring, training, promotion, and pay.

Strong opinions about affirmative action. Affirmative action programs ensure that minorities are represented within the organization in approximately the same proportion as in the surrounding community. In the Winston-Salem Police Department, of the 30 recruits in the Basic Law Enforcement Training classes, 24 are white men, two are Hispanic men, two are black women, one is a white woman, and one is an American Indian man.

Unfortunately, affirmative action programs have been plagued by two problems. The first involves quotas. In the beginning, many firms pledged to recruit and hire a certain number of minority members by a specific date. To achieve this goal, they were forced to consider only minority applicants for job openings; if they hired nonminority workers, they would be defeating their own purpose. However, the courts have ruled that such quotas are unconstitutional even though their purpose is commendable. They are, in fact, a form of discrimination called *reverse discrimination.*

The second problem is that although most such programs have been reasonably successful, not all businesspeople are in favor of affirmative action programs. Managers not committed to these programs can "play the game" and still discriminate against workers. To help solve this problem, Congress created (and later strengthened) the **Equal Employment Opportunity Commission (EEOC)**, a government agency with the power to investigate complaints of employment discrimination and sue firms that practice it.

The threat of legal action has persuaded some corporations to amend their hiring and promotional policies, but the discrepancy between men's and women's salaries still exists, as illustrated in Figure 2.4. For more than 50 years, women have consistently earned only about 77 cents for each dollar earned by men.

Training Programs for the Hard-Core Unemployed

For some firms, social responsibility extends far beyond placing a help-wanted advertisement in the local newspaper. These firms have assumed the task of helping the **hard-core unemployed**, workers with little education or vocational training and a long history of unemployment. For example, a few years ago, General Mills helped establish Siyeza, a frozen soul-food processing plant in North Minneapolis. Through the years, Siyeza has provided stable, high-quality full-time jobs for a permanent core of 80 unemployed or underemployed minority inner-city residents. In addition, groups of up to 100 temporary employees are called in when needed. In the past, such workers often were turned down routinely by personnel managers, even for the most menial jobs.

Obviously, such workers require training; just as obviously, this training can be expensive and time-consuming. To share the costs, business and community leaders have joined together in a number of cooperative programs. One particularly successful partnership is the **National Alliance of Business (NAB)**, a joint business–government program to train the hard-core unemployed. The alliance's 5,000 members include companies of all sizes and industries, their CEOs and senior executives, as well as educators and community leaders. NAB, founded in 1968 by President Lyndon Johnson and Henry Ford II, is a major national business organization focusing on education and workforce issues.

Equal Employment Opportunity Commission (EEOC) a government agency with the power to investigate complaints of employment discrimination and the power to sue firms that practice it

hard-core unemployed workers with little education or vocational training and a long history of unemployment

National Alliance of Business (NAB) a joint business–government program to train the hard-core unemployed

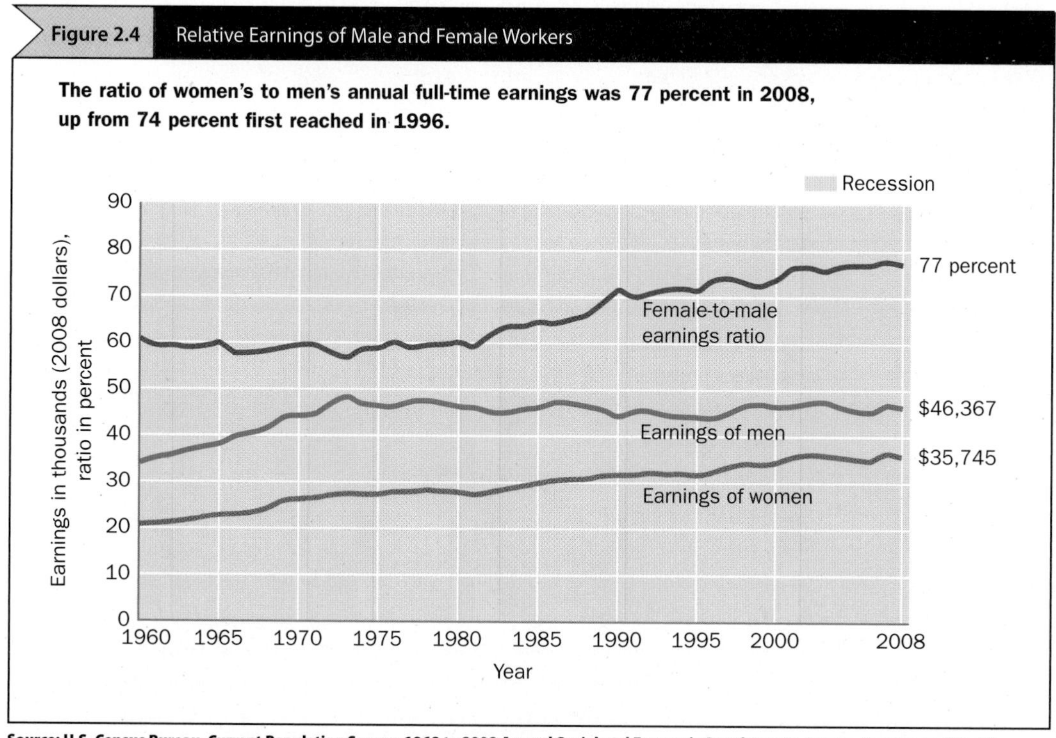

Figure 2.4 Relative Earnings of Male and Female Workers

The ratio of women's to men's annual full-time earnings was 77 percent in 2008, up from 74 percent first reached in 1996.

Source: U.S. Census Bureau, Current Population Survey, 1968 to 2008 Annual Social and Economic Supplements, *Income, Poverty, and Health Insurance Coverage in the United States: 2008*, issued August 2009, U.S. Census Bureau, U.S. Department of Commerce, 11, http://www.census.gov/prod/2009pubs/p60-236.pdf (accessed April 29, 2010).

Describe the major types of pollution, their causes, and their cures.

Concern for the Environment

The social consciousness of responsible business managers, the encouragement of a concerned government, and an increasing concern on the part of the public have led to a major effort to reduce environmental pollution, conserve natural resources, and reverse some of the worst effects of past negligence in this area. **Pollution** is the contamination of water, air, or land through the actions of people in an industrialized society. For several decades, environmentalists have been warning us about the dangers of industrial pollution. Unfortunately, business and government leaders either ignored the problem or were not concerned about it until pollution became a threat to life and health in America. Today, Americans expect business and government leaders to take swift action to clean up our environment—and to keep it clean.

Effects of Environmental Legislation

As in other areas of concern to our society, legislation and regulations play a crucial role in pollution control. The laws outlined in Table 2.5 reflect the scope of current environmental legislation: laws to promote clean air, clean water, and even quiet work and living environments. Of major importance was the creation of the Environmental Protection Agency (EPA), the federal agency charged with enforcing laws designed to protect the environment.

pollution the contamination of water, air, or land through the actions of people in an industrialized society

When they are aware of a pollution problem, many firms respond to it rather than wait to be cited by the EPA. Other owners and managers, however, take the position that environmental standards are too strict. (Loosely translated, this means that compliance with present standards is too expensive.) Consequently, it often

Table 2.5 Summary of Major Environmental Laws

Legislation	Major Provisions
National Environmental Policy Act (1970)	Established the Environmental Protection Agency (EPA) to enforce federal laws that involve the environment
Clean Air Amendment (1970)	Provided stringent automotive, aircraft, and factory emission standards
Water Quality Improvement Act (1970)	Strengthened existing water pollution regulations and provided for large monetary fines against violators
Resource Recovery Act (1970)	Enlarged the solid-waste disposal program and provided for enforcement by the EPA
Water Pollution Control Act Amendment (1972)	Established standards for cleaning navigable streams and lakes and eliminating all harmful waste disposal by 1985
Noise Control Act (1972)	Established standards for major sources of noise and required the EPA to advise the Federal Aviation Administration on standards for airplanes
Clean Air Act Amendment (1977)	Established new deadlines for cleaning up polluted areas; also required review of existing air-quality standards
Resource Conservation and Recovery Act (1984)	Amended the original 1976 act and required federal regulation of potentially dangerous solid-waste disposal
Clean Air Act Amendment (1987)	Established a national air-quality standard for ozone
Oil Pollution Act (1990)	Expanded the nation's oil-spill prevention and response activities; also established the Oil Spill Liability Trust Fund
Clean Air Act Amendments (1990)	Required that motor vehicles be equipped with onboard systems to control about 90 percent of refueling vapors
Food Quality Protection Act (1996)	Amended the Federal Insecticide, Fungicide and Rodenticide Act and the Federal Food Drug and Cosmetic Act; the requirements included a new safety standard—reasonable certainty of no harm—that must be applied to all pesticides used on foods
American Recovery and Reinvestment Act (2009)	Provided $7.22 billion to the EPA to protect and promote "green" jobs and a healthier environment

has been necessary for the EPA to take legal action to force firms to install antipollution equipment and to clean up waste storage areas.

Experience has shown that the combination of environmental legislation, voluntary compliance, and EPA action can succeed in cleaning up the environment and keeping it clean. However, much still remains to be done.

Water Pollution The Clean Water Act has been credited with greatly improving the condition of the waters in the United States. This success comes largely from the control of pollutant discharges from industrial and wastewater treatment plants. Although the quality of our nation's rivers, lakes, and streams has improved significantly in recent years, many of these surface waters remain severely polluted. Currently, one of the most serious water-quality problems results from the high level of toxic pollutants found in these waters.

Among the serious threats to people posed by water pollutants are respiratory irritation, cancer, kidney and liver damage, anemia, and heart failure. Toxic pollutants also damage fish and other forms of wildlife. In fish, they cause tumors or reproductive problems; shellfish and wildlife living in or drinking from toxin-laden waters also have suffered genetic defects. Recently, the Pollution Control Board of Kerala in India ordered Coca-Cola to close its major bottling plant. For years, villagers in the nearby areas had accused Coke of depleting local groundwater and producing other local pollution. The village council president said, "We are happy that the government is finally giving justice to the people who are affected by the plant."

One of the worst environmental disasters in 2010 was the explosion of the *Deepwater Horizon*, in which 11 people died. The British Petroleum (BP) catastrophe led to an oil spill in the Gulf of Mexico that contaminated a vast area of the United States marine environment. It caused a serious impact on wildlife, the local fishing industry, and regional tourism. British Petroleum was held liable for property damaged by the oil spill and the cleanup efforts; loss of income or earning capacity; loss of income to boat owners, hotel owners, and restaurant owners; removal and cleanup costs of property; and claims of bodily injury caused by the spill.

The task of water cleanup has proved to be extremely complicated and costly because of pollution runoff and toxic contamination. Yet, improved water quality is not only necessary, it is also achievable. Consider Cleveland's Cuyahoga River. A few years ago, the river was so contaminated by industrial wastes that it burst into flames one hot summer day! Now, after a sustained community cleanup effort, the river is pure enough for fish to thrive in.

Another serious issue is acid rain, which is contributing significantly to the deterioration of coastal waters, lakes, and marine life in the eastern United States. Acid rain forms when sulfur emitted by smokestacks in

SPoTLIGHT

Recession and Responsibility

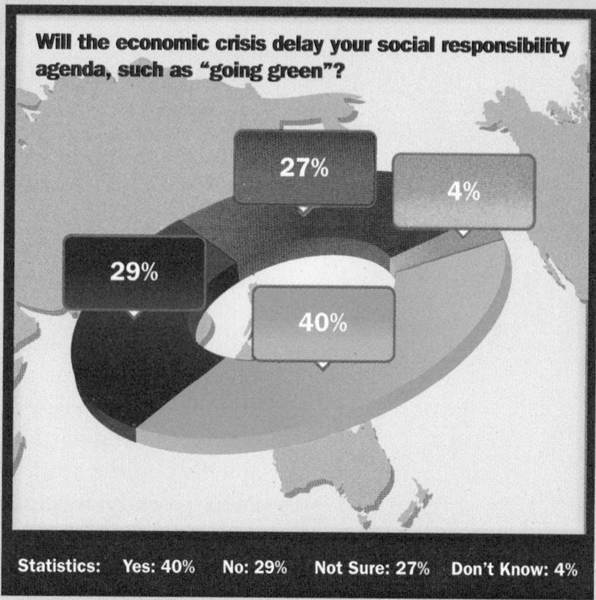

Source: Booz & Co. survey of 828 chief executive officers and managers. Margin of error: 3+/− percentage points.

Corporate concern for the environment. Motorola Co-CEO Sanjay Jha helps clear brush at the Old School Forest Preserve in Libertyville, Illinois, as part of the company's fourth Annual Global Day of Services. Employees from 41 countries volunteered in their communities, with their focus on the environment.

industrialized areas combines with moisture in the atmosphere to form acids that are spread by winds. The acids eventually fall to Earth in rain, which finds its way into streams, rivers, and lakes. The acid-rain problem has spread rapidly in recent years, and experts fear that the situation will worsen if the nation begins to burn more coal to generate electricity. To solve the problem, investigators first must determine where the sulfur is being emitted. The costs of this vital investigation and cleanup are going to be high. The human costs of having ignored the problem so long may be higher still.

Air Pollution Aviation emissions are a potentially significant and growing percentage of greenhouse gases that contribute to global warming. Aircraft emissions are significant for several reasons. First, jet aircraft are the main source of human emissions deposited directly into the upper atmosphere, where they may have a greater warming effect than if they were released at Earth's surface. Second, carbon dioxide—the primary aircraft emission—is the main focus of international concern. For example, it survives in the atmosphere for nearly 100 years and contributes to global warming, according to the Intergovernmental Panel on Climate Change. The carbon dioxide emissions from worldwide aviation roughly equal those of some industrialized countries. Third, carbon dioxide emissions combined with other gases and particles emitted by jet aircraft could have two to four times as great an effect on the atmosphere as carbon dioxide alone. Fourth, the Intergovernmental Panel recently concluded that the rise in aviation emissions owing to the growing demand for air travel would not be fully offset by reductions in emissions achieved solely through technological improvements.

Usually, two or three factors combine to form air pollution in any given location. The first factor is large amounts of carbon monoxide and hydrocarbons emitted by motor vehicles concentrated in a relatively small area. The second is the smoke and other pollutants emitted by manufacturing facilities. These two factors can be eliminated in part through pollution control devices on cars, trucks, and smokestacks.

A third factor that contributes to air pollution—one that cannot be changed—is the combination of weather and geography. The Los Angeles Basin, for example, combines just the right weather and geographic conditions for creating dense smog. Los Angeles has strict regulations regarding air pollution. Even so, Los Angeles still struggles with air pollution problems because of uncontrollable conditions.

How effective is air pollution control? The EPA estimates that the Clean Air Act and its amendments will eventually result in the removal of 56 billion pounds of pollution from the air each year, thus measurably reducing lung disease, cancer, and other serious health problems caused by air pollution. Other authorities note that we have already seen improvement in air quality. A number of cities have cleaner air today than they did 30 years ago. Even in southern California, bad air-quality days have dropped to less than 40 days a year, about 60 percent lower than that observed just a decade ago. Numerous chemical companies have recognized that they must take responsibility for operating their plants in an environmentally safe manner; some now devote considerable capital to purchasing antipollution devices. For example, 3M's pioneering Pollution Prevention Pays (3P) program, designed to find ways to avoid the generation of pollutants, marked its 30th anniversary in 2005. Since 1975, more than 5,600 employee-driven 3P projects have prevented the generation of more than 2.2 billion pounds of pollutants and produced first-year savings of nearly $1 billion.

Land Pollution Air and water quality may be improving, but land pollution is still a serious problem in many areas. The fundamental issues are (1) how to restore damaged or contaminated land at a reasonable cost and (2) how to protect unpolluted land from future damage.

The land pollution problem has been worsening over the past few years because modern technology has continued to produce increasing amounts of chemical and radioactive waste. U.S. manufacturers produce an estimated 40 to 60 million tons of contaminated oil, solvents, acids, and sludge each year. Service businesses, utility companies, hospitals, and other industries also dump vast amounts of wastes into the environment.

Individuals in the United States contribute to the waste-disposal problem, too. A shortage of landfills, owing to stricter regulations, makes garbage disposal a serious problem in some areas. Incinerators help to solve the landfill-shortage problem, but they bring with them their own problems. They reduce the amount of garbage but also leave tons of ash to be buried—ash that often has a higher concentration of toxicity than the original garbage. Other causes of land pollution include strip mining of coal, nonselective cutting of forests, and development of agricultural land for housing and industry.

To help pay the enormous costs of cleaning up land polluted with chemicals and toxic wastes, Congress created a $1.6 billion Superfund in 1980. Originally, money was to flow into the Superfund from a tax paid by 800 oil and chemical companies that produce toxic waste. The EPA was to use the money in the Superfund to finance the cleanup of hazardous waste sites across the nation. To replenish the Superfund, the EPA had two options: It could sue companies guilty of dumping chemicals at specific waste sites, or it could negotiate with guilty companies and thus completely avoid the legal system. During the 1980s, officials at the EPA came under fire because they preferred negotiated settlements. Critics referred to these settlements as "sweetheart deals" with industry. They felt that the EPA should be much more aggressive in reducing land pollution. Of course, most corporate executives believe that cleanup efficiency and quality might be improved if companies were more involved in the process. Many firms, including Delphi Automotive Systems Corporation and 3M, have modified or halted the production and sale of products that have a negative impact on the environment. For example, after tests showed that ScotchGuard does not decompose in the environment, 3M announced a voluntary end to production of the 40-year-old product, which had generated $300 million in sales.

Noise Pollution Excessive noise caused by traffic, aircraft, and machinery can do physical harm to human beings. Research has shown that people who are exposed to loud noises for long periods of time can suffer permanent hearing loss. The Noise Control Act of 1972 established noise emission standards for aircraft and airports, railroads, and interstate motor carriers. The act also provided funding for noise research at state and local levels.

Noise levels can be reduced by two methods. The source of noise pollution can be isolated as much as possible. (Thus, many metropolitan airports are located outside the cities.) Engineers can also modify machinery and equipment to reduce noise levels. If it is impossible to reduce industrial noise to acceptable levels, workers should be required to wear earplugs to guard them against permanent hearing damage.

Who Should Pay for a Clean Environment?

Governments and businesses are spending billions of dollars annually to reduce pollution—more than $45 billion to control air pollution, $33 billion to control water pollution, and $12 billion to treat hazardous wastes. To make matters worse, much of the money required to purify the environment is supposed to come from already depressed industries, such as the chemical industry. A few firms have discovered that it is cheaper to pay a fine than to install expensive equipment for pollution control.

Entrepreneurial SUCCESS

Recycling Entrepreneurs

As Yale University undergraduates, Rich Littlehale and Bob Casey wondered what to do with their old cell phones and other electronic devices. Some were broken, but some still worked, even if the technology was outdated. The two friends realized that if they could persuade people to recycle gadgets instead of throwing them away, they would be helping the environment. The more they researched the situation, the more it seemed like a good business opportunity as well as a good way to solve a growing problem.

Casey and Littlehale named their new company TwigTek and began contacting firms that refurbish and resell used devices as well as firms that reclaim recyclable parts from unusable electronics. Then they set up collection boxes near Yale's New Haven campus as drop-off points for unwanted devices. However, volume was lower than they had hoped, so the co-founders made two key changes. First, they set up a Web site, YouRenew.com, to make the process more convenient. Second, they began paying consumers for unwanted devices.

© Bakalusha/Shutterstock.com

These two changes made all the difference. Today TwigTek has a staff of 15, buys back thousands of devices every month for recycling, and donates part of the profits to environmental groups. What about competition? Co-founder Casey observes: "Less than 10 percent of unwanted devices are recycled, so our biggest competition is the trash can."

Sources: Cara Baruzzi, "Growing 'Green' Start-up Focused on Recycling Is Poised to Expand," *New Haven Register,* December 13, 2009, http://www.nhregister.com/articles/2009/12/13/business/doc4b22f9ae0706d548182201.txt; Cara Baruzzi, "New Haven Company Proves It Pays to Recycle," *New Haven Register,* April 14, 2009, http://www.nhregister.com/articles/2009/04/14/business/c1-_renew14.txt; "Student Electronics Recycling Entrepreneurs 'Graduate' from Start-up Status into New Space," *EDC New Haven,* November 30, 2009, http://www.prlog.org/10432966-student-electronics-recycling-entrepreneurs-graduate-from-startup-status-into-new-space.html; Alex Zurita, "The Land of Misfit Electronics," *NBC Connecticut,* June 23, 2009, http://www.nbcconnecticut.com.

Who, then, will pay for the environmental cleanup? Many business leaders offer one answer—tax money should be used to cleanup the environment and to keep it clean. They reason that business is not the only source of pollution, so business should not be forced to absorb the entire cost of the cleanup. Environmentalists disagree. They believe that the cost of proper treatment and disposal of industrial wastes is an expense of doing business. In either case, consumers probably will pay a large part of the cost—either as taxes or in the form of higher prices for goods and services.

10

Identify the steps a business must take to implement a program of social responsibility.

Implementing a Program of Social Responsibility

A firm's decision to be socially responsible is a step in the right direction—but only the first step. The firm then must develop and implement a program to reach this goal. The program will be affected by the firm's size, financial resources, past record in the area of social responsibility, and competition. Above all, however, the program must have the firm's total commitment or it will fail.

Developing a Program of Social Responsibility

An effective program for social responsibility takes time, money, and organization. In most cases, developing and implementing such a program will require four steps: securing the commitment of top executives, planning, appointing a director, and preparing a social audit.

Commitment of Top Executives Without the support of top executives, any program will soon falter and become ineffective. For example, the Boeing Company's Ethics and Business Conduct Committee is responsible for the ethics program. The committee is appointed by the Boeing board of directors, and its members include the company chairman and CEO, the president and chief operating officer, the presidents of the operating groups, and senior vice presidents. As evidence of their commitment to social responsibility, top managers should develop a policy statement that outlines key areas of concern. This statement sets a tone of positive support and later will serve as a guide for other employees as they become involved in the program.

Planning Next, a committee of managers should be appointed to plan the program. Whatever form their plan takes, it should deal with each of the issues described in the top managers' policy statement. If necessary, outside consultants can be hired to help develop the plan.

Appointment of a Director After the social responsibility plan is established, a top-level executive should be appointed to implement the organization's plan. This individual should be charged with recommending specific policies and helping individual departments to understand and live up to the social responsibilities the firm has assumed. Depending on the size of the firm, the director may require a staff to handle the program on a day-to-day basis. For example, at the Boeing Company, the director of ethics and business conduct administers the ethics and business conduct program.

The Social Audit At specified intervals, the program director should prepare a social audit for the firm. A **social audit** is a comprehensive report of what an organization has done and is doing with regard to social issues that affect it. This document provides the information the firm needs to evaluate and revise its social responsibility program. Typical subject areas include human resources, community involvement, the quality and safety of products, business practices, and efforts to reduce pollution and improve the environment. The information included in a social audit should be as accurate and as quantitative as possible, and the audit should reveal both positive and negative aspects of the program.

Today, many companies listen to concerned individuals within and outside the company. For example, the Boeing Ethics Line listens to and acts on concerns expressed by employees and others about possible violations of company policies, laws, or regulations, such as improper or unethical business practices, as well as health, safety, and environmental issues. Employees are encouraged to communicate their concerns, as well as ask questions about ethical issues. The Ethics Line is available to all Boeing employees, including Boeing subsidiaries. It is also available to concerned individuals outside the company.

Funding the Program

We have noted that social responsibility costs money. Thus, just like any other corporate undertaking, a program to improve social responsibility must be funded. Funding can come from three sources:

1. Management can pass the cost on to consumers in the form of higher prices.
2. The corporation may be forced to absorb the cost of the program if, for example, the competitive situation does not permit a price increase. In this case, the cost is treated as a business expense, and profit is reduced.
3. The federal government may pay for all or part of the cost through tax reductions or other incentives.

social audit a comprehensive report of what an organization has done and is doing with regard to social issues that affect it

return to inside business

Divine Chocolate

Divine Chocolate makes more than premium chocolate—it makes a difference in the everyday lives of the thousands of cocoa farmers who are part-owners, as members of Ghana's Kuapa Kokoo cooperative. The farmers are guaranteed a high price for the Fairtrade-certified cocoa beans they sell to Divine Chocolate. They also share in the profits from sales of Divine Chocolate products and have a say in how the company is run.

Day by day, more retailers are stocking Divine Chocolate products and the company is gaining wider recognition for its top-quality chocolate and its unique background. Customers who buy the company's chocolate bars not only enjoy the rich taste, they feel good about supporting a socially responsible business that has been a force for positive change in villages throughout Ghana.

Questions

1. Does Divine Chocolate appear to be closer to the economic or the socioeconomic model of social responsibility, as shown in Table 2.3?
2. Kuapa Kokoo now owns 45 percent of the U.K. Divine Chocolate and 33 percent of the U.S. Divine Chocolate. Do you think it should own at least half of each company? Why or why not?

Sources: Leonie Nimmo and Dan Welch, "Chocolate Revolution from the World's Favourite Treat," *The Guardian (UK)*, October 14, 2009, http://www.guardian.co.uk/environment/blog/oct/14/chocolate-week-fairtrade-ethical-living; Kiri Blakeley, "Entrepreneurs: Saving the World, One Chocolate Bar at a Time," *Forbes.com*, May 15, 2009, http://www.forbes.com/2009/05/14/small-business-ceo-forbes-woman-entrepreneurs-food.html; http://www.divinechocolate.com; http://www.divinechocolateusa.com.

CHAPTER REVIEW

Summary

1 Understand what is meant by *business ethics.*

Ethics is the study of right and wrong and of the morality of choices. Business ethics is the application of moral standards to business situations.

2 Identify the types of ethical concerns that arise in the business world.

Ethical issues arise often in business situations out of relationships with investors, customers, employees, creditors, or competitors. Businesspeople should make every effort to be fair, to consider the welfare of customers and others within the firm, to avoid conflicts of interest, and to communicate honestly.

3 Discuss the factors that affect the level of ethical behavior in organizations.

Individual, social, and opportunity factors all affect the level of ethical behavior in an organization. Individual factors include knowledge level, moral values and attitudes, and personal goals. Social factors include cultural norms and the actions and values of co-workers and significant others. Opportunity factors refer to the amount of leeway that exists in an organization for employees to behave unethically if they choose to do so.

4 Explain how ethical decision making can be encouraged.

Governments, trade associations, and individual firms can establish guidelines for defining ethical behavior. Governments can pass stricter regulations. Trade associations provide ethical guidelines for their members. Companies provide codes of ethics—written guides to acceptable and ethical behavior as defined by an organization—and create an atmosphere in which ethical behavior is encouraged. An ethical employee working in an unethical environment may resort to whistle-blowing to bring a questionable practice to light.

5 Describe how our current views on the social responsibility of business have evolved.

In a socially responsible business, management realizes that its activities have an impact on society and considers that impact in the decision-making process. Before the 1930s, workers, consumers, and government had very little influence on business activities; as a result, business leaders gave little thought to social responsibility. All this changed with the Great Depression. Government regulations, employee demands, and consumer awareness combined to create a demand that businesses act in socially responsible ways.

6 Explain the two views on the social responsibility of business and understand the arguments for and against increased social responsibility.

The basic premise of the economic model of social responsibility is that society benefits most when business is left alone to produce profitable goods and services. According to the socioeconomic model, business has as much responsibility to society as it has to its owners. Most managers adopt a viewpoint somewhere between these two extremes.

7 Discuss the factors that led to the consumer movement and list some of its results.

Consumerism consists of all activities undertaken to protect the rights of consumers. The consumer movement generally has demanded—and received—attention from business in the areas of product safety, product information, product choices through competition, and the resolution of complaints about products and business practices. Although concerns over consumer rights have been around to some extent since the early 19th century, the movement became more powerful in the 1960s when President John F. Kennedy initiated the Consumer Bill of Rights. The six basic rights of consumers include the right to safety, the right to be informed, the right to choose, the right to be heard, and the rights to consumer education and courteous service.

8 Analyze how present employment practices are being used to counteract past abuses.

Legislation and public demand have prompted some businesses to correct past abuses in employment practices—mainly with regard to minority groups. Affirmative action and training of the hard-core unemployed are two types of programs that have been used successfully.

9 Describe the major types of pollution, their causes, and their cures.

Industry has contributed to noise pollution and pollution of our land and water through the dumping of wastes, and to air pollution through vehicle and smokestack emissions. This contamination can be cleaned up and controlled, but the big question is: Who will pay? Present cleanup efforts are funded partly by government tax revenues, partly by business, and in the long run by consumers.

10 Identify the steps a business must take to implement a program of social responsibility.

A program to implement social responsibility in a business begins with total commitment by top management. The program should be planned carefully, and a capable director should be appointed to implement it. Social audits should be prepared periodically as a means of evaluating and revising the program. Programs may be funded through price increases, reduction of profit, or federal incentives.

Key Terms

You should now be able to define and give an example relevant to each of the following terms:

ethics (39)
business ethics (39)
Sarbanes-Oxley Act of 2002 (43)
code of ethics (44)
whistle-blowing (44)
social responsibility (47)
caveat emptor (51)
economic model of social responsibility (52)
socioeconomic model of social responsibility (52)
consumerism (54)
minority (56)
affirmative action program (58)
Equal Employment Opportunity Commission (EEOC) (59)
hard-core unemployed (59)
National Alliance of Business (NAB) (59)
pollution (60)
social audit (65)

Review Questions

1. Why might an individual with high ethical standards act less ethically in business than in his or her personal life?
2. How would an organizational code of ethics help to ensure ethical business behavior?
3. How and why did the American business environment change after the Great Depression?
4. What are the major differences between the economic model of social responsibility and the socioeconomic model?
5. What are the arguments for and against increasing the social responsibility of business?
6. Describe and give an example of each of the six basic rights of consumers.
7. There are more women than men in the United States. Why, then, are women considered a minority with regard to employment?
8. What is the goal of affirmative action programs? How is this goal achieved?
9. What is the primary function of the Equal Employment Opportunity Commission?
10. How do businesses contribute to each of the four forms of pollution? How can they avoid polluting the environment?
11. Our environment can be cleaned up and kept clean. Why haven't we simply done so?
12. Describe the steps involved in developing a social responsibility program within a large corporation.

Discussion Questions

1. When a company acts in an ethically questionable manner, what types of problems are caused for the organization and its customers?
2. How can an employee take an ethical stand regarding a business decision when his or her superior already has taken a different position?
3. Overall, would it be more profitable for a business to follow the economic model or the socioeconomic model of social responsibility?
4. Why should business take on the task of training the hard-core unemployed?
5. To what extent should the blame for vehicular air pollution be shared by manufacturers, consumers, and government?
6. Why is there so much government regulation involving social responsibility issues? Should there be less?

Video Case 2.1

Scholfield Honda—Going Green with Honda

Signs of green marketing can be found everywhere today: reusable shopping bags are the rule rather than the exception, organic and natural products fill grocers' shelves, and socially responsible companies are increasing their efforts to reduce pollution, conserve water and energy, and recycle waste paper, plastic, and other reusable materials.

Of course, some companies have always been ahead of the curve. Since the early 1970s, Honda has been producing the low-emissions, fuel-efficient Civic model, and the company has never strayed from its roots. Today's Honda line consists of four classes of vehicles: Good, Better, Best, and Ultimate. Its regular gas cars are Good, with about 30 mpg; hybrids are Better at about 45 mpg; and its Best solution is a natural gas-powered Civic GX, which gets about 220 miles to a tank. Honda also has Ultimate solutions in the works, such as the new Honda FCX Clarity—a hydrogen fuel cell car that uses hydrogen and oxygen to create electricity. Although the Civic GX and Clarity models are available to consumers, neither vehicle is practical for the average driver as fueling stations are scarce.

Alternative energy vehicles are making their way to the Midwest. Lee Lindquist, an alternative fuels specialist at Scholfield Honda in Wichita, Kansas, was researching alternative fuel vehicles for a local Sierra Club meeting when he learned that municipalities in New York and California used the natural gas Civic GX to address air-quality issues. Although Lee recognized that his own Wichita market was not teeming with green consumers, he knew that people needed ways to combat rising fuel prices—so he proposed the Civic GX for use at his dealership.

Lee's boss was skeptical of the idea. Although management was open to clever ways to promote the dealership, owner Roger Scholfield did not want to risk muddying the waters with a new and somewhat impractical vehicle. Nevertheless, he agreed to offer the car to his fleet and corporate customers, and in time fate offered another opportunity for Scholfield Honda to go green.

In May 2007, a devastating tornado hit the nearby town of Greensburg, Kansas, leveling the area. Once again Lee Lindquist approached his boss. This time, he proposed donating both a Honda Civic GX and a natural-gas fueling station to Greensburg as a way of helping the town rebuild. Upon careful reflection, Roger realized that Lee's idea would benefit his dealership through good publicity and higher awareness of alternative fuel vehicles. Scholfield made the Civic model and fuel station available to Greensburg residents free of charge, and the dealership has been on the green bandwagon ever since.

Although there are more cost-effective ways of advertising, Roger Scholfield notes that customers are becoming more interested in alternative fuel vehicles since he donated the Civic GX. In addition, his dealership has generated plenty of goodwill in the press and among local residents—Scholfield Honda has developed a good reputation for its commitment to the environment and the people of Greensburg, even opening a "Honda Green Zone" conference room on the premises. The room can hold several hundred people. It includes a digital projector, sound system, and kitchenette and is available free to local firms and organizations for meetings and conferences. Its chairs, tables, tiles, and flooring are all made from recycled materials.[17]

Questions

1. How would you rate Scholfield Honda's sense of social responsibility? Does the dealership meet all the criteria for a socially responsible company?
2. What is Scholfield Honda's primary ethical responsibility in situations where a proposed green initiative is cost-prohibitive or even detrimental to the company's bottom line?
3. Should the government regulate companies' claims that their products are green? Should official classifications for environmental friendliness be defined?

Case 2.2

Belu Water Aims to Change the World

Reed Paget was a journalist and documentary filmmaker when, in 2001, he covered the launch of the United Nations' Global Compact. Paget was deeply impressed by this environmental initiative's call to "use capitalism to change the world." What better mechanism is there for change, he thought, than business, with its wide financial and entrepreneurial resources and its risk-taking mind-set?

Although he had no business experience, Paget was determined to start a company in the United Kingdom that would be both socially responsible and environmentally friendly. When he learned that a quarter of the world's people have no access to clean water, he decided to create a bottled water company, both to alert the public to the global water crisis and to show that bottled water could be manufactured and marketed in an environmentally sustainable way. Finally, Paget determined that all his company's profits would be donated to clean-water projects.

With start-up funding from the Idyll Foundation, a team of friends, and a stack of business how-to books, Paget sat down to develop a brand name, find a bottle design, work out a manufacturing deal, and find customers. Coming up with a name that was not already trademarked was a challenge, but the team settled on "Belu" (pronounced "belloo") to evoke the color of water and the idea of beauty. A deal with an upscale designer yielded an affordable glass bottle design. After taste-test visits to more than 70 sources of water around the United Kingdom, Paget selected Wenlock Water, a supplier of natural mineral water located in the Shropshire hills. Not only was the water great; it was more ecologically friendly for a U.K. company than bottling and shipping water from springs in the mountains of France, which is what competitor Evian does.

A marketing firm helped Belu land its first customer, the Waitrose supermarket chain. With additional funding to pay for the initial run of glass bottles, Belu delivered its first order in May 2004. Soon the company put up a Web site, obtained further funding, and secured distribution through Tesco, the leading U.K. supermarket chain. Sales increased as Belu, positioned as the first bottled water that does not contribute to climate change, began to prove its appeal to consumers.

Another breakthrough came when the company found a manufacturer to produce corn-based bottles for its water. The bottles are completely stable on store shelves but biodegrade back to soil in just eight weeks, under the right conditions of heat and humidity and with a little help from microorganisms. Although this compostable bottle is more costly than traditional plastic or glass bottles, the use of eco-friendly packaging is important to Belu and its customers.

Bottled water is a multibillion-dollar industry worldwide, with huge profit potential. Still, Belu faces intense competition from a number of multinational giants as well as from firms that serve local areas. One major rival is Nestlé, which owns such water brands as Perrier, Pellegrino, and Nestlé Pure Life™. Another is Group Danone, which owns Evian and Volvic, among other brands. Belu must also consider competition from tap water and from beverages such as soft drinks and juices, which can be substituted for bottled water.

Thanks to its positioning on the basis of social responsibility and sustainability, Belu Water™ now reaches more than 500,000 consumers each month. Through a charity called WaterAid, the company has brought clean water, wells, and hand pumps to more than 20,000 people in India and Mali, with expectations of helping at least ten times this number in the coming years. It uses clean electricity, offsets its remaining carbon emissions, and has won numerous awards, including Social Enterprise of the Year and Social Entrepreneur of the Year (in partnership with Schwab Foundation). Backed by smart marketing, Belu will keep growing sales and generating more profits to help more people in the future.[18]

For more information about this organization, go to http://www.belu.org.

Questions

1. Belu Water gives all its profits away and is the first firm to package water in corn-based bottles. Do you think its levels of eco-consciousness and social responsibility set a realistic model of environmental performance for other manufacturing companies? Why or why not?
2. Why does Belu Water produce a saleable product instead of just asking the public to donate money for clean-water projects?
3. Do you agree with Reed Paget that business is ideally suited to "change the world"? Explain your answer.

Building Skills for Career Success

❶ JOURNALING FOR SUCCESS

Discovery statement: This chapter was devoted mostly to business ethics, ethical concerns that arise in the business world, personal ethics, and social responsibility of business.

Assume that you are an accountant at ABC Corporation, where you question the company's accounting practices. What legal and managerial changes would you suggest to prevent the use of accounting tricks to manipulate corporate earnings?

Assignment

1. Assume that your manager refuses to incorporate any of your suggestions. Would you blow the whistle? Why or why not?
2. Suppose that you blow the whistle and get fired. Which law might protect your rights, and how would you proceed to protect yourself?

❷ EXPLORING THE INTERNET

Socially responsible business behavior can be as simple as donating unneeded older computers to schools, mentoring interested learners in good business practices, or supplying public speakers to talk about career opportunities. Students, as part of the public at large, perceive a great deal of information about a company, its employees, and its owners by the positive social actions taken, and perhaps even more by actions not taken. Microsoft donates millions of dollars of computers and software to educational institutions every year. Some people consider this level of corporate giving to be insufficient given the scale of the wealth of the corporation. Others believe that firms have no obligation to give back any more than they wish and that recipients should be grateful. Visit the text Web site for updates to this exercise.

Assignment

1. Select any firm involved in high technology and the Internet such as Microsoft or IBM. Examine its Web site and report its corporate position on social responsibility and giving as it has stated it. What activities is it involved in? What programs does it support, and how does it support them?
2. Search the Internet for commentary on business social responsibility, form your own opinions, and then evaluate the social effort demonstrated by the firm you have selected. What more could the firm have done?

❸ DEVELOPING CRITICAL-THINKING SKILLS

Recently, an article entitled "Employees Coming to Terms with Moral Issues on the Job" appeared in a big-city newspaper. It posed the following situations:

You are asked to work on a project you find morally wrong.

Important tasks are left undone because a co-worker spends more time planning a social event than working on a proposal.

Your company is knowingly selling defective merchandise to customers.

Unfortunately, many employees currently are struggling with such issues. The moral dilemmas that arise when employees find their own ethical values incompatible with the work they do every day are causing a lot of stress in the workplace, and furthermore, these dilemmas are not being discussed. There exists an ethics gap. You already may have faced a similar situation in your workplace.

Assignment

1. In small groups with your classmates, discuss your answers to the following questions:
   a. If you were faced with any of the preceding situations, what would you do?
   b. Would you complete work you found morally unacceptable, or would you leave it undone and say nothing?
   c. If you spoke up, what would happen to you or your career? What would be the risk?
   d. What are your options?
   e. If you were a manager rather than a lower-level employee, would you feel differently and take a different approach to the issue? Why?
2. In a written report, summarize what you learned from this discussion.

❹ BUILDING TEAM SKILLS

A firm's code of ethics outlines the kinds of behaviors expected within the organization and serves as a guideline for encouraging ethical behavior in the workplace. It reflects the rights of the firm's workers, shareholders, and consumers.

Assignment

1. Working in a team of four, find a code of ethics for a business firm. Start the search by asking firms in your community for a copy of their codes, by visiting the library, or by searching and downloading information from the Internet.
2. Analyze the code of ethics you have chosen, and answer the following questions:
   a. What does the company's code of ethics say about the rights of its workers, shareholders, consumers, and suppliers? How does the code reflect the company's attitude toward competitors?
   b. How does this code of ethics resemble the information discussed in this chapter? How does it differ?
   c. As an employee of this company, how would you personally interpret the code of ethics? How might the code influence your behavior within the workplace? Give several examples.

❺ RESEARCHING DIFFERENT CAREERS

Business ethics has been at the heart of many discussions over the years and continues to trouble employees and shareholders. Stories about dishonesty and wrongful behavior in the workplace appear on a regular basis in newspapers and on the national news.

Assignment

Prepare a written report on the following:

1. Why can it be so difficult for people to do what is right?
2. What is your personal code of ethics? Prepare a code outlining what you believe is morally right. The document should include guidelines for your personal behavior.
3. How will your code of ethics affect your decisions about:
   a. The types of questions you should ask in a job interview?
   b. Selecting a company in which to work?

Exploring Global Business

细节更细腻
moretosee.com
AQUOS
视界更宽广

3

© Newscom

Learning Objectives

What you will be able to do once you complete this chapter:

1. Explain the economic basis for international business.
2. Discuss the restrictions nations place on international trade, the objectives of these restrictions, and their results.
3. Outline the extent of international business and the world economic outlook for trade.
4. Discuss international trade agreements and international economic organizations working to foster trade.
5. Define the methods by which a firm can organize for and enter into international markets.
6. Describe the various sources of export assistance.
7. Identify the institutions that help firms and nations finance international business.

FYI

Did You Know?

Once a small firm in South Korea exporting food products to China, Samsung Electronics now makes more television sets than any other manufacturer on the planet and rings in $110 billion in annual sales.

inside business

Samsung Electronics Shines in the Global Spotlight

In the 40 years since Samsung Electronics made its first television set, the South Korean company has more than lived up to the shining success suggested by its name (which translates as *three stars*). Samsung started as a small firm specializing in exporting food products to China and later branched out into the insurance industry. By 1970, the unit that would become Samsung Electronics was manufacturing black and white televisions and was readying plans to produce additional household and business products for the global marketplace.

Today Samsung Electronics has grown into an international corporation offering everything from cameras and computers to cell phones and semiconductors, even dishwashers and disk drives. It makes more television sets than any other manufacturer on the planet and has long been the market leader in memory chips for computers. It sells more than 200 million cell phones every year, putting it second only to Finland's Nokia in worldwide output. With $110 billion in annual sales and 164,000 employees, Samsung Electronics is a shining star of the global economy.

The electronics industry is intensely competitive, with local firms and global giants, such as Apple, Hewlett-Packard, Intel, and Motorola, fighting for sales on every continent. In fact, Samsung Electronics' main rival in LCD (liquid crystal display) screens is LG, another South Korean company that has prospered by expanding worldwide. Despite its strong competitive position, however, Samsung Electronics is not immune to world economic troubles, and it lost money for a brief period during the recent downturn. Yet, because the company owns and operates its own factories, it was able to control costs and reduce production as soon as the economy started to slow.

To keep its business growing, Samsung Electronics pursues innovation through research and development centers in the United States, Europe, India, and China. It also participates in joint ventures that tackle cutting-edge manufacturing challenges. For example, it is partnered with Sony to jointly own and operate three South Korean factories that produce advanced flat-panel television displays. Looking ahead to a greener future, Samsung Electronics is designing products that are easier on the environment, cutting greenhouse gas emissions, and helping suppliers do business in more sustainable ways.[1]

Samsung Electronics is just one of a growing number of foreign companies, large and small, that are doing business with firms in other countries. Some companies, such as Coca-Cola, sell to firms in other countries; others, such as Pier 1 Imports, buy goods around the world to import into the United States. Whether they buy or sell products across national borders, these companies are all contributing to the volume of international trade that is fueling the global economy.

Theoretically, international trade is every bit as logical and worthwhile as interstate trade between, say, California and Washington. Yet, nations tend to restrict the import of certain goods for a variety of reasons. For example, in the early 2000s, the United States restricted the import of Mexican fresh tomatoes because they were undercutting price levels of domestic fresh tomatoes.

Despite such restrictions, international trade has increased almost steadily since World War II. Many of the industrialized nations have signed trade agreements intended to eliminate problems in international business and to help less-developed nations participate in world trade. Individual firms around the world have seized the opportunity to compete in foreign markets by exporting products and increasing foreign production, as well as by other means.

Signing the Trade Act of 2002, President George W. Bush remarked, "Trade is an important source of good jobs for our workers and a source of higher growth for our economy. Free trade is also a proven strategy for building global prosperity and adding to the momentum of political freedom. Trade is an engine of economic growth. In our lifetime, trade has helped lift millions of people and whole nations out of poverty and put them on the path of prosperity".[2] In his national best seller, *The World Is Flat,* Thomas L. Friedman states, "The flattening of the world has presented us with new opportunities, new challenges, new partners but, also, alas new dangers, particularly as Americans it is imperative that we be the best global citizens that we can be—because in a flat world, if you don't visit a bad neighborhood, it might visit you."

We describe international trade in this chapter in terms of modern specialization, whereby each country trades the surplus goods and services it produces most efficiently for products in short supply. We also explain the restrictions nations place on products and services from other countries and present some of the possible advantages and disadvantages of these restrictions. We then describe the extent of international trade and identify the organizations working to foster it. We describe several methods of entering international markets and the various sources of export assistance available from the federal government. Finally, we identify some of the institutions that provide the complex financing necessary for modern international trade.

1

Explain the economic basis for international business.

The Basis for International Business

International business encompasses all business activities that involve exchanges across national boundaries. Thus, a firm is engaged in international business when it buys some portion of its input from, or sells some portion of its output to, an organization located in a foreign country. (A small retail store may sell goods produced in some other country. However, because it purchases these goods from American distributors, it is not engaged in international trade.)

international business all business activities that involve exchanges across national boundaries

absolute advantage the ability to produce a specific product more efficiently than any other nation

comparative advantage the ability to produce a specific product more efficiently than any other product

Absolute and Comparative Advantage

Some countries are better equipped than others to produce particular goods or services. The reason may be a country's natural resources, its labor supply, or even customs or a historical accident. Such a country would be best off if it could specialize in the production of such products so that it can produce them most efficiently. The country could use what it needed of these products and then trade the surplus for products it could not produce efficiently on its own.

Saudi Arabia thus has specialized in the production of crude oil and petroleum products; South Africa, in diamonds; and Australia, in wool. Each of these countries is said to have an absolute advantage with regard to a particular product. An **absolute advantage** is the ability to produce a specific product more efficiently than any other nation.

One country may have an absolute advantage with regard to several products, whereas another country may have no absolute advantage at all. Yet it is still worthwhile for these two countries to specialize and trade with each other. To see why this is so, imagine that you are the president of a successful manufacturing firm and that you can accurately type 90 words per minute. Your assistant can type 80 words per minute but would run the business poorly. Thus, you have an absolute advantage over your assistant in both typing and managing. However, you cannot afford to type your own letters because your time is better spent in managing the business. That is, you have a **comparative advantage** in managing. A comparative advantage is the ability to produce a specific product more efficiently than any other product.

Exploiting absolute advantage. Saudi Arabia and Siberia have long specialized in the production of crude oil and petroleum products. Because of their natural oil resources, Siberia, Saudi Arabia, and other countries in the Middle East enjoy an absolute advantage—their ability to produce petroleum products more efficiently than any other area of the world.

SPOTLIGHT

The Growing Deficit

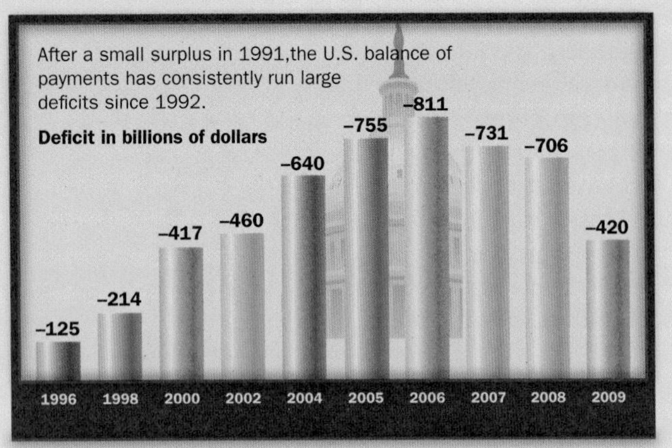

Source: U.S. Department of Commerce, Bureau of Economic Analysis, http://bea.gov/newsreleases/rels.htm, April 22, 2010.

Your assistant, on the other hand, has a comparative advantage in typing because he or she can do that better than managing the business. Thus, you spend your time managing, and you leave the typing to your assistant. Overall, the business is run as efficiently as possible because you are each working in accordance with your own comparative advantage.

The same is true for nations. Goods and services are produced more efficiently when each country specializes in the products for which it has a comparative advantage. Moreover, by definition, every country has a comparative advantage in some product. The United States has many comparative advantages—in research and development, high-technology industries, and identifying new markets, for instance.

Exporting and Importing

Suppose that the United States specializes in producing corn. It then will produce a surplus of corn, but perhaps it will have a shortage of wine. France, on the other hand, specializes in producing wine but experiences a shortage of corn. To satisfy both needs—for corn and for wine—the two countries should trade with each other. The United States should export corn and import wine. France should export wine and import corn.

Exporting is selling and shipping raw materials or products to other nations. The Boeing Company, for example, exports its airplanes to a number of countries for use by their airlines. Figure 3.1 shows the top ten merchandise-exporting states in this country.

exporting selling and shipping raw materials or products to other nations

Figure 3.1 The Top Ten Merchandise-Exporting States

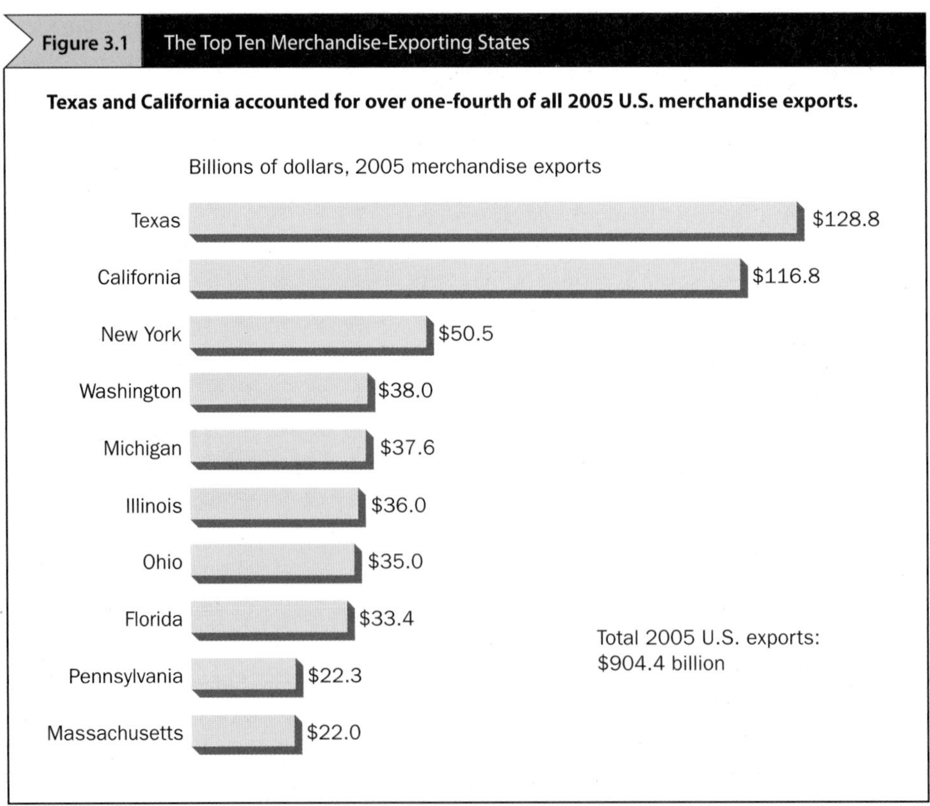

Source: http://www.ita.doc.gov/td/industry/otea/state/2005_year_end_dollar_value_05.html (accessed May 23, 2010).

Importing is purchasing raw materials or products in other nations and bringing them into one's own country. Thus, buyers for Macy's department stores may purchase rugs in India or raincoats in England and have them shipped back to the United States for resale.

Importing and exporting are the principal activities in international trade. They give rise to an important concept called the *balance of trade*. A nation's **balance of trade** is the total value of its exports minus the total value of its imports over some period of time. If a country imports more than it exports, its balance of trade is negative and is said to be *unfavorable*. (A negative balance of trade is unfavorable because the country must export money to pay for its excess imports.)

In 2009, the United States imported $1,933 billion worth of goods and services and exported $1,555 billion worth. It thus had a trade deficit of $378 billion. A **trade deficit** is a negative balance of trade (see Figure 3.2). However,

importing purchasing raw materials or products in other nations and bringing them into one's own country

balance of trade the total value of a nation's exports minus the total value of its imports over some period of time

trade deficit a negative balance of trade

Figure 3.2 U.S. International Trade in Goods and Services

If a country imports more goods than it exports, the balance of trade is negative, as it was in the United States from 1987 to 2007.

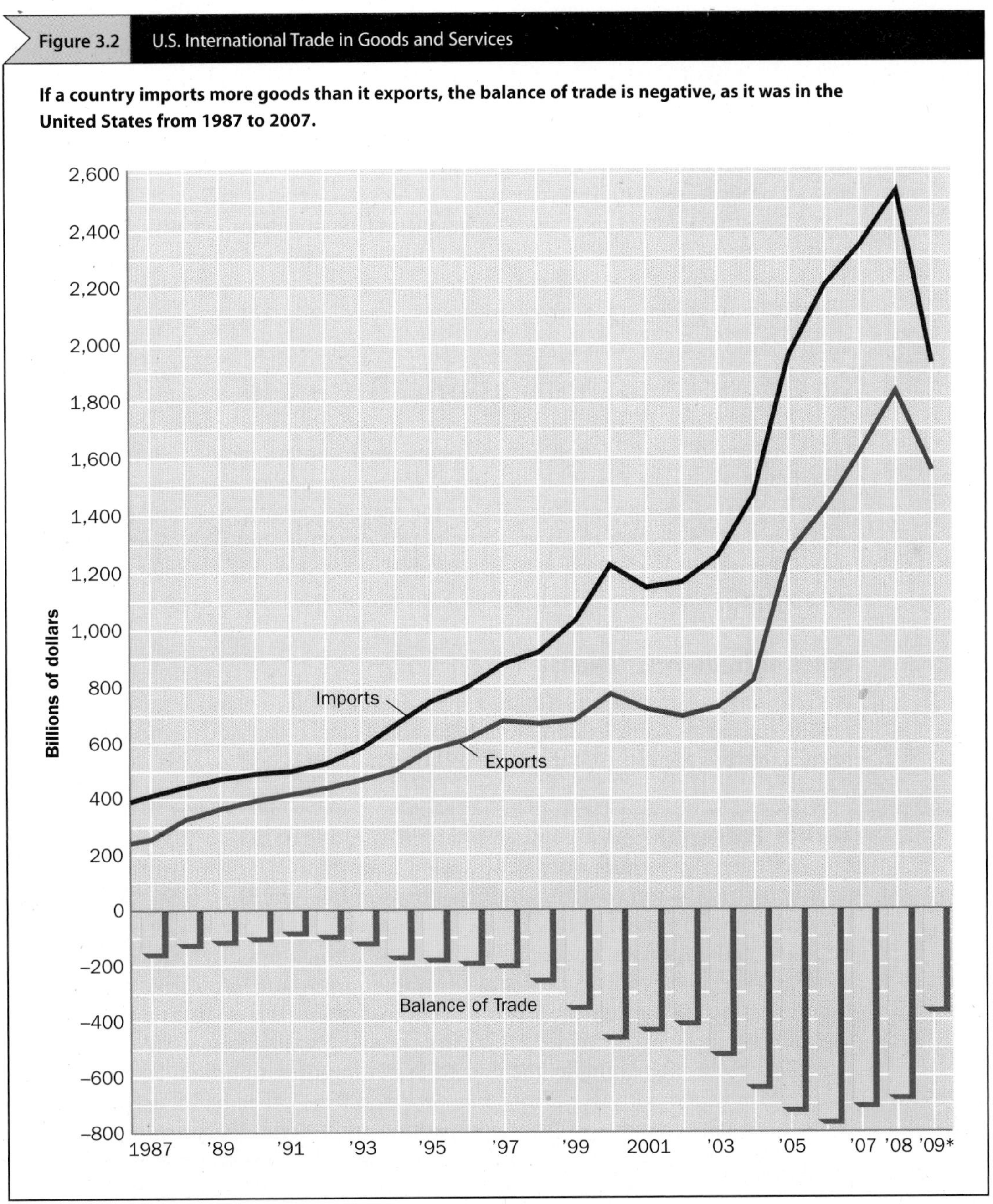

*Preliminary

Source: U.S. Department of Commerce, International Trade Administration, U.S. Bureau of Economic Analysis, http://bea.gov/international/bp_web/simple.cfm?anon=90730&table_id=1&area_id=3 (accessed July 25, 2010).

the United States has consistently enjoyed a large and rapidly growing surplus in services. For example, in 2009, the United States imported $371 billion worth of services and exported $509 billion worth, thus creating a favorable balance of $138 billion.[3]

Question: *Are trade deficits bad?*

Answer: In testimony before the Senate Finance Committee, Daniel T. Griswold, associate director of the Center for Trade Policy at the Cato Institute, remarked, "The trade deficit is not a sign of economic distress, but of rising domestic demand and investment. Imposing new trade barriers will only make Americans worse off while leaving the trade deficit virtually unchanged."

On the other hand, when a country exports more than it imports, it is said to have a *favorable* balance of trade. This has consistently been the case for Japan over the last two decades or so.

A nation's **balance of payments** is the total flow of money into a country minus the total flow of money out of that country over some period of time. Balance of payments, therefore, is a much broader concept than balance of trade. It includes imports and exports, of course. However, it also includes investments, money spent by foreign tourists, payments by foreign governments, aid to foreign governments, and all other receipts and payments.

A continual deficit in a nation's balance of payments (a negative balance) can cause other nations to lose confidence in that nation's economy. Alternatively, a continual surplus may indicate that the country encourages exports but limits imports by imposing trade restrictions.

2

Discuss the restrictions nations place on international trade, the objectives of these restrictions, and their results.

Restrictions to International Business

Specialization and international trade can result in the efficient production of want-satisfying goods and services on a worldwide basis. As we have noted, international business generally is increasing. Yet the nations of the world continue to erect barriers to free trade. They do so for reasons ranging from internal political and economic pressures to simple mistrust of other nations. We examine first the types of restrictions that are applied and then the arguments for and against trade restrictions.

Types of Trade Restrictions

Nations generally are eager to export their products. They want to provide markets for their industries and to develop a favorable balance of trade. Hence, most trade restrictions are applied to imports from other nations.

Tariffs Perhaps the most commonly applied trade restriction is the customs (or import) duty. An **import duty** (also called a **tariff**) is a tax levied on a particular foreign product entering a country. For example, the United States imposes a 2.2 percent import duty on fresh Chilean tomatoes, an 8.7 percent duty if tomatoes are dried and packaged, and nearly 12 percent if tomatoes are made into ketchup or salsa. The two types of tariffs are revenue tariffs and protective tariffs; both have the effect of raising the price of the product in the importing nations, but for different reasons. *Revenue tariffs* are imposed solely to generate income for the government. For example, the United States imposes a duty on Scotch whiskey solely for revenue purposes. *Protective tariffs,* on the other hand, are imposed to protect a domestic industry from competition by keeping the price of competing imports level with or higher than the price of similar domestic products. Because fewer units of the product will be sold at the increased price, fewer units will be imported. The French and Japanese agricultural sectors would both shrink drastically if their nations abolished the protective tariffs that keep the price of

balance of payments the total flow of money into a country minus the total flow of money out of that country over some period of time

import duty (tariff) a tax levied on a particular foreign product entering a country

imported farm products high. Today, U.S. tariffs are the lowest in history, with average tariff rates on all imports under 3 percent.

Some countries rationalize their protectionist policies as a way of offsetting an international trade practice called *dumping*. **Dumping** is the exportation of large quantities of a product at a price lower than that of the same product in the home market.

Thus, dumping drives down the price of the domestic item. Recently, for example, the Pencil Makers Association, which represents eight U.S. pencil manufacturers, charged that low-priced pencils from Thailand and the People's Republic of China were being sold in the United States at less than fair value prices. Unable to compete with these inexpensive imports, several domestic manufacturers had to shut down. To protect themselves, domestic manufacturers can obtain an antidumping duty through the government to offset the advantage of the foreign product. In 2010, for example, the U.S. Department of Commerce imposed antidumping duties of up to 99 percent on a variety of steel products imported from China, following allegations by U.S. Steel Corp. and other producers that the products were being dumped at unfair prices.

The United States-Brazil cotton dispute. After a series of fruitless discussions between the United States and Brazil, the World Trade Organization ruled that the United States and European Union have been dumping cotton in developing countries, hurting poor farmers in the developing country.

Nontariff Barriers A **nontariff barrier** is a nontax measure imposed by a government to favor domestic over foreign suppliers. Nontariff barriers create obstacles to the marketing of foreign goods in a country and increase costs for exporters. The following are a few examples of government-imposed nontariff barriers:

- An **import quota** is a limit on the amount of a particular good that may be imported into a country during a given period of time. The limit may be set in terms of either quantity (so many pounds of beef) or value (so many dollars' worth of shoes). Quotas also may be set on individual products imported from specific countries. Once an import quota has been reached, imports are halted until the specified time has elapsed.
- An **embargo** is a complete halt to trading with a particular nation or of a particular product. The embargo is used most often as a political weapon. At present, the United States has import embargoes against Iran and North Korea—both as a result of extremely poor political relations.
- A **foreign-exchange control** is a restriction on the amount of a particular foreign currency that can be purchased or sold. By limiting the amount of foreign currency importers can obtain, a government limits the amount of goods importers can purchase with that currency. This has the effect of limiting imports from the country whose foreign exchange is being controlled.
- A nation can increase or decrease the value of its money relative to the currency of other nations. **Currency devaluation** is the reduction of the value of a nation's currency relative to the currencies of other countries.

Devaluation increases the cost of foreign goods, whereas it decreases the cost of domestic goods to foreign firms. For example, suppose that the British pound is worth \$2. In this case, an American-made \$2,000 computer can be purchased for £1,000. However, if the United Kingdom devalues the pound so that it is worth only \$1, that same computer will cost £2,000. The increased cost, in pounds, will reduce the import of American computers—and all foreign goods—into England.

On the other hand, before devaluation, a £500 set of English bone china will cost an American \$1,000. After the devaluation, the set of china will cost only \$500. The

dumping exportation of large quantities of a product at a price lower than that of the same product in the home market

nontariff barrier a nontax measure imposed by a government to favor domestic over foreign suppliers

import quota a limit on the amount of a particular good that may be imported into a country during a given period of time

embargo a complete halt to trading with a particular nation or in a particular product

foreign-exchange control a restriction on the amount of a particular foreign currency that can be purchased or sold

currency devaluation the reduction of the value of a nation's currency relative to the currencies of other countries

Restrictions or not, international business is booming. Globalization is the reality of our time. As trade barriers decrease, ever-increasing numbers of U.S. companies are entering the global marketplace, creating more choices for consumers.

decreased cost will make the china—and all English goods—much more attractive to U.S. purchasers. Bureaucratic red tape is more subtle than the other forms of nontariff barriers. Yet it can be the most frustrating trade barrier of all. A few examples are the unnecessarily restrictive application of standards and complex requirements related to product testing, labeling, and certification.

Another type of nontariff barrier is related to cultural attitudes. Cultural barriers can impede acceptance of products in foreign countries. For example, illustrations of feet are regarded as despicable in Thailand. When customers are unfamiliar with particular products from another country, their general perceptions of the country itself affect their attitude toward the product and help to determine whether they will buy it. Because Mexican cars have not been viewed by the world as being quality products, Volkswagen, for example, may not want to advertise that some of its models sold in the United States are made in Mexico. Many retailers on the Internet have yet to come to grips with the task of designing an online shopping site that is attractive and functional for all global customers.

Reasons for Trade Restrictions

Various reasons are given for trade restrictions either on the import of specific products or on trade with particular countries. We have noted that political considerations usually are involved in trade embargoes. Other frequently cited reasons for restricting trade include the following:

- *To equalize a nation's balance of payments.* This may be considered necessary to restore confidence in the country's monetary system and in its ability to repay its debts.
- *To protect new or weak industries.* A new, or *infant*, industry may not be strong enough to withstand foreign competition. Temporary trade restrictions may be used to give it a chance to grow and become self-sufficient. The problem is that once an industry is protected from foreign competition, it may refuse to grow, and "temporary" trade restrictions will become permanent. For example, a recent report by the Government Accountability Office (GAO), the congressional investigative agency, has accused the federal government of routinely imposing quotas on foreign textiles without "demonstrating the threat of serious damage" to U.S. industry. The GAO said that the Committee for the Implementation of Textile Agreements sometimes applies quotas even though it cannot prove the textile industry's claims that American companies have been hurt or jobs have been eliminated.
- *To protect national security.* Restrictions in this category generally apply to technological products that must be kept out of the hands of potential enemies. For example, strategic and defense-related goods cannot be exported to unfriendly nations.
- *To protect the health of citizens.* Products may be embargoed because they are dangerous or unhealthy (e.g., farm products contaminated with insecticides).
- *To retaliate for another nation's trade restrictions.* A country whose exports are taxed by another country may respond by imposing tariffs on imports from that country.
- *To protect domestic jobs.* By restricting imports, a nation can protect jobs in domestic industries. However, protecting these jobs can be expensive. For example, protecting 9,000 jobs in the U.S. carbon-steel industry costs $6.8 billion, or $750,000 per job. In addition, Gary Hufbauer and Ben Goodrich, economists at the Institute for International Economics, estimate that the tariffs could

temporarily save 3,500 jobs in the steel industry, but at an annual cost to steel users of $2 billion, or $584,000 per job saved. Yet recently the United States imposed tariffs of up to 616 percent on steel pipes imported from China, South Korea, and Mexico. Similarly, it is estimated that we spent more than $100,000 for every job saved in the apparel manufacturing industry—jobs that seldom paid more than $35,000 a year.

Reasons Against Trade Restrictions

Trade restrictions have immediate and long-term economic consequences—both within the restricting nation and in world trade patterns. These include the following:

- *Higher prices for consumers.* Higher prices may result from the imposition of tariffs or the elimination of foreign competition, as described earlier. For example, imposing quota restrictions and import protections adds $25 billion annually to U.S. consumers' apparel costs by directly increasing costs for imported apparel.
- *Restriction of consumers' choices.* Again, this is a direct result of the elimination of some foreign products from the marketplace and of the artificially high prices that importers must charge for products that are still imported.
- *Misallocation of international resources.* The protection of weak industries results in the inefficient use of limited resources. The economies of both the restricting nation and other nations eventually suffer because of this waste.
- *Loss of jobs.* The restriction of imports by one nation must lead to cutbacks—and the loss of jobs—in the export-oriented industries of other nations. Furthermore, trade protection has a significant effect on the composition of employment. U.S. trade restrictions—whether on textiles, apparel, steel, or automobiles—benefit only a few industries while harming many others. The gains in employment accrue to the protected industries and their primary suppliers, and the losses are spread across all other industries. A few states gain employment, but many other states lose employment.

The Extent of International Business

3

Outline the extent of international business and the world economic outlook for trade.

Restrictions or not, international business is growing. Although the worldwide recessions of 1991 and 2001–2002 slowed the rate of growth, and the 2008–2009 global economic crisis caused the sharpest decline in more than 70 years, globalization is a reality of our time. In the United States, international trade now accounts for over one-fourth of GDP. As trade barriers decrease, new competitors enter the global marketplace, creating more choices for consumers and new opportunities for job seekers. International business will grow along with the expansion of commercial use of the Internet.

The World Economic Outlook for Trade

Although the global economy continued to grow robustly until 2007 economic performance was not equal: growth in the advanced economies slowed and then stopped in 2009, whereas emerging and developing economies continued to grow. Looking ahead, the International Monetary Fund (IMF), an international bank with 186 member nations, expected growth to continue in 2010 and 2011 in both advanced and emerging developing economies.[4]

Although the U.S. economy had been growing steadily since 2000 and recorded the longest peacetime expansion in the nation's history, the worldwide recession which began in December 2007 has slowed the rate of growth. The IMF estimated that the U.S. economy grew by less than half of 1 percent in 2008 and, because of subprime mortgage lending and other global financial problems, declined 2.5 percent in 2009. International experts expected global economic growth of 3.9 percent in 2010 and 4.3 percent in 2011, despite the high oil prices.

Canada and Western Europe Our leading export partner, Canada, is projected to show a growth rate of 2.6 percent in 2010 and 3.6 percent in 2011. The euro area, which declined by 3.9 percent in 2009, grew by 1.0 percent in 2010, and is expected to grow 1.6 percent in 2011. The United Kingdom and smaller European countries, such as Austria, the Netherlands, Sweden, and Switzerland, are expected to experience a recession.

Mexico and Latin America Our second-largest export customer, Mexico, suffered its sharpest recession ever in 1995, and experienced another major setback in 2009. However, its growth rate in 2010 and 2011 is expected to be 4.0 percent and 4.7 percent, respectively. Brazil escaped the recent global economic crisis with only minor setbacks: its growth in 2008 was more than 5 percent, and in 2009 it declined only 0.4 percent. Growth of about 4.7 percent and 3.7 percent is expected in 2010 and 2011, respectively. In general, the Latin American and the Caribbean economies are recovering at a robust pace.

Japan Japan's economy is regaining momentum. Stronger consumer demand and business investment make Japan less reliant on exports for growth. The IMF estimates the growth for Japan at 1.7 percent in 2010 and 2.2 percent in 2011.

Other Asian Countries The economic growth in Asia remained strong in 2008 and 2009 despite the global recession. Growth was led by China, where its economy expanded by 8.7 percent in 2009, and is expected to grow at 10 percent and 9.7 percent in 2010 and 2011, respectively. Growth in India slowed modestly to 5.6 percent in 2009, but is predicted to grow at 7.7 percent and 7.8 percent in 2010 and 2011, respectively. Growth in Indonesia, Malaysia, the Philippines, Thailand, and Vietnam is expected at 4.7 percent and 5.3 percent in 2010 and 2011, respectively. In short, the key emerging economies in Asia are leading the global recovery.

China's emergence as a global economic power has been among the most dramatic economic developments of recent decades. From 1980 to 2004, China's economy averaged a real GDP growth rate of 9.5 percent and became the world's sixth-largest economy. China's total share in world trade expanded from 1 percent in 1980 to almost 6 percent in 2003. By 2004, China had become the third-largest trading nation in dollar terms, behind the United States and Germany and just ahead of Japan.[5]

Emerging Europe The year 2007 marked the sixth consecutive year during which emerging Europe grew much faster than Western Europe, but growth in many countries was uneven. The global economic crisis that plagued this region finally came to an end in 2009, and most countries in the region are expected to see positive growth in 2010 and 2011.

Commonwealth of Independent States The growth in this region is expected to be 3.8 percent in 2010 and 4.0 percent in 2011. Strong growth is expected to continue in Azerbaijan and Armenia, whereas growth is projected to remain stable in Moldova, Tajikistan, and Uzbekistan.

After World War II, trade between the United States and the communist nations of Central and Eastern Europe was minimal. The United States maintained high tariff barriers on imports from most of these countries and also restricted their exports. However, since the disintegration of the Soviet Union and the collapse of communism, trade between the United States and Central and Eastern Europe has expanded substantially.

The countries that made the transition from communist to market economies quickly have recorded positive growth for several years—those that did not continue to struggle. Among the nations that have enjoyed several years of positive economic growth are the member countries of the Central European Free Trade Association: Hungary, the Czech Republic, Poland, Slovenia, and Slovakia.

U.S. exports to Central and Eastern Europe and Russia will increase, as will U.S. investment in these countries, as demand for capital goods and technology opens new markets for U.S. products. There already has been a substantial expansion in trade between the United States and the Czech Republic, Slovakia, Hungary, and Poland. Table 3.1 shows the growth rates from 2008 to 2011 for most regions of the world.

Exports and the U.S. Economy In 2008, U.S. exports supported more than 10.3 million full- and part-time jobs during a historic time, when exports as a percentage of GDP reached the highest levels since 1916. This new record, 12.7 percent of GDP, shows that U.S. businesses have great opportunities in the global marketplace. Even though the global economic crisis caused the number of jobs supported by exports to decline sharply to 8.5 million in 2009, globalization represents a huge opportunity for all countries—rich or poor. The 15-fold increase in trade volume over the past 55 years has been one of the most important factors in the rise of living standards around the world. During this time, exports have become increasingly important to the U.S. economy. Exports as a percentage of U.S. GDP have increased steadily since 1985, except in the 2001 and 2008 recessions. Our exports to developing and newly industrialized countries are on the rise. Table 3.2 shows the value of U.S. merchandise exports to, and imports from, each of the nation's ten major trading partners. Note that Canada and Mexico are our best partners for our exports; China and Canada, for imports.

Figure 3.3 shows the U.S. goods export and import shares in 2009. Major U.S. exports and imports are manufactured goods, agricultural products, and mineral fuels.

Table 3.1 Global Growth Remains Sluggish

Growth has been led by developing countries and emerging markets.

	Annual Percent Change			
	2008	2009	Projected 2010	Projected 2011
World	3.0	0.8	3.9	4.3
United States	0.4	−2.5	2.7	2.4
Euro area	0.6	−3.9	1.0	1.6
United Kingdom	0.5	−4.8	1.3	2.7
Japan	−1.2	−5.3	1.7	2.2
Canada	0.4	−2.6	2.6	3.6
Other advanced economies	1.7	−1.3	3.3	3.6
Newly industrialized Asian economies	1.7	−1.2	4.8	4.7
Developing countries and emerging markets	6.1	2.1	6.0	6.3
Africa	5.2	1.9	4.3	5.3
Developing Asia	7.9	6.5	8.4	8.4
Commonwealth of Independent States	5.5	−7.5	3.8	4.0
Middle East	5.3	2.2	4.5	4.8
Western Hemisphere	4.2	−2.3	3.7	3.8

Source: *International Monetary Fund: World Economic Outlook* by International Monetary Fund. Copyright 2008 by International Monetary Fund. Reproduced with permission of International Monetary Fund via Copyright Clearance Center. http://www.imf.org/external/pubs/ft/weo/2010/update/01/index.htm (accessed April 19, 2010).

Table 3.2 Value of U.S. Merchandise Exports and Imports, 2009

Rank/Trading Partner	Exports ($ billions)	Rank/Trading Partner	Imports ($ billions)
1/Canada	204.7	1/China	296.4
2/Mexico	129.0	2/Canada	224.9
3/China	69.6	3/Mexico	176.5
4/Japan	51.2	4/Japan	95.9
5/United Kingdom	45.7	5/Germany	71.3
6/Germany	43.3	6/United Kingdom	47.5
7/Netherlands	32.3	7/South Korea	39.2
8/South Korea	28.6	8/France	34.0
9/France	26.5	9/Taiwan	28.4
10/Brazil	26.2	10/Venezuela	28.1

Source: U.S. Department of Commerce, International Trade Administration, http://www.census.gov/foreign-trade/statistics/highlights/top/top0912yr.html (accessed April 19, 2010).

4

Discuss international trade agreements and international economic organizations working to foster trade.

International Trade Agreements

The General Agreement on Tariffs and Trade and the World Trade Organization

General Agreement on Tariffs and Trade (GATT) an international organization of 153 nations dedicated to reducing or eliminating tariffs and other barriers to world trade

At the end of World War II, the United States and 22 other nations organized the body that came to be known as GATT. The **General Agreement on Tariffs and Trade (GATT)** was an international organization of 153 nations dedicated to reducing or eliminating tariffs and other barriers to world trade. These 153 nations accounted for more than 97 percent of the world's merchandise trade (see Figure 3.4). GATT, headquartered in Geneva, Switzerland, provided a forum for tariff negotiations and a means for settling international trade disputes and problems. *Most-favored-nation status* (MFN) was the famous principle of GATT. It meant that each GATT member nation was to be treated equally by all contracting nations. Therefore, MFN ensured

Figure 3.3 U.S. Goods Export and Import Shares in 2009

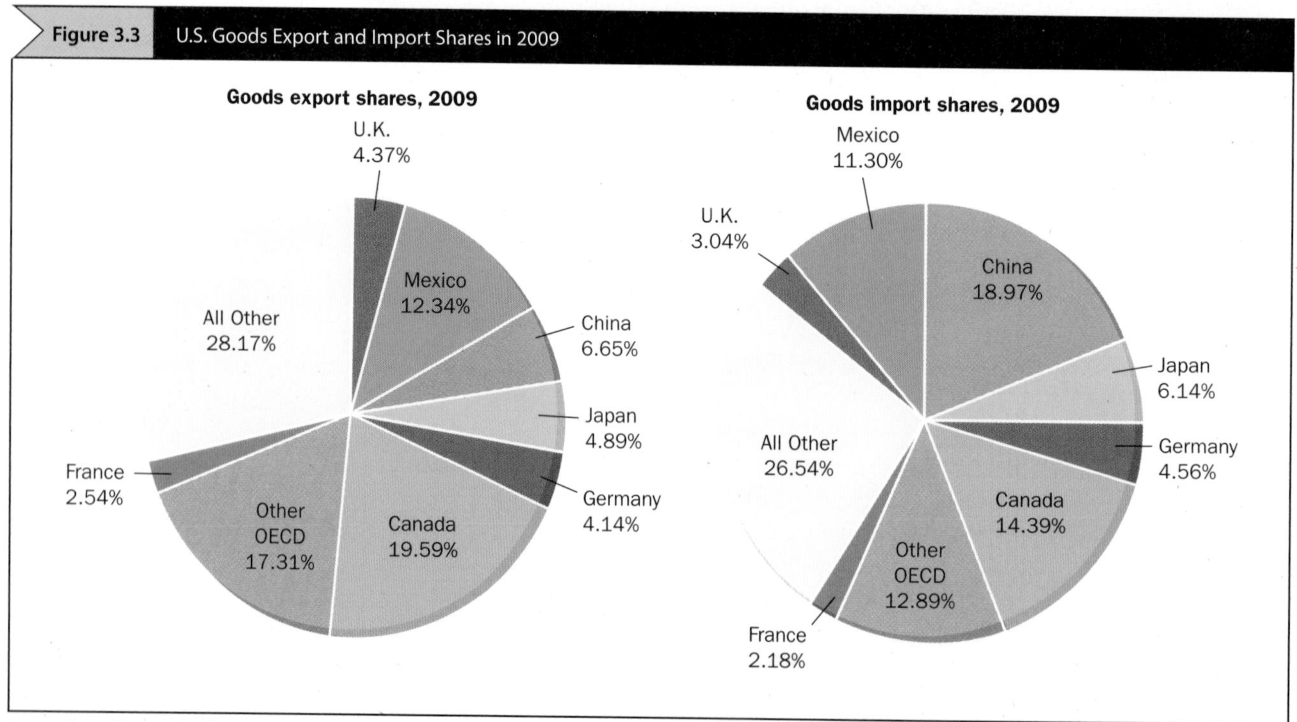

Source: Federal Reserve Bank of St. Louis, *National Economic Trends*, May 2010, 18.

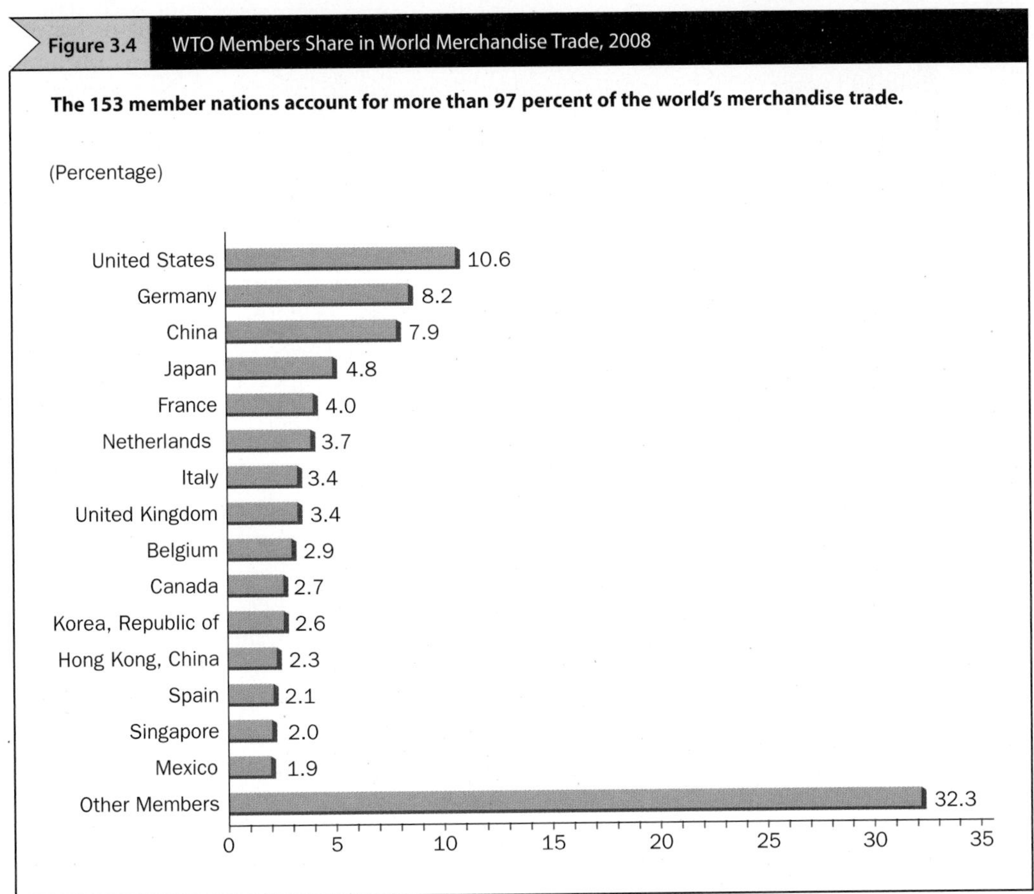

Source: http://www.wto.org (accessed on May 25, 2010).

that any tariff reductions or other trade concessions were extended automatically to all GATT members. From 1947 to 1994, the body sponsored eight rounds of negotiations to reduce trade restrictions. Three of the most fruitful were the Kennedy Round, the Tokyo Round, and the Uruguay Round.

The Kennedy Round (1964–1967) In 1962, the U.S. Congress passed the Trade Expansion Act. This law gave President John F. Kennedy the authority to negotiate reciprocal trade agreements that could reduce U.S. tariffs by as much as 50 percent. Armed with this authority, which was granted for a period of five years, President Kennedy called for a round of negotiations through GATT.

These negotiations, which began in 1964, have since become known as the Kennedy Round. They were aimed at reducing tariffs and other barriers to trade in both industrial and agricultural products. The participants succeeded in reducing tariffs on these products by an average of more than 35 percent. However, they were less successful in removing other types of trade barriers.

The Tokyo Round (1973–1979) In 1973, representatives of approximately 100 nations gathered in Tokyo for another round of GATT negotiations. The *Tokyo Round* was completed in 1979. The participants negotiated tariff cuts of 30 to 35 percent, which were to be implemented over an eight-year period. In addition, they were able to remove or ease such nontariff barriers as import quotas, unrealistic quality standards for imports, and unnecessary red tape in customs procedures.

The Uruguay Round (1986–1993) In 1986, the *Uruguay Round* was launched to extend trade liberalization and widen the GATT treaty to include textiles, agricultural products, business services, and intellectual-property rights.

This most ambitious and comprehensive global commercial agreement in history concluded overall negotiations on December 15, 1993, with delegations on hand from 109 nations. The agreement included provisions to lower tariffs by greater than one-third, to reform trade in agricultural goods, to write new rules of trade for intellectual property and services, and to strengthen the dispute-settlement process. These reforms were expected to expand the world economy by an estimated $200 billion annually.

The Uruguay Round also created the **World Trade Organization (WTO)** on January 1, 1995. The WTO was established by GATT to oversee the provisions of the Uruguay Round and resolve any resulting trade disputes. Membership in the WTO obliges 153 member nations to observe GATT rules. The WTO has judicial powers to mediate among members disputing the new rules. It incorporates trade in goods, services, and ideas and exerts more binding authority than GATT.

The Doha Round (2001) On November 14, 2001, in Doha, Qatar, the WTO members agreed to further reduce trade barriers through multilateral trade negotiations over the next three years. This new round of negotiations focuses on industrial tariffs and nontariff barriers, agriculture, services, and easing trade rules. U.S. exporters of industrial and agricultural goods and services should have improved access to overseas markets. The Doha Round has set the stage for WTO members to take an important step toward significant new multilateral trade liberalization. It is a difficult task, but the rewards—lower tariffs, more choices for consumers, and further integration of developing countries into the world trading system—are sure to be worth the effort. Some experts suggest that U.S. exporters of industrial and agricultural goods and services should have improved access to overseas markets, whereas others disagree. Negotiations between the developed and developing countries continue.

World Trade and Global Economic Crisis

After the sharpest decline in more than 70 years, world trade was set to rebound in 2010 by growing at 9.5 percent, according to the WTO economists. According to WTO Director-General Pascal Lamy, "WTO rules and principles have assisted governments in keeping markets open and they now provide a platform for which trade can grow as the global economy improves. We see the light at the end of the tunnel and trade promises to be an important part of the recovery. But we must avoid derailing any economic revival through protectionism."[6]

Exports from developed economies are expected to rise by 7.5 percent in 2010, whereas exports from the rest of the world, including developing economies and the Commonwealth of Independent States, should increase by 11 percent as the world emerges from recession. This strong expansion will help recover some, but not all, of the loss in 2009, when the global economic crisis caused a 12.2 percent decline in the volume of global trade—the largest such decline since World War II.

International Economic Organizations Working to Foster Trade

The primary objective of the WTO is to remove barriers to trade on a worldwide basis. On a smaller scale, an **economic community** is an organization of nations formed to promote the free movement of resources and products among its members and to create common economic policies. A number of economic communities now exist.

- The European Union (EU), also known as the *European Economic Community* and the *Common Market*, was formed in 1957 by six countries—France, the Federal Republic of Germany, Italy, Belgium, the Netherlands, and Luxembourg. Its objective was freely conducted commerce among these nations and others that might later join. As shown in Figure 3.5, many more nations have joined the EU since then.

World Trade Organization (WTO) powerful successor to GATT that incorporates trade in goods, services, and ideas

economic community an organization of nations formed to promote the free movement of resources and products among its members and to create common economic policies

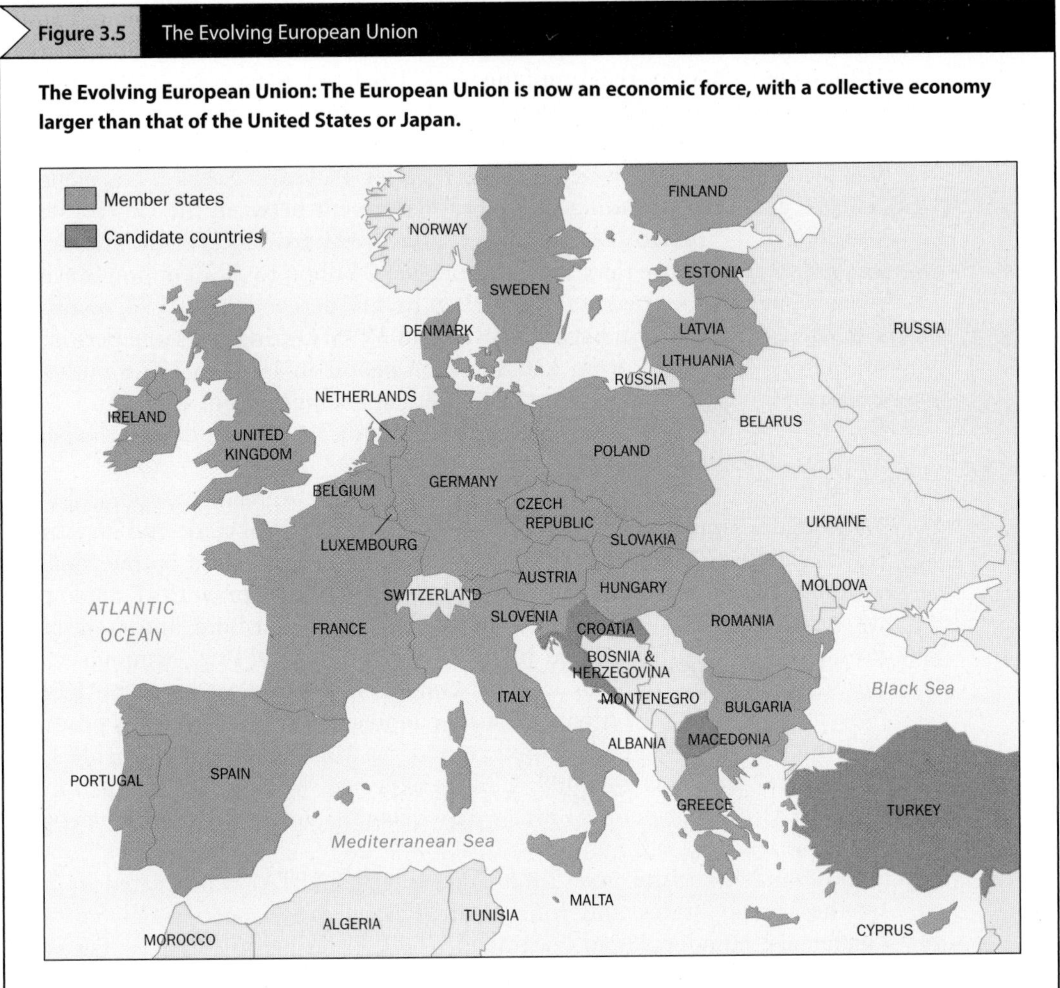

Figure 3.5 The Evolving European Union

The Evolving European Union: The European Union is now an economic force, with a collective economy larger than that of the United States or Japan.

Source: http://europa.eu/abc/european_countries/index_en.htm (accessed May 25, 2010).

- On January 1, 2007, the 25 nations of the EU became the EU27 as Bulgaria and Romania became new members. The EU, with a population of nearly half a billion, is now an economic force with a collective economy larger than much of the United States or Japan.

In celebrating the EU's 50th anniversary in 2007, the president of the European Commission, Jose Manuel Durao Barraso, declared, "Let us first recognize 50 years of achievement. Peace, liberty, and prosperity, beyond the dreams of even the most optimistic founding fathers of Europe. In 1957, 15 of our 27 members were either under dictatorship or were not allowed to exist as independent countries. Now we are all prospering democracies. The EU of today is around 50 times more prosperous and with three times the population of the EU of 1957."

Since January 2002, 15 member nations of the EU have been participating in the new common currency, the euro. The euro is the single currency of the European Monetary Union nations. However, three EU members, Denmark, the United Kingdom, and Sweden, still keep their own currencies.

- A second community in Europe, the *European Economic Area* (EEA), became effective in January 1994. This pact consists of Iceland, Norway, Liechtenstein, and the 27 member nations of the EU. The EEA, encompassing an area inhabited by more than 500 million people, allows for the free movement of goods throughout all 30 countries.

- The *North American Free Trade Agreement* (NAFTA) joined the United States with its first- and second-largest export trading partners, Canada and Mexico. Implementation of NAFTA on January 1, 1994, created a market of more than 454 million people. This market consists of Canada (population 34 million), the United States (309 million), and Mexico (111 million). According to the Office of the U.S. Trade Representative, after 14 years, NAFTA has achieved its core goals of expanding trade and investment between the United States, Canada, and Mexico. For example, from 1993 to 2007, trade among the NAFTA nations more than tripled, from $297 billion to $930 billion. Business investment in the Untied States has risen by 117 percent since 1993, compared to a 45 percent increase between 1979 and 1993. During the same period, the U.S. employment rose from 110.8 million people in 1993 to 137.6 million in 2007, an increase of 24 percent. The average unemployment rate was 5.1 percent in the period 1994 to 2007, compared with 7.1 percent during the period 1980 to 1993.[7]

  NAFTA is built on the Canadian Free Trade Agreement, signed by the United States and Canada in 1989, and on the substantial trade and investment reforms undertaken by Mexico since the mid-1980s. Initiated by the Mexican government, formal negotiations on NAFTA began in June 1991 among the three governments. The support of NAFTA by President Bill Clinton, past U.S. Presidents Ronald Reagan and Jimmy Carter, and Nobel Prize–winning economists provided the impetus for U.S. congressional ratification of NAFTA in November 1993. NAFTA will gradually eliminate all tariffs on goods produced and traded among Canada, Mexico, and the United States to provide for a totally free-trade area by 2009. Chile is expected to become the fourth member of NAFTA, but political forces may delay its entry into the agreement for several years.
- The *Central American Free Trade Agreement* (CAFTA) was created in 2003 by the United States and four Central American countries—El Salvador, Guatemala, Honduras, and Nicaragua. The CAFTA became CAFTA-DR when the Dominican Republic joined the group in 2007. On January 1, 2009, Costa Rica joined CAFTA-DR as the sixth member. CAFTA-DR creates the third-largest U.S. export market in Latin America, behind only Mexico and Brazil. The United States exported $22.4 billion in goods to the five Central American countries and the Dominican Republic in 2007. U.S. exports to the CAFTA-DR countries increased by 14.4 percent in 2008.[8]
- The *Association of Southeast Asian Nations*, with headquarters in Jakarta, Indonesia, was established in 1967 to promote political, economic, and social cooperation among its seven member countries: Indonesia, Malaysia, the Philippines, Singapore, Thailand, Brunei, and Vietnam. With the three new members, Cambodia, Laos, and Myanmar, this region is already our fifth-largest trading partner. The ten-member region, with a population of 592 million, has $1.5 trillion in GDP and accounts for more than $169 million worth of trade with the United States.[9]
- The *Pacific Rim*, referring to countries and economies bordering the Pacific Ocean, is an informal, flexible term generally regarded as a reference to East Asia, Canada, and the United States. At a minimum, the Pacific Rim includes Canada, Japan, China, Taiwan, and the United States.
- The *Commonwealth of Independent States* was established in December 1991 by the newly independent states as an association of 11 republics of the former Soviet Union.
- The *Caribbean Basin Initiative* (CBI) is an inter-American program led by the United States to give economic assistance and trade preferences to the Caribbean and Central American countries. CBI provides duty-free access to the U.S. market for most products from the region and promotes private-sector development in member nations.

- The *Common Market of the Southern Cone* (MERCOSUR) was established in 1991 under the Treaty of Asuncion to unite Argentina, Brazil, Paraguay, and Uruguay as a free-trade alliance; Colombia, Ecuador, Peru, Bolivia, and Chile joined later as associates. The alliance represents more than 267 million consumers—67 percent of South America's population, making it the third-largest trading block behind NAFTA and the EU. Like NAFTA, MERCOSUR promotes "the free circulation of goods, services and production factors among the countries" and established a common external tariff and commercial policy.
- The *Organization of Petroleum Exporting Countries* was founded in 1960 in response to reductions in the prices that oil companies were willing to pay for crude oil. The organization was conceived as a collective bargaining unit to provide oil-producing nations with some control over oil prices.
- The *Organization for Economic Cooperation and Development* (OECD) is a group of 30 industrialized market-economy countries of North America, Europe, the Far East, and the South Pacific. OECD, headquartered in Paris, was established in 1961 to promote economic development and international trade.

Celebrating the 18th anniversary. The MERCOSUR alliance represents more than 267 million consumers—67 percent of South America's population, making it the third-largest trading block. Here, Paraguayan President Fernando Lugo speaks during a ceremony celebrating the 18th anniversary of the creation of the MERCOSUR trade block.

Methods of Entering International Business

5 Define the methods by which a firm can organize for and enter into international markets.

A firm that has decided to enter international markets can do so in several ways. We will discuss several different methods. These different approaches require varying degrees of involvement in international business. Typically, a firm begins its international operations at the simplest level. Then, depending on its goals, it may progress to higher levels of involvement.

Licensing

Licensing is a contractual agreement in which one firm permits another to produce and market its product and use its brand name in return for a royalty or other compensation. For example, Yoplait yogurt is a French yogurt licensed for production in the United States. The Yoplait brand maintains an appealing French image, and in return, the U.S. producer pays the French firm a percentage of its income from sales of the product.

Licensing is especially advantageous for small manufacturers wanting to launch a well-known domestic brand internationally. For example, all Spalding sporting products are licensed worldwide. The licensor, the Questor Corporation, owns the Spalding name but produces no goods itself. Licensing thus provides a simple method for expanding into a foreign market with virtually no investment. On the other hand, if the licensee does not maintain the licensor's product standards, the product's image may be damaged. Another possible disadvantage is that a licensing arrangement may not provide the original producer with any foreign marketing experience.

Exporting

A firm also may manufacture its products in its home country and export them for sale in foreign markets. As with licensing, exporting can be a relatively low-risk method of entering foreign markets. Unlike licensing, however, it is not a simple method; it opens up several levels of involvement to the exporting firm.

licensing a contractual agreement in which one firm permits another to produce and market its product and use its brand name in return for a royalty or other compensation

Going for SUCCESS

LEGO Builds on Licensing for Global Growth

Over the past 15 years, Luke Skywalker, Batman, and Spider-Man have all helped fuel the global growth of Denmark's LEGO Group. Founded in 1932 to market wooden toys, LEGO patented its now iconic interlocking plastic bricks in 1958. The brick system became an instant sensation.

Decades later, with high-tech toys such as robots and video games crowding store shelves, LEGO executives began looking for a way to connect the timeless appeal of their bricks to pop-culture trends worldwide. The answer: licensing. The first license they arranged was with Lucasfilm, covering popular characters such as Luke Skywalker and R2-D2, as well as spaceships and weapons in LEGO form, based on the blockbuster Star Wars films. These licensed products became so popular in so many countries that LEGO pursued additional licenses.

Today the company offers all kinds of licensed products featuring fictional favorites, such as Harry Potter, Indiana Jones, Batman, Spider-Man, and SpongeBob SquarePants. LEGO's license with Walt Disney allows it to market plastic blocks and figures based on Toy Story, Cars, and Prince of Persia. Even as many competitors struggled during the recent economic turmoil, LEGO has prospered because more than half of its global sales come from products linked to such brand licenses.

© tavi/Shutterstock.com

Sources: Lauren McKay, "Where Does Innovation Come From?" *CRM Magazine*, January 2010, 24ff; "Toymaker Grows by Listening to Customers," *Advertising Age*, November 9, 2009, 15; "LEGO: Always Listening," *Advertising Age*, October 19, 2009, 4; "Disney, LEGO Strike Licensing Deal," *Triangle Business Journal*, February 16, 2009, http://triangle.bizjournals.com; LEGO Web site and company profile, http://www.lego.com.

At the most basic level, the exporting firm may sell its products outright to an *export–import merchant*, which is essentially a merchant wholesaler. The merchant assumes all the risks of product ownership, distribution, and sale. It may even purchase the goods in the producer's home country and assume responsibility for exporting the goods. An important and practical issue for domestic firms dealing with foreign customers is securing payment. This is a two-sided issue that reflects the mutual concern rightly felt by both parties to the trade deal: The exporter would like to be paid before shipping the merchandise, whereas the importer obviously would prefer to know that it has received the shipment before releasing any funds. Neither side wants to take the risk of fulfilling its part of the deal only to discover later that the other side has not. The result would lead to legal costs and complex, lengthy dealings that would waste everyone's resources. This mutual level of mistrust, in fact, makes good business sense and has been around since the beginning of trade centuries ago. The solution then was the same as it still is today—for both parties to use a mutually trusted go-between who can ensure that the payment is held until the merchandise is in fact delivered according to the terms of the trade contract. The go-between representatives employed by the importer and exporter are still, as they were in the past, the local domestic banks involved in international business.

letter of credit issued by a bank on request of an importer stating that the bank will pay an amount of money to a stated beneficiary

Exporting to international markets. American companies may manufacture their products in the United States and export them for sale in foreign markets. Exporting can be a relatively low-risk method of entering foreign markets.

© Ben Jeayes/Shutterstock.com

Here is a simplified version of how it works. After signing contracts detailing the merchandise sold and terms for its delivery, an importer will ask its local bank to issue a **letter of credit** for the amount of money needed to pay for the merchandise. The letter of credit is issued "in favor of the exporter," meaning that the funds are tied specifically to the trade contract involved. The importer's bank forwards the letter of credit to the exporter's bank, which also normally deals in international transactions. The exporter's bank then notifies the exporter that a letter of credit has been received in its name, and the exporter can go ahead with the shipment. The carrier transporting the merchandise provides the exporter with evidence of the shipment in a document called a **bill of lading**. The exporter signs over title to the merchandise (now in transit) to its bank by delivering signed copies of the bill of lading and the letter of credit.

In exchange, the exporter issues a **draft** from the bank, which orders the importer's bank to pay for the merchandise. The draft, bill of lading, and letter of credit are sent from the exporter's bank to the importer's bank. Acceptance by the importer's bank leads to return of the draft and its sale by the exporter to its bank, meaning that the exporter receives cash and the bank assumes the risk of collecting the funds from the foreign bank. The importer is obliged to pay its bank on delivery of the merchandise, and the deal is complete.

In most cases, the letter of credit is part of a lending arrangement between the importer and its bank. Of course, both banks earn fees for issuing letters of credit and drafts and for handling the import–export services for their clients. Furthermore, the process incorporates the fact that both importer and exporter will have different local currencies and might even negotiate their trade in a third currency. The banks look after all the necessary exchanges. For example, the vast majority of international business is negotiated in U.S. dollars, even though the trade may be between countries other than the United States. Thus, although the importer may end up paying for the merchandise in its local currency and the exporter may receive payment in another local currency, the banks involved will exchange all necessary foreign funds in order to allow the deal to take place.

bill of lading document issued by a transport carrier to an exporter to prove that merchandise has been shipped

draft issued by the exporter's bank, ordering the importer's bank to pay for the merchandise, thus guaranteeing payment once accepted by the importer's bank

Alternatively, the exporting firm may ship its products to an *export–import agent*, which arranges the sale of the products to foreign intermediaries for a commission or fee. The agent is an independent firm—like other agents—that sells and may perform other marketing functions for the exporter. The exporter, however, retains title to the products during shipment and until they are sold.

An exporting firm also may establish its own *sales offices*, or *branches*, in foreign countries. These installations are international extensions of the firm's distribution system. They represent a deeper involvement in international business than the other exporting techniques we have discussed—and thus they carry a greater risk. The exporting firm maintains control over sales, and it gains both experience in and knowledge of foreign markets. Eventually, the firm also may develop its own sales force to operate in conjunction with foreign sales offices.

Joint Ventures

A *joint venture* is a partnership formed to achieve a specific goal or to operate for a specific period of time. A joint venture with an established firm in a foreign country provides immediate market knowledge and access, reduced risk, and control over product attributes. However, joint-venture agreements established across national borders can become extremely complex. As a result, joint-venture agreements generally require a very high level of commitment from all the parties involved.

A joint venture may be used to produce and market an existing product in a foreign nation or to develop an entirely new product. Recently, for example, Archer Daniels Midland Company (ADM), one of the world's leading food processors, entered into a joint venture with

GE venturing into a joint venture. In 2010, GE Oil and Gas and Triveni Engineering & Industries Limited have signed a joint venture agreement to design, manufacture, supply, sell, and service advanced technology steam turbines in India. The joint venture, which will benefit from a full technology transfer and ongoing R&D support from GE, will use Triveni's Bangalore facility for turbine manufacturing.

Gruma SA, Mexico's largest corn flour and tortilla company. Besides a 22 percent stake in Gruma, ADM also received stakes in other joint ventures operated by Gruma. One of them will combine both companies' U.S. corn flour operations, which account for about 25 percent of the U.S. market. ADM also has a 40 percent stake in a Mexican wheat flour mill. ADM's joint venture increased its participation in the growing Mexican economy, where ADM already produces corn syrup, fructose, starch, and wheat flour.

Totally Owned Facilities

At a still deeper level of involvement in international business, a firm may develop *totally owned facilities*, that is, its own production and marketing facilities in one or more foreign nations. This *direct investment* provides complete control over operations, but it carries a greater risk than the joint venture. The firm is really establishing a subsidiary in a foreign country. Most firms do so only after they have acquired some knowledge of the host country's markets.

Direct investment may take either of two forms. In the first, the firm builds or purchases manufacturing and other facilities in the foreign country. It uses these facilities to produce its own established products and to market them in that country and perhaps in neighboring countries. Firms such as General Motors, Union Carbide, and Colgate-Palmolive are multinational companies with worldwide manufacturing facilities. Colgate-Palmolive factories are becoming *Eurofactories*, supplying neighboring countries as well as their own local markets.

A second form of direct investment in international business is the purchase of an existing firm in a foreign country under an arrangement that allows it to operate independently of the parent company. When Sony Corporation (a Japanese firm) decided to enter the motion picture business in the United States, it chose to purchase Columbia Pictures Entertainment, Inc., rather than start a new motion picture studio from scratch.

Strategic Alliances

A **strategic alliance**, the newest form of international business structure, is a partnership formed to create competitive advantage on a worldwide basis. Strategic alliances are very similar to joint ventures. The number of strategic alliances is growing at an estimated rate of about 20 percent per year. In fact, in the automobile and computer industries, strategic alliances are becoming the predominant means of competing. International competition is so fierce and the costs of competing on a global basis are so high that few firms have all the resources needed to do it alone. Thus, individual firms that lack the internal resources essential for international success may seek to collaborate with other companies.

An example of such an alliance is the New United Motor Manufacturing, Inc. (NUMMI), formed by Toyota and General Motors to make automobiles of both firms. This enterprise united the quality engineering of Japanese cars with the marketing expertise and market access of General Motors.[10]

Trading Companies

A **trading company** provides a link between buyers and sellers in different countries. A trading company, as its name implies, is not involved in manufacturing or owning assets related to manufacturing. It buys products in one country at the lowest price consistent with quality and sells to buyers in another country. An important function of trading companies is taking title to products and performing all the activities necessary to move the products from the domestic country to a foreign country. For example, large grain-trading companies operating out of home offices both in the United States and overseas control a major portion of the world's trade in basic food commodities. These trading companies sell homogeneous

strategic alliance a partnership formed to create competitive advantage on a worldwide basis

trading company provides a link between buyers and sellers in different countries

agricultural commodities that can be stored and moved rapidly in response to market conditions.

Countertrade

In the early 1990s, many developing nations had major restrictions on converting domestic currency into foreign currency. Therefore, exporters had to resort to barter agreements with importers. **Countertrade** is essentially an international barter transaction in which goods and services are exchanged for different goods and services. Examples include Saudi Arabia's purchase of ten 747 jets from Boeing with payment in crude oil and Philip Morris' sale of cigarettes to Russia in return for chemicals used to make fertilizers.

Multinational Firms

A **multinational enterprise** is a firm that operates on a worldwide scale without ties to any specific nation or region. The multinational firm represents the highest level of involvement in international business. It is equally "at home" in most countries of the world. In fact, as far as the operations of the multinational enterprise are concerned, national boundaries exist only on maps. It is, however, organized under the laws of its home country.

Table 3.3 shows the ten largest foreign and U.S. public multinational companies; the ranking is based on a composite score reflecting each company's best three out of four rankings for sales, profits, assets, and market value. Table 3.4 describes steps in entering international markets.

Career SUCCESS

Volunteer Abroad to Prepare to Work Abroad

If your career plans include getting a job abroad, consider doing volunteer work in another country before you graduate. By volunteering abroad, you can feel good about helping people and communities in need while you polish your communication skills and add to your résumé.

Although you will not be paid, you will have countless opportunities to learn about the world and yourself as you confront unfamiliar situations and new challenges. Later, when you are in the market for a full-time job, even a brief international volunteer stint is likely to make your employment application stand out and demonstrate your interest in working overseas.

Whether you volunteer in your chosen field or work for a charity or cause you believe in, you will return with new insights and ideas. Jonathan King was a biology major at West Virginia University when he went to Africa through Amizade, a not-for-profit organization that tackles projects such as building community clinics and new schools. Despite the initial culture shock, King says he benefited from the experience of volunteering in hospitals and orphanages—and he plans to go back.

In addition to Amizade, other groups that offer international volunteer programs for college students include Habitat for Humanity, Global Volunteers, and EarthWatch Institute. Check on your campus for more information about these and other opportunities to make a difference while preparing for future work abroad.

Sources: "Where to Find a Voluntourism Program," *Washington Post*, December 13, 2009, http://www.washingtonpost.com; Chloe White Kennedy, "Collegians Help Pay for School Costs in Ghana," *Knoxville News (TN)*, November 26, 2009, http://www.knoxnews.com; Morgan Young, "A Real Culture Shock," *The Daily Athenaeum (West Virginia University)*, September 3, 2009, http://www.thedaonline.com/news/a-real-culture-shock-1.349936.

Table 3.3 The Ten Largest Foreign and U.S. Multinational Corporations

2009 Rank	Company	Business	Country	Revenue ($ millions)
1	Royal Dutch/Shell Group	Energy	Netherlands/ United Kingdom	458,361
2	ExxonMobil	Energy	United States	442,851
3	Walmart Stores	General merchandiser	United States	405,607
4	BP	Energy	United Kingdom	367,053
5	Chevron	Energy	United States	263,159
6	Total	Energy	France	234,674
7	Conoco Phillips	Energy	United States	230,764
8	ING Group	Financial services	Netherlands	226,577
9	Sinopec	Energy	China	207,815
10	Toyota Motor	Automobiles	Japan	204,352

Source: http://money.cnn.com/magazines/fortune/global500/2009/snapshots/6752.html (accessed May 23, 2010).

countertrade an international barter transaction

multinational enterprise a firm that operates on a worldwide scale without ties to any specific nation or region

Table 3.4 Steps in Entering International Markets

Step	Activity	Marketing Tasks
1	Identify exportable products.	Identify key selling features. Identify needs that they satisfy. Identify the selling constraints that are imposed.
2	Identify key foreign markets for the products.	Determine who the customers are. Pinpoint what and when they will buy. Do market research. Establish priority, or "target," countries.
3	Analyze how to sell in each priority market (methods will be affected by product characteristics and unique features of country/market).	Locate available government and private-sector resources. Determine service and backup sales requirements.
4	Set export prices and payment terms, methods, and techniques.	Establish methods of export pricing. Establish sales terms, quotations, invoices, and conditions of sale. Determine methods of international payments, secured and unsecured.
5	Estimate resource requirements and returns.	Estimate financial requirements. Estimate human resources requirements (full- or part-time export department or operation?). Estimate plant production capacity. Determine necessary product adaptations.
6	Establish overseas distribution network.	Determine distribution agreement and other key marketing decisions (price, repair policies, returns, territory, performance, and termination). Know your customer (use U.S. Department of Commerce international marketing services).
7	Determine shipping, traffic, and documentation procedures and requirements.	Determine methods of shipment (air or ocean freight, truck, rail). Finalize containerization. Obtain validated export license. Follow export-administration documentation procedures.
8	Promote, sell, and be paid.	Use international media, communications, advertising, trade shows, and exhibitions. Determine the need for overseas travel (when, where, and how often?). Initiate customer follow-up procedures.
9	Continuously analyze current marketing, economic, and political situations.	Recognize changing factors influencing marketing strategies. Constantly re-evaluate.

Source: U.S. Department of Commerce, International Trade Administration, Washington, DC.

According to the chairman of the board of Dow Chemical Company, a multinational firm of U.S. origin, "The emergence of a world economy and of the multinational corporation has been accomplished hand in hand." He sees multinational enterprises moving toward what he calls the "anational company," a firm that has no nationality but belongs to all countries. In recognition of this movement, there already have been international conferences devoted to the question of how such enterprises would be controlled.

Table 3.5	U.S. Government Export Assistance Programs	
1	U.S. Export Assistance Centers, http://www.sba.gov/oit/export/useac.html	Provides assistance in export marketing and trade finance
2	International Trade Administration, http://www.ita.doc.gov/	Offers assistance and information to exporters through its domestic and overseas commercial officers
3	U.S. and Foreign Commercial Services, http://www.export.gov/	Helps U.S. firms compete more effectively in the global marketplace and provides information on foreign markets
4	Advocacy Center, http://www.ita.doc.gov/advocacy	Facilitates advocacy to assist U.S. firms competing for major projects and procurements worldwide
5	Trade Information Center, http://www.ita.doc.gov/td/tic/	Provides U.S. companies information on federal programs and activities that support U.S. exports
6	STAT-USA/Internet, http://www.stat-usa.gov/	Offers a comprehensive collection of business, economic, and trade information on the Web
7	Small Business Administration, http://www.sba.gov/oit/	Publishes many helpful guides to assist small- and medium-sized companies
8	National Trade Data Bank, http://www.stat-usa.gov/tradtest.nsf	Provides international economic and export-promotion information supplied by more than 20 U.S. agencies

6

Describe the various sources of export assistance.

Sources of Export Assistance

In September 1993, President Bill Clinton announced the *National Export Strategy* (NES) to revitalize U.S. exports. Under the NES, the *Trade Promotion Coordinating Committee* (TPCC) assists U.S. firms in developing export-promotion programs. The export services and programs of the 19 TPCC agencies can help American firms to compete in foreign markets and create new jobs in the United States. Table 3.5 provides an overview of selected export assistance programs.

These and other sources of export information enhance the business opportunities of U.S. firms seeking to enter expanding foreign markets. Another vital energy factor is financing.

7

Identify the institutions that help firms and nations finance international business.

Financing International Business

International trade compounds the concerns of financial managers. Currency exchange rates, tariffs and foreign exchange controls, and the tax structures of host nations all affect international operations and the flow of cash. In addition, financial managers must be concerned both with the financing of their international operations and with the means available to their customers to finance purchases.

Fortunately, along with business in general, a number of large banks have become international in scope. Many have established branches in major cities around the world. Thus, like firms in other industries, they are able to provide their services where and when they are needed. In addition, financial assistance is available from U.S. government and international sources.

Several of today's international financial organizations were founded many years ago to facilitate free trade and the exchange of currencies among nations. Some, such as the Inter-American Development Bank, are supported internationally and focus on developing countries. Others, such as the Export-Import Bank, are operated by one country but provide international financing.

Sustaining the Planet

Selling Eco-Friendly Goods, Services, and Technologies

Since 1994, the Export-Import Bank's Environmental Export Financing Program has been promoting sustainability by helping U.S. businesses obtain the funding they need to sell their eco-friendly goods, services, and technologies to overseas buyers around the world. Take a look: http://www.exim.gov/products/policies/environment/index.cfm.

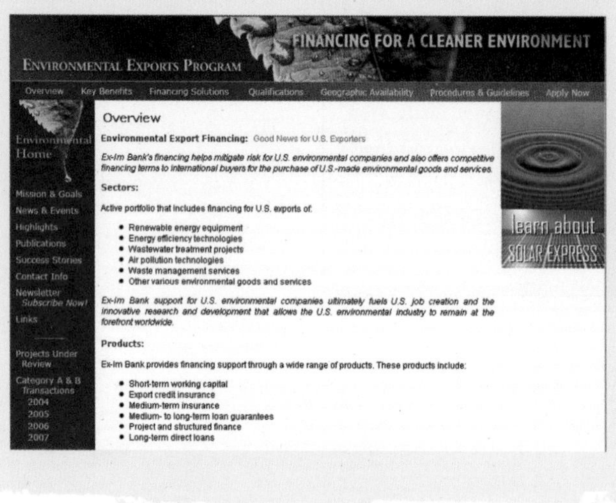

The Export-Import Bank of the United States

The **Export-Import Bank of the United States**, created in 1934, is an independent agency of the U.S. government whose function is to assist in financing the exports of American firms. *Ex-Im Bank*, as it is commonly called, extends and guarantees credit to overseas buyers of American goods and services and guarantees short-term financing for exports. It also cooperates with commercial banks in helping American exporters to offer credit to their overseas customers.

According to Fred P. Hochberg, chairman and president of Ex-Im Bank, "Working with private lenders we are helping U.S. exporters put Americans to work producing the high quality goods and services that foreign buyers prefer. As part of President Obama's National Export Initiative, Ex-Im Bank's export financing is contributing to the goal of doubling of U.S. exports within the next five years."

Multilateral Development Banks

A **multilateral development bank (MDB)** is an internationally supported bank that provides loans to developing countries to help them grow. The most familiar is the World Bank, which operates worldwide. Established in 1944 and headquartered in Washington, DC, the bank provides low-interest loans, interest-free credits, and grants to developing countries. In 2009, the World Bank provided $46.9 billion for 303 projects in developing countries. Its more than 1,800 projects include providing credit in Bosnia and Herzegovina, raising AIDS-prevention awareness in Guinea, supporting the education of girls in Bangladesh, improving health care delivery in Mexico, and helping India rebuild Gujarat after a devastating earthquake.[11] Four other MDBs operate primarily in Central and South America, Asia, Africa, and Eastern and Central Europe. All five are supported by the industrialized nations, including the United States.

The *Inter-American Development Bank* (IDB), the oldest and largest regional bank, was created in 1959 by 19 Latin American countries and the United States. The bank, which is headquartered in Washington, DC, makes loans and provides technical advice and assistance to countries. Today, the IDB is owned by 48 member states.

With 67 member nations, the *Asian Development Bank* (ADB), created in 1966 and headquartered in the Philippines, promotes economic and social progress in Asian and Pacific regions. The U.S. government is the second-largest contributor to the ADB's capital, after Japan.

The *African Development Bank* (AFDB), also known as *Banque Africaines de Development*, was established in 1964 with headquarters in Abidjan, Ivory Coast. Its members include 53 African and 24 non-African countries from the Americas, Europe, and Asia. The AFDB's goal is to foster the economic and social development of its African members. The bank pursues this goal through loans, research, technical assistance, and the development of trade programs.

Established in 1991 to encourage reconstruction and development in the Eastern and Central European countries, the London-based *European Bank*

Export-Import Bank of the United States an independent agency of the U.S. government whose function is to assist in financing the exports of American firms

multilateral development bank (MDB) an internationally supported bank that provides loans to developing countries to help them grow

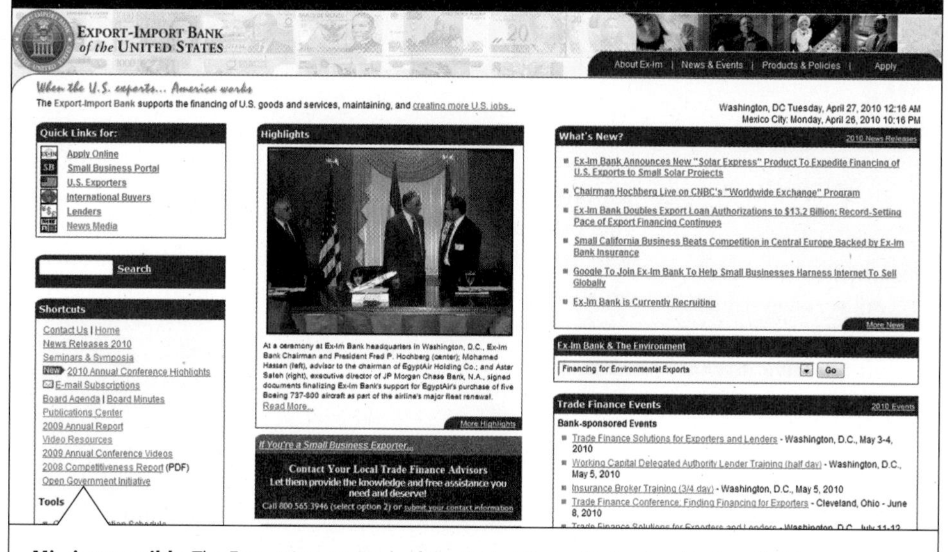

Mission possible. The Export-Import Bank of the United States (Ex-Im Bank) is the official export credit agency of the United States. Ex-Im Bank's mission is to assist in financing U.S. goods and services to international markets. With more than 70 years of experience, Ex-Im Bank has supported more than $400 billion of U.S. exports, primarily to developing markets worldwide.

for Reconstruction and Development is owned by 61 countries and 2 intergovernmental institutions. Its loans are geared toward developing market-oriented economies and promoting private enterprise.

The International Monetary Fund

The **International Monetary Fund (IMF)** is an international bank with 186 member nations that makes short-term loans to developing countries experiencing balance-of-payment deficits. This financing is contributed by member nations, and it must be repaid with interest. Loans are provided primarily to fund international trade. Created in 1945 and headquartered in Washington, DC, the bank's main goals are to:

- promote international monetary cooperation,
- facilitate the expansion and balanced growth of international trade,
- promote exchange rate stability,
- assist in establishing a multilateral system of payments, and
- make resources available to members experiencing balance-of-payment difficulties.

International Monetary Fund (IMF) an international bank with 186 member nations that makes short-term loans to developing countries experiencing balance-of-payment deficits

return to inside business

Samsung

From its modest roots as a food exporter, Samsung Electronics has grown into a world-class powerhouse that exports more than $50 billion worth of products every year. During the past decade, the company has increased total revenue fivefold, and CEO Lee Yoon-Woo recently set the ambitious goal of achieving $400 billion in annual sales by 2020.

Meanwhile, the ever-higher buying power of consumers in South Korea is attracting competitors from abroad, adding to the competitive pressure on Samsung Electronics in its home country. When Apple began exporting iPhones to South Korea, Samsung Electronics fought back by reducing the price of its touch-screen phones—which, in turn, cut into its profit margins. Can the company maintain its competitive momentum and continue as a shining star in the crowded global marketplace?

Questions

1. How much should Samsung Electronics rely on joint ventures and strategic alliances as it seeks to reach $400 billion in revenue by 2020?
2. According to the case, is Samsung Electronics a multinational enterprise? Explain your answer.

CHAPTER REVIEW

SUMMARY

Summary

1 Explain the economic basis for international business.

International business encompasses all business activities that involve exchanges across national boundaries. International trade is based on specialization, whereby each country produces the goods and services that it can produce more efficiently than any other goods and services. A nation is said to have a comparative advantage relative to these goods. International trade develops when each nation trades its surplus products for those in short supply.

A nation's balance of trade is the difference between the value of its exports and the value of its imports. Its balance of payments is the difference between the flow of money into and out of the nation. Generally, a negative balance of trade is considered unfavorable.

2 Discuss the restrictions nations place on international trade, the objectives of these restrictions, and their results.

Despite the benefits of world trade, nations tend to use tariffs and nontariff barriers (import quotas, embargoes, and other restrictions) to limit trade. These restrictions typically are justified as being needed to protect a nation's economy, industries, citizens, or security. They can result in the loss of jobs, higher prices, fewer choices in the marketplace, and the misallocation of resources.

3 Outline the extent of international business and the world economic outlook for trade.

World trade is generally increasing. Trade between the United States and other nations is increasing in dollar value but decreasing in terms of our share of the world market. Exports as a percentage of U.S. GDP have increased steadily since 1985, except in the 2001 and 2008 recessions.

4 Discuss international trade agreements and international economic organizations working to foster trade.

The General Agreement on Tariffs and Trade (GATT) was formed to dismantle trade barriers and provide an environment in which international business can grow. Today, the World Trade Organization (WTO) and various economic communities carry on this mission. These world economic communities include the European Union, the NAFTA, the CAFTA, the Association of Southeast Asian Nations, the Pacific Rim, the Commonwealth of Independent States, the Caribbean Basin Initiative, the Common Market of the Southern Cone, the Organization of Petroleum Exporting Countries, and the Organization for Economic Cooperation and Development.

5 Define the methods by which a firm can organize for and enter into international markets.

A firm can enter international markets in several ways. It may license a foreign firm to produce and market its products. It may export its products and sell them through foreign intermediaries or its own sales organization abroad, or it may sell its exports outright to an export–import merchant. It may enter into a joint venture with a foreign firm. It may establish its own foreign subsidiaries, or it may develop into a multinational enterprise.

Generally, each of these methods represents an increasingly deeper level of involvement in international business, with licensing being the simplest and the development of a multinational corporation the most involved.

6 Describe the various sources of export assistance.

Many government and international agencies provide export assistance to U.S. and foreign firms. The export services and programs of the 19 agencies of the U.S. Trade Promotion Coordinating Committee (TPCC) can help U.S. firms to compete in foreign markets and create new jobs in the United States. Sources of export assistance include U.S. Export Assistance Centers, the International Trade Administration, U.S. and Foreign Commercial Services, Export Legal Assistance Network, Advocacy Center, National Trade Data Bank, and other government and international agencies.

7 Identify the institutions that help firms and nations finance international business.

The financing of international trade is more complex than that of domestic trade. Institutions such as the Ex-Im Bank and the International Monetary Fund have been established to provide financing and ultimately to increase world trade for American and international firms.

Key Terms

You should now be able to define and give an example relevant to each of the following terms:

international business (73)
absolute advantage (73)
comparative advantage (73)
exporting (74)
importing (75)
balance of trade (75)
trade deficit (75)
balance of payments (76)
import duty (tariff) (76)
dumping (77)
nontariff barrier (77)
import quota (77)
embargo (77)
foreign-exchange control (77)
currency devaluation (77)
General Agreement on Tariffs and Trade (GATT) (82)
World Trade Organization (WTO) (84)
economic community (84)
licensing (87)
letter of credit (88)
bill of lading (89)
draft (89)
strategic alliance (90)
trading company (90)
countertrade (91)
multinational enterprise (91)
Export-Import Bank of the United States (94)
multilateral development bank (MDB) (94)
International Monetary Fund (IMF) (95)

Review Questions

1. Why do firms engage in international trade?
2. What is the difference between an absolute and a comparative advantage in international trade? How are both types of advantages related to the concept of specialization?
3. What is a favorable balance of trade? In what way is it "favorable"?
4. List and briefly describe the principal restrictions that may be applied to a nation's imports.
5. What reasons are generally given for imposing trade restrictions?
6. What are the general effects of import restrictions on trade?
7. Define and describe the major objectives of the WTO and the international economic communities.
8. Which nations are the principal trading partners of the United States? What are the major U.S. imports and exports?
9. The methods of engaging in international business may be categorized as either direct or indirect. How would you classify each of the methods described in this chapter? Why?
10. In what ways is a multinational enterprise different from a large corporation that does business in several countries?
11. List some key sources of export assistance. How can these sources be useful to small business firms?
12. In what ways do the Ex-Im Bank, multilateral development banks, and the IMF enhance international trade?

Discussion Questions

1. The United States restricts imports but, at the same time, supports the WTO and international banks whose objective is to enhance world trade. As a member of Congress, how would you justify this contradiction to your constituents?
2. What effects might the devaluation of a nation's currency have on its business firms, its consumers, and the debts it owes to other nations?
3. Should imports to the United States be curtailed by, say, 20 percent to eliminate our trade deficit? What might happen if this were done?
4. When should a firm consider expanding from strictly domestic trade to international trade? When should it consider becoming further involved in international trade? What factors might affect the firm's decisions in each case?
5. How can a firm obtain the expertise needed to produce and market its products in, for example, the EU?

Video Case 3.1

Evo: Creatively Exceeding Customer Expectations Here and Abroad

Evo is proof that a company does not have to be large or operate worldwide in order to run a successful global business. Based in Seattle, Evo is an online and brick-and-mortar retailer of skiing, wakeboarding, skateboarding, and snowboarding equipment and clothing that recently reached $10 million in annual sales. It employs about 70 people and has been growing more than 70 percent a year since moving beyond founder Bryce Phillips' apartment eight years ago.

Evo now maintains a 40,000-square-foot distribution center and a busy Seattle store, along with a highly successful retail Web site, EvoGear.com. It is through the Web site that Evo started the global side of its operations, serving customers as far away as Bahrain, Turkey, Bali, Europe, and Australia and New Zealand. Because taxes, duties, exchange rates, and shipping requirements are so complex, for now customers in countries other than the United States and Canada must call the company's customer-service line to personally place their orders and arrange shipping and payment individually. Although for the present these customers account for a very small percentage of Evo's annual orders (5 percent including Canada), the company's managers hope that the growth of e-commerce will eventually ease order-handling and payment procedures enough to let this side of the business grow.

Another factor that might continue to limit Evo's international growth in the meantime is the business practices of Evo's suppliers. Most of these equipment manufacturers want to protect their own brands, so they restrict the amount of their products that any one retailer can sell to avoid saturating markets and to keep competition fair. Thus, Evo sometimes has to turn down requests for particular products, though the company hopes that this problem too will some day be overcome. For now the firm is able to keep its customer-service lines open for less than 24 hours a day and still remain accessible to most of its international callers.

The firm does not have plans to open any overseas operations because its shipping partners are already located everywhere that Evo needs assistance abroad. Most of the company's overseas suppliers have offices or representatives in the United States, so Evo team members usually travel only within the country for trade shows and the like. One exception is founder Bryce Phillips himself.

Evo has recently begun offering extreme skiing, snowboarding, and surfing expeditions to its customers through a new operation called EvoTrip. By outsourcing the logistics of these trips to a separate international travel company called JustFares.com, Evo is able to focus on choosing destinations like Japan, Indonesia, Switzerland, and South America, many of which Phillips has visited and enjoyed, and arranging for professional athletes to accompany each group. Each of these trips, Phillips feels, is an opportunity for Evo's "ambassadors" to seamlessly spread the word about the company to potential new customers in every country they visit.

Despite management's conviction that its domestic business probably brings a better return on investment for now than its global operations, Evo can still proudly call itself a multinational firm.[12]

Questions

1. Do you think Evo's decision not to set up any physical operations overseas is a good one? Why or why not?
2. What political and economic challenges could EvoTrip encounter in other countries?
3. Would you recommend that Evo expand the international side of its business? If so, how, and if not, why not?

Case 3.2

Global Profits Are a Menu Mainstay at McDonald's

Few U.S. businesses are as international as McDonald's, the Illinois-based fast-food giant that began as an all-American hamburger place. With $22 billion in annual revenue, McDonald's now rings the world with 32,400 restaurants and serves 60 million customers every day. Although the United States accounts for 35 percent of McDonald's global revenue, Europe accounts for 41 percent and the Asia/Pacific, Middle East, and Africa regions account for 19 percent.

Hamburgers are, of course, the main attraction in many McDonald's restaurants: worldwide, the company sells more than four million burgers every day. However, one of McDonald's key strengths is its ability to adapt to local tastes. In Japan, McDonald's sells Cheese Katsu sandwiches, featuring fried pork and cheese. In the Middle East, it sells McArabia pita sandwiches filled with grilled chicken or spiced beef. In France, it sells Croque McDo sandwiches with melted cheese and ham. In India, it sells vegetarian McAloo Tikki burgers. In Mexico, it sells McMolletes sandwiches made with refried beans and cheese.

Being a global business also helps McDonald's weather the economic ups and downs of different regions. At one point during the recent recession, its Asian revenue grew almost twice as quickly as its European revenue, both of which balanced the smaller increase in U.S. sales. Worldwide, McDonald's owns some of its restaurants and also sells franchise licenses to firms that open restaurants under the McDonald's brand name. In some markets, the company operates restaurants in joint ventures with local firms. For example, in India, it has one joint venture with a local firm to operate restaurants in the west and south and a second joint venture with a different company to operate restaurants in the east and the north.

The company is also building its global business by attracting more customers during different "dayparts," such as at breakfast time and in the late-night hours. A growing number of its global units stay open 24 hours a day for customer convenience. McDonald's has introduced a steady stream of breakfast, beverage, snack, and sandwich items to encourage repeat visits from customers at all income levels.

On the high end, McDonald's is doing well with its McCafés, which serve mochas and other gourmet coffees in a separate area of selected McDonald's units. As the company opens new restaurants and remodels existing restaurants, it is adding more McCafés in U.S. and European markets. The Angus Burger is another popular premium menu item. Both McCafé coffees and Angus Burgers appeal to customers willing to pay a little more to splurge on high quality. At the same time, the items on McDonald's budget menus are priced to appeal to customers who keep a close rein on their wallets.

Being a major power in global business means McDonald's must think carefully about the value of the different currencies its restaurants take in. Outside the United States, much of its revenue is rung up in euros, British pounds, Australian dollars, and Canadian dollars. As a result, McDonald's pays close attention to swings in foreign-exchange rates as it manages its financial affairs.

McDonald's is stepping up its involvement in sustainability all around the world. It has increased its use of packaging made from renewable materials and boosted recycling efforts to keep waste out of landfills. It has also been building eco-friendly restaurants in North and South America as well as in Europe to test green construction methods and cut back on energy and water usage. The company's social responsibility menu includes supporting the Ronald McDonald House charities and offering a range of organic foods and beverages plus healthy snack choices.

From India to Ireland, Argentina to Australia, McDonald's is poised for continued growth in sales and profits as it expands its restaurant empire and cooks up new products for customers to enjoy around the clock and around the world.[13]

Questions

1. What are the advantages and disadvantages of McDonald's ringing up sales in so many foreign currencies worldwide?
2. Why would McDonald's use two joint ventures to operate restaurants in different regions of India?
3. Discuss how being a multinational enterprise, with a presence in more than 170 countries, helps McDonald's build its business regardless of the short-term global economic outlook.

Building Skills for Career Success

❶ JOURNALING FOR SUCCESS

Discovery statement: This chapter was designed to excite you about international business and how trade among nations affects our daily lives.

Assignment

1. Assume that your friend, who recently lost his job in the automobile industry, is critical of imported Toyotas, Hondas, and Volkswagens. How would you respond to his resentment of imported goods?
2. What specific reasons will you offer to your friend in support of the fact that international trade is beneficial to society as a whole?
3. Ask your friend what might be some consequences if the trade among nations was banned.

❷ EXPLORING THE INTERNET

A popular question debated among firms actively involved on the Internet is whether there exists a truly global Internet-based customer, irrespective of any individual culture, linguistic, or nationality issues. Does this Internet-based universal customer see the Internet and products sold there in pretty much the same way? If so, then one model might fit all customers. For example, although Yahoo.com translates its Web pages so that they are understood around the world, the pages look pretty much the same regardless of which international site you use. Is this good strategy, or should the sites reflect local customers differently? Visit the text Web site for updates to this exercise.

Assignment

1. Examine a Web site such as Yahoo! (http://www.yahoo.com) and its various international versions that operate in other languages around the world. Compare their similarities and differences as best you can, even if you do not understand the individual languages.
2. After making your comparison, do you now agree that there are indeed universal Internet products and customers? Explain your decision.

❸ DEVELOPING CRITICAL-THINKING SKILLS

Suppose that you own and operate an electronics firm that manufactures transistors and integrated circuits. As foreign competitors enter the market and undercut your prices, you realize that your high labor costs are hindering your ability to compete. You are concerned about what to do and are open for suggestions. Recently, you have been trying to decide whether to move your plant to Mexico, where labor is cheaper.

Assignment

1. Questions you should consider in making this decision include the following:
   a. Would you be better off to build a new plant in Mexico or to buy an existing building?
   b. If you could find a Mexican electronics firm similar to yours, would it be wiser to try to buy it than to start your own operation?
   c. What are the risks involved in directly investing in your own facility in a foreign country?
   d. If you did decide to move your plant to Mexico, how would you go about it? Are there any government agencies that might offer you advice?
2. Prepare a two-page summary of your answers to these questions.

❹ BUILDING TEAM SKILLS

The North American Free Trade Agreement among the United States, Mexico, and Canada went into effect on January 1, 1994. It has made a difference in trade among the countries and has affected the lives of many people.

Assignment

1. Working in teams and using the resources of your library, investigate NAFTA. Answer the following questions:
   a. What are NAFTA's objectives?
   b. What are its benefits?
   c. What impact has NAFTA had on trade, jobs, and travel?
   d. Some Americans were opposed to the implementation of NAFTA. What were their objections? Have any of these objections been justified?
   e. Has NAFTA influenced your life? How?
2. Summarize your answers in a written report. Your team also should be prepared to give a class presentation.

❺ RESEARCHING DIFFERENT CAREERS

Today, firms around the world need employees with special skills. In some countries, such employees are not always available, and firms then must search abroad for qualified applicants. One way they can do this is through global workforce databases. As business and trade operations continue to grow globally, you may one day find yourself working in a foreign country, perhaps for an American company doing business there or for a foreign company. In what foreign country would you like to work? What problems might you face?

Assignment

1. Choose a country in which you might like to work.
2. Research the country. The National Trade Data Bank is a good place to start. Find answers to the following questions:
   a. What language is spoken in this country? Are you proficient in it? What would you need to do if you are not proficient?
   b. What are the economic, social, and legal systems like in this nation?
   c. What is its history?
   d. What are its culture and social traditions like? How might they affect your work or your living arrangements?
3. Describe what you have found out about this country in a written report. Include an assessment of whether you would want to work there and the problems you might face if you did.

Running a Business PART 1

Graeter's

Let's Go Get a Graeter's!

Only a tiny fraction of family-owned businesses are still viable four generations after their founding, but happily for lovers of premium-quality ice cream, Graeter's is one of them.

Graeter's, now a $20 million firm, was founded in Cincinnati in 1870 by a young couple named Charlie and Regina Graeter, who made ice cream and chocolate candies in the back room of their shop, sold them in the front room, and lived upstairs. Refrigeration was unknown at the time, and ice cream was a novelty. Regina carried on the business for more than 30 years after her husband's death, at a time when women didn't run companies, opening not only a factory but also 20 additional stores. Her sons followed her into the firm, and three of her great-grandsons now share the responsibility for continuing to bring the company's original dense and creamy ice cream recipe to an ever-growing customer base.

The company currently operates a few dozen stores in Cincinnati and several neighboring cities, and its products are also available in hundreds of supermarkets thanks to distribution through big supermarket chains like Kroger's. Graeter's is currently building an additional factory to support its continued expansion, and it even operates a retail Web site where customers can order ice cream shipped anywhere in the continental United States, via UPS, guaranteed frozen on arrival.

SIMPLE SECRETS OF SUCCESS

Several factors make Graeter's unique and account for its long success. Perhaps the most important is product quality. Throughout its history, Graeter's has focused on using a unique manufacturing process that produces its signature ice cream flavors in small batches of about two gallons every 20 minutes. "Our competition is making thousands and thousands of gallons a day," says Chip Graeter, the company's vice president of retail stores. "We are making hundreds of gallons a day at the most. All of our ice cream is packed by hand, so it's a very laborious process." Graeter's "French pot" manufacturing method ensures that very little air gets into the product, producing the same creamy texture all ice cream used to have but few other brands can still achieve. The product is so dense that each pint of Graeter's weighs nearly a pound.

Another success factor is the use of simple, fresh ingredients. Fresh eggs, high-grade chocolate, pure cane sugar, and the choicest raspberries, strawberries, and other fruits in season are among the basic ingredients, and the company gets its milk and cream only from local farmers who guarantee their cows are not fed artificial growth hormones. (These hormones are believed to have environmental effects and health effects on humans.) "We use a really great grade of chocolate," says Bob Graeter, vice president of manufacturing. "We don't cut corners on that. . . . Specially selected great black raspberries, strawberries, blueberries, cherries, go into our ice cream because we feel that we want to provide flavor not from artificial or unnatural ingredients but from really quality ripe rich fruits."

WELCOMING CHANGE

Finally, while many things about Graeter's—like its recipes—have stayed simple, its recent expansion and future growth plans have resulted from something quite new to the firm: outside advice. The current generation of owners hired management consultants to help them achieve the kind of productivity increases that allowed for greatly increased capacity so that when Kroger's, for instance, suggested expanding Graeter's to a chain of supermarkets Kroger owns in Denver, the company could quickly ramp up production to fill the increased orders.

In recent years, change has come quickly to this small firm, which prospered for three prior generations by staying essentially the same. But, says Bob Graeter, success does require balancing consistency—what he calls "preserving the core"—with innovation. "If you just preserve the core," he says, "ultimately you stagnate. And if you are constantly stimulating progress and looking for new ideas, well, then you risk losing what was important. . . . Part of your secret to long-term success is knowing what your core is and holding to that. Once you know what you're really all about and what is most important to you, you can change everything else." One of those "important" things is giving back to the community and its families via local charities and other initiatives. Graeter's recently celebrated a new store opening by making a cash donation to the local public library, for instance, and has given a research foundation for pediatric brain cancer the proceeds from sales of a limited-time flavor created by the winner of a special drawing created for the purpose.

DEFINING THE COMPETITIVE LANDSCAPE

The company recognizes that while it produces a premium product in the ice cream category, its competition includes offerings other than ice cream. "We would be compared to Ben & Jerry's and Haagen Dazs," says Bob Graeter. "From a sales standpoint and from a shelf-space allocation, that is how [supermarkets] rank us, but . . . in my opinion that is really not our competition. Our competition is the upscale treats. It's like New York Cheesecake. That is our competition in my opinion. What is it that you are going to have when you want that indulgence, when you are willing to spend a thousand calories on dessert? It's going to be something that is fabulous. Graeter's in Cincinnati is synonymous with ice cream. People will say, 'Let's go get a Graeter's.' They don't say, 'Let's go get an ice cream.'"[14]

Questions

1. Think about the elements of Graeter's business that have stayed the same over its long history and those that have changed. Do you think the company's owners have chosen the right factors to change over time? Why or why not?
2. Which view of social responsibility does Graeter's management appear to take—the economic view or the socioeconomic view? What evidence in the case supports your answer?
3. Do you agree with Bob Graeter about what the company's real competition is? Why or why not?

To access the online *Interactive Business Plan,* go to www.cengagebrain.com.

A *business plan* is a carefully constructed guide for a person starting a business. The purpose of a well-prepared business plan is to show how practical and attainable the entrepreneur's goals are. It also serves as a concise document that potential investors can examine to see if they would like to invest or assist in financing a new venture. A business plan should include the following 12 components:

- Introduction
- Executive summary
- Benefits to the community
- Company and industry
- Management team
- Manufacturing and operations plan
- Labor force
- Marketing plan
- Financial plan
- Exit strategy
- Critical risks and assumptions
- Appendix

A brief description of each of these sections is provided in Chapter 5 (see also Table 5.4 on page 148).

This is the first of seven exercises that appear at the ends of each of the seven major parts in this textbook. The goal of these exercises is to help you work through the preceding components to create your own business plan. For example, in the exercise for this part, you will make decisions and complete the research that will help you to develop the introduction for your business plan and the benefits to the community that your business will provide. In the exercises for Parts 2 through 7, you will add more components to your plan and eventually build a plan that actually could be used to start a business. The flowchart shown in Figure 3.6 gives an overview of the steps you will be taking to prepare your business plan.

THE FIRST STEP: CHOOSING YOUR BUSINESS

One of the first steps for starting your own business is to decide what type of business you want to start. Take some time to think about this decision. Before proceeding, answer the following questions:

- Why did you choose this type of business?
- Why do you think this business will be successful?
- Would you enjoy owning and operating this type of business?

Warning: Do not rush this step. This step often requires much thought, but it is well worth the time and effort. As an added bonus, you are more likely to develop a quality business plan if you really want to open this type of business.

Now that you have decided on a specific type of business, it is time to begin the planning process. The goal for this part is to complete the introduction and benefits-to-the-community components of your business plan.

Before you begin, it is important to note that the business plan is not a document that is written and then set aside. It is a living document that an entrepreneur should refer to continuously in order to ensure that plans are being carried through appropriately. As the entrepreneur begins to execute the plan, he or she should monitor the business environment continuously and make changes to the plan to address any challenges or opportunities that were not foreseen originally.

Throughout this course, you will, of course, be building your knowledge about business. Therefore, it will be appropriate for you to continually revisit parts of the plan that you have already written in order to refine them based on your more comprehensive knowledge. You will find that writing your plan is not a simple matter of starting at the beginning and moving chronologically through to the end. Instead, you probably will find yourself jumping around the various components, making refinements as you go. In fact, the second component—the executive summary—should be written last, but because of its comprehensive nature and its importance to potential investors, it appears after the introduction in the final business plan. By the end of this course, you should be able to put the finishing touches on your plan, making sure that all the parts create a comprehensive and sound whole so that you can present it for evaluation.

THE INTRODUCTION COMPONENT

1.1. Start with the cover page. Provide the business name, street address, telephone number, Web address (if any), name(s) of owner(s) of the business, and the date the plan is issued.

1.2. Next, provide background information on the company and include the general nature of the business: retailing, manufacturing, or service; what your product or service is; what is unique about it; and why you believe that your business will be successful.

1.3. Then include a summary statement of the business's financial needs, if any. You probably will need to revise your financial needs summary after you complete a detailed financial plan later in Part 6.

1.4. Finally, include a statement of confidentiality to keep important information away from potential competitors.

Figure 3.6 Business Plan

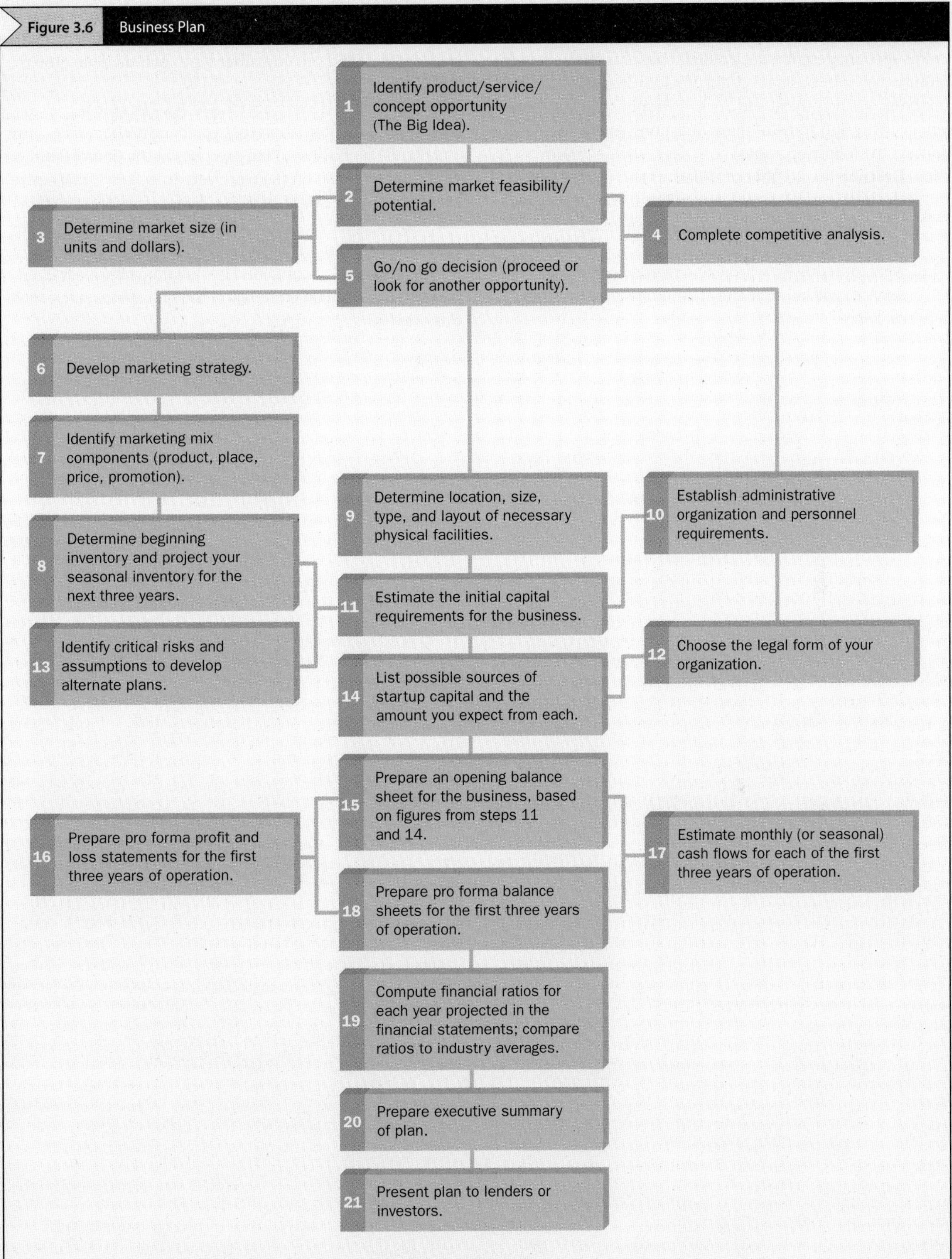

Source: Hatten, Timothy, *Small Business Management*, Fifth Edition. Copyright © 2012 Cengage Learning.

THE BENEFITS-TO-THE-COMMUNITY COMPONENT

In this section, describe the potential benefits to the community that your business could provide. Chapter 2 in your textbook, "Being Ethical and Socially Responsible," can help you in answering some of these questions. At the very least, address the following issues:

1.5. Describe the number of skilled and nonskilled jobs the business will create, and indicate how purchases of supplies and other materials can help local businesses.
1.6. Next, describe how providing needed goods or services will improve the community and its standard of living.
1.7. Finally, state how your business can develop new technical, management, or leadership skills; offer attractive wages; and provide other types of individual growth.

REVIEW OF BUSINESS PLAN ACTIVITIES

Read over the information that you have gathered. Because the Building a Business Plan exercises at the end of Parts 2 through 7 are built on the work you do in Part 1, make sure that any weaknesses or problem areas are resolved before continuing. Finally, write a brief statement that summarizes all the information for this part of the business plan.

The information contained in "Building a Business Plan" will also assist you in completing the online *Interactive Business Plan*.

PART 2

Business Ownership and Entrepreneurship

©AP Images SouthtownStar, Joseph P. Meier

In Part 2 of *Business,* we look at a very practical aspect of business: How businesses are owned. Issues related to ownership are particularly interesting in today's world, where large global businesses coexist with small businesses. In addition, because the majority of businesses are small, we look at specific issues related to small business.

4 Choosing a Form of Business Ownership

© Alan Berner/Seattle Times/MCT/Newscom

Learning Objectives

What you will be able to do once you complete this chapter:

1. Describe the advantages and disadvantages of sole proprietorships.
2. Explain the different types of partners and the importance of partnership agreements.
3. Describe the advantages and disadvantages of partnerships.
4. Summarize how a corporation is formed.
5. Describe the advantages and disadvantages of a corporation.
6. Examine special types of corporations, including S-corporations, limited-liability companies, and not-for-profit corporations.
7. Discuss the purpose of a cooperative, joint venture, and syndicate.
8. Explain how growth from within and growth through mergers can enable a business to expand.

inside business

How Mint.com Makes Money from Money Management

Before he turned 30, Aaron Patzer made a mint by helping people do a better job of managing their money. Patzer came up with the idea for Mint.com in 2006, when he was trying to organize his personal finances. He found existing software programs and online banking systems cumbersome, time-consuming, and costly. So Patzer quit his job and began designing a free Web site where consumers could track all their accounts and, with a click, see where their money was going.

Patzer planned to make money by analyzing users' financial data and suggesting money-saving solutions from credit card companies, banks, and insurance firms that would pay a referral fee whenever a Mint.com user opened an account. He had started small businesses before and knew that incorporating would be an advantage because it would limit the financial liability for Patzer and his investors.

Six months later, Patzer sought funding from investors and venture capital firms to prepare for the launch. Many expressed doubt that consumers would trust their private data to a tiny, unknown start-up. However, the venture capital firm First Round Capital was intrigued by the way Patzer's site would solve a common consumer problem. After watching a demonstration and studying the business plan, the firm invested $325,000 and raised an additional $400,000 from other investors. One of the firm's partners joined Mint.com's board of directors and another became an expert advisor.

The venture capitalists' connections in the tech world helped Patzer contain a crisis that could have crippled Mint.com in its early months. The site had just won an award and as thousands of new users tried to log on, a software glitch knocked the servers out of commission. First Round Capital's partners called their contacts at the software company and made a personal appeal for assistance. Hours later, Mint.com was back in business.

By 2010, Mint.com had raised more than $30 million in investment capital, had more than a million customers, and was adding more than 3,000 new users every day. Patzer then faced the most important decision of his business career. Competitor Intuit, which makes Quicken and Quickbooks software, wanted to buy Mint.com. Should he sell?[1]

FYI

Did You Know?

Founder Aaron Patzer raised more than $30 million in venture capital to grow his corporation, Mint.com.

Aaron Patzer started Mint.com with one basic goal: Help people manage their personal finances. To meet this need, Patzer developed a software program that now helps more than a million users track $175 billion in transactions and $47 billion in assets. More importantly, Mint.com has identified more than $300 million in potential savings for the corporation's users.[2] Pretty impressive achievements for a firm that began in 2006. Patzer chose to incorporate his business because this type of business ownership would limit the financial liability for both Patzer and his investors. While some would-be business owners think that if they incorporate, their business will automatically be successful, the fact is that there's more to increasing sales and earning profits than the type of ownership you choose. In today's competitive business world, any corporation, sole proprietorship, or partnership must produce products or services that customers want. And that's what Mint.com does best. The typical Mint.com user finds $1,000 in savings the first time they visit the firm's Web site at http://www.mint.com.[3]

Many people dream of opening a business, and one of the first decisions they must make is what form of ownership to choose. We begin this chapter by describing the three common forms of business ownership: sole proprietorships, partnerships, and corporations. We discuss how these types of businesses are formed and note the advantages and disadvantages of each. Next, we consider several types of business ownership usually chosen for special purposes, including S-corporations, limited-liability companies, not-for-profit corporations, cooperatives, joint ventures, and syndicates. We conclude the chapter with a discussion of how businesses can grow through internal expansion or through mergers with other companies.

1

Describe the advantages and disadvantages of sole proprietorships.

Sole Proprietorships

A **sole proprietorship** is a business that is owned (and usually operated) by one person. Although a few sole proprietorships are large and have many employees, most are small. Sole proprietorship is the simplest form of business ownership and the easiest to start. In most instances, the owner (the *sole* proprietor) simply decides that he or she is in business and begins operations. Some of today's largest corporations, including Ford Motor Company, H.J. Heinz Company, and Procter & Gamble Company, started out as tiny—and in many cases, struggling—sole proprietorships.

As you can see in Figure 4.1, there are approximately 22 million nonfarm sole proprietorships in the United States. They account for 71 percent of the country's business firms. Although the most popular form of ownership when compared with partnerships and corporations, they rank last in total sales revenues. As shown in Figure 4.2, sole proprietorships account for just over $1 trillion, or about 4 percent of total annual sales.

Sole proprietorships are most common in retailing, service, and agriculture. Thus, the clothing boutique, corner grocery, television-repair shop down the street, and small, independent farmers are likely to be sole proprietorships.

Advantages of Sole Proprietorships

Most of the advantages of sole proprietorships arise from the two main characteristics of this form of ownership: simplicity and individual control.

Figure 4.1 Relative Percentages of Nonfarm Sole Proprietorships, Partnerships, and Corporations in the United States

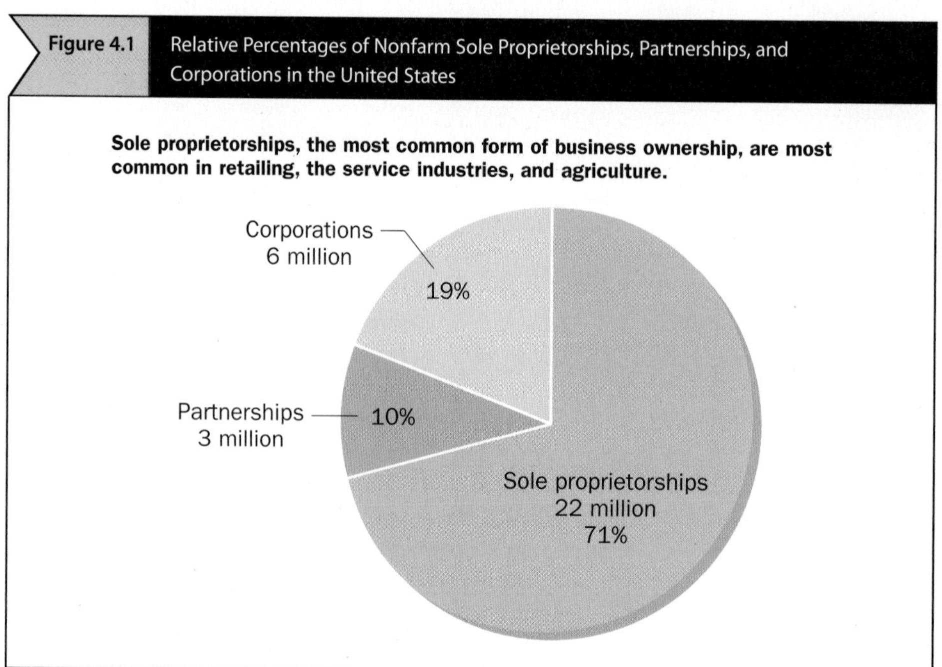

Source: U.S. Bureau of the Census, *Statistical Abstract of the United States* (Washington, DC: Bureau of the Census, 2010), table 729 (http://www.census.gov).

sole proprietorship a business that is owned (and usually operated) by one person

Ease of Start-Up and Closure Sole proprietorship is the simplest and cheapest way to start a business. Often, start-up requires no contracts, agreements, or other legal documents. Thus, a sole proprietorship can be, and most often is, established without the services of an attorney. The legal requirements often are limited to registering the name of the business and obtaining any necessary licenses or permits.

If the enterprise does not succeed, the firm can be closed as easily as it was opened. Creditors must be paid, of course, but generally, the owner does not have to go through any legal procedure before hanging up an "Out of Business" sign.

Pride of Ownership A successful sole proprietor is often very proud of her or his accomplishments—and rightfully so. In almost every case, the owner deserves a great deal of credit for assuming the risks and solving the day-to-day problems associated with operating sole proprietorships. Unfortunately, the reverse is also true. When the business fails, it is often the sole proprietor who is to blame.

Retention of All Profits Because all profits become the personal earnings of the owner, the owner has a strong incentive to succeed. This direct financial reward attracts many entrepreneurs to the sole proprietorship form of business and, if the business succeeds, is a source of great satisfaction.

No Special Taxes Profits earned by a sole proprietorship are taxed as the personal income of the owner. As a result, sole proprietors must report certain financial information on their personal income tax returns and make estimated quarterly tax payments to the federal government. Thus, a sole proprietorship does not pay the special state and federal income taxes that corporations pay.

Flexibility of Being Your Own Boss A sole proprietor is completely free to make decisions about the firm's operations. Without asking or waiting for anyone's approval, a sole proprietor can switch from retailing to wholesaling, move a shop's location, open a new store, or close an old one. Suppose that the sole proprietor of an appliance

Figure 4.2 Total Sales Receipts of American Businesses

Although corporations account for only about 19 percent of U.S. businesses, they bring in 83 percent of sales receipts.

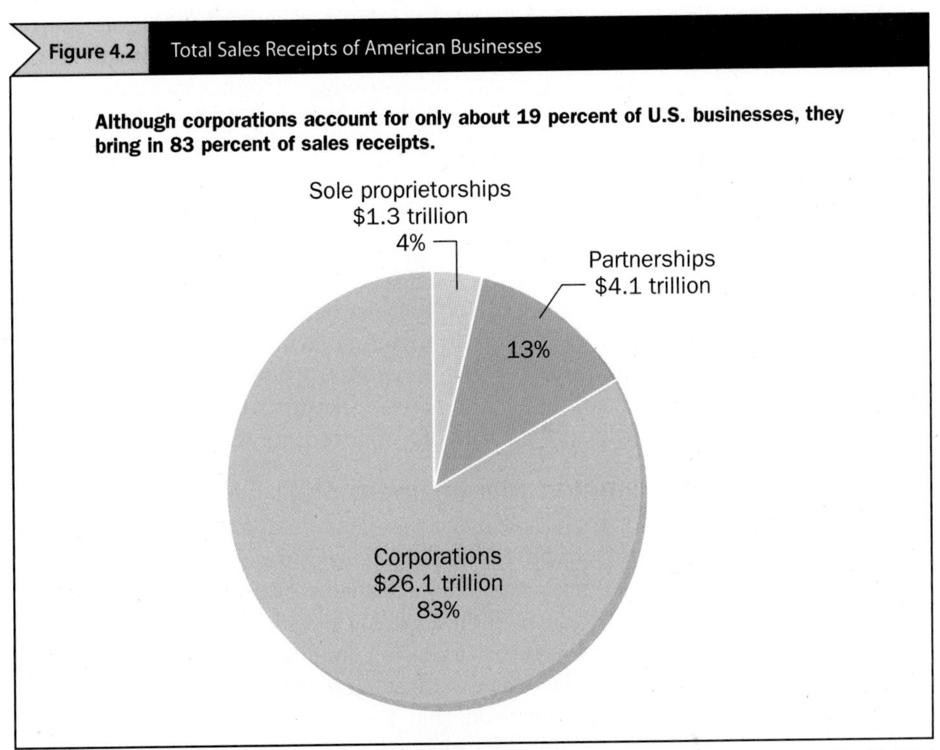

Source: U.S. Bureau of the Census, *Statistical Abstract of the United States* (Washington, DC: Bureau of the Census, 2010), table 729 (http://www.census gov).

store finds that many customers now prefer to shop on Sunday afternoons. He or she can make an immediate change in business hours to take advantage of this information (provided that state laws allow such stores to open on Sunday). The manager of a store in a large corporate chain such as Best Buy Company may have to seek the approval of numerous managers and company officials before making such a change.

Disadvantages of Sole Proprietorships

The disadvantages of a sole proprietorship stem from the fact that these businesses are owned by one person. Some capable sole proprietors experience no problems. Individuals who start out with few management skills and little money are most at risk for failure.

Unlimited Liability **Unlimited liability** is a legal concept that holds a business owner personally responsible for all the debts of the business. There is legally no difference between the debts of the business and the debts of the proprietor. If the business fails, or if the business is involved in a lawsuit and loses, the owner's personal property—including savings and other assets—can be seized (and sold if necessary) to pay creditors.

Unlimited liability is perhaps the major factor that tends to discourage would-be entrepreneurs with substantial personal wealth from using the sole proprietor form of business organization.

Lack of Continuity Legally, the sole proprietor *is* the business. If the owner retires, dies, or is declared legally incompetent, the business essentially ceases to exist. In many cases, however—especially when the business is a profitable enterprise—the owner's heirs take it over and either sell it or continue to operate it. The business also can suffer if the sole proprietor becomes ill and cannot work for an extended period of time. If the owner, for example, has a heart attack, there is often no one who can step in and manage the business. An illness can be devastating if the sole proprietor's personal skills are what determine if the business is a success or a failure.

unlimited liability a legal concept that holds a business owner personally responsible for all the debts of the business

Lack of Money Banks, suppliers, and other lenders usually are unwilling to lend large sums of money to sole proprietorships. Only one person—the sole proprietor—can be held responsible for repaying such loans, and the assets of most sole proprietors usually are limited. Moreover, these assets may have been used already as the basis for personal borrowing (a home mortgage or car loan) or for short-term credit from suppliers. Lenders also worry about the lack of continuity of sole proprietorships: Who will repay a loan if the sole proprietor dies? Finally, many lenders are concerned about the large number of sole proprietorships that fail—a topic discussed in Chapter 5.

The limited ability to borrow money can prevent a sole proprietorship from growing. It is the main reason that many business owners, when in need of relatively large amounts of capital, change from a sole proprietorship to a partnership or corporate form of ownership.

A builder with a dream. As a homebuilder, Shelley Reynolds, owner and president of Reynolds Signature Homes, has faced new challenges since the downturn in home sales that began three years ago. In most areas of the United States, there are fewer homeowners that can qualify for home mortgages, which makes it hard for business owners like Reynolds to construct upscale homes and sell them for a profit.

Limited Management Skills The sole proprietor is often the sole manager—in addition to being the only salesperson, buyer, accountant, and, on occasion, janitor. Even the most experienced business owner is unlikely to have expertise in all these areas. Unless he or she obtains the necessary expertise by hiring employees, assistants, or consultants, the business can suffer in the areas in which the owner is less knowledgeable. For the many sole proprietors who cannot hire the help they need, there just are not enough hours in the day to do everything that needs to be done.

Entrepreneurial SUCCESS

Student Business Incubators

Whether you're starting a new venture or expanding an existing company, you may be able to get expert help, office space, and even some funding without leaving your campus, if your school has a student business incubator. A growing number of colleges and universities are setting up incubators to help student entrepreneurs choose an appropriate form of business ownership and proceed to develop, test, implement, and refine their business ideas in a supportive environment.

The incubator at the University of Northern Iowa, for instance, invites student entrepreneurs to apply for a semester of on-campus assistance, including legal and accounting services, management training, and access to seed funds. Carlos Arguello was the first student entrepreneur to "graduate" from this incubator, working with his mother to successfully launch the Spanish-language newspaper *La Prensa* in northern Iowa.

At the University of Wisconsin-Madison, student entrepreneurs compete for six spaces in the on-campus incubator by submitting a written application and making a presentation to the Student Business Incubator Board. At the University of Michigan, the TechArb incubator houses up to 12 student-owned high-tech businesses at a time. One recent tenant was Mobil33t, which designed the iPhone app DoGood to encourage people to do a good deed every day. Can an incubator set you on the path toward entrepreneurial success?

Sources: Nathan Bomey, "University of Michigan Strikes Deal to Establish Permanent Student Business Incubator," *AnnArbor.com*, November 5, 2009, http://www.annarbor.com/business-review/university-of-michigan-strikes-deal-to-establish-permanent-student-business-incubator/; University of Wisconsin-Madison Student Business Incubator, http://www.asm.wisc.edu/sbi.html; University of Northern Iowa Student Business Incubator, http://www.bcs.uni.edu/jpec/sbi.htm.

Difficulty in Hiring Employees The sole proprietor may find it hard to attract and keep competent help. Potential employees may feel that there is no room for advancement in a firm whose owner assumes all managerial responsibilities. And when those who *are* hired are ready to take on added responsibility, they may find that the only way to do so is to quit the sole proprietorship and go to work for a larger firm or start up their own businesses. The lure of higher salaries and increased benefits (especially health insurance) also may cause existing employees to change jobs.

Beyond the Sole Proprietorship

Like many others, you may decide that the major disadvantage of a sole proprietorship is the limited amount that one person can do in a workday. One way to reduce the effect of this disadvantage (and retain many of the advantages) is to have more than one owner.

Partnerships

2

Explain the different types of partners and the importance of partnership agreements.

A person who would not think of starting and running a business alone may enthusiastically seize the opportunity to enter into a business partnership. The U.S. Uniform Partnership Act defines a **partnership** as a voluntary association of two or more persons to act as co-owners of a business for profit. For example, in 1990, two young African-American entrepreneurs named Janet Smith and Gary Smith started Ivy Planning Group—a company that provides strategic planning and performance measurement for clients. Today, more than 20 years later, the company has evolved into a multimillion-dollar company that has hired a diverse staff of employees and provides cultural diversity training for *Fortune* 1,000 firms, large not-for-profit organizations, and government agencies. In recognition of its efforts, Ivy Planning Group has been honored by DiversityBusiness.com as one of the top 50 minority-owned companies and by *Black Enterprise* and *Working Mother* magazines. And both Janet Smith and Gary Smith—Ivy Planning Group's founders—have been named "1 of 50 Most Influential Minorities in Business" by Minority Business and Professionals Network.[4]

As shown in Figures 4.1 and 4.2, there are approximately 3 million partnerships in the United States, and this type of ownership accounts for about $4.1 trillion in sales receipts each year. Note, however, that this form of ownership is much less common than the sole proprietorship or the corporation. In fact, as Figure 4.1 shows, partnerships

partnership a voluntary association of two or more persons to act as co-owners of a business for profit

represent only about 10 percent of all American businesses. Although there is no legal maximum on the number of partners a partnership may have, most have only two. Large accounting, law, and advertising partnerships, however, are likely to have multiple partners. Regardless of the number of people involved, a partnership often represents a pooling of special managerial skills and talents; at other times, it is the result of a sole proprietor's taking on a partner for the purpose of obtaining more capital.

Types of Partners

All partners are not necessarily equal. Some may be active in running the business, whereas others may have a limited role.

General Partners A **general partner** is a person who assumes full or shared responsibility for operating a business. General partners are active in day-to-day business operations, and each partner can enter into contracts on behalf of the other partners. He or she also assumes unlimited liability for all debts, including debts incurred by any other general partner without his or her knowledge or consent. A *general partnership* is a business co-owned by two or more general partners who are liable for everything the business does. To avoid future liability, a general partner who withdraws from the partnership must give notice to creditors, customers, and suppliers.

general partner a person who assumes full or shared responsibility for operating a business

limited partner a person who contributes capital to a business but has no management responsibility or liability for losses beyond the amount he or she invested in the partnership

master limited partnership (MLP) a business partnership that is owned and managed like a corporation but often taxed like a partnership

Limited Partners A **limited partner** is a person who invests money in a business but who has no management responsibility or liability for losses beyond his or her investment in the partnership. A *limited partnership* is a business co-owned by one or more general partners who manage the business and limited partners who invest money in it. Limited partnerships may be formed to finance real estate, oil and gas, motion picture, and other business ventures. Typically, the general partner or partners collect management fees and receive a percentage of profits. Limited partners receive a portion of profits and tax benefits.

Because of potential liability problems, special rules apply to limited partnerships. These rules are intended to protect customers and creditors who deal with limited partnerships. For example, prospective partners in a limited partnership must file a formal declaration, usually with the secretary of state, that describes the essential details of the partnership and the liability status of each partner involved in the business. At least one general partner must be responsible for the debts of the limited partnership. Also, some states prohibit the use of the limited partner's name in the partnership's name.

A special type of limited partnership is referred to as a *master limited partnership*. A **master limited partnership (MLP)** (sometimes referred to as a *publicly traded partnership*, or PTP) is a business partnership that is owned and managed like a corporation but often taxed like a partnership. This special ownership arrangement has a major advantage. Units of ownership in MLPs can be sold to investors to raise capital and often are traded on organized security exchanges. Because MLP units can be traded on an exchange, investors can sell their units of ownership at any time, hopefully for a profit. For more information on MLPs, visit the National Association of Publicly Traded Partnerships Web site at http://www.naptp.org.

Originally, there were tax advantages to forming an MLP because profits from this special type of partnership were reported as personal income. MLPs thus avoided the double taxation paid on corporate income. Today, the Internal Revenue Service has limited many of the tax advantages of MLPs. While there are exceptions, most MLPs typically are in natural resources, energy, or real estate-related businesses.[5]

Often two heads are better than one! Kevin and Mellisa Berger recently purchased and remodeled the Zesto Drive In in Jefferson City, Missouri. Today many married couples—like the Bergers—form a special type of partnership with each partner using his or her own unique skills and talents to build a successful business.

The Partnership Agreement

Articles of partnership refers to an agreement listing and explaining the terms of the partnership. Although both oral and written partnership agreements are legal and can be enforced in the courts, a written agreement has an obvious advantage. It is not subject to lapses of memory.

Figure 4.3 shows a typical partnership agreement. The partnership agreement should state who will make the final decisions, what each partner's duties will be, and the investment each partner will make. The partnership agreement also should state how much profit or loss each partner receives or is responsible for. Finally, the partnership agreement should state what happens if a partner wants to dissolve the partnership or dies. Although the people involved in a partnership can draft their own agreement, most experts recommend consulting an attorney.

When entering into a partnership agreement, partners would be wise to let a neutral third party—a consultant, an accountant, a lawyer, or a mutual friend—assist with any disputes that might arise.

Figure 4.3 Articles of Partnership

The articles of partnership is a written or oral agreement that lists and explains the terms of a partnership.

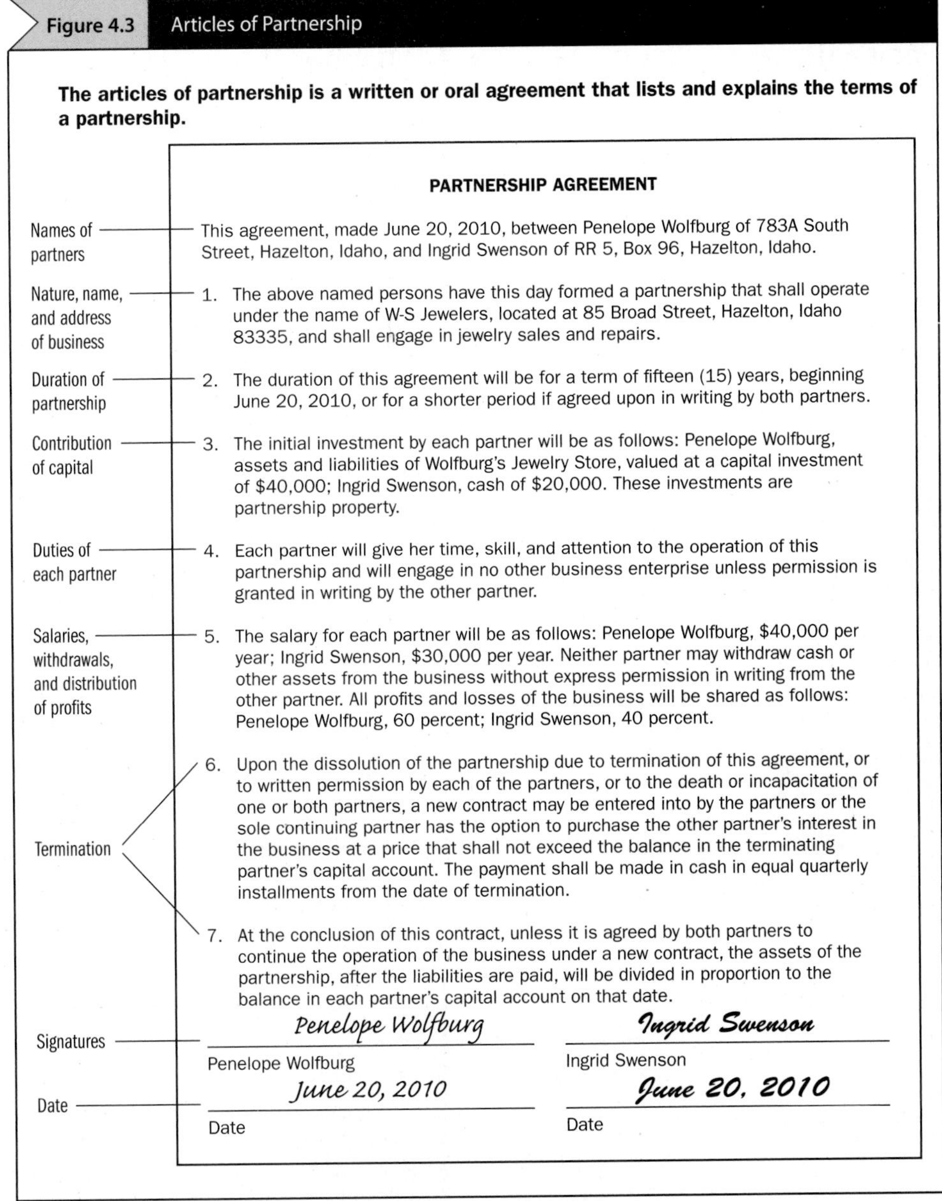

PARTNERSHIP AGREEMENT

Names of partners — This agreement, made June 20, 2010, between Penelope Wolfburg of 783A South Street, Hazelton, Idaho, and Ingrid Swenson of RR 5, Box 96, Hazelton, Idaho.

Nature, name, and address of business — 1. The above named persons have this day formed a partnership that shall operate under the name of W-S Jewelers, located at 85 Broad Street, Hazelton, Idaho 83335, and shall engage in jewelry sales and repairs.

Duration of partnership — 2. The duration of this agreement will be for a term of fifteen (15) years, beginning June 20, 2010, or for a shorter period if agreed upon in writing by both partners.

Contribution of capital — 3. The initial investment by each partner will be as follows: Penelope Wolfburg, assets and liabilities of Wolfburg's Jewelry Store, valued at a capital investment of $40,000; Ingrid Swenson, cash of $20,000. These investments are partnership property.

Duties of each partner — 4. Each partner will give her time, skill, and attention to the operation of this partnership and will engage in no other business enterprise unless permission is granted in writing by the other partner.

Salaries, withdrawals, and distribution of profits — 5. The salary for each partner will be as follows: Penelope Wolfburg, $40,000 per year; Ingrid Swenson, $30,000 per year. Neither partner may withdraw cash or other assets from the business without express permission in writing from the other partner. All profits and losses of the business will be shared as follows: Penelope Wolfburg, 60 percent; Ingrid Swenson, 40 percent.

Termination — 6. Upon the dissolution of the partnership due to termination of this agreement, or to written permission by each of the partners, or to the death or incapacitation of one or both partners, a new contract may be entered into by the partners or the sole continuing partner has the option to purchase the other partner's interest in the business at a price that shall not exceed the balance in the terminating partner's capital account. The payment shall be made in cash in equal quarterly installments from the date of termination.

7. At the conclusion of this contract, unless it is agreed by both partners to continue the operation of the business under a new contract, the assets of the partnership, after the liabilities are paid, will be divided in proportion to the balance in each partner's capital account on that date.

Signatures — *Penelope Wolfburg* Penelope Wolfburg — *Ingrid Swenson* Ingrid Swenson

Date — *June 20, 2010* Date — *June 20, 2010* Date

3

Describe the advantages and disadvantages of partnerships.

Advantages of Partnerships

Partnerships have many advantages. The most important are described below.

Ease of Start-Up Partnerships are relatively easy to form. As with a sole proprietorship, the legal requirements often are limited to registering the name of the business and obtaining any necessary licenses or permits. It may not even be necessary to prepare written articles of partnership, although doing so is generally a good idea.

Availability of Capital and Credit Because partners can pool their funds, a partnership usually has more capital available than a sole proprietorship does. This additional capital, coupled with the general partners' unlimited liability, can form the basis for a better credit rating. Banks and suppliers may be more willing to extend credit or approve larger loans to such a partnership than to a sole proprietor. This does not mean that partnerships can borrow all the money they need. Many partnerships have found it hard to get long-term financing simply because lenders worry about the possibility of management disagreements and lack of continuity.

Personal Interest General partners are very concerned with the operation of the firm—perhaps even more so than sole proprietors. After all, they are responsible for the actions of all other general partners, as well as for their own. The pride of ownership from solving the day-to-day problems of operating a business—with the help of another person(s)—is a strong motivating force and often makes all the people involved in the partnership work harder to become more successful.

Combined Business Skills and Knowledge Partners often have complementary skills. The weakness of one partner—in manufacturing, for example—may be offset by another partner's strength in that area. Moreover, the ability to discuss important decisions with another concerned individual often relieves some pressure and leads to more effective decision making.

Two entrepreneurs with one goal. The goal for Matt Flannery (right) and Premal Shah (left) when they co-founded Kiva.org was to create an organization that would connect people, through lending, for the sake of alleviating poverty. Have the two partners been successful? You bet—at the beginning of 2010, Kiva.org had facilitated over $100 million in loans. For more information about Kiva.org or to become a lender and get involved, go to http://www.kiva.org.

Retention of Profits As in a sole proprietorship, all profits belong to the owners of the partnership. The partners share directly in the financial rewards and therefore are highly motivated to do their best to make the firm succeed. As noted, the partnership agreement should state how much profit or loss each partner receives or is responsible for.

No Special Taxes Although a partnership pays no income tax, the Internal Revenue Service requires partnerships to file an annual information return that states the names and addresses of all partners involved in the business. The return also must provide information about income and expenses and distributions made to each partner. Then each partner is required to report his or her share of profit (or loss) from the partnership business on his or her individual tax return and is taxed on his or her share of the profit—in the same way a sole proprietor is taxed.

Disadvantages of Partnerships

Although partnerships have many advantages when compared with sole proprietorships and corporations, they also have some disadvantages, which anyone thinking of forming a partnership should consider.

Unlimited Liability As we have noted, each *general* partner has unlimited liability for all debts of the business. Each partner is legally and personally responsible for the debts, taxes, and actions of any other partner conducting partnership business, even if that partner did not incur those debts or do anything wrong. General partners thus run the risk of having to use their personal assets to pay creditors. *Limited* partners, however, risk only their original investment.

Today, many states allow partners to form a *limited-liability partnership* (LLP), in which a partner may have limited-liability protection from legal action resulting from the malpractice or negligence of the other partners. Most states that allow LLPs restrict this type of ownership to certain types of professionals such as accountants, architects, attorneys, and similar professionals. (Note the difference between a limited partnership and a limited-liability partnership. A limited partnership must have at least one general partner that has unlimited liability. On the other hand, all partners in a limited-liability partnership may have limited liability *for the malpractice of the other partners.*)

SPOTLIGHT

Where the jobs are!

Source: The U.S. Census Bureau, *Statistical Abstract of the United States*, 2010, table 742.

Management Disagreements What happens to a partnership if one of the partners brings a spouse or a relative into the business? What happens if a partner wants to withdraw more money from the business? Notice that each of the preceding situations—and for that matter, most of the other problems that can develop in a partnership—involves one partner doing something that disturbs the other partner(s). This human factor is especially important because business partners—with egos, ambitions, and money on the line—are especially susceptible to friction. When partners begin to disagree about decisions, policies, or ethics, distrust may build and get worse as time passes—often to the point where it is impossible to operate the business successfully.

Lack of Continuity Partnerships are terminated if any one of the general partners dies, withdraws, or is declared legally incompetent. However, the remaining partners can purchase that partner's ownership share. For example, the partnership agreement may permit surviving partners to continue the business after buying a deceased partner's interest from his or her estate. However, if the partnership loses an owner whose specific management or technical skills cannot be replaced, it is not likely to survive.

Frozen Investment It is easy to invest money in a partnership, but it is sometimes quite difficult to get it out. This is the case, for example, when remaining partners are unwilling to buy the share of the business that belongs to a partner who retires or wants to relocate to another city. To avoid such difficulties, the partnership agreement should include some procedure for buying out a partner.

In some cases, a partner must find someone outside the firm to buy his or her share. How easy or difficult it is to find an outsider depends on how successful the business is and how willing existing partners are to accept a new partner.

Beyond the Partnership

The main advantages of a partnership over a sole proprietorship are the added capital and management expertise of the partners. However, some of the basic disadvantages of the sole proprietorship also plague the general partnership. One disadvantage in particular—unlimited liability—can cause problems for a partner with substantial personal wealth. A third form of business ownership, the corporation, overcomes this disadvantage.

4

Summarize how a corporation is formed.

Corporations

Back in 1837, William Procter and James Gamble—two sole proprietors—formed a partnership called Procter & Gamble (P&G) and set out to compete with 14 other soap and candle makers in Cincinnati, Ohio. Then, in 1890, Procter & Gamble incorporated to raise additional capital for expansion that eventually allowed the company to become a global giant. Today, 4 billion times a day, Procter & Gamble brands touch the lives of people in 180 countries around the globe.[6] Like many large corporations, P&G's market capitalization is greater than the gross domestic product of many countries. Although this corporation is a corporate giant, the firm's executives and employees believe it also has a responsibility to be an ethical corporate citizen. For example, P&G's purpose statement (or mission) is

> *We will provide branded products and services of superior quality and value that improve the lives of the world's consumers, now and for generations to come. As a result, consumers will reward us with leadership sales, profit and value creation, allowing our people, our shareholders and the communities in which we live and work to prosper.*[7]

In today's competitive environment, it's common to hear of large companies that are profitable. It is less common to hear of profitable companies that are held in high regard because they are good corporate citizens.

While not all sole proprietorships and partnerships become corporations, there are reasons why business owners choose the corporate form of ownership. Let's begin with a definition of a corporation. Perhaps the best definition of a corporation was given by Chief Justice John Marshall in a famous Supreme Court decision in 1819. A corporation, he said, "is an artificial person, invisible, intangible, and existing only in contemplation of the law." In other words, a **corporation** (sometimes referred to as a *regular* or *C-corporation*) is an artificial person created by law, with most of the legal rights of a real person. These include:

- The right to start and operate a business
- The right to buy or sell property
- The right to borrow money
- The right to sue or be sued
- The right to enter into binding contracts

corporation an artificial person created by law with most of the legal rights of a real person, including the rights to start and operate a business, to buy or sell property, to borrow money, to sue or be sued, and to enter into binding contracts

stock the shares of ownership of a corporation

stockholder a person who owns a corporation's stock

Would you believe a major corporation was started in this building? The building in this photo was once used by Bill Hewlett and Dave Packard as a research lab, development workshop, and manufacturing facility. Their efforts paid off, and today Hewlett-Packard Corporation is one of the world's leading technology companies. By the way, this building is now a historic landmark and is considered to be the birthplace of Silicon Valley.

© David Paul Morris/Getty Images

Unlike a real person, however, a corporation exists only on paper. There are approximately 6 million corporations in the United States. They comprise about 19 percent of all businesses, but they account for 83 percent of sales revenues (see Figures 4.1 and 4.2). Table 4.1 lists the seven largest U.S. industrial corporations, ranked according to sales.

Corporate Ownership

The shares of ownership of a corporation are called **stock.** The people who own a corporation's stock—and thus own part of the corporation—are called **stockholders.** Once a corporation has been formed, it may sell its stock

Table 4.1	The Seven Largest U.S. Industrial Corporations, Ranked by Sales Revenues		
Rank	**Company**	**Revenues ($ millions)**	**Profits ($ millions)**
1	ExxonMobil	442,851.0	45,220.0
2	Walmart Stores	405,607.0	13,400.0
3	Chevron	263,159.0	23,931.0
4	ConocoPhillips	230,764.0	−16,998.0
5	General Electric	183,207.0	17,410.0
6	General Motors	148,979.0	−30,860.0
7	Ford Motor	146,277.0	−14,672.0

Source: *Fortune* Web site at http://www.fortune.com (accessed March 16, 2010). September 12, 2008. Copyright © 2008. Reprinted by permission.

to individuals or other companies that want to invest in the corporation. It also may issue stock as a reward to key employees in return for certain services or as a return to investors in place of cash payments.

A **closed corporation** is a corporation whose stock is owned by relatively few people and is not sold to the general public. As an example, DeWitt and Lila Wallace owned virtually all the stock of Reader's Digest Association, making it one of the largest corporations of this kind. A person who wishes to sell the stock of a closed corporation generally arranges to sell it privately to another stockholder or a close acquaintance.

Although founded in 1921 as a closed corporation, the Reader's Digest Association became an open corporation when it sold stock to investors for the first time in 1990. (*Note:* In 2007, Reader's Digest Association became a closed corporation once again after the firm was purchased by a group of investors.)

An **open corporation** is one whose stock can be bought and sold by any individual. Examples of open corporations include General Electric, Microsoft, and Johnson & Johnson.

Forming a Corporation

Although you may think that incorporating a business guarantees success, it does not. There is no special magic about placing the word *Incorporated* or the abbreviation *Inc.* after the name of a business. Unfortunately, like sole proprietorships or partnerships, incorporated businesses can go broke. The decision to incorporate a business therefore should be made only after carefully considering whether the corporate form of ownership suits your needs better than the sole proprietorship or partnership forms.

If you decide that the corporate form is the best form of organization for you, most experts recommend that you begin the incorporation process by consulting a lawyer to be sure that all legal requirements are met. While it may be possible to incorporate a business without legal help, it is well to keep in mind the old saying, "A man who acts as his own attorney has a fool for a client." Table 4.2 lists some aspects of starting and running a business that may require legal help.

Where to Incorporate A business is allowed to incorporate in any state that it chooses. Most small- and medium-sized businesses are incorporated in the state where they do the most business. The founders of larger corporations or of those that will do business nationwide often compare the benefits that various states provide to corporations. The decision on where to incorporate usually is based on two factors: (1) the cost of incorporating in one state compared with the cost in another state and (2) the advantages and disadvantages of each state's corporate laws and tax structure. Some states are more hospitable than others, and some offer fewer restrictions, lower taxes, and other benefits to attract new firms. Delaware and Nevada are often chosen by corporations that do business in more than one state because of their corporation-friendly laws.[8]

closed corporation a corporation whose stock is owned by relatively few people and is not sold to the general public

open corporation a corporation whose stock can be bought and sold by any individual

Table 4.2	Ten Aspects of Business that May Require Legal Help
1. Choosing either the sole proprietorship, partnership, corporate, or some special form of ownership	6. Filing for licenses or permits at the local, state, and federal levels
2. Constructing a partnership agreement	7. Purchasing an existing business or real estate
3. Incorporating a business	8. Creating valid contracts
4. Registering a corporation's stock	9. Hiring employees and independent contractors
5. Obtaining a trademark, patent, or copyright	10. Extending credit and collecting debts

An incorporated business is called a **domestic corporation** in the state in which it is incorporated. In all other states where it does business, it is called a **foreign corporation**. Sears Holdings Corporation, the parent company of Sears and Kmart, is incorporated in Delaware, where it is a domestic corporation. In the remaining 49 states, Sears is a foreign corporation. Sears must register in all states where it does business and also pay taxes and annual fees to each state. A corporation chartered by a foreign government and conducting business in the United States is an **alien corporation**. Volkswagen AG, Sony Corporation, and the Royal Dutch/Shell Group are examples of alien corporations.

The Corporate Charter Once a home state has been chosen, the incorporator(s) submits *articles of incorporation* to the secretary of state. When the articles of incorporation are approved, they become a contract between a corporation and the state in which the state recognizes the formation of the artificial person that is the corporation. Usually, the articles of incorporation include the following information:

- The firm's name and address
- The incorporators' names and addresses
- The purpose of the corporation
- The maximum amount of stock and types of stock to be issued
- The rights and privileges of stockholders
- The length of time the corporation is to exist

To help you to decide if the corporate form of organization is the right choice, you may want to review the material available on the Yahoo! Small Business Web site (http://smallbusiness.yahoo.com). Once at the site, click on Resources. In addition, before making a decision to organize your business as a corporation, you may want to consider two additional areas: stockholders' rights and the importance of the organizational meeting.

Stockholders' Rights There are two basic types of stock. Owners of **common stock** may vote on corporate matters. Generally, an owner of common stock has one vote for each share owned. However, any claims of common-stock owners on profits and assets of the corporation are subordinate to the claims of others. The owners of **preferred stock** usually have no voting rights, but their claims on dividends are paid before those of common-stock owners. Although large corporations may issue both common and preferred stock, generally small corporations issue only common stock.

Perhaps the most important right of owners of both common and preferred stock is to share in the profit earned by the corporation through the payment of dividends. A **dividend** is a distribution of earnings to the stockholders of a corporation. Other rights include receiving information about the corporation, voting on changes to the corporate charter, and attending the corporation's annual stockholders' meeting, where they may exercise their right to vote.

Because common stockholders usually live all over the nation, very few actually may attend a corporation's annual meeting. Instead, they vote by proxy. A **proxy** is a legal form listing issues to be decided at a stockholders' meeting and enabling

domestic corporation a corporation in the state in which it is incorporated

foreign corporation a corporation in any state in which it does business except the one in which it is incorporated

alien corporation a corporation chartered by a foreign government and conducting business in the United States

common stock stock owned by individuals or firms who may vote on corporate matters but whose claims on profits and assets are subordinate to the claims of others

preferred stock stock owned by individuals or firms who usually do not have voting rights but whose claims on dividends are paid before those of common-stock owners

dividend a distribution of earnings to the stockholders of a corporation

proxy a legal form listing issues to be decided at a stockholders' meeting and enabling stockholders to transfer their voting rights to some other individual or individuals

stockholders to transfer their voting rights to some other individual or individuals. The stockholder can register a vote and transfer voting rights simply by signing and returning the form. Today, most corporations also allow stockholders to exercise their right to vote by proxy by accessing the Internet or using a toll-free phone number.

Organizational Meeting As the last step in forming a corporation, the incorporators and original stockholders meet to adopt corporate by-laws and elect their first board of directors. (Later, directors will be elected or reelected at the corporation's annual meetings.) The board members are directly responsible to the stockholders for the way they operate the firm.

Corporate Structure

The organizational structure of most corporations is more complicated than that of a sole proprietorship or partnership. This is especially true as the corporation begins to grow and expand. In a corporation, both the board of directors and the corporate officers are involved in management.

Three corporate executives with a mission. At a recent press conference, PepsiCo announced that it will acquire its two anchor bottlers in order to provide enhanced customer service and drive the company's efforts to increase innovation. In this photo, Indra Nooyi, Chairperson of the Board and Chief Executive Officer of PepsiCo (center), is pictured with Robert Pohlad, Chairman of PepsiAmericas (left), and Eric Foss, Chairperson of the Pepsi Bottling Group.

Board of Directors As an artificial person, a corporation can act only through its directors, who represent the corporation's stockholders. The **board of directors** is the top governing body of a corporation and is elected by the stockholders. Board members can be chosen from within the corporation or from outside it. *Note:* For a small corporation, only one director is required in many states although you can choose to have more.

Directors who are elected from within the corporation are usually its top managers—the president and executive vice presidents, for example. Those elected from outside the corporation generally are experienced managers or entrepreneurs with proven leadership ability and/or specific talents the organization seems to need. In smaller corporations, majority stockholders usually serve as board members.

The major responsibilities of the board of directors are to set company goals and develop general plans (or strategies) for meeting those goals. The board also is responsible for the firm's overall operation.

Corporate Officers **Corporate officers** are appointed by the board of directors. Although a small corporation may not have all of the following officers, the chairman of the board, president, executive vice presidents, corporate secretary, and treasurer are all corporate officers. They help the board to make plans, carry out strategies established by the board, hire employees, and manage day-to-day business activities. Periodically (usually each month), they report to the board of directors. And at the annual meeting, the directors report to the stockholders. In theory, then, the stockholders are able to control the activities of the entire corporation through its directors because they are the group that elects the board of directors (see Figure 4.4).

board of directors the top governing body of a corporation, the members of which are elected by the stockholders

corporate officers the chairman of the board, president, executive vice presidents, corporate secretary, treasurer, and any other top executive appointed by the board of directors

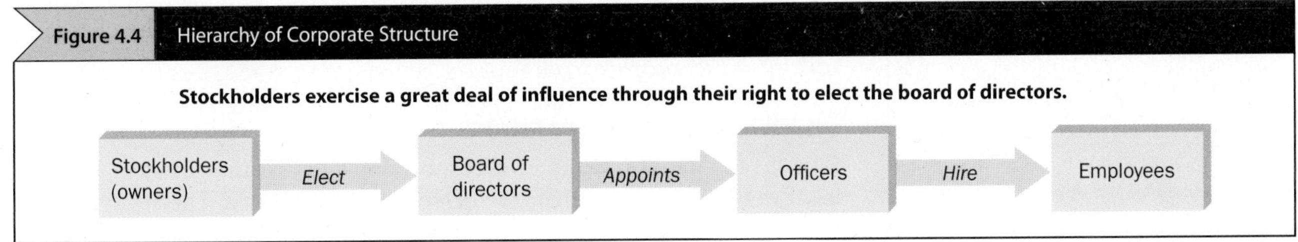

Figure 4.4 Hierarchy of Corporate Structure

5

Describe the advantages and disadvantages of a corporation.

Advantages of Corporations

Back in October 2000, Manny Ruiz decided that it was time to start his own company. With the help of a team of media specialists, he founded Hispanic PR Wire. In a business where hype is the name of the game, Hispanic PR Wire is the real thing and has established itself as the nation's premier news distribution service reaching U.S. Hispanic media and opinion leaders. Today, the business continues to build on its early success.[9] Mr. Ruiz chose to incorporate this business because it provided a number of advantages that other forms of business ownership did not offer. Typical advantages include limited liability, ease of raising capital, ease of transfer of ownership, perpetual life, and specialized management.

Limited Liability One of the most attractive features of corporate ownership is **limited liability**. With few exceptions, each owner's financial liability is limited to the amount of money he or she has paid for the corporation's stock. This feature arises from the fact that the corporation is itself a legal person, separate from its owners. If a corporation fails or is involved in a lawsuit and loses, creditors have a claim only on the corporation's assets, not on the owners' (stockholders') personal assets. Because it overcomes the problem of unlimited liability connected with sole proprietorships and general partnerships, limited liability is one of the chief reasons why entrepreneurs often choose the corporate form of organization.

limited liability a feature of corporate ownership that limits each owner's financial liability to the amount of money that he or she has paid for the corporation's stock

Ease of Raising Capital The corporation is by far the most effective form of business ownership for raising capital. Like sole proprietorships and partnerships, corporations can borrow from lending institutions. However, they also can raise additional sums of money by selling stock. Individuals are more willing to invest in corporations than in other forms of business because of limited liability, and they can sell their stock easily—hopefully for a profit.

Where did all these products come from? One company—the 3M Company—is known for its financial commitment to funding research to develop innovative products. One of the advantages of the corporate form of ownership is that a company like 3M can sell stock to raise the money needed to begin operations, to fund expansion, *and* to pay for new product research and development.

© Adrian Brown/Sipa Press/Newscom

Ease of Transfer of Ownership Accessing a brokerage firm Web site or a telephone call to a stockbroker is all that is required to put most stock up for sale. Willing buyers are available for most stocks at the market price. Ownership is transferred when the sale is made, and practically no restrictions apply to the sale and purchase of stock issued by an open corporation.

Perpetual Life Since it is essentially a legal "person," a corporation exists independently of its owners and survives them. The withdrawal, death, or incompetence of a key executive or owner does not cause the corporation to be terminated. Sears, Roebuck and Co. incorporated in 1893 and is one of the nation's largest retailing corporations, even though its original cofounders, Richard Sears and Alvah Roebuck, have been dead for decades.

Specialized Management Typically, corporations are able to recruit more skilled, knowledgeable, and talented managers than proprietorships and partnerships. This is so because they pay bigger salaries, offer excellent fringe benefits, and are large enough to offer considerable opportunity for advancement. Within the corporate structure, administration, human resources, finance, marketing, and operations are placed in the charge of experts in these fields.

Disadvantages of Corporations

Like its advantages, many of a corporation's disadvantages stem from its legal definition as an artificial person or legal entity. The most serious disadvantages are described in the following text. (See Table 4.3 for a

Table 4.3 Some Advantages and Disadvantages of a Sole Proprietorship, Partnership, and Corporation

	Sole Proprietorship	General Partnership	Regular C-Corporation
Protecting against liability for debts	Difficult	Difficult	Easy
Raising money	Difficult	Difficult	Easy
Ownership transfer	Difficult	Difficult	Easy
Preserving continuity	Difficult	Difficult	Easy
Government regulations	Few	Few	Many
Formation	Easy	Easy	Difficult
Income taxation	Once	Once	Twice

comparison of some of the advantages and disadvantages of a sole proprietorship, general partnership, and corporation.)

Difficulty and Expense of Formation Forming a corporation can be a relatively complex and costly process. The use of an attorney is usually necessary to complete the legal forms that are submitted to the secretary of state. Application fees, attorney's fees, registration costs associated with selling stock, and other organizational costs can amount to thousands of dollars for even a medium-sized corporation. The costs of incorporating, in terms of both time and money, discourage many owners of smaller businesses from forming corporations.

Government Regulation and Increased Paperwork A corporation must meet various government standards before it can sell its stock to the public. Then it must file many reports on its business operations and finances with local, state, and federal governments. In addition, the corporation must make periodic reports to its stockholders about various aspects of the business. To prepare all the necessary reports, even small corporations often need the help of an attorney, certified public accountant, and other professionals on a regular basis. In addition, a corporation's activities are restricted by law to those spelled out in its charter.

Conflict Within the Corporation Because a large corporation may employ thousands of employees, some conflict is inevitable. For example, the pressure to increase sales revenue, reduce expenses, and increase profits often leads to increased stress and tension for both managers and employees. This is especially true when a corporation operates in a competitive industry, attempts to develop and market new products, or must downsize the workforce to reduce employee salary expense during an economic crisis.

Double Taxation Corporations must pay a tax on their profits. In addition, stockholders must pay a personal income tax on profits received as dividends. Corporate profits thus are taxed twice—once as corporate income and a second time as the personal income of stockholders. *Note:* Both the S-corporation and the limited-liability company discussed in the next section eliminate the disadvantage of double taxation because they are taxed like a partnership. These special types of ownership still provide limited liability for the personal assets of the owners.

Lack of Secrecy Because open corporations are required to submit detailed reports to government agencies and to stockholders, they cannot keep their operations confidential. Competitors can study these corporate reports and then use the information to compete more effectively. In effect, every public corporation has to share some of its secrets with its competitors.

6

Examine special types of corporations, including S-corporations, limited-liability companies, and not-for-profit corporations.

Special Types of Business Ownership

In addition to the sole proprietorship, partnership, and the regular corporate form of organization, some entrepreneurs choose other forms of organization that meet their special needs. Additional organizational options include S-corporations, limited-liability companies, and not-for-profit corporations.

S-Corporations

If a corporation meets certain requirements, its directors may apply to the Internal Revenue Service for status as an S-corporation. An **S-corporation** is a corporation that is taxed as though it were a partnership. In other words, the corporation's income is taxed only as the personal income of its stockholders. Corporate profits or losses "pass through" the business and are reported on the owners' personal income tax returns.

To qualify for the special status of an S-corporation, a firm must meet the following criteria:[10]

S-corporation a corporation that is taxed as though it were a partnership

limited-liability company (LLC) a form of business ownership that combines the benefits of a corporation and a partnership while avoiding some of the restrictions and disadvantages of those forms of ownership

1. No more than 100 stockholders are allowed.
2. Stockholders must be individuals, estates, or certain trusts.
3. There can be only one class of outstanding stock.
4. The firm must be a domestic corporation eligible to file for S-corporation status.
5. There can be no partnerships, corporations, or nonresident-alien stockholders.
6. All stockholders must agree to the decision to form an S-corporation.

Becoming an S-corporation can be an effective way to avoid double taxation while retaining the corporation's legal benefit of limited liability.

American Girl: A limited-liability company. A limited-liability company (LLC) doesn't have to be small. The truth is that even large companies like American Girl often choose the LLC form of business ownership. American Girl, LLC, chose this type of business ownership because it provided limited liability for investors and avoided some of the restrictions and disadvantages of other forms of business ownership.

© Kim Karpeles/Alamy

Limited-Liability Companies

A new form of ownership called a *limited-liability company* has been approved in all 50 states—although each state's laws may differ. A **limited-liability company (LLC)** is a form of business ownership that combines the benefits of a corporation and a partnership while avoiding some of the restrictions and disadvantages of those forms of ownership. Chief advantages of an LLC are as follows:

1. LLCs with at least two members are taxed like a partnership and thus avoid the double taxation imposed on most corporations. LLCs with just one member are taxed like a sole proprietorship. LLCs can even elect to be taxed as a corporation if there are benefits to offset the corporate double taxation.
2. Like a corporation, it provides limited-liability protection for acts and debts of the LLC. An LLC thus extends the concept of personal-asset protection to small business owners.
3. The LLC type of organization provides more management flexibility when compared with corporations. A corporation, for example, is required to hold annual meetings and record meeting minutes; an LLC is not.

Although many experts believe that the LLC is nothing more than a variation of the S-corporation, there is a difference. An LLC is not restricted to 100 stockholders—a common drawback of the S-corporation. LLCs are also less restricted and have more flexibility than S-corporations in terms of who can become an owner. Although the owners of an LLC may file the required articles of organization in any state, most choose to file in their home state—the state where they do most of their business. For more information about the benefits of forming an LLC, go to http://www.llc.com.

Because of the increased popularity of the LLC form of organization, experts are predicting that LLCs may become one of the most popular forms of business ownership available. For help in understanding the differences between a regular corporation, S-corporation, and limited-liability company, see Table 4.4.

Not-for-Profit Corporations

A **not-for-profit corporation** (sometimes referred to as *non-profit*) is a corporation organized to provide a social, educational, religious, or other service rather than to earn a profit. Various charities, museums, private schools, colleges, and charitable organizations are organized in this way, primarily to ensure limited liability.

While the process used to organize a not-for-profit corporation is similar to the process used to create a regular corporation, each state does have different laws. In fact, many of the requirements are different than the requirements for establishing a regular corporation. Once approved by state authorities, not-for-profit corporations must meet specific Internal Revenue Service guidelines in order to obtain tax-exempt status.

Today, there is a renewed interest in not-for-profits because these organizations are formed to improve communities and change lives. For example, Habitat for Humanity is a not-for-profit corporation and was formed to provide homes for qualified lower income people who cannot afford housing. Even though this corporation may receive more money than it spends, any surplus funds are "reinvested" in building activities to provide low-cost housing to qualified individuals. Other examples of not-for-profit corporations include the SeaWorld and Busch Gardens Conservation Fund, the Girl Scouts, the Bill and Melinda Gates Foundation, and many local not-for-profits designed to meet specific needs within a community.

From a career standpoint, you should realize that many not-for-profit corporations operate in much the same way as a for-profit business. While many not-for-profit corporations rely on volunteers to perform services, larger organizations do have paid employees. These employees are responsible for making sure the not-for-profit corporation achieves its goals and objectives, ensuring accountability for finances and donations, and monitoring activities to improve performance of both paid employees and volunteers. If interested in a career in the non-profit sector, why not volunteer your time and effort in a local not-for-profit organization to see if you enjoy this type of challenge.

Table 4.4 Some Advantages and Disadvantages of a Regular Corporation, S-Corporation, and Limited-Liability Company

	Regular C-Corporation	S-Corporation	Limited-Liability Company
Double taxation	Yes	No	No
Limited liability and personal asset protection	Yes	Yes	Yes
Management and ownership flexibility	No	No	Yes
Restrictions on the number of owners/ stockholders	No	Yes	No
Internal Revenue Service tax regulations	Many	Many	Fewer

not-for-profit corporation a corporation organized to provide a social, educational, religious, or other service rather than to earn a profit

Career SUCCESS

Choosing a Career in Not-for-Profit Corporations

If you're looking to make a difference, consider a career in the world of not-for-profit corporations. Such organizations exist to offer social, educational, religious, or other services, rather than striving for profitability. Although employees may receive lower salaries than they would in for-profit businesses, many find not-for-profit corporations rewarding places to develop their personal and professional skills.

Ginny Wiedower, who graduated from the University of Central Arkansas with a B.A. in public relations and writing, worked for several businesses before joining Goodwill Industries of Arkansas in Little Rock as director of marketing and communications. Goodwill helps low-income and disabled people improve their situations through job training and employment opportunities.

"Goodwill is the first non-profit [not-for-profit] that I've worked for," Ginny says, "and during my time here I've realized that this is really where I want to be, in the non-profit sector." She likes being able to help people "grow and really reach their highest potential." Now Ginny's career goal is to become the executive director of a local not-for-profit corporation.

Thousands of college graduates have chosen careers in education after being trained by the not-for-profit corporation Teach for America. For example, once Boston College graduate Kilian Betlach completed his training, he taught in a California middle school and then joined a not-for-profit policy group that works to improve the U.S. education system. Is a career in the not-for-profit sector in your future?

Sources: Jeff Hankins, "The New Influentials in Their 20s," *Arkansas Business*, November 9, 2009, 18ff; Amanda Paulson, "The Approach of Teach for America," *Christian Science Monitor*, March 27, 2009, http://www.csmonitor.com/USA/Education/2009/0327/p13s02-ussc.html; Kate Stanton and Lizzy Berryman, "New Grads Increasingly Turning to Jobs in Service, Volunteer Sectors," *PBS Online NewsHour*, March 16, 2009, http://www.pbs.org/newshour/updates/business/jan-june09/service_03-16.html.

7

Discuss the purpose of a cooperative, joint venture, and syndicate.

Cooperatives, Joint Ventures, and Syndicates

Today, three additional types of business organizations—cooperatives, joint ventures, and syndicates—are used for special purposes. Each of these forms of organization is unique when compared with more traditional forms of business ownership.

Cooperatives

A **cooperative** is an association of individuals or firms whose purpose is to perform some business function for its members. The cooperative can perform its function more effectively than any member could by acting alone. For example, cooperatives purchase goods in bulk and distribute them to members; thus, the unit cost is lower than it would be if each member bought the goods in a much smaller quantity.

Although cooperatives are found in all segments of our economy, they are most prevalent in agriculture. Farmers use cooperatives to purchase supplies, to buy services such as trucking and storage, and to process and market their products. Ocean Spray Cranberries, Inc., for example, is a cooperative of some 600 cranberry growers and about 50 citrus growers spread throughout the country.[11]

cooperative an association of individuals or firms whose purpose is to perform some business function for its members

Joint Ventures

A **joint venture** is an agreement between two or more groups to form a business entity in order to achieve a specific goal or to operate for a specific period of time. Both the scope of the joint venture and the liabilities of the people or businesses involved usually are limited to one project. Once the goal is reached, the period of time elapses, or the project is completed, the joint venture is dissolved.

Corporations, as well as individuals, may enter into joint ventures. Major oil producers often have formed a number of joint ventures to share the extremely high cost of exploring for offshore petroleum deposits. And many U.S. companies are forming joint ventures with foreign firms in order to enter new markets around the globe. For example, Walmart has joined forces with India's Bharti Enterprises to establish wholesale cash-and-carry stores that sell directly to local retailers in different cities and towns in India. Plans are for each store to offer an assortment of approximately 6,000 items including food and nonfood items at competitive wholesale prices, allowing retailers and small business owners to lower their cost of operation. The first cash-and-carry store was named Best Price Modern Wholesale and opened in Amritsar, India, in May 2009. Over the next seven years, the joint venture plans to open 10 to 15 cash-and-carry stores that will employ approximately 5,000 people.[12]

Sustaining the Planet

Get Your Daily Dose of Sustainability News

What steps are small businesses, major corporations, and not-for-profit corporations worldwide taking to achieve a more sustainable and earth-friendly future? Find out by clicking to get your daily dose of sustainability news, analysis, and videos at the *Environmental Leader* Web site. Take a look: http://www.environmentalleader.com.

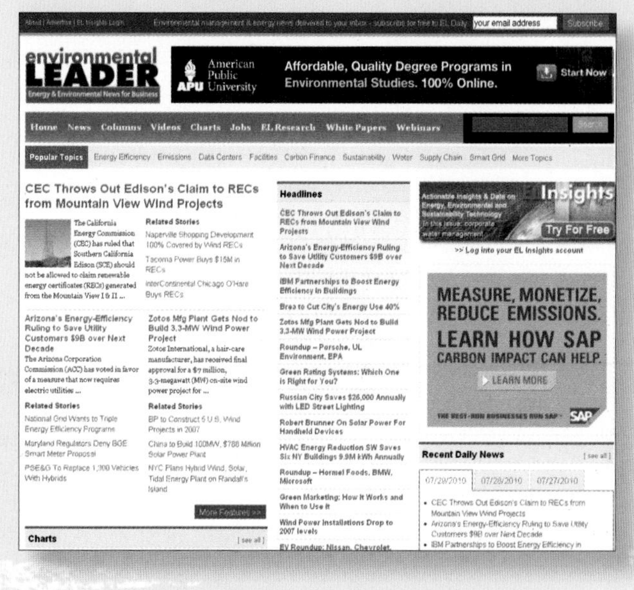

Syndicates

A **syndicate** is a temporary association of individuals or firms organized to perform a specific task that requires a large amount of capital. The syndicate is formed because no one person or firm is willing to put up the entire amount required for the undertaking. Like a joint venture, a syndicate is dissolved as soon as its purpose has been accomplished.

Syndicates are used most commonly to underwrite large insurance policies, loans, and investments. To share the risk of default, banks have formed syndicates to provide loans to developing countries. Stock brokerage firms usually join together in the same way to market a new issue of stock. For example, three Wall Street firms—Bank of America, JPMorgan Chase & Co., and Goldman Sachs—formed a syndicate to sell shares of stock in Symetra—a Washington-based insurance company. With the help of the syndicate, Symetra was able to raise $365 million in 2010.[13] (An *initial public offering* is the term used to describe the first time a corporation sells stock to the general public.)

joint venture an agreement between two or more groups to form a business entity in order to achieve a specific goal or to operate for a specific period of time

syndicate a temporary association of individuals or firms organized to perform a specific task that requires a large amount of capital

Corporate Growth

8

Explain how growth from within and growth through mergers can enable a business to expand.

Growth seems to be a basic characteristic of business. One reason for seeking growth has to do with profit: A larger firm generally has greater sales revenue and thus greater profit. Another reason is that in a growing economy, a business that does not grow is actually shrinking relative to the economy. A third reason is that business growth is a means by which some executives boost their power, prestige, and reputation.

Growth poses new problems and requires additional resources that first must be available and then must be used effectively. The main ingredient in growth is capital—and as we have noted, capital is most readily available to corporations.

A tasty partnership for growth. When Starbucks formed a partnership with All Nippon Airways, passengers were delighted. In this photo, Starbucks Chairperson and CEO Howard Schultz shakes hands with Shinichiro Ito, Chairperson of the Japanese air carrier. This partnership is good for both firms. Simply put: Starbucks sells more product and obtains more brand recognition; All Nippon Airways adds another perk to enhance the customer's travel experience.

Growth from Within

Most corporations grow by expanding their present operations. Some introduce and sell new but related products. Others expand the sale of present products to new geographic markets or to new groups of consumers in geographic markets already served. Although Walmart was started by Sam Walton in 1962 with one discount store, today Walmart has over 8,400 stores in the United States and 14 other countries and has long-range plans for expanding into additional international markets.[14]

Growth from within, especially when carefully planned and controlled, can have relatively little adverse effect on a firm. For the most part, the firm continues to do what it has been doing, but on a larger scale. For instance, Larry Ellison, co-founder and CEO of Oracle Corporation of Redwood Shores, California, built the firm's annual revenues up from a mere $282 million in 1988 to approximately $23 billion today.[15] Much of this growth has taken place over the last ten years as Oracle capitalized on its global leadership in information management software.

Growth Through Mergers and Acquisitions

Another way a firm can grow is by purchasing another company. The purchase of one corporation by another is called a **merger**. An *acquisition* is essentially the same thing as a merger, but the term usually is used in reference to a large corporation's purchases of other corporations. Although most mergers and acquisitions are friendly, hostile takeovers also occur. A **hostile takeover** is a situation in which the management and board of directors of a firm targeted for acquisition disapprove of the merger.

When a merger or acquisition becomes hostile, a corporate raider—another company or a wealthy investor—may make a tender offer or start a proxy fight to gain control of the target company. A **tender offer** is an offer to purchase the stock of a firm targeted for acquisition at a price just high enough to tempt stockholders to sell their shares. Corporate raiders also may initiate a proxy fight. A **proxy fight** is a technique used to gather enough stockholder votes to control a targeted company.

If the corporate raider is successful and takes over the targeted company, existing management usually is replaced. Faced with this probability, existing management may take specific actions, sometimes referred to as "poison pills," "shark repellents," or "porcupine provisions," to maintain control of the firm and avoid the hostile takeover. Whether mergers are friendly or hostile, they are generally classified as *horizontal, vertical,* or *conglomerate* (see Figure 4.5).

merger the purchase of one corporation by another

hostile takeover a situation in which the management and board of directors of a firm targeted for acquisition disapprove of the merger

tender offer an offer to purchase the stock of a firm targeted for acquisition at a price just high enough to tempt stockholders to sell their shares

proxy fight a technique used to gather enough stockholder votes to control a targeted company

Horizontal Mergers A *horizontal merger* is a merger between firms that make and sell similar products or services in similar markets. The merger between Merck and Schering-Plough is an example of a horizontal merger because both firms are in the pharmaceutical industry. This type of merger tends to reduce the number of firms in an industry—and thus may reduce competition. Most horizontal mergers are reviewed carefully by federal agencies before they are approved in order to protect competition in the marketplace.

Vertical Mergers A *vertical merger* is a merger between firms that operate at different but related levels in the production and marketing of a product. Generally, one

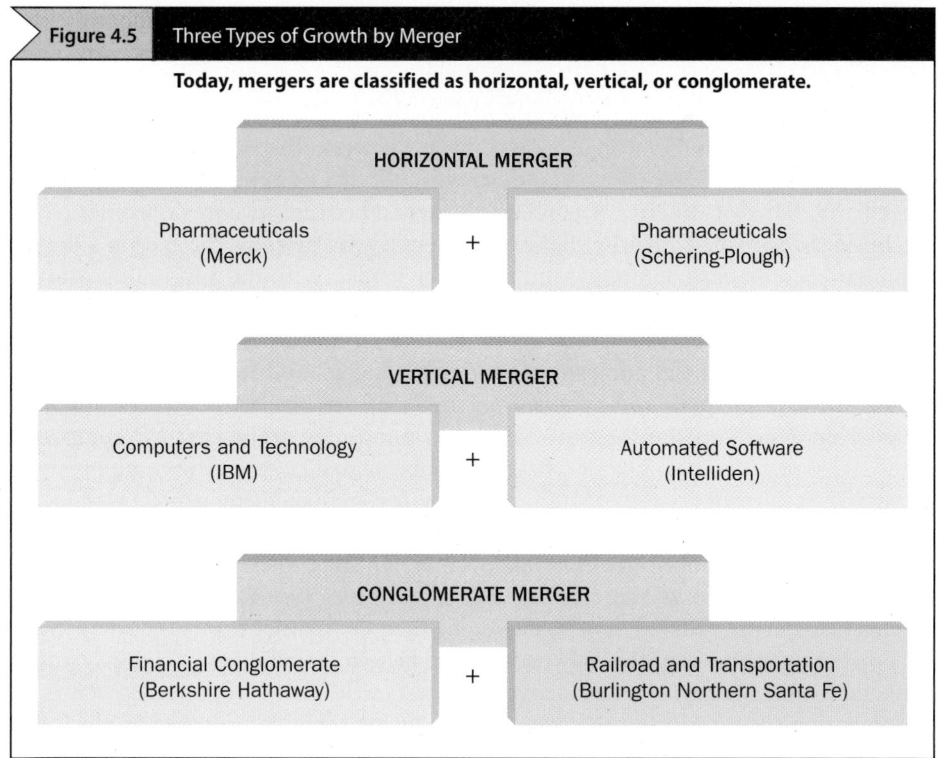

Figure 4.5 Three Types of Growth by Merger

of the merging firms is either a supplier or a customer of the other. A vertical merger occurred when IBM acquired Intelliden. At the time of the 2010 merger, Intelliden, a privately held company based in Menlo Park, California, was a leading provider of intelligent network automation software that enables organizations to manage their computer systems and network services. By acquiring Intelliden's automation software technology, IBM will be able to help clients improve network service availability and reduce errors and downtime for its customers. Rather than develop its own automated software, IBM simply purchased the Intelliden company.[16]

Conglomerate Mergers A *conglomerate merger* takes place between firms in completely different industries. One of the largest conglomerate mergers in recent history occurred when Berkshire Hathaway acquired Burlington Northern Santa Fe Railway. While both companies were recognized as successful companies that have a history of increasing sales revenues and profits, they operate in different industries. The Berkshire Hathaway–Burlington Northern Santa Fe merger was friendly because it was beneficial for both firms.

Merger and Acquisition Trends During an Economic Crisis

While there have always been mergers and acquisitions, the recent economic crisis has changed the dynamics of how and why firms merge. Recently, mergers and acquisitions have been fueled by the desire of financially secure firms to take over firms in financial trouble. For a firm experiencing financial difficulties, a merger or acquisition is often a better option than bankruptcy. During the recent economic crisis, this trend was especially evident in the financial services and banking industry. For example, Wachovia was purchased by Wells Fargo in order to avoid a Wachovia bank failure or a government takeover of Wachovia's assets and loan portfolio. In other cases, the FDIC and the Comptroller of the Currency seized bank assets and sold them to the highest bidder. Bank seizure by the federal government is important because it provides a way for the government to step in and protect depositors from a bank failure.

In other situations, a financially secure firm will purchase a company experiencing financial problems because it is a good investment. Consider why Bank of America acquired Merrill Lynch. Merrill Lynch's survival as a viable company was threatened because of mounting dollar losses from mortgage defaults the firm experienced during the economic crisis. In just one week, the value of Merrill's stock shares dropped over 35 percent. And there was talk of a possible bankruptcy. On the other hand, Bank of America was relatively strong because its core consumer banking business remained healthy. Bank of America was already the nation's largest retail bank, credit card company, and mortgage lender. With the $50 billion acquisition of Merrill Lynch, it also became the nation's largest retail brokerage firm—a goal Bank of America had been trying to achieve on its own for years.[17]

Economists, financial analysts, corporate managers, and stockholders still hotly debate whether mergers and acquisitions are good for the economy—or for individual companies—in the long run. Takeover advocates argue that for companies that have been taken over, the purchasers have been able to make the company more profitable and productive by installing a new top-management team, by reducing expenses, and by forcing the company to concentrate on one main business.

Takeover opponents argue that takeovers do nothing to enhance corporate profitability or productivity. These critics argue that threats of takeovers have forced managers to devote valuable time to defending their companies from takeover. Finally, the opposition argues that the only people who benefit from takeovers are investment bankers, brokerage firms, and takeover "artists," who receive financial rewards by manipulating corporations rather than by producing tangible products or services.

Most experts now predict that mergers and acquisitions after the economic crisis will be the result of cash-rich companies looking to acquire businesses that will enhance their position in the marketplace. Analysts also anticipate more mergers that involve companies or investors from other countries. Regardless of the companies involved or where the companies are from, future mergers and acquisitions will be driven by solid business logic and the desire to compete in the international marketplace.

Whether they are sole proprietorships, partnerships, corporations, or some other form of business ownership, most U.S. businesses are small. In the next chapter, we focus on these small businesses. We examine, among other things, the meaning of the word *small* as it applies to business and the place of small business in the American economy.

return to inside business

MINT.COM

Aaron Patzer didn't set out to become a multimillionaire when he founded Mint.com. He was filling a need by offering a quick and easy way for consumers to manage their money. When Intuit made an acquisition offer, Patzer deliberated for months and finally agreed to sell. Intuit paid $170 million for Mint.com and, as part of the deal, invited Patzer to head its personal finance division, including the Quicken software and Web site. All of Mint.com's employees were offered jobs with Intuit, and all accepted.

Backed by Intuit's strength and resources, Patzer is currently applying his entrepreneurial skills to the challenge of growing his division. What does it feel like to be a senior executive in a major corporation rather than the founder of a start-up corporation? "I now have one boss as opposed to the five bosses I had on the board of directors before, and all the investors," he says.

Questions

1. Is Intuit's acquisition of Mint.com a horizontal, vertical, or conglomerate merger? How do you know?
2. What does Aaron Patzer mean when he says that at Intuit he has one boss, whereas at Mint .com, his bosses were the board of directors and all the investors?

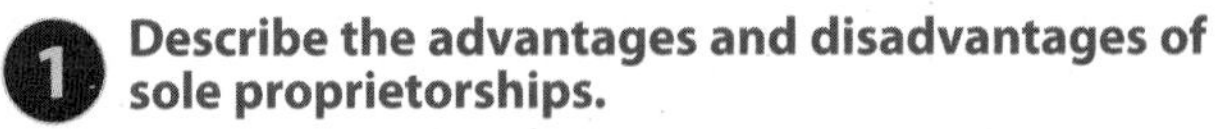

Summary

CHAPTER REVIEW

1 Describe the advantages and disadvantages of sole proprietorships.

In a sole proprietorship, all business profits become the property of the owner, but the owner is also personally responsible for all business debts. A successful sole proprietorship can be a great source of pride for the owner. When comparing different types of business ownership, the sole proprietorship is the simplest form of business to enter, control, and leave. It also pays no special taxes. Perhaps for these reasons, 71 percent of all American business firms are sole proprietorships. Sole proprietorships nevertheless have disadvantages, such as unlimited liability and limits on one person's ability to borrow or to be an expert in all fields. As a result, this form of ownership accounts for only 4 percent of total revenues when compared with partnerships and corporations.

2 Explain the different types of partners and the importance of partnership agreements.

Like sole proprietors, general partners are responsible for running the business and for all business debts. Limited partners receive a share of the profit in return for investing in the business. However, they are not responsible for business debts beyond the amount they have invested. It is also possible to form a master limited partnership (MLP) and sell units of ownership to raise capital. Regardless of the type of partnership, it is always a good idea to have a written agreement (or articles of partnership) setting forth the terms of a partnership.

3 Describe the advantages and disadvantages of partnerships.

Although partnership eliminates some of the disadvantages of sole proprietorship, it is the least popular of the major forms of business ownership. The major advantages of a partnership include ease of start-up, availability of capital and credit, personal interest, combined skills and knowledge, retention of profits, and possible tax advantages. The effects of management disagreements are one of the major disadvantages of a partnership. Other disadvantages include unlimited liability (in a general partnership), lack of continuity, and frozen investment. By forming a limited partnership, the disadvantage of unlimited liability may be eliminated for the limited partner(s). This same disadvantage may be eliminated for partners that form a limited-liability partnership (LLP). Of course, special requirements must be met if partners form either the limited partnership or the limited-liability partnership.

4 Summarize how a corporation is formed.

A corporation is an artificial person created by law, with most of the legal rights of a real person, including the right to start and operate a business, to own property, to borrow money, to be sued or sue, and to enter into contracts. With the corporate form of ownership, stock can be sold to individuals to raise capital. The people who own a corporation's stock—and thus own part of the corporation—are called stockholders. Generally, corporations are classified as closed corporations (few stockholders) or open corporations (many stockholders).

The process of forming a corporation is called incorporation. Most experts believe that the services of a lawyer are necessary when making decisions about where to incorporate and about obtaining a corporate charter, issuing stock, holding an organizational meeting, and all other legal details involved in incorporation. In theory, stockholders are able to control the activities of the corporation because they elect the board of directors who appoint the corporate officers.

5 Describe the advantages and disadvantages of a corporation.

Perhaps the major advantage of the corporate form is limited liability—stockholders are not liable for the corporation's debts beyond the amount they paid for its stock. Other important advantages include ease of raising capital, ease of transfer of ownership, perpetual life, and specialized management. A major disadvantage of a large corporation is double taxation: All profits are taxed once as corporate income and again as personal income because stockholders must pay a personal income tax on the profits they receive as dividends. Other disadvantages include difficulty and expense of formation, government regulation, conflict within the corporation, and lack of secrecy.

6 Examine special types of corporations, including S-corporations, limited-liability companies, and not-for-profit corporations.

S-corporations are corporations that are taxed as though they were partnerships but that enjoy the benefit of limited liability. To qualify as an S-corporation, a number of criteria must be met. A limited-liability company (LLC) is a form of business ownership that provides limited liability and has fewer restrictions. LLCs with at least two members are taxed like a partnership and thus avoid the double taxation imposed on most corporations. LLCs with just one member are taxed like a sole proprietorship. When compared with a regular corporation or an S-corporation, an LLC is more flexible. Not-for-profit corporations are formed to provide social services and to improve communities and change lives rather than to earn profits.

7 Discuss the purpose of a cooperative, joint venture, and syndicate.

Three additional forms of business ownership—the cooperative, joint venture, and syndicate—are used by their owners to meet special needs. A cooperative is an association of individuals or firms whose purpose is to perform some business function for its members. A joint venture is formed when two or more groups form a business entity in order to achieve a specific goal or to operate for a specific period of time. Once the goal is reached, the period of time elapses, or the project is completed, the joint venture is dissolved. A syndicate is a temporary association of individuals or firms organized to perform a specific task that requires large amounts of capital. Like a joint venture, a syndicate is dissolved as soon as its purpose has been accomplished.

Explain how growth from within and growth through mergers can enable a business to expand.

A corporation may grow by expanding its present operations or through a merger or an acquisition. Although most mergers are friendly, hostile takeovers also occur. A hostile takeover is a situation in which the management and board of directors of a firm targeted for acquisition disapprove of the merger. Mergers generally are classified as horizontal, vertical, or conglomerate.

During the recent economic crisis, mergers and acquisitions have been fueled by the desire of financially secure firms to take over firms in financial trouble. For a firm experiencing financial trouble, a merger or acquisition is often a better option than bankruptcy. In other situations, a financially secure firm will purchase a company experiencing financial problems because it is a good investment.

While economists, financial analysts, corporate managers, and stockholders debate the merits of mergers, some trends should be noted. First, experts predict that future mergers will be the result of cash-rich companies looking to acquire businesses that will enhance their position in the marketplace. Second, more mergers are likely to involve foreign companies or investors. Third, mergers will be driven by business logic and the desire to compete in the international marketplace.

Key Terms

You should now be able to define and give an example relevant to each of the following terms:

sole proprietorship (108)
unlimited liability (110)
partnership (111)
general partner (112)
limited partner (112)
master limited partnership (MLP) (112)
corporation (116)
stock (116)
stockholder (116)
closed corporation (117)
open corporation (117)
domestic corporation (118)
foreign corporation (118)
alien corporation (118)
common stock (118)
preferred stock (118)
dividend (118)
proxy (118)
board of directors (119)
corporate officers (119)
limited liability (120)
S-corporation (122)
limited-liability company (LLC) (122)
not-for-profit corporation (123)
cooperative (124)
joint venture (125)
syndicate (125)
merger (126)
hostile takeover (126)
tender offer (126)
proxy fight (126)

Review Questions

1. What is a sole proprietorship? What are the major advantages and disadvantages of this form of business ownership?
2. How does a partnership differ from a sole proprietorship? Which disadvantages of sole proprietorship does the partnership tend to eliminate or reduce?
3. What is the difference between a general partner and a limited partner?
4. What issues should be included in a partnership agreement? Why?
5. Explain the difference between
   a. an open corporation and a closed corporation.
   b. a domestic corporation, a foreign corporation, and an alien corporation.
6. Outline the incorporation process, and describe the basic corporate structure.
7. What rights do stockholders have?
8. What are the primary duties of a corporation's board of directors? How are directors selected?
9. What are the major advantages and disadvantages associated with the corporate form of business ownership?
10. How do an S-corporation and a limited-liability company differ?
11. Explain the difference between a regular corporation and a not-for-profit corporation.
12. Why are cooperatives formed? Explain how they operate.
13. In what ways are joint ventures and syndicates alike? In what ways do they differ?
14. What is a hostile takeover? How is it related to a tender offer and a proxy fight?
15. Describe the three types of mergers.

Discussion Questions

1. If you were to start a business, which ownership form would you choose? What factors might affect your choice?
2. Why might an investor choose to become a partner in a limited-liability partnership (LLP) business instead of purchasing the stock of an open corporation?
3. Discuss the following statement: "Corporations are not really run by their owners."
4. What kinds of services do not-for-profit corporations provide? Would a career in a not-for-profit corporation appeal to you?
5. Is growth a good thing for all firms? How does management know when a firm is ready to grow?

Video Case 4.1

Annie's Homegrown: A Corporation with Entrepreneurial Spirit

When Annie Withey's first husband suggested she create a snack food to go into the resalable bag he'd invented, the 21-year-old newlywed developed an all-natural, cheddar cheese-flavored popcorn. The bag never made it to market, but Annie's popcorn, called Smartfood, became one of the fastest-selling snack foods in U.S. history. In fact, in 1989 PepsiCo Inc's Frito-Lay division bought the brand for about $15 million.

Annie, an organic farmer and mother of two children, cashed out stock worth $1 million and created the all-natural white-cheddar macaroni and cheese product she had been thinking about for some time. She and her husband initially marketed it by knocking on supermarket doors and canvassing ski lodges, outdoor folk concerts, store parking lots, and wherever people gathered. Thus Annie's Homegrown, a pioneering entrepreneurial company in the natural and organic food industry, was born.

This venture was also a success for Annie, and even though her firm has gone on to become part of a larger conglomerate, Annie remains the entrepreneurial heart of the brand. "I learned a lot and took a lot with me," says Annie of her early experience running the operation. Now she delegates day-to-day management, as well as public appearances, to others, and concentrates on what she does best—creating new recipes and providing inspiration to her co-workers. Being a public figure? "That's just not me," she says. "I'm not very good at making presentations and selling," she feels.

Annie's Homegrown offers 80 natural and organic pasta and canned products, as well as snack crackers and a microwaveable version of its now-famous macaroni and cheese, designed for college dorm room convenience. Its products are found in Costco and Target, as well as in 18,000 grocery and 6,000 natural food stores nationwide. Yet Annie's still has only about 3 percent of the macaroni and cheese market compared with the leader, Kraft, which has 80 percent.

"We could never compete directly," says CEO John Foraker. "We appeal to a consumer who is less price conscious and willing to pay more to feel good about what they eat." Because Annie's mac and cheese also costs 30 percent more than Kraft's, the company's marketing focuses on product attributes. The nation's leading brand of organic and natural pasta meals and snacks, Annie's Homegrown represents what *Customer Relationship Magazine* calls "an unmistakable shift toward organic products, green marketing, and sustainability efforts." Annie's story, well known to many of the company's customers, also helps build loyalty to the company's brands.

But for Annie Withey, becoming successful meant taking some risks. Annie had to personally guarantee all loans to her company early on. "Your entire career and reputation are on the line," says company president Paul Nardone. But Annie has always trusted her instincts, and events have usually proven her right. She is "our moral compass," says Nardone, and a continuing inspiration. By 1998 a capital infusion from two small food companies, Consorzio and Fantastic Foods, was helping fuel growth, but choosing the right investment company would become critical to the company's long-term expansion goals.

CEO Foraker says Solera Capital LLC, a $250 million private-equity firm run by women, was looking to enter the fast-growing organic food market and took a majority stake in the company with an initial $20 million investment in 2002. "It's a perfect fit," says Molly Ashby, Solera's chief executive officer. It's a great brand, very authentic, with tremendous crossover into both mainstream and natural markets. The remaining interest in the company is held by Withey, current management, and a small group of founding investors. Solera recently bought Consorzio and Fantastic Foods and combined them with Annie's Homegrown to form Homegrown Naturals Inc., based in Napa, California.

As founder, Annie Withey has assumed the role of "inspirational president." She still writes the text on every product box, and Bernie the Bunny, inspired by her brother's illustration, still appears on every package. As she continues to fill the role of creative leader of the company she started, Annie has been described as its "quality gatekeeper" and a humble person whose creative instincts are "right on." When customers write or e-mail to suggest new products, each idea is still considered, and the "real" Annie never gets tired of hearing how much people enjoy her products.[18]

Questions

1. What personal traits does Annie Withey exhibit that entrepreneurs need to succeed? How have her personal characteristics helped shape the success of her business?
2. How did the company evolve from a small business into a multimillion dollar leader in the natural organic food industry? What long-term growth strategies is the company pursuing as it moves into the future?
3. Explore Annie's Web site at http://www.annies.com. What unique features did you find? How does this Web site support Annie's mission?

Case 4.2

The Conglomerate Success of Berkshire Hathaway

When Warren Buffett started his first partnership more than 50 years ago, he never dreamed he would wind up putting together a wildly diverse collection of businesses under one corporate umbrella. Originally, Buffett set up a series of partnerships with family and friends to pool cash for buying big blocks of stock in companies he had researched. Not all of Buffett's stock picks paid off, but many were so successful that Buffett quickly earned a worldwide reputation for savvy investing.

Always looking for a good investment, Buffett turned his attention to the prospects of Berkshire Hathaway, a struggling textile manufacturer based in New Bedford, Massachusetts. Seeing value in the company's heritage and its plans for making synthetic fibers, Buffett began buying its stock. Once he controlled the mills, Buffett put one of Berkshire Hathaway's executives in charge. This was Buffett's pattern over and over as he built a conglomerate by adding to his company's portfolio of businesses. He provided the financial backing, but he didn't meddle in the day-to-day management decisions of the corporations he purchased.

Berkshire Hathaway became the corporate vehicle through which Buffett acquired a variety of companies. In the early days, he pursued insurance firms, banks, and publishing companies. He continued buying year after year, adding See's Candies to his conglomerate and, later, GEICO insurance, sticking to his tried-and-true formula of investing in companies with long-term profit potential and strong competitive positions.

Living in Omaha, Buffett couldn't help but notice the success of the Nebraska Furniture Mart, a superstore that annually sold $100 million worth of furniture. The family-owned business was a fierce competitor and a major regional power in furniture retailing. Although Buffett had tried, unsuccessfully, to buy the store, he never gave up. During the 1980s, he again approached the retailer. This time he pointed out all the financial benefits of being part of Berkshire Hathaway and emphasized his hands-off approach to ownership. Berkshire Hathaway won the deal.

Today Berkshire Hathaway has more than six dozen companies in its diverse portfolio. Although it still owns some of the companies it acquired decades ago, the portfolio has changed a bit over the years. GEICO, the third-largest U.S. auto insurance firm, has been a member of the conglomerate since 1996. Berkshire Hathaway also owns the General Re insurance firm. Among the retailing businesses it owns are Jordan Furniture, Star Furniture, Helzberg Diamond Shops, and the Pampered Chef direct-seller of kitchen tools. In addition, it owns the ice-cream franchising company Dairy Queen; Benjamin Moore paint; Johns Manville building products; and Shaw Industries, which makes tufted broadloom carpeting.

Berkshire Hathaway has expanded into transportation, as well. Its NetJets was a pioneer in offering companies and individuals the opportunity to own a fraction of a private jet, so they can enjoy the convenience of flying whenever and wherever they want. In 2009, the conglomerate paid $26 billion for Burlington Northern Santa Fe Corp., a railroad that serves western and southwestern states. This acquisition, labeled "brilliant" by a railway competitor because it was completed just as the industry began to rebound from recession, gave Buffett access to years of details about the size, volume, and destination of train shipments. By analyzing this information, Buffett spotted clues that helped him fine-tune his investments.

The annual meeting held by Berkshire Hathaway is unlike any stockholder gathering on Earth. The more-than-35,000 people in attendance spend hours browsing and buying from exhibits set up by the conglomerate's companies. Stockholders are encouraged to bring the details of their car insurance and let GEICO give them quotes on the spot, including a small ownership discount. Nebraska Furniture Mart promotes a special stockholders' weekend of sales, as do other Berkshire Hathaway-owned retailers in the area. The annual meeting is such a high-profile event that it merits coverage by the *New York Times*, CNBC, and *Fortune* magazine, among many other major media outlets. What will Berkshire Hathaway's next acquisition target be?[19]

Questions

1. Why would Berkshire Hathaway own a number of furniture retailers? Outline the possible advantages and disadvantages.
2. Do you think Berkshire Hathaway should allow stockholders to suggest or vote on potential acquisitions via proxy or at the annual meeting? Why or why not?
3. How much influence are Berkshire Hathaway's stockholders likely to have (or want) over the management of the conglomerate or one of the conglomerate's companies? Explain.

Building Skills for Career Success

❶ JOURNALING FOR SUCCESS

Today, many people work for a sole proprietorship, partnership, or corporation. Still others decide to become entrepreneurs and start their own business.

Assignment

1. Assume that you are now age 25 and have graduated from college. Would you prefer to work in someone else's business or one that you would start? Explain your answer.
2. Assuming that you have decided to start your own small business, what special skills and experience will you need to be successful? (*Note:* You may want to talk with someone who owns a business before answering this question.)
3. Now describe where and how you could obtain the skills and experience you need to be successful.
4. What type of business ownership would you choose for your business?

❷ EXPLORING THE INTERNET

Arguments about mergers and acquisitions often come down to an evaluation of who benefits and by how much. Sometimes the benefits include access to new products, talented management, new customers, or new sources of capital. Often, the debate is complicated by the involvement of firms based in different countries.

The Internet is a fertile environment for information and discussion about mergers. The firms involved will provide their view about who will benefit and why it is either a good thing or not. Journalists will report facts and offer commentary as to how they see the future result of any merger, and of course, chat rooms located on the Web sites of many journals promote discussion about the issues. Visit the text Web site for updates to this exercise.

Assignment

1. Using an Internet search engine such as Google or Yahoo!, locate two or three sites providing information about a recent merger (use a keyword such as *merger* or *acquisition*).
2. After examining these sites and reading journal articles, report information about the merger, such as the dollar value, the reasons behind the merger, and so forth.
3. Based on your assessment of the information you have read, do you think the merger is a good idea or not for the firms involved, the employees, the investors, the industry, and society as a whole? Explain your reasoning.

❸ DEVELOPING CRITICAL-THINKING SKILLS

Suppose that you are a person who has always dreamed of owning a business but never had the money to open one. Since you were old enough to read a recipe, your mother allowed you to help in the kitchen. Most of all, you enjoyed baking and decorating cakes. You liked using your imagination to create cakes for special occasions. By the time you were in high school, you were baking and decorating wedding cakes for a fee. Also assume that after high school you started working full time as an adjuster for an insurance company. Your schedule now allows little time for baking and decorating cakes. Finally, assume that you inherited $250,000 and that changes at your job have created undue stress in your life. What should you do?

Assignment

1. Discuss the following points:
   a. What career options are available to you?
   b. If you decide to open your own business, what form of ownership would be best for your business?
   c. What advantages and disadvantages apply to your preferred form of business ownership?
2. Prepare a two-page report summarizing your findings.

❹ BUILDING TEAM SKILLS

Using the scenario in Exercise 3, suppose that you have decided to quit your job as an insurance adjuster and open a bakery. Your business is now growing, and you have decided to add a full line of catering services. This means more work and responsibility. You will need someone to help you, but you are undecided about what to do. Should you hire an employee or find a partner? If you add a partner, what type of decisions should be made to create a partnership agreement?

Assignment

1. In a group, discuss the following questions:
   a. What are the advantages and disadvantages of adding a partner versus hiring an employee?
   b. Assume that you have decided to form a partnership. What articles should be included in a partnership agreement?
   c. How would you go about finding a partner?
2. Summarize your group's answers to these questions, and present them to your class.
3. As a group, prepare an articles-of-partnership agreement. Be prepared to discuss the pros and cons of your group's agreement with other groups from your class, as well as to examine their agreements.

❺ RESEARCHING DIFFERENT CAREERS

Many people spend their entire lives working in jobs that they do not enjoy. Why is this so? Often, it is because they have taken the first job they were offered without giving it much thought. How can you avoid having this happen to you? First, you should determine your "personal profile" by identifying and analyzing your own strengths, weaknesses, things you enjoy, and things you dislike. Second, you should identify the types of jobs that fit your profile. Third, you should identify and research the companies that offer those jobs.

Assignment

1. Take two sheets of paper and draw a line down the middle of each sheet, forming two columns on each page. Label column 1 "Things I Enjoy or Like to Do," column 2 "Things I Do Not Like Doing," column 3 "My Strengths," and column 4 "My Weaknesses."
2. Record data in each column over a period of at least one week. You may find it helpful to have a relative or friend give you input.
3. Summarize the data, and write a profile of yourself.
4. Take your profile to a career counselor at your college or to the public library and ask for help in identifying jobs that fit your profile. Your college may offer testing to assess your skills and personality. The Internet is another resource.
5. Research the companies that offer the types of jobs that fit your profile.
6. Write a report on your findings.

Small Business, Entrepreneurship, and Franchises

©iStockphoto.com/mangostock

Learning Objectives

What you will be able to do once you complete this chapter:

1. Define what a small business is and recognize the fields in which small businesses are concentrated.
2. Identify the people who start small businesses and the reasons why some succeed and many fail.
3. Assess the contributions of small businesses to our economy.
4. Judge the advantages and disadvantages of operating a small business.
5. Explain how the Small Business Administration helps small businesses.
6. Appraise the concept and types of franchising.
7. Analyze the growth of franchising and franchising's advantages and disadvantages.

FYI

Did You Know?

Today, Five Guys Burgers and Fries has more than 600 franchised restaurants in North America, a number that will double in the near future as franchisees continue to open units.

inside business

Franchising Feeds Growth of Five Guys Burgers and Fries

Five Guys Burgers and Fries has a simple recipe for success in the hotly competitive casual restaurant industry: Serve up popularly priced, generously sized meals in a family-friendly atmosphere. Founders Jerry and Janie Murrell opened their first burger place in 1986 near Arlington, Virginia. Naming the growing chain for their five sons, the husband-and-wife team eventually opened four more restaurants in Virginia.

The Murrells limited their menu to all-American favorites such as juicy hamburgers with a choice of 15 free toppings, crispy fries, hot dogs, grilled cheese sandwiches, and soft drinks with free refills. They cooked every order individually and used only fresh, high-quality ingredients for the best flavor. For example, they refused to use frozen meat, cooked their fries in pure peanut oil for extra crunch, and ordered hamburger buns baked to their own specifications. The owners were so focused on flavor that they tested dozens of condiments and brands to find the very tastiest. The combination of quality food and friendly service set the restaurants apart from the many competitors in the burger world.

By 2002, sales were stronger than ever, and the five-restaurant chain had attracted a loyal following of burger lovers from all around the metropolitan DC area. To expand more quickly, Five Guys added franchising to its business menu, charging entrepreneurs a one-time fee and a small percentage of each restaurant's revenue in exchange for the right to use the brand, its menu, and its proven processes and procedures. Within 18 months, Five Guys had 300 franchised restaurants. Today, it has more than 600 franchised restaurants in North America, a number that will double in the near future as franchisees continue to open units.

Because quality and service are so important to the company's success, all Five Guys restaurants receive two visits a week from mystery shoppers who check that their orders are cooked properly and the service is friendly. When a restaurant scores high on these evaluations, each staff member receives a cash bonus. Instead of paying for splashy ad campaigns, Five Guys spends $8 million or more yearly on such employee rewards—an important investment in maintaining the company's image and competitive edge.[1]

Just as Jerry and Janie Murrell's empire grew from one restaurant in Arlington, Virginia, most businesses start small. Unlike Murrell's empire, most small businesses that survive usually stay small. They provide a solid foundation for our economy—as employers, as suppliers and purchasers of goods and services, and as taxpayers.

In this chapter, we do not take small businesses for granted. Instead, we look closely at this important business sector—beginning with a definition of small business, a description of industries that often attract small businesses, and a profile of some of the people who start small businesses. Next, we consider the importance of small businesses in our economy. We also present the advantages and disadvantages of smallness in business. We then describe services provided by the Small Business Administration, a government agency formed to assist owners and managers of small businesses. We conclude the chapter with a discussion of the pros and cons of franchising, an approach to small-business ownership that has become very popular in the last 40 years.

1

Define what a small business is and recognize the fields in which small businesses are concentrated.

Small Business: A Profile

The Small Business Administration (SBA) defines a **small business** as "one which is independently owned and operated for profit and is not dominant in its field." How small must a firm be not to dominate its field? That depends on the particular industry it is in. The SBA has developed the following specific "smallness" guidelines for the various industries, as shown in Table 5.1.[2] The SBA periodically revises and simplifies its small-business size regulations.

Annual sales in millions of dollars may not seem very small. However, for many firms, profit is only a small percentage of total sales. Thus, a firm may earn only $40,000 or $50,000 on yearly sales of $1 million—and that *is* small in comparison with the profits earned by most medium-sized and large firms. Moreover, most small firms have annual sales well below the maximum limits in the SBA guidelines.

The Small-Business Sector

In the United States, it typically takes four days and $210 to establish a business as a legal entity. The steps include registering the name of the business, applying for tax IDs, and setting up unemployment and workers' compensation insurance. In Japan, however, a typical entrepreneur spends more than $3,500 and 31 days to follow 11 different procedures (see Table 5.2).

A surprising number of Americans take advantage of their freedom to start a business. There are, in fact, about 29.6 million businesses in this country. Only just over 17,000 of these employ more than 500 workers—enough to be considered large.

Interest in owning or starting a small business has never been greater than it is today. During the last decade, the number of small businesses in the United States has increased 49 percent. For the last few years, new-business formation in the United States has broken successive records, except during the 2001–2002 and 2008 recessions. Recently, nearly 627,200 new businesses were incorporated. Furthermore, part-time entrepreneurs have increased fivefold in recent years; they now account for one-third of all small businesses.[3]

According to a recent study, 70 percent of new businesses survive at least two years, about 50 percent survive at least five years, and 31 percent survive at least seven years.[4] The primary reason for these failures is mismanagement resulting

Table 5.1 Industry Group-Size Standards

Small-business size standards are usually stated in number of employees or average annual sales. In the United States, 99.7 percent of all businesses are considered small.

Industry Group	Size Standard
Manufacturing, mining industries	500 employees
Wholesale trade	100 employees
Agriculture	$750,000
Retail trade	$7 million
General and heavy construction (except dredging)	$33.5 million
Dredging	$20 million
Special trade contractors	$14 million
Travel agencies	$3.5 million (commissions and other income)
Business and personal services except	$7 million
• Architectural, engineering, surveying, and mapping services	$4.5 million
• Dry cleaning and carpet cleaning services	$4.5 million

Source: http://www.sba.gov/contractingopportunities/officials/size/summaryofssi/index.html (accessed June 13, 2010).

small business one that is independently owned and operated for profit and is not dominant in its field

Table 5.2 Establishing a Business Around the World

The entrepreneurial spirit provides the spark that enriches the U.S. economy. The growth will continue if lawmakers resist the urge to overregulate entrepreneurs and provide policies that foster free enterprise.

	Number of Procedures	Time (days)	Cost (US$)	Minimum Capital (% per capita income)
Australia	2	2	402	0
Belgium	7	56	2,633	75.1
Canada	2	3	127	0
Denmark	4	4	0	52.3
France	10	53	663	32.1
Germany	9	45	1,341	103.8
Greece	16	45	8,115	145.3
Ireland	3	12	2,473	0
Italy	9	23	4,565	49.6
Japan	11	31	3,518	71.3
Netherlands	7	11	3,276	70.7
New Zealand	3	3	28	0
Norway	4	24	1,460	33.1
Portugal	11	95	1,360	43.4
Spain	11	115	2,366	19.6
Sweden	3	16	190	41.4
Switzerland	6	20	3,228	33.8
United Kingdom	6	18	264	0
United States	5	4	210	0

Sources: World Bank (2004); as found in *Inside the Vault*, Federal Reserve Bank of St. Louis, Fall 2004, 1.

from a lack of business know-how. The makeup of the small-business sector thus is constantly changing. Despite the high failure rate, many small businesses succeed modestly. Some, like Apple Computer, Inc., are extremely successful—to the point where they can no longer be considered small. Taken together, small businesses are also responsible for providing a high percentage of the jobs in the United States. According to some estimates, the figure is well over 50 percent.

Industries that Attract Small Businesses

Some industries, such as auto manufacturing, require huge investments in machinery and equipment. Businesses in such industries are big from the day they are started—if an entrepreneur or group of entrepreneurs can gather the capital required to start one.

By contrast, a number of other industries require only a low initial investment and some special skills or knowledge. It is these industries that tend to attract new businesses. Growing industries, such as outpatient-care facilities, are attractive because of their profit potential. However, knowledgeable entrepreneurs choose areas with which they are familiar, and these are most often the more established industries.

Small enterprise spans the gamut from corner newspaper vending to the development of optical fibers. The owners of small businesses sell gasoline, flowers, and coffee to go. They publish magazines, haul freight, teach languages, and program computers. They make wines, movies, and high-fashion clothes. They build new homes and restore old ones. They fix appliances, recycle metals, and sell used cars. They drive cabs and fly planes. They make us well when we are ill, and they sell us the products of corporate giants. In fact, 74 percent of real estate, rental, and leasing industries; 61 percent of the businesses in the leisure and hospitality services; and

86 percent of the construction industries are dominated by small businesses.[5] The various kinds of businesses generally fall into three broad categories of industry: distribution, service, and production.

Distribution Industries This category includes retailing, wholesaling, transportation, and communications—industries concerned with the movement of goods from producers to consumers. Distribution industries account for approximately 33 percent of all small businesses. Of these, almost three-quarters are involved in retailing, that is, the sale of goods directly to consumers. Clothing and jewelry stores, pet shops, bookstores, and grocery stores, for example, are all retailing firms. Slightly less than one-quarter of the small distribution firms are wholesalers. Wholesalers purchase products in quantity from manufacturers and then resell them to retailers.

Service Industries This category accounts for more than 48 percent of all small businesses. Of these, about three-quarters provide such nonfinancial services as medical and dental care; watch, shoe, and TV repairs; haircutting and styling; restaurant meals; and dry cleaning. About 8 percent of the small service firms offer financial services, such as accounting, insurance, real estate, and investment counseling. An increasing number of self-employed Americans are running service businesses from home.

Production Industries This last category includes the construction, mining, and manufacturing industries. Only about 19 percent of all small businesses are in this group, mainly because these industries require relatively large initial investments. Small firms that do venture into production generally make parts and subassemblies for larger manufacturing firms or supply special skills to larger construction firms.

2

Identify the people who start small businesses and the reasons why some succeed and many fail.

The People in Small Businesses: the Entrepreneurs

The entrepreneurial spirit is alive and well in the United States. A recent study revealed that the U.S. population is quite entrepreneurial when compared with those of other countries. More than 70 percent of Americans would prefer being an entrepreneur to working for someone else. This compares with 46 percent of adults in Western Europe and 58 percent of adults in Canada. Another study on entrepreneurial activity for 2002 found that of 36 countries studied, the United States was in the top third in entrepreneurial activity and was the leader when compared with Japan, Canada, and Western Europe.[6]

Small businesses typically are managed by the people who started and own them. Most of these people have held jobs with other firms and still could be so employed if they wanted. Yet owners of small businesses would rather take the risk of starting and operating their own firms, even if the money they make is less than the salaries they otherwise might earn.

Researchers have suggested a variety of personal factors as reasons why people go into business for themselves. These are discussed below.

Meet Sir Richard Branson, founder and chairperson of the Virgin Group. Born in 1950, Richard set up *Student* magazine at age 16. Then, at age 20, he founded Virgin as a small mail-order record retailer. Today, Virgin is a leading venture capital organization and is one of the world's most recognized and respected brands. Sir Branson established Branson School of Entrepreneurship to identify and support the most promising young entrepreneurs to launch successful businesses of their own.

Characteristics of Entrepreneurs

Entrepreneurial spirit is the desire to create a new business. For example, Nikki Olyai always knew that she wanted to create and develop her own business. Her father, a successful businessman in Iran, was her role model. She came to the United States at the age of 17 and lived with a host family in Salem, Oregon, attending high school there. Undergraduate and graduate degrees in computer science led her to start Innovision Technologies while she held two other jobs to keep the business going and took care of her four-year-old son. Recently, Nikki Olyai's business was honored by the Women's Business Enterprise National Council's "Salute to Women's Business Enterprises" as one of 11 top successful firms. For three consecutive years, her firm was selected as a "Future 50 of Greater Detroit Company."

Other Personal Factors

Other personal factors in small-business success include

- Independence
- A desire to determine one's own destiny
- A willingness to find and accept a challenge
- Family background (In particular, researchers think that people whose families have been in business, successfully or not, are most apt to start and run their own businesses.)
- Age (Those who start their own businesses also tend to cluster around certain ages—more than 70 percent are between 24 and 44 years of age; see Figure 5.1.)

Motivation

There must be some motivation to start a business. A person may decide that he or she simply has "had enough" of working and earning a profit for someone else. Another may lose his or her job for some reason and decide to start the business he or she has always wanted rather than to seek another job. Still another person may have an idea for a new product or a new way to sell an existing product. Or the opportunity to go into business may arise suddenly, perhaps as a result of a hobby. For example, Cheryl Strand started baking and decorating cakes from her home while working full time as a word processor at Clemson University. Her cakes became so popular that she soon found herself working through her lunch breaks and late into the night to meet customer demand.

Women as Small-Business Owners

- Women are 51 percent of the U.S. population, and according to the SBA, they owned at least 50 percent of all small businesses in 2008.
- Women already own 66 percent of the home-based businesses in this country, and the number of men in home-based businesses is growing rapidly.

Figure 5.1 How Old Is the Average Entrepreneur?

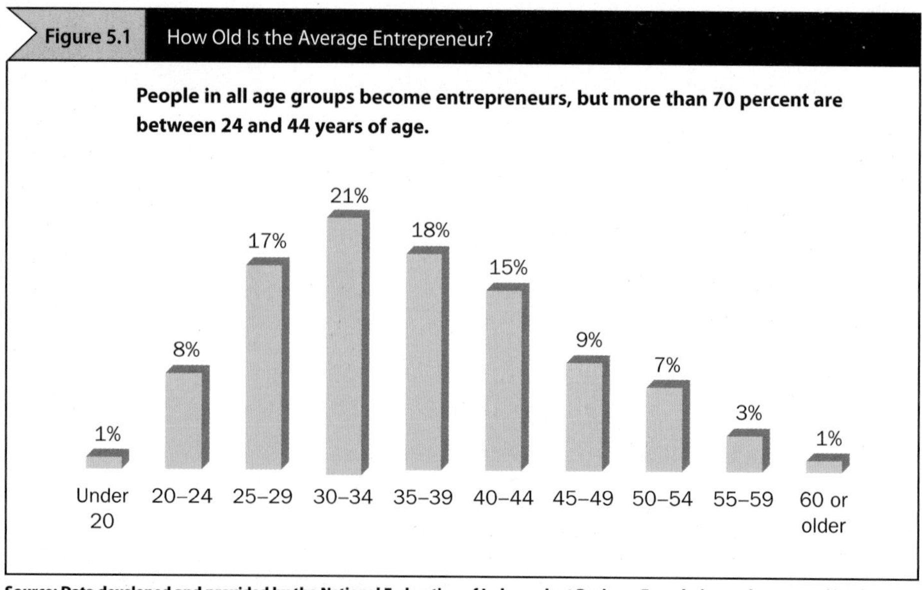

Source: Data developed and provided by the National Federation of Independent Business Foundation and sponsored by the American Express Travel Related Services Company, Inc.

- According to the SBA, 9.1 million women-owned businesses in the United States provide almost 27.5 million jobs and generate $3.6 trillion in sales.
- Women-owned businesses in the United States have proven that they are more successful; more than 40 percent have been in business for 12 years or more.
- According to Dun and Bradstreet, women-owned businesses are financially sound and credit-worthy, and their risk of failure is lower than average.
- Compared to other working women, self-employed women are older, better educated, and have more managerial experience.
- Just over one-half of small businesses are home based, and 91 percent have no employees. About 60 percent of home-based businesses are in service industries, 16 percent in construction, 14 percent in retail trade, and the rest in manufacturing, finance, transportation, communications, wholesaling, and other industries.[7]

Leanna Archer—A child entrepreneur. Thirteen-year-old Leanna Archer, child entrepreneur, owner, and CEO of Leanna's Hair Inc., developed and runs her own natural hair care products company, which she founded at age nine in New York. She invented a line of five green hair care products whose profits she plans to use for tuition at Harvard University.

Teenagers as Small-Business Owners

High-tech teen entrepreneurship is definitely exploding. "There's not a period in history where we've seen such a plethora of young entrepreneurs," comments Nancy F. Koehn, associate professor of business administration at Harvard Business School. Still, teen entrepreneurs face unique pressures in juggling their schoolwork, their social life, and their high-tech workload. Some ultimately quit school, whereas others quit or cut back on their business activities. Consider Brian Hendricks at Winston Churchill High School in Potomac, Maryland. He is the founder of StartUpPc and VB Solutions, Inc. StartUpPc, founded in 2001, sells custom-built computers and computer services for home users, home offices, small businesses, and students. Brian's services include design, installation of systems, training, networking, and on-site technical support. In October 2002, Brian founded VB Solutions, Inc., which develops and customizes Web sites and message boards. The firm sets up advertising contracts and counsels Web site owners on site improvements. The company has designed corporate ID kits, logos, and Web sites for clients from all over the world. Brian learned at a very young age that working for yourself is one of the best jobs available. According to Brian, a young entrepreneur must possess "the five P's of entrepreneurship"—planning, persistence, patience, people, and profit. Brian knows what it takes to be a successful entrepreneur. His accolades include Junior Achievement's "National Youth Entrepreneur of the Year" and SBA's 2005 "Young Entrepreneur of the Year" awards.[8]

In some people, the motivation to start a business develops slowly as they gain the knowledge and ability required for success as a business owner. Knowledge and ability—especially, management ability—are probably the most important factors involved. A new firm is very much built around the entrepreneur. The owner must be able to manage the firm's finances, its personnel (if there are any employees), and its day-to-day operations. He or she must handle sales, advertising, purchasing, pricing, and a variety of other business functions. The knowledge and ability to do so are acquired most often through experience working for other firms in the same area of business.

Why Some Entrepreneurs and Small Businesses Fail

Small businesses are prone to failure. Capital, management, and planning are the key ingredients in the survival of a small business, as well as the most common reasons for failure. Businesses can experience a number of money-related problems.

Table 5.3 U.S. Business Start-ups, Closures, and Bankruptcies

	New	Closures	Bankruptcies
2009	NA	NA	60,840
2008	627,200[e]	595,600[e]	43,546
2007	663,100[e]	571,300[e]	28,322
2006	670,058	599,333	19,695
2005	644,122	565,745	39,201

e = Advocacy estimate. For a discussion of methodology, see Brian Headd, 2005 (http://www.sba.gov/advo/research/rs258tot.pdf).
NA = Not available.

Source: Small Business Administration, Office of Advocacy, *Frequently Asked Questions*, July 2009, http://www.sba.gov/advo (accessed June 13, 2010).

It may take several years before a business begins to show a profit. Entrepreneurs need to have not only the capital to open a business but also the money to operate it in its possibly lengthy start-up phase. One cash flow obstacle often leads to others. Moreover, a series of cash flow predicaments usually ends in a business failure. This scenario is played out all too often by small and not-so-small start-up Internet firms that fail to meet their financial backers' expectations and so are denied a second wave of investment dollars to continue their drive to establish a profitable online firm. According to Maureen Borzacchiello, co-owner of Creative Display Solutions, a trade show products company, "Big businesses such as Bear Stearns, Fannie Mae and Freddie Mac, and AIG can get bailouts, but small-business owners are on their own when times are tough and credit is tight."

Many entrepreneurs lack the management skills required to run a business. Money, time, personnel, and inventory all need to be managed effectively if a small business is to succeed. Starting a small business requires much more than optimism and a good idea.

Success and expansion sometimes lead to problems. Frequently, entrepreneurs with successful small businesses make the mistake of overexpansion. Fast growth often results in dramatic changes in a business. Thus, the entrepreneur must plan carefully and adjust competently to new and potentially disruptive situations.

Every day, and in every part of the country, people open new businesses. For example, 627,200 new businesses recently opened their doors. At the same time, however, 595,600 businesses closed their business and 60,840 businesses (in 2009) declared bankruptcy (see Table 5.3).[9] Although many fail, others represent well-conceived ideas developed by entrepreneurs who have the expertise, resources, and determination to make their businesses succeed. As these well-prepared entrepreneurs pursue their individual goals, our society benefits in many ways from their work and creativity. Billion-dollar companies such as Apple Computer, McDonald's Corporation, and Procter & Gamble are all examples of small businesses that expanded into industry giants.

3

Assess the contributions of small businesses to our economy.

The Importance of Small Businesses in Our Economy

This country's economic history abounds with stories of ambitious men and women who turned their ideas into business dynasties. The Ford Motor Company started as a one-man operation with an innovative method for industrial production. L.L. Bean, Inc., can trace its beginnings to a basement shop in Freeport, Maine. Both Xerox and Polaroid began as small firms with a better way to do a job. Indeed, every year since 1963, the President of the United States has proclaimed National Small Business Week to recognize the contributions of small businesses to the economic well-being of America.

Providing Technical Innovation

Invention and innovation are part of the foundations of our economy. The increases in productivity that have characterized the past 200 years of our history are all rooted in one principal source: new ways to do a job with less effort for less money. Studies show that the incidence of innovation among small-business workers is significantly higher than among workers in large businesses. Small firms produce two-and-a-half times as many innovations as large firms relative to the number of persons employed. In fact, small firms employ 40 percent of all high-tech workers such as scientists, engineers, and computer specialists. No wonder small firms produce 13 to 14 times more patents per employee than large patenting firms.

Consider Waymon Armstrong, the owner of a small business that uses computer simulations to help government and other clients prepare for and respond to natural disasters, medical emergencies, and combat. In presenting the 2010 National Small Business Person of the Year award, Karen Mills, Administrator of the U.S. Small Business Administration, said, "Waymon Armstrong is a perfect example of the innovation, inspiration, and determination that exemplify America's most successful entrepreneurs. He believed in his brainchild to the point where he deferred his own salary for three years to keep it afloat. When layoffs loomed for his staff after 9/11, their loyalty and belief in the company was so great that they were willing to work without pay for four months."

"Waymon's commitment to his employees and to his business—Engineering & Computer Simulations, Inc.—demonstrates the qualities that make small businesses such a powerful force for job creation in the American economy and in their local communities," said Mills. "It's the same qualities that will lead us to economic recovery. We are especially proud that his company benefited from two grants under SBA's Small Business Innovation and Research Program."[10]

According to the U.S. Office of Management and Budget, more than half the major technological advances of the 20th century originated with individual inventors and small companies. Even just a sampling of those innovations is remarkable:

- Air conditioning
- Airplane
- Automatic transmission
- FM radio
- Heart valve
- Helicopter
- Instant camera
- Insulin
- Jet engine
- Penicillin
- Personal computer
- Power steering

Perhaps even more remarkable—and important—is that many of these inventions sparked major new U.S. industries or contributed to an established industry by adding some valuable service.

Innovate or die contest. Aquaduct is the brainchild of five California-based design students who want to provide clean water to 1.1 billion people in the world who don't have access to clean drinking water. This pedal-powered bike transports and filters water without burning fossil fuels or wood, thus reducing CO_2 emissions.

Providing Employment

Small firms traditionally have added more than their proportional share of new jobs to the economy. Seven out of the ten industries that added the most new jobs were small-business-dominated industries. Small businesses creating the most new jobs recently included business services, leisure and hospitality services, and special trade contractors. Small firms hire a larger proportion of employees who are younger workers, older workers, women, or workers who

Getting personal. For those who like dealing with people, small business is the place to be. Here, a business-owner-manager provides personal service to a happy customer.

prefer to work part time. Furthermore, small businesses provide 67 percent of workers with their first jobs and initial on-the-job training in basic skills. According to the SBA, small businesses represent 99.7 percent of all employers, employ more than 50 percent of the private workforce, and provide about two-thirds of the net new jobs added to our economy.[11] Small businesses thus contribute significantly to solving unemployment problems.

The business cycle, as discussed in Chapter 1, is an important factor in the net creation or loss of jobs. During the 2008–2009 recession, businesses with fewer than 20 employees began losing jobs as early as mid-2007. From 2008 to mid-2009, these smallest businesses accounted for 24 percent of the net job losses, while those with 20–499 employees accounted for 36 percent; the remaining 40 percent of job losses were in larger firms with more than 500 employees.[12]

Providing Competition

Small businesses challenge larger, established firms in many ways, causing them to become more efficient and more responsive to consumer needs. A small business cannot, of course, compete with a large firm in all respects. However, a number of small firms, each competing in its own particular area and its own particular way, together have the desired competitive effect. Thus, several small janitorial companies together add up to reasonable competition for the no-longer-small ServiceMaster.

Filling Needs of Society and Other Businesses

Small firms also provide a variety of goods and services to each other and to much larger firms. Sears, Roebuck & Co. purchases merchandise from approximately 12,000 suppliers—and most of them are small businesses. General Motors relies on more than 32,000 companies for parts and supplies and depends on more than 11,000 independent dealers to sell its automobiles and trucks. Large firms generally buy parts and assemblies from smaller firms for one very good reason: It is less expensive than manufacturing the parts in their own factories. This lower cost eventually is reflected in the price that consumers pay for their products.

It is clear that small businesses are a vital part of our economy and that, as consumers and as members of the labor force, we all benefit enormously from their existence. Now let us look at the situation from the viewpoint of the owners of small businesses.

4

Judge the advantages and disadvantages of operating a small business.

The Pros and Cons of Smallness

Do most owners of small businesses dream that their firms will grow into giant corporations—managed by professionals—while they serve only on the board of directors? Or would they rather stay small, in a firm where they have the opportunity (and the responsibility) to do everything that needs to be done? The answers depend on the personal characteristics and motivations of the individual owners. For many, the advantages of remaining small far outweigh the disadvantages.

Advantages of Small Business

Small-business owners with limited resources often must struggle to enter competitive new markets. They also have to deal with increasing international competition. However, they enjoy several unique advantages.

Personal Relationships with Customers and Employees For those who like dealing with people, small business is the place to be. The owners of retail shops get to know many of their customers by name and deal with them on a personal basis. Through such relationships, small-business owners often become involved in the social, cultural, and political life of the community.

Relationships between owner-managers and employees also tend to be closer in smaller businesses. In many cases, the owner is a friend and counselor as well as the boss.

These personal relationships provide an important business advantage. The personal service small businesses offer to customers is a major competitive weapon—one that larger firms try to match but often cannot. In addition, close relationships with employees often help the small-business owner to keep effective workers who might earn more with a larger firm.

Sustaining the Planet

Tips from the Environmental Protection Agency

The Environmental Protection Agency's Small Business Gateway offers a multitude of resources and ideas for small businesses going green. The site offers links to state and local environmental experts plus the latest information about complying with environmental laws and regulations. Take a look: http://www.epa.gov/smallbusiness/.

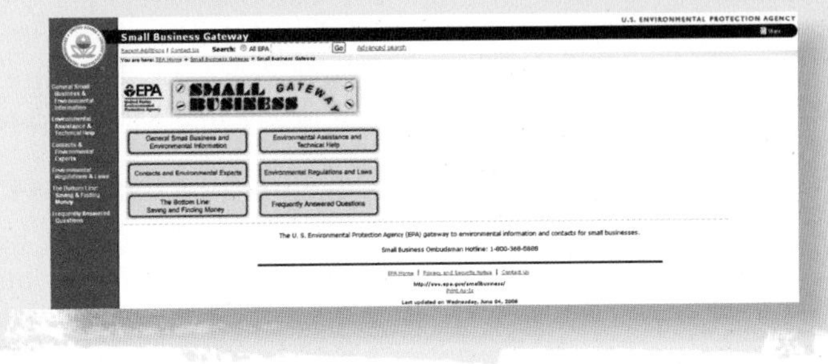

Ability to Adapt to Change Being his or her own boss, the owner-manager of a small business does not need anyone's permission to adapt to change. An owner may add or discontinue merchandise or services, change store hours, and experiment with various price strategies in response to changes in market conditions. And through personal relationships with customers, the owners of small businesses quickly become aware of changes in people's needs and interests, as well as in the activities of competing firms.

Simplified Record Keeping Many small firms need only a simple set of records. Record keeping might consist of a checkbook, a cash-receipts journal in which to record all sales, and a cash-disbursements journal in which to record all amounts paid out. Obviously, enough records must be kept to allow for producing and filing accurate tax returns.

Independence Small-business owners do not have to punch in and out, bid for vacation times, take orders from superiors, or worry about being fired or laid off. They are the masters of their own destinies—at least with regard to employment. For many people, this is the prime advantage of owning a small business.

Other Advantages According to the SBA, the most profitable companies in the United States are small firms that have been in business for more than ten years and employ fewer than 20 people. Small-business owners also enjoy all the advantages of sole proprietorships, which were discussed in Chapter 4. These include being able to keep all profits, the ease and low cost of going into business and (if necessary) going out of business, and being able to keep business information secret.

Disadvantages of Small Business

Personal contacts with customers, closer relationships with employees, being one's own boss, less cumbersome record-keeping chores, and independence are the bright side of small business. In contrast, the dark side reflects problems unique to these firms.

Risk of Failure As we have noted, small businesses (especially new ones) run a heavy risk of going out of business—about two out of three close their doors within the first six years. Older, well-established small firms can be hit hard by a business recession mainly because they do not have the financial resources to weather an extended difficult period.

Limited Potential Small businesses that survive do so with varying degrees of success. Many are simply the means of making a living for the owner and his or her family. The owner may have some technical skill—as a hair stylist or electrician, for example—and may have started a business to put this skill to work. Such a business is unlikely to grow into big business. In addition, employees' potential for advancement is limited.

Limited Ability to Raise Capital Small businesses typically have a limited ability to obtain capital. Figure 5.2 shows that most small-business financing comes out of the owner's pocket. Personal loans from lending institutions provide only about one-fourth of the capital required by small businesses. About 50 percent of all new firms begin with less than $30,000 in total capital, according to Census Bureau and Federal Reserve surveys. In fact, almost 36 percent of new firms begin with less than $20,000, usually provided by the owner or family members and friends.[13]

Although every person who considers starting a small business should be aware of the hazards and pitfalls we have noted, a well-conceived business plan may help to avoid the risk of failure. The U.S. government is also dedicated to helping small businesses make it. It expresses this aim most actively through the SBA.

Developing a Business Plan

Lack of planning can be as deadly as lack of money to a new small business. Planning is important to any business, large or small, and never should be overlooked or taken lightly. A **business plan** is a carefully constructed guide for the person starting a business. Consider it as a tool with three basic purposes: communication, management, and planning. As a communication tool, a business plan serves as a concise document that potential investors can examine to see if they would like to invest or assist in financing a new venture. It shows whether a business has the potential to make a profit. As a management tool, the business plan helps to track, monitor, and evaluate the progress. The business plan is a living document; it is modified as the entrepreneur gains knowledge and experience. It also serves to establish time

business plan a carefully constructed guide for the person starting a business

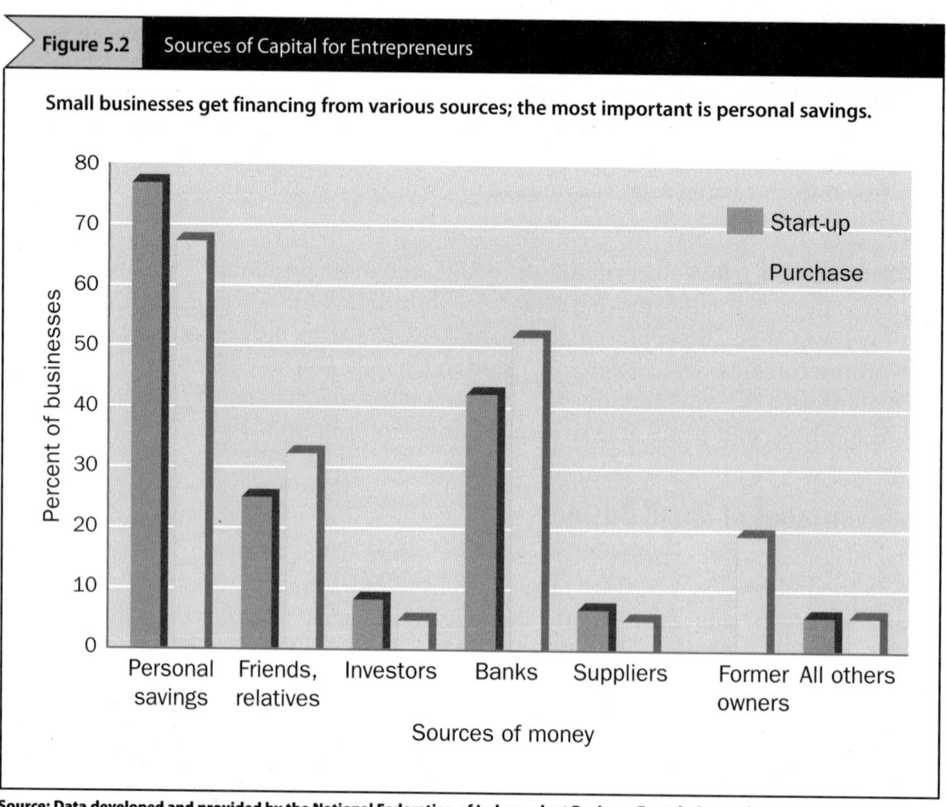

Source: Data developed and provided by the National Federation of Independent Business Foundation and sponsored by the American Express Travel Related Services Company, Inc.

Entrepreneurial SUCCESS

Prep Your Elevator Pitch

Imagine that you've just stepped into an elevator with a potential investor. You have a mere 60 seconds to pitch your business idea before the ride is over and the doors open. Are you ready?

Successful entrepreneurs are always perfecting their "elevator pitch," a quick, to-the-point summary of the business proposition. In just a minute or two, you should be able to clearly and succinctly explain what your business is about and the opportunity or problem you're addressing. Practice until you can project confidence and high energy without appearing rushed or overly aggressive. Just as important, a good elevator pitch should end with a "call to action," such as asking for a meeting to discuss more details.

© Comstock/Photolibrary

"Entrepreneur Idol" Jordan Leahy knows how to make every second count. A student at the University of Wisconsin–Whitewater, Leahy recently won the Northwestern University "elevator pitch" competition with a one-minute summary of his newest business venture. In addition to a cash prize, Leahy won an internship at a venture-capital firm. The day after his win, he received a call from one of the judges, a potential investor who requested more details about the business idea. That's the point of having your elevator pitch ready: "You never know when or where you'll meet your next investor," Leahy explains.

Sources: Scott Austin, "How to Pitch a Venture Capitalist on a Napkin," *Wall Street Journal Blog*, January 11, 2010, http://blogs.wsj.com/venturecapital/2010/01/11/how-to-pitch-a-venture-capitalist-on-a-napkin/?mod=rss_WSJBlog; "UW-Whitewater Student Entrepreneur Wins 'Entrepreneur Idol' Elevator Pitch Competition," *WisBusiness.com (Wisconsin)*, November 24, 2009, http://www.wisbusiness.com/index.iml?Article=177894; Scott Andron, "Entrepreneurs Seek Success in a Minute," *Miami Herald*, November 20, 2009, http://www.miamiherald.com/business/small-business/story/1342790.html; Daisy Wademan Dowling, "How to Perfect an Elevator Pitch about Yourself," *Harvard Business Review Blog*, May 4, 2009, http://blogs.harvardbusiness.org/dowling/2009/05/how-to-perfect-an-elevator-pit.html.

lines and milestones and allows comparison of growth projections against actual accomplishments. Finally, as a planning tool, the business plan guides a businessperson through the various phases of business. For example, the plan helps to identify obstacles to avoid and to establish alternatives. According to Robert Krummer, Jr., chairman of First Business Bank in Los Angeles, "The business plan is a necessity. If the person who wants to start a small business can't put a business plan together, he or she is in trouble."

Components of a Business Plan

Table 5.4 shows the 12 sections that a business plan should include. Each section is further explained at the end of each of the seven major parts in the text. The goal of each end-of-the-part exercise is to help a businessperson create his or her own business plan. When constructing a business plan, the businessperson should strive to keep it easy to read, uncluttered, and complete. Like other busy executives, officials of financial institutions do not have the time to wade through pages of extraneous data. The business plan should answer the four questions banking officials and investors are most interested in: (1) What exactly is the nature and mission of the new venture? (2) Why is this new enterprise a good idea? (3) What are the businessperson's goals? (4) How much will the new venture cost?

The great amount of time and consideration that should go into creating a business plan probably will end up saving time later. For example, Sharon Burch, who was running a computer software business while earning a degree in business administration, had to write a business plan as part of one of her courses. Burch has said, "I wish I'd taken the class before I started my business. I see a lot of things I could have done differently. But it has helped me since because I've been using the business plan as a guide for my business." Table 5.5 provides a business plan checklist. Accuracy and realistic expectations are crucial to an effective business plan. It is unethical to deceive loan officers, and it is unwise to deceive yourself.

Table 5.4 Components of a Business Plan

1. *Introduction.* Basic information such as the name, address, and phone number of the business; the date the plan was issued; and a statement of confidentiality to keep important information away from potential competitors.
2. *Executive Summary.* A one- to two-page overview of the entire business plan, including a justification why the business will succeed.
3. *Benefits to the Community.* Information on how the business will have an impact on economic development, community development, and human development.
4. *Company and Industry.* The background of the company, choice of the legal business form, information on the products or services to be offered, and examination of the potential customers, current competitors, and the business's future.
5. *Management Team.* Discussion of skills, talents, and job descriptions of management team, managerial compensation, management training needs, and professional assistance requirements.
6. *Manufacturing and Operations Plan.* Discussion of facilities needed, space requirements, capital equipment, labor force, inventory control, and purchasing requirement.
7. *Labor Force.* Discussion of the quality of skilled workers available and the training, compensation, and motivation of workers.
8. *Marketing Plan.* Discussion of markets, market trends, competition, market share, pricing, promotion, distribution, and service policy.
9. *Financial Plan.* Summary of the investment needed, sales and cash flow forecasts, breakeven analysis, and sources of funding.
10. *Exit Strategy.* Discussion of a succession plan or going public. Who will take over the business?
11. *Critical Risks and Assumptions.* Evaluation of the weaknesses of the business and how the company plans to deal with these and other business problems.
12. *Appendix.* Supplementary information crucial to the plan, such as résumés of owners and principal managers, advertising samples, organization chart, and any related information.

Source: Adapted from Timothy S. Hatten, *Small Business Management: Entrepreneurship and Beyond,* 4th ed. Copyright © 2009 by Houghton Mifflin Company, 93–118. Reprinted with permission.

Table 5.5 Business Plan Checklist

1. Does the executive summary grab the reader's attention and highlight the major points of the business plan?
2. Does the business-concept section clearly describe the purpose of the business, the customers, the value proposition, and the distribution channel and convey a compelling story?
3. Do the industry and market analyses support acceptance and demand for the business concept in the marketplace and define a first customer in depth?
4. Does the management team plan persuade the reader that the team could implement the business concept successfully? Does it assure the reader that an effective infrastructure is in place to facilitate the goals and operations of the company?
5. Does the product/service plan clearly provide details on the status of the product, the time line for completion, and the intellectual property that will be acquired?
6. Does the operations plan prove that the product or service could be produced and distributed efficiently and effectively?
7. Does the marketing plan successfully demonstrate how the company will create customer awareness in the target market and deliver the benefit to the customer?
8. Does the financial plan convince the reader that the business model is sustainable—that it will provide a superior return on investment for the investor and sufficient cash flow to repay loans to potential lenders?
9. Does the growth plan convince the reader that the company has long-term growth potential and spin-off products and services?
10. Does the contingency and exit-strategy plan convince the reader that the risk associated with this venture can be mediated? Is there an exit strategy in place for investors?

Source: Kathleen R. Allen, *Launching New Ventures: An Entrepreneurial Approach,* 4th ed. Copyright © 2006 by Houghton Mifflin Company, 197. Reprinted with permission.

Explain how the Small Business Administration helps small businesses.

Small Business Administration (SBA) a governmental agency that assists, counsels, and protects the interests of small businesses in the United States

The Small Business Administration

The **Small Business Administration (SBA)**, created by Congress in 1953, is a governmental agency that assists, counsels, and protects the interests of small businesses in the United States. It helps people get into business and stay in business. The agency provides assistance to owners and managers of prospective, new, and established small businesses. Through more than 1,000 offices and resource centers throughout the nation, the SBA provides both financial assistance and management counseling. Recently, the SBA provided training, technical assistance, and education to more than 3 million small businesses. It helps small firms to bid for and obtain government contracts, and it helps them to prepare to enter foreign markets.

SBA Management Assistance

Statistics show that most failures in small business are related to poor management. For this reason, the SBA places special emphasis on improving the management ability of the owners and managers of small businesses. The SBA's Management Assistance Program is extensive and diversified. It includes free individual counseling, courses, conferences, workshops, and a wide range of publications. Recently, the SBA provided management and technical assistance to nearly 1 million small businesses through its 1,100 Small Business Development Centers and 12,400 volunteers from the Service Corps of Retired Executives.[14]

Management Courses and Workshops The management courses offered by the SBA cover all the functions, duties, and roles of managers. Instructors may be teachers from local colleges and universities or other professionals, such as management consultants, bankers, lawyers, and accountants. Fees for these courses are quite low. The most popular such course is a general survey of eight to ten different areas of business management. In follow-up studies, businesspeople may concentrate in-depth on one or more of these areas depending on their particular strengths and weaknesses. The SBA occasionally offers one-day conferences. These conferences are aimed at keeping owner-managers up-to-date on new management developments, tax laws, and the like. The Small Business Training Network (SBTN) is an online training network consisting of 83 SBA-run courses, workshops, and resources. Some of the most requested courses include Entrepreneurship, Starting and Managing Your Own Business, Developing a Business Plan, Managing the Digital Enterprise, Identify Your Target Market, and Analyze Profitability. Find out more at http://www.sba.gov/training. Recently, more than 240,000 small-business owners benefited from SBA's free online business courses.

SCORE The **Service Corps of Retired Executives (SCORE)**, created in 1964, is a group of more than 12,400 businesspeople including more than 2,000 women who volunteer their services to small businesses through the SBA. The collective experience of SCORE volunteers spans the full range of American enterprise. These volunteers have worked for such notable companies as Eastman Kodak, General Electric, IBM, and Procter & Gamble. Experts in areas of accounting, finance, marketing, engineering, and retailing provide counseling and mentoring to entrepreneurs.

A small-business owner who has a particular problem can request free counseling from SCORE. An assigned counselor visits the owner in his or her establishment and, through careful observation, analyzes the business situation and the problem. If the problem is complex, the counselor may call on other volunteer experts to assist. Finally, the counselor offers a plan for solving the problem and helping the owner through the critical period.

Consider the plight of Elizabeth Halvorsen, a mystery writer from Minneapolis. Her husband had built up the family advertising and graphic arts firm for 17 years when he was called in 1991 to serve in the Persian Gulf War. The only one left behind who could run the business was Mrs. Halvorsen, who admittedly had no business experience. Enter SCORE. With a SCORE management expert at her side, she kept the business on track. In 2009, SCORE volunteers served more than 523,800 small-business people like Mrs. Halvorsen through its 800 branches. The 12,400 counselors provided 203,000 face-to-face counseling sessions, 119,000 online counseling sessions, and more than 49,500 online workshops to more than 201,000 workshop participants. Since its inception, SCORE has assisted more than 8.5 million small-business people with online and face-to-face small business counseling.[15]

Service Corps of Retired Executives (SCORE) a group of businesspeople who volunteer their services to small businesses through the SBA

Going for SUCCESS

Building a Business with SCORE's Help

Tony Clarke was looking to start a microbrewery in San Diego. Janice Selfridge wanted to get her Beacon, New York, art conservation company ready for future growth. Both succeeded in building their businesses with the expert advice and guidance of SCORE volunteers.

Tony Clarke is a former Navy pilot with a taste for handcrafted artisanal beers. When Clarke retired, he decided to brew and sell his own beers. He visited the SBA Web site in search of information about preparing a business plan and noticed a link to get assistance from SCORE. Clarke began attending SCORE workshops and receiving free individualized counseling from a local SCORE volunteer. "It was through SCORE that I met a lender who was open to financing a start-up," he says. Today Clarke's Airedale Brewing Company is growing quickly, selling specialty beers and ales through local taverns, hotels, restaurants, and liquor stores.

Janice Selfridge's Hudson Valley Fine Art Conservators is another SCORE success story. Selfridge used her background in fine art to start a business restoring historic paintings and frames. Her customers are individuals and museums that need paintings or frames cleaned and repaired. Over the course of a year, SCORE counselors helped Selfridge sharpen her management skills and plan for marketing to attract new customers. With help from SCORE, Selfridge's company is on the road to higher revenues and profits.

Sources: "Airdale Brewing Company: SCORE Helps Former Navy Pilot Reach His Dream of Becoming a Microbrewer," *SCORE Success Stories*, May 7, 2009, http://www.score.org/success_airdale.html; "The Beer Necessities," *Riviera*, May/June 2009, 110; "Success Stories: Airdale Brewing Company," *SCORE San Diego Chapter*, n.d., https://www.score-sandiego.org/about_successstory.asp?ID=10 (accessed July 26, 2010); http://www.airdalebrewing.com/about.shtml; "Garrison Fine Art Restorer Janice Selfridge Receives Putnam SCORE Award," *Putnam Country News & Recorder*, April 8, 2009, 11.

Help for Minority-Owned Small Businesses

Americans who are members of minority groups have had difficulty entering the nation's economic mainstream. Raising money is a nagging problem for minority business owners, who also may lack adequate training. Members of minority groups are, of course, eligible for all SBA programs, but the SBA makes a special effort to assist those minority groups who want to start small businesses or expand existing ones. For example, the Minority Business Development Agency awards grants to develop and increase business opportunities for members of racial and ethnic minorities.

Helping women become entrepreneurs is also a special goal of the SBA. Emily Harrington, one of nine children, was born in Manila, the Philippines. She arrived in the United States in 1972 as a foreign-exchange student. Convinced that there was a market for hard-working, dedicated minorities and women, she launched Qualified Resources, Inc. *Inc.* magazine selected her firm as one of "America's Fastest Growing Private Companies" just six years later. Harrington credits the SBA with giving her the technical support that made her first loan possible. Finding a SCORE counselor who worked directly with her, she refined her business plan until she got a bank loan. Before contacting the SBA, Harrington was turned down for business loans "by all the banks I approached," even though she worked as a manager of loan credit and collection for a bank. Later, Emily Harrington was SBA's winner of the local, regional, and national Small Business Entrepreneurial Success Award for Rhode Island, the New England region, and the nation! For several years in a row, Qualified Resources, Inc., was named one of the fastest growing private companies in Rhode Island. Now with more than 100 Women's Business Centers, entrepreneurs like Harrington can receive training and technical assistance, access to credit and capital, federal contracts, and international markets. The SBA's Online Women's Business Center (http://www.sba.gov/aboutsba/sbaprograms/onlinewbc/index.html) is a state-of-the-art Internet site to help women expand their businesses. This free, interactive Web site offers women information about business principles and practices, management techniques, networking, industry news, market research and technology training, online counseling, and hundreds of links to other sites, as well as information about the many SBA services and resources available to them.

Small-Business Institutes **Small-business institutes (SBIs)**, created in 1972, are groups of senior and graduate students in business administration who provide management counseling to small businesses. SBIs have been set up on more than 520 college campuses as another way to help business owners. The students work in small groups guided by faculty advisers and SBA management-assistance experts. Like SCORE volunteers, they analyze and help solve the problems of small-business owners at their business establishments.

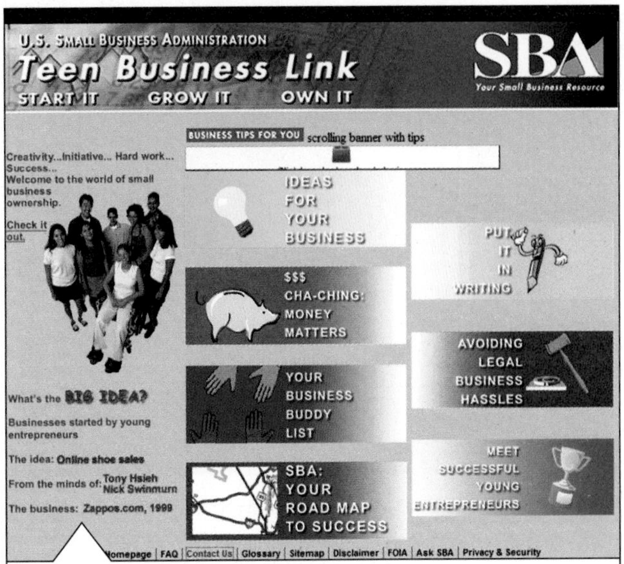

The SBA's Teen Business Link. This link provides information to young entrepreneurs about starting a business and other important business start-up questions.

Courtesy of U.S. Small Business Administration (www.sba.gov)

Small-Business Development Centers **Small-business development centers (SBDCs)** are university-based groups that provide individual counseling and practical training to owners of small businesses. SBDCs draw from the resources of local, state, and federal governments, private businesses, and universities. These groups can provide managerial and technical help, data from research studies, and other types of specialized assistance of value to small businesses. In 2010, there were more than 1,100 SBDC locations, primarily at colleges and universities, assisting people such as Kathleen DuBois. After scribbling a list of her abilities and the names of potential clients on a napkin in a local restaurant, Kathleen DuBois decided to start her own marketing firm. Beth Thornton launched her engineering firm after a discussion with a colleague in the ladies room of the Marriott. When Richard Shell was laid off after 20 years of service with Nisource (Columbia Gas), he searched the Internet tirelessly before finding the right franchise option. Introduced by mutual friends, Jim Bostic and Denver McMillion quickly connected, built a high level of trust, and combined their diverse professional backgrounds to form a manufacturing company. Although these entrepreneurs took different routes in starting their new businesses in West Virginia, all of them turned to the West Virginia Small Business Development Center for the technical assistance to make their dreams become a reality.

SBA Publications The SBA issues management, marketing, and technical publications dealing with hundreds of topics of interest to present and prospective managers of small firms. Most of these publications are available from the SBA free of charge. Others can be obtained for a small fee from the U.S. Government Printing Office.

SBA Financial Assistance

Small businesses seem to be constantly in need of money. An owner may have enough capital to start and operate the business. But then he or she may require more money to finance increased operations during peak selling seasons, to pay for required pollution control equipment, to finance an expansion, or to mop up after a natural disaster such as a flood or a terrorist attack. For example, the Supplemental Terrorist Activity Relief program has made $3.7 billion in loans to 8,202 small businesses harmed or disrupted by the September 11 terrorist attacks. In October 2005, the SBA guaranteed loans of up to $150,000 to small businesses affected by Hurricanes Katrina and Rita. Since the 2005 hurricanes, SBA has made more than $4.9 billion in disaster loans to 102,903 homeowners and renters in the Gulf region. Businesses in the area received 16,828 business disaster loans with disbursements worth $1.5 billion.[16] In 2010, the SBA offered economic injury loans to fishing and fishing-dependent small businesses as a result of the Deepwater BP spill that shut down commercial and recreational fishing waters. According to the SBA Administrator Karen Mills, "SBA remains committed to taking every step to help small businesses deal with the financial challenges they are facing as a result of the Deepwater

small-business institutes (SBIs) groups of senior and graduate students in business administration who provide management counseling to small businesses

small-business development centers (SBDCs) university-based groups that provide individual counseling and practical training to owners of small businesses

Making music at the Modesto Academy of Music & Design. After giving private piano lessons for more than 25 years, Pam Tallman of Modesto, California, used an SBA loan to help finance the purchase of a building to open the academy. The school offers music, art, design, and computer classes for students aged two years and older.

BP oil spill."[17] The SBA offers special financial-assistance programs that cover all these situations. However, its primary financial function is to guarantee loans to eligible businesses.

Regular Business Loans Most of the SBA's business loans are actually made by private lenders such as banks, but repayment is partially guaranteed by the agency. That is, the SBA may guarantee that it will repay the lender up to 90 percent of the loan if the borrowing firm cannot repay it. Guaranteed loans approved on or after October 1, 2002, may be as large as $1.5 million (this loan limit may be increased in the future). The average size of an SBA-guaranteed business loan is about $300,000, and its average duration is about eight years.

Small-Business Investment Companies **Venture capital** is money that is invested in small (and sometimes struggling) firms that have the potential to become very successful. In many cases, only a lack of capital keeps these firms from rapid and solid growth. The people who invest in such firms expect that their investments will grow with the firms and become quite profitable.

The popularity of these investments has increased over the past 30 years, but most small firms still have difficulty obtaining venture capital. To help such businesses, the SBA licenses, regulates, and provides financial assistance to **small-business investment companies (SBICs)**.

An SBIC is a privately owned firm that provides venture capital to small enterprises that meet its investment standards. Such firms as America Online, Apple Computer, Federal Express, Compaq Computer, Intel Corporation, Outback Steakhouse, and Staples, Inc., all were financed through SBICs during their initial growth period. SBICs are intended to be profit-making organizations. The aid that SBA offers allows them to invest in small businesses that otherwise would not attract venture capital. Since Congress created the program in 1958, SBICs have financed more than 102,000 small businesses for a total of about $50.6 billion. In 2009, SBIC benefited 1,477 businesses, and 24 percent of these firms were less than two years old.[18]

State of Small Business During the Recession

Celebrating the 47th annual observance of National Small Business Week in May 2010, President Obama stated,

> *Our nation is still emerging from one of the worst recessions in our history, and small businesses were among the hardest hit. From mom-and-pop stores to high tech start-ups, countless small businesses have been forced to lay off employees or shut their doors entirely. In these difficult times, we must do all we can to help these firms recover from the recession and put Americans back to work. Our government cannot guarantee a company's success, but it can help create market conditions that allow small businesses to thrive.*
>
> *My Administration is committed to helping small businesses drive our economy toward recovery and long-term growth. The American Recovery and Reinvestment Act has supported billions of dollars in loans and Federal contracts for small businesses across the country. The Affordable Care Act makes it easier for small business owners to provide health insurance to their employees, and gives entrepreneurs the security they need to innovate and take risks. We have enacted new tax cuts and tax credits for small firms. Still, we must do more to empower these companies. Small businesses are the engine of our prosperity*

venture capital money that is invested in small (and sometimes struggling) firms that have the potential to become very successful

small-business investment companies (SBICs) privately owned firms that provide venture capital to small enterprises that meet their investment standards

and a proud reflection of our character. A healthy small business sector will give us vibrant communities, cutting-edge technology, and an American economy that can compete and win in the 21st century.[19]

As if the recession was not enough, in the states near the Gulf of Mexico, many small businesses suffered financial losses following the April 20, 2010, Deepwater BP oil spill that shut down commercial and recreational fishing along the coasts. According to the SBA Administrator, Karen Mills, "With the region still recovering from previous devastation and the national recession of the last couple of years, it's critical that we take every step we can to provide small businesses with resources to make it through this latest crisis so that they can continue to drive local economic growth and provide good-paying jobs." The SBA is offering working capital loans up to $2 million at an interest rate of 4 percent with terms up to 30 years.[20]

We have discussed the importance of the small-business segment of our economy. We have weighed the advantages and drawbacks of operating a small business as compared with a large one. But is there a way to achieve the best of both worlds? Can one preserve one's independence as a business owner and still enjoy some of the benefits of "bigness"? Let's take a close look at franchising.

6

Appraise the concept and types of franchising.

Franchising

A **franchise** is a license to operate an individually owned business as if it were part of a chain of outlets or stores. Often, the business itself is also called a *franchise*. Among the most familiar franchises are McDonald's, H&R Block, AAMCO Transmissions, GNC (General Nutrition Centers), and Dairy Queen. Many other franchises carry familiar names; this method of doing business has become very popular in the last 30 years or so. It is an attractive means of starting and operating a small business.

What Is Franchising?

Franchising is the actual granting of a franchise. A **franchisor** is an individual or organization granting a franchise. A **franchisee** is a person or organization purchasing a franchise. The franchisor supplies a known and advertised business name, management skills, the required training and materials, and a method of doing business. The franchisee supplies labor and capital, operates the franchised business, and agrees to abide by the provisions of the franchise agreement. Table 5.6 lists the basic franchisee rights and obligations that would be covered in a typical franchise agreement.

Types of Franchising

Franchising arrangements fall into three general categories. In the first approach, a manufacturer authorizes a number of retail stores to sell a certain brand-name item. This type of franchising arrangement, one of the oldest, is prevalent in sales of passenger cars and trucks, farm equipment, shoes, paint, earth-moving equipment, and petroleum. About 90 percent of all gasoline is sold through franchised, independent retail service stations, and franchised dealers handle virtually all sales of new cars and trucks. In the second type of franchising arrangement, a producer licenses distributors to sell a given product to retailers. This arrangement is common in the soft drink industry. Most national manufacturers of soft drink syrups—The Coca-Cola Company, Dr. Pepper/Seven-Up Companies, PepsiCo, Royal Crown Companies, Inc.—franchise independent bottlers who then serve retailers. In a third form of franchising, a franchisor supplies brand names, techniques, or other services instead of a complete product. Although the franchisor may provide certain production and distribution services, its primary role is the careful development and control of marketing strategies. This approach to franchising, which is the most typical today, is used by Holiday Inns, Howard Johnson Company, AAMCO Transmissions, McDonald's, Dairy Queen, Avis, Hertz Corporation, KFC (Kentucky Fried Chicken), and SUBWAY, to name but a few.

franchise a license to operate an individually owned business as though it were part of a chain of outlets or stores

franchising the actual granting of a franchise

franchisor an individual or organization granting a franchise

franchisee a person or organization purchasing a franchise

Table 5.6 Basic Rights and Obligations Delineated in a Franchise Agreement

Franchisee rights include:
1. use of trademarks, trade names, and patents of the franchisor.
2. use of the brand image and the design and decor of the premises developed by the franchisor.
3. use of the franchisor's secret methods.
4. use of the franchisor's copyrighted materials.
5. use of recipes, formulae, specifications, processes, and methods of manufacture developed by the franchisor.
6. conducting the franchised business upon or from the agreed premises strictly in accordance with the franchisor's methods and subject to the franchisor's directions.
7. guidelines established by the franchisor regarding exclusive territorial rights.
8. rights to obtain supplies from nominated suppliers at special prices.
Franchisee obligations include:
1. to carry on the business franchised and no other business upon the approved and nominated premises.
2. to observe certain minimum operating hours.
3. to pay a franchise fee.
4. to follow the accounting system laid down by the franchisor.
5. not to advertise without prior approval of the advertisements by the franchisor.
6. to use and display such point-of-sale advertising materials as the franchisor stipulates.
7. to maintain the premises in good, clean, and sanitary condition and to redecorate when required to do so by the franchisor.
8. to maintain the widest possible insurance coverage.
9. to permit the franchisor's staff to enter the premises to inspect and see if the franchisor's standards are being maintained.
10. to purchase goods or products from the franchisor or his designated suppliers.
11. to train the staff in the franchisor's methods to ensure that they are neatly and appropriately clothed.
12. not to assign the franchise contract without the franchisor's consent.

Source: Excerpted from the SBA's "Is Franchising for Me?" http://www.sba.gov (accessed June 10, 2010).

Analyze the growth of franchising and franchising's advantages and disadvantages.

The Growth of Franchising

Franchising, which began in the United States around the time of the Civil War, was used originally by large firms, such as the Singer Sewing Company, to distribute their products. Franchising has been increasing steadily in popularity since the early 1900s, primarily for filling stations and car dealerships; however, this retailing strategy has experienced enormous growth since the mid-1970s. The franchise proliferation generally has paralleled the expansion of the fast-food industry. As Table 5.7 shows, three of *Entrepreneur* magazine's top-rated franchises for 2010 were in this category.

Of course, franchising is not limited to fast foods. Hair salons, tanning parlors, and dentists and lawyers are expected to participate in franchising arrangements in growing numbers. Franchised health clubs, pest exterminators, and campgrounds are already widespread, as are franchised tax preparers and travel agencies. The real estate industry also has experienced a rapid increase in franchising.

Also, franchising is attracting more women and minority business owners in the United States than ever before. One reason is that special outreach programs designed to encourage franchisee diversity have developed. Consider Angela Trammel, a young mother of two. She had been laid off from her job at the Marriott after 9/11. Since she was a member of a Curves Fitness Center and liked the concept of empowering women to become physically fit, she began researching the cost of purchasing a Curves franchise and ways to finance the business. "I was online looking for financing, and I linked to Enterprise Development Group in Washington, DC. I knew that they had diverse clients." The cost for the franchise was $19,500, but it took $60,000 to open the doors to her fitness center. "Applying for a loan

Table 5.7 Entrepreneur's Top Ten Franchises in 2010

Rank	Franchise	Total Investment ($)	Franchise Fee ($)	Royalty Fee	Net Worth Requirement ($)	Cash Requirement ($)	Comments
1	SUBWAY	84,300–258,300	15,000	8%	—	84,300–258,000	20-year renewable term
2	McDonald's	1,057,200–1,885,000	45,000	>12.5%	—	500,000	20-year renewable term
3	7-Eleven Inc.	30,800–604,500	10,000–611,600	Varies	127,000	—	15-year renewable term
4	Hampton Inn/ Hampton Inn & Suites	3,716,000–13,148,800	50,000	5%	—	—	22-year renewable term
5	Supercuts	112,550–243,200	22,500	6%	300,000	100,000	Conditional, renewable term
6	H&R Block	34,438–110,033	—	Varies	—	—	—
7	Dunkin' Donuts	358,200–1,980,300	80,000	5.9%	1,500,000	750,000	—
8	Jani-King	13,150–93,150	8,600–16,300	10%	—	—	20-year renewable term
9	Servpro	127,300–174,700	40,000	3–10%	100,000	60,000	5-year renewable term
10	ampm Mini Market	1,786,929–7,596,688	30,000–70,000	5%	—	700,000–1,000,000	20-year renewable term

Source: http://www.entrepreneur.com/franchise500 (accessed August 26, 2010), with permission of Entrepreneur.com, Inc. ©2010 by Entrepreneur.com, Inc. All rights reserved.

to start the business was much harder than buying a house," said Trammel. Just three years later, Angela and her husband, Ernest, own three Curves Fitness Centers with 12 employees. Recently, since giving birth to her third child, she has found the financial freedom and flexibility needed to care for her busy family. In fact, within a three-year period, the Trammels grew their annual household income from $80,000 to $250,000.[21] Franchisors such as Wendy's, McDonald's, Burger King, and Church's Chicken all have special corporate programs to attract minority and women franchisees. Just as important, successful women and minority franchisees are willing to get involved by offering advice and guidance to new franchisees.

Herman Petty, the first African-American McDonald's franchisee, remembers that the company provided a great deal of help while he worked to establish his first units. In turn, Petty traveled to help other black franchisees, and he invited new franchisees to gain hands-on experience in his Chicago restaurants before starting their own establishments. Petty also organized a support group, the National Black McDonald's Operators Association, to help black franchisees in other areas. Today, this support group has 33 local chapters and more than 330 members across the country. "We are really concentrating on helping our operators to be successful both operationally and financially," says Craig Welburn, the McDonald's franchisee who leads the group.

Dual-branded franchises, in which two franchisors offer their products together, are a new small-business trend. For example, in 1993, pleased with the success of its first cobranded restaurant with Texaco in Beebe, Arkansas, McDonald's now has more than 400 cobranded restaurants in the United States. Also, an agreement between franchisors Doctor's Associates, Inc., and TCBY Enterprises, Inc., now allows franchisees to sell SUBWAY sandwiches and TCBY yogurt in the same establishment.

Are Franchises Successful?

Franchising is designed to provide a tested formula for success, along with ongoing advice and training. The success rate for businesses owned and operated by franchisees is significantly higher than the success rate for other independently owned small businesses. In a recent nationwide Gallup poll of 944 franchise owners, 94 percent of franchisees indicated that they were very or somewhat successful, only 5 percent believed that they were very unsuccessful or somewhat unsuccessful, and 1 percent did not know. Despite these impressive statistics, franchising is not a guarantee of success for either franchisees or franchisors. Too rapid expansion, inadequate capital or management skills, and a host of other problems can cause failure for both franchisee and franchisor. Thus, for example, the Dizzy Dean's Beef and Burger franchise is no longer in business. Timothy Bates, a Wayne State University economist, warns, "Despite the hype that franchising is the safest way to go when starting a new business, the research just doesn't bear that out." Just consider Boston Chicken, which once had more than 1,200 restaurants before declaring bankruptcy in 1998.

How sweet it is. Cold Stone Creamery opened its first store in 1988 and started franchising in 1995. Today, about 1,400 stores have opened in the United States, Puerto Rico, Guam, Japan, and Korea. In 2006, Cold Stone was ranked #11 in *Entrepreneur* magazine's Fastest Growing Franchising.

Advantages of Franchising

Franchising plays a vital role in our economy and soon may become the dominant form of retailing. Why? Because franchising offers advantages to both the franchisor and the franchisee.

To the Franchisor The franchisor gains fast and well-controlled distribution of its products without incurring the high cost of constructing and operating its own outlets. The franchisor thus has more capital available to expand production and to use for advertising. At the same time, it can ensure, through the franchise agreement, that outlets are maintained and operated according to its own standards.

The franchisor also benefits from the fact that the franchisee—a sole proprietor in most cases—is likely to be very highly motivated to succeed. The success of the franchise means more sales, which translate into higher royalties for the franchisor.

To the Franchisee The franchisee gets the opportunity to start a business with limited capital and to make use of the business experience of others. Moreover, an outlet with a nationally advertised name, such as Radio Shack, McDonald's, or Century 21 Real Estate, has guaranteed customers as soon as it opens.

If business problems arise, the franchisor gives the franchisee guidance and advice. This counseling is primarily responsible for the very high degree of success enjoyed by franchises. In most cases, the franchisee does not pay for such help.

The franchisee also receives materials to use in local advertising and can take part in national promotional campaigns sponsored by the franchisor. McDonald's and its franchisees, for example, constitute one of the nation's top 20 purchasers of advertising. Finally, the franchisee may be able to minimize the cost of advertising, supplies, and various business necessities by purchasing them in cooperation with other franchisees.

Disadvantages of Franchising

The main disadvantage of franchising affects the franchisee, and it arises because the franchisor retains a great deal of control. The franchisor's contract can dictate every aspect of the business: decor, design of employee uniforms, types of signs, and all the details of business operations. All Burger King French fries taste the same because all Burger King franchisees have to make them the same way.

Contract disputes are the cause of many lawsuits. For example, Rekha Gabhawala, a Dunkin' Donuts franchisee in Milwaukee, alleged that the franchisor was forcing her out of business so that the company could profit by reselling the downtown franchise to someone else; the company, on the other hand, alleged that Gabhawala breached the contract by not running the business according to company standards. In another case, Dunkin' Donuts sued Chris Romanias, its franchisee in Pennsylvania, alleging that Romanias intentionally underreported gross sales to the company. Romanias, on the other hand, alleged that Dunkin' Donuts, Inc., breached the contract because it failed to provide assistance in operating the franchise. Other franchisees claim that contracts are unfairly tilted toward the franchisors. Yet others have charged that they lost their franchise and investment because their franchisor would not approve the sale of the business when they found a buyer.

To arbitrate disputes between franchisors and franchisees, the National Franchise Mediation Program was established in 1993 by 30 member firms, including Burger King Corporation, McDonald's Corporation, and Wendy's International, Inc. Negotiators have since resolved numerous cases through mediation. Recently, Carl's Jr. brought in one of its largest franchisees to help set its system straight, making most franchisees happy for the first time in years. The program also helped PepsiCo settle a long-term contract dispute and renegotiate its franchise agreements.

Because disagreements between franchisors and franchisees have increased in recent years, many franchisees have been demanding government regulation of franchising. In 1997, to avoid government regulation, some of the largest franchisors proposed a new self-policing plan to the Federal Trade Commission.

Franchise holders pay for their security, usually with a one-time franchise fee and continuing royalty and advertising fees, collected as a percentage of sales. As Table 5.7 shows, a SUBWAY franchisee pays an initial franchise fee of $15,000 and an annual fee of 8 percent of gross sales. In Table 5.7, you can see how much money a franchisee needs to start a new franchise for selected organizations. In some fields, franchise agreements are not uniform. One franchisee may pay more than another for the same services.

Even success can cause problems. Sometimes a franchise is so successful that the franchisor opens its own outlet nearby, in direct competition—although franchisees may fight back. For example, a court recently ruled that Burger King could not enter into direct competition with the franchisee because the contract was not specific on the issue. A spokesperson for one franchisor contends that the company "gives no geographical protection" to its franchise holders and thus is free to move in on them. Franchise operators work hard. They often put in 10- and 12-hour days, six days a week. The International Franchise Association advises prospective franchise purchasers to investigate before investing and to approach buying a franchise cautiously. Franchises vary widely in approach as well as in products. Some, such as Dunkin' Donuts and Baskin-Robbins, demand long hours. Others, such as Great Clips hair salons and Albert's Family Restaurants, are more appropriate for those who do not want to spend many hours at their stores.

The growth of franchising. Franchising is designed to provide a tested formula for success, along with ongoing advice and training. The franchisor, such as TGIF or KFC, supplies a known and advertised business name, management skills, the required training and materials, and a method of doing business. Franchising, however, is not a guarantee of success for either franchisees or franchisors.

Global Perspectives in Small Business

For small American businesses, the world is becoming smaller. National and international economies are growing more and more interdependent as political leadership and national economic directions change and trade barriers diminish or disappear. Globalization and instant worldwide communications are rapidly shrinking distances at the same time that they are expanding business opportunities. According to a recent study, the Internet is increasingly important to small-business strategic thinking, with more than 50 percent of those surveyed indicating that the Internet represented their most favored strategy for growth. This was more than double the next-favored choice, strategic alliances reflecting the opportunity to reach both global and domestic customers. The Internet and online payment systems enable even very small businesses to serve international customers. In fact, technology now gives small businesses the leverage and power to

SPoTLIGHT

SUBWAY's Foreign Franchising Around the World

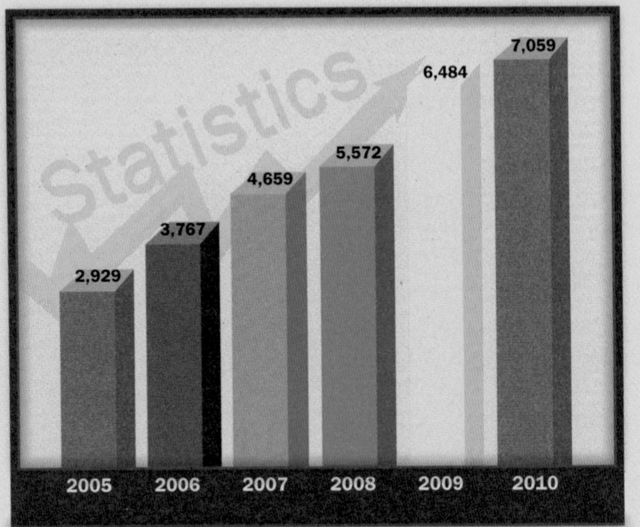

Source: http://www.entrepreneur.com/franchises/subway/282839-0.html (accessed August 26, 2010).

reach markets that were once limited solely to large corporations. No wonder the number of businesses exporting their goods and services has tripled since 1990, with two-thirds of that boom coming from companies with fewer than 20 employees.[22]

The SBA offers help to the nation's small-business owners who want to enter the world markets. The SBA's efforts include counseling small firms on how and where to market overseas, matching U.S. small-business executives with potential overseas customers, and helping exporters to secure financing. The agency brings small U.S. firms into direct contact with potential overseas buyers and partners. The SBA International Trade Loan program provides guarantees of up to $1.75 million in loans to small-business owners. These loans help small firms in expanding or developing new export markets. The U.S. Commercial Service, a Commerce Department division, aids small and medium-sized businesses in selling overseas. The division's global network includes more than 100 offices in the United States and 151 others in 80 countries around the world.[23]

Consider Daniel J. Nanigian, President of Nanmac Corporation in Framingham, Massachusetts. This company manufactures temperature sensors used in a wide range of industrial applications. With an export strategy aimed at growing revenues in diverse foreign markets including China, the Nanmac Corporation experienced explosive growth in 2009. The company nearly doubled its sales from $2.7 million in 2008 to $5.1 million in 2009. The company's international sales, at $300,000 in 2004, reached $700,000 in 2009 and were expected to reach $1.7 million in 2010. Its administrative, sales, and manufacturing employees have increased by 80 percent.

The company has a strong presence in China and is expanding in other markets, as well, including Latin America, Singapore, and Russia. Under Nanigian's guidance, the company has developed creative solutions and partnerships to help maximize its presence internationally. As part of its China strategy, Nanmac partners with distributors, recruits European and in-country sales representatives, uses a localized Chinese Web site, and relies for advice on the export assistance programs of the Massachusetts Small Business Development Center Network's Massachusetts Export Center. The strategy, along with travel to China to conduct technical training seminars and attend trade shows and technical conferences, has helped to grow Nanmac's Chinese client list from 1 in 2003 to more than 30 accounts today. Mr. Nanigian received SBA's 2010 Small Business Exporter of the Year Award.[24]

International trade will become more important to small-business owners as they face unique challenges in the new century. Small businesses, which are expected to remain the dominant form of organization in this country, must be prepared to adapt to significant demographic and economic changes in the world marketplace.

This chapter ends our discussion of American business today. From here on, we shall be looking closely at various aspects of business operations. We begin, in the next chapter, with a discussion of management—what management is, what managers do, and how they work to coordinate the basic economic resources within a business organization.

return to inside business

Five Guys Burgers and Fries

Five Guys Burgers and Fries will only consider prospective franchisees who have strong personal finances and sufficient capital to open and operate at least five restaurants in their territory. Franchisees must also have a solid business background and previous management experience. Above all, franchisees must be completely committed to the company's standards of food quality and customer service. To ensure that every unit from Swampscott to Seattle cooks up the same juicy burgers and friendly service, the company awards cash bonuses to the staff of restaurants that earn high scores in twice-weekly checks by mystery shoppers.

For long-term growth, Five Guys is planning to build on its current franchising success by expanding in the European market. Will the company's restaurants be as popular overseas as they have been with U.S. burger lovers and franchisees?

Questions

1. If you were working on a business plan for opening a Five Guys franchise in your area, what critical risks would you list? How would you plan to deal with those risks?
2. Do you agree with Five Guys' policy of spending millions to reward good customer service rather than promoting itself through traditional advertising campaigns?

SUMMARY

Summary

1 Define what a small business is and recognize the fields in which small businesses are concentrated.

A small business is one that is independently owned and operated for profit and is not dominant in its field. There are about 23 million businesses in this country, and more than 90 percent of them are small businesses. Small businesses employ more than half the nation's workforce, even though about 70 percent of new businesses can be expected to fail within five years. More than half of all small businesses are in retailing and services.

2 Identify the people who start small businesses and the reasons why some succeed and many fail.

Such personal characteristics as independence, desire to create a new enterprise, and willingness to accept a challenge may encourage individuals to start small businesses. Various external circumstances, such as special expertise or even the loss of a job, also can supply the motivation to strike out on one's own. Poor planning and lack of capital and management experience are the major causes of small-business failures.

3 Assess the contributions of small businesses to our economy.

Small businesses have been responsible for a wide variety of inventions and innovations, some of which have given rise to new industries. Historically, small businesses have created the bulk of the nation's new jobs. Further, they have mounted effective competition to larger firms. They provide things that society needs, act as suppliers to larger firms, and serve as customers of other businesses, both large and small.

4 Judge the advantages and disadvantages of operating a small business.

The advantages of smallness in business include the opportunity to establish personal relationships with customers and employees, the ability to adapt to changes quickly, independence, and simplified record keeping. The major disadvantages are the high risk of failure, the limited potential for growth, and the limited ability to raise capital.

5 Explain how the Small Business Administration helps small businesses.

The Small Business Administration (SBA) was created in 1953 to assist and counsel the nation's millions of small-business owners. The SBA offers management courses and workshops; managerial help, including one-to-one counseling through SCORE; various publications; and financial assistance through guaranteed loans and SBICs. It places special emphasis on aid to minority-owned businesses, including those owned by women.

6 Appraise the concept and types of franchising.

A franchise is a license to operate an individually owned business as though it were part of a chain. The franchisor provides a known business name, management skills, a method of doing business, and the training and required materials. The franchisee contributes labor and capital, operates the franchised business, and agrees to abide by the provisions of the franchise agreement. There are three major categories of franchise agreements.

7 Analyze the growth of franchising and franchising's advantages and disadvantages.

Franchising has grown tremendously since the mid-1970s. The franchisor's major advantage in franchising is fast and well-controlled distribution of products with minimal capital outlay. In return, the franchisee has the opportunity to open a business with limited capital, to make use of the business experience of others, and to sell to an existing clientele. For this, the franchisee usually must pay both an initial franchise fee and a continuing royalty based on sales. He or she also must follow the dictates of the franchise with regard to operation of the business.

Worldwide business opportunities are expanding for small businesses. The SBA assists small-business owners in penetrating foreign markets. The next century will present unique challenges and opportunities for small-business owners.

Key Terms

You should now be able to define and give an example relevant to each of the following terms:

small business (137)
business plan (146)
Small Business Administration (SBA) (148)
Service Corps of Retired Executives (SCORE) (149)
small-business institutes (SBIs) (151)
small-business development centers (SBDCs) (151)
venture capital (152)
small-business investment companies (SBICs) (152)
franchise (153)
franchising (153)
franchisor (153)
franchisee (153)

Review Questions

1. What information would you need to determine whether a particular business is small according to SBA guidelines?
2. Which two areas of business generally attract the most small businesses? Why are these areas attractive to small business?
3. Distinguish among service industries, distribution industries, and production industries.
4. What kinds of factors encourage certain people to start new businesses?
5. What are the major causes of small-business failure? Do these causes also apply to larger businesses?
6. Briefly describe four contributions of small business to the American economy.
7. What are the major advantages and disadvantages of smallness in business?
8. What are the major components of a business plan? Why should an individual develop a business plan?
9. Identify five ways in which the SBA provides management assistance to small businesses.
10. Identify two ways in which the SBA provides financial assistance to small businesses.
11. Why does the SBA concentrate on providing management and financial assistance to small businesses?
12. What is venture capital? How does the SBA help small businesses to obtain it?
13. Explain the relationships among a franchise, the franchisor, and the franchisee.
14. What does the franchisor receive in a franchising agreement? What does the franchisee receive? What does each provide?
15. Cite one major benefit of franchising for the franchisor. Cite one major benefit of franchising for the franchisee.

Discussion Questions

1. Most people who start small businesses are aware of the high failure rate and the reasons for it. Why, then, do some take no steps to protect their firms from failure? What steps should they take?
2. Are the so-called advantages of small business really advantages? Wouldn't every small-business owner like his or her business to grow into a large firm?
3. Do average citizens benefit from the activities of the SBA, or is the SBA just another way to spend our tax money?
4. Would you rather own your own business independently or become a franchisee? Why?

Video Case 5.1

Murray's Cheese: More Cheese Please

Murray's Cheese began in New York's Greenwich Village in 1940, as a wholesale butter and egg shop owned by a Jewish veteran of the Spanish Civil War named Murray Greenberg. When the current president Rob Kaufelt purchased the shop in 1991, it was little more than a local hole-in-the-wall. Kaufelt and his staff made the decision to focus on high-quality gourmet cheeses from around the world. Today, people come from all over to sample Murray's cheeses and to take classes or attend its Cheese U bootcamp to learn about cheese. Although Murray's has extended its product line to include gourmet meats, crackers, olives, and dried fruit, cheese remains its core product. In fact, Murray's Cheese has been voted by *Forbes* as "the best cheese shop" and it is expanding to three other stores. Its success prompted Kroger to seek it out as a partner in its chain of supermarkets, a step that included intensively training Kroger employees in the fine points of selling Murray's products and the creation of a 300-page cheese service guide for them.

"We are little and they are very big," says Murray's managing director, Liz Thorpe, in speaking of Kroger. "So it's a very interesting model for us. We've begun operating cheese shops in Kroger delis that are similar to our New York shops. This allows us to bring our knowledge and expertise on sourcing, production selection, education, and customer service to a different format.... We're actually going to be opening 50 of these shops in the next 36 months."

Murray's is still small, with about 70 employees, and has an advertising budget of zero dollars. Instead of advertising, Murray's relies on providing great customer service and creating positive word of mouth to promote its products and to secure its reputation. Personal selling is key. The company recruits salespeople who are passionate about both cheese and people and trains them carefully. The key is to inform customers about the store's many unique products and persuade them to taste and then purchase. The staff enjoys listening to customers, gaining an understanding of their interests, and trying to find the right product to satisfy their needs. Their efforts often succeed in getting customers to purchase more and to make repeat buys.

All customers get to taste free samples of cheese before they buy it. "We like knowing the folks who walk in our door and having everyone taste the cheese," said the managing director. "It's part of the shopping experience. That said, we are getting more sophisticated about how we communicate with people. E-mail marketing continues to be really critical, and we're starting to take advantage of social networking outlets like Twitter. For people who are into cheese and into Murray's, it's a great way for them to be directly tapped into knowing what's going on right this second."

What continues to appeal to sophisticated shoppers about Murray's is that cheese is an affordable luxury. A wine and cheese party for a dozen people, for instance, can fit almost any budget, and Murray's salespeople are happy to provide suggestions and samples to assist in the selection. Murray's manager also credits popular media like the Food Network with helping to popularize food in general, and cheese in particular. After all, he says, cheeses "don't have to be improved upon or fortified. They are naturally good for you."[25]

Questions

1. How does Murray's overcome one of the most common limitations facing small companies, its nonexistent advertising budget?
2. What are some of the advantages of being a small business that Murray's can (or does) take advantage of? What disadvantages might it face as a small firm?
3. Do you think the partnership with Kroger will have a negative or a positive effect on the unique experience customers expect from Murray's? Why?

Case 5.2

Tumbleweed Tiny House Company

The average American home is between 2,000 and 2,500 square feet in size. Jay Shafer's handcrafted 89-square-foot house on wheels is so small he can almost parallel-park it. Ecological concerns have combined with an uncertain real estate market to give a big boost to the small-house movement, which promotes simple living in tiny spaces. A growing number of people are happily living in houses ranging from just 70 to 800 square feet, small enough to fit on a flatbed truck and pull into a field or farmstead.

One of the pioneer builders of such tiny homes is the Tumbleweed Tiny House Company, the brainchild of Shafer, a 40-something professor-turned-designer who has lived in three of his own creations over the last several years. His young do-it-yourself company, until recently a one-person operation, builds and provides plans for several different models and sizes of tiny houses. The homes are fully equipped but scaled-down, with kitchens and baths, windowed sleeping lofts under peaked roofs, front porches, and lots of ingenious storage space. The houses are designed to hook up to public water and waste lines; many buyers use them as primary homes, but they can also serve as studios, guest rooms, weekend getaways, or home offices.

Shafer was inspired to found the company about 15 years ago, when he was teaching drawing at the University of Iowa. "I was living in an average-sized apartment and I realized I just didn't need so much space," he says. After a false start living in an uninsulated Airstream trailer, he decided to build his own 100-square-foot house from scratch. He parked it on a friend's farm because minimum-size housing standards prevented him from putting it on a city lot. Not long after, Gregory Paul Johnson, a friend who later founded the Small House Society, asked Shafer to build him a similar home, and Tumbleweed Tiny House Company was born.

Shafer and his company have been featured in *This Old House* magazine, *The New York Times*, *USA Today*, *Time*, *The Los Angeles Times*, *The Wall Street Journal*, numerous public radio programs, and *The Oprah Winfrey Show*. He has sold more than a dozen homes and 50 sets of plans for the different models on view at his Web site; plans cost about $1,000 a set and the houses cost from $20,000 to $90,000 to build (the services of a professional contractor are recommended). Shafer also conducts workshops on tiny-house living, sometimes travels around the country with his house, and maintains a blog and active discussion board on his Web site.

He has big plans for Tumbleweed, but rapid expansion doesn't fit his very personal business philosophy. "We are still in our infancy and still building our foundation for growth," he explains on his Web site. "We have a business plan that we are adhering to. Everything in due time." Among his future dreams are finding partners to represent Tumbleweed homes (real estate license required), partners to build them (licensed contractors only need apply), and makers of products like solar panels and lumber for incorporation into his homes (but nothing that would require redesigning any Tumbleweed products). In the long term, Shafer would even like to see a whole village of Tumbleweed homes, "even if it's just three houses." For now, though, like its products, Tumbleweed remains a small and very carefully built affair.[26]

For more information about this company, go to http://www.tumbleweedhouses.com.

Questions

1. Do you think Shafer's plan to grow his small business slowly is a good one? Why or why not?
2. What economic and social factors seem to have aided Tumbleweed's success so far? Which potential business challenges should Shafer consider as he plans for the future?
3. Do you think a company like Tumbleweed could go global? Why or why not?

Building Skills for Career Success

❶ JOURNALING FOR SUCCESS

Discovery statement: One of the objectives in this chapter was to make you aware of the advantages and disadvantages of owning a franchise.

Assignment

1. Assume that after evaluating your skills, experience, and financial situation, you have decided to purchase a franchise in your community. Identify and describe sources where you can obtain information on what the franchise package should contain.
2. List at least five reasons why you should choose franchising rather than starting a new, independent business.
3. Identify issues you need to be aware of as a franchisee.
4. Make a list of possible advantages and disadvantages of the franchise you are considering. What are your rights and your obligations as a franchisee?

❷ EXPLORING THE INTERNET

Perhaps the most challenging difficulty for small businesses is operating with scarce resources, especially people and money. To provide information and point small-business operators in the right direction, many Internet sites offer helpful products and services. Although most are sponsored by advertising and may be free of charge, some charge a fee, and others are a combination of both. The SBA within the U.S. Department of Commerce provides a wide array of free information and resources. You can find your way to the SBA through http://www.sbaonline.sba.gov or http://www.sba.gov. Visit the text Web site for updates to this exercise.

Assignment

1. Describe the various services provided by the SBA site.
2. What sources of funding are there?
3. What service would you like to see improved? How?

❸ DEVELOPING CRITICAL-THINKING SKILLS

Small businesses play a vital role in our economy. They not only contribute to technological innovation and to the creation of many new jobs but also ensure that customers have an alternative to the products and services offered by large firms. In addition, by making parts for large firms at a lower cost than the large firms could make the parts themselves, they help to keep the lid on consumer prices. Regardless of our need for them, many small businesses fail within their first five years. Why is this so?

Assignment

1. Identify several successful small businesses in your community.
2. Identify one small business that has failed.
3. Gather enough information about those businesses to answer the following questions:
   a. What role do small businesses play in your community?
   b. Why are they important?
   c. Why did the business fail?
   d. What was the most important reason for its failure?
   e. How might the business have survived?
4. Summarize what you have learned about the impact of small businesses on your community. Give the summary to your instructor.

❹ BUILDING TEAM SKILLS

A business plan is a written statement that documents the nature of a business and how that business intends to achieve its goals. Although entrepreneurs should prepare a business plan *before* starting a business, the plan also serves as an effective guide later on. The plan should concisely describe the business's mission, the amount of capital it requires, its target market, competition, resources, production plan, marketing plan, organizational plan, assessment of risk, and financial plan.

Assignment

1. Working in a team of four students, identify a company in your community that would benefit from using a business plan, or create a scenario in which a hypothetical entrepreneur wants to start a business.
2. Using the resources of the library or the Internet and/or interviews with business owners, write a business plan incorporating the information in Table 5.4.
3. Present your business plan to the class.

❺ RESEARCHING DIFFERENT CAREERS

Many people dream of opening and operating their own businesses. Are you one of them? To be successful, entrepreneurs must have certain characteristics; their profiles generally differ from those of people who work for someone else. Do you know which personal characteristics make some entrepreneurs succeed and others fail? Do you fit the successful entrepreneur's profile? What is your potential for opening and operating a successful small business?

Assignment

1. Use the resources of the library or the Internet to establish what a successful entrepreneur's profile is and to determine whether your personal characteristics fit that profile. Internet addresses that can help you are http://www.smartbiz.com/sbs/arts/ieb1.html and http://www.sba.gov (see "Start your Business" and "FAQ"). These sites have quizzes online that can help you to assess your personal characteristics. The SBA also has helpful brochures.
2. Interview several small-business owners. Ask them to describe the characteristics they think are necessary for being a successful entrepreneur.
3. Using your findings, write a report that includes the following:
   a. A profile of a successful small-business owner
   b. A comparison of your personal characteristics with the profile of the successful entrepreneur
   c. A discussion of your potential as a successful small-business owner

Running a Business PART 2

Graeter's

Graeter's: A Fourth-Generation Family Business

Graeter's, headquartered in Cincinnati, is a small, privately owned fourth-generation family business that has been making premium ice cream for about 140 years. Though the company has grown and expanded, particularly in the last ten years (it is now worth $20 million), its small-batch manufacturing remains similar to an original handmade process, and each machine still churns out only about two gallons every 20 minutes. Compared to the competition, which mass produces its ice cream, Graeter's takes time with every batch and packs it by hand. Two brothers and a cousin, all great-grandsons of the founders, share responsibility for the firm's day-to-day operations and its future direction.

"Even though I have the title of CEO, in a family business titles don't mean a whole lot," says CEO Richard Graeter II. "The functions that I am doing now as CEO, I was doing as executive vice president for years . . . . It really was and remains a partnership with my two cousins . . . . Our fathers brought us into the business at an early age . . . . One summer I was on the maintenance crew, another summer I worked at the store, another summer I worked up in the bakery, and my cousins all did the same thing. We were just around this business all of our lives. I think most important is we saw our fathers and their dedication and the fact that, you know, they came home later, they came home tired, they got up early and went to work before we ever got up to go to school in the morning, and you see that dedication and appreciate that—that is what keeps your business going."

GROWING THE BUSINESS

From one small store in 1870, Graeter's has expanded to a few dozen small stores in Ohio, Kentucky, Indiana, Texas, and Colorado; an online retail operation that ships ice cream overnight to 48 states; and multi-state distribution to about 1,700 supermarkets through big supermarket chains like Kroger's. The kitchen in the back of the original store has grown to three factories; the newest is an $11 million Cincinnati plant being built to support the expanded distribution the company is planning. Because the new factory will create 50 new jobs, the city helped pay for the land and lent money for the construction.

What Graeter's no longer has, however, is a franchise operation. It had licensed a handful of franchise operators over the past 20 years, which were quite successful, and at one time the owners thought of franchising as a good expansion strategy. One franchise operation had even opened its own factory. Recently, however, the company repurchased all the stores of its last remaining franchisee. "When you think about Graeter's," says the CEO, "the core of Graeter's is the quality of the product. You can't franchise your core. So by franchising our manufacturing, that created substantial risk for the organization, because the customer doesn't know that it is a franchise . . . . They know it is Graeter's. . . . You really have to rely on the intention and goodwill of the individual franchisees to make the product the way you would make it, and that is not an easy thing to guarantee."[27]

Questions

1. Graeter's current management team—Richard, Robert, and Chip Graeter—took the business over from their parents, who did not have a formal succession plan in place to indicate who would do what. Do you think the current team should have such a plan specifying who is to step into the business, when, and with what responsibilities? Why or why not?
2. Graeter's has recently hired management consultants to help improve its hiring and training processes and especially to assist in the continued expansion of its distribution chain. "I think my cousins and I all have come to realize we can't do it alone," says the CEO. Why do you think the management team made this decision? Does bringing these outsiders into the firm make Graeter's less of a family company than it has been?
3. Do you think Graeter's made the right decision to close its franchise operation? Why or why not?

Building a Business Plan PART 2

To access the online *Interactive Business Plan*, go to www.cengagebrain.com.

After reading Part 2, "Business Ownership and Entrepreneurship," you should be ready to tackle the company and industry component of your business plan. In this section, you will provide information about the background of the company, choice of the legal business form, information on the product or services to be offered, and descriptions of potential customers, current competitors, and the business's future. Chapter 4 in your textbook, "Choosing a Form of Business Ownership," and Chapter 5, "Small Business, Entrepreneurship, and Franchises," can help you to answer some of the questions in this part of the business plan.

THE COMPANY AND INDUSTRY COMPONENT

The company and industry analysis should include the answers to at least the following questions:

2.1. What is the legal form of your business? Is your business a sole proprietorship, a partnership, or a corporation?
2.2. What licenses or permits will you need, if any?
2.3. Is your business a new independent business, a takeover, an expansion, or a franchise?
2.4. If you are dealing with an existing business, how did your company get to the point where it is today?
2.5. What does your business do, and how does it satisfy customers' needs?
2.6. How did you choose and develop the products or services to be sold, and how are they different from those currently on the market?
2.7. What industry do you operate in, and what are the industry-wide trends?
2.8. Who are the major competitors in your industry?
2.9. Have any businesses recently entered or exited? Why did they leave?
2.10. Why will your business be profitable, and what are your growth opportunities?
2.11. Does any part of your business involve e-business?

REVIEW OF BUSINESS PLAN ACTIVITIES

Make sure to check the information you have collected, make any changes, and correct any weaknesses before beginning Part 3. *Reminder:* Review the answers to questions in the preceding part to make sure that all your answers are consistent throughout the business plan. Finally, write a summary statement that incorporates all the information for this part of the business plan.

The information contained in "Building a Business Plan" will also assist you in completing the online *Interactive Business Plan.*

PART 3

Management and Organization

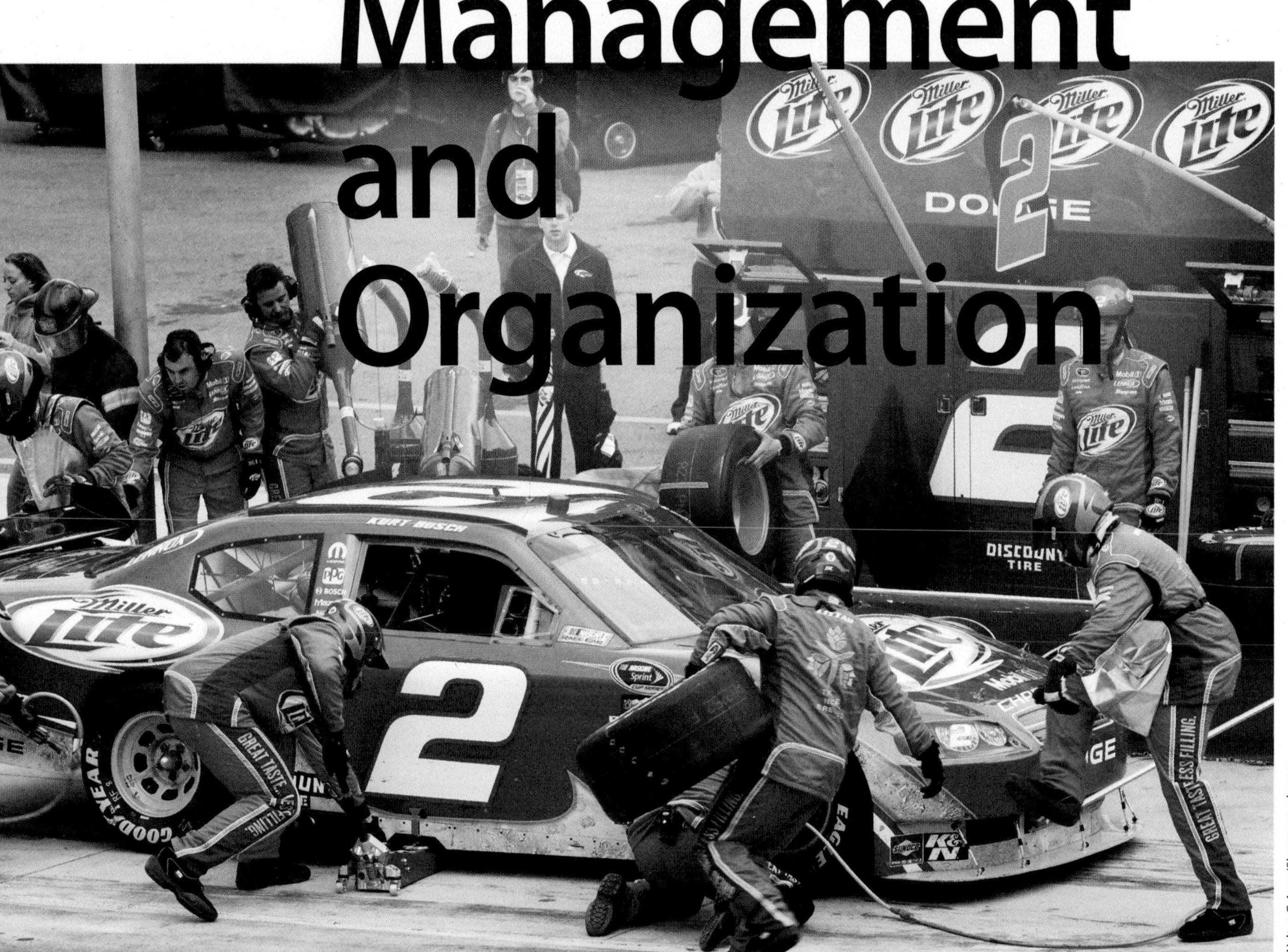

© Walter G Arce/Shutterstock.com

This part of the book deals with the organization—the "thing" that is a business. We begin with a discussion of the management functions involved in developing and operating a business. Next, we analyze the organization's elements and structure. Then we consider a firm's operations that are related to the production of goods and services.

Understanding the Management Process

6

© Monkey Business Images/Shutterstock.com

Learning Objectives

What you will be able to do once you complete this chapter:

1. Define what management is.
2. Describe the four basic management functions: planning, organizing, leading and motivating, and controlling.
3. Distinguish among the various kinds of managers in terms of both level and area of management.
4. Identify the key management skills of successful managers.
5. Explain the different types of leadership.
6. Discuss the steps in the managerial decision-making process.
7. Describe how organizations benefit from total quality management.

inside business

Procter & Gamble Succeeds Through Excellent Management

For decades, the five values of integrity, leadership, ownership, trust, and a passion for winning have guided the management of Procter & Gamble (P&G) toward long-term success. The Cincinnati-based company was founded in 1837 by William Procter and his brother-in-law, James Gamble, as a manufacturer of candles and soap. Today, P&G has grown into an $80 billion corporation with 135,000 employees worldwide and more than 100 brands, 22 of which each bring in more than $1 billion in annual sales. Soaps such as Ivory and Safeguard remain an important part of P&G's global empire, along with other well-known brands such as Bounty, Crest, Iams, Pampers, and Tide.

During good times and bad, facing crisis or opportunity, P&G's managers have relied on the company's five values, as well as on their expertise and experience, to make decisions and plans that keep sales and profits growing. Managers at all levels aim for a high level of personal and professional leadership. They understand the importance of acting ethically and believe in being held accountable for their actions. They also strive to maintain P&G's competitive advantage by continuously innovating to meet the needs of customers today and tomorrow.

When CEO Robert McDonald set the aggressive goal of extending the company's reach to serve one billion additional consumers by 2015, he and his managers formulated a variety of short- and long-term plans to achieve that goal. One plan calls for developing a higher number of new products and introducing them more quickly than in the past. Another plan details how the company will digitize documents to improve communications and get data more quickly to decision makers all over the world. In addition, managers for each brand and each country's operations have their own plans for expanding sales and attracting new customers.

To ensure continued success, P&G's top 42 executives meet every week to dissect the company's results, review future plans, and identify problem areas for immediate management attention. The executive team closely tracks the performance of the corporation's most promising middle managers and senior managers—throughout the world—and plans future assignments to round out these leaders' skills and knowledge to keep P&G growing in the decades to come.[1]

FYI

Did You Know?

Procter & Gamble employs 135,000 people worldwide, rings up $80 billion in annual revenue, and owns 22 billion-dollar brands.

The leadership employed at Procter & Gamble illustrates that management can be one of the most exciting and rewarding professions available today. Depending on its size, a firm may employ a number of specialized managers who are responsible for particular areas of management, such as marketing, finance, and operations. That same organization also includes managers at several levels within the firm. In this chapter, we define *management* and describe the four basic management functions of planning, organizing, leading and motivating, and controlling. Then we focus on the types of managers with respect to levels of responsibility and areas of expertise. Next, we focus on the skills of effective managers and the different roles managers must play. We examine several styles of leadership and explore the process by which managers make decisions. We also describe how total quality management can improve customer satisfaction.

1

Define what management is.

What Is Management?

Management is the process of coordinating people and other resources to achieve the goals of an organization. As we saw in Chapter 1, most organizations make use of four kinds of resources: material, human, financial, and informational (see Figure 6.1).

Material resources are the tangible, physical resources an organization uses. For example, General Motors uses steel, glass, and fiberglass to produce cars and trucks on complex machine-driven assembly lines. A college or university uses books, classroom buildings, desks, and computers to educate students. And the Mayo Clinic uses beds, operating room equipment, and diagnostic machines to provide health care.

Perhaps the most important resources of any organization are its *human resources*—people. In fact, some firms live by the philosophy that their employees are their most important assets. One such firm is Southwest Airlines. Southwest treats its employees with the same respect and attention it gives its passengers. Southwest selectively seeks employees with upbeat attitudes and promotes from within 80 percent of the time. In decision making, everyone who will be affected is encouraged to get involved in the process. In an industry in which deregulation, extreme price competition, and fluctuating fuel costs have eliminated several major competitors, Southwest keeps growing and making a profit because of its employees. Many experts would agree with Southwest's emphasis on employees. Some managers believe that the way employees are developed and managed may have more impact on an organization than other vital components such as marketing, sound financial decisions about large expenditures, production, or use of technology.

management the process of coordinating people and other resources to achieve the goals of an organization

Financial resources are the funds an organization uses to meet its obligations to investors and creditors. A 7-Eleven convenience store obtains money from customers at the checkout counters and uses a portion of that money to pay its suppliers. Citicorp, a large New York bank, borrows and lends money. Your college obtains money in the form of tuition, income from its endowments, and state and federal grants. It uses the money to pay utility bills, insurance premiums, and professors' salaries.

Human resources. In most organizations, effective management of human resources is absolutely critical.

Finally, many organizations increasingly find that they cannot afford to ignore *information*. External environmental conditions—including the economy, consumer markets, technology, politics, and cultural forces—are all changing so rapidly that a business that does not adapt probably will not survive. To adapt to change, the business must know what is changing and how it is changing. Most companies gather information about their competitors to increase their knowledge about changes in their industry and to learn from other companies' failures and successes.

Figure 6.1 The Four Main Resources of Management

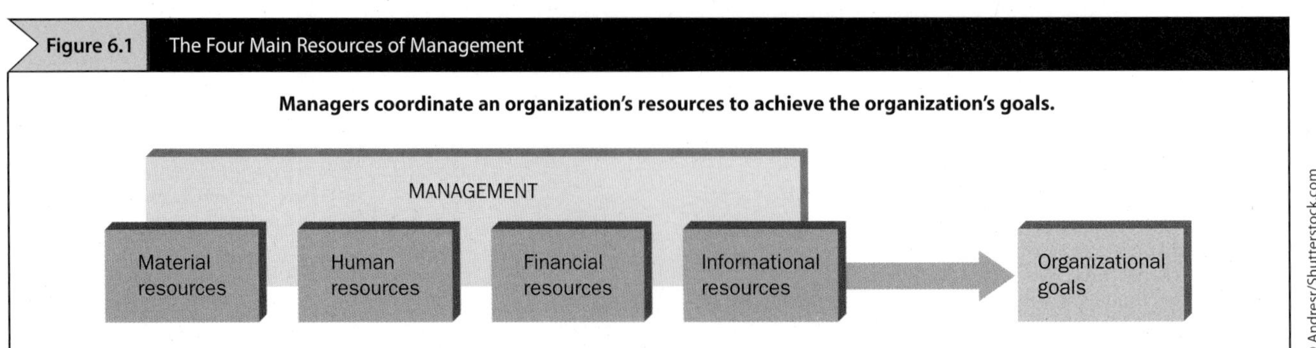

It is important to realize that the four types of resources described earlier are only general categories of resources. Within each category are hundreds or thousands of more specific resources. It is this complex mix of specific resources—and not simply "some of each" of the four general categories—that managers must coordinate to produce goods and services.

Another interesting way to look at management is in terms of the different functions managers perform. These functions have been identified as planning, organizing, leading and motivating employees, and controlling. We look at each of these management functions in the next section.

Basic Management Functions

2

Describe the four basic management functions: planning, organizing, leading and motivating, and controlling.

Pharmaceutical company Eli Lilly recently made a decision to focus on the emerging market of China. The company reorganized its structure so that one of its six units would handle emerging markets, doubled its employee count from 1,100 to 2,200, and began construction on a second manufacturing plant in Suzhou, China. The company also implemented a partnering strategy in China to handle research and development. Eli Lilly's key strategies include maximizing their core assets, accelerating new product launches, capitalizing on longer product life-cycles in areas like China, and establishing local alliances to access fast-growing market segments.[2]

Management functions such as those just described do not occur according to some rigid, preset timetable. Managers do not plan in January, organize in February, lead and motivate in March, and control in April. At any given time, managers may engage in a number of functions simultaneously. However, each function tends to lead naturally to others. Figure 6.2 provides a visual framework for a more detailed discussion of the four basic management functions. How well managers perform these key functions determines whether a business is successful.

Planning

Planning, in its simplest form, is establishing organizational goals and deciding how to accomplish them. It is often referred to as the "first" management function because all other management functions depend on planning. Organizations such as Starbucks, Houston Community Colleges, and Facebook begin the planning process by developing a mission statement.

An organization's **mission** is a statement of the basic purpose that makes that organization different from others. Starbucks' mission statement, for example, is "to inspire and nurture the human spirit—one person, one cup, and one neighborhood at a time." Houston Community College's mission is to provide an education for local citizens. Facebook's mission statement is "to give people the power to share and make the world more open and connected."[3] Once an organization's mission has been described in a mission statement, the next step is to engage in strategic planning.

Figure 6.2 The Management Process

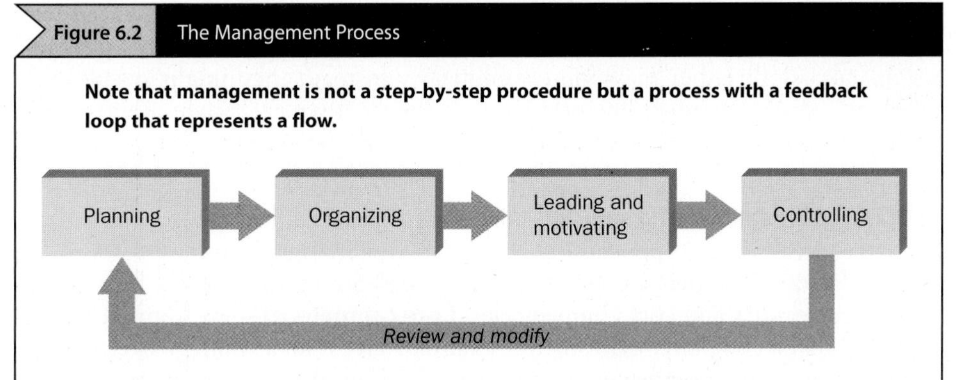

planning establishing organizational goals and deciding how to accomplish them

mission a statement of the basic purpose that makes an organization different from others

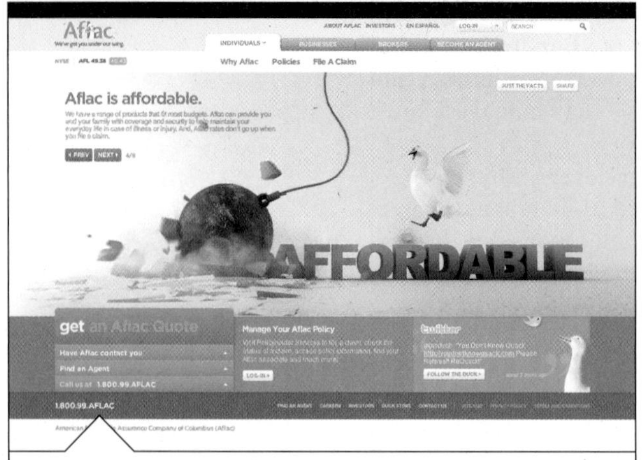

Mission statement. The mission statement of Aflac Insurance is "to combine aggressive strategic marketing with quality products and services at competitive prices to provide the best insurance value for consumers."

Strategic Planning Process The **strategic planning process** involves establishing an organization's major goals and objectives and allocating resources to achieve them. Top management is responsible for strategic planning, although customers, products, competitors, and company resources are some of the factors that are analyzed in the strategic planning process.

In today's rapidly changing business environment, constant internal or external changes may necessitate changes in a company's goals, mission, or strategy. The time line for strategic plans is generally one to two years and can be as long as ten years. Strategic plans should be flexible and include action items, such as outlining how plans will be implemented.

Establishing Goals and Objectives A **goal** is an end result that an organization is expected to achieve over a one- to ten-year period. An **objective** is a specific statement detailing what the organization intends to accomplish over a shorter period of time.

Goals and objectives can deal with a variety of factors, such as sales, company growth, costs, customer satisfaction, and employee morale. Whereas a small manufacturer may focus primarily on sales objectives for the next six months, a large firm may be more interested in goals that impact several years in the future. Starbucks, for example, has established several goals under its "Shared Planet" program to be completed in the next few years, specifically in the areas of ethical sourcing, environmental stewardship, and community involvement. By 2015, Starbucks hopes to purchase 100 percent of its coffee from ethical sources or farmers who grow their coffee responsibly without permanently harming the environment. The company also hopes to combat climate change by encouraging farmers to prevent deforestation through the use of incentive programs. Starbucks hopes to develop a recyclable cup by 2012. Also, the company hopes to use their stores to lead volunteer programs in each store's community.[4] Finally, goals are set at every level of an organization. Every member of an organization—the president of the company, the head of a department, and an operating employee at the lowest level—has a set of goals that he or she hopes to achieve.

The goals developed for these different levels must be consistent. However, it is likely that some conflict will arise. A production department, for example, may have a goal of minimizing costs. One way to do this is to produce only one type of product and offer "no frills." Marketing may have a goal of maximizing sales. One way to implement this goal is to offer customers a wide range of products and options. As part of goal setting, the manager who is responsible for *both* departments must achieve some sort of balance between conflicting goals. This balancing process is called *optimization.*

The optimization of conflicting goals requires insight and ability. Faced with the marketing-versus-production conflict just described, most managers probably would not adopt either viewpoint completely. Instead, they might decide on a reasonably diverse product line offering only the most widely sought-after options. Such a compromise would seem to be best for the whole organization.

SWOT Analysis **SWOT analysis** is the identification and evaluation of a firm's strengths, weaknesses, opportunities, and threats. Strengths and weaknesses are internal factors that affect a company's capabilities. Strengths refer to a firm's favorable characteristics and core competencies. **Core competencies** are approaches and processes that a company performs well that may give it an advantage over its competitors. These core competencies may help the firm attract financial and human

strategic planning process the establishment of an organization's major goals and objectives and the allocation of resources to achieve them

goal an end result that an organization is expected to achieve over a one- to ten-year period

objective a specific statement detailing what an organization intends to accomplish over a shorter period of time

SWOT analysis the identification and evaluation of a firm's strengths, weaknesses, opportunities, and threats

core competencies approaches and processes that a company performs well that may give it an advantage over its competitors

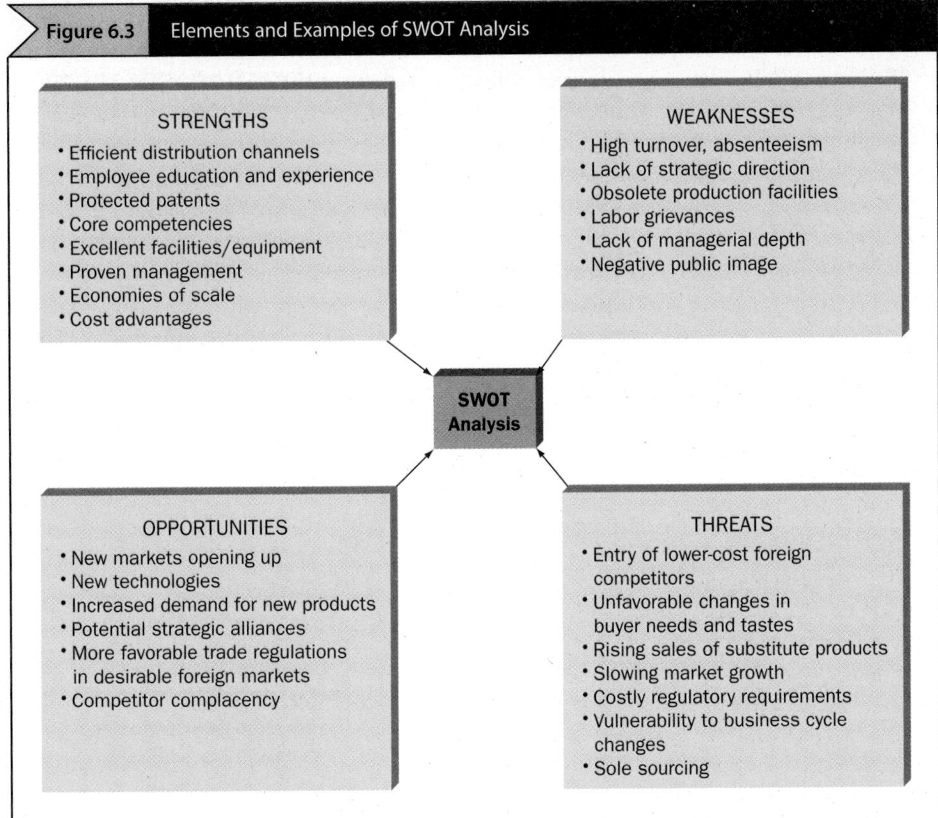

resources and be more capable of producing products that better satisfy customers. Weaknesses refer to any internal limitations a company faces in developing or implementing plans. At times, managers have difficulty identifying and understanding the negative effects of weaknesses in their organizations.

External opportunities and threats exist independently of the firm. Opportunities refer to favorable conditions in the environment that could produce rewards for the organization. That is, opportunities are situations that exist but must be exploited for the firm to benefit from them. Threats, on the other hand, are conditions or barriers that may prevent the firm from reaching its objectives. Opportunities and threats can stem from many sources within the business environment. For example, competitor's actions, new laws, economic changes, or new technology can be threats. Threats for some firms may be opportunities for others. Examples of strengths, weaknesses, opportunities, and threats are shown in Figure 6.3.

Types of Plans Once goals and objectives have been set for the organization, managers must develop plans for achieving them. A **plan** is an outline of the actions by which an organization intends to accomplish its goals and objectives. Just as it has different goals and objectives, the organization also develops several types of plans, as shown in Figure 6.4.

Resulting from the strategic planning process, an organization's **strategic plan** is its broadest plan, developed as a guide for major policy setting and decision-making. Strategic plans are set by the board of directors and top management and are generally designed to achieve the organization's long-term goals. Thus, a firm's strategic plan defines what business the company is in or wants to be in and the kind of company it is or wants to be. When top management at the world's biggest retailer, Walmart, wanted to manage their stores more efficiently, they decided to focus on three priorities—growth, leverage, and returns—in order to provide more value for customers and shareholders. First, management consolidated the company's logistics, real estate, and store operations. Then, stores in the United

plan an outline of the actions by which an organization intends to accomplish its goals and objectives

strategic plan an organization's broadest plan, developed as a guide for major policy setting and decision making

Figure 6.4 Types of Plans

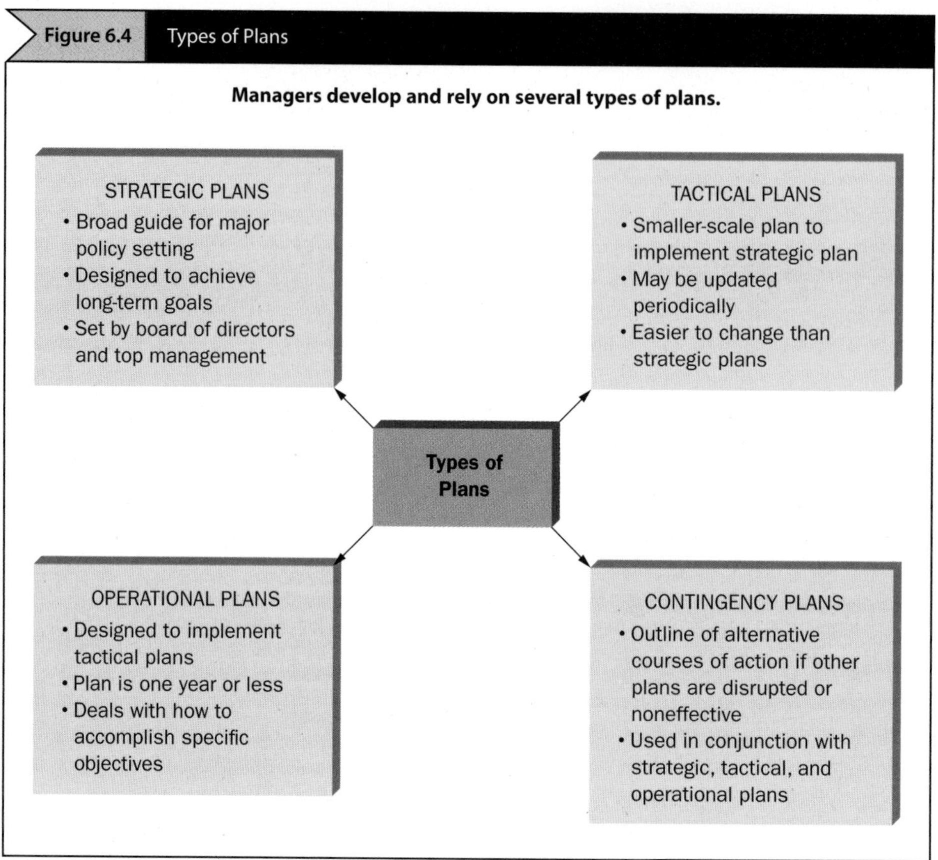

States were divided into three new business units: Walmart West, Walmart South, and Walmart North. Finally, a new division called Global.com was created to regulate global e-commerce and business. This long-term strategy has been adopted to facilitate the company's future growth as it expands.[5]

The Internet has challenged traditional strategic thinking. For example, reluctant to move from a face-to-face sales approach to a less personal Web site approach, Allstate has created an Internet presence to support its established sales force.

In addition to strategic plans, most organizations also employ several narrower kinds of plans. A **tactical plan** is a smaller scale plan developed to implement a strategy. Most tactical plans cover a one- to three-year period. If a strategic plan will take five years to complete, the firm may develop five tactical plans, one covering each year. Tactical plans may be updated periodically as dictated by conditions and experience. Their more limited scope permits them to be changed more easily than strategies. Volkswagen, for example, recently began constructing a new assembly plant in Guangzhou, China. The 300,000-unit plant is expected to begin operations in 2013, and is expected to increase Volkswagen's sales and market penetration in southern China, which is currently dominated by Toyota, Honda, and Nissan. This tactical plan is part of Volkwagen's recent strategic plan to achieve annual sales of more than 2 million units in southern China by 2018. China is currently Volkwagen's largest market, with nearly 1.5 million units of annual sales, more than the company's market in Germany or the United States. The automobile manufacturer hopes that this newest assembly plant will help Volkswagen achieve its long-term goal.[6]

tactical plan a smaller scale plan developed to implement a strategy

operational plan a type of plan designed to implement tactical plans

An **operational plan** is a type of plan designed to implement tactical plans. Operational plans are usually established for one year or less and deal with how to accomplish the organization's specific objectives. Procter & Gamble has adopted the *Go-to-Market plan* in order to speed up the availability of products to retailers and thus to consumers. The strategic and tactical plans have been kept in mind in

Going for SUCCESS

Be Prepared with a Contingency Plan

Managers have to be prepared for all kinds of twists and turns as they move their organizations toward the future in today's highly dynamic business environment. Strategic, tactical, and operational plans are vital for keeping the company on track toward its long-term and short-term goals. However, the future doesn't always unfold the way managers expect. That's why successful companies formulate a variety of contingency plans to deal with possible problems due to economic volatility, extreme weather conditions, prolonged power outages, a pandemic, fire or flood, or other major challenges.

The Danish toymaker Lego, for example, has used contingency plans to effectively adapt to a range of economic circumstances. First, its top managers take a close look at several possible economic scenarios and estimate how each might disrupt Lego's performance. Next, they create contingency plans to minimize the disruption under each scenario. Then every month, the managers meet to review key economic indicators, examine Lego's performance in the context of these trends, and determine whether and when to put one of their contingency plans into operation. Thanks to good contingency planning, Lego has been able to preserve profits even during periods of economic turmoil.

Sources: Joann S. Lublin and Dana Mattioli, "Strategic Plans Lose Favor," *The Wall Street Journal*, January 25, 2010, http://www.wsj.com; "Managing in the Fog," *The Economist*, February 28, 2009, 67–68; Phyllis Furman, "In Case of Emergency: Business Contingency Plan Needed," *New York Daily News*, July 27, 2009, http://www.nydailynews.com/money/2009/07/27/2009-07-27_getting_ready_for_the_day_after.html?page=0.

order to achieve this plan. It includes making significant changes in the way that Procter & Gamble distributes its products.[7]

Regardless of how hard managers try, sometimes business activities do not go as planned. Today, most corporations also develop contingency plans along with strategies, tactical plans, and operational plans. A **contingency plan** is a plan that outlines alternative courses of action that may be taken if an organization's other plans are disrupted or become ineffective.

Organizing the Enterprise

After goal setting and planning, the manager's second major function is organization. **Organizing** is the grouping of resources and activities to accomplish some end result in an efficient and effective manner. Consider the case of an inventor who creates a new product and goes into business to sell it. At first, the inventor will do everything on his or her own—purchase raw materials, make the product, advertise it, sell it, and keep business records. Eventually, as business grows, the inventor will need help. To begin with, he or she might hire a professional sales representative and a part-time bookkeeper. Later, it also might be necessary to hire sales staff, people to assist with production, and an accountant. As the inventor hires new personnel, he or she must decide what each person will do, to whom each person will report, and how each person can best take part in the organization's activities. We discuss these and other facets of the organizing function in much more detail in Chapter 7.

Leading and Motivating

The leading and motivating function is concerned with the human resources within an organization. Specifically, **leading** is the process of influencing people to work toward a common goal. **Motivating** is the process of providing reasons for people to work in the best interests of an organization. Together, leading and motivating are often referred to as **directing**.

We have already noted the importance of an organization's human resources. Because of this importance, leading and motivating are critical activities. Obviously, different people do things for different reasons—that is, they have

contingency plan a plan that outlines alternative courses of action that may be taken if an organization's other plans are disrupted or become ineffective

organizing the grouping of resources and activities to accomplish some end result in an efficient and effective manner

leading the process of influencing people to work toward a common goal

motivating the process of providing reasons for people to work in the best interests of an organization

directing the combined processes of leading and motivating

Creating a satisfying work environment. At Google's Kirkland Washington facility, employees eat for free.

different *motivations*. Some are interested primarily in earning as much money as they can. Others may be spurred on by opportunities to get promoted. Part of a manager's job, then, is to determine what factors motivate workers and to try to provide those incentives to encourage effective performance. Jeffrey R. Immelt, GE's chairperson and CEO, has worked to transform GE into a leader in essential themes tied to world development, such as emerging markets, environmental solutions, demographics, and digital connections. He believes in giving freedom to his teams and wants them to come up with their own solutions. However, he does not hesitate to intervene if the situation demands. He believes that a leader's primary role is to teach, and he makes people feel that he is willing to share what he has learned. Immelt also laid the vision for GE's ambitious "ecomagination initiative" and has been named one of the "World's Best CEOs" three times by *Barron's*.[8] A lot of research has been done on both motivation and leadership. As you will see in Chapter 10, research on motivation has yielded very useful information. However, research on leadership has been less successful. Despite decades of study, no one has discovered a general set of personal traits or characteristics that makes a good leader. Later in this chapter, we discuss leadership in more detail.

Controlling Ongoing Activities

Controlling is the process of evaluating and regulating ongoing activities to ensure that goals are achieved. To see how controlling works, consider a rocket launched by NASA to place a satellite in orbit. Do NASA personnel simply fire the rocket and then check back in a few days to find out whether the satellite is in place? Of course not. The rocket is monitored constantly, and its course is regulated and adjusted as needed to get the satellite to its destination.

The control function includes three steps (see Figure 6.5). The first is *setting standards* with which performance can be compared. The second is *measuring*

controlling the process of evaluating and regulating ongoing activities to ensure that goals are achieved

Figure 6.5 The Control Function

The control function includes three steps: setting standards, measuring actual performance, and taking corrective action.

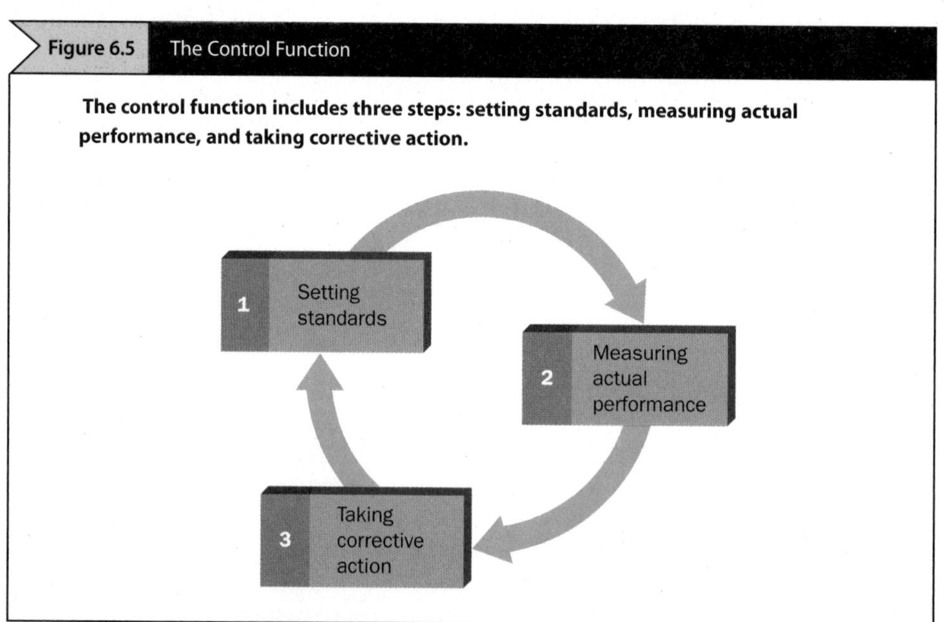

actual performance and comparing it with the standard. The third is *taking corrective action* as necessary. Notice that the control function is circular in nature. The steps in the control function must be repeated periodically until the goal is achieved. For example, suppose that Southwest Airlines establishes a goal of increasing profits by 12 percent. To ensure that this goal is reached, Southwest's management might monitor its profit on a monthly basis. After three months, if profit has increased by 3 percent, management might be able to assume that plans are going according to schedule. In this case, it is likely that no action will be taken. However, if profit has increased by only 1 percent after three months, some corrective action is needed to get the firm on track. The particular action that is required depends on the reason for the small increase in profit.

Kinds of Managers

3

Distinguish among the various kinds of managers in terms of both level and area of management.

Managers can be classified in two ways: according to their level within an organization and according to their area of management. In this section, we use both perspectives to explore the various types of managers.

Levels of Management

For the moment, think of an organization as a three-story structure (as illustrated in Figure 6.6). Each story corresponds to one of the three general levels of management: top managers, middle managers, and first-line managers.

Top Managers A **top manager** is an upper-level executive who guides and controls an organization's overall fortunes. Top managers constitute a small group. In terms of planning, they are generally responsible for developing the organization's mission. They also determine the firm's strategy. It takes years of hard work, long hours, and perseverance, as well as talent and no small share of good luck, to reach the ranks of top management in large companies. Common job titles associated with top managers are president, vice president, chief executive officer (CEO), and chief operating officer (COO).

Figure 6.6 Management Levels Found in Most Companies

The coordinated effort of all three levels of managers is required to implement the goals of any company.

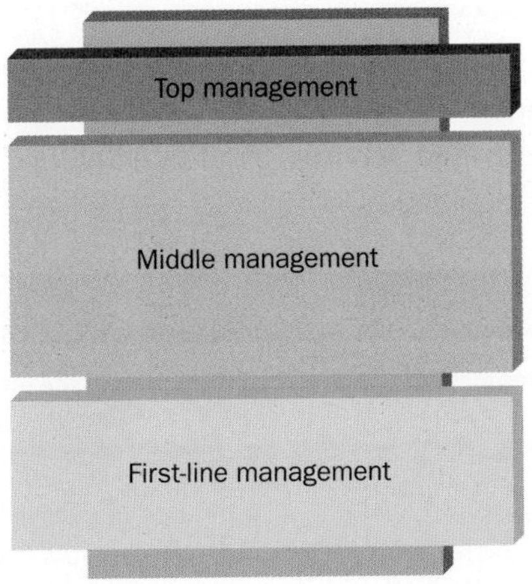

Top management

Middle management

First-line management

top manager an upper-level executive who guides and controls the overall fortunes of an organization

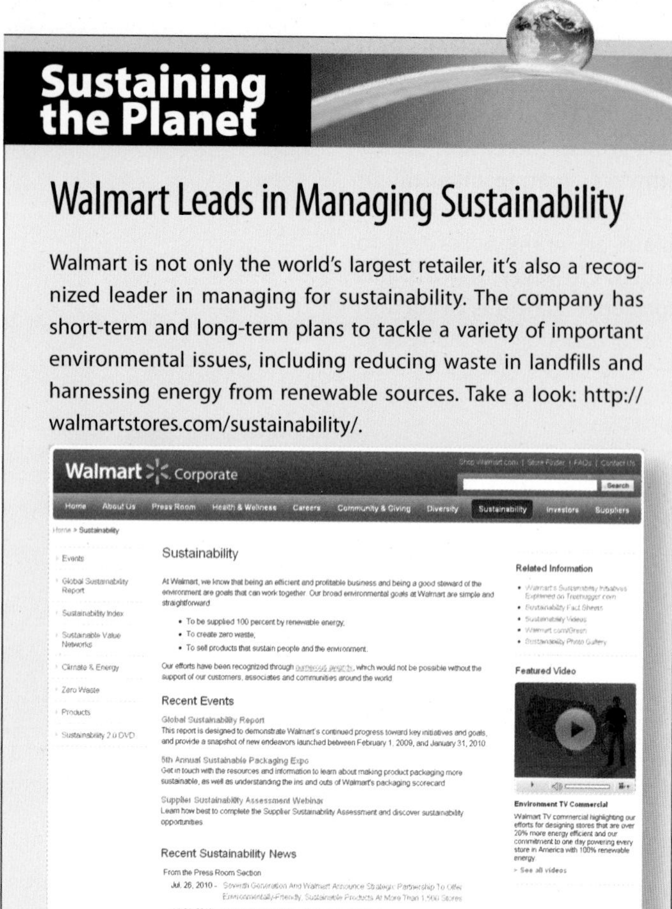

Middle Managers Middle managers probably make up the largest group of managers in most organizations. A **middle manager** is a manager who implements the strategy and major policies developed by top management. Middle managers develop tactical plans and operational plans, and they coordinate and supervise the activities of first-line managers. Titles at the middle-management level include division manager, department head, plant manager, and operations manager.

First-Line Managers A **first-line manager** is a manager who coordinates and supervises the activities of operating employees. First-line managers spend most of their time working with and motivating their employees, answering questions, and solving day-to-day problems. Most first-line managers are former operating employees who, owing to their hard work and potential, were promoted into management. Many of today's middle and top managers began their careers on this first management level. Common titles for first-line managers include office manager, supervisor, and foreman.

Areas of Management Specialization

Organizational structure can also be divided into areas of management specialization (see Figure 6.7). The most common areas are finance, operations, marketing, human resources, and administration. Depending on its mission, goals, and objectives, an organization may include other areas as well—research and development (R&D), for example.

middle manager a manager who implements the strategy and major policies developed by top management

first-line manager a manager who coordinates and supervises the activities of operating employees

financial manager a manager who is primarily responsible for an organization's financial resources

operations manager a manager who manages the systems that convert resources into goods and services

Financial Managers A **financial manager** is primarily responsible for an organization's financial resources. Accounting and investment are specialized areas within financial management. Because financing affects the operation of the entire firm, many of the CEOs and presidents of this country's largest companies are people who got their "basic training" as financial managers.

Operations Managers An **operations manager** manages the systems that convert resources into goods and services. Traditionally, operations management has

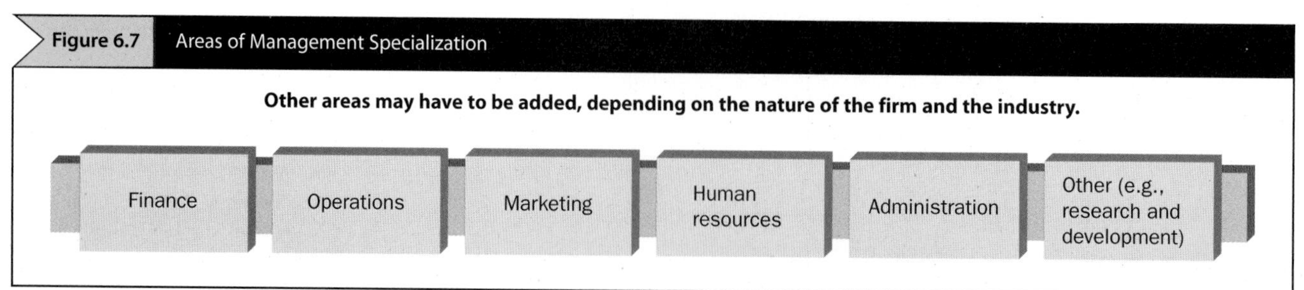

Figure 6.7 Areas of Management Specialization

been equated with manufacturing—the production of goods. However, in recent years, many of the techniques and procedures of operations management have been applied to the production of services and to a variety of nonbusiness activities. As with financial management, operations management has produced a large percentage of today's company CEOs and presidents.

Managers work in teams. Managers from various specializations work together in teams to generate favorable outcomes.

Marketing Managers A **marketing manager** is responsible for facilitating the exchange of products between an organization and its customers or clients. Specific areas within marketing are marketing research, product management, advertising, promotion, sales, and distribution. A sizable number of today's company presidents have risen from the ranks of marketing management.

Human Resources Managers A **human resources manager** is charged with managing an organization's human resources programs. He or she engages in human resources planning; designs systems for hiring, training, and evaluating the performance of employees; and ensures that the organization follows government regulations concerning employment practices. Some human resources managers make effective use of technology. For example, more than 1 million job openings are posted on Monster.com, which attracts about 15 million visitors monthly.[9]

Administrative Managers An **administrative manager** (also called a *general manager*) is not associated with any specific functional area but provides overall administrative guidance and leadership. A hospital administrator is an example of an administrative manager. He or she does not specialize in operations, finance, marketing, or human resources management but instead coordinates the activities of specialized managers in all these areas. In many respects, most top managers are really administrative managers.

Whatever their level in the organization and whatever area they specialize in, successful managers generally exhibit certain key skills and are able to play certain managerial roles. However, as we shall see, some skills are likely to be more critical at one level of management than at another.

marketing manager a manager who is responsible for facilitating the exchange of products between an organization and its customers or clients

human resources manager a person charged with managing an organization's human resources programs

Key Skills of Successful Managers

4

Identify the key management skills of successful managers.

As shown in Figure 6.8, managers need a variety of skills, including conceptual, analytic, interpersonal, technical, and communication skills.

Conceptual Skills

Conceptual skills involve the ability to think in abstract terms. Conceptual skills allow a manager to see the "big picture" and understand how the various parts of an organization or idea can fit together. These skills are useful in a wide range of situations, including the optimization of goals described earlier.

Analytic Skills

Employers expect managers to use **analytic skills** to identify problems correctly, generate reasonable alternatives, and select the "best" alternatives to solve problems. Top-level managers especially need these skills because they need to discern the important issues from the less important ones, as well as recognize the underlying

administrative manager a manager who is not associated with any specific functional area but who provides overall administrative guidance and leadership

conceptual skills the ability to think in abstract terms

analytic skills the ability to identify problems correctly, generate reasonable alternatives, and select the "best" alternatives to solve problems

Figure 6.8 Key Skills of Successful Managers

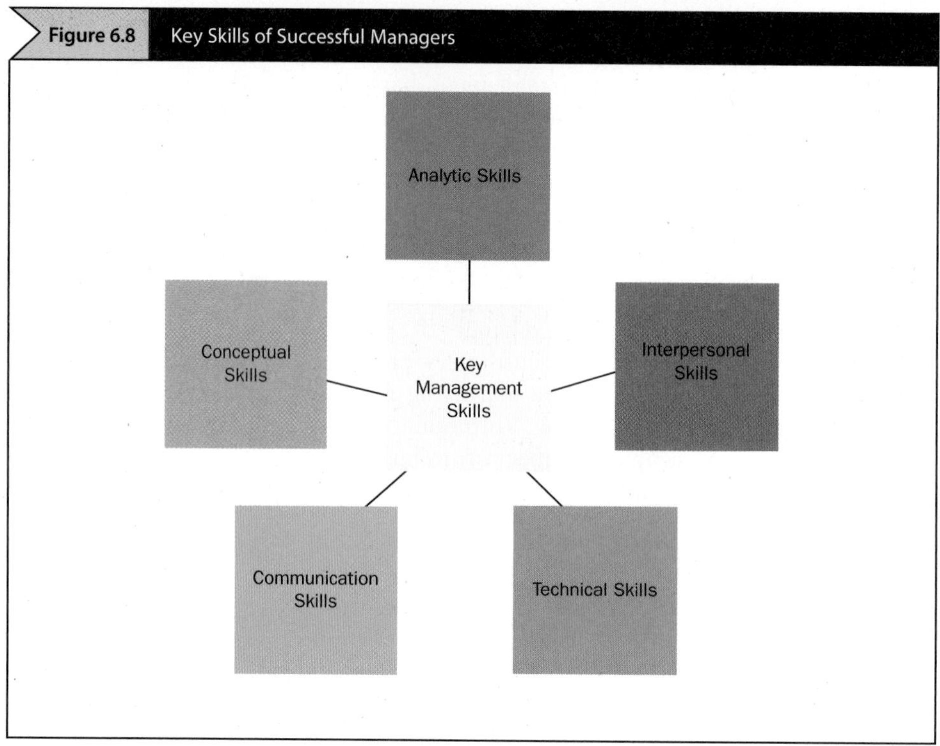

reasons for different situations. Managers who use these skills not only address a situation but also correct the initial event or problem that caused it to occur. Thus, these skills are vital to run a business efficiently and logically.

Interpersonal Skills

Interpersonal skills involve the ability to deal effectively with other people, both inside and outside an organization. Examples of interpersonal skills are the ability to relate to people, understand their needs and motives, and show genuine compassion. One reason why Steve Jobs, founder of Apple, has been so successful is his ability to motivate his employees and to inspire their loyalty to his vision for the firm. Although it is obvious that a CEO such as Steve Jobs must be able to work with employees throughout the organization, what is not so obvious is that middle and first-line managers must also possess interpersonal skills. For example, a first-line manager on an assembly line at Procter & Gamble must rely on employees to manufacture Tide detergent. The better the manager's interpersonal skills, the more likely the manager will be able to lead and motivate those employees. When all other things are equal, the manager who is able to exhibit these skills will be more successful than the arrogant and brash manager who does not care about others.

Technical Skills

Technical skills involve specific skills needed to accomplish a specialized activity. For example, the skills engineers and machinists need to do their jobs are technical skills. First-line managers (and, to a lesser extent, middle managers) need the technical skills relevant to the activities they manage. Although these managers may not perform the technical tasks themselves, they must be able to train subordinates, answer questions, and otherwise provide guidance and direction. A first-line manager in the accounting department of the Hyatt Corporation, for example, must be able to perform computerized accounting transactions and help employees complete the same accounting task. In general, top managers do

interpersonal skills the ability to deal effectively with other people

technical skills specific skills needed to accomplish a specialized activity

not rely on technical skills as heavily as managers at other levels. Still, understanding the technical side of a business is an aid to effective management at every level.

Communication Skills

Communication skills, both oral and written, involve the ability to speak, listen, and write effectively. Managers need both oral and written communication skills. Because a large part of a manager's day is spent conversing with others, the ability to speak *and* listen is critical. Oral communication skills are used when a manager makes sales presentations, conducts interviews, and holds press conferences. Written communication skills are important because a manager's ability to prepare letters, e-mails, memos, sales reports, and other written documents may spell the difference between success and failure. In order to further communicate within an organization, most managers should know how to use a computer to prepare written and statistical reports and to communicate with other managers and employees.

Managerial skills. An effective manager must be able to integrate and simultaneously employ several skills in order to be successful.

Leadership

5

Explain the different types of leadership.

Leadership has been defined broadly as the ability to influence others. A leader can use his or her power to affect the behavior of others. Leadership is different from management in that a leader strives for voluntary cooperation, whereas a manager may have to depend on coercion to change employee behavior.

communication skills the ability to speak, listen, and write effectively

leadership the ability to influence others

autocratic leadership task-oriented leadership style in which workers are told what to do and how to accomplish it; workers have no say in the decision-making process

Formal and Informal Leadership

Some experts make distinctions between formal leadership and informal leadership. Formal leaders have legitimate power of position. They have *authority* within an organization to influence others to work for the organization's objectives. Informal leaders usually have no such authority and may or may not exert their influence in support of the organization. Both formal and informal leaders make use of several kinds of power, including the ability to grant rewards or impose punishments, the possession of expert knowledge, and personal attraction or charisma. Informal leaders who identify with the organization's goals are a valuable asset to any organization. However, a business can be brought to its knees by informal leaders who turn work groups against management.

Styles of Leadership

For many years, leadership was viewed as a combination of personality traits, such as self-confidence, concern for people, intelligence, and dependability. Achieving a consensus on which traits were most important was difficult, however, so attention turned to styles of leadership behavior. In recent years, several styles of leadership have emerged, including *autocratic, participative,* and *entrepreneurial*.

Top management. Apple CEO, Steve Jobs, presents an iPhone 4 to Russian President Dmitry.

SPOTLIGHT

What Are the Top-Ranked Traits of Successful Female Leaders?

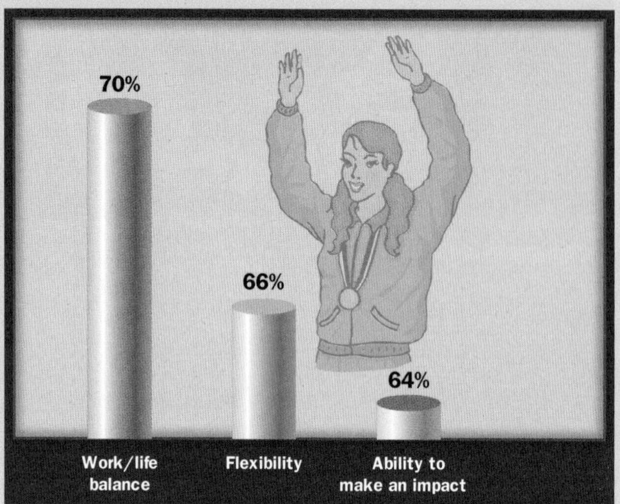

Source: Accenture survey of 1,000 full-time female workers 22–35 years old. Margin of error ±3 percentage points. Multiple responses allowed.

Autocratic leadership is very task oriented. Decisions are made confidently, with little concern about employee opinions. Employees are told exactly what is expected from them and given specific guidelines, rules, and regulations on how to achieve their tasks. At one time, managers at UPS used autocratic leadership. Managers at Hyundai USA also successfully employ the authoritarian leadership style.[10]

Participative leadership is common in today's business organizations. Participative leaders consult workers before making decisions. This helps workers understand which goals are important and fosters a sense of ownership and commitment to reach those goals. Participative leaders can be classified into three groups: consultative, consensus, and democratic. *Consultative leaders* discuss issues with workers but retain the final authority for decision making. *Consensus leaders* seek input from almost all workers and make final decisions based on their support. *Democratic leaders* give final authority to the group. They collect opinions and base their decisions on the vote of the group. Google co-founders Larry Page and Sergey Brin are known for their democratic decision-making styles.[11] Communication is active upward and downward in participative organizations. Coaching, collaborating, and negotiating are important skills for participative leaders.

participative leadership leadership style in which all members of a team are involved in identifying essential goals and developing strategies to reach those goals

entrepreneurial leadership personality-based leadership style in which the manager seeks to inspire workers with a vision of what can be accomplished to benefit all stakeholders

Entrepreneurial leadership is personality dependent. Although each entrepreneur is different, this leadership style is generally task-oriented, driven, charismatic, and enthusiastic.[12] The entrepreneurial personality tends to take initiative, venture into new areas, be visionary, and focus on the next deal. Their enthusiasm energizes and inspires their people. Entrepreneurial leaders take responsibility for the success or failure of their firm, and often don't understand why their employees don't always share their passion for their work.[13]

Leadership style. Apple CEO, Steve Jobs, has a leadership style that helps to create an environment that nurtures and enhances the creation of technology-based products, many of which become highly successful.

Which Leadership Style Is the Best?

Today, most management experts agree that no "best" managerial leadership style exists. Each of the styles described—autocratic, participative, and entrepreneurial—has advantages and disadvantages. Participative leadership can motivate employees to work effectively because they are implementing their own decisions. However, the decision-making process in participative leadership takes time that subordinates could be devoting to the work itself. Table 6.1 presents tips for effective leadership. Most of these tips are consistent with the participative leadership style.

Although hundreds of research studies have been conducted to prove which leadership style is best, there are no definite conclusions. The "best" leadership seems to occur when the leader's style matches the situation. Each of the leadership styles can be effective in the right situation. The *most* effective

Table 6.1	Tips for Successful Leadership
1.	Walk the talk. Make your actions consistent with your words.
2.	Be truthful, fair, and respectful, and honor confidences.
3.	Demonstrate a vision and values worth following.
4.	Co-workers make mistakes. So do you. Admit to them and learn from them.
5.	Be open to what others have to offer. Ask questions and take time to listen to co-workers.
6.	Know your weaknesses, so you can build a team to make up for them.
7.	All work and no fun can reduce productivity.
8.	Help workers do their best by encouraging them to grow and learn.
9.	Never publicly blame anyone but yourself.
10.	Stay positive and expect it of your people. Negativity leads downhill fast.
11.	Involve people in decisions—especially those regarding change.
12.	Be open to new ways of doing things. Embrace change—it's inevitable.
13.	Recognize and celebrate individual and team successes, both big and not so big.
14.	Embrace and benefit from diversity.
15.	Empower your workers. They will have greater self-respect, responsibility, and accountability.
16.	Take your work, but not yourself, seriously.

style depends on interaction among employees, characteristics of the work situation, and the manager's personality.

6

Discuss the steps in the managerial decision-making process.

Managerial Decision Making

Decision making is the act of choosing one alternative from a set of alternatives.[14] In ordinary situations, decisions are made casually and informally. We encounter a problem, mull it over, settle on a solution, and go on. Managers, however, require a more systematic method for solving complex problems. As shown in Figure 6.9, managerial decision making involves four steps: (1) identifying the problem or opportunity, (2) generating alternatives, (3) selecting an alternative, and (4) implementing and evaluating the solution.

Identifying the Problem or Opportunity

A **problem** is the discrepancy between an actual condition and a desired condition—the difference between what is occurring and what one wishes would occur. For example, a marketing manager at Campbell Soup Company has a problem if sales revenues for Campbell's Hungry Man frozen dinners are declining (the actual condition). To solve this problem, the marketing manager must take steps to increase sales revenues (desired condition). Most people consider a problem to be "negative;" however, a problem also can be "positive." A positive problem should be viewed as an "opportunity."

Although accurate identification of a problem is essential before it can be solved or turned into an opportunity, this stage of decision making creates many difficulties

Figure 6.9 Major Steps in the Managerial Decision-Making Process

Managers require a systematic method for solving problems in a variety of situations.

Identifying the problem or opportunity → Generating alternatives → Selecting an alternative → Implementing and evaluating the solution

decision making the act of choosing one alternative from a set of alternatives

problem the discrepancy between an actual condition and a desired condition

for managers. Sometimes managers' preconceptions of the problem prevent them from seeing the actual situation. They produce an answer before the proper question has been asked. In other cases, managers overlook truly significant issues by focusing on unimportant matters. Also, managers may mistakenly analyze problems in terms of symptoms rather than underlying causes.

Effective managers learn to look ahead so that they are prepared when decisions must be made. They clarify situations and examine the causes of problems, asking whether the presence or absence of certain variables alters a situation. Finally, they consider how individual behaviors and values affect the way problems or opportunities are defined.

Generating Alternatives

After a problem has been defined, the next task is to generate alternatives. The more important the decision, the more attention that must be devoted to this stage. Managers should be open to fresh, innovative ideas as well as obvious answers.

Certain techniques can aid in the generation of creative alternatives. Brainstorming, commonly used in group discussions, encourages participants to produce many new ideas. During brainstorming, other group members are not permitted to criticize or ridicule. Another approach, developed by the U.S. Navy, is called "Blast! Then Refine." Group members tackle a recurring problem by erasing all previous solutions and procedures. The group then re-evaluates its original objectives, modifies them if necessary, and devises new solutions. Other techniques—including trial and error—are also useful in this stage of decision making.

Selecting an Alternative

Final decisions are influenced by a number of considerations, including financial constraints, human and informational resources, time limits, legal obstacles, and political factors. Managers must select the alternative that will be most effective and practical. Starbucks, for example, was experiencing high profits a few years ago as it continued to expand to more than 17,000 stores. However, the recession eventually caught up with the company, as more of its customers turned to less expensive options offered by competition such as McDonald's and Dunkin' Donuts, and the costs of its numerous failing stores added up. In an effort to turn Starbucks around, Howard Schultz, the man who bought the first six stores in 1987, returned to the CEO position and rehired many of the original top management staff to help lead the company's renovation. Starbucks then began an extensive process of closing low-producing stores and laying off workers, as management tried to return the company's focus back to urban areas. New stores were no longer cookie cutouts of each other, but instead were each specifically targeted to their community, with the product offering and store appearance varying by location. Many new locations didn't even carry the Starbucks name, such as the 15th Avenue Coffee and Tea in Seattle. One year later, Starbucks' net income had nearly quadrupled as it began to see the effects of its changes.[15]

At times, two or more alternatives or some combination of alternatives will be equally appropriate. Managers may choose solutions to problems on several levels. The coined word *satisfice* describes solutions that are only adequate and not ideal. When lacking time or information, managers often make decisions that "satisfice." Whenever possible, managers should try to investigate alternatives carefully and select the ideal solution.

Implementing and Evaluating the Solution

Implementation of a decision requires time, planning, preparation of personnel, and evaluation of results. Managers usually deal with unforeseen consequences even when they have carefully considered the alternatives.

Ethical Challenges & SUCCESSFUL SOLUTIONS

Through Social Media, Do Workers Create Problems for Their Employers?

How should managers handle an employee's use of social media such as Twitter, blogs, and Facebook? Despite the growing popularity of tweeting, blogging, and connecting with others on Facebook, LinkedIn, and other sites, some companies are concerned that employees will inadvertently disclose proprietary information or become involved in controversial conversations that could harm the company's image. Another reason for discouraging social media use is to keep employees focused on business activities during the workday.

Employers in a few industries—such as financial services—are required to monitor business-related messages that employees post on social-media sites to ensure that communications comply with government regulations. In most cases, however, companies are free to set their own policies regarding the use of social media.

© E.D. Torial / Alamy

A growing number of firms are encouraging employees to interact with each other and with customers and suppliers using social media, as long as they follow specific guidelines. For example, IBM's policy requires employees to use respectful language, obey copyright laws, and indicate that their views are personal rather than corporate. Kodak's employees must disclose their affiliation when discussing anything related to the company's business and are not allowed to reveal any confidential information. The social-media policy of online retailer Zappos is short and to the point: "Be real and use your best judgment."

Sources: Tamara Schweitzer, "Do You Need a Social Media Policy?" *Inc.*, January 25, 2010, http://www.inc.com/articles/2010/01/need-a-social-media-policy.html; David Scheer, "Brokers' Facebook, Twitter Posts Must Be Tracked by Employers," *BusinessWeek*, January 25, 2010, http://www.businessweek.com; Charlene Li, *Open Leadership* (San Francisco, CA: Jossey-Bass, 2010), chap. 5; Stephen Baker, "Beware Social Media Snake Oil," *BusinessWeek*, December 14, 2009, 48–51.

The final step in managerial decision making entails evaluating a decision's effectiveness. If the alternative that was chosen removes the difference between the actual condition and the desired condition, the decision is considered effective. If the problem still exists, managers may select one of the following choices:

- Decide to give the chosen alternative more time to work.
- Adopt a different alternative.
- Start the problem identification process all over again.

Failure to evaluate decisions adequately may have negative consequences. For example, Toyota suffered negative consequences after its focus on rapid growth led to a series of recalls that damaged the company's reputation for quality. In 2002, Toyota executives announced plans to become the largest automaker by attaining 15 percent of the global market share for automobiles. Although the company reached their goal less than eight years later, their choice to cut costs by switching to less-expensive suppliers for parts led to recent issues with faulty accelerator pedals. These issues temporarily stopped production in several countries and caused Toyota to recall over eight million vehicles worldwide, making it the largest automobile recall in history.[16]

Managing Total Quality

7

Describe how organizations benefit from total quality management.

The management of quality is a high priority in some organizations today. Major reasons for a greater focus on quality include foreign competition, more demanding customers, and poor financial performance resulting from reduced market shares

Total quality management. Starbucks CEO Howard Schultz, who espouses the importance and methods of total quality management, addresses the company's shareholders.

and higher costs. Over the last few years, several U.S. firms have lost the dominant competitive positions they had held for decades.

Total quality management is a much broader concept than just controlling the quality of the product itself (which is discussed in Chapter 8). **Total quality management (TQM)** is the coordination of efforts directed at improving customer satisfaction, increasing employee participation, strengthening supplier partnerships, and facilitating an organizational atmosphere of continuous quality improvement. For TQM programs to be effective, management must address each of the following components:

- *Customer satisfaction.* Ways to improve include producing higher-quality products, providing better customer service, and showing customers that the company cares.
- *Employee participation.* This can be increased by allowing employees to contribute to decisions, develop self-managed work teams, and assume responsibility for improving the quality of their work.
- *Strengthening supplier partnerships.* Developing good working relationships with suppliers can ensure that the right supplies and materials will be delivered on time at lower costs.
- *Continuous quality improvement.* This should not be viewed as achievable through one single program that has a target objective. A program based on continuous improvement has proven to be the most effective long-term approach.

One tool that is used for TQM is called benchmarking. **Benchmarking** is the process of evaluating the products, processes, or management practices of another organization for the purpose of improving quality. The focal organization may be superior in safety, customer service, productivity, innovativeness, or in some other way.

For example, competitor's products might be disassembled and evaluated, or wage and benefit plans might be surveyed to measure compensation packages against the labor market. The four basic steps of benchmarking are identifying objectives, forming a benchmarking team, collecting data, analyzing data, and acting on the results. Best practices may be discovered in any industry or organization.

Although many factors influence the effectiveness of a TQM program, two issues are crucial. First, top management must make a strong commitment to a TQM program by treating quality improvement as a top priority and giving it frequent attention. Firms that establish a TQM program but then focus on other priorities will find that their quality-improvement initiatives will fail. Second, management must coordinate the specific elements of a TQM program so that they work in harmony with each other.

Although not all U.S. companies have TQM programs, these programs provide many benefits. Overall financial benefits include lower operating costs, higher return on sales and on investments, and an improved ability to use premium pricing rather than competitive pricing. Motorola has successfully implemented a TQM program, which helps the company reduce defects and keep up with its competitors technologically.[17]

total quality management (TQM) the coordination of efforts directed at improving customer satisfaction, increasing employee participation, strengthening supplier partnerships, and facilitating an organizational atmosphere of continuous quality improvement

benchmarking a process used to evaluate the products, processes, or management practices of another organization that is superior in some way in order to improve quality

return to inside business

Procter & Gamble

Procter & Gamble (P&G) has passed its 170th birthday, yet in its long and successful history, the company has had only 12 CEOs, always chosen from the ranks of its top managers rather than brought in from the outside. The latest is Robert McDonald, who says that one of his most important management responsibilities is ensuring "continuity with change" to keep the company growing as quickly as it did under the previous CEO.

McDonald has reaffirmed the company's commitment to its mission of providing "branded products and services of superior quality and value that improve the lives of the world's consumers, now and for generations to come." Now P&G's managers are being challenged, as a team, to apply all of their technical, conceptual, and interpersonal skills to make progress toward McDonald's long-term goal of profitable growth through the addition of one billion new customers by 2015.

Questions

1. CEO Robert McDonald has created a computerized "dashboard" for managers to monitor the company's actual financial performance as it happens. What effect do you think this will have on the management process at P&G?
2. How does P&G's mission guide managers in preparing and implementing strategic, tactical, and operational plans for the future?

SUMMARY

Summary

CHAPTER REVIEW

1 Define what management is.

Management is the process of coordinating people and other resources to achieve an organization's goals. Managers are concerned with four types of resources—material, human, financial, and informational.

2 Describe the four basic management functions: planning, organizing, leading and motivating, and controlling.

Managers perform four basic functions. Management functions do not occur according to some rigid, preset timetable, though. At any time, managers may engage in a number of functions simultaneously. However, each function tends to lead naturally to others. First, managers engage in planning—determining where the firm should be going and how best to get there. One method of planning that can be used is SWOT analysis, which identifies and evaluates a firm's strengths, weaknesses, opportunities, and threats. Three types of plans, from the broadest to the most specific, are strategic plans, tactical plans, and operational plans. Managers also organize resources and activities to accomplish results in an efficient and effective manner, and they lead and motivate others to work in the best interests of the organization. In addition, managers control ongoing activities to keep the organization on course. There are three steps in the control function: setting standards, measuring actual performance, and taking corrective action.

3 Distinguish among the various kinds of managers in terms of both level and area of management.

Managers—or management positions—may be classified from two different perspectives. From the perspective of level within the organization, there are top managers, who control the fortunes of the organization; middle managers, who implement strategies and major policies; and first-line managers, who supervise the activities of operating employees. From the viewpoint of area of management, managers most often deal with the areas of finance, operations, marketing, human resources, and administration.

4 Identify the key management skills of successful managers.

Managers need a variety of skills in order to run a successful and efficient business. Conceptual skills are used to think in abstract terms or see the "big picture." Analytic skills are used to identify problems correctly, generate reasonable alternatives, and select the "best" alternatives to solve problems. Interpersonal skills are used to deal effectively with other people, both inside and outside an organization. Technical skills are needed to accomplish a specialized activity, whether they are used to actually do the task or used to train and assist employees. Communication skills are used to speak, listen, and write effectively.

5 Explain the different types of leadership.

Managers' effectiveness often depends on their styles of leadership—that is, their ability to influence others, either formally or informally. Autocratic leaders are very task oriented; they tell their employees exactly what is expected from them and give them specific instructions on how to do their assigned tasks. Participative leaders consult their employees before making decisions and can be classified into three groups: consultative, consensus, and democratic. Entrepreneurial leaders are different depending on their personalities, but they are generally enthusiastic and passionate about their work and tend to take initiative.

6 Discuss the steps in the managerial decision-making process.

Decision making, an integral part of a manager's work, is the process of developing a set of possible alternative solutions to a problem and choosing one alternative from among the set. Managerial decision making involves four steps: Managers must accurately identify problems, generate several possible solutions, choose the solution that will be most effective under the circumstances, and implement and evaluate the chosen course of action.

7 Describe how organizations benefit from total quality management.

Total quality management (TQM) is the coordination of efforts directed at improving customer satisfaction, increasing employee participation, strengthening supplier partnerships, and facilitating an organizational atmosphere of continuous quality improvement. Another tool used for TQM is benchmarking, which is used to evaluate the products, processes, or management practices of another organization that is superior in some way in order to improve quality. The five basic steps in benchmarking are identifying objectives, forming a benchmarking team, collecting data, analyzing data, and acting on the results. To have an effective TQM program, top management must make a strong, sustained commitment to the effort and must be able to coordinate all the program's elements so that they work in harmony. Overall financial benefits of TQM include lower operating costs, higher return on sales and on investment, and an improved ability to use premium pricing rather than competitive pricing.

Key Terms

You should now be able to define and give an example relevant to each of the following terms:

management (168)
planning (169)
mission (169)
strategic planning process (170)
goal (170)
objective (170)
SWOT analysis (170)
core competencies (170)
plan (171)
strategic plan (171)
tactical plan (172)
operational plan (172)
contingency plan (173)
organizing (173)
leading (173)
motivating (173)
directing (173)
controlling (174)
top manager (175)
middle manager (176)
first-line manager (176)
financial manager (176)
operations manager (176)
marketing manager (177)
human resources manager (177)
administrative manager (177)
conceptual skills (177)
analytic skills (177)
interpersonal skills (178)
technical skills (178)
communication skills (179)
leadership (179)
autocratic leadership (179)
participative leadership (180)
entrepreneurial leadership (180)
decision making (181)
problem (181)
total quality management (TQM) (184)
benchmarking (184)

Review Questions

1. Define the term *manager* without using the word *management* in your definition.
2. Identify and describe the basic management functions.
3. What are the major elements of SWOT analysis?
4. How do a strategic plan, a tactical plan, and an operational plan differ? What do they all have in common?
5. What exactly does a manager organize and for what reason?
6. Why are leadership and motivation necessary in a business in which people are paid for their work?
7. Explain the steps involved in the control function.
8. How are the two perspectives on kinds of managers—that is, level and area—different from each other?
9. What skills should a manager possess in order to be successful?
10. Compare and contrast the major styles of leadership.
11. Discuss what happens during each of the four steps of the managerial decision-making process.
12. What are the major benefits of a total quality management program?

Discussion Questions

1. Does a healthy firm (one that is doing well) have to worry about effective management? Explain.
2. What might be the mission of a neighborhood restaurant? Of the Salvation Army? What might be reasonable objectives for these organizations?
3. Which of the management functions and skills do not apply to the owner-operator of a sole proprietorship?
4. Which leadership style might be best suited to each of the three general levels of management within an organization?
5. According to this chapter, the leadership style that is *most* effective depends on interaction among the employees, characteristics of the work situation, and the manager's personality. Do you agree or disagree? Explain your answer.
6. Do you think that people are really as important to an organization as this chapter seems to indicate?
7. As you learned in this chapter, managers often work long hours at a hectic pace. Would this type of career appeal to you? Explain your answer.

Video Case 6.1

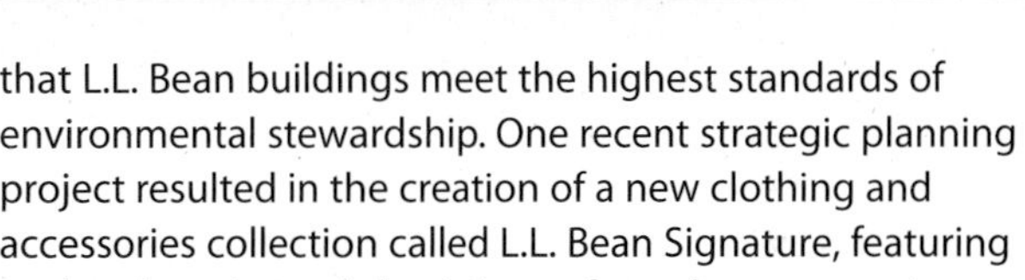

L.L. Bean Relies on Its Core Values and Effective Leadership

L.L. Bean's first product was a waterproof boot, designed by Maine outdoorsman Leon Leonwood Bean, who promised complete customer satisfaction. One hundred pairs were sold—and 90 pairs were returned because of a defect. Bean refunded the customers' money and went to work perfecting the product, now one of the most popular in the firm's long and successful history.

L.L. Bean began in 1912 as a tiny mail-order company and has grown to include 14 retail stores in ten states, an online store, and a popular catalog showcasing many of the company's 20,000 items, including high-quality clothing, accessories, outdoor gear, luggage, linens, and furniture. It is still privately owned and family run and has had just three presidents in its history—L.L. Bean himself, his grandson Leon Gorman, and now Chris McCormick, the first nonfamily member to lead the firm. New England is the core of L.L. Bean's market, and its selling cycle accelerates sharply every year around the winter holidays. Headquartered in Freeport, Maine, near its original store, the company reports annual sales of over $1.5 billion.

Managers at L.L. Bean today have many opportunities for using their planning, organizing, leading, and controlling skills. During the preholiday selling season, for instance, temporary workers hired to handle the increased workload bring the normal staff of about 4,600 to almost double its size, so managers have to reorganize the teams of 25 to 30 front-line employees who work in the call centers. Regular employees not currently in leadership positions are asked to head the teams of temps, ensuring they have an experienced person to help them develop their skills and perform to expectations. This organizing strategy works so well that many temps return year after year.

Planning skills come to the fore when top management decides when and where to open new retail stores, whether to expand the number of outlet stores offering discontinued items and overstocks, and how much to invest in ensuring that L.L. Bean buildings meet the highest standards of environmental stewardship. One recent strategic planning project resulted in the creation of a new clothing and accessories collection called L.L. Bean Signature, featuring updated versions of classic items from the company's 100-year heritage.

With respect to the control function, managers assess employee performance with a continuous evaluation process. Corporate-level goals are broken down to the level of the individual store and employee. If something isn't on track, the supervisor is expected to let the employee know and help figure out a solution. However, control at L.L. Bean is not entirely a top-down process. Employees are encouraged to develop their own personal goals, such as learning a new skill or gaining a better appreciation of the way L.L. Bean makes business decisions. Managers help them find ways to meet these personal objectives as well, through a temporary reassignment within the firm or participation in a special company project.

L.L. Bean has a strong collaborative work culture in which it is equally important to work through your supervisor, your co-workers, and your subordinates. That means everyone is a leader to some extent. Formal management candidates are asked to demonstrate both analytical and interpersonal skills and to model the company's six core values: outdoor heritage, integrity, service, respect, perseverance, and safe and healthy living. In the early days of the company, L.L. Bean lived above the store and would come downstairs in the middle of the night to help a customer who rang the bell. "A customer is the most important person ever in this office—in person or by mail," he was fond of saying. So, true to his beliefs, leadership style continues to revolve around serving the customer's needs. As one L.L. Bean manager said, the company is all about salespeople and customer service representatives so that they can better serve customers.[18]

Questions

1. What style of leadership do you think most L.L. Bean managers probably employ?
2. To produce hot water in L.L. Bean's flagship store, the company recently installed a solar hot water system that will offset almost 11,000 pounds of carbon dioxide emissions every year. Suggest some of the questions the company's managers might have asked at each level of planning (strategic, tactical, operational, and contingency) for this project.
3. Which managerial role or roles do you think the leaders of L.L. Bean's temp teams fill?

Case 6.2 DocuSign Changes Its Decision-Making to Cope with Crisis

What happens to decision making when a fast-growing company suddenly faces a crisis that could cloud its financial future? This happened to DocuSign, Inc., a Seattle-based provider of fully automated electronic signature services. The company offers software products that allow companies to transmit documents online and gather e-signatures quickly, cost-effectively, and securely. DocuSign's customers include companies in the financial services, e-commerce, mortgage, real estate, travel, and insurance industries. Since its founding in 2003, the firm has executed more than 58 million electronic signatures using desktop computers, laptops, cell phones, and other mobile devices.

Not long ago, however, DocuSign's executives faced a big problem. Many of its major customers at that time were mortgage lenders and college loan companies, which relied heavily on its e-signature services to speed the loan-approval process for their customers. However, poor economic conditions and increased regulation threatened to slow or even shut down these companies' spending, imperiling DocuSign's rapid growth and its revenue stream. "We were faced with large market shifts in two of our top segments," said the CEO, "both out of our control, and both within a 60-day period."

Instead of closeting themselves in a conference room to work out a solution to the crisis, top managers called a town-hall style meeting of the entire company. Gathering their 40 employees together, they described the new market conditions they faced, outlined what the situation meant for DocuSign, and asked everyone for input to help devise solutions to the problem. "We went straight to the people that deal with these customers on a daily basis, and that's our employees," the CEO remembers.

This approach to shared decision making, implemented during a time of crisis, was effective in helping the company fend off the threats to its growth and pursue promising business opportunities. The firm began holding monthly company-wide meetings in which employees brainstormed new ways to assess the effect of changing market conditions. Top management also created smaller groups of employees and gave them responsibility for specific tasks such as bringing new products to market.

During the next year, as employees rose to the challenge of shared responsibility for decision making, the company was able to identify and start relationships with a number of lucrative new clients. It created a new marketing program to focus potential customers' attention on the environmental benefits of shifting to paperless transactions and e-signatures instead of printing mountains of paper contracts and agreements. The marketing program also emphasized the cost benefits of completing transactions electronically rather than relying on expensive overnight delivery of legal documents when signatures were required.

As a result of this change in decision making, the company came out of the crisis with a secure enough financial future to obtain more than $12 million in additional venture capital, enabling it to continue its growth. Just as important, since the crisis was averted, employees have continued to take an active role in formulating and guiding DocuSign's business strategy. "You empower these people by telling them the truth and being open and honest with them," the CEO says. However, he goes on to say, "We don't always want to get into a situation where our employees think that our senior management team doesn't have any input or doesn't have options. There's a balance there."[19] For more information about the company, go to http://www.docusign.com.

Questions

1. How closely did DocuSign's top managers follow the steps in management decision making as outlined in the chapter? Explain your answer.
2. Was the idea of involving both employees and managers in decision-making an effective solution to the crisis DocuSign faced? What are the advantages and disadvantages of continuing to involve employees in decision-making now that the crisis has been averted?
3. Have you ever participated in a group decision-making situation, whether at work or in any organization to which you've belonged? Did it follow the stages of decision making outlined in the chapter, and how effective was it in solving a problem or resolving a crisis? What would you do differently, having read the chapter?

Building Skills for Career Success

1 JOURNALING FOR SUCCESS

Discovery statement: This chapter discussed the critical management function of leading and motivating others to work in the best interests of an organization. Think about your current job or a job that you had previously.

Assignment

1. Who is the most outstanding leader with whom you have worked?
2. What was his or her position and in what capacity did you work with the person?
3. What are this person's outstanding leadership qualities?
4. Select the most outstanding leadership quality from question 3 and provide an example that demonstrates this quality.
5. Do most of your co-workers view this person as being an outstanding leader, too? Explain.

2 EXPLORING THE INTERNET

Most large companies call on a management consulting firm for a variety of services, including employee training, help in the selection of an expensive purchase such as a computer system, recruitment of employees, and direction in reorganization and strategic planning.

Large consulting firms generally operate globally and provide information to companies considering entry into foreign countries or business alliances with foreign firms. They use their Web sites, along with magazine-style articles, to celebrate achievements and present their credentials to clients. Business students can acquire an enormous amount of up-to-date information in the field of management by perusing these sites.

Assignment

1. Explore each of the following Web sites:

   Accenture: http://www.accenture.com
   BearingPoint (formerly KPMG Consulting):
   http://www.bearingpoint.com
   Cap Gemini Ernst & Young: http://www.capgemini.com

   Visit the text Web site for updates to this exercise.

2. Judging from the articles and notices posted, what are the current areas of activities of one of these firms?
3. Explore one of these areas in more detail by comparing postings from each firm's site. For instance, if "global business opportunities" appears to be a popular area of management consulting, how has each firm distinguished itself in this area? Who would you call first for advice?
4. Given that consulting firms are always trying to fill positions for their clients and to meet their own recruitment needs, it is little wonder that employment postings are a popular area on their sites. Examine these in detail. Based on your examination of the site and the registration format, what sort of recruit are they interested in?

3 DEVELOPING CRITICAL-THINKING SKILLS

As defined in the chapter, an organization's mission is a statement of the basic purpose that makes the organization different from others. Clearly, a mission statement, by indicating the purpose of a business, directly affects the company's employees, customers, and stockholders.

Assignment

1. Find the mission statements of three large corporations in different industries. The Internet is one source of mission statements. For example, you might search these sites:

   http://www.kodak.com
   http://www.benjerry.com
   http://www.usaa.com

2. Compare the mission statements on the basis of what each reflects about the company's philosophy and its concern for employees, customers, and stockholders.
3. Which company would you like to work for and why?
4. Prepare a report on your findings.

4 BUILDING TEAM SKILLS

Over the past few years, an increasing number of employees, stockholders, and customers have been demanding to know what their companies are about. As a result, more companies have been taking the time to analyze their operations and to prepare mission statements that focus on the purpose of the company. The mission statement is becoming a critical planning tool for successful companies. To make effective decisions, employees must understand the purpose of their company.

Assignment

1. Divide into teams and write a mission statement for one of the following types of businesses:

   Food service, restaurant
   Banking
   Airline
   Auto repair
   Cabinet manufacturing

2. Discuss your mission statement with other teams. How did the other teams interpret the purpose of your company? What is the mission statement saying about the company?
3. Write a one-page report on what you learned about developing mission statements.

CHAPTER REVIEW

❺ RESEARCHING DIFFERENT CAREERS

A successful career requires planning. Without a plan, or roadmap, you will find it very difficult, if not impossible, to reach your desired career destination. The first step in planning is to establish your career goal. You then must set objectives and develop plans for accomplishing those objectives. This kind of planning takes time, but it will pay off later.

Assignment

Complete the following statements:

1. My career goal is to

____
____
____
____

This statement should encapsulate what you want to accomplish over the long run. It may include the type of job you want and the type of business or industry you want to work in. Examples include the following:

- My career goal is to work as a top manager in the food industry.
- My career goal is to supervise aircraft mechanics.
- My career goal is to win the top achievement award in the advertising industry.

2. My career objectives are to

____
____
____
____

Objectives are benchmarks along the route to a career destination. They are more specific than a career goal. A statement about a career objective should specify what you want to accomplish, when you will complete it, and any other details that will serve as criteria against which you can measure your progress. Examples include the following:

- My objective is to enroll in a management course at Main College in the spring semester 2012.
- My objective is to earn an A in the management course at Main College in the spring semester 2012.
- My objective is to be promoted to supervisor by January 1, 2013.
- My objective is to prepare a status report by September 30 covering the last quarter's activities by asking Charlie in Quality Control to teach me the procedures.

3. Exchange your goal and objectives statements with another class member. Can your partner interpret your objectives correctly? Are the objectives concise and complete? Do they include criteria against which you can measure your progress? If not, discuss the problem and rewrite the objective.

Creating a Flexible Organization

7

© Ryan McVay/Riser/Getty Images

Learning Objectives

What you will be able to do once you complete this chapter:

1. Understand what an organization is and identify its characteristics.
2. Explain why job specialization is important.
3. Identify the various bases for departmentalization.
4. Explain how decentralization follows from delegation.
5. Understand how the span of management describes an organization.
6. Describe the four basic forms of organizational structure.
7. Describe the effects of corporate culture.
8. Understand how committees and task forces are used.
9. Explain the functions of the informal

FYI

inside business

Did You Know?

A British soap maker and a Dutch margarine company merged to form Unilever, which is now the world's third-largest manufacturer of consumer goods.

Unilever Restructures Using Mobile Technology

Unilever, formed from the merger of a British soap maker and a Dutch margarine company in 1930, has grown into a global powerhouse selling 400 brands in 150 nations. Today, the company is the world's third-largest manufacturer of consumer goods, with more than $57 billion in annual sales and a workforce of 174,000. Among Unilever's best-known brands are Axe (personal care), Ben & Jerry's (ice cream), Dove (soap), Lipton (tea), Sunsilk (hair care), and Surf (laundry).

To manage operations on six continents, Unilever organizes its employees by location, product, and function. The CEO directly supervises the top executives responsible for managing three key regions: the Americas; Western Europe; and Asia, Africa, and Central and Eastern Europe. Also reporting to the CEO is the global president of foods, personal care, and home care (the company's three main product categories). In addition, the heads of three vital functions—finance, human resources, and research and development—report directly to the CEO.

Unilever's organizing principle is that "work can be done anywhere, anytime as long as business needs are being fully met," according to the senior vice president of human resources and communications for the Americas. As a result, the company classifies workers according to three categories of where they work. A *resident employee* works mainly in a single Unilever office or facility. A *mobile employee* works at different locations, spending some time at a company facility and some time at a customer's facility. An *off-site employee* telecommutes from home or works on-site at a partner business rather than in a Unilever facility.

To direct, coordinate, and control the activities of Unilever's highly mobile workforce, managers rely on teleconferencing, Internet phone services, and other communication technologies. To encourage teamwork and accommodate the visits of mobile and off-site employees, the company is reconfiguring major facilities to enlarge areas for collaboration and reduce areas set aside for individual work. This movement toward "agile space" has saved Unilever 40 percent on office costs. Just as important, it has enhanced the company's overall flexibility as the workforce becomes increasingly mobile to meet the challenges of today's global marketplace.[1]

To survive and to grow, companies such as Unilever must constantly look for ways to improve their methods of doing business. Managers at Unilever, like those at many other organizations, deliberately reorganized the company to achieve its goals and to create satisfying products that foster long-term customer relationships.

When firms are organized, or reorganized, the focus is sometimes on achieving low operating costs. Other firms, such as Nike, emphasize providing high-quality products to ensure customer satisfaction. A firm's organization influences its performance. Thus, the issue of organization is important.

We begin this chapter by examining the business organization—what it is and how it functions in today's business environment. Next, we focus one by one on five characteristics that shape an organization's structure. We discuss job specialization within a company, the grouping of jobs into manageable units or departments, the delegation of power from management to workers, the span of management, and establishment of a chain of command. Then we step back for an overall view of organizational structure, describe the effects of corporate culture, and focus in on how committees and task forces are used. Finally, we look at the network of social interactions—the informal organization—that operates within the formal business structure.

What Is an Organization?

1

Understand what an organization is and identify its characteristics.

We used the term *organization* throughout Chapter 6 without really defining it mainly because its everyday meaning is close to its business meaning. Here, however, let us agree that an **organization** is a group of two or more people working together to achieve a common set of goals. A neighborhood dry cleaner owned and operated by a husband-and-wife team is an organization. IBM and Home Depot, which employ thousands of workers worldwide, are also organizations in the same sense. Although each corporation's organizational structure is more complex than the dry-cleaning establishment, all must be organized to achieve their goals.

An inventor who goes into business to produce and market a new invention hires people, decides what each will do, determines who will report to whom, and so on. These activities are the essence of organizing, or creating, the organization. One way to create this "picture" is to create an organization chart.

Developing Organization Charts

An **organization chart** is a diagram that represents the positions and relationships within an organization. An example of an organization chart is shown in Figure 7.1. Each rectangle represents a particular position or person in the organization. At the top is the president, at the next level are the vice presidents. The solid vertical lines connecting the vice presidents to the president indicate that the vice presidents are in the chain of command. The **chain of command** is the line of authority that extends from the highest to the lowest levels of the organization. Moreover, each vice president reports directly to the president. Similarly, the plant managers, regional sales managers, and accounting department manager report to the vice presidents. The chain of command can be short or long. For example, at Royer's Roundtop Café, an independent restaurant in Roundtop, Texas, the chain of command is very short. Bud Royer, the owner, is responsible only to himself and can alter his hours or change his menu quickly. On the other hand, the chain of command at McDonald's is long. Before making certain types of changes, a McDonald's franchisee seeks permission from regional management, which, in turn, seeks approval from corporate headquarters.

In the chart, the connections to the directors of legal services, public affairs, and human resources are shown as broken lines; these people are not part of the direct chain of command. Instead, they hold *advisory*, or *staff*, positions. This difference will be examined later in this chapter when we discuss line-and-staff positions.

Most smaller organizations find organization charts useful. They clarify positions and report relationships for everyone in the organization, and they help managers to track growth and change in the organizational structure. However, many large organizations, such as ExxonMobil, Kellogg's, and Procter & Gamble, do not maintain complete, detailed charts for two reasons. First, it is difficult to chart even a few dozen positions accurately, much less the thousands that characterize larger firms. Second, larger organizations are almost always changing parts of their structure. An organization chart would be outdated before it was completed. However, organization must exist even without a chart in order for a business to be successful. Technology is helping large companies implement up-to-date organization charts.

organization a group of two or more people working together to achieve a common set of goals

organization chart a diagram that represents the positions and relationships within an organization

chain of command the line of authority that extends from the highest to the lowest levels of an organization

Major Considerations for Organizing a Business

When a firm is started, management must decide how to organize the firm. These decisions focus on job design, departmentalization, delegation, span of management, and chain of command. In the next several sections, we discuss major issues associated with these dimensions.

Figure 7.1 A Typical Corporate Organization Chart

A company's organization chart represents the positions and relationships within the organization and shows the managerial chains of command.

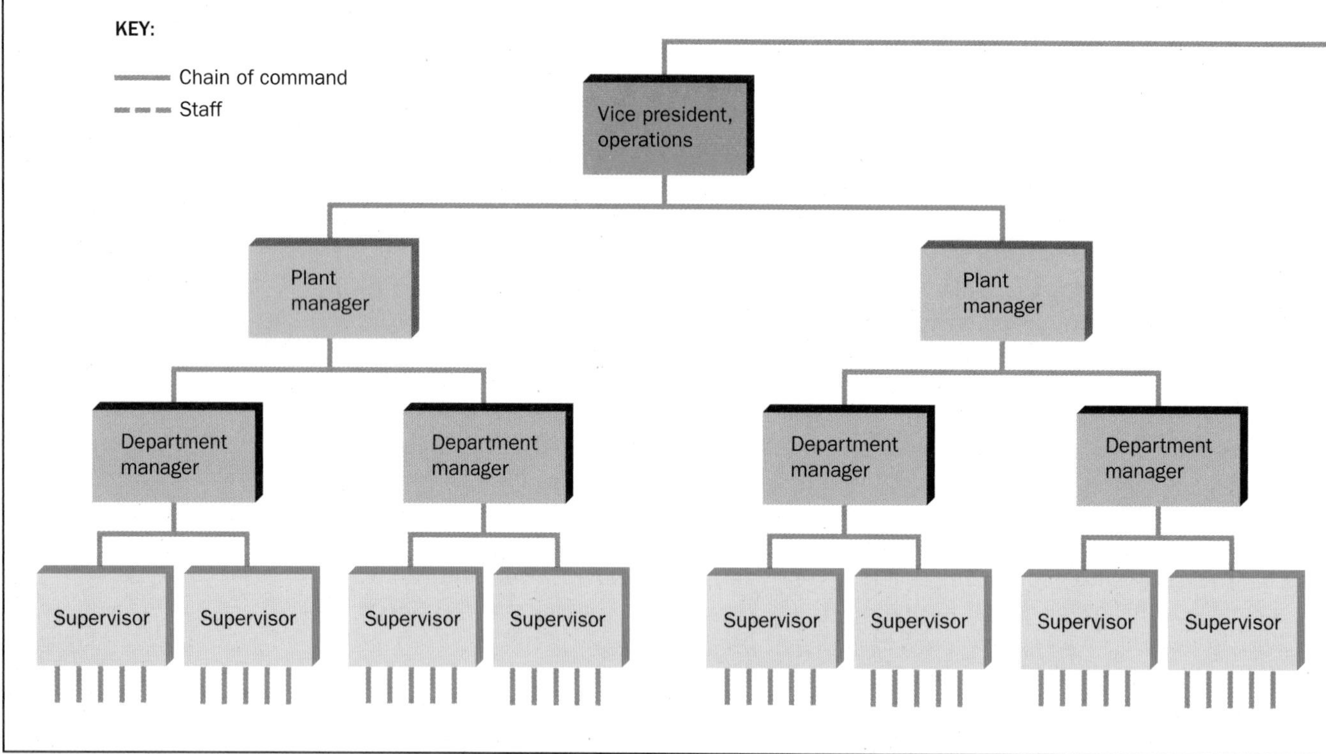

2

Explain why job specialization is important.

Job Design

In Chapter 1, we defined *specialization* as the separation of a manufacturing process into distinct tasks and the assignment of different tasks to different people. Here we are extending that concept to *all* the activities performed within an organization.

Job Specialization

Job specialization is the separation of all organizational activities into distinct tasks and the assignment of different tasks to different people. Adam Smith, the 18th-century economist whose theories gave rise to capitalism, was the first to emphasize the power of specialization in his book, *The Wealth of Nations*. According to Smith, the various tasks in a particular pin factory were arranged so that one worker drew the wire for the pins, another straightened the wire, a third cut it, a fourth ground the point, and a fifth attached the head. Smith claimed that ten men were able to produce 48,000 pins per day. Before specialization, they could produce only 200 pins per day because each worker had to perform all five tasks!

The Rationale for Specialization

job specialization the separation of all organizational activities into distinct tasks and the assignment of different tasks to different people

For a number of reasons, some job specialization is necessary in every organization because the "job" of most organizations is too large for one person to handle. In a firm such as DaimlerChrysler, thousands of people are needed to manufacture

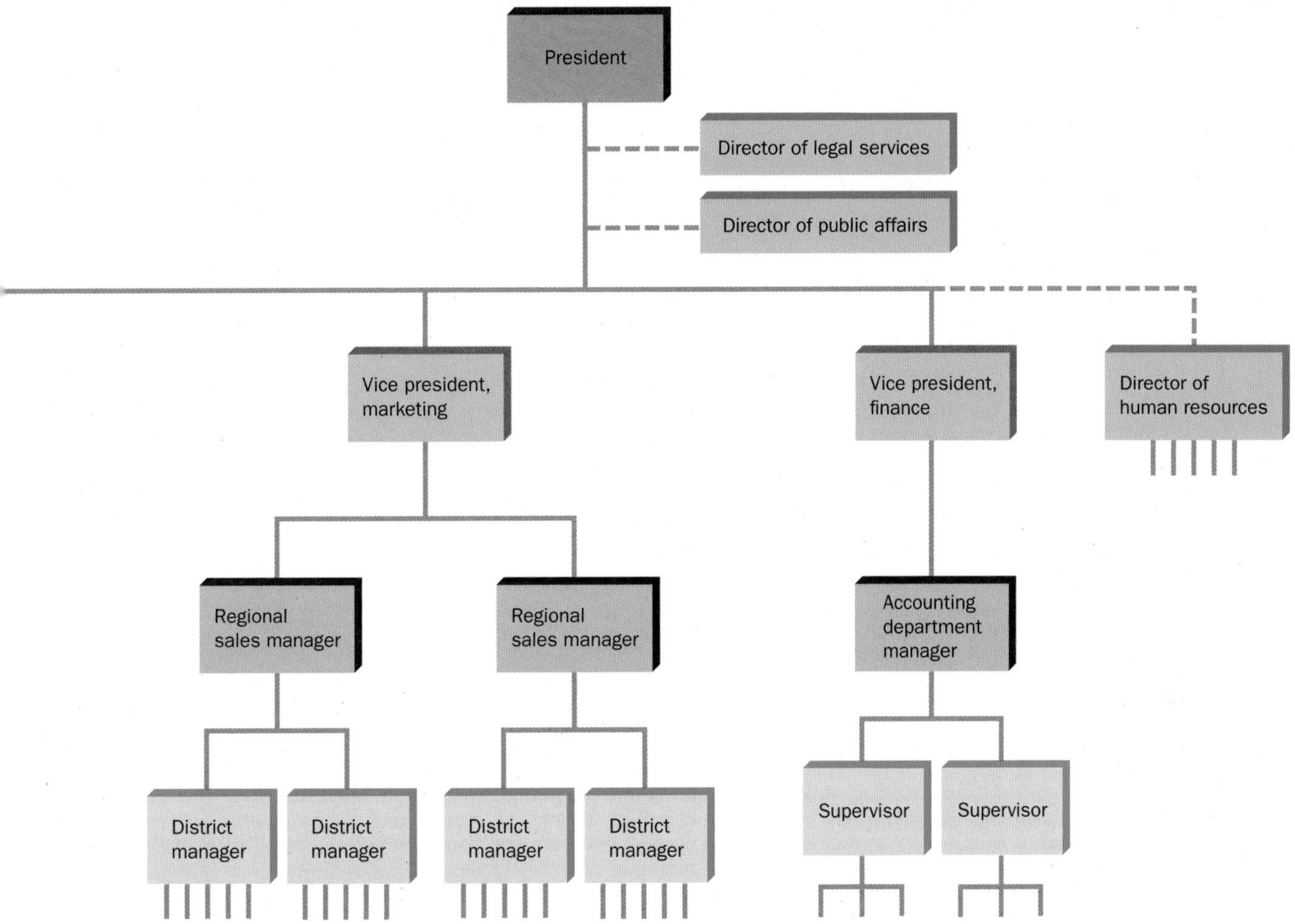

President

Director of legal services

Director of public affairs

Vice president, marketing

Vice president, finance

Director of human resources

Regional sales manager

Regional sales manager

Accounting department manager

District manager

District manager

District manager

District manager

Supervisor

Supervisor

automobiles. Others are needed to sell the cars, control the firm's finances, and so on.

Second, when a worker has to learn one specific, highly specialized task, that individual should be able to learn it very efficiently. Third, a worker repeating the same job does not lose time changing from operations, as the pin workers did when producing complete pins. Fourth, the more specialized the job, the easier it is to design specialized equipment. And finally, the more specialized the job, the easier is the job training.

Job specialization. This designer at Puma has a highly specialized job that includes the evaluation of proposed designs of specific types of athletic shoes.

Alternatives to Job Specialization

Unfortunately, specialization can have negative consequences as well. The most significant drawback is the boredom and dissatisfaction employees may feel when repeating the same job. Bored employees may be absent from work frequently, may not put much effort into their work, and may even sabotage the company's efforts to produce quality products.

To combat these problems, managers often turn to job rotation. **Job rotation** is the systematic shifting of employees from one job to another. For example, a worker may be assigned a different job every week for a four-week period and then return to the first job in the fifth week. Job rotation provides a variety of tasks so that workers are less likely to become bored and dissatisfied. Pharmaceutical company Eli Lilly, for example, uses a form of job rotation for its managers in which it gives them short-term assignments outside their field of expertise to further develop their skills.[2]

Two other approaches—job enlargement and job enrichment—also can provide solutions to the problems caused by job specialization. These topics, along with other methods used to motivate employees, are discussed in Chapter 11.

3

Identify the various bases for departmentalization.

Departmentalization

After jobs are designed, they must be grouped together into "working units," or departments. This process is called *departmentalization.* More specifically, **departmentalization** is the process of grouping jobs into manageable units. Several departmentalization bases are used commonly. In fact, most firms use more than one. Today, the most common bases for organizing a business into effective departments are by function, by product, by location, and by customer.

By Function

Departmentalization by function groups jobs that relate to the same organizational activity. Under this scheme, all marketing personnel are grouped together in the marketing department, all production personnel in the production department, and so on.

Most smaller and newer organizations departmentalize by function. Supervision is simplified because everyone is involved in the same activities, and coordination is easy. The disadvantages of this method of grouping jobs are that it can lead to slow decision making and that it tends to emphasize the department over the whole organization.

job rotation the systematic shifting of employees from one job to another

departmentalization the process of grouping jobs into manageable units

departmentalization by function grouping jobs that relate to the same organizational activity

departmentalization by product grouping activities related to a particular product or service

departmentalization by location grouping activities according to the defined geographic area in which they are performed

By Product

Departmentalization by product groups activities related to a particular good or service. This approach is used often by older and larger firms that produce and sell a variety of products. Each department handles its own marketing, production, financial management, and human resources activities.

Departmentalization by product makes decision making easier and provides for the integration of all activities associated with each product. However, it causes some duplication of specialized activities—such as finance—from department to department. Moreover, the emphasis is placed on the product rather than on the whole organization.

Departmentalization. These employees are co-workers in an information technology department.

© iStockphoto.com/Catherine Yeulet

By Location

Departmentalization by location groups activities according to the defined geographic area in which they are performed. Departmental areas may range from whole countries (for international firms) to regions within countries (for national firms) to areas of several city blocks (for police departments organized into precincts). Departmentalization by location allows the organization to respond readily to the unique demands or requirements of different locations. Nevertheless, a large administrative staff and an elaborate control system may be needed to coordinate operations in many locations.

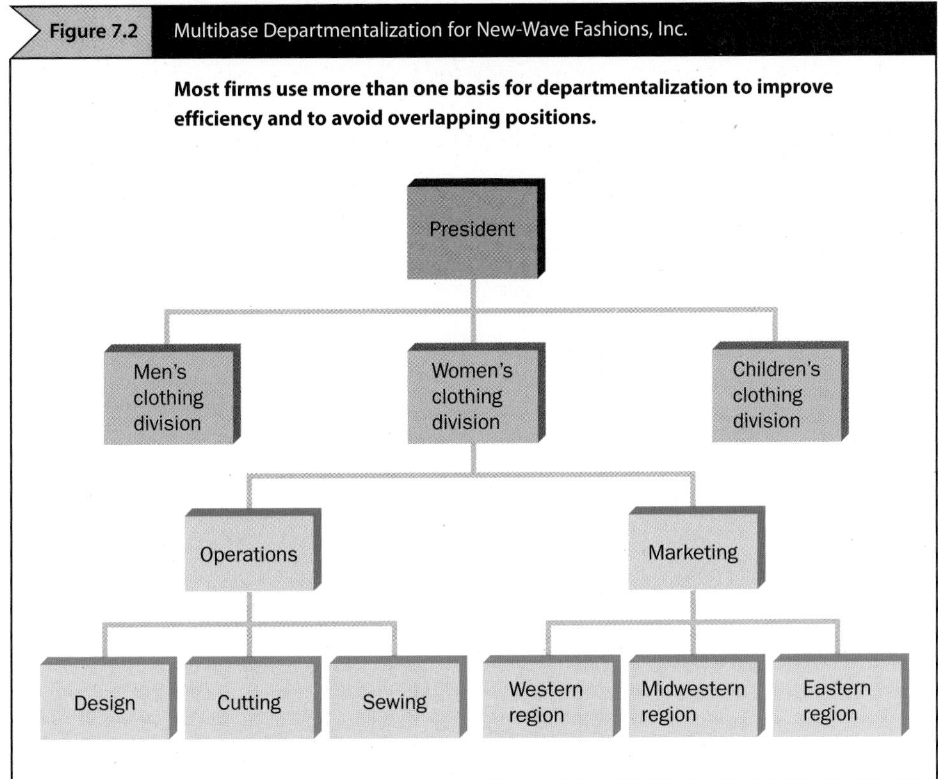

Figure 7.2 Multibase Departmentalization for New-Wave Fashions, Inc.

Most firms use more than one basis for departmentalization to improve efficiency and to avoid overlapping positions.

By Customer

Departmentalization by customer groups activities according to the needs of various customer populations. A local Chevrolet dealership, for example, may have one sales staff to deal with individual consumers and a different sales staff to work with corporate fleet buyers. The obvious advantage of this approach is that it allows the firm to deal efficiently with unique customers or customer groups. The biggest drawback is that a larger-than-usual administrative staff is needed.

Combinations of Bases

Many organizations use more than one of these departmentalization bases.

Take a moment to examine Figure 7.2. Notice that departmentalization by customer is used to organize New-Wave Fashions, Inc., into three major divisions: men's, women's, and children's clothing. Then functional departmentalization is used to distinguish the firm's production and marketing activities. Finally, location is used to organize the firm's marketing efforts.

Delegation, Decentralization, and Centralization

Explain how decentralization follows from delegation.

The third major step in the organizing process is to distribute power in the organization. **Delegation** assigns part of a manager's work and power to other workers. The degree of centralization or decentralization of authority is determined by the overall pattern of delegation within the organization.

Delegation of Authority

Because no manager can do everything, delegation is vital to completion of a manager's work. Delegation is also important in developing the skills and abilities of subordinates. It allows those who are being groomed for higher-level positions to play increasingly important roles in decision making.

departmentalization by customer grouping activities according to the needs of various customer populations

delegation assigning part of a manager's work and power to other workers

Figure 7.3 Steps in the Delegation Process

To be successful, a manager must learn how to delegate. No one can do everything alone.

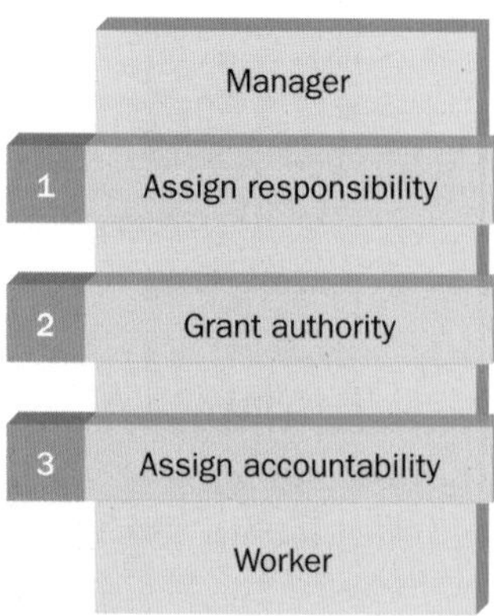

responsibility the duty to do a job or perform a task

authority the power, within an organization, to accomplish an assigned job or task

accountability the obligation of a worker to accomplish an assigned job or task

decentralized organization an organization in which management consciously attempts to spread authority widely in the lower levels of the organization

centralized organization an organization that systematically works to concentrate authority at the upper levels of the organization

Steps in Delegation The delegation process generally involves three steps (see Figure 7.3). First, the manager must *assign responsibility*. **Responsibility** is the duty to do a job or perform a task. In most job settings, a manager simply gives the worker a job to do. Typical job assignments might range from having a worker prepare a report on the status of a new quality control program to placing the person in charge of a task force. Second, the manager must *grant authority*. **Authority** is the power, within the organization, to accomplish an assigned job or task. This might include the power to obtain specific information, order supplies, authorize relevant expenditures, or make certain decisions. Finally, the manager must *create accountability*. **Accountability** is the obligation of a worker to accomplish an assigned job or task.

Note that accountability is created, but it cannot be delegated. Suppose that you are an operations manager for Target and are responsible for performing a specific task. You, in turn, delegate this task to someone else. You nonetheless remain accountable to your immediate supervisor for getting the task done properly. If the other person fails to complete the assignment, you—not the person to whom you delegated the task—will be held accountable.

Delegation. Delegation allows subordinates to develop the skills and abilities required for higher-level positions.

Barriers to Delegation For several reasons, managers may be unwilling to delegate work. Many managers are reluctant to delegate because they want to be sure that the work gets done. Another reason for reluctance stems from the opposite situation. The manager fears that the worker will do the work well and attract the approving notice of higher-level managers. Finally, some managers do not delegate because they are so disorganized that they simply are not able to plan and assign work effectively.

Decentralization of Authority

The pattern of delegation throughout an organization determines the extent to which that organization is decentralized or centralized. In a **decentralized organization**, management consciously attempts to spread authority widely across various organization levels. A **centralized organization**, on the other hand, systematically works to

Going for SUCCESS

Google Changes Corporate Culture at Web Speed

Why would a highly successful business like Google deliberately change its corporate culture? One reason is to keep up with the ever-changing business environment—or, better yet, to stay one or two steps ahead.

As a long-time leader in the fast-moving world of information technology, Google knows that speed and innovation are critical to maintaining its competitive edge. Throughout the company's history, employees have been encouraged to come up with unconventional new ideas for catapulting Google into the future. These days, employees are invited to present their best ideas in regular meetings with the company's co-founders and top management, a change that allows for direct feedback and speedier decision making.

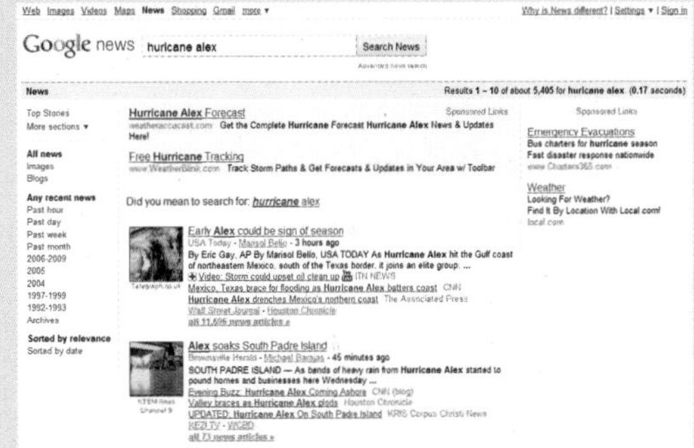

© Courtesy of Google, Inc.

Another reason to change the corporate culture is to maintain the nimbleness and entrepreneurial drive of a scrappy start-up even as the company grows and matures. Because Google is now a global corporation with 20,000 employees, it is "actively trying to prevent middle-agedom," the CEO says.

In a change to its culture, Google has increased the number of small teams working on new ideas and now allows each team considerable freedom and resources for its projects. In another cultural change, some teams are located hundreds or thousands of miles from Google's California headquarters. This means teams have the opportunity to develop ideas in some detail before asking managers and colleagues for constructive criticism and assistance.

Sources: Jonathan Tombes, "Editor's Letter: Google and Other Crazies," *Communications Technology*, January 15, 2010, http://www.cable360.net/ct/sections/columns/editorsletter/39258.html; "Creative Tension: Google's Corporate Culture," *The Economist*, September 19, 2009, 67EU; Jonathan V. Last, "Googling Google," *Weekly Standard*, October 12, 2009, http://www.weeklystandard.com/Content/Public/Articles/000/000/017/033pmaeg.asp; Google Corporate Culture, http://www.google.com/corporate/culture.html.

concentrate authority at the upper levels. For example, many publishers of college-level textbooks are centralized organizations, with authority concentrated at the top. Large organizations may have characteristics of both decentralized and centralized organizations.

A number of factors can influence the extent to which a firm is decentralized. One is the external environment in which the firm operates. The more complex and unpredictable this environment, the more likely it is that top management will let lower-level managers make important decisions. After all, lower-level managers are closer to the problems. Another factor is the nature of the decision itself. The riskier or more important the decision, the greater is the tendency to centralize decision making. A third factor is the abilities of lower-level managers. If these managers do not have strong decision-making skills, top managers will be reluctant to decentralize. And, in contrast, strong lower-level decision-making skills encourage decentralization. Finally, a firm that traditionally has practiced centralization or decentralization is likely to maintain that posture in the future.

In principle, neither decentralization nor centralization is right or wrong. What works for one organization may or may not work for another. Kmart Corporation and McDonald's are very successful—and both practice centralization. But decentralization has worked very well for General Electric and Sears. Every organization must assess its own situation and then choose the level of centralization or decentralization that will work best.

span of management (or span of control) the number of workers who report directly to one manager

The Span of Management

5

Understand how the span of management describes an organization.

The fourth major step in organizing a business is establishing the **span of management** (or **span of control**), which is the number of workers who report directly to one manager. For hundreds of years, theorists have searched for an ideal span of management. When it became apparent that there is no perfect number of subordinates for a manager to supervise, they turned their attention to the general issue of whether the span should be wide or narrow. This issue is complicated because the span of management may change by department within the same organization.

Wide and Narrow Spans of Management

A *wide* span of management exists when a manager has a larger number of subordinates. A *narrow* span exists when the manager has only a few subordinates. Several factors determine the span that is better for a particular manager (see Figure 7.4). Generally, the span of control may be wide when (1) the manager and the subordinates are very competent, (2) the organization has a well-established set of standard operating procedures, and (3) few new problems are expected to arise. The span should be narrow when (1) workers are physically located far from one another, (2) the manager has much work to do in addition to supervising workers, (3) a great deal of interaction is required between supervisor and workers, and (4) new problems arise frequently.

Organizational Height

The span of management has an obvious impact on relations between managers and workers. It has a more subtle but equally important impact on the height of the organization. **Organizational height** is the number of layers, or levels, of management in a firm. The span of management plays a direct role in determining the height of the organization (see Figure 7.4). If spans of management are wider, fewer levels are needed, and the organization is *flat*. If spans of management generally are narrow, more levels are needed, and the resulting organization is *tall*.

Figure 7.4 The Span of Management

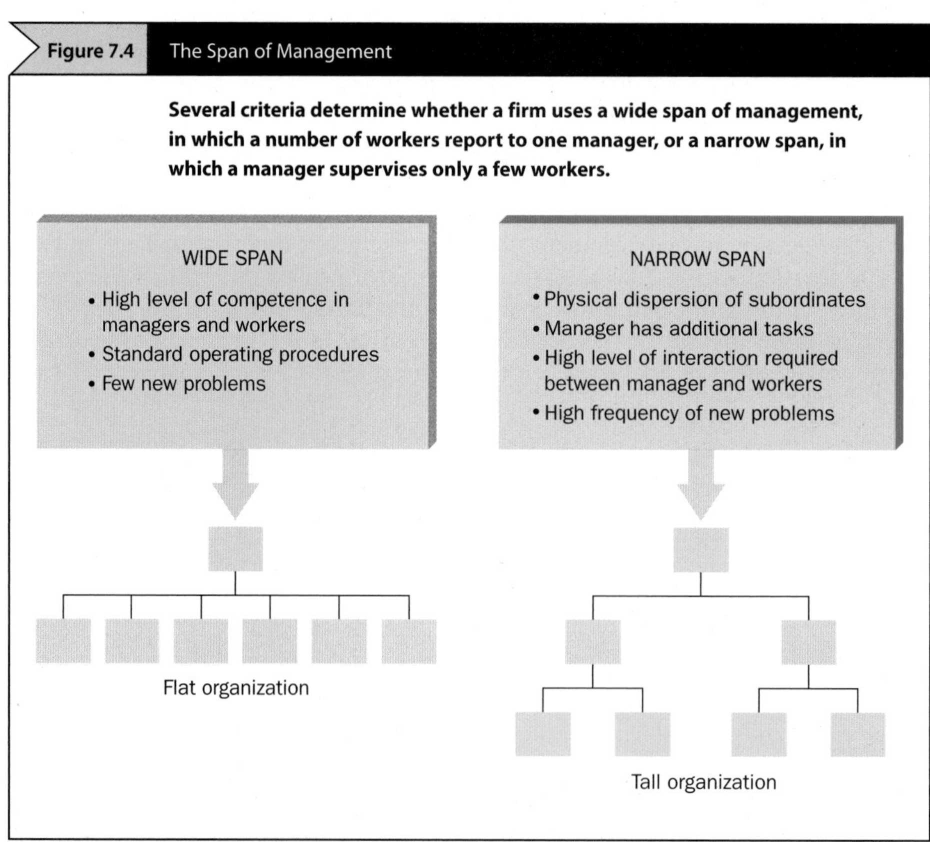

organizational height the number of layers, or levels, of management in a firm

Career
SUCCESS

Your Green Career Path?

If you want to pursue a green career path, you have more choices and opportunities than ever before, extending up to the very top of the management ranks. The post of chief sustainability officer (CSO) is the newest C-level position in the organizational hierarchy—a green management job that reports directly to the president or chief executive officer.

AT&T, Google, Dow Chemical, DuPont, and many other businesses have appointed a CSO to plan and coordinate company-wide environmental initiatives, ensure proper compliance with government regulations, and manage internal and external communications about sustainability issues. Just as important, the CSO is responsible for inserting sustainability into corporate strategy and making it part of the business case for new goods and services. Some colleges, universities, and municipalities are hiring sustainability officers to handle such diverse issues as switching to clean power sources, improving recycling programs, reducing waste, and minimizing the environmental impact of buildings, supplies, and operations.

Rather than isolate responsibility for sustainability in a single top-management role, companies are increasingly adding sustainability to job descriptions throughout the organization. As Levi Strauss's vice president for social and environmental sustainability explains: "We're successful when sustainability gets embedded in all the roles in the company."

Sources: Henry Fountain, "Sustainability Comes of Age," *New York Times Education Life Supplement*, January 3, 2010, 20; Tiffany Hsu, "Eco-officers Are Moving into Executive Suites," *Los Angeles Times*, December 30, 2009, http://www.latimes.com/business/la-fi-green-officers30-2009dec30,0,3283781.story; Geoff Colvin, "Linda Fisher, C-Suite Strategies," *Fortune*, November 23, 2009, 45ff.

In a taller organization, administrative costs are higher because more managers are needed. Communication among levels may become distorted because information has to pass up and down through more people. When companies are cutting costs, one option is to decrease organizational height in order to reduce related administrative expenses. For example, when cosmetics provider Avon experienced declining sales, the company began a series of long and extensive restructuring programs, with the first beginning in 2005 and the second beginning in 2009. The programs focused on increasing efficiency and organizational effectiveness. While the original restructuring plan saved the company approximately $200 million per year, the newer plan has saved the company an estimated $350 million per year.[3] Although flat organizations avoid these problems, their managers may perform more administrative duties simply because there are fewer managers. Wide spans of management also may require managers to spend considerably more time supervising and working with subordinates.

6

Describe the four basic forms of organizational structure.

Forms of Organizational Structure

Up to this point, we have focused our attention on the major characteristics of organizational structure. In many ways, this is like discussing the parts of a jigsaw puzzle one by one. It is now time to put the puzzle together. In particular, we discuss four basic forms of organizational structure: line, line-and-staff, matrix, and network.

The Line Structure

The simplest and oldest form of organizational structure is the **line structure**, in which the chain of command goes directly from person to person throughout the organization. Thus, a straight line could be drawn down through the levels of management, from the chief executive down to the lowest level in the organization. In a small retail store, for example, an hourly employee might report to an assistant manager, who reports to a store manager, who reports to the owner.

Managers within a line structure, called **line managers**, make decisions and give orders to subordinates to achieve the organization's goals. A line structure's simplicity and clear chain of command allow line managers to make decisions

line structure an organizational structure in which the chain of command goes directly from person to person throughout the organization

line manager a position in which a person makes decisions and gives orders to subordinates to achieve the organization's goals

quickly with direct accountability because the decision-maker only has one supervisor to report to.

The downside of a line structure, however, is that line managers are responsible for many activities, and therefore must have a wide range of knowledge about all of them. While this may not be a problem for small organizations with a lower volume of activities, in a larger organization, activities become more numerous and complex, thus making it more difficult for line managers to fully understand what they are in charge of. Therefore, line managers in a larger organization would have a hard time making an educated decision without expert advice from outside sources. As a result, line structures are not very effective in medium- or large-size organizations, but are very popular in small organizations.

Line-and-staff organization structure. Ronald McDonald occupies a staff position and does not have direct authority over other employees at McDonald's. The other individuals shown here occupy line positions and do have direct authority over some of the other McDonald's employees.

© Feature Photo Service/McDonald's

The Line-and-Staff Structure

A **line-and-staff structure** not only utilizes the chain of command from a line structure but also provides line managers with specialists, called staff managers. Therefore, this structure works much better for medium- and large-size organizations than line management alone. **Staff managers** provide support, advice, and expertise to line managers, thus eliminating the previous drawback of line structures. Staff managers are not part of the chain of command like line managers are, but they do have authority over their assistants (see Figure 7.5).

line-and-staff structure an organizational structure that utilizes the chain of command from a line structure in combination with the assistance of staff managers

staff manager a position created to provide support, advice, and expertise within an organization

Figure 7.5 Line and Staff Managers

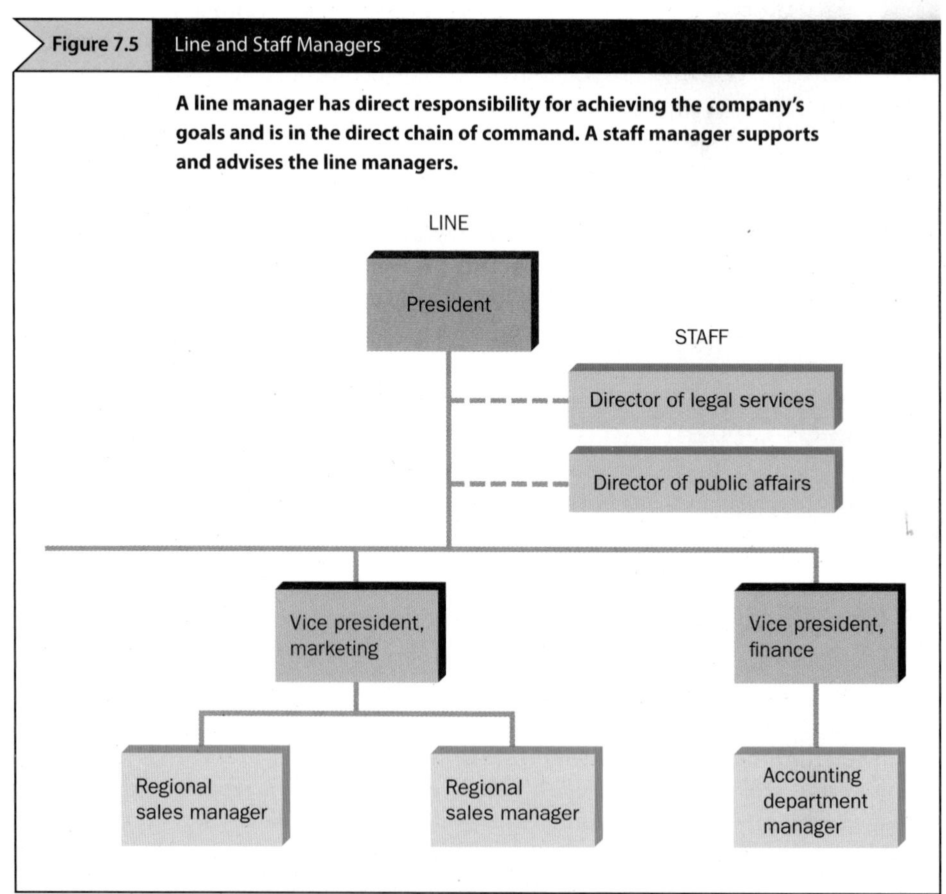

Both line and staff managers are needed for effective management, but the two positions differ in important ways. The basic difference is in terms of authority. Line managers have *line authority*, which means that they can make decisions and issue directives relating to the organization's goals. Staff managers seldom have this kind of authority. Instead, they usually have either advisory authority or functional authority. *Advisory authority* is the expectation that line managers will consult the appropriate staff manager when making decisions. Functional authority is stronger. *Functional authority* is the authority of staff managers to make decisions and issue directives about their areas of expertise. For example, a legal adviser for Nike can decide whether to retain a particular clause in a contract but not product pricing.

For a variety of reasons, conflict between line managers and staff managers is fairly common in business. Staff managers often have more formal education and sometimes are younger (and perhaps more ambitious) than line managers. Line managers may perceive staff managers as a threat to their own authority and thus may resent them. For their part, staff managers may become annoyed or angry if their expert recommendations—for example, in public relations or human resources management—are not adopted by line management.

Fortunately, there are several ways to minimize the likelihood of such conflict. One way is to integrate line and staff managers into one team. Another is to ensure that the areas of responsibility of line and staff managers are clearly defined. Finally, line and staff managers both can be held accountable for the results of their activities.

The Matrix Structure

When the matrix structure is used, individuals report to more than one superior at the same time. The **matrix structure** combines vertical and horizontal lines of authority, which is why it is called a matrix structure. The matrix structure occurs when product departmentalization is superimposed on a functionally departmentalized organization. In a matrix organization, authority flows both down and across. Martha Stewart Living Omnimedia, for example, utilizes the matrix structure to combine the management of its functional departments (publishing, Internet, broadcasting, and merchandising) with its product departments (food, crafts, entertaining, gardening, etc.).[4] Another example of a matrix organization could be an automobile manufacturer, whose company may be divided into functional departments, such as production, sales, marketing, distribution, and accounting, which co-manage with product departments (the vehicle models).

To understand the structure of a matrix organization, consider the usual functional arrangement, with people working in departments such as engineering, finance, and marketing. Now suppose that we assign people from these departments to a special group that is working on a new project as a team—a cross-functional team. A **cross-functional team** consists of individuals with varying specialties, expertise, and skills that are brought together to achieve a common task. Frequently, cross-functional teams are charged with the responsibility of developing new products. For example, Ford Motor Company assembled a special project team to design and manufacture its global cars. The manager in charge of a team is usually called a *project manager*. Any individual who is working with the team reports to *both* the project manager and the individual's superior in the functional department (see Figure 7.6).

Cross-functional team projects may be temporary, in which case the team is disbanded once the mission is accomplished, or they may be permanent. These teams often are empowered to make major decisions. When a cross-functional team is employed, prospective team members may receive special training because effective teamwork can require different skills. For cross-functional teams to be

matrix structure an organizational structure that combines vertical and horizontal lines of authority, usually by superimposing product departmentalization on a functionally departmentalized organization

cross-functional team a team of individuals with varying specialties, expertise, and skills that are brought together to achieve a common task

SPOTLIGHT

Top-Ranked Barriers to Women in the Workplace

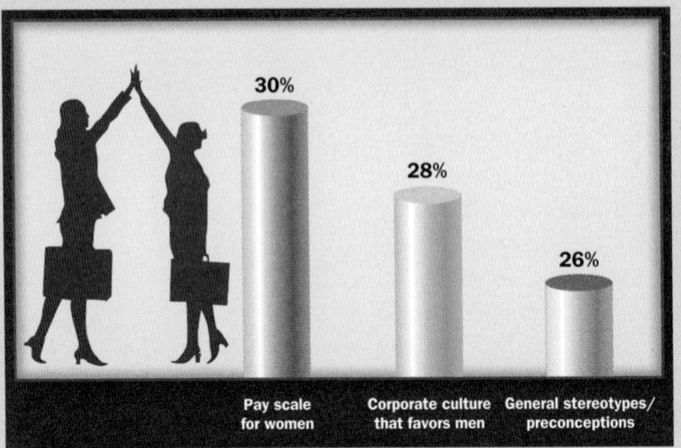

Source: Accenture survey of 1,000 full-time female workers 22 to 35 years old.

successful, team members must be given specific information on the job each performs. The team also must develop a sense of cohesiveness and maintain good communications among its members.

Matrix structures offer advantages over other organizational forms. Added flexibility is probably the most obvious advantage. The matrix structure also can increase productivity, raise morale, and nurture creativity and innovation. In addition, employees experience personal development through doing a variety of jobs.

The matrix structure also has disadvantages. Having employees report to more than one supervisor can cause confusion about who is in charge. Like committees, teams may take longer to resolve problems and issues than individuals working alone. Other difficulties include personality clashes, poor communication, undefined individual roles, unclear responsibilities, and finding ways to reward individual and team performance simultaneously. Because more managers and support staff may be needed, a matrix structure may be more expensive to maintain.

Figure 7.6 A Matrix Structure

A matrix is usually the result of combining product departmentalization with function departmentalization. It is a complex structure in which employees have more than one supervisor.

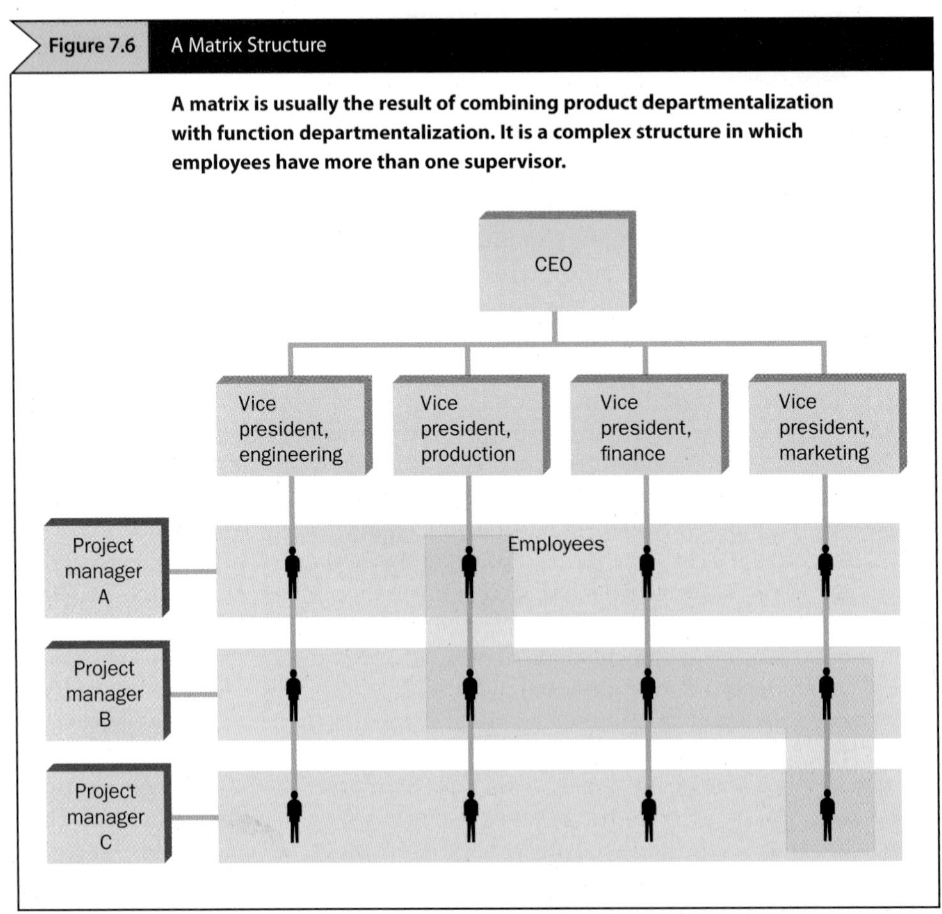

Source: Ricky W. Griffin, *Management*, 10th ed. Copyright © 2011 by South-Western/Cengage Learning, Mason, OH. Adapted with permission.

The Network Structure

In a **network structure** (sometimes called a *virtual organization*), administration is the primary function performed, and other functions such as engineering, production, marketing, and finance are contracted out to other organizations. Frequently, a network organization does not manufacture the products it sells. This type of organization has a few permanent employees consisting of top management and hourly clerical workers. Leased facilities and equipment, as well as temporary workers, are increased or decreased as the organization's needs change. Thus, there is rather limited formal structure associated with a network organization.

An obvious strength of a network structure is flexibility that allows the organization to adjust quickly to changes. Some of the challenges faced by managers in network-structured organizations include controlling the quality of work performed by other organizations, low morale and high turnover among hourly workers, and the vulnerability associated with relying on outside contractors.

7

Describe the effects of corporate culture.

Corporate Culture

Most managers function within a corporate culture. A **corporate culture** is generally defined as the inner rites, rituals, heroes, and values of a firm. An organization's culture has a powerful influence on how employees think and act. It also can determine public perception of the organization.

Corporate culture generally is thought to have a very strong influence on a firm's performance over time. Hence, it is useful to be able to assess a firm's corporate culture. Common indicators include the physical setting (building, office layouts), what the company says about its corporate culture (in advertising and news releases), how the company greets guests (does it have formal or informal reception areas?), and how employees spend their time (working alone in an office or working with others).

Goffee and Jones have identified four distinct types of corporate cultures (see Figure 7.7). One is called the *networked culture*, characterized by a base of trust and friendship among employees, a strong commitment to the organization, and an informal environment. The *mercenary culture* embodies the feelings of passion, energy, sense of purpose, and excitement for one's work. The term *mercenary* does not imply that employees are motivated to work only for the money, but this is part of it. In this culture, employees are very intense, focused, and determined to win. In the *fragmented culture*, employees do not become friends, and they work "at" the organization, not "for" it. Employees have a high degree of autonomy, flexibility, and equality. The *communal culture* combines the positive traits of the networked culture and the mercenary culture—those of friendship, commitment, high focus on performance, and high energy. People's lives revolve around the product in this culture, and success by anyone in the organization is celebrated by all.[5]

Some experts believe that cultural change is needed when a company's environment changes, when the industry becomes more competitive, the company's performance is mediocre, and when the company is growing or is about to become a truly large organization. For example, top executives at Dell Computer allocated considerable time and

network structure an organizational structure in which administration is the primary function, and most other functions are contracted out to other firms

corporate culture the inner rites, rituals, heroes, and values of a firm

Corporate culture. Food and fun are part of the corporate culture at Google.

Sustaining the Planet

GE's Environmental Stewardship

General Electric views sustainability as essential to being a good corporate citizen. The company has woven environmental stewardship into the fabric of its organizational structure and made sustainability an integral part of its corporate culture. Take a look: http://www.ge.com/citizenship/index.html.

resources to develop a strong, positive corporate culture aimed at increasing employee loyalty and the success of the company. Organizations in the future will look quite different. Experts predict that tomorrow's businesses will comprise small, task-oriented work groups, each with control over its own activities. These small groups will be coordinated through an elaborate computer network and held together by a strong corporate culture. Businesses operating in fast-changing industries will require leadership that supports trust and risk taking. Creating a culture of trust in an organization can lead to increases in growth, profit, productivity, and job satisfaction. A culture of trust can retain the best people, inspire customer loyalty, develop new markets, and increase creativity.

Another area where corporate culture plays a vital role is the integration of two or more companies. Business leaders often cite the role of corporate cultures in the integration process as one of the primary factors affecting the success of a merger or acquisition. Experts note that corporate culture is a way of conducting business both within the company and externally. If two merging companies do not address differences in corporate culture, they are setting themselves up for missed expectations and possibly failure.

Figure 7.7 Types of Corporate Cultures

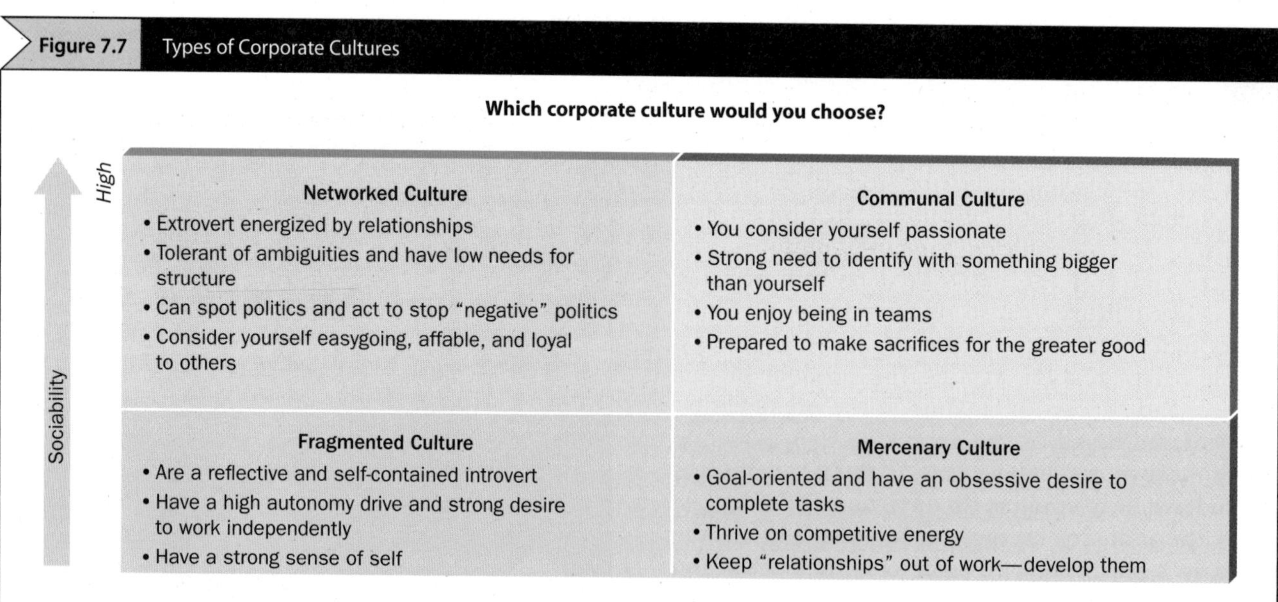

Source: "Types of Corporate Culture," in Rob Goffee and Gareth Jones, *The Character of a Corporation* (New York: HarperCollins, 1998). Copyright © 1998 by Rob Goffee and Gareth Jones. Permission granted by Rob Goffee and Gareth Jones by arrangement with The Helen Rees Literary Agency.

8

Understand how committees and task forces are used.

Committees and Task Forces

Today, business firms use several types of committees that affect organizational structure. An **ad hoc committee** is created for a specific short-term purpose, such as reviewing the firm's employee benefits plan. Once its work is finished, the ad hoc committee disbands. A **standing committee** is a relatively permanent committee charged with performing a recurring task. A firm might establish a budget review committee, for example, to review departmental budget requests on an ongoing basis. Finally, a **task force** is a committee established to investigate a major problem or pending decision. A firm contemplating a merger with another company might form a task force to assess the pros and cons of the merger.

Committees offer some advantages over individual action. Their several members are able to bring information and knowledge to the task at hand. Furthermore, committees tend to make more accurate decisions and to transmit their results through the organization more effectively. However, committee deliberations take longer than individual actions. In addition, unnecessary compromise may take place within the committee, or the opposite may occur, as one person dominates (and thus negates) the committee process.

ad hoc committee a committee created for a specific short-term purpose

standing committee a relatively permanent committee charged with performing some recurring task

task force a committee established to investigate a major problem or pending decision

9

Explain the functions of the informal organization and the grapevine in a business.

The Informal Organization and the Grapevine

So far, we have discussed the organization as a formal structure consisting of interrelated positions. This is the organization that is shown on an organization chart. There is another kind of organization, however, that does not show up on any chart. We define this **informal organization** as the pattern of behavior and interaction that stems from personal rather than official relationships. Firmly embedded within every informal organization are informal groups and the notorious grapevine.

An **informal group** is created by the group members themselves to accomplish goals that may or may not be relevant to the organization. Workers may create an informal group to go bowling, form a union, get a particular manager fired or transferred, or meet for lunch. The group may last for several years or a few hours.

Informal groups can be powerful forces in organizations. They can restrict output, or they can help managers through tight spots. They can cause disagreement and conflict, or they can help to boost morale and job satisfaction. They can show new people how to contribute to the organization, or they can help people to get away with substandard performance. Clearly, managers should be aware of these informal groups. Those who make the mistake of fighting the informal organization have a major obstacle to overcome.

informal organization the pattern of behavior and interaction that stems from personal rather than official relationships

informal group a group created by the members themselves to accomplish goals that may or may not be relevant to an organization

grapevine the informal communications network within an organization

The **grapevine** is the informal communications network within an organization. It is completely separate from—and sometimes much faster than—the organization's formal channels of communication. Formal communications usually follow a path that parallels the organizational chain of command. Information can be transmitted through the grapevine in any direction—up, down, diagonally, or horizontally across the organizational structure. Subordinates may pass information to their bosses, an executive may relay something to a maintenance worker, or there may be an exchange of information between people who work in totally unrelated departments. Grapevine information may be concerned with topics ranging from the latest management decisions to gossip.

How should managers treat the grapevine? Certainly, it would be a mistake to try to eliminate it. People working together, day in and day out, are going to communicate.

Informal groups. Informal groups can be a source of information and camaraderie for participants. These groups can create both challenges and benefits for an organization.

A more rational approach is to recognize its existence. For example, managers should respond promptly and aggressively to inaccurate grapevine information to minimize the damage that such misinformation might do. Moreover, the grapevine can come in handy when managers are on the receiving end of important communications from the informal organization.

In the next chapter, we apply these and other management concepts to an extremely important business function: the production of goods and services.

return to inside business

Unilever

The mission of Unilever is to "add vitality to life through meeting everyday needs for nutrition, hygiene, and personal care with brands that help people look good, feel good, and get more out of life." Meeting customer needs on the local level requires some degree of decentralization so everyday decisions can be made quickly. At the same time, Unilever has centralized functions such as global research and development. By streamlining the chain of command for its 6,000 research and development specialists, the company has improved efficiency while speeding up innovation.

Unilever uses structural flexibility to its advantage in other ways, as well. After acquiring Ben & Jerry's the company created a separate board of directors to preserve the ice cream company's unique social-responsibility values and corporate culture. Over the years, this structure has enabled Ben & Jerry's to expand internationally without losing the personality that loyal customers like as much as the quirky flavors.

Questions

1. In Unilever's structure, research and development report directly to the CEO. Do you think managers in this function are considered line or staff? Explain your answer.
2. When Unilever created a separate board of directors for Ben & Jerry's, was it acting to centralize or decentralize authority? What are the implications for decision-making at Ben & Jerry's?

SUMMARY

CHAPTER REVIEW

Summary

1 Understand what an organization is and identify its characteristics.

An organization is a group of two or more people working together to achieve a common set of goals. The relationships among positions within an organization can be illustrated by means of an organization chart. Five specific characteristics—job design, departmentalization, delegation, span of management, and chain of command—help to determine what an organization chart and the organization itself look like.

2 Explain why job specialization is important.

Job specialization is the separation of all the activities within an organization into smaller components and the assignment of those different components to different people. Several factors combine to make specialization a useful technique for designing jobs, but high levels of specialization may cause employee dissatisfaction and boredom. One technique for overcoming these problems is job rotation.

3 Identify the various bases for departmentalization.

Departmentalization is the grouping of jobs into manageable units. Typical bases for departmentalization are by function, product, location, or customer. Because each of these bases provides particular advantages, most firms—especially larger ones—use a combination of different bases in different organizational situations.

4 Explain how decentralization follows from delegation.

Delegation is the assigning of part of a manager's work to other workers. It involves the following three steps: (1) assigning responsibility, (2) granting authority, and

(3) creating accountability. A decentralized firm is one that delegates as much power as possible to people in the lower management levels. In a centralized firm, on the other hand, power is systematically retained at the upper levels.

5 Understand how the span of management describes an organization.

The span of management is the number of workers who report directly to a manager. Spans generally are characterized as wide (many workers per manager) or narrow (few workers per manager). Wide spans generally result in flat organizations (few layers of management); narrow spans generally result in tall organizations (many layers of management).

6 Describe the four basic forms of organizational structure.

There are four basic forms of organizational structure. The line structure is the oldest and most simple structure, in which the chain of command goes in a straight line from person to person down through the levels of management. The line-and-staff structure is similar to the line structure, but adds specialists called staff managers to assist the line managers in decision making. The line structure works most efficiently for smaller organizations, whereas the line-and-staff structure is used by medium- and large-size organizations. The matrix structure may be visualized as product departmentalization superimposed on functional departmentalization. With the matrix structure, an employee on a cross-functional team reports to both the project manager and the individual's supervisor in a functional department. In an organization with a network structure, the primary function performed internally is administration, and other functions are contracted out to other firms.

7 Describe the effects of corporate culture.

Corporate culture has both internal and external effects on an organization. An organization's culture can influence the way employees think and act, and it can also determine the public's perception of the organization. Corporate culture can affect a firm's performance over time, either negatively or positively. Creating a culture of trust, for example, can lead to increased growth, profits, productivity, and job satisfaction, while retaining the best employees, inspiring customer loyalty, developing new markets, and increasing creativity. In addition, when two or more companies undergo the integration process, their different or similar corporate cultures can affect the success of a merger or acquisition.

8 Understand how committees and task forces are used.

Committees and task forces are used to develop organizational structure within an organization. An ad hoc committee is created for a specific short-term purpose, whereas a standing committee is relatively permanent. A task force is created to investigate a major problem or pending decision.

9 Explain the functions of the informal organization and the grapevine in a business.

Informal groups are created by group members to accomplish goals that may or may not be relevant to the organization, and they can be very powerful forces. The grapevine—the informal communications network within an organization—can be used to transmit information (important or gossip) through an organization much faster than through the formal communication network. Information transmitted through the grapevine can go in any direction across the organizational structure, skipping up or down levels of management and even across departments.

Key Terms

You should now be able to define and give an example relevant to each of the following terms:

organization (193)
organization chart (193)
chain of command (193)
job specialization (194)
job rotation (196)
departmentalization (196)
departmentalization by function (196)
departmentalization by product (196)
departmentalization by location (196)
departmentalization by customer (197)
delegation (197)
responsibility (198)
authority (198)
accountability (198)
decentralized organization (198)
centralized organization (198)
span of management (or span of control) (199)
organizational height (200)
line structure (201)
line manager (201)
line-and-staff structure (202)
staff manager (202)
matrix structure (203)
cross-functional team (203)
network structure (205)
corporate culture (205)
ad hoc committee (207)
standing committee (207)
task force (207)
informal organization (207)
informal group (207)
grapevine (207)

Review Questions

1. In what way do organization charts create a picture of an organization?
2. What is the chain of command in an organization?
3. What determines the degree of specialization within an organization?
4. Describe how job rotation can be used to combat the problems caused by job specialization.
5. What are the major differences among the four departmentalization bases?
6. Why do most firms employ a combination of departmentalization bases?
7. What three steps are involved in delegation? Explain each.
8. How does a firm's top management influence its degree of centralization?
9. How is organizational height related to the span of management?
10. What are the key differences between line and staff positions?
11. Contrast line-and-staff and matrix forms of organizational structure.
12. What is corporate culture? Describe the major types.
13. Which form of organizational structure probably would lead to the strongest informal organization? Why?
14. What is the role of the informal organization?

Discussion Questions

1. How does the corporate culture of a local Best Buy store compare to that of a local McDonald's?
2. Which kinds of firms probably would operate most effectively as centralized firms? As decentralized firms?
3. How do decisions concerning span of management and the use of committees affect organizational structure?
4. How might a manager go about formalizing the informal organization?

Video Case 7.1

At Numi Organic Tea, Teams and Organizational Culture Are Critical

You might expect a company specializing in marketing organic teas to have a distinctive corporate culture. In the case of Numi Organic Tea, a progressive seller of premium organic and Fair Trade teas based in Oakland, California, you'd be right.

With a relatively small staff of about 50 people and a recent growth rate of 180 percent a year, Numi needs to remain nimble and responsive. Its founders, the brother-and-sister team of Ahmed and Reem Rahim, were inspired to create a tea company after Ahmed had spent some years operating tea houses in Europe while Reem studied art in the United States. Combining both their interests led to a unique firm dedicated to quality, sustainability, and community. Numi occupies offices that include a tea garden where employees often gather to relax, and it has won awards for many achievements including its unique teas, its innovative packaging, and its commitment to the environment. Numi's 25 different tea and flowering tea products and gift packs are sold in Whole Foods and Safeway markets, as well as in individual natural food and grocery stores throughout the United States, and in 20 other countries overseas.

The prevailing attitude in the company, which maintains a blog and a presence on Facebook and MySpace, is a can-do, team-oriented spirit. Because it's a small firm where everyone works hard, Numi can't afford rapid employee turnover and the time that would be lost in recruiting, interviewing, and training. Employees are thus carefully chosen for their willingness to do whatever it takes to get the job done and to remain upbeat and positive despite the occasional stress of working for a small company with customers around the world. Workers must also be able to devote long hours when necessary and share the company's goals.

Employees in Numi's distribution center, for instance, recently found themselves under pressure because it was taking nearly two weeks to fill international orders. With a new manager and a new focus on everyone's understanding how each job fit into the big picture, however, a sense of teamwork began to grow. Soon each employee had been trained to perform all the critical tasks in order fulfillment, so instead of working in isolation they were able to pitch in during crunch times. Their new flexibility reduced lead times for overseas orders to about five days and cut the time for domestic orders in half. Sometimes the team can ship them the same day.

At Numi, managers who communicate well and who are out working alongside their staff are the norm. They must also communicate well with customers and demonstrate a high level of emotional maturity. Some meet with their teams on a regular basis, to review project status against deadlines and due dates and to make changes in workload and procedures where necessary. The company offers flex-time to help employees retain a balance between their work and personal life, and when things get overwhelming at the office, there's always the tea garden and a freshly brewed cup of organic tea.[6]

Questions

1. Numi's customer service manager, Cindy Graffort, says the company is like a "living, breathing organism." What does she mean? How does the company's culture reflect this belief?
2. Numi's distribution manager, Dannielle Oviedo, says her philosophy of management means she gets involved in what her team is doing: "I do what I ask folks to do." Do you think she is a good delegator? Why or why not?
3. What can you infer about Numi's basis for departmentalization and its chain of command?

Case 7.2

HP's Corporate Challenge: To Remain Agile and Responsive in an Ever-Changing Environment

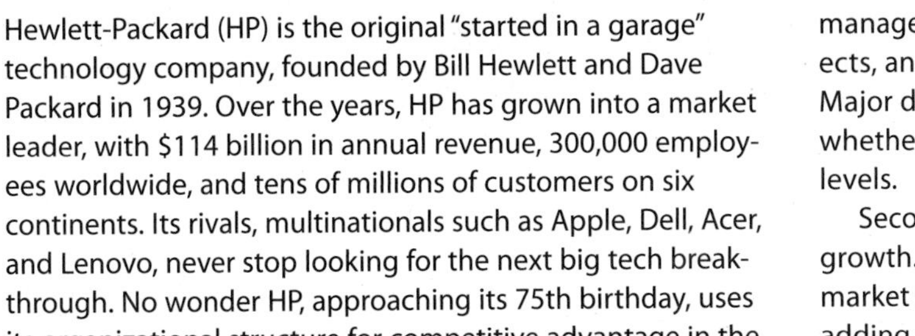

Hewlett-Packard (HP) is the original "started in a garage" technology company, founded by Bill Hewlett and Dave Packard in 1939. Over the years, HP has grown into a market leader, with $114 billion in annual revenue, 300,000 employees worldwide, and tens of millions of customers on six continents. Its rivals, multinationals such as Apple, Dell, Acer, and Lenovo, never stop looking for the next big tech breakthrough. No wonder HP, approaching its 75th birthday, uses its organizational structure for competitive advantage in the 21st-century race for higher sales and profits.

The company has seven divisions, organized according to product or function: Services, Enterprise Storage and Servers, HP Software, the Personal Systems Group, the Imaging and Printing Group, HP Financial Services, and Corporate Investments. Within each division are business units organized by product. For example, the services division contains four main units (infrastructure technology outsourcing, applications services, business process outsourcing, and technology services). Each unit hires managers and employees with the particular skills, experience, and training appropriate for the services it offers.

Some HP business units are organized by customer and by product within a division. The Personal Systems Group, for example, includes one unit that focuses on commercial PCs and one that focuses on consumer PCs. Establishing these as separate business units allows HP to address differences in products and customers' needs while sharing expertise within the division. For efficiency, some functions straddle divisions and serve multiple units. The company recently consolidated its data-center operations and now has six megacenters instead of 85 smaller centers for data management.

Through its organizational structure, HP seeks to achieve two key objectives. First, knowing that technological change can occur at any time and move in unexpected directions, the company is determined to remain agile and adaptable. Its structure leaves day-to-day planning, decisions, and implementation in the hands of each unit's managers, allowing them to satisfy customers, initiate projects, and respond to environmental shifts without delay. Major decisions that affect the overall organization, such as whether to acquire another company, are made at higher levels.

Second, the company uses its structure to support growth. Eyeing a larger share of the $1.7 trillion global market for information technology, HP has been steadily adding to its portfolio of goods and services. Some of this expansion has occurred through acquisition. During the past few years, HP has bought EDS, 3Com, and Palm, among other businesses, and merged their operations into the appropriate corporate divisions. Palm, a pioneer of handheld computing devices and maker of smart-phones, was integrated into HP's Personal Systems Group to enhance that division's technical capabilities in preparation for future growth.

Innovation has been woven into the fabric of HP's corporate culture since the early days. The company is famous for investing billions of dollars annually to research new technology and develop new products. Although senior managers don't want to stifle innovation by imposing too many limits, they have very clear expectations for research projects. "The key change we made was to take our brilliant scientists and sharpen their focus around a much smaller pool of big bets," explains the head of HP Labs. Researchers know that "every single [project] must have the potential to [generate] $1 billion-plus in revenue for HP." As a result, instead of pursuing as many as 150 projects at any given time, researchers now concentrate their efforts on the most promising two dozen projects.

Top managers are also involved in coordinating the overall efforts of employees that serve their very largest customers. For example, HP has a $3 billion contract to handle information technology operations for Procter & Gamble on an outsourcing basis. The head of the HP division visits with Procter & Gamble's senior managers six times a year to jointly evaluate performance. HP's CEO also joins the conversation at least twice a year. "When you have the CEO of a company sitting across the table saying, 'We're going to deliver this,' you know they're going to deliver," says a senior Procter & Gamble executive.[7]

Questions

1. How is corporate culture likely to affect HP's ability to integrate acquired companies into its organizational structure?
2. Analyze HP's use of departmentalization. Why are its choices appropriate for a technology company?
3. Analyze HP's approach to delegation and decentralization. Are its choices appropriate for a technology company? Why or why not?

Building Skills for Career Success

❶ JOURNALING FOR SUCCESS

Discovery statement: This chapter described the powerful influence that a corporate culture has on an organization.

Assume that after leaving school, you are hired by your "dream company."

Assignment

1. What are the major corporate culture dimensions of your dream company?
2. Before accepting a job at your "dream company," how will you find out about the company's corporate culture?
3. From Figure 7.7, identify the type of corporate culture that you prefer and explain why.
4. Thinking back to previous jobs that you have had, describe the worst corporate culture you have ever experienced.

❷ EXPLORING THE INTERNET

After studying the various organizational structures described in this chapter and the reasons for employing them, you may be interested in learning about the organizational structures in place at large firms. As noted in the chapter, departmentalization typically is based on function, product, location, and customer. Many large firms use a combination of these organizational structures successfully. You can gain a good sense of which organizational theme prevails in an industry by looking at several corporate sites.

Assignment

1. Explore the Web site of any large firm that you believe is representative of its industry, and find its organization chart or a description of its organization. Create a brief organization chart from the information you have found.
2. Describe the bases on which this firm is departmentalized.

❸ DEVELOPING CRITICAL-THINKING SKILLS

A firm's culture is a reflection of its most basic beliefs, values, customs, and rituals. Because it can have a powerful influence on how employees think and act, this culture also can have a powerful influence on a firm's performance. The influence may be for the better, of course, as in the case of Southwest Airlines, or it may be for the worse, as in the case of a bureaucratic organization whose employees feel hopelessly mired in red tape. When a company is concerned about mediocre performance and declining sales figures, its managers would do well to examine the cultural environment to see what might be in need of change.

Assignment

1. Analyze the cultural environment in which you work. (If you have no job, consider your school as your workplace and your instructor as your supervisor.) Ask yourself and your co-workers (or classmates) the following questions and record the answers:
   a. Do you feel that your supervisors welcome your ideas and respect them even when they may disagree with them? Do you take pride in your work? Do you feel that your work is appreciated? Do you think that the amount of work assigned to you is reasonable? Are you compensated adequately for your work?
   b. Are you proud to be associated with the company? Do you believe what the company says about itself in its advertisements? Are there any company policies or rules, written or unwritten, that you feel are unfair? Do you think that there is an opportunity for you to advance in this environment?
   c. How much independence do you have in carrying out your assignments? Are you ever allowed to act on your own, or do you feel that you have to consult with your supervisor on every detail?
   d. Do you enjoy the atmosphere in which you work? Is the physical setting pleasant? How often do you laugh in an average workday? How well do you get along with your supervisor and co-workers?
   e. Do you feel that the company cares about you? Will your supervisor give you time off when you have some pressing personal need? If the company had to downsize, how do you think you would be treated?

2. Using the responses to these questions, write a two-page paper describing how the culture of your workplace affects your performance and the overall performance of the firm. Point out the cultural factors that have the most beneficial and negative effects. Include your thoughts on how negative effects could be reversed.

4 BUILDING TEAM SKILLS

An organization chart is a diagram showing how employees and tasks are grouped and how the lines of communication and authority flow within an organization. These charts can look very different depending on a number of factors, including the nature and size of the business, the way it is departmentalized, its patterns of delegating authority, and its span of management.

Assignment

1. Working in a team, use the following information to draw an organization chart: The KDS Design Center works closely with two home-construction companies, Amex and Highmass. KDS's role is to help customers select materials for their new homes and to ensure that their selections are communicated accurately to the builders. The company is also a retailer of wallpaper, blinds, and drapery. The retail department, the Amex accounts, and the Highmass accounts make up KDS's three departments. The company has the following positions: President, executive vice president, managers, 2 appointment coordinators, 2 Amex coordinators, 2 Highmass coordinators, 2 consultants/designers for the Amex and Highmass accounts, 15 retail positions, and 4 payroll and billing personnel.
2. After your team has drawn the organization chart, discuss the following:
   a. What type of organizational structure does your chart depict? Is it a bureaucratic, matrix, cluster, or network structure? Why?
   b. How does KDS use departmentalization?
   c. To what extent is authority in the company centralized or decentralized?
   d. What is the span of management within KDS?
   e. Which positions are line positions and which are staff? Why?
3. Prepare a three-page report summarizing what the chart revealed about relationships and tasks at the KDS Design Center and what your team learned about the value of organization charts. Include your chart in your report.

5 RESEARCHING DIFFERENT CAREERS

In the past, company loyalty and the ability to assume increasing job responsibility usually ensured advancement within an organization. While the reasons for seeking advancement (the desire for a better-paying position, more prestige, and job satisfaction) have not changed, the qualifications for career advancement have. In today's business environment, climbing the corporate ladder requires packaging and marketing yourself. To be promoted within your company or to be considered for employment with another company, it is wise to improve your skills continually. By taking workshops and seminars or enrolling in community college courses, you can keep up with the changing technology in your industry. Networking with people in your business or community can help you to find a new job. Most jobs are filled through personal contacts, who you know can be important.

A list of your accomplishments on the job can reveal your strengths and weaknesses. Setting goals for improvement helps to increase your self-confidence.

Be sure to recognize the signs of job dissatisfaction. It may be time to move to another position or company.

Assignment

Are you prepared to climb the corporate ladder? Do a self-assessment by analyzing the following areas and summarize the results in a two-page report.

1. Skills
   - What are your most valuable skills?
   - What skills do you lack?
   - Describe your plan for acquiring new skills and improving your skills.
2. Networking
   - How effective are you at using a mentor?
   - Are you a member of a professional organization?
   - In which community, civic, or church groups are you participating?
   - Whom have you added to your contact list in the last six weeks?
3. Accomplishments
   - What achievements have you reached in your job?
   - What would you like to accomplish? What will it take for you to reach your goal?
4. Promotion or new job
   - What is your likelihood for getting a promotion?
   - Are you ready for a change? What are you doing or willing to do to find another job?

Producing Quality Goods and Services

8

Learning Objectives

What you will be able to do once you complete this chapter:

1. Explain the nature of production.
2. Outline how the conversion process transforms raw materials, labor, and other resources into finished products or services.
3. Describe how research and development lead
4. Discuss the components involved in planning the production process.
5. Explain how purchasing, inventory control, scheduling, and quality control affect production.
6. Summarize how productivity and technology

FYI

Did You Know?

With factories or offices in nearly every country on Earth, Nestlé rings up more than $100 billion in global revenue and employs 280,000 people worldwide.

inside business

Nestlé Plans Ahead for Quality Production

From chocolate bars to coffee to cat food, quality food manufacturing is always on the menu at Switzerland's Nestlé. Among the company's best-known brands are Nescafé, Nesquik, Kit Kat, Häagen-Dazs, Lean Cuisine, Juicy Juice, Purina, and Fancy Feast. Nestlé's U.S. sales top $10 billion, and its global sales exceed $100 billion. The company employs 280,000 people worldwide and manufactures foods and beverages on every continent.

Whereas some big companies outsource most of their production to other firms, Nestlé generally handles its own. As a result, management can tightly control every aspect of the operation, from the careful selection of ingredients and the maintenance of equipment to the timing and quality of production and packaging. Sometimes Nestlé partners with a local manufacturer for competitive reasons, such as speeding a new product to market. Still, "we invariably find that we are much more cost-effective in-house than out-of-house," a Nestlé executive explains.

To be more responsive to customers' needs and tap the resources of local suppliers, Nestlé prefers to locate production in or near the markets it serves. It operates 26 manufacturing plants in the United States alone, including a state-of-the-art facility recently opened in Anderson, Indiana. The 900,000-square-foot plant makes liquid Nesquik and Coffee-Mate products using ultra-high-temperature processing and cutting-edge packaging technology. In the past, Nestlé had to keep these dairy products chilled after production to maintain quality and freshness. Now, thanks to the new production process, the products are "shelf stable" and can be distributed and stored without special refrigeration, adding to their convenience.

Sustainability is also on Nestlé's menu. As it builds new plants and updates existing facilities, the company has been incorporating numerous features that help the environment by conserving energy, reducing harmful emissions, and cutting waste. For example, the Anderson, Indiana, plant was designed to meet the U.S. Green Building Council's energy and environmental guidelines for sustainability. When Nestlé expanded its Solon, Ohio, plant, the company substituted landfill gas for most of the natural gas used to power production. In the process of making its products greener, Nestlé is redesigning some packaging to increase the amount of biodegradable materials used. Small wonder that Nestlé has become known for its social responsibility, not just its quality.[1]

There's a good chance when you saw the name Nestlé in the opening case for this chapter you thought about chocolate milk or chocolate candy—products you see everyday. However, this company is so much more. Consider three factors about Nestlé. First, the company is profitable because it produces products that customers want or need. Like most companies, it wants to increase sales and profits, but it all starts with the customer. Second, Nestlé is concerned with quality. The manufacturing process begins with the selection of suppliers to get just the right ingredients. Then each step of the production process is examined to make sure that quality is a high priority. Finally, Nestlé is a socially responsible company. Among the company's top concerns are its employees, the environment, and giving something back to the communities in which it operates. Today, it is quite common to hear of profitable companies. It is less common to hear of profitable companies that are held in high regard by their competitors. And yet, Nestlé has managed to do both—earn both profits and respect. Nestlé is an excellent example of what this chapter's content—the production of quality goods and services—is all about.

We begin this chapter with an overview of operations management—the activities required to produce goods and services that meet the needs of customers. In this section, we also discuss the role of manufacturing in the U.S. economy, competition in the global marketplace, and careers in operations management. Next, we describe the conversion process that makes production possible and also note the growing role of services in our economy. Then we examine more closely three important aspects of operations management: developing ideas for new products, planning for production, and effectively controlling operations after production has begun. We close the chapter with a look at the productivity trends and the ways that productivity can be improved through the use of technology.

1

Explain the nature of production.

What Is Production?

Have you ever wondered where a new pair of Levi jeans comes from? Or a new Mitsubishi flat-screen television, Izod pullover sweater, or Uniroyal tire for your car? Even factory service on a Hewlett-Packard computer or a Maytag clothes dryer would be impossible if it weren't for the activities described in this chapter. In fact, these products and services and millions of others like them would not exist if it weren't for production activities.

Let's begin this chapter by reviewing what an operating manager does. In Chapter 6, we described an *operations manager* as a person who manages the systems that convert resources into goods and services. This area of management is usually referred to as **operations management**, which consists of all the activities managers engage in to produce goods and services.

operations management all activities managers engage in to produce goods and services

To produce a product or service successfully, a business must perform a number of specific activities. For example, suppose that Chevrolet has an idea for a new version of the sporty Camaro that will cost approximately $30,000. Marketing research must determine not only if customers are willing to pay the price for this product but also what special features they want. Then Chevrolet's operations managers must turn the idea into reality.

Chevrolet's managers cannot just push the "start button" and immediately begin producing the new automobile. Production must be planned. As you will see, planning takes place both *before* anything is produced and *during* the production process.

Managers also must concern themselves with the control of operations to ensure that the organization's goals are achieved. For a product such as Chevrolet's Camaro, control of operations involves a number of important issues, including product quality, performance standards, the amount of inventory of both raw materials and finished products, and production costs.

We discuss each of the major activities of operations management later in this chapter. First, however, let's take a closer look at American manufacturers and how they compete in the global marketplace.

Where did these blue toy rabbits come from? Answer: China. In today's competitive global marketplace, many products like these stuffed animals are manufactured in China and then shipped to nations around the globe. Today, people in all nations want to sell the products and services they produce to customers in their own nation and to customers in the global marketplace. In fact, experts say the world has become a smaller place because of increased global trade.

How American Manufacturers Compete in the Global Marketplace

After World War II, the United States became the most productive country in the world. For almost 30 years, until the late 1970s, its leadership was never threatened. By then, however, manufacturers in Japan, Germany, Great Britain, Taiwan, Korea, Sweden, and other industrialized nations were offering U.S. firms increasing competition. Now the Chinese are manufacturing everything from sophisticated electronic equipment and automobiles to less expensive everyday items—often at a lower cost than the same goods can be manufactured in other countries.

When assessing manufacturing in the United States, there is both good and bad news. First, the bad news: The number of Americans employed in the manufacturing sector has decreased. Currently, approximately 12 million U.S. workers are employed in manufacturing jobs—down from just over 19 million back in 1979.[2] Many of the manufacturing jobs that were lost were outsourced to low-wage workers in nations where there are few labor and environmental regulations. Finally, the number of unemployed factory workers increased during the recent economic crisis because of decreased consumer demand for manufactured goods. As a result of the previously noted factors, manufacturing accounts for only about 11 percent of the current work force.[3] Since 1979, 7 million jobs have been lost, and many of those jobs aren't coming back.

Now, the good news. The United States remains the largest manufacturing country in the world—producing approximately 20 percent of total global manufacturing output.[4] As a result, the manufacturing sector is still a very important part of the U.S. economy. Although the number of manufacturing jobs has declined, productivity has increased. At least two very important factors account for increases in productivity: First, innovation—finding a better way to produce products—is the key factor that has enabled American manufacturers to compete in the global marketplace. Often, innovation is the result of manufacturers investing money to purchase new, state-of-the-art equipment that helps employees improve productivity. Second, today's workers in the manufacturing sector are highly skilled in order to operate sophisticated equipment. Simply put, Americans are making more goods, but with fewer employees.

Even more good news. Many American manufacturers that outsourced work to factories in foreign nations are once again beginning to manufacture goods in the United States. For example, General Electric (GE) built a new plant in Louisville, Kentucky, to manufacture hybrid electric water heaters. Before the Kentucky plant was built, the water heaters were manufactured in China.[5] Increasing labor costs in foreign nations, faster product development when goods are produced in the United States, the ability to quickly customize existing products to meet customer needs, and federal and state subsidies all help account for this trend in U.S. manufacturing.

Although the global marketplace has never been more competitive, the most successful U.S. firms have focused on the following:

1. Motivating employees to cooperate with management and improve productivity.
2. Reducing costs by selecting suppliers that offer higher quality raw materials and components at reasonable prices.
3. Using computer-aided and flexible manufacturing systems that allow a higher degree of customization.
4. Improving control procedures to help ensure lower manufacturing costs.
5. Using green manufacturing to conserve natural resources and sustain the planet.

Although competing in the global economy is a major challenge, it is a worthwhile pursuit. For most firms, competing in the global marketplace is not only profitable but also an essential activity that requires the cooperation of everyone within the organization.

Careers in Operations Management

Although it is hard to provide information about specific career opportunities in operations management, some generalizations do apply to this management area. First, you must appreciate the manufacturing process and the steps required to produce a product or service. A basic understanding of mass production and the difference between an analytical process and a synthetic process is essential. **Mass production** is a manufacturing process that lowers the cost required to produce a large number of identical or similar products over a long period of time. An **analytical process** breaks raw materials into different component parts. For example, a barrel of crude oil refined by Marathon Oil Corporation—a Texas-based oil and chemical refiner—can be broken down into gasoline, oil, and lubricants and many other petroleum by-products. A **synthetic process** is just the opposite of the analytical one; it combines raw materials or components to create a finished product. Black & Decker uses a synthetic process when it combines plastic, steel, rechargeable batteries, and other components to produce a cordless drill.

mass production a manufacturing process that lowers the cost required to produce a large number of identical or similar products over a long period of time

analytical process a process in operations management in which raw materials are broken into different component parts

synthetic process a process in operations management in which raw materials or components are combined to create a finished product

Once you understand that operations managers are responsible for producing tangible products or services that customers want, you must determine how you fit into the production process. Today's successful operations managers must:

1. Be able to motivate and lead people.
2. Understand how technology can make a manufacturer more productive and efficient.
3. Appreciate the control processes that help lower production costs and improve product quality.
4. Understand the relationship between the customer, the marketing of a product, and the production of a product.

If operations management seems like an area you might be interested in, why not do more career exploration? You could take an operations management course if your college or university offers one, or you could obtain a part-time job during the school year or a summer job in a manufacturing company.

2

Outline how the conversion process transforms raw materials, labor, and other resources into finished products or services.

The Conversion Process

The purpose of manufacturing is to provide utility to customers. **Utility** is the ability of a good or service to satisfy a human need. Although there are four types of utilities—form, place, time, and possession—operations management focuses primarily on form utility. **Form utility** is created by people converting raw materials, finances, and information into finished products. The other types of utility—place, time, and possession—are discussed in Chapter 12.

But how does the conversion take place? How does Kellogg's convert grain, sugar, salt, and other ingredients; money from previous sales and stockholders' investments; production workers and managers; and economic and marketing forecasts into Frosted Flakes cereal products? How does New York Life Insurance convert office buildings, insurance premiums, actuaries, and mortality tables into life insurance policies? They do so through the use of a conversion process like the one illustrated in Figure 8.1. As indicated by our New York Life Insurance example, the conversion process is not limited to manufacturing products. The conversion process also can be used to produce services.

utility the ability of a good or service to satisfy a human need

form utility utility created by people converting raw materials, finances, and information into finished products

Manufacturing Using a Conversion Process

The conversion of resources into products and services can be described in several ways. We limit our discussion here to three: the focus or major resource used in the conversion process, its magnitude of change, and the number of production processes employed.

Focus By the *focus* of a conversion process, we mean the resource or resources that make up the major or most important *input*. The resources are financial, material, information, and people—the same resources discussed in Chapters 1 and 6. For a bank such as Citibank, financial resources are the major resource. A chemical and energy company such as Chevron concentrates on material resources. Your college or university is concerned primarily with information. And temporary employment services, such as Manpower, Inc., focus on the use of human resources.

Magnitude of Change The *magnitude* of a conversion process is the degree to which the resources are physically changed. At one extreme lie such processes as the one by which the Glad Products Company produces Glad

Many parts equal one automobile. The conversion process required to manufacture a complicated product like an automobile requires a number of steps *and*, in most cases, 4,000 to 5,000 different parts. In this photo, Derek Hurlburt uses high-tech machinery to bolt the wheels on a new Chevrolet Camaro at the General Motors of Canada plant in Oshawa, Ontario, Canada.

Figure 8.1 The Conversion Process

The conversion process converts ideas and resources into useful goods and services. The ability to create ideas and to produce products and services is a crucial step in the economic development of any nation.

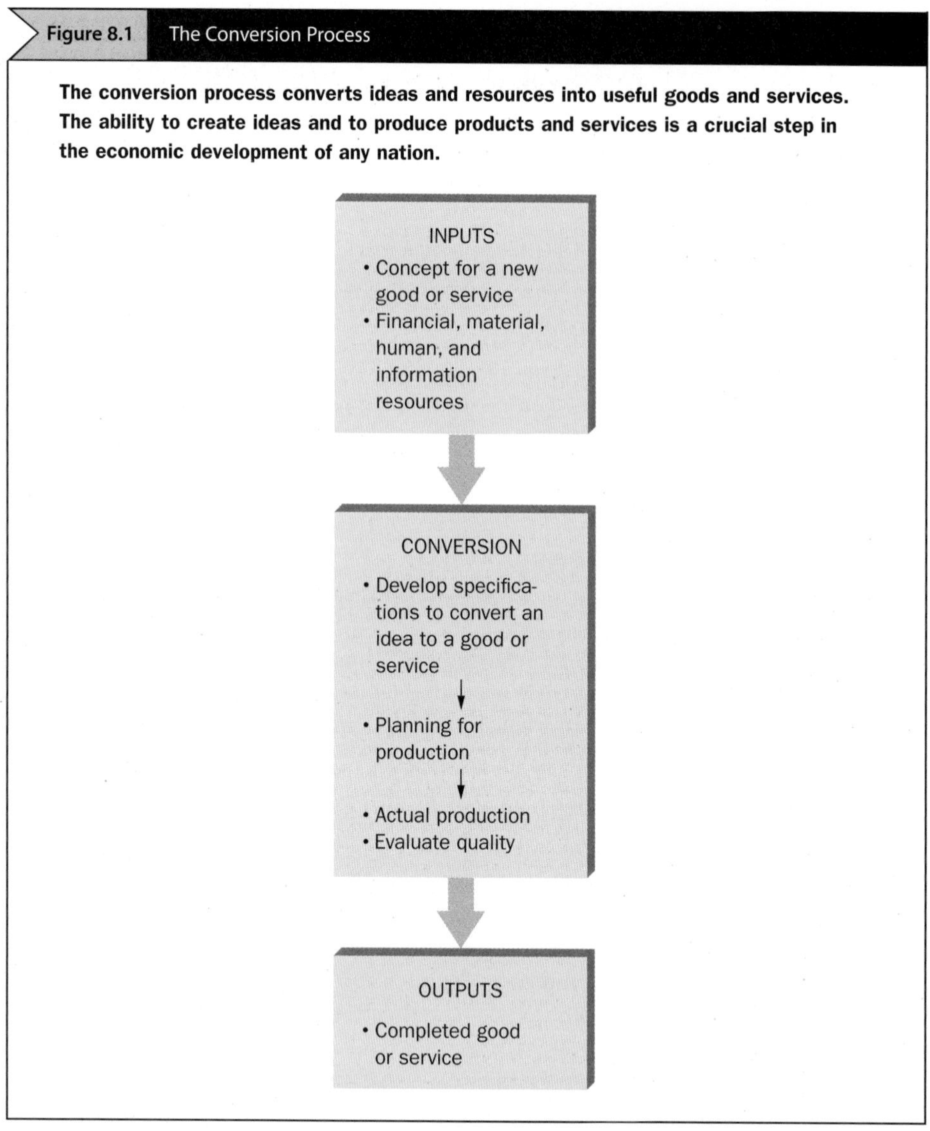

Cling Wrap. Various chemicals in liquid or powder form are combined to produce long, thin sheets of plastic Glad Cling Wrap. Here, the original resources are totally unrecognizable in the finished product. At the other extreme, Southwest Airlines produces *no* physical change in its original resources. The airline simply provides a service and transports people from one place to another.

Number of Production Processes A single firm may employ one production process or many. In general, larger firms that make a variety of products use multiple production processes. For example, GE manufactures some of its own products, buys other merchandise from suppliers, and operates multiple divisions including a finance division, a lighting division, an entertainment division, a medical equipment division, and other divisions responsible for the products and services that customers associate with the GE name. Smaller firms, by contrast, may use one production process. For example, Texas-based Advanced Cast Stone, Inc., manufactures one basic product: building materials made from concrete.

The Increasing Importance of Services

The application of the basic principles of operations management to the production of services has coincided with a dramatic growth in the number and diversity of service businesses. In 1900, only 28 percent of American workers were employed in service firms. By 1950, this figure had grown to 40 percent, and by 2010, it had risen to 86 percent.[6] In fact, the American economy is now characterized as a **service economy** (see Figure 8.2). A service economy is one in which more effort is devoted to the production of services than to the production of goods.

Today, the managers of restaurants, laundries, real estate agencies, banks, movie theaters, airlines, travel bureaus, and other service firms have realized that they can benefit from the experience of manufacturers. Yet the production of services is very different from the production of manufactured goods in the following four ways:

1. Services are consumed immediately and, unlike manufactured goods, cannot be stored. For example, a hair stylist cannot store completed haircuts.
2. Services are provided when and where the customer desires the service. In many cases, customers will not travel as far to obtain a service.
3. Services are usually labor-intensive because the human resource is often the most important resource used in the production of services.
4. Services are intangible, and it is therefore more difficult to evaluate customer satisfaction.[7]

Although it is often more difficult to measure customer satisfaction, today's successful service firms work hard at providing the services customers want. Compared with manufacturers, service firms often listen more carefully to customers and respond more quickly to the market's changing needs. For example, Maggiano's Little Italy restaurant is a chain of eating establishments owned by Brinker International. This restaurant prides itself on customer service and wants customers to have an enjoyable dining experience. In order to continuously improve customer service, the restaurant encourages diners to complete online surveys that prompt diners to evaluate the

Sustaining the Planet

Sustainable Manufacturing Clearing-House

The U.S. Department of Commerce has set up a Web site to serve as a clearing-house for information about federal programs and resources that support sustainable manufacturing. The site is searchable by industry or by sustainability issue, and visitors can sign up to receive free e-mail updates. Take a look: http://www.trade.gov/competitiveness/sustainablemanufacturing/index.asp.

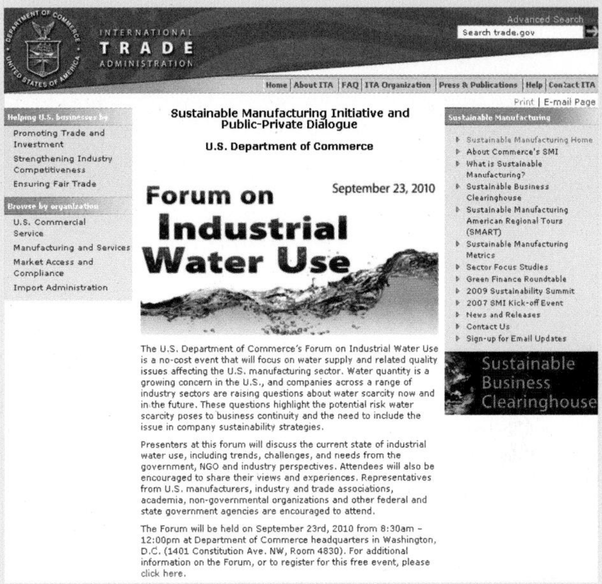

Figure 8.2 Service Industries

The growth of service firms has increased so dramatically that we now live in what is referred to as a service economy.

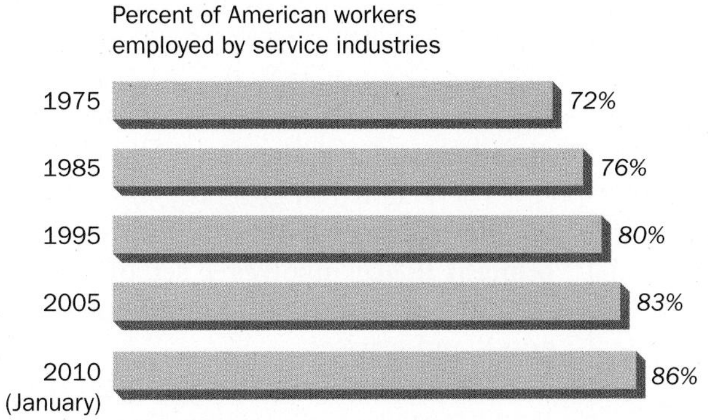

Percent of American workers employed by service industries

Year	Percent
1975	72%
1985	76%
1995	80%
2005	83%
2010 (January)	86%

Source: U.S. Bureau of Labor Statistics Web site, http://www.bls.gov (accessed May 1, 2010).

service economy an economy in which more effort is devoted to the production of services than to the production of goods

Ethical Challenges &

SUCCESSFUL SOLUTIONS

Ecotourism Services

From boat trips to the remote Galapagos Islands to hikes through the rugged Canadian backcountry, ecotourism to regions of natural beauty is a fast-growing segment of the service economy. Specialized service businesses—large and small—have sprung up to cater to the needs of adventurous travelers who want to visit pristine places all over the planet.

Yet the ecotourism boom has intensified the controversy over bringing travelers to ecologically sensitive destinations. Some people worry that increased tourism will overwhelm fragile ecosystems, increase pollution, and lead to overcommercialization. Proponents say ecotourism attracts much-needed economic development, with more job opportunities and more money to preserve the unique character of scenic areas.

Many local governments strive for balance by limiting the number of tourists at sensitive sites and setting environmental-protection standards for travel firms. Some ecotourism services showcase their ethical side by going beyond the basics. Lindblad Expeditions, for example, donates to conservation groups in the Galapagos and other areas where it operates. Karisia, a safari firm in Kenya, gets visitors out of gas-guzzling all-terrain vehicles with tours on mountain bikes and on foot. "The idea is to get people to appreciate nature through traveling here and supporting the local communities, so they in turn become inspired to protect the animals and everything around them," says one of the owners.

Sources: Lucy Siegle, "Is It Possible to Be an Eco-Friendly Tourist?" *The Observer (UK)*, November 22, 2009, http://www.guardian.co.uk; Simon Horsford, "Hump Day," *Time International*, August 24, 2009, 49; Lindblad Expeditions, http://www.expeditions.com.

food, atmosphere, service, and other variables. The information from the surveys is then used to fine-tune the way Maggiano's meets its customers' needs.

research and development (R&D) a set of activities intended to identify new ideas that have the potential to result in new goods and services

Now that we understand something about the production process that is used to transform resources into goods and services, we can consider three major activities involved in operations management: product development, planning for production, and operations control.

3

Describe how research and development lead to new products and services.

Where Do New Products and Services Come From?

No firm can produce a product or service until it has an idea. In other words, someone first must come up with a new way to satisfy a need—a new product or an improvement in an existing product. Both Apple's iPad and Amazon's Kindle began as an idea. Although no one can predict with 100 percent accuracy what types of products will be available in the next five years, it is safe to say that companies will continue to introduce new products that will change our everyday lives.

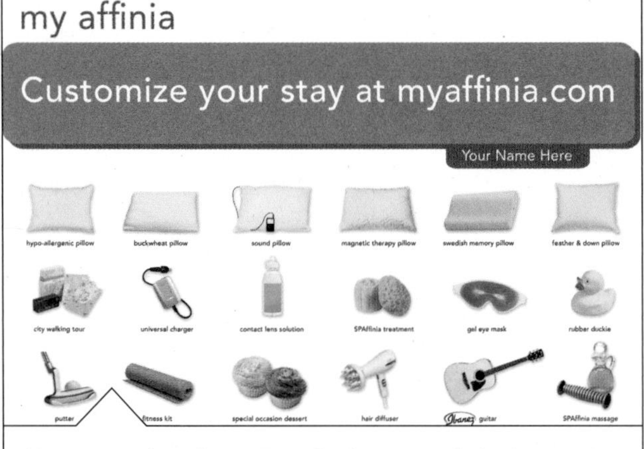

Home away from home. To make their guests feel at home, Affinia Hotels has developed a revolutionary new customer service program that allows guests to customize every aspect of their stay. Using the new online service, guests can pre-select "just the right features" that help make their stay perfect and at the same time build repeat business for this upscale hotel chain.

© AP Images/PRNewsFoto/Affinia Hotels

Research and Development

How did we get the iPad and the Kindle? We got them as a result of people working with new ideas that developed into useful products. In the same way, scientists and researchers working in businesses, colleges, and universities have produced many of the newer products we already take for granted.

These activities generally are referred to as *research and development*. For our purposes, **research and development (R&D)** involves a set of activities intended to identify new ideas that have the potential to result in new goods and services.

Today, business firms use three general types of R&D activities. *Basic research* consists of activities aimed at uncovering new knowledge. The goal of basic research is scientific advancement, without regard for its potential use in the development of goods and services. *Applied research*, in contrast, consists of activities geared toward discovering new knowledge with some potential use. *Development and implementation* involves research activities undertaken specifically to put new or existing knowledge to use in producing goods and services. The 3M Company has always been known for its development and implementation research activities. Currently, the company employs 6,700 researchers worldwide and has invested more than $6.9 billion over the last five years to develop new products designed to make people's lives easier and safer.[8]

Zero calories but *great* taste. The goal for The Coca-Cola Company was to develop a soft drink that had real Coke taste, but zero calories. As a result of hard work by the company's product research and development team, Coca-Cola Zero is one of the most successful new products in the company's history. Today, the company sells more than 600 million cases of Coca-Cola Zero each year in more than 130 countries.

Product Extension and Refinement

When a brand-new product is first marketed, its sales are zero and slowly increase from that point. If the product is successful, annual sales increase more and more rapidly until they reach some peak. Then, as time passes, annual sales begin to decline, and they continue to decline until it is no longer profitable to manufacture the product. (This rise-and-decline pattern, called the *product life-cycle*, is discussed in more detail in Chapter 13.)

If a firm sells only one product, when that product reaches the end of its life-cycle, the firm will die, too. To stay in business, the firm must, at the very least, find ways to refine or extend the want-satisfying capability of its product. Consider television sets. Since they were introduced in the late 1930s, television sets have been constantly *refined* so that they now provide clearer, sharper pictures with less dial adjusting. During the same time, television sets also were extended. There are television-only sets and others that include DVD players. There are even television sets that allow their owners to access the Internet. And the latest development—high-definition television—has already become the standard.

For most firms, extension and refinement are expected results of their research, development, and implementation activities. Often, product extensions and refinements result from the application of new knowledge to existing products. Each refinement or extension results in an essentially "new" product whose sales make up for the declining sales of a product that was introduced earlier. When consumers discovered that the original five varieties of Campbell's Soup were of the highest quality, as well as inexpensive, the soups were an instant success. Although one of the most successful companies at the beginning of the 1900s, Campbell's had to continue to innovate, refine, and extend its product line. For example, many consumers in the United States live in what is called an on-the-go society. To meet this need, Campbell's Soup has developed ready-to-serve products that can be popped into a microwave at work or school.

A new product or a product extension? Actually, the answer is both. For Apple, the iPad is a new product based on improved technology. For Netflix, the ability to download a movie to an iPad is a product extension and a new way to distribute rental movies. As a result, both companies have been able to increase sales and profits.

How Do Managers Plan Production?

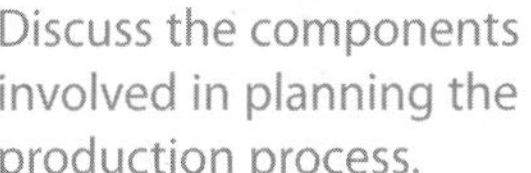

Discuss the components involved in planning the production process.

Only a few of the many ideas for new products, refinements, and extensions ever reach the production stage. For those ideas that do, however, the next step is planning for production. Once a new product idea has been identified, planning for

Figure 8.3 Planning for Production

Once research and development identifies an idea that meets customer needs, manufacturers then use three additional phases to convert the idea to an actual product or service.

1. Research and development identifies an idea for a new product or service.
2. Design planning develops a plan to convert the idea into a new product or service.
3. Facilities planning identifies a site where the good or service can be produced.
4. Operational planning decides on the amount of products or services that will be produced within a specific time period.

design planning the development of a plan for converting an idea into an actual product or service

product line a group of similar products that differ only in relatively minor characteristics

Automated assembly lines: The key to increasing both quality and productivity. The hot, dirty job of welding, which is key to many manufacturing and construction tasks, is changing. Today, welders are becoming operators of robots that can weld quicker and with more precision. To help companies plan for the future, Lincoln Electric, the company that produces this robotic rapid arc welder, opened a 100,000 square foot automation center where customers can see the latest in manufacturing technology.

© AP images/Tony Dejak

production involves three different phases: design planning, facilities planning, and operational planning (see Figure 8.3).

Design Planning

When the R&D staff at Hewlett-Packard recommended to top management that the firm produce and market an affordable netbook computer, the company could not simply swing into production the next day. Instead, a great deal of time and energy had to be invested in determining what the new computer would look like, where and how it would be produced, and what options would be included. These decisions are a part of design planning. **Design planning** is the development of a plan for converting an idea into an actual product or service. The major decisions involved in design planning deal with product line, required capacity, and use of technology.

Product Line A **product line** is a group of similar products that differ only in relatively minor characteristics. During the design-planning stage, a computer manufacturer such as Hewlett-Packard must determine how many different models to produce and what major options to offer. Likewise, a restaurant chain such as Pizza Hut must decide how many menu items to offer.

An important issue in deciding on the product line is to balance customer preferences and production requirements. For this reason, marketing managers play an important role in making product-line decisions. Typically, marketing personnel want a "long" product line that offers customers many options. Because a long product line with more options gives customers greater choice, it is easier to sell products that meet the needs of individual customers. On the other hand, production personnel generally want a "short" product line with fewer options because products are easier to produce. In many cases, the actual choice between a long and short product line involves balancing customer preferences with the cost and problems associated with a more complex production process.

Once the product line has been determined, each distinct product within the product line must be designed. **Product design** is the process of creating a set of specifications from which a product can be produced. When designing a new product, specifications are extremely important. For example, product engineers for Whirlpool Corporation must make sure that a new frost-free refrigerator keeps food frozen in the freezer compartment. At the same time, they must make sure that lettuce and tomatoes do not freeze in the crisper section of the refrigerator. The need for a complete product design is fairly obvious; products that work cannot be manufactured without it. But services should be designed carefully as well—and *for the same reason.*

Required Production Capacity **Capacity** is the amount of products or services that an organization can produce in a given period of time. (For example, the capacity of a Panasonic assembly plant might be 1.3 million high-definition televisions per year.) Operations managers—again working with the firm's marketing managers—must determine the required capacity. This, in turn, determines the size of the production facility. If the facility is built with too much capacity, valuable resources (plant, equipment, and money) will lie idle. If the facility offers insufficient capacity, additional capacity may have to be added later when it is much more expensive than in the initial building stage.

Capacity means about the same thing to service businesses. For example, the capacity of a restaurant such as the Hard Rock Cafe in Nashville, Tennessee, is the number of customers it can serve at one time. As with the manufacturing facility described earlier, if the restaurant is built with too much capacity—too many tables and chairs—valuable resources will be wasted. If the restaurant is too small, customers may have to wait for service; if the wait is too long, they may leave and choose another restaurant.

Use of Technology During the design-planning stage, management must determine the degree to which *automation* and *technology* will be used to produce a product or service. Here, there is a trade-off between high initial costs and low operating costs (for automation) and low initial costs and high operating costs (for human labor). Ultimately, management must choose between a labor-intensive technology and a capital-intensive technology. A **labor-intensive technology** is a process in which people must do most of the work. Housecleaning services and the New York Yankees baseball team, for example, are labor-intensive. A **capital-intensive technology** is a process in which machines and equipment do most of the work. A Sony automated assembly plant is capital-intensive.

Facilities Planning

Once initial decisions have been made about a new product line, required capacity, and the use of technology, it is time to determine where the products or services are going to be produced. Generally, a business will choose to produce a new product in an existing factory as long as (1) the existing factory has enough capacity to handle customer demand for both the new product and established products and (2) the cost of refurbishing an existing factory is less than the cost of building a new one.

After exploring the capacity of existing factories, management may decide to build a new production facility. Once again, a number of decisions must be made. Should all the organization's production capacity be placed in one or two large facilities? Or should it be divided among several smaller facilities? In general, firms that market a wide variety of products find it more economical to have a number of smaller facilities. Firms that produce only a small number of products tend to have fewer but larger facilities.

product design the process of creating a set of specifications from which a product can be produced

capacity the amount of products or services that an organization can produce in a given time

labor-intensive technology a process in which people must do most of the work

capital-intensive technology a process in which machines and equipment do most of the work

SPoTLIGHT

Manufacturing Employment

The bar chart below represents the percentage of U.S. manufacturing employees when compared to the nation's entire workforce.

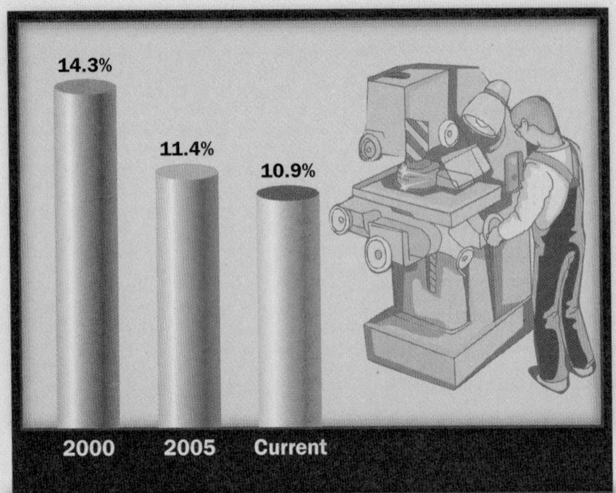

Source: 2010 Statistical Abstract of the United States, Table 607.

In determining where to locate production facilities, management must consider a number of variables, including the following:

- Locations of major customers and suppliers.
- Availability and cost of skilled and unskilled labor.
- Quality of life for employees and management in the proposed location.
- The cost of land and construction to build a new facility.
- Local and state taxes, environmental regulations, and zoning laws.
- The amount of financial support and subsidies, if any, offered by local and state governments.
- Special requirements, such as great amounts of energy or water used in the production process.

The choice of a location often involves balancing the most important variables for each production facility. Before making a final decision about where a proposed plant will be located and how it will be organized, two other factors—human resources and plant layout—should be examined.

Human Resources Several issues involved in facilities planning and site selection fall within the province of the human resources manager. Thus, at this stage, human resources and operations managers work closely together. For example, suppose that a U.S. firm such as Reebok wants to lower labor costs by constructing a sophisticated production plant in China. The human resources manager will have to recruit managers and employees with the appropriate skills who are willing to relocate to a foreign country, develop training programs for local Chinese workers, or both.

plant layout the arrangement of machinery, equipment, and personnel within a production facility

A big product! The Boeing facility in Everett, Washington, is an example of a fixed-position production layout and is used to build some of the world's largest airliners. When the fixed-position layout is used, the product is not moved until it is finished because it is easier to move people, machinery, and parts to where they are needed when building a jet airliner or other large products.

Plant Layout **Plant layout** is the arrangement of machinery, equipment, and personnel within a production facility. Three general types of plant layout are used (see Figure 8.4).

The *process layout* is used when different operations are required for creating small batches of different products or working on different parts of a product. The plant is arranged so that each operation is performed in its own particular area. An auto repair facility at a local automobile dealership provides an example of a process layout. The various operations may be engine repair, bodywork, wheel alignment, and safety inspection. If you take your Lincoln Navigator for a wheel alignment, your car "visits" only the area where alignments are performed.

A *product layout* (sometimes referred to as an *assembly line*) is used when all products undergo the same operations in the same sequence. Workstations are arranged to match the sequence of operations, and work flows from station to station. An assembly line is the best example of a product layout. For example, California-based Maxim

Figure 8.4 Facilities Planning

The process layout is used when small batches of different products are created or when working on different parts of a product. The product layout (assembly line) is used when all products undergo the same operations in the same sequence. The fixed-position layout is used in producing a product too large to move.

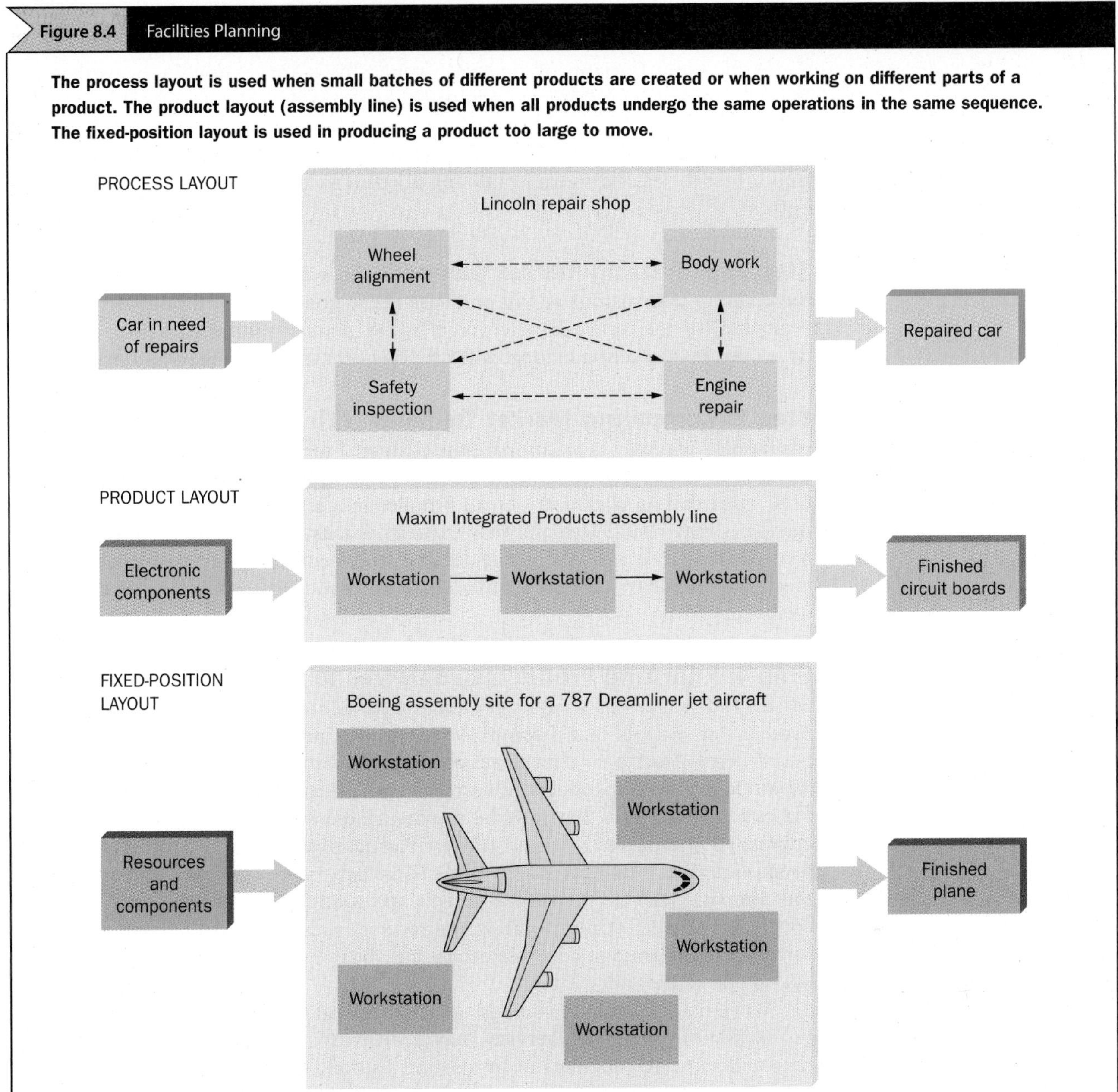

Integrated Products, Inc., uses a product layout to manufacture components for consumer and business electronic products.

A *fixed-position layout* is used when a very large product is produced. Aircraft manufacturers and shipbuilders apply this method because of the difficulty of moving a large product such as an airliner or a ship. The product remains stationary, and people and machines are moved as needed to assemble the product. Boeing, for example, uses the fixed-position layout to build 787 Dreamliner jet aircraft at its Everett, Washington, manufacturing facility.

Operational Planning

The objective of operational planning is to decide on the amount of products or services each facility will produce during a specific period of time. Four steps are required.

planning horizon the period during which an operational plan will be in effect

Step 1: Selecting a Planning Horizon A **planning horizon** is simply the time period during which an operational plan will be in effect. A common planning horizon for production plans is one year. Then, before each year is up, management must plan for the next.

A planning horizon of one year generally is long enough to average out seasonal increases and decreases in sales. At the same time, it is short enough for planners to adjust production to accommodate long-range sales trends. Firms that operate in a rapidly changing business environment with many competitors may find it best to select a shorter planning horizon to keep their production planning current.

Step 2: Estimating Market Demand The *market demand* for a product is the quantity that customers will purchase at the going price. This quantity must be estimated for the time period covered by the planning horizon. Sales projections developed by marketing managers are the basis for market-demand estimates.

Step 3: Comparing Market Demand with Capacity The third step in operational planning is to compare the estimated market demand with the facility's capacity to satisfy that demand. (Remember that capacity is the amount of products or services that an organization can produce in a given time period.) One of three outcomes may result: Demand may exceed capacity, capacity may exceed demand, or capacity and demand may be equal. If they are equal, the facility should be operated at full capacity. However, if market demand and capacity are not equal, adjustments may be necessary.

Step 4: Adjusting Products or Services to Meet Demand The biggest reason for changes to a firm's production schedule is changes in the amount of products or services that a company sells to its customers. For example, Indiana-based Berry Plastics uses an injection-molded manufacturing process to produce all kinds of plastic products. One particularly successful product line for Berry Plastics is drink cups that can be screen-printed to promote a company or the company's products or services.[9] If Berry Plastics obtains a large contract to provide promotional cups to a large fast-food chain such as Whataburger or McDonald's, the company may need to work three shifts a day, seven days a week, until the contract is fulfilled. Unfortunately, the reverse is also true. If the company's sales force does not generate new sales, there may be only enough work for the employees on one shift.

When market demand exceeds capacity, several options are available to a firm. Production of products or services may be increased by operating the facility overtime with existing personnel or by starting a second or third work shift. For manufacturers, another response is to subcontract or outsource a portion of the work to other manufacturers. If the excess demand is likely to be permanent, the firm may expand the current facility or build another facility.

What happens when capacity exceeds market demand? Again, there are several options. To reduce output temporarily, workers may be laid off and part of the facility shut down, or the facility may be operated on a shorter-than-normal workweek for as long as the excess capacity persists. To adjust to a permanently decreased demand, management may shift the excess capacity of a manufacturing facility to the production of other goods or services. The most radical adjustment is to eliminate the excess capacity by selling unused manufacturing facilities.

5

Explain how purchasing, inventory control, scheduling, and quality control affect production.

Operations Control

We have discussed the development of an idea for a product or service and the planning that translates that idea into the reality. Now we are ready to push the "start button" to begin the production process. In this section, we examine four important areas of operations control: purchasing, inventory control, scheduling, and quality control (see Figure 8.5).

Figure 8.5 Four Aspects of Operations Control

Implementing the operations control system in any business requires the effective use of purchasing, inventory control, scheduling, and quality control.

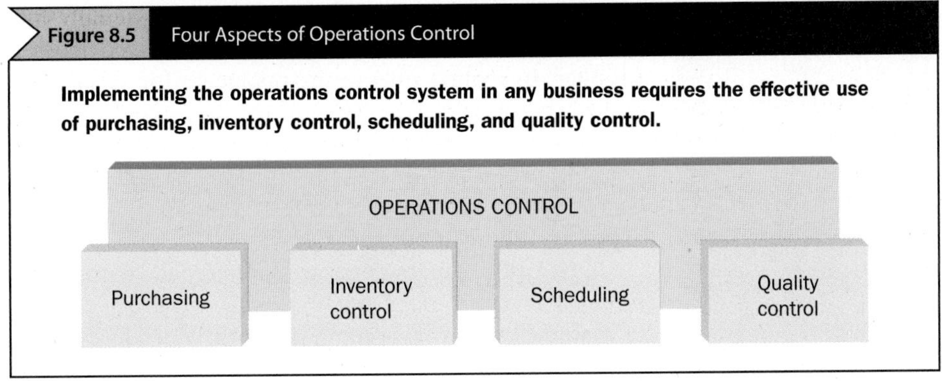

Purchasing

Purchasing consists of all the activities involved in obtaining required materials, supplies, components (or subassemblies), and parts from other firms. Levi Strauss, for example, must purchase denim cloth, thread, and zippers before it can produce a single pair of jeans. For all firms, the purchasing function is far from routine, and its importance should not be underestimated. For some products, purchased materials make up more than 50 percent of their wholesale costs.

The objective of purchasing is to ensure that required materials are available when they are needed, in the proper amounts, and at minimum cost. Generally, the company with purchasing needs and suppliers must develop a working relationship built on trust. In addition to a working relationship built on trust, many companies believe that purchasing is one area where they can promote diversity. For example, AT&T developed a Supplier Diversity Program that includes minorities, women, and disabled veteran business enterprises in 1968. Today, more than 40 years later, goals for the AT&T program include purchasing a total of 21.5 percent of all products and services from these three groups. As a result of its Supplier Diversity Program, the company is now recognized as one of the nation's leading companies in supplier diversity.[10]

Purchasing personnel should constantly be on the lookout for new or backup suppliers, even when their needs are being met by their present suppliers, because problems such as strikes and equipment breakdowns can cut off the flow of purchased materials from a primary supplier at any time.

The choice of suppliers should result from careful analysis of a number of factors. The following are especially critical:

- *Price.* Comparing prices offered by different suppliers is always an essential part of selecting a supplier. Even tiny differences in price add up to enormous sums when large quantities are purchased.
- *Quality.* Purchasing specialists always try to buy materials at a level of quality in keeping with the type of product being manufactured. The minimum acceptable quality is usually specified by product designers.
- *Reliability.* An agreement to purchase high-quality materials at a low price is the purchaser's dream. However, the dream becomes a nightmare if the supplier does not deliver.
- *Credit terms.* Purchasing specialists should determine if the supplier demands immediate payment or will extend credit. Also, does the supplier offer a cash discount or reduction in price for prompt payment?
- *Shipping costs.* Low prices and favorable credit terms offered by a supplier can be wiped out when the buyer must pay the shipping costs. Above all, the question of who pays the shipping costs should be answered before any supplier is chosen.

Inventory Control

Can you imagine what would happen if a Coca-Cola manufacturing plant ran out of the company's familiar red-and-white aluminum cans? It would be impossible to complete the manufacturing process and ship the cases of Coke to retailers.

purchasing all the activities involved in obtaining required materials, supplies, components, and parts from other firms

When inventory is very important! While most people regard a cell phone as a convenient way to stay in touch with friends, relatives, and business associates, this inventory—10,000 ready-to-use cell phones—is being shipped to people who have experienced the trauma caused by earthquakes. An effective inventory control system helps speed the phones to the people who need them to communicate with family and friends.

Management would be forced to shut the assembly line down until the next shipment of cans arrived from a supplier. In reality, operations managers for Coca-Cola realize the disasters that a shortage of needed materials can cause and will avoid this type of problem if at all possible. The simple fact is that shutdowns are expensive because costs such as rent, wages, insurance, and other expenses still must be paid.

Operations managers are concerned with three types of inventories. A *raw-materials inventory* consists of materials that will become part of the product during the production process. The *work-in-process inventory* consists of partially completed products. The *finished-goods inventory* consists of completed goods. Each type of inventory also has a *holding cost*, or storage cost, and a *stock-out cost*, the cost of running out of inventory. **Inventory control** is the process of managing inventories in such a way as to minimize inventory costs, including both holding costs and potential stock-out costs.

Today, computer systems are being used to keep track of inventories and alert managers to impending stock-outs. One of the most sophisticated methods of inventory control used today is materials requirements planning. **Materials requirements planning (MRP)** is a computerized system that integrates production planning and inventory control. One of the great advantages of an MRP system is its ability to juggle delivery schedules and lead times effectively. For a complex product such as an automobile, it is virtually impossible for individual managers to oversee the hundreds of parts that go into the finished product. However, a manager using an MRP system can arrange both order and delivery schedules so that materials, parts, and supplies arrive when they are needed.

Two extensions of MRP are used by manufacturing firms today. The first is known as *manufacturing resource planning*, or simply *MRP II*. The primary difference between the two systems is that MRP involves just production and inventory personnel, whereas MRP II involves the entire organization. Thus, MRP II provides a single common set of facts that can be used by all the organization's managers to make effective decisions. The second extension of MRP is known as *enterprise resource planning* (ERP). The primary difference between ERP and the preceding methods is that ERP software is more sophisticated and can monitor not only inventory and production processes but also quality, sales, and even such variables as inventory at a supplier's location.

Because large firms can incur huge inventory costs, much attention has been devoted to inventory control. The just-in-time system being used by some businesses is one result of all this attention. A **just-in-time inventory system** is designed to ensure that materials or supplies arrive at a facility just when they are needed so that storage and holding costs are minimized. The customer must specify what will be needed, when, and in what amounts. The supplier must be sure that the right supplies arrive at the agreed-upon time and location. For example, managers using a just-in-time inventory system at a Ford assembly plant determine the number of automobiles that will be assembled in a specified time period. Then Ford purchasing personnel order just the parts needed to produce those automobiles. In turn, suppliers deliver the parts in time or when they are needed on the assembly line.

Without proper inventory control, it is impossible for operations managers to schedule the work required to produce goods that can be sold to customers.

inventory control the process of managing inventories in such a way as to minimize inventory costs, including both holding costs and potential stock-out costs

materials requirements planning (MRP) a computerized system that integrates production planning and inventory control

just-in-time inventory system a system designed to ensure that materials or supplies arrive at a facility just when they are needed so that storage and holding costs are minimized

scheduling the process of ensuring that materials and other resources are at the right place at the right time

Scheduling

Scheduling is the process of ensuring that materials and other resources are at the right place at the right time. The materials and resources may be moved from a warehouse to the workstations, they may move from station to station along an

assembly line, or they may arrive at workstations "just in time" to be made part of the work-in-process there.

As our definition implies, both place and time are important to scheduling. The *routing* of materials is the sequence of workstations that the materials will follow. Assume that Drexel-Heritage—one of America's largest and oldest furniture manufacturers—is scheduling production of an oval coffee table made from cherry wood. Operations managers route the needed materials (wood, screws, packaging materials, etc.) through a series of individual workstations along an assembly line. At each workstation, a specific task is performed, and then the partially finished coffee table moves to the next workstation. When routing materials, operations managers are especially concerned with the sequence of each step of the production process. For the coffee table, the top and legs must be cut to specifications before the wood is finished. (If the wood were finished before being cut, the finish would be ruined, and the coffee table would have to be stained again.)

When scheduling production, managers also are concerned with timing. The *timing* function specifies when the materials will arrive at each station and how long they will remain there. For the cherry coffee table, it may take workers 30 minutes to cut the table top and legs and another 30 minutes to drill the holes and assemble the table. Before packaging the coffee table for shipment, it must be finished with cherry stain and allowed to dry. This last step may take as long as three days depending on weather conditions and humidity. Only after the product is completely dry can the coffee table be packaged and shipped to wholesalers and retailers.

Regardless of whether the finished product requires a simple or complex production process, operations managers are responsible for monitoring schedules—called *follow-up*—to ensure that the work flows according to a timetable. For complex products, many operations managers prefer to use Gantt charts or the PERT technique.

Scheduling Through Gantt Charts Developed by Henry L. Gantt, a **Gantt chart** is a graphic scheduling device that displays the tasks to be performed on the vertical axis and the time required for each task on the horizontal axis. Gantt charts do the following:

- Allow you to determine how long a project should take.
- Lay out the order in which tasks need to be completed.
- Determine the resources needed.
- Monitor progress of different activities required to complete the project.

A Gantt chart that describes the activities required to build three dozen golf carts is illustrated in Figure 8.6. Gantt charts usually are not suitable for scheduling extremely complex situations. Nevertheless, using them forces a manager to plan the steps required to get a job done and to specify time requirements for each part of the job.

Scheduling via PERT Another technique for scheduling a complex project and maintaining control of the schedule is **PERT (Program Evaluation and Review Technique)**. To use PERT, we begin by identifying all the major *activities* involved in the project. For example, the activities involved in producing your textbook are illustrated in Figure 8.7.

All events are arranged in a sequence. In doing so, we must be sure that an event that must occur before another event in the actual process also occurs before that event on the PERT chart. For example, the manuscript must be edited before the type is set. Next, we use arrows to connect events that must occur in sequence. We then estimate the time required for each activity and mark it near the corresponding arrow. The sequence of production activities that take the longest time from start to finish is called the *critical path*. The activities on this path determine the minimum time in which the process can be completed. These activities are the ones that must

Gantt chart a graphic scheduling device that displays the tasks to be performed on the vertical axis and the time required for each task on the horizontal axis

PERT (Program Evaluation and Review Technique) a scheduling technique that identifies the major activities necessary to complete a project and sequences them based on the time required to perform each one

Figure 8.6 A Gantt Chart

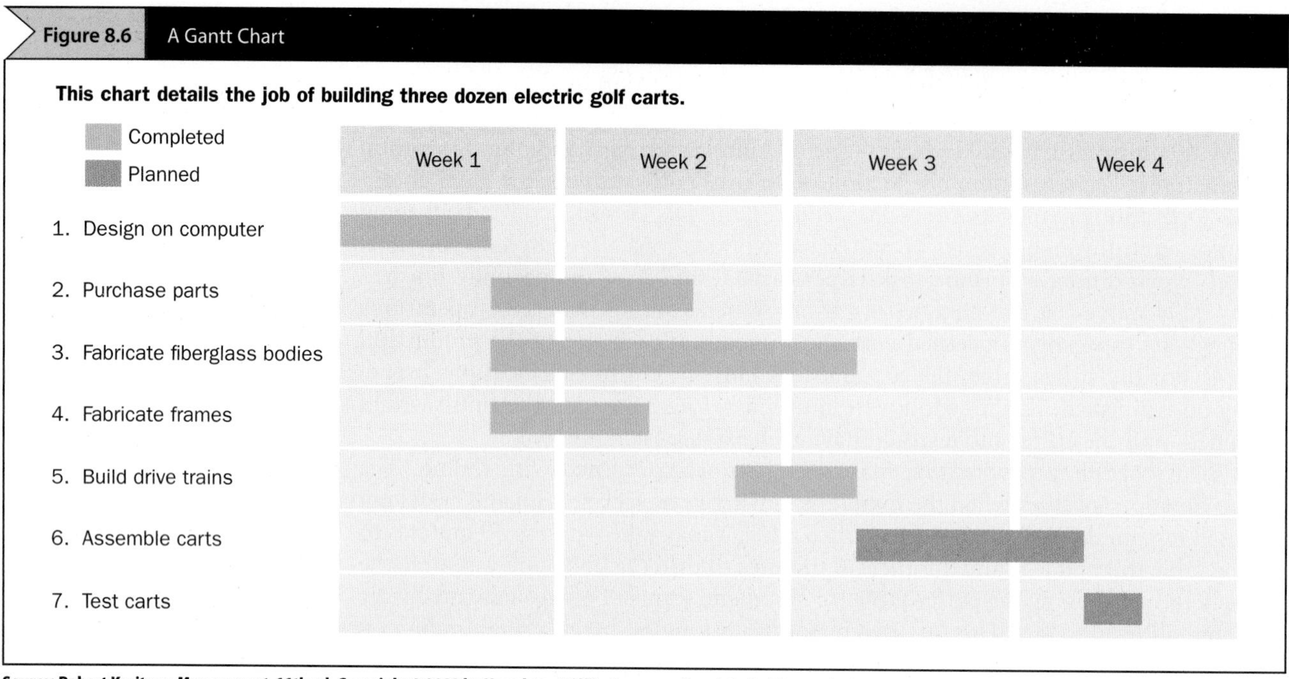

Source: Robert Kreitner, *Management*, 11th ed. Copyright © 2009 by Houghton Mifflin Company. Reprinted with permission.

Figure 8.7 Simplified PERT Diagram for Producing this Book

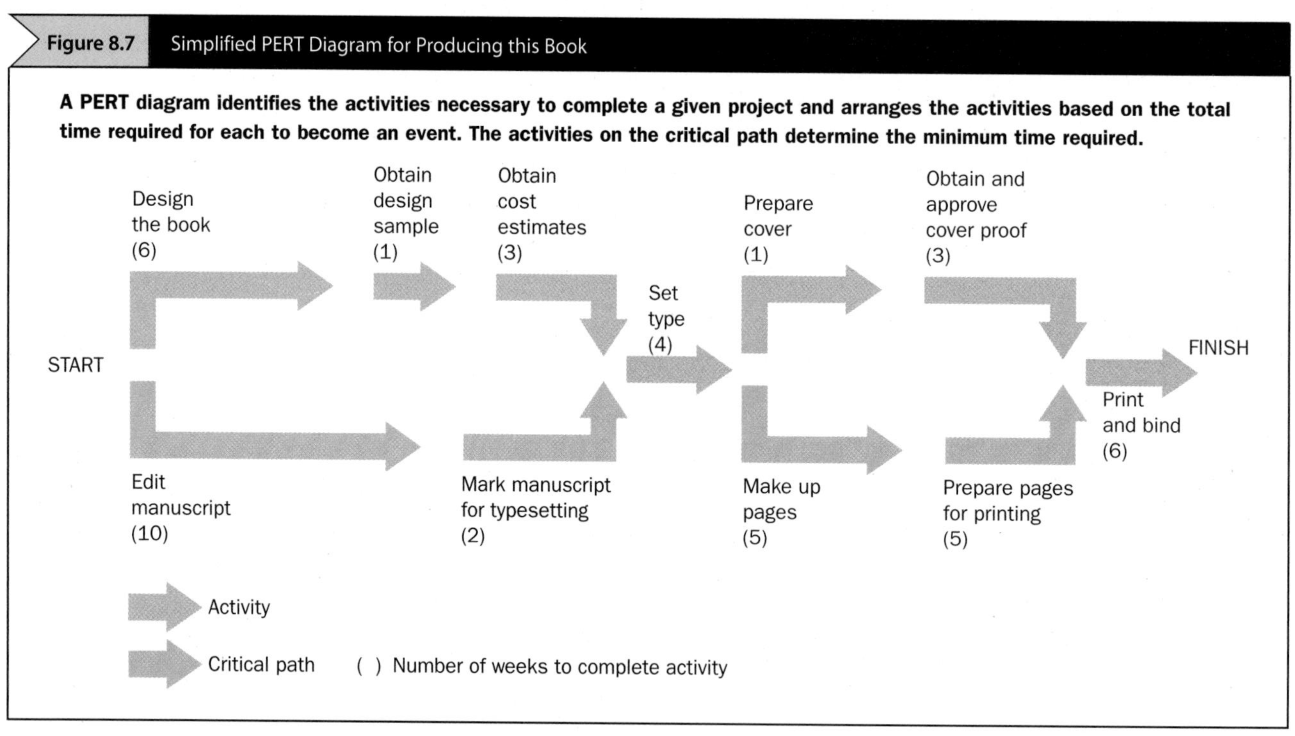

be scheduled and controlled carefully. A delay in any one of them will cause a delay in completion of the project as a whole.

Quality Control

Malcolm Baldrige National Quality Award an award given by the U.S. president to organizations that apply and are judged to be outstanding in specific managerial tasks that lead to improved quality for both products and services

As mentioned earlier in this chapter, American business firms that compete in the very competitive global marketplace have taken another look at the importance of improving quality. Today, there is even a national quality award. The **Malcolm Baldrige National Quality Award** is given by the U.S. president to organizations that apply and are judged to be outstanding in specific managerial tasks that lead to improved quality for both products and services. Past winners include Ritz-Carlton Hotels, Boeing, Motorola, Honeywell Federal Manufacturing & Technologies, Cargill Corn Milling North America, Richland Community College (part of the Dallas Community College District), and many others. For many organizations, using the Baldrige criteria results in

- better employee relations,
- higher productivity,
- greater customer satisfaction,
- increased market share, and
- improved profitability.[11]

Although winning the "Baldrige" can mean prestige and lots of free media coverage, the winners all have one factor in common: They use quality control to improve their firm's products or services.

Quality control is the process of ensuring that goods and services are produced in accordance with design specifications. The major objective of quality control is to see that the organization lives up to the standards it has set for itself on quality. Some firms, such as Mercedes-Benz, have built their reputations on quality. Customers pay more for their products in return for assurances of high quality. Other firms adopt a strategy of emphasizing lower prices along with reasonable (but not particularly high) quality.

Many U.S. firms use two systems to gather statistical information about the quality of their products and study the way they operate. **Statistical process control (SPC)** is a system that uses sampling to obtain data that are plotted on control charts and graphs to see if the production process is operating as it should and to pinpoint problem areas. **Statistical quality control (SQC)**, a similar technique, is a set of specific statistical techniques used to monitor all aspects of the production process to ensure that both work-in-process and finished products meet the firm's quality standards. A firm can use the information provided by both these techniques to correct problems in the production process and to improve the quality of its products.

Quality matters! SC Johnson was started in 1886 as a parquet flooring company. Today, more than 125 years later, the company is one of the world's most trusted manufacturers of household products like Windex. The company's success is tied to its quest for quality in all of the products it produces. In this photo, an employee examines the finished product to make sure small details like labels and packaging meet the company's stringent quality standards.

Inspection Increased effort is also being devoted to **inspection**, which is the examination of the quality of work-in-process. Inspections are performed at various times during production. Purchased materials may be inspected when they arrive at the production facility. Subassemblies and manufactured parts may be inspected before they become part of a finished product. In addition, finished goods may be inspected before they are shipped to customers. Items that are within design specifications continue on their way. Those that are not within design specifications are removed from production.

Improving Quality Through Employee Participation Over the years, more and more managers have realized that quality is an essential "ingredient" of the good or service being provided. This view of quality provides several benefits. The number of defects decreases, which causes profits to increase. Furthermore, making products right the first time reduces many of the rejects and much of the rework. In addition, making employees responsible for quality often eliminates the need for inspection. An employee is encouraged to accept full responsibility for the quality of his or her work.

The use of a **quality circle**, a team of employees who meet on company time to solve problems of product quality, is another way manufacturers are achieving better quality at the operations level. Quality circles have been used

quality control the process of ensuring that goods and services are produced in accordance with design specifications

statistical process control (SPC) a system that uses sampling to obtain data that are plotted on control charts and graphs to see if the production process is operating as it should and to pinpoint problem areas

statistical quality control (SQC) a set of specific statistical techniques used to monitor all aspects of the production process to ensure that both work-in-process and finished products meet the firm's quality standards

inspection the examination of the quality of work-in-process

quality circle a team of employees who meet on company time to solve problems of product quality

successfully in companies such as IBM, Northrop Grumman Corporation, Lockheed Martin, and GE.

Total quality management (TQM) can also be used to improve quality of a firm's products or services. As noted in Chapter 6, a TQM program coordinates the efforts directed at improving customer satisfaction, increasing employee participation, strengthening supplier partnerships, and facilitating an organizational atmosphere of continuous quality improvement. Firms such as American Express, AT&T, Motorola, and Hewlett-Packard all have used TQM to improve product quality and, ultimately, customer satisfaction.

Another technique that businesses may use to improve not only quality but also overall performance is Six Sigma. **Six Sigma** is a disciplined approach that relies on statistical data and improved methods to eliminate defects for a firm's products and services. Although many experts agree that Six Sigma is similar to TQM and other methods used to improve quality, Six Sigma often has more top-level support, much more teamwork, and a new corporate attitude or culture. The companies that developed, refined, and have the most experience with Six Sigma are Motorola, GE, and Honeywell. Although each of these companies is a corporate giant, the underlying principles of Six Sigma can be used by all firms regardless of size.[12]

World Quality Standards: ISO 9000 and ISO 14000 Different companies have different perceptions of quality. Without a common standard of quality, however, customers may be at the mercy of manufacturers and vendors. As the number of companies competing in the world marketplace has increased, so has the seriousness of this problem. To deal with the problem of standardization, the International Organization for Standardization, a nongovernmental organization with headquarters in Geneva, Switzerland, was created. The **International Organization for Standardization (ISO)** is a network of national standards institutes and similar organizations from 161 different countries that is charged with developing standards for quality products and services that are traded throughout the globe. According to the organization,

> *ISO's work makes a positive difference to the world we live in. ISO standards add value to all types of business operations. They contribute to making the development, manufacturing and supply of products and services more efficient, safer and cleaner. They make trade between countries easier and fairer. ISO standards also serve to safeguard consumers and users of products and services in general, as well as making their lives simpler.*[13]

Standardization is achieved through consensus agreements between national delegations representing all the economic stakeholders—suppliers, customers, and often governments. The member organization for the United States is the American National Standards Institute located in Washington, D.C.

In 1987, the panel published ISO 9000 (*iso* is Greek for "equal"), which sets the guidelines for quality procedures that businesses must use to receive certification. Certification by independent auditors and laboratory testing services serves as evidence that a company meets the standards for quality control procedures in design, production processes, and product testing.

Although certification is not a legal requirement to do business globally, the organization's 161 member countries have approved the ISO standards. In fact, ISO standards are so prevalent around the globe that many customers refuse to do business with noncertified companies. As an added bonus, companies completing the certification process often discover new, cost-efficient ways to improve their existing quality-control programs.

As a continuation of this standardization process, the International Organization for Standardization has developed ISO 14000. ISO 14000 is a family of international standards for incorporating environmental concerns into operations and product standards. As with ISO 9000 certification, ISO 14000

Six Sigma a disciplined approach that relies on statistical data and improved methods to eliminate defects for a firm's products and services

International Organization for Standardization (ISO) a network of national standards institutes and similar organizations from 161 different countries that is charged with developing standards for quality products and services that are traded throughout the globe

Entrepreneurial
SUCCESS

Small Manufacturers Achieve Big Productivity Gains

Even the smallest manufacturer can boost productivity with careful planning for product design, facilities, and site selection. For example, family-owned Ingrained Style Furniture, based in Calgary, Canada, recently purchased new equipment for computer-assisted product design. The company, which makes high-quality home furnishings, has only five employees. Yet its owner chose to borrow $300,000 to buy the new high-tech machinery, even though orders were slowing due to an economic downturn. Why? "We are looking at a fourfold increase in productivity from that machinery," the owner says—a whopping improvement in productivity that is helping the company continue its long-term record of growth and profitability while maintaining top quality.

Mole Hollow Candles is a small Massachusetts business that produces hand-dipped candles for sale across the United States. For many years, the company ran a factory and separate warehouse in central Massachusetts. Then new owners bought Mole Hollow Candles. The new owners analyzed every aspect of the operation and, over time, determined that they could improve productivity by moving to a larger facility with manufacturing and distribution activities under one roof. Just as important, the new site accommodates larger trucks and is much closer to major highways than the previous facilities, smoothing the way for speedier receipt of raw materials and distribution of finished products.

Sources: Craig S. Semon, "An American Light," *Telegram (Worcester, MA)*, February 9, 2010, http://www.telegram.com/article/20100209/NEWS/2090342/1002/BUSINESS; Denise Deveau, "Small Businesses Getting the Skinny on Lean Manufacturing," *CBC News*, October 15, 2009, http://www.cbc.ca/money/story/2009/10/05/f-small-business-lean-manufacturing.html#ixzz0eyOZYPlq; Joel Schlesinger, "Credit Crunch Puts Pressure on Small Business; Furniture Firm Plans for Growth Even in Downturn," *Calgary Herald*, January 19, 2009, http://www.canada.com/calgaryherald/news/calgarybusiness/story.html?id=ba68926c-2893-4edc-8873-626be5462d49.

requires that a company's procedures be documented by independent auditors. It also requires that a company develop an environmental management system that will help it to achieve environmental goals, objectives, and targets. Both the ISO 9000 and ISO 14000 family of standards are updated periodically. For example, ISO 9001:2008 reflects new standards for quality when compared with the original ISO standards.

6 Summarize how productivity and technology are related.

Improving Productivity with Technology

No coverage of production and operations management would be complete without a discussion on productivity. Productivity concerns all managers, but it is especially important to operations managers, the people who must oversee the creation of a firm's goods or services. We define **productivity** as the average level of output per worker per hour. Hence, if each worker at plant A produces 75 units per day and each worker at plant B produces only 70 units per day, the workers at plant A are more productive. If one bank teller serves 25 customers per hour and another serves 28 per hour, the second teller is more productive.

Productivity Trends

Overall productivity growth for the U.S. business sector averaged 3.9 percent for the period 1979–2008.[14] More specifically, productivity in 2008 increased 1.2 percent.[15] (*Note:* At the time of publication, 2008 was the last year that complete statistics were available.) Although a 1.2 percent increase in U.S. productivity in 2008 does not compare with the nation's average productivity gains for the period between 1979 and 2008, it does compare favorably with 16 other nations that the U.S. Bureau of Labor Statistics tracks each year. By comparison, productivity in 2008 decreased in 12 of the 17 economies. Only 5 of the 17 countries had productivity increases. Among these five, both the United States and the Republic of Korea led other nations with a productivity increase of 1.2 percent.[16]

productivity the average level of output per worker per hour

Several factors have been cited as possible causes for the small increase in America's productivity growth rate. First, the economic crisis that accompanied the downturn in the home construction and automobile industries and the crisis in banking and finance have caused many businesses to reduce the rate of investment in new equipment and technology. As workers have had to use increasingly outdated equipment, their ability to increase productivity has declined.

Another important factor that has hurt the U.S. productivity growth rate is the tremendous growth of the service sector in the United States. Although this sector grew in the number of employees and economic importance, its productivity levels did not grow as fast. Today, many economic experts agree that improving service-sector productivity can lead to higher overall productivity growth for the nation.

Finally, increased government regulation is frequently cited as a factor affecting productivity. Federal agencies such as the Occupational Safety and Health Administration, the Environmental Protection Agency, and the Food and Drug Administration are increasingly regulating business practices. Often, the time employees spend complying with government reporting requirements can reduce productivity growth rates. Even though executives, managers, and business owners often cite increased regulation from all levels of government as a reason for low productivity, the general public believes there is need for effective government regulations that improve working conditions, product safety, and the environment. For example, the recent British Petroleum oil spill in the Gulf of Mexico and its effect on nearby beaches and wetlands may have been prevented or at least reduced if there had been more government regulation of off-shore drilling. Although there are two sides to the regulatory argument, it may be beneficial to take a new look at existing and proposed regulations to ensure all the regulations are needed and compliance is no more time-consuming and expensive than absolutely necessary.

Improving Productivity Growth Rates

Several techniques and strategies have been suggested to improve current productivity growth rates. For example:

- Government policies that may be hindering productivity growth could be eliminated or at least modified.
- Increased employee motivation and participation can enhance productivity.
- Increased cooperation between labor and management could be fostered to improve productivity.
- Investing more money in facilities, equipment, technology and automation, and employee training could improve productivity.

The Impact of Computers and Robotics on Productivity

Automation is the total or near-total use of machines to do work. The rapid increase in automated procedures has been made possible by the microprocessor, a silicon chip that led to the production of desktop computers for businesses, homes, and schools. In factories, microprocessors are used in robotics and in computer manufacturing systems.

Robotics **Robotics** is the use of programmable machines to perform a variety of tasks by manipulating materials and tools. Robots work quickly, accurately, and steadily. For example, Illumina, Inc., a San Diego company, uses robots to perform medical laboratory tests. The information then is sold to some of the world's largest pharmaceutical companies, where it is used to alter existing prescription drugs, develop new drug therapies, and customize diagnoses and treatments for all kinds of serious diseases. As an added bonus, Illumina's

automation the total or near-total use of machines to do work

robotics the use of programmable machines to perform a variety of tasks by manipulating materials and tools

robots can work 24 hours a day at much lower costs than if human lab workers performed the same tests.[17]

Robots are especially effective in tedious, repetitive assembly-line jobs, as well as in handling hazardous materials. They are also useful as artificial "eyes" that can check the quality of products as they are being processed on the assembly lines. To date, the automotive industry has made the most extensive use of robotics, but robots also have been used to mine coal, inspect the inner surfaces of pipes, assemble computer components, provide certain kinds of patient care in hospitals, and clean and guard buildings at night.

Computer Manufacturing Systems People are quick to point out how computers have changed their everyday lives, but most people do not realize the impact computers have had on manufacturing. In simple terms, the factory of the future has already arrived. For most manufacturers, the changeover began with the use of computer-aided design and computer-aided manufacturing. **Computer-aided design (CAD)** is the use of computers to aid in the development of products. Ford speeds up car design, Canon designs new photocopiers, and American Greetings creates new birthday cards by using CAD. **Computer-aided manufacturing (CAM)** is the use of computers to plan and control manufacturing processes. A well-designed CAM system allows manufacturers to become much more productive. Not only are a greater number of products produced, but speed and quality also increase. Toyota, Hasbro, Oneida, and Apple Computer all have used CAM to increase productivity.

If you are thinking that the next logical step is to combine the CAD and CAM computer systems, you are right. Today, the most successful manufacturers use CAD and CAM together to form a computer-integrated manufacturing system. Specifically, **computer-integrated manufacturing (CIM)** is a computer system that not only helps to design products but also controls the machinery needed to produce the finished product. For example, Liz Claiborne, Inc., uses CIM to design clothing, to establish patterns for new fashions, and then to cut the cloth needed to produce the finished product. Other advantages of using CIM include improved flexibility, more efficient scheduling, and higher product quality—all factors that make a production facility more competitive in today's global economy.

Flexible Manufacturing Systems Manufacturers have known for a number of years that the old-style, mass-production, and traditional assembly lines used to manufacture products present a number of problems. For example, although traditional assembly lines turn out extremely large numbers of identical products economically, the system requires expensive, time-consuming retooling of equipment whenever a new product is to be manufactured. This type of manufacturing is often referred to as a continuous process. **Continuous process** is a manufacturing process in which a firm produces the same product(s) over a long period of time. Now it is possible to use flexible manufacturing systems to solve such problems. A **flexible manufacturing system (FMS)** combines electronic machines and computer-integrated manufacturing in a single production system. Instead of having to spend vast amounts of time and effort to retool the traditional mechanical equipment on an assembly line for each new product, an FMS is rearranged simply by reprogramming electronic machines. Because FMSs require less time and expense to reprogram than traditional systems, manufacturers can produce smaller batches of a variety of products without raising the production cost. Flexible manufacturing is sometimes referred to as an intermittent process. An **intermittent process** is a manufacturing process in which a firm's manufacturing machines and equipment are changed to produce different products. When compared with the continuous process (longer production runs), an intermittent process has a shorter production run.

computer-aided design (CAD) the use of computers to aid in the development of products

computer-aided manufacturing (CAM) the use of computers to plan and control manufacturing processes

computer-integrated manufacturing (CIM) a computer system that not only helps to design products but also controls the machinery needed to produce the finished product

continuous process a manufacturing process in which a firm produces the same product(s) over a long period of time

flexible manufacturing system (FMS) a single production system that combines electronic machines and computer-integrated manufacturing

intermittent process a manufacturing process in which a firm's manufacturing machines and equipment are changed to produce different products

For most manufacturers, the driving force behind FMSs is the customer. In fact, the term *customer-driven production* is often used by operations managers to describe a manufacturing system that is driven by customer needs and what customers want to buy. For example, advanced software and a flexible manufacturing system have enabled Dell Computer to change to a more customer-driven manufacturing process. The process starts when a customer phones a sales representative on a toll-free line or accesses Dell's Web site. Then the representative or the customer enters the specifications for the new product directly into a computer. The order then is sent to a nearby plant. Once the order is received, a team of employees, with the help of a reprogrammable assembly line, can build the product just the way the customer wants it. Products include desktop computers, notebook computers, and other Dell equipment.[18] Although the costs of designing and installing an FMS such as this are high, the electronic equipment is used more frequently and efficiently than the machinery on a traditional assembly line.

Technological Displacement Automation is increasing productivity by cutting manufacturing time, reducing error, and simplifying retooling procedures. However, many of the robots being developed for use in manufacturing will not replace human employees. Rather, these robots will work with employees in making their jobs easier and help to prevent accidents. In the future, most experts agree that, because U.S. manufacturers will continue to innovate, workers who have manufacturing jobs will be highly skilled and can work with the automated and computer-assisted manufacturing systems. Those that don't possess high-tech skills will be dispensable and unemployed. Many workers will be faced with the choice of retraining for new jobs or seeking jobs in other sectors of the economy. Government, business, and education will have to cooperate to prepare workers for new roles in an automated workplace.

The next chapter discusses many of the issues caused by technological displacement. In addition, a number of major components of human resources management are described, and we see how managers use various reward systems to boost motivation, productivity, and morale.

return to inside business

Nestlé

All around the world, supermarket shelves are packed with foods made by Nestlé for consumers and their furry friends. The company originally made baby formula and, applying its expertise in production, soon expanded into dairy products, coffee, chocolate bars, and pet food. Now, more than a century after Henri Nestlé founded the company in Switzerland, its U.S. food manufacturing plants are earning ISO certifications in environmental management systems, food safety management, and occupational health and safety. The plants also follow the Nestlé Continuous Excellence program to ensure higher quality through such initiatives as Six Sigma.

Nestlé takes a long-term view when planning for production. It recently began distributing the first of 12 million cocoa trees to farmers in Ivory Coast, where the company gets much of its cocoa. Over the next decade, these new trees will produce more and higher-quality beans for the farmers, increasing their income and improving the supply of cocoa for Nestlé.

Questions

1. How does the purchasing function affect the quality of a product like Nestlé's Kit Kat chocolate bars?
2. What benefits would a global corporation such as Nestlé be likely to gain by having all its U.S. plants qualify for ISO certification?

SUMMARY

Summary

1 Explain the nature of production.

Operations management consists of all the activities that managers engage in to create goods and services. Operations are as relevant to service organizations as to manufacturing firms. Generally, three major activities are involved in producing goods or services: product development, planning for production, and operations control. Today, U.S. manufacturers are forced to compete in an ever-smaller world to meet the needs of more-demanding customers. As a result, U.S. manufacturers have used innovation to improve productivity. Because of innovation, fewer workers are needed, but those workers who are needed possess the skills to use automation and technology. In an attempt to regain a competitive edge, manufacturers have taken another look at the importance of improving quality and meeting the needs of their customers. They also have used new techniques to motivate employees, reduced costs, used computer-aided and flexible manufacturing systems, improved control procedures, and used green manufacturing. Competing in the global economy is not only profitable but also an essential activity that requires the cooperation of everyone within an organization.

2 Outline how the conversion process transforms raw materials, labor, and other resources into finished products or services.

A business transforms resources into goods and services in order to provide utility to customers. Utility is the ability of a good or service to satisfy a human need. Form utility is created by people converting raw materials, finances, and information into finished products. Conversion processes vary in terms of the major resources used to produce goods and services (focus), the degree to which resources are changed (magnitude of change), and the number of production processes that a business uses. The application of the basic principles of operations management to the production of services has coincided with the growth and importance of service businesses in the United States.

3 Describe how research and development lead to new products and services.

Operations management often begins with product R&D. The results of R&D may be entirely new products or extensions and refinements of existing products. R&D activities are classified as basic research (aimed at uncovering new knowledge), applied research (discovering new knowledge with some potential use), and development and implementation (using new or existing knowledge to produce goods and services). If a firm sells only one product, when that product reaches the end of its life-cycle, the firm will die, too. To stay in business, the firm must, at the very least, find ways to refine or extend the want-satisfying capability of its product.

4 Discuss the components involved in planning the production process.

Planning for production involves three major phases: design planning, facilities planning, and operational planning. First, design planning is undertaken to address questions related to the product line, required production capacity, and the use of technology. Then production facilities, human resources, and plant layout must be considered. Operational planning focuses on the use of production facilities and resources. The steps for operational planning include (1) selecting a planning horizon, (2) estimating market demand, (3) comparing market demand with capacity, and (4) adjusting production of products or services to meet demand.

5 Explain how purchasing, inventory control, scheduling, and quality control affect production.

The major areas of operations control are purchasing, inventory control, scheduling, and quality control. Purchasing involves selecting suppliers. The choice of suppliers should result from careful analysis of a number of factors, including price, quality, reliability, credit terms, and shipping costs. Inventory control is the management of stocks of raw materials, work-in-process, and finished goods to minimize the total inventory cost. Today, most firms use a computerized system to maintain inventory records. In addition, many firms use a just-in-time inventory system, in which materials or supplies arrive at a facility just when they are needed so that storage and holding costs are minimized. Scheduling ensures that materials and other resources are at the right place at the right time. Both Gantt charts and PERT can be used to improve a firm's ability to schedule the production of products. Quality control guarantees that products meet the design specifications for those products. The major objective of quality control is to see that the organization lives up to the standards it has set for itself on quality. A number of different activities can be used to improve quality.

6 Summarize how productivity and technology are related.

Productivity is the average level of output per worker per hour. From 1979 to 2008, U.S. productivity growth averaged a 3.9 percent increase. More specifically, productivity in 2008 increased 1.2 percent. Although a 1.2 percent increase in U.S. productivity in 2008 does not compare with the nation's average productivity gains for the period between 1979 and 2008, it does compare favorably with the 16 other nations that the U.S. Bureau of Labor Statistics tracks each year. Several factors have been cited as possible causes for lower productivity growth, and managers have begun to explore solutions for overcoming them. Possible solutions include less government regulation, increased cooperation between management and labor, increased employee motivation and participation, and additional investment by business to fund new or renovated facilities, equipment, employee training, and the use of automation and technology.

Automation, the total or near-total use of machines to do work, has for some years been changing the way work is done in factories. A growing number of industries are using programmable machines called robots to perform tasks that are tedious or hazardous to human beings. Computer-aided design, computer-aided manufacturing, and computer-integrated manufacturing use computers to help design and manufacture products. FMS combines electronic machines and computer-integrated manufacturing to produce smaller batches of products more efficiently than on the traditional assembly line. Instead of having to spend vast amounts of time and effort to retool the traditional mechanical equipment on an assembly line for each new product, an FMS is rearranged simply by reprogramming electronic machines.

Key Terms

You should now be able to define and give an example relevant to each of the following terms:

operations management (217)
mass production (218)
analytical process (218)
synthetic process (218)
utility (219)
form utility (219)
service economy (221)
research and development (R&D) (222)
design planning (224)
product line (224)
product design (225)
capacity (225)
labor-intensive technology (225)
capital-intensive technology (225)
plant layout (226)
planning horizon (227)
purchasing (229)
inventory control (230)
materials requirements planning (MRP) (230)
just-in-time inventory system (230)
scheduling (230)
Gantt chart (231)
PERT (Program Evaluation and Review Technique) (231)
Malcolm Baldrige National Quality Award (232)
quality control (233)
statistical process control (SPC) (233)
statistical quality control (SQC) (233)
inspection (233)
quality circle (233)
Six Sigma (234)
International Organization for Standardization (ISO) (234)
productivity (235)
automation (236)
robotics (236)
computer-aided design (CAD) (237)
computer-aided manufacturing (CAM) (237)
computer-integrated manufacturing (CIM) (237)
continuous process (237)
flexible manufacturing system (FMS) (237)
intermittent process (237)

Review Questions

1. List all the activities involved in operations management.
2. What is the difference between an analytical and a synthetic manufacturing process? Give an example of each type of process.
3. In terms of focus, magnitude, and number, characterize the production processes used by a local pizza parlor, a dry-cleaning establishment, and an auto repair shop.
4. Describe how research and development leads to new products.
5. Explain why product extension and refinement are important.
6. What are the major elements of design planning?
7. What factors should be considered when selecting a site for a new manufacturing facility?
8. What is the objective of operational planning? What four steps are used to accomplish this objective?
9. If you were an operations manager, what would you do if market demand exceeded the production capacity of your manufacturing facility? What action would you take if the production capacity of your manufacturing facility exceeded market demand?
10. Why is selecting a supplier so important?
11. What costs must be balanced and minimized through inventory control?
12. How can materials requirements planning (MRP), manufacturing resource planning (MRP II), and enterprise resource planning (ERP) help to control inventory and a company's production processes?
13. How does the just-in-time-inventory system help to reduce inventory costs?

14. Explain in what sense scheduling is a *control* function of operations managers.
15. How can management and employees use statistical process control, statistical quality control, inspection, and quality circles to improve a firm's products?
16. How might productivity be measured in a restaurant? In a department store? In a public school system?
17. How can CIM and FMS help a manufacturer to produce products?

Discussion Questions

1. Why would Rubbermaid—a successful U.S. company—need to expand and sell its products to customers in foreign countries?
2. Do certain kinds of firms need to stress particular areas of operations management? Explain.
3. Is it really necessary for service firms to engage in research and development? In planning for production and operations control?
4. How are the four areas of operations control interrelated?
5. In what ways can employees help to improve the quality of a firm's products?
6. Is operations management relevant to nonbusiness organizations such as colleges and hospitals? Why or why not?

Video Case 8.1

Burton Snowboards' High-Quality Standards

"The people at Burton are a powerful, inspiring, and fun group, and I will miss that," said the recently departing CEO of Vermont's fabled Burton Snowboards. In fact, the company's nearly 900 employees are some of the many reasons the firm has grown to be the world's leading snowboard and accessories company. Many are snowboard enthusiasts, not least among them Jake Burton Carpenter, founder and currently interim CEO. Despite his management responsibilities, Jake still rides a snowboard about 100 days of the year, sometimes to test new products, but sometimes just for fun. "There are a lot of vibrant folks," at the company "and it rubs off on you," he says.

The company began as an entrepreneurial venture housed in a barn in 1977. Jake, who says he was a failure in shop class while in school, handmade his own boards for a sport that had few followers and was yet to be recognized. Snowboarding has since come a long way, having made its Olympic debut during the 1998 Winter Games at Nagano, Japan. Burton Snowboards has grown, too. With world headquarters in Burlington, the company operates a factory in Austria and stores in Chicago, Los Angeles, New York, Wrentham (MA), Orlando, and of course Burlington, as well as in Tokyo and Innsbruck (Austria). It also works with thousands of retail dealers in more than 30 countries around the world and offers products for sale online as well.

A major factor in the company's success is the high-quality standards to which it has adhered from its very beginning. These have made Burton Snowboards a premium supplier whose name is synonymous with quality. Its snowboards are made to exacting specifications from wood, fiberglass, and steel, not cheaper foam materials, and with unrelenting attention to every step, including the finishing details. "We don't cut corners," says a company spokesperson, though that sometimes means its products will cost a bit more than competitors'. The prevailing philosophy at the firm is that "you get what you pay for," and by listening to its core customers, who fall between 12 and 35 years of age, Burton remains confident that its high standards meet the expectations of those for whom snowboarding is not just a sport but also a lifestyle. "We've always based our decisions around snowboarders and what's best for them," says Jake.

Quality is further assured by the company's policy of redesigning every product every year in order to retain its position as "an innovator, not an imitator" and to keep up with changing customers' needs and desires as well as with competitors' efforts to grow their own market share. One such threat comes from ski companies that have decided to move into the snowboarding industry. Burton's managers credit much of the company's success to its ability to respond well to change. According to Jake, "As a company we've always thrived on opportunity."

One new opportunity the firm faces is the need to control its production costs without sacrificing quality. Burton recently announced that it is closing its Burlington factory and will manufacture exclusively at the Austrian plant it has operated for the past 25 years. "It costs us significantly more to produce a board in Vermont than we are capable of selling it for," a company statement said, "and sadly, this is not sustainable in the current economy." Nearly 400 employees will remain at the Burlington facility, however, which has "excelled at prototyping and developing product" in the past and will still carry that responsibility. "Here in Vermont," said the then-CEO, "we will continue to focus on advanced product development, which will allow us to bring the latest snowboard technology to riders faster than ever before."[19]

Questions

1. About 40 people will lose their jobs when Burton closes its Burlington factory, and the company is working with the state of Vermont to provide them with help in finding new employment. How do you think the factory closing might affect the productivity of the remaining headquarters staff? What impact could it have on product quality?
2. Do you think there will be an impact on quality when the design and development staff are separated from the factory floor by so many miles? Why or why not?
3. Can you reconcile the company's focus on product quality with its decision to concentrate manufacturing in a place where it's less expensive to operate? If so, how, and if not, why not?

Case 8.2 Toyota's Quality Crisis

Toyota Motor Corp., once the role model for world-class manufacturing, is facing a quality crisis. With over $200 billion in annual sales and 320,000 employees worldwide, the Japan-based automaker has been driving hard for higher market share. However, after a string of recalls involving millions of vehicles, Toyota is now playing catch-up in the very area in which it has long prided itself—product quality. It also faces serious questions about its slow response to reports of defects.

Production efficiency has long been central to Toyota's culture and its financial strength. Its just-in-time inventory system, which minimizes holding costs, has been copied by manufacturers all over the world. Still, during the past decade alone, the company has boosted its bottom line by building new factories and wringing billions of dollars in savings from its production process. It has reduced the number of parts in its cars, redesigned components to be cheaper and lighter, and increased the speed at which designs are finalized and moved into production. Asked about the effect on quality, a Toyota vice president in North America commented: "It's not true that by reducing cost you automatically reduce quality. Every automaker has to stay competitive relative to price."

Yet in 2005 and again in 2006, Toyota recalled millions of vehicles. After that series of recalls, the company announced a quality-improvement plan based on its famous Toyota Way. One tenet of the Toyota Way is mutual ownership of problems, with quality circles designated to deal with difficulties as they arise. A second is the need to solve problems at their source, which allows factory workers to stop the production line if necessary to address a problem. The third is an urgent and constant drive to improve work processes, fueled by employee suggestions.

In 2008, Toyota's president acknowledged that the company needed to improve internal communications. "When Toyota was a small company," he said, "we could expressly communicate" about quality problems and solutions. "But now that Toyota is so big, we've realized that we have not adequately communicated."

Quality problems surfaced again in 2009, when Toyota learned that a number of vehicles sold in Europe had faulty gas pedals that could lead to sudden acceleration, a serious safety problem. Although Toyota sent its European distributors a bulletin about the problem, it didn't notify U.S. dealers or regulators. That September, the U.S. National Highway Traffic Safety Administration put pressure on Toyota to recall cars because of "unintended acceleration" problems, some reportedly linked to fatal accidents. However, the company didn't announce its gas-pedal fix until November and didn't actually issue the recall until January 2010.

With U.S. regulators and the car-buying public expressing outrage at the slow speed of Toyota's response, Congress held hearings on the matter in March 2010. Toyota's president testified and offered a public apology. Toyota's top U.S. official, asked about the gas-pedal problem, told legislators: "We did not hide it. But it was not properly shared."

The crisis deepened in April when U.S. regulators, after reviewing documents turned over by Toyota, said they would slap the automaker with a multimillion-dollar fine for delaying the recall. For its part, Toyota blamed poor communication. Only weeks after the Congressional hearings, Toyota's president told securities analysts: "Once we thoroughly explored and tried to identify the root cause, we came to realize the problem was . . . with communications [rather] than with quality itself." A company statement, issued the same day, reinforced this explanation: "We have publicly acknowledged on several occasions that the company did a poor job of communicating during the period preceding our recent recalls."

Right after the recalls, *Consumer Reports* suspended its "buy" recommendations on the eight Toyota models involved. The magazine, which many consumers consult before buying cars and trucks, later issued a rare "don't buy" warning on one of Toyota's Lexus GX SUVs, expressing concern about the possibility of a rollover during emergency driving maneuvers. What can Toyota do to steer out of its quality crisis?[20]

Questions

1. Although the Toyota Way relates to quality control, can it be applied to the company's communications about quality? Explain your answer.
2. Evaluate this Toyota executive's quote: "Every automaker has to stay competitive relative to price." What are the implications for the company's management of productivity?
3. What do you think Toyota needs to do to restore its reputation for quality?

Building Skills for Career Success

❶ JOURNALING FOR SUCCESS

Today, people purchase all kinds of products ranging from inexpensive, everyday items to expensive, sophisticated products including electronics, automobiles, and even housing. In each case, customers like to think they are "getting their money's worth" when they purchase a product or service.

Assignment

1. Describe a recent purchase that you made. Be sure to include the cost and why you made the purchase.
2. Given the cost of the product or service, were you satisfied? Why?
3. Do you think that the quality of this product or service was acceptable or unacceptable?
4. How could the manufacturer or provider of the service improve the quality of the product or service?

❷ EXPLORING THE INTERNET

Improvements in the quality of products and services is an ever-popular theme in business management. Besides the obvious increase to profitability to be gained by such improvements, a company's demonstration of its continuous search for ways to improve operations can be a powerful statement to customers, suppliers, and investors. Two of the larger schools of thought in this field are Six Sigma and Total Quality Management.

Assignment

1. Use Internet search engines to find more information about each of these topics.
2. From the information on the Internet, can you tell whether there is any real difference between these two approaches?
3. Describe one success story of a firm that realized improvement by adopting either approach.

❸ DEVELOPING CRITICAL-THINKING SKILLS

Plant layout—the arrangement of machinery, equipment, and personnel within a production facility—is a critical ingredient in a company's success. If the layout is inefficient, productivity and, ultimately, profits will suffer. The purpose of the business dictates the type of layout that will be most efficient. There are three general types: process layout, product layout, and fixed-position layout.

Assignment

1. For each of the following businesses, identify the best type of layout:

   One-hour dry cleaner
   Health club
   Auto repair shop
   Fast-food restaurant
   Shipyard that builds supertankers
   Automobile assembly plant
2. Prepare a two-page report explaining why you chose these layouts and why proper plant layout is important.

❹ BUILDING TEAM SKILLS

Suppose that you are planning to build a house in the country. It will be a brick, one-story structure of approximately 2,000 square feet, centrally heated and cooled. It will have three bedrooms, two bathrooms, a family room, a dining room, a kitchen with a breakfast nook, a study, a utility room, an entry foyer, a two-car garage, a covered patio, and a fireplace. Appliances will operate on electricity and propane fuel. You have received approval and can be connected to the cooperative water system at any time. Public sewerage services are not available; therefore, you must rely on a septic system. You want to know how long it will take to build the house.

Assignment

1. Identify the major activities involved in the project and sequence them in the proper order.
2. Estimate the time required for each activity.
3. Working in a group, prepare a PERT diagram to show the steps involved in building your house.
4. Present your PERT diagram to the class and ask for comments and suggestions.

❺ RESEARCHING DIFFERENT CAREERS

Because service businesses are now such a dominant part of our economy, job seekers sometimes overlook the employment opportunities available in production. Two positions often found in these plants are quality-control inspector and purchasing agent.

Assignment

1. Using the *Occupational Outlook Handbook* at your local library or on the Internet (http://stats.bls.gov/oco/home.htm), find the following information for the jobs of quality-control inspector and purchasing agent:

   Nature of work, including main activities and responsibilities
   Job outlook
   Earnings
   Training, qualifications, and advancement.
2. Look for other production jobs that may interest you and compile the same sort of information about them.
3. Summarize in a two-page report the key things you learned about jobs in production.

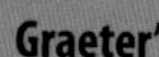

Graeter's Leadership and Management Efforts Enhance Performance

Graeter's, the premier ice-cream maker based in Cincinnati, is a special organization. A small company ($20 million in annual sales) currently unfolding ambitious plans for national expansion, it is also a fourth-generation family firm with an entrepreneurial spirit. Even though it is currently undergoing changes as monumental as building a new factory and preparing to quadruple production, Graeter's still clings fiercely to its original small-batch production method for making rich, creamy ice cream by hand from a simple recipe of natural ingredients. "What is unique to Graeter's, I believe, is that they are just the best out there," says one food industry analyst.

A FAMILY AFFAIR

Graeter's top-management team consists of CEO Richard Graeter II and his two cousins, (brothers) Bob and Chip Graeter. All are great grandsons of the original founders. As vice president of manufacturing, Bob is responsible for sourcing the fresh fruits, cream, eggs, sugar, and top-quality chocolates that go into Graeter's products, whereas Chip oversees the 45 company-owned retail stores in Cincinnati and neighboring cities. A controller and vice president of sales and marketing are also on the team. All three Graeters grew up by working their way through various jobs within the company, sometimes making packing boxes and stamping the names of flavors on ice-cream containers. "I think I always knew that I'd be here," says Richard. "Looking back, I can't imagine not being here. It is just such a part of who I am." On the other hand, he observes, "It can be challenging to work with your family. My father and I didn't always see things the same way. But on the other hand, there is a lot of strength in the family relationship... we certainly had struggles, and family businesses do struggle, especially with transition ... but we found people to help us, including lawyers, accountants, and a family-business psychologist."

Richard describes the current management structure as "an equal partnership" of himself and his two cousins. He says of their collaborative decision-making process, "Every major decision, we make on a consensus basis. That doesn't mean we don't have a different point of view from time to time, but... we learn to see each other's view and discuss, debate, and get down to a decision that all of us support. The other thing that we have learned to do, something that is a little different than our parents' generation [did], is bring in outside people into the... executive level of the management team.... We now work with a couple of consultants to help us plan our strategy to look for a new vision, to develop training programs... all those systems that big companies have."

Says another of the company's managers about problem solving and decision making at Graeter's, "If I can get the right resources in the room, there is no problem that cannot be solved.... Sometimes that means the operators on the floor... because they are in touch with what is really going on. So I ask a lot of questions. I understand what the barriers are, and I find resources to come to a solution." A team of technicians meets with their manager twice a day. "We get in a room for half an hour and I go around the room and I say, 'What did you see today? What did you learn today? What kind of problems do you see? What could we do about that?'"

EMBRACING OPPORTUNITIES FOR GROWTH

Change has come quickly to Graeter's, not all of it anticipated. After three generations of local mom-and-pop style operations, the company is poised for what it hopes will be rapid nationwide expansion of its supermarket distribution operation, which currently puts Graeter's ice cream in the freezers of about 1,700 Kroger's supermarkets in the Midwest, Texas, and Colorado. A new factory to help increase production was already being built when an unexpected opportunity arose: to buy out the last franchise company operating Graeter's retail stores and take over the franchisor's factory as well. The management team jumped at the chance. "A few months ago our strategy was just operate one plant," says Richard. "Now our strategy is, adapt to the opportunity that came along... we are operating three plants. The goal is to keep all of your assets deployed productively, so if we have these three plants, what is the most we can do out of those plants to be generating product and profit? One example would be supplying restaurants in other cities, which we really weren't considering originally because our new plant was really geared for pints, but if we have this excess capacity, the smart thing to do is figure out what we can do with that."

As the company looks forward to the possibility of opening Graeter's stores as far away as Dallas, Los Angeles, and New York, the management team is carefully considering the risk. "Our family has always been contented to make a little less profit in order to ensure our long-term survival," says Richard. "It is a trait that we intend to drum into the fifth generation the same way that our fathers drummed it into us."[21]

Questions

1. What do you think is Graeter's current basis of departmentalization? Do you think this basis might change as Graeter's begins to expand across the country?
2. How would you describe the decision-making process at Graeter's?
3. How many types of planning can you observe in the case? How well do you think Graeter's team handles the planning function of management?

Building a Business Plan PART 3

Now you should be ready to provide evidence that you have a management team with the necessary skills and experience to execute your business plan successfully. Only a competent management team can transform your vision into a successful business. You also should be able to describe your manufacturing and operations plans. The three chapters in Part 3 of your textbook, "Understanding the Management Process," "Creating a Flexible Organization," and "Producing Quality Goods and Services," should help you in answering some of the questions in this part of the business plan.

THE MANAGEMENT TEAM COMPONENT

The management team component should include the answers to at least the following questions:

3.1. How is your team balanced in technical, conceptual, interpersonal, and other special skills needed in your business?

3.2. What will be your style of leadership?

3.3. How will your company be structured? Include a statement of the philosophy of management and company culture.

3.4. What are the key management positions, compensation, and key policies?

3.5. Include a job description for each management position and specify who will fill that position. *Note:* Prepare an organization chart and provide the résumé of each key manager for the appendix.

3.6. What other professionals, such as a lawyer, an insurance agent, a banker, and a certified public accountant, will you need for assistance?

THE MANUFACTURING AND OPERATIONS PLAN COMPONENT

If you are in a manufacturing business, now is a good time to describe your manufacturing and operations plans, space requirements, equipment, labor force, inventory control, and purchasing requirements. Even if you are in a service-oriented business, many of these questions still may apply.

The manufacturing and operations plan component should include the answers to at least the following questions:

3.7. What are the advantages and disadvantages of your planned location in terms of

- Wage rates
- Unionization
- Labor pool
- Proximity to customers and suppliers
- Types of transportation available
- Tax rates
- Utility costs
- Zoning requirements

3.8. What facilities does your business require? Prepare a floor plan for the appendix. Will you rent, lease, or purchase the facilities?

3.9. Will you make or purchase component parts to be assembled into the finished product? Make sure to justify your "make-or-buy decision."

3.10. Who are your potential subcontractors and suppliers?

3.11. How will you control quality, inventory, and production? How will you measure your progress?

3.12. Is there a sufficient quantity of adequately skilled people in the local labor force to meet your needs?

REVIEW OF BUSINESS PLAN ACTIVITIES

Be sure to go over the information you have gathered. Check for any weaknesses and resolve them before beginning Part 4. Also, review all the answers to the questions in Parts 1, 2, and 3 to be certain that they are consistent throughout the entire business plan. Finally, write a brief statement that summarizes all the information for this part of the business plan.

The information contained in "Building a Business Plan" will also assist you in completing the online *Interactive Business Plan*.

PART 4

Human Resources

© ColorBlind Images/Iconica/Getty Images

This part of *Business* is concerned with the most important and least predictable of all resources—people. We begin by examining the human resources efforts that organizations use to hire, develop, and retain their best employees. Then we discuss employee motivation and satisfaction. Finally, we look at organized labor and probe the sometimes controversial relationship between business management and labor unions.

Attracting and Retaining the Best Employees

9

© Jon Feingersh/Iconica/Getty Images

Learning Objectives

What you will be able to do once you complete this chapter:

1. Describe the major components of human resources management.
2. Identify the steps in human resources planning.
3. Describe cultural diversity and understand some of the challenges and opportunities associated with it.
4. Explain the objectives and uses of job analysis.
5. Describe the processes of recruiting, employee selection, and orientation.
6. Discuss the primary elements of employee compensation and benefits.
7. Explain the purposes and techniques of employee training and development.
8. Discuss performance appraisal techniques and performance feedback.
9. Outline the major legislation affecting human resources management.

inside business

Wegmans Has "a Propensity to Serve"

After more than nine decades of business success, Wegmans has proven itself to be much more than a profitable, family-owned grocery retailer. It has also gained widespread recognition as one of the best employers in the United States.

Wegmans started as a small fruit-and-vegetable store in 1916 and has since expanded from its base in Rochester, New York, to become a regional chain that stretches across the Northeast and rings up $5 billion in annual sales. The first Wegmans supermarket was large for its time, with about 20,000 square feet. Today, a typical Wegmans store covers 145,000 square feet and includes a pharmacy, bakery, café, and florist. Keeping a busy supermarket of that size running smoothly requires hundreds of full- and part-time managers and employees. Because the company operates 75 stores, many open around the clock, it also needs a full complement of headquarters and warehouse staff to support its retail operations.

Wegmans currently has a total workforce of 37,000; by 2020, it expects to have 60,000 employees. Employees are more than statistics for Wegmans—they are a vital competitive advantage. The company is particular about who it hires. It seeks out talented applicants who have top-notch skills and "a propensity to serve." Believing in the business possibilities of diversity, Wegmans deliberately reaches out to a broad population of potential employees, a strategy that has won awards locally and nationally.

High turnover is the norm for the supermarket industry, but not at Wegmans. More than 4,000 of its employees have been with the firm for 15 years (and sometimes longer). Wegmans works hard to retain employees by providing the training they need to be successful, respecting their abilities, challenging them to do their best, and giving them the power to satisfy customers. The company offers an excellent package of pay and benefits, and it regularly surveys its employees to learn what they think of its policies and practices. Small wonder that the last time Wegmans opened a new store, it was bombarded with 6,147 applications for 550 positions.[1]

FYI

Did You Know?

Wegmans, a family-owned retailer with 37,000 employees and $5 billion in annual sales, has made 13 consecutive appearances on *Fortune*'s yearly list of "100 Best Companies to Work For."

Wegmans devotes considerable time and resources to hire the right people and to take actions to make them satisfied with their jobs. We begin our study of human resources management (HRM) with an overview of how businesses acquire, maintain, and develop their human resources. After listing the steps by which firms match their human resources needs with the supply available, we explore several dimensions of cultural diversity. Then we examine the concept of job analysis. Next, we focus on a firm's recruiting, selection, and orientation procedures as the means of acquiring employees. We also describe forms of employee compensation that motivate employees to remain with a firm and to work effectively. Then we discuss methods of employee training, management development, and performance appraisal. Finally, we consider legislation that affects HRM practices.

Describe the major components of human resources management.

Human Resources Management: An Overview

The human resource is not only unique and valuable but also an organization's most important resource. It seems logical that an organization would expend a great deal of effort to acquire and make full use of such a resource. This effort is known as *human resources management.* It also has been called *staffing* and *personnel management.*

Human resources management (HRM) consists of all the activities involved in acquiring, maintaining, and developing an organization's human resources. As the definition implies, HRM begins with acquisition—getting people to work for the organization. The acquisition process can be quite competitive for certain types of qualified employees. Next, steps must be taken to keep these valuable resources. (After all, they are the only business resources that can leave an organization.) Finally, the human resources should be developed to their full capacity.

HRM Activities

Each of the three phases of HRM—acquiring, maintaining, and developing human resources—consists of a number of related activities. Acquisition, for example, includes planning, as well as the various activities that lead to hiring new personnel. Altogether this phase of HRM includes five separate activities:

- *Human resources planning*—determining the firm's future human resources needs
- *Job analysis*—determining the exact nature of the positions
- *Recruiting*—attracting people to apply for positions
- *Selection*—choosing and hiring the most qualified applicants
- *Orientation*—acquainting new employees with the firm

Maintaining human resources consists primarily of encouraging employees to remain with the firm and to work effectively by using a variety of HRM programs, including the following:

- *Employee relations*—increasing employee job satisfaction through satisfaction surveys, employee communication programs, exit interviews, and fair treatment
- *Compensation*—rewarding employee effort through monetary payments
- *Benefits*—providing rewards to ensure employee well-being

The development phase of HRM is concerned with improving employees' skills and expanding their capabilities. The two important activities within this phase are:

- *Training and development*—teaching employees new skills, new jobs, and more effective ways of doing their present jobs
- *Performance appraisal*—assessing employees' current and potential performance levels

These activities are discussed in more detail shortly, when we have completed this overview of HRM.

Responsibility for HRM

In general, HRM is a shared responsibility of line managers and staff HRM specialists. In very small organizations, the owner handles all or most HRM activities. As a firm grows in size, a human resources manager is hired to take over staff responsibilities. In firms as large as Disney, HRM activities tend to be very highly specialized. There are separate groups to deal with compensation, benefits, training and development, and other staff activities.

Specific HRM activities are assigned to those who are in the best position to perform them. Human resources planning and job analysis usually are done by

human resources management (HRM) all the activities involved in acquiring, maintaining, and developing an organization's human resources

staff specialists, with input from line managers. Similarly, recruiting and selection are handled by staff experts, although line managers are involved in hiring decisions. Orientation programs are devised by staff specialists and carried out by both staff specialists and line managers. Compensation systems (including benefits) most often are developed and administered by the HRM staff. However, line managers recommend pay increases and promotions. Training and development activities are the joint responsibility of staff and line managers. Performance appraisal is the job of the line manager, although HRM personnel design the firm's appraisal system in many organizations.

2

Identify the steps in human resources planning.

Human Resources Planning

Human resources planning is the development of strategies to meet a firm's future human resources needs. The starting point is the organization's overall strategic plan. From this, human resources planners can forecast future demand for human resources. Next, the planners must determine whether the needed human resources will be available. Finally, they have to take steps to match supply with demand.

Forecasting Human Resources Demand

Planners should base forecasts of the demand for human resources on as much relevant information as available. The firm's overall strategic plan will provide information about future business ventures, new products, and projected expansions or contractions of specific product lines. Information on past staffing levels, evolving technologies, industry staffing practices, and projected economic trends also can be helpful.

HRM staff use this information to determine both the number of employees required and their qualifications. Planners use a wide range of methods to forecast specific personnel needs. For example, with one simple method, personnel requirements are projected to increase or decrease in the same proportion as sales revenue. Thus, if a 30 percent increase in sales volume is projected over the next two years, then up to a 30 percent increase in personnel requirements may be expected for the same period. (This method can be applied to specific positions as well as to the workforce in general. It is not, however, a very precise forecasting method.) At the other extreme are elaborate, computer-based personnel planning models used by some large firms such as ExxonMobil Corporation.

human resources planning the development of strategies to meet a firm's future human resources needs

replacement chart a list of key personnel and their possible replacements within a firm

Forecasting Human Resources Supply

The forecast of the supply of human resources must take into account both the present workforce and any changes that may occur within it. For example, suppose that planners project that in five years a firm that currently employs 100 engineers will need to employ a total of 200 engineers. Planners simply cannot assume that they will have to hire 100 engineers; during that period, some of the firm's present engineers are likely to be promoted, leave the firm, or move to other jobs within the firm. Thus, planners may project the supply of engineers in five years at 87, which means that the firm will have to hire a total of 113 new engineers. When forecasting supply, planners should analyze the organization's existing employees to determine who can be retrained to perform the required tasks.

Two useful techniques for forecasting human resources supply are the replacement chart and the skills inventory. A **replacement chart** is a list of key personnel and their

Rewarding employees. Appropriate employee rewards help to attract and retain employees.

Are You Looking for a Green Collar Job?

Where are the green jobs of today and tomorrow? The Green Collar Association offers information about a wide variety of careers in sustainability, including in renewable energy, clean transportation, land management, and environmental engineering. It also posts job openings and links to resources for researching green jobs. Take a look: http://www.greencollar.org.

possible replacements within a firm. The chart is maintained to ensure that top-management positions can be filled fairly quickly in the event of an unexpected death, resignation, or retirement. Some firms also provide additional training for employees who might eventually replace top managers.

A **skills inventory** is a computerized data bank containing information on the skills and experience of all present employees. It is used to search for candidates to fill available positions. For a special project, a manager may be seeking a current employee with specific information technology skills, at least six years of experience, and fluency in French. The skills inventory can quickly identify employees who possess such qualifications. Skill-assessment tests can be administered inside an organization, or they can be provided by outside vendors. For example, SkillView Technologies, Inc., and Bookman Testing Services, Inc., are third-party information technology skill-assessment providers.

Matching Supply with Demand

Once they have forecasted the supply and demand for personnel, planners can devise a course of action for matching the two. When demand is predicted to be greater than supply, they must make plans to recruit new employees. The timing of these actions depends on the types of positions to be filled. Suppose that we expect to open another plant in five years that will need, along with other employees, a plant manager and 25 maintenance workers. We probably can wait quite a while before we begin to recruit maintenance personnel. However, because the job of a plant manager is so critical, we may start searching for the right person for that position immediately.

When supply is predicted to be greater than demand, the firm must take steps to reduce the size of its workforce. When the oversupply is expected to be temporary, some employees may be *laid off*—dismissed from the workforce until they are needed again.

Perhaps the most humane method for making personnel cutbacks is through attrition. *Attrition* is the normal reduction in the workforce that occurs when employees leave a firm. Over the last five years, Ford, for example, has cut its number of hourly workers by more than 50 percent. Tens of thousands of employees left the company through a combination of involuntary layoffs, buyouts, and normal attrition, which allowed the company to cut salary costs and avoid declaring bankruptcy during the recent recession.[2]

Early retirement is another option. Under early retirement, people who are within a few years of retirement are permitted to retire early with full benefits. Depending on the age makeup of the workforce, this may or may not reduce the staff enough.

As a last resort, unneeded employees are sometimes simply *fired*. However, because of its negative impact, this method generally is used only when absolutely necessary.

skills inventory a computerized data bank containing information on the skills and experience of all present employees

Cultural Diversity in Human Resources

3

Describe cultural diversity and understand some of the challenges and opportunities associated with it.

Today's workforce is made up of many types of people. Firms can no longer assume that every employee has similar beliefs or expectations. Whereas North American white males may believe in challenging authority, Asians tend to respect and defer to it. In Hispanic cultures, people often bring music, food, and family members to work, a custom that U.S. businesses traditionally have not allowed. A job applicant who will not make eye contact during an interview may be rejected for being unapproachable, when, according to his or her culture, he or she was just being polite.

Because a larger number of women, minorities, and immigrants have entered the U.S. workforce, the workplace is more diverse. It is estimated that women make up about 47 percent of the U.S. workforce; African Americans and Hispanics each make up about 11 and 14 percent of U.S. workers, respectively.[3]

Cultural (or workplace) diversity refers to the differences among people in a workforce owing to race, ethnicity, and gender. Increasing cultural diversity is forcing managers to learn to supervise and motivate people with a broader range of value systems. The high proportion of women in the workforce, combined with a new emphasis on participative parenting by men, has brought many family-related issues to the workplace. Today's more educated employees also want greater independence and flexibility. In return for their efforts, they want both compensation and a better quality of life.

Although cultural diversity presents a challenge, managers should view it as an opportunity rather than a limitation. When managed properly, cultural diversity can provide advantages for an organization. Table 9.1 shows several benefits that creative management of cultural diversity can offer. A firm that manages diversity properly can develop cost advantages over other firms. Moreover, organizations that manage diversity creatively are in a much better position to attract the best personnel. A culturally diverse organization may gain a marketing edge because it understands different cultural groups. Proper guidance and management of diversity in an organization also can improve the level of creativity. Culturally diverse people frequently are more flexible in the types of positions they will accept.

Because cultural diversity creates challenges along with advantages, it is important for an organization's employees to understand it. To accomplish this goal, numerous U.S. firms have trained their managers to respect and manage diversity.

cultural (workplace) diversity differences among people in a workforce owing to race, ethnicity, and gender

Table 9.1	Advantages of Cultural Diversity
Cost	As organizations become more diverse, the cost of doing a poor job of integrating workers will increase. Companies that handle this well thus can create cost advantages over those that do a poor job. In addition, companies also experience cost savings by hiring people with knowledge of various cultures as opposed to having to train Americans, for example, about how Germans do business.
Resource acquisition	Companies develop reputations as being favorable or unfavorable prospective employers for women and ethnic minorities. Those with the best reputations for managing diversity will win the competition for the best personnel.
Marketing edge	For multinational organizations, the insight and cultural sensitivity that members with roots in other countries bring to marketing efforts should improve these efforts in important ways. The same rationale applies to marketing subpopulations domestically.
Flexibility	Culturally diverse employees often are open to a wider array of positions within a company and are more likely to move up the corporate ladder more rapidly, given excellent performance.
Creativity	Diversity of perspectives and less emphasis on conformity to norms of the past should improve the level of creativity.
Problem solving	Differences within decision-making and problem-solving groups potentially produce better decisions through a wider range of perspectives and more thorough critical analysis of issues.
Bilingual skills	Cultural diversity in the workplace brings with it bilingual and bicultural skills, which are very advantageous to the ever-growing global marketplace. Employees with knowledge about how other cultures work not only can speak to them in their language but also can prevent their company from making embarrassing moves owing to a lack of cultural sophistication. Thus, companies may seek job applicants with a background in cultures in which the company does business.

Sources: Taylor H. Cox and Stacy Blake, "Managing Cultural Diversity: Implications for Organizational Competitiveness," Academy of Management Executive 5(3):46, 1991; Ricky Griffin and Gregory Moorhead, *Organizational Behavior* (Mason, OH: South-Western/Cengage Learning, 2010), 40; and Richard L. Daft, *Management* (Mason, OH: South-Western/Cengage Learning, 2010), 348–349.

The value of cultural diversity. Organizations that are dedicated to diversity gain significant benefits from their efforts.

Diversity training programs may include recruiting minorities, training minorities to be managers, training managers to view diversity positively, teaching English as a second language, and facilitating support groups for immigrants. Many companies are realizing the necessity of having diversity training span beyond just racial issues. For example, companies such as PricewaterhouseCoopers and PepsiCo require annual diversity training and use company-sanctioned global employee-resource groups.[4] Companies such as these are continuously expanding their business worldwide and therefore need to meld a cohesive workforce from a labor pool whose demographics are constantly becoming more diverse.

A diversity program will be successful only if it is systematic, is ongoing, and has a strong, sustained commitment from top leadership. Cultural diversity is here to stay. Its impact on organizations is widespread and will continue to grow within corporations. Management must learn to overcome the obstacles and capitalize on the advantages associated with culturally diverse human resources.

Explain the objectives and uses of job analysis.

Job Analysis

There is no sense in hiring people unless we know what we are hiring them for. In other words, we need to know the nature of a job before we can find the right person to do it.

Job analysis is a systematic procedure for studying jobs to determine their various elements and requirements. Consider the position of a clerk, for example. In a large corporation, there may be 50 kinds of clerk positions. They all may be called "clerks," but each position may differ from the others in the activities performed, the level of proficiency required for each activity, and the particular set of qualifications that the position demands. These distinctions are the focus of job analysis. Some companies, such as HR.BLR.COM, help employers with preparing the material for job analysis and keeping them updated about state and federal HR employment laws. They provide employers with easy-to-use online service for the resources needed for HR success.[5]

The job analysis for a particular position typically consists of two parts—a job description and a job specification. A **job description** is a list of the elements that make up a particular job. It includes the duties to be performed, the working conditions, the responsibilities, and the tools and equipment that must be used on the job (see Figure 9.1).

A **job specification** is a list of the qualifications required to perform a particular job, such as certain skills, abilities, education, and experience. When attempting to hire a financial analyst, the Bank of America might use the following job specification: "Requires eight to ten years of financial experience, a broad-based financial background, strong customer focus, the ability to work confidently with the client's management team, strong analytical skills. Must have strong Excel and Word skills. Personal characteristics should include strong desire to succeed, impact performer (individually and as a member of a team), positive attitude, high energy level and ability to influence others."

The job analysis is not only the basis for recruiting and selecting new employees; it is also used in other areas of HRM, including evaluation and the determination of equitable compensation levels.

job analysis a systematic procedure for studying jobs to determine their various elements and requirements

job description a list of the elements that make up a particular job

job specification a list of the qualifications required to perform a particular job

Describe the processes of recruiting, employee selection, and orientation.

Recruiting, Selection, and Orientation

In an organization with jobs waiting to be filled, HRM personnel need to (1) find candidates for the jobs and (2) match the right candidate with each job. Three activities are involved: recruiting, selection, and new employee orientation.

Figure 9.1 Job Description and Job Specification

This job description explains the job of sales coordinator and lists the responsibilities of the position. The job specification is contained in the last paragraph.

SOUTH-WESTERN
JOB DESCRIPTION

TITLE:	Georgia Sales Coordinator	**DATE:**	3/25/11
DEPARTMENT:	College, Sales	**GRADE:**	12
REPORTS TO:	Regional Manager	**EXEMPT/NONEXEMPT:**	Exempt

BRIEF SUMMARY:
Supervise one other Georgia-based sales representative to gain supervisory experience. Captain the four members of the outside sales rep team that are assigned to territories consisting of colleges and universities in Georgia. Oversee, coordinate, advise, and make decisions regarding Georgia sales activities. Based upon broad contact with customers across the state and communication with administrators of schools, the person will make recommendations regarding issues specific to the needs of higher education in the state of Georgia such as distance learning, conversion to the semester system, potential statewide adoptions, and faculty training.

PRINCIPAL ACCOUNTABILITIES:
1. Supervises/manages/trains one other Atlanta-based sales rep.
2. Advises two other sales reps regarding the Georgia schools in their territories.
3. Increases overall sales in Georgia as well as his or her individual sales territory.
4. Assists regional manager in planning and coordinating regional meetings and Atlanta conferences.
5. Initiates a dialogue with campus administrators, particularly in the areas of the semester conversion, distance learning, and faculty development.

DIMENSIONS:
This position will have one direct report in addition to the leadership role played within the region. Revenue most directly impacted will be within the individually assigned territory, the supervised territory, and the overall sales for the state of Georgia.

KNOWLEDGE AND SKILLS:
Must have displayed a history of consistently outstanding sales in personal territory. Must demonstrate clear teamwork and leadership skills and be willing to extend beyond the individual territory goals. Should have a clear understanding of the company's systems and product offerings in order to train and lead other sales representatives. Must have the communication skills and presence to communicate articulately with higher education administrators and to serve as a bridge between the company and higher education in the state.

Recruiting

recruiting the process of attracting qualified job applicants

external recruiting the attempt to attract job applicants from outside an organization

Recruiting is the process of attracting qualified job applicants. Because it is a vital link in a costly process (the cost of hiring an employee can be several thousand dollars), recruiting needs to be a systematic process. One goal of recruiters is to attract the "right number" of applicants. The right number is enough to allow a good match between applicants and open positions but not so many that matching them requires too much time and effort. For example, if there are five open positions and five applicants, the firm essentially has no choice. It must hire those five applicants (qualified or not), or the positions will remain open. At the other extreme, if several hundred job seekers apply for the five positions, HRM personnel will have to spend weeks processing their applications.

Recruiters may seek applicants outside the firm, within the firm, or both. The source used depends on the nature of the position, the situation within the firm, and sometimes the firm's established or traditional recruitment policies.

Recruiting. This ad from Manpower is used to recruit temporary employees by stressing the potential for career advancement through part-time or temporary work experience.

External Recruiting **External recruiting** is the attempt to attract job applicants from outside an organization. External recruiting may include recruiting via newspaper advertising, employment agencies, and online employment organizations; recruiting on college campuses; soliciting recommendations from present

Career
SUCCESS

What Can a Career Coach Do for You?

Whether you are hunting for your first job, getting ready to change jobs, or testing the waters in a new industry, consider consulting a career coach. Like a sports coach, a career coach can offer good advice and provide guidance from the sidelines as you take the field and move ahead with key career decisions.

Working with a career coach can open the door to new career possibilities, help you focus your networking efforts, and provide feedback to polish your interviewing skills. Career coaches can also offer insights into what recruiters look for when they read résumés and recommend ways to demonstrate the value of your skills and education to a potential employer. To get the most from coaching, have your résumé handy, prepare questions in advance, and take notes as your coach makes suggestions.

Although you should expect to pay an experienced, professional career coach, do not rule out the idea of asking a trusted mentor to coach you through an important career decision, as a favor. Depending on your goals, you may decide on a single coaching session or meet more than once to continue the discussion. No career coach will hand you a listing of job openings, but you should come away with a definite direction for your job search and more confidence in your abilities.

Sources: Nick Corcodilos, "When Someone You Respect Offers to Be Your Career Coach, What's the Best Response?" *Seattle Times NW Jobs*, February 28, 2010, http://blog.marketplace.nwsource.com/careercenter/when_someone_you_respect_offers_to_be_your_career_coach_whats_the_best_response.html?cmpid=2694; Karina Diaz Cano, "Is a Career Coach Really Worth the Investment?" *The Wall Street Journal*, May 28, 2009, http://blogs.wsj.com/laidoff/2009/05/28/is-a-career-coach-really-worth-the-investment/tab/article.

employees; and conducting "open houses." The biggest of the online job-search sites is Monster.com, which has almost all the *Fortune* 500 companies, as well as small- and medium-sized businesses, as clients. In addition, many people simply apply at a firm's employment office.

Clearly, it is best to match the recruiting means with the kind of applicant being sought. For example, private employment agencies most often handle professional people, whereas public employment agencies (operated by state or local governments) are more concerned with operations personnel. We might approach a private agency when looking for a vice president but contact a public agency to hire a machinist. Procter & Gamble hires graduates directly out of college. It picks the best and brightest—those not "tainted" by another company's culture. It promotes its own "inside" people. This policy makes sure that the company retains the best and brightest and trains new recruits. Procter & Gamble pays competitively and offers positions in many countries. Employee turnover is very low.[6]

The primary advantage of external recruiting is that it brings in people with new perspectives and varied business backgrounds. A disadvantage of external recruiting is that it is often expensive, especially if private employment agencies must be used. External recruiting also may provoke resentment among present employees.

Internal Recruiting **Internal recruiting** means considering present employees as applicants for available positions. Generally, current employees are considered for *promotion* to higher-level positions. However, employees may be considered for *transfer* from one position to another at the same level. Among leading companies, 85 percent of CEOs are promoted from within. In the companies that hire CEOs from outside, 40 percent of the CEOs are gone after 18 months.[7]

internal recruiting considering present employees as applicants for available positions

Promoting from within provides strong motivation for current employees and helps the firm to retain quality personnel. General Electric, ExxonMobil, and Eastman Kodak are companies dedicated to promoting from within. The practice of *job posting*, or informing current employees of upcoming openings, may be a

Going for SUCCESS

Salesforce.com Uses Social Networking to Recruit

Recruiting is a highly social activity at California-based Salesforce.com. The high-tech company, which rings up $1 billion in annual revenue from Web-based software for sales management and other corporate functions, has nearly 3,000 employees worldwide. However, product demand is so strong that the company must add hundreds of new jobs every year to keep up with the fast pace of business growth. To fill all these jobs, Salesforce.com attracts applicants by posting openings and promoting itself as an employer on a multitude of social media.

For example, Salesforce.com has a Twitter account (http://twitter.com/salesforcejobs) devoted to external recruiting. Its managers use this account to post brief messages about internship opportunities, on-campus recruitment visits, and other activities designed to attract qualified applicants. Knowing many job-seekers network on LinkedIn (http://www.linkedin.com), Salesforce.com also lists openings there, providing a detailed job description, company description, and the specific skills required for each position. Interested applicants can click the "apply now" button to complete an application and submit a résumé without leaving their keyboards.

Using blogs and other social media, Salesforce.com invites its workforce to suggest good candidates for open positions. Of the 1,000 new employees hired during the past two years, 40 percent came through employee referrals. The company knows that its success can continue only if its employees succeed. That is why the top human resources executive holds the title of "Senior Vice President of Employee Success."

Sources: Milton Moskowitz, Robert Levering, and Christopher Tkaczyk, "100 Best Companies to Work For: No. 43, Salesforce.com," *Fortune*, February 8, 2010, 82; Steve Hamm, "The King of the Cloud," *BusinessWeek*, November 30, 2009, 77; http://www.salesforce.com.

company policy or required by union contract. The primary disadvantage of internal recruiting is that promoting a current employee leaves another position to be filled. Not only does the firm still incur recruiting and selection costs, but it also must train two employees instead of one.

In many situations it may be impossible to recruit internally. For example, a new position may be such that no current employee is qualified, or the firm may be growing so rapidly that there is no time to reassign positions that promotion or transfer requires.

Selection

Selection is the process of gathering information about applicants for a position and then using that information to choose the most appropriate applicant. Note the use of the word *appropriate*. In selection, the idea is not to hire the person with the *most* qualifications but rather the applicant who is *most appropriate*. The selection of an applicant is made by line managers responsible for the position. However, HRM personnel usually help by developing a pool of applicants and by expediting the assessment of these applicants. Common means of obtaining information about applicants' qualifications are employment applications, interviews, references, and assessment centers.

Employment Applications An employment application is useful in collecting factual information on a candidate's education, work experience, and personal history (see Figure 9.2). The data obtained from applications usually are used for two purposes: to identify applicants who are worthy of further scrutiny and to familiarize interviewers with their backgrounds.

Many job candidates submit résumés, and some firms require them. A *résumé* is a one- or two-page summary of the candidate's background and qualifications. It may include a description of the type of job the applicant is seeking. A résumé may be sent to a firm to request consideration for available jobs, or it may be submitted along with an employment application.

To improve the usefulness of information, HRM specialists ask current employees about factors in their backgrounds most related to their current jobs. Then these

selection the process of gathering information about applicants for a position and then using that information to choose the most appropriate applicant

Figure 9.2 Typical Employment Application

Employers use applications to collect factual information on a candidate's education, work experience, and personal history.

3M Employment Application
Form 14650 - D

3M Staffing Resource Center
3M Center, Building 224-1W-02
P.O. Box 33224
St. Paul, MN 55133-3224

No. 109060

Personal Data *(Print or Type)*

Name — Last / First

Present Address — Street Address / City, State and Zip / Internet e-mail Address

Permanent Address — *Leave blank if same as above* — Street Address / City, State and Zip

Job Interest — Position applied for / Salary desired
Type of position applied for: ☐ Regular ☐ Part-time ☐ Temporary ☐ Summer ☐ ____

Authorization to Work
It is unlawful for 3M to hire individuals that are not authorized to work in the citizens or aliens that are authorized to work in the United States. If you rec offer, before you will be placed on the payroll, you will be required to docum that is authorized to work in the United States.
Are you a United States citizen or a lawful permanent resident? ☐ Yes
If your answer is No, what type of Visa and employment authorization do y

Education History

Schools Attended (Last School First)	Attendance Dates Mo./Yr. From - To	Grad. Date
Name of School (City, State)	-	
	-	
	-	
	-	
High School or GED		

Additional Education Information
(If additional space is needed, attach separate page)
Faculty person who knows you best (name, telephone)
Memberships in professional or honorary societies and any other extracurricular activities
Post graduate research, title and description
Publications/Patents Issued

Please Open Folder and Complete Additional Info

Printed with soy inks on Torchglow Opaque (made of 50% recycled fiber

General Information and Job Requirements
Are you willing to → Work Shifts ☐ Yes ☐ No | Work overtime ☐ Yes ☐ No | Work a schedule other than M/F ☐ Yes ☐ No | Work a rotation work schedule ☐ Yes ☐ No
Travel ☐ Yes ___% ☐ No | List any restrictions regarding relocation | Are you willing to relocate? ☐ Yes ☐ No
If you wish to indicate that you were referred to 3M by any of the following, please check appropriate box and specify
☐ Employment advertisement (Name of publication) ☐ Employment agency (Name of agency) ☐ 3M Employee (Name) ☐ Other
Are you under 18? ☐ Yes ☐ No | Have you ever ☐ been employed by 3M or any 3M Subsidiary ☐ previously applied to 3M or any 3M Subsidiary | If so, please check appropriate box and specify location, date, employee number - (include last two 3M performance reviews if appropriate and available.) | Date/Employee Number

Employment Record

List most current or recent employer first, include periods of unemployment, include U.S. Military Service (show rank/rate at discharge, but not type of discharge). Include previous 3M experience (summer/part time jobs and Cooperative Education assignments and any volunteer experience which relates to the position you are applying for).

Employer (company name) | Immediate supervisor's name | Your job title
Street Address | Employment dates (mo. and yr.) From To | Salary Begin End
City, State, Zip Code | Reason for leaving or why do you want to leave?
Company's Product or Service | Summarize your job duties

Employer (company name) | Immediate supervisor's name | Your job title
Street Address | Employment dates (mo. and yr.) From To | Salary Begin End
City, State, Zip Code | Reason for leaving
Company's Product or Service | Summarize your job duties

Employer (company name) | Immediate supervisor's name | Your job title
Street Address | Employment dates (mo. and yr.) From To | Salary Begin End
City, State, Zip Code | Reason for leaving
Company's Product or Service | Summarize your job duties

Employer (company name) | Immediate supervisor's name | Your job title
Street Address | Employment dates (mo. and yr.) From To | Salary Begin End
City, State, Zip Code | Reason for leaving
Company's Product or Service | Summarize your job duties

Additional Information
(Please include any additional information you think might be helpful to use in considering you for employment, such as additional work experience, activities, accomplishments, etc.)

Source: **Courtesy of 3M.**

factors are included on the applications and may be weighted more heavily when evaluating new applicants' qualifications.

Employment Tests Tests administered to job candidates usually focus on aptitudes, skills, abilities, or knowledge relevant to the job. Such tests (basic computer skills tests, for example) indicate how well the applicant will do the job. Occasionally, companies use general intelligence or personality tests, but these are seldom helpful in predicting specific job performance. However, *Fortune* 500 companies, as well as an increasing number of medium- and small-sized companies, are using predictive behavior personality tests as administration costs decrease.

At one time, a number of companies were criticized for using tests that were biased against certain minority groups—in particular, African Americans. The test results were, to a great extent, unrelated to job performance. Today, a firm must be able to prove that a test is not discriminatory by demonstrating that it accurately measures one's ability to perform. Applicants who believe that they have been discriminated against through an invalid test may file a complaint with the Equal Employment Opportunity Commission (EEOC).

Interviews The interview is perhaps the most widely used selection technique. Job candidates are interviewed by at least one member of the HRM staff and by the person for whom they will be working. Candidates for higher-level jobs may meet with a department head or vice president over several interviews.

Interviews provide an opportunity for applicants and the firm to learn more about each other. Interviewers can pose problems to test the candidate's abilities, probe employment history, and learn something about the candidate's attitudes and motivation. The candidate has a chance to find out more about the job and potential co-workers.

SPOTLIGHT

When Should a Job Candidate Ask About Salary?

Source: Accountemps survey of 150 senior executives.

Unfortunately, interviewing may be the stage at which discrimination begins. For example, suppose that a female applicant mentions that she is the mother of small children. Her interviewer may assume that she would not be available for job-related travel. In addition, interviewers may be unduly influenced by such factors as appearance, or they may ask different questions of different applicants so that it becomes impossible to compare candidates' qualifications. Table 9.2 contains interview questions that are difficult to answer.

Some of these problems can be solved through better interviewer training and use of structured interviews. In a *structured interview*, the interviewer asks only a prepared set of job-related questions. The firm also may consider using several different interviewers for each applicant, but this is likely to be costly.

References A job candidate generally is asked to furnish the names of references—people who can verify background information and provide personal evaluations. Naturally, applicants tend to list only references who are likely to say good things. Thus, personal evaluations obtained from references may not be of much value. However, references are often contacted to verify such information as previous job responsibilities and the reason an applicant left a former job.

Assessment Centers An assessment center is used primarily to select current employees for promotion to higher-level positions. Typically, a group of employees is sent to the center for a few days. While there, they participate in activities designed to simulate the management environment and to predict managerial effectiveness. Trained observers make recommendations regarding promotion possibilities. Although this technique is gaining popularity, the expense involved limits its use.

Job interview. Interviews are a normal part of the recruiting process. They can occur in a variety of locations through several different formats.

Table 9.2 Interview Questions that May Be Difficult to Answer

1. Tell me about yourself.
2. What do you know about our organization?
3. What can you do for us? Why should we hire you?
4. What qualifications do you have that make you feel that you will be successful in your field?
5. What have you learned from the jobs that you have held?
6. If you could write your own ticket, what would be your ideal job?
7. What are your special skills, and how did you acquire them?
8. Have you had any special accomplishments in your lifetime that you are particularly proud of?
9. Why did you leave your most recent job?
10. How do you spend your spare time? What are your hobbies?
11. What are your strengths and weaknesses?
12. Discuss five major accomplishments.
13. What kind of box would you like? Why?
14. If you could spend a day with someone you have known or known of, who would it be?
15. What personality characteristics rub you the wrong way?
16. How do you show your anger? What type of things make you angry?
17. With what type of person do you spend the majority of your time?
18. What activities have you ever quit?
19. Define cooperation.

Sources: Adapted from Susan D. Greene and Melanie C. L. Martel, *The Ultimate Job Hunter's Guidebook*, 5th ed. Copyright © 2008 by Houghton Mifflin Company, 196–197. Used with permission.

Orientation

Once all information about job candidates has been collected and analyzed, the company extends a job offer. If it is accepted, the candidate becomes an employee.

Soon after a candidate joins a firm, he or she goes through the firm's orientation program. **Orientation** is the process of acquainting new employees with an organization. Orientation topics range from the location of the company cafeteria to career paths within the firm. The orientation itself may consist of a half-hour informal presentation by a human resources manager, or it may be an elaborate program involving dozens of people and lasting several days or weeks.

6

Discuss the primary elements of employee compensation and benefits.

Compensation and Benefits

An effective employee reward system must (1) enable employees to satisfy basic needs, (2) provide rewards comparable with those offered by other firms, (3) be distributed fairly within the organization, and (4) recognize that different people have different needs.

A firm's compensation system can be structured to meet the first three of these requirements. The fourth is more difficult because it must account for many variables. Most firms offer a number of benefits that, taken together, generally help to provide for employees' varying needs.

Compensation Decisions

Compensation is the payment employees receive in return for their labor. Its importance to employees is obvious. Because compensation may account for up to 80 percent of a firm's operating costs, it is equally important to the management. Therefore, the firm's **compensation system**, the policies and strategies that determine employee compensation, must be designed carefully to provide for employees' needs while keeping labor costs within reasonable limits. For most firms, designing an effective compensation system requires three separate management decisions—wage level, wage structure, and individual wages.

orientation the process of acquainting new employees with an organization

compensation the payment employees receive in return for their labor

compensation system the policies and strategies that determine employee compensation

Wage Level Management first must position the firm's general pay level relative to pay levels of comparable firms. Most firms choose a pay level near the industry average. However, a firm that is not in good financial shape may pay less than average, and large, prosperous organizations may pay more than average.

To determine the average pay for a job, the firm may use wage surveys. A **wage survey** is a collection of data on prevailing wage rates within an industry or a geographic area. Such surveys are compiled by industry associations, local governments, personnel associations, and (occasionally) individual firms.

Wage Structure Next, management must decide on relative pay levels for all the positions within the firm. Will managers be paid more than secretaries? Will secretaries be paid more than custodians? The result of this set of decisions is often called the firm's *wage structure.*

The wage structure almost always is developed on the basis of a job evaluation. **Job evaluation** is the process of determining the relative worth of the various jobs within a firm. Most observers probably would agree that a secretary should make more money than a custodian, but how much more? Job evaluation should provide the answer to this question.

A number of techniques may be used to evaluate jobs. The simplest is to rank all the jobs within the firm according to value. A more frequently used method is based on the job analysis. Points are allocated to each job for each of its elements and requirements. For example, "college degree required" might be worth 50 points, whereas the need for a high school education might count for only 25 points. The more points a job is allocated, the more important it is presumed to be (and the higher its level in the firm's wage structure).

Individual Wages Finally, the company must determine the specific payments individual employees will receive. Consider the case of two secretaries working side by side. Job evaluation has been used to determine the relative level of secretarial pay within the firm's wage structure. However, suppose that one secretary has 15 years of experience and can type 80 words per minute accurately and the other has two years of experience and can type only 55 words per minute; in most firms, these two people would not receive the same pay. Instead, a wage range would be established for the secretarial position. In this case, the range might be \$8.50 to \$12.50 per hour. The more experienced and proficient secretary then would be paid an amount near the top of the range (say, \$12.25 per hour); the less experienced secretary would receive an amount that is lower but still within the range (say, \$8.75 per hour).

Two wage decisions come into play here. First, the employee's initial rate must be established. It is based on experience, other qualifications, and expected performance. Later, the employee may be given pay increases based on seniority and performance.

Comparable Worth

One reason women in the workforce are paid less may be that a proportion of women occupy female-dominated jobs—nurses, secretaries, and medical records analysts, for example—that require education, skills, and training equal to higher-paid positions but are undervalued. **Comparable worth** is a concept that seeks equal compensation for jobs that require about the same level of education, training, and skill. Several states have enacted laws requiring equal pay for comparable work in government positions. Critics of comparable worth argue that the market has determined the worth of jobs and laws should not tamper with the market's pricing mechanism. The Equal Pay Act, discussed later in this chapter, does not address the issue of comparable worth. Critics also argue that inflating salaries artificially for female-dominated occupations encourages women to keep these jobs rather than seek out higher-paying jobs.

wage survey a collection of data on prevailing wage rates within an industry or a geographic area

job evaluation the process of determining the relative worth of the various jobs within a firm

comparable worth a concept that seeks equal compensation for jobs requiring about the same level of education, training, and skills

Types of Compensation

Compensation can be paid in a variety of forms. Most forms of compensation fall into the following categories: hourly wage, weekly or monthly salary, commissions, incentive payments, lump-sum salary increases, and profit sharing.

Hourly Wage An **hourly wage** is a specific amount of money paid for each hour of work. People who earn wages are paid their hourly wage for the first 40 hours worked in any week. They are then paid one-and-one-half times their hourly wage for time worked in excess of 40 hours (i.e., they are paid "time-and-a-half" for overtime). Workers in retailing and fast-food chains, on assembly lines, and in clerical positions usually are paid an hourly wage.

Weekly or Monthly Salary A **salary** is a specific amount of money paid for an employee's work during a set calendar period, regardless of the actual number of hours worked. Salaried employees receive no overtime pay, but they do not lose pay when they are absent from work. Most professional and managerial positions are salaried.

Commissions A **commission** is a payment that is a percentage of sales revenue. Sales representatives and sales managers often are paid entirely through commissions or through a combination of commissions and salary.

Incentive Payments An **incentive payment** is a payment in addition to wages, salary, or commissions. Incentive payments are really extra rewards for outstanding job performance. They may be distributed to all employees or only to certain employees. Some firms distribute incentive payments to all employees annually. The size of the payment depends on the firm's earnings and, at times, on the particular employee's length of service with the firm. Firms sometimes offer incentives to employees who exceed specific sales or production goals, a practice called *gain sharing*.

To avoid yearly across-the-board salary increases, some organizations reward outstanding workers individually through *merit pay*. This pay-for-performance approach allows management to control labor costs while encouraging employees to work more efficiently. An employee's merit pay depends on his or her achievements relative to those of others.

Lump-Sum Salary Increases In traditional reward systems, an employee who receives an annual pay increase is given part of the increase in each pay period. For example, suppose that an employee on a monthly salary gets a 10 percent annual pay hike. He or she actually receives 10 percent of the former monthly salary added to each month's paycheck for a year. Companies that offer a **lump-sum salary increase** give the employee the option of taking the entire pay raise in one lump sum. The employee then draws his or her "regular" pay for the rest of the year. The lump-sum payment typically is treated as an interest-free loan that must be repaid if the employee leaves the firm during the year.

Profit-Sharing **Profit-sharing** is the distribution of a percentage of a firm's profit among its employees. The idea is to motivate employees to work effectively by giving them a stake in the company's financial success. Some firms—including Sears, Roebuck—have linked their profit-sharing plans to employee retirement programs; that is, employees receive their profit-sharing distributions, with interest, when they retire.

Employee Benefits

An **employee benefit** is a reward in addition to regular compensation that is provided indirectly to employees. Employee benefits consist mainly of services (such as insurance) that are paid for partially or totally by employers and employee

hourly wage a specific amount of money paid for each hour of work

salary a specific amount of money paid for an employee's work during a set calendar period, regardless of the actual number of hours worked

commission a payment that is a percentage of sales revenue

incentive payment a payment in addition to wages, salary, or commissions

lump-sum salary increase an entire pay raise taken in one lump sum

profit-sharing the distribution of a percentage of a firm's profit among its employees

employee benefit a reward in addition to regular compensation that is provided indirectly to employees

expenses (such as college tuition) that are reimbursed by employers. Currently, the average cost of these benefits is 29.3 percent of an employee's total compensation, which includes wages plus benefits.[8] Thus, a person who received total compensation (including benefits) of $50,000 a year earned $33,350 in wages and received an additional $14,650 in benefits.

Employee benefits. Companies vary among themselves on the types of employee benefits provided. For example, some provide child-care services.

Types of Benefits Employee benefits take a variety of forms. *Pay for time not worked* covers such absences as vacation time, holidays, and sick leave. *Insurance packages* may include health, life, and dental insurance for employees and their families. Some firms pay the entire cost of the insurance package, and others share the cost with the employee. The costs of *pension and retirement programs* also may be borne entirely by the firm or shared with the employee.

Some benefits are required by law. For example, employers must maintain *workers' compensation insurance,* which pays medical bills for injuries that occur on the job and provides income for employees who are disabled by job-related injuries. Employers must also pay for *unemployment insurance* and contribute to each employee's federal *Social Security* account.

Other benefits provided by employers include tuition-reimbursement plans, credit unions, child-care services, company cafeterias, exercise rooms, and broad stock-option plans available to all employees. Some companies offer special benefits to U.S. military reservists who are called up for active duty.

Some companies offer unusual benefits to attract and retain employees. Paychex, a payroll-processing company, gives awards of up to $300 to its employees for participating in healthy activities, such as receiving flu shots, going to the dentist, attending exercise classes, running a race, and riding their bike to work. MITRE, a non-profit technology services provider, rewards its employees who want to further their education by giving them money to go toward getting a Master's degree or a PhD. Employees at SC Johnson have access to an on-site concierge service that will run errands for them, such as mailing packages, getting groceries, and changing their car's oil. Intel offers all its full-time employees in the United States and Canada an eight-week paid sabbatical every seven years. SAS, which is highly ranked in *Fortune* magazine's "Top 100 Companies to Work For," offers unlimited sick days, a medical center that provides free services, a free 66,000-square-foot fitness center and natatorium, a lending library, on-site saunas, discounted massages, classes on Wii bowling, and even a summer camp for children of employees. Google is known for its unusual perks and fun activities, which include foosball, pool, volleyball, video games, ping pong, and gymnasiums that offer yoga and dance classes.[9]

Flexible Benefit Plans Through a **flexible benefit plan**, an employee receives a predetermined amount of benefit dollars and may allocate those dollars to various categories of benefits in the mix that best fits his or her needs. Some flexible benefit plans offer a broad array of benefit options, including health care, dental care, life insurance, accidental death and dismemberment coverage for both the worker and dependents, long-term disability coverage, vacation benefits, retirement savings, and dependent-care benefits. Other firms offer limited options, primarily in health and life insurance and retirement plans.

flexible benefit plan compensation plan whereby an employee receives a predetermined amount of benefit dollars to spend on a package of benefits he or she has selected to meet individual needs

Although the cost of administering flexible plans is high, a number of organizations, including Quaker Oats and Coca-Cola, have implemented this option for several reasons. Because employees' needs are so diverse, flexible plans help firms to offer benefit packages that more specifically meet their employees' needs. Flexible plans can, in the long run, help a company to contain costs because a specified amount is allocated to cover the benefits of each employee. Furthermore, organizations that offer flexible plans with many choices may be perceived as being employee-friendly. Thus, they are in a better position to attract and retain qualified employees.

7

Explain the purposes and techniques of employee training and development.

Training and Development

Training and development are extremely important at the Container Store. Because great customer service is so important, every first-year full-time salesperson receives about 185 hours of formal training as opposed to the industry standard, which is approximately seven hours. Training and development continue throughout a person's career. Each store has a full-time trainer called the *super sales trainer*. This trainer provides product training, sales training, and employee-development training. A number of top managers believe that the financial and human resources invested in training and development are well worth it.

Both training and development are aimed at improving employees' skills and abilities. However, the two are usually differentiated as either employee training or management development. **Employee training** is the process of teaching operations and technical employees how to do their present jobs more effectively and efficiently. **Management development** is the process of preparing managers and other professionals to assume increased responsibility in both present and future positions. Thus, training and development differ in who is being taught and the purpose of the teaching. However, both are necessary for personal and organizational growth. Companies that hope to stay competitive typically make huge commitments to employee training and development. Internet-based e-learning is growing. Driven by cost, travel, and time savings, online learning alone (and in conjunction with face-to-face situations) is a strong alternative strategy. Development of a training program usually has three components: analysis of needs, determination of training and development methods, and creation of an evaluation system to assess the program's effectiveness.

employee training the process of teaching operations and technical employees how to do their present jobs more effectively and efficiently

management development the process of preparing managers and other professionals to assume increased responsibility in both present and future positions

Analysis of Training Needs

When thinking about developing a training program, managers first must determine if training is needed and, if so, what types of training needs exist. At times, what at first appears to be a need for training is actually, on assessment, a need for motivation. Training needs can vary considerably. For example, some employees may need training to improve their technical skills, or they may need training about organizational procedures. Training also may focus on business ethics, product information, or customer service. Because training is expensive, it is critical that the correct training needs be identified.

Training. Organizations train employees using a variety of methods and during a variety of time periods.

© Monkey Business Images

Training and Development Methods

A number of methods are available for employee training and management development. Some of these methods may be more suitable for one or the other, but most can be applied to both training and management development.

- *On-the-job methods.* The trainee learns by doing the work under the supervision of an experienced employee.
- *Simulations.* The work situation is simulated in a separate area so that learning takes place away from the day-to-day pressures of work.
- *Classroom teaching and lectures.* You probably already know these methods quite well.

- *Conferences and seminars.* Experts and learners meet to discuss problems and exchange ideas.
- *Role-playing.* Participants act out the roles of others in the organization for better understanding of those roles (primarily a management development tool).

Evaluation of Training and Development

Training and development are very expensive. The training itself costs quite a bit, and employees are usually not working—or are working at a reduced load and pace—during training sessions. To ensure that training and development are cost-effective, the managers responsible should evaluate the company's efforts periodically.

The starting point for this evaluation is a set of verifiable objectives that are developed before the training is undertaken. Suppose that a training program is expected to improve the skills of machinists. The objective of the program might be stated as follows: "At the end of the training period, each machinist should be able to process 30 parts per hour with no more than one defective part per 90 parts completed." This objective clearly specifies what is expected and how training results may be measured or verified. Evaluation then consists of measuring machinists' output and the ratio of defective parts produced after the training.

The results of training evaluations should be made known to all those involved in the program—including trainees and upper management. For trainees, the results of evaluations can enhance motivation and learning. For upper management, the results may be the basis for making decisions about the training program itself.

8

Discuss performance appraisal techniques and performance feedback.

Performance Appraisal

Performance appraisal is the evaluation of employees' current and potential levels of performance to allow managers to make objective human resources decisions. The process has three main objectives. First, managers use performance appraisals to let workers know how well they are doing and how they can do better in the future. Second, a performance appraisal provides an effective basis for distributing rewards, such as pay raises and promotions. Third, performance appraisal helps the organization monitor its employee selection, training, and development activities. If large numbers of employees continually perform below expectations, the firm may need to revise its selection process or strengthen its training and development activities. Most performance appraisal processes include a written document. An example appears in Figure 9.3.

Common Evaluation Techniques

The various techniques and methods for appraising employee performance are either objective or judgmental in nature.

Objective Methods Objective appraisal methods use some measurable quantity as the basis for assessing performance. Units of output, dollar volume of sales, number of defective products, and number of insurance claims processed are all objective, measurable quantities. Thus, an employee who processes an average of 26 insurance claims per week is given a higher evaluation than one whose average is 19 claims per week.

Such objective measures may require some adjustment for the work environment. Suppose that the first of our insurance claims' processors works in New York City and the second works in rural Iowa. Both must visit each client because they are processing homeowners' insurance claims. The difference in their average weekly output may be entirely because of the long distances the Iowan must travel to visit clients. In this case, the two workers may very well be equally competent and motivated. Thus, a manager must take into account circumstances that may be hidden by a purely statistical measurement.

performance appraisal the evaluation of employees' current and potential levels of performance to allow managers to make objective human resources decisions

Figure 9.3 Performance Appraisal

3M **Contribution and Development Summary**
FORM 37450 - B

Employee Name	Employee Number	Job Title
Department		Location
Coach/Supervisor(s) Name(s)		Review Period From :

Major Job Responsibilities

Goals/Expectations | **Contributions/R**

Contribution (To be completed by coach/supervisor)

- ☐ Good Level of Contribution for this year
- ☐ Unsatisfactory Level of Contribution for this year
- ☐ Exceptional

Development Summary

Areas of Strength	Development Priorities

Career Interests

Next job	Longer Range

Current Mobility

- ☐ **0** - Currently Unable to Relocate
- ☐ **1** - Position In Home Country Only (Use if Home Country is Outside U.S.)
- ☐ **2** - Position Within O.U.S. Region (e: Nordic, SEA...)
- ☐ **3** - Position Within O.U.S. Area (ex: Europe, Asia)
- ☐ **4** - Position In U.S.
- ☐ **5** - Position Anywhere In The World

Development

- ☐ **W** - Well placed. Development plans achievable in current role for at least the next year
- ☐ **C** - Ready now for a move to a different job for career broadening experience
- ☐ **I** - Ready now for a move to a different job involving increased responsibility
- ☐ **X** - Not well placed. Action required to resolve placement issues.

Comments on Development

Employee Comments

Coach/Supervisor Comments | **Other Supervisor (if applicable) and/or Reviewer**

Signatures

Coach/Supervisor	Date	Other Coach/Supervisor or Reviewer	Date
Employee			Date

page 4

Source: Courtesy of 3M.

Judgmental Methods Judgmental appraisal methods are used much more frequently than objective methods. They require that the manager judge or estimate the employee's performance level. However, judgmental methods are not capricious. These methods are based on employee ranking or rating scales. When ranking is used, the manager ranks subordinates from best to worst. This approach has a number of drawbacks, including the lack of any absolute standard. Use of rating scales is the most popular judgmental appraisal technique. A *rating scale* consists of a number of statements; each employee is rated on the degree to which the statement applies. For example, one statement might be, "This employee always does high-quality work." The supervisor would give the employee a rating, from 5 down to 1, corresponding to gradations ranging from "strongly agree" to "strongly disagree." The ratings on all the statements are added to obtain the employee's total evaluation.

Avoiding Appraisal Errors Managers must be cautious if they are to avoid making mistakes when appraising employees. It is common to overuse one portion of an evaluation instrument, thus overemphasizing some issues and underemphasizing others. A manager must guard against allowing an employee's poor performance on one activity to influence his or her judgment of that subordinate's work on other activities. Similarly, putting too much weight on recent performance distorts an employee's evaluation. For example, if the employee is being rated on performance over the last year, a manager should not permit last month's disappointing performance to overshadow the quality of the work done in the first 11 months of the year. Finally, a manager must guard against discrimination on the basis of race, age, gender, religion, national origin, or sexual orientation.

Performance Feedback

No matter which appraisal technique is used, the results should be discussed with the employee soon after the evaluation is completed. The manager should explain the basis for present rewards and should let the employee know what he or she can do to be recognized as a better performer in the future. The information provided to an employee in such discussions is called *performance feedback*, and the process is known as a *performance feedback interview.*

There are three major approaches to performance feedback interviews: tell-and-sell, tell-and-listen, and problem solving. In a *tell-and-sell* feedback interview, the superior tells the employee how good or bad the employee's performance has been and then attempts to persuade the employee to accept the evaluation. Because the employee has no input into the evaluation, the tell-and-sell interview can lead to defensiveness, resentment, and frustration on the part of the subordinate. The employee may not accept the results of the interview and may not be committed to achieving the goals that are set.

With the *tell-and-listen* approach, the supervisor tells the employee what has been right and wrong with the employee's performance and then gives the employee a chance to respond. The subordinate may simply be given an opportunity to react to the supervisor's statements or may be permitted to offer a full self-appraisal, challenging the supervisor's assessment.

In the *problem-solving* approach, employees evaluate their own performance and set their own goals for future performance. The supervisor is more a colleague than a judge and offers comments and advice in a noncritical manner. An active and open dialogue ensues in which goals for improvement are mutually established. The problem-solving interview is most likely to result in the employee's commitment to the established goals.

To avoid some of the problems associated with the tell-and-sell interview, supervisors sometimes use a mixed approach. The mixed interview uses the tell-and-sell approach to communicate administrative decisions and the problem-solving approach to discuss employee-development issues and future performance goals.[10]

An appraisal approach that has become popular is called a *360-degree evaluation.* A 360-degree evaluation collects anonymous reviews about an employee from his or her peers, subordinates, and supervisors and then compiles these reviews into a feedback report that is given to the employee. Companies that invest significant resources in employee-development efforts are especially likely to use 360-degree evaluations. An employee should not be given a feedback report without first having a one-on-one meeting with his or her supervisor. The most appropriate way to introduce a 360-degree evaluation system in

A 360-degree evaluation. As part of the review process at companies like Johnson & Johnson, IBM, and Xerox, managers first gather information about an employee from peers, subordinates, and supervisors, and then compile these reviews into a feedback report that is given to the employee.

a company is to begin with upper-level management. Then managers should be trained on how to interpret feedback reports so that they can coach their employees on how to use the feedback to achieve higher-level job-related skills and behaviors.[11]

Finally, we should note that many managers find it difficult to discuss the negative aspects of an appraisal. Unfortunately, they may ignore performance feedback altogether or provide it in a very weak and ineffectual manner. In truth, though, most employees have strengths that can be emphasized to soften the discussion of their weaknesses. An employee may not even be aware of the weaknesses and their consequences. If such weaknesses are not pointed out through performance feedback, they cannot possibly be eliminated. Only through tactful, honest communication can the results of an appraisal be fully used.

9

Outline the major legislation affecting human resources management.

The Legal Environment of HRM

Legislation regarding HRM practices has been passed mainly to protect the rights of employees, to promote job safety, and to eliminate discrimination in the workplace. The major federal laws affecting HRM are described in Table 9.3.

Table 9.3 Federal Legislation Affecting Human Resources Management

Law	Purpose
National Labor Relations Act (1935)	Established a collective-bargaining process in labor–management relations as well as the National Labor Relations Board (NLRB).
Fair Labor Standards Act (1938)	Established a minimum wage and an overtime pay rate for employees working more than 40 hours per week.
Labor–Management Relations Act (1947)	Provides a balance between union power and management power; also known as the Taft–Hartley Act.
Equal Pay Act (1963)	Specifies that men and women who do equal jobs must be paid the same wage.
Title VII of the Civil Rights Act (1964)	Prohibits discrimination in employment practices based on sex, race, color, religion, or national origin.
Age Discrimination in Employment Act (1967–1986)	Prohibits personnel practices that discriminate against people aged 40 years and older; the 1986 amendment eliminated a mandatory retirement age.
Occupational Safety and Health Act (1970)	Regulates the degree to which employees can be exposed to hazardous substances and specifies the safety equipment that the employer must provide.
Employment Retirement Income Security Act (1974)	Regulates company retirement programs and provides a federal insurance program for retirement plans that go bankrupt.
Worker Adjustment and Retraining Notification (WARN) Act (1988)	Requires employers to give employees 60 days notice regarding plant closure or layoff of 50 or more employees.
Americans with Disabilities Act (1990)	Prohibits discrimination against qualified individuals with disabilities in all employment practices, including job-application procedures, hiring, firing, advancement, compensation, training, and other terms, conditions, and privileges of employment.
Civil Rights Act (1991)	Facilitates employees' suing employers for sexual discrimination and collecting punitive damages.
Family and Medical Leave Act (1993)	Requires an organization with 50 or more employees to provide up to 12 weeks of leave without pay on the birth (or adoption) of an employee's child or if an employee or his or her spouse, child, or parent is seriously ill.
Affordable Care Act (2010)	Requires an organization with 50 or more employees to make health insurance available to employees or pay an assessment and gives employees the right to buy health insurance from another provider if an organization's health insurance is too expensive.

National Labor Relations Act and Labor–Management Relations Act

These laws are concerned with dealings between business firms and labor unions. This general area is, in concept, a part of HRM. However, because of its importance, it is often treated as a separate set of activities. We discuss both labor–management relations and these two acts in detail in Chapter 11.

Fair Labor Standards Act

This act, passed in 1938 and amended many times since, applies primarily to wages. It established minimum wages and overtime pay rates. Many managers and other professionals, however, are exempt from this law. Managers, for example, seldom get paid overtime when they work more than 40 hours a week.

Equal Pay Act

Passed in 1963, this law overlaps somewhat with Title VII of the Civil Rights Act (see next section). The Equal Pay Act specifies that men and women who are doing equal jobs must be paid the same wage. Equal jobs are jobs that demand equal effort, skill, and responsibility and are performed under the same conditions. Differences in pay are legal if they can be attributed to differences in seniority, qualifications, or performance. However, women cannot be paid less (or more) for the same work solely because they are women.

Civil Rights Acts

Title VII of the Civil Rights Act of 1964 applies directly to selection and promotion. It forbids organizations with 15 or more employees to discriminate in those areas on the basis of sex, race, color, religion, or national origin. The purpose of Title VII is to ensure that employers make personnel decisions on the basis of employee qualifications only. As a result of this act, discrimination in employment (especially against African Americans) has been reduced in this country.

The EEOC is charged with enforcing Title VII. A person who believes that he or she has been discriminated against can file a complaint with the EEOC. The commission then investigates the complaint and, if it finds that the person has, in fact, been the victim of discrimination, the commission can take legal action on his or her behalf.

The Civil Rights Act of 1991 facilitates an employee's suing and collecting punitive damages for sexual discrimination. Discriminatory promotion and termination decisions as well as on-the-job issues, such as sexual harassment, are covered by this act.

Age Discrimination in Employment Act

The general purpose of this act, which was passed in 1967 and amended in 1986, is the same as that of Title VII—to eliminate discrimination. However, as the name implies, the Age Discrimination in Employment Act is concerned only with discrimination based on age. It applies to companies with 20 or more employees. In particular, it outlaws personnel practices that discriminate against people aged 40 years or older. (No federal law forbids discrimination against people younger than 40 years, but several states have adopted age discrimination laws that apply to a variety of age groups.) Also outlawed are company policies that specify a mandatory retirement age. Employers must base employment decisions on ability and not on a number.

Occupational Safety and Health Act

Passed in 1970, this act is mainly concerned with issues of employee health and safety. For example, the act regulates the degree to which employees can be exposed to hazardous substances. It also specifies the safety equipment that the employer must provide.

Americans with Disabilities Act. A major element in the ADA focuses on providing access to accommodate employees with disabilities.

The Occupational Safety and Health Administration (OSHA) was created to enforce this act. Inspectors from OSHA investigate employee complaints regarding unsafe working conditions. They also make spot checks on companies operating in particularly hazardous industries, such as chemical and mining industries, to ensure compliance with the law. A firm found to be in violation of federal standards can be heavily fined or shut down. Nonetheless, many people feel that issuing OSHA violations is not enough to protect workers from harm.

Employee Retirement Income Security Act

This act was passed in 1974 to protect the retirement benefits of employees. It does not require that firms provide a retirement plan. However, it does specify that if a retirement plan is provided, it must be managed in such a way that the interests of employees are protected. It also provides federal insurance for retirement plans that go bankrupt.

Affirmative Action

Affirmative action is not one act but a series of executive orders issued by the President of the United States. These orders established the requirement for affirmative action in personnel practices. This stipulation applies to all employers with 50 or more employees holding federal contracts in excess of $50,000. It prescribes that such employers (1) actively encourage job applications from members of minority groups and (2) hire qualified employees from minority groups who are not fully represented in their organizations. Many firms that do not hold government contracts voluntarily take part in this affirmative action program.

Americans with Disabilities Act

The Americans with Disabilities Act (ADA) prohibits discrimination against qualified individuals with disabilities in all employment practices—including job-application procedures, hiring, firing, advancement, compensation, training, and other terms and conditions of employment. All private employers and government agencies with 15 or more employees are covered by the ADA. Defining who is a qualified individual with a disability is, of course, difficult. Depending on how *qualified individual with a disability* is interpreted, up to 43 million Americans can be included under this law. This law also mandates that all businesses that serve the public must make their facilities accessible to people with disabilities.

ADA not only protects individuals with obvious physical disabilities but also safeguards those with less visible conditions, such as heart disease, diabetes, epilepsy, cancer, AIDS, and mental illnesses. Because of this law, many organizations no longer require job applicants to pass physical examinations as a condition of employment.

Employers are required to provide disabled employees with reasonable accommodation. *Reasonable accommodation* is any modification or adjustment to a job or work environment that will enable a qualified employee with a disability to perform a central job function. Examples of reasonable accommodation include making existing facilities readily accessible to and usable by an individual confined to a wheelchair. Reasonable accommodation also might mean restructuring a job, modifying work schedules, acquiring or modifying equipment, providing qualified readers or interpreters, or changing training programs.

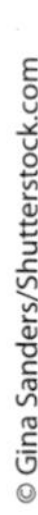

return to inside business

Wegmans

Wegmans has become a regional supermarket success by using its employees as a competitive advantage. Other supermarkets may stock many of the same national brands, but they do not have the talented workforce that Wegmans has recruited and trained to work with the public and behind the scenes. The company sifts through stacks of résumés, asks employees for referrals, and conducts round after round of interviews until it finds the right candidates for each job.

Putting good people on the payroll is only the start. Family-owned Wegmans wants its workforce to share the company's "family" feeling and feel empowered to do what's right for the customer. Every week, human resources personnel fan out to visit the stores and listen to employees' ideas and concerns. "Just as we engage our customers, we want to let our employees know that they're valued," explains the company's top human resources executive.

Questions

1. Although in business for nearly 100 years, Wegmans has never had to downsize or lay off workers. How would you use the concepts of human resources planning to explain this accomplishment?
2. If you were a recruiter for Wegmans, what questions would you ask in a job interview to determine whether a candidate has "a propensity to serve"?

SUMMARY

Summary

1 Describe the major components of human resources management.

Human resources management (HRM) is the set of activities involved in acquiring, maintaining, and developing an organization's human resources. Responsibility for HRM is shared by specialized staff and line managers. HRM activities include human resources planning, job analysis, recruitment, selection, orientation, compensation, benefits, training and development, and performance appraisal.

2 Identify the steps in human resources planning.

Human resources planning consists of forecasting the human resources that a firm will need and those that it will have available and then planning a course of action to match supply with demand. Layoffs, attrition, early retirement, and (as a last resort) firing are ways to reduce the size of the workforce. Supply is increased through hiring.

3 Describe cultural diversity and understand some of the challenges and opportunities associated with it.

Cultural diversity refers to the differences among people in a workforce owing to race, ethnicity, and gender. With an increasing number of women, minorities, and immigrants entering the U.S. workforce, management is faced with both challenges and competitive advantages. Some organizations are implementing diversity-related training programs and working to make the most of cultural diversity. With proper guidance and management, a culturally diverse organization can prove beneficial to all involved.

4 Explain the objectives and uses of job analysis.

Job analysis provides a job description and a job specification for each position within a firm. A job description is a list of the elements that make up a particular job. A job specification is a list of qualifications required to perform a particular job. Job analysis is used in evaluation and in the determination of compensation levels and serves as the basis for recruiting and selecting new employees.

5 Describe the processes of recruiting, employee selection, and orientation.

Recruiting is the process of attracting qualified job applicants. Candidates for open positions may be recruited from within or outside a firm. In the selection process, information about candidates is obtained from applications, résumés, tests, interviews, references, or assessment centers. This information then is used to select the most appropriate candidate for the job. Newly hired employees will then go through a formal or an informal orientation program to acquaint themselves with the firm.

6 Discuss the primary elements of employee compensation and benefits.

Compensation is the payment employees receive in return for their labor. In developing a system for paying employees, management must decide on the firm's general wage level (relative to other firms), the wage structure within the firm, and individual wages. Wage surveys and job analyses are useful in making these decisions. Employees may be paid hourly wages, salaries, or commissions. They also may receive incentive payments, lump-sum salary increases, and profit-sharing payments. Employee benefits, which are nonmonetary rewards to employees, add about 28 percent to the cost of compensation.

7 Explain the purposes and techniques of employee training and development.

Employee-training and management-development programs enhance the ability of employees to contribute to a firm. When developing a training program, the company should analyze training needs and then select training methods. Because training is expensive, an organization should periodically evaluate the effectiveness of its training programs.

8 Discuss performance appraisal techniques and performance feedback.

Performance appraisal, or evaluation, is used to provide employees with performance feedback, to serve as a basis for distributing rewards, and to monitor selection and training activities. Both objective and judgmental appraisal techniques are used. Their results are communicated to employees through three performance feedback approaches: tell-and-sell, tell-and-listen, and problem solving.

9 Outline the major legislation affecting human resources management.

A number of laws have been passed that affect HRM practices and that protect the rights and safety of employees. Some of these are the National Labor Relations Act of 1935, the Labor–Management Relations Act of 1947, the Fair Labor Standards Act of 1938, the Equal Pay Act of 1963, Title VII of the Civil Rights Act of 1964, the Age Discrimination in Employment Acts of 1967 and 1986, the Occupational Safety and Health Act of 1970, the Employment Retirement Income Security Act of 1974, the Worker Adjustment and Retraining Notification Act of 1988, the Americans with Disabilities Act of 1990, the Civil Rights Act of 1991, and the Family and Medical Leave Act of 1993.

Key Terms

You should now be able to define and give an example relevant to each of the following terms:

human resources management (HRM) (250)
human resources planning (251)
replacement chart (251)
skills inventory (252)
cultural (workplace) diversity (253)
job analysis (254)
job description (254)
job specification (254)
recruiting (255)
external recruiting (255)
internal recruiting (256)
selection (257)
orientation (260)
compensation (260)
compensation system (260)
wage survey (261)
job evaluation (261)
comparable worth (261)
hourly wage (262)
salary (262)
commission (262)
incentive payment (262)
lump-sum salary increase (262)
profit-sharing (262)
employee benefit (262)
flexible benefit plan (263)
employee training (264)
management development (264)
performance appraisal (265)

Review Questions

1. List the three main HRM activities and their objectives.
2. In general, on what basis is responsibility for HRM divided between staff and line managers?
3. How is a forecast of human resources demand related to a firm's organizational planning?
4. How do human resources managers go about matching a firm's supply of workers with its demand for workers?
5. What are the major challenges and benefits associated with a culturally diverse workforce?
6. How are job analysis, job description, and job specification related?
7. What are the advantages and disadvantages of external recruiting and of internal recruiting?
8. In your opinion, what are the two best techniques for gathering information about job candidates?
9. Why is orientation an important HRM activity?
10. Explain how the three wage-related decisions result in a compensation system.

11. How is a job analysis used in the process of job evaluation?
12. Suppose that you have just opened a new Ford sales showroom and repair shop. Which of your employees would be paid wages, which would receive salaries, and which would receive commissions?
13. What is the difference between the objective of employee training and the objective of management development?
14. Why is it so important to provide feedback after a performance appraisal?

Discussion Questions

1. How accurately can managers plan for future human resources needs?
2. How might an organization's recruiting and selection practices be affected by the general level of employment?
3. Are employee benefits really necessary? Why?
4. As a manager, what actions would you take if an operations employee with six years of experience on the job refused ongoing training and ignored performance feedback?
5. Why are there so many laws relating to HRM practices? Which are the most important laws, in your opinion?

Video Case 9.1

Whirlpool's Award-Winning Diversity Program Is Facilitated Through Employee Network

In today's global marketplace, managers interact with people of different cultures, languages, beliefs, and values. Whirlpool Corporation has shown that a diverse workforce can be a powerful advantage.

Since its establishment in 1911, Whirlpool, headquartered in Michigan, has grown into a global corporation with manufacturing locations on every major continent and annual revenues in excess of $19 billion. Approximately 60 percent of Whirlpool's 70,000+ employees work outside North America. The development of this broad workforce is aided by the company's award-winning diversity program, which gathers workers into support groups based on personal affiliations. To enter the program, workers join a particular employee network of their choosing, such as the Hispanic network, the young professionals network, the Asian or African American networks, the women's network, the Native American network, or the Pride network, which includes gay, lesbian, bisexual, and transgender (GLBT) employees.

These networks give employees access to a world of new career resources and training opportunities. For instance, according to the company's Web site, "Our primary objective is to become the employer of choice for GLBT and affirming employees." Despite the program's obvious focus on employee well-being, leaders at Whirlpool say the networks also offer a competitive advantage in global marketing. "Having diverse people making decisions and giving input to the factors that we consider on a daily basis is extremely important to the business," according to the company's vice president of consumer and appliance care, Kathy Nelson. "It's important because we need to make sure that the people who are making business decisions are reflective of who our consumers are."

This belief is fully in keeping with the company's Diversity Mission Statement, expressed by Chairman and CEO Jeff Fettig: "We best serve the unique needs of our customers through diverse, inclusive, and engaged employees who truly reflect our global customer base."[12]

Questions

1. What are the three main objectives of Whirlpool's diversity networks?
2. What challenges do managers face in establishing a diverse workplace, and how might they respond to these challenges?
3. Do you think formation of Whirlpool's employee networks is the best way to promote a positive culture of diversity? Explain.

Case 9.2

Domino's Pizza Franchisee Finds Sharing Success Promotes Success

Turnover—the rate at which employees leave their jobs—is notoriously high in the fast-food industry. According to the National Restaurant Association, more than half of all managers in limited-service restaurants change jobs each year, and turnover among lower-level employees is even higher. So it is rare to find a pizza franchise in which employees are so loyal that they name their children after the boss. But that is exactly the kind of thing that happens at Dave Melton's Domino's Pizza franchises.

Melton has been a Domino's franchisee since 1989 and now operates six Domino's units in New York City and Connecticut. A newspaper reporter recently found Melton preparing his Domino's stores for Super Bowl Sunday. He had his entire staff of about 100 employees working in the stores, plus 12 former employees who were happy to come back and help on the chain's busiest day of the year. Melton knew business would be "crazy" for the two-and-a-half hours of the game, but he was confident, too. Most of his team had been with him long enough to have worked through the Super Bowl together several times already.

All of Melton's managers started as minimum-wage delivery workers who worked their way up and have now been with him for at least six years, some for twice as long. They earn as much as $80,000, partly by sharing in the profits of their stores, which each ring up about $1 million in annual sales. Regular employees are just as committed to their jobs as the store managers. On average, Melton's hourly employees remain on his payroll for eight years. Several of his employees have gone on to follow in Melton's footsteps by becoming Domino's franchisees and hiring employees of their own.

Why is turnover so low at Dave Melton's Domino's units? Workers say they are treated with dignity and respect. For instance, Melton and his wife encouraged one kitchen worker to take a city food safety course. "I was a little skeptical," she said. "I don't like tests. But I took it and I passed. I did well. I got a raise and I got a bonus for passing the test." And, following one of his basic employment policies, Melton promoted her to assistant manager. Another employee, an immigrant from Pakistan, started as a delivery worker and now manages one of Melton's stores. Someday he hopes to open his own. "My No. 1 career goal is to be in my own business and bring my family here," he said. And then there's the employee from Burkina Faso, who has been with Melton for many years and named his son after him.

How does Melton account for his success at retaining people in such a fluid industry? Domino's provides its franchise operators with at least a week of management training and continued support, but Melton's results are special. He admits his first year as a franchise operator was filled with hiring mistakes, often the result of hasty decisions. Some employees were disruptive, argued with customers, had high absentee rates, and even stole from the firm. Melton quickly learned how to do better. "You are on your feet," he says of the jobs in his business. "It is long hours. It takes a certain kind of person to love it"—someone who can work fast and cheerfully.

Most of Melton's hires now are referrals from current employees, who come from many countries, and he devotes time to training them, setting goals with them, sharing information about how the stores are faring, and paying bonuses for outstanding work. "My role is being a resource, providing motivation, inspiration, and compensation," he says. "This is one of the places where so many people get their first experience in America. It is fun exposing them to the way capitalism and business in America works."[13] For more information about this company, go to http://www.dominosbiz.com.

Questions

1. What are some of the strategies Dave Melton uses to retain good employees?
2. What do you think are the advantages of Dave Melton's hiring strategies? Can you think of any disadvantages?
3. What effect do you think Dave Melton's compensation methods have on his firm's success?

Building Skills for Career Success

❶ JOURNALING FOR SUCCESS

Discovery statement: This chapter discussed human resources management from an organizational and business perspective.

Assignment

1. Assuming that you are currently in school and that you plan to begin a new job when you have completed your studies, at what point will you begin looking for a job? Explain why.
2. How will you find out about job openings?
3. What types of information will be important to you when considering whether to interview for a specific position?
4. What sources of information will you use to prepare for an interview with a specific organization?

❷ EXPLORING THE INTERNET

Although you may believe that your formal learning will end when you graduate and enter the working world, it will not. Companies both large and small spend billions of dollars annually in training employees and updating their knowledge and skills. Besides supporting employees who attend accredited continuing-education programs, companies also may provide more specialized in-house course work on new technologies, products, and markets for strategic planning. The Internet is an excellent search tool to find out about course work offered by private training organizations, as well as by traditional academic institutions. Learning online is a fast-growing alternative, especially for busy employees requiring updates to skills in the information technology field, where software knowledge must be refreshed continuously. Visit the text Web site for updates to this exercise.

Assignment

1. Visit the Web sites of several academic institutions and examine their course work offerings. Also examine the offerings of some of the following private consulting firms:

   Learning Tree International: http://www.learningtree.com
   Accenture: http://www.accenture.com
   KPMG: http://www.kpmg.com
   Ernst & Young: http://www.ey.com/global

2. What professional continuing-education training and services are provided by any one of the academic institutions whose site you have visited?
3. What sort of training is offered by one of the preceding consulting firms?
4. From the company's point of view, what is the total real cost of a day's worth of employee training? What is the money value of one day of study for a full-time college student? Can you explain why firms are willing to pay higher starting salaries for employees with higher levels of education?
5. The American Society for Training & Development (http://www.astd.org/) and the Society for Human Resource Management (http://www.shrm.org/) are two good sources of information about online training programs. Describe what you found out at these and other sites providing online learning solutions.

❸ DEVELOPING CRITICAL-THINKING SKILLS

Suppose that you are the manager of the six supervisors described in the following list. They have all just completed two years of service with you and are eligible for an annual raise. How will you determine who will receive a raise and how much each will receive?

- Joe Garcia has impressed you by his above-average performance on several difficult projects. Some of his subordinates, however, do not like the way he assigns jobs. You are aware that several family crises have left him short of cash.
- Sandy Vance meets her goals, but you feel that she could do better. She is single, likes to socialize, and at times arrives late for work. Several of her subordinates have low skill levels, but Sandy feels that she has explained their duties to them adequately. You believe that Sandy may care more about her friends than about coaching her subordinates. Her workers never complain and appear to be satisfied with their jobs.
- Paul Steiberg is not a good performer, and his work group does not feel that he is an effective leader. You also know that his group is the toughest one to manage. The work is hard and dirty. You realize that it would be very difficult to replace him, and you therefore do not want to lose him.
- Anna Chen runs a tight ship. Her subordinates like her and feel that she is an excellent leader. She listens to them and supports them. Recently, her group won the TOP (The Outstanding Performance) Award. Anna's husband is CEO of a consulting firm, and as far as you know, she is not in financial need.
- Jill Foster has completed every assignment successfully. You are impressed by this, particularly because she has a very difficult job. You recently learned that she spends several hours every week on her own taking classes to improve her skills. Jill seems to be motivated more by recognition than by money.
- Fred Hammer is a jolly person who gets along with everyone. His subordinates like him, but you do not think that he is getting the job done to your expectations. He has missed a critical delivery date twice, and this cost the firm over $5,000 each time. He recently divorced his wife and is having an extremely difficult time meeting his financial obligations.

Assignment

1. You have $25,000 available for raises. As you think about how you will allot the money, consider the following:
   a. What criteria will you use in making a fair distribution?
   b. Will you distribute the entire $25,000? If not, what will you do with the remainder?
2. Prepare a four-column table in the following manner:
   a. In column 1, write the name of the employee.
   b. In column 2, write the amount of the raise.
   c. In column 3, write the percentage of the $25,000 the employee will receive.
   d. In column 4, list the reasons for your decision.

❹ BUILDING TEAM SKILLS

The New Therapy Company is soliciting a contract to provide five nursing homes with physical, occupational, speech, and respiratory therapy. The therapists will float among the five nursing homes. The therapists have not yet been hired, but the nursing homes expect them to be fully trained and ready to go to work in three months. The previous therapy company lost its contract because of high staff turnover owing to "burnout" (a common problem in this type of work), high costs, and low-quality care. The nursing homes want a plan specifying how the New Therapy Company will meet staffing needs, keep costs low, and provide high-quality care.

Assignment

1. Working in a group, discuss how the New Therapy Company can meet the three-month deadline and still ensure that the care its therapists provide is of high quality. Also discuss the following:
   a. How many of each type of therapist will the company need?
   b. How will it prevent therapists from "burning out"?
   c. How can it retain experienced staff and still limit costs?
   d. Are promotions available for any of the staff? What is the career ladder?
   e. How will the company manage therapists at five different locations? How will it keep in touch with them (computer, voice mail, or monthly meetings)? Would it make more sense to have therapists work

permanently at each location rather than rotate among them?

f. How will the company justify the travel costs? What other expenses might it expect?

2. Prepare a plan for the New Therapy Company to present to the nursing homes.

❺ RESEARCHING DIFFERENT CAREERS

A résumé provides a summary of your skills, abilities, and achievements. It also may include a description of the type of job you want. A well-prepared résumé indicates that you know what your career objectives are, shows that you have given serious thought to your career, and tells a potential employer what you are qualified to do. The way a résumé is prepared can make a difference in whether you are considered for a job.

Assignment

1. Prepare a résumé for a job that you want using the information in Appendix A (see text Web site).
   a. First, determine what your skills are and decide which skills are needed to do this particular job.
   b. Decide which type of format—chronological or functional—would be most effective in presenting your skills and experience.
   c. Keep the résumé to one page, if possible (definitely no more than two pages). (Note that portfolio items may be attached for certain types of jobs, such as artwork.)
2. Have several people review the résumé for accuracy.
3. Ask your instructor to comment on your résumé.

Motivating and Satisfying Employees and Teams

10

Learning Objectives

What you will be able to do once you complete this chapter:

1. Explain what motivation is.
2. Understand some major historical perspectives on motivation.
3. Describe three contemporary views of motivation: equity theory, expectancy theory, and goal-setting theory.
4. Explain several techniques for increasing employee motivation.
5. Understand the types, development, and uses of teams.

FYI

inside business

Did You Know?

GE rings up $160 billion in annual revenue and invests more than $1 billion yearly in developing its global workforce.

General Electric Invests in Employee Motivation

General Electric (GE) knows that an engaged, energetic, and educated workforce is the lifeblood of its business. That's why GE puts a premium on motivating and satisfying its employees. The Connecticut-based multinational rings up $160 billion in annual revenue from a variety of goods and services, everything from jet engines and credit cards to gas turbines and digital X-ray equipment. It employs 300,000 people worldwide, with more than half its employees located outside the United States.

GE offers a wide range of advancement possibilities, encourages its workforce to learn through formal training and development courses, and offers many paths to achieve a balance between personal and professional objectives. "We believe that life at GE leaves you a better person than when you first walked through our doors," says the CEO. "Our culture is all about providing anyone who works here with the opportunities to exercise their responsibility, creativity, and integrity while growing themselves, their careers, and our business."

Once employees join GE, their careers can blossom in surprising ways as they earn the right to advance within their own business units or transfer to other divisions to round out their skills and experience. They also have access to GE's extensive training and development resources, which are under the direction of the chief learning officer. In all, GE budgets $1 billion every year for training programs, a sizable commitment to investing in the motivation and education of its workforce.

Newly hired managers know that they will be challenged and rewarded with a combination of classroom training and rotating work assignments. Employees and mid-career managers can choose from a long list of courses in general business operations and specific functional and technical skills. Experienced managers being groomed for executive positions are invited to high-level seminars at GE's John F. Welch Leadership Development Center, named for one of the company's most influential CEOs. In addition to the educational aspects of such training programs, participants are motivated by the ability to test their capabilities in responding to new goals, tapping a wider pool of resources, and interacting with colleagues from different business units.[1]

To achieve its goals, any organization—whether it is GE, FedEx, or a local convenience store—must be sure that its employees have more than the right raw materials, adequate facilities, and equipment that works. The organization also must ensure that its employees are *motivated*. To some extent, a high level of employee motivation derives from effective management practices.

In this chapter, after first explaining what motivation is, we present several views of motivation that have influenced management practices over the years: Taylor's ideas of scientific management, Mayo's Hawthorne Studies, Maslow's hierarchy of needs, Herzberg's motivation–hygiene theory, McGregor's Theory X and Theory Y, Ouchi's Theory Z, and reinforcement theory. Then, turning our attention to contemporary ideas, we examine equity theory, expectancy theory, and goal-setting theory. Finally, we discuss specific techniques managers can use to foster employee motivation and satisfaction.

motivation the individual internal process that energizes, directs, and sustains behavior; the personal "force" that causes you or me to behave in a particular way

Explain what motivation is.

What Is Motivation?

A *motive* is something that causes a person to act. A successful athlete is said to be "highly motivated." A student who avoids work is said to be "unmotivated." We define **motivation** as the individual internal process that energizes, directs, and sustains behavior. It is the personal "force" that causes you or me to act in a

Table 10.1 The Ten Best Companies to Work For

Rank	Company Name	Number of Employees
1	SAS	5,487
2	Edward Jones	37,079
3	Wegmans Food Markets	36,770
4	Google	N/A
5	Nugget Market	1,342
6	Dreamworks Animation SKG	1,825
7	Netapp	5,033
8	Boston Consulting Group	1,737
9	Qualcomm	12,255
10	Camden Property Trust	1,743

Source: "Top 100 Companies to Work For," *Fortune*, February 8, 2010, 75–77.

particular way. For example, although job rotation may increase your job satisfaction and your enthusiasm for your work so that you devote more energy to it, job rotation may not have the same impact on me.

Morale is an employee's attitude or feelings about the job, about superiors, and about the firm itself. To achieve organizational goals effectively, employees need more than the right raw materials, adequate facilities, and efficient equipment. High morale results mainly from the satisfaction of needs on the job or as a result of the job. One need that might be satisfied on the job is the need *to be recognized* as an important contributor to the organization. A need satisfied as a result of the job is the need for *financial security*. High morale, in turn, leads to dedication and loyalty, as well as to the desire to do the job well. Low morale, however, can lead to shoddy work, absenteeism, and high turnover rates as employees leave to seek more satisfying jobs with other firms. A study conducted by the Society for Human Resource Management showed that 75 percent of all employees are actively or passively seeking new employment opportunities. To offset this turnover trend, companies are creating work environments focused on increasing employee satisfaction. One obvious indicator of satisfaction at a specific organization is whether employees like working there and whether other people want to work there. Table 10.1 shows the top ten best companies to work for, partially determined by measures of employee satisfaction.

Motivation, morale, and the satisfaction of employees' needs are thus intertwined. Along with productivity, they have been the subject of much study since the end of the 19th century. We continue our discussion of motivation by outlining some landmarks of the early research.

Historical Perspectives on Motivation

2

Understand some major historical perspectives on motivation.

Researchers often begin a study with a fairly narrow goal in mind. After they develop an understanding of their subject, however, they realize that both their goal and their research should be broadened. This is exactly what happened when early research into productivity blossomed into the more modern study of employee motivation.

Scientific Management

Toward the end of the 19th century, Frederick W. Taylor became interested in improving the efficiency of individual workers. This interest, which stemmed from his own experiences in manufacturing plants, eventually led to **scientific management**, the application of scientific principles to management of work and workers.

One of Taylor's first jobs was with the Midvale Steel Company in Philadelphia, where he developed a strong distaste for waste and inefficiency. He also observed a

morale an employee's feelings about his or her job and superiors and about the firm itself

scientific management the application of scientific principles to management of work and workers

Employee satisfaction? Employee satisfaction was not of much concern at this automotive production plant in 1914. Today, however, employee satisfaction is a major consideration in many business organizations.

practice he called "soldiering." Workers "soldiered," or worked slowly, because they feared that if they worked faster, they would run out of work and lose their jobs. Taylor realized that managers were not aware of this practice because they had no idea what the workers' productivity levels *should* be.

Taylor later left Midvale and spent several years at Bethlehem Steel. While there, he made his most significant contribution to the field of motivation. He suggested that each job should be broken down into separate tasks. Then management should determine (1) the best way to perform each task and (2) the job output to expect when employees performed the tasks properly. Next, management should carefully choose the best person for each job and train that person in how to do the job properly. Finally, management should cooperate with workers to ensure that jobs were performed as planned.

Taylor also developed the idea that most people work only to earn money. He therefore reasoned that pay should be tied directly to output. The more a person produced, the more he or she should be paid. This gave rise to the **piece-rate system**, under which employees are paid a certain amount for each unit of output they produce. Under Taylor's piece-rate system, each employee was assigned an output quota. Those exceeding the quota were paid a higher per-unit rate for all units they produced (see Figure 10.1). Today, the piece-rate system is still used by some manufacturers and by farmers who grow crops that are harvested by farm laborers.

When Taylor's system was put into practice at Bethlehem Steel, the results were dramatic. Average earnings per day for steel handlers rose from $1.15 to $1.88. (Do not let the low wages that prevailed at the time obscure the fact that this was an increase of better than 60 percent!) The average amount of steel handled per day increased from 16 to 57 tons.

Taylor's revolutionary ideas had a profound impact on management practice. However, his view of motivation was soon recognized as overly simplistic and narrow. It is true that most people expect to be paid for their work, but it is also true that people work for a variety of reasons other than pay. Therefore, simply increasing a person's pay may not increase that person's motivation or productivity.

piece-rate system a compensation system under which employees are paid a certain amount for each unit of output they produce

Figure 10.1 Taylor's Piece-Rate System

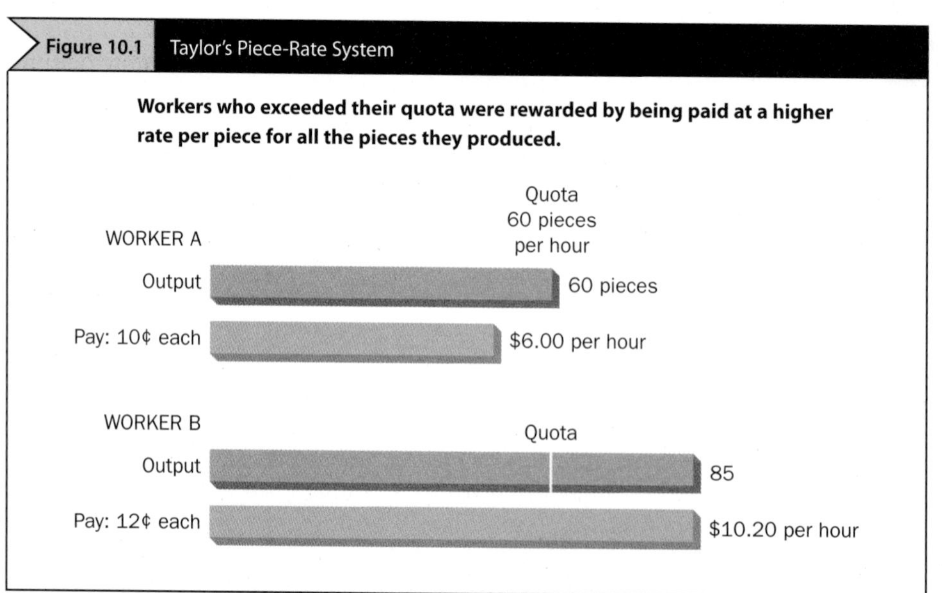

The Hawthorne Studies

Between 1927 and 1932, Elton Mayo conducted two experiments at the Hawthorne plant of the Western Electric Company in Chicago. The original objective of these studies, now referred to as the *Hawthorne Studies,* was to determine the effects of the work environment on employee productivity.

In the first set of experiments, lighting in the workplace was varied for one group of workers but not for a second group. Then the productivities of both groups were measured to determine the effect of light. To the amazement of the researchers, productivity increased for both groups. For the group whose lighting was varied, productivity remained high until the light was reduced to the level of moonlight!

The second set of experiments focused on the effectiveness of the piece-rate system in increasing the output of groups of workers. Researchers expected that output would increase because faster workers would put pressure on slower workers to produce more. Again, the results were not as expected. Output remained constant no matter what "standard" rates management set.

The researchers came to the conclusion that *human factors* were responsible for the results of the two experiments. In the lighting experiments, researchers had given both groups of workers a *sense of involvement* in their jobs merely by asking them to participate in the research. These workers—perhaps for the first time—felt as though they were an important part of the organization. In the piece-rate experiments, each group of workers informally set the acceptable rate of output for the group. To gain or retain the *social acceptance* of the group, each worker had to produce at that rate. Slower or faster workers were pressured to maintain the group's pace.

The Hawthorne Studies showed that such human factors are at least as important to motivation as pay rates. From these and other studies, the *human relations movement* in management was born. Its premise was simple: Employees who are happy and satisfied with their work are motivated to perform better. Hence, management is best served by providing a work environment that maximizes employee satisfaction.

Maslow's Hierarchy of Needs

Abraham Maslow, an American psychologist whose best-known works were published in the 1960s and 1970s, developed a theory of motivation based on a hierarchy of needs. A **need** is a personal requirement. Maslow assumed that humans are "wanting" beings who seek to fulfill a variety of needs. He observed that these needs can be arranged according to their importance in a sequence now known as **Maslow's hierarchy of needs** (see Figure 10.2).

Figure 10.2 Maslow's Hierarchy of Needs

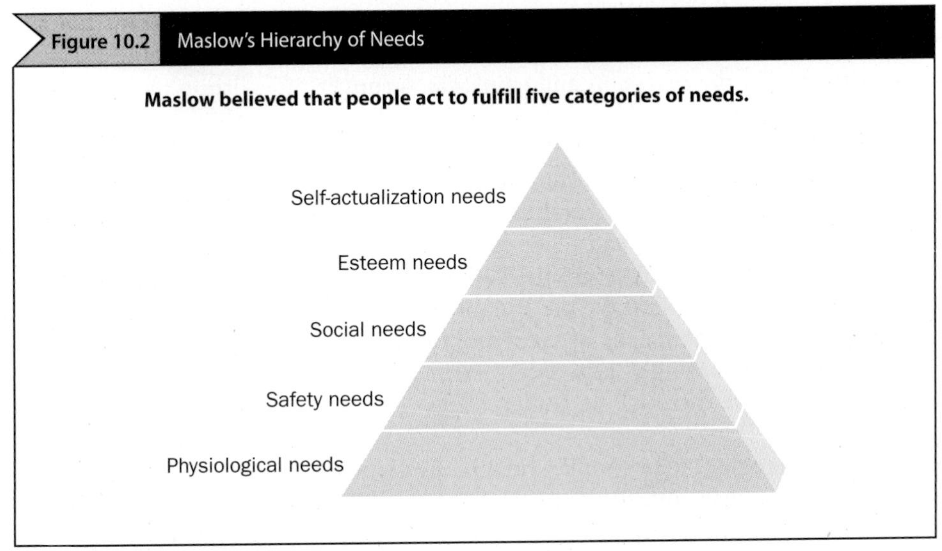

need a personal requirement

Maslow's hierarchy of needs a sequence of human needs in the order of their importance

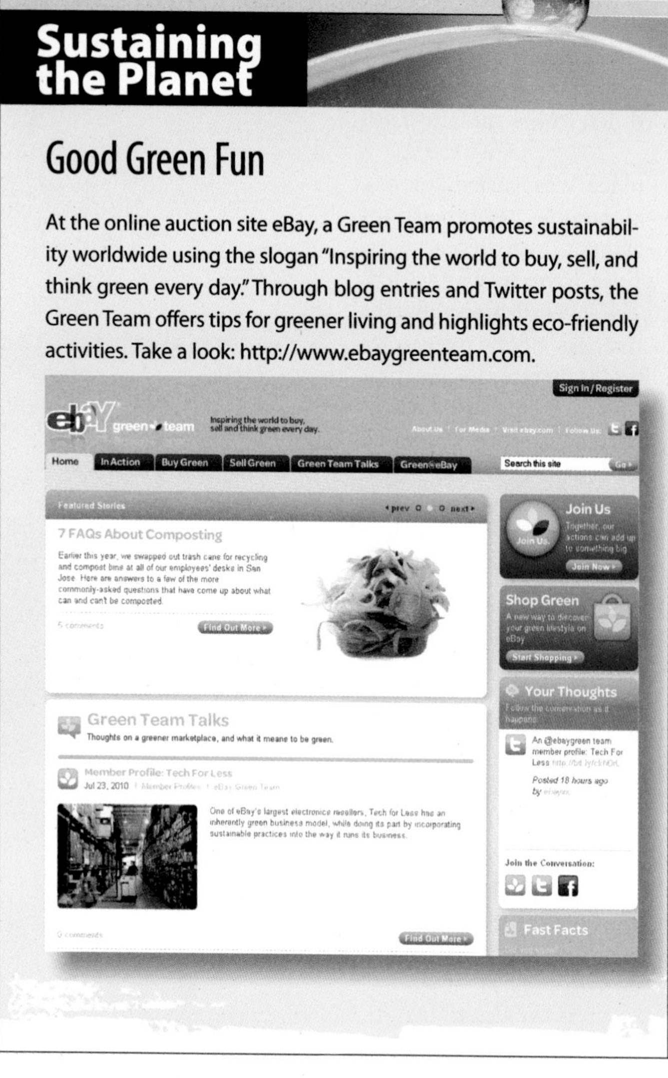

Sustaining the Planet

Good Green Fun

At the online auction site eBay, a Green Team promotes sustainability worldwide using the slogan "Inspiring the world to buy, sell, and think green every day." Through blog entries and Twitter posts, the Green Team offers tips for greener living and highlights eco-friendly activities. Take a look: http://www.ebaygreenteam.com.

At the most basic level are **physiological needs**, the things we require to survive. They include food and water, clothing, shelter, and sleep. In the employment context, these needs usually are satisfied through adequate wages.

At the next level are **safety needs**, the things we require for physical and emotional security. Safety needs may be satisfied through job security, health insurance, pension plans, and safe working conditions. Many companies are facing increasing insurance premiums for employee health care. Both GE and Hershey recently endured strikes centered on the issue of increased health care costs. Reduced health care coverage is a threat to employees' need for safety. Some companies are trying to find unique solutions to the health care question. For example, SAS, a software company recently ranked as the number one company to work for by *Fortune*, covers 90 percent of its employees' health care premiums and maintains its own medical center that provides several services at no cost to employees.[2]

Next are the **social needs**, the human requirements for love and affection and a sense of belonging. To an extent, these needs can be satisfied through relationships in the work environment and the informal organization. However, social networks beyond the workplace—with family and friends, for example—are needed, too. Restaurant chain Texas Roadhouse uses fun corporate retreats to help employees meet their social needs. The company regularly holds retreats that are fun and exciting. During the company's most recent retreat, several of their top-performing employees went to New York, where they watched a meat-cutting contest at Rockefeller Plaza and spent a day at Ellis Island. Although the recession caused many companies to cancel retreats in order to save money, Texas Roadhouse CEO G. J. Hart believes the company retreats are beneficial because motivating and caring for employees results in much happier restaurant guests. This mentality seems to be working, as evidenced by the chain opening 20 new restaurants during the recession and employee turnover rates dropping by 80 percent in the past ten years.[3]

At the level of **esteem needs**, we require respect and recognition from others and a sense of our own accomplishment and worth (self-esteem). These needs may be satisfied through personal accomplishment, promotion to more responsible jobs, various honors and awards, and other forms of recognition.

At the top of the hierarchy are the **self-actualization needs**, the need to grow, develop, and become all that we are capable of being. These are the most difficult needs to satisfy, and the means of satisfying them tend to vary with the individual. For some people, learning a new skill, starting a new career after retirement, or becoming "the best there is" at some endeavor may be the way to realize self-actualization.

Maslow suggested that people work to satisfy their physiological needs first, then their safety needs, and so on up the "needs ladder." In general, they are motivated by the needs at the lowest level that remain unsatisfied. However, needs at one

physiological needs the things we require for survival

safety needs the things we require for physical and emotional security

social needs the human requirements for love and affection and a sense of belonging

esteem needs our need for respect, recognition, and a sense of our own accomplishment and worth

self-actualization needs the need to grow and develop and to become all that we are capable of being

level do not have to be satisfied completely before needs at the next higher level come into play. If the majority of a person's physiological and safety needs are satisfied, that person will be motivated primarily by social needs. However, any physiological and safety needs that remain unsatisfied also will be important.

Maslow's hierarchy of needs provides a useful way of viewing employee motivation, as well as a guide for management. By and large, American business has been able to satisfy workers' basic needs, but the higher-order needs present more of a challenge. These needs are not satisfied in a simple manner, and the means of satisfaction vary from one employee to another.

Esteem needs. Employee recognition helps to satisfy esteem needs. Recognition of this type shows respect for an individual and his or her accomplishments.

Herzberg's Motivation–Hygiene Theory

In the late 1950s, Frederick Herzberg interviewed approximately 200 accountants and engineers in Pittsburgh. During the interviews, he asked them to think of a time when they had felt especially good about their jobs and their work. Then he asked them to describe the factor or factors that had caused them to feel that way. Next, he did the same regarding a time when they had felt especially bad about their work. He was surprised to find that feeling good and feeling bad resulted from entirely different sets of factors; that is, low pay may have made a particular person feel bad, but it was some factor other than high pay that made that person feel good.

Satisfaction and Dissatisfaction Before Herzberg's interviews, the general assumption was that employee satisfaction and dissatisfaction lay at opposite ends of the same scale. People felt satisfied, dissatisfied, or somewhere in between. However, Herzberg's interviews convinced him that satisfaction and dissatisfaction may be different dimensions altogether. One dimension might range from satisfaction to no satisfaction, and the other might range from dissatisfaction to no dissatisfaction. In other words, the opposite of satisfaction is not dissatisfaction. The idea that satisfaction and dissatisfaction are separate and distinct dimensions is referred to as the **motivation–hygiene theory** (see Figure 10.3).

Figure 10.3 Herzberg's Motivation–Hygiene Theory

Herzberg's theory takes into account that there are different dimensions to job satisfaction and dissatisfaction and that these factors do not overlap.

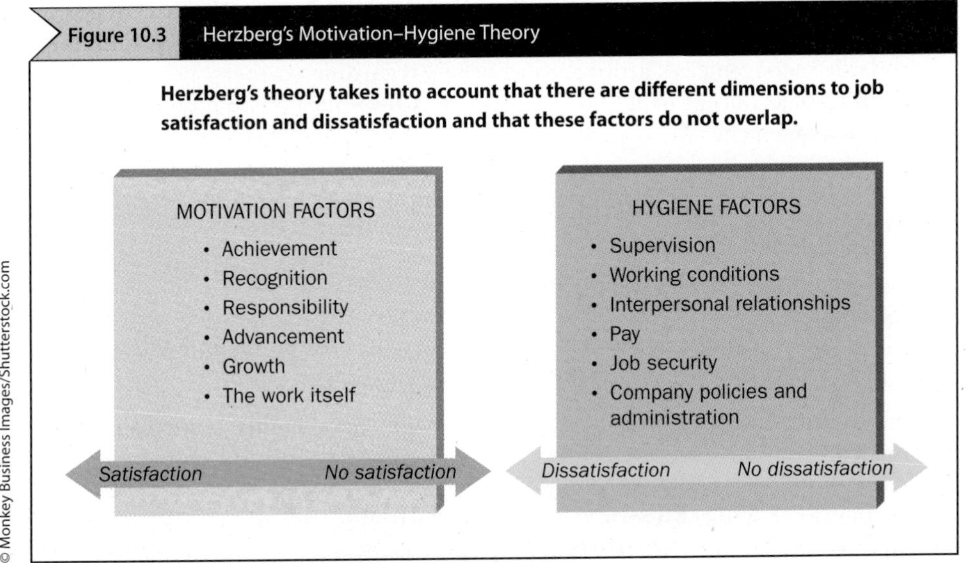

motivation–hygiene theory the idea that satisfaction and dissatisfaction are separate and distinct dimensions

Motivation–hygiene theory. Companies sometimes use travel awards as incentives for better employee performance. According to the motivation-hygiene theory, when an incentive for higher performance is not provided, is that a dissatisfier?

The job factors that Herzberg found most frequently associated with satisfaction were achievement, recognition, responsibility, advancement, growth, and the work itself. These factors generally are referred to as **motivation factors** because their presence increases motivation. However, their absence does not necessarily result in feelings of dissatisfaction. When motivation factors are present, they act as *satisfiers*.

Job factors cited as causing dissatisfaction were supervision, working conditions, interpersonal relationships, pay, job security, company policies, and administration. These factors, called **hygiene factors**, reduce dissatisfaction when they are present to an acceptable degree. However, they do not necessarily result in high levels of motivation. When hygiene factors are absent, they act as *dissatisfiers*.

Using Herzberg's Motivation–Hygiene Theory

Herzberg provides explicit guidelines for using the motivation–hygiene theory of employee motivation. He suggests that the hygiene factors must be present to ensure that a worker can function comfortably. He warns, however, that a state of *no dissatisfaction* never exists. In any situation, people always will be dissatisfied with something.

According to Herzberg, managers should make hygiene as positive as possible, but then should expect only short-term, rather than long-term, improvement in motivation. Managers must focus instead on providing those motivation factors that presumably will enhance motivation and long-term effort.

We should note that employee pay has more effect than Herzberg's theory indicates. He suggests that pay provides only short-term change and not true motivation. Yet, in many organizations, pay constitutes a form of recognition and reward for achievement—and recognition and achievement are both motivation factors. The effect of pay may depend on how it is distributed. If a pay increase does not depend on performance (as in across-the-board or cost-of-living raises), it may not motivate people. However, if pay is increased as a form of recognition (as in bonuses or incentives), it may play a powerful role in motivating employees to higher performance.

Theory X and Theory Y

The concepts of Theory X and Theory Y were advanced by Douglas McGregor in his book *The Human Side of Enterprise*. They are, in essence, sets of assumptions that underlie management's attitudes and beliefs regarding workers' behavior.[4]

Theory X is a concept of employee motivation generally consistent with Taylor's scientific management. Theory X assumes that employees dislike work and will function effectively only in a highly controlled work environment.

Theory X is based on the following assumptions:

1. People dislike work and try to avoid it.
2. Because people dislike work, managers must coerce, control, and frequently threaten employees to achieve organizational goals.
3. People generally must be led because they have little ambition and will not seek responsibility; they are concerned mainly about security.

The logical outcome of such assumptions will be a highly controlled work environment—one in which managers make all the decisions and employees take all the orders.

On the other hand, **Theory Y** is a concept of employee motivation generally consistent with the ideas of the human relations movement. Theory Y assumes

motivation factors job factors that increase motivation, although their absence does not necessarily result in dissatisfaction

hygiene factors job factors that reduce dissatisfaction when present to an acceptable degree but that do not necessarily result in high levels of motivation

Theory X a concept of employee motivation generally consistent with Taylor's scientific management; assumes that employees dislike work and will function only in a highly controlled work environment

Theory Y a concept of employee motivation generally consistent with the ideas of the human relations movement; assumes that employees accept responsibility and work toward organizational goals, and by doing so they also achieve personal rewards

Table 10.2 Theory X and Theory Y Contrasted

Area	Theory X	Theory Y
Attitude toward work	Dislike	Involvement
Control systems	External	Internal
Supervision	Direct	Indirect
Level of commitment	Low	High
Employee potential	Ignored	Identified
Use of human resources	Limited	Not limited

that employees accept responsibility and work toward organizational goals, and by doing so they also achieve personal rewards. Theory Y is based on the following assumptions:

1. People do not naturally dislike work; in fact, work is an important part of their lives.
2. People will work toward goals to which they are committed.
3. People become committed to goals when it is clear that accomplishing the goals will bring personal rewards.
4. People often seek out and willingly accept responsibility.
5. Employees have the potential to help accomplish organizational goals.
6. Organizations generally do not make full use of their human resources.

Obviously, this view is quite different from—and much more positive than—that of Theory X. McGregor argued that most managers behave in accordance with Theory X, but he maintained that Theory Y is more appropriate and effective as a guide for managerial action (see Table 10.2).

The human relations movement and Theories X and Y increased managers' awareness of the importance of social factors in the workplace. However, human motivation is a complex and dynamic process to which there is no simple key. Neither money nor social factors alone can provide the answer. Rather, a number of factors must be considered in any attempt to increase motivation.

Theory Z

William Ouchi, a management professor at UCLA, studied business practices in American and Japanese firms. He concluded that different types of management systems dominate in these two countries.[5] In Japan, Ouchi found what he calls *type J* firms. They are characterized by lifetime employment for employees, collective (or group) decision making, collective responsibility for the outcomes of decisions, slow evaluation and promotion, implied control mechanisms, nonspecialized career paths, and a holistic concern for employees as people.

American industry is dominated by what Ouchi calls *type A* firms, which follow a different pattern. They emphasize short-term employment, individual decision making, individual responsibility for the outcomes of decisions, rapid evaluation and promotion, explicit control mechanisms, specialized career paths, and a segmented concern for employees only as employees.

A few very successful American firms represent a blend of the type J and type A patterns. These firms, called *type Z* organizations, emphasize long-term employment, collective decision making, individual responsibility for the outcomes of decisions, slow evaluation and promotion, informal control along with some formalized measures, moderately specialized career paths, and a holistic concern for employees.

Ouchi's **Theory Z** is the belief that some middle ground between his type A and type J practices is best for American business (see Figure 10.4). A major part of Theory Z is the emphasis on participative decision making. The focus is on "we" rather than on "us versus them." Theory Z employees and managers view the

Theory Z the belief that some middle ground between type A and type J practices is best for American business

Figure 10.4 The Features of Theory Z

The best aspects of Japanese and American management theories combine to form the nucleus of Theory Z.

TYPE J FIRMS
(Japanese)

- Lifetime employment
- Collective decision making
- Collective responsibility
- Slow promotion
- Implied control mechanisms
- Nonspecialized career paths
- Holistic concern for employees

TYPE Z FIRMS
(Best choice for American firms)

- Long-term employment
- Collective decision making
- Individual responsibility
- Slow promotion
- Informal control
- Moderately specialized career paths
- Holistic concern for employees

TYPE A FIRMS
(American)

- Short-term employment
- Individual decision making
- Individual responsibility
- Rapid promotion
- Explicit control mechanisms
- Specialized career paths
- Segmented concern for employees

organization as a family. This participative spirit fosters cooperation and the dissemination of information and organizational values.

Reinforcement Theory

Reinforcement theory is based on the premise that behavior that is rewarded is likely to be repeated, whereas behavior that is punished is less likely to recur. A *reinforcement* is an action that follows directly from a particular behavior. It may be a pay raise after a particularly large sale to a new customer or a reprimand for coming to work late.

Reinforcements can take a variety of forms and can be used in a number of ways. A *positive reinforcement* is one that strengthens desired behavior by providing a reward. For example, many employees respond well to praise; recognition from their supervisors for a job done well increases (strengthens) their willingness to perform well in the future. A *negative reinforcement* strengthens desired behavior by eliminating an undesirable task or situation. Suppose that a machine shop must be cleaned thoroughly every month—a dirty, miserable task. During one particular month when the workers do a less-than-satisfactory job at their normal work assignments, the boss requires the workers to clean the factory rather than bringing in the usual private maintenance service. The employees will be motivated to work harder the next month to avoid the unpleasant cleanup duty again.

Punishment is an undesired consequence of undesirable behavior. Common forms of punishment used in organizations include reprimands, reduced pay, disciplinary layoffs, and termination (firing). Punishment often does more harm than good. It tends to create an unpleasant environment, fosters hostility and resentment, and suppresses undesirable behavior only until the supervisor's back is turned.

Managers who rely on *extinction* hope to eliminate undesirable behavior by not responding to it. The idea is that the behavior eventually will become "extinct." Suppose, for example, that an employee writes memo after memo to his or her manager about insignificant events. If the manager does not respond to any of these memos, the employee probably will stop writing them, and the behavior will be squelched.

reinforcement theory a theory of motivation based on the premise that rewarded behavior is likely to be repeated, whereas punished behavior is less likely to recur

The effectiveness of reinforcement depends on which type is used and how it is timed. One approach may work best under certain conditions, although some situations lend themselves to the use of more than one approach. Generally, positive reinforcement is considered the most effective, and it is recommended when the manager has a choice.

Continual reinforcement can become tedious for both managers and employees, especially when the same behavior is being reinforced over and over again in the same way. At the start, it may be necessary to reinforce a desired behavior every time it occurs. However, once a desired behavior has become more or less established, occasional reinforcement seems to be most effective.

Contemporary Views on Motivation

3

Describe three contemporary views of motivation: equity theory, expectancy theory, and goal-setting theory.

Maslow's hierarchy of needs and Herzberg's motivation–hygiene theory are popular and widely known theories of motivation. Each is also a significant step up from the relatively narrow views of scientific management and Theories X and Y. However, they do have one weakness: Each attempts to specify *what* motivates people, but neither explains *why* or *how* motivation develops or is sustained over time. In recent years, managers have begun to explore three other models that take a more dynamic view of motivation. These are equity theory, expectancy theory, and goal-setting theory.

Equity Theory

The **equity theory** of motivation is based on the premise that people are motivated to obtain and preserve equitable treatment for themselves. As used here, *equity* is the distribution of rewards in direct proportion to each employee's contribution to the organization. Everyone need not receive the same rewards, but the rewards should be in accordance with individual contributions.

According to this theory, we tend to implement the idea of equity in the following way: First, we develop our own input-to-outcome ratio. *Inputs* are the time, effort, skills, education, experience, and so on, that we contribute to the organization. *Outcomes* are the rewards we get from the organization, such as pay, benefits, recognition, and promotions. Next, we compare this ratio with what we perceive as the input-to-outcome ratio for some other person. It might be a co-worker, a friend who works for another firm, or even an average of all the people in our organization. This person is called the *comparison other*. Note that our perception of this person's input-to-outcome ratio may be absolutely correct or completely wrong. However, we believe that it is correct.

If the two ratios are roughly the same, we feel that the organization is treating us equitably. In this case, we are motivated to leave things as they are. However, if our ratio is the higher of the two, we feel underrewarded and are motivated to make changes. We may (1) decrease our own inputs by not working so hard, (2) try to increase our total outcome by asking for a raise in pay, (3) try to get the comparison other to increase some inputs or receive decreased outcomes, (4) leave the work situation, or (5) do a new comparison with a different comparison other.

Equity theory is most relevant to pay as an outcome. Because pay is a very real measure of a person's worth to an organization, comparisons involving pay are a natural part of organizational life. Managers can try to avoid problems arising from inequity by making sure that rewards are distributed on the basis of performance and that everyone clearly understands the basis for his or her own pay.

Expectancy Theory

Expectancy theory, developed by Victor Vroom, is a very complex model of motivation based on a deceptively simple assumption. According to expectancy theory, motivation depends on how much we want something and on how likely we think we are to get it (see Figure 10.5). Consider, for example, the case of three sales representatives who are candidates for promotion to one sales manager's job. Bill has had a very good sales year and always gets good performance evaluations. However, he is not sure that he wants the job because it involves a great deal of travel, long working hours, and much stress and pressure. Paul wants the job badly but does not think he has much chance of getting it. He has had a terrible sales year and gets only mediocre performance evaluations from his present boss. Susan wants the

equity theory a theory of motivation based on the premise that people are motivated to obtain and preserve equitable treatment for themselves

expectancy theory a model of motivation based on the assumption that motivation depends on how much we want something and on how likely we think we are to get it

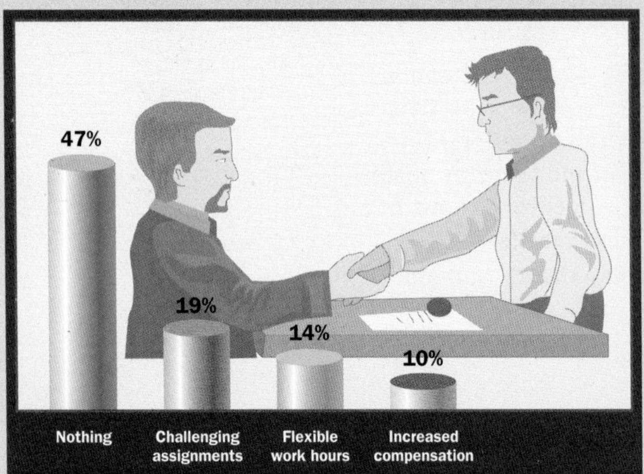

Source: Dice salary survey of 16,908 technology workers.

job as much as Paul, and she thinks that she has a pretty good shot at it. Her sales have improved significantly this past year, and her evaluations are the best in the company.

Expectancy theory would predict that Bill and Paul are not very motivated to seek the promotion. Bill does not really want it, and Paul does not think that he has much of a chance of getting it. Susan, however, is very motivated to seek the promotion because she wants it and thinks that she can get it.

Expectancy theory is complex because each action we take is likely to lead to several different outcomes; some we may want, and others we may not want. For example, a person who works hard and puts in many extra hours may get a pay raise, be promoted, and gain valuable new job skills. However, that person also may be forced to spend less time with his or her family and be forced to cut back on his or her social life.

For one person, the promotion may be paramount, the pay raise and new skills fairly important, and the loss of family and social life of negligible importance. For someone else, the family and social life may be most important, the pay raise of moderate importance, the new skills unimportant, and the promotion undesirable because of the additional hours it would require. The first person would be motivated to work hard and put in the extra hours, whereas the second person would not be motivated at all to do so. In other words, it is the entire bundle of outcomes—and the individual's evaluation of the importance of each outcome—that determines motivation.

Expectancy theory is difficult to apply, but it does provide several useful guidelines for managers. It suggests that managers must recognize that (1) employees work for a variety of reasons; (2) these reasons, or expected outcomes, may change over time; and (3) it is necessary to clearly show employees how they can attain the outcomes they desire.

Goal-Setting Theory

Goal-setting theory suggests that employees are motivated to achieve goals that they and their managers establish together. The goal should be very specific, moderately difficult, and one the employee will be committed to achieve.[6] Rewards should

goal-setting theory a theory of motivation suggesting that employees are motivated to achieve goals that they and their managers establish together

Figure 10.5 Expectancy Theory

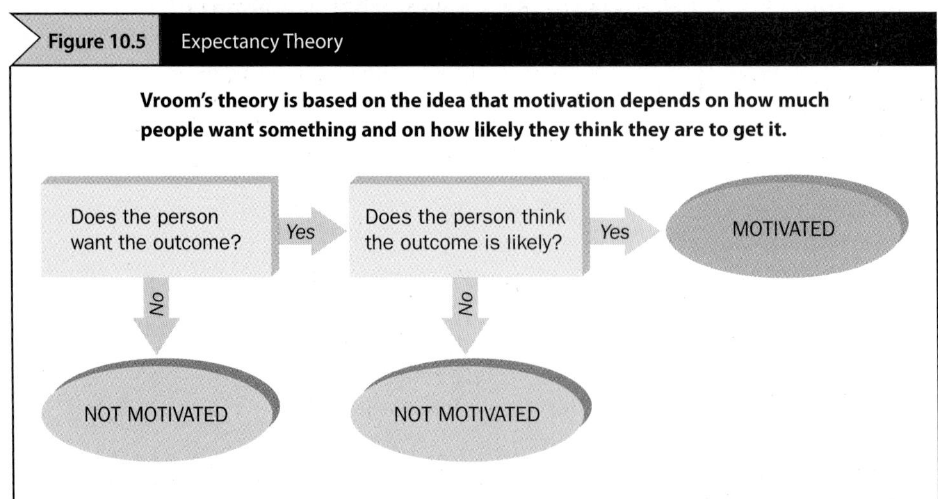

be tied directly to goal achievement. Using goal-setting theory, a manager can design rewards that fit employee needs, clarify expectations, maintain equity, and provide reinforcement. A major benefit of this theory is that it provides a good understanding of the goal the employee has to achieve and the rewards that will accrue to the employee if the goal is accomplished.

Key Motivation Techniques

4

Explain several techniques for increasing employee motivation.

Today, it takes more than a generous salary to motivate employees. Increasingly, companies are trying to provide motivation by satisfying employees' less-tangible needs. At times, businesses use simple, low- or no-cost approaches such as those listed in Table 10.3 to motivate workers. Organizations also use more complex approaches. In this section, we discuss several specific techniques that help managers to boost employee motivation and job satisfaction.

Table 10.3 No-Cost/Low-Cost Motivation Techniques
1. Acknowledge and celebrate birthdays and other important events.
2. Allow an employee to choose his/her next assignment.
3. Call an employee to your office to thank him or her (do not discuss any other issue).
4. In the department newsletter, publish a "kudos" column and ask for nominations throughout the department.
5. Nominate the employee for a formal award program.
6. Plan a surprise achievement celebration for an employee or group of employees.
7. Pop in at the first meeting of a special project team and express your appreciation for their involvement.
8. Send a letter to all team members at the conclusion of a project, thanking them for their participation.
9. When you hear a positive remark about someone, repeat it to that person as soon as possible in person or electronically.
10. Widely publicize suggestions used and their positive impact on your department.
11. Support flexible work schedules.
12. Ask the employee to be a mentor to a new hire.
13. Put up a bulletin board in your department and post letters of thanks from customers.
14. Take the opportunity to learn what your people are working on and recognize their efforts.
15. Interview your people and capture their wisdom. Compile the quotes and stories in a booklet and hand it out to employees.
16. Send a letter of praise to the employee's spouse/family.
17. Honor employee subgroups in your department with their own day or week (e.g., Administrative Staff Week, Custodian Week) and present them with flowers, candy, breakfast, and so on.
18. Recognize highly skilled employees with increased responsibility that will develop new skills that may be helpful for advancement.
19. Pass around an office trophy to the employee of the week or other traveling awards.
20. Volunteer to do an employee's least favorite task.
21. Wash the employee's car.
22. Give the person tickets to a ball game, golf lessons, movie tickets, a book by his or her favorite author, "Lunch on me" coupons, and so on.
23. Reserve the best parking spot for employees who have done something truly worthwhile.
24. Send a handwritten note or praise about a specific action, not "thanks for all you do."
25. Create a yearbook for your team with pictures and stories of accomplishments during the year.
26. Copy senior management on your thank-you note to the employee, to advise them of an employee's efforts/accomplishments.
27. Introduce employees to key suppliers, customers, or someone in senior management.
28. Reward ideas even if they fail.
29. Set aside a public space inside your firm as a "wall of fame" and place photos of employees who have accomplished something truly special along with the details of what they did to earn that space.
30. Say, "Thank you."

Sources: Texas A&M University Human Resources Department, http://employees.tamu.edu/docs/employment/classComp;/614recognitionIdeas.pdf; HRWorld, http://www.hrworld.com/features/25-employee-rewards/; Michigan Office of Great Workplace Development, http://www.michigan.gov/documents/firstgentlemen/50_242400_7.pdf.

Setting and achieving goals. Abbott provides hybrid cars to its sales force in order to help achieve environmental goals set by this company.

Management by Objectives

Management by objectives (MBO) is a motivation technique in which managers and employees collaborate in setting goals. The primary purpose of MBO is to clarify the roles employees are expected to play in reaching the organization's goals.

By allowing individuals to participate in goal setting and performance evaluation, MBO increases their motivation. Most MBO programs consist of a series of five steps. The first step in setting up an MBO program is to secure the acceptance of top management. It is essential that top managers endorse and participate in the program if others in the firm are to accept it. The commitment of top management also provides a natural starting point for educating employees about the purposes and mechanics of MBO.

Next, preliminary goals must be established. Top management also plays a major role in this activity because the preliminary goals reflect the firm's mission and strategy. The intent of an MBO program is to have these goals filter down through the organization.

The third step, which actually consists of several smaller steps, is the heart of MBO:

1. The manager explains to each employee that he or she has accepted certain goals for the group (the manager as well as the employees) and asks the individual to think about how he or she can help to achieve these goals.
2. The manager later meets with each employee individually. Together they establish goals for the employee. Whenever possible, the goals should be measurable and should specify the time frame for completion (usually one year).
3. The manager and the employee decide what resources the employee will need to accomplish his or her goals.

As the fourth step, the manager and each employee meet periodically to review the employee's progress. They may agree to modify certain goals during these meetings if circumstances have changed. For example, a sales representative may have accepted a goal of increasing sales by 20 percent. However, an aggressive competitor may have entered the marketplace, making this goal unattainable. In light of this circumstance, the goal may be revised downward to 10 or 15 percent.

The fifth step in the MBO process is evaluation. At the end of the designated time period, the manager and each employee meet again to determine which of the individual's goals were met and which were not met, and why. The employee's reward (in the form of a pay raise, praise, or promotion) is based primarily on the degree of goal attainment.

As with every other management method, MBO has advantages and disadvantages. MBO can motivate employees by involving them actively in the life of the firm. The collaboration on goal setting and performance appraisal improves communication and makes employees feel that they are an important part of the organization. Periodic review of progress also enhances control within an organization. A major problem with MBO is that it does not work unless the process begins at the top of an organization. In some cases, MBO results in excessive paperwork. Also, a manager may not like sitting down and working out goals with subordinates and may instead just assign them goals. Finally, MBO programs prove difficult to implement unless goals are quantifiable.

management by objectives (MBO) a motivation technique in which managers and employees collaborate in setting goals

job enrichment a motivation technique that provides employees with more variety and responsibility in their jobs

Job Enrichment

Job enrichment is a method of motivating employees by providing them with variety in their tasks while giving them some responsibility for, and control over,

Entrepreneurial SUCCESS

Employee Empowerment Powers Bonobos' Growth

Although Andy Dunn and Brian Spaly named their e-business Bonobos, they do not monkey around when it comes to employee motivation. Bonobos, co-founded by roommates at Stanford Business School, is a fast-growing young company that manufactures and sells men's clothing. These entrepreneurs continued success depends on the ability of their employees to make the most of every opportunity, solve problems quickly, and turn first-time buyers into loyal repeat customers through outstanding service.

The co-founders have motivation on their mind from the moment they sit down to design a new job or enrich an existing job. Their goal, says Dunn, is to create "an environment where people can come alive every day" and be empowered to deliver the best possible service. The first step is to seek out highly qualified candidates who possess skills and expertise that complement the company's strengths. Dunn begins job interviews with one simple statement: "I am not good at what you do, and I need your help."

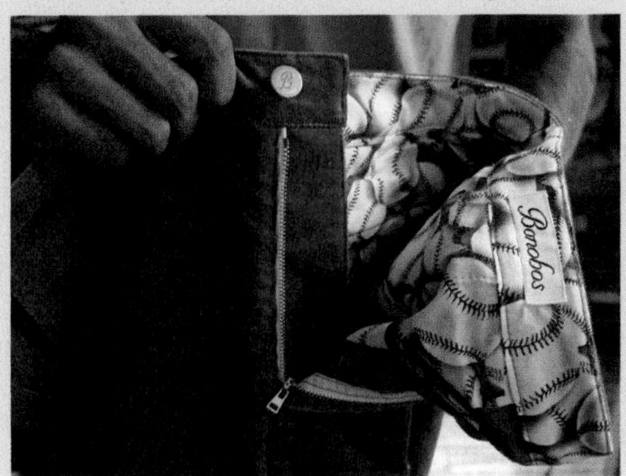

© AP Images/Kathy Willens

Because the high-energy culture encourages delegation at all organizational levels, Bonobos prepares new hires with training and on-the-job coaching so that they can make informed decisions on their own. Employees are motivated by being respected by their managers and peers, challenged to do their best, and delegated responsibility for meeting their objectives. Only with such empowerment can Bonobos keep growing and offering the kind of exceptional service that sets it apart from its competition.

Sources: "To Recruit the Best, Admit Weaknesses," *BusinessWeek*, December 29, 2009, http://www.businessweek.com/smallbiz/content/dec2009/sb20091224_646669.htm; Bambi Francisco Roizen, "Can Friends Be Business Partners?" *VatorNews*, November 10, 2009, http://vator.tv/news/show/2009-11-10-can-friends-be-business-partners; Matt Kinsey, "Bonobos: An America's Hottest Brands Case Study," *Advertising Age*, November 16, 2009, http://www.adage.com.

their jobs. At the same time, employees gain new skills and acquire a broader perspective about how their individual work contributes to the goals of the organization. Earlier in this chapter, we noted that Herzberg's motivation–hygiene theory is one rationale for the use of job enrichment; that is, the added responsibility and control that job enrichment confers on employees increases their satisfaction and motivation. For example, engineers at Google get to spend 20 percent of their time at work on projects of their choosing.[7] This type of enrichment can motivate employees and create a variety of benefits for the company. At times, **job enlargement**, expanding a worker's assignments to include additional but similar tasks, can lead to job enrichment. Job enlargement might mean that a worker on an assembly line who used to connect three wires to components moving down the line now connects five wires. Unfortunately, the added tasks often are just as routine as those the worker performed before the change. In such cases, enlargement may not be effective.

job enlargement expanding a worker's assignments to include additional but similar tasks

Whereas job enlargement does not really change the routine and monotonous nature of jobs, job enrichment does. Job enrichment requires that added tasks give an employee more responsibility for what he or she does. It provides workers with both more tasks to do and more control over how they perform them. In particular, job enrichment removes many controls from jobs, gives workers more authority, and assigns work in com-

© Casper Hedberg/Bloomberg via Getty Images

Job enrichment. Volvo was one of the first automobile companies to deviate from the traditional assembly line system and adopt a more employee-centric approach for manufacturing automobiles.

plete, natural units. Moreover, employees frequently are given fresh and challenging job assignments. By blending more planning and decision making into jobs, job enrichment gives work more depth and complexity.

Job redesign is a type of job enrichment in which work is restructured in ways that cultivate the worker–job match. Job redesign can be achieved by combining tasks, forming work groups, or establishing closer customer relationships. Employees often are more motivated when jobs are combined because the increased variety of tasks presents more challenge and therefore more reward. Work groups motivate employees by showing them how their jobs fit within the organization as a whole and how they contribute to its success. Establishing client relationships allows employees to interact directly with customers. This type of redesign not only adds a personal dimension to employment but also provides workers with immediate and relevant feedback about how they are doing their jobs.

Job enrichment works best when employees seek more challenging work. Of course, not all workers respond positively to job-enrichment programs. Employees must desire personal growth and have the skills and knowledge to perform enriched jobs. Lack of self-confidence, fear of failure, and distrust of management's intentions are likely to lead to ineffective performance on enriched jobs. In addition, some workers do not view their jobs as routine and boring, and others even prefer routine jobs because they find them satisfying. Companies that use job enrichment as an alternative to specialization also face extra expenses, such as the cost of retraining. Another motivation for job redesign is to reduce employees' stress at work. A job redesign that carefully matches worker to job can prevent stress-related injuries, which constitute about 60 to 80 percent of all work-related injuries.

Behavior Modification

Behavior modification is a systematic program of reinforcement to encourage desirable behavior. Behavior modification involves both rewards to encourage desirable actions and punishments to discourage undesirable actions. However, studies have shown that rewards, such as compliments and expressions of appreciation, are much more effective behavior modifiers than punishments, such as reprimands and scorn.

When applied to management, behavior modification strives to encourage desirable organizational behavior. Use of this technique begins with identification of a *target behavior*—the behavior that is to be changed. (It might be low production levels or a high rate of absenteeism, for example.) Existing levels of this behavior are then measured. Next, managers provide positive reinforcement in the form of a reward when employees exhibit the *desired behavior* (such as increased production or less absenteeism). The reward might be praise or a more tangible form of recognition, such as a gift, meal, or trip. Apple Company created the Corporate Gifting and Rewards Program in order to give companies the ability to reward their staff with iPods, iPod accessories, and iTunes gift cards.[8] Finally, the levels of the target behavior are measured again to determine whether the desired changes have been achieved. If they have been achieved, the reinforcement is maintained. However, if the target behavior has not changed significantly in the desired direction, the reward system must be changed to one that is likely to be more effective. The key is to devise effective rewards that will not only modify employees' behavior in desired ways but also motivate them. To this end, experts suggest that management should reward quality, loyalty, and productivity.

Flextime

To most people, a work schedule means the standard nine-to-five, 40-hour work week. In reality, though, many people have work schedules that are quite different from this. SC Johnson's Flexible Work Schedule Program allows employees to create their own work schedule around their personal lives.[9] Police officers, firefighters, restaurant personnel, airline employees, and medical personnel usually have work schedules that are far from standard. Some manufacturers also rotate personnel

job redesign a type of job enrichment in which work is restructured to cultivate the worker–job match

behavior modification a systematic program of reinforcement to encourage desirable behavior

from shift to shift. Many professional people—such as managers, artists, and lawyers—need more than 40 hours each week to get their work done.

The needs and lifestyles of today's workforce are changing. Dual-income families make up a much larger share of the workforce than ever before, and women are one of its fastest-growing sectors. In addition, more employees are responsible for the care of elderly relatives. Recognizing that these changes increase the demand for family time, many employers are offering flexible work schedules that not only help employees to manage their time better but also increase employee motivation and job satisfaction.

Flextime is a system in which employees set their own work hours within certain limits determined by employers. Typically, the firm establishes two bands of time: the *core time,* when all employees must be at work, and the *flexible time,* when employees may choose whether to be at work. The only condition is that every employee must work a total of eight hours each day. For example, the hours between 9 and 11 a.m. and 1 and 3 p.m. might be core times, and the hours between 6 and 9 a.m., 11 a.m. and 1 p.m., and 3 and 6 p.m. might be flexible times. This would give employees the option of coming in early and getting off early, coming in later and leaving later, or taking an extra long lunch break. But flextime also ensures that everyone is present at certain times, when conferences with supervisors and department meetings can be scheduled. Another type of flextime allows employees to work a 40-hour work week in four days instead of five. Workers who put in ten hours a day instead of eight get an extra day off each week. More than three-quarters of companies currently offer flextime.[10]

At times, smaller firms use flextime to attract and retain employees, especially when they cannot match the salaries and benefit package provided by larger companies. Other companies view flextime as an entitlement, given out on a case-by-case basis. For example, Sodexo, a provider of food and facilities management solutions, allows employees with a history of good work performance to propose a flexible schedule to their managers, who then monitor the new schedule through a trial period and semiannual performance reviews. Flextime has been used not only by corporations but also by local governments. For example, the "Flex in the City" event in Houston, Texas, began a few years ago in an effort to lighten the city's congested commutes. The two-week program involving over 200 companies has been held every year since then and is estimated to reduce workers' stress by 58 percent while nearly doubling their productivity.[11]

flextime a system in which employees set their own work hours within employer-determined limits

part-time work permanent employment in which individuals work less than a standard work week

The sense of independence and autonomy employees gain from having a say in what hours they work can be a motivating factor. In addition, employees who have enough time to deal with non-work issues often work more productively and with greater satisfaction when they are on the job. Two common problems associated with using flextime are (1) supervisors sometimes find their jobs complicated by having employees who come and go at different times and (2) employees without flextime sometimes resent co-workers who have it.

Part-Time Work and Job Sharing

Part-time work is permanent employment in which individuals work less than a standard work week. The specific number of hours worked varies, but part-time jobs are structured so that all responsibilities can be completed in the number of hours an employee works. Part-time work is of special interest to parents who want more time with their children and people who simply desire more leisure time. One disadvantage of part-time work is that it often does not provide the benefits that come with a full-time position. This is not, however, the

Part-time work. UPS employs both full- and part-time workers.

case at Starbucks, where approximately 80 percent of its employees work part-time. Starbucks does not treat its part-time employees any differently from its full-time employees; all receive the same access to numerous benefits, which even includes a free pound of coffee every week.[12]

Job sharing (sometimes referred to as *work sharing*) is an arrangement whereby two people share one full-time position. One job sharer may work from 8 a.m. to noon, and the other may work from 1 to 5 p.m., or they may alternate workdays. Dr. Jennifer Stahl and Dr. Suzy McNulty, two pediatricians in California, recently established their own practice where they can share their work. Dr. Stahl and Dr. McNulty each work two-and-a-half days a week doing clinical duties, and while one of them is working, the other remains on-call in case of an emergency. Any additional paperwork is done when they are not busy with their children, usually in the evenings from home or during a child's practice. They divide the management-related work based on their individual skills: Dr. Stahl handles accounting and marketing, whereas Dr. McNulty takes care of human resources and information technology. Not only do they share their job, but their employees share jobs with each other. This way, everyone has more time to spend with their families.[13] Job sharing combines the security of a full-time position with the flexibility of a part-time job. For firms, job sharing provides a unique opportunity to attract highly skilled employees who might not be available on a full-time basis. In addition, companies can save on expenses by reducing the cost of benefits and avoiding the disruptions of employee turnover. For employees, opting for the flexibility of job sharing may mean giving up some of the benefits received for full-time work. In addition, job sharing is difficult if tasks are not easily divisible or if two people do not work or communicate well with one another.

Telecommuting

A growing number of companies allow **telecommuting**, working at home all the time or for a portion of the work week. Personal computers, modems, fax machines, voice mail, cellular phones, and overnight couriers all facilitate the work-at-home trend. Working at home means that individuals can set their own hours and have more time with their families.

Companies that allow telecommuting experience several benefits, including increased productivity, lower real estate and travel costs, reduced employee absenteeism and turnover, increased work/life balance, improved morale, and access to additional labor pools. Telecommuting also helps improve the community by decreasing air pollutants, reducing traffic congestion, and lowering consumption of fossil fuels, which can give a company a green factor. Also, by having fewer employees commuting to work, the Reason Public Policy Institute estimates that approximately 350 lives are saved per year. Of all the companies that give employees the option to telecommute or work from home, Deloitte is ranked number one with 93 percent of its employees classified as "regular" telecommuters.[14]

Among the disadvantages of telecommuting are feelings of isolation, putting in longer hours, and being distracted by family or household responsibilities. Although most bosses say that they trust their staff to work from home, many think that home workers are work-shy and less productive than office-based staff. A survey conducted in the United Kingdom found that up to 38 percent of managers surveyed believe that home workers are less productive, and 22 percent think that working from home is an excuse for time off. In addition, some supervisors have difficulty monitoring productivity.[15]

Cisco, for example, is an industry leader at providing a virtual work environment. Approximately 85 percent of the company's 37,000-member U.S. workforce connects to the company remotely on a regular basis. Cisco's employees use many of the company's own products, including WebEx and TelePresence, which allow employees to attend meetings, do training, and hold video conferences online. Cisco's telecommuting program has boosted employee satisfaction, reduced turnover, and earned the company numerous sustainability awards. Telecommuting

job sharing an arrangement whereby two people share one full-time position

telecommuting working at home all the time or for a portion of the work week

has saved the company over $277 million and lowers employees' fuel costs by an estimated $10 million annually.[16]

Employee Empowerment

Many companies are increasing employee motivation and satisfaction through the use of empowerment. **Empowerment** means making employees more involved in their jobs and in the operations of the organization by increasing their participation in decision making. With empowerment, control no longer flows exclusively from the top level of the organization downward. Empowered employees have a voice in what they do and how and when they do it. In some organizations, employees' input is restricted to individual choices, such as when to take breaks. In other companies, their responsibilities may encompass more far-reaching issues. For example, at W. L. Gore & Associates, a product-development company, workers are "associates" and never referred to as "employees." Gore's unique lattice management structure creates a nonhierarchical system free from traditional bosses or managers. At Gore, there is no assigned authority, and people become a leader by gaining the respect of their peers. Everyone owns a part of the company through the corporate stock plan. Associates at Gore are never told what to do or given assignments. Instead, they are encouraged to work on their own projects, developing innovative new products and technologies. It is this unique corporate culture at Gore that inspires their associates to explore, discover, and invent.[17]

For empowerment to work effectively, management must be involved. Managers should set expectations, communicate standards, institute periodic evaluations, and guarantee follow-up. If effectively implemented, empowerment can lead to increased job satisfaction, improved job performance, higher self-esteem, and increased organizational commitment. Obstacles to empowerment include resistance on the part of management, distrust of management on the part of workers, insufficient training, and poor communication between management and employees.

Employee Ownership

Some organizations are discovering that a highly effective technique for motivating employees is **employee ownership**—that is, employees own the company they work for by virtue of being stockholders. Employee-owned businesses directly reward employees for success. When the company enjoys increased sales or lower costs, employees benefit directly. The National Center for Employee Ownership, an organization that studies employee-owned American businesses, reports that employee stock ownership plans (ESOPs) provide considerable employee incentive and increase employee involvement and commitment. In the United States today, about 13.7 million employees participate in 11,400 ESOPs and stock bonus plans.[18] As a means to motivate top executives and, frequently, middle-ranking managers who are working long days for what are generally considered poor salaries, some firms provide stock options as part of the employee compensation package. The option is simply the right to buy shares of the firm within a prescribed time at a set price. If the firm does well and its stock price rises past the set price (presumably because of all the work being done by the employee), the employee can exercise the option and immediately sell the stock and cash in on the company's success.

The difficulties of such companies as United Airlines have damaged the idea of employee ownership. United Airlines' ESOP failed to solve problems between employees and management. In addition, Lowe's, the home-improvement retailer, recently stopped its long-running and mostly successful ESOP and transferred the remaining money into 401(k) plans.

empowerment making employees more involved in their jobs by increasing their participation in decision making

employee ownership a situation in which employees own the company they work for by virtue of being stockholders

5 Understand the types, development, and uses of teams.

Teams and Teamwork

The concepts of teams and teamwork may be most commonly associated with sports, but they are also integral parts of business organizations. This organizational structure is popular because it encourages employees to participate more fully in business decisions. The growing number of companies organizing their workforces into teams reflects an effort to increase employee productivity and creativity because team members are working on specific goals and are given greater autonomy. This leads to greater job satisfaction as employees feel more involved in the management process.[19]

What Is a Team?

In a business organization, a **team** is two or more workers operating as a coordinated unit to accomplish a specific task or goal.[20] A team may be assigned any number of tasks or goals, from development of a new product to selling that product. A team can also be created to identify or solve a problem that an organization is experiencing. Toyota, for example, assembled a team of seven experts in the fields of business, transportation, automobile safety, and technology to help the company after an unprecedented number of vehicles needed to be recalled because of the possibility of sudden acceleration. The team analyzed the company from top to bottom, evaluating Toyota's quality-control methods to figure out how unsafe acceleration problems in certain vehicles went unnoticed during development and testing.[21] Although teamwork may seem like a simple concept learned on soccer or football fields, teams function as a microcosm of the larger organization. Therefore, it is important to understand the types, development, and general nature of teams.

Types of Teams

There are several types of teams within businesses that function in specific ways to achieve different purposes, including problem-solving teams, self-managed teams, cross-functional teams, and virtual teams.

Problem-Solving Teams The most common type of team in business organizations is the **problem-solving team**. It is generally used temporarily in order to bring knowledgeable employees together to tackle a specific problem. Once the problem is solved, the team typically is disbanded.

In some extraordinary cases, an expert team may be needed to generate groundbreaking ideas. A **virtuoso team** consists of exceptionally highly skilled and talented individuals brought together to produce significant change. As with other kinds of problem-solving teams, virtuoso teams are usually assembled on a temporary basis. Instead of being task-oriented, they focus on producing ideas and provoking change that could have an effect on the company and its industry. Because of the high skill level of their members, virtuoso teams can be difficult to manage. Unlike traditional teams, virtuoso teams place an emphasis on individuality over teamwork, which can cause further conflict. However, their conflicts usually are viewed as competitive and therefore productive in generating the most substantial ideas.[22]

Self-Managed Work Teams **Self-managed teams** are groups of employees with the authority and skills to manage themselves. Experts suggest that workers on self-managed teams are more motivated and satisfied because they have more task variety and job control. On many work teams, members rotate through all the jobs for which the team is responsible. Some organizations cross-train the entire team so that everyone can perform everyone else's job. In a traditional business structure, management is responsible for hiring and firing employees, establishing budgets, purchasing supplies, conducting performance reviews, and taking corrective action. When self-managed teams are in place, they take over some or all of these management functions. Xerox, Procter & Gamble, Ferrari, and numerous other companies have used self-managed teams successfully. The major advantages and disadvantages of self-managed teams are mentioned in Figure 10.6.

Cross-Functional Teams Traditionally, businesses have organized employees into departments based on a common function or specialty. However, increasingly, business organizations are faced with projects that require a diversity of skills not

team two or more workers operating as a coordinated unit to accomplish a specific task or goal

problem-solving team a team of knowledgeable employees brought together to tackle a specific problem

virtuoso team a team of exceptionally highly skilled and talented individuals brought together to produce significant change

self-managed teams groups of employees with the authority and skills to manage themselves

Figure 10.6 Advantages and Disadvantages of Self-Managed Teams

While self-managed teams provide advantages, managers must recognize their disadvantages.

ADVANTAGES	DISADVANTAGES
• Boosts employee morale	• Additional training costs
• Increases productivity	• Teams may be disorganized
• Aids innovation	• Conflicts may arise
• Reduces employee boredom	• Leadership role may be unclear

available within a single department. A **cross-functional team** consists of individuals with varying specialties, expertise, and skills that are brought together to achieve a common task. For example, a purchasing agent might create a cross-functional team with representatives from various departments to gain insight into useful purchases for the company. This structure avoids departmental separation and allows greater efficiency when there is a single goal. Although cross-functional teams are not necessarily self-managed, most self-managed teams are cross-functional. They can also be cross-divisional, such as at Dow Chemical Company, which created a cross-divisional team at their West Alexandria plant to improve energy efficiency. The team was able to look throughout the plant's divisions to find ways to save energy, including turning off unnecessary equipment and optimizing various processes, which resulted in 14 percent annual energy savings.[23] Cross-functional teams can also include a variety of people from outside the company, such as the cross-functional team of ergonomists, users, and university scientists that developed a new natural ergonomic keyboard for Microsoft.[24] Because of their speed, flexibility, and increased employee satisfaction, it is likely that the use of cross-functional teams will increase.

cross-functional team a team of individuals with varying specialties, expertise, and skills that are brought together to achieve a common task

virtual team a team consisting of members who are geographically dispersed but communicate electronically

Virtual Teams With the advent of sophisticated communications technology, it is no longer necessary for teams to be geographically close. A **virtual team** consists of members who are geographically dispersed but communicate electronically. In fact, team members may never meet in person but rely solely on e-mail, teleconferences, faxes, voice mail, and other technological interactions. In the modern global environment, virtual teams connect employees on a common task across continents, oceans, time zones, and organizations. For example, Mozilla, the software provider responsible for Firefox, regularly requests the help of volunteers to test and improve their products virtually. Some of these volunteers become employees of the organization based on their performance in the project they did.[25] In some cases, the physical distances between participants and the lack of face-to-face interaction can be difficult when deadlines approach or communication is not clear.

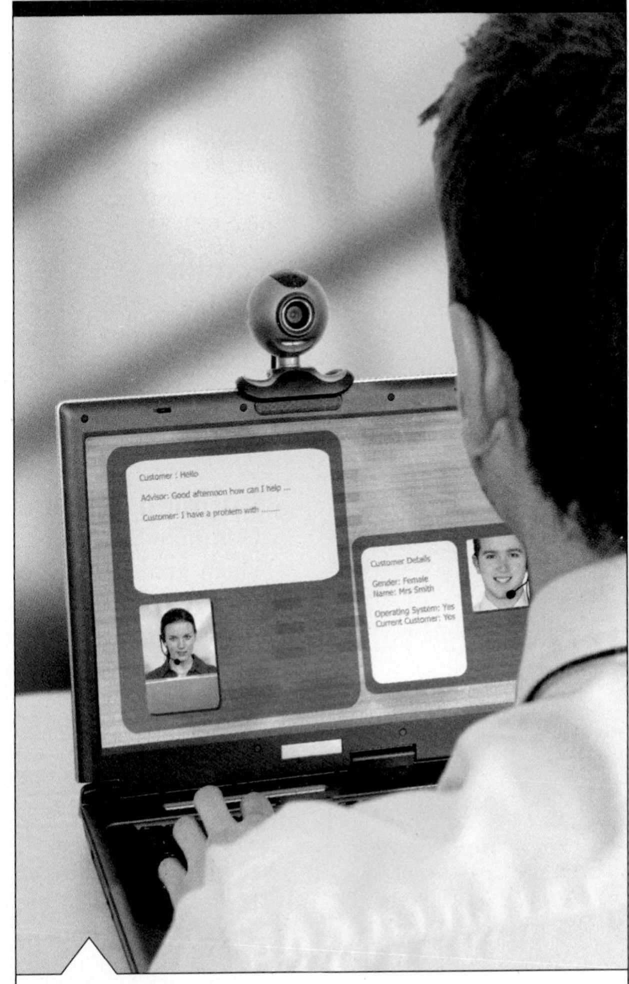

Virtual team. Virtual team members work together online.

Going for SUCCESS

Paid Volunteerism Is Good for Everybody!

A growing number of companies are increasing workforce motivation and satisfaction—and making a difference in local communities—by giving employees paid time off to do volunteer work. For example, the global accounting firm PricewaterhouseCoopers encourages employees to give back to their communities by paying them for up to ten hours of volunteering annually in charities, education, and civic projects. With a 60 percent participation rate in its volunteer programs, PricewaterhouseCoopers has found that employees feel particularly good about using their personal and professional skills to help the communities in which they live and work.

Merck, one of the giants of the pharmaceutical industry, will pay its 100,000 employees to volunteer for up to 20 hours a year on non-profit projects of their choice. Umpqua Bank will pay full-time employees for up to 40 hours annually to volunteer with community-development programs such as Habitat for Humanity or help young people through Big Brothers Big Sisters and other non-profit groups.

W. Rogers Company, which builds water treatment plants, encourages involvement in the community by paying employees for up to ten hours of volunteer work every year. The CEO emphasizes that volunteerism "builds employee morale, increases retention, and is an opportunity for team building and for leadership development. Some of our employees have truly developed into better leaders by serving on various non-profit boards and committees."

Sources: Quoted in Lee Ann Walton, "Businesses Find Benefits in Volunteering," *Business Lexington*, March 4, 2010, http://www.bizlex.com; Chris Jarvis, "Six Essential Strengths of an Employee Volunteer Program," *Fast Company blog*, June 11, 2009, http://www.fastcompany.com/blog/chris-jarvis/innovative-thinking-corporate-volunteering/six-essential-strengths-employee-volunt; Tony Di Domizio, "Business Outlook: Merck Looks Ahead," *The Reporter (Pennsylvania)*, February 23, 2010, http://www.thereporteronline.com; http://www.umpquabank.com.

Developing and Using Effective Teams

When a team is first developed, it takes time for the members to establish roles, relationships, delegation of duties, and other attributes of an effective team. As a team matures, it passes through five stages of development, as shown in Figure 10.7.

Forming In the first stage, *forming*, team members are introduced to one another and begin to develop a social dynamic. The members of the team are still unsure about how to relate to one another, what behaviors are considered acceptable, and what the ground rules are for the team. Through group member interaction over time, team members become more comfortable and a group dynamic begins to emerge.

Storming During the *storming* stage, the interaction may be volatile and the team may lack unity. Because the team is still relatively new, this is the stage at which goals and objectives begin to develop. Team members will brainstorm to develop ideas and plans and establish a broad-ranging agenda. It is important at this stage for team members to grow more comfortable around the others so that they can contribute openly. At this time, the leadership role likely will be formally undefined. A team member may emerge as the informal leader. The success or failure of the ideas in storming determines how long the team will take to reach the next stage.

Norming After storming and the first large burst of activity, the team begins to stabilize during the *norming* stage. During this process, each person's role within the group starts to become apparent, and members begin to recognize the roles of others. A sense of unity will become stronger. If it has not occurred already, an identified leader will emerge. The group still may be somewhat volatile at this point and may regress back to the second stage if any conflict, especially over the leadership role, occurs.

Figure 10.7 Stages of Team Development

When attempting to develop teams, managers must understand that multiple stages are generally required.

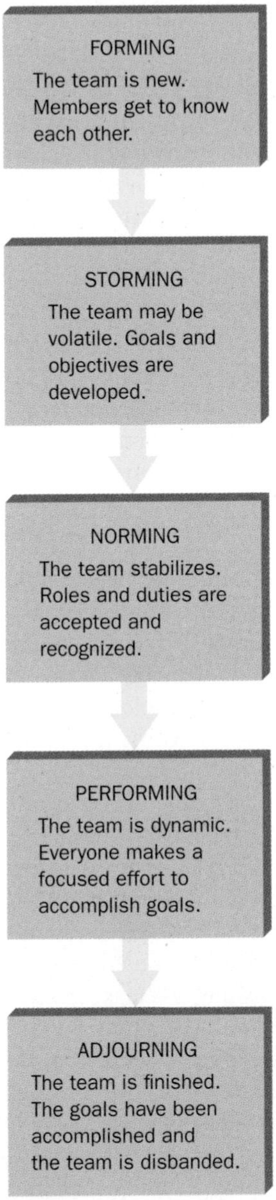

FORMING
The team is new. Members get to know each other.

STORMING
The team may be volatile. Goals and objectives are developed.

NORMING
The team stabilizes. Roles and duties are accepted and recognized.

PERFORMING
The team is dynamic. Everyone makes a focused effort to accomplish goals.

ADJOURNING
The team is finished. The goals have been accomplished and the team is disbanded.

Performing The fourth stage, *performing*, is when the team achieves its full potential. It is usually slow to develop and occurs when the team begins to focus strongly on the assigned task and away from team-development issues. The members of the team work in harmony under the established roles to accomplish the necessary goals.

Adjourning In the final stage, *adjourning*, the team is disbanded because the project has been completed. Team members may be reassigned to other teams or tasks. This stage does not always occur if the team is placed together for a task with no specific date of completion. For example, a marketing team for Best Buy may continue to develop promotional efforts for a store even after a specific promotional task has been accomplished. This stage is especially common in problem-solving teams that are dismantled after the assigned problem has been resolved.

Roles Within a Team

Within any team, each member has a role to play in helping the team attain its objectives. Each of these roles adds important dimensions to team member interactions. The group member who pushes forward toward goals and places the objective first plays the *task-specialist role* by concentrating fully on the assigned task. In a cross-functional team, this might be the person with the most expertise relating to the current task. The *socioemotional role* is played by the individual who supports and encourages the emotional needs of the other members. This person places the team members' personal needs over the task of the team. Although this may sound unimportant, the socioemotional member's dedication to team cohesiveness will lead to greater unity and higher productivity. The leader of the team, and possibly others as well, will play a *dual role*. This dual role is a combination of both the socioemotional and task-specialist roles because this individual focuses on both the task and the team. The team leader might not always play a dual role, but the team is likely to be most successful when he or she does. Sometimes an individual assumes the *nonparticipant role*. This role behavior is characterized by a person who does not contribute to accomplishing the task and does not provide favorable input with respect to team members' socioemotional needs.

Team Cohesiveness

Developing a unit from a diverse group of personalities, specialties, backgrounds, and work styles can be challenging and complicated. In a cohesive team, the members get along and are able to accomplish their tasks effectively. There are factors that affect cohesiveness within a team. Teams generally are ideal when they contain 5 to 12 people. Teams with fewer than 5 people often fail to accomplish tasks and generate a variety of ideas. Teams with more than 12 are too large because members do not develop relationships, may feel intimidated to speak, or may disconnect. It also may be beneficial to have team members introduce themselves and describe their past work experiences. This activity will foster familiarity and shared experiences. One of the most reliable ways to build cohesiveness within a team is through competition with other teams. When two teams are competing for a single prize or recognition, they are forced to put aside conflict and accomplish their goal. By adding an incentive to finishing the task, the team automatically becomes more goal oriented. Also, a favorable appraisal from an outsider may strengthen team cohesiveness. Because the team is being praised as a group, team members recognize their contribution as a unit. Teams are also more successful when goals have been agreed up on. A team that is clear about its objective will focus more on accomplishing it. Frequent interaction also builds cohesiveness as relationships strengthen and familiarity increases.

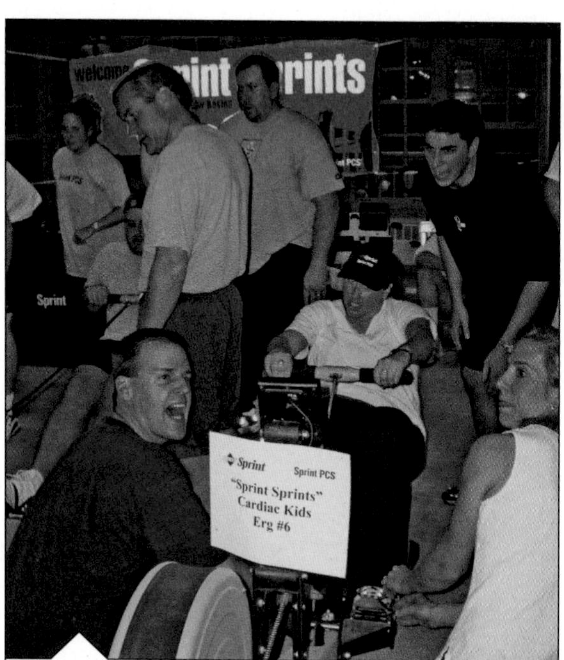

Team building. Employees at Sprint paticipate in team sports, which helps them improve their overall ability to engage in productive team work.

© Susan Van Etten

Team Conflict and How to Resolve It

Conflict occurs when a disagreement arises between two or more team members. Conflict traditionally has been viewed as negative; however, if handled properly, conflict can work to improve a team. For example, if two team members disagree about a certain decision, both may analyze the situation more closely to determine the best choice. As long as conflict is handled in a respectful and professional manner, it can improve the quality of work produced. However, if conflict turns hostile and affects the work environment, then steps must be taken to arrive at a suitable compromise. Compromises can be difficult in a business organization because neither party ends up getting everything he or she wants. The best solution is a middle-ground alternative in which each party is satisfied to some degree. It is best to avoid attempting to minimize or ignore conflicts within a group because this may cause the conflict to grow as members concentrate on the problem instead of the task. However the conflict is resolved, it is important to remember that conflict must be acknowledged if it is to either be resolved or serve a constructive purpose.

Benefits and Limitations of Teams

Teamwork within a company has been credited as a key to reducing turnover and costs and increasing production, quality, and customer service. There is also evidence that working in teams leads to higher levels of job satisfaction among employees and a harmonious work environment. Thus, an increasingly large number of companies are considering teams as a viable organizational structure. However, the process of reorganizing into teams can be stressful and time consuming with no guarantee that the team will develop effectively. If a team lacks cohesiveness and is unable to resolve conflict, the company may experience lower productivity.

return to inside business

General Electric

GE has long been recognized as a leader in developing corporate leaders, with a world-renowned training and development program that inspires professional growth and high performance. Career-long learning is not the only reason that GE is a talent magnet. It also uses flextime, telecommuting, empowerment, and other techniques to increase motivation and satisfaction in its global workforce.

Given the fast pace of change within the business environment, GE is now emphasizing "more networking, more managing in volatility," says the CEO. This affects the company's approach to teamwork as well as its development programs. To maintain its competitive edge, GE is motivating employees and managers by giving them the skills and the opportunities to tackle difficult business challenges in collaboration with managers and colleagues they respect.

Questions

1. Even with a $1 billion training budget, GE cannot afford to give every employee and manager exactly the same educational experiences. What do you think GE should do to avoid diminishing employee motivation in this situation?
2. How can GE use its training and development programs to enhance teamwork?

CHAPTER REVIEW

Summary

1 Explain what motivation is.

Motivation is the individual internal process that energizes, directs, and sustains behavior. Motivation is affected by employee morale—that is, the employee's feelings about the job, superiors, and the firm itself. Motivation, morale, and job satisfaction are closely related.

2 Understand some major historical perspectives on motivation.

One of the first approaches to employee motivation was Frederick Taylor's scientific management, the application of scientific principles to the management of work and workers. Taylor believed that employees work only for money and that they must be closely supervised and managed. This thinking led to the piece-rate system, under which employees are paid a certain amount for each unit they produce. The Hawthorne Studies attempted to determine the effects of the work environment on productivity. Results of these studies indicated that human factors affect productivity more than do physical aspects of the workplace.

Maslow's hierarchy of needs suggests that people are motivated by five sets of needs. In ascending order of importance, these motivators are physiological, safety, social, esteem, and self-actualization needs. People are motivated by the lowest set of needs that remains unfulfilled. As needs at one level are satisfied, people try to satisfy needs at the next level.

Frederick Herzberg found that job satisfaction and dissatisfaction are influenced by two distinct sets of factors. Motivation factors, including recognition and responsibility, affect an employee's degree of satisfaction, but their absence does not necessarily cause dissatisfaction. Hygiene factors, including pay and working conditions, affect an employee's degree of dissatisfaction but do not affect satisfaction.

Theory X is a concept of motivation that assumes that employees dislike work and will function effectively only in a highly controlled work environment. Thus, to achieve an organization's goals, managers must coerce, control, and threaten employees. This theory generally is consistent with Taylor's ideas of scientific management. Theory Y is more in keeping with the results of the Hawthorne Studies and the human relations movement. It suggests that employees can be motivated to behave as responsible members of the organization. Theory Z emphasizes long-term employment, collective decision making, individual responsibility for the outcomes of decisions, informal control, and a holistic concern for employees. Reinforcement theory is based on the idea that people will repeat behavior that is rewarded and will avoid behavior that is punished.

3 Describe three contemporary views of motivation: equity theory, expectancy theory, and goal-setting theory.

Equity theory maintains that people are motivated to obtain and preserve equitable treatment for themselves. Expectancy theory suggests that our motivation depends on how much we want something and how likely we think we are to get it. Goal-setting theory suggests that employees are motivated to achieve a goal that they and their managers establish together.

4 Explain several techniques for increasing employee motivation.

Management by objectives (MBO) is a motivation technique in which managers and employees collaborate in setting goals. MBO motivates employees by getting them more involved in their jobs and in the organization as a whole. Job enrichment seeks to motivate employees by varying their tasks and giving them more responsibility for and control over their jobs. Job enlargement, expanding a worker's assignments to include additional tasks, is one aspect of job enrichment. Job redesign is a type of job enrichment in which work is restructured to improve the worker–job match.

Behavior modification uses reinforcement to encourage desirable behavior. Rewards for productivity, quality, and loyalty change employees' behavior in desired ways and also increase motivation.

Allowing employees to work more flexible hours is another way to build motivation and job satisfaction. Flextime is a system of work scheduling that allows workers to set their own hours as long as they fall within the limits established by employers. Part-time work is permanent employment in which individuals work less than a standard work week. Job sharing is an arrangement whereby two people share one full-time position. Telecommuting allows employees to work at home all or part of the work week. All these types of work arrangements give employees more time outside the workplace to deal with family responsibilities or to enjoy free time.

Employee empowerment, self-managed work teams, and employee ownership are also techniques that boost employee motivation. Empowerment increases employees' involvement in their jobs by increasing their decision-making authority. Self-managed work teams are groups of employees with the authority and skills to manage themselves. When employees participate in ownership programs, such as employee stock ownership plans (ESOPs), they have more incentive to make the company succeed and therefore work more effectively.

5 Understand the types, development, and uses of teams.

A large number of companies use teams to increase their employees' productivity. In a business organization, a team is a group of workers functioning together as a unit to complete a common goal or purpose.

There are several types of teams within businesses that function in specific ways to achieve different purposes. A problem-solving team is a team of knowledgeable employees brought together to tackle a specific problem. A virtuoso team is a team of highly skilled and talented individuals brought together to produce significant change. A virtual team is a team consisting of members who are geographically dispersed but communicate electronically. A cross-functional team is a team of individuals with varying specialties, expertise, and skills.

The five stages of team development are forming, storming, norming, performing, and adjourning. As a team develops, it should become more productive and unified. The four roles within teams are task specialist, socioemotional, dual, and nonparticipative. Each of these roles plays a specific part in the team's interaction. For a team to be successful, members must learn how to resolve and manage conflict so that the team can work cohesively to accomplish goals.

Key Terms

You should now be able to define and give an example relevant to each of the following terms:

motivation (278)
morale (279)
scientific management (279)
piece-rate system (280)
need (281)
Maslow's hierarchy of needs (281)
physiological needs (282)
safety needs (282)
social needs (282)
esteem needs (282)
self-actualization needs (282)
motivation–hygiene theory (283)
motivation factors (284)
hygiene factors (284)
Theory X (284)
Theory Y (284)
Theory Z (285)
reinforcement theory (286)
equity theory (287)
expectancy theory (287)
goal-setting theory (288)
management by objectives (MBO) (290)
job enrichment (290)
job enlargement (291)
job redesign (292)
behavior modification (292)
flextime (293)
part-time work (293)
job sharing (294)
telecommuting (294)
empowerment (295)
employee ownership (295)
team (296)
problem-solving team (296)
virtuoso team (296)
self-managed teams (296)
cross-functional team (297)
virtual team (297)

Review Questions

1. How do scientific management and Theory X differ from the human relations movement and Theory Y?
2. How did the results of the Hawthorne Studies influence researchers' thinking about employee motivation?
3. What are the five sets of needs in Maslow's hierarchy? How are a person's needs related to motivation?
4. What are the two dimensions in Herzberg's theory? What kinds of elements affect each dimension?
5. What is the fundamental premise of reinforcement theory?
6. According to equity theory, how does an employee determine whether he or she is being treated equitably?
7. According to expectancy theory, what two variables determine motivation?
8. Identify and describe the major techniques for motivating employees.
9. Describe the steps involved in the MBO process.
10. What are the objectives of MBO? What do you think might be its disadvantages?
11. How does employee participation increase motivation?
12. Describe the steps involved in the process of behavior modification.
13. Identify and describe the major types of teams.
14. What are the major benefits and limitations associated with the use of self-managed teams?
15. Explain the major stages of team development.

Discussion Questions

1. How might managers make use of Maslow's hierarchy of needs in motivating employees? What problems would they encounter?
2. Do the various theories of motivation contradict each other or complement each other? Explain.
3. What combination of motivational techniques do you think would result in the best overall motivation and reward system?
4. Reinforcement theory and behavior modification have been called demeaning because they tend to treat people "like mice in a maze." Do you agree?
5. In what ways are team cohesiveness and team conflict related?

Video Case 10.1 At L.L. Bean, Everyone Is Family

From a tiny mail-order company begun 100 years ago, L.L. Bean has grown into a well-known retail firm with net sales of over $1.5 billion a year. It encompasses 14 stores in 10 states, continues its ever-popular catalog, has a thriving online store, and sells some 20,000 high-quality items, including clothing for the whole family, accessories, outdoor and camping gear, and even luggage, linens, and furniture. Employees at L.L. Bean share a sense of purpose that closely reflects the values of the company's founders and managers, making them feel like they are part of a large family.

Although its online store has grown enormously in popularity, the company continues to field a huge number of mail and telephone orders year-round, which puts employees in constant direct contact with customers. The company has a world-class training program, so employees' skills are not an issue. In addition, employees' motivation brought the company to the top of *BusinessWeek's* list of companies with outstanding customer service. Why are they so motivated? "Our frontline employees are the face of L.L. Bean and the voice of L.L. Bean to our customers," says the company's vice president of e-commerce, "so they need to feel that they're supported in making the right decisions on behalf of the customer and the company." Describing the way many other firms require their telephone call center employees to bring in a supervisor to resolve customers' problems, the vice president explains why L.L. Bean does things differently. "We expect that the person you talk to on the phone will make it right. Other places you have to say, 'Let me talk to your supervisor,' and we really can't stand that. We look on elevated calls as a bad thing."

Empowering employees to resolve customer problems on their own not only speeds the handling of calls and leaves L.L. Bean's customers more satisfied, it also increases employees' decision-making authority and the pride and satisfaction they feel in their work. The company offers annual bonuses and profit sharing for all year-round employees. However, as one company executive explained, the sense of ownership Bean employees feel in the company isn't founded on money. "It's definitely not based on that kind of incentive. . . . We select employees based on their ability to feel that kind of ownership, based on their investment in delivering the right customer experience. . . . They have this sort of underlying sense of values that drives them to deliver and . . . act as if they are an owner of the company. I talk about that a lot with my frontline employees."

Communication at the firm goes both ways. L.L. Bean employees also know they are empowered to speak up when they think a product or a business process can be improved. As one manager says, "They would be very clear to the chain of command that 'this doesn't work, and you need to change it so that it better suits the customer.'"

Other ways in which L.L. Bean rewards its employees are the company-owned fitness centers, walking trails, and sporting camps for fishing, kayaking, and skiing that encourage everyone at the firm to stay healthy and active. Ergonomic workstations bring the company's commitment to its employees' well-being right to their desks. During his tenure as president, in fact, Leon Gorman defined the company's stakeholders as including not just customers, stockholders, vendors, communities, and the natural environment, but employees as well. Benefits, wages, discounts, and pensions are competitive, even generous. Some employees have worked for the company for as long as 30 years, and nearly 800 applicants turned out for 130 jobs created by the opening of a new L.L. Bean store in upstate New York. It all comes back to what Gorman calls the power of L.L.'s personality: "His personal charisma, based on down-home honesty, a true love for the outdoors, and a genuine enthusiasm for people inspired all who worked for him." In that respect, the founder's legacy is very much alive today.[26]

Questions

1. What role do you think empowerment plays at L.L. Bean?
2. Because the company's retail Web site has proven to be so successful, L.L. Bean recently announced the closing of one of its four call centers, but the 220 employees there will have the option to work at another site or telecommute. What net effect do you think closing of the call center will have on employee morale and motivation?
3. What else could L.L. Bean do to motivate its employees?

Case 10.2 Why Do So Many People Want to Work at Google?

Imagine having a job where you could get generous pay, free gourmet lunches and dinners, free any-time snacks, a pet center, free gym membership, a game room, an on-site massage therapist and doctor, hair styling, generous vacation and maternity benefits, parental leave, adoption benefits, paid take-out meals for new parents, stock options, tuition reimbursement, free shuttle to the office, reimbursement toward the purchase of a hybrid or an electric car, telecommuting, on-site oil change and car wash, dry cleaning, fitness classes, bike repair, a sauna, roller hockey, an outdoor volleyball court, and much, much more.

That's life at Google, the Internet's dominant search company and one of the trendiest and fastest-growing businesses in the world. The company, based in Mountain View, California, boasts an informal, dynamic, and collaborative culture "unlike any in corporate America." With people's pet dogs happily roaming the shared work spaces, it is clearly unlike most office environments. Google's CEO explains on the company Web site that "the goal is to strip away everything that gets in our employees' way. . . . Let's face it: programmers want to program, they don't want to do their laundry. So we make it easy for them to do both."

Although a few perks are available only at headquarters, employees at all the company's offices can customize their benefits, including traditional health and dental coverage plans, life insurance, and retirement and savings plans, into a package that works for each individual and family. These benefits make for happy and productive employees, many of whom have become millionaires as the company's stock has appreciated in value. All these perks are one of the reasons that *Fortune* magazine includes Google on its list of 100 best places to work in the United States.

Because it must compete directly for top-notch talent with other high-tech firms like Yahoo!, eBay, Facebook, and Amazon.com, Google is committed to retaining those who fit well with its "Google-y" culture, that is, people who are "fairly flexible, adaptable and not focusing on titles and hierarchy, and just get stuff done," according to the company's chief culture officer. The company even conducts an annual "happiness survey" to find out how committed to Google its employees are, why, and what matters to them and their managers. The results are funneled into the company's continuing focus on career development and growth.

Can a company ever provide too many benefits? Google might be about to find out. It recently announced a major and widely unpopular change in one of its most enviable perks—access to its on-site day-care facilities. Saying the move was a response to a two-year waiting list for entry into the program, which it called "inequitable," the company sharply raised the fee for using the service to well above the market rate (from $33,000 to $57,000 a year for two children). It also started charging families several hundred dollars to stay on the waiting list. The list promptly shrank by more than half. After parents protested the price increase, the company scaled it back slightly and changed the company that operates the day-care program, but let the basic outline of its decision stand. It also offers five free days of backup child-care services per year to California employees whose regular day-care arrangements fall through unexpectedly.

Today, Google has trimmed a few of its traditional perks but still offers a lengthy menu of choices. It has not changed its long-standing policy of allowing engineers to devote up to one full workday each week to projects they themselves choose. With the freedom to pursue unusual and creative ideas during company time, engineers can work on their own or team up with colleagues to experiment with new technologies. The next big Google breakthrough might very well grow out of an unofficial project initiated by an engineer taking advantage of his or her right to doodle around with something new during spare moments on the job.[27]

Questions

1. What does Google gain by offering these generous benefits? Do you think there is any downside to offering so many?
2. Which of Google's benefits appeal to you? Why? Are there any benefits you think the company does not need to offer? Why or why not?
3. What do you think will be the long-term effect of Google's changed child-care benefit? Is it a good idea for companies to reduce or withdraw such benefits?

Building Skills for Career Success

1 JOURNALING FOR SUCCESS

Discovery statement: Many managers use special techniques to foster employee motivation and satisfaction.

Assignment

1. Thinking about your current job (or your most recent job), what types of motivation techniques are being used?
2. How well does each technique work on you and on your co-workers?
3. Thinking about the first job that you will take after completing your studies, what types of motivation techniques will be most effective in motivating you to truly excel in your new position? Explain why.
4. Do you expect that most of your co-workers will be motivated by the same techniques that motivate you? Explain.

2 EXPLORING THE INTERNET

There are few employee incentives as motivating as owning "a piece of the action." Either through profit sharing or equity, many firms realize that the opportunity to share in the wealth generated by their effort is a primary force to drive employees toward better performance and a sense of ownership. The Foundation for Enterprise Development (http://www.fed.org/) is a non-profit organization dedicated to helping entrepreneurs and executives use employee ownership and equity compensation as a fair and effective means of motivating the workforce and improving corporate performance. You can learn more about this approach at the foundation's Web site. Visit the text Web site for updates to this exercise.

Assignment

1. Describe the content and services provided by the Foundation for Enterprise Development through its Web site.
2. Do you agree with this orientation toward motivation of employees/owners, or does it seem contrived to you? Discuss.
3. How else might employees be motivated to improve their performance?

❸ DEVELOPING CRITICAL-THINKING SKILLS

This chapter has described several theories managers can use as guidelines in motivating employees to do the best job possible for the company. Among these theories are Maslow's hierarchy of needs, equity theory, expectancy theory, and goal-setting theory. How effective would each of these theories be in motivating you to be a more productive employee?

Assignment

1. Identify five job needs that are important to you.
2. Determine which of the theories mentioned above would work best to satisfy your job needs.
3. Prepare a two-page report explaining how you reached these conclusions.

❹ BUILDING TEAM SKILLS

By increasing employees' participation in decision making, empowerment makes workers feel more involved in their jobs and the operations of the organization. Although empowerment may seem like a commonsense idea, it is a concept not found universally at the workplace. If you had empowerment in your job, how would you describe it?

Assignment

1. Brainstorm to explore the concept of empowerment.
   a. Write each letter of the word *empowerment* in a vertical column on a sheet of paper or on the classroom chalkboard.
   b. Think of several words that begin with each letter.
   c. Write the words next to the appropriate letter.
2. Formulate a statement by choosing one word from each letter that best describes what empowerment means to you.
3. Analyze the statement.
   a. How relevant is the statement for you in terms of empowerment? Or empowerment in your workplace?
   b. What changes must occur in your workplace for you to have empowerment?
   c. How would you describe yourself as an empowered employee?
   d. What opportunities would empowerment give to you in your workplace?
4. Prepare a report of your findings.

❺ RESEARCHING DIFFERENT CAREERS

Because a manager's job varies from department to department within firms, as well as among firms, it is virtually impossible to write a generic description of a manager's job. If you are contemplating becoming a manager, you may find it very helpful to spend time on the job with several managers learning firsthand what they do.

Assignment

1. Make an appointment with managers in three firms, preferably firms of different sizes. When you make the appointments, request a tour of the facilities.
2. Ask the managers the following questions:
   a. What do you do in your job?
   b. What do you like most and least about your job? Why?
   c. What skills do you need in your job?
   d. How much education does your job require?
   e. What advice do you have for someone thinking about pursuing a career in management?
3. Summarize your findings in a two-page report. Include answers to these questions:
   a. Is management a realistic field of study for you? Why?
   b. What might be a better career choice? Why?

11 Enhancing Union–Management Relations

© AP Images/Carlos Osorio

Learning Objectives

What you will be able to do once you complete this chapter:

1. Explain how and why labor unions came into being.
2. Discuss the sources of unions' negotiating power and trends in union membership.
3. Identify the main focus of several major pieces of labor–management legislation.
4. Enumerate the steps involved in forming a union and show how the National Labor Relations Board is involved in the process.
5. Describe the basic elements of the collective-bargaining process.
6. Identify the major issues covered in a union–management contract.
7. Explain the primary bargaining tools available to unions and management.

FYI

inside business

Southwest Airlines and Its Pilots' Union Strike a Good Deal

How does a union navigate contract negotiations with the management of an airline that issues stock under the symbol of LUV? The Southwest Airlines Pilots' Association (SWAPA) was founded in 1978, just seven years after Southwest Airlines first took to the Texas skies. The fledgling airline with the friendly attitude was already successful, having flown 5 million passengers and gone public by 1977.

When SWAPA was originally established, it represented 112 pilots. Now, more than 30 years later, the union represents more than 5,900 of the company's pilots. Unaffiliated with other labor organizations, SWAPA's mission is to provide a secure and rewarding career for its members by negotiating contracts with Southwest Airlines' management, defending its members' contractual rights, and promoting pilot professionalism and safety.

SWAPA's negotiations with Southwest Airlines are subject to the Railway Labor Act, legislation aimed at avoiding disruptions in interstate commerce. Under this law, the pilots' contract with the airline never actually expires, although it can be amended starting on certain dates. The pilots continue to fly under the terms of the current contract while union and airline negotiators hold discussions, which can last for months or even years.

For example, when the SWAPA pilots' contract became amendable in 2006, both sides began talking about several key issues, including salary increases, retirement contributions, and work schedules. They continued negotiating as the economy went into recession, and finally reached a tentative agreement by June 2009. However, SWAPA members rejected it by a small margin, sending union and management back to the bargaining table. A few months later, union members overwhelmingly approved a new agreement that called for pilots to receive retroactive pay increases for 2007 and 2008, linked pay to airline profitability in 2009 and 2010, and set the next amendment date in 2011.

After the pilots approved the contract, the airline's CEO praised SWAPA members as "the hardest working and most productive in the business" and said they "deserve a contract that reflects this, yet is still in keeping with the current uncertain economic outlook." The union pointed to the contract's positive points and said it would press for improvements during the 2011 amendment talks.[1]

Did You Know?

Since the Southwest Airlines Pilots' Association was founded as an independent labor union in 1978, its membership has grown from 112 to 5,900 pilots.

Southwest Airlines, like a number of other business organizations, has been unionized for years, and both management and the unions have experienced ups and downs. Many businesses today have highly cooperative relationships with labor unions. A **labor union** is an organization of workers acting together to negotiate their wages and working conditions with employers. In the United States, nonmanagement employees have the legal right to form unions and to bargain, as a group, with management. The result of the bargaining process is a *labor contract*, a written agreement that is in force for a set period of time (usually one to three years). The dealings between labor unions and business management, both in the bargaining process and beyond it, are called **union–management relations** or, more simply, **labor relations**.

labor union an organization of workers acting together to negotiate their wages and working conditions with employers

union–management (labor) relations the dealings between labor unions and business management both in the bargaining process and beyond it

Because labor and management have different goals, they tend to be at odds with each other. However, these goals must be attained by the same means—through the production of goods and services. At contract bargaining sessions, the two groups must work together to attain their goals. Perhaps mainly for this reason, antagonism now seems to be giving way to cooperation in union–management relations.

We open this chapter by reviewing the history of labor unions in this country. Then we turn our attention to organized labor today, noting current membership trends and union–management partnerships and summarizing important labor-relations laws. We discuss the unionization process, why employees join unions, how a union is formed, and what the National Labor Relations Board does. Then, collective-bargaining procedures are explained. Next, we consider issues in union–management contracts, including employee pay, working hours, security, management rights, and grievance procedures. We close with a discussion of various labor and management negotiating techniques: strikes, slowdowns and boycotts, lockouts, mediation, and arbitration.

1

Explain how and why labor unions came into being.

The Historical Development of Unions

Until the middle of the 19th century, there was very little organization of labor in this country. Groups of workers occasionally did form a **craft union**, an organization of skilled workers in a single craft or trade. These alliances were usually limited to a single city, and they often lasted only a short time. In 1786, the first-known strike in the United States involved a group of Philadelphia printers who stopped working over demands for higher wages. When the employers granted the printers a pay increase, the group disbanded.

Early History

In the mid-1800s, improved transportation opened new markets for manufactured goods. Improved manufacturing methods made it possible to supply those markets, and American industry began to grow. The Civil War and the continued growth of the railroads after the war led to further industrial expansion.

Large-scale production required more and more skilled industrial workers. As the skilled labor force grew, craft unions emerged in the more industrialized areas. From these craft unions, three significant labor organizations evolved. (See Figure 11.1 for a historical overview of unions and their patterns of membership.)

Knights of Labor The first significant national labor organization to emerge was the Knights of Labor, which was formed as a secret society in 1869 by Uriah Stephens, a utopian reformer and abolitionist from Philadelphia. Membership

Figure 11.1 Historical Overview of Unions

The total number of members for all unions generally rose between 1869, when the first truly national union was organized, and 1980. The dates of major events in the history of labor unions are singled out along the line of membership change.

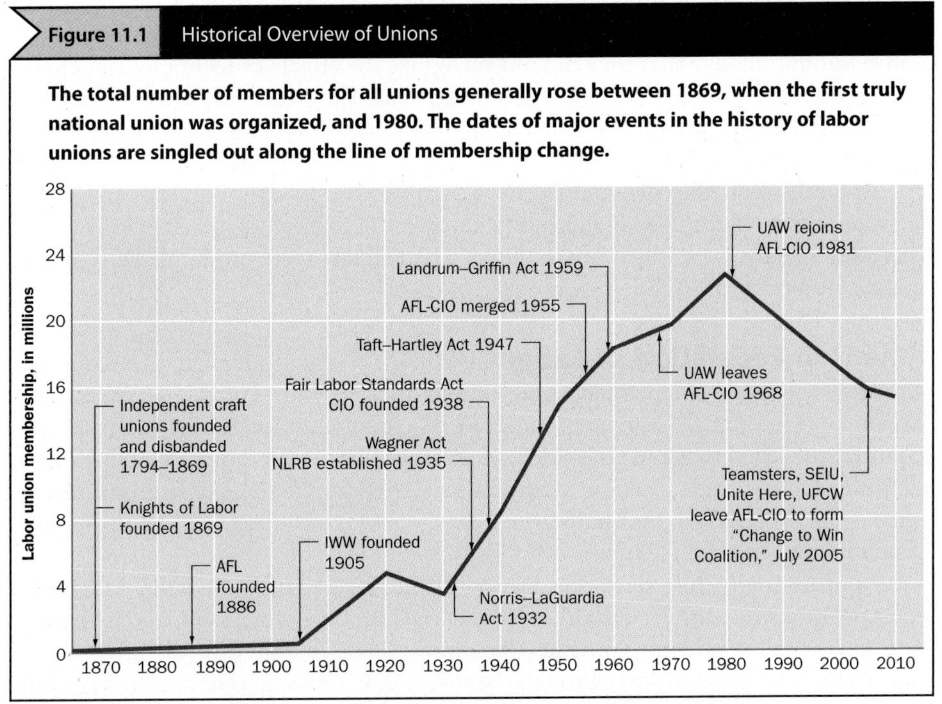

Source: U.S. Bureau of Labor Statistics, Union Membership, http://www.bls.gov (accessed April 29, 2010).

craft union an organization of skilled workers in a single craft or trade

Going for SUCCESS

Players' Unions in the Big Leagues

Unions have been part of professional sports for more than 125 years. The Brotherhood of Professional Base Ball Players was the first to represent the interests of major-league players, starting in 1885. Although several other unions sprang up early in the 20th century, the first collective-bargaining agreement between players and team owners was not negotiated until the 1960s, when the Major League Baseball Players Association was formed. This initial contract raised the minimum player salary to $10,000. Later, the union would negotiate the right to send grievances to arbitration, to have players share in licensing revenues, and other issues important to its members.

Players in other big-league sports also have union representation. Under the hoops and behind the scenes, the National Basketball Players Association, founded in 1954, negotiates with team owners over issues such as pay, retirement benefits, health benefits, and expense reimbursement. It also helps players with insurance arrangements, provides extra security if needed, and arranges charity appearances. On the gridiron, the National Football League Players Association, established in 1956, has negotiated over diverse issues such as salary caps, working conditions, and players' safety. On and off the ice, the National Hockey League Players' Association, based in Toronto and founded in 1967, has negotiated collective-bargaining agreements covering everything from wages and benefits to sharing in revenue from the sale of player trading cards.

Sources: Paul Angilly, "Panini, Upper Deck Each Get NHL Deals," *Bristol Press (Bristol, CT)*, March 28, 2010, http://www.bristolpress.com; http://www.nbpa.org; http://www.nflplayers.com; http://www.nhlpa.com; http://mlbplayers.mlb.com.

reached approximately 700,000 by 1886. One major goal of the Knights was to eliminate the depersonalization of the worker, which resulted from mass-production technology. Another was to improve the moral standards of both employees and society. To the detriment of the group, its leaders concentrated so intently on social and economic change that they did not recognize the effects of technological change. Moreover, they assumed that all employees had the same goals as the Knights' leaders—social and moral reform. The major reason for the demise of the Knights was the Haymarket riot of 1886.

At a rally (called to demand a reduction in the length of a work day from ten to eight hours) in Chicago's Haymarket Square, a bomb exploded. Several police officers and civilians were killed or wounded. The Knights were not implicated directly, but they quickly lost public favor.

American Federation of Labor In 1886, several leaders of the Knights of Labor joined with independent craft unions to form the *American Federation of Labor* (AFL). Samuel Gompers, one of AFL's founders, became its first president. Gompers believed that the goals of the union should be those of its members rather than those of its leaders. The AFL did not seek to change the existing business system, as the Knights of Labor had. Instead, its goal was to improve its members' living standards within the system.

Another major difference between the Knights of Labor and the AFL was in their positions regarding strikes. A **strike** is a temporary work stoppage by employees, calculated to add force to their demands. The Knights did not favor the use of strikes, whereas the AFL strongly believed that striking was an effective labor weapon. The AFL also believed that organized labor should play a major role in

strike a temporary work stoppage by employees, calculated to add force to their demands

politics. As we will see, the AFL is still very much a part of the American labor scene.

Unacceptable employment practices. An 11-year-old girl works alongside adult co-workers in a Tennessee textile mill, 1910.

Industrial Workers of the World The *Industrial Workers of the World* (IWW) was created in 1905 as a radical alternative to the AFL. Among its goals was the overthrow of capitalism. This revolutionary stance prevented the IWW from gaining much of a foothold. Perhaps its major accomplishment was to make the AFL seem, by comparison, less threatening to the general public and to business leaders.

Evolution of Contemporary Labor Organizations

Between 1900 and 1920, both business and government attempted to keep labor unions from growing. This period was plagued by strikes and violent confrontations between management and unions. In steelworks, garment factories, and auto plants, clashes took place in which striking union members fought bitterly against non-union workers, police, and private security guards.

The AFL continued to be the major force in organized labor. By 1920, its membership included 75 percent of all those who had joined unions. Throughout its existence, however, the AFL had been unsure of the best way to deal with unskilled and semiskilled workers. Most of its members were workers skilled in specific crafts or trades. However, technological changes during World War I had brought about a significant increase in the number of unskilled and semiskilled employees in the workforce. These people sought to join the AFL, but they were not well-received by its established membership.

Some unions within the AFL did recognize the need to organize unskilled and semiskilled workers, and they began to penetrate the auto and steel industries. The type of union they formed was an **industrial union**, an organization of both skilled and unskilled workers in a single industry. Soon workers in the rubber, mining, newspaper, and communications industries were also organized into unions. Eventually, these unions left the AFL and formed the *Congress of Industrial Organizations* (CIO).

During the same time (the late 1930s), there was a major upswing in rank-and-file membership in the AFL, the CIO, and independent unions. Strong union leadership, the development of effective negotiating tactics, and favorable legislation combined to increase total union membership to 9 million in 1940. At this point, the CIO began to rival the AFL in size and influence. There was another bitter rivalry: The AFL and CIO often clashed over which of them had the right to organize and represent particular groups of employees.

Since World War II, the labor scene has gone through a number of changes. For one thing, during and after the war years there was a downturn in public opinion regarding unions. A few isolated but very visible strikes during the war caused public sentiment to shift against unionism. Perhaps the most significant occurrence, however, was the merger of the AFL and the CIO. After years of bickering, the two groups recognized that they were wasting effort and resources by fighting each other and that a merger would greatly increase the strength of both. The merger took place on December 5, 1955. The resulting organization, called the *AFL–CIO*, had a membership of as many as 16 million workers, which made it the largest labor organization of its kind in the world. Its first president was George Meany, who served until 1979.

industrial union an organization of both skilled and unskilled workers in a single industry

Organized Labor Today

2

Discuss the sources of unions' negotiating power and trends in union membership.

The power of unions to negotiate effectively with management is derived from two sources. The first is their membership. The more workers a union represents within an industry, the greater is its clout in dealing with firms operating in that industry.

SPoTLIGHT

Where Are the Union Members?

For the first time, there are more union members in government jobs than in company jobs.

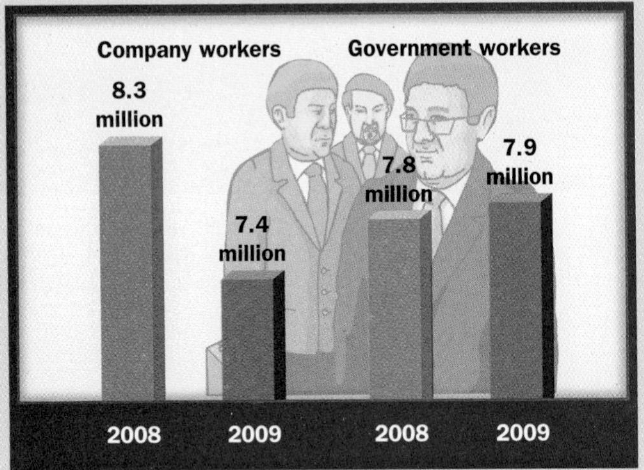

Source: Bureau of Labor Statistics.

The second source of union power is the group of laws that guarantee unions the right to negotiate and, at the same time, regulate the negotiating process.

Union Membership

Approximately 12.3 percent of the nation's workers belong to unions.[2] Union membership is concentrated in a few industries and job categories. Within these industries, though, unions wield considerable power.

The AFL–CIO is still the largest union organization in this country, boasting approximately 11.5 million members. Those represented by the AFL–CIO include actors, barbers, construction workers, carpenters, retail clerks, musicians, teachers, postal workers, painters, steel and iron workers, firefighters, bricklayers, and newspaper reporters.

One of the largest unions not associated directly with the AFL–CIO is the *Teamsters Union*. The Teamsters originally were part of the AFL–CIO, but in 1957 they were expelled for corrupt and illegal practices. The union started out as an organization of professional drivers, but it has begun recently to recruit employees in a wide variety of jobs. Current membership is about 1.4 million workers.

The *United Steelworkers* (USW) and the *United Auto Workers* (UAW) are two of the largest industrial unions. The USW membership has risen to over 1 million workers. It is known as the dominant union in paper and forestry products, steel, aluminum, tire and rubber, mining, glass, chemicals, petroleum, and other basic resource industries. The UAW represents employees in the automobile industry. The UAW, too, originally was part of the AFL–CIO, but it left the parent union—of its own accord—in 1968. Currently, the UAW has about 990,000 members. For a while, the Teamsters and the UAW formed a semistructured partnership called the *Alliance for Labor Action*. This partnership was dissolved eventually, and the UAW again became part of the AFL–CIO in 1981.

Membership Trends

The proportion of union members relative to the size of the nation's workforce has declined over the last 30 years. Moreover, total union membership has dropped since 1980 despite steadily increasing membership in earlier years (see Figure 11.1).

To a great extent, this decline in membership is caused by changing trends in business, such as the following:

- Heavily unionized industries either have been decreasing in size or have not been growing as fast as non-unionized industries. For example, cutbacks in the steel industry have tended to reduce union membership. At the same time, the growth of high-tech industries has increased the ranks of non-union workers.
- Many firms have moved from the heavily unionized Northeast and Great Lakes regions to the less-unionized southeast and southwest regions—the so-called Sunbelt. At the relocated plants, formerly unionized firms tend to hire non-union workers.
- The largest growth in employment is occurring in the service industries, and these industries typically are not unionized.
- Some U.S. companies have moved their manufacturing operations to other countries where less-unionized labor is employed.

- Management is providing benefits that tend to reduce employees' need for unionization.
  - Increased employee participation and better wages and working conditions are goals of unions.
  - When these benefits are already supplied by management, workers are less likely to join existing unions or start new ones. The number of elections to vote on forming new unions has declined. The unions usually win about half the elections.
- According to Alan Greenspan, former chairman of the Federal Reserve, American labor laws and culture allow for the quicker displacement of unneeded workers and their replacement with those in demand, whereas labor laws in other countries tend to take longer for the change to occur.

It remains to be seen whether unions will be able to regain the prominence and power they enjoyed between the world wars and during the 1950s. There is little doubt, however, that they will remain a powerful force in particular industries.

Union–management partnerships. The United Auto Workers president and a top Ford Motor executive are guiding their organizations toward a partnership aimed at having at least 25 percent of Ford vehicles powered partially by electricity.

Union–Management Partnerships

For most of the 20th century, unions represented workers with respect to wages and working conditions. To obtain rights for workers and recognition for themselves, unions engaged in often-antagonistic collective-bargaining sessions and strikes. At the same time, management traditionally protected its own rights of decision making, workplace organization, and strategic planning. Increasingly, however, management has become aware that this traditionally adversarial relationship does not result in the kind of high-performance workplace and empowered workforce necessary to succeed in today's highly competitive markets. For their part, unions and their members acknowledge that most major strikes result in failures that cost members thousands of jobs and reduce the unions' credibility. Today, instead of maintaining an "us versus them" mentality, many unions are becoming partners with management and cooperating to enhance the workplace, empower workers, increase production, improve quality, and reduce costs. According to the Department of Labor, the number of union–management partnerships in the United States is increasing.

Union–management partnerships can be initiated by union leaders, employees, or management. *Limited partnerships* center on accomplishing one specific task or project, such as the introduction of teams or the design of training programs. For example, Levi Strauss formed a limited partnership with its employees, who are members of the Amalgamated Clothing and Textile Workers Union, to help the company in setting up team operations in its non-union plants. *Long-range strategic partnerships* focus on sharing decision-making power for a whole range of workplace and business issues. Long-range partnerships sometimes begin as limited ones and develop slowly over time.

Although strategic union–management partnerships vary, most of them have several characteristics in common. First, strategic partnerships focus on developing cooperative relationships between unions and management instead of arguing over contractual rights. Second, partners work toward mutual gain, in which the organization becomes more competitive, employees are better off, and unions are stronger as a result of the partnership. Finally, as already noted, strategic partners engage in joint decision making on a broad array of issues. These issues include performance expectations, organizational structure, strategic alliances, new technology, pay and benefits, employee security and involvement, union–management roles, product development, and education and training.

Good labor–management relations can help everyone to deal with new and difficult labor issues as they develop. For example, many companies hope that their union–management partnerships will be strong enough to deal with the critical issue of rising health care costs. Unions work hard to protect their members from having to pay an increased percentage of health care costs, and they have experienced some success, in that an average union worker pays about 16 percent of his or her health care premiums compared with a non-union worker's contribution of about 33 percent.[3] Strong union–management partnerships will play a vital role in resolving health care issues.

Union–management partnerships have many potential benefits for management, workers, and unions. For management, partnerships can result in lower costs, increased revenue, improved product quality, and greater customer satisfaction. For workers, benefits may include increased response to their needs, more decision-making opportunities, less supervision, more responsibility, and increased job security. Unions can gain credibility, strength, and increased membership.

Among the many organizations that have found union–management partnerships beneficial is Saturn. The labor–management partnership between the Saturn Corporation and the UAW is one of the boldest experiments in U.S. industrial relations today. It was created through a joint design effort that included the UAW as a full partner in decisions regarding product, technology, suppliers, retailers, site selection, business planning, training, quality systems, job design, and manufacturing systems. This partnership has resulted in a dense communications network throughout the company's management system as well as improvement in quality performance.

3

Identify the main focus of several major pieces of labor–management legislation.

Labor–Management Legislation

As we have noted, business opposed early efforts to organize labor. The federal government generally supported anti-union efforts through the court system, and in some cases federal troops were used to end strikes. Gradually, however, the government began to correct this imbalance through the legislative process.

Norris–LaGuardia Act

The first major piece of legislation to secure rights for unions, the *Norris–LaGuardia Act* of 1932, was considered a landmark in labor–management relations. This act made it difficult for businesses to obtain court orders that banned strikes, picketing, or union membership drives. Previously, courts had issued such orders readily as a means of curbing these activities.

National Labor Relations Act

The *National Labor Relations Act*, also known as the *Wagner Act*, was passed by Congress in 1935. It established procedures by which employees decide whether they want to be represented by a union. If workers choose to be represented, the Wagner Act requires management to negotiate with union representatives. Before this law was passed, union efforts sometimes were interpreted as violating the Sherman Act (1890) because they were viewed as attempts to monopolize. The Wagner Act also forbid certain unfair labor practices on the part of management, such as firing or punishing workers because they were pro-union, spying on union meetings, and bribing employees to vote against unionization.

Finally, the Wagner Act established the **National Labor Relations Board (NLRB)** to enforce the provisions of the law. The NLRB is concerned primarily with (1) overseeing the elections in which employees decide whether they will be represented by a union and (2) investigating complaints lodged by unions or employees. For example, New York University (NYU) graduate teaching and research assistants organized themselves as a union under the UAW. Initially, the NLRB voted to recognize the union, and the students negotiated a 40 percent stipend increase and gained health care benefits. The NLRB later reversed its decision, stating that the graduate students were not employees of the college and should not be recognized as a union. The students went on strike when NYU chose not to renew their union contract and extended offers to students on an individual basis. However, NYU graduate employees recently filed a request with the NLRB to hold another union election and negotiate a contract with NYU once again.[4]

National Labor Relations Board (NLRB) the federal agency that enforces the provisions of the Wagner Act

Fair Labor Standards Act

In 1938, Congress enacted the *Fair Labor Standards Act*. One major provision of this act permits the federal government to set a minimum wage. The first minimum wage, which was set in the late 1930s and did not include farm workers and retail employees, was $0.25 an hour. Today, the minimum wage is $7.25 an hour. Some employees, such as farm workers, are still exempt from the minimum-wage provisions. The act also requires that employees be paid overtime rates for work in excess of 40 hours a week. Finally, it prohibits the use of child labor.

Labor–Management Relations Act

The legislation of the 1930s sought to discourage unfair practices on the part of employers. Recall from Figure 11.1 that union membership grew from approximately 2 million in 1910 to almost 12 million by 1945. Unions represented over 35 percent of all nonagricultural employees in 1945. As union membership and power grew, however, the federal government began to examine the practices of labor. Several long and bitter strikes, mainly in the coal mining and trucking industries, in the early 1940s led to a demand for legislative restraint on unions. As a result, in 1947 Congress passed the *Labor–Management Relations Act*, also known as the *Taft–Hartley Act*, over President Harry Truman's veto.

The Taft–Hartley Act's objective is to provide a balance between union power and management authority. It lists unfair labor practices that unions are forbidden to use. These include refusal to bargain with management in good faith, charging excessive membership dues, harassing non-union workers, and using various means of coercion against employers.

The Taft–Hartley Act also gives management more rights during union organizing campaigns. For example, management may outline for employees the advantages and disadvantages of union membership, as long as the information it presents is accurate. The act gives the President of the United States the power to obtain a temporary injunction to prevent or stop a strike that endangers national health and safety. An **injunction** is a court order requiring a person or group either to perform some act or to refrain from performing some act. Finally, the Taft–Hartley Act authorized states to enact laws to allow employees to work in a unionized firm without joining the union. About 20 states (many in the south) have passed such *right-to-work laws*.

Landrum–Griffin Act

In the 1950s, Senate investigations and hearings exposed racketeering in unions and uncovered cases of bribery, extortion, and embezzlement among union leaders. It was discovered that a few union leaders had taken union funds for personal use and accepted payoffs from employers for union protection. Some were involved in arson, blackmail, and murder. Public pressure for reform resulted in the 1959 *Landrum–Griffin Act*.

This law was designed to regulate the internal functioning of labor unions. Provisions of the law require unions to file annual reports with the U.S. Department of Labor regarding their finances, elections, and various decisions made by union officers. The Landrum–Griffin Act also ensures that each union member has the right to seek, nominate, and vote for each elected position in his or her union. It provides safeguards governing union funds, and it requires management and unions to report the lending of management funds to union officers, union members, or local unions.

The various pieces of legislation we have reviewed here effectively regulate much of the relationship between labor and management after a union has been established. The next section demonstrates that forming a union is also a carefully regulated process.

injunction a court order requiring a person or group either to perform some act or to refrain from performing some act

The Unionization Process

Enumerate the steps involved in forming a union and show how the National Labor Relations Board is involved in the process.

Before a union can be formed at a particular firm, some employees of the firm must be interested in being represented by a union. Then, they must take a number of steps to formally declare their desire for a union. To ensure fairness, most of the steps in this unionization process are supervised by the NLRB.

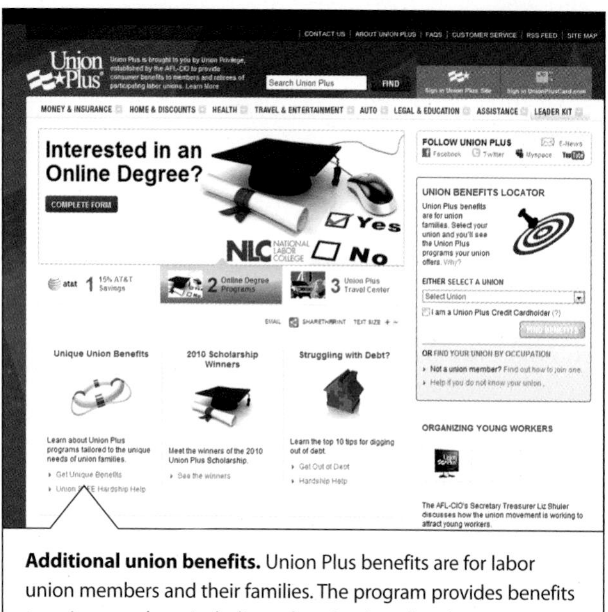

Additional union benefits. Union Plus benefits are for labor union members and their families. The program provides benefits to union members, including education benefits, discounts on consumer services and goods, financial services, grants, and more.

© Courtesy of Union Privilege

Why Some Employees Join Unions

Obviously, employees start or join a union for a variety of reasons. One commonly cited reason is to combat alienation. Some employees—especially those whose jobs are dull and repetitive—may perceive themselves as merely parts of a machine. They may feel that they lose their individual or social identity at work. Union membership is one way to establish contact with others in a firm.

Another common reason for joining a union is the perception that union membership increases job security. No one wants to live in fear of arbitrary or capricious dismissal from a job. Unions actually have only limited ability to guarantee a member's job, but they can help to increase job security by enforcing seniority rules.

Employees may also join a union because of dissatisfaction with one or more elements of their jobs. If they are unhappy with their pay, benefits, or working conditions, they may look to a union to correct the perceived deficiencies.

Some people join unions because of their personal backgrounds. For example, a person whose parents are strong believers in unions might be inclined to feel just as positive about union membership.

In some situations, employees must join a union to keep their jobs. Many unions try, through their labor contracts, to require that a firm's new employees join the union after a specified probationary period. Under the Taft–Hartley Act, states may pass right-to-work laws prohibiting this practice.

Steps in Forming a Union

The first step in forming a union is the *organizing campaign* (see Figure 11.2). Its primary objective is to develop widespread employee interest in having a union. To kick off the campaign, a national union may send organizers to the firm to stir this

Figure 11.2 Steps in Forming a Union

The unionization process consists of a campaign, signing of authorization cards, a formal election, and certification of the election by the NLRB.

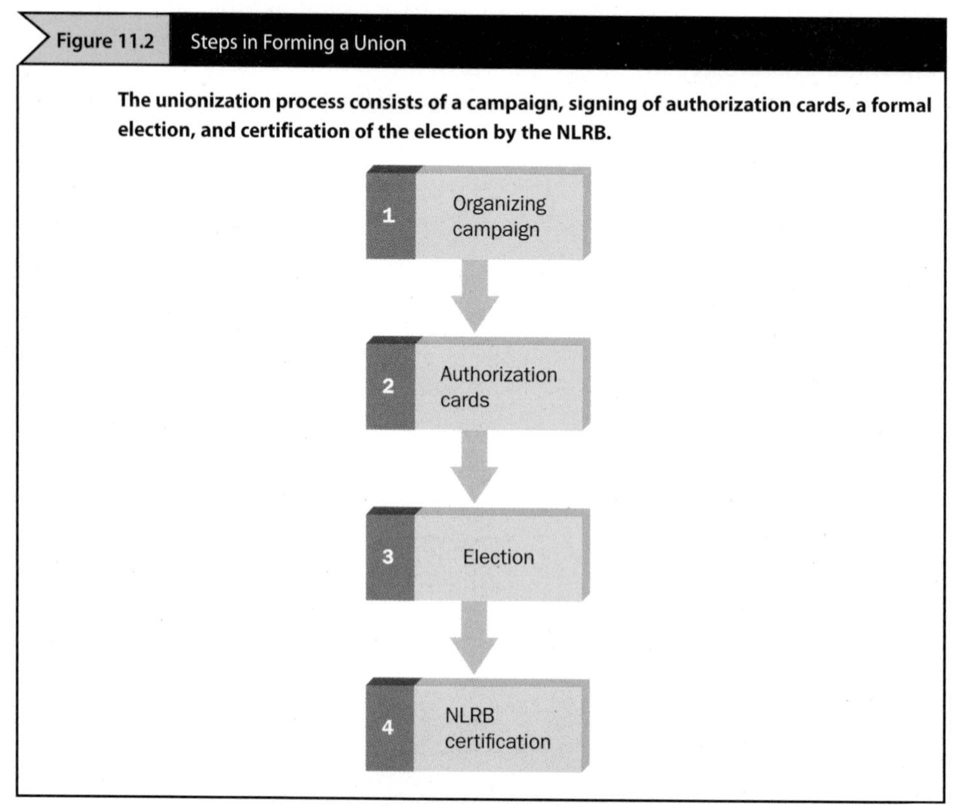

interest. Alternatively, the employees themselves may decide that they want a union. Then they contact the appropriate national union and ask for organizing assistance.

The organizing campaign can be quite emotional, and it may lead to conflict between employees and management. On the one hand, the employees who want the union will be dedicated to its creation. On the other hand, management will be extremely sensitive to what it sees as a potential threat to its power and control.

At some point during the organizing campaign, employees are asked to sign *authorization cards* (see Figure 11.3) to indicate—in writing—their support for the union. Because of various NLRB rules and regulations, both union organizers and company management must be very careful in their behavior during this authorization drive. For example, employees cannot be asked to sign the cards when they are supposed to be working. Management may not indicate in any way that employees' jobs or job security will be in jeopardy if they do sign the cards.

If at least 30 percent of the eligible employees sign authorization cards, the organizers generally request that the firm recognize the union as the employees' bargaining representative. Usually the firm rejects this request, and a *formal election* is held to decide whether to have a union. This election usually involves secret ballots and is conducted by the NLRB. The outcome of the election is determined by a simple majority of eligible employees who choose to vote.

If the union obtains a majority, it becomes the official bargaining agent for its members, and the final step, *NLRB certification*, takes place. The union may immediately begin the process of negotiating a labor contract with management. If the union is voted down, the NLRB will not allow another election for one year.

Figure 11.3 Sample Authorization Card

Unions must have written authorization to represent employees.

OBLIGATION OF

"I ________________________ (PLEASE PRINT NAME), in the presence of members of the ____________ promise and agree to conform to and abide by the Constitution and laws of the ____________ and its Local Unions. I will further the purpose for which the ____________ is instituted. I will bear true allegiance to it and will not sacrifice its interest in any manner."

____
(TO BE SIGNED BY APPLICANT — PLEASE DO NOT PRINT)

PRINT OR TYPE IN BLACK INK ONLY

SEX — MALE ☐ FEMALE ☐

LAST NAME	FIRST	INITIAL	SOCIAL SECURITY NO.
ADDRESS (STREET & NUMBER)			DATE OF BIRTH
CITY & STATE (OR PROVINCE)		POSTAL CODE	TELEPHONE NO.
PRESENT EMPLOYER			DATE HIRED
CLASSIFICATION			DATE OF THIS APPLICATION

Have you ever been a member of ? YES ☐ NO ☐ If so, where? LOCAL NO. ________ STATE ________

PORTION BELOW TO BE FILLED IN BY L.U. SECRETARY

LOCAL UNION NO.	DATE OF INITIATION	TYPE OF MEMBERSHIP	CARD NO.

Several factors can complicate the unionization process. For example, the **bargaining unit**, which is the specific group of employees that the union is to represent, must be defined. Union organizers may want to represent all hourly employees at a particular site (such as all workers at a manufacturing plant), or they may wish to represent only a specific group of employees (such as all electricians in a large manufacturing plant).

Another issue that may have to be resolved is that of **jurisdiction**, which is the right of a particular union to organize particular groups of workers (such as nurses). When jurisdictions overlap or are unclear, the employees themselves may decide who will represent them. In some cases, two or more unions may be trying to organize some or all of the employees of a firm. Then, the election choices may be union A, union B, or no union at all.

The Role of the NLRB

As we have demonstrated, the NLRB is heavily involved in the unionization process. Generally, the NLRB is responsible for overseeing the organizing campaign, conducting the election (if one is warranted), and certifying the election results.

During the organizing campaign, both employers and union organizers can take steps to educate employees regarding the advantages and disadvantages of having a union. However, neither is allowed to use underhanded tactics or to distort the truth. If violations occur, the NLRB can stop the questionable behavior, postpone the election, or set aside the results of an election that has already taken place.

The NLRB usually conducts the election within 45 days of receiving the required number of signed authorization cards from the organizers. A very high percentage of the eligible voters generally participate in the election, and it is held at the workplace during normal working hours. In certain cases, however, a mail ballot or some other form of election may be called for.

Certification of the election involves counting the votes and considering challenges to the election. After the election results are announced, management and the union organizers have five days to challenge the election. The basis for a challenge might be improper conduct before the election or participation by an ineligible voter. After considering any challenges, the NLRB passes final judgment on the election results.

When union representation is established, union and management get down to the serious business of contract negotiations.

bargaining unit the specific group of employees represented by a union

jurisdiction the right of a particular union to organize particular groups of workers

collective bargaining the process of negotiating a labor contract with management

5

Describe the basic elements of the collective-bargaining process.

Collective Bargaining

Once certified by the NLRB, a new union's first task is to establish its own identity and structure. It immediately signs up as many members as possible. Then, in an internal election, members choose officers and representatives. A negotiating committee is also chosen to begin **collective bargaining**, the process of negotiating a labor contract with management.

Union–management negotiation issues. Compensation and employee benefits are often the major issues that company and union leaders negotiate.

© AP Images/M. Spencer Green

The First Contract

To prepare for its first contract session with management, the negotiating committee decides on its position on the various contract issues and determines the issues that are most important to the union's members. For example, the two most pressing concerns might be a general wage increase and an improved benefits package.

The union then informs management that it is ready to begin negotiations, and the two parties agree on a time and location. Both sides continue to prepare for the session up to the actual date of the negotiations.

Negotiations are occasionally held on company premises, but it is more common for the parties to meet away from the workplace—perhaps in a local hotel. The union typically is represented by the negotiating committee and one or more officials from the regional or national union office. The firm normally is represented by managers from the industrial-relations, operations, human resources management, and legal departments. Each side is required by law to negotiate in good faith and not to stall or attempt to extend the bargaining proceedings unnecessarily.

The union normally presents its contract demands first. Management then responds to the demands, often with a counterproposal. The bargaining may move back and forth, from proposal to counterproposal, over a number of meetings. Throughout the process, union representatives constantly keep their members informed of what is going on and how the negotiating committee feels about the various proposals and counterproposals.

Each side clearly tries to "get its own way" as much as possible, but each also recognizes the need for compromise. For example, the union may begin the negotiations by demanding a wage increase of $1 per hour but may be willing to accept 60 cents per hour. Management initially may offer 40 cents but may be willing to pay 75 cents. Eventually, the two sides will agree on a wage increase of between 60 and 75 cents per hour.

If an agreement cannot be reached, the union may strike. However, strikes are rare during a union's first contract negotiations. In most cases, the negotiating teams are able to agree on an initial contract without recourse to a strike.

The final step in collective bargaining is **ratification**, which is approval of the contract by a vote of the union membership. If the membership accepts the terms of the contract, it is signed and becomes a legally binding agreement. If the contract is not ratified, the negotiators must go back and try to iron out a more acceptable agreement.

Later Contracts

A labor contract may cover a period of one to three years or more, but every contract has an expiration date. As that date approaches, both management and the union begin to prepare for new contract negotiations. Now, however, the entire process is likely to be much thornier than the first negotiation.

For one thing, the union and the firm have "lived with each other" for several years, during which some difficulties may have emerged. Each side may see certain issues as being of critical importance—issues that provoke a great deal of emotion at the bargaining table and often are difficult to resolve. Also, each side has learned from the earlier negotiations. Each may take a harder line on certain issues and be less willing to compromise.

The contract deadline itself also produces tension. As the expiration date of the existing contract draws near, each side feels a pressure—real or imagined—to reach an agreement. This pressure may nudge the negotiators toward an agreement, but it also can have the opposite effect, making an accord more difficult to reach. Moreover, at some point during the negotiations, union leaders are likely to take a *strike vote*. This vote reveals whether union members are willing to strike in the event that a new contract is not negotiated before the old one expires. In almost all cases, this vote supports a strike. Thus, the threat of a strike may add to the pressure mounting on both sides as they go about the business of negotiating.

Union–Management Contract Issues

6

Identify the major issues covered in a union–management contract.

As you might expect, many diverse issues are negotiated by unions and management and are incorporated into a labor contract. Unions tend to emphasize issues related to members' income, their standard of living, and the strength of the union. Management's primary goals are to retain as much control as possible over the firm's operations and to maximize its strength relative to that of the union. The balance of power between union and management varies from firm to firm.

Employee Pay

An area of bargaining central to union–management relations is employee pay. Three separate issues are usually involved: the forms of pay, the magnitude of pay, and the means by which the magnitude of pay will be determined.

ratification approval of a labor contract by a vote of the union membership

Forms of Pay The primary form of pay is direct compensation—the wage or salary and benefits an employee receives in exchange for his or her contribution to the organization. Because direct compensation is a fairly straightforward issue, negotiators often spend much more of their time developing a benefits package for employees. Because the range of benefits and their costs have escalated over the years, this element of pay has become increasingly important and complex.

We discussed the various employee benefits in Chapter 9. Of these, health, life, disability, and dental insurance are important benefits that unions try to obtain for their members. As the costs of health care continue to increase, insurance benefits are costing employers more, and many are trying to pass a higher portion of this increased cost on to their employees. Deferred compensation, in the form of pension or retirement programs, is also a common focal point. Decisions about deferred compensation can have a long-lasting impact on a company.

Other benefits commonly dealt with in the bargaining process include paid vacation time, holidays, and a policy on paid sick leave. Obviously, unions argue for as much paid vacation and holiday time as possible and for liberal sick-leave policies. Management naturally takes the opposite position.

Magnitude of Pay Of considerable importance is the *magnitude*, or amount, of pay that employees receive as both direct and indirect compensation. The union attempts to ensure that pay is on par with that received by other employees in the same or similar industries, both locally and nationally. The union also attempts to include in the contract clauses that provide pay increases over the life of the agreement. The most common is the *cost-of-living clause*, which ties periodic pay increases to increases in the cost of living, as defined by various economic statistics or indicators.

Of course, the magnitude of pay is also affected by the organization's ability to pay. If the firm has posted large profits recently, the union may expect large pay increases for its members. If the firm has not been very profitable, the union may agree to smaller pay hikes or even to a pay freeze. In an extreme situation (e.g., when the firm is bordering on bankruptcy), the union may agree to pay cuts. Very stringent conditions usually are included in any agreement to a pay cut.

Bargaining with regard to magnitude also revolves around employee benefits. At one extreme, unions seek a wide range of benefits, entirely or largely paid for by the firm. At the other extreme, management may be willing to offer the benefits package but may want its employees to bear most of the cost. Again, factors such as equity (with similar firms and jobs) and ability to pay enter into the final agreement.

Pay Determinants Negotiators also address the question of how individual pay will be determined. For management, the ideal arrangement is to tie wages to each employee's productivity. As we have seen, this method of payment tends to motivate and reward effort. Unions, on the other hand, feel that this arrangement can create unnecessary competition among employees. They generally argue that employees should be paid—at least in part—according to seniority. **Seniority** is the length of time an employee has worked for an organization.

Determinants regarding benefits are also negotiated. For example, management may want to provide profit-sharing benefits only to employees who have worked for the firm for a specified number of years. The union may want these benefits provided to all employees.

Working Hours

The number of working hours is another important issue in contract negotiations. The matter of overtime is of special interest. Federal law defines **overtime** as time worked in excess of 40 hours in one week. It also specifies that overtime pay must be at least one-and-one-half times the normal hourly wage. Unions may also attempt to negotiate overtime rates for all hours worked beyond eight hours in a single day. Similarly, the union may attempt to obtain higher overtime rates (say, twice the normal hourly wage) for weekend or holiday work. Still another issue is an upper limit to overtime, beyond which employees can refuse to work.

seniority the length of time an employee has worked for an organization

overtime time worked in excess of 40 hours in one week (under some union contracts, time worked in excess of eight hours in a single day)

Ethical Challenges & SUCCESSFUL SOLUTIONS

How Much Say Should Unions Have?

Unions want to protect their members' interests, but how much say should they have in corporate decisions? This is an important consideration for companies with workforces that are partly or completely unionized, especially when mergers and acquisitions are in the works. Unions have publicly expressed concern about some recent airline mergers, bringing up issues such as loss of seniority and reduced benefits.

Other acquisitions have provoked union objections, as well. For example, the Communications Workers of America spoke out when Verizon Communications agreed to sell its landline phone business to Frontier Communications. Verizon viewed the $8.6 billion deal, involving 4.8 million landlines in 14 states, as a way to divest a slow-growing division. For its part, Frontier saw an opportunity to significantly increase its geographic reach and its revenue.

For months after the deal was announced, the union held demonstrations to capture the attention of federal and state regulators. It argued that Frontier would have so much debt that it would eventually have to lay off employees. The union also said that Frontier would not have the resources to invest in service upgrades. Frontier said the deal would help its financial situation and promised to honor Verizon's contracts with the union. State regulators eventually approved the deal. But how much influence should unions have over these kinds of corporate decisions?

Sources: Eric Eyre, "PSC Orders Verizon to Put Aside Millions for Customer Service," *Charleston Gazette (West Virginia)*, May 10, 2010, http://wvgazette.com; "Verizon, Frontier Assail Union's Latest Move," *Charleston Gazette*, May 3, 2010, http://wvgazette.com; Roger Cheng, "Union Pushes Back on Verizon," *The Wall Street Journal*, April 12, 2010, http://www.wsj.com; Carrie Jones, "Rally Protests Verizon-Frontier Deal," *WSAZ NewsChannel 3*, January 10, 2010, http://www.wsaz.com; Jeremy Edwards, "Communication Workers Protest Verizon-Frontier Merger," *WSAZ NewsChannel 3*, April 15, 2010, http://www.wsaz.com.

In firms with two or more work shifts, workers on less-desirable shifts are paid a premium for their time. Both the amount of the premium and the manner in which workers are chosen for (or choose) particular shifts are negotiable issues. Other issues related to working hours are the work starting times and the length of lunch periods and coffee breaks.

job security protection against the loss of employment

union security protection of the union's position as the employees' bargaining agent

closed shop a workplace in which workers must join the union before they are hired; outlawed by the Taft–Hartley Act

Security

Security actually covers two issues. One is the job security of the individual worker; the other is the security of the union as the bargaining representative of the firm's employees.

Job security is protection against the loss of employment. It is a major concern of individuals. As we noted earlier, the desire for increased job security is a major reason for joining unions in the first place. In the typical labor contract, job security is based on seniority. If employees must be laid off or dismissed, those with the least seniority are the first to go. Some of the more senior employees may have to move to lower-level jobs, but they remain employed.

Union security is protection of the union's position as the employees' bargaining agent. Union security is frequently a more volatile issue than job security. Unions strive for as much security as possible, but management tends to see an increase in union security as an erosion of its control.

Using a strike to negotiate. A strike can increase public support for a union's position and decrease a firm's ability to operate effectively.

Union security arises directly from its membership. The greater the ratio of union employees to non-union employees, the more secure the union is. In contract negotiations, unions thus attempt to establish various union membership conditions. The most restrictive of these is the **closed shop**, in which workers must join the union before they are hired. This condition was outlawed by the Taft–Hartley Act, but several other arrangements, including the following, are subject to negotiation:

- The **union shop**, in which new employees must join the union after a specified probationary period
- The **agency shop**, in which employees can choose not to join the union but must pay dues to the union anyway (The idea is that non-union employees benefit from union activities and should help to support them.)
- The **maintenance shop**, in which an employee who joins the union must remain a union member as long as he or she is employed by the firm

Management Rights

Of particular interest to the firm are those rights and privileges that are to be retained by management. For example, the firm wants as much control as possible over whom it hires, how work is scheduled, and how discipline is handled. The union, in contrast, would like some control over these and other matters affecting its members. It is interesting that some unions are making progress toward their goal of playing a more direct role in corporate governance. Some union executives have, in fact, been given seats on corporate boards of directors.

union shop a workplace in which new employees must join the union after a specified probationary period

agency shop a workplace in which employees can choose not to join the union but must pay dues to the union anyway

maintenance shop a workplace in which an employee who joins the union must remain a union member as long as he or she is employed by the firm

grievance procedure a formally established course of action for resolving employee complaints against management

shop steward an employee elected by union members to serve as their representative

Grievance Procedures

A **grievance procedure** is a formally established course of action for resolving employee complaints against management. Virtually every labor contract contains a grievance procedure. Procedures vary in scope and detail, but they may involve the four steps described below (see Figure 11.4).

Original Grievance The process begins with an employee who believes that he or she has been treated unfairly in violation of the labor contract. For example, an employee may be entitled to a formal performance review after six months on the job. If no such review is conducted, the employee may file a grievance. To do so, the employee explains the grievance to a **shop steward**, an employee elected by union

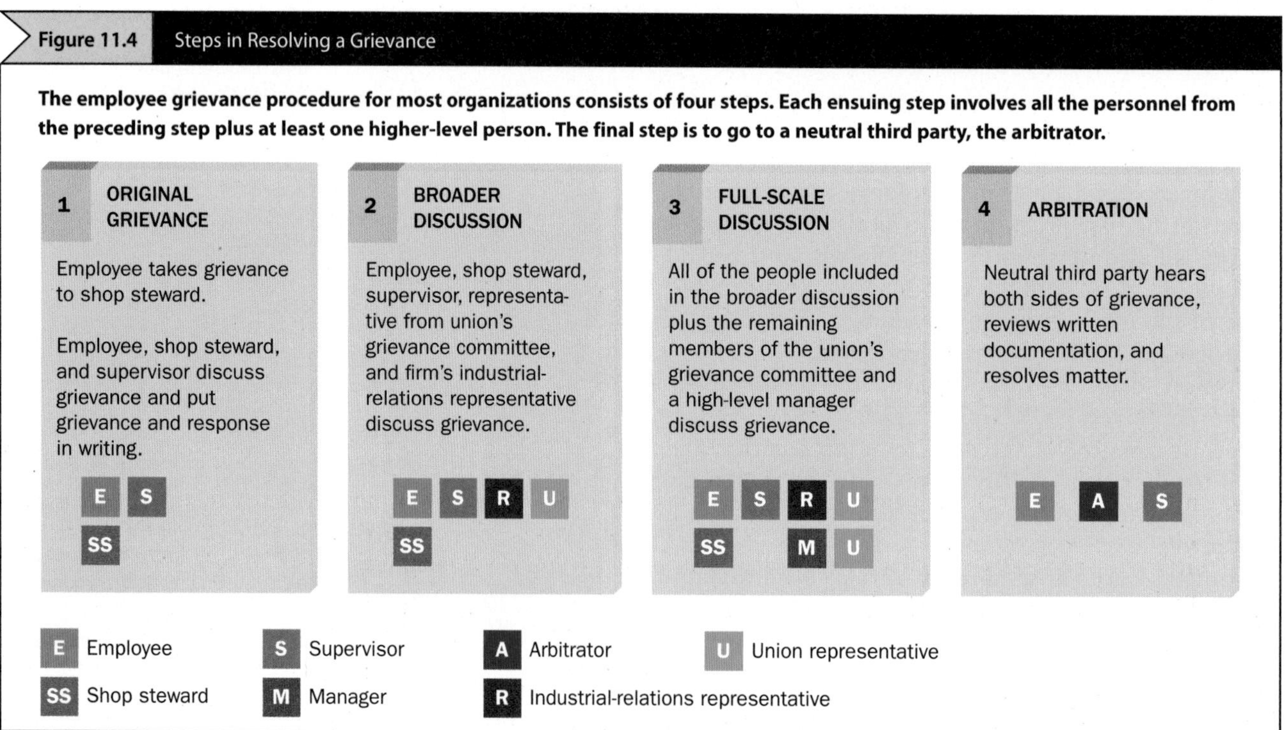

members to serve as their representative. The employee and the steward then discuss the grievance with the employee's immediate supervisor. Both the grievance and the supervisor's response are put in writing.

Broader Discussion In most cases, the problem is resolved during the initial discussion with the supervisor. If it is not, a second discussion is held. Now the participants include the original parties (employee, supervisor, and steward), a representative from the union's grievance committee, and the firm's industrial-relations representative. Again, a record is kept of the discussion and its results.

Full-Scale Discussion If the grievance is still not resolved, a full-scale discussion is arranged. This discussion includes everyone involved in the broader discussion, as well as all remaining members of the union's grievance committee and another high-level manager. As usual, all proceedings are put in writing. All participants are careful not to violate the labor contract during this attempt to resolve the complaint.

Arbitration The final step in a grievance procedure is **arbitration**, in which a neutral third party hears the two sides of a dispute and renders a binding decision. As in a court hearing, each side presents its case and has the right to cross-examine witnesses. In addition, the arbitrator reviews the written documentation of all previous steps in the grievance procedure. Both sides may then give summary arguments and/or present briefs. The arbitrator then decides whether a provision of the labor contract has been violated and proposes a remedy. The arbitrator cannot make any decision that would add to, detract from, or modify the terms of the contract. If it can be proved that the arbitrator exceeded the scope of his or her authority, either party may appeal the decision to the courts.

What actually happens when union and management "lock horns" over all the issues we have mentioned? We can answer this question by looking now at the negotiating tools each side can wield.

Union and Management Negotiating Tools

Explain the primary bargaining tools available to unions and management.

Management and unions can draw on certain tools to influence each other during contract negotiations. Both sides may use advertising and publicity to gain support for their respective positions. The most extreme tools are strikes and lockouts, but there are other, milder techniques as well.

Strikes

Unions only go out on strike in a very few instances. These almost always occur after an existing labor contract has expired. (In 2009, there were only five major strikes in the United States, which was the lowest number since strikes began to be documented by the government in 1947.)[5] Even then, if new contract negotiations seem to be proceeding smoothly, a union does not actually start a strike. The union does take a strike vote, but the vote may be used primarily to show members' commitment to a strike if negotiations fail.

The main objective of a strike is to put financial pressure on the company to encourage management to meet union demands. The recent strike at Boeing Company, where 27,000 union members walked off their jobs in a dispute over job security, pay, and benefits, cost the company about $100 million a day in lost revenue. Thirty-two days after the strike began, Boeing Company and the Machinists Union agreed to resume negotiations.[6] When union members do go out on strike, it is usually because negotiations seem to be stalled. A strike is simply a work stoppage: The employees do not report for work. In addition, striking workers engage in **picketing**, marching back and forth in front of a place of employment with signs informing the public that a strike is in progress. In doing so, they hope that (1) the

arbitration the step in a grievance procedure in which a neutral third party hears the two sides of a dispute and renders a binding decision

picketing marching back and forth in front of a place of employment with signs informing the public that a strike is in progress

public will be sympathetic to the strikers and will not patronize the struck firm, (2) nonstriking employees of the firm will honor the picket line and not report to work, and (3) members of other unions will not cross the picket line (e.g., to make deliveries) and thus will further restrict the operations of the struck firm. Unions may also engage in informational picketing to let companies know of their dissatisfaction. Philadelphia, for example, experienced major problems when nearly 5,000 members of the Transport Workers Union went on a six-day strike. The strike shut down most of the city's subways, buses, and trolleys, causing its almost 1 million daily commuters to rely on taxis, cars, and their own feet. The striking workers were angry over contract negotiations that reduced pensions and caused disagreements on some work rule issues.[7]

Obviously, strikes are expensive to both the firm and the strikers. The firm loses business and earnings during the strike, and the striking workers lose the wages they would have earned if they had been at their jobs. During a strike, unions try to provide their members with as much support as possible. Larger unions are able to put a portion of their members' dues into a *strike fund*. The fund is used to provide financial support for striking union members. At times, workers may go out on a **wildcat strike**, which is a strike that has not been approved by the union. In this situation, union leaders typically work with management to convince the strikers to return to work.

Slowdowns and Boycotts

Almost every labor contract contains a clause that prohibits strikes during the life of the contract. (This is why strikes, if they occur, usually take place after a contract has expired.) However, a union may strike a firm while the contract is in force if members believe that management has violated its terms. Workers also may engage in a **slowdown**, a technique whereby workers report to their jobs but work at a pace that is slower than normal.

A **boycott** is a refusal to do business with a particular firm. Unions occasionally bring this strategy to bear by urging members (and sympathizers) not to purchase the products of a firm with which they are having a dispute. The Major League Baseball players' union joined a growing number of organizations that boycotted Arizona after the state passed a law that gave police unprecedented powers to determine anyone's immigration status. In addition to expressing their disapproval of the law, many big-league teams vowed they would not attend the 2011 All-Star Game, scheduled to be held in Arizona, unless it was moved to another state.[8] A *primary boycott*, aimed at the employer directly involved in the dispute, can be a powerful weapon. A *secondary boycott*, aimed at a firm doing business with the employer, is prohibited by the Taft–Hartley Act. Cesar Chavez, a migrant worker who founded the United Farm Workers Union, used boycotts to draw attention to the low pay and awful conditions endured by produce pickers.

wildcat strike a strike not approved by the strikers' union

slowdown a technique whereby workers report to their jobs but work at a slower pace than normal

boycott a refusal to do business with a particular firm

lockout a firm's refusal to allow employees to enter the workplace

Picketing. Picketing is used to publicize that a strike is occurring. In this illustration, hospital workers are picketing to inform the public that they are on strike because they have been working without a contract for over six months.

© AP Images/Matt Rourke

Lockouts and Strikebreakers

Management's most potent weapon is the lockout. In a **lockout**, the firm refuses to allow employees to enter the workplace. Like strikes, lockouts are expensive for both the firm and its employees. For this reason, they are only used rarely and in certain circumstances. A firm that produces perishable goods, for example, may use a lockout if management believes that its employees will soon go on strike. The idea is to stop production in time to ensure minimal spoilage of finished goods or work-in-process.

Management also may attempt to hire strikebreakers. A **strikebreaker** is a non-union employee who performs the job of a striking union member. Hiring strikebreakers can result in violence when picketing employees confront the non-union workers at the entrance to the struck facility. The firm also faces the problem of finding qualified replacements for the striking workers. Sometimes management personnel take over the jobs of strikers. Managers at telephone companies have handled the switchboards on more than one occasion.

Mediation and Arbitration

Strikes, strikebreaking, lockouts, and boycotts all pit one side against the other. Ultimately, one side "wins" and the other "loses." Unfortunately, the negative effects of such actions—including resentment, fear, and distrust—may linger for months or years after a dispute has been resolved.

More productive techniques that are being used increasingly are mediation and arbitration. Either one may come into play before a labor contract expires or after some other strategy, such as a strike, has proved ineffective.

Mediation is the use of a neutral third party to assist management and the union during their negotiations. This third party (the mediator) listens to both sides, trying to find common ground for agreement. The mediator also tries to facilitate communication between the two sides, to promote compromise, and generally to keep the negotiations moving. At first the mediator may meet privately with each side. Eventually, however, his or her goal is to get the two to settle their differences. The Federal Mediation and Conciliation Service (FMCS) is an independent government agency that handles mediation for labor disputes. The FMCS resolved a strike led by employees of aircraft maker Hawker Beechcraft by helping the company and the Machinists Union reach a tentative contract deal after several days of negotiations.[9] The agency handles 4,800 collective-bargaining negotiations per year, with 86 percent of those mediations reaching an agreement from both parties. The agency reports to have saved businesses and workers approximately $18 billion during 1999–2009, showing the benefits of mediation for both parties.[10]

Unlike mediation, the *arbitration* step is a formal hearing. Just as it may be the final step in a grievance procedure, it also may be used in contract negotiations (perhaps after mediation attempts) when the two sides cannot agree on one or more issues. Here, the arbitrator hears the formal positions of both parties on outstanding, unresolved issues. The arbitrator then analyzes these positions and makes a decision on the possible resolution of the issues. If both sides have agreed in advance that the arbitration will be *binding*, they must accept the arbitrator's decision.

If mediation and arbitration are unsuccessful, then, under the provisions of the Taft–Hartley Act, the President of the United States can obtain a temporary injunction to prevent or stop a strike if it would jeopardize national health or security.

This chapter ends our discussion of human resources. Next, we examine the marketing function of business. We begin in Chapter 12 by discussing the meaning of the term *marketing*.

Sustaining the Planet

The Sierra Club and Green Jobs

The Sierra Club, dedicated to environmental protection, is promoting green jobs by working with legislators to build a greener economy, working with labor unions to ensure fair treatment of employees in green jobs, and encouraging the creation of green jobs to clean up the planet. Take a look: http://www.sierraclub.org/greenjobs/default.aspx.

strikebreaker a non-union employee who performs the job of a striking union member

mediation the use of a neutral third party to assist management and the union during their negotiations

return to inside business

Southwest Airlines Pilots' Association

The Southwest Airlines Pilots' Association (SWAPA) engages in collective bargaining on behalf of its members, the pilots who fly for Southwest Airlines. Among the issues it negotiates with airline management are pilot pay, retirement benefits, and flexible work schedules. Although SWAPA is not part of any national or international union, it joins with the Coalition of Airline Pilots Associations to communicate its views on airline safety and security to federal legislators and regulators.

Because SWAPA's relations with Southwest Airlines are governed by the Railway Labor Act, certain negotiating tools (such as strikes) are not permitted. When the pilots failed to ratify a tentative contract agreement in 2009, neither the union nor the airline threatened to take any extreme measures. Instead, they reopened talks and, weeks later, hammered out a deal that ultimately was approved, with 87 percent of the union members voting to ratify the new agreement.

Questions

1. How would you describe relations between Southwest Airlines and its pilots' union? Do you think the two sides should aim for speedier negotiations, considering that the 2006 contract talks stretched over nearly three years?
2. Do you agree that airline pilots should not be allowed to strike? Explain your answer.

CHAPTER REVIEW

SUMMARY

Summary

1 Explain how and why labor unions came into being.

A labor union is an organization of workers who act together to negotiate wages and working conditions with their employers. Labor relations are the dealings between labor unions and business management.

The first major union in the United States was the Knights of Labor, formed in 1869 to eliminate the depersonalization of workers. The Knights were followed in 1886 by the American Federation of Labor (AFL). The goal of the AFL was to improve its members' living standards without changing the business system. In 1905, the radical Industrial Workers of the World (IWW) was formed; its goal was to overthrow capitalism. Of these three, only the AFL remained when the Congress of Industrial Organizations (CIO) was founded as a body of industrial unions between World War I and World War II. After years of competing, the AFL and CIO merged in 1955. The largest union not affiliated with the AFL–CIO is the Teamsters Union.

2 Discuss the sources of unions' negotiating power and trends in union membership.

The power of unions to negotiate with management comes from two sources. The first is the size of their membership. The second is the groups of laws that guarantee unions the right to negotiate and that regulate the negotiation process. At present, union membership accounts for less than 15 percent of the American workforce, and it seems to be decreasing for various reasons. Nonetheless, unions wield considerable power in many industries—those in which their members comprise a large proportion of the workforce.

Many unions today are entering into partnerships with management rather than maintaining their traditional adversarial position. Unions and management cooperate to increase production, improve quality, lower costs, empower workers, and enhance the workplace. Limited partnerships center on accomplishing one specific task or project. Long-range strategic partnerships focus on sharing decision-making power for a range of workplace and business matters.

3 Identify the main focus of several major pieces of labor–management legislation.

Important laws that affect union power are the Norris–LaGuardia Act (limits management's ability to obtain injunctions against unions), the Wagner Act (forbids certain unfair labor practices by management), the Fair Labor Standards Act (allows the federal government to set the minimum wage and to mandate overtime rates), the Taft–Hartley Act (forbids certain unfair practices by unions), and the Landrum–Griffin Act (regulates the internal functioning of labor unions). The National Labor Relations Board (NLRB), a federal agency that oversees union–management relations, was created by the Wagner Act.

Enumerate the steps involved in forming a union and show how the National Labor Relations Board is involved in the process.

Attempts to form a union within a firm begin with an organizing campaign to develop widespread employee interest in having a union. Next, employees sign authorization cards, indicating in writing their support for the union. The third step is to hold a formal election to decide whether to have a union. Finally, if the union obtains a majority, it receives NLRB certification, making it the official bargaining agent for its members. The entire process is supervised by the NLRB, which oversees the organizing campaign, conducts the election, and certifies the election results.

Describe the basic elements of the collective-bargaining process.

Once a union is established, it may negotiate a labor contract with management through the process of collective bargaining. First, the negotiating committee decides on its position on the various contract issues. The union informs management that it is ready to begin negotiations, and a time and place are set. The union is represented by the negotiating committee, and the organization is represented by managers from several departments in the company. Each side is required to negotiate in good faith and not to stall or attempt to extend the bargaining unnecessarily. The final step is ratification, which is approval of the contract by a vote of the union membership.

Identify the major issues covered in a union–management contract.

As the expiration date of an existing contract approaches, management and the union begin to negotiate a new contract. Contract issues include employee pay and benefits, working hours, job and union security, management rights, and grievance procedures.

Explain the primary bargaining tools available to unions and management.

Management and unions can use certain tools to sway one another—and public opinion—during contract negotiations. Advertising and publicity help each side to gain support. When contract negotiations do not run smoothly, unions may apply pressure on management through strikes, slowdowns, or boycotts. Management may counter by imposing lockouts or hiring strikebreakers. Less drastic techniques for breaking contract deadlocks are mediation and arbitration. In both, a neutral third party is involved in the negotiations.

Key Terms

You should now be able to define and give an example relevant to each of the following terms:

labor union (308)
union–management (labor) relations (308)
craft union (309)
strike (310)
industrial union (311)
National Labor Relations Board (NLRB) (314)
injunction (315)
bargaining unit (318)
jurisdiction (318)
collective bargaining (318)
ratification (319)
seniority (320)
overtime (320)
job security (321)
union security (321)
closed shop (321)
union shop (322)
agency shop (322)
maintenance shop (322)
grievance procedure (322)
shop steward (322)
arbitration (323)
picketing (323)
wildcat strike (324)
slowdown (324)
boycott (324)
lockout (324)
strikebreaker (325)
mediation (325)

Review Questions

1. Briefly describe the history of unions in the United States.
2. Describe the three characteristics common to most union–management partnerships. Discuss the benefits of union–management partnerships to management, unions, and workers.
3. How has government regulation of union–management relations evolved during this century?
4. For what reasons do employees start or join unions?
5. Describe the process of forming a union, and explain the role of the National Labor Relations Board (NLRB) in this process.
6. List the major areas that are negotiated in a labor contract.
7. Explain the three issues involved in negotiations concerning employee pay.
8. What is the difference between job security and union security? How do unions attempt to enhance union security?
9. What is a grievance? Describe the typical grievance procedure.
10. What are the steps involved in collective bargaining?
11. Why are strikes and lockouts relatively rare nowadays?
12. What are the objectives of picketing?
13. In what ways do the techniques of mediation and arbitration differ?

Discussion Questions

1. Do unions really derive their power mainly from their membership and labor legislation? What are some other sources of union power?
2. Which labor contract issues are likely to be the easiest to resolve? Which are likely to be the most difficult?
3. Discuss the following statement: Union security means job security for union members.
4. How would you prepare for labor contract negotiations as a member of management? As head of the union negotiating committee?
5. Under what circumstances are strikes and lockouts justified in place of mediation or arbitration?

Video Case 11.1

Understanding Labor Unions with the Writers Guild of America

Most people probably don't think "Hollywood" when they think "unions." Perhaps they think of truck drivers, teachers, autoworkers, electricians, and other members of powerful and well-known labor unions. But in fact, the Writers Guild of America (WGA) is a long-standing and potent force in the media business and has been protecting and advocating for creative workers across the United States for over 50 years.

The Guild consists of two separate unions that are loosely linked but often act together—the Writers Guild East and the Writers Guild West. It's a not-for-profit organization whose members include thousands of graphic artists and writers for motion pictures, television, radio, newscasts, and increasingly the Internet. One direct result of the three-month writers' strike in 2008 was the Guild's extension of its jurisdiction to include Internet content, and the organization is now in the process of developing rules to protect and govern its members' work online. The Guild has created the position of New Media Project Manager for this purpose.

As one writer associated with a late-night TV talk show observed, in the entertainment business "all ideas start with the writer. Without writers you don't have a business at all—we start the ball rolling." That's the kind of pride in authorship that members of the Guild readily feel with the power of their union behind them.

The main purpose of the Writers Guild union is to protect its members, ensuring they get proper credit for their work and are properly paid. Compensation for scriptwriters consists of two parts: up-front money, which is paid on delivery of the work, and residuals, which are continuing payments made when the work is reused—for instance, when a show is rerun or goes into syndication. One way the Guild protects members is by receiving their residuals directly from the networks and other broadcasters, so it can check their accuracy before turning the money over to the individual writer who earned it. The Guild maintains a complex monitoring system that allows it to track reruns and verify payments and crediting. When something goes wrong—if someone isn't properly paid or credited—the Guild will step in on the writer's behalf. In the event of disagreements, the Guild will take the case to arbitration to ensure the writer gets what he or she has earned.

Most networks are closed shops, meaning writers must belong to the union to work there. In return, the Guild provides benefits like health care plans and pensions. Members' income can range widely, so the Guild makes special efforts to draw them together and develop the kind of solidarity that can make picketing and strikes effective. Recently, for instance, almost 1,000 WGA members filed a class-action lawsuit against two leading talent agencies claiming age discrimination. A $4.5 million settlement fund was the result.

Picketing has been successful, too. WGA picket lines recently won members protection against employers' ability to fire workers at will (employment at will means an employee can be fired at any time for almost any reason and with few legal rights). And strikes, while costly to all parties, can get good, if imperfect, results for union members. The 2008 writers' strike, for instance, sought a penny increase in the fee writers earned from the sale of movie videos and a percentage of the income from foreign sales of films (many U.S. films earn even more money abroad than they do at home). After three long months of a strike that disrupted the fall seasons of many top-rated TV shows and left other workers associated with those shows temporarily out of work, the strike ended with the achievement of only one of the goals—the percentage of foreign sales. Union officials were satisfied that the deal made everyone at least a little bit happy, and from that perspective it was a good outcome.

The WGA continues to support creative workers in the entertainment area. Writers Guild West recently came out in support of Hollywood's composers and lyricists, who are currently not unionized but are seeking entry to Teamsters Local 399. "We're very supportive," said a Guild spokesperson. "We consider composers and lyricists our colleagues, and we believe they deserve the benefits of a union contract."[11]

Questions

1. Should union members in nonessential industries like entertainment have the right to strike when their actions may put others out of work as well?
2. Do you think a labor dispute outcome that leaves both sides partly satisfied is a good outcome? Why or why not?
3. Union membership in the United States has been on a slow decline for about 30 years. What factors do you think account for this drop?

Case 11.2

When Nurses and Hospitals Don't Agree

What happens when unionized nurses and hospital administrators do not agree? Not long ago, the California Nurses Association threatened a one-day strike against dozens of California hospitals. The union wanted to call attention to its serious concerns about hospitals' preparations for protecting nurses against the potentially deadly H1N1 swine flu. At the time, 200 people in California had died from the flu strain, and hospitals around the state were coping with an influx of patients suffering from swine flu. The union was also in the middle of negotiating a new contract for its members, seeking higher pay and higher staffing levels than specified in the previous contract, which had expired months earlier.

Only days before the strike was scheduled to take place, however, it was called off as union negotiators and hospital administrators sat down with a federal mediator and worked to resolve their differences. The two sides were able to reach an agreement, and the union's members ratified the contract, which included extra safety precautions to protect nurses against swine flu.

This is only one example of how complex the negotiations can be when nurses' unions and hospital management disagree. Adding to the challenge, the U.S. health care system is currently facing two conflicting issues: a shortage of nurses and pressure to contain costs while providing proper medical care. The quality of care is, in fact, an important consideration for both sides, especially in light of research published by the National Bureau of Economic Research. Covering 50 nurses' strikes in New York state hospitals over 20 years, the study found higher mortality rates and higher readmission rates among patients hospitalized during the strikes, even when hospitals hired replacement nurses to cover for those on the picket line.

Because the stakes are so high, some nurses' unions are banding together to boost their advocacy efforts. In 2009, the California Nurses Association, the Massachusetts Nurses Association, and the United American Nurses merged to create National Nurses United, a union which has 150,000 members nationwide. The union's top priority is to lobby for a higher ratio of nurses to patients.

Strikes are not the only way a nurses' union can put the spotlight on their concerns. When members of the Washington State Nursing Association were unhappy with proposed contract changes that could limit rest breaks, the nurses walked an informational picket line outside the Providence Sacred Heart Medical Center. The nurses were worried about fatigue affecting the quality of care, and they wanted to ensure that they had a full ten minutes of break time every four hours to rest. Rather than call a strike, nurses carried explanatory picket signs outside the hospital before and after their regular shifts. This nurses' union also set up an informational picket line when its contract negotiations with Tacoma General Hospital were stalled over pay increases and changes to retirement programs.

Sometimes nurses' unions and hospital administrators disagree on other issues. The Pennsylvania Association of Staff Nurses and Allied Professionals decided to strike Temple University Hospital in Pennsylvania after working without a contract for months. One of the key reasons was to protest a clause preventing union leaders and members from publicly criticizing hospital administration and staff. The hospital's CEO said the "non-disparagement" clause would not prevent nurses from alerting administrators to concerns about patient care. Other issues included pay, retirement programs, and college-tuition benefits for the children of hospital workers. The hospital hired 850 temporary nurses to maintain staffing levels during the strike, which lasted for a month. At the end, union and hospital negotiators bargained for days about the issues that had divided them, reached an agreement acceptable to both sides, and the union promptly ratified the new multiyear contract.[12]

Questions

1. Identify the major issues that have led to disagreements between nurses' unions and hospitals. Which do you think are most important for each side, and why?
2. Why would a nurses' union choose an informational picket instead of a strike when it wants to call attention to important contract issues?
3. Should U.S. lawmakers forbid nurses' unions from striking unless mediation and arbitration fail to settle their disputes with management?

Building Skills for Career Success

❶ JOURNALING FOR SUCCESS

Discovery statement: This chapter focused on the unionization process and why employees join unions.

Assignment

1. What are the major reasons for joining and being a part of a labor union?
2. Under what conditions would you like to be a union member?
3. Are there any circumstances under which a striking union member should cross a picket line and go back to work? Explain.
4. Will the unions in the United States grow or decline over the next decade? Why?

❷ EXPLORING THE INTERNET

Union Web sites provide a wealth of information about union activities and concerns. Just as a corporate home page gives a firm the opportunity to describe its mission and goals and present its image to the world, so too does a Web site allow a union to speak to its membership as well as to the public at large. Visit the text Web site for updates to this exercise.

Assignment

1. Visit the following Web sites:

   AFL–CIO: http://www.aflcio.com
   United Auto Workers: http://www.uaw.org
2. What are the mission statements of these unions?
3. Briefly describe your impression of the areas of interest to union members.
4. What is your impression of the tone of these Web sites? Do they differ in any way from a typical business Web site?

❸ DEVELOPING CRITICAL-THINKING SKILLS

Recently, while on its final approach to an airport in Lubbock, Texas, a commercial airliner encountered a flock of ducks. The flight crew believed that one or more of the ducks hit the aircraft and were ingested into the plane's main engine. The aircraft landed safely and taxied to the terminal. The flight crew advised the maintenance and operations crews of the incident. Operations grounded the plane until it could be inspected, but because of the time of day, maintenance personnel available to perform the inspection were in short supply. A supervisor, calling from an overtime list, made calls until contacting two available off-duty mechanics. They worked on overtime pay to perform the inspection and return the aircraft to a safe flying status. Several days after the inspection, a mechanic on the overtime list who was not home when the supervisor called complained that she had been denied overtime. This union member believed that the company owed her overtime pay for the same number of hours worked by a mechanic who performed the actual inspection. The company disagreed. What options are available to resolve this conflict?

Assignment

1. Using the following questions as guidelines, determine how this dispute can be resolved.
   a. What options are available to the unhappy mechanic? What process must she pursue? How does this process work?
   b. Do you believe that the mechanic should receive pay for the time she did not work? Justify your answer.
   c. What do you think was the final outcome of this conflict?
2. Prepare a report describing how you would resolve this situation.

❹ BUILDING TEAM SKILLS

For more than a century, American unions have played an important role in the workplace, striving to improve the working conditions and quality of life of employees. Today, federal laws cover many of the workers' rights that unions first championed. For this reason, some people believe that unions are no longer necessary. According to some experts, however, as technology changes the workplace and as cultural diversity and the number of part-time workers increase, unions will increase their memberships and become stronger as we move into the new century. What do you think?

Assignment

1. Form a "pro" group and a "con" group and join one of them.
2. Debate whether unions will be stronger or weaker in the next century.
3. Record the key points for each side.
4. Summarize what you learned about unions and their usefulness in a report, and state your position on the debated issue.

❺ RESEARCHING DIFFERENT CAREERS

When applying for a job, whether mailing or faxing in your résumé, you should always include a letter of application, or a cover letter, as it is often called. A well-prepared cover letter should convince the prospective employer to read your résumé and to phone you for an interview. The letter should describe the job you want and your qualifications for the job. It should also let the firm know where you can be reached to set up an appointment for an interview.

Assignment

1. Prepare a letter of application to use with the résumé you prepared in Chapter 9. (An example appears in Appendix A online.)
2. After having several friends review your letter, edit it carefully.
3. Ask your instructor to comment on your letter.

Graeter's: Where Tenure Is "a Proud Number"

Although you might think working for an ice-cream company would be motivating under almost any circumstances, Graeter's doesn't take its employees' commitment for granted. Including full-time and part-time seasonal workers, Graeter's employs about 800 hourly workers in nearly 30 retail stores in Cincinnati and surrounding areas. Over the last few years, it has benefitted from tightening up some of its long-standing human resource management (HRM) procedures, including those for hiring and evaluating employees.

IMPROVING TRAINING AND PERFORMANCE MEASUREMENT

According to an HR consultant who works with top management at this fourth-generation family-owned firm, in past years the company ran more or less on unquestioned directives from the top down. There was a Laissez-Faire attitude, and goals and measurement systems weren't strongly emphasized. "If [employees] came in and they made ice cream, if they made enough for the week, for the day, that was enough," says the consultant. Now "that has really radically changed. If you walk around now we have measurement systems up. People understand what their expectation is, and we have defined the behaviors that are acceptable and not acceptable within the company. We communicate that. We teach and educate people. We've done a lot of work in retail about exceptional customer service and what that looks like and how you do that.... Employees are going to engage you... and you are going to have a good time."

Turnover is low. "We don't hire based on race," says David Blink, the company's controller. "We don't hire based on gender. We hire based on potential... We are looking for people who are conscientious about their work, who do a good job, who show up every day. We are a fun place to work.... We have turnover based on seasonal work only because we hire a lot of college kids [and] high school kids that are here for the summer and then they come back for the holidays." Each store is staffed with a manager and an assistant manager as well as team leaders. Some employees spend their entire working careers with Graeter's and eventually retire from the firm.

RAISING THE BAR FOR PRODUCTION

Graeter's looks for people with baking industry skills for its factories, which recently grew from one to three as the company has undertaken a major and possibly nationwide expansion of its supermarket distribution system. Higher production goals have given newly empowered factory employees achievements to boast about on the slogan T-shirts they wear. Employee suggestions for improvement pour in, and morale is going up. Employees also wear badges with their names and the number of years they have worked for the firm, "and that is a proud number," says Blink. Some factory employees have been with Graeter's for 25 years, a milestone that merits a party. Birthdays and anniversaries are also celebrated with flair.

BENEFITS THAT PAY

The benefits package is competitive. Graeter's offers its employees profit sharing, and it has made a profit every year. It also has a 401k retirement plan that matches employees' contributions and a rolling allowance for paid time off that is separate from paid vacations and based on the employee's tenure with the firm. The health care plan covers 65 percent of employees' medical expenses; dental insurance, life insurance, and short- and long-term disability insurance are offered. Employees who don't use the company's insurance plan (because they are covered by a spouse's plan, for instance) are rewarded with a stipend. Store employees wear uniforms for which the company pays as well.

ADDING EXECUTIVES BECAUSE "YOU CAN'T DO IT ALONE"

Hiring at the executive level is largely the province of CEO Richard Graeter II, who, like his cousins Robert (vice president of manufacturing) and Chip (vice president of retail stores), is a great grandson of the 140-year-old company's founders. The company has adopted ambitious expansion plans and has taken advantage of the unexpected opportunity to purchase several Graeter's stores and a factory from the last of its franchisees, increasing its production capacity overnight. Therefore, the management team has also grown, altering the structure of the growing firm.

"In the last few months," says Richard, "I have hired a vice president of sales and marketing... we now work with a food broker... we hired a vice president of finance, basically a CFO [chief financial officer] because we are big enough to support that. Actually when we bought the franchisee we kept his entire team, so we added another vice president of sales for the Columbus area. We elevated our director of sales to a vice president level here in Cincinnati, and I think we are going to find someone to be our marketing director, which is a position we've never had on our staff before.... Identifying the gaps in your executive team and your talent pool, and going out and finding people to fill those gaps, is probably one of my most critical functions in addition to looking out to define the strategic direction of the company. I've got some wonderful people on the team now, and they are really helping us make the jump from a small business to a medium-sized business.... People at that level, you've got to pay them well. It's worth it, though.... They can command the kind of salary they do because they bring the talent you need to navigate the waters."

"You can't do it alone," Richard concludes. "That is the other thing that I think my cousins and I all have come to realize; we can't do it alone. Our fathers and aunt and the folks that came before them... they did it all, from figuring out where to build the next store to hanging up the laundry at the end of the day." But now, as the company's growth begins to surge, "you need to rely on talent that is beyond just you."[13]

Questions

1. If you were a Graeter's human resource executive, would you expect to do more internal recruiting or external recruiting for the company's retail stores? Why?
2. Graeter's controller believes the company "must be doing something right" because employee turnover is low. What are some of the factors that might be contributing to Graeter's low turnover?
3. Graeter's is currently a non-union company. How might the experience of working there change if a union were to be introduced?

Building a Business Plan PART 4

To access the online *Interactive Business Plan*, go to www.cengagebrain.com.

In this section of your business plan, you will expand on the type and quantity of employees that will be required to operate the business. Your human resources requirements are determined by the type of business and by the size and scale of your operation. From the preceding section, you should have a good idea of how many people you will need. Part 4 of your textbook, "Human Resources," especially Chapters 9 and 10, should help you in answering some of the questions in this part of the business plan.

THE HUMAN RESOURCES COMPONENT

To ensure successful performance by employees, you must inform workers of their specific job requirements. Employees must know what is expected of the job, and they are entitled to expect regular feedback on their work. It is vital to have a formal job description and job specification for every position in your business. Also, you should establish procedures for evaluating performance.

The labor force component should include the answers to at least the following questions:

4.1. How many employees will you require, and what qualifications should they have—including skills, experience, and knowledge? How many jobs will be full-time? Part-time?
4.2. Will you have written job descriptions for each position?
4.3. Have you prepared a job-application form? Do you know what can legally be included in it?
4.4. What criteria will you use in selecting employees?
4.5. Have you made plans for the orientation process?
4.6. Who will do the training?
4.7. What can you afford to pay in wages and salaries? Is this in line with the going rate in your region and industry?
4.8. Who will evaluate your employees?
4.9. Will you delegate any authority to employees?
4.10. Have you developed a set of disciplinary rules?
4.11. Do you plan to interview employees when they resign?

REVIEW OF BUSINESS PLAN ACTIVITIES

Remember that your employees are the company's most valuable and important resource. Therefore, make sure that you expend a great deal of effort to acquire and make full use of this resource. Check and resolve any issues in this component of your business plan before beginning Part 5. Again, make sure that your answers to the questions in each part are consistent with the entire business plan. Finally, write a brief statement that summarizes all the information for this part of the business plan.

The information contained in "Building a Business Plan" will also assist you in completing the online *Interactive Business Plan*.

PART 5

Marketing

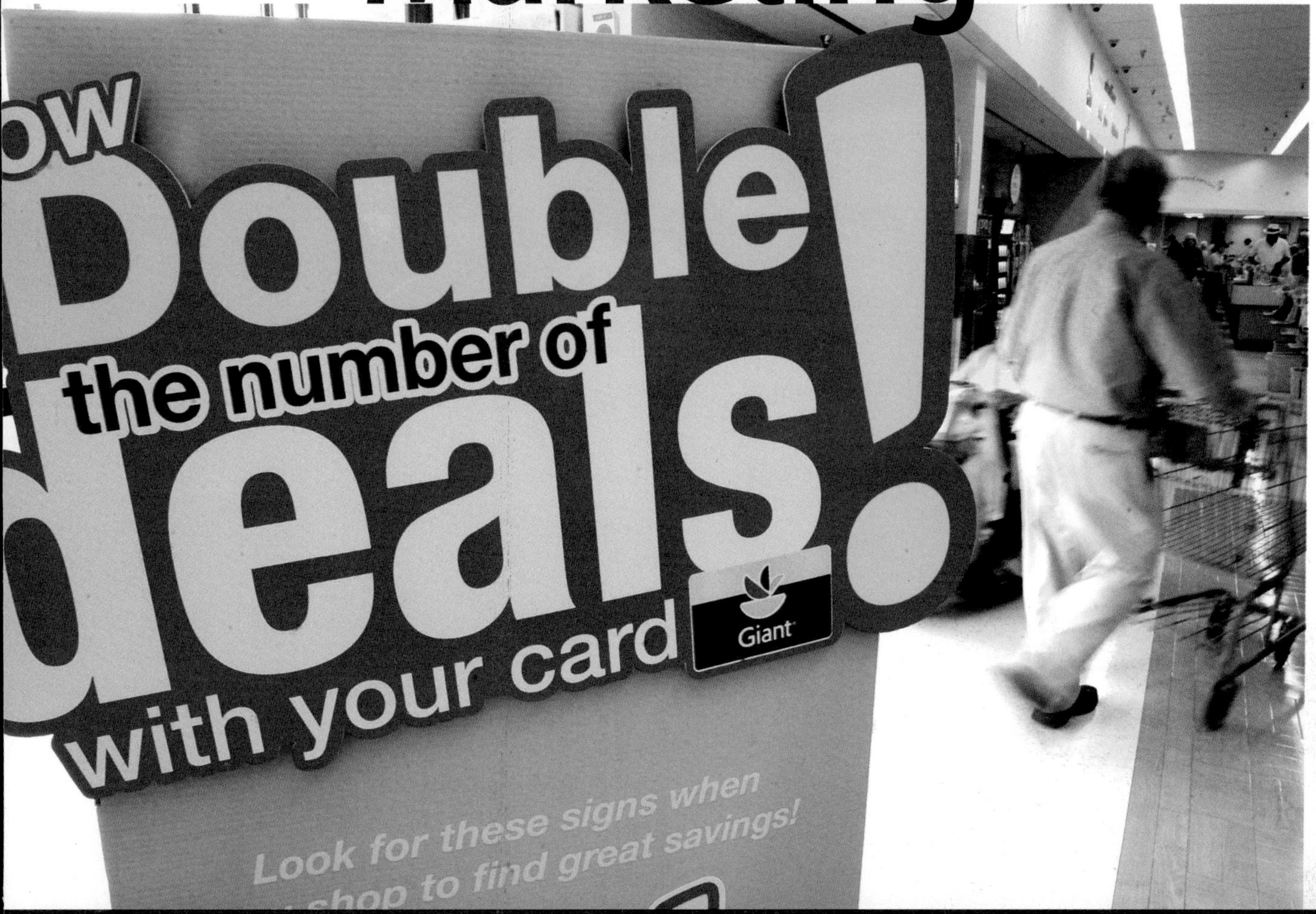

© Mark Gail/The Washington Post/Getty Images

The business activities that make up a firm's marketing efforts are those most directly concerned with satisfying customers' needs. In this part, we explore these activities in some detail. Initially, we discuss markets, marketing mixes, marketing environment forces, marketing plans, and buying behavior. Then, we discuss the four elements that together make up a marketing mix: product, price, distribution, and promotion.

12

Building Customer Relationships Through Effective Marketing

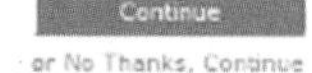

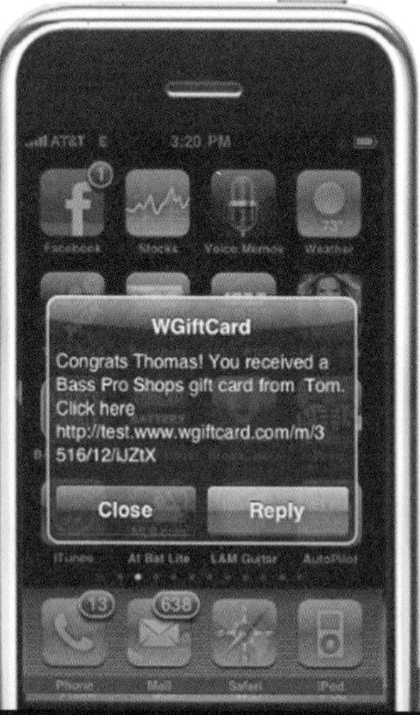

© AP Images/PRNewsFoto/Transaction Wireless

Learning Objectives

What you will be able to do once you complete this chapter:

1. Understand the meaning of *marketing* and the importance of management of customer relationships.
2. Explain how marketing adds value by creating several forms of utility.
3. Trace the development of the marketing concept and understand how it is implemented.
4. Understand what markets are and how they are classified.
5. Identify the four elements of the marketing mix and be aware of their importance in
6. Explain how the marketing environment affects strategic market planning.
7. Understand the major components of a marketing plan.
8. Describe how market measurement and sales forecasting are used.
9. Distinguish between a marketing information system and marketing research.
10. Identify the major steps in the consumer buying decision process and the sets of factors that may influence this process.

inside business

FYI

Gotta Have the New iWhats-It!

Since it began marketing computers in 1976, Apple has made top-quality user experience its top priority. The company's earliest computers—such as the Apple II and the small, boxy Macintosh—may seem chunky and slow by comparison to today's slim, stylish, and speedy Apple models. However, they were as innovative for their time as the iPod digital media player was when it was introduced in 2001 and the iPad tablet computer was when it debuted in 2010. Even the company's chain of retail stores broke new ground for the way customers try and buy electronics.

Today, Apple rings up $43 billion in annual revenue worldwide from a wide range of electronics products. Every year, it sells 10 million Macintosh computers and 8 million iPod digital media gadgets. Apple's best-selling item is the iPhone, a touch-screen smart-phone that can do everything from playing music and taking photos to checking e-mail and surfing YouTube. One of Apple's newer products, the touch-screen iPad tablet, sold a whopping 1 million units in just 28 days.

Apple's wildly successful digital entertainment store, iTunes, has sold more than 10 billion songs since opening its virtual doors in 2003. Its App Store, which offers downloadable software to enhance the utility of iPhones and iPods, has also been extremely successful, serving up more than 2 billion downloads since 2008. Small wonder that competitors such as Nokia have followed Apple's lead and set up their own application stores to supplement smart-phone sales.

Through its international Apple Store retail chain, the company presents its ever-expanding line of electronics products in style. Instead of keeping products locked away, Apple displays them in the open so customers can stop by, test the keyboards or screens, and see exactly how things work before they buy. Every Apple store contains a Genius Bar tech support counter where customers can get answers to questions, take classes to learn each product's functions, and have their products serviced. It is all part of Apple's bid to make the user experience as friendly and satisfying as possible.[1]

Did You Know?

Apple rings up $43 billion in annual revenue, selling 10 million Macintosh computers, 8 million iPods, and 20 million iPhones every year.

Numerous organizations, like Apple, use marketing efforts to provide customer satisfaction and value. Understanding customers' needs, such as "what's cool," is crucial to provide customer satisfaction. Although marketing encompasses a diverse set of decisions and activities performed by individuals as well as both business and nonbusiness organizations, marketing always begins and ends with the customer. The American Marketing Association defines **marketing** as "The activity, set of institutions, and processes for creating, communicating, delivering, and exchanging offerings that have value for customers, clients, partners, and society at large."[2] The marketing process involves eight major functions and numerous related activities (see Table 12.1). All these functions are essential if the marketing process is to be effective.

In this chapter, we examine marketing activities that add value to products. We trace the evolution of the marketing concept and describe how organizations practice it. Next, our focus shifts to market classifications and marketing strategy. We analyze the four elements of a marketing mix and also discuss uncontrollable factors in the marketing environment. Then we examine the major components of a marketing plan. We consider tools for strategic market planning, including market measurement, sales forecasts, marketing information systems, and marketing research. Last, we look at the forces that influence consumer and organizational buying behavior.

marketing the activity, set of institutions, and processes for creating, communicating, delivering, and exchanging offerings that have value for customers, clients, partners, and society at large

Table 12.1 Major Marketing Functions
Exchange functions: All companies—manufacturers, wholesalers, and retailers—buy and sell to market their merchandise.
1. Buying includes obtaining raw materials to make products, knowing how much merchandise to keep on hand, and selecting suppliers.
2. Selling creates possession utility by transferring the title of a product from seller to customer.
Physical distribution functions: These functions involve the flow of goods from producers to customers. Transportation and storage provide time utility and place utility and require careful management of inventory.
3. Transporting involves selecting a mode of transport that provides an acceptable delivery schedule at an acceptable price.
4. Storing goods is often necessary to sell them at the best selling time.
Facilitating functions: These functions help the other functions to take place.
5. Financing helps at all stages of marketing. To buy raw materials, manufacturers often borrow from banks or receive credit from suppliers. Wholesalers may be financed by manufacturers, and retailers may receive financing from the wholesaler or manufacturer. Finally, retailers often provide financing to customers.
6. Standardization sets uniform specifications for products or services. Grading classifies products by size and quality, usually through a sorting process. Together, standardization and grading facilitate production, transportation, storage, and selling.
7. Risk taking—even though competent management and insurance can minimize risks—is a constant reality of marketing because of such losses as bad-debt expense, obsolescence of products, theft by employees, and product-liability lawsuits.
8. Gathering market information is necessary for making all marketing decisions.

1

Understand the meaning of *marketing* and the importance of management of customer relationships.

Managing Customer Relationships

Marketing relationships with customers are the lifeblood of all businesses. Maintaining positive relationships with customers is an important goal for marketers. The term **relationship marketing** refers to "marketing decisions and activities focused on achieving long-term, satisfying relationships with customers." Relationship marketing continually deepens the buyer's trust in the company, which, as the customer's loyalty grows, increases a company's understanding of the customer's needs and desires. Successful marketers respond to customers' needs and strive to continually increase value to buyers over time. Eventually, this interaction becomes a solid relationship that allows for cooperation and mutual trust. Sears, for example, offers Shop Your Way Rewards, a card-based program that provides incentives for frequent shoppers at any Sears or Kmart store, as well as their online sites. Members of this program receive rewards totaling 1 percent of their purchases, which can be used in a store, spent online, or saved for later use. Members are allowed to return any items they purchase without presenting a receipt, can take part in exclusive promotional events, and are also entered to win prizes. Such initiatives give stores the opportunity to build stronger relationships with customers.[3]

Building long-term customer relationships. Airlines, like many other organizations, spend considerable resources to develop and maintain long-term customer relationships.

© AP Images/PRNewsFoto/Virgin America

To build long-term customer relationships, marketers are increasingly turning to marketing research and information technology. **Customer relationship management (CRM)** focuses on using information about customers to create marketing strategies that develop and sustain desirable customer relationships. By increasing customer value over time, organizations try to retain and increase long-term profitability through customer loyalty.

Managing customer relationships requires identifying patterns of buying behavior and using this information to focus on the most promising and profitable customers. Companies must be sensitive to customers' requirements and desires and establish communication to build customers' trust and loyalty. In some instances, it may be more profitable for a company to focus on satisfying a valuable existing customer than to attempt to attract a new one who may never develop the same level of loyalty. This involves determining how much the customer will spend over his or her lifetime. The **customer lifetime value** is a measure of a customer's worth (sales minus costs) to a business during one's lifetime.[4] However, there are also intangible benefits of retaining lifetime-value customers, such as their ability to provide feedback to a company and refer new customers of similar value. The amount of money a company is willing to spend to retain such customers is also a factor. In general, when marketers focus on customers chosen for their lifetime value, they earn higher profits in future periods than when they focus on customers selected for other reasons.[5] Because the loss of a potential lifetime customer can result in lower profits, managing customer relationships has become a major focus of marketers.

relationship marketing establishing long-term, mutually satisfying buyer–seller relationships

customer relationship management (CRM) using information about customers to create marketing strategies that develop and sustain desirable customer relationships

customer lifetime value a measure of a customer's worth (sales minus costs) to a business over one's lifetime

Utility: The Value Added by Marketing

2

Explain how marketing adds value by creating several forms of utility.

As defined in Chapter 8, **utility** is the ability of a good or service to satisfy a human need. A lunch at a Pizza Hut, an overnight stay at a Holiday Inn, and a Mercedes S500L all satisfy human needs. Thus, each possesses utility. There are four kinds of utility.

Form utility is created by converting production inputs into finished products. Marketing efforts may influence form utility indirectly because the data gathered as part of marketing research are frequently used to determine the size, shape, and features of a product.

The three kinds of utility that are created directly by marketing are place, time, and possession utility. **Place utility** is created by making a product available at a location where customers wish to purchase it. A pair of shoes is given place utility when it is shipped from a factory to a department store.

Time utility is created by making a product available when customers wish to purchase it. For example, Halloween costumes may be manufactured in April but not displayed until late September, when consumers start buying them. By storing the costumes until they are wanted, the manufacturer or retailer provides time utility.

Possession utility is created by transferring title (or ownership) of a product to a buyer. For a product as simple as a pair of shoes, ownership usually is transferred by means of a sales slip or receipt. For such products as automobiles and homes, the transfer of title is a more complex process. Along with the title to its products, the seller transfers the right to use that product to satisfy a need (see Figure 12.1).

utility the ability of a good or service to satisfy a human need

form utility utility created by converting production inputs into finished products

place utility utility created by making a product available at a location where customers wish to purchase it

time utility utility created by making a product available when customers wish to purchase it

possession utility utility created by transferring title (or ownership) of a product to a buyer

Place, time, and possession utility have real value in terms of both money and convenience. This value is created and added to goods and services through a wide variety of marketing activities—from research indicating what customers want to product warranties ensuring that customers get what they pay for. Overall, these marketing activities account for about half of every dollar spent by consumers. When they are part of an integrated marketing program that delivers maximum utility to the customer, many would agree that they are worth the cost.

Place, time, and possession utility are only the most fundamental applications of marketing activities. In recent years, marketing activities have been influenced by a broad business philosophy known as the *marketing concept*.

Place and time utility. Marketing adds value by making the product available where and when customers want to purchase it.

Figure 12.1 Types of Utility

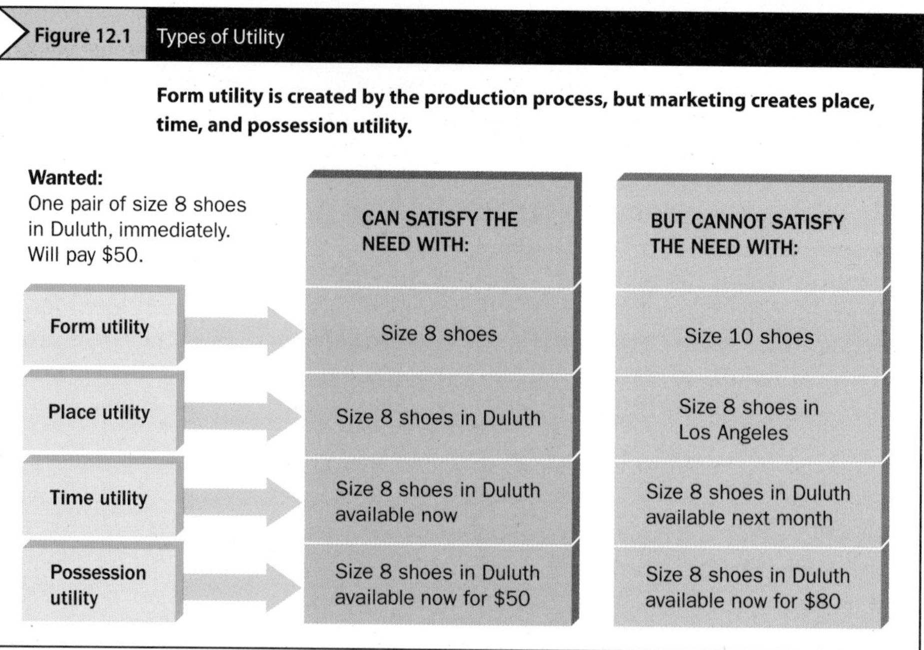

3

Trace the development of the marketing concept and understand how it is implemented.

The Marketing Concept

The **marketing concept** is a business philosophy that a firm should provide goods and services that satisfy customers' needs through a coordinated set of activities that allow the firm to achieve its objectives. Thus, initially, the firm must communicate with potential customers to assess their product needs. Then, the firm must develop a good or service to satisfy those needs. Finally, the firm must continue to seek ways to provide customer satisfaction. This process is an application of the marketing concept or marketing orientation. Ben & Jerry's, for example, constantly assesses customer demand for ice cream and sorbet. On its Web site, it maintains a "flavor

The marketing concept. Being focused on the customer and providing customer satisfaction is at the heart of the marketing concept.

© Stew Leonard's

marketing concept a business philosophy that a firm should provide goods and services that satisfy customers' needs through a coordinated set of activities that allow the firm to achieve its objectives

graveyard" listing combinations that were tried and ultimately failed. It also notes its top ten flavors each month. Thus, the marketing concept emphasizes that marketing begins and ends with customers.

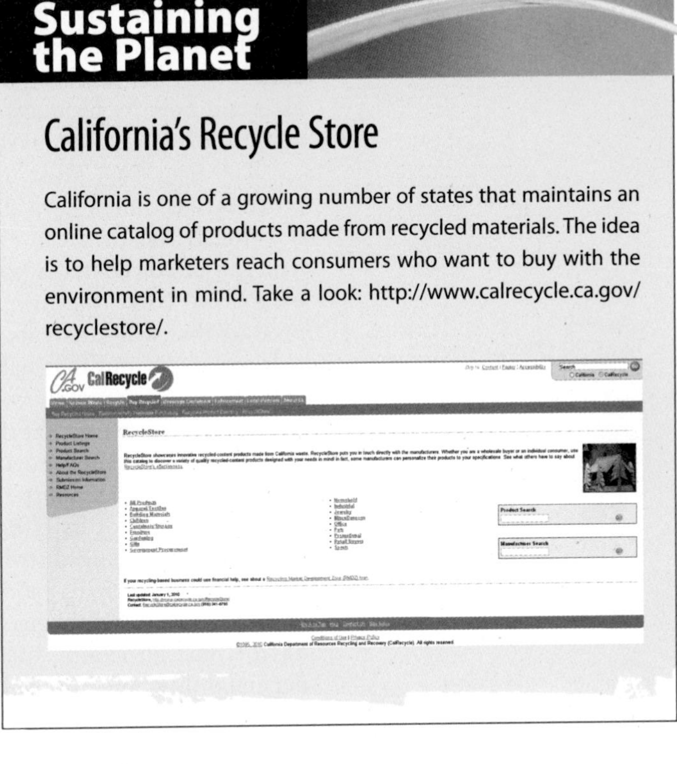

Sustaining the Planet

California's Recycle Store

California is one of a growing number of states that maintains an online catalog of products made from recycled materials. The idea is to help marketers reach consumers who want to buy with the environment in mind. Take a look: http://www.calrecycle.ca.gov/recyclestore/.

Evolution of the Marketing Concept

From the start of the Industrial Revolution until the early 20th century, business effort was directed mainly toward the production of goods. Consumer demand for manufactured products was so great that manufacturers could almost bank on selling everything they produced. Business had a strong *production orientation*, in which emphasis was placed on increased output and production efficiency. Marketing was limited to taking orders and distributing finished goods.

In the 1920s, production caught up with and began to exceed demand. Now producers had to direct their efforts toward selling goods rather than just producing goods that consumers readily bought. This new *sales orientation* was characterized by increased advertising, enlarged sales forces, and, occasionally, high-pressure selling techniques. Manufacturers produced the goods they expected consumers to want, and marketing consisted primarily of promoting products through personal selling and advertising, taking orders, and delivering goods.

During the 1950s, however, businesspeople started to realize that even enormous advertising expenditures and the most thoroughly proven sales techniques were not enough. Something else was needed if products were to sell as well as expected. It was then that business managers recognized that they were not primarily producers or sellers but rather were in the business of satisfying customers' needs. Marketers realized that the best approach was to adopt a customer orientation—in other words, the organization had to first determine what customers need and then develop goods and services to fill those particular needs (see Table 12.2).

All functional areas—research and development, production, finance, human resources, and, of course, marketing—are viewed as playing a role in providing customer satisfaction.

Implementing the Marketing Concept

The marketing concept has been adopted by many of the most successful business firms. Some firms, such as Ford Motor Company and Apple Computer, have gone through minor or major reorganizations in the process. Because the marketing concept is essentially a business philosophy, anyone can say, "I believe in it." To make it work, however, management must fully adopt and then implement it.

Table 12.2 Evolution of Customer Orientation

Business managers recognized that they were not primarily producers or sellers but were rather in the business of satisfying customers' wants.

Production Orientation	Sales Orientation	Customer Orientation
Take orders	Increase advertising	Determine customer needs
Distribute goods	Enlarge sales force	Develop products to fill these needs
	Intensify sales techniques	Achieve the organization's goals

To implement the marketing concept, a firm first must obtain information about its present and potential customers. The firm must determine not only what customers' needs are but also how well these needs are being satisfied by products currently in the market—both its own products and those of competitors. It must ascertain how its products might be improved and what opinions customers have about the firm and its marketing efforts.

The firm then must use this information to pinpoint the specific needs and potential customers toward which it will direct its marketing activities and resources. (Obviously, no firm can expect to satisfy all needs. Also, not every individual or firm can be considered a potential customer for every product manufactured or sold by a firm.) Next, the firm must mobilize its marketing resources to (1) provide a product that will satisfy its customers, (2) price the product at a level that is acceptable to buyers and that will yield an acceptable profit, (3) promote the product so that potential customers will be aware of its existence and its ability to satisfy their needs, and (4) ensure that the product is distributed so that it is available to customers where and when needed.

Finally, the firm must again obtain marketing information—this time regarding the effectiveness of its efforts. Can the product be improved? Is it being promoted properly? Is it being distributed efficiently? Is the price too high or too low? The firm must be ready to modify any or all of its marketing activities based on information about its customers and competitors. Sears' Kenmore brand, for example, has become an iconic American brand of appliances, known for its high quality, dependability, and innovation. However, as the brand neared its 85-year mark, managers at Sears noticed that the aging brand was not in very high demand among the younger population. The company decided to rebrand Kenmore, modernizing it with a focus on sophisticated, contemporary styling and increased energy efficiency. Sears decided to market its new brand's vision mostly to women in their 20s to 50s, specifically "savvy moms" and young first-time home buyers. The company launched a new advertising campaign, with television advertisements, as well as online advertisements on Facebook, YouTube, and Twitter. All advertisements featured real customers or actual engineers at Kenmore, and used the tagline "Kenmore, That's Genius." Sears also launched the Kenmore.com site, where customers could view and purchase Kenmore products and use the "help me choose" tool to help them find the best model for their needs. Sears hopes that this rebranding will help Kenmore appeal to the younger generations as the market adjusts.[6]

4

Understand what markets are and how they are classified.

Markets and Their Classification

A **market** is a group of individuals or organizations, or both, that need products in a given category and that have the ability, willingness, and authority to purchase such products. The people or organizations must want the product. They must be able to purchase the product by exchanging money, goods, or services for it. They must be willing to use their buying power. Finally, they must be socially and legally authorized to purchase the product.

Markets are broadly classified as consumer or business-to-business markets. These classifications are based on the characteristics of the individuals and organizations within each market. Because marketing efforts vary depending on the intended market, marketers should understand the general characteristics of these two groups.

Consumer markets consist of purchasers and/or household members who intend to consume or benefit from the purchased products and who do not buy products to make profits. *Business-to-business markets*, also called *industrial markets*, are grouped broadly into producer, reseller, governmental, and institutional categories. These markets purchase specific kinds of products for use in making other products for resale or for day-to-day operations. *Producer markets* consist of individuals and business organizations that buy certain products to use in the manufacture of other products. *Reseller markets* consist of intermediaries such as wholesalers and retailers, who buy finished products and sell them for a profit. *Governmental markets* consist

market a group of individuals or organizations, or both, that need products in a given category and that have the ability, willingness, and authority to purchase such products

of federal, state, county, and local governments. They buy goods and services to maintain internal operations and to provide citizens with such products as highways, education, water, energy, and national defense. Governmental purchases total billions of dollars each year. *Institutional markets* include churches, not-for-profit private schools and hospitals, civic clubs, fraternities and sororities, charitable organizations, and foundations. Their goals are different from such typical business goals as profit, market share, or return on investment.

Segmentation based on gender. This Maybelline product is aimed specifically at women.

Developing Marketing Strategies

A **marketing strategy** is a plan that will enable an organization to make the best use of its resources and advantages to meet its objectives. A marketing strategy consists of (1) the selection and analysis of a target market and (2) the creation and maintenance of an appropriate **marketing mix**, a combination of product, price, distribution, and promotion developed to satisfy a particular target market.

Target Market Selection and Evaluation

A **target market** is a group of individuals or organizations, or both, for which a firm develops and maintains a marketing mix suitable for the specific needs and preferences of that group. In selecting a target market, marketing managers examine potential markets for their possible effects on the firm's sales, costs, and profits. The managers attempt to determine whether the organization has the resources to produce a marketing mix that meets the needs of a particular target market and whether satisfying these needs is consistent with the firm's overall objectives. They also analyze the strengths and number of competitors already marketing to people in this target market. Marketing managers may define a target market as a sizable number of people or a relatively small group. The Nissan Cube, for example, definitely has features to attract the teens and early 20-somethings, including an upgraded Rockford Fosgate subwoofer, an interface system for the iPod, smaller cup holders for energy drinks, and the option to add more than 40 accessories. Nissan also ensured that its promotion, price, and distribution were appropriate for this target market. The price point for the Cube starts at just under $14,000. Ideas for promoting this vehicle came straight from U.S. college students who competed to have their marketing strategy adopted by Nissan and are part of this vehicle's target market.[7] On the other hand, Rolls-Royce targets its automobiles toward a small, very exclusive market: wealthy people who want the ultimate in prestige in an automobile. Other companies target multiple markets with different products, prices, distribution systems, and promotion for each one. Nike uses this strategy, marketing different types of shoes to meet specific needs of cross-trainers, rock climbers, basketball players, aerobics enthusiasts, and other athletic-shoe buyers. When selecting a target market, marketing managers generally take either the undifferentiated approach or the market segmentation approach.

Undifferentiated Approach A company that designs a single marketing mix and directs it at the entire market for a particular product is using an **undifferentiated approach** (see Figure 12.2). This approach assumes that individual customers in the target market for a specific kind of product have similar needs and that the organization therefore can satisfy most customers with a single marketing mix. This single marketing mix consists of one type of product with little or no variation, one price, one promotional program aimed at everyone, and one distribution system to reach all customers in the total market. Products that can be marketed successfully with the undifferentiated approach include staple food items, such as sugar and salt, and certain kinds of farm produce. An undifferentiated approach is useful in only a limited number of situations because for most product categories buyers have

marketing strategy a plan that will enable an organization to make the best use of its resources and advantages to meet its objectives

marketing mix a combination of product, price, distribution, and promotion developed to satisfy a particular target market

target market a group of individuals or organizations, or both, for which a firm develops and maintains a marketing mix suitable for the specific needs and preferences of that group

undifferentiated approach directing a single marketing mix at the entire market for a particular product

Figure 12.2 General Approaches for Selecting Target Markets

The undifferentiated approach assumes that individual customers have similar needs and that most customers can be satisfied with a single marketing mix. When customers' needs vary, the market segmentation approach—either concentrated or differentiated—should be used.

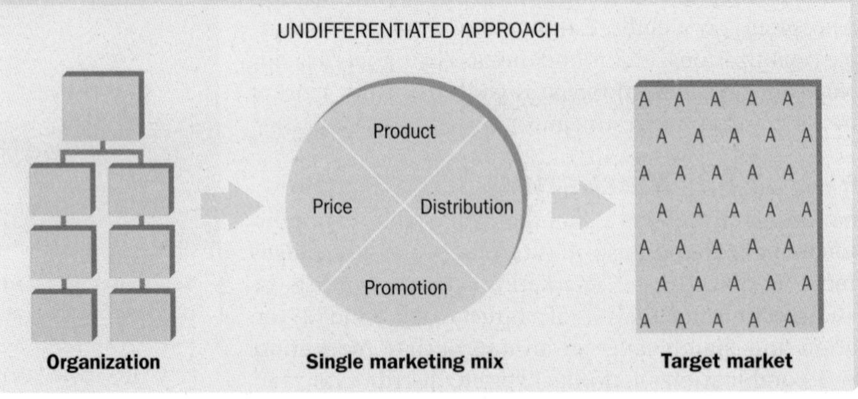

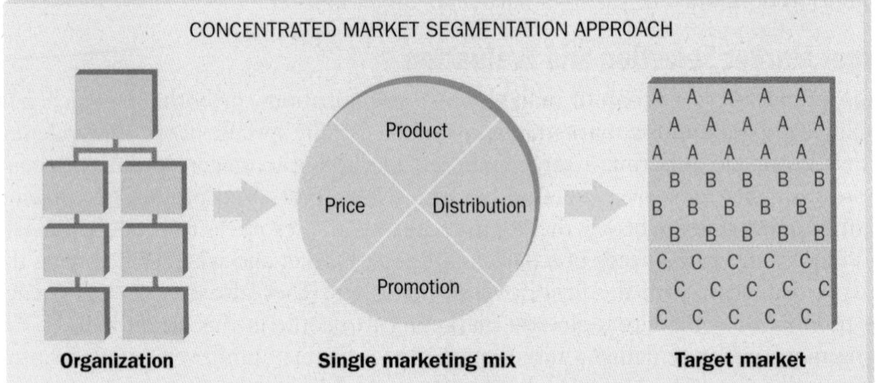

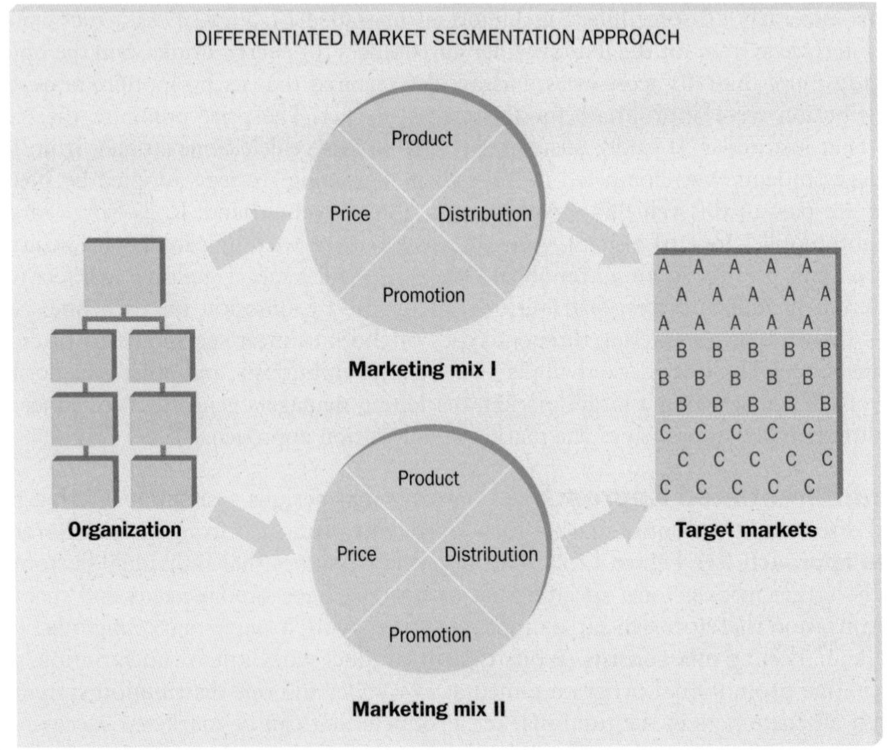

NOTE: The letters in each target market represent potential customers. Customers that have the same letters have similar characteristics and similar product needs.

Source: William M. Pride and O. C. Ferrell, *Marketing: Concepts and Strategies*, 16th ed. (Mason, OH: South-Western/Cengage Learning, 2012). Adapted with permission.

different needs. When customers' needs vary, a company should use the market segmentation approach.

Market Segmentation Approach A firm that is marketing 40-foot yachts would not direct its marketing effort toward every person in the total boat market. Some might want a sailboat or a canoe. Others might want a speedboat or an outboard-powered fishing boat. Still others might be looking for something resembling a small ocean liner. Marketing efforts directed toward such boat buyers would be wasted.

Instead, the firm would direct its attention toward a particular portion, or *segment*, of the total market for boats. A **market segment** is a group of individuals or organizations within a market that shares one or more common characteristics. The process of dividing a market into segments is called **market segmentation**. As shown in Figure 12.2, there are two types of market segmentation approaches: concentrated and differentiated. When an organization uses *concentrated* market segmentation, a single marketing mix is directed at a single market segment. If *differentiated* market segmentation is used, multiple marketing mixes are focused on multiple market segments.

Undifferentiated approach. The producer of Morton Salt uses an undifferentiated approach because people's needs for salt are homogeneous.

In our boat example, one common characteristic, or *basis*, for segmentation might be "end use of a boat." The firm would be interested primarily in the market segment whose uses for a boat could lead to the purchase of a 40-foot yacht. Another basis for segmentation might be income, still another might be geographic location. Each of these variables can affect the type of boat an individual might purchase. When choosing a basis for segmentation, it is important to select a characteristic that relates to differences in people's needs for a product. The yacht producer, for example, would not use religion to segment the boat market because people's needs for boats do not vary based on religion.

Marketers use a wide variety of segmentation bases. Bases most commonly applied to consumer markets are shown in Table 12.3. Each may be used as a single basis for market segmentation or in combination with other bases. OfficeMax, for example, is typically considered to be in a not-so-dazzling industry with a very broad definition for its target market (people and businesses that need office supplies). Therefore, the company recently decided to completely reposition itself. No longer a dull office

Table 12.3 Common Bases of Market Segmentation

Demographic	Psychographic	Geographic	Behavioristic
Age	Personality attributes	Region	Volume usage
Gender	Motives	Urban, suburban, rural	End use
Race	Lifestyles	Market density	Benefit expectations
Ethnicity		Climate	Brand loyalty
Income		Terrain	Price sensitivity
Education		City size	
Occupation		County size	
Family size		State size	
Family life cycle			
Religion			
Social class			

Source: William M. Pride and O. C. Ferrell, *Marketing: Concepts and Strategies*, 16th ed. (Mason, OH: South-Western/Cengage Learning, 2012). Adapted with permission.

market segment a group of individuals or organizations within a market that share one or more common characteristics

market segmentation the process of dividing a market into segments and directing a marketing mix at a particular segment or segments rather than at the total market

Figure 12.3 The Marketing Mix and the Marketing Environment

The marketing mix consists of elements that the firm controls—product, price, distribution, and promotion. The firm generally has no control over forces in the marketing environment.

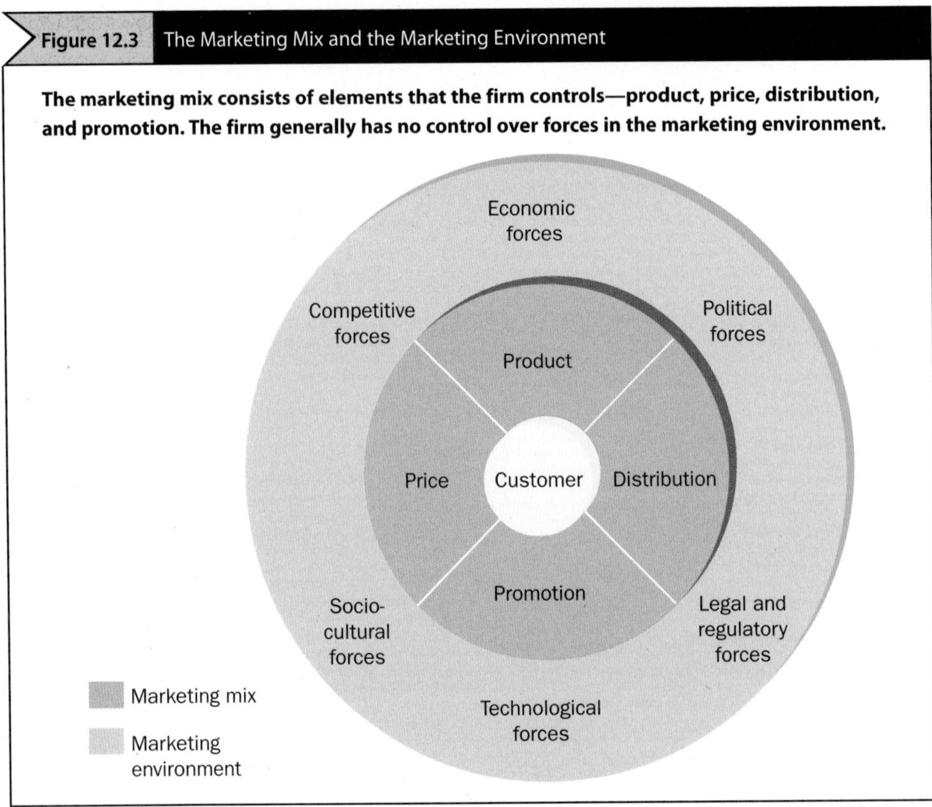

Source: William M. Pride and O. C. Ferrell, *Marketing: Concepts and Strategies,* 16th ed. (Mason, OH: South-Western/Cengage Learning, 2012). Adapted with permission.

supply store, it is now a fun, more intimate, retail outlet that appeals to women. The company repositioned itself through its campaign called "Life Is Beautiful, Work Can Be Too," which featured stylish new private-label product lines, a spiced up catalog, and appearances at venues like Mercedes-Benz Fashion Week in New York. OfficeMax has made a huge effort to separate itself from other office supply stores by further defining its target market and centering all of its marketing around "her."[8]

5

Identify the four elements of the marketing mix and be aware of their importance in developing a marketing strategy.

Creating a Marketing Mix

A business firm controls four important elements of marketing that it combines in a way that reaches the firm's target market. These are the *product* itself, the *price* of the product, the means chosen for its *distribution*, and the *promotion* of the product. When combined, these four elements form a marketing mix (see Figure 12.3). Nissan, for example, recently released the LEAF and developed a marketing mix that included an affordable, zero-emission electric vehicle with seating for five; a price starting at just over $25,000; distribution through straightforward online reservations and orders; and promotion through an extensive and interactive global tour, which included 63 stops in the United States.[9]

A firm can vary its marketing mix by changing any one or more of these ingredients. Thus, a firm may use one marketing mix to reach one target market and a second, somewhat different, marketing mix to reach another target market. For example, most automakers produce several different types and models of vehicles and aim them at different market segments based on the potential customers' age, income, and other factors.

The *product* ingredient of the marketing mix includes decisions about the product's design, brand name, packaging, warranties, and the like. When McDonald's decides on brand names, package designs, sizes of orders, flavors of sauces, and recipes, these choices are all part of the product ingredient.

The *pricing* ingredient is concerned with both base prices and discounts of various kinds. Pricing decisions are intended to achieve particular goals, such as

Ethical Challenges & SUCCESSFUL SOLUTIONS

Limits to Online Privacy?

Can online targeting go too far? When consumers do an online search or download a digital coupon, marketers can follow their electronic movements. For example, Jackson Hewitt recently offered digital coupons for its tax preparation services. Each coupon's bar code was unique, allowing the company's ad agency to track an individual consumer's search history leading up to the download.

The purpose of tracking online behavior is to do a better job of targeting communications and tailoring offers to customers' needs and interests. However, consumers are not always aware of exactly what information is being gathered and how it will be used. This raises questions about the limits of online privacy.

"Imagine that you were walking through a shopping mall, and there was someone that was walking behind you . . . taking notes on everywhere you went," says the head of the Federal Trade Commission. Moreover, the data would be available "to every shop or anyone who was interested, for a small fee." Privacy advocates also worry about identity theft and about the possibility of "online redlining," marketers restricting access to products based on what consumers do or say on the Internet. As experts debate the limits of online privacy, regulators are formulating new privacy protections and industry groups are developing new ways for consumers to opt out of tracking systems if they choose.

Sources: Wendy Davis, "Report: Marketers Limit Behavioral Targeting Due to Privacy Worries," *MediaPost*, May 2, 2010, http://www.mediapost.com; Bob Garfield, "FTC Privacy Review Could Mean Trouble for Online Marketing," *Advertising Age*, April 19, 2010, http://www.adage.com; Stephanie Clifford, "Web Coupons Know Lots About You, and They Tell," *New York Times*, April 16, 2010, http://www.nytimes.com; Laurie Burkitt, "Ad Industry to Regulators: We Can Take Care of Ourselves," *Forbes*, April 14, 2010, http://www.forbes.com; Steve Lohr, "How Privacy Vanishes Online," *New York Times*, March 16, 2010, http://www.nytimes.com.

to maximize profit or even to make room for new models. The rebates offered by automobile manufacturers are a pricing strategy developed to boost low auto sales. Product and pricing are discussed in detail in Chapter 13.

The *distribution* ingredient involves not only transportation and storage but also the selection of intermediaries. How many levels of intermediaries should be used in the distribution of a particular product? Should the product be distributed as widely as possible or should distribution be restricted to a few specialized outlets in each area? Video rental retailers have had to make numerous decisions regarding distribution. Currently, vending machines like Redbox make up 19 percent of the video rental market, mail rental services like Netflix have 36 percent, and brick-and-mortar stores like Blockbuster own 45 percent. Fifteen years ago, almost all videos were distributed through brick-and-mortar stores. Distribution decisions and activities are discussed in more detail in Chapter 14.[10]

The *promotion* ingredient focuses on providing information to target markets. The major forms of promotion are advertising, personal selling, sales promotion, and public relations. These four forms are discussed in Chapter 15.

These ingredients of the marketing mix are controllable elements. A firm can vary each of them to suit its organizational goals, marketing goals, and target markets. As we extend our discussion of marketing strategy, we will see that the marketing environment includes a number of *uncontrollable* elements.

6

Explain how the marketing environment affects strategic market planning.

Marketing Strategy and the Marketing Environment

The marketing mix consists of elements that a firm controls and uses to reach its target market. In addition, the firm has control over such organizational resources as finances and information. These resources may be used to accomplish marketing goals, too. However, the firm's marketing activities are also affected by a number of external—and generally uncontrollable—forces. As Figure 12.3 illustrates, the following forces make up the external *marketing environment*:

- *Economic forces*—the effects of economic conditions on customers' ability and willingness to buy

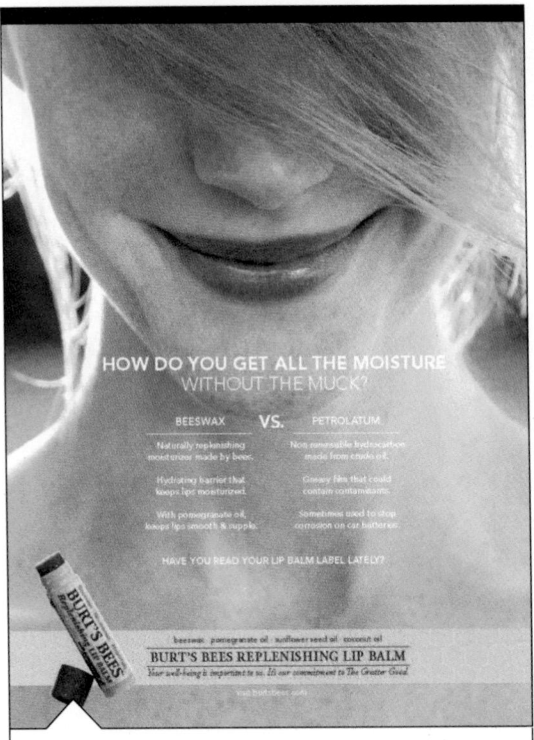

Developing a marketing mix. The maker of this product has developed a marketing mix (product, price, distribution, and promotion) specifically for this product.

- *Sociocultural forces*—influences in a society and its culture that result in changes in attitudes, beliefs, norms, customs, and lifestyles
- *Political forces*—influences that arise through the actions of elected and appointed officials
- *Competitive forces*—the actions of competitors, who are in the process of implementing their own marketing plans
- *Legal and regulatory forces*—laws that protect consumers and competition and government regulations that affect marketing
- *Technological forces*—technological changes that can create new marketing opportunities or cause products to become obsolete almost overnight

These forces influence decisions about marketing-mix ingredients. Changes in the environment can have a major impact on existing marketing strategies. In addition, changes in environmental forces may lead to abrupt shifts in customers' needs. Consider the effect technological forces have had on printed newspapers: years ago, very few people would have predicted that consumers would one day have no need for their daily newspaper. However, that day has come; with 24-hour up-to-the-second news online, fewer people are buying newspapers. Consumers want today's news now and are able to access it, most of the time for free, from computers, smart-phones, and other devices with Internet access.[11]

Understand the major components of a marketing plan.

Developing a Marketing Plan

A **marketing plan** is a written document that specifies an organization's resources, objectives, marketing strategy, and implementation and control efforts to be used in marketing a specific product or product group. The marketing plan describes the firm's current position or situation, establishes marketing objectives for the product, and specifies how the organization will attempt to achieve these objectives. Marketing plans vary with respect to the time period involved. Short-range plans are for one year or less, medium-range plans cover from over one year to five years, and long-range plans cover periods of more than five years.

Although time-consuming, developing a clear, well-written marketing plan is important. The plan will be used for communication among the firm's employees. It covers the assignment of responsibilities, tasks, and schedules for implementation. It specifies how resources are to be allocated to achieve marketing objectives. It helps marketing managers monitor and evaluate the performance of the marketing strategy. Because the forces of the marketing environment are subject to change, marketing plans have to be updated frequently. Disney, for example, recently made changes to its marketing plans by combining all activities and licensing associated with the Power Rangers, Winnie the Pooh, and Disney Princess into one marketing plan with a $500 million budget. The primary goal is to send consistent messages about branding to customers. As the new marketing plan is implemented, Disney will have to respond quickly to customers' reactions and make adjustments to the plan. The major components of a marketing plan are shown in Table 12.4.

marketing plan a written document that specifies an organization's resources, objectives, strategy, and implementation and control efforts to be used in marketing a specific product or product group

Describe how market measurement and sales forecasting are used.

Market Measurement and Sales Forecasting

Measuring the sales potential of specific types of market segments helps an organization to make some important decisions, such as the feasibility of entering new segments. The organization can also decide how best to allocate its marketing resources

© AP Images/PRNewsFoto/Burt's Bees

and activities among market segments in which it is already active. All such estimates should identify the relevant time frame. As with marketing plans, these estimates may be short-range plans, covering periods of less than one year; medium-range plans, covering one to five years; or long-range plans, covering more than five years. The estimates should also define the geographic boundaries of the forecast. For example, sales potential can be estimated for a city, county, state, or group of nations. Finally, analysts should indicate whether their estimates are for a specific product item, a product line, or an entire product category.

A **sales forecast** is an estimate of the amount of a product that an organization expects to sell during a certain period of time based on a specified level of marketing effort. Managers in different divisions of an organization rely on sales forecasts when they purchase raw materials, schedule production, secure financial resources, consider plant or equipment purchases, hire personnel, and plan inventory levels. Because the accuracy of a sales forecast is so important, organizations often use several forecasting methods, including executive judgments, surveys of buyers or sales personnel, time-series analyses, correlation analyses, and market tests. The specific methods used depend on the costs involved, type of product, characteristics of the market, time span of the forecast, purposes for which the forecast is used, stability of historical sales data, availability of the required information, and expertise and experience of forecasters.

SPOTLIGHT

When You Are 12–17 Years Old, What Is a Necessity?

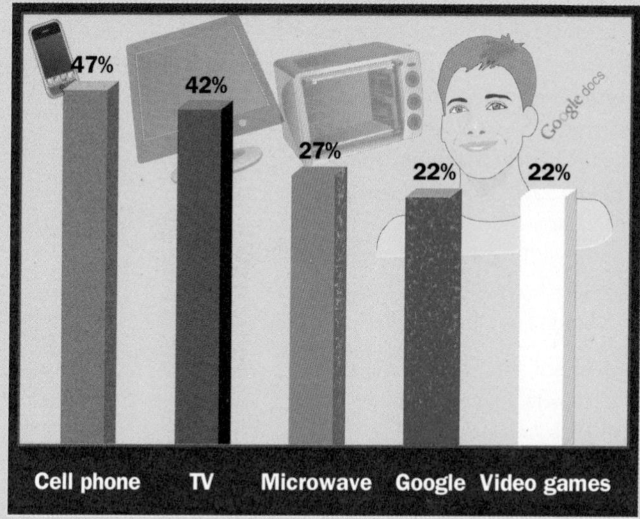

Source: Information from Lemelson-MIT Invention Index Survey of 500 teens.

Table 12.4 Components of the Marketing Plan

Plan Component	Component Summary	Highlights
Executive summary	One- to two-page synopsis of the entire marketing plan	
Environmental analysis	Information about the company's current situation with respect to the marketing environment	1. Assessment of marketing environment factors 2. Assessment of target market(s) 3. Assessment of current marketing objectives and performance
SWOT analysis	Assessment of the organization's strengths, weaknesses, opportunities, and threats	1. Strengths 2. Weaknesses 3. Opportunities 4. Threats
Marketing objectives	Specification of the firm's marketing objectives	Qualitative measures of what is to be accomplished
Marketing strategies	Outline of how the firm will achieve its objectives	1. Target market(s) 2. Marketing mix
Marketing implementation	Outline of how the firm will implement its marketing strategies	1. Marketing organization 2. Activities and responsibilities 3. Implementation timetable
Evaluation and control	Explanation of how the firm will measure and evaluate the results of the implemented plan	1. Performance standards 2. Financial controls 3. Monitoring procedures (audits)

Source: William M. Pride and O. C. Ferrell, *Marketing: Concepts and Strategies*, 16th ed. (Mason, OH: South-Western/Cengage Learning, 2012). Reprinted with permission.

sales forecast an estimate of the amount of a product that an organization expects to sell during a certain period of time based on a specified level of marketing effort

Career
SUCCESS

Marketing Yourself via Webcam

How can you market yourself during a webcam job interview? All kinds of companies are saving money and time by interviewing candidates via webcam. Recruiters for Zappos, the online retailer, screen applicants by calling them on Skype. While they listen to candidates talk, they also learn a lot by observing body language and facial expressions.

If you're asked to participate in a webcam interview, use the following tips to get ready.

- Check that your computer, camera, and microphone are all in working order.
- Plan to sit facing a good light source so that your face can be seen.
- Tidy up the area visible on camera and remove any inappropriate or distracting decorations.
- Close the windows to keep out street noise and close the doors for privacy. You want recruiters to focus on you, not on pets or people who happen to wander in during the interview.
- Plan to make a good impression by wearing appropriate business attire.
- Anticipate questions you might be asked and rehearse brief but meaty answers.

Do a run-through with a friend to be sure that you look professional on-screen and that your answers can be heard. Remember, your interview may be replayed several times before managers make any hiring decisions. Are you ready for your webcam close-up?

9

Distinguish between a marketing information system and marketing research.

Marketing Information

The availability and use of accurate and timely information are critical to make effective marketing decisions. A wealth of marketing information is obtainable. There are two general ways to obtain it: through a marketing information system and through marketing research.

Marketing Information Systems

A **marketing information system** is a system for managing marketing information that is gathered continually from internal and external sources. Most of these systems are computer based because of the amount of data the system must accept, store, sort, and retrieve. *Continual* collection of data is essential if the system is to incorporate the most up-to-date information.

In concept, the operation of a marketing information system is not complex. Data from a variety of sources are fed into the system. Data from *internal* sources include sales figures, product and marketing costs, inventory levels, and activities of the sales force. Data from *external* sources relate to the organization's suppliers, intermediaries, and customers; competitors' marketing activities; and economic conditions. All these data are stored and processed within the marketing information system. Its output is a flow of information in the form that is most useful for making marketing decisions. This information might include daily sales reports by territory and product, forecasts of sales or buying trends, and reports on changes in market share for the major brands in a specific industry. Both the information outputs and their form depend on the requirements of the personnel in the organization. Anheuser-Busch, for example, uses a system called BudNet that compiles information about past sales at individual stores, inventory, competitors' displays and prices, and a host of other information collected by distributors' sales representatives on handheld computers. BudNet allows

marketing information system a system for managing marketing information that is gathered continually from internal and external sources

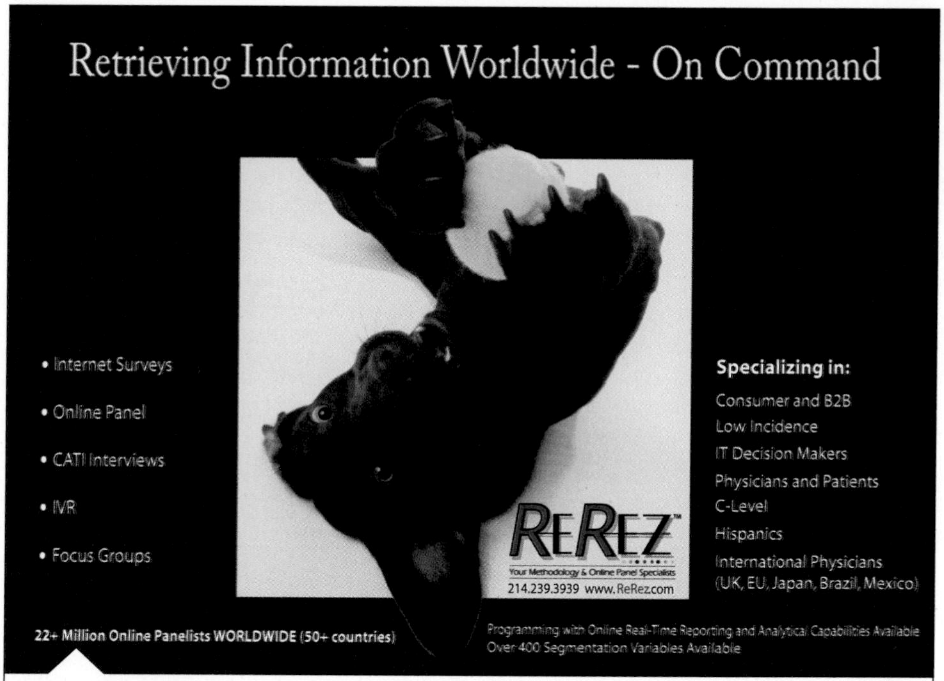

Retrieving Information Worldwide - On Command

- Internet Surveys
- Online Panel
- CATI Interviews
- IVR
- Focus Groups

ReRez™
Your Methodology & Online Panel Specialists
214.239.3939 www.ReRez.com

Specializing in:
Consumer and B2B
Low Incidence
IT Decision Makers
Physicians and Patients
C-Level
Hispanics
International Physicians (UK, EU, Japan, Brazil, Mexico)

22+ Million Online Panelists WORLDWIDE (50+ countries)

Programming with Online Real-Time Reporting and Analytical Capabilities Available
Over 400 Segmentation Variables Available

Marketing research. Marketing research service companies provide a variety of marketing research services to organizations that have information needs.

Courtesy of ReRez

managers to respond quickly to changes in social trends or competitors' strategies with an appropriate promotional message, package, display, or discount.[12]

Marketing Research

Marketing research is the process of systematically gathering, recording, and analyzing data concerning a particular marketing problem. Thus, marketing research is used in specific situations to obtain information not otherwise available to decision makers. It is an intermittent, rather than a continual, source of marketing information.

JCPenney, for example, conducted extensive research to learn more about a core segment of shoppers who were not being adequately reached by department stores: middle-income mothers between 35 and 54 years old. The research involved asking 900 women about their casual clothes preferences. Later, the firm conducted in-depth interviews with 30 women about their clothing needs, feelings about fashion, and shopping experiences. The research helped the company recognize that this "missing middle" segment of shoppers was frustrated with the choices and quality of the clothing available in their price range and stressed out by the experience of shopping for clothes for themselves. Armed with this information, JCPenney launched two new lines of moderately priced, quality casual women's clothing, including one by designer Nicole Miller.[13] A study by SPSS Inc. found that the most common reasons for conducting marketing research surveys included determining satisfaction (43 percent); product development (29 percent); branding (23 percent); segmentation (18 percent); awareness, trend tracking, and concept testing (18 percent); and business markets (11 percent).[14]

Table 12.5 outlines a six-step procedure for conducting marketing research. This procedure is particularly well-suited to test new products, determine various characteristics of consumer markets, and evaluate promotional activities. Food-processing companies, such as Kraft Foods and Kellogg's, use a variety of marketing research methods to avoid costly mistakes in introducing the wrong products, not to mention introducing products in the wrong way or at the wrong time. They have been particularly interested in using marketing research to learn more about the African-American and Hispanic markets. Understanding of the food preferences, loyalties, and purchase motivators of these groups enables companies to serve them better.

marketing research the process of systematically gathering, recording, and analyzing data concerning a particular marketing problem

Table 12.5 The Six Steps of Marketing Research

Step	Description
1. Define the problem.	In this step, the problem is stated clearly and accurately to determine what issues are involved in the research, what questions to ask, and what types of solutions are needed. This is a crucial step that should not be rushed.
2. Make a preliminary investigation.	The objective of preliminary investigation is to develop both a sharper definition of the problem and a set of tentative answers. The tentative answers are developed by examining internal information and published data and by talking with persons who have some experience with the problem. These answers will be tested by further research.
3. Plan the research.	At this stage, researchers know what facts are needed to resolve the identified problem and what facts are available. They make plans on how to gather needed but missing data.
4. Gather factual information.	Once the basic research plan has been completed, the needed information can be collected by mail, telephone, or personal interviews; by observation; or from commercial or government data sources. The choice depends on the plan and the available sources of information.
5. Interpret the information.	Facts by themselves do not always provide a sound solution to a marketing problem. They must be interpreted and analyzed to determine the choices available to management.
6. Reach a conclusion.	Sometimes the conclusion or recommendation becomes obvious when the facts are interpreted. However, in other cases, reaching a conclusion may not be so easy because of gaps in the information or intangible factors that are difficult to evaluate. If and when the evidence is less than complete, it is important to say so.

Using Technology to Gather and Analyze Marketing Information

Technology is making information for marketing decisions increasingly accessible. The ability of firms to track the purchase behaviors of customers electronically and to better determine what they want is changing the nature of marketing. The integration of telecommunications with computing technology provides marketers with access to accurate information not only about customers and competitors but also about industry forecasts and business trends. Among the communication tools that are radically changing the way marketers obtain and use information are databases, online information services, and the Internet.

A *database* is a collection of information arranged for easy access and retrieval. Using databases, marketers tap into internal sales reports, newspaper articles, company news releases, government economic reports, bibliographies, and more. Many marketers use commercial databases, such as LEXIS-NEXIS, to obtain useful information for marketing decisions. Many of these commercial databases are available in printed form (for a fee), online (for a fee), or on purchasable CD-ROMs. Other marketers develop their own databases in-house. Some firms sell their databases to other organizations. *Reader's Digest*, for example, markets a database that provides information on 100 million households. Dunn & Bradstreet markets a database that includes information on the addresses, phone numbers, and contacts of businesses located in specific areas.

Information provided by a single firm on household demographics, purchases, television viewing behavior, and responses to promotions such as coupons and free samples is called *single-source data*. For example, Behavior Scan, offered by Information Resources, Inc., screens about 60,000 households in 26 U.S. markets. This single-source information service monitors household televisions and records the programs and commercials viewed. When buyers from these households shop in stores equipped with scanning registers, they present Hotline cards (similar to credit cards) to cashiers. This enables each customer's identification to be coded electronically so that the firm can track each product purchased and store the information in a database.

Online information services offer subscribers access to e-mail, Web sites, files for downloading (such as with Acrobat Reader), news, databases, and research materials. By subscribing to mailing lists, marketers can receive electronic newsletters and participate in online discussions with other network users. This ability to communicate online with customers, suppliers, and employees improves the capability of a firm's marketing information system and helps the company track its customers' changing desires and buying habits.

The *Internet* has evolved as a powerful communication medium, linking customers and companies around the world via computer networks with e-mail, forums, Web pages, and more. Growth in Internet use has given rise to an entire industry that makes marketing information easily accessible to both companies and customers. Among the many Web pages useful for marketing research are the home pages of Nielsen marketing research and *Advertising Age*. While most Web pages are open to all Internet users, some companies, such as U.S. West and Turner Broadcasting System, also maintain internal Web pages, called *intranets,* that allow employees to access internal data and facilitate communication among departments.

Table 12.6 contains a variety of sources of secondary information, which is existing information that has been gathered by other organizations. Many of these sources are available through Web sites. As can be seen in Table 12.6, secondary information can be obtained from a variety of sources including government sources, trade associations, general publications and news sources, and corporate information.

A tool that has recently gained popularity as a means of marketing research is social media. There are many companies that have begun using various social media outlets to solicit feedback from customers on the company's existing or upcoming products. Not all information that a company receives will be solicited, however. A part of being involved in social media is exposing your company to unwanted or

Table 12.6 Sources of Secondary Information

Source	URL
Government sources	
Economic census	http://www.census.gov/econ/census07/
Export.gov—country and industry market research	http://www.export.gov/mrktresearch/index.asp
National Technical Information Services	http://www.ntis.gov/
STAT-USA	http://www.stat-usa.gov/
Strategis—Canadian trade	http://strategis.ic.gc.ca/engdoc/main.html
Trade associations and shows	
American Society of Association Executives	http://www.asaecenter.org/
Directory of Associations	http://www.marketingsource.com/associations/
Trade Show News Network	http://www.tsnn.com/
Magazines, newspapers, video, and audio news programming	
Blinkx	http://www.blinkx.com/
FindArticles.com	http://findarticles.com/p/articles/tn_bus/?tag=trunk
Google Video Search	http://video.google.com/
Media Jumpstation	http://www.directcontactpr.com/jumpstation/
Google News Directory	http://www.google.com/Top/News/
Yahoo! Video Search	http://video.search.yahoo.com/
Corporate information	
Annual Report Service	http://www.annualreportservice.com/
Bitpipe	http://www.bitpipe.com/
Business Wire—press releases	http://www.businesswire.com/
Hoover's Online	http://www.hoovers.com/
Open Directory Project	http://dmoz.org/
PR Newswire—press releases	http://www.prnewswire.com/

Source: Adapted from "Data Collection: Low-Cost Secondary Research," ***KnowThis.com*****, http://www.knowthis.com/principles-of-marketing-tutorials/data-collection-low-cost-secondary-research/ (accessed September 10, 2010).**

negative information from the general public. Nevertheless, these comments need to be regarded as useful and viable information from a marketing research standpoint. Customer complaints are opportunities for improvement; if handled correctly, they can be an invaluable source of data.

10

Identify the major steps in the consumer buying decision process and the sets of factors that may influence this process.

Types of Buying Behavior

Buying behavior may be defined as the decisions and actions of people involved in buying and using products.[15] **Consumer buying behavior** refers to the purchasing of products for personal or household use, not for business purposes. **Business buying behavior** is the purchasing of products by producers, resellers, governmental units, and institutions. Because a firm's success depends greatly on buyers' reactions to a particular marketing strategy, it is important to understand buying behavior. Marketing managers are better able to predict customer responses to marketing strategies and to develop a satisfying marketing mix if they are aware of the factors that affect buying behavior.

Consumer Buying Behavior

Consumers' buying behaviors differ when they buy different types of products. For frequently purchased low-cost items, a consumer uses routine response behavior involving very little search or decision-making effort. The buyer uses limited decision making for purchases made occasionally or when more information is needed about an unknown product in a well-known product category. When buying an unfamiliar, expensive item or one that is seldom purchased, the consumer engages in extensive decision making.

A person deciding on a purchase goes through some or all of the steps shown in Figure 12.4. First, the consumer acknowledges that a problem exists. A problem is usually the lack of a product or service that is desired or needed. Then, the buyer looks for information, which may include brand names, product characteristics, warranties, and other features. Next, the buyer weighs the various alternatives he or she has discovered and then finally makes a choice and acquires the item. In the after-purchase stage, the consumer evaluates the suitability of the product. This

Recognizing a problem. Some advertisements, such as this one for Olay Definity, are aimed at a particular stage of the consumer buying-decision process. This ad is meant to stimulate the problem-recognition stage of the buying-decision process.

Image courtesy of The Advertising Archives

buying behavior the decisions and actions of people involved in buying and using products

consumer buying behavior the purchasing of products for personal or household use, not for business purposes

business buying behavior the purchasing of products by producers, resellers, governmental units, and institutions

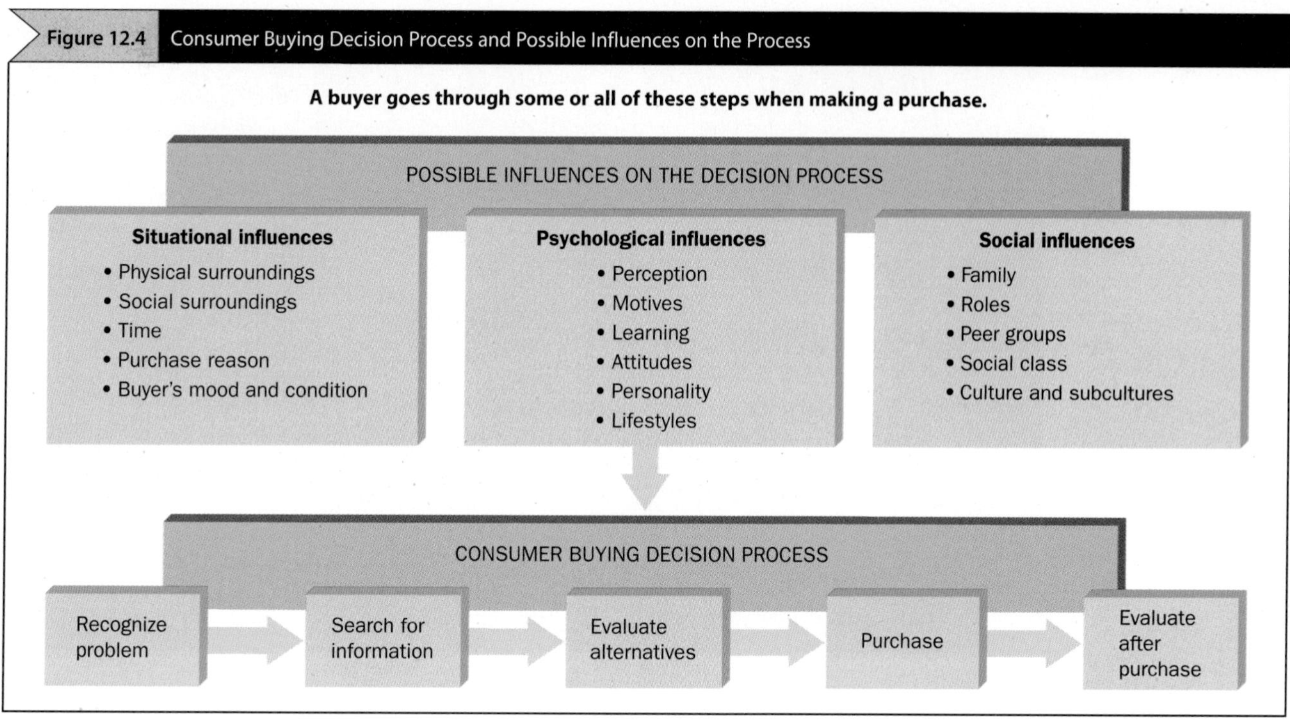

Consumer Buying Decision Process and Possible Influences on the Process

Source: William M. Pride and O. C. Ferrell, *Marketing: Concepts and Strategies*, 16th ed. (Mason, OH: South-Western/Cengage Learning, 2012). Adapted with permission.

judgment will affect future purchases. As Figure 12.4 shows, the buying process is influenced by situational factors (physical surroundings, social surroundings, time, purchase reason, and buyer's mood and condition), psychological factors (perception, motives, learning, attitudes, personality, and lifestyle), and social factors (family, roles, reference groups, online social networks, social class, culture, and subculture).

Consumer buying behavior is also affected by the ability to buy or one's buying power, which is largely determined by income. As every taxpayer knows, not all income is available for spending. For this reason, marketers consider income in three different ways. **Personal income** is the income an individual receives from all sources *less* the Social Security taxes the individual must pay. **Disposable income** is personal income *less* all additional personal taxes. These taxes include income, estate, gift, and property taxes levied by local, state, and federal governments. About 3 percent of all disposable income is saved. **Discretionary income** is disposable income *less* savings and expenditures on food, clothing, and housing. Discretionary income is of particular interest to marketers because consumers have the most choice in spending it. Consumers use their discretionary income to purchase items ranging from automobiles and vacations to movies and pet food.

Business Buying Behavior

Business buyers consider a product's quality, its price, and the service provided by suppliers. Business buyers are usually better informed than consumers about products and generally buy in larger quantities. In a business, a committee or a group of people, rather than just one person, often decides on purchases. Committee members must consider the organization's objectives, purchasing policies, resources, and personnel. Business buying occurs through description, inspection, sampling, or negotiation. A number of organizations buy a variety of products online.

personal income the income an individual receives from all sources *less* the Social Security taxes the individual must pay

disposable income personal income *less* all additional personal taxes

discretionary income disposable income *less* savings and expenditures on food, clothing, and housing

return to inside business

Apple

Apple, a pioneer of the personal computer, has always been interested in making its products user-friendly. In the days when computers were room-size and had numbers instead of names, Apple stood out by making easy-to-use desktop computers with easy-to-remember names. Thanks to savvy marketing and positive word of mouth, Apple's products are now in such high demand that many customers camp out in front of Apple Stores to be the first to buy new items.

When Apple launched its first touch-screen iPhone, it sold 1 million units in 74 days. A few years later, its touch-screen iPad tablet computer reached the 1-million mark in just 28 days. Initial response to the iPad was so strong, in fact, that Apple struggled to meet demand and had to temporarily delay release of the new product outside of the United States. What exciting new innovations are in Apple's marketing plans for the coming years?

Questions

1. How is Apple adding value by creating form, place, time, and possession utility?
2. What do you see as Apple's strengths, weaknesses, opportunities, and threats? How might this SWOT analysis affect Apple's marketing of new products?

CHAPTER REVIEW

SUMMARY

Summary

1 Understand the meaning of *marketing* and the importance of management of customer relationships.

Marketing is an organizational function and a set of processes for creating, communicating, and delivering value to customers and for managing customer relationships in ways that benefit the organization and its stakeholders. Maintaining positive relationships with customers is crucial. Relationship marketing is establishing long-term, mutually satisfying buyer–seller relationships. Customer relationship management uses information about customers to create marketing strategies that develop and sustain desirable customer relationships. Managing customer relationships requires identifying patterns of buying behavior and focusing on the most profitable customers. Customer lifetime value is a combination of purchase frequency, average value of purchases, and brand-switching patterns over the entire span of a customer's relationship with the company.

2 Explain how marketing adds value by creating several forms of utility.

Marketing adds value in the form of utility or the power of a product or service to satisfy a need. It creates place utility by making products available where customers want them, time utility by making products available when customers want them, and possession utility by transferring the ownership of products to buyers.

3 Trace the development of the marketing concept and understand how it is implemented.

From the Industrial Revolution until the early 20th century, businesspeople focused on the production of goods; from the 1920s to the 1950s, the emphasis moved to the selling of goods. During the 1950s, however, businesspeople recognized that their enterprises involved not only producing and selling products but also satisfying customers' needs. They began to implement the marketing concept, a business philosophy that involves the entire organization in the dual processes of meeting the customers' needs and achieving the organization's goals.

Implementation of the marketing concept begins and ends with customers—first to determine what customers' needs are and then to evaluate how well the firm is meeting these needs.

4 Understand what markets are and how they are classified.

A market consists of people with needs, the ability to buy, and the desire and authority to purchase. Markets are classified as consumer and industrial (producer, reseller, governmental, and institutional) markets.

5 Identify the four elements of the marketing mix and be aware of their importance in developing a marketing strategy.

A marketing strategy is a plan for the best use of an organization's resources to meet its objectives.

Developing a marketing strategy involves selecting and analyzing a target market and creating and maintaining a marketing mix that will satisfy the target market. A target market is chosen through either the undifferentiated approach or the market segmentation approach. A market segment is a group of individuals or organizations within a market that have similar characteristics and needs. Businesses that use an undifferentiated approach design a single marketing mix and direct it at the entire market for a particular product. The market segmentation approach directs a marketing mix at a segment of a market.

The four elements of a firm's marketing mix are product, price, distribution, and promotion. The product ingredient includes decisions about the product's design, brand name, packaging, and warranties. The pricing ingredient is concerned with both base prices and various types of discounts. Distribution involves not only transportation and storage but also the selection of intermediaries. Promotion focuses on providing information to target markets. The elements of the marketing mix can be varied to suit broad organizational goals, marketing objectives, and target markets.

6 Explain how the marketing environment affects strategic market planning.

To achieve a firm's marketing objectives, marketing-mix strategies must begin with an assessment of the marketing environment, which, in turn, will influence decisions about marketing-mix ingredients. Marketing activities are affected by a number of external forces that make up the marketing environment. These forces include economic forces, sociocultural forces, political forces, competitive forces, legal and regulatory forces, and technological forces. Economic forces affect customers' ability and willingness to buy. Sociocultural forces are societal and cultural factors, such as attitudes, beliefs, and lifestyles, that affect customers' buying choices. Political forces and legal and regulatory forces influence marketing planning through laws that protect consumers and regulate competition. Competitive forces are the actions of competitors who are implementing their own marketing plans. Technological forces can create new marketing opportunities or quickly cause a product to become obsolete.

7 Understand the major components of a marketing plan.

A marketing plan is a written document that specifies an organization's resources, objectives, strategy, and implementation and control efforts to be used in marketing a specific product or product group. The marketing plan describes a firm's current position, establishes marketing objectives, and specifies the methods the organization will use to achieve these objectives. Marketing plans can be short-range plans, covering one year or less; medium-range plans, covering two to five years; or long-range plans, covering periods of more than five years.

8 Describe how market measurement and sales forecasting are used.

Market measurement and sales forecasting are used to estimate sales potential and predict product sales in specific market segments.

9 Distinguish between a marketing information system and marketing research.

Strategies are monitored and evaluated through marketing research and the marketing information system that stores and processes internal and external data in a form that aids marketing decision making. A marketing information system is a system for managing marketing information that is gathered continually from internal and external sources. Marketing research is the process of systematically gathering, recording, and analyzing data concerning a particular marketing problem. It is an intermittent rather than a continual source of marketing information. Technology is making information for marketing decisions more accessible. Electronic communication tools can be very useful for accumulating accurate information with minimal customer interaction. Information technologies that are changing the way marketers obtain and use information are databases, online information services, and the Internet. Some companies are using social media to obtain feedback from customers.

10 Identify the major steps in the consumer buying decision process and the sets of factors that may influence this process.

Buying behavior consists of the decisions and actions of people involved in buying and using products. Consumer buying behavior refers to the purchase of products for personal or household use. Organizational buying behavior is the purchase of products by producers, resellers, governments, and institutions. Understanding buying behavior helps marketers to predict how buyers will respond to marketing strategies. The consumer buying decision process consists of five steps, that is, recognizing the problem, searching for information, evaluating alternatives, purchasing, and evaluating after purchase. Factors affecting the consumer buying decision process fall into three categories: situational influences, psychological influences, and social influences.

Key Terms

You should now be able to define and give an example relevant to each of the following terms:

marketing (335)
relationship marketing (337)
customer relationship management (CRM) (337)
customer lifetime value (337)
utility (337)
form utility (337)
place utility (337)
time utility (337)
possession utility (337)
marketing concept (338)
market (340)
marketing strategy (341)
marketing mix (341)
target market (341)
undifferentiated approach (341)
market segment (343)
market segmentation (343)
marketing plan (346)
sales forecast (347)
marketing information system (348)
marketing research (349)
buying behavior (352)
consumer buying behavior (352)
business buying behavior (352)
personal income (353)
disposable income (353)
discretionary income (353)

Review Questions

1. How, specifically, does marketing create place, time, and possession utility?
2. What is relationship marketing?
3. How is a marketing-oriented firm different from a production-oriented firm or a sales-oriented firm?
4. What are the major requirements for a group of individuals and organizations to be a market? How does a consumer market differ from a business-to-business market?
5. What are the major components of a marketing strategy?
6. What is the purpose of market segmentation? What is the relationship between market segmentation and the selection of target markets?
7. What are the four elements of the marketing mix? In what sense are they "controllable"?
8. Describe the forces in the marketing environment that affect an organization's marketing decisions.
9. What is a marketing plan, and what are its major components?
10. What major issues should be specified before conducting a sales forecast?
11. What is the difference between a marketing information system and a marketing research project? How might the two be related?
12. What new information technologies are changing the ways that marketers keep track of business trends and customers?
13. What are the major sources of secondary information?
14. Why do marketers need to understand buying behavior?
15. How are personal income, disposable income, and discretionary income related? Which is the best indicator of consumer purchasing power?

Discussion Questions

1. What problems might face a company that focuses mainly on its most profitable customers?
2. In what way is each of the following a marketing activity?
   a. The provision of sufficient parking space for customers at a suburban shopping mall.
   b. The purchase by a clothing store of seven dozen sweaters in assorted sizes and colors.
   c. The inclusion of a longer and more comprehensive warranty on an automobile.
3. How might adoption of the marketing concept benefit a firm? How might it benefit the firm's customers?
4. Is marketing information as important to small firms as it is to larger firms? Explain.
5. How does the marketing environment affect a firm's marketing strategy?

Video Case 12.1

E*Trade Builds Long-Term Customer Relationships

Even if you are not an active investor, you probably already know e*Trade, the online investing service, from its wildly successful series of funny television commercials. The ads feature an irreverent talking baby wielding a laptop and boasting about his investing expertise to all his admiring baby friends. The commercials were inspired by e*Trade's desire to come up with a marketing message that would not only be memorable and funny but would also create an overall sense of unity in its marketing efforts. (Before the baby appeared, each new advertisement was a start-from-scratch proposition.)

The theme of ease of use that the baby conveys has proven effective through several e*Trade advertising campaigns and Super Bowl spots. The ads' light-hearted appeal has also helped the company strengthen its brand name, particularly among hard-to-reach and highly desirable 20-somethings. Even the outtake reels have proven popular, and an online "Baby Mail" campaign in which viewers can insert their own words or their own pictures and share them with friends has successfully extended the marketing message from television to the Internet and from passive to interactive. "We are one of the largest online advertisers," says the company's senior vice president of marketing. "And we're an online company, so it stands to reason that we'd find different types of interactive ways to be able to reach consumers through the Internet as well."

E*Trade is a publicly traded financial and banking services company that encourages customers to take control of their own financial futures with an array of quick and easy-to-use online tools, products, and services. These are available online and also through a network of customer service representatives reachable both via telephone and in person at one of e*Trade's 28 retail branches across the United States. Mobile applications for the iPhone and the BlackBerry include access to a stripped-down e*Trade Web site and target both experienced and novice investors. Securities can be traded instantaneously (when the stock exchanges are open; otherwise, the next trading day) or when a particular security meets the customer's desired buy or sell price.

E*Trade can accommodate customers' long- and short-term financial goals and prides itself on its ability to offer customers exactly what they need, often by replicating, as nearly as possible, the experience of talking to a financial advisor. Even if a user is just looking for information about investing, the company's online Investor Resource Center provides free educational articles, brief three-minute videos, webinars, and seminars about many different types of investment topics, from basic to sophisticated, as well as access to independent research about investment options. "Education has become a really major component for us and for our customers," says one of the company's vice presidents. A new feedback link on the company's Web site allows users to tell e*Trade what they like or don't like about a page on the Resource Center so improvements can be made. "It's really a core lesson in listening to your customers, what they want, and not always thinking that you know what they want," says a company executive.

Meanwhile, e*Trade's baby is unlikely to grow up very soon. "When people see that baby," says a company executive, "they stop their DVRs and they watch. I think the real challenge for us is being able to blend the combination of humor, magic, and the overall value proposition and message in a way that none of it gets buried."[16]

Questions

1. How does e*Trade manage its customer relationships?
2. How many different kinds of utility does e*Trade provide for its customers?
3. Why are young adults a desirable target market for a company like e*Trade?

Case 12.2

PepsiCo Tailors Tastes to Tantalize Tastebuds of Target Markets

PepsiCo, the world's leading snack marketer, aims to gobble up more market share through careful targeting and creative marketing. Most of PepsiCo's sales come from North and South America, where it has traditionally been a strong competitor. Among its ever-expanding pantry of brands, 19 are already billion-dollar businesses, including Pepsi-Cola, Diet Pepsi, and Mountain Dew soft drinks; Lay's, Doritos, and Tostitos chips; Lipton teas; Tropicana fruit drinks; Gatorade sports drinks; Quaker foods; and Aquafina bottled waters.

The company faces aggressive competition from Coca-Cola and Draft Foods, both of which are making marketing waves in the Americas, across Europe, and in Asia. It must also deal with a variety of local brands that, in some cases, have large and loyal customer bases. Therefore, PepsiCo's marketers constantly research customers' needs and study the influence of environmental forces so that they can develop the right marketing mix for the right market.

One global trend that PepsiCo's marketers have identified is increased interest in healthier eating. Several years ago, the U.K. government mounted a campaign warning consumers of the dangers of high salt intake and urged them to change their diets. In response, PepsiCo slashed the amount of sodium in its locally popular Walkers snacks by 25 percent. With U.S. health experts also calling for lower salt in processed foods, PepsiCo is now reducing the level of salt in many other snacks worldwide. It is also lightening up on fats and sugar and making nutrition labeling more prominent so that consumers can make educated choices. "What we want to do with our 'fun for you' products is to make them the healthiest 'fun for you' products," says the CEO.

Another trend that PepsiCo's marketers noticed is sharply higher use of digital media among teenagers and young adults, a large and lucrative target market for snacks and beverages. As a result, PepsiCo has stepped up its use of the Internet, blogs, Twitter, Facebook, and YouTube to communicate with and influence these consumers. Its Dewmocracy campaigns, for example, invite customers to vote online for their favorite new Mountain Dew flavors. It has also run contests asking customers to create and submit homemade television commercials for Doritos chips. After posting the finalists online for public viewing and voting, PepsiCo airs the winning advertisements during the Super Bowl, giving winners cash prizes and their 30 seconds of fame.

PepsiCo's recent Refresh Project, one of its more unusual marketing efforts, combined digital marketing with social responsibility. During the year-long program, PepsiCo invited consumers to apply online for grants to make a difference in their community. Every month, the public voted on which grants they thought were most deserving of funding. In all, PepsiCo awarded nearly $20 million in grants, got tens of thousands of customers interested in the project, and earned positive publicity for its good works. Of course, PepsiCo hoped that customers would also notice and respond to its social responsibility when they were making buying decisions about snacks and beverages.

These days, PepsiCo is keeping up a steady stream of new product introductions, based on marketing research that helps it understand the preferences of customers in each country. For example, catering to Russian palates, it offers Lay's chips flavored with red caviar. In China, its Cao Ben Le drinks feature herb flavors that local customers favor. In Japan, knowing that its customers look forward to seasonal variety, the company has launched a series of limited-edition soft drinks such as Pepsi Baobab (with the tang of African fruit flavor). In India, it markets Nimbooz by 7Up, its unique twist on a traditional lemon drink. What will PepsiCo do next in its quest to satisfy its global customer base?[17]

Questions

1. What is PepsiCo's approach to target marketing?
2. How are forces in the marketing environment affecting PepsiCo's marketing strategy?
3. Which influences on consumer buying behavior should PepsiCo pay particular attention to, and why?

Building Skills for Career Success

1 JOURNALING FOR SUCCESS

Discovery statement: This chapter emphasized the importance of keeping the customer at the core of every marketing decision.

Assignment

1. Think about the businesses from which you have purchased goods or services. Select the organization that you believe has adopted the marketing concept. Discuss the reasons why you believe that this company has adopted the marketing concept.
2. Describe the marketing mix this company has created for the brand that you purchase from this company.
3. Which two companies are the strongest competitors of this organization? Explain why.
4. Besides competition, which environmental forces have the greatest impact on this company for which you are a customer?
5. Calculate your customer lifetime value to this company. After recording your customer lifetime value, describe how you calculated it.

2 EXPLORING THE INTERNET

Consumer products companies with a variety of famous brand names known around the world are making their presence known on the Internet through Web sites and online banner advertising. The giants in consumer products include U.S.-based Procter & Gamble (http://www.pg.com/), Swiss-based Nestlé (http://www.nestle.com/), and U.K.-based Unilever (http://www.unilever.com/).

According to a spokesperson for the Unilever Interactive Brand Center in New York, the firm is committed to making the Internet part of its marketing strategy. The center carries out research and development and serves as a model for others now in operation in the Netherlands and Singapore. Information is shared with interactive marketers assigned to specific business units. Eventually, centers will be established globally, reflecting the fact that most of Unilever's $52 billion in sales takes place in about 100 countries around the world.

Unilever's view that online consumer product sales are the way of the future was indicated by online alliances established with Microsoft Network, America Online, and NetGrocer.com. Creating an online dialogue with consumers on a global scale is no simple task. Cultural differences are often subtle and difficult to explain but nonetheless are perceived by the viewers interacting with a site. Unilever's Web site, which is its connection to customers all over the world, has a global feel to it. The question is whether it is satisfactory to each target audience. Visit the text Web site for updates to this exercise.

Assignment

1. Examine the Unilever, Procter & Gamble, and Nestlé sites and describe the features that you think would be most interesting to consumers.
2. Describe the features you do not like and explain why.
3. Do you think that the sites can contribute to better consumer buyer behavior? Explain your thinking.

❸ DEVELOPING CRITICAL-THINKING SKILLS

Market segmentation is the process of breaking down a larger target market into smaller segments. One common base of market segmentation is demographics. Demographics for the consumer market, which consists of individuals and household members who buy goods for their own use, include criteria such as age, gender, race, religion, income, family size, occupation, education, social class, and marital status. Liz Claiborne, Inc., retailer of women's apparel, uses demographics to target a market it calls *Liz Lady*. The company knows Liz Lady's age, income range, professional status, and family status, and it uses this profile to make marketing decisions.

Assignment

1. Identify a company that markets to the consumer.
2. Identify the company's major product.
3. Determine the demographics of one of the company's markets.
   a. From the list that follows, choose the demographics that apply to this market. (Remember that the demographics chosen must relate to the interest, need, and ability of the customer to purchase the product.)
   b. Briefly describe each demographic characteristic.

Consumer	Market	Description
Age		
Gender		
Race		
Ethnicity		
Income		
Occupation		
Family size		
Education		
Religion		
Homeowner		
Marital status		
Social class		

4. Summarize your findings in a statement that describes the target market for the company's product.

❹ BUILDING TEAM SKILLS

Review the text definitions of *market* and *target market*. Markets can be classified as consumer or industrial. Buyer behavior consists of the decisions and actions of those involved in buying and using products or services. By examining aspects of a company's products, you usually can determine the company's target market and the characteristics important to members of that target market.

Assignment

1. Working in teams of three to five, identify a company and its major products.
2. List and discuss characteristics that customers may find important. These factors may include price, quality, brand name, variety of services, salespeople, customer service, special offers, promotional campaign, packaging, convenience of use, convenience of purchase, location, guarantees, store/office decor, and payment terms.
3. Write a description of the company's primary customer (target market).

❺ RESEARCHING DIFFERENT CAREERS

Before interviewing for a job, you should learn all you can about the company. With this information, you will be prepared to ask meaningful questions about the firm during the interview, and the interviewer no doubt will be impressed with your knowledge of the business and your interest in it. To find out about a company, you can conduct some market research.

Assignment

1. Choose at least two local companies for which you might like to work.
2. Contact your local Chamber of Commerce. (The Chamber of Commerce collects information about local businesses, and most of its services are free.) Ask for information about the companies.
3. Call the Better Business Bureau in your community and ask if there are any complaints against the companies.
4. Prepare a report summarizing your findings.

Creating and Pricing Products that Satisfy Customers

© AP Images/Paul Sakuma

13

Learning Objectives

What you will be able to do once you complete this chapter:

1. Explain what a product is and how products are classified.
2. Discuss the product life-cycle and how it leads to new-product development.
3. Define *product line* and *product mix* and distinguish between the two.
4. Identify the methods available for changing a product mix.
5. Explain the uses and importance of branding, packaging, and labeling.
6. Describe the economic basis of pricing and the means by which sellers can control prices and buyers' perceptions of prices.
7. Identify the major pricing objectives used by businesses.
8. Examine the three major pricing methods that firms employ.
9. Explain the different strategies available to companies for setting prices.
10. Describe three major types of pricing associated with business products

FYI

inside business

Did You Know?

By its tenth anniversary, Threadless was ringing up more than $30 million in annual sales and attracting 300 new T-shirt designs every day.

Customers Design the Products at Threadless

Loyal customers are also loyal designers at Threadless, a fast-growing T-shirt company based in Chicago. The idea for Threadless grew out of Jake Nickell's hobby of creating digital designs for T-shirts. In 2000, after one of his designs won a contest, 20-year-old Nickell teamed up with his friend Jacob DeHart to start a new business. Their unique marketing twist was that the T-shirts they sold would feature digital designs submitted and selected by customers through online voting.

The first contest, which offered a grand prize of two free T-shirts, drew dozens of entries. Threadless printed and sold 24 copies each of the five top vote getters. Soon the company began paying $100 for each winning design, an amount it gradually raised above $2,000. By 2002, Threadless had 10,000 customers voting on designs and was selling $100,000 worth of T-shirts. By 2010, annual sales had skyrocketed beyond $30 million, and customers were submitting 300 designs per *day*.

Threadless starts a new design competition every Monday. It encourages designers to show off their best work and stir up voter excitement by using social media such as Facebook and Twitter. The designs that receive the best scores are moved into production. Several weeks later, the new T-shirts appear for sale on the Threadless home page, and designers jump back into the process to promote their winning work. This constant stream of new designs and new T-shirts brings customers back again and again to vote and to buy.

By marketing only designs that customers approve with their votes, Threadless keeps costs down and profit margins high. Sooner or later, all of its T-shirts sell out, and customers can vote to have sold-out designs reprinted. Although Threadless operates two small outlet stores as well as its Web site, its products aren't widely available, which only enhances the value that customers perceive in its products.

To accommodate its increasingly international customer base, Threadless translates its Web content into French, German, and Spanish. Already, overseas sales account for 40 percent of Threadless's revenue. Watch for more growth as Threadless expands into shirts with hoods, art prints, and other products featuring designs created by loyal—and talented—customers.[1]

A **product**, like a Threadless T-shirt, is everything one receives in an exchange, including all tangible and intangible attributes and expected benefits. An Apple iPod purchase, for example, includes not only the iPod itself but also earphones, instructions, and a warranty. A car includes a warranty, an owner's manual, and perhaps free emergency road service for a year. Some of the intangibles that may go with an automobile include the status associated with ownership and the memories generated from past rides. Developing and managing products effectively are crucial to an organization's ability to maintain successful marketing mixes.

A product may be a good, a service, or an idea. A *good* is a real, physical thing that we can touch, such as a Classic Sport football. A *service* is the result of applying human or mechanical effort to a person or thing. Basically, a *service* is a change we pay others to make for us. A real estate agent's services result in a change in the ownership of real property. A barber's services result in a change in your appearance. An *idea* may take the form of philosophies, lessons, concepts, or advice. Often ideas are included with a good or service. Thus, we might buy a book (a good) that provides ideas on how to lose weight. Alternatively, we might join Weight Watchers for ideas on how to lose weight and for help (services) in doing so.

product everything one receives in an exchange, including all tangible and intangible attributes and expected benefits; it may be a good, a service, or an idea

We look first in this chapter at products. We examine product classifications and describe the four stages, or life-cycles, through which every product moves. Next, we illustrate how firms manage products effectively by modifying or deleting existing products and by developing new products. We also discuss branding, packaging, and labeling of products. Then our focus shifts to pricing. We explain competitive factors that influence sellers' pricing decisions and also explore buyers' perceptions of prices. After considering organizational objectives that can be accomplished through pricing, we outline several methods for setting prices. Finally, we describe pricing strategies by which sellers can reach target markets successfully.

Classification of Products

1

Explain what a product is and how products are classified.

Different classes of products are directed at particular target markets. A product's classification largely determines what kinds of distribution, promotion, and pricing are appropriate in marketing the product.

Products can be grouped into two general categories: consumer and business (also called *business-to-business* or *industrial products*). A product purchased to satisfy personal and family needs is a **consumer product**. A product bought for resale, for making other products, or for use in a firm's operations is a **business product**. The buyer's use of the product determines the classification of an item. Note that a single item can be both a consumer and a business product. A broom is a consumer product if you use it in your home. However, the same broom is a business product if you use it in the maintenance of your business. After a product is classified as a consumer or business product, it can be categorized further as a particular type of consumer or business product.

consumer product a product purchased to satisfy personal and family needs

business product a product bought for resale, for making other products, or for use in a firm's operations

convenience product a relatively inexpensive, frequently purchased item for which buyers want to exert only minimal effort

shopping product an item for which buyers are willing to expend considerable effort on planning and making the purchase

specialty product an item that possesses one or more unique characteristics for which a significant group of buyers is willing to expend considerable purchasing effort

Consumer Product Classifications

The traditional and most widely accepted system of classifying consumer products consists of three categories: convenience, shopping, and specialty products. These groupings are based primarily on characteristics of buyers' purchasing behavior.

A **convenience product** is a relatively inexpensive, frequently purchased item for which buyers want to exert only minimal effort. Examples include bread, gasoline, newspapers, soft drinks, and chewing gum. The buyer spends little time in planning the purchase of a convenience item or in comparing available brands or sellers.

A **shopping product** is an item for which buyers are willing to expend considerable effort on planning and making the purchase. Buyers allocate ample time for comparing stores and brands with respect to prices, product features, qualities, services, and perhaps warranties. Appliances, upholstered furniture, men's suits, bicycles, and cellular phones are examples of shopping products. These products are expected to last for a fairly long time and thus are purchased less frequently than convenience items.

A **specialty product** possesses one or more unique characteristics for which a group of buyers is willing to expend considerable purchasing effort. Buyers actually plan the purchase of a specialty product; they know exactly what they want and will not accept a substitute. In searching for specialty products, purchasers do not compare alternatives. Examples include unique sports cars, a specific type of antique dining table, a rare imported beer, or perhaps special handcrafted stereo speakers.

Specialty products. Most cars are classified as shopping products. However, a few automobiles, such as the Bentley, are extremely expensive, have distinctive styling and amenities, and are distributed exclusively through just a few dealers. These distinctive vehicles are specialty products.

Component parts. Tires and tire rims are component parts used in the production of vehicles.

One problem with this approach to classification is that buyers may behave differently when purchasing a specific type of product. Thus, a single product can fit into more than one category. To minimize this problem, marketers think in terms of how buyers are most likely to behave when purchasing a specific item.

Business Product Classifications

Based on their characteristics and intended uses, business products can be classified into the following categories: raw materials, major equipment, accessory equipment, component parts, process materials, supplies, and services.

A **raw material** is a basic material that actually becomes part of a physical product. It usually comes from mines, forests, oceans, or recycled solid wastes. Raw materials are usually bought and sold according to grades and specifications.

Major equipment includes large tools and machines used for production purposes. Examples of major equipment are lathes, cranes, and stamping machines. Some major equipment is custom-made for a particular organization, but other items are standardized products that perform one or several tasks for many types of organizations.

Accessory equipment is standardized equipment used in a firm's production or office activities. Examples include hand tools, fax machines, fractional horsepower motors, and calculators. Compared with major equipment, accessory items are usually much less expensive and are purchased routinely with less negotiation.

A **component part** becomes part of a physical product and is either a finished item ready for assembly or a product that needs little processing before assembly. Although it becomes part of a larger product, a component part can often be identified easily. Clocks, tires, computer chips, and switches are examples of component parts.

A **process material** is used directly in the production of another product. Unlike a component part, however, a process material is not readily identifiable in the finished product. Like component parts, process materials are purchased according to industry standards or to the specifications of the individual purchaser. Examples include industrial glue and food preservatives.

A **supply** facilitates production and operations but does not become part of a finished product. Paper, pencils, oils, and cleaning agents are examples.

A **business service** is an intangible product that an organization uses in its operations. Examples include financial, legal, online, janitorial, and marketing research services. Purchasers must decide whether to provide their own services internally or to hire them from outside the organization.

raw material a basic material that actually becomes part of a physical product; usually comes from mines, forests, oceans, or recycled solid wastes

major equipment large tools and machines used for production purposes

accessory equipment standardized equipment used in a firm's production or office activities

component part an item that becomes part of a physical product and is either a finished item ready for assembly or a product that needs little processing before assembly

process material a material that is used directly in the production of another product but is not readily identifiable in the finished product

supply an item that facilitates production and operations but does not become part of a finished product

business service an intangible product that an organization uses in its operations

2

Discuss the product life-cycle and how it leads to new-product development.

The Product Life-Cycle

In a way, products are like people. They are born, they live, and they die. Every product progresses through a **product life-cycle**, a series of stages in which a product's sales revenue and profit increase, reach a peak, and then decline. A firm must be able to launch, modify, and delete products from its offering of products in response to changes in product life-cycles. Otherwise, the firm's profits will disappear, and the firm will fail. Depending on the product, life-cycle stages will vary in length. In this section, we discuss the stages of the life-cycle and how marketers can use this information.

product life-cycle a series of stages in which a product's sales revenue and profit increase, reach a peak, and then decline

Figure 13.1 Product Life-Cycle

The graph shows sales volume and profits during the life-cycle of a product.

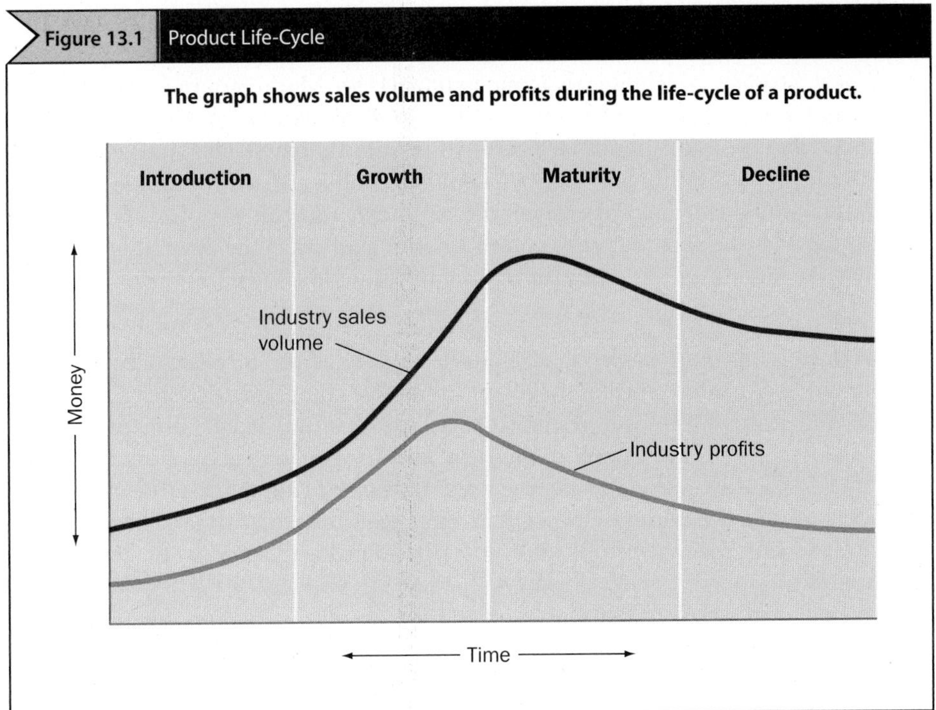

Source: William M. Pride and O. C. Ferrell, *Marketing: Concepts and Strategies*, 16th ed. (Mason, OH: South-Western/Cengage Learning, 2012). Adapted with permission.

Stages of the Product Life-Cycle

Generally, the product life-cycle is assumed to be composed of four stages—introduction, growth, maturity, and decline—as shown in Figure 13.1. Some products progress through these stages rapidly, in a few weeks or months. Others may take years to go through each stage. The Rubik's Cube had a relatively short life-cycle. In contrast, Parker Brothers' Monopoly game, which was introduced over 70 years ago, is still going strong.

Introduction In the *introduction stage,* customer awareness and acceptance of the product are low. Sales rise gradually as a result of promotion and distribution activities; initially, however, high development and marketing costs result in low profit or even in a loss. There are relatively few competitors. The price is sometimes high, and purchasers are primarily people who want to be "the first" to own the new product. The marketing challenge at this stage is to make potential customers aware of the product's existence and its features, benefits, and uses. Apple, for example, recently introduced the iPad, a highly portable tablet computer. The iPad was described as revolutionary by many—combining the touch screen and features of an iPod Touch with the hard drive space of a Mac computer. In addition, the product can function as an e-reader, able to display electronic books. Apple created a new iBooks application for their iPad, where customers can purchase and download books from a large electronic library. With the release of the iPad, Apple further improved their market penetration in the personal computer market while also entering the e-reader market. The product's starting price of $499, although high compared to its e-reader market competitors, reflected the iPad's impressive additional features. The product's

Product life-cycle. The iPad is currently in the introduction stage of the product life-cycle, but as more competitors release similar products, it will move into the growth stage.

introduction was a success, with Apple selling its one-millionth iPad just 28 days after the product was introduced to the market.[2]

A new product is seldom an immediate success. Marketers must watch early buying patterns carefully and be prepared to modify the new product promptly if necessary. The product should be priced to attract the particular market segment that has the greatest desire and ability to buy the product. Plans for distribution and promotion should suit the targeted market segment. As with the product itself, the initial price, distribution channels, and promotional efforts may need to be adjusted quickly to maintain sales growth during the introduction stage.

Growth In the *growth stage,* sales increase rapidly as the product becomes well-known. Other firms have probably begun to market competing products. The competition and lower unit costs (owing to mass production) result in a lower price, which reduces the profit per unit. Note that industry profits reach a peak and begin to decline during this stage. To meet the needs of the growing market, the originating firm offers modified versions of its product and expands its distribution. For example, the 3M Company, the maker of Post-it Notes, has developed a variety of sizes, colors, and designs.

Management's goal in the growth stage is to stabilize and strengthen the product's position by encouraging brand loyalty. To beat the competition, the company may further improve the product or expand the product line to appeal to additional market segments. Apple, for example, has introduced several variations of its wildly popular iPod MP3 player. The iPod Shuffle is the smallest and most affordable version, whereas the iPod Nano offers song, photo, and video support in a thin, lightweight version that has a built-in video camera. The iPod Classic provides up to 160 GB of hard drive space, the most of any of the versions. The iPod Touch has a large, vibrant touch screen and an additional Wi-Fi connection that can use GPS technology and download applications. Apple has expanded its iTunes Music Store to include downloadable versions of popular TV shows that can be purchased per episode or as an entire season, exclusive music video downloads, and movies that can be purchased or rented online. Apple greatly expanded its product mix with the release of the iPhone, a combination iPod Touch and cell phone. Continuous product innovation and service expansion have helped to expand Apple's market penetration in the competitive MP3 player market.[3]

Management also may compete by lowering prices if increased production efficiency has resulted in savings for the company. As the product becomes more widely accepted, marketers may be able to broaden the network of distributors. Marketers can also emphasize customer service and prompt credit for defective products. During this period, promotional efforts attempt to build brand loyalty among customers.

Maturity Sales are still increasing at the beginning of the *maturity stage,* but the rate of increase has slowed. Later in this stage, the sales curve peaks and begins to decline. Industry profits decline throughout this stage. Product lines are simplified, markets are segmented more carefully, and price competition increases. The increased competition forces weaker competitors to leave the industry. Refinements and extensions of the original product continue to appear on the market.

During a product's maturity stage, its market share may be strengthened by redesigned packaging or style changes. In addition, consumers may be encouraged to use the product more often or in new ways. Pricing strategies are flexible during this stage. Markdowns and price incentives are not uncommon, although price increases may work to offset production and distribution costs. Marketers may offer incentives and assistance of various kinds to dealers to encourage them to support mature products, especially in the face of competition from private-label brands. New promotional efforts and aggressive personal selling may be necessary during this period of intense competition.

Decline During the *decline stage,* sales volume decreases sharply. Profits continue to fall. The number of competing firms declines, and the only survivors in the marketplace are firms that specialize in marketing the product. Production and marketing costs become the most important determinant of profit.

When a product adds to the success of the overall product line, the company may retain it; otherwise, management must determine when to eliminate the product. A product usually declines because of technological advances or environmental factors or because consumers have switched to competing brands. Therefore, few changes are made in the product itself during this stage. Instead, management may raise the price to cover costs, reprice to maintain market share, or lower the price to reduce inventory. Similarly, management will narrow distribution of the declining product to the most profitable existing markets. During this period, the company probably will not spend heavily on promotion, although it may use some advertising and sales incentives to slow the product's decline. The company may choose to eliminate less-profitable versions of the product from the product line or may decide to drop the product entirely. General Motors (GM), for example, recently had to discontinue its Hummer brand. The company originally tried to sell the brand to a Chinese manufacturer, but the deal fell through, and GM had to begin phasing out Hummer vehicles. Although the brand had several loyal customers, GM claimed declining sales, the recession, and increased customer value of sustainability as reasons for the discontinuation. The CEO of GM himself acknowledged that the brand had developed a negative stigma as being a gas-guzzling icon of wealth and didn't think the brand could be salvaged.[4]

Using the Product Life-Cycle

Marketers should be aware of the life-cycle stage of each product for which they are responsible. Moreover, they should try to estimate how long the product is expected to remain in that stage. Both must be taken into account in making decisions about the marketing strategy for a product. If a product is expected to remain in the maturity stage for a long time, a replacement product might be introduced later in the maturity stage. If the maturity stage is expected to be short, however, a new product should be introduced much earlier. In some cases, a firm may be willing to take the chance of speeding up the decline of existing products. In other situations, a company will attempt to extend a product's life-cycle. For example, General Mills has extended the life of Bisquick baking mix (launched in the mid-1930s) by improving the product's formulation significantly and creating and promoting a variety of uses.

Product Line and Product Mix

3

Define *product line* and *product mix* and distinguish between the two.

A **product line** is a group of similar products that differ only in relatively minor characteristics. Generally, the products within a product line are related to each other in the way they are produced, marketed, or used. Procter & Gamble, for example, manufactures and markets several shampoos, including Prell, Head & Shoulders, and Ivory.

Many organizations tend to introduce new products within existing product lines. This permits them to apply the experience and knowledge they have acquired to the production and marketing of new products. Other firms develop entirely new product lines.

An organization's **product mix** consists of all the products the firm offers for sale. For example, Procter & Gamble, which acquired Gillette, has over 85 brands that fall into one of three product line categories: beauty and grooming, health and well-being, and household care.[5] Two "dimensions" are often applied to a firm's product mix. The *width* of the mix is the number of product lines it contains. The *depth* of the mix is the average number of individual products within each line. These are general measures; we speak of a *broad* or a *narrow* mix rather than a mix of exactly three or five product lines. Some organizations provide broad product mixes to be competitive.

product line a group of similar products that differ only in relatively minor characteristics

product mix all the products a firm offers for sale

4

Identify the methods available for changing a product mix.

Managing the Product Mix

To provide products that satisfy people in a firm's target market or markets and that also achieve the organization's objectives, a marketer must develop, adjust, and maintain an effective product mix. Seldom can the same product mix be effective for long. Because customers' product preferences and attitudes change, their desire for a product may diminish or grow. In some cases, a firm needs to alter its product mix to adapt to competition. A marketer may have to eliminate a product from the mix because one or more competitors dominate that product's specific market segment. Similarly, an organization may have to introduce a new product or modify an existing one to compete more effectively. A marketer may also expand the firm's product mix to take advantage of excess marketing and production capacity. For example, both Coca-Cola and Pepsi have expanded their lines by adding to their existing brands and acquiring new brands as well. In response to the increasing popularity of energy drinks, Coca-Cola acquired the Full Throttle brand, whereas Pepsi acquired AMP. In an effort to seem more health conscious, both companies came out with new sugar-free or zero-calorie soda products, along with more juice brands. Coca-Cola contains brands such as Minute Maid, Simply Orange, and FUZE, whereas Pepsi contains Tropicana, Ocean Spray, Dole, and SoBe. For tea and coffee brands, Coca-Cola has Nestea and Caribou Iced Coffee, whereas Pepsi has partnerships with Lipton and Starbucks. Both companies are also involved in the fast-growing sports drink category, with Coca-Cola's POWERADE and Pepsi's Gatorade and Propel among the top competitors. Coca-Cola even has a brand in the alcohol category: BACARDI Mixers.[6] For whatever reason a product mix is altered, the product mix must be managed to bring about improvements in the mix. There are three major ways to improve a product mix: change an existing product, delete a product, or develop a new product.

product modification the process of changing one or more of a product's characteristics

Product lines. Burberry produces several product lines including shoes, handbags, sunglasses, watches, and apparel.

Image courtesy of The Advertising Archives

Managing Existing Products

A product mix can be changed by deriving additional products from existing ones. This can be accomplished through product modifications and by line extensions.

Product Modifications **Product modification** refers to changing one or more of a product's characteristics. For this approach to be effective, several conditions must be met. First, the product must be modifiable. Second, existing customers must be able to perceive that a modification has been made, assuming that the modified item is still directed at the same target market. Third, the modification should make the product more consistent with customers' desires so that it provides greater satisfaction. For example, Energizer increased its product's durability by using better materials—a larger cathode and anode interface—that make batteries last longer.

Existing products can be altered in three primary ways: in quality, function, and aesthetics. *Quality modifications* are changes that relate to a product's dependability and durability and are usually achieved by alterations in the materials or production process. *Functional modifications* affect a product's versatility, effectiveness, convenience, or safety; they usually require redesign of the product. Typical product categories that have undergone extensive functional modifications include home appliances, office and farm equipment, and consumer electronics. *Aesthetic modifications* are directed at changing the sensory appeal of a product by altering its taste, texture, sound, smell, or visual characteristics. Because a buyer's purchasing decision is affected by how a product looks, smells, tastes, feels, or sounds, an aesthetic modification may have a definite impact on purchases. Through aesthetic modifications, a firm can differentiate its product from competing brands and perhaps gain a sizable market share if customers find the modified product more appealing.

Product modification. Consider how laundry equipment has been modified many times to improve its quality, improve and add features, and make it more attractive.

© AP Images/PRNewsFoto/Whirlpool Corporation

Line Extensions A **line extension** is the development of a product closely related to one or more products in the existing product line but designed specifically to meet somewhat different customer needs. For example, Nabisco extended its cookie line to include Reduced Fat Oreos and Double Stuf Oreos.

Many of the so-called new products introduced each year are in fact line extensions. Line extensions are more common than new products because they are a less-expensive, lower-risk alternative for increasing sales. A line extension may focus on a different market segment or be an attempt to increase sales within the same market segment by more precisely satisfying the needs of people in that segment. Line extensions are also used to take market share from competitors.

Deleting Products

To maintain an effective product mix, an organization often has to eliminate some products. This is called **product deletion**. A weak product costs a firm time, money, and resources that could be used to modify other products or develop new ones. In addition, when a weak product generates an unfavorable image among customers, the negative image may rub off on other products sold by the firm.

Most organizations find it difficult to delete a product. Some firms drop weak products only after they have become severe financial burdens. A better approach is to conduct some form of systematic review of the product's impact on the overall effectiveness of a firm's product mix. Such a review should analyze a product's contribution to a company's sales for a given period. It should include estimates of future sales, costs, and profits associated with the product and a consideration of whether changes in the marketing strategy could improve the product's performance.

A product-deletion program can definitely improve a firm's performance. Condé Nast, for example, recently discontinued its *Gourmet* magazine. The magazine, which had been around since 1940, was experiencing declining ad sales and suffering from the move to digital media. However, Condé Nast plans to continue the brand in book publishing and television programming as well as online.[7]

Developing New Products

Developing and introducing new products frequently is time-consuming, expensive, and risky. Thousands of new products are introduced annually. Depending on how we define it, the failure rate for new products ranges between 60 and 75 percent. Although developing new products is risky, failing to introduce new products can be just as hazardous. Successful new products bring a number of benefits to an organization, including survival, profits, a sustainable competitive advantage, and a favorable public image. Consider the numerous ways that the producers of the products in Table 13.1 have benefited.

New products are generally grouped into three categories on the basis of their degree of similarity to existing products. *Imitations* are products designed to be similar to—and to compete with—existing products of other firms. Examples are the various brands of whitening toothpastes that were developed to compete with Rembrandt. *Adaptations*

line extension development of a new product that is closely related to one or more products in the existing product line but designed specifically to meet somewhat different customer needs

product deletion the elimination of one or more products from a product line

Table 13.1 Top Ten New Products of the Decade

Rank	Product Name	Year Introduced
1	iPod	2001
2	Wii	2006
3	Axe	2002
4	$5 Footlong	2008
5	Activia	2006
6	Mini Cooper	2002
7	Crest Whitestrips	2000
8	Guitar Hero	2005
9	Toyota Prius	2000
10	7 For All Mankind	2000

Source: ***Advertising Age*****, December 14, 2008, 16.**

are variations of existing products that are intended for an established market. Product refinements and extensions are the adaptations considered most often, although imitative products may also include some refinement and extension. *Innovations* are entirely new products. They may give rise to a new industry or revolutionize an existing one. The introduction of digital music, for example, has brought major changes to the recording industry. Innovative products take considerable time, effort, and money to develop. They are therefore less common than adaptations and imitations. As shown in Figure 13.2, the process of developing a new product consists of seven phases.

New-product development. New-product ideas can come from numerous sources, including a company's own scientists, such as this scientist at Procter & Gamble.

© Tom Uhlman/Bloomberg via Getty Images

Idea Generation Idea generation involves looking for product ideas that will help a firm to achieve its objectives. Although some organizations get their ideas almost by chance, firms trying to maximize product-mix effectiveness usually develop systematic approaches for generating new-product ideas. Ideas may come from managers, researchers, engineers, competitors, advertising agencies, management consultants, private research organizations, customers, salespersons, or top executives. For example, Fahrenheit 212 serves as an "idea factory" that provides ready-to-go product ideas, including market potential analysis, to its clients, which include Procter & Gamble, Coca-Cola, Hershey, Samsung, Starbucks, Capital One Financial, General Mills, Nestlé, Clorox, and Adidas.[8]

Screening During screening, ideas that do not match organizational resources and objectives are rejected. In this phase, a firm's managers consider whether the organization has personnel with the expertise to develop and market the proposed product. Management may reject a good idea because the company lacks the necessary skills and abilities. The largest number of product ideas are rejected during the screening phase.

Concept Testing Concept testing is a phase in which a product idea is presented to a small sample of potential buyers through a written or oral description (and

Figure 13.2 Phases of New-Product Development

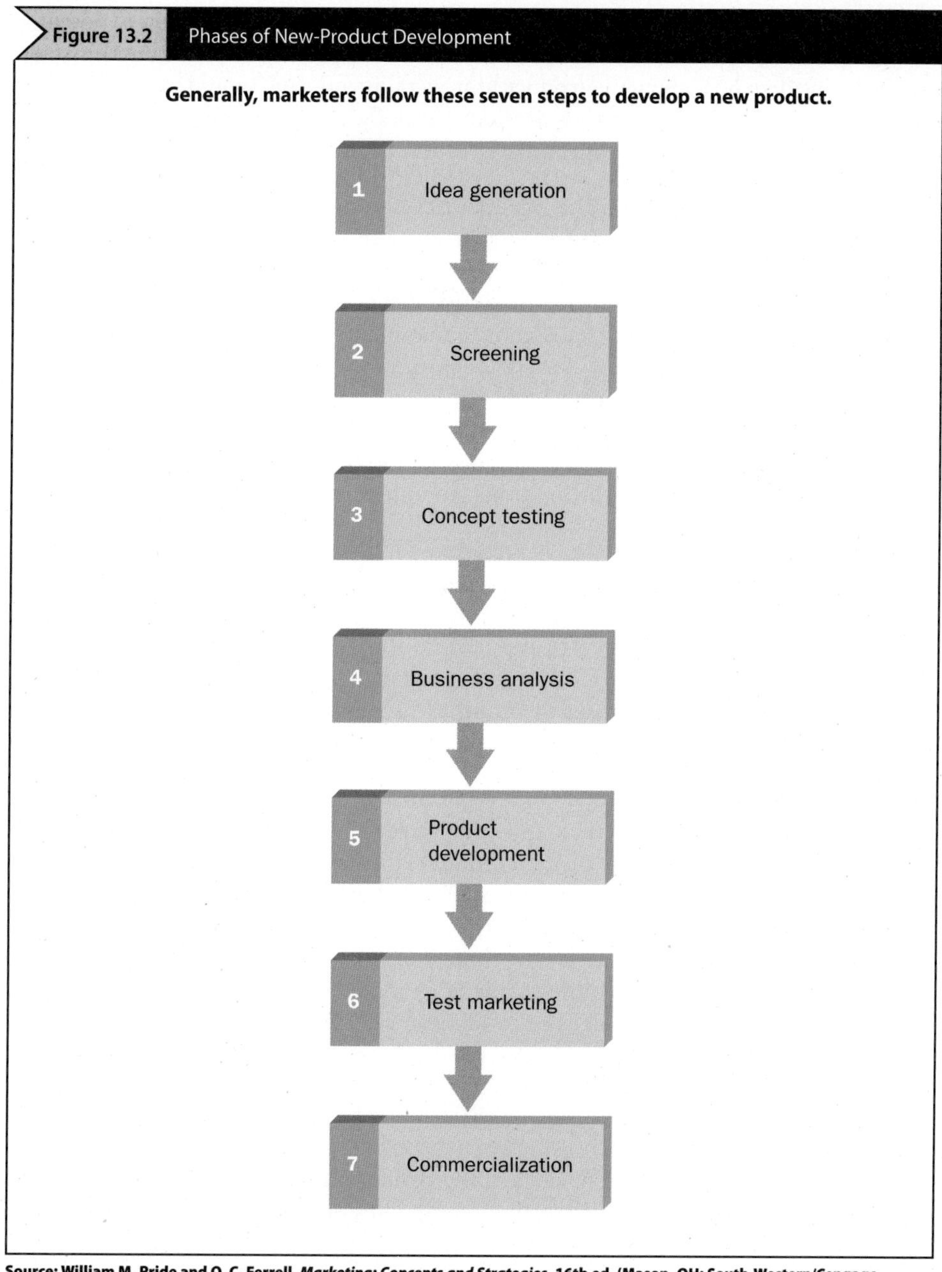

Source: William M. Pride and O. C. Ferrell, *Marketing: Concepts and Strategies*, 16th ed. (Mason, OH: South-Western/Cengage Learning, 2012). Adapted with permission.

perhaps a few drawings) to determine their attitudes and initial buying intentions regarding the product. For a single product idea, an organization can test one or several concepts of the same product. Concept testing is a low-cost means for an organization to determine consumers' initial reactions to a product idea before investing considerable resources in product research and development (R&D). Product development personnel can use the results of concept testing to improve product attributes and product benefits that are most important to potential customers. The types of questions asked vary considerably depending on the type of product idea being tested. The following are typical questions:

- Which benefits of the proposed product are especially attractive to you?
- Which features are of little or no interest to you?
- What are the primary advantages of the proposed product over the one you currently use?
- If this product were available at an appropriate price, how often would you buy it?
- How could this proposed product be improved?

Business Analysis Business analysis provides tentative ideas about a potential product's financial performance, including its probable profitability. During this stage, the firm considers how the new product, if it were introduced, would affect the firm's sales, costs, and profits. Marketing personnel usually work up preliminary sales and cost projections at this point, with the help of R&D and production managers.

Product Development In the product development phase, the company must find out first if it is technically feasible to produce the product and then if the product can be made at costs low enough to justify a reasonable price. If a product idea makes it to this point, it is transformed into a working model, or *prototype*. For example, Aptera, a California-based vehicle manufacturer, recently developed a prototype electric vehicle called the 2e. The 2e is an innovative three-wheeled, two-seat vehicle that uses an electric motor with phosphate-based lithium-ion batteries. The 2e is expected to operate at about 200 MPG and travel about 100 miles on a single charge.[9] Often, this step is time-consuming and expensive for the organization. If a product successfully moves through this step, then it is ready for test marketing.

Test Marketing Test marketing is the limited introduction of a product in several towns or cities chosen to be representative of the intended target market. Its aim is to determine buyers' probable reactions. The product is left in the test markets long enough to give buyers a chance to repurchase the product if they are so inclined. Marketers can experiment with advertising, pricing, and packaging in different test areas and can measure the extent of brand awareness, brand switching, and repeat purchases that result from alterations in the marketing mix.

Commercialization During commercialization, plans for full-scale manufacturing and marketing must be refined and completed, and budgets for the project must be prepared. In the early part of the commercialization phase, marketing management analyzes the results of test marketing to find out what changes in the marketing mix are needed before the product is introduced. The results of test marketing may tell the marketers, for example, to change one or more of the product's physical attributes, to modify the distribution plans to include more retail outlets, to alter promotional efforts, or to change the product's price. Products are usually not introduced nationwide overnight. Most new products are marketed in stages, beginning in selected geographic areas and expanding into adjacent areas over a period of time.

Why Do Products Fail?

Despite this rigorous process for developing product ideas, most new products end up as failures. In fact, many well-known companies have produced market failures (see Table 13.2).

Table 13.2 Examples of Product Failures

Company	Product
Gillette	For Oily Hair shampoo
3M	Floptical storage disk
IncrEdibles Breakaway Foods	Push n' Eat
General Mills	Betty Crocker MicroRave Singles
Adams (Pfizer)	Body Smarts nutritional bars
General Motors	Corp. Cadillac Allante luxury sedan
Anheuser-Busch	Bud Dry and Michelob Dry beer
Coca-Cola	Surge Citrus drink
Heinz	Ketchup Salsa
Noxema	Noxema Skin Fitness

Sources: http://www.newproductworks.com (accessed January 23, 2006); Robert M. McMath, "Copycat Cupcakes Don't Cut It," *American Demographics*, January 1997, 60; Eric Berggren and Thomas Nacher, "Why Good Ideas Go Bust," *Management Review*, February 2000, 32–36.

Why does a new product fail? Mainly because the product and its marketing program are not planned and tested as completely as they should be. For example, to save on development costs, a firm may market-test its product but not its entire marketing mix. Alternatively, a firm may market a new product before all the "bugs" have been worked out. Or, when problems show up in the testing stage, a firm may try to recover its product development costs by pushing ahead with full-scale marketing anyway. Finally, some firms try to market new products with inadequate financing.

brand a name, term, symbol, design, or any combination of these that identifies a seller's products as distinct from those of other sellers

brand name the part of a brand that can be spoken

brand mark the part of a brand that is a symbol or distinctive design

5

Explain the uses and importance of branding, packaging, and labeling.

Branding, Packaging, and Labeling

Three important features of a product (particularly a consumer product) are its brand, package, and label. These features may be used to associate a product with a successful product line or to distinguish it from existing products. They may be designed to attract customers at the point of sale or to provide information to potential purchasers. Because the brand, package, and label are very real parts of the product, they deserve careful attention during product planning.

trademark a brand name or brand mark that is registered with the U.S. Patent and Trademark Office and thus is legally protected from use by anyone except its owner

trade name the complete and legal name of an organization

manufacturer (or producer) brand a brand that is owned by a manufacturer

store (or private) brand a brand that is owned by an individual wholesaler or retailer

What Is a Brand?

A **brand** is a name, term, symbol, design, or any combination of these that identifies a seller's products and distinguishes it from other sellers' products. A **brand name** is the part of a brand that can be spoken. It may include letters, words, numbers, or pronounceable symbols, such as the ampersand in *Procter & Gamble.* A **brand mark**, on the other hand, is the part of a brand that is a symbol or distinctive design, such as the Nike "swoosh." A **trademark** is a brand name or brand mark that is registered with the U.S. Patent and Trademark Office and thus is legally protected from use by anyone except its owner. A **trade name** is the complete and legal name of an organization, such as Pizza Hut or Cengage Learning (the publisher of this text).

Types of Brands

Brands are often classified according to who owns them: manufacturers or stores. A **manufacturer** (or **producer**) **brand**, as the name implies, is a brand that is owned by a manufacturer. Many foods (Frosted Flakes), major appliances (Whirlpool), gasolines (Exxon), automobiles (Honda), and clothing (Levi's) are sold as manufacturers' brands. Some consumers prefer manufacturer brands because they are usually nationally known, offer consistent quality, and are widely available.

A **store** (or **private**) **brand** is a brand that is owned by an individual wholesaler or retailer. Among the better-known store brands are Kenmore and Craftsman, both owned by Sears, Roebuck. Owners of store brands claim that they can offer lower prices, earn greater profits, and improve customer loyalty with their own brands. Some companies that manufacture private brands also produce their own manufacturer brands. They often find such operations profitable because they can use excess capacity and at the same time avoid most marketing costs. Many private-branded grocery products are produced by companies that specialize in making private-label products. About 25 percent of products sold in supermarkets are private-branded items.[10]

Consumer confidence is the most important element in the success of a branded product, whether the brand is owned by a producer or by a retailer. Because branding identifies each product completely, customers can easily repurchase products that provide satisfaction, performance, and quality. Moreover, they can just as easily avoid or ignore products that do not. In supermarkets, the products most likely to keep their shelf space are the brands with large market shares and strong customer loyalty.

Private brand. A number of supermarkets, like Kroger, develop numerous private-branded products.

A **generic product** (sometimes called a **generic brand**) is a product with no brand at all. Its plain package carries only the name of the product—applesauce, peanut butter, potato chips, or whatever. Generic products, available in supermarkets since 1977, sometimes are made by the major producers that manufacture name brands. Even though generic brands may have accounted for as much as 10 percent of all grocery sales several years ago, they currently represent less than one-half of 1 percent.

Benefits of Branding

Both buyers and sellers benefit from branding. Because brands are easily recognizable, they reduce the amount of time buyers must spend shopping; buyers can quickly identify the brands they prefer. Choosing particular brands, such as Tommy Hilfiger, Polo, Nautica, and Nike, can be a way of expressing oneself. When buyers are unable to evaluate a product's characteristics, brands can help them to judge the quality of the product. For example, most buyers are not able to judge the quality of stereo components but may be guided by a well-respected brand name. Brands can symbolize a certain quality level to a customer, allowing that perception of quality to represent the actual quality of the item. Brands thus help to reduce a buyer's perceived risk of purchase. Finally, customers may receive a psychological reward that comes from owning a brand that symbolizes status. The Lexus brand is an example.

Because buyers are already familiar with a firm's existing brands, branding helps a firm to introduce a new product that carries the same brand name. Branding aids sellers in their promotional efforts because promotion of each branded product indirectly promotes other products of the same brand. H.J. Heinz, for example, markets many products with the Heinz brand name, such as ketchup, vinegar, vegetarian beans, gravies, barbecue sauce, and steak sauce. Promotion of one Heinz product indirectly promotes the others.

One chief benefit of branding is the creation of **brand loyalty**, the extent to which a customer is favorable toward buying a specific brand. The stronger the brand loyalty, the greater is the likelihood that buyers will consistently choose the brand. For example, Toyota is expected to survive as a company, despite the massive recalls affecting several million vehicles, because of its historically high perceived brand quality. Even though this is a huge mark against the brand, the company is relying on its loyalists and previously perceived brand quality to survive.[11] There are three levels of brand loyalty: recognition, preference, and insistence. *Brand recognition* is the level of loyalty at which customers are aware that the brand exists and will purchase it if their preferred brands are unavailable or if they are unfamiliar with available brands. This is the weakest form of brand loyalty. *Brand preference* is the level of brand loyalty at which a customer prefers one brand over competing brands. However, if the preferred brand is unavailable, the customer is willing to substitute another brand. *Brand insistence* is the strongest level of brand loyalty. Brand-insistent customers strongly prefer a specific brand and will not buy substitutes. Brand insistence is the least common type of brand loyalty. Partly owing to marketers' increased dependence on discounted prices, coupons, and other short-term promotions, and partly because of the enormous array of new products with similar characteristics, brand loyalty in general seems to be declining.

Brand equity is the marketing and financial value associated with a brand's strength in a market. Although difficult to measure, brand equity represents the value of a brand to an organization. The top ten most highly valued brands in the world are shown in Table 13.3. The four major factors that contribute to brand equity are brand awareness, brand associations, perceived brand quality, and brand loyalty. Brand awareness leads to brand familiarity, and buyers are more likely to select a familiar

generic product (or brand) a product with no brand at all

brand loyalty extent to which a customer is favorable toward buying a specific brand

brand equity marketing and financial value associated with a brand's strength in a market

Table 13.3 Top Ten Most Valuable Brands in the World

Brand	Brand Value (in billion $)
Coca-Cola	68.7
IBM	60.2
Microsoft	56.6
GE	47.8
Nokia	34.9
McDonald's	32.3
Google	32.0
Toyota	31.3
Intel	30.6
Disney	28.4

Source: "Best Global Brands," *Interbrand*, http://www.interbrand.com/best_global_brands.aspx (accessed October 15, 2009).

Career
SUCCESS

Building Your Personal Brand

What does your personal brand stand for? This is a key issue as you begin or continue your career. To stand out in the minds of employers and stand for positive qualities such as professionalism, think about the brand image you want to communicate. You're not a generic product—you're a unique individual with specific credentials, educational accomplishments, and work experiences that make you valuable as an employee. Your personal interests and your professional connections are also important aspects of your brand.

Here are tips for building your personal brand to enhance your job search:

- *Polish your résumé.* This is often the first contact a potential employer will have with your brand, so be sure you highlight your strengths.
- *Pay attention to appearance.* What you wear to an interview or a job fair is part of your packaging.
- *Plan your introduction.* When a recruiter says, "Tell me about yourself," be prepared to use this as an opportunity to communicate your brand identity.
- *Build your brand online.* Remember that "any information you have on the Internet shapes your personal brand, whether it's on a blog, Facebook, MySpace, [or] articles about you," says the director of Stanford University's Career Development Center. Build your brand with links to professional Web sites and comments on industry doings, while protecting your brand by deleting inappropriate photos and messages.

© iStockphoto.com/nicole waring

Sources: Stephanie Weber, "As Personal Branding Rises, a Search for Balance," *Stanford Daily (Stanford, CA)*, May 12, 2010, http://www.stanforddaily.com; Jerry S. Wilson, "Transitioning Your Personal Brand," *BusinessWeek*, April 27, 2010, http://www.businessweek.com; Andrea Mora, "Tips for Creating Your Own Professional Brand," *Daily Aztec (San Diego, CA)*, April 29, 2010, http://www.thedailyaztec.com.

brand than an unfamiliar one. The associations linked to a brand can connect a personality type or lifestyle with a particular brand. For example, customers associate Michelin tires with protecting family members; a De Beers diamond with a loving, long-lasting relationship ("A Diamond Is Forever"); and Dr Pepper with a unique taste. When consumers are unable to judge for themselves the quality of a product, they may rely on their perception of the quality of the product's brand. Finally, brand loyalty is a valued element of brand equity because it reduces both a brand's vulnerability to competitors and the need to spend tremendous resources to attract new customers; it also provides brand visibility and encourages retailers to carry the brand. Companies have much work to do in establishing new brands to compete with well-known brands. For example, Coca-Cola decided that it would be a better business decision to buy the established brand Glaceau than to create a new brand of its own. The company acquired Glaceau, which included the Vitaminwater and Smartwater brands, to strengthen Coca-Cola's water and energy drink product line.[12]

Marketing on the Internet is sometimes best done in collaboration with a better-known Web brand. For instance, Tire Rack, Razor Gator, Audible.com, and Shutterfly all rely on partnerships with Internet retail giant Amazon to increase their sales. Amazon provides special sections on its Web site to promote its partners and their products. As with its own products, Amazon gives users the ability to post online

Image courtesy of The Advertising Archives

Building brand equity. Toyota is attempting to build brand equity by promoting favorable brand associations.

reviews of its partners' products or to add them to an Amazon "wish list" that can be saved or e-mailed to friends. Amazon even labels its partners as "Amazon Trusted" when customers browse their sites, giving even these well-known real-world companies credibility in the online marketplace.[13]

Choosing and Protecting a Brand

A number of issues should be considered when selecting a brand name. The name should be easy for customers to say, spell, and recall. Short, one-syllable names such as *Tide* often satisfy this requirement. Letters and numbers are used to create such brands as Volvo's S60 sedan or RIM's BlackBerry 8100. Words, numbers, and letters are combined to yield brand names such as Motorola's RAZR V3 phone or BMW's Z4 Roadster. The brand name should suggest, in a positive way, the product's uses, special characteristics, and major benefits and should be distinctive enough to set it apart from competing brands. Choosing the right brand name has become a challenge because many obvious product names already have been used.

It is important that a firm select a brand that can be protected through registration, reserving it for exclusive use by that firm. Some brands, because of their designs, are infringed on more easily than others. Although registration protects trademarks domestically for ten years and can be renewed indefinitely, a firm should develop a system for ensuring that its trademarks will be renewed as needed. To protect its exclusive right to the brand, the company must ensure that the selected brand will not be considered an infringement on any existing brand already registered with the U.S. Patent and Trademark Office. This task may be complicated by the fact that infringement is determined by the courts, which base their decisions on whether a brand causes consumers to be confused, mistaken, or deceived about the source of the product. McDonald's is one company that aggressively protects its trademarks against infringement; it has brought charges against a number of companies with *Mc* names because it fears that the use of the prefix will give consumers the impression that these companies are associated with or owned by McDonald's.

A firm must guard against having its brand name become a generic term that refers to a general product category. Generic terms cannot be legally protected as exclusive brand names. For example, names such as *yo-yo, aspirin, escalator,* and *thermos*—all exclusively brand names at one time—eventually were declared generic terms that refer to product categories. As such, they can no longer be protected. To ensure that a brand name does not become a generic term, the firm should spell the name with a capital letter and use it as an adjective to modify the name of the general product class, as in Jell-O Brand Gelatin. An organization can deal directly with this problem by advertising that its brand is a trademark and should not be used generically. Firms also can use the registered trademark symbol® to indicate that the brand is trademarked.

Branding Strategies

The basic branding decision for any firm is whether to brand its products. A producer may market its products under its own brands, private brands, or both. A retail store may carry only producer brands, its own brands, or both. Once either type of firm decides to brand, it chooses one of two branding strategies: individual branding or family branding.

Individual branding is the strategy in which a firm uses a different brand for each of its products. For example, Procter & Gamble uses individual branding for its line of bar soaps, which includes Ivory, Camay, Zest, Safeguard, Coast, and Olay. Individual branding offers two major advantages. A problem with one product will not affect the good name of the firm's other products, and the different brands can be directed toward different market

individual branding the strategy in which a firm uses a different brand for each of its products

segments. For example, Marriott's Fairfield Inns are directed toward budget-minded travelers, whereas Marriott Hotels are aimed toward upscale customers.

Family branding is the strategy in which a firm uses the same brand for all or most of its products. Sony, Dell, IBM, and Xerox use family branding for their entire product mixes. A major advantage of family branding is that the promotion of any one item that carries the family brand tends to help all other products with the same brand name. In addition, a new product has a head start when its brand name is already known and accepted by customers.

Brand Extensions

A **brand extension** occurs when an organization uses one of its existing brands to brand a new product in a different product category. For example, Procter & Gamble employed a brand extension when it named a new product Ivory Body Wash. A brand extension should not be confused with a line extension. A *line extension* refers to using an existing brand on a new product in the same product category, such as a new flavor or new sizes. For example, when the makers of Tylenol introduced Extra Strength Tylenol PM, the new product was a line extension because it was in the same product category. One thing marketers must be careful of, however, is extending a brand too many times or extending too far outside the original product category, which may weaken the brand. For example, Kellogg's extended its brand name to a line of hip-hop street clothing that was later named one of the worst brand extensions that year.[14]

Packaging

Packaging consists of all the activities involved in developing and providing a container with graphics for a product. The package is a vital part of the product. It can make the product more versatile, safer, or easier to use. Through its shape, appearance, and printed message, a package can influence purchasing decisions.

family branding the strategy in which a firm uses the same brand for all or most of its products

brand extension using an existing brand to brand a new product in a different product category

packaging all the activities involved in developing and providing a container with graphics for a product

Packaging Functions Effective packaging means more than simply putting products in containers and covering them with wrappers. The basic function of packaging materials is to protect the product and maintain its functional form. Fluids such as milk, orange juice, and hair spray need packages that preserve and protect them; the packaging should prevent damage that could affect the product's usefulness and increase costs. Because product tampering has become a problem for marketers of many types of goods, several packaging techniques have been developed to counter this danger. Some packages are also designed to foil shoplifting.

Another function of packaging is to offer consumer convenience. For example, small, aseptic packages—individual-serving boxes or plastic bags that contain liquids and do not require refrigeration—appeal strongly to children and to young adults with active lifestyles. The size or shape of a package may relate to the product's storage, convenience of use, or replacement rate. Small, single-serving cans of vegetables, for instance, may prevent waste and make storage easier. A third function of packaging is to promote a product by communicating its features, uses, benefits, and image. Sometimes a firm develops a reusable package to make its product more desirable. For example, the Cool Whip package doubles as a food-storage container.

Package design. Parent's Choice Baby Food, made by PBM Products, employs reusable plastic tubs that are designed to be sturdy, spill less, and keep its contents fresh longer.

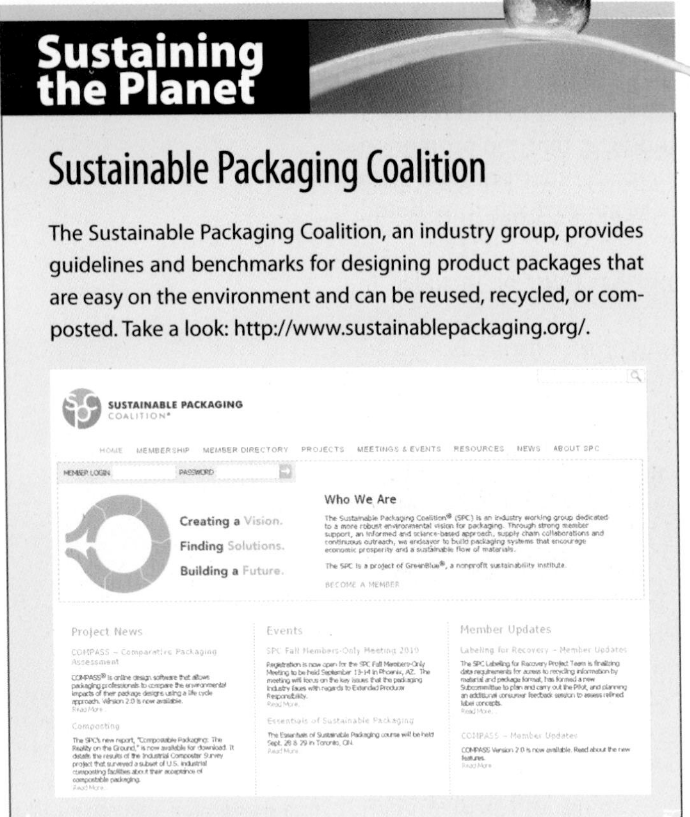

Sustaining the Planet

Sustainable Packaging Coalition

The Sustainable Packaging Coalition, an industry group, provides guidelines and benchmarks for designing product packages that are easy on the environment and can be reused, recycled, or composted. Take a look: http://www.sustainablepackaging.org/.

Package Design Considerations Many factors must be weighed when developing packages. Obviously, one major consideration is cost. Although a number of packaging materials, processes, and designs are available, some are rather expensive. Although U.S. buyers have shown a willingness to pay more for improved packaging, there are limits.

Marketers also must decide whether to package the product in single or multiple units. Multiple-unit packaging can increase demand by increasing the amount of the product available at the point of consumption (in the home, for example). However, multiple-unit packaging does not work for infrequently used products because buyers do not like to tie up their dollars in an excess supply or to store those products for a long time. However, multiple-unit packaging can make storage and handling easier (as in the case of six-packs used for soft drinks); it can also facilitate special price offers, such as two-for-one sales. In addition, multiple-unit packaging may increase consumer acceptance of a product by encouraging the buyer to try it several times. On the other hand, customers may hesitate to try the product at all if they do not have the option to buy just one.

Marketers should consider how much consistency is desirable among an organization's package designs. To promote an overall company image, a firm may decide that all packages must be similar or include one major element of the design. This approach, called *family packaging,* is sometimes used only for lines of products, as with Campbell's soups, Weight Watchers entrées, and Planters nuts. The best policy is sometimes no consistency, especially if a firm's products are unrelated or aimed at vastly different target markets.

Packages also play an important promotional role. Through verbal and nonverbal symbols, the package can inform potential buyers about the product's content, uses, features, advantages, and hazards. Firms can create desirable images and associations by choosing particular colors, designs, shapes, and textures. Many cosmetics manufacturers, for example, design their packages to create impressions of richness, luxury, and exclusiveness. The package performs another promotional function when it is designed to be safer or more convenient to use, especially if such features help to stimulate demand.

Packaging also must meet the needs of intermediaries. Wholesalers and retailers consider whether a package facilitates transportation, handling, and storage. Resellers may refuse to carry certain products if their packages are cumbersome.

Finally, firms must consider the issue of environmental responsibility when developing packages. Companies must balance consumers' desires for convenience against the need to preserve the environment. About one-half of all garbage consists of discarded plastic packaging, such as plastic soft drink bottles and carryout bags. Plastic packaging material is not biodegradable, and paper necessitates destruction of valuable forest lands. Consequently, many companies are exploring packaging alternatives and recycling more materials. Last year, Naked Juice became the first beverage with national distribution to produce its packaging completely from recycled plastic.[15]

Labeling

Labeling is the presentation of information on a product or its package. The *label* is the part that contains the information. This information may include the brand name and mark, the registered trademark symbol ®, the package size and contents, product claims, directions for use and safety precautions, a list of ingredients, the name and address of the manufacturer, and the Universal Product Code (UPC) symbol, which is used for automated checkout and inventory control.

A number of federal regulations specify information that *must* be included in the labeling for certain products. For example,

- Garments must be labeled with the name of the manufacturer, country of manufacture, fabric content, and cleaning instructions.
- Food labels must contain the most common term for ingredients.
- Any food product for which a nutritional claim is made must have nutrition labeling that follows a standard format.
- Food product labels must state the number of servings per container, the serving size, the number of calories per serving, the number of calories derived from fat, and the amounts of specific nutrients.
- Non-edible items such as shampoos and detergents must carry safety precautions as well as instructions for their use.

Such regulations are aimed at protecting customers from both misleading product claims and the improper (and thus unsafe) use of products. A product that has come under fire in 2010 is the printer cartridge. Consumers are pushing for more disclosure on labels about the amount of ink in each cartridge. Currently, it is difficult for consumers to compare offerings and prices without knowing the amount of ink contained in each cartridge. Companies have responded by saying ink does not fall under the Fair Packaging and Labeling Act. This dispute is currently under review.[16]

Labels also may carry the details of written or express warranties. An **express warranty** is a written explanation of the producer's responsibilities in the event that a product is found to be defective or otherwise unsatisfactory. As a result of consumer discontent (along with some federal legislation), firms have begun to simplify the wording of warranties and to extend their duration. The L.L.Bean warranty states, "Our products are guaranteed to give 100 percent satis-faction in every way. Return anything purchased from us at any time if it proves otherwise. We will replace it, refund your purchase price or credit your credit card, as you wish."

Pricing Products

A product is a set of attributes and benefits that has been carefully designed to satisfy its market while earning a profit for its seller. No matter how well a product is designed, however, it cannot help an organization to achieve its goals if it is priced incorrectly. Few people will purchase a product with too high a price, and a product with too low a price will earn little or no profit. Somewhere between too high and too low there is a "proper," effective price for each product. Let's take a closer look at how businesses go about determining a product's right price.

The Meaning and Use of Price

The **price** of a product is the amount of money a seller is willing to accept in exchange for the product at a given time and under given circumstances. At times, the price results from negotiations between buyer and seller. In many business situations, however, the price is fixed by the seller. Suppose that a seller sets a price of $10 for a particular product. In essence, the seller is saying, "Anyone who wants this product can have it here and now in exchange for $10."

6

Describe the economic basis of pricing and the means by which sellers can control prices and buyers' perceptions of prices.

labeling the presentation of information on a product or its package

express warranty a written explanation of the producer's responsibilities in the event that a product is found to be defective or otherwise unsatisfactory

price the amount of money a seller is willing to accept in exchange for a product at a given time and under given circumstances

Price competition. Price competition is common among general merchandise retailers such as supermarkets and discount stores.

Each interested buyer then makes a personal judgment regarding the product's utility, often in terms of some dollar value. A particular person who feels that he or she will get at least $10 worth of want satisfaction (or value) from the product is likely to buy it. If that person can get more want satisfaction by spending $10 in some other way, however, he or she will not buy the product.

Price thus serves the function of *allocator*. First, it allocates goods and services among those who are willing and able to buy them. (As we noted in Chapter 1, the answer to the economic question "For whom to produce?" depends primarily on prices.) Second, price allocates financial resources (sales revenue) among producers according to how well they satisfy customers' needs. Third, price helps customers to allocate their own financial resources among various want-satisfying products.

Supply and Demand Affects Prices

In Chapter 1, we defined the **supply** of a product as the quantity of the product that producers are willing to sell at each of various prices. We can draw a graph of the supply relationship for a particular product, say, jeans (see the left graph in Figure 13.3). Note that the quantity supplied by producers *increases* as the price increases along this *supply curve.*

As defined in Chapter 1, the **demand** for a product is the quantity that buyers are willing to purchase at each of various prices. We can also draw a graph of the demand relationship (see the center graph in Figure 13.3). Note that the quantity demanded by purchasers *increases* as the price decreases along the *demand curve*. The buyers and sellers of a product interact in the marketplace. We can show this interaction by superimposing the supply curve onto the demand curve for our product, as shown in the right graph in Figure 13.3. The two curves intersect at point *E*, which represents a quantity of 15 million pairs of jeans and a price of $30 per pair. Point *E* is on the *supply curve;* thus, producers are willing to supply 15 million pairs at $30 each. Point *E* is also on the demand curve; thus, buyers are

supply the quantity of a product that producers are willing to sell at each of various prices

demand the quantity of a product that buyers are willing to purchase at each of various prices

Figure 13.3 Supply and Demand Curves

Supply curve (*left*): The upward slope means that producers will supply more jeans at higher prices. Demand curve (*center*): The downward slope (to the right) means that buyers will purchase fewer jeans at higher prices. Supply and demand curves together (*right*): Point *E* indicates equilibrium in quantity and price for both sellers and buyers.

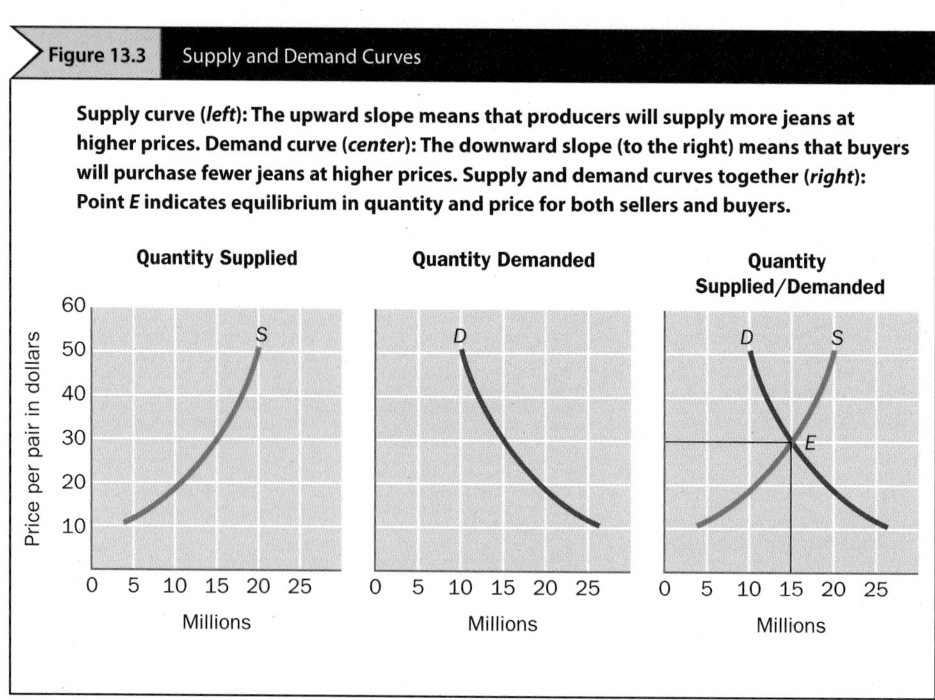

willing to purchase 15 million pairs at $30 each. Point *E* represents *equilibrium.* If 15 million pairs are produced and priced at $30, they all will be sold. In addition, everyone who is willing to pay $30 will be able to buy a pair of jeans.

Price and Non-Price Competition

Before a product's price can be set, an organization must determine the basis on which it will compete—whether on price alone or some combination of factors. The choice influences pricing decisions as well as other marketing-mix variables.

Price competition occurs when a seller emphasizes a product's low price and sets a price that equals or beats competitors' prices. To use this approach most effectively, a seller must have the flexibility to change prices often and must do so rapidly and aggressively whenever competitors change their prices. Price competition allows a marketer to set prices based on demand for the product or in response to changes in the firm's finances. Competitors can do likewise, however, which is a major drawback of price competition. They, too, can quickly match or outdo an organization's price cuts. In addition, if circumstances force a seller to raise prices, competing firms may be able to maintain their lower prices. For example, when increasing numbers of coffee sellers entered the market, competition increased. Starbucks needed to counter the widespread perception that it was the home of the $4 cup of coffee, especially during the economic downturn. In order to compete with McDonald's inexpensive coffee, Starbucks cut its coffee prices and started selling discounted breakfast foods for $3.95, including coffee.[17]

The Internet makes price comparison relatively easy for users. This ease of price comparison helps to drive competition. Examples of Web sites where customers can compare prices include http://mysimon.com, http://pricescan.com, http://bizrate.com, http://pricegrabber.com, http://pricecomparison.com, http://shopping.yahoo.com, http://nextag.com, and http://froogle.google.com.

Non-price competition is competition based on factors other than price. It is used most effectively when a seller can make its product stand out from the competition by distinctive product quality, customer service, promotion, packaging, or other features. Buyers must be able to perceive these distinguishing characteristics and consider them desirable. Once customers have chosen a brand for non-price reasons, they may not be attracted as easily to competing firms and brands. In this way, a seller can build customer loyalty to its brand. A method of non-price competition, **product differentiation**, is the process of developing and promoting differences between one's product and all similar products. Apple, for example, is known for producing products that demand a premium price because of the capabilities and service that comes with its products. One writer went as far as to say that Linux will not be able to compete with the Apple iPad because it lacks the "magic" that Apple products have. It is difficult to define and therefore imitate Apple's magic; it is a combination of several qualities including the appearance of its products, ease of use, and product integration.[18]

Buyers' Perceptions of Price

In setting prices, managers should consider the price sensitivity of people in the target market. How important is price to them? Is it always "very important?" Members of one market segment may be more influenced by price than members of another. For a particular product, the price may be a bigger factor to some buyers than to others. For example, buyers may be more sensitive to price when purchasing gasoline than when purchasing running shoes.

Buyers will accept different ranges of prices for different products; that is, they will tolerate a narrow range for certain items and a wider range for others. Consider the wide range of prices that consumers pay for soft drinks—from 15 cents per ounce at the movies down to 1.5 cents per ounce on sale at the grocery store. Management should be aware of these limits of acceptability and the products to which they apply. The firm also should take note of buyers' perceptions of a given product in relation to competing products. A premium price may be appropriate if a

price competition an emphasis on setting a price equal to or lower than competitors' prices to gain sales or market share

non-price competition competition based on factors other than price

product differentiation the process of developing and promoting differences between one's product and all similar products

product is considered superior to others in its category or if the product has inspired strong brand loyalty. On the other hand, if buyers have even a hint of a negative view of a product, a lower price may be necessary.

Sometimes buyers relate price to quality. They may consider a higher price to be an indicator of higher quality. Managers involved in pricing decisions should determine whether this outlook is widespread in the target market. If it is, a higher price may improve the image of a product and, in turn, make the product more desirable.

7

Identify the major pricing objectives used by businesses.

Pricing Objectives

Before setting prices for a firm's products, management must decide what it expects to accomplish through pricing. That is, management must set pricing objectives that are in line with both organizational and marketing objectives. Of course, one objective of pricing is to make a profit, but this may not be a firm's primary objective. One or more of the following factors may be just as important.

Survival

A firm may have to price its products to survive—either as an organization or as a player in a particular market. This usually means that the firm will cut its price to attract customers, even if it then must operate at a loss. Obviously, such a goal hardly can be pursued on a long-term basis, for consistent losses would cause the business to fail. Even Abercrombie and Fitch (A&F) had to resort to price reductions on its luxury priced clothing to stay in business during the recent economic downturn. Last year, A&F's first quarter result was a loss of almost $27 million, compared to the previous year's income of over $62 million. This drastic difference forced the retailer to adjust prices to better complement customer's smaller budgets.[19]

Pricing objectives associated with product quality. Ikea's pricing objectives focus on value, or the product quality relative to the price.

Profit Maximization

Many firms may state that their goal is to maximize profit, but this goal is impossible to define (and thus impossible to achieve). What, exactly, is the *maximum* profit? How does a firm know when it has been reached? Firms that wish to set profit goals should express them as either specific dollar amounts, or percentage increases, over previous profits.

Target Return on Investment

The *return on investment* (ROI) is the amount earned as a result of that investment. Some firms set an annual percentage ROI as their pricing goal. ConAgra, the company that produces Healthy Choice meals and a multitude of other products, has a target after-tax ROI of 20 percent.

Market-Share Goals

A firm's *market share* is its proportion of total industry sales. Some firms attempt, through pricing, to maintain or increase their market shares. Both U.S. cola giants try to gain market share through aggressive pricing and other marketing efforts.

Status-Quo Pricing

In pricing their products, some firms are guided by a desire to avoid "making waves," or to maintain the status quo. This is especially true in industries that depend

Photo courtesy of Susan Van Etten

on price stability. If such a firm can maintain its profit or market share simply by meeting the competition—charging about the same price as competitors for similar products—then it will do so.

Pricing Methods

8

Examine the three major pricing methods that firms employ.

Once a firm has developed its pricing objectives, it must select a pricing method to reach that goal. Two factors are important to every firm engaged in setting prices. The first is recognition that the market, and not the firm's costs, ultimately determines the price at which a product will sell. The second is awareness that costs and expected sales can be used only to establish some sort of *price floor,* the minimum price at which the firm can sell its product without incurring a loss. In this section, we look at three kinds of pricing methods: cost-based, demand-based, and competition-based pricing.

Cost-Based Pricing

Using the simplest method of pricing, *cost-based pricing,* the seller first determines the total cost of producing (or purchasing) one unit of the product. The seller then adds an amount to cover additional costs (such as insurance or interest) and profit. The amount that is added is called the **markup**. The total of the cost plus the markup is the product's selling price.

A firm's management can calculate markup as a percentage of its total costs. Suppose, for example, that the total cost of manufacturing and marketing 1,000 DVD players is $100,000, or $100 per unit. If the manufacturer wants a markup that is 20 percent above its costs, the selling price will be $100 plus 20 percent of $100, or $120 per unit.

Markup pricing is easy to apply, and it is used by many businesses (mostly retailers and wholesalers). However, it has two major flaws. The first is the difficulty of determining an effective markup percentage. If this percentage is too high, the product may be overpriced for its market; then too few units may be sold to return the total cost of producing and marketing the product. In contrast, if the markup percentage is too low, the seller is "giving away" profit it could have earned simply by assigning a higher price. In other words, the markup percentage needs to be set to account for the workings of the market, and that is very difficult to do.

The second problem with markup pricing is that it separates pricing from other business functions. The product is priced *after* production quantities are determined, *after* costs are incurred, and almost without regard for the market or the marketing mix. To be most effective, the various business functions should be integrated. *Each* should have an impact on all marketing decisions.

Cost-based pricing can also be facilitated through the use of breakeven analysis. For any product, the **breakeven quantity** is the number of units that must be sold for the total revenue (from all units sold) to equal the total cost (of all units sold). **Total revenue** is the total amount received from the sales of a product. We can estimate projected total revenue as the selling price multiplied by the number of units sold.

The costs involved in operating a business can be broadly classified as either fixed or variable costs. A **fixed cost** is a cost incurred no matter how many units of a product are produced or sold. Rent, for example, is a fixed cost; it remains the same whether 1 or 1,000 units are produced. A **variable cost** is a cost that depends on the number of units produced. The cost of fabricating parts for a stereo receiver is a variable cost. The more units produced, the more parts that will be needed, and thus the higher cost of fabricating parts. The **total cost** of producing a certain number of units is the sum of the fixed costs and the variable costs attributed to those units.

If we assume a particular selling price, we can find the breakeven quantity either graphically or by using a formula. Figure 13.4 graphs the total revenue earned and the total cost incurred by the sale of various quantities of a hypothetical product. With fixed costs of $40,000, variable costs of $60 per unit, and a selling price

markup the amount a seller adds to the cost of a product to determine its basic selling price

breakeven quantity the number of units that must be sold for the total revenue (from all units sold) to equal the total cost (of all units sold)

total revenue the total amount received from sales of a product

fixed cost a cost incurred no matter how many units of a product are produced or sold

variable cost a cost that depends on the number of units produced

total cost the sum of the fixed costs and the variable costs attributed to a product

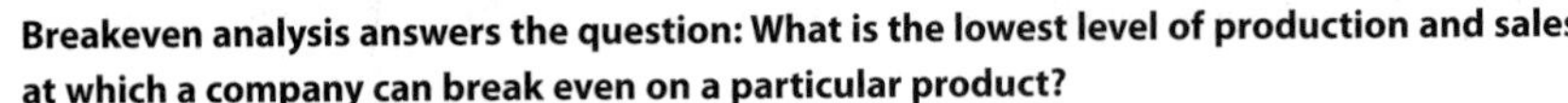
Figure 13.4 Breakeven Analysis

Breakeven analysis answers the question: What is the lowest level of production and sales at which a company can break even on a particular product?

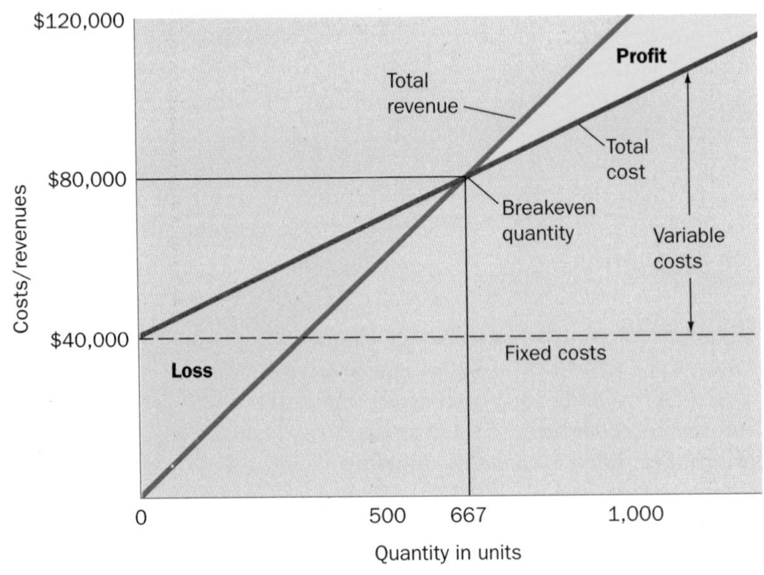

of $120, the breakeven quantity is 667 units. To find the breakeven quantity, first deduct the variable cost from the selling price to determine how much money the sale of one unit contributes to offsetting fixed costs. Then divide that contribution into the total fixed costs to arrive at the breakeven quantity. (The breakeven quantity in Figure 13.4 is the quantity represented by the intersection of the total revenue and total cost axes.) If the firm sells more than 667 units at $120 each, it will earn a profit. If it sells fewer units, it will suffer a loss.

Demand-Based Pricing

Rather than basing the price of a product on its cost, companies sometimes use a pricing method based on the level of demand for the product: *demand-based pricing*. This method results in a high price when product demand is strong and a low price when demand is weak. Some long-distance telephone companies use demand-based pricing. Buyers of new cars that are in high demand, such as the Chevrolet Camaro, Dodge Charger, Ford Mustang GT, and Toyota Prius, pay sticker prices plus a premium. To use this method, a marketer estimates the amount of a product that customers will demand at different prices and then chooses the price that generates the highest total revenue. Obviously, the effectiveness of this method depends on the firm's ability to estimate demand accurately.

Demand-based pricing. Many airlines employ demand-based pricing. The price of an airline ticket will usually be higher when demand for that specific flight is higher.

A firm may favor a demand-based pricing method called *price differentiation* if it wants to use more than one price in the marketing of a specific product. Price differentiation can be based on such considerations as time of the purchase, type of customer, or type of distribution channel. For example, Florida hotel accommodations are more expensive in winter than in summer, a home owner pays more for air conditioner filters than does an apartment complex owner purchasing the same size filters in greater quantity, and Christmas tree ornaments usually are cheaper on December 26 than on December 16. For price differentiation to work correctly, the company first must be able to segment a market on the basis of different strengths of demand. The company must then be able to keep the segments separate enough so that those who buy at lower prices cannot sell to buyers in segments that are charged a higher price. This isolation can be accomplished, for example, by selling to geographically separated segments.

Compared with cost-based pricing, demand-based pricing places a firm in a better position to attain higher profit levels, assuming that buyers value the product at levels sufficiently above the product's cost. To use demand-based pricing, however, management must be able to estimate demand at different price levels, which may be difficult to do accurately.

Competition-Based Pricing

In using *competition-based pricing,* an organization considers costs and revenue secondary to competitors' prices. The importance of this method increases if competing products are quite similar and the organization is serving markets in which price is the crucial variable of the marketing strategy. A firm that uses competition-based pricing may choose to be below competitors' prices, slightly above competitors' prices, or at the same level. The price that your bookstore paid to the publishing company of this text was determined using competition-based pricing. Competition-based pricing can help to attain a pricing objective to increase sales or market share. Competition-based pricing may also be combined with other cost approaches to arrive at profitable levels.

Pricing Strategies

9

Explain the different strategies available to companies for setting prices.

A *pricing strategy* is a course of action designed to achieve pricing objectives. Generally, pricing strategies help marketers to solve the practical problems of setting prices. The extent to which a business uses any of the following strategies depends on its pricing and marketing objectives, the markets for its products, the degree of product differentiation, the product's life-cycle stage, and other factors. Figure 13.5 contains a list of the major types of pricing strategies. We discuss these strategies in the remainder of this section.

New-Product Pricing

The two primary types of new-product pricing strategies are price skimming and penetration pricing. An organization can use either one, or even both, over a period of time.

Figure 13.5 Types of Pricing Strategies

Price Skimming Some consumers are willing to pay a high price for an innovative product either because of its novelty or because of the prestige or status that ownership confers. **Price skimming** is the strategy of charging the highest possible price for a product during the introduction stage of its life-cycle. The seller essentially "skims the cream" off the market, which helps to recover the high costs of R&D more quickly. In addition, a skimming policy may hold down demand for the product, which is helpful if the firm's production capacity is limited during the introduction stage. The greatest disadvantage is that a skimming price may make the product appear lucrative to potential competitors, who then may attempt to enter that market.

Penetration Pricing At the opposite extreme, **penetration pricing** is the strategy of setting a low price for a new product. The main purpose of setting a low price is to build market share for the product quickly. The seller hopes that the building of a large market share quickly will discourage competitors from entering the market. If the low price stimulates sales, the firm also may be able to order longer production runs, which result in lower production costs per unit. A disadvantage of penetration pricing is that it places a firm in a less-flexible position. It is more difficult to raise prices significantly than it is to lower them.

Differential Pricing

An important issue in pricing decisions is whether to use a single price or different prices for the same product. A single price is easily understood by both employees and customers. Since many salespeople and customers do not like having to negotiate a price, having a single price reduces the chance of a marketer developing an adversarial relationship with a customer.

Differential pricing means charging different prices to different buyers for the same quality and quantity of product. For differential pricing to be effective, the market must consist of multiple segments with different price sensitivities. When this method is employed, caution should be used to avoid confusing or antagonizing customers. Differential pricing can occur in several ways, including negotiated pricing, secondary-market pricing, periodic discounting, and random discounting.

Negotiated Pricing **Negotiated pricing** occurs when the final price is established through bargaining between the seller and the customer. Negotiated pricing occurs in a number of industries and at all levels of distribution. Even when there is a predetermined stated price or a price list, manufacturers, wholesalers, and retailers still may negotiate to establish the final sales price. Consumers commonly negotiate prices for houses, cars, and used equipment.

Secondary-Market Pricing **Secondary-market pricing** means setting one price for the primary target market and a different price for another market. Often the price charged in the secondary market is lower. However, when the costs of serving a secondary market are higher than normal, secondary-market customers may have to pay a higher price. Examples of secondary markets include a geographically isolated domestic market, a market in a foreign country, and a segment willing to purchase a product during off-peak times (such as "early bird" diners at restaurants and off-peak users of cellular phones).

Periodic Discounting **Periodic discounting** is the temporary reduction of prices on a patterned or systematic basis. For example, many retailers have annual holiday sales, and some women's apparel stores have two seasonal sales each year—a winter sale in the last two weeks of January and a summer sale in the first two weeks of July.

price skimming the strategy of charging the highest possible price for a product during the introduction stage of its life-cycle

penetration pricing the strategy of setting a low price for a new product

negotiated pricing establishing a final price through bargaining

secondary-market pricing setting one price for the primary target market and a different price for another market

periodic discounting temporary reduction of prices on a patterned or systematic basis

From the marketer's point of view, a major problem with periodic discounting is that customers can predict when the reductions will occur and may delay their purchases until they can take advantage of the lower prices.

Random Discounting To alleviate the problem of customers' knowing when discounting will occur, some organizations employ **random discounting**. That is, they reduce their prices temporarily on a nonsystematic basis. When price reductions of a product occur randomly, current users of that brand are unlikely to predict when the reductions will occur; therefore, they will not delay their purchases in anticipation of buying the product at a lower price. Marketers also use random discounting to attract new customers.

random discounting temporary reduction of prices on an unsystematic basis

odd-number pricing the strategy of setting prices using odd numbers that are slightly below whole-dollar amounts

multiple-unit pricing the strategy of setting a single price for two or more units

reference pricing pricing a product at a moderate level and positioning it next to a more expensive model or brand

bundle pricing packaging together two or more complementary products and selling them for a single price

Psychological Pricing

Psychological pricing strategies encourage purchases based on emotional responses rather than on economically rational responses. These strategies are used primarily for consumer products rather than business products.

Odd-Number Pricing Many retailers believe that consumers respond more positively to odd-number prices such as $4.99 than to whole-dollar prices such as $5. **Odd-number pricing** is the strategy of setting prices using odd numbers that are slightly below whole-dollar amounts. Nine and five are the most popular ending figures for odd-number prices.

Sellers who use this strategy believe that odd-number prices increase sales. The strategy is not limited to low-priced items. Auto manufacturers may set the price of a car at $11,999 rather than $12,000. Odd-number pricing has been the subject of various psychological studies, but the results have been inconclusive.

Multiple-Unit Pricing Many retailers (and especially supermarkets) practice **multiple-unit pricing**, setting a single price for two or more units, such as two cans for 99 cents rather than 50 cents per can. Especially for frequently purchased products, this strategy can increase sales. Customers who see the single price and who expect eventually to use more than one unit of the product regularly purchase multiple units to save money.

Reference Pricing **Reference pricing** means pricing a product at a moderate level and positioning it next to a more expensive model or brand in the hope that the customer will use the higher price as a reference price (i.e., a comparison price). Because of the comparison, the customer is expected to view the moderate price favorably. When you go to Sears to buy a DVD recorder, a moderately priced DVD recorder may appear especially attractive because it offers most of the important attributes of the more expensive alternatives on display and at a lower price.

Bundle Pricing **Bundle pricing** is the packaging together of two or more products, usually of a complementary nature, to be sold for a single price. To be attractive to customers, the single price usually is considerably less than the sum of the prices of the individual products.

Bundle pricing. Bundle pricing is commonly used in food pricing. Food service providers combine numerous services and sell them for a single-bundle price.

Being able to buy the bundled combination of products in a single transaction may be of value to the customer as well. Bundle pricing is used commonly for banking and travel services, computers, and automobiles with option packages. Bundle pricing can help to increase customer satisfaction. By bundling slow-moving products with ones with a higher turnover, an organization can stimulate sales and increase its revenues. Selling products as a package rather than individually also may result in cost savings. As regulations in the telecommunications industry continue to evolve, many experts agree that telecom services will be provided together using bundled pricing in the near future. The new term *all-distance* has emerged; however, the bundling of services goes beyond just combined pricing for local and long-distance services. Verizon, for example, is offering the Verizon Triple Play plan that gives customers unlimited local, long-distance, wireless, high speed Internet, and DirectTV for a bundled price of about $85 per month.[20]

Everyday Low Prices (EDLPs) To reduce or eliminate the use of frequent short-term price reductions, some organizations use an approach referred to as **everyday low prices (EDLPs)**. When EDLPs are used, a marketer sets a low price for its products on a consistent basis rather than setting higher prices and frequently discounting them. EDLPs, though not deeply discounted, are set far enough below competitors' prices to make customers feel confident that they are receiving a fair price. EDLPs are employed by retailers such as Walmart and by manufacturers such as Procter & Gamble. A company that uses EDLPs benefits from reduced promotional costs, reduced losses from frequent markdowns, and more stability in its sales. A major problem with this approach is that customers have mixed responses to it. In some instances, customers simply do not believe that EDLPs are what they say they are but are instead a marketing gimmick.

Customary Pricing In **customary pricing**, certain goods are priced primarily on the basis of tradition. Examples of customary, or traditional, prices would be those set for candy bars and chewing gum.

Product-Line Pricing

Rather than considering products on an item-by-item basis when determining pricing strategies, some marketers employ product-line pricing. *Product-line pricing* means establishing and adjusting the prices of multiple products within a product line. Product-line pricing can provide marketers with flexibility in price setting. For example, marketers can set prices so that one product is quite profitable, whereas another increases market share by virtue of having a lower price than competing products.

When marketers employ product-line pricing, they have several strategies from which to choose. These include captive pricing, premium pricing, and price lining.

Captive Pricing When **captive pricing** is used, the basic product in a product line is priced low, but the price on the items required to operate or enhance it are set at a higher level. Some razors are relatively inexpensive, but the razor blade replacement cartridges are priced to be highly profitable for the manufacturer. It is estimated that if a person replaces the cartridges as suggested by the manufacturer, the annual cost to the consumer will exceed $50.

Premium Pricing **Premium pricing** occurs when the highest-quality product or the most-versatile version of similar products in a product line is given the highest price. Other products in the line are priced to appeal to price-sensitive shoppers or to those who seek product-specific features. Marketers that use premium pricing often

everyday low prices (EDLPs) setting a low price for products on a consistent basis

customary pricing pricing on the basis of tradition

captive pricing pricing the basic product in a product line low, but pricing related items at a higher level

premium pricing pricing the highest-quality or most-versatile products higher than other models in the product line

Entrepreneurial SUCCESS

New Day, New Deal

Small businesses are getting big attention on dozens of "deal-a-day" Web sites such as Groupon and Group Swoop. The idea is to promote one eye-catching local discount every day, with one important catch: The deal is valid only if a minimum number of consumers click to buy. The deal sites keep a commission on each sale, which entrepreneurs must factor into their pricing plans.

Small businesses see these daily-deal sites as a good way to introduce their products to a large number of new customers. Mission Minis, a San Francisco bakery specializing in tiny cupcakes, recently offered a half-price deal on Groupon. Although the owner set the minimum number of customers at 100, more than 3,000 consumers had clicked to buy by the end of the day. The unexpectedly strong response caught the bakery by surprise. Scrambling to keep up with demand, bakers had to buy additional ingredients twice a day for the first few weeks. Despite the higher costs and the strain on the workforce, the owner says the deal was worthwhile because many customers came back to buy cupcakes at full price.

Satisfying deal-a-day buyers today can lead to profits tomorrow. More than 80 percent of the customers who responded to a deal for MindBody Fitness in Washington, D.C., purchased additional services at regular prices. Endeavor Personal Concierge in Chicago found that 25 percent of its deal-a-day buyers turned into repeat customers, a good deal for all.

Sources: Angela Kilduff, "Collective Buys by Groupon and Others = Customers + More," *Mission Local (San Francisco)*, May 11, 2010, http://missionlocal.org; Kunur Patel, "Groupon Takes Coupons into the Social-Media Age," *Advertising Age*, December 21, 2009, http://www.adage.com.

realize a significant portion of their profits from premium-priced products. Examples of product categories in which premium pricing is common are small kitchen appliances, beer, ice cream, and television cable service.

Price Lining **Price lining** is the strategy of selling goods only at certain predetermined prices that reflect definite price breaks. For example, a shop may sell men's ties only at $22 and $37. This strategy is used widely in clothing and accessory stores. It eliminates minor price differences from the buying decision—both for customers and for managers who buy merchandise to sell in these stores.

Promotional Pricing

Price, as an ingredient in the marketing mix, often is coordinated with promotion. The two variables sometimes are so interrelated that the pricing policy is promotion oriented. Examples of promotional pricing include price leaders, special-event pricing, and comparison discounting.

Price Leaders Sometimes a firm prices a few products below the usual markup, near cost, or below cost, which results in prices known as **price leaders**. This type of pricing is used most often in supermarkets and restaurants to attract customers by giving them especially low prices on a few items. Management hopes that sales of regularly priced products will more than offset the reduced revenues from the price leaders.

Special-Event Pricing To increase sales volume, many organizations coordinate price with advertising or sales promotions for seasonal or special situations. **Special-event pricing** involves advertised sales or price cutting linked to a holiday, season, or event. If the pricing objective is survival, then special sales events may be designed to generate the necessary operating capital.

price lining the strategy of selling goods only at certain predetermined prices that reflect definite price breaks

price leaders products priced below the usual markup, near cost, or below cost

special-event pricing advertised sales or price cutting linked to a holiday, season, or event

SPoTLIGHT

Which Online Content Are People Willing to Pay for?

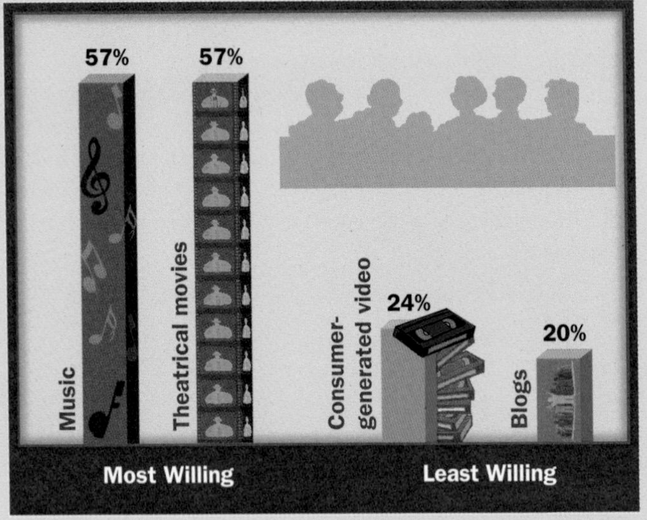

Source: Data from Nielsen survey of 27,548 consumers in 54 countries.

Comparison Discounting **Comparison discounting** sets the price of a product at a specific level and simultaneously compares it with a higher price. The higher price may be the product's previous price, the price of a competing brand, the product's price at another retail outlet, or a manufacturer's suggested retail price. Customers may find comparative discounting informative, and it can have a significant impact on them. However, because this pricing strategy on occasion has led to deceptive pricing practices, the Federal Trade Commission has established guidelines for comparison discounting. If the higher price against which the comparison is made is the price formerly charged for the product, sellers must have made the previous price available to customers for a reasonable period of time. If sellers present the higher price as the one charged by other retailers in the same trade area, they must be able to demonstrate that this claim is true. When they present the higher price as the manufacturer's suggested retail price, then the higher price must be similar to the price at which a reasonable proportion of the product was sold. Some manufacturers' suggested retail prices are so high that very few products actually are sold at those prices. In such cases, it would be deceptive to use comparison discounting.

10

Describe three major types of pricing associated with business products.

Pricing Business Products

Many of the pricing issues discussed thus far in this chapter deal with pricing in general. However, setting prices for business products can be different from setting prices for consumer products owing to several factors such as size of purchases, transportation considerations, and geographic issues. We examine three types of pricing associated with business products: geographic pricing, transfer pricing, and discounting.

Geographic Pricing

Geographic pricing strategies deal with delivery costs. The pricing strategy that requires the buyer to pay the delivery costs is called *FOB origin pricing*. It stands for "free on board at the point of origin," which means that the price does not include freight charges, and thus the buyer must pay the transportation costs from the seller's warehouse to the buyer's place of business. *FOB destination* indicates that the price does include freight charges, and thus the seller pays these charges.

Transfer Pricing

When one unit in an organization sells a product to another unit, **transfer pricing** occurs. The price is determined by calculating the cost of the product. A transfer price can vary depending on the types of costs included in the calculations. The choice of the costs to include when calculating the transfer price depends on the company's management strategy and the nature of the units' interaction. An organization also must ensure that transfer pricing is fair to all units involved in the purchases.

comparison discounting setting a price at a specific level and comparing it with a higher price

transfer pricing prices charged in sales between an organization's units

Table 13.4	Discounts Used for Business Markets	
Type	Reasons for Use	Examples
Trade (functional)	To attract and keep effective resellers by compensating them for performing certain functions, such as transportation, warehousing, selling, and providing credit.	A college bookstore pays about one-third less for a new textbook than the retail price a student pays.
Quantity	To encourage customers to buy large quantities when making purchases and, in the case of cumulative discounts, to encourage customer loyalty.	Numerous companies serving business markets allow a 2 percent discount if an account is paid within ten days.
Seasonal	To allow a marketer to use resources more efficiently by stimulating sales during off-peak periods.	Florida hotels provide companies holding national and regional sales meetings with deeply discounted accommodations during the summer months.
Allowance	In the case of a trade-in allowance, to assist the buyer in making the purchase and potentially earn a profit on the resale of used equipment; in the case of a promotional allowance, to ensure that dealers participate in advertising and sales support programs.	A farm equipment dealer takes a farmer's used tractor as a trade-in on a new one. Nabisco pays a promotional allowance to a supermarket for setting up and maintaining a large end-of-aisle display for a two-week period.

Source: William M. Pride and O. C. Ferrell, *Foundations of Marketing* (Mason, OH: South-Western/Cengage Learning, 2011), 279.

Discounting

A **discount** is a deduction from the price of an item. Producers and sellers offer a wide variety of discounts to their customers, including trade, quantity, cash, and seasonal discounts as well as allowances. *Trade discounts* are discounts from the list prices that are offered to marketing intermediaries, or middlemen. *Quantity discounts* are discounts given to customers who buy in large quantities. The seller's per-unit selling cost is lower for larger purchases. *Cash discounts* are discounts offered for prompt payment. A seller may offer a discount of "2/10, net 30," meaning that the buyer may take a 2 percent discount if the bill is paid within ten days and that the bill must be paid in full within 30 days. A *seasonal discount* is a price reduction to buyers who purchase out of season. This discount lets the seller maintain steadier production during the year. An *allowance* is a reduction in price to achieve a desired goal. Trade-in allowances, for example, are price reductions granted for turning in used equipment, like aircraft, when purchasing new equipment. Table 13.4 describes some of the reasons for using these discounting techniques as well as some examples.

discount a deduction from the price of an item

return to inside business

Threadless

"Why wouldn't you want to make the products that people want you to make?" asks Jake Nickell, co-founder of Threadless. That's exactly how the company manages its product mix. Customers submit and vote on new T-shirt designs, and then Threadless selects the highest-scoring designs for production. This compresses the new-product development process into a matter of weeks and prevents expensive product failures.

Threadless now sells 100,000 T-shirts every month featuring artwork created and approved by its customers. Customers are loyal because they know that their design ideas and their votes really count. Not long ago, Threadless began marketing iPhone cases designed by—of course—its customers. What will its customers/designers think of next?

Questions

1. Would you classify Threadless's T-shirts as convenience products, shopping products, or specialty products? Explain your answer.
2. How is the life-cycle of a sold-out T-shirt likely to be affected when customers vote for reprinting that design? What are the marketing implications for Threadless?

Summary

1 Explain what a product is and how products are classified.

A product is everything one receives in an exchange, including all attributes and expected benefits. The product may be a manufactured item, a service, an idea, or some combination of these.

Products are classified according to their ultimate use. Classification affects a product's distribution, promotion, and pricing. Consumer products, which include convenience, shopping, and specialty products, are purchased to satisfy personal and family needs. Business products are purchased for resale, for making other products, or for use in a firm's operations. Business products can be classified as raw materials, major equipment, accessory equipment, component parts, process materials, supplies, and services.

2 Discuss the product life-cycle and how it leads to new-product development.

Every product moves through a series of four stages—introduction, growth, maturity, and decline—which together form the product life-cycle. As the product progresses through these stages, its sales and profitability increase, peak, and then decline. Marketers keep track of the life-cycle stage of products in order to estimate when a new product should be introduced to replace a declining one.

3 Define *product line* and *product mix* and distinguish between the two.

A product line is a group of similar products marketed by a firm. The products in a product line are related to each other in the way they are produced, marketed, and used. The firm's product mix includes all the products it offers for sale. The width of a mix is the number of product lines it contains. The depth of the mix is the average number of individual products within each line.

4 Identify the methods available for changing a product mix.

Customer satisfaction and organizational objectives require marketers to develop, adjust, and maintain an effective product mix. Marketers may improve a product mix by changing existing products, deleting products, and developing new products.

New products are developed through a series of seven steps. The first step, idea generation, involves the accumulation of a pool of possible product ideas. Screening, the second step, removes from consideration those product ideas that do not mesh with organizational goals or resources. Concept testing, the third step, is a phase in which a small sample of potential buyers is exposed to a proposed product through a written or oral description in order to determine their initial reaction and buying intentions. The fourth step, business analysis, generates information about the potential sales, costs, and profits. During the development step, the product idea is transformed into mock-ups and actual prototypes to determine if the product is technically feasible to build and can be produced at reasonable costs. Test marketing is an actual launch of the product in several selected cities. Finally, during commercialization, plans for full-scale production and marketing are refined and implemented. Most product failures result from inadequate product planning and development.

5 Explain the uses and importance of branding, packaging, and labeling.

A brand is a name, term, symbol, design, or any combination of these that identifies a seller's products as distinct from those of other sellers. Brands can be classified as manufacturer brands, store brands, or generic brands. A firm can choose between two branding strategies—individual branding or family branding. Branding strategies are used to associate (or *not* associate) particular products with existing products, producers, or intermediaries. Packaging protects goods, offers consumer convenience, and enhances marketing efforts by communicating product features, uses, benefits, and image. Labeling provides customers with product information, some of which is required by law.

6 Describe the economic basis of pricing and the means by which sellers can control prices and buyers' perceptions of prices.

Under the ideal conditions of pure competition, an individual seller has no control over the price of its products. Prices are determined by the workings of supply and demand. In our real economy, however, sellers do exert some control, primarily through product differentiation. Product differentiation is the process of developing and promoting differences between one's product and all similar products. Firms also attempt to gain some control over pricing through advertising. A few large sellers have considerable control over prices because each controls a large proportion of the total supply of the product. Firms must consider the relative importance of price to buyers in the target market before setting prices. Buyers' perceptions of prices are affected by the importance of the product to them, the range of prices they consider acceptable, their perceptions of competing products, and their association of quality with price.

Identify the major pricing objectives used by businesses.

Objectives of pricing include survival, profit maximization, target return on investment, achieving market goals, and maintaining the status quo. Firms sometimes have to price products to survive, which usually requires cutting prices to attract customers. ROI is the amount earned as a result of the investment in developing and marketing the product. The firm sets an annual percentage ROI as the pricing goal. Some firms use pricing to maintain or increase their market share. And in industries in which price stability is important, firms often price their products by charging about the same as competitors.

Examine the three major pricing methods that firms employ.

The three major pricing methods are cost-based pricing, demand-based pricing, and competition-based pricing. When cost-based pricing is employed, a proportion of the cost is added to the total cost to determine the selling price. When demand-based pricing is used, the price will be higher when demand is higher, and the price will be lower when demand is lower. A firm that uses competition-based pricing may choose to price below competitors' prices, at the same level as competitors' prices, or slightly above competitors' prices.

Explain the different strategies available to companies for setting prices.

Pricing strategies fall into five categories: new-product pricing, differential pricing, psychological pricing, product-line pricing, and promotional pricing. Price skimming and penetration pricing are two strategies used for pricing new products. Differential pricing can be accomplished through negotiated pricing, secondary-market pricing, periodic discounting, and random discounting. The types of psychological pricing strategies are odd-number pricing, multiple-unit pricing, reference pricing, bundle pricing, everyday low prices, and customary pricing. Product-line pricing can be achieved through captive pricing, premium pricing, and price lining. The major types of promotional pricing are price-leader pricing, special-event pricing, and comparison discounting.

Describe three major types of pricing associated with business products.

Setting prices for business products can be different from setting prices for consumer products as a result of several factors, such as size of purchases, transportation considerations, and geographic issues. The three types of pricing associated with the pricing of business products are geographic pricing, transfer pricing, and discounting.

Key Terms

You should now be able to define and give an example relevant to each of the following terms:

product (362)
consumer product (363)
business product (363)
convenience product (363)
shopping product (363)
specialty product (363)
raw material (364)
major equipment (364)
accessory equipment (364)
component part (364)
process material (364)
supply (364)
business service (364)
product life-cycle (364)
product line (367)
product mix (367)
product modification (368)
line extension (369)
product deletion (369)
brand (373)
brand name (373)
brand mark (373)
trademark (373)
trade name (373)
manufacturer (or producer) brand (373)
store (or private) brand (373)
generic product (or brand) (374)
brand loyalty (374)
brand equity (374)
individual branding (376)
family branding (377)
brand extension (377)
packaging (377)
labeling (379)
express warranty (379)
price (379)
supply (380)
demand (380)
price competition (381)
non-price competition (381)
product differentiation (381)
markup (383)
breakeven quantity (383)
total revenue (383)
fixed cost (383)
variable cost (383)
total cost (383)
price skimming (386)
penetration pricing (386)
negotiated pricing (386)
secondary-market pricing (386)
periodic discounting (386)
random discounting (387)
odd-number pricing (387)
multiple-unit pricing (387)
reference pricing (387)
bundle pricing (387)
everyday low prices (EDLPs) (388)
customary pricing (388)
captive pricing (388)
premium pricing (388)
price lining (389)
price leaders (389)
special-event pricing (389)
comparison discounting (390)
transfer pricing (390)
discount (391)

CHAPTER REVIEW

Review Questions

1. What does the purchaser of a product obtain besides the good, service, or idea itself?
2. What are the products of (a) a bank, (b) an insurance company, and (c) a university?
3. What major factor determines whether a product is a consumer or a business product?
4. Describe each of the classifications of business products.
5. What are the four stages of the product life-cycle? How can a firm determine which stage a particular product is in?
6. What is the difference between a product line and a product mix? Give an example of each.
7. Under what conditions does product modification work best?
8. Why do products have to be deleted from a product mix?
9. Why must firms introduce new products?
10. Briefly describe the seven new-product development stages.
11. What is the difference between manufacturer brands and store brands? Between family branding and individual branding?
12. What is the difference between a line extension and a brand extension?
13. How can packaging be used to enhance marketing activities?
14. For what purposes is labeling used?
15. What is the primary function of prices in our economy?
16. Compare and contrast the characteristics of price and non-price competition.
17. How might buyers' perceptions of price influence pricing decisions?
18. List and briefly describe the five major pricing objectives.
19. What are the differences among markup pricing, pricing by breakeven analysis, and competition-based pricing?
20. In what way is demand-based pricing more realistic than markup pricing?
21. Why would a firm use competition-based pricing?
22. What are the five major categories of pricing strategies? Give at least two examples of specific strategies that fall into each category.
23. Identify and describe the main types of discounts that are used in the pricing of business products.

Discussion Questions

1. Why is it important to understand how products are classified?
2. What factors might determine how long a product remains in each stage of the product life-cycle? What can a firm do to prolong each stage?
3. Some firms do not delete products until they become financially threatening. What problems may result from relying on this practice?
4. Which steps in the evolution of new products are most important? Which are least important? Defend your choices.
5. Do branding, packaging, and labeling really benefit consumers? Explain.
6. To what extent can a firm control its prices in our market economy? What factors limit such control?
7. Under what conditions would a firm be most likely to use non-price competition?
8. Can a firm have more than one pricing objective? Can it use more than one of the pricing methods discussed in this chapter? Explain.
9. What are the major disadvantages of price skimming?
10. What is an "effective" price?
11. Under what conditions would a business most likely decide to employ one of the differential pricing strategies?
12. For what types of products are psychological pricing strategies most likely to be used?

Video Case 13.1

From Artistic Roots, Blu Dot Styles Marketing Strategy

When a trio of college friends with backgrounds in art and architecture started moving into their first apartments in the late 1990s, they were frustrated to find that when it came to furniture, they couldn't afford what they liked and didn't like what they could afford. Happily for many future furniture shoppers, however, this frustration led the three to found Blu Dot, a Minneapolis-based furniture design and manufacturing company that has flourished and grown.

Blu Dot specializes in the creation of furniture that is attractive, high quality, and affordable. Its modern, streamlined pieces use off-the-shelf materials and simple manufacturing processes that keep the company's costs and prices down. The company also contracts with suppliers that make industrial rather than consumer products, because they use more efficient and cost-effective processes and technology. These strategies, plus designs that pack flat and are easy to ship, allow the firm to combine what Maurice Blanks, one of the founders, describes as the affordability of the low end of the market and the craftsmanship of the high end. Anyone can design a $600 or $700 coffee table, Blu Dot believes. It's the $99 one the company is aiming for that's more of a challenge.

The company sells seven product lines—tables, storage, accessories, desks, beds, seating, and shelving. Its pricing strategy for each of these is straightforward. Managers add their fixed and variable costs, plus the markup they believe they'll need to keep the business functioning. They then usually look at what competitors are doing with similar products and try to identify three or four different pieces of pricing information to help them settle on a profitable price. The company also uses some creative pricing strategies to make its margins. For instance, one coffee table in a set might have a higher markup, whereas another has a slightly lower one for more price-conscious customers. Overall, then, the target margins are often met.

Blu Dot thinks of its total product offering as consisting of three interdependent elements: the core product, its supplemental features, and its symbolic or experiential value. Although some customers are attracted by the design aspects of the products, others are more concerned with value. That's one reason the company recently introduced a separate brand, called +oo ("too"), and priced it slightly below the original Blu Dot line. These items have been marketed through Urban Outfitters, and Blu Dot has adjusted the prices over time after seeing how sales progressed. Co-founder John Christakos likens Blu Dot's pricing practice to cooking, in that both are processes that allow for fine-tuning as events develop.

In an interesting recent promotion that flirted with the price of zero, Blu Dot celebrated the opening of its new store in New York's hip SoHo district by leaving 25 brand-new units of its iconic "Real Good Chair," normally priced at $129, on various street corners in the city. Most of the chairs were equipped with GPS devices that allowed the company's marketing agency to trace the chairs to those who "rescued" them and brought them home. The company's Web site proclaims that all the chairs found good homes, and those "scavengers" who agreed to chat with the firm about its products received a second free chair in thanks.[21]

Questions

1. What challenges does Blu Dot face in selling consumer products (as opposed to business products)?
2. Do you think the product life-cycle is an important marketing concept in developing and managing Blu Dot products? Why or why not?
3. Describe the product mix and the role different product lines play in Blu Dot's marketing strategy.

Case 13.2

Apple iPhone Pricing Dials Up Customer Demand

Days before the first Apple iPhones went on sale, thousands of buyers lined up outside Apple stores, eager to try the new cell phone's large, user-friendly touch-screen and multimedia capabilities. Like Apple's iconic iPod media player, instantly identifiable because of its sleek case and white ear buds, the stylish iPhone became a must-have status symbol for tech-savvy consumers across the United States. However, despite a major promotional campaign, widespread media coverage, many rave reviews, and a fast-growing customer base, the iPhone became the focus of criticism and controversy within two months of its release.

Apple has traditionally set high prices for its new products. One purpose of pricing in this way is to reinforce the brand's high-end positioning and special cachet. Another is to start recouping development costs and build profits from the very start of each product's life. This pricing strategy has worked with the company's Macintosh computers, iPods, and iPads, allowing Apple to increase both revenues and profits year after year.

The iPhone was initially priced at $599, not including the cost of monthly phone service through an exclusive deal with AT&T. Two months later, in a break from its usual pattern, Apple abruptly slashed the iPhone's price by $200. Although electronic products often drop in price over time, they rarely sell for so much less so soon after introduction. This time, Apple had its eye on the year-end holidays, believing that setting a more affordable price during the fall would put the iPhone within reach of a larger number of gift-giving buyers. The company also saw an opportunity to achieve its objective of selling 10 million iPhones worldwide within 18 months of the product's launch (which it did).

Apple's pricing decision provoked angry protests from customers who protested that they had overpaid for a cutting-edge product that was going mainstream more quickly than expected. With Apple on the spot, CEO Steve Jobs quickly conceded that customers had a point. "Our early customers trusted us, and we must live up to that trust with our actions in moments like these," he said in a statement posted on Apple's Web site. To avoid alienating early buyers, the company offered a $100 Apple store credit to each customer who had purchased an iPhone before the price cut. Although this policy also drew criticism—because the credit had no value except toward the purchase of something from Apple—the pricing controversy lost steam after a few weeks.

Intense competition from multinational rivals such as Nokia, Samsung, and Research in Motion (maker of Blackberry) has been a major influence on smart-phone pricing. As Apple launches new iPhone models with more features and more power, it sets prices that are considerably lower than when the product was originally introduced years ago. The lower-priced iPhones have become enormously successful, sparking excitement and prompting long lines at Apple stores worldwide. During one recent three-month period, Apple sold more than 8 million iPhones, thanks to particularly strong demand in Asia and Europe. Just as the iPod attracted many first-time Apple buyers, the iPhone's unique appeal and new, more affordable price tag have brought in new customers and given loyal customers another reason to buy from Apple.

The buzz from the iPhone, the iPad, and other products has also boosted demand for Apple's line of Macintosh computers and allowed the company to gain significant market share in that industry. Higher sales of Apple's entire product mix have also resulted in record-setting company profits and helped the company expand into new markets. Just as important, all these innovations have polished the Apple brand and added to its trend-setting image—which, in turn, allows the company to charge premium prices when it launches new products.[22]

Questions

1. What was Apple's primary pricing objective when it introduced the iPhone? What was its primary objective in cutting the product's price just two months after introduction?
2. How much weight does Apple appear to have given to its evaluation of competitive pricing?
3. Do you agree with Apple's decision to switch away from price skimming after the iPhone's introduction? Defend your answer.

Building Skills for Career Success

❶ JOURNALING FOR SUCCESS

Discovery statement: This chapter explained the importance of product branding.

Assignment

1. Thinking about the brands of products that you use, to which brand are you the most loyal? Explain the functional benefits of this brand.
2. Beyond the functional benefits, what does this brand mean to you?
3. Under what set of circumstances would you be willing to change to another competing brand?
4. Discuss how you first began to use this brand.

❷ EXPLORING THE INTERNET

The Internet has quickly taken comparison shopping to a new level. Several Web sites such as http://bizrate.com, http://pricescan.com, and http://mysimon.com have emerged boasting that they can find the consumer the best deal on any product. From computers to watches, these sites offer unbiased price and product information to compare virtually any product. Users may read reviews about products as well as provide their own input from personal experience. Some of these sites also offer special promotions and incentives in exchange for user information. Visit the text Web site for updates to this exercise.

Assignment

1. Search all three of the Web sites listed above for the same product.
2. Did you notice any significant differences between the sites and the information they provide?
3. What percentage of searches do you think lead to purchases as opposed to browsing? Explain your answer.
4. Which site are you most likely to use on a regular basis? Why?
5. In what ways do these Web sites contribute to price competition?

❸ DEVELOPING CRITICAL-THINKING SKILLS

A feature is a characteristic of a product or service that enables it to perform its function. Benefits are the results a person receives from using a product or service. For example, a toothpaste's stain-removing formula is a feature; the benefit to the user is whiter teeth. Although features are valuable and enhance a product, benefits motivate people to buy. The customer is more interested in how the product can help (the benefits) than in the details of the product (the features).

Assignment

1. Choose a product and identify its features and benefits.
2. Divide a sheet of paper into two columns. In one column, list the features of the product. In the other column, list the benefits each feature yields to the buyer.
3. Prepare a statement that would motivate you to buy this product.

❹ BUILDING TEAM SKILLS

In his book, *The Post-Industrial Society*, Peter Drucker wrote:

> *Society, community, and family are all conserving institutions. They try to maintain stability and to prevent, or at least slow down, change. But the organization of the post-capitalist society of organizations is a destabilizer. Because its function is to put knowledge to work—on tools, processes, and products; on work; on knowledge itself—it must be organized for constant change. It must be organized for innovation.*
>
> *New product development is important in this process of systematically abandoning the past and building a future. Current customers can be sources of ideas for new products and services and ways of improving existing ones.*

Assignment

1. Working in teams of five to seven, brainstorm ideas for new products or services for your college.
2. Construct questions to ask currently enrolled students (your customers). Sample questions might include:
   a. Why did you choose this college?
   b. How can this college be improved?
   c. What products or services do you wish were available?
3. Conduct the survey and review the results.
4. Prepare a list of improvements and/or new products or services for your college.

❺ RESEARCHING DIFFERENT CAREERS

Standard & Poor's Industry Surveys, designed for investors, provides insight into various industries and the companies that compete within those industries. The "Basic Analysis" section gives overviews of industry trends and issues. The other sections define some basic industry terms, report the latest revenues and earnings of more than 1,000 companies, and occasionally list major reference books and trade associations.

Assignment

1. Identify an industry in which you might like to work.
2. Find the industry in *Standard & Poor's*. (*Note: Standard & Poor's* uses broad categories of industry. For example, an apparel or home-furnishings store would be included under "Retail" or "Textiles.")
3. Identify the following:
   a. Trends and issues in the industry
   b. Opportunities and/or problems that might arise in the industry in the next five years
   c. Major competitors within the industry (These companies are your potential employers.)
4. Prepare a report of your findings.

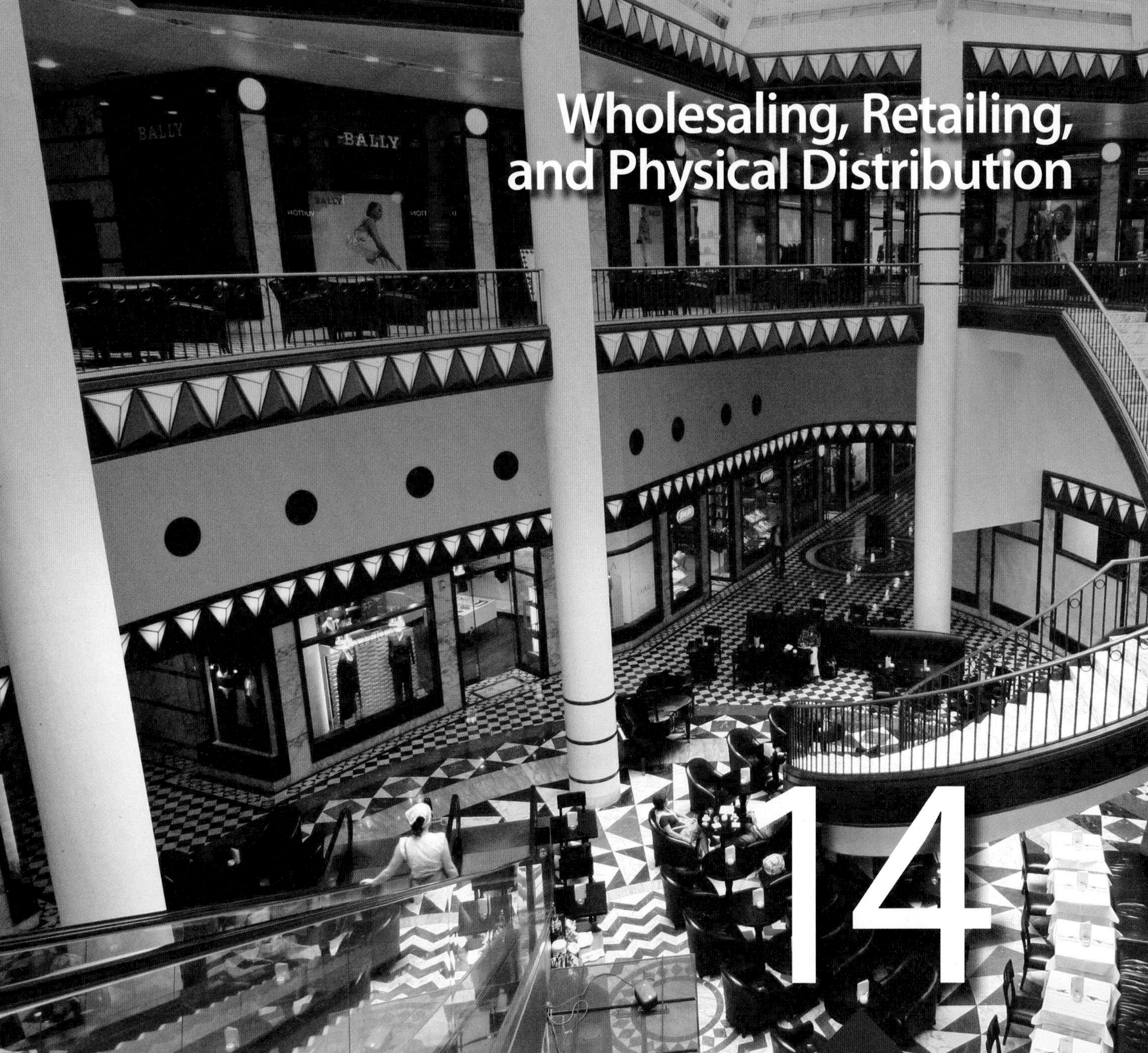

Wholesaling, Retailing, and Physical Distribution

14

Learning Objectives

What you will be able to do once you complete this chapter:

1. Identify the various channels of distribution that are used for consumer and industrial products.
2. Explain the concept of market coverage.
3. Understand how supply-chain management facilitates partnering among channel members.
4. Describe what a vertical marketing system is and identify the types of vertical marketing systems.
5. Discuss the need for wholesalers and describe the services they provide to retailers and manufacturers.
6. Identify and describe the major types of wholesalers.
7. Distinguish among the major types of retailers.
8. Identify the categories of shopping centers and the factors that determine how shopping centers are classified.
9. Explain the five most important physical distribution activities.

FYI

Did You Know?

Founded in 1996, GameStop now rings up $9 billion in annual sales through 6,450 stores in 17 countries.

inside business

GameStop's Game Plan for Global Retailing

From Dallas, Texas, to Dee Why, Australia, GameStop is a big player in video-game retailing. The company, based in Grapevine, Texas, was founded in 1996 and now rings up $9 billion in annual sales through 6,450 stores in 17 countries. GameStop targets three customer segments: enthusiasts who want the newest or hottest consoles and games, consumers who are casual game-players, and consumers who give games or accessories as gifts. Its game plan for global success is based on an ever-changing store assortment of new and used games and game consoles.

Under GameStop's trade-in program, customers who bring in used games, consoles, or accessories can receive store credit toward the purchase of other merchandise. GameStop ships used items to one of its three refurbishment centers to be tested, fixed if necessary, repackaged, and sent back to the stores for resale. This trade-in program stimulates a steady stream of store traffic and adds to GameStop's inventory. Just as important, it boosts GameStop's profitability, because gross margins on sales of used merchandise are much higher than on sales of new merchandise. In fact, 25 percent of GameStop's revenue and 45 percent of its profits now come from retailing used games.

Thanks to its sophisticated information system, GameStop knows exactly which items are in demand in each location. Analyzing what sells where (and how quickly) also helps the company allocate supplies of new games and consoles. To ensure that new products reach store shelves as quickly as possible, GameStop has one distribution center devoted to handling new items and a second distribution center that handles all other merchandise. The company monitors daily sales in each store and automatically ships replenishment stock twice a week, freeing store staff to concentrate on serving customers.

GameStop has been building up its online presence to cater to consumers who prefer to buy with a click. Its Web site provides previews of soon-to-be-released games, invites customers to pre-order new games, and offers downloads of new and classic games, some for sale and some for free. Although digital downloads are increasingly popular, GameStop believes that its in-store retailing strength will keep the company ahead of the game for years to come.[1]

Some companies, like GameStop, use a particular approach to distribution and marketing channels that gives them a sustainable competitive advantage. More than 2 million firms in the United States help to move products from producers to consumers. Store chains such as Dollar General Stores, Starbucks, Sears, and Walmart operate retail outlets where consumers make purchases. Some retailers, such as Avon Products and Amway, send their salespeople to the homes of customers. Other retailers, such as Lands' End and L.L.Bean, sell through both catalogs and online. Still others, such as Amazon, sell online to customers.

In addition, there are more than half a million wholesalers that sell merchandise to other firms. Most consumers know little about these firms, which work "behind the scenes" and rarely sell directly to consumers. These and other intermediaries are concerned with the transfer of both products and ownership. They thus help to create the time, place, and possession utilities that are critical to marketing. As we will see, they also perform a number of services for their suppliers and their customers.

In this chapter, we initially examine various channels of distribution that products follow as they move from producer to ultimate user. Then we discuss wholesalers and retailers within these channels. Next, we examine the types of shopping centers. Finally, we explore the physical distribution function and the major modes of transportation that are used to move goods.

Channels of Distribution

A **channel of distribution**, or **marketing channel**, is a sequence of marketing organizations that directs a product from the producer to the ultimate user. Every marketing channel begins with the producer and ends with either the consumer or the business user.

A marketing organization that links a producer and user within a marketing channel is called a **middleman** or **marketing intermediary**. For the most part, middlemen are concerned with the transfer of *ownership* of products. A **merchant middleman** (or, more simply, a *merchant*) is a middleman that actually takes title to products by buying them. A **functional middleman**, on the other hand, helps in the transfer of ownership of products but does not take title to the products.

1

Identify the various channels of distribution that are used for consumer and industrial products.

Channels for Consumer Products

Different channels of distribution generally are used to move consumer and business products. The four most commonly used channels for consumer products are illustrated in Figure 14.1.

Producer to Consumer This channel, often called the *direct channel,* includes no marketing intermediaries. Practically all services and a few consumer goods are distributed through a direct channel. Examples of marketers that sell goods directly to consumers include Dell Computer, Mary Kay Cosmetics, and Avon Products.

Producers sell directly to consumers for several reasons. They can better control the quality and price of their products. They do not have to pay (through discounts) for the services of intermediaries. They can maintain closer ties with customers.

Figure 14.1 Distribution Channels

Producers use various channels to distribute their products.

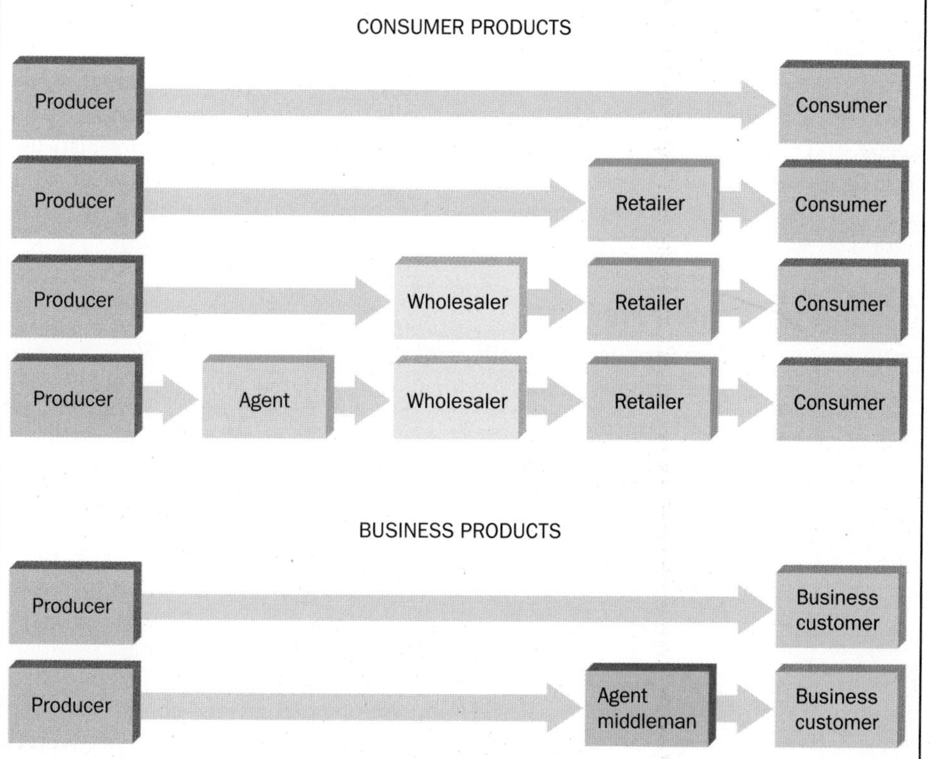

CONSUMER PRODUCTS

Producer → Consumer

Producer → Retailer → Consumer

Producer → Wholesaler → Retailer → Consumer

Producer → Agent → Wholesaler → Retailer → Consumer

BUSINESS PRODUCTS

Producer → Business customer

Producer → Agent middleman → Business customer

channel of distribution (or marketing channel) a sequence of marketing organizations that directs a product from the producer to the ultimate user

middleman (or marketing intermediary) a marketing organization that links a producer and user within a marketing channel

merchant middleman a middleman that actually takes title to products by buying them

functional middleman a middleman that helps in the transfer of ownership of products but does not take title to the products

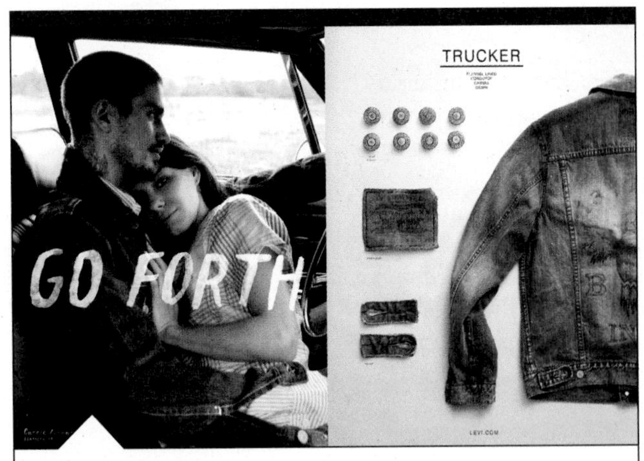

Marketing channels for consumer products. Clothing like Levi's products is often distributed through the producer-retailer consumer channel.

Producer to Retailer to Consumer A **retailer** is a middleman that buys from producers or other middlemen and sells to consumers. Producers sell directly to retailers when retailers (such as Walmart) can buy in large quantities. This channel is used most often for products that are bulky, such as furniture and automobiles, for which additional handling would increase selling costs. It is also the usual channel for perishable products, such as fruits and vegetables, and for high-fashion products that must reach the consumer in the shortest possible time.

Producer to Wholesaler to Retailer to Consumer This channel is known as the *traditional channel* because many consumer goods (especially convenience goods) pass through wholesalers to retailers. A **wholesaler** is a middleman that sells products to other firms. These firms may be retailers, industrial users, or other wholesalers. A producer uses wholesalers when its products are carried by so many retailers that the producer cannot deal with all of them. For example, the maker of Wrigley's gum uses this type of channel.

Producer to Agent to Wholesaler to Retailer to Consumer Producers may use agents to reach wholesalers. Agents are functional middlemen who do not take title to products and are compensated by commissions paid by producers. Often these products are inexpensive, frequently purchased items. For example, to reach a large number of potential customers, a small manufacturer of gas-powered lawn edgers might choose to use agents to market its product to wholesalers, which, in turn, sell the lawn edgers to a large number of retailers. This channel is also used for highly seasonal products (such as Christmas tree ornaments) and by producers that do not have their own sales forces.

Multiple Channels for Consumer Products

Often, a manufacturer uses different distribution channels to reach different market segments. A manufacturer uses multiple channels, for example, when the same product is sold to consumers and business customers. Multiple channels are also used to increase sales or to capture a larger share of the market. With the goal of selling as much merchandise as possible, Firestone markets its tires through its own retail outlets as well as through independent dealers.

Channels for Business Products

Producers of business products generally tend to use short channels. We will outline the two that are used most commonly, which are illustrated in Figure 14.1.

Producer to Business User In this direct channel, the manufacturer's own sales force sells directly to business users. Heavy machinery, airplanes, and major equipment usually are distributed in this way. The very short channel allows the producer to provide customers with expert and timely services, such as delivery, machinery installation, and repairs.

Producer to Agent Middleman to Business User Manufacturers use this channel to distribute such items as operating supplies, accessory equipment, small tools, and standardized parts. The agent is an independent intermediary between the producer and the user. Generally, agents represent sellers.

retailer a middleman that buys from producers or other middlemen and sells to consumers

wholesaler a middleman that sells products to other firms

Level of Market Coverage

2 Explain the concept of market coverage.

The level of market coverage refers to the number of wholesalers and the number of retailers that are used for a specific geographic area. There are three levels of market coverage: intensive distribution, selective distribution, and exclusive distribution. Figure 14.2 shows examples of products that are likely to be distributed through each of these levels of market coverage.

Intensive distribution is the use of all available outlets for a product. The producer that wants to give its product the widest possible exposure in the marketplace chooses intensive distribution. The manufacturer saturates the market by selling to any intermediary of good financial standing that is willing to stock and sell the product. For the consumer, intensive distribution means being able to shop at a convenient store and spend a minimum amount of time buying the product. Companies such as Procter & Gamble that produce consumer packaged items rely on intensive distribution for many of their products because consumers want ready availability.

Selective distribution is the use of only a portion of the available outlets for a product in each geographic area. Examples include the launch of Apple's iPhone, distributed in AT&T and Apple retail stores in the United States, and perfumes distributed through large department and specialty perfume stores. The majority of perfumes and colognes use selective distribution to maintain a particular image. For example, eBay was recently fined by a Parisian court for selling certain brands of perfume on its Web site, such as Christian Dior, Givenchy, and Kenzo. These companies are trying to protect their brand's image by only selling through select retail outlets.[2]

Selective distribution. Coach brand products are distributed through selective distribution.

Image courtesy of The Advertising Archives

Figure 14.2 Levels of Market Coverage

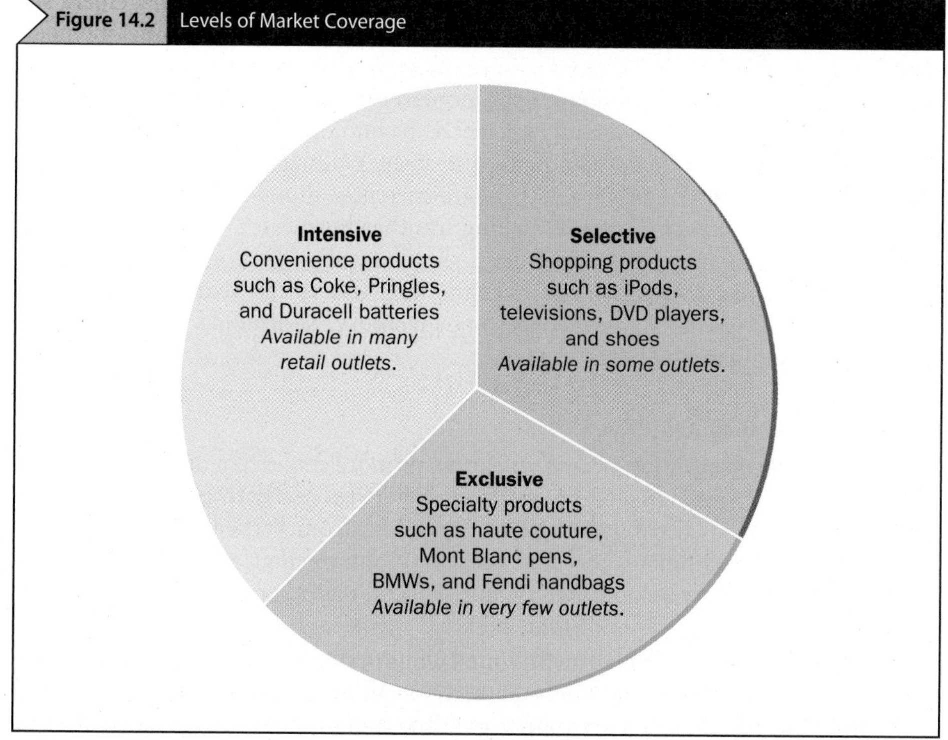

Source: William M. Pride and O. C. Ferrell, *Foundations of Marketing* (Mason, OH: South-Western/Cengage Learning, 2011), 319.

intensive distribution the use of all available outlets for a product

selective distribution the use of only a portion of the available outlets for a product in each geographic area

Exclusive distribution is the use of only a single retail outlet for a product in a large geographic area. Exclusive distribution usually is limited to very prestigious products. The producer usually places many requirements (such as inventory levels, sales training, service quality, and warranty procedures) on exclusive dealers. For example, Patek Philippe watches, which may sell for $10,000 or more, are available in only a few select locations.

3

Understand how supply-chain management facilitates partnering among channel members.

Partnering Through Supply-Chain Management

Supply-chain management is a long-term partnership among channel members working together to create a distribution system that reduces inefficiencies, costs, and redundancies while creating a competitive advantage and satisfying customers. Supply-chain management requires cooperation throughout the entire marketing channel, including manufacturing, research, sales, advertising, and shipping. Supply chains focus not only on producers, wholesalers, retailers, and customers but also on component-parts suppliers, shipping companies, communication companies, and other organizations that participate in product distribution. Suppliers are having a greater impact on determining what items retail stores carry. This phenomenon, called *category management,* is becoming common for mass merchandisers, supermarkets, and convenience stores. Through category management, the retailer asks a supplier in a particular category how to stock the shelves. Many retailers and suppliers claim this process delivers maximum efficiency.

Traditionally, buyers and sellers have been adversarial when negotiating purchases. Supply-chain management, however, encourages cooperation in reducing the costs of inventory, transportation, administration, and handling; in speeding order-cycle times; and in increasing profits for all channel members. When buyers, sellers, marketing intermediaries, and facilitating agencies work together, customers' needs regarding delivery, scheduling, packaging, and other requirements are better met. Home Depot, North America's largest home-improvement retailer, is working to help its suppliers improve productivity and thereby supply Home Depot with better-quality products at lower costs. The company has even suggested a cooperative partnership with its competitors so that regional trucking companies making deliveries to all these organizations can provide faster, more efficient delivery.

Technology has enhanced the implementation of supply-chain management significantly. Through computerized integrated information sharing, channel members reduce costs and improve customer service. At Walmart, for example, supply-chain management has almost eliminated the occurrence of out-of-stock items. Using barcode and electronic data interchange (EDI) technology, stores, warehouses, and suppliers communicate quickly and easily to keep Walmart's shelves stocked with items customers want. Furthermore, there are currently about 400 electronic trading communities made up of businesses selling to other businesses, including auctions, exchanges, e-procurement hubs, and multi-supplier online catalogs. As many major industries transform their processes over the next five to ten years, the end result will be increased productivity by reducing inventory, shortening cycle time, and removing wasted human effort.

exclusive distribution the use of only a single retail outlet for a product in a large geographic area

supply-chain management long-term partnership among channel members working together to create a distribution system that reduces inefficiencies, costs, and redundancies while creating a competitive advantage and satisfying customers

vertical channel integration the combining of two or more stages of a distribution channel under a single firm's management

Describe what a vertical marketing system is and identify the types of vertical marketing systems.

Vertical Marketing Systems

Vertical channel integration occurs when two or more stages of a distribution channel are combined and managed by one firm. A **vertical marketing system (VMS)** is a centrally managed distribution channel resulting from vertical channel integration. This merging eliminates the need for certain intermediaries. One member of a marketing channel may assume the responsibilities of another member, or it actually may purchase the operations of that member. PepsiCo, for example, recently purchased PepsiAmericas and The Pepsi Bottling Group, both of which own and operate local bottling and distribution organizations. Although the purchase may trigger antitrust concerns, it represents a new strategy among beverage manufacturers to better control the distribution and marketing of all of their drink products, not just

vertical marketing system (VMS) a centrally managed distribution channel resulting from vertical channel integration

sodas, as consumers increasingly buy other beverages, such as energy drinks, juices, and flavored waters.[3] Total vertical integration occurs when a single management controls all operations from production to final sale. Oil companies that own wells, transportation facilities, refineries, terminals, and service stations exemplify total vertical integration.

There are three types of VMSs: administered, contractual, and corporate. In an *administered VMS,* one of the channel members dominates the other members, perhaps because of its large size. Under its influence, the channel members collaborate on production and distribution. A powerful manufacturer, such as Procter & Gamble, receives a great deal of cooperation from intermediaries that carry its brands. Although the goals of the entire system are considered when decisions are made, control rests with individual channel members, as in conventional marketing channels. Under a *contractual VMS,* cooperative arrangements and the rights and obligations of channel members are defined by contracts or other legal measures. In a *corporate VMS,* actual ownership is the vehicle by which production and distribution are joined. For example, The Limited established a corporate VMS that operates corporate-owned production facilities and retail stores. Most VMSs are organized to improve distribution by combining individual operations.

Discuss the need for wholesalers and describe the services they provide to retailers and manufacturers.

Marketing Intermediaries: Wholesalers

Wholesalers may be the most misunderstood of marketing intermediaries. Producers sometimes try to eliminate them from distribution channels by dealing directly with retailers or consumers. Yet wholesalers provide a variety of essential marketing services. Although wholesalers can be eliminated, their functions cannot be eliminated. These functions *must* be performed by other channel members or by consumers. Eliminating a wholesaler may or may not cut distribution costs.

Justifications for Marketing Intermediaries

The press, consumers, public officials, and other marketers often charge wholesalers, at least in principle, with inefficiency and parasitism. Consumers in particular feel strongly that the distribution channel should be made as short as possible. They assume that the fewer the intermediaries in a distribution channel, the lower the price of the product will be.

Those who believe that the elimination of wholesalers will bring about lower prices, however, do not recognize that the services wholesalers perform are still needed. Those services simply are provided by other means, and consumers still bear the costs. Moreover, all manufacturers operating without wholesalers would have to keep extensive records and employ enough personnel to deal with a multitude of retailers individually. Even with direct distribution, products might be considerably more expensive because prices would reflect the costs of producers' inefficiencies. Figure 14.3 shows that 16 contacts could result from the efforts of four buyers purchasing the products of four producers. With the assistance of an intermediary, only eight contacts would be necessary.

To illustrate further the useful role of wholesalers in the marketing system, assume that all wholesalers in the candy industry were abolished. With thousands of candy retailers to contact, candy manufacturers would be making an extremely large number of sales calls just to maintain the present level of product visibility. Hershey Foods, for example, would have to set up warehouses all over the country, organize a fleet of trucks, purchase and maintain thousands of vending machines, and deliver all its own candy. Sales and distribution costs for candy would soar. Candy producers would be contacting and shipping products to thousands of small businesses instead of to a limited number of large wholesalers and retailers. The outrageous costs of this inefficiency would be passed on to consumers. Candy bars would be more expensive and likely available through fewer retailers.

Wholesalers often are more efficient and economical not only for manufacturers, but also for consumers. Because pressure to eliminate them comes from both

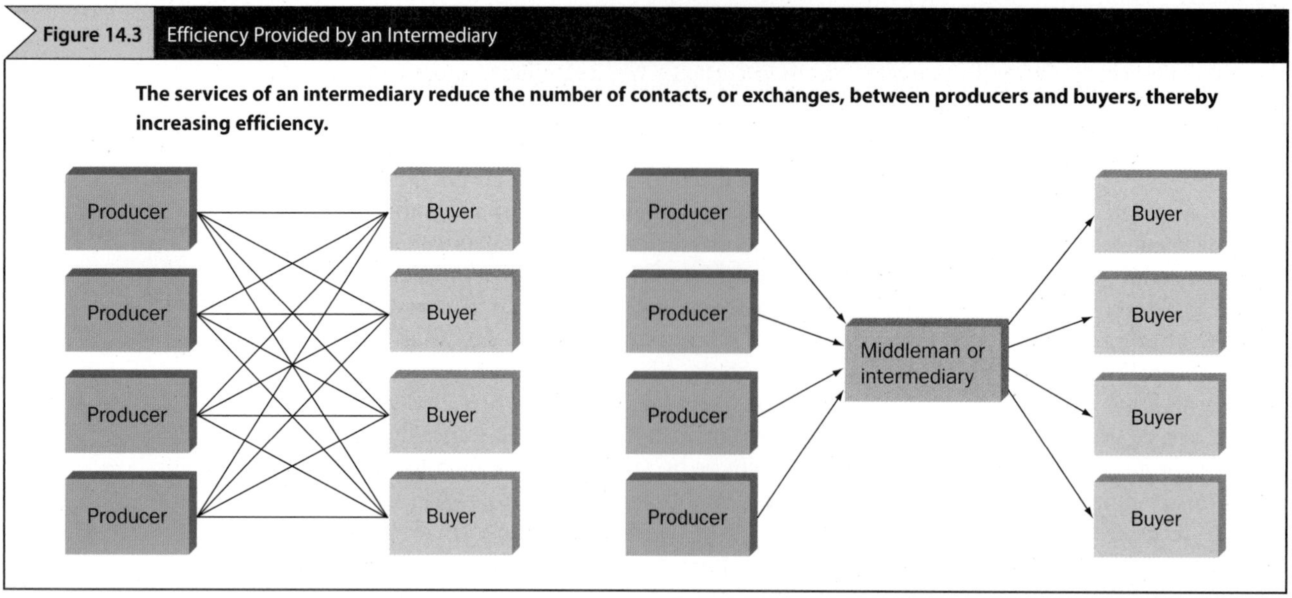

Figure 14.3 Efficiency Provided by an Intermediary

Source: William M. Pride and O.C. Ferrell, *Marketing: Concepts and Strategies*, 16 ed. (Mason, OH: South-Western/Cengage Learning, 2012). Adapted with permission.

ends of the marketing channel, wholesalers should perform only those functions that are genuinely in demand. To stay in business, wholesalers also should take care to be efficient and productive and to provide high-quality services to other channel members.

Wholesalers' Services to Retailers

Wholesalers help retailers by buying in large quantities and then selling to retailers in smaller quantities and by delivering goods to retailers. They also stock—in one place—the variety of goods that retailers otherwise would have to buy from many producers. Wholesalers provide assistance in three other vital areas: promotion, market information, and financial aid.

Promotion Some wholesalers help to promote the products they sell to retailers. These services are usually either free or performed at cost. Wholesalers, for example, are major sources of display materials designed to stimulate impulse buying. They also may help retailers to build effective window, counter, and shelf displays. Some may even assign their own employees to work on the retail sales floor during special promotions.

Market Information Wholesalers are a constant source of market information. Wholesalers have numerous contacts with local businesses and distant suppliers. In the course of these dealings, they accumulate information about consumer demand, prices, supply conditions, new developments within the trade, and even industry personnel. This information may be relayed to retailers informally through the wholesaler's sales force. Some wholesalers also provide information to their customers through Web sites.

Information regarding industry sales and competitive prices is especially important to all firms. Dealing with a number of suppliers and many retailers, a wholesaler is a natural clearinghouse for such information. Most wholesalers are willing to pass information on to their customers.

Financial Aid Most wholesalers provide a type of financial aid that retailers often take for granted. By making prompt and frequent deliveries, wholesalers enable retailers to keep their own inventory investments small in relation to sales. Such indirect financial aid reduces the amount of operating capital that retailers need.

Wholesalers' Services to Manufacturers

Some of the services that wholesalers perform for producers are similar to those they provide to retailers. Others are quite different.

Providing an Instant Sales Force A wholesaler provides its producers with an instant sales force so that producers' sales representatives need not call on retailers. This can result in enormous savings for producers. For example, Lever Brothers and General Foods would have to spend millions of dollars each year to field a sales force large enough to call on all the retailers that sell their numerous products. Instead, these producers rely on wholesalers to sell and distribute their products to many retailers. These producers do have sales forces, though, that call on wholesalers and large retailers.

Reducing Inventory Costs Wholesalers purchase goods in sizable quantities from manufacturers and store these goods for resale. By doing so, they reduce the amount of finished-goods inventory that producers must hold and thereby reduce the cost of carrying inventories.

Assuming Credit Risks When producers sell through wholesalers, it is the wholesalers who extend credit to retailers, make collections from retailers, and assume the risks of non-payment. These services reduce the producers' cost of extending credit to customers and the resulting bad-debt expense.

merchant wholesaler a middleman that purchases goods in large quantities and then sells them to other wholesalers or retailers and to institutional, farm, government, professional, or industrial users

Furnishing Market Information Just as they do for retailers, wholesalers supply market information to the producers they serve. Valuable information accumulated by wholesalers may concern consumer demand, the producers' competition, and buying trends.

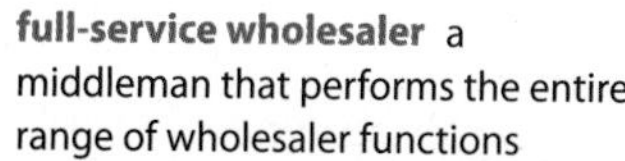

Identify and describe the major types of wholesalers.

Types of Wholesalers

Wholesalers generally fall into three categories: merchant wholesalers; commission merchants, agents, and brokers; and manufacturers' sales branches and sales offices. Of these, merchant wholesalers constitute the largest portion. They account for about four-fifths of all wholesale establishments and employees.

Merchant Wholesalers A **merchant wholesaler** is a middleman that purchases goods in large quantities and then sells them to other wholesalers or retailers and to institutional, farm, government, professional, or industrial users. Merchant wholesalers usually operate one or more warehouses at which they receive, take title to, and store goods. These wholesalers are sometimes called *distributors* or *jobbers*.

full-service wholesaler a middleman that performs the entire range of wholesaler functions

Most merchant wholesalers are businesses composed of salespeople, order takers, receiving and shipping clerks, inventory managers, and office personnel. The successful merchant wholesaler must analyze available products and market needs. It must be able to adapt the type, variety, and quality of its products to changing market conditions.

Merchant wholesalers may be classified as full-service or limited-service wholesalers, depending on the number of services they provide. A **full-service wholesaler** performs the entire range of wholesaler functions described earlier in this section. These functions include delivering goods, supplying, warehousing, arranging for credit, supporting promotional activities, and providing general customer assistance.

General merchandise wholesaler. A general merchandise wholesaler carries a broad product mix.

© Daleen Loest/Shutterstock.com

Under this broad heading are the general-merchandise wholesaler, limited-line wholesaler, and specialty-line wholesaler. A **general-merchandise wholesaler** deals in a wide variety of products, such as drugs, hardware, nonperishable foods, cosmetics, detergents, and tobacco. A **limited-line wholesaler** stocks only a few product lines but carries numerous product items within each line. A **specialty-line wholesaler** carries a select group of products within a single line. Food delicacies such as shellfish represent the kind of product handled by this type of wholesaler.

In contrast to a full-service wholesaler, a **limited-service wholesaler** assumes responsibility for a few wholesale services only. Other marketing tasks are left to other channel members or consumers. This category includes cash-and-carry wholesalers, truck wholesalers, drop shippers, and mail-order wholesalers.

Commission Merchants, Agents, and Brokers Commission merchants, agents, and brokers are functional middlemen. Functional middlemen do not take title to products. They perform a small number of marketing activities and are paid a commission that is a percentage of the sales price.

A **commission merchant** usually carries merchandise and negotiates sales for manufacturers. In most cases, commission merchants have the power to set the prices and terms of sales. After a sale is made, they either arrange for delivery or provide transportation services.

An **agent** is a middleman that expedites exchanges, represents a buyer or a seller, and often is hired permanently on a commission basis. When agents represent producers, they are known as *sales agents* or *manufacturer's agents*. As long as the products represented do not compete, a sales agent may represent one or several manufacturers on a commission basis. The agent solicits orders for the manufacturers within a specific territory. As a rule, the manufacturers ship the merchandise and bill the customers directly. The manufacturers also set the prices and other conditions of the sales. What do the manufacturers gain by using a sales agent? The sales agent provides immediate entry into a territory, regular calls on customers, selling experience, and a known, predetermined selling expense (a commission that is a percentage of sales revenue).

A **broker** is a middleman that specializes in a particular commodity, represents either a buyer or a seller, and is likely to be hired on a temporary basis. However, food brokers, which sell grocery products to resellers, generally have long-term relationships with their clients. Brokers may perform only the selling function, or both buying and selling, using established contacts or special knowledge of their fields.

Manufacturers' Sales Branches and Sales Offices A **manufacturer's sales branch** is, in essence, a merchant wholesaler that is owned by a manufacturer. Sales branches carry inventory, extend credit, deliver goods, and offer help in promoting products. Their customers are retailers, other wholesalers, and industrial purchasers.

Because sales branches are owned by producers, they stock primarily the goods manufactured by their own firms. Selling policies and terms usually are established centrally and then transmitted to branch managers for implementation.

A **manufacturer's sales office** is essentially a sales agent owned by a manufacturer. Sales offices may sell goods manufactured by their own firms as well as certain products of other manufacturers that complement their own product lines. For example, Hiram Walker & Sons imports wine from Spain to increase the number of products its sales offices can offer to customers.

general-merchandise wholesaler a middleman that deals in a wide variety of products

limited-line wholesaler a middleman that stocks only a few product lines but carries numerous product items within each line

specialty-line wholesaler a middleman that carries a select group of products within a single line

limited-service wholesaler a middleman that assumes responsibility for a few wholesale services only

commission merchant a middleman that carries merchandise and negotiates sales for manufacturers

agent a middleman that expedites exchanges, represents a buyer or a seller, and often is hired permanently on a commission basis

broker a middleman that specializes in a particular commodity, represents either a buyer or a seller, and is likely to be hired on a temporary basis

manufacturer's sales branch essentially a merchant wholesaler that is owned by a manufacturer

manufacturer's sales office essentially a sales agent owned by a manufacturer

Distinguish among the major types of retailers.

Marketing Intermediaries: Retailers

Retailers are the final link between producers and consumers. Retailers may buy from either wholesalers or producers. They sell not only goods but also such services as auto repairs, haircuts, and dry cleaning. Some retailers sell both. Sears, Roebuck and Company sells consumer goods, financial services, and repair services for home appliances bought at Sears.

Of approximately 2.6 million retail firms in the United States, about 90 percent have annual sales of less than $1 million. On the other hand, some large retail organizations realize well over $1 million in sales revenue per day. Table 14.1 lists the ten largest retail organizations and their approximate sales revenues and yearly profits.

Retailing. Retailing occurs in brick-and-mortar establishments, online, at home, and in the workplace.

Classes of In-Store Retailers

One way to classify retailers is by the number of stores owned and operated by the firm. An **independent retailer** is a firm that operates only one retail outlet. Approximately three-fourths of retailers are independent. One-store operators, like all small businesses, generally provide personal service and a convenient location.

A **chain retailer** is a company that operates more than one retail outlet. By adding outlets, chain retailers attempt to reach new geographic markets. As sales increase, chains usually buy merchandise in larger quantities and thus take advantage of quantity discounts. They also wield more power in their dealings with suppliers. About one-fourth of retail organizations operate chains.

Another way to classify in-store retailers is by store size and the kind and number of products carried. Let's take a closer look at store types based on these dimensions.

Department Stores These large retail establishments consist of several sections, or departments, that sell a wide assortment of products. According to the U.S. Bureau of the Census, a **department store** is a retail store that (1) employs 25 or more persons and (2) sells at least home furnishings, appliances, family apparel, and household linens and dry goods, each in a different part of the store. Marshall Field's in Chicago (and several other cities), Harrods in London, and Au Printemps in Paris are examples of large department stores. Sears, Roebuck and JCPenney are also department stores. Traditionally, department stores have been service oriented. Along with the goods they sell, these retailers provide credit, delivery, personal assistance, liberal return policies, and pleasant shopping atmospheres.

Discount Stores A **discount store** is a self-service general-merchandise outlet that sells products at lower-than-usual prices. These stores can offer lower prices by operating on smaller markups, by locating large retail showrooms in low-rent areas,

Table 14.1 Top Ten Largest U.S. Retailers

Rank	Company	Revenues (000)	Earnings (000)	No. of Stores
1	Walmart	$405,607,000	$13,400,000	7,873
2	CVS Caremark	$ 87,471,900	$ 3,212,100	6,981
3	Kroger	$ 76,000,000	$ 1,249,000	3,654
4	Costco	$ 72,483,020	$ 1,282,725	544
5	Home Depot	$ 71,288,000	$ 2,260,000	2,274
6	Target	$ 64,948,000	$ 2,214,000	1,682
7	Walgreens	$ 59,034,000	$ 2,157,000	6,934
8	Lowe's	$ 48,230,000	$ 2,157,000	1,649
9	Sears Holdings	$ 46,770,000	$ 53,000	3,918
10	Best Buy	$ 45,015,000	$ 1,003,000	3,942

Source: "Top 100 Retailers," *Stores*, July 2009, http://www.stores.org/2009/Top-100-Retailers. Reprinted with permission from Wrights Reprints.

independent retailer a firm that operates only one retail outlet

chain retailer a company that operates more than one retail outlet

department store a retail store that (1) employs 25 or more persons and (2) sells at least home furnishings, appliances, family apparel, and household linens and dry goods, each in a different part of the store

discount store a self-service general-merchandise outlet that sells products at lower-than-usual prices and by offering minimal customer services. To keep prices low, discount stores operate on the basic principle of high turnover of such items as appliances, toys, clothing, automotive products, and sports equipment. To attract customers, many discount stores also offer some food and household items at low prices. Popular discount stores include Kmart, Walmart, Dollar General, and Target.

As competition among discount stores has increased, some discounters have improved their services, store environments, and locations. As a consequence, many of the better-known discount stores have assumed the characteristics of department stores. This upgrading has boosted their prices and blurred the distinction between some discount stores and department stores.

Catalog and Warehouse Showrooms A **catalog showroom** is a retail outlet that displays well-known brands and sells them at discount prices through catalogs within the store. Colorful catalogs are available in the showroom (and sometimes by mail). The customer selects the merchandise, either from the catalog or from the showroom display. The customer fills out an order form provided by the store and hands the form to a clerk. The clerk retrieves the merchandise from a warehouse room that is adjacent to the selling area. Service Merchandise is a catalog showroom.

A **warehouse showroom** is a retail facility with five basic characteristics: (1) a large, low-cost building; (2) warehouse materials-handling technology; (3) vertical merchandise displays; (4) a large on-premises inventory; and (5) minimal service. Some of the best-known showrooms are operated by big furniture retailers. These operations employ few personnel and offer few services. Most customers carry away purchases in the manufacturer's carton, although some warehouse showrooms will deliver for a fee.

Convenience Stores A **convenience store** is a small food store that sells a limited variety of products but remains open well beyond normal business hours. Almost 70 percent of convenience store customers live within a mile of the store. White Hen Pantry, 7-Eleven, Circle K, and Open Pantry stores, for example, are found in some areas, as are independent convenience stores. There are over 117,000 convenience stores in the United States.[4] Their limited product mixes and higher prices keep convenience stores from becoming a major threat to other grocery retailers.

Supermarkets A **supermarket** is a large self-service store that sells primarily food and household products. It stocks canned, fresh, frozen, and processed foods; paper products; and cleaning supplies. Supermarkets also may sell such items as housewares, toiletries, toys and games, drugs, stationery, books and magazines, plants and flowers, and a few clothing items.

Supermarkets are large-scale operations that emphasize low prices and one-stop shopping for household needs. A supermarket has annual sales of at least $2 million. Current top-ranking supermarkets include Kroger, Albertson's, Safeway, Winn-Dixie, and A&P. Many of these supermarket chains are finding it difficult to compete with superstores such as Walmart Supercenters and are experiencing minuscule profit margins. Walmart, for example, expects to generate in its "supermarket-type" stores more revenue than the top three U.S. supermarket chains—Kroger, Albertson's, and Safeway—combined.

Superstores A **superstore** is a large retail store that carries not only food and nonfood products ordinarily found in supermarkets but also additional product lines—housewares, hardware, small appliances, clothing, personal-care products, garden products, and automotive merchandise. Superstores also provide a number of services to entice customers. Typically, these include automotive repair, snack bars and restaurants, film developing, and banking.

catalog showroom a retail outlet that displays well-known brands and sells them at discount prices through catalogs within the store

warehouse showroom a retail facility in a large, low-cost building with a large on-premises inventory and minimal service

convenience store a small food store that sells a limited variety of products but remains open well beyond normal business hours

supermarket a large self-service store that sells primarily food and household products

superstore a large retail store that carries not only food and nonfood products ordinarily found in supermarkets but also additional product lines

advertising in the promotion mix. We discuss different types of advertising, the process of developing an advertising campaign, and social and legal concerns in advertising.

Next, we consider several categories of personal selling, noting the importance of effective sales management. We also look at sales promotion—why firms use it and which sales promotion techniques are most effective. Then we explain how public relations can be used to promote an organization and its products. Also, we illustrate how these four promotional methods are combined in an effective promotion mix. Finally, we discuss the criticisms of promotion.

What Is Integrated Marketing Communications?

1 Describe integrated marketing communications.

Integrated marketing communications is the coordination of promotion efforts to ensure their maximal informational and persuasive impact on customers. A major goal of integrated marketing communications is to send a consistent message to customers. Integrated marketing communications provides an organization with a way to coordinate and manage its promotional efforts to ensure that customers do receive consistent messages. This approach fosters not only long-term customer relationships but also the efficient use of promotional resources.

The concept of integrated marketing communications has been increasingly accepted for several reasons. Mass-media advertising, a very popular promotional method in the past, is used less today because of its high costs and less-predictable audience sizes. Marketers now can take advantage of more precisely targeted promotional tools, such as cable TV, direct mail, DVDs, the Internet, special-interest magazines, and podcasts. Database marketing is also allowing marketers to be more precise in targeting individual customers. Until recently, suppliers of marketing communications were specialists. Advertising agencies provided advertising campaigns, sales promotion companies provided sales promotion activities and materials, and public-relations organizations engaged in public-relations efforts. Today, a number of promotion-related companies provide one-stop shopping to the client seeking advertising, sales promotion, and public relations, thus reducing coordination problems for the sponsoring company. Because the overall costs of marketing communications are significant, management demands systematic evaluations of communications efforts to ensure that promotional resources are being used efficiently. Although the fundamental role of promotion is not changing, the specific communication vehicles employed and the precision with which they are used are changing.

The Role of Promotion

2 Understand the role of promotion.

Promotion is commonly the object of two misconceptions. Often, people take note of highly visible promotional activities, such as advertising and personal selling, and conclude that these make up the entire field of marketing. People also sometimes consider promotional activities to be unnecessary, expensive, and the cause of higher prices. Neither view is accurate.

The role of promotion is to facilitate exchanges directly or indirectly by informing individuals, groups, or organizations and influencing them to accept a firm's products or to have more positive feelings about the firm. To expedite changes directly, marketers convey information about a firm's goods, services, and ideas to particular market segments. To bring about exchanges indirectly, marketers address interest groups (such as environmental and consumer groups), regulatory agencies, investors, and the general public concerning a company and its products. The broader role of promotion, therefore, is to maintain positive relationships between a company and various groups in the marketing environment.

Marketers frequently design promotional communications, such as advertisements, for specific groups, although some may be directed at wider audiences. Several different messages may be communicated simultaneously to different market segments. For example, ExxonMobil Corporation may address customers about a

integrated marketing communications coordination of promotion efforts to ensure their maximal informational and persuasive impact on customers

Career SUCCESS

Help Wanted: Marketing Communications

Thanks to global competition and shifts in technology and media, more jobs are opening up in marketing communications. Although the recent recession thinned the ranks at many advertising agencies, jobs are available in promotions, public relations, sales, and other areas. According to the *Occupational Outlook Handbook*, marketing-communications employment will increase by 13 percent through 2018. How can you prepare for a career in this exciting field?

Whether you're aiming for a creative job such as copywriting, a high-contact position in personal selling, or a behind-the-scenes role in direct mail, you'll need excellent interpersonal skills to exchange ideas with colleagues and connect with customers. More than ever before, marketing- communications jobs demand critical thinking as well as technical skills. You'll also have to keep up with digital developments. Even if you're not going to be a Web master, you should know a little something about the latest tools and media used in marketing communications.

© iStockphoto.com/Inga Ivanova

If you aspire to become a chief marketing officer, you'll need to polish your conceptual skills. Start now by studying customer needs, tracking environmental trends, and analyzing innovative communications to see what makes them effective. No matter what area of marketing communications you want to work in, the key to getting ahead is "having a positive attitude and being able and willing to put in the effort," says Bridget Soden of the Creative Vortex marketing agency.

Sources: Christopher S. Rugaber, "Millions of Jobs that Were Cut Won't Likely Return," *Associated Press*, May 13, 2010, http://www.usatoday.com/money/economy/2010-05-13-jobs-gone_N.htm; Don Stefanovich, "Industry Artists Stress Networking, Share Career Experiences During Comm Week," *Daily Titan* (California State University-Fullerton), April 28, 2010, http://www.dailytitan.com; Carlos Cata and Scott Davis, "Traditional CMO Roles Won't Position Your Company or Your Career for Growth," *Advertising Age*, May 10, 2010, http://www.adage.com; "Advertising, Marketing, Promotions, Public Relations, and Sales Managers," *Occupational Outlook Handbook 2010–2011 Edition*, U.S. Department of Labor Bureau of Labor Statistics, December 17, 2009, http://www.bls.gov/oco/ocos020.htm#outlook.

new motor oil, inform investors about the firm's financial performance, and update the general public on the firm's environmental efforts.

Marketers must plan, implement, and coordinate promotional communications carefully to make the best use of them. The effectiveness of promotional activities depends greatly on the quality and quantity of information available to marketers about the organization's marketing environment (see Figure 15.1). If a marketer wants to influence customers to buy a certain product, for example, the firm must know who these customers are and how they make purchase decisions for that type of product. Marketers must gather and use information about particular audiences to communicate successfully with them. At times, two or more firms partner in joint promotional efforts.

The Promotion Mix: An Overview

Marketers can use several promotional methods to communicate with individuals, groups, and organizations. The methods that are combined to promote a particular product make up the promotion mix for that item.

Advertising, personal selling, sales promotion, and public relations are the four major elements in an organization's promotion mix (see Figure 15.2) While it is possible that only one ingredient may be used, it is likely that two, three, or four of these ingredients will be used together in a promotion mix, depending on the type of product and target market involved.

advertising a paid nonpersonal message communicated to a select audience through a mass medium

personal selling personal communication aimed at informing customers and persuading them to buy a firm's products

Advertising is a paid nonpersonal message communicated to a select audience through a mass medium. Advertising is flexible enough that it can reach a very large target group or a small, carefully chosen one. **Personal selling** is personal communication aimed at informing customers and persuading them to buy a firm's products. It is more expensive to reach a consumer through personal selling than

Figure 15.1 Information Flows Into and Out of an Organization

A promotional activity's effectiveness depends on the information available to marketers.

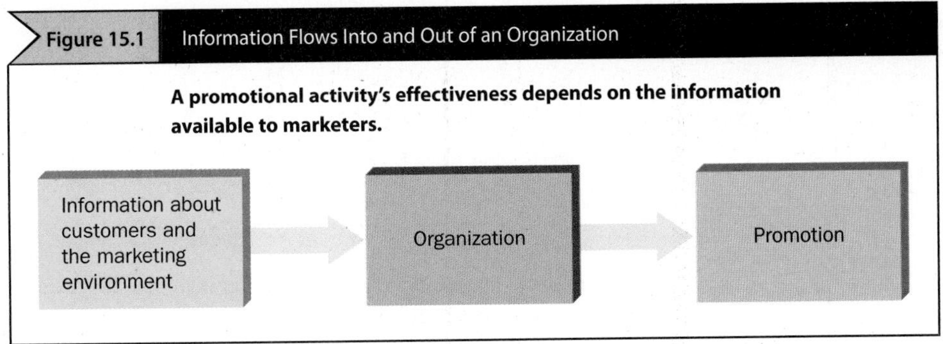

Source: William M. Pride and O. C. Ferrell, *Marketing: Concepts and Strategies*, 16th ed. (Mason, OH: South-Western/Cengage Learning, 2012). Adapted with permission.

Figure 15.2 Possible Ingredients of a Promotion Mix

Depending on the type of product and target market involved, one or more of these ingredients are used in a promotion mix.

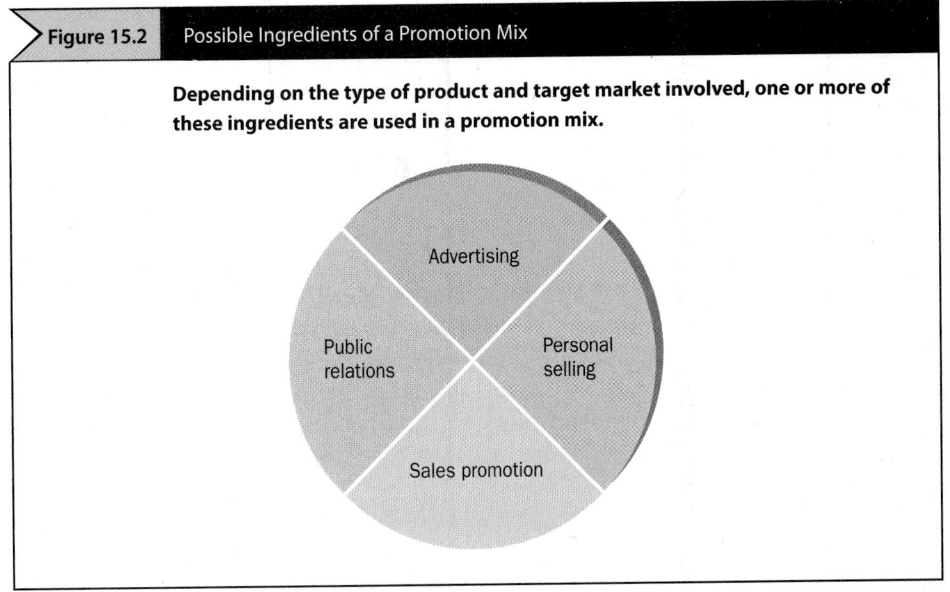

Source: William M. Pride and O. C. Ferrell, *Marketing: Concepts and Strategies*, 16th ed. (Mason, OH: South-Western/Cengage Learning, 2012). Adapted with permission.

through advertising, but this method provides immediate feedback and often is more persuasive than advertising. **Sales promotion** is the use of activities or materials as direct inducements to customers or salespersons. It adds extra value to the product or increases the customer's incentive to buy the product. **Public relations** is a broad set of communication activities used to create and maintain favorable relationships between an organization and various public groups, both internal and external. There are a variety of public relations activities that can be very effective.

sales promotion the use of activities or materials as direct inducements to customers or salespersons

3

Explain the purposes of the three types of advertising.

Advertising

Last year, organizations spent over $300 billion on advertising in the United States.[2] Figure 15.3 shows the proportion of total advertising dollars spent on selected media.

Types of Advertising by Purpose

Depending on its purpose and message, advertising may be classified into one of three groups: primary demand, selective demand, or institutional.

public relations communication activities used to create and maintain favorable relations between an organization and various public groups, both internal and external

primary-demand advertising advertising aimed at increasing the demand for all brands of a product within a specific industry

Primary-Demand Advertising **Primary-demand advertising** is advertising aimed at increasing the demand for *all* brands of a product within a specific industry. Trade and industry associations, such as the California Milk Processor Board ("Got Milk?"), are the major users of primary-demand advertising. Their advertisements

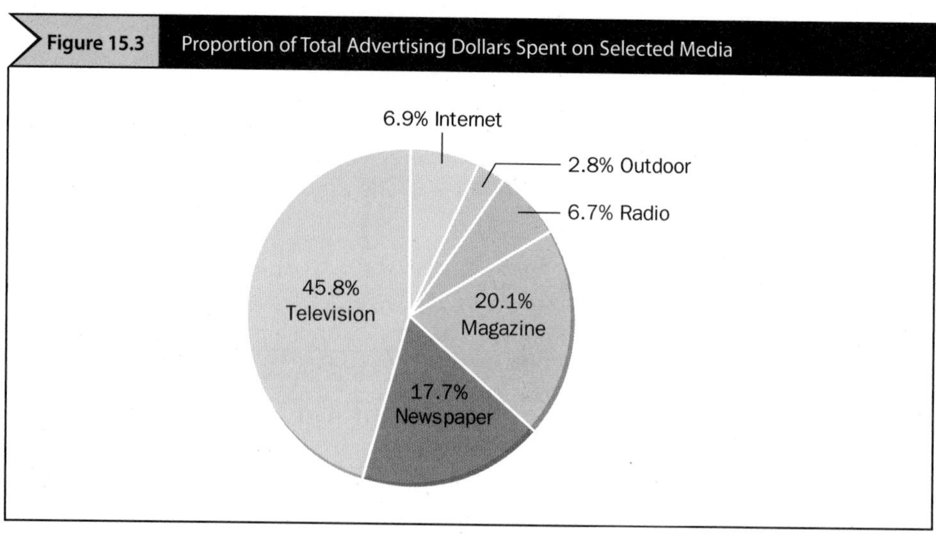

Source: "Spending Fell Only 2.7% in '08, the Real Issue '09," *Advertising Age*, June 22, 2009, 12–13.

selective-demand (or brand) advertising advertising that is used to sell a particular brand of product

institutional advertising advertising designed to enhance a firm's image or reputation

promote broad product categories, such as beef, milk, pork, potatoes, and prunes, without mentioning specific brands.

Selective-demand advertising. This advertisement promotes a specific brand, indicating that the maker of Jamba Juice is attempting to stimulate selective demand.

Selective-Demand Advertising **Selective-demand (or brand) advertising** is advertising that is used to sell a particular brand of product. It is by far the most common type of advertising, and it accounts for the lion's share of advertising expenditures. Producers use brand-oriented advertising to convince us to buy everything from Orbit gum to Buicks.

Selective advertising that aims at persuading consumers to make purchases within a short time is called *immediate-response advertising*. Most local advertising is of this type. Often local advertisers promote products with immediate appeal. Selective advertising aimed at keeping a firm's name or product before the public is called *reminder advertising*.

Comparative advertising, which has become more popular over the last three decades, compares specific characteristics of two or more identified brands. Of course, the comparison shows the advertiser's brand to be as good as or better than the other identified competing brands. Comparisons often are based on the outcome of surveys or research studies. Although competing firms act as effective watchdogs against each other's advertising claims, consumers themselves sometimes become rather guarded concerning claims based on "scientific studies" and various statistical manipulations. Comparative advertising is unacceptable or illegal in a number of countries.

Institutional Advertising **Institutional advertising** is advertising designed to enhance a firm's image or reputation. Many public utilities and larger firms, such as AT&T and the major oil companies, use part of their advertising dollars to build goodwill rather than to stimulate sales directly. A positive public image helps an organization to attract not only customers but also employees and investors.

Advertising Media

4

Describe the advantages and disadvantages of the major advertising media.

The **advertising media** are the various forms of communication through which advertising reaches its audience. The major media are newspapers, magazines, direct mail, Yellow Pages, out-of-home displays, television, radio, the Internet, and social media. Figure 15.3 shows the proportion of ad dollars spent on selected media.

Newspapers Approximately 85 percent of newspaper advertising is purchased by local retailers. Retailers use newspaper advertising extensively because it is relatively inexpensive compared with other media. Moreover, since most newspapers provide local coverage, advertising dollars are not wasted in reaching people outside the organization's market area. It is also timely. Ads usually can be placed just a few days before they are to appear.

There are some drawbacks, however, to newspaper advertising. It has a short life span; newspapers generally are read through once and then discarded. Color reproduction in newspapers is usually not high quality; thus, most ads are run in black and white. Finally, marketers cannot target specific demographic groups through newspaper ads because newspapers are read by such a broad spectrum of people.

Magazines The amount of money companies spend on magazine advertising has been flat over the last few years. However, advertisers can reach very specific market segments through ads in special-interest magazines. A boat manufacturer has a ready-made consumer audience in subscribers to *Yachting* or *Sail.* Producers of photographic equipment advertise in *Travel & Leisure* or *Popular Photography.* A number of magazines such as *Time* and *Cosmopolitan* publish regional editions, which provide advertisers with geographic flexibility as well.

Magazine advertising is more prestigious than newspaper advertising, and it allows for high-quality color reproduction. In addition, magazine advertisements have a longer life span than those in other media. Issues of *National Geographic,* for example, may be kept for months or years, and the ads they contain may be viewed repeatedly.

The major disadvantages of magazine advertising are high cost and lack of timeliness. Because magazine ads normally must be prepared two to three months in advance, they cannot be adjusted to reflect the latest market conditions. Magazine ads—especially full-color ads—are also expensive. Although the cost of reaching a thousand people may compare favorably with that of other media, the cost of a full-page four-color ad can be very high—$287,440 in *Time.*[3]

Direct Mail **Direct-mail advertising** is promotional material mailed directly to individuals. Direct mail is the most selective medium; mailing lists are available (or can be compiled) to reach almost any target audience, from airplane enthusiasts to zoologists. The effectiveness of direct-mail advertising can be measured because the advertiser has a record of who received the advertisements and can track who responds to the ads.

Some organizations are using direct e-mail. To avoid customers receiving unwanted e-mail, a firm should ask customers to complete a request form in order to receive promotional e-mail from the company.

The success of direct-mail advertising depends to some extent on maintaining appropriate and current mailing lists. A direct-mail campaign may fail if the mailing list is outdated and the mailing does not reach the right people. In addition, this medium is relatively costly.

Yellow Pages Advertising **Yellow Pages advertising** appears in over 6,000 editions of telephone directories that are distributed to millions of customers annually. Approximately 85 percent of Yellow Pages advertising is used by local advertisers as opposed to national advertisers.

advertising media the various forms of communication through which advertising reaches its audience

direct-mail advertising promotional material mailed directly to individuals

Yellow Pages advertising simple listings or display advertisements presented under specific product categories appearing in print and online telephone directories

Sustaining the Planet

Go Postal for Greener Direct-Mail Advertising

Companies that use direct-mail advertising to connect with their customers will find lots of good tips for greener campaigns at the U.S. Postal Service Web site. Take a look: http://www.usps.com/green/ideas.htm.

Customers use Yellow Pages advertising to save time in finding products, to find information quickly, and to learn about products and marketers. It is estimated that approximately 60 percent of adults read Yellow Pages advertising at least once a week. Unlike other types of advertising media, Yellow Pages advertisements are purchased for one year and cannot be changed. Advertisers often pay for their Yellow Pages advertisements through monthly charges on their telephone statements.

Out-of-Home Advertising **Out-of-home advertising** consists of short promotional messages on billboards, posters, signs, and transportation vehicles.

Sign and billboard advertising allows the marketer to focus on a particular geographic area; it is also fairly inexpensive. However, because most outdoor promotion is directed toward a mobile audience, the message must be limited to a few words. The medium is especially suitable for products that lend themselves to pictorial display.

Television Television ranks number one in total advertising expenditures. Approximately 99 percent of American homes have at least one television set that is watched an average of 7 hours and 40 minutes each day. The average U.S. household can receive 28 TV channels, including cable and pay stations, and about 80 percent of households receive basic cable/satellite television. Television obviously provides advertisers with considerable access to consumers.

out-of-home advertising short promotional messages on billboards, posters, signs, and transportation vehicles

Television advertising is the primary medium for larger firms whose objective is to reach national or regional markets. A national advertiser may buy *network time,* which means that its message usually will be broadcast by hundreds of local stations affiliated with the network. However, the opportunity to reach extremely large television audiences has been reduced by the increased availability and popularity of cable channels and home videos. Both national and local firms may buy *local time* on a single station that covers a particular geographic area.

Out-of-home advertising. Promotion messages on buses are examples of out-of-home advertising.

Advertisers may *sponsor* an entire show, participate with other sponsors of a show, or buy *spot time* for a single 10-, 20-, 30-, or 60-second commercial during or between programs. To an extent, they may select their audience by choosing the day of the week and the approximate time of day their ads will be shown. Anheuser-Busch advertises Budweiser Beer during TV football games because the majority of viewers are men, who are likely to buy beer.

Marketers also can employ *product placement,* which is paying a fee to have a product appear in a television program or movie. The product might appear on a table or counter, or one or more of the actors might be using it. Through channel switching and personal video recorders such as TiVo, television viewers can avoid watching regular television commercials. By placing the product directly into the program, viewers are likely to be exposed to the product. Product placement continues to be a stable advertising method for many marketers, especially in popular season premiere episodes. For example, when the hit Fox show *24* premiered its fourth season, the four-hour long episode integrated products from Apple, Pontiac, Ford, Chevy, and Sprint within its storyline. Such product placement increases viewers' interest in the product, causing some to visit the company's Web site for more information, and others to go one step further and buy the products.[4] Recently, researchers reported that 95 percent of viewers who own a DVR still watch TV live and that, when they watch recorded TV, they skip commercials only 6.5 percent of the time.

SPOTLIGHT

Attitudes Toward Super Bowl Commercials

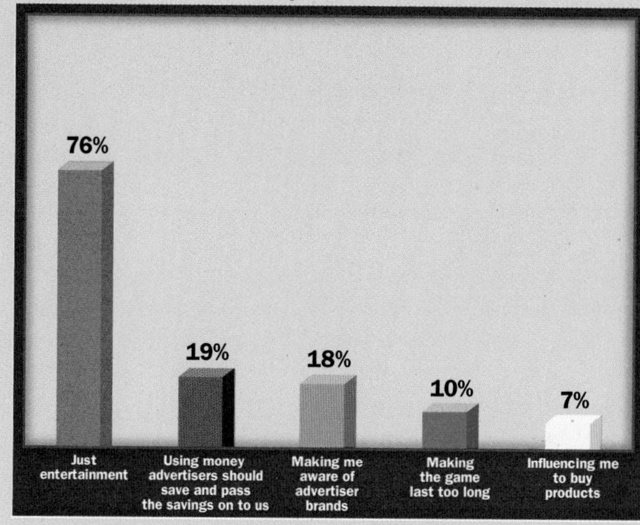

Source: National Retail Federation survey of 9,578 adults 18 and older.

Another option available to television advertisers is the infomercial. An **infomercial** is a program-length televised commercial message resembling an entertainment or consumer affairs program. Infomercials for products such as exercise equipment tell customers why they need the product, what benefits it provides, in what ways it outperforms its competitors, and how much it costs. Although initially aired primarily over cable television, today infomercials are becoming more common on network and local TV as well. Currently, infomercials are responsible for marketing over $1 billion worth of products annually. Even some *Fortune* 500 companies are using them.

Television advertising rates are based on the number of people expected to be watching when the commercial is aired. In 2010, the cost of a 30-second Super Bowl commercial was just over $3 million. Advertisers typically spend over $500,000 for a 30-second television commercial during a top-rated prime-time program.[5]

Radio Like magazine advertising, radio advertising offers selectivity. Radio stations develop programming for—and are tuned in by—specific groups of listeners. There are almost half a billion radios in the United States (about six per household), which makes radio the most accessible medium.

Radio advertising can be less expensive than in other media. Actual rates depend on geographic coverage, the number of commercials contracted for, the time period specified, and whether the station broadcasts on AM, FM, or both. Even small retailers are able to afford radio advertising, and a radio advertiser can schedule and change ads on short notice. The disadvantages of using radio are the absence of visual images and (because there are so many stations) the small audience size.

Internet Spending on Internet advertising has increased significantly. Internet advertising can take a variety of forms. The *banner ad* is a rectangular graphic that appears at the top of a Web site. Many Web sites are able to offer free services because they are supported by banner advertisements. Advertisers can use animation and interactive capabilities to draw more attention to their ads. Yahoo! even invites its users to participate in surveys evaluating the banner ads on its home page. Another type of advertising is *sponsorship* (or *cobranded* ads). These ads

infomercial a program-length televised commercial message resembling an entertainment or consumer affairs program

Ethical Challenges &

SUCCESSFUL SOLUTIONS

How Many Times Can a Company Violate a Customer's Trust? Only Once!

The line between digital content and digital advertising is blurring as marketers strive to engage their audiences on media Web sites and in social media. Online audiences can't always tell when a message is non-commercial digital content—such as a magazine or newspaper feature, a personal blog post, an ordinary tweet, or a consumer-generated video—and when it's actually an advertising message. For example, the *Los Angeles Times* embeds links to product pages and retail sites within some non-news articles posted online. The newspaper explains that these e-commerce links, which are visually distinct from the content, "serve as both a reader service and a revenue opportunity for the company."

However, experts are concerned that audiences may get the wrong impression when they click. Media sites "need consumers to trust them," says journalism professor Cecelia Friend, "and misleading them with content that looks like information but turns out to be advertising undermines that trust."

Now industry groups such as the American Society of Magazine Editors have created ethical codes calling for digital advertising to be clearly labeled as such. The Federal Trade Commission has also issued guidelines requiring bloggers, Twitter users, and Web sites to alert the audience when a message is promotional. Because disclosure is difficult in 140-character Twitter messages, the Word of Mouth Marketing Association recommends that marketing tweets include the tag #spon or #paid.

Sources: Susan Currie Sivek, "The Ethics of Digital Magazine Advertising," *Media Shift: Public Broadcasting Service*, April 28, 2010, http://www.pbs.org; Stephanie Clifford, "*Los Angeles Times* Adds Paid Links in Articles," *New York Times*, April 27, 2010, http://www.nytimes.com; Mark Milian, "What's A #spon Tweet? It's a Twitter Ad, Silly," *Los Angeles Times Technology*, February 18, 2010, http://latimesblogs.latimes.com; Kayleen Schaefer, "New F.T.C. Rules Have Bloggers and Twitterers Mulling," *New York Times*, October 14, 2009, http://www.nytimes.com.

integrate a company's brand with editorial content. The goal of this type of ad is to get users to strongly identify the advertiser with the site's mission. For example, many food brands such as Kraft advertise on http://Allrecipes.com. This site allows users to share and browse thousands of recipes. Kraft offers its own recipes on the site, and they all include its products. There are also banner ads for Kraft on other recipes, reminding the user of Kraft cheese while they read a recipe for cheese dip. Many Internet advertisers choose to purchase keywords on popular search engines such as Google, Yahoo!, and MSN. For example, Kellogg purchased the word *cereal* on Google so that every time someone conducts a search using that word, a link to Kellogg's Web site appears. *Interstitial* ads pop up to display a product. For example, users of http://www.Hulu.com can watch any of the available TV episodes and movies free of charge by viewing commercials periodically throughout each video.

Social Media In the last few years, the use of social media as an advertising medium has increased dramatically. This is largely due to the perception that marketers can target, interact, and connect more personally with their customers through the different social-media outlets as opposed to more traditional media. Many companies offer customers the ability to follow them on Twitter, become their fan on Facebook, or connect with them on LinkedIn in order to receive information on the company. Many businesses post ads throughout the social-networking sites. Some companies also host their own branded sites that incorporate aspects and features of other social-media outlets but focus solely on their brands and products.

Despite the emphasis placed on advertising through social media, there are drawbacks that companies need to be aware of. The same characteristics that allow companies to target their audience through these sites also restrict the number of contacts that can be made per message. While a single television ad can reach millions of viewers at once, an interactive ad can only reach the person sitting at the computer. In addition, because social media is a relatively new form of advertising, marketers are still unsure as to the best way to use the medium or how to measure the return on investment. Social media also requires a large time commitment. Since everything happens in real time, companies need to have dedicated social-media representatives who monitor activity, respond accordingly as things occur, and continually check for the next big trend in social media.

Major Steps in Developing an Advertising Campaign

5 Identify the major steps in developing an advertising campaign.

An advertising campaign is developed in several stages. These stages may vary in number and the order in which they are implemented depending on the company's resources, products, and audiences. The development of a campaign in any organization, however, will include the following steps in some form:

1. Identify and Analyze the Target Audience The target audience is the group of people toward which a firm's advertisements are directed. To pinpoint the organization's target audience and develop an effective campaign, marketers must analyze such information as the geographic distribution of potential customers; their age, sex, race, income, and education; and their attitudes toward both the advertiser's product and competing products. How marketers use this information will be influenced by the features of the product to be advertised and the nature of the competition. Precise identification of the target audience is crucial to the proper development of subsequent stages and, ultimately, to the success of the campaign itself. NutriSystem Silver, for example, is a weight loss program just for men over the age of 60, and it is targeted through advertisements that use older sports celebrities, such as ex-NFL coach Don Shula, who have had success using the program.[6]

2. Define the Advertising Objectives The goals of an advertising campaign should be stated precisely and in measurable terms. The objectives should include the firm's current position, indicate how far and in what direction from that original reference point the company wishes to move, and specify a definite period of time for the achievement of the goals. Advertising objectives that focus on sales will stress increasing sales by a certain percentage or dollar amount or expanding the firm's market share. Communication objectives will emphasize increasing product or brand awareness, improving consumer attitudes, or conveying product information.

Target audience. Is this ad aimed at everyone? It's unlikely. Most ads are aimed at a specific target audience and not at everyone.

3. Create the Advertising Platform An advertising platform includes the important selling points or features that an advertiser wishes to incorporate into the advertising campaign. These features should be important to customers in their selection and use of a product, and, if possible, they should be features that competing products lack. Although research into what consumers view as important issues is expensive, it is the most productive way to determine which issues to include in an advertising platform. A recent advertising campaign by Miller Lite, for example, pokes fun at other light beers, reminding its male target audience that they shouldn't have to sacrifice great taste when they get a light beer.[7]

4. Determine the Advertising Appropriation The advertising appropriation is the total amount of money designated for advertising in a given period.

This stage is critical to the campaign's success because advertising efforts based on an inadequate budget will understimulate customer demand, and a budget too large will waste a company's resources. Advertising appropriations may be based on last year's (or next year's forecasted) sales, on what competitors spend on advertising, or on executive judgment. Table 15.1 shows the nation's top 20 advertising spenders. Procter & Gamble is traditionally one of the top spenders.

5. Develop the Media Plan A media plan specifies exactly which media will be used in the campaign and when advertisements will appear. Although cost-effectiveness is not easy to measure, the primary concern of the media planner is to reach the largest number of persons in the target audience for each dollar spent. In addition to cost, media planners must consider the location and demographics of people in the advertising target, the content of the message, and the characteristics of the audiences reached by various media. The media planner begins with general media decisions, selects subclasses within each medium, and finally chooses particular media vehicles for the campaign.

6. Create the Advertising Message The content and form of a message are influenced by the product's features, the characteristics of people in the target audience, the objectives of the campaign, and the choice of media. An advertiser must consider these factors when choosing words and illustrations that will be meaningful and appealing to persons in the advertising target. The copy, or words, of an advertisement will vary depending on the media choice but should attempt to move the audience through attention, interest,

Table 15.1 Who Spends the Most on Advertising?

Rank	Company	Advertising Expenditures (in millions)	Sales (in millions)	Advertising Expenditure as a Percentage of Sales
1	Procter & Gamble Co.	$ 4,828	$ 33,005	14.7
2	Verizon Communications	3,700	93,775	3.9
3	AT&T	3,073	124,028	2.5
4	General Motors Corp.	2,901	75,382	3.8
5	Johnson & Johnson	2,529	32,309	7.8
6	Unilever	2,423	19,420	12.5
7	Walt Disney Co.	2,218	28,506	7.8
8	Time Warner	2,208	38,808	5.7
9	General Electric Co.	2,019	85,300	2.4
10	Sears Holdings Corp.	1,865	41,534	4.5
11	Ford Motor Co.	1,856	60,376	3.1
12	GlaxoSmithKline	1,827	18,081	10.1
13	Toyota Motor Co.	1,690	60,977	2.8
14	L'Oréal	1,673	6,132	27.3
15	Walmart Stores	1,660	302,599	0.5
16	Bank of America Corp.	1,650	67,549	2.4
17	Anheuser-Busch InBev	1,587	23,568	6.7
18	Sprint Nextel Corp.	1,500	35,635	4.2
19	Sony Corp.	1,465	18,651	7.9
20	JPMorgan Chase & Co.	1,357	49,854	2.7

Source: Reprinted with permission from the June 22, 2009, issue of *Advertising Age*. Copyright Craine Communications Inc., 2009.

desire, and action. Artwork and visuals should complement copy by attracting the audience's attention and communicating an idea quickly. Creating a cohesive advertising message is especially difficult for a company such as eBay that offers such a broad mix of products. eBay developed a "whatever it is" campaign that features a variety of consumers of every age using a variety of products (a car, a television, a dress, and a laptop) all shaped like the letters "it." The tagline, "Whatever *it* is, you can get it on eBay," emphasizes the massive range of products available from the site and effectively showcases the service that the company provides its cutomers.

7. Execute the Campaign Execution of an advertising campaign requires extensive planning, scheduling, and coordinating because many tasks must be completed on time. Many people and firms, such as production companies, research organizations, media firms, printers, photoengravers, and commercial artists, may contribute to a campaign. Advertising managers constantly must assess the quality of the work and take corrective action when necessary. Situations may also arise that require a change in plans. Florida's tourism marketing committee, Visit Florida, for example, pulled the plug on its "Coast is Clear" ad campaign after the BP oil leak progressed further than state officials anticipated. The ads, which were meant to assure tourists that the Florida coast wouldn't be affected by an oil leak, had to be pulled as the oil leak went on longer than expected.[8]

8. Evaluate Advertising Effectiveness A campaign's success should be measured in terms of its original objectives before, during, and/or after the campaign. An advertiser should at least be able to estimate whether sales or market share went up because of the campaign or whether any change occurred in customer attitudes or brand awareness. Data from past and current sales and responses to coupon offers and customer surveys administered by research organizations are some of the ways in which advertising effectiveness can be evaluated.

Advertising Agencies

Advertisers can plan and produce their own advertising with help from media personnel, or they can hire advertising agencies. An **advertising agency** is an independent firm that plans, produces, and places advertising for its clients. Many large ad agencies offer help with sales promotion and public relations as well. The media usually pay a commission of 15 percent to advertising agencies. Thus, the cost to the agency's client can be quite moderate. The client may be asked to pay for selected services that the agency performs. Other methods for compensating agencies are also used.

Firms that do a lot of advertising may use both an in-house advertising department and an independent agency. This approach gives the firm the advantage of being able to call on the agency's expertise in particular areas of advertising. An agency also can bring a fresh viewpoint to a firm's products and advertising plans.

Personal Selling

6

Recognize the various kinds of salespersons, the steps in the personal-selling process, and the major sales management tasks.

Personal selling is the most adaptable of all promotional methods because the person who is presenting the message can modify it to suit the individual buyer. However, personal selling is also the most expensive method of promotion.

Most successful salespeople are able to communicate with others on a one-to-one basis and are strongly motivated. They strive to have a thorough knowledge of the products they offer for sale, and they are willing and able to deal with the details involved in handling and processing orders. Sales managers tend to emphasize these qualities when recruiting and hiring.

Many selling situations demand the face-to-face contact and adaptability of personal selling. This is especially true of industrial sales, in which a single purchase

advertising agency an independent firm that plans, produces, and places advertising for its clients

Personal selling. As a major promotion-mix ingredient, personal selling is very flexible and can occur in stores, factories, offices, homes, or on the phone and can be expensive.

may amount to millions of dollars. Obviously, sales of that size must be based on carefully planned sales presentations, personal contact with customers, and thorough negotiations.

Kinds of Salespersons

Because most businesses employ different salespersons to perform different functions, marketing managers must select the kinds of sales personnel that will be most effective in selling the firm's products. Salespersons may be identified as order-getters, order-takers, and support personnel. A single individual can, and often does, perform all three functions.

Order-Getters An **order-getter** is responsible for what is sometimes called **creative selling**—selling a firm's products to new customers and increasing sales to current customers. An order-getter must perceive buyers' needs, supply customers with information about the firm's product, and persuade them to buy the product. Order-getting activities may be separated into two groups. In current-customer sales, salespeople concentrate on obtaining additional sales or leads for prospective sales from customers who have purchased the firm's products at least once. In new-business sales, sales personnel seek out new prospects and convince them to make an initial purchase of the firm's product. The real estate, insurance, appliance, heavy industrial machinery, and automobile industries in particular depend on new-business sales.

Order-Takers An **order-taker** handles repeat sales in ways that maintain positive relationships with customers. An order-taker sees that customers have products when and where they are needed and in the proper amounts. *Inside order-takers* receive incoming mail and telephone orders in some businesses; salespersons in retail stores are also inside order-takers. *Outside* (or *field*) *order-takers* travel to customers. Often, the buyer and the field salesperson develop a mutually beneficial relationship of placing, receiving, and delivering orders. Both inside and outside order-takers are active salespersons and often produce most of their companies' sales.

Support Personnel **Sales support personnel** aid in selling but are more involved in locating *prospects* (likely first-time customers), educating customers, building goodwill for the firm, and providing follow-up service. The most common categories of support personnel are missionary, trade, and technical salespersons.

A **missionary salesperson**, who usually works for a manufacturer, visits retailers to persuade them to buy the manufacturer's products. If the retailers agree, they buy the products from wholesalers, who are the manufacturer's actual customers. Missionary salespersons often are employed by producers of medical supplies and pharmaceuticals to promote these products to retail druggists, physicians, and hospitals.

A **trade salesperson**, who generally works for a food producer or processor, assists customers in promoting products, especially in retail stores. A trade salesperson may obtain additional shelf space for the products, restock shelves, set up displays, and distribute samples. Because trade salespersons usually are order-takers as well, they are not strictly support personnel.

A **technical salesperson** assists a company's current customers in technical matters. He or she may explain how to use a product, how it is made, how to install it, or how a system is designed. A technical salesperson should be formally educated in science or engineering. Computers, steel, and chemicals are some of the products handled by technical salespeople.

order-getter a salesperson who is responsible for selling a firm's products to new customers and increasing sales to present customers

creative selling selling products to new customers and increasing sales to present customers

order-taker a salesperson who handles repeat sales in ways that maintain positive relationships with customers

sales support personnel employees who aid in selling but are more involved in locating prospects, educating customers, building goodwill for the firm, and providing follow-up service

missionary salesperson a salesperson—generally employed by a manufacturer—who visits retailers to persuade them to buy the manufacturer's products

trade salesperson a salesperson—generally employed by a food producer or processor—who assists customers in promoting products, especially in retail stores

technical salesperson a salesperson who assists a company's current customers in technical matters

Marketers usually need sales personnel from several of these categories. Factors that affect hiring and other personnel decisions include the number of customers and their characteristics; the product's attributes, complexity, and price; the distribution channels used by the company; and the company's approach to advertising.

The Personal-Selling Process

No two selling situations are exactly alike, and no two salespeople perform their jobs in exactly the same way. Most salespeople, however, follow the six-step procedure illustrated in Figure 15.4.

Prospecting The first step in personal selling is to research potential buyers and choose the most likely customers, or prospects. Sources of prospects include business associates and customers, public records, telephone and trade-association directories, and company files. The salesperson concentrates on those prospects who have the financial resources, willingness, and authority to buy the product.

Figure 15.4 The Six Steps of the Personal-Selling Process

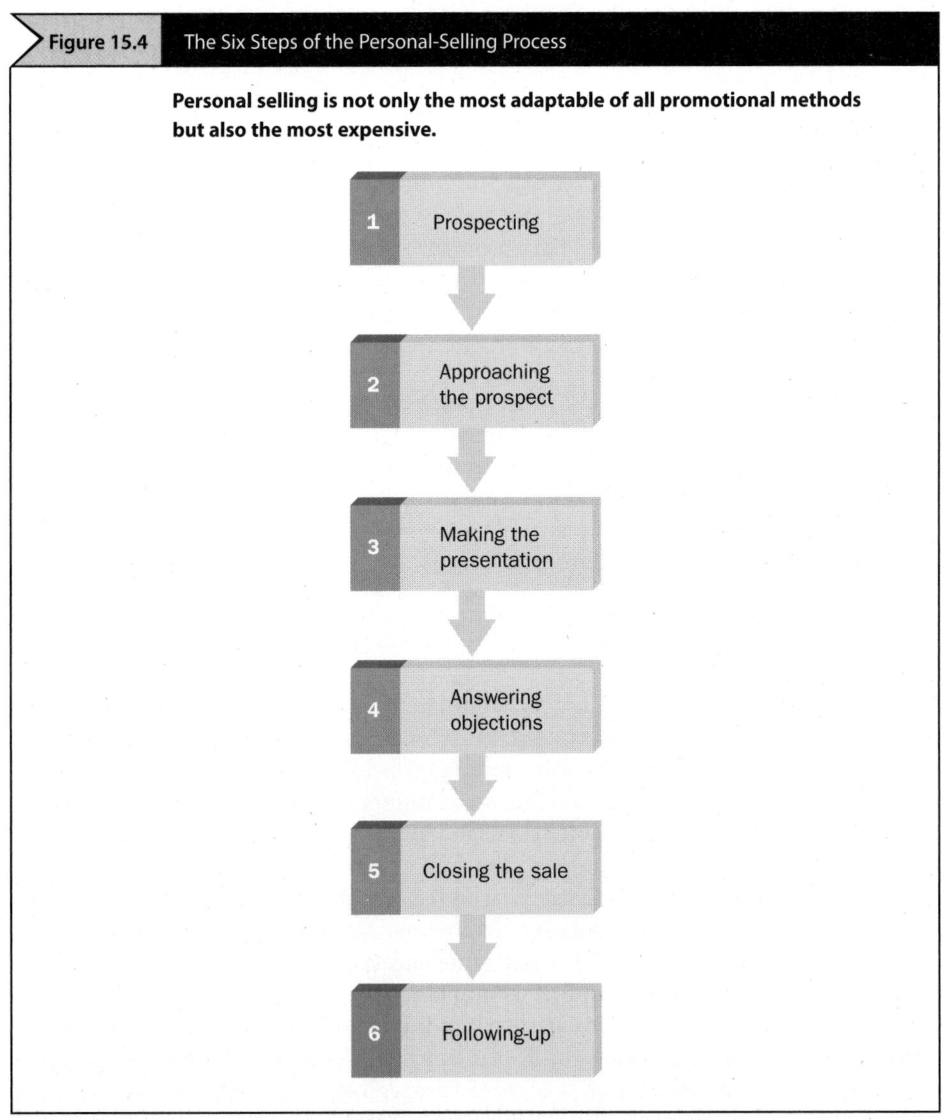

Source: William M. Pride and O. C. Ferrell, *Marketing: Concepts and Strategies,* 16th ed. (Mason, OH: South-Western/Cengage Learning, 2012). Adapted with permission.

Approaching the Prospect First impressions are often lasting impressions. Thus, the salesperson's first contact with the prospect is crucial to successful selling. The best approach is one based on knowledge of the product, of the prospect's needs, and of how the product can meet those needs. Salespeople who understand each customer's particular situation are likely to make a good first impression—and to make a sale.

Making the Presentation The next step is actual delivery of the sales presentation. In many cases, this includes demonstrating the product. The salesperson points out the product's features, its benefits, and how it is superior to competitors' merchandise. If the product has been used successfully by other firms, the salesperson may mention this as part of the presentation.

During a demonstration, the salesperson may suggest that the prospect try out the product personally. The demonstration and product trial should underscore specific points made during the presentation.

Answering Objections The prospect is likely to raise objections or ask questions at any time. This gives the salesperson a chance to eliminate objections that might prevent a sale, to point out additional features, or to mention special services the company offers.

Closing the Sale To close the sale, the salesperson asks the prospect to buy the product. This is considered the critical point in the selling process. Many experienced salespeople make use of a *trial closing,* in which they ask questions based on the assumption that the customer is going to buy the product. The questions "When would you want delivery?" and "Do you want the standard model or the one with the special options package?" are typical of trial closings. They allow the reluctant prospect to make a purchase without having to say, "I'll take it."

Following-Up The salesperson must follow-up after the sale to ensure that the product is delivered on time, in the right quantity, and in proper operating condition. During follow-up, the salesperson also makes it clear that he or she is available in case problems develop. Follow-up leaves a good impression and eases the way toward future sales. Hence, it is essential to the selling process. The salesperson's job does not end with a sale. It continues as long as the seller and the customer maintain a working relationship.

Managing Personal Selling

A firm's success often hinges on the competent management of its sales force. Although some companies operate efficiently without a sales force, most firms rely on a strong sales force—and the sales revenue it brings in—for their success.

Sales managers have responsibilities in a number of areas. They must set sales objectives in concrete, quantifiable terms and specify a certain period of time and a certain geographic area. They must adjust the size of the sales force to meet changes in the firm's marketing plan and the marketing environment. Sales managers must attract and hire effective salespersons. They must also develop a training program and decide where, when, how, and for whom to conduct the training. They must formulate a fair and adequate compensation plan to keep qualified employees. They must motivate salespersons to boost their productivity. They must define sales territories and determine scheduling and routing of the sales force. Finally, sales managers must evaluate the operation as a whole through sales reports, communications with customers, and invoices.

Sales Promotion

7 Describe sales promotion objectives and methods.

Sales promotion consists of activities or materials that are direct inducements to customers or salespersons. Are you a member of an airline frequent-flyer program? Did you recently receive a free sample in the mail or at a supermarket? Have you recently received a rebate from a manufacturer? Do you use coupons? All these are examples of sales promotion efforts. Sales promotion techniques often are used to enhance and supplement other promotional methods. They can have a significant impact on sales.

The dramatic increase in spending for sales promotion shows that marketers have recognized the potential of this promotional method. Many firms now include numerous sales promotion efforts as part of their overall promotion mix.

Sales Promotion Objectives

Sales promotion activities may be used singly or in combination, both offensively and defensively, to achieve one goal or a set of goals. Marketers use sales promotion activities and materials for a number of purposes, including

1. To attract new customers
2. To encourage trial of a new product
3. To invigorate the sales of a mature brand
4. To boost sales to current customers
5. To reinforce advertising
6. To increase traffic in retail stores
7. To steady irregular sales patterns
8. To build up reseller inventories
9. To neutralize competitive promotional efforts
10. To improve shelf space and displays

Any sales promotion objectives should be consistent with the organization's general goals and with its marketing and promotional objectives.

Sales Promotion Methods

Most sales promotion methods can be classified as promotional techniques for either consumer sales or trade sales. A **consumer sales promotion method** attracts consumers to particular retail stores and motivates them to purchase certain new or established products. A **trade sales promotion method** encourages wholesalers and retailers to stock and actively promote a manufacturer's product. Incentives such as money, merchandise, marketing assistance, and gifts are commonly awarded to resellers who buy products or respond positively in other ways. Of the combined dollars spent on sales promotion and advertising last year, about one-half was spent on trade promotions, one-fourth on consumer promotions, and one-fourth on advertising.

A number of factors enter into marketing decisions about which and how many sales promotion methods to use. Of greatest importance are the objectives of the promotional effort. Product characteristics—size, weight, cost, durability, uses, features, and hazards—and target market profiles—age, gender, income, location, density, usage rate, and buying patterns—likewise must be considered. Distribution channels and availability of appropriate resellers also influence the choice of sales promotion methods, as do the competitive and regulatory forces in the environment. Let's now discuss a few important sales promotion methods.

Rebates A **rebate** is a return of part of the product's purchase price. Usually, the refund is offered by the producer to consumers who send in a coupon along with a specific proof of purchase. Rebating is a relatively low-cost promotional method. Once used mainly to help launch new product items, it is now applied

consumer sales promotion method a sales promotion method designed to attract consumers to particular retail stores and to motivate them to purchase certain new or established products

trade sales promotion method a sales promotion method designed to encourage wholesalers and retailers to stock and actively promote a manufacturer's product

rebate a return of part of the product's purchase price

Coupons. Tyson offers coupons to encourage consumers to try their products and to increase the quantity purchased.

to a wide variety of products. Some automakers offer rebates on their vehicles because they have found that many car customers are more likely to purchase a car with a rebate than the same car with a lower price and no rebate. One problem with rebates is that many people perceive the redemption process as too complicated. Only about half of individuals who purchase rebated products actually apply for the rebates.

Coupons A **coupon** reduces the retail price of a particular item by a stated amount at the time of purchase. Coupons may be worth anywhere from a few cents to a few dollars. They are made available to customers through newspapers, magazines, direct mail, online, and shelf dispensers in stores. Some coupons are precisely targeted at customers. Cellfire, for example, is a Web site that provides its users with access to coupons that can be downloaded to their cell phone or added to a specific store's savings card for free. Other companies, such as Target and Old Navy, offer coupons on their Web sites that can be used online, or redeemed at a store by printing the coupon or even downloading it to a cell phone. Approximately 89 percent of coupons are distributed through traditional newspaper inserts, but digital coupons offered through the Internet and mobile phones are becoming increasingly popular.[9]

Although coupon use had been declining steadily for several years, the recent recession caused coupon usage to increase. Last year, businesses issued 367 billion coupons, the highest level in 30 years. Consumers redeemed 3.3 billion coupons, a 27 percent increase over the previous year, making it the first time in 17 years that consumers used more coupons than they did the year before.[10] The largest number of coupons distributed are for household cleaners, condiments, frozen foods, medications and health aids, and paper products. Stores in some areas even deduct double or triple the value of manufacturers' coupons from the purchase price as a sales promotion technique of their own. Coupons also may offer free merchandise, either with or without an additional product purchase.

Samples A **sample** is a free product given to customers to encourage trial and purchase. Marketers use free samples to stimulate trial of a product, increase sales volume in the early stages of a product's life-cycle, and obtain desirable distribution. Samples may be offered via online coupons, direct mail, or in stores. Many customers prefer to receive their samples by mail. It is the most expensive sales promotion technique. Although it is used often to promote new products, it can also be used to promote established brands. For example, cosmetics companies may use samples to attract customers. Coca-Cola often gives out free samples of products such as Vitamin Water at business conventions, concerts, and sporting events. In designing a free sample, organizations must consider such factors as seasonal demand for the product, market characteristics, and prior advertising.

Distribution of free samples through Web sites such as http://StartSampling.com is growing. Consumers choose the free samples they would like to receive and request delivery. The online company manages the packaging and distribution of the samples.

Premiums A **premium** is a gift that a producer offers a customer in return for buying its product. They are used to attract competitors' customers, introduce different sizes of established products, add variety to other promotional efforts, and stimulate consumer loyalty. Creativity is essential when using premiums; to stand out and achieve a significant number of redemptions, the premium must match both

coupon an offer that reduces the retail price of a particular item by a stated amount at the time of purchase

sample a free product given to customers to encourage trial and purchase

premium a gift that a producer offers a customer in return for buying its product

the target audience and the brand's image. Examples include a service station giving a free car wash with a fill-up, a free toothbrush available with a tub of toothpaste, and a free plastic storage box given with the purchase of Kraft Cheese Singles. Premiums also must be easily recognizable and desirable. Premiums are placed on or inside packages and also can be distributed through retailers or through the mail.

Trade show. Trade shows provide an opportunity to make products visible to a large number of people. Samsung is able to promote its product to many participants at the Consumer Electronics Show in Las Vegas.

© Newscom

Frequent-User Incentives A **frequent-user incentive** is a program developed to reward customers who engage in repeat (frequent) purchases. Such programs are used commonly by service businesses such as airlines, hotels, and auto rental agencies. Frequent-user incentives foster customer loyalty to a specific company or group of cooperating companies because the customer is given an additional reason to continue patronizing the business. For example, most major airlines offer frequent-flyer programs that reward customers who have flown a specified number of miles with free tickets for additional travel. There is significant evidence that airline miles are highly valued by customers. Now, more frequent-flyer miles are awarded to customers of non-airline companies than to airline customers to stimulate customer loyalty. Research shows that 93 percent of people with household incomes above $100,000 participate in frequent-user programs, whereas only 58 percent of people with incomes below $50,000 participate.[11]

Point-of-Purchase Displays A **point-of-purchase display** is promotional material placed within a retail store. The display is usually located near the product being promoted. It actually may hold merchandise (as do L'eggs hosiery displays), or it may simply inform customers about what the product offers and encourage them to buy it. Most point-of-purchase displays are prepared and set up by manufacturers and wholesalers.

Trade Shows A **trade show** is an industry-wide exhibit at which many sellers display their products. Some trade shows are organized exclusively for dealers—to permit manufacturers and wholesalers to show their latest lines to retailers. Others are promotions designed to stimulate consumer awareness and interest. Among the latter are boat shows, home shows, and flower shows put on each year in large cities.

Buying Allowances A **buying allowance** is a temporary price reduction to resellers for purchasing specified quantities of a product. For example, a laundry detergent manufacturer might give retailers $1 for each case of detergent purchased. A buying allowance may serve as an incentive to resellers to handle new products and may stimulate purchase of items in large quantities. While the buying allowance is simple, straightforward, and easily administered, competitors can respond quickly by offering a better buying allowance.

Cooperative Advertising **Cooperative advertising** is an arrangement whereby a manufacturer agrees to pay a certain amount of a retailer's media cost for advertising the manufacturer's products. To be reimbursed, a retailer must show proof that the advertisements actually did appear. A large percentage of all cooperative advertising dollars is spent on newspaper advertisements. However, not all retailers take advantage of available cooperative advertising offers because some cannot afford to advertise or choose not to do so.

frequent-user incentive a program developed to reward customers who engage in repeat (frequent) purchases

point-of-purchase display promotional material placed within a retail store

trade show an industry-wide exhibit at which many sellers display their products

buying allowance a temporary price reduction to resellers for purchasing specified quantities of a product

cooperative advertising an arrangement whereby a manufacturer agrees to pay a certain amount of a retailer's media cost for advertising the manufacturer's product

8

Understand the types and uses of public relations.

Public Relations

As noted earlier, public relations is a broad set of communication activities used to create and maintain favorable relationships between an organization and various public groups, both internal and external. These groups can include customers, employees, stockholders, suppliers, educators, the media, government officials, and society in general.

Types of Public-Relations Tools

Organizations use a variety of public-relations tools to convey messages and to create images. Public-relations professionals prepare written materials such as brochures, newsletters, company magazines, annual reports, and news releases. They also create corporate-identity materials such as logos, business cards, signs, and stationery. Speeches are another public-relations tool. Speeches can affect an organization's image and therefore must convey the desired message clearly.

Another public-relations tool is event sponsorship, in which a company pays for all or part of a special event such as a concert, sports competition, festival, or play. Sponsoring special events is an effective way for organizations to increase brand recognition and receive media coverage with comparatively little investment. The Big Apple Barbeque Block Party, for example, is a weekend-long event that occurs every June in New York's Madison Square Park, and features free live music and cooking demonstrations. Barbeque enthusiasts can purchase plates of food from some of the country's top pitmasters, and all proceeds go to the Madison Square Park Conservancy, which maintains the park. Several companies sponsor this event to help promote their brand and the event's charity, including Coca-Cola, Ikea, Heartland Brewery, and Weber Grills.[12]

publicity communication in news-story form about an organization, its products, or both

news release a typed page of about 300 words provided by an organization to the media as a form of publicity

feature article a piece (of up to 3,000 words) prepared by an organization for inclusion in a particular publication

captioned photograph a picture accompanied by a brief explanation

press conference a meeting at which invited media personnel hear important news announcements and receive supplementary textual materials and photographs

Some public-relations tools traditionally have been associated specifically with publicity, which is a part of public relations. **Publicity** is communication in news-story form about an organization, its products, or both. Publicity is transmitted through a mass medium, such as newspapers or radio, at no charge. Organizations use publicity to provide information about products; to announce new product launches, expansions, or research; and to strengthen the company's image. Public-relations personnel sometimes organize events, such as grand openings with prizes and celebrities, to create news stories about a company.

The most widely used type of publicity is the **news release**. It is generally one typed page of about 300 words provided by an organization to the media as a form of publicity. The release includes the firm's name, address, phone number, and contact person. Table 15.2 lists some of the issues news releases can address. There are also several other kinds of publicity-based public-relations tools. A **feature article**, which may run as long as 3,000 words, is usually written for inclusion in a particular publication. For example, a software firm might send an article about its new product to a computer magazine. A **captioned photograph**, a picture accompanied by a brief explanation, is an effective way to illustrate a new or improved product. A **press conference** allows invited media personnel to hear important news announcements and to receive supplementary textual materials and photographs. Finally, letters to the editor, special newspaper or magazine editorials, films, and tapes may be prepared and distributed to appropriate media for possible use.

Event sponsorship. Event sponsorship is a public relations tool. It can be tied in with advertising, personal selling, and sales promotion.

The Uses of Public Relations

Public relations can be used to promote people, places, activities, ideas, and even countries. Public relations focuses on enhancing the reputation of the total organization by making people aware of a company's products,

Table 15.2 Possible Issues for News Releases	
Use of new information technology	Packaging changes
Support of a social cause	New products
Improved warranties	Creation of new software
Reports on industry conditions	Research developments
New uses for established products	Company's history and development
Product endorsements	Launching of new Web site
Winning of quality awards	Award of contracts
Company name changes	Opening of new markets
Interviews with company officials	Improvements in financial position
Improved distribution policies	Opening of an exhibit
Global business initiatives	History of a brand
Sponsorship of events	Winners of company contests
Visits by celebrities	Logo changes
Reports of new discoveries	Speeches of top management
Innovative marketing activities	Merit awards to the organization
Economic forecasts	Anniversaries of inventions

brands, or activities and by creating specific company images such as that of innovativeness or dependability. Many organizations utilize social media to further connect to consumers, including YouTube channels, Facebook Fan Pages, and Twitter accounts. Social media use facilitates customer relationships and feedback, while also further publicizing the organization's news, events, promotions, and products. Mercedes-Benz, for example, operates a YouTube channel, where users can watch videos describing the company's models, recent events, TV ads, and innovative technology. The company also manages a Facebook fan page.[13]

Promotion Planning

9

Identify the factors that influence the selection of promotion-mix ingredients.

A **promotional campaign** is a plan for combining and using the four promotional methods—advertising, personal selling, sales promotion, and public relations—in a particular promotion mix to achieve one or more marketing goals. When selecting promotional methods to include in promotion mixes, it is important to coordinate promotional elements to maximize the total informational and promotional impact on customers. Integrated marketing communication requires a marketer to look at the broad perspective when planning promotional programs and coordinating the total set of communication functions.

In planning a promotional campaign, marketers must answer these two questions:

1. What will be the role of promotion in the overall marketing mix?
2. To what extent will each promotional method be used in the promotion mix?

The answer to the first question depends on the firm's marketing objectives because the role of each element of the marketing mix—product, price, distribution, and promotion—depends on these detailed versions of the firm's marketing goals. The answer to the second question depends on the answer to the first, as well as on the target market.

promotional campaign a plan for combining and using the four promotional methods—advertising, personal selling, sales promotion, and publicity—in a particular promotion mix to achieve one or more marketing goals

Promotion and Marketing Objectives

Promotion naturally is better suited to certain marketing objectives than to others. For example, promotion can do little to further a marketing objective such as "reduce delivery time by one-third." It can, however, be used to inform customers that delivery is faster. Let's consider some objectives that *would* require the use of promotion as a primary ingredient of the marketing mix.

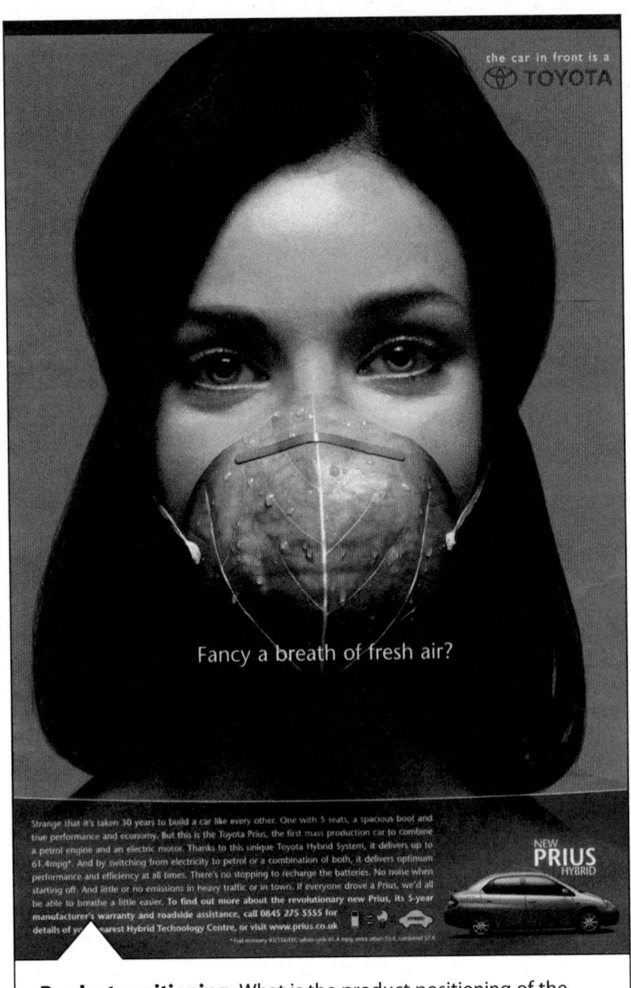

Product positioning. What is the product positioning of the Prius?

Providing Information This is, of course, the main function of promotion. It may be used to communicate to target markets the availability of new products or product features. It may alert them to special offers or give the locations of retailers that carry a firm's products. In other words, promotion can be used to enhance the effectiveness of each of the other ingredients of the marketing mix.

Increasing Market Share Promotion can be used to convince new customers to try a product while maintaining the product loyalty of established customers. Comparative advertising, for example, is directed mainly at those who might—but presently do not—use a particular product. Advertising that emphasizes the product's features also assures those who *do* use the product that they have made a smart choice.

Positioning the Product The sales of a product depend, to a great extent, on its competition. The stronger the competition, the more difficult it is to maintain or increase sales. For this reason, many firms go to great lengths to position their products in the marketplace. **Positioning** is the development of a product image in buyers' minds relative to the images they have of competing products.

Promotion is the prime positioning tool. A marketer can use promotion to position a brand away from competitors to avoid competition. Promotion also may be used to position one product directly against another product. For example, in hopes of providing legitimate competition to Apple's iPhone, Motorola is offering the Droid. There is no doubt is its advertising which phone it is competing against. With statements about its competition like "iDon't have a real keyboard, iDon't allow open development, and iDon't take pictures in the dark," it is very clear that the Droid is positioned head to head with the iPhone.[14]

Stabilizing Sales Special promotional efforts can be used to increase sales during slack periods, such as the "off season" for certain sports equipment. By stabilizing sales in this way, a firm can use its production facilities more effectively and reduce both capital costs and inventory costs. Promotion is also used frequently to increase the sales of products that are in the declining stage of their life-cycle. The objective is to keep them going for a little while longer.

Developing the Promotion Mix

Once the role of promotion is established, the various methods of promotion may be combined in a promotional campaign. As in so many other areas of business, promotion planning begins with a set of specific objectives. The promotion mix then is designed to accomplish these objectives.

Marketers often use several promotion mixes simultaneously if a firm sells multiple products. The selection of promotion-mix ingredients and the degree to which

positioning the development of a product image in buyers' minds relative to the images they have of competing products

they are used depend on the organization's resources and objectives, the nature of the target market, the characteristics of the product, and the feasibility of various promotional methods.

The amount of promotional resources available in an organization influences the number and intensity of promotional methods that marketers can use. A firm with a limited budget for promotion probably will rely on personal selling because the effectiveness of personal selling can be measured more easily than that of advertising. An organization's objectives also have an effect on its promotional activities. A company wishing to make a wide audience familiar with a new convenience item probably will depend heavily on advertising and sales promotion. If a company's objective is to communicate information to consumers—on the features of countertop appliances, for example—then the company may develop a promotion mix that includes some advertising, some sales promotion to attract consumers to stores, and much personal selling.

The size, geographic distribution, and socioeconomic characteristics of the target market play a part in the composition of a product's promotion mix. If the market is small, personal selling probably will be the most important element in the promotion mix. This is true of organizations that sell to small industrial markets and businesses that use only a few wholesalers to market their products. Companies that need to contact millions of potential customers, however, will emphasize sales promotion and advertising because these methods are relatively inexpensive. The age, income, and education of the target market also will influence the choice of promotion techniques. For example, with less-educated consumers, personal selling may be more effective than ads in newspapers or magazines.

In general, industrial products require a considerable amount of personal selling, whereas consumer goods depend on advertising. This is not true in every case, however. The price of the product also influences the composition of the promotion mix. Because consumers often want the advice of a salesperson on an expensive product, high-priced consumer goods may call for more personal selling. Similarly, advertising and sales promotion may be more crucial to marketers of seasonal items because having a year-round sales force is not always appropriate.

The cost and availability of promotional methods are important factors in the development of a promotion mix. Although national advertising and sales promotion activities are expensive, the cost per customer may be quite small if the campaign succeeds in reaching large numbers of people. In addition, local advertising outlets—newspapers, magazines, radio and television stations, and outdoor displays—may not be that costly for a small local business. In some situations, a firm may find that no available advertising medium reaches the target market effectively.

Criticisms of Promotion

10

Identify and explain the criticisms of promotion.

Even though promotional activities can help customers to make informed purchasing decisions, social scientists, consumer groups, government agencies, and members of society in general have long criticized promotion. There are two main reasons for such criticism: Promotion does have some flaws, and it is a highly visible business activity that pervades our daily lives. Although people almost universally complain that there is simply too much promotional activity, several more specific issues have been raised. Promotional efforts have been called deceptive. Promotion has been blamed for increasing prices. Other criticisms of promotion are that it manipulates consumers into buying products they do not need, that it leads to a more materialistic society, that customers do not benefit sufficiently from promotion to justify its high costs, and that promotion is used to market potentially harmful products. These issues are discussed in Table 15.3.

Table 15.3	Criticisms of Promotion
Issue	**Discussion**
Is promotion deceptive?	Although no longer widespread, some deceptive promotion still occurs; laws, government regulations, and industry self-regulation have helped to decrease intentionally deceptive promotion; however, customers may be unintentionally misled because some words have diverse meanings.
Does promotion increase prices?	When promotion stimulates demand, higher production levels may result in lower per-unit production costs which keeps prices lower; when demand is not stimulated, however, prices increase owing to the added costs of promotion; promotion fuels price competition, which helps to keep prices lower.
Does promotion create needs?	Many marketers capitalize on people's needs by basing their promotional appeals on these needs; however, marketers do not actually create these needs. If there were no promotion, people would still have basic needs such as those suggested by Maslow.
Does promotion encourage materialism?	Because promotion creates awareness and visibility for products, it may contribute to materialism in the same way that movies, sports, theater, art, and literature may contribute to materialism; if there were no promotion, it is likely that there would still be materialism among some groups, as evidenced by the existence of materialism among some ancient groups of people.
Does promotion help customers without costing too much?	Customers learn about products and services through promotion, allowing them to make more intelligent buying decisions.
Should potentially harmful products be promoted?	Some critics suggest that the promotion of possibly unhealthy products should not be allowed at all; others argue that as long as it is legal to sell such products, promoting those products should be allowed.

Source: William M. Pride and O. C. Ferrell, *Foundations of Marketing* (Mason, OH: South-Western/Cengage Learning, 2011), 389.

return to inside business

Panera Bread

When Panera Bread was just starting out, its first cafés served a few dozen customers per day. Now the company serves 6 million customers every week and opens the doors to a new café every five days. It announces grand openings with a combination of local advertising, direct mail to nearby residents and businesses, and publicity to spread the word through local media coverage.

Throughout the day, Panera's employees walk through the cafés offering bite-size samples of fresh-from-the-oven baked goods so customers can taste new menu items before they buy. The company also uses point-of-purchase displays to inform customers about special services such as catering. With so many competitors jockeying for market share, Panera knows that satisfied customers are ultimately the key ingredient in sparking positive word of mouth about the brand.

Questions

1. What is Panera's promotion mix, and why is it appropriate for the company's situation?
2. How would you suggest that Panera evaluate the effectiveness of its advertising? Be specific.

CHAPTER REVIEW

SUMMARY

Summary

1 Describe integrated marketing communications.

Integrated marketing communications is the coordination of promotion efforts to achieve the maximum informational and persuasive impact on customers.

2 Understand the role of promotion.

Promotion is communication about an organization and its products that is intended to inform, persuade, or remind target-market members. The major ingredients of a promotion mix are advertising, personal selling, sales promotion, and public relations. The role of promotion is to facilitate exchanges directly or indirectly and to help an organization maintain favorable relationships with groups in the marketing environment.

3 Explain the purposes of the three types of advertising.

Advertising is a paid nonpersonal message communicated to a specific audience through a mass medium. Primary-demand advertising promotes the products of an entire industry rather than just a single brand.

Selective-demand advertising promotes a particular brand of product. Institutional advertising is image-building advertising for a firm.

4 Describe the advantages and disadvantages of the major advertising media.

The major advertising media are newspapers, magazines, direct mail, out-of-home displays, television, radio, the Internet, and social media. Newspapers are relatively inexpensive compared with other media, reach only people in the market area, and are timely. Disadvantages include a short life span, poor color reproduction, and an inability to target specific demographic groups. Magazine advertising can be quite prestigious. In addition, it can reach very specific market segments, can provide high-quality color reproduction, and has a relatively long life span. Major disadvantages are high cost and lack of timeliness. Direct mail is the most selective medium, and its effectiveness is measured easily. The disadvantage of direct mail is that if the mailing list is outdated and the advertisement does not reach the right people, then the campaign cannot be successful. Yellow Pages advertising allows customers who use it to save time in finding products, to find information quickly, and to learn about products and marketers. Unlike other types of advertising media, Yellow Pages advertisements are purchased for one year and cannot be changed. Out-of-home advertising allows marketers to focus on a particular geographic area and is relatively inexpensive. Messages, though, must be limited to a few words because the audience is usually moving.

Television accounts for the largest share of advertising expenditures. Television offers marketers the opportunity to broadcast a firm's message nationwide. However, television advertising can be very expensive and has a short life span. In addition, cable channels and home videos have reduced the likelihood of reaching extremely large audiences. Radio advertising offers selectivity, can be less expensive than other media, and is flexible for scheduling purposes. Radio's limitations include no visual presentation and fragmented, small audiences. Benefits of using the Internet as an advertising medium include the growing number of people using the Internet, which means a growing audience, and the ability to precisely target specific customers. Disadvantages include the relatively simplistic nature of the ads that can be produced, especially in comparison with television, and the lack of evidence that net browsers actually pay attention to the ads. Social media appear to allow marketers the ability to target, interact, and connect more personally with customers through sites such as Twitter, Facebook, and brand-specific Web sites. Drawbacks are that the audience is restricted to followers, marketers are still unsure of the usefulness and return on investment, and companies must have employees dedicated to real-time activity.

5 Identify the major steps in developing an advertising campaign.

An advertising campaign is developed in several stages. A firm's first task is to identify and analyze its advertising target. The goals of the campaign also must be clearly defined. Then the firm must develop the advertising platform, or statement of important selling points, and determine the size of the advertising budget. The next steps are to develop a media plan, to create the advertising message, and to execute the campaign. Finally, promotion managers must evaluate the effectiveness of the advertising efforts before, during, and/or after the campaign.

6 Recognize the various kinds of salespersons, the steps in the personal-selling process, and the major sales management tasks.

Personal selling is personal communication aimed at informing customers and persuading them to buy a firm's products. It is the most adaptable promotional method because the salesperson can modify the message to fit each buyer. Three major kinds of salespersons are order-getters, order-takers, and support personnel. The six steps in the personal-selling process are prospecting, approaching the prospect, making the presentation, answering objections, closing the sale, and following-up. Sales managers are involved directly in setting sales force objectives; recruiting, selecting, and training salespersons; compensating and motivating sales personnel; creating sales territories; and evaluating sales performance.

7 Describe sales promotion objectives and methods.

Sales promotion is the use of activities and materials as direct inducements to customers and salespersons. The primary objective of sales promotion methods is to enhance and supplement other promotional methods. Methods of sales promotion include rebates, coupons, samples, premiums, frequent-user incentives, point-of-purchase displays, trade shows, buying allowances, and cooperative advertising.

8 Understand the types and uses of public relations.

Public relations is a broad set of communication activities used to create and maintain favorable relationships between an organization and various public groups, both internal and external. Organizations use a variety of public-relations tools to convey messages and create images. Brochures, newsletters, company magazines, and annual reports are written public-relations tools. Speeches, event sponsorship, and publicity are other public-relations tools. Publicity is communication in news-story form about an organization, its products, or both. Types of publicity include news releases, feature articles, captioned photographs, and press conferences. Public relations can be used to promote people, places, activities, ideas, and even countries. It can be used to enhance the reputation of an organization and also to reduce the unfavorable effects of negative events.

9 Identify the factors that influence the selection of promotion-mix ingredients.

A promotional campaign is a plan for combining and using advertising, personal selling, sales promotion, and publicity to achieve one or more marketing goals. Campaign objectives are developed from marketing objectives. Then the promotion mix is developed based on the organization's promotional resources and objectives, the nature of the target market, the product characteristics, and the feasibility of various promotional methods.

10 Identify and explain the criticisms of promotion.

Promotion activities can help consumers to make informed purchasing decisions, but they also have evoked many criticisms. Promotion has been accused of deception. Although some deceiving or misleading promotions do exist, laws, government regulation, and industry self-regulation minimize deceptive promotion. Promotion has been blamed for increasing prices, but it usually tends to lower them. When demand is high, production and marketing costs decrease, which can result in lower prices. Promotion also helps to keep prices lower by facilitating price competition. Other criticisms of promotional activity are that it manipulates consumers into buying products they do not need, that it leads to a more materialistic society, and that consumers do not benefit sufficiently from promotional activity to justify its high cost. Finally, some critics of promotion suggest that potentially harmful products, especially those associated with violence, sex, and unhealthy activities, should not be promoted at all.

Key Terms

You should now be able to define and give an example relevant to each of the following terms:

promotion (430)
promotion mix (430)
integrated marketing communications (431)
advertising (432)
personal selling (432)
sales promotion (433)
public relations (433)
primary-demand advertising (433)
selective-demand (or brand) advertising (434)
institutional advertising (434)
advertising media (435)
direct-mail advertising (435)
Yellow Pages advertising (435)
out-of-home advertising (436)
infomercial (437)
advertising agency (441)
order-getter (442)
creative selling (442)
order-taker (442)
sales support personnel (442)
missionary salesperson (442)
trade salesperson (442)
technical salesperson (442)
consumer sales promotion method (445)
trade sales promotion method (445)
rebate (445)
coupon (446)
sample (446)
premium (446)
frequent-user incentive (447)
point-of-purchase display (447)
trade show (447)
buying allowance (447)
cooperative advertising (447)
publicity (448)
news release (448)
feature article (448)
captioned photograph (448)
press conference (448)
promotional campaign (449)
positioning (450)

Review Questions

1. What is integrated marketing communications, and why is it becoming increasingly accepted?
2. Identify and describe the major ingredients of a promotion mix.
3. What is the major role of promotion?
4. How are selective-demand, institutional, and primary-demand advertising different from one another? Give an example of each.
5. List the four major print media, and give an advantage and a disadvantage of each.
6. Which types of firms use radio, television, and the Internet?
7. Outline the main steps involved in developing an advertising campaign.
8. Why would a firm with its own advertising department use an ad agency?
9. Identify and give examples of the three major types of salespersons.
10. Explain how each step in the personal-selling process leads to the next step.
11. What are the major tasks involved in managing a sales force?
12. What are the major differences between consumer and trade sales promotion methods? Give examples of each.
13. What is cooperative advertising? What sorts of firms use it?

14. What is the difference between publicity and public relations? What is the purpose of each?
15. Why is promotion particularly effective in positioning a product? In stabilizing or increasing sales?
16. What factors determine the specific promotion mix that a firm should use?
17. Is promotion deceptive? What is your evidence that it is or is not deceptive?

Discussion Questions

1. Discuss the pros and cons of comparative advertising from the viewpoint of (a) the advertiser, (b) the advertiser's competitors, and (c) the target market.
2. Which kinds of advertising—in which media—influence you most? Why?
3. Which kinds of retail outlets or products require mainly order-taking by salespeople?
4. A number of companies have shifted a portion of their promotion dollars from advertising to trade sales promotion methods. Why?
5. Why would a producer offer refunds or cents-off coupons rather than simply lowering the price of its products?
6. How can public-relations efforts aimed at the general public help an organization?
7. Why do firms use event sponsorship?
8. What kind of promotion mix might be used to extend the life of a product that has entered the declining stage of its product life-cycle?

Video Case 15.1

L.L.Bean Employs a Variety of Promotion Methods to Communicate with Customers

Perhaps best known for its beloved mail-order catalog, L.L.Bean was recently placed near the top of Photobrand's list of New England's most powerful brands, beating Ethan Allen and Yankee Candle. L.L.Bean has grown from its founding as a one-product firm in 1912 to a national brand with 14 stores in 10 different states and a thriving online store. Net sales are over $1.5 billion a year.

Marketing communications are more sophisticated now than they were when L. L. Bean created his first product, a waterproof boot, and publicized it with a homemade brochure. In its early days, the firm thrived on word-of-mouth communication about its reliability and the expert advice of its founder, himself an avid outdoorsman. Determined to build his company and his mailing list, L. L. Bean poured all the company's profits into advertising and talked about the company with one and all. Said one neighbor at the time, "If you drop in just to shake his hand, you get home to find his catalog in your mailbox."

Now the company makes use of marketing database systems to manage and update its mailing lists. The L.L.Bean catalog swelled in size in the 1980s and 1990s, but it has slimmed down as the company's Web site has taken over some of the task of promoting the company's products. Still a major communication tool for the firm, the catalog is also a multiple-industry award-winner. The company uses computer-modeling tools to help it identify what customers want and sends them only the catalogs they desire. Still, says the vice president of stores, "What we find is most customers want some sort of touch point," and the catalog remains very popular.

Online orders recently surpassed mail and phone orders for the first time in the company's history. The relationship between the catalog and the Web site is complicated. As L.L.Bean's vice president for e-commerce explains, customers have begun to shift much of their buying to the Internet, but they still rely on the catalog to browse, plan, and get ideas. Customers take their L.L.Bean catalogs "to soccer games, they read them in the car," she says. "What's changed is what they do next"—often they go online to find more details about an item or to place an order.

L.L.Bean still places print advertising, sometimes small ads that simply offer a free catalog or remind customers that they already have the catalog at home. Since the catalog is expensive to produce, the company tries to support it with other marketing media so it doesn't get lost among all the other messages demanding customers' attention.

A big and growing area for the company's promotion efforts is the Internet, where it uses banner ads on popular sites like Hulu.com that let customers click through to the L.L.Bean online store. It also maintains a Facebook page, a Twitter account, and a YouTube channel. The company invests heavily in television advertising as well, particularly around the holidays. Local TV ads are concentrated in the areas around the company's retail stores.

L.L.Bean doesn't take the wide familiarity of its brand for granted. It also promotes its name through partnerships with environmentally conscious companies and organizations and through charitable giving, mainly to organizations committed to maintaining and protecting Earth's natural resources. The company recognizes, however, that a good product is at the heart of its success. "We really want to sell a good product, and we really guarantee that product," says the company's vice president of e-commerce. "We want to keep . . . the customer happy and keep that customer coming back to L.L.Bean over and over."[15]

Questions

1. What are the ingredients of L.L.Bean's promotion mix?
2. L.L.Bean is reaching into "alternative" promotions, including outfitting Weather Channel meteorologists around the United States and emblazoning its name on the tarp used by the Red Sox baseball team to protect the field during rain delays. What other kinds of promotional activities do you think would suit the company's outdoors image?
3. Do you think L.L.Bean's Web site will ever entirely take the place of its mail-order catalog? Why or why not?

Case 15.2

Mother and Son Team Flourish at Columbia Sportswear

Gert Boyl is "one tough mother." Not only is she the chairperson of the board for Columbia Sportswear, but she has also been its advertising spokeswoman. Gert assumed control of Columbia Sportswear 35 years ago after her husband Neil passed away unexpectedly. Gert, with her son Tim's help, reported for duty a mere four days after Neil's death to take the reins of the struggling company—a company that has flourished under their tough leadership.

Founded by Gert Boyle's parents in 1938, Columbia Sportswear is a global leader in the design, marketing, and distribution of active outdoor apparel and footwear. The $1.2 billion company employs more than 2,700 people and markets its products in 100 countries through more than 13,000 retailers as well as its own stores and Web site. As one of the world's largest outerwear brands and the leading seller of skiwear in the United States, the company has developed an international reputation for quality, performance, and value.

Columbia Sportswear has worked hard over the years to develop its image of offering high-quality products. It promotes itself and its products by sponsoring outdoorsy events such as bass-fishing contests, marathons, kayaking events, and snowboarding competitions. In addition, the company uses print and television advertising, plus a strong public-relations program, to promote its brand and its quality products.

One of its most successful ad campaigns featured Gert and her son, Tim Boyle, as an outgrowth of their relationship since they began running the company together. According to people who know them, Tim and his mother have argued from the beginning about how to run Columbia Sportswear. A director of the company says, "Tim and Gert are a lot like the Jack Lemmon and Walter Matthau characters in *The Odd Couple*. They complain all the time, and yet they cherish each other."

Over 20 years ago, Borders, Perrin & Norrander, the company's former advertising agency, came up with an idea to use the relationship between Gert and her son to develop an identity for the company—an identity beyond technical claims about product quality. They developed an ad campaign that portrays Gert as "one tough mother," who uses her son to demonstrate that Columbia Sportswear clothes will protect whoever wears them under any weather conditions. Gert appears as a hard-driving mother who refuses to accept anything but the highest quality of products, for both her son and her company. The ads were so successful at positioning and promoting Columbia Sportswear's products that Gert and Tim became the company's ad staples.

Showing Gert put her son through a series of catastrophic tests to demonstrate product durability reinforced the brand's quality and unique positioning. In one commercial, Gert drives an SUV with Tim strapped on top through a series of severe weather situations to show that this clothing is protecting him. The ending scene is a close-up of the jacket he is wearing with the tagline "Tested Tough." This theme is continued through a series of commercials that depict Tim in a number of cold-weather survival situations, such as being dropped on the top of a snow-covered mountain by a helicopter piloted by Gert. In all cases, Tim is unharmed and Gert is unconcerned—all because he is wearing Columbia Sportswear clothing.

One of the company's classic commercials shows Gert in a biker bar. The audio track says, "In a world of rugged individuals, only one is the toughest mother of them all. Mother Gert Boyle—maker of tough mother jeans." The audience sees a close-up of Gert with a "Born to Nag" tattoo on her bicep before the spot ends with a product shot of Columbia jeans. More recently, the company has continued its irreverent approach to communications with print and television ads focused on new products such as the Bugathermo heated boot for winter. With U.S. sales continuing to rise, and a pipeline of new products to put through their paces, Columbia Sportswear is living up to the tough standards that Gert has always set.[16]

Questions

1. What are the characteristics of Columbia's target audience, and how do these appear to be affecting its advertising?
2. What are the major objectives of Columbia Sportswear's promotion program?
3. What recommendations would you make to strengthen Columbia's promotional activities?

Building Skills for Career Success

❶ JOURNALING FOR SUCCESS

Discovery statement: As this chapter showed, advertising is an important part of an organization's promotional mix.

Assignment

1. During the last year, you have been exposed to a number of television advertisements. Identify and describe what you believe to be the best TV commercial that you have experienced over the last year.
2. Why did you feel that this ad is the very best?
3. Describe the content of this advertisement in as much detail as possible, and explain what you can recall about this television advertisement.

❷ EXPLORING THE INTERNET

As a promotional tool, the Internet stands alone among all media for cost-effectiveness and variety. A well-designed company Web site can enhance most of the promotional strategies discussed in this chapter. It can provide consumers with advertising copy and sales representatives with personal-selling support services and information any time on-demand. In addition, many companies use the Internet for sales promotion. For instance, most newspapers and magazines provide sample articles in the hope that interested readers eventually will become subscribers. Moreover, virtually all software companies present demonstration editions of their products for potential customers to explore and test.

Assignment

1. Visit two of the following Web sites and examine the promotional activities taking place there. Note the sort of promotion being used and its location within the site. Also visit the text Web site for updates to this exercise.

   http://www.wsj.com
   http://www.businessweek.com
   http://www.forbes.com

2. Describe the promotional tools exhibited on one of these sites.
3. What would you recommend the company do to improve the site?

❸ DEVELOPING CRITICAL-THINKING SKILLS

Obviously, salespeople must know the products they are selling, but to give successful sales presentations, they also must know their competition. Armed with information about competing products, they are better able to field prospective customers' questions and objections regarding their own products.

Assignment

1. Choose a product or service offered by one company and gather samples of the competitors' sales literature.
2. After examining the competitors' sales literature, answer the following questions:
   a. What type of literature do the competitors use to advertise their product or service? Do they use full-color brochures?
   b. Do they use videotapes?
   c. Do they offer giveaways or special discounts?
3. Compare the product or service you chose with what the competition is selling.
4. Compile a list of all the strengths and weaknesses you have discovered.

❹ BUILDING TEAM SKILLS

The cost of promotional methods is an important factor in a promotional campaign. Representatives who sell advertising space for magazines, newspapers, radio stations, and television stations can quote the price of the medium to the advertiser. The advertiser then can use cost per thousand persons reached (CPM) to compare the cost efficiency of advertising in the same medium.

Assignment

1. Working in teams of five to seven, choose one of these media: local television stations, newspapers, or radio stations. You can choose magazines if your library has a copy of *Standard Rate and Data Service.*
2. Using the following equation, compare the CPM of advertising in whatever local medium you chose:

$$\textbf{CPM} = \frac{\textbf{price of the medium to the advertiser} \times \textbf{1,000}}{\textbf{circulation}}$$

3. Report your team's findings to the class.

❺ RESEARCHING DIFFERENT CAREERS

There are many sources available online containing occupational and career materials. Search for trade and professional magazines and journals about specific occupations and industries that you are interested in. Familiarize yourself with the concerns and activities of potential employers by skimming their annual reports and other publicly distributed materials. Publicly traded companies often have a link to this data on their Web site. Another potentially useful source of information is to visit the Web sites of some of the key companies in the industry you are researching. Checking their Web sites for current industry news, challenges, and developments can provide a good insight into the nature of the industry.

Assignment

1. Choose a specific occupation.
2. Conduct an Internet search of the occupation.
3. Prepare a list of sources where information about the occupation you selected can be found.

Graeter's Is "Synonymous with Ice Cream"

When a 140-year-old company finally redesigns its logo, that's big news. Graeter's, the beloved Cincinnati-based maker of premium, hand-packed ice cream, is still managed by direct descendants of its founders. Its new logo is just one part of a major rebranding effort to support the company's first big planned expansion. "If we don't continue to improve and innovate, somebody will come and do it better than us," says Chip Graeter, the company's vice president of retail stores. "And we don't want that to happen."

QUALITY BUILDS THE BRAND

Graeter's considers as its competitors not only Häagen-Dazs and Ben & Jerry's, national premium ice-cream brands that have much bigger marketing budgets, but also all kinds of premium-quality desserts and edible treats. Taking that wide-angle view means its competition is both broad and fierce. One thing the company is firm about, however, is maintaining the quality of its dense, creamy product (it's so dense that one pint of Graeter's ice cream weighs about a pound). Graeter's quality standards call for adhering to its simple, original family recipe—which now includes more all-natural ingredients, like beet juice instead of food dye and dairy products from hormone-free cows—and an original, artisanal production process that yields only about two gallons per machine every 20 minutes. "We were always all-natural," says CEO Richard Graeter II, "but now we're being militant about it."

That hard-earned premium quality is what built the Graeter's brand from its earliest days when refrigeration was unknown and ice cream was a true novelty. Today, "Graeter's in Cincinnati is synonymous with ice cream," says a company executive. "People will say, 'Let's go get a Graeter's.' They don't say, 'Let's go get an ice cream.'" Quality is also what the current management team hopes will propel Graeter's beyond its current market, which consists of a few dozen company-owned retail stores in Ohio, Missouri, Kentucky, and nearby states, and the freezer cases of about 1,700 supermarkets and grocery stores, particularly the Kroger chain. Graeter's is also on the menu in some fine restaurants and country clubs. The company operates an online store and will ship ice cream overnight via UPS to any of the 48 continental states (California is its biggest shipping market). Graeter's also sells a limited line of candies, cakes, and other bakery goods, and its ice-cream line includes smoothies and sorbets.

EXPANDING TO NEW MARKETS

Graeter's ambitious expansion plans are backed by a recent increase in production capacity from one factory to three (one of the new factories was built, and the other purchased). The plans call for distributing Graeter's delectable, seasonal flavors to even more supermarkets and grocery stores, and for gradually opening new retail stores, perhaps as far away as Los Angeles and New York. The Kroger chain is Graeter's biggest distribution partner. Of the tens of thousands of brands Kroger carries, says the chain, pricey Graeter's commands the strongest brand loyalty. It was through Kroger, in fact, that Graeter's managers hit upon the idea of conducting a trial expansion to Denver, a new market for the brand.

Kroger owns the King Soopers chain of grocery stores in Denver, and research showed that more Denver ice-cream buyers choose premium brands than cheaper choices, suggesting that Graeter's might do well there. So Graeter's chose 12 flavors to send to 30 King Soopers stores in Denver as a test market, with the goal of selling two or three gallons a week. The test was an unqualified success. Within a few weeks, the company was selling an average of five gallons a week per store.

"I'd like to be coast to coast," admits Graeter's CEO. In fact, the management team would like to explore selling Graeter's in Canada, perhaps within the next five years. "The challenge, of course, is to preserve the integrity of the product as we grow. But we have done that for more than 100 years, and I'd argue that it's better now than ever."

PROMOTING THE BRAND

Graeter's had already gotten a big free boost from a positive mention on the *Oprah Winfrey Show* in 2002, when the influential talk-show host called it the best ice cream she had ever tasted. "We were shipping about 40 orders a day," says CEO Richard Graeter II. "After her show, the next day we probably shipped 400." National attention continues with occasional exposure on the Food Network, the Fine Living Channel, the Travel Channel, and even the History Channel. "How does that happen?" asks one of the firm's executives. "It happens because we have a product and a process and a growth that is exciting."

Still, says George Denman, the company's vice president of sales and marketing, Graeter's faces the same challenge in new markets as any "small, regional niche player" and one with a limited marketing budget: "establishing a relationship with the consumer, building brand awareness [through] trial and repeat . . . .So obviously when we roll into a marketplace one of the first things we do is we demo the product. We get it out in front of the consumer and get them to taste it, because the product sells itself." The company has also been reducing its price to distributors, who pass the savings along to stores that can then advertise that Graeter's pints are on sale. "If a consumer has maybe been buying Ben & Jerry's and never considered ours, because maybe that dollar price point difference was too high, this gives her the opportunity to try us. And once she tries us, we know we've brand-switched that consumer right then," says Denman.

MARKETING COMMUNICATIONS

Through its Cincinnati-based ad agency, Graeter's does some local advertising, including attractive point-of-sale displays in supermarkets and grocery stores and some radio ads, occasional print ads, and billboards. The company launches small-scale promotions for the introduction of a new flavor or to celebrate National Ice Cream Month or other occasions. However, brand loyalty for this family business has grown mostly through word of mouth that endures across generations. "We are the beneficiary of that loyalty that our customers have built up over so many years, multiple generations," says one of the company's executives. "Our customers have told us they were introduced to the product through their grandmother, or a special time . . . . They don't come to our stores because they have to; they come because they want to."

"We use the traditional [marketing] methods," says Denman. "We are also doing nontraditional methods. We are looking at electronic couponing, where consumers will be able to go to our Web site as a new consumer . . . and secure a dollar-off coupon to try Graeter's, just for coming to our Web site or joining up on Facebook. We've done loyalty programs with Kroger where they have actually direct-mailed loyal consumers and offered . . . discounts as well . . . . So far it's worked well for us. We've had to go back and look at the return on investment on each of these programs and cut some things out and improve on some other things, but in the end we have been very pleased with the results."

"QUALITY . . . WE NEVER CHANGED"

"We ship our product, and that was something that for the first hundred years you never thought about. I mean, who would think about shipping ice cream from Cincinnati to California? But it is our number-one market for shipping, so all those things you can change," says Richard Graeter, the CEO. "The most important thing, the quality of the product and how we make it, that we never changed."[17]

Questions

1. How might Graeter's capitalize on its valuable capacity for word-of-mouth promotion in expanding to new markets where, despite some national publicity like the *Oprah Winfrey Show*, its name is still not widely known?
2. Graeter's ice-cream line includes smoothies and sorbets. Do you think it should consider other brand extensions such as yogurt, low-fat ice cream, coffee drinks, or other related products? Why or why not?
3. What are the elements of Graeter's marketing mix? Which are most likely to be affected by external forces in the marketing environment?

Building a Business Plan PART 5

To access the online *Interactive Business Plan*, go to www.cengagebrain.com.

This part is one of the most important components of your business plan. In this part, you will present the facts that you have gathered on the size and nature of your market(s). State market size in dollars and units. How many units and what is the dollar value of the products you expect to sell in a given time period? Indicate your primary and secondary sources of data and the methods you used to estimate total market size and your market share. Part 5 of your textbook covers all marketing-related topics. These chapters should help you to answer the questions in this part of the business plan.

THE MARKETING PLAN COMPONENT

The marketing plan component is and should be unique to your business. Many assumptions or projections used in the analysis may turn out differently; therefore, this component should be flexible enough to be adjusted as needed. The marketing plan should include answers to at least the following questions:

5.1. What are your target markets, and what common identifiable need(s) can you satisfy?

5.2. What are the competitive, legal, political, economic, technological, and sociocultural factors affecting your marketing efforts?

5.3. What are the current needs of each target market? Describe the target market in terms of demographic, geographic, psychographic, and product-usage characteristics. What changes in the target market are anticipated?

5.4. What advantages and disadvantages do you have in meeting the target market's needs?

5.5. How will your product distribution, promotion, and price satisfy customer needs?

5.6. How effectively will your products meet these needs?

5.7. What are the relevant aspects of consumer behavior and product use?

5.8. What are your company's projected sales volume, market share, and profitability?

5.9. What are your marketing objectives? Include the following in your marketing objectives:

- Product introduction, improvement, or innovation
- Sales or market share
- Profitability
- Pricing
- Distribution
- Advertising (Prepare advertising samples for the appendix.)

Make sure that your marketing objectives are clearly written, measurable, and consistent with your overall marketing strategy.

5.10. How will the results of your marketing plan be measured and evaluated?

REVIEW OF BUSINESS PLAN ACTIVITIES

Remember that even though it will be time-consuming, developing a clear, well-written marketing plan is important. Therefore, make sure that you have checked the plan for any weaknesses or problems before proceeding to Part 6. Also, make certain that all your answers to the questions in this and other parts are consistent throughout the business plan. Finally, write a brief statement that summarizes all the information for this part of the business plan.

The information contained in this section will also assist you in completing the online *Interactive Business Plan*.

PART 6

Information for Business Strategy and Decision Making

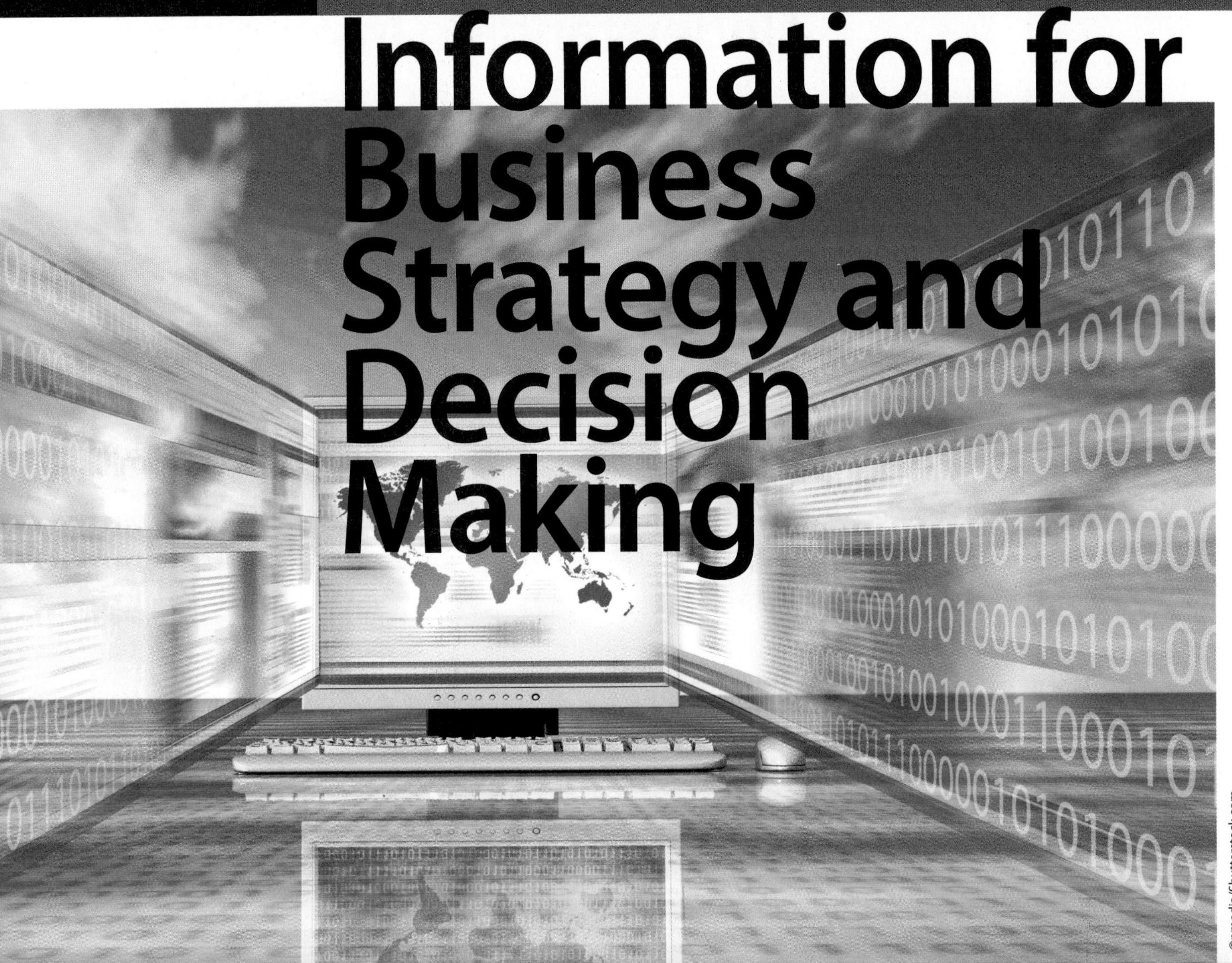

©nmedia/Shutterstock.com

In this part of the book, we focus on information, one of the four essential resources on which all businesses rely. First, we discuss the information necessary for effective decision making, where it can be found, how it is organized, and how it can be used throughout an organization by those who need it. We also investigate the world of e-business in Chapter 16. In Chapter 17, we then examine the role of accounting and how financial information is collected, stored, processed, presented, and used to better control managerial decision making.

Understanding Information and e-Business

16

© MCT/Newscom

Learning Objectives

What you will be able to do once you complete this chapter:

1. Examine how information can reduce risk when making a decision.
2. Discuss management's information requirements.
3. Outline the five functions of an information system.
4. Describe how computers and technology help improve productivity, decision making, communications, sales, and recruiting and training.
5. Analyze how computers and technology change the way information is acquired, organized, and used.
6. Explain the meaning of e-business.
7. Describe the fundamental models of e-business.
8. Explore the factors that will affect the future of e-business.

inside business

Net-a-Porter Builds Its Luxury e-Business

Net-a-Porter got its start in 2000, as the global economy was moving into recession and many young e-businesses were struggling or failing. Founder Natalie Massenet was a London-based fashion editor who had just discovered the convenience of online shopping. When she clicked around trying to buy a pair of expensive designer jeans, however, she was surprised to find no way to buy high-end fashions and accessories online.

That's when Massenet decided to start an e-business. She chose the name Net-a-Porter as a play on the French phrase *pret-a-porter*, "ready to wear." Massenet planned a Web site as upscale and glamorous as the world of designer fashion. Each Monday morning she would upload a glitzy new weekly "edition" of her pick of the latest couture collections, complete with tips on what to wear with what—and when.

Believing that affluent, style-conscious women would welcome personalized service, Massenet arranged same-day courier service to deliver Net-a-Porter purchases to homes and offices in central London. (Customers outside London receive their packages via commercial express delivery.) Purchases are packed in chic black boxes to reinforce the e-business's luxury positioning, and Net-a-Porter pays for shipping if customers return or exchange a purchase.

When Net-a-Porter opened its virtual doors, the e-business success was far from assured. Skeptics doubted that women would pay thousands of dollars without seeing the clothing or shoes in person and trying things on. Massenet proved them wrong. She launched Net-a-Porter with a line-up of leading brands such as Jimmy Choo, and her careful attention to service quickly earned her a loyal following. Later, Net-a-Porter expanded with a New York office to serve the U.S. market, including same-day delivery to buyers in central New York City. In 2009, it opened an outlet site featuring designer styles at discount prices.

Together, Net-a-Porter.com and Theoutnet.com now ring up more than $180 million in annual sales to customers in 170 countries. In 2010, Net-a-Porter was acquired by Richemont, the Swiss company that owns Cartier and other luxury brands. Massenet remains executive chairperson, working with Richemont to continue improving the shopping experience for its customers worldwide.[1]

FYI

Did You Know?

Net-a-Porter.com and its outlet site, Theoutnet.com, ring up more than $180 million in annual sales to customers in 170 countries.

According to the traditional view of retailing, you can't sell expensive, designer fashions on a Web site. And yet, Natalie Massenet—the entrepreneur profiled in the Inside Business opening case—proved the experts were wrong. More than ten years ago, she started Net-a-Porter with one goal in mind: Offer high-quality designer clothing to very selective customers. Today Massenet's Internet businesses generate $180 million in annual sales to customers in 170 countries. Because the company offers its customers the latest clothing designs and provides excellent customer service, repeat customers visit the Web site on a regular basis to purchase the clothes created by only the best designers. She also made sure that customers receive excellent customer service and information that helps them find just the right type of clothing for all occasions. Simply put, providing information to its customers has helped Net-a-Porter become a very successful online retailer in a very competitive high-fashion world.

To improve the decision-making process, the information used by both individuals and business firms must be relevant or useful to meet a specific need. Using relevant information results in better decisions.

Relevant information → Better intelligence and knowledge → Better decisions

For businesses, better intelligence and knowledge that lead to better decisions are especially important because they can provide a *competitive edge* over competitors and improve a firm's *profits*. We begin this chapter by describing why employees need information.

The first three major sections in this chapter answer the following questions:

- How can information reduce risk when making a decision?
- What is a management information system?
- How do employees use a management information system?

Next, we discuss how computers, the Internet, and software—all topics covered in this chapter—are used to obtain the information needed to make decisions and improve productivity on a daily basis. In the last part of this chapter, we take a close look at how firms conduct business on the Internet and what growth opportunities and challenges affect both new and existing e-business firms.

1

Examine how information can reduce risk when making a decision.

How Can Information Reduce Risk When Making a Decision?

As we noted in Chapter 1, information is one of the four major resources (along with material, human, and financial resources) managers must have to operate a business. Although a successful business uses all four resources efficiently, it is information that helps managers reduce risk when making a decision.

Information and Risk

Theoretically, with accurate and complete information, there is no risk whatsoever. On the other hand, a decision made without any information is a gamble. These two extreme situations are rare in business. For the most part, business decision makers see themselves located someplace between either extreme. As illustrated in Figure 16.1, when the amount of available information is high, there is less risk; when the amount of available information is low, there is more risk.

Suppose that a marketing manager for Procter & Gamble (P&G) responsible for the promotion of a well-known shampoo such as Pantene Pro-V has called a meeting of her department team to consider the selection of a new magazine advertisement. The company's advertising agency has submitted two new advertisements in sealed envelopes. Neither the manager nor any of her team has seen them before. Only one selection will be made for the new advertising campaign. Which advertisement should be chosen?

Without any further information, the team might as well make the decision by flipping a coin. If, however, team members were allowed to open the envelopes and

Figure 16.1 The Relationship Between Information and Risk

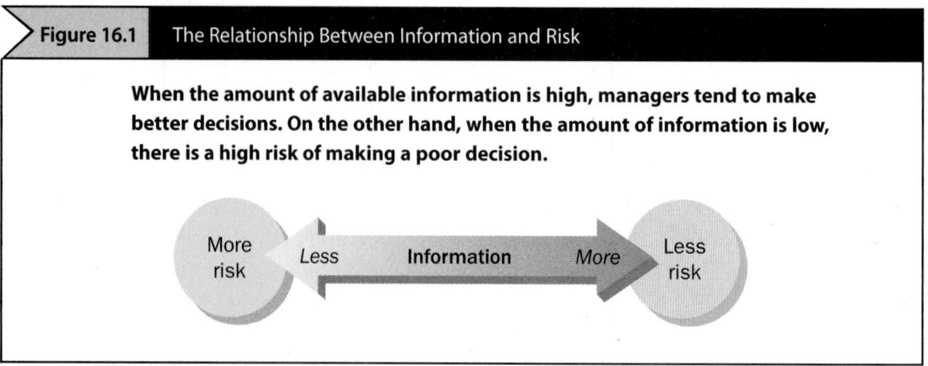

examine the advertisements, they would have more information. If, in addition to allowing them to examine the advertisements, the marketing manager circulated a report containing the reactions of a group of target consumers to each of the two advertisements, the team would have even more information with which to work. Thus, information, when understood properly, produces knowledge and empowers managers and employees to make better decisions.

Information Rules

Marketing research continues to show that discounts influence almost all car buyers. Simply put, if dealers lower their prices, they will sell more cars. This relationship between buyer behavior and price can be thought of as an information rule that usually will guide the marketing manager correctly. An information rule emerges when research confirms the same results each time that it studies the same or a similar set of circumstances.

Because of the volume of information they receive each day and their need to make decisions on a daily basis, businesspeople try to accumulate information rules to shorten the time they spend analyzing choices. Information rules are the "great simplifiers" for all decision makers. Business research is continuously looking for new rules that can be put to good use and looking to discredit old ones that are no longer valid. This ongoing process is necessary because business conditions rarely stay the same for very long.

The Difference Between Data and Information

Many people use the terms *data* and *information* interchangeably, but the two differ in important ways. **Data** are numerical or verbal descriptions that usually result from some sort of measurement. (The word *data* is plural; the singular form is datum.) Your current wage level, the amount of last year's after-tax profit for Motorola, and the current retail prices of Honda automobiles are all data. Most people think of data as being numerical only, but they can be nonnumerical as well. A description of an individual as a "tall, athletic person with short, dark hair" certainly would qualify as data.

data numerical or verbal descriptions that usually result from some sort of measurement

information data presented in a form that is useful for a specific purpose

Information is data presented in a form that is useful for a specific purpose. Suppose that a human resources manager wants to compare the wages paid to male and female employees over a period of five years. The manager might begin with a stack of computer printouts listing every person employed by the firm, along with each employee's current and past wages. The manager would be hard pressed to make any sense of all the names and numbers. Such printouts consist of data rather than information.

Now suppose that the manager uses a computer to graph the average wages paid to men and to women in each of the five years. The result is information because the manager can use it for the purpose at hand—to compare wages paid to men with those paid to women over the five-year period. For a manager, information presented in a practical, useful form such as a graph simplifies the decision-making process.

The average company maintains a great deal of data that can be transformed into information. Typical data include records pertaining to personnel, inventory, sales, and accounting. Often each type of data is stored in individual departments within an organization. However, the data can be used more effectively when they are organized

Is there a database in that box? No, it's an IBM z9 mainframe computer. IBM computers are often used by large companies to store, update, and process the information used by people throughout an organization. The z9 IBM mainframe computer is one of the most sophisticated, secure computing systems ever built and is equipped with 18 billion transistors—three for every person on the planet.

into a database. A **database** is a single collection of data and information stored in one place that can be used by people throughout an organization to make decisions. Although databases are important, the way the data and information are used is even more important—and more valuable to the firm. As a result, management information experts now use the term **knowledge management (KM)** to describe a firm's procedures for generating, using, and sharing the data and information. Typically, data, information, databases, and KM all become important parts of a firm's management information system.

2

Discuss management's information requirements.

What Is a Management Information System?

A **management information system (MIS)** is a system that provides managers and employees with the information they need to perform their jobs as effectively as possible. The purpose of an MIS (sometimes referred to as an information technology system or simply IT system) is to distribute timely and useful information from both internal and external sources to the managers and employees who need it (see Figure 16.2). Today, most medium-sized to large business firms have an information technology (IT) officer. An **information technology (IT) officer** is a manager at the executive level who is responsible for ensuring that a firm has the equipment necessary to provide the information the firm's employees and managers need to make effective decisions.

Today's typical MIS is built around a computerized system of record-keeping and communications software so that it can provide information based on a wide variety of data. After all, the goal is to provide needed information to all employees and managers.

A Firm's Information Requirements

Employees and managers have to plan for the future, implement their plans in the present, and evaluate results against what has been accomplished in the past. Of course, the specific types of information they need depend on their work area and on their level within the firm.

Today, many firms are organized into five areas of management: *finance, operations, marketing, human resources,* and *administration.* Managers in each of these areas need specific information in order to make decisions.

database a single collection of data and information stored in one place that can be used by people throughout an organization to make decisions

knowledge management (KM) a firm's procedures for generating, using, and sharing the data and information

management information system (MIS) a system that provides managers and employees with the information they need to perform their jobs as effectively as possible

information technology (IT) officer a manager at the executive level who is responsible for ensuring that a firm has the equipment necessary to provide the information the firm's employees and managers need to make effective decisions

Figure 16.2 Management Information System (MIS)

After an MIS is installed, employers and managers can get information directly from the MIS without having to go through other people in the organization.

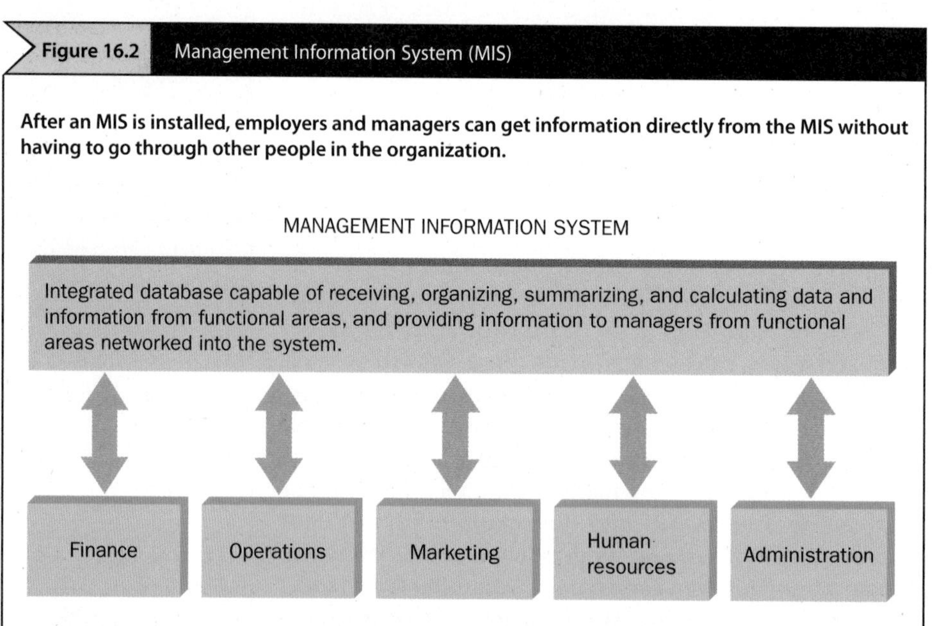

Source: Ricky W. Griffin, *Management*, 10/e (Mason, OH: Cengage Learning, 2011). Reprinted by permission.

- *Financial managers* obviously are most concerned with their firm's finances. They study its debts and receivables, cash flow, future capitalization needs, financial statements, and other accounting information. Of equal importance to financial managers is information about the present state of the economy, interest rates, and predictions of business conditions in the future.
- *Operations managers* are concerned with present and future sales levels, current inventory levels of work in process and finished goods, and the availability and cost of the resources required to produce products and services. They also must keep abreast of any innovative production technology that might be useful to the firm.
- *Marketing managers* need to have detailed information about their firm's products and the products offered by competitors. Such information includes pricing strategies, new promotional campaigns, and products that competitors are test marketing. Information concerning the firm's customers, current and projected market share, and new and pending product legislation is also important to marketing managers.

Numbers and charts. What does it all mean? Good question. The fact is that few managers and employees would be able to perform their jobs without accurate and up-to-date information. Because it is so important, most organizations invest large amounts of money to ensure that the firm's employees have access to the information they need to make decisions on a daily basis.

- *Human resources managers* must be aware of anything that pertains to the firm's employees. Key examples include current wage levels and benefits packages both within the firm and in firms that compete for valuable employees, current legislation and court decisions that affect employment practices, union activities, and the firm's plans for growth, expansion, or mergers.
- *Administrative managers* are responsible for the overall management of the organization. Thus, they are concerned with the coordination of information—just as they are concerned with the coordination of material, human, and financial resources.

First, administrators must ensure that all employees have access to the information they need to do their jobs.

Second, administrative managers must also ensure that the information is used in a consistent manner throughout the firm. Suppose, for example, that General Electric (GE) is designing a new plant that will open in five years. GE's management will want answers to many questions: Is the capacity of the plant consistent with marketing plans based on sales projections? Will human resources managers be able to staff the plant on the basis of employment forecasts? And do sales projections indicate enough income to cover the expected cost of the plant?

Third, administrative managers must make sure that all managers and employees are able to use the IT that is available. Certainly, this requires that all employees receive the skills training required to use the firm's MIS. Finally, administrative managers must commit to the costs of updating the firm's MIS and providing additional training when necessary.

Size and Complexity of the System

An MIS must be tailored to the needs of the organization it serves. In some firms, a tendency to save on initial costs may result in a system that is too small or overly simple. Such a system generally ends up serving only one or two management levels or a single department. Managers in other departments "give up" on the system as soon as they find that it cannot process their data.

Almost as bad is an MIS that is too large or too complex for the organization. Unused capacity and complexity do nothing but increase the cost of owning and operating the system. In addition, a system that is difficult to use probably will not be used at all.

Outline the five functions of an information system.

How Do Employees Use a Management Information System?

To provide information, a management information system (MIS) must perform five specific functions. It must (1) collect data, (2) store the data, (3) update the data, (4) process the data into information, and (5) present the information to users (see Figure 16.3).

Step 1: Collecting Data

A firm's employees, with the help of an MIS system, must gather the data needed to establish the firm's *data bank*. The data bank should include all past and current data that may be useful in managing the firm. Clearly, the data entered into the system must be *relevant* to the needs of the firm's managers. And perhaps most important, the data must be *accurate*. Irrelevant data are simply useless; inaccurate data can be disastrous. There are two data sources: *internal* and *external*.

Internal Sources of Data Typically, most of the data gathered for an MIS come from internal sources. The most common internal sources of information are managers and employees, company records and reports, and minutes of meetings.

Past and present accounting data can also provide information about the firm's transactions with customers, creditors, and suppliers. Sales reports are a source of data on sales, pricing strategies, and the effectiveness of promotional campaigns.

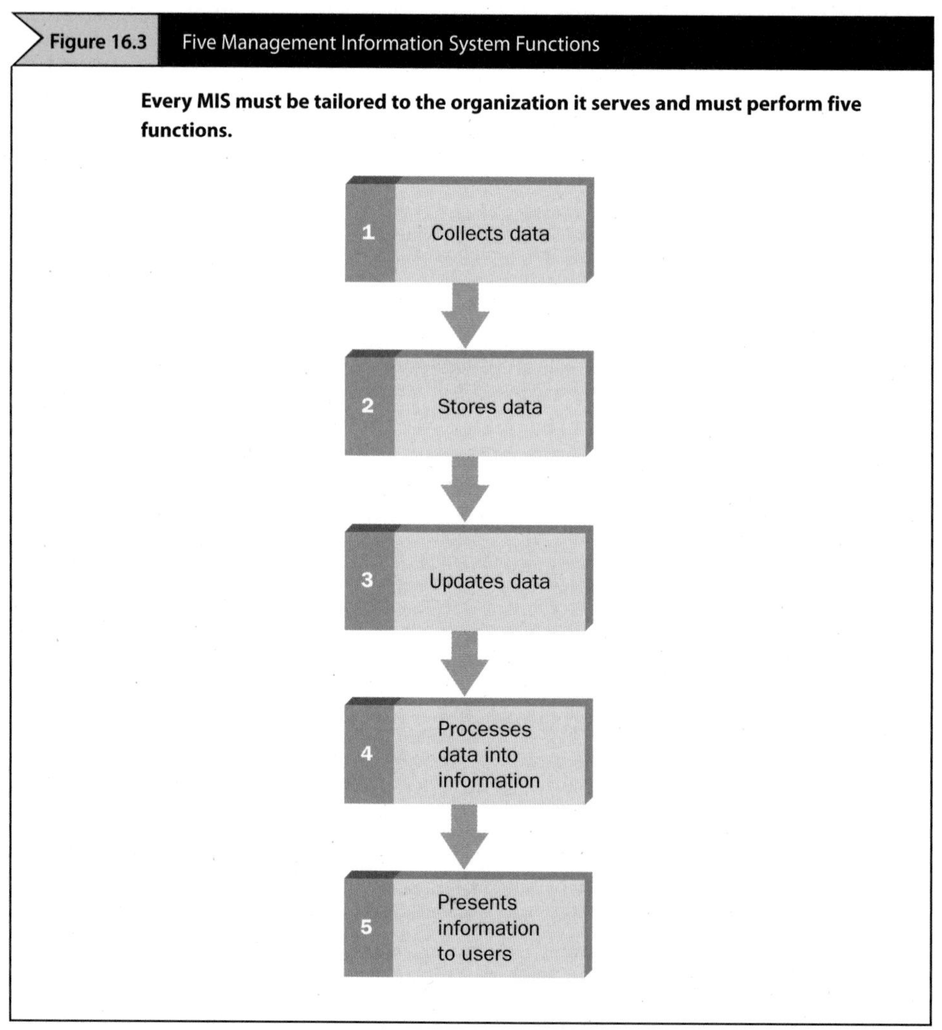

Figure 16.3 Five Management Information System Functions

Every MIS must be tailored to the organization it serves and must perform five functions.

Human resources records are useful as a source of data on wage and benefits levels, hiring patterns, employee turnover, and other personnel variables.

Present and past production forecasts also should be included in the firm's data bank, along with data indicating how well these forecasts predicted actual events. Specific plans and management decisions—regarding capital expansion and new product development, for example—should be incorporated into the MIS system.

SPOTLIGHT

More Computers in Record Numbers

In an attempt to gather information, individuals and businesses are purchasing more computers in record numbers. (Numbers represent actual sales or sales projections for computers around the globe—in millions.)

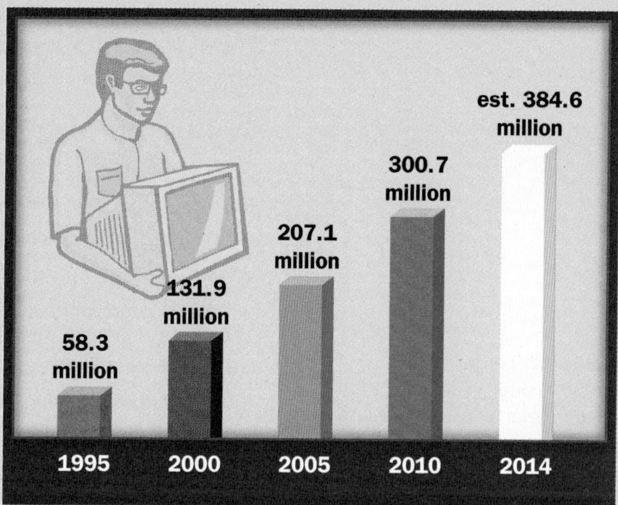

Source: The Computer Industry Almanac, Inc. Web site at http://www.c-i-a.com (accessed May 25, 2010).

External Sources of Data External sources of data include customers, suppliers, bankers, trade and business publications, industry conferences, online computer services, government sources, and firms that specialize in gathering data for organizations. For example, a marketing research company may acquire forecasts pertaining to product demand, consumer tastes, and other marketing variables. Suppliers are also an excellent source of information about the future availability and costs of raw materials and component parts. Bankers often can provide valuable economic insights and projections. The information furnished by trade and business publications and industry conferences is usually concerned as much with future projections as with present conditions. Legal issues and court decisions that may affect a firm are discussed occasionally in local newspapers and, more often, in specialized publications such as *The Wall Street Journal, Fortune,* and *BusinessWeek*. Government publications such as the *Monthly Labor Review* and the *Federal Reserve Bulletin* are also quite useful as sources of external data, as are a number of online computer services.

Whether the source of the data is internal or external, always remember the following three cautions:

1. The cost of obtaining data from some external sources, such as marketing research firms, can be quite high.
2. Outdated or incomplete data usually yield inaccurate information.
3. Although computers generally do not make mistakes, the people who use them can make or cause errors. When data (or information) and your judgment disagree, always check the data.

Step 2: Storing Data

An MIS must be capable of storing data until they are needed. Typically, the method chosen to store data depends on the size and needs of the organization. Small businesses may enter data and then store them directly on the hard drive inside an employee's computer. Generally, medium-sized to large businesses store data in a larger computer system and provide access to employees through a computer network. Today, networks take on many configurations and are designed by specialists who work with a firm's IT personnel to decide on what's best for the company.

Step 3: Updating Data

Today, an MIS must be able to update stored data regularly to ensure that the information presented to managers and employees is accurate, complete, and up-to-date. The frequency with which the data are updated depends on how fast they change and how often they are used. When it is vital to have current data, updating may occur as soon as the new data are available. For example, Giant Food, a grocery store chain operating in the eastern part of the United States, has cash registers that automatically transmit data on each item sold to a central computer. The computer adjusts the store's inventory records accordingly. In some systems, the computer may even be programmed to reorder items whose inventories fall below some specified level. Data and information may also be entered into a firm's data bank at certain intervals—every 24 hours, weekly, or monthly.

Step 4: Processing Data

Some data are used in the form in which they are stored, whereas other data require processing to extract, highlight, or summarize the information they contain. **Data processing** is the transformation of data into a form that is useful for a specific purpose.

For verbal data, this processing consists mainly of extracting the pertinent material from storage and combining it into a report. Most business data, however, are in the form of numbers—large groups of numbers, such as daily sales totals or production costs for a specific product. Fortunately, computers can be programmed to process such large volumes of numbers quickly. While such groups of numbers may be difficult to handle and to comprehend, their contents can be summarized through the use of statistics. A **statistic** is a measure that summarizes a particular characteristic of an entire group of numbers.

data processing the transformation of data into a form that is useful for a specific purpose

statistic a measure that summarizes a particular characteristic of an entire group of numbers

Why visual displays are important! Visual displays, like the bar chart in this photo, are often more interesting than if the same information was described in a written report. Here, food costs (as a percent of budget) for people in different countries are illustrated using a bar chart. Because it's easier to compare data when visual displays are used, the eye can quickly pick out the most important information.

© AP Images/PRNewsFoto/National Corn Growers Association

Step 5: Presenting Information

An MIS must be capable of presenting information in a usable form. That is, the method of presentation—reports, tables, graphs, or charts, for example—must be appropriate for the information itself and for the uses to which it will be put.

Business Reports Verbal information may be presented in list or paragraph form. Employees often are asked to prepare formal business reports. A typical business report includes (1) an introduction, (2) the body of the report, (3) the conclusions, and (4) the recommendations.

The *introduction*, which sets the stage for the remainder of the report, describes the problem to be studied in the report, identifies the research techniques that were used, and previews the material that will be presented in the report. The *body* of the report should objectively describe the facts that were discovered in the process of completing the report. The body also should provide a foundation for the conclusions and the recommendations. The *conclusions* are statements of fact that describe the finding contained in the report. They should be specific, practical, and based on the evidence contained in the report. The *recommendations* section presents suggestions on how the problem might be solved. Like the conclusions, the recommendations should be specific, practical, and based on the evidence.

Visual Displays and Tables A visual display can also be used to present information and may be a diagram that represents several items of information in a manner that makes comparison easier. Figure 16.4 illustrates examples of visual displays generated by a computer. Typical visual displays include:

- Graphs
- Bar charts
- Pie charts

A tabular display is used to present verbal or numerical information in columns and rows. It is most useful in presenting information about two or more related variables. A table, for example, can be used to illustrate the number of salespeople in each region of the country, sales for different types of products, and total sales for all products (see Table 16.1). Information that is to be manipulated—for example, to calculate loan payments—is usually displayed in tabular form.

Tabular displays generally have less impact than visual displays. However, displaying the information that could be contained in a multicolumn table such as Table 16.1 would require several bar or pie charts.

Figure 16.4 Typical Visual Displays Used in Business Presentations

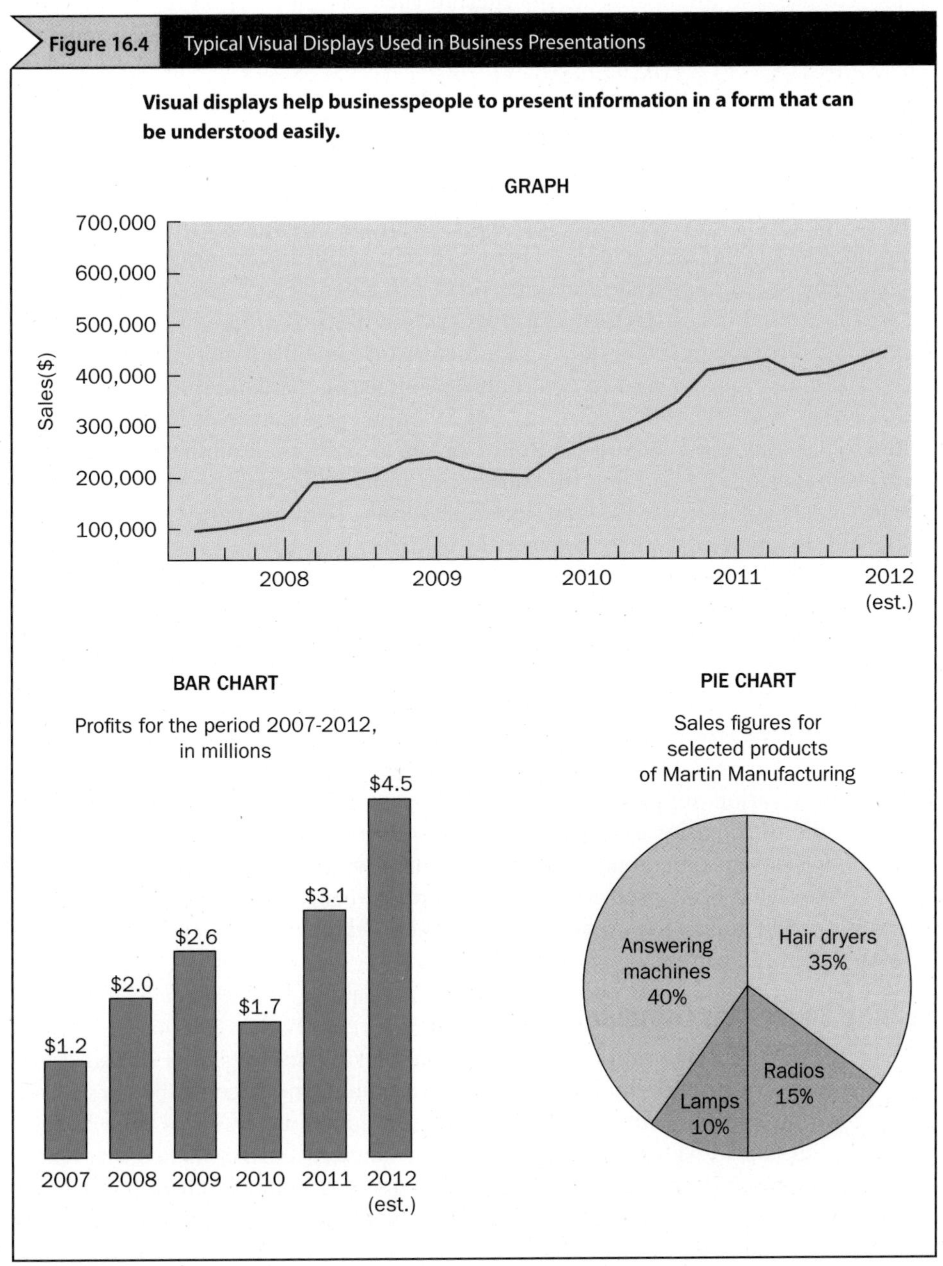

Table 16.1 Typical Three-Column Table Used in Business Presentations			
Tables are most useful for displaying information about two or more variables.			
All-Star Technology Projected Sales			
Section of the Country	Number of Salespeople	Consumer Products ($)	Industrial Products ($)
Eastern territory	15	1,500,000	3,500,000
Midwestern territory	20	2,000,000	5,000,000
Western territory	10	1,000,000	4,000,000
TOTAL	45	4,500,000	12,500,000

Describe how computers and technology help improve productivity, decision making, communications, sales, and recruiting and training.

Improving Productivity with the Help of Computers and Technology

In this section, we examine several solutions to challenges created when a firm or its employees use computers and the Internet. In each case, a solution is always evaluated in terms of its costs and compared with the benefits a firm receives, generally referred to as a *cost/benefit analysis*. Typical areas of concern for a business include decision making, communications, sales, recruiting and training employees, business software applications, and virtual offices.

Making Smart Decisions

How do managers and employees sort out relevant and useful information from the spam, junk mail, and useless data? Three different applications can actually help to improve and speed the decision-making process for people at different levels within an organization. First, a **decision-support system (DSS)** is a type of computer program which provides relevant data and information to help a firm's employees make decisions. It also can be used to determine the effect of changing different variables and answer "what if" type questions. For example, a manager at Michigan-based Pulte Homes may use a DSS to determine prices for new homes built in an upscale, luxury subdivision. By entering the number of homes that will be built along with different costs associated with land, labor, materials, building permits, promotional costs, and all other costs, a DSS can help to determine a base price for each new home. It is also possible to increase or decrease the building costs and determine new home prices for each set of assumptions with a DSS. Although similar to a DSS, an **executive information system (EIS)** is a computer-based system that facilitates and supports the decision-making needs of top managers and senior executives by providing easy access to both internal and external information.

An **expert system** is a type of computer program that uses artificial intelligence to imitate a human's ability to think. An expert system uses a set of rules that analyze information supplied by the user about a particular activity or problem. Based on the information supplied, the expert system then provides recommendations or suggests specific actions in order to help make decisions. Expert systems, for example, have been used to schedule manufacturing tasks, diagnose illnesses, determine credit limits for credit-card customers, evaluate loan applications, and develop electronic games.

decision-support system (DSS) a type of computer program that provides relevant data and information to help a firm's employees make decisions

executive information system (EIS) a computer-based system that facilitates and supports the decision-making needs of top managers and senior executives by providing easy access to both internal and external information

expert system a type of computer program that uses artificial intelligence to imitate a human's ability to think

Helping Employees Communicate

One of the first business applications of computer technology was e-mail. Once software was chosen and employees trained, communications could be carried out globally within and outside a firm at any time, 24 hours a day, seven days a week. Today, e-mail is also being used as a direct link between businesses and customers. For example, many brokerage and financial firms like Charles Schwab and Fidelity Investments use e-mail to stay in contact with customers and promote different investment products.

Today, employers expect that their employees will be able to use e-mail to communicate with other employees and customers. Although it takes practice, the following seven tips will help you improve your ability to effectively use e-mails.

1. *Most Important:* Think about what you are really saying in an e-mail. Don't put something in an e-mail that you wouldn't say face-to-face to another person. In addition, remember that it is very easy for the reader to forward your e-mail to everyone in the company—even when it was meant for just the original reader.
2. Write perfect subject lines. After your name, the subject line is often the next information the reader sees. Make sure your subject line captures the reader's attention.
3. Talk about one subject in an e-mail. Including more than one idea, concept, or issue in an e-mail can make your e-mail confusing.
4. Keep e-mails short. Long e-mails with long sentences intimidate readers. Often, readers skip important information and miss the most important point because they get tired of reading.
5. Be careful when using all caps. Using ALL CAPS is like shouting and should only be used when you really want to emphasize an important point.
6. Do not use the reply all option unless everyone needs to see your response. Send your response to only the people who really need to see it.
7. Don't hit the send button until you are ready to send the e-mail. Often, people accidentally hit the send button before they are finished writing an e-mail. A better approach is to leave the address line blank until you have finished and reread your e-mail. Once completed, enter the address of the recipients(s) and hit send.

Groupware is one of the latest types of software that facilitates the management of large projects among geographically dispersed employees, as well as such group activities as problem solving and brainstorming. Suppose that the home office of a software development firm in a major city has been hired to prepare customized software for a client in another city. The project team leader uses groupware to establish guidelines for the project, check availability of employees around the world, give individuals specific work assignments, and set up a schedule for work completion, testing, and final installation on the client's computer. The team leader is able to monitor work progress and may intervene if asked or if problems develop. When needed, people from various locations, possessing an array of knowledge and skills, can be called to the "workspace" created on the computer system for their contribution. When the work is finally completed, it can be forwarded to the client's computer and installed.

Besides being useful in project management, groupware provides an opportunity to establish a collaborative learning system to help solve a specific problem. A **collaborative learning system** is a work environment that allows problem-solving participation by all team members. By posting a question or problem on the groupware site, the team leader invites members, who may be located anywhere in the world, to submit messages that can help to move the group toward a solution.

Assisting the Firm's Sales Force

Internet-based software application programs, sometimes referred to as customer relationship management programs, focus on the special information needs of sales personnel. For example, sales force automation programs support sales representatives with organized databases of information such as names of clients, status of pending orders, and sales leads and opportunities, as well as any related advice or recommendations from other company personnel. Consider what happens when a sales representative for the pharmaceutical division of a company such as Johnson & Johnson is planning to visit doctors, health care providers, and hospitals in the Chicago area. A sales force automation software program can provide information about what the results were of the last contacts, who else in the pharmaceutical firm has interacted with the client, and previous purchases the client has made.

groupware one of the latest types of software that facilitates the management of large projects among geographically dispersed employees as well as such group activities as problem solving and brainstorming

collaborative learning system a work environment that allows problem solving participation by all team members

Entrepreneurial SUCCESS

Apps Become Big Business

Apps—small software programs that users download to run on cell phones and iPods—are becoming big business. Some apps, such as the game Trism, are just for fun; some, such as Recorder, which records voices with the touch of a button, have both business and personal uses.

In the past 18 months, more than 3 billion apps for iPhones and iPods have been downloaded from Apple's App Store. With Microsoft, Google, and many other companies setting up sites featuring apps for handheld wireless devices, experts see app sales soaring to $30 billion within a few years. No wonder thousands of entrepreneurs are busy developing and marketing apps for consumer and business use.

Steve Demeter, who created Trism for the iPhone, is a successful app entrepreneur. He began as a software developer for a major bank but spent nights and weekends writing and polishing the code for Trism. After his game was ready for release, Demeter submitted it for App Store approval and sent copies to influential reviewers. The game was an instant sensation, generating thousands of dollars in sales in its first two months. Now Demeter is a full-time app developer, with a number of promising ideas in the works. He tells budding app entrepreneurs to ask themselves: "Does my app convey something unique and interesting in 10 to 15 seconds?"

© AP Images/PRNewsFoto/Apple

Sources: Bill Shea, "New iPad May Fuel 'Gold Rush' for App Makers," *Crain's Detroit Business*, February 1, 2010, 1; Douglas MacMillan, Peter Burrows, and Spencer E. Ante, "Inside the App Economy," *BusinessWeek*, October 22, 2009, http://www.businessweek.com/magazine/content/09_44/b4153044881892.htm; Gary Marshall, "App Store Millionaires Share Their Secrets," *Tech Radar*, February 5, 2009, http://www.techradar.com/news/phone-and-communications/other-phones/app-store-millionaires-share-their-secrets-524586; Kira Bindrim, "Big App-le, indeed: Rush Is on," *Crain's New York Business*, October 19, 2009, 2.

As sales representatives complete their visits, information about what was learned should be entered into the sales force automation system as soon as possible so that everyone can use the latest information.

Recruiting and Training Employees

A common icon on most corporate Web sites is a link to "Careers" or "Employment Opportunities." Firms looking for people with specialized skills can post their employee needs on their Web sites and reach potential candidates from around the globe. This is an extremely important method of recruiting employees for positions where labor shortages are common and individuals with the *right* skills are in high demand.

Furthermore, software programs can help large firms such as GE, ExxonMobil, and General Mills to establish a database of potential employees. This is an especially important function for a firm that receives thousands of unsolicited employment applications from people all over the world. The cost of organizing and processing this information is high, but software can reduce this expense when compared with a paper-based system.

Large and midsize companies also spend a great deal of money on educational and training programs for employees. By distributing information about the firm, products and services, new procedures, and general information to employees through the Internet for reading and study at convenient times and places, firms can reduce training costs dramatically. Often, these sites may be needed only on rare occasions; however, it is important that employees know that the information exists and where it is. Furthermore, revision and distribution of changes to this type of information are much easier if the information is provided on the company's Web site.

Telecommuting, Virtual Offices, and Technology

Today more and more employees are using telecommuting, virtual offices, and technology to perform typical work activities. In Chapter 10, *telecommuting* was defined as employees working at home all the time or for a portion of the work week. Although we do not want to cover the same topic again, it is important to understand how technology enables workers to work any place—at home, in an airport, in a hotel room, or even in an automobile. Simply put: The ability to use technology—computers, e-mail, software, the Internet, and phones—makes telecommuting and virtual offices a reality. Although there are different definitions of a virtual office, for our purposes a **virtual office** allows employees to work at any place where they have access to computers, software, and other technology that enables them to perform their normal work activities.

For both employees and employers, the chief benefits of telecommuting and virtual offices include:

- Higher job satisfaction and increased productivity.
- Greater independence and flexible work hours.
- Reduced commuting costs and time required to commute to an office.
- Lower employee turnover.
- New employment opportunities for employees with physical disabilities, new mothers, and people living in remote areas.

Improving productivity is just a handheld device away. In a competitive business environment, a company's sales representatives must stay in contact with their customers. In this photo, a sales representative is text messaging information about current inventory levels and product availability to one of his customers.

© Vicki Beaver

Although experts predict that the use of telecommuting, virtual offices, and technology will all increase in the future, there are certain factors to consider that can create problems for employees working in a virtual office. Typical challenges include feelings of isolation and exploitation, working too many hours, lack of support from managers, inability to access needed files and information, and fear of performance evaluations. Still, employers have found that if the right person is selected, the benefits of telecommuting and virtual offices outweigh the disadvantages. The key is often finding the right person.

Business Applications Software

Early software typically performed a single function. Today, however, *integrated* software combines many functions in a single package. Integrated packages allow for the easy *linking* of text, numerical data, graphs, photographs, and even audiovisual clips. A business report prepared using the Microsoft Office package, for instance, can include all these components.

Integration offers at least two other benefits. Once data have been entered into an application in an integrated package, the data can be used in another integrated package without having to reenter the data again. In addition, once a user learns one application, it is much easier to learn another application in an integrated package. From a career standpoint, you should realize that employers will assume that you possess, or will possess after training, a high degree of working comfort with several of the software applications described in Table 16.2.

Computer Backup and Disaster Recovery

Anyone who has ever used a computer understands how frustrating it can be when data and information are lost. For individuals, the frustration often turns to anger, but life goes on. For a business, lost data and information can threaten the very existence of the firm and its ability to operate on a day-to-day basis. In fact, the majority

virtual office allows employees to work at any place where they have access to computers, software, and other technology that enables them to perform their normal work activities

Table 16.2	Current Business Application Software Used to Improve Productivity
Word processing	Users can prepare and edit written documents and store them in the computer or on a memory device.
Desktop publishing	Users can combine text and graphics in reports, newsletters, and pamphlets in professional reports.
Accounting	Users can record routine financial transactions and prepare financial reports at the end of the accounting period.
Database management	Users can electronically store large amounts of data and transform the data into information.
Graphics	Users can display and print pictures, drawings, charts, and diagrams.
Spreadsheets	Users can organize numerical data into a grid of rows and columns.

of businesses lose some data and information because of computer viruses, hackers, power failures, equipment breakdowns, defective software, and even floods, tornadoes, hurricanes, ice storms, and other natural disasters every year. Although many business owners think it won't happen to their firm, the risk is real. According to Symantec, a leading security software company, "the average small or midsize business has experienced three technology failures in the past 12 months, with the leading causes being virus or hacker attacks, power outages, and natural disasters. The cost of these outages: an estimated $15,000 per day."[2]

To avoid losing data and information stored on a computer system, most firms begin by creating backup files. **Computer backup** is a process of storing data, information, and computer systems on secondary computer systems that can be accessed if a firm's main computer system fails. Although no single set of guidelines will protect every business, computer experts recommend the following:[3]

- *Schedule data and information backups.* Although both manual and automated backup procedures can be established, automated procedures are usually preferred because manual systems are time-consuming and can be prone to errors.
- *Backup computer systems.* A business must also backup the computer systems that are needed to access recovered data and information.
- *Keep backups off-site.* A separate location for backup files is always recommended because of the possibility of a fire, flood, or other natural disaster destroying your primary computer system.
- *Test backup systems.* It is not enough to just develop a plan for data, information, and computer systems recovery. The plan must be tested on a regular basis to make sure that it works.

computer backup a process of storing data, information, and computer systems on secondary computer systems that can be accessed if a firm's main computer system fails

information society a society in which large groups of employees generate or depend on information to perform their jobs

Finally, a decision must be made to determine who is responsible for computer backup and disaster recovery. Many businesses choose to make their employees responsible for computer backup and disaster recovery. Other businesses choose outside vendors that will provide these important services for a fee. Regardless, the important point to remember is that a plan for computer backup and disaster recovery must be developed and then used to protect important data, information, and computer systems.

Analyze how computers and technology change the way information is acquired, organized, and used.

Using Computers and the Internet to Obtain Information

We live in a rapidly changing **information society**—that is, a society in which large groups of employees generate or depend on information to perform their jobs. Today, businesses are using the Internet to find and distribute information to global users. The Internet is also used for communicating between the firm's employees and its customers. Finally, businesses use the Internet to gather information about competitors' products, prices, and other business strategies. Clearly, the Internet is here to stay.

The Internet and Networks

The **Internet** is a worldwide network of computers linked through telecommunications. Enabling users around the world to communicate with each other electronically, the Internet provides access to a huge array of information sources. The Internet's most commonly used network for finding information is the World Wide Web. The **World Wide Web** (or more simply, **the Web**) is the Internet's multimedia environment of audio, visual, and text data. Today, connections to the Internet include simple telephone lines or faster digital subscriber lines (DSLs) and cabled broadband that carry larger amounts of data at quicker transfer speeds. **Broadband technology** is a general term referring to higher speed Internet connections that deliver data, voice, and video material. With new wireless technology, it is possible to access the Internet by using your laptop computer, cellular phone, and other wireless communications devices.

In addition to business sites, the World Wide Web has a wide array of government and institutional sites that provide information to a firm's employees and the general public. There are also online sites available for most of the popular business periodicals.

An **intranet** is a smaller version of the Internet for use within a firm. Using a series of customized Web pages, employees can quickly find information about their firm as well as connect to external sources. For instance, an employee might use the intranet to access the firm's policy documents on customer warranties or even take a company-designed course on new products and how to introduce them to customers. Generally, intranet sites are protected, and users must supply both a user name and a password to gain access to a company's intranet site. *Note:* Although the term *intranet* was popular in the 1990s, it was often confused with the Internet. Although still used today, many computer experts use the term *LAN* (which stands for local-area network) to describe intranet applications used within a company. More information about different types of computer networks, including LANs, is provided below.

Both the Internet and intranets are examples of a computer network. A **computer network** is a group of two or more computers linked together that allows users to share data and information. Today, two basic types of networks affect the way employees and the general public obtain data and information. A **wide-area network (WAN)** is a network that connects computers over a large geographic area, such as a city, a state, or even the world. The world's most popular WAN is the Internet.[4] In addition to the Internet, other WANs include private corporate networks (sometimes referred to as virtual private networks, or VPNs) and research networks. A **local-area network (LAN)** is a network that connects computers that are in close proximity to each other, such as an office building or a college campus. LANs allow users to share files, printers, games, or other applications.[5] Typically, LANs also allow users to connect to the Internet.

Accessing the Internet

In order to access the Internet or a computer network, computers and software must be standardized. Establishing standards is vital to ensuring that a Hewlett-Packard computer in McPherson, Kansas, can "talk" with a Dell computer in San Francisco, California.

The search for available information often begins with a specific Web site address or a search engine. Every Web site on the Internet is identified by its Uniform Resource Locator (URL), which acts as its address. To connect to a site, you enter its URL in your Web browser. A Web browser such as Windows Internet Explorer or Mozilla Firefox is software that helps users to navigate around the Internet and connect to different Web sites. The URLs of most corporate sites are similar to the organizations' real names. For instance, you can reach IBM by entering http://www.ibm.com. The first part of the entry, *http*, sets the software protocols

Internet a worldwide network of computers linked through telecommunications

World Wide Web (the Web) the Internet's multimedia environment of audio, visual, and text data

broadband technology a general term referring to higher speed Internet connections that deliver data, voice, and video material

intranet a smaller version of the Internet for use within a firm's computer network

computer network a group of two or more computers linked together that allows users to share data and information

wide-area network (WAN) a network that connects computers over a large geographic area, such as a city, a state, or even the world

local-area network (LAN) a network that connects computers that are in close proximity to each other, such as an office building or a college campus

for proper transfer of information between your computer and the one at the site to which you are connecting. *Http* stands for *HyperText Transfer Protocol.* Both http and www are frequently omitted from a URL because your computer adds them automatically when you enter the rest of the address. *HyperText* refers to words or phrases highlighted or underlined on a Web page; when you select these, they link you to other Web sites.

To find a particular Web site, you can take advantage of several free search programs available on the Web, such as Google, Yahoo!, and AltaVista. To locate a search engine, enter its URL in your browser. Some URLs for popular search engines are http://www.altavista.com, http://www.google.com, and http://www .yahoo.com.

The home page for many search engines provides a short list of primary topic divisions, such as careers, news, shopping, yellow pages, and weather, as well as a search window where you can enter the particular topic you are looking for.

Creating Web Sites

Today, employees and the general public connect to the Internet, enter a Web address, or use a search engine to access information. That information is presented on a Web site created and maintained by business firms; agencies of federal, state, or local governments; or educational or similar organizations. Because a Web site should provide accurate information, great care is required when creating a Web site. Generally, once a *template* or structure for the Web page has been created, content such as text or images can be inserted or changed readily, allowing the site to remain current.

What the Web site says about a company is important and should be developed carefully to portray the "right" image. Therefore, it is understandable that a firm without the internal human resources to design and launch its Web site will turn to

Often the search for information begins with a search engine like Yahoo! Internet search engines make finding information on the Internet easy. With a click of your computer's mouse, you can find the latest news stories, information about products and services, investment research, and even information about new movies and the current weather.

Table 16.3	Tips for Web Site Development	
Whether you build your site from scratch, use a Web design software program, or hire outside professionals, make sure that your Web site conveys not only the "right" image but also useful information about your company or organization.		
1.	Develop a theme.	A Web site is like a book and needs a theme to tie ideas together and tell an interesting story.
2.	Determine how much information to include on your site.	Get a handle on the type and amount of information that will be contained on your site. Although it is tempting to include everything, you must be selective.
3.	Plan the layout of your site.	Think about how you want your site to look. Web sites that combine color, art, and links to narrative material are the most useful.
4.	Add graphics.	Obtain graphics that illustrate the types of data and information contained on your site. Choose colors and photographs carefully to make sure that they add rather than detract from the site.
5.	Outline the material for each page.	Generally, the opening, or home, page contains basic information with links to additional pages that provide more detailed information.
6.	Develop plans to update the site.	It is important to develop a plan to update your site on a regular basis. Too often, sites are "forgotten" and contain dated or inaccurate material.
7.	Make sure that your site is easy to use.	Stand back and take a look at your site. Is your site confusing, or does it provide a road map to get from point A to point B? If you have trouble getting information, others will too.

the talents of creative experts available through Web consulting firms. Regardless of whether the Web site is developed by the firm's employees or outside consultants, the suggestions listed in Table 16.3 should be considered when creating materials for a firm's Web site.

Once a Web site is established, most companies prefer to manage their sites on their own computers. An alternative approach is to pay a hosting service that often will provide guaranteed user accessibility, e-business shopping software, site-updating services, and other specialized services.

Defining e-Business

6

Explain the meaning of e-business.

In Chapter 1, we defined *business* as the organized effort of individuals to produce and sell, for a profit, the products and services that satisfy society's needs. In a simple sense, then, **e-business**, or **electronic business**, can be defined as the organized effort of individuals to produce and sell, for a profit, the products and services that satisfy society's needs *through the facilities available on the Internet*. As you will see in the remainder of this chapter, e-business is transforming key business activities.

Organizing e-Business Resources

As noted in Chapter 1, to be organized, a business must combine *human, material, informational,* and *financial resources*. This is true of e-business, too (see Figure 16.5), but in this case, the resources may be more specialized than in a typical business. For example, people who can design, create, and maintain Web sites are only a fraction of the specialized human resources required by e-businesses. Material resources must include specialized computers, sophisticated equipment and software, and high-speed Internet connections. Computer programs that track the number of customers who view a firm's Web site are generally among

e-business (electronic business) the organized effort of individuals to produce and sell, for a profit, the products and services that satisfy society's needs through the facilities available on the Internet

Figure 16.5 Combining e-Business Resources

While all businesses use four resources (human, material, informational, and financial), these resources typically are more specialized when used in an e-business.

HUMAN RESOURCES		INFORMATIONAL RESOURCES
• Web site designers • Programmers • Web masters	→ BUSINESS ←	• Customer tracking systems • Order fulfillment and tracking systems • Online content-monitoring systems
MATERIAL RESOURCES		**FINANCIAL RESOURCES**
• Computers • Software • High-speed Internet connection lines	→ BUSINESS ←	• Investors interested in supporting e-business firms • Electronic payment from customers

outsourcing the process of finding outside vendors and suppliers that provide professional help, parts, or materials at a lower cost

One way to reduce customer service costs. Many American companies are outsourcing customer service to high-tech companies in India. The main reason: lower labor costs for educated and affordable customer service representatives. In this photo, future customer service employees attend a class at Infosys Technologies' training center at its sprawling corporate campus in Mysore, India.

the specialized informational resources required. Financial resources, the money required to start and maintain the firm and allow it to grow, usually reflect greater participation by individual entrepreneurs and investors willing to invest in a high-tech firm instead of conventional financial sources such as banks.

In an effort to reduce the cost of specialized resources that are used in e-business, many firms have turned to outsourcing. **Outsourcing** is the process of finding outside vendors and suppliers that provide professional help, parts, or materials at a lower cost. For example, a firm that needs specialized software to complete a project may turn to an outside firm located in another part of the United States, India, or an Eastern European country.

Satisfying Needs Online

Think for a moment about this question: "Why do people use the Internet?" For most people, the Internet can be used to purchase products or services and as a source of information and interaction with other people. Today, more people use the Internet to satisfy these needs than ever before. Let's start with two basic assumptions.

- The Internet has created some new customer needs that did not exist before creation of the Internet.
- e-Businesses can satisfy those needs, as well as more traditional ones.

Restoration Hardware (http://www.restorationhardware.com), for instance, gives customers anywhere in the world access to the same virtual store of hardware and decorative items. And at eBay's global auction site, customers can, for a small fee, buy and sell almost anything. In each of these examples, customers can use the Internet to purchase a product or service.

Ethical Challenges & SUCCESSFUL SOLUTIONS

The Ethics of Ethical Hacking

Can hacking be ethical? That's the question at the heart of the debate over ethical hacking, in which security experts test the vulnerability of a computer network to outside attacks by criminal or malicious hackers. The goal of ethical hacking is to identify a network's weak points and strengthen defenses against data corruption or theft.

Many companies use ethical hacking to guard against criminal hacking. NCR, one of the world's largest ATM manufacturers, funds ethical-hacking research to stop would-be hackers and viruses before crimes occur. NCR worked with the University of Abertay, Dundee in Scotland to create undergraduate and graduate courses in ethical hacking. The U.S. Department of Defense requires its computer security professionals to meet specific guidelines for analyzing and responding to unauthorized network entry. One way to meet those requirements is by becoming a Certified Ethical Hacker.

However, is it ethical for security researchers at universities or independent companies to use hacking as they study system intrusions? One university researcher says that his actions in detecting and halting a particular hacking attack could be misconstrued as illegal. Rather than wait for government authorities to go through the lengthy process of investigating and taking action, the researcher decided he had to move quickly to identify the firms at risk and stop the damage, even before he received official permission. "We are studying criminal activity, and some of the things we do can't be distinguished from the criminals themselves," the researcher says. Do you think this kind of hacking is ethical?

Sources: Elizabeth Montalbano, "DoD Approves Ethical Hacker Certification," *InformationWeek*, March 2, 2010, http://www.informationweek.com; Alan Cane, "Data Fills the Airwaves—But Who Is Listening In?" *Financial Times*, June 18, 2009, 4; "NCR, University Join to Fight ATM Fraud," *American Banker*, August 10, 2009, 6; Jon Brodkin, "The Legal Risks of Ethical Hacking," *Network World*, April 24, 2009, http://www.networkworld.com.

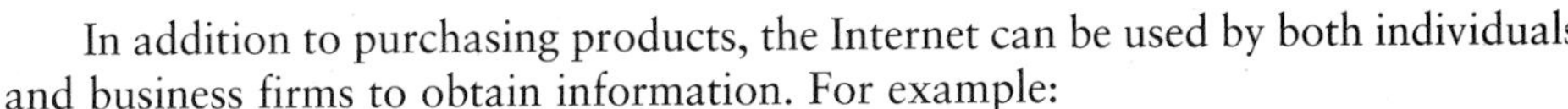

In addition to purchasing products, the Internet can be used by both individuals and business firms to obtain information. For example:

- Internet users can access newspapers, magazines, and radio and television programming at a time and place convenient to them.
- The Internet provides the opportunity for two-way interaction between an Internet firm and the viewer. A Web site like http://CNN.com and other news-content sites encourage dialogue among users in chat rooms and exchanges with the writers of articles posted to the site.
- Customers can respond to information on the Internet by requesting more information about a product or posing specific questions, which may lead to purchasing a product or service.
- Finally, the Internet allows customers to choose the content they are offered. Knowing the interests of a customer allows an Internet firm to direct appropriate, smart advertising to a specific customer. For example, someone wanting to read articles about the New York Yankees might be a potential customer for products and services related to baseball. For the advertiser, knowing that its advertisements are being directed to the most likely customers represents a better way to spend advertising dollars.

Creating e-Business Profit

Business firms can increase profits either by increasing sales revenue or by reducing expenses through a variety of e-business activities.

Increasing Sales Revenue Each source of sales revenue flowing into a firm is referred to as a **revenue stream**. One way to increase revenues is to sell merchandise on the Internet. Online merchants can reach a global customer base 24 hours a day, seven days a week because the opportunity to shop on the Internet is virtually unrestricted. However, shifting revenues earned from customers inside a real store to revenues earned from these same customers online does not create any real new revenue for a firm. The goal is to find *new customers* and generate *new sales* so that *total revenues are increased.*

revenue stream a source of revenue flowing into a firm

Got something to sell, then use eBay. For many consumers, the search for that hard-to-find item starts with accessing the eBay Web site. Started one weekend in 1995 when Pierre Omidyar wrote the software code for an auction Web site, eBay is now the world's largest online marketplace that enables trade on a local, national, and international basis.

© Vicki Beaver

Intelligent information systems also can help to generate sales revenue for Internet firms such as Amazon.com. Such systems store information about each customer's purchases, along with a variety of other information about the buyer's preferences. Using this information, the system can assist the customer the next time he or she visits the Web site. For example, if the customer has bought a Taylor Hicks or Carrie Underwood CD in the past, the system might suggest CDs by similar artists who have appeared on the popular televised talent-search program *American Idol*.

Although some customers in certain situations may not make a purchase online, the existence of the firm's Web site and the services and information it provides may lead to increased sales in the firm's physical stores. For example, http://Honda.com can provide basic comparative information for shoppers so that they are better prepared for their visit to an automobile showroom.

In addition to selling products or services online, e-business revenue streams are created by advertising placed on Web pages and by subscription fees charged for access to online services and content. For example, Hoover's Online (http://www.hoovers.com), a comprehensive source for company and industry information, makes some of its online content free for anyone who visits the site, but more detailed data are available only by paid subscription. In addition, it receives revenue from companies that are called sponsors, who advertise their products and services on Hoover's Web site.

Many Internet firms that distribute news, magazine and newspaper articles, and similar content generate revenue from commissions earned from sellers of products linked to the site. Online shopping malls, for example, now provide groups of related vendors of electronic equipment and computer hardware and software with a new method of selling their products and services. In many cases, the vendors share online sales revenues with the site owners.

Reducing Expenses Reducing expenses is the second major way in which e-business can help to increase profitability. Providing online access to information that customers want can reduce the cost of dealing with customers. Sprint Nextel (http://www.sprint.com), for instance, is just one company that maintains an extensive Web site where potential customers can learn more about cell phone products and services and current customers can access personal account information, send e-mail questions to customer service, and purchase additional products or services. With such extensive online services, Sprint Nextel does not have to maintain as many physical store locations as it would without these online services. We examine more examples of how e-business contributes to profitability throughout this chapter, especially as we focus on some of the business models for activity on the Internet.

Fundamental Models of e-Business

7

Describe the fundamental models of e-business.

One way to get a better sense of how businesses are adapting to the opportunities available on the Internet is to identify e-business models. A **business model** represents a group of common characteristics and methods of doing business to generate sales revenues and reduce expenses. Each of the models discussed in the following text represents a primary e-business model. Regardless of the type of business model, planning often depends on if the e-business is a new firm or an existing firm adding an online presence—see Figure 16.6. It also helps to remember the definition of e-business that was included at the beginning of the last section. Finally, keep in mind that to generate sales revenues and earn profits, a business—especially an e-business—must meet the needs of its customers.

Business-to-Business (B2B) Model

Many e-businesses can be distinguished from others simply by their customer focus. For instance, some firms use the Internet mainly to conduct business with other

Figure 16.6 Planning for a New Internet Business or Building an Online Presence for an Existing Business

The approach taken to creating an e-business plan will depend on whether you are establishing a new Internet business or adding an online component to an existing business.

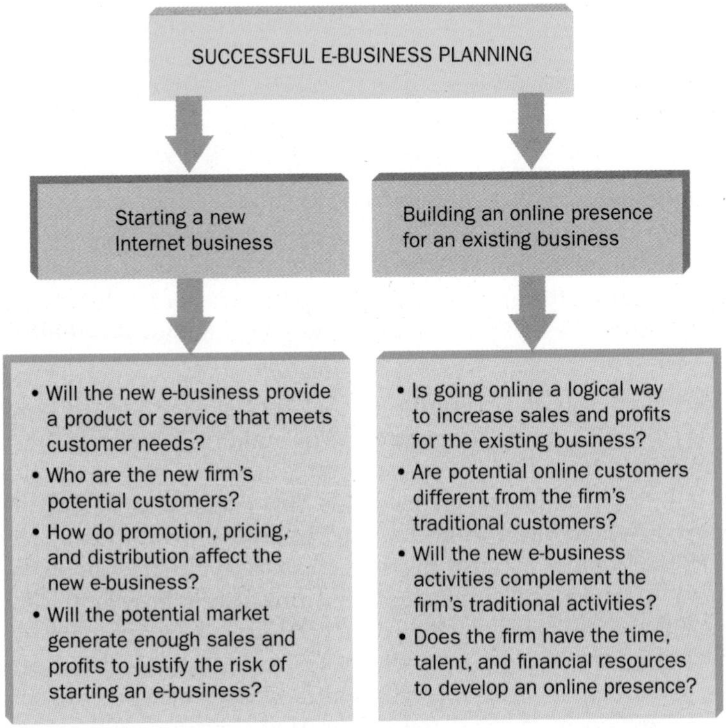

SUCCESSFUL E-BUSINESS PLANNING

Starting a new Internet business

- Will the new e-business provide a product or service that meets customer needs?
- Who are the new firm's potential customers?
- How do promotion, pricing, and distribution affect the new e-business?
- Will the potential market generate enough sales and profits to justify the risk of starting an e-business?

Building an online presence for an existing business

- Is going online a logical way to increase sales and profits for the existing business?
- Are potential online customers different from the firm's traditional customers?
- Will the new e-business activities complement the firm's traditional activities?
- Does the firm have the time, talent, and financial resources to develop an online presence?

business model represents a group of common characteristics and methods of doing business to generate sales revenues and reduce expenses

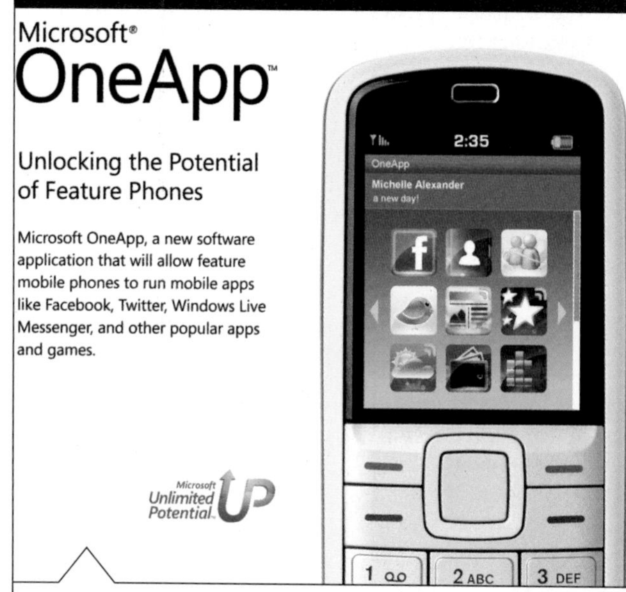

Microsoft's OneApp technology unlocks the potential of new phones. Using Microsoft's software application, cell phone users can access Facebook, Twitter, and Windows Live Messenger; pay bills; and get the latest news. What's nice about OneApp is that Microsoft (and programmers working with Microsoft) adds new applications for e-business on a regular basis.

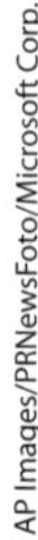

businesses. These firms are generally referred to as having a **business-to-business** (or **B2B**) **model**.

When examining B2B firms, two clear types emerge. In the first type, the focus is simply on facilitating sales transactions between businesses. For example, Dell manufactures computers to specifications that customers enter on the Dell Web site. A large portion of Dell's online orders are from corporate clients who are well-informed about the products they need and are looking for fairly priced, high-quality computer products that will be delivered quickly. Basically, by building only what is ordered, Dell reduces storage and carrying costs and rarely is stuck with unsold inventory. By dealing directly with Dell, customers eliminate costs associated with wholesalers and retailers, thereby helping to reduce the price they pay for equipment.

A second, more complex type of B2B model involves a company and its suppliers. Today, suppliers use the Internet to bid on products and services they wish to sell to a customer and learn about the customer's rules and procedures that must be followed. For example, Ford has developed a B2B model to link thousands of suppliers that sell the automobile maker parts worth billions of dollars each year. Although the B2B site is expensive to start and maintain, there are significant savings for Ford. Given the potential savings, it is no wonder that many other manufacturers and their suppliers are beginning to use the same kind of B2B systems that are used by the automakers. In fact, suppliers know that to be a "preferred" supplier for a large firm that may purchase large quantities of parts, supplies, or raw materials, they must be tied into the purchaser's B2B system.

Business-to-Consumer (B2C) Model

In contrast to the B2B model, firms such as Barnesandnoble.com and Landsend.com clearly are focused on individual consumers. These companies are referred to as having a **business-to-consumer** (or **B2C**) **model**. In a B2C situation, understanding how consumers behave online is critical to a firm's success. Typically, a business firm that uses a B2C model must answer the following questions:

- Will consumers use Web sites merely to simplify and speed up comparison shopping?
- Will consumers purchase services and products online or end up buying at a traditional retail store?
- What sorts of products and services are best suited for online consumer shopping?

In addition to providing round-the-clock global access to all kinds of products and services, B2C firms often attempt to build long-term relationships with their customers. Often, firms will make a special effort to make sure that the customer is satisfied and that problems, if any, are solved quickly. Specialized software also can help build good customer relationships. Tracking the decisions and buying preferences as customers navigate a Web site, for instance, helps management to make well-informed decisions about how best to serve such customers. In essence, this is Orbitz.com's online selling approach. By tracking and analyzing customer data, Orbitz can provide individualized service to its customers. Although a "little special attention" may increase the cost of doing business for a B2C firm, the customer's repeated purchases will repay the investment many times over.

business-to-business (or B2B) model a model used by firms that conduct business with other businesses

business-to-consumer (or B2C) model a model used by firms that focus on conducting business with individual consumers

Table 16.4	Other Business Models that Perform Specialized e-Business Activities
Although modified versions of B2B or B2C, these business models perform specialized e-business activities to generate revenues.	
Advertising e-business model	Advertisements that are displayed on a firm's Web site in return for a fee. Examples include pop-up and banner advertisements on search engines and other popular Internet sites.
Brokerage e-business model	Online marketplaces where buyers and sellers are brought together to facilitate exchange of goods and services. Examples include eBay (http://www.ebay.com), which provides a site for buying and selling virtually anything.
Consumer-to-consumer model	Peer-to-peer software that allows individuals to share information over the Internet. Examples include LimeWire (http://www.limewire.com), which allows users to exchange digital media files.
Subscription and pay-per-view e-business models	Content that is available only to users who pay a fee to gain access to a Web site. Examples include investment information provided by Standard & Poor's (http://www2.standardandpoors.com) and business research provided by Forrester Research, Inc. (http://www.forrester.com).

Today, B2B and B2C models are the most popular business models for e-business. And yet, there are other business models that perform specialized e-business activities to generate revenues. Most of the business models described in Table 16.4 are modified versions of the B2B and B2C models.

The Future of Computer Technology, the Internet, and e-Business

8

Explore the factors that will affect the future of e-business.

Since the beginning of commercial activity on the Internet, developments in computer technology and e-business have been rapid and formidable with spectacular successes such as Google, eBay, and Yahoo! However, the slowdown in e-business activity that began in 2000 caused a shakeout of excessive optimism in this new-business environment. Once again, a larger-than-usual number of technology companies and e-business firms struggled or even failed during the economic crisis that began in fall 2007. Today, most firms involved in computer technology and e-business use a more intelligent approach to development. The long-term view held by the vast majority of analysts is that the Internet and e-business will continue to expand along with related computer technologies. For example, according to Forrester Research, Inc., the popularity and growth of consumer broadband access to the Internet have pushed marketers to allocate more money to interactive marketing that utilizes computer technology to understand the customer's purchasing decisions. As a result, Forrester predicts that advertisers will spend more than $61 billion on interactive marketing by 2012.[6]

Internet Growth Potential

To date, only a small percentage of the global population uses the Internet. In 2010, estimates suggest that about 1.8 billion of the nearly 7 billion people in the world use the Web.[7] Clearly, there is much more growth opportunity. Americans comprise 12 percent of all users.[8] Of the 307 million people making up the American population, 223 million use the Internet. With approximately 73 percent of the American population already being Internet users, potential growth in the United States is limited.[9] On the other hand, the number of Internet users in the world's developing countries is expected to increase dramatically. There will also be additional growth as more people begin to use smart-phones and mobile devices. Because of worldwide growth and an increase in wireless computing devices, Computer Industry Almanac projects that worldwide users will exceed 2.1 billion by 2012.[10]

Firms that adapt existing business models to an online environment will continue to dominate development. For example, books, CDs, clothing, hotel

A new way to sell, market, train, and communicate. ReadyTalk allows users to use its Web meeting software to "meet" with clients located any place in the world. The software is easy to use and can be used for Web seminars, online meetings, and conference calls. Sessions can also be recorded for future use, which can save users both time and money.

accommodations, car rentals, and travel reservations are products and services well-suited to online buying and selling. These products or services will continue to be sold in the traditional way, as well as in a more cost-effective and efficient fashion over the Internet.

Although the number of global Internet users is expected to increase by 2012, that's only part of the story. Perhaps the more important question is why people are using the Internet. Internet users may want to obtain information about a firm's products or services. As mentioned earlier in this chapter, all experts agree that the number of businesses using the e-business B2B or B2C models to sell products or services or to provide customers with information is increasing. All experts agree that this trend will continue. In addition to obtaining information about products or services, many people use the Internet to become part of a social network. In addition to advertising through social media—a topic discussed in the marketing chapters—the Internet is often used to promote social network sites. A **social network site** is a Web site (often called a social site) that functions like an online community of Internet users where you can share your personal profile, messages, and photographs with family and friends. All social sites also provide users with a method to meet other people and gather and share information about special interests, hobbies, religion, and politics. Businesses like Dell Computer, Starbucks, and Macy's also use social sites to post information about products and services and obtain information from customers. The most common social networking sites include Facebook, MySpace, and Twitter. Some social sites, like LinkedIn, can also be useful when you are looking for employment or developing a network of professionals to help you advance your career. *CAUTION:* Prospective employers often use information on social sites to learn about future employees. Reading profiles and viewing photographs has become standard procedure for human resources departments in many companies. Therefore, think before you post inappropriate language or photographs on your social site.

Ethical and Legal Concerns

The social and legal concerns for the Internet and e-business extend beyond those shared by all businesses. Essentially, the Internet is a new "frontier" without borders and without much control by governments or other organizations.

Ethics and Social Responsibility Socially responsible and ethical behavior by individuals and businesses on the Internet are major concerns. For example, **spamming**, the sending of massive amounts of unsolicited e-mails, is an ethical issue. Sorting through what many recipients view as *junk e-mail* is, if nothing else, a waste of resources that costs the individual time and their employer money.

Another ethically questionable practice in cyberspace is the unauthorized access and use of information discovered through computerized tracking of users once they are connected to the Internet. Essentially, a user may visit a Web page and unknowingly receive a small piece of software code called a **cookie**. This cookie can track where the user goes on the Internet and measure how long the user stays at any particular Web site. Although this type of software may produce valuable customer information, it also can be viewed as an invasion of privacy, especially since users may not even be aware that their movements are being monitored.

Besides the unauthorized use of cookies to track online behavior, there are several other threats to users' privacy and confidentiality. Monitoring an employee's **log-file records**, which record the Web sites visited, may be intended to help employers

social network site a Web site (often called a social site) that functions like an online community of Internet users where you can share your profile, messages, and photographs with family and friends

spamming the sending of massive amounts of unsolicited e-mails

cookie a small piece of software sent by a Web site that tracks an individual's Internet use

log-file records files that store a record of the Web sites visited

police unauthorized Internet use on company time. However, the same records can also give a firm the opportunity to observe what otherwise might be considered private and confidential information. Today, legal experts suggest that, at the very least, employers need to disclose the level of surveillance to their employees and consider the corporate motivation for monitoring employees' behavior.

Some firms also practice data mining. **Data mining** refers to the practice of searching through data records looking for useful information. Customer registration forms typically require a variety of information before a user is given access to a site. When this is combined with customer-transaction records, data mining analysis can provide what might be considered private and confidential information about individuals or groups. For instance, assume an individual frequents a Web site that provides information about a life-threatening disease. If this information is sent to an insurance company, the company might refuse to insure this individual, thinking that there is a higher risk associated with someone who wants more information about this disease.

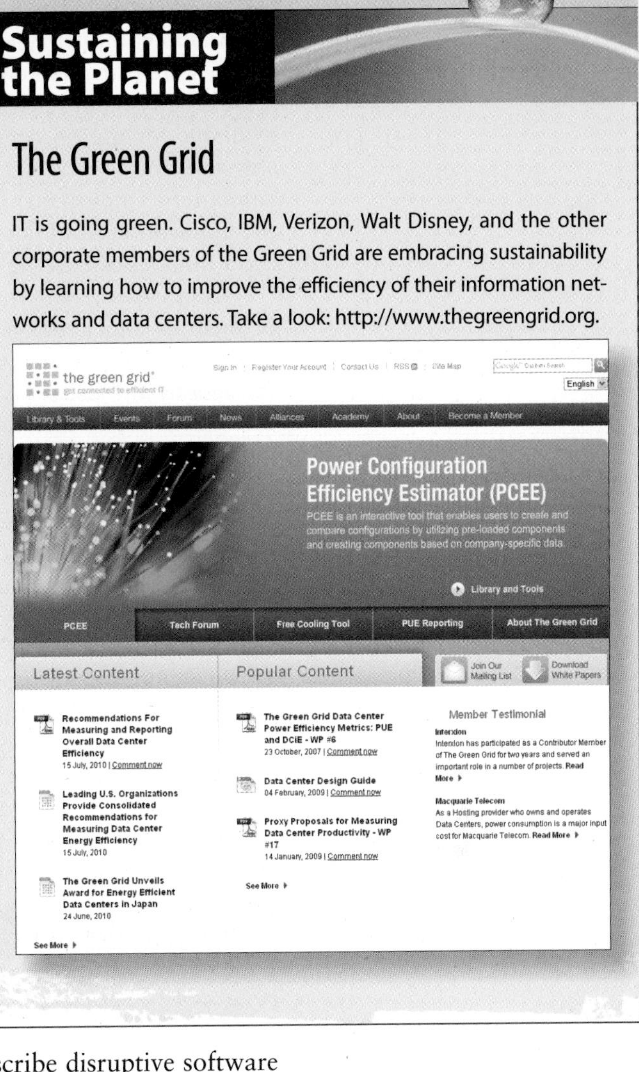

Internet Crime Because the Internet is often regarded as an unregulated frontier, both individuals and business users must be particularly aware of online risks and dangers. For example, a general term that describes software designed to infiltrate a computer system without the user's consent is **malware**. Malware is often based on the creator's criminal or malicious intent and can include computer viruses, spyware, deceptive adware, and other software capable of criminal activities. A more specific term used to describe disruptive software is computer virus. A **computer virus**, which can originate anywhere in the world, is a software code designed to disrupt normal computer activities. The potentially devastating effects of both malware and computer viruses have given rise to a software security industry.

In addition to the risk of computer viruses, identity theft is one of the most common computer crimes that affects both individuals and business users. A 2010 study conducted by Javelin Strategy and Research determined that more than 11 million Americans were victims of identity theft in just one year.[11] Most consumers are also concerned about fraud. Because the Internet allows easy creation of Web sites, access from anywhere in the world, and anonymity for the creator, it is almost impossible to know with certainty that the Web site, organization, or individuals that you believe you are interacting with are what they seem. The Javelin study also indicated that the total cost associated with identity theft *and* fraud amounted to more than $54 billion during the same 12-month period.[12] As always, caveat emptor ("let the buyer beware") is a good suggestion to follow whether on the Internet or not.

Future Challenges for Computer Technology and e-Business

Today, there is more information available than ever before. Although individuals and business users may think we are at the point of information overload, the amount of information will only increase in the future. In order to obtain more information in the future, both individuals and business users must consider the cost of obtaining information and computer technology. For a business, the ability to obtain information or sell products or services with the click of a computer mouse is

data mining the practice of searching through data records looking for useful information

malware a general term that describes software designed to infiltrate a computer system without the user's consent

computer virus a software code designed to disrupt normal computer operations

expensive. In an effort to reduce expenses, some companies are using cloud computing. **Cloud computing** is a type of computer usage in which services stored on the Internet are provided to users on a temporary basis. When cloud computing is used, a third party makes processing power, software applications, databases, and storage available for use on-demand from anywhere, via the Internet. Instead of running software and storing data on their employer's computer network or their individual computers, employees log onto the third party's system and use (and pay for) only the applications and data storage they actually need. In addition to just cost, there are a number of external and internal factors that a business must consider.

Although the environmental forces at work are complex, it is useful to think of them as either *internal* or *external* forces that affect computer technology and e-business. Internal environmental forces are those that are closely associated with the actions and decisions taking place within a firm. As shown in Figure 16.7, typical internal forces include a firm's planning activities, organization structure, human resources, management decisions, information database, and available financing. A shortage of skilled employees needed for a specialized project, for instance, can undermine a firm's ability to sell its services to clients. Unlike the external environmental forces affecting the firm, internal forces such as this one are more likely to be under the direct control of management. In this case, management can either hire the needed staff or choose to pass over a prospective project. In addition to the obvious internal factors that affect how a computer technology company or e-business firm operates, a growing number of firms are concerned about how their e-business activities affect the environment. The term **green IT** is now used to describe all of a firm's activities to support a healthy environment and sustain the planet. Many offices, for example, are reducing the amount of paper they use by storing data and information on computers.

In contrast, external environmental forces are factors affecting e-business planning that originate from outside the organization. These forces are unlikely

Figure 16.7 Internal and External Forces that Affect an e-Business

Today, managers and employees of an e-business must respond to internal forces within the organization and external forces outside the organization.

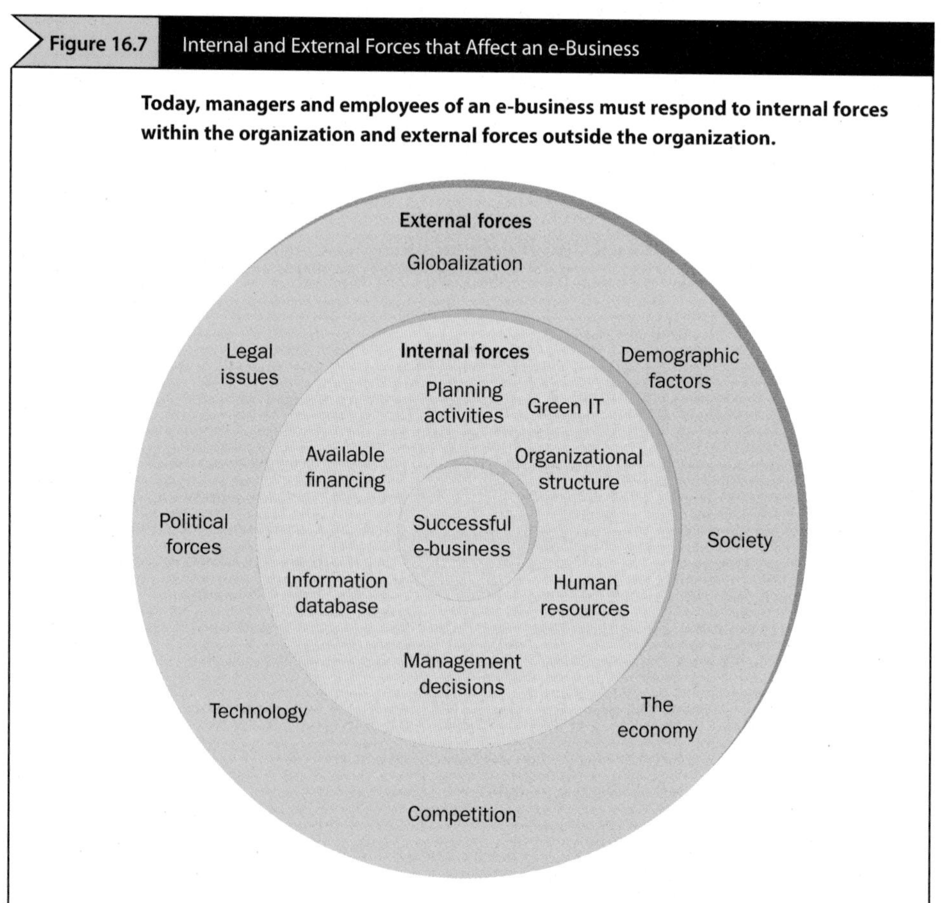

cloud computing a type of computer usage in which services stored on the Internet are provided to users on a temporary basis

green IT a term used to describe all of a firm's activities to support a healthy environment and sustain the planet

to be controllable by an e-business firm. Instead, managers and employees of an e-business firm generally will react to these forces, attempting to shield the organization from any undue negative effects and finding ways to take advantage of opportunities in the ever-changing e-business environment. The primary external environmental forces affecting e-business planning include globalization, demographic, societal, economic, competitive, technological, and political and legal forces.

In this chapter, we have explored a business firm's need for information and how a computer, the Internet, and technology can help people to obtain the information they need. We also examined how e-business is changing the way that firms do business. In Chapter 17, we examine the accounting process, which is a major source of information for business.

return to inside business

Net-a-Porter

Fashionistas seeking the trendy new look by Chloé, Stella McCartney, or Marc Jacobs depend on Net-a-Porter for instant access to high fashion. This e-business pioneered luxury apparel retailing on the Internet, pampering its customers with hand delivery and free returns. Founder Natalie Massenet remembers: "A lot of people said, 'It won't work, people won't buy a £5,000 dress online,' but this was the way I wanted to shop. I love fashion and I wanted it to come to me."

Net-a-Porter's success caught the attention of Richemont, which took a minority stake in the e-business in 2002 and purchased the rest eight years later. Today, its U.K. and U.S. sites, including the outlet site, feature more than 300 fashion brands and attract up to 3 million visitors every month. Combining personalized service with extras such as video runway shows and weekly fashion reports has made Net-a-Porter a must-click online destination for customers who want to stay in vogue.

Questions

1. Of the environmental forces affecting e-business, which seem to have had the most influence on Net-a-Porter's success, and why?
2. This chapter mentions two ways that e-businesses can increase profits. Net-a-Porter has concentrated on increasing sales revenue. How might Net-a-Porter reduce expenses without sacrificing the personal service that built its reputation?

Summary

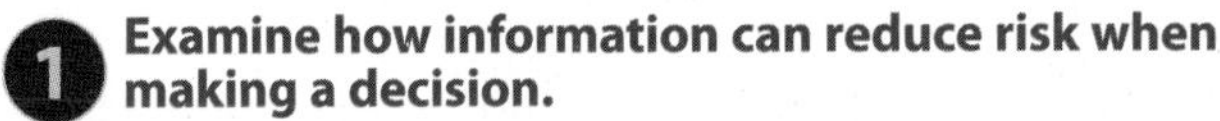

1 Examine how information can reduce risk when making a decision.

The more information a manager has, the less risk there is that a decision will be incorrect. Information produces knowledge and empowers managers and employees to make better decisions. Without accurate and timely information, individual performance will be undermined. Consequently, so will the performance of the entire organization. Because of the volume of information they receive each day and their need to make decisions on a daily basis, businesspeople use information rules to shorten the time spent analyzing choices. Information rules emerge when business research confirms the same results each time it studies the same or a similar set of circumstances. Although many people use the terms *data* and *information* interchangeably, there is a difference. Data are numerical or verbal descriptions that usually result from some sort of measurement. Information is data presented in a form that is useful for a specific purpose. A database is a single collection of data and information stored in one place that can be used by people throughout an organization to make decisions. Although databases are important, the way the data and information are used is even more important. As a result, management information experts now use the term *knowledge management* (KM) to incorporate a firm's procedures for generating, using, and sharing the data and information contained in the firm's databases.

2 Discuss management's information requirements.

A management information system (MIS) is a means of providing managers with the information they need to perform their jobs as effectively as possible. The purpose of an MIS (sometimes referred to as an information technology system or simply IT system) is to distribute timely and useful information from both internal and external sources to the decision makers who need it. The specific types of information managers need depend on their area of management and level within the firm. The size and complexity of an MIS must be tailored to the information needs of the organization it serves.

 Outline the five functions of an information system.

The five functions performed by an MIS system are collecting data, storing data, updating data, processing data into information, and presenting information. Data may be collected from such internal sources as company records, reports, and minutes of meetings, as well as from the firm's managers. External sources include customers, suppliers, bankers, trade and business publications, industry conferences, online computer services, and information-gathering organizations. An MIS must be able to store data until they are needed and to update them regularly to ensure that the information presented to managers is accurate, complete, and timely. Data processing is the MIS function that transforms stored data into a form useful for a specific purpose. Large groups of numerical data are usually processed into summary numbers called statistics. Finally, the processed data (which now can be called information) must be presented for use. Verbal information generally is presented in the form of a report. Numerical information most often is displayed in graphs, charts, or tables.

 Describe how computers and technology help improve productivity, decision making, communications, sales, and recruiting and training.

Today, many employees use computers and the Internet to improve productivity and performance and communicate with other employees while at the office or away from the office. Three different applications—decision-support systems, executive information systems, and expert systems—can help managers and employees to speed and improve the decision-making process. Another application in the workplace is electronic mail, or simply e-mail, which provides for communication within and outside the firm at any time, 24 hours a day, seven days a week. An extension of e-mail is groupware, which is software that facilitates the management of large projects among geographically dispersed employees as well as such group activities as problem solving and brainstorming. The Internet and a sales force automation software program can provide a database of information that can be used to assist a sales representative. The Internet also can be used to improve employee training and recruitment while lowering costs. Now, with the help of technology, more and more employees are telecommuting and using virtual offices. A number of software applications—word processing, desktop publishing, accounting, database management, graphics, and spreadsheets—can all help employees improve productivity. Today, business firms have systems in place to backup important data and information.

5 Analyze how computers and technology change the way information is acquired, organized, and used.

We live in an information society—one in which large groups of employees generate or depend on information to perform their jobs. To find needed information, many businesses and individuals use the Internet. The Internet is a worldwide network of computers linked through telecommunications. Firms also can use an intranet (local-area network) to distribute information within the firm. Both the Internet and intranets are examples of a computer network. A computer network is a group of two or more computers linked together to allow users to share data and information. Today, two basic types—local-area networks (LANs) and wide-area networks (WANs)—affect the way employees and the general public obtain data and information. Today, employees and the general public connect to the Internet, enter a Web address, or use a Web search engine to access information. That information is presented on a Web site created and maintained by business firms; agencies of federal, state, and local governments; or educational or similar organizations. Because a Web site should provide accurate information, great care is required when creating a Web site.

6 Explain the meaning of e-business.

e-Business, or electronic business, can be defined as the organized effort of individuals to produce and sell, for a profit, the goods and services that satisfy society's needs *through the facilities available on the Internet.* The human, material, information, and financial resources that any business requires are highly specialized for e-business. In an effort to reduce the cost of e-business resources, many firms have turned to outsourcing.

Using e-business activities, it is possible to satisfy new customer needs created by the Internet as well as traditional ones in unique ways. Meeting customer needs is especially important when an e-business is trying to earn profits by increasing sales and reducing expenses. Each source of revenue flowing into the firm is referred to as a revenue stream.

7 Describe the fundamental models of e-business.

e-Business models focus attention on the identity of a firm's customers. Firms that use the Internet mainly to conduct business with other businesses generally are referred to as having a business-to-business, or B2B, model. When examining B2B firms, two clear types emerge. In the first type of B2B, the focus is simply on facilitating sales transactions between businesses. A second, more complex type of the B2B model involves a company and its suppliers. In contrast to the focus of the B2B model, firms such as Amazon or eBay clearly are focused on individual buyers and so are referred to as having a business-to-consumer, or B2C, model. In a B2C situation, understanding how consumers behave online is critical to the firm's success. Successful B2C firms often make a special effort to build long-term relationships with their customers. While B2B and B2C models are the most popular e-business models, there are other models that perform specialized e-business activities to generate revenues (see Table 16.4).

8 Explore the factors that will affect the future of e-business.

Because of the advent of commercial activity on the Internet, developments in e-business have been rapid and formidable. Today, most firms involved in e-business use a more intelligent approach to development. The long-term view held by the vast majority of analysts is that the Internet will continue to expand along with related technologies. While approximately 73 percent of Americans now have access to the Internet, it is expected that worldwide users will exceed 2.1 billion by 2012. When you consider the future of computer technology, the Internet, and e-business, social networks, ethics and social responsibility, and Internet crime are all factors that must be considered in the future. Although the environmental forces at work are complex, it is useful to think of them as either internal or external forces that affect an e-business. Internal environmental forces are those that are closely associated with the actions and decisions taking place within a firm. In contrast, external environmental forces are those factors affecting an e-business originating outside an organization.

Key Terms

You should now be able to define and give an example relevant to each of the following terms:

data (465)
information (465)
database (466)
knowledge management (KM) (466)
management information system (MIS) (466)
information technology (IT) officer (466)
data processing (470)
statistic (470)
decision-support system (DSS) (472)
executive information system (EIS) (472)
expert system (472)
groupware (473)
collaborative learning system (473)
virtual office (475)
computer backup (476)
information society (476)
Internet (477)
World Wide Web (the Web) (477)
broadband technology (477)
intranet (477)
computer network (477)
wide-area network (WAN) (477)
local-area network (LAN) (477)
e-business (electronic business) (479)
outsourcing (480)
revenue stream (481)
business model (483)
business-to-business (or B2B) model (484)
business-to-consumer (or B2C) model (484)
social network site (486)
spamming (486)
cookie (486)
log-file records (486)
data mining (487)
malware (487)
computer virus (487)
cloud computing (488)
green IT (488)

Review Questions

1. In your own words, describe how information reduces risk when you make a personal or work-related decision.
2. What are information rules? How do they simplify the process of making decisions?
3. What is the difference between data and information? Give one example of accounting data and one example of accounting information.
4. List the five functions of an MIS.
5. What are the components of a typical business report?
6. Describe the three types of computer applications that help employees, managers, and executives make smart decisions.
7. How can computers and software help the firm's employees communicate, increase sales, and recruit and train employees?
8. Explain the differences between the Internet and an intranet. What types of information does each of these networks provide?

9. What is the difference between a wide-area network (WAN) and a local-area network (LAN)?
10. What factors should be considered when a firm is developing a Web page?
11. What are the four major factors contained in the definition of e-business?
12. How do e-businesses generate revenue streams?
13. What are the two fundamental e-business models?
14. Give an example of an unethical use of computer technology by a business.
15. What is the difference between internal and external forces that affect an e-business? How do they change the way an e-business operates?

Discussion Questions

1. Do managers really need all the kinds of information discussed in this chapter? If not, which kinds can they do without?
2. How can confidential data and information (such as the wages of individual employees) be kept confidential and yet still be available to managers who need them?
3. Why are computers so well suited to management information systems (MISs)? What are some things computers *cannot* do in dealing with data and information?
4. How could the Internet help you to find information about employment opportunities at Coca-Cola, Johnson & Johnson, or Microsoft? Describe the process you would use to access this information.
5. Can advertising provide enough revenue for an e-business to succeed in the long run?
6. Is outsourcing good for an e-business firm? The firm's employees? Explain your answer.
7. What distinguishes a B2B from a B2C e-business model?

Video Case 16.1

How E*Trade Uses e-Business

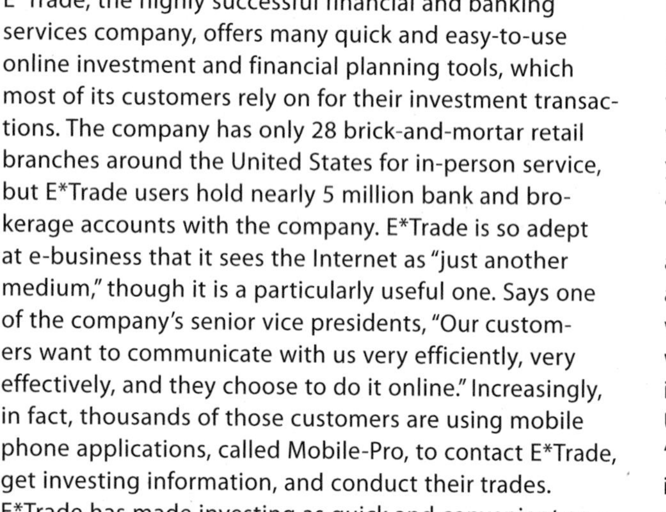

E*Trade, the highly successful financial and banking services company, offers many quick and easy-to-use online investment and financial planning tools, which most of its customers rely on for their investment transactions. The company has only 28 brick-and-mortar retail branches around the United States for in-person service, but E*Trade users hold nearly 5 million bank and brokerage accounts with the company. E*Trade is so adept at e-business that it sees the Internet as "just another medium," though it is a particularly useful one. Says one of the company's senior vice presidents, "Our customers want to communicate with us very efficiently, very effectively, and they choose to do it online." Increasingly, in fact, thousands of those customers are using mobile phone applications, called Mobile-Pro, to contact E*Trade, get investing information, and conduct their trades. E*Trade has made investing as quick and convenient as accessing the company's Web site from a computer, but now more portable.

"We have industry-leading applications (for) the high-active trader to the new-to-online-investing," says another senior vice president, "letting those customers invest with confidence regardless of who they are. I think that becomes a real differentiator for us as a company. . . . We're the first one to offer the ability for a customer to trade on a BlackBerry, and today, our biggest growth area has been with the iPhone." E*Trade was also the first online investing company to build an iPad application. "We had it out there for our customers, day one, when Apple released the iPad. . . . We've seen many customers switch their accounts over to E*Trade because we had this app starting day one." The company is very pleased with customers' response to its phone apps, which were designed to be very similar in look and feel. "If you've used one," says the firm, "you can virtually use almost any of them."

Investment tools available from E*Trade's Web site around the clock include trading charts, streaming news and stock quotes, live "watch" lists, and screening tools, as well as a new customer-feedback link. Global markets on which E*Trade's customers can buy and sell securities are in Canada, France, Germany, Hong Kong, Japan, and the United Kingdom. As one of the company's executives says, "It's not really about finding the trade, but it's about finding it first. So we've got to deliver speed and reliability on a particular platform." Securities trade instantaneously online when the stock exchanges are open, on the next trading day if not, or when a particular security meets the customer's stated buy or sell price. If a customer has a problem or question, E*Trade maintains customer service teams and an online customer service center 24 hours a day, seven days a week.

SmartMoney magazine recently gave E*Trade its highest rating for excellence based on its trading tools, banking services, and customer service. Barron's also gave the firm high marks for trade experience and technology, usability, customer service, and cost. Because it doesn't sell any of its own investment vehicles, E*Trade is able to offer fair and competitive pricing, including special prices for high-volume traders. Its well-organized Web site also provides a wide array of free research and educational materials for investors of all types, from the novice to the very experienced, and in different formats including webinars, short videos, written articles, and other resources that users can access at their own convenience, whether they want to start investing, diversify their portfolio, or plan their retirement as an employee or a small-business owner. "At E*Trade you'll never stop learning," says the Web site, "and that's a good thing."[13]

Questions

1. Each year E*Trade helps millions of individuals evaluate and invest in publicly traded companies. It also operates a Corporate Services business that helps firms, from start-ups to *Fortune* 500 companies, manage their stock plans. What type of business model(s) is E*Trade using?
2. What are some of the ways in which E*Trade works to strengthen its competitive position as an e-business?
3. What are some of the advantages offered by E*Trade's mobile apps? How do these capitalize on the capabilities of the Internet?

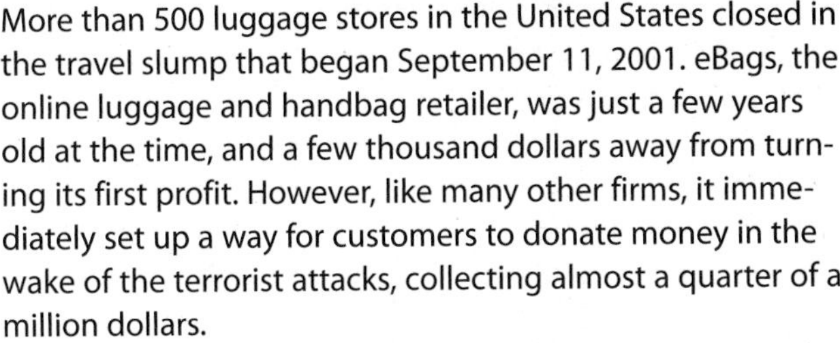

Case 16.2

How eBags Does e-Business

More than 500 luggage stores in the United States closed in the travel slump that began September 11, 2001. eBags, the online luggage and handbag retailer, was just a few years old at the time, and a few thousand dollars away from turning its first profit. However, like many other firms, it immediately set up a way for customers to donate money in the wake of the terrorist attacks, collecting almost a quarter of a million dollars.

"We were about four days into it," remembers co-founder Jon Nordmark, "when we realized 'Oh my God, we're not getting any orders.'" As fellow co-founder and senior vice president Peter Cobb describes the situation, the fall off in travel hurt luggage sales, and troubled economic times compounded the firm's bad news. "We were really just in a foxhole waiting for nuclear winter to end," he says.

The company moved fast, however, expanding its product offerings to include "day" bags such as briefcases, backpacks, purses, and laptop carriers. Another strength was its policy of drop shipping, ordering from suppliers only when customers order from eBags and letting suppliers ship products directly to customers. As a result, eBags avoids the usual retail problem of needing to have a lot of stock on hand to meet demand. "This drop ship model is the reason we're alive," Cobb says. "We don't have to spend tens of millions [of dollars] buying products and putting them in a warehouse." Thanks to quick action and good business planning, the company managed to turn a profit that year and never looked back.

Today, eBags is a $100 million company with about 100 employees and has sold over 7 million bags since its founding. As the biggest online retailer of luggage and bags of all kinds and a leader in the use of Internet technology, it offers 40,000 different products from 520 brands. Inspired by its fund-raising success after 9/11, the company also continues its commitment to the community, giving more than $500,000 to breast cancer research and donating thousands of bags and packs to foster children around the United States.

As eBags has grown, it's become more sophisticated in its use of technology. For example, the company segments its database of 1 million customers and can target individuals in different groups with personalized messages based on their previous purchases and other details. It also offers its products through eBay and other online channels.

Hallmarks of eBags' award-winning Web site are multiple photographs of each product, full-color images in every available color instead of mere swatches, and videos starring employees who seek out and interview up-and-coming New York and Los Angeles designers to showcase their products on the site. Google Maps help shoppers locate other new designers around the country. Specialized search tools locate specific products, like airline-approved carry-on luggage. Unlimited customer reviews—as many as 4,000 for one popular product and more than 1.5 million overall—encourage customers to rate products and read others' comments. Visitors can even post their own videos. "What we're really saying is, 'It's your whiteboard,'" says Cobb.

The company developed most of these interactive software applications in-house. They're costly to maintain, requiring a staff of 40 people and an annual budget of about $10 million. However, eBags believes they contribute directly to sales, which doubled in one recent year and continue to grow. "It is important for us to have unlimited customer reviews, so we do it ourselves," says Cobb. "An outside vendor might limit you to 100 customer reviews. When you go outside, you tend to be forced to cut corners on innovation—you have to dilute the customer experience to be like everyone else."[14]

For more information about this company, go to http://www.ebags.com.

Questions

1. What are some of the reasons eBags has grown to be so successful?
2. What information do you think a company like eBags collects from its Web site? How might eBags use such data to improve its customer service and its business performance?
3. eBags was one of the first online stores to allow customer reviews on its Web site, and now sells its in-house technology to non-competing retailers. What other steps do you think an e-business like eBags might take to keep growing in the future?

Building Skills for Career Success

1 JOURNALING FOR SUCCESS

Today, more and more people use the Internet to purchase products or services. And yet, many people are reluctant to make online purchases because of identity and privacy issues. Still others are "afraid" of the technology.

Assignment

1. Have you ever used the Internet to purchase a product or service? If you answered yes, why did you purchase online as compared with purchasing the same product or service in a traditional retail store?
2. In your own words, describe whether the online shopping experience was a pleasant one. What factors contributed to your level of satisfaction or dissatisfaction?
3. If you answered no, describe why you prefer to shop in a traditional retail store as compared with shopping on the Web.

2 EXPLORING THE INTERNET

Computer technology is a fast-paced, highly competitive industry in which product life cycles sometimes are measured in months or even weeks. To keep up with changes and trends in hardware and software, MIS managers routinely must scan computer publications and Web sites that discuss new products.

A major topic of interest among MIS managers is groupware, software that facilitates the management of large projects among geographically dispersed employees, as well as group activities such as problem solving and brainstorming.

Assignment

1. Use a search engine and enter the keyword "groupware" to locate companies that provide this type of software. Try the demonstration edition of the groupware if it is available or read case studies where groupware has been used to manage a large project.
2. Based on your research of this business application, why do you think groupware is growing in popularity?
3. Describe the structure of one of the groupware programs you examined as well as your impressions of its value to users.

3 DEVELOPING CRITICAL-THINKING SKILLS

To stay competitive in the marketplace, businesses must process data into information and make sure that information is readily available to decision makers. For this, many businesses rely on a management information system (MIS). The purpose of an MIS is to provide managers with accurate, complete, and timely information so that they can perform their jobs as effectively as possible. Because an MIS must fit the needs of the firm it serves, these systems vary in the way they collect, store, update, and process data and present information to users.

Assignment

1. Select a local company large enough to have an MIS. Set up an interview with the person responsible for managing the flow of information within the company.
2. Prepare a list of questions you will ask during the interview. Structure the questions around the five basic functions of an MIS. Some sample questions follow:
   a. *Collecting data*. What types of data are needed? How often are data collected? What sources produce the data? How do you ensure that the data are accurate?
   b. *Storing data*. How are data stored?
   c. *Updating data*. What is the process for updating?
   d. *Processing data*. Can you show me some examples of the types of data that will be processed into information? How is the processing done?
   e. *Presenting information*. Would you show me some examples (reports, tables, graphs, charts) of how the information is presented to various decision makers and tell me why that particular format is used?
3. At the end of the interview, ask the interviewee to predict how the system will change in the next three years.
4. In a report, describe what you believe the strengths and weaknesses of this firm's MIS are. In addition, describe the most important thing you learned from the interview.

4 BUILDING TEAM SKILLS

To provide marketing managers with information about consumer reactions to a particular product or service, business researchers often conduct focus groups. The participants in these groups are representative of the target market for the product or service under study. The leader poses questions and lets members of the group express their feelings and ideas about the product or service. The ideas are recorded, transcribed, and analyzed.

Assignment

1. Working in a small team, select a product or service to research—for example, your college's food service or bookstore or a new item you would like to see stocked in your local grocery store.
2. Create a list of questions that can be used to generate discussion about the product or service with focus-group members.
3. Form a focus group of five to seven people representative of the market for the product or service your team has selected.

4. During the group sessions, record the input. Later, transcribe it into printed form, analyze it, and process it into information. On the basis of this information, make recommendations for improving the product or service.
5. In a report, describe your team's experiences in forming the focus groups and the value of focus groups in collecting data. Use the report as the basis for a three- to five-minute class presentation.

5 RESEARCHING DIFFERENT CAREERS

Firms today expect employees to be proficient in using computers and computer software. Typical business applications include e-mail, word processing, spreadsheets, and graphics. By improving your skills in these areas, you can increase your chances not only of being employed but also of being promoted once you are employed.

Assignment

1. Assess your computer skills by placing a check in the appropriate column in the following table:

	Skill Level			
Software	None	Low	Average	High
e-Mail				
Word processing				
Desktop publishing				
Accounting				
Database management				
Graphics				
Spreadsheet				
Groupware				
Internet research				

2. Describe your self-assessment in a written report. Specify the skills in which you need to become more proficient, and outline a plan for doing this.

17

Using Accounting Information

© iStockphoto.com/Kenishirotie

Learning Objectives

What you will be able to do once you complete this chapter:

1. Explain why accurate accounting information and audited financial statements are important.
2. Identify the people who use accounting information and possible careers in the accounting industry.
3. Discuss the accounting process.
4. Read and interpret a balance sheet.
5. Read and interpret an income statement.
6. Describe business activities that affect a firm's cash flow.
7. Summarize how managers evaluate the financial health of a business.

FYI

Did You Know?

In the United States, Deloitte rings up $10 billion in annual revenue and employs more than 40,000 people, including 9,000 CPAs.

inside business

Deloitte Digs Deep into Financial Data

The global accounting powerhouse Deloitte Touche Tohmatsu may have a long name, but it has an even longer history of success. From its earliest 19th-century roots in England, Deloitte has expanded to dozens of nations, with 169,000 employees providing accounting, auditing, consulting, and tax services for clients in many industries. Today, Deloitte's annual worldwide revenue exceeds $26 billion. In the United States, the firm rings up $10 billion in annual revenue and maintains a workforce of more than 40,000 people, including 9,000 certified public accountants (CPAs).

Deloitte has been hired by many well-known U.S. corporations, including Microsoft and H&R Block, to dig deep into their financial data and processes and help them prepare complete and accurate reports about their financial situations, as required by law. Thanks to its global presence, Deloitte has the capabilities and experience to help multinational corporations comply with the accounting and tax regulations of their home countries and the countries in which they do business.

In addition, Deloitte has conducted extensive research into illegal accounting scams, such as reporting nonexistent sales, so it can advise top executives and boards of directors about preventing these kinds of frauds. It also offers consulting services to help companies improve their operations, analyze and manage business risks, and implement new information technology systems. Although most of the firm's work goes on behind the scenes, one of its highest-profile jobs is totaling Grammy votes for the Recording Academy.

Only by attracting, training, and retaining top-notch personnel can Deloitte continue its long tradition of accounting excellence. Its CEO explains: "We work in a highly competitive, knowledge-based profession where having the best resources and the most intellectual capital is a critical determinant of our success." That's why Deloitte's recruiters are always on the road, visiting colleges, universities, and community colleges to identify talented candidates and describe the challenges and rewards of an accounting career. Deloitte has been acclaimed for its long-standing commitment to diversity, which includes such initiatives as mentoring programs for minority and women professionals. Whether the economy is up or down, clients are counting on Deloitte to meet their accounting needs.[1]

For Barry Salzberg, CEO of Deloitte Touche Tohmatsu, Deloitte was his first professional job back in 1977. Now, 32 years later, he is running an accounting firm known around the globe. According to Salzberg, the reason he stayed is "because of what Deloitte offers—an opportunity culture, in which *everyone* has a shot."[2] Deloitte is proud of its people culture where employees from all kinds of backgrounds find a culture in which they have the freedom and flexibility to grow while helping their clients solve their toughest accounting problems. The fact is that without accounting information, managers can't make decisions, investors can't evaluate potential investments, and lenders and suppliers can't extend credit to a business firm. Although accurate accounting information has always been important, it is even more important now in the wake of the recent accounting scandals and the crisis in the banking and financial industries.

Many people have the idea that accountants spend their day working with endless columns of numbers in a small office locked away from other people. In fact, accountants do spend a lot of time at their desks, but their job entails far more than just adding or subtracting numbers. Accountants are expected to share their ideas and the information they possess with people who need the information.

We begin this chapter by looking at why accounting information is important, the recent problems in the accounting industry, and attempts to improve financial reporting. Then we look at how managers, employees, individuals, and groups outside a firm use accounting information. We also identify different types of accountants and career opportunities in the accounting industry. Next, we focus on the accounting process and the basics of an accounting system. We also examine the three most important financial statements: the balance sheet, the income statement, and the statement of cash flows. Finally, we show how ratios are used to measure specific aspects of a firm's financial health.

Why Accounting Information Is Important

1

Explain why accurate accounting information and audited financial statements are important.

Accounting is the process of systematically collecting, analyzing, and reporting financial information. Today, it is impossible to manage a business without accurate and up-to-date information supplied by the firm's accountants. Just for a moment, think about the following three questions:

1. How much profit did a business earn last year?
2. How much tax does a business owe the Internal Revenue Service?
3. How much cash does a business have to pay lenders and suppliers?

In each case, the firm's accountants and its accounting system provide the answers to these questions and many others. Although accounting information can be used to answer questions about what has happened in the past, it can also be used to help make decisions about the future. For these reasons, accounting is one of the most important areas within a business organization.

Because the information provided by a firm's accountants and its accounting system is so important, managers and other groups interested in a business firm's financial records must be able to "trust the numbers." Unfortunately, a large number of accounting scandals have caused people to doubt not only the numbers but also the accounting industry.

Recent Accounting Scandals

Which of the following firms has been convicted or accused of accounting fraud?

a. Enron
b. Lehman Brothers
c. Fannie Mae
d. AIG
e. All of the above

accounting the process of systematically collecting, analyzing, and reporting financial information

Unfortunately, the answer to the question is e—all of the above. Each company is a major U.S. business that has been plagued by accounting problems. These problems led to bankruptcy for Enron and Lehman Brothers and a massive federal bailout for mortgage giant Fannie Mae and insurance giant AIG. The accounting problems at these companies—and similar problems at even more companies—have forced many investors, lenders and suppliers, and government regulators to question the motives behind fraudulent and unethical accounting practices.

Today, much of the pressure on corporate executives to "cook" the books is driven by the desire to look good to Wall Street analysts and investors. Every three months companies report their revenues, expenses, profits, and projections for the future. If a company meets or exceeds "the street's" expectations, everything is usually fine. However, if a company

This photo says it all! Because a number of the firms listed on this protestor's sign were forced to file for bankruptcy protection or experienced financial difficulties during the recent economic crisis, employees, lenders, and investors made new demands for more financial disclosure and improved accounting procedures.

reports financial numbers that are lower than expected, the company's stock value can drop dramatically. An earnings report that is lower by even a few pennies per share than what is expected can cause a company's stock value to drop immediately by as much as 20 to 30 percent or more. Greed—especially when salary and bonuses are tied to a company's stock value—is another factor that can lead some corporate executives to use questionable accounting methods to inflate a firm's sales revenues and profit amount.

Unfortunately, the ones hurt when companies (and their accountants) report inaccurate or misleading accounting information often are not the high-paid corporate executives. In many cases, it's the employees who lose their jobs, as well as the money they invested in the company's retirement program. In addition, investors, lenders, and suppliers who relied on fraudulent accounting information in order to make a decision to invest in or lend money to the company also usually experience a loss.

In an indirect way, the recent accounting scandals underscore how important accurate accounting information is for a corporation. To see how the auditing process can improve accounting information, read the next section.

Why Audited Financial Statements Are Important

Assume that you are a bank officer responsible for evaluating business loan applications. How do you make a decision to approve or reject a loan request? In this situation, most bank officers rely on the information contained in the firm's balance sheet, income statement, and statement of cash flows, along with other information provided by the prospective borrower. In fact, most lenders insist that these financial statements be audited by a CPA. An **audit** is an examination of a company's financial statements and the accounting practices that produced them. The purpose of an audit is to make sure that a firm's financial statements have been prepared in accordance with **generally accepted accounting principles (GAAPs)**. GAAPs have been developed to provide an accepted set of guidelines and practices for U.S. companies reporting financial information and the accounting profession. At the time of publication, the Financial Accounting Standards Board (FASB), which establishes and improves accounting standards for U.S. companies, is working toward establishing a new set of standards that combines GAAPs with the International Financial Reporting Standards (IFRS) to create one set of accounting standards that can be used by both U.S. and multinational firms. Created by the International Accounting Standards Board, IFRS are now used in more than 100 different countries around the world. For multinational firms, the benefits of global accounting standards are huge because preparing financial statements and accounting records that meet global standards saves both time and money. According to many accounting experts, it's not a question of whether IFRS guidelines will be adopted in the United States but when.[3]

If an accountant determines that a firm's financial statements present financial information fairly and conform to GAAPs, then he or she will issue the following statement:

> *In our opinion, the financial statements . . . present fairly, in all material respects . . . in conformity with generally accepted accounting principles.*

Although an audit and the resulting report do not *guarantee* that a company has not "cooked" the books, it does imply that, on the whole, the company has followed GAAPs. Bankers, creditors, investors, and government agencies are willing to rely on an auditor's opinion because of the historically ethical reputation and independence of auditors and accounting firms. Finally, it should be noted that without the audit function and GAAPs, there would be very little oversight or supervision. The validity of a firm's financial statements and its accounting records would drop quickly, and firms would find it difficult to obtain debt financing, acquire goods and services from suppliers, find investor financing, or prepare documents requested by government agencies.

audit an examination of a company's financial statements and the accounting practices that produced them

generally accepted accounting principles (GAAPs) an accepted set of guidelines and practices for companies reporting financial information and for the accounting profession

Reform: The Sarbanes-Oxley Act of 2002

According to John Bogle, founder of Vanguard Mutual Funds, "Investing is an act of faith. Without that faith—that reported numbers reflect reality, that companies are being run honestly, that Wall Street is playing it straight, and that investors aren't being hoodwinked—our capital markets simply can't function."[4] In reality, what Mr. Bogle says is true. To help ensure that corporate financial information is accurate and in response to the many accounting scandals that surfaced in the last few years, Congress enacted the Sarbanes-Oxley Act. Key components include the following:[5]

- The Securities and Exchange Commission (SEC) is required to establish a full-time five-member federal oversight board that will police the accounting industry.
- Chief executive and financial officers are required to certify periodic financial reports and are liable for intentional violations of securities reporting requirements.
- Accounting firms are prohibited from providing many types of non-audit and consulting services to the companies they audit.
- Auditors must maintain financial documents and audit work papers for five years.
- Auditors, accountants, and employees can be imprisoned for up to 20 years and subject to fines for destroying financial documents and willful violations of the securities laws.
- A public corporation must change its lead auditing firm every five years.
- There is added protection for whistle-blowers who report violations of the Sarbanes-Oxley Act.

Sustaining the Planet

The Global Reporting Initiative

Just as corporations follow a standardized accounting framework for their financial statements, the Global Reporting Initiative wants corporations worldwide to use a standardized framework for reporting their sustainability programs and achievements. Take a look: http://www.globalreporting.org.

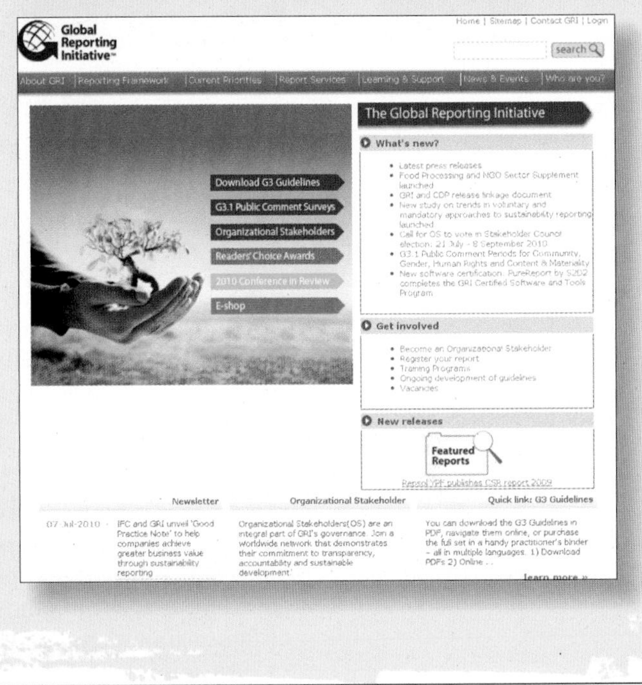

© 2007 GRI

Although most people welcome the Sarbanes-Oxley Act, complex rules make compliance more expensive and time-consuming for corporate management and more difficult for accounting firms. Yet, most people agree that the cost of compliance is justified. As you read the next section, you will see the importance of maintaining accurate accounting information.

Who Uses Accounting Information

2 Identify the people who use accounting information and possible careers in the accounting industry.

Managers and employees, lenders, suppliers, stockholders, and government agencies all rely on the information contained in three financial statements, each no more than one page in length. These three reports—the balance sheet, the income statement, and the statement of cash flows—are concise summaries of a firm's activities during a specific time period. Together they represent the results of perhaps tens of thousands of transactions that have occurred during the accounting period. Moreover, the form of the financial statements is pretty much the same for all businesses, from a neighborhood video store or small dry cleaner to giant conglomerates such as Home Depot, Boeing, and Bank of America. This information has a variety of uses both within the firm and outside it. However, first and foremost, accounting information is management information.

Why do stockholders attend annual meetings? There are many reasons why stockholders—the actual owners of a corporation—attend an annual meeting. For starters, most stockholders want to learn more about the company. Others want to vote in person for the board of directors and approve or reject major corporate actions. Still other stockholders want a chance to ask questions about the corporation's future plans.

The People Who Use Accounting Information

The primary users of accounting information are *managers*. The firm's accounting system provides information that can be compiled for the entire firm—for each product; for each sales territory, store, or salesperson; for each division or department; and generally in any way that will help those who manage the organization. At a company such as Kraft Foods, for example, financial information is gathered for all its hundreds of food products: Maxwell House Coffee, A1 Steak Sauce, Chips Ahoy Cookies, Jell-O Desserts, Kool Aid, and so on. The president of the company is interested in total sales for all these products. The vice president for marketing for Maxwell House Coffee is interested in national sales. The northeastern sales manager might want to look at sales figures for Kool Aid in New England. For a large, complex organization like Kraft, the accounting system must enable managers to get the information they need.

Much of this accounting information is *proprietary;* it is not divulged to anyone outside the firm. This type of information is used by a firm's managers and employees to plan and set goals, organize, lead and motivate, and control—all the management functions that were described in Chapter 6.

To see how important accounting is, just think about what happens when an employee or a manager asks a supervisor for a new piece of equipment or a salary increase. Immediately, everyone involved in the decision begins discussing how much it will cost and what effect it will have on the firm's profits, sales, and expenses. It is the firm's accounting system that provides the answers to these important questions. In addition to proprietary information used inside the firm, certain financial information must be supplied to lenders, suppliers, stockholders, potential investors, government agencies, and other stakeholders. For more information about the type of information these individuals and organizations need, take a look at Table 17.1.

An important function of accountants is to ensure that such information is accurate and thorough enough to satisfy these outside groups.

Different Types of Accounting

Although many people think that all accountants do the same tasks, there are special areas of expertise within the accounting industry. In fact, accounting is usually broken down into two broad categories: managerial and financial.

Table 17.1 Users of Accounting Information

The primary users of accounting information are a company's managers and employees, although individuals and organizations outside the company also require information on its finances.

Management and Employees	Lenders and Suppliers	Stockholders and Potential Investors	Government Agencies
• Plan and set goals • Organize • Lead and motivate • Control	• Evaluate credit applicants before committing to short- or long-term financing • Evaluate the risk of non-payment before selling goods or services to a firm	• Evaluate the financial health of the firm before purchasing stocks or bonds • Evaluate the risk associated with investing in a company's stocks, bonds, or securities	• Confirm tax liabilities • Confirm payroll deductions • Approve new issues of stocks and bonds

Managerial accounting provides managers and employees within the organization with the information needed to make decisions about a firm's financing, investing, marketing, and operating activities. By using managerial accounting information, both managers and employees can evaluate how well they have done in the past and what they can expect in the future. **Financial accounting**, on the other hand, generates financial statements and reports for interested people outside of an organization. Typically, stockholders, financial analysts, bankers, lenders, suppliers, government agencies, and other interested groups use the information provided by financial accounting to determine how well a business firm has achieved its goals. In addition to managerial and financial accounting, additional special areas of accounting include the following:

- *Cost accounting*—determining the cost of producing specific products or services
- *Tax accounting*—planning tax strategy and preparing tax returns for firms or individuals
- *Government accounting*—providing basic accounting services to ensure that tax revenues are collected and used to meet the goals of state, local, and federal agencies
- *Not-for-profit accounting*—helping not-for-profit organizations to account for all donations and expenditures

Accounting information you can use. To find out more about the accounting profession, career paths, mentoring opportunities, and up-to-date information about the CPA exam, go to the American Institute of CPAs' Web site at http://www.aicpa.org.

Careers in Accounting

Wanted: An individual with at least two years of college accounting courses. Must be honest, dependable, and willing to complete all routine accounting activities for a manufacturing business. Salary dependent on experience.

Want a job? Positions such as the one described in this newspaper advertisement are increasingly becoming available to those with the required training. According to the *Occupational Outlook Handbook*, published by the Department of Labor, job opportunities for accountants, as well as auditors in the accounting area, are expected to experience much faster-than-average employment growth between now and the year 2018. According to a recent salary survey conducted by the National Association of Colleges and Employers, starting salaries for accountants with a bachelor's degree average $48,993 a year.[6] Job applicants with a two-year degree or with some college accounting courses make less, but still higher than the starting salaries for other entry-level positions.

Accounting can be an exciting and rewarding career—one that offers higher-than-average starting salaries. To be successful in the accounting industry, employees must

- Be responsible, honest, and ethical.
- Have a strong background in financial management.
- Know how to use a computer and software to process data into accounting information.
- Be able to communicate with people who need accounting information.

Today, accountants generally are classified as either private accountants or public accountants. A *private accountant* is employed by a specific organization. A medium-sized or a large firm may employ one or more private accountants to design its accounting information system, manage its accounting department, and provide managers with accounting information, advice, and assistance.

managerial accounting provides managers and employees with the information needed to make decisions about a firm's financing, investing, marketing, and operating activities

financial accounting generates financial statements and reports for interested people outside an organization

SPOTLIGHT

Starting Salaries for Certified Public Accountants (CPAs)

It takes a lot of time and energy to find the right accounting position, but the salary is worth it. Below are starting salaries for CPAs.

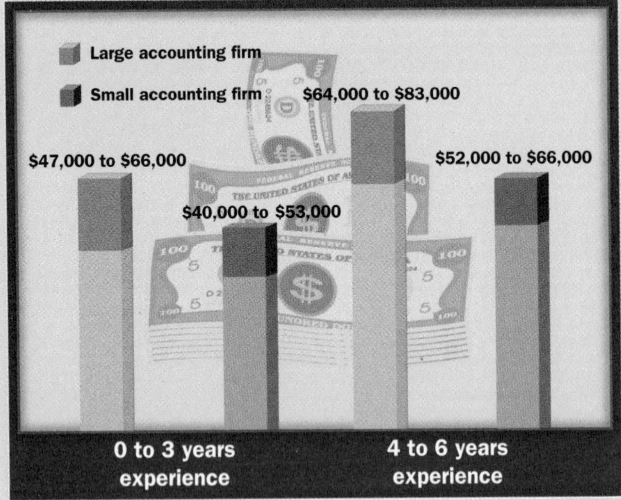

Source: The AICPA Web site at http://www.aicpa.org (accessed April 12, 2010).

Individuals, self-employed business owners, and smaller firms that do not require their own full-time accountants can hire the services of public accountants. A *public accountant* works on a fee basis for clients and may be self-employed or be the employee of an accounting firm. Accounting firms range in size from one-person operations to huge international firms with hundreds of accounting partners and thousands of employees. Today, the largest accounting firms, sometimes referred to as the "Big Four," are PricewaterhouseCoopers, Ernst & Young, KPMG, and Deloitte Touche Tohmatsu.

Typically, public accounting firms include on their staffs at least one **certified public accountant (CPA)**, an individual who has met state requirements for accounting education and experience and has passed a rigorous accounting examination. The AICPA uniform CPA examination covers four areas: (1) regulation, taxation, business law, ethics, and professional and legal responsibilities; (2) auditing; (3) business environment and concepts; and (4) financial accounting and reporting. More information about general requirements and the CPA profession can be obtained by contacting the AICPA at http://www.aicpa.org.[7] State requirements usually include a college degree or a specified number of hours of college course work and generally from one to three years of on-the-job experience. Details regarding specific state requirements for practice as a CPA can be obtained by contacting the state's board of accountancy.

Once an individual becomes a CPA, he or she must participate in continuing-education programs to maintain state certification. These specialized programs are designed to provide the current training needed in today's changing business environment.

Certification as a CPA brings both status and responsibility. In addition to auditing a corporation's financial statements, typical services performed by CPAs include planning and preparing tax returns, determining the true cost of producing and marketing a firm's goods or services, and compiling the financial information needed to make major management decisions. Fees for the services provided by CPAs generally range from $50 to $300 an hour.

certified public accountant (CPA) an individual who has met state requirements for accounting education and experience and has passed a rigorous accounting examination prepared by the AICPA

certified management accountant (CMA) an accountant who has met the requirements for education and experience, passed a rigorous exam, and is certified by the Institute of Management Accountants

In addition to CPAs, there are also certified management accountants (CMAs). A **certified management accountant (CMA)** is an accountant who has met the requirements for education and experience, passed a rigorous exam, and is certified by the Institute of Management Accountants. The CMA exam is designed to develop and measure not only accounting skills but also decision-making, financial planning, analysis, and critical-thinking skills. For more information about the CMA exam, visit the Institute of Management Accountants Web site at http://www.imanet.org. Although both CPAs and CMAs can work for the public, a CMA is more likely to work within a large organization. In addition, both types of accountants are excellent career choices.

3

Discuss the accounting process.

The Accounting Process

In Chapter 16, *information* was defined as data presented in a form that is useful for a specific purpose. In this section, we examine accounting as the system for transforming raw financial *data* into useful financial *information*. Then, in the next sections, we describe the three most important financial statements—the balance sheet, income statement, and statement of cash flows—provided by the accounting process.

Career SUCCESS

More Accountants and Auditors Needed!

U.S. businesses and not-for-profit organizations will soon need the services of many more accountants and auditors. The *Occupational Outlook Handbook* forecasts a 22 percent increase in the number of accountants and auditors needed in the nation's workforce by 2018—a higher-than-average occupational growth rate.

Already, the "Big Four" (Deloitte Touche Tohmatsu, Ernst & Young, KPMG, and PricewaterhouseCoopers) are actively recruiting to fill open positions and prepare for the coming boom in demand for such services. All four appear on *Fortune*'s annual list of 100 Best Companies to Work for in America, as well as *BusinessWeek*'s annual list of Best Places to Launch a Career.

Here's a taste of what the Big Four are doing to attract, develop, and retain career-minded accountants and auditors. Deloitte (http://www.deloitte.com) has created Deloitte University, a $300 million state-of-the-art learning center for companywide technical and leadership training. Ernst & Young (http://www.ey.com) has a wide variety of international assignments to develop, challenge, and motivate its personnel. KPMG (http://www.kpmg.com) encourages work-life balance by granting employees sabbatical leaves for up to three months at 20 percent pay. PricewaterhouseCoopers (http://www.pwc.com) provides on-the-job coaching and networking opportunities to help employees sharpen their skills, learn from experts throughout the organization, and identify new job opportunities internally. Is a Big Four career in your future?

Sources: Alison Maitland, "A Different Way of Working," *Financial Times*, March 22, 2010, http://www.ft.com; Milton Moskowitz, Robert Levering, and Christopher Tkaczyk, "100 Best Companies to Work for in America," *Fortune*, February 8, 2010, 75–88; Lindsey Gerdes, "Best Places to Launch a Career," *BusinessWeek*, September 14, 2009, 32ff; "Accountants and Auditors," *Occupational Outlook Handbook*, December 17, 2009, http://www.bls.gov/oco/ocos001.htm.

The Accounting Equation

The accounting equation is a simple statement that forms the basis for the accounting process. This important equation shows the relationship between a firm's assets, liabilities, and owners' equity.

- **Assets** are the resources a business owns—cash, inventory, equipment, and real estate.
- **Liabilities** are the firm's debts—what it owes to others.
- **Owners' equity** is the difference between total assets and total liabilities—what would be left for the owners if the firm's assets were sold and the money used to pay off its liabilities.

The relationship between assets, liabilities, and owners' equity is shown by the following **accounting equation**:

Assets = liabilities + owners' equity

Whether a business is a small corner grocery store or a giant corporation such as General Mills, its assets must equal the sum of its liabilities and owners' equity. To use this equation, a firm's accountants must record raw data—that is, the firm's day-to-day financial transactions—using the double-entry system of bookkeeping. The **double-entry bookkeeping system** is a system in which each financial transaction is recorded as two separate accounting entries to maintain the balance shown in the accounting equation. With the double-entry system, an accountant can use the steps in the accounting cycle to generate accounting information and financial statements.

The Accounting Cycle

In the typical accounting system, raw data are transformed into financial statements in five steps. The first three—analyzing, recording, and posting—are performed on a regular basis throughout the accounting period. The last two—preparation of the

assets the resources that a business owns

liabilities a firm's debts and obligations

owners' equity the difference between a firm's assets and its liabilities

accounting equation the basis for the accounting process: *assets = liabilities + owners' equity*

double-entry bookkeeping system a system in which each financial transaction is recorded as two separate accounting entries to maintain the balance shown in the accounting equation

trial balance and preparation of the financial statements and closing the books—are performed at the end of the accounting period.

Analyzing Source Documents Basic accounting data are contained in *source documents,* the receipts, invoices, sales slips, and other documents that show the dollar amounts of day-to-day business transactions. The accounting cycle begins with the analysis of each of these documents. The purpose of the analysis is to determine which accounts are affected by the documents and how they are affected.

Recording Transactions Every financial transaction then is recorded in a journal—a process called *journalizing*. Transactions must be recorded in the firm's general journal or in specialized journals. The *general journal* is a book of original entry in which typical transactions are recorded in order of their occurrence. An accounting system also may include *specialized journals* for specific types of transactions that occur frequently. Thus, a retail store might have journals for cash receipts, cash disbursements, purchases, and sales in addition to its general journal.

Posting Transactions After the information is recorded in the general journal and specialized journals, it is transferred to the general ledger. The *general ledger* is a book of accounts containing a separate sheet or section for each account. Today, most businesses use a computer and software to record accounting entries in the general journal or specialized journals and then to post journal entries to the general ledger.

Preparing the Trial Balance A **trial balance** is a summary of the balances of all general ledger accounts at the end of the accounting period. To prepare a trial balance, the accountant determines and lists the balances for all ledger accounts. If the trial balance totals are correct and the accounting equation is still in balance, the accountant can prepare the financial statements. If not, a mistake has occurred somewhere, and the accountant must find it and correct it before proceeding.

Preparing Financial Statements and Closing the Books The firm's financial statements are prepared from the information contained in the trial balance. This information is presented in a standardized format to make the statements as accessible as possible to the various people who may be interested in the firm's financial affairs—managers, employees, lenders, suppliers, stockholders, potential investors, and government agencies. A firm's financial statements are prepared at least once a year and included in the firm's annual report. An **annual report** is a report distributed to stockholders and other interested parties that describes a firm's operating activities and its financial condition. Most firms also have financial statements prepared semiannually, quarterly, or monthly.

Once these statements have been prepared and checked, the firm's books are "closed" for the accounting period, and a *postclosing* trial balance is prepared. Unlike the trial balance just described, the postclosing trial balance generally is prepared after *all* accounting work is completed for one accounting period. If the postclosing trial balance totals agree, the accounting equation is still in balance at the end of the cycle. Only then can a new accounting cycle begin for the next accounting period.

With this brief information about the steps of the accounting cycle in mind, let's now examine the three most important financial statements generated by the accounting process: the balance sheet, the income statement, and the statement of cash flows.

trial balance a summary of the balances of all general ledger accounts at the end of the accounting period

annual report a report distributed to stockholders and other interested parties that describes a firm's operating activities and its financial condition

The Balance Sheet

4

Read and interpret a balance sheet.

Question: *Where could you find the total amount of assets, liabilities, and owners' equity for Hershey Foods Corporation?*

Answer: The firm's balance sheet.

A **balance sheet** (sometimes referred to as a **statement of financial position**) is a summary of the dollar amounts of a firm's assets, liabilities, and owners' equity accounts at the end of a specific accounting period. The balance sheet must demonstrate that assets are equal to liabilities plus owners' equity. Most people think of a balance sheet as a statement that reports the financial condition of a business firm such as the Home Depot or Hershey Foods Corporation, but balance sheets apply to individuals, too. For example, Marty Campbell graduated from college three years ago and obtained a position as a sales representative for an office supply firm. After going to work, he established a checking and savings account and purchased an automobile, stereo, television, and a few pieces of furniture. Marty paid cash for some purchases, but he had to borrow money to pay for the larger ones. Figure 17.1 shows Marty's current personal balance sheet.

Marty Campbell's assets total $26,500, and his liabilities amount to $10,000. Although the difference between total assets and total liabilities is referred to as *owners' equity* or *stockholders' equity* for a business, it is normally called *net worth* for an individual. As reported on Marty's personal balance sheet, net worth is $16,500. The total assets ($26,500) and the total liabilities *plus* net worth ($26,500) are equal. Thus, the accounting equation (Assets = liabilities + owners' equity) is still in balance.

Figure 17.1 Personal Balance Sheet

Often individuals determine their net worth, or owners' equity, by subtracting the value of their liabilities from the value of their assets.

Marty Campbell
Personal Balance Sheet
December 31, 20XX

ASSETS		
Cash	$ 2,500	
Savings account	5,000	
Automobile	15,000	
Stereo	1,000	
Television	500	
Furniture	2,500	
TOTAL ASSETS		$26,500
LIABILITIES		
Automobile loan	$ 9,500	
Credit card balance	500	
TOTAL LIABILITIES		$10,000
NET WORTH (Owners' Equity)		16,500
TOTAL LIABILITIES AND NET WORTH		$26,500

balance sheet (or statement of financial position) a summary of the dollar amounts of a firm's assets, liabilities, and owners' equity accounts at the end of a specific accounting period

Figure 17.2 shows the balance sheet for Northeast Art Supply, a small corporation that sells picture frames, paints, canvases, and other artists' supplies to retailers in New England. Note that assets are reported at the top of the statement, followed by liabilities and stockholders' equity. Let's work through the different accounts in Figure 17.2 from top to bottom.

Assets

On a balance sheet, assets are listed in order from the *most liquid* to the *least liquid*. The **liquidity** of an asset is the ease with which it can be converted into cash.

Current Assets **Current assets** are assets that can be converted quickly into cash or that will be used in one year or less. Because cash is the most liquid asset, it is listed first. Next are *marketable securities*—stocks, bonds, and other investments—that can be converted into cash in a matter of days.

Next are the firm's receivables. Its *accounts receivable,* which result from allowing customers to make credit purchases, generally are paid within 30 to 60 days. However, the firm expects that some of these debts will not be collected. Thus, it has reduced its accounts receivables by a 5 percent *allowance for doubtful accounts.* The firm's *notes receivable* are receivables for which customers have signed promissory notes. They generally are repaid over a longer period of time than the firm's accounts receivable.

Northeast's *merchandise inventory* represents the value of goods on hand for sale to customers. Since Northeast Art Supply is a wholesale operation, the inventory listed in Figure 17.2 represents finished goods ready for sale to retailers. For a manufacturing firm, merchandise inventory also may represent raw materials that will become part of a finished product or work that has been partially completed but requires further processing.

Northeast's last current asset is *prepaid expenses,* which are assets that have been paid for in advance but have not yet been used. An example is insurance premiums. They are usually paid at the beginning of the policy year. The unused portion (say, for the last four months of the time period covered by the policy) is a prepaid expense. For Northeast Art, all current assets total $182,000.

Fixed Assets **Fixed assets** are assets that will be held or used for a period longer than one year. They generally include land, buildings, and equipment used in the continuing operation of the business. Although Northeast owns no land or buildings, it does own delivery equipment that originally cost $110,000. It also owns furniture and store equipment that originally cost $62,000.

Note that the values of both fixed assets are decreased by their *accumulated depreciation.* **Depreciation** is the process of apportioning the cost of a fixed asset over the period during which it will be used, that is, its useful life. The depreciation amount allotted to each year is an expense for that year, and the value of the asset must be reduced by the amount of depreciation expense. In the case of Northeast's delivery equipment, $20,000 of its value has been depreciated (or used up) since it was purchased. Its value at this time is thus $110,000 less $20,000, or $90,000. In a similar fashion, the original value of furniture and store equipment ($62,000) has been reduced by depreciation totaling $15,000. Furniture and store equipment now has a reported value of $47,000. For Northeast Art, all fixed assets total $137,000.

Intangible Assets **Intangible assets** are assets that do not exist physically but that have a value based on the rights or privileges they confer on a firm. They include patents, copyrights, trademarks, and goodwill. By their nature, intangible assets are long-term assets—they are of value to the firm for a number of years.

Northeast Art Supply lists two intangible assets. The first is a *patent* for a special oil paint that the company purchased from the inventor. The firm's accountants

liquidity the ease with which an asset can be converted into cash

current assets assets that can be converted quickly into cash or that will be used in one year or less

fixed assets assets that will be held or used for a period longer than one year

depreciation the process of apportioning the cost of a fixed asset over the period during which it will be used

intangible assets assets that do not exist physically but that have a value based on the rights or privileges they confer on a firm

Figure 17.2 Business Balance Sheet

A balance sheet (sometimes referred to as a statement of financial position) summarizes a firm's accounts at the end of an accounting period, showing the various dollar amounts that enter into the accounting equation. Note that assets ($340,000) equal liabilities plus owners' equity ($340,000).

NORTHEAST ART SUPPLY, INC.

Balance Sheet
December 31, 20XX

ASSETS			
Current assets			
Cash		$ 59,000	
Marketable securities		10,000	
Accounts receivable	$ 40,000		
Less allowance for doubtful accounts	2,000	38,000	
Notes receivable		32,000	
Merchandise inventory		41,000	
Prepaid expenses		2,000	
Total current assets			$182,000
Fixed assets			
Delivery equipment	$110,000		
Less accumulated depreciation	20,000	$ 90,000	
Furniture and store equipment	$62,000		
Less accumulated depreciation	15,000	47,000	
Total fixed assets			137,000
Intangible assets			
Patents		$ 6,000	
Goodwill		15,000	
Total intangible assets			21,000
TOTAL ASSETS			$340,000
LIABILITIES AND STOCKHOLDERS' EQUITY			
Current liabilities			
Accounts payable	$ 35,000		
Notes payable	25,675		
Salaries payable	4,000		
Taxes payable	5,325		
Total current liabilities		$ 70,000	
Long-term liabilities			
Mortgage payable on store equipment	$ 40,000		
Total long-term liabilities		$ 40,000	
TOTAL LIABILITIES			$110,000
Stockholders' equity			
Common stock (25,000×$6)		$ 150,000	
Retained earnings		80,000	
TOTAL OWNERS' EQUITY			230,000
TOTAL LIABILITIES AND OWNERS' EQUITY			$340,000

estimate that the patent has a current market value of $6,000. The second intangible asset, *goodwill,* is the value of a firm's reputation, location, earning capacity, and other intangibles that make the business a profitable concern. Goodwill normally is not listed on a balance sheet unless the firm has been purchased from previous owners. In such a case, the new owners actually have paid an additional amount over and above the fair market value of the firm's assets for goodwill. Goodwill exists because most businesses are worth more as going concerns than as a collection of assets. Northeast Art's accountants included a $15,000 amount for goodwill. The firm's intangible assets total $21,000. Now it is possible to total all three types of assets for Northeast Art. As calculated in Figure 17.2, total assets are $340,000.

Liabilities and Owners' Equity

The liabilities and the owners' equity accounts complete the balance sheet. The firm's liabilities are separated into two categories—current and long-term liabilities.

Current Liabilities A firm's **current liabilities** are debts that will be repaid in one year or less. Northeast Art Supply purchased merchandise from its suppliers on credit. Thus, its balance sheet includes an entry for accounts payable. *Accounts payable* are short-term obligations that arise as a result of a firm making credit purchases.

Notes payable are obligations that have been secured with promissory notes. They are usually short-term obligations, but they may extend beyond one year. Only those that must be paid within the year are listed under current liabilities.

Northeast also lists *salaries payable* and *taxes payable* as current liabilities. These are both expenses that have been incurred during the current accounting period but will be paid in the next accounting period. For Northeast Art, current liabilities total $70,000.

Long-Term Liabilities **Long-term liabilities** are debts that need not be repaid for at least one year. Northeast lists only one long-term liability—a $40,000 *mortgage payable* for store equipment. As you can see in Figure 17.2, Northeast's current and long-term liabilities total $110,000.

Owners' or Stockholders' Equity For a sole proprietorship or partnership, the owners' equity is shown as the difference between assets and liabilities. In a partnership, each partner's share of the ownership is reported separately in each owner's name. For a corporation, the owners' equity usually is referred to as *stockholders' equity*. The dollar amount reported on the balance sheet is the total value of stock plus retained earnings that have accumulated to date. **Retained earnings** are the portion of a business's profits not distributed to stockholders.

The original investment by the owners of Northeast Art Supply was $150,000 and was obtained by selling 25,000 shares at $6 per share. In addition, $80,000 of Northeast's earnings has been reinvested in the business since it was founded. Thus, owners' equity totals $230,000.

As the two grand totals in Figure 17.2 show, Northeast's assets and the sum of its liabilities and owners' equity are equal—at $340,000. The accounting equation (Assets = liabilities + owners' equity) is still in balance.

current liabilities debts that will be repaid in one year or less

long-term liabilities debts that need not be repaid for at least one year

retained earnings the portion of a business's profits not distributed to stockholders

Read and interpret an income statement.

The Income Statement

Question: *Where can you find the profit or loss amount for Gap Inc.?*

Answer: The firm's income statement.

income statement a summary of a firm's revenues and expenses during a specified accounting period

An **income statement** is a summary of a firm's revenues and expenses during a specified accounting period—one month, three months, six months, or a year. The income statement is sometimes called the *earnings statement* or *the statement of*

Figure 17.3 Personal Income Statement

By subtracting expenses from income, anyone can construct a personal income statement and determine if he or she has a surplus or deficit at the end of each month.

Marty Campbell
Personal Income Statement
For the month ended December 31, 20XX

INCOME (Take-home pay)		$1,900
LESS MONTHLY EXPENSES		
Automobile loan	$ 250	
Credit card payment	100	
Apartment rent	500	
Utilities	200	
Food	250	
Clothing	100	
Recreation & entertainment	250	
TOTAL MONTHLY EXPENSES		1,650
CASH SURPLUS (or profit)		$ 250

income and expenses. Let's begin our discussion by constructing a personal income statement for Marty Campbell. Having worked as a sales representative for an office supply firm for the past three years, Marty now earns $33,600 a year, or $2,800 a month. After deductions, his take-home pay is $1,900 a month. As illustrated in Figure 17.3, Marty's typical monthly expenses include payments for an automobile loan, credit card purchases, apartment rent, utilities, food, clothing, and recreation and entertainment.

Although the difference between income and expenses is referred to as *profit* or *loss* for a business, it is normally referred to as a *cash surplus* or *cash deficit* for an individual. Fortunately for Marty, he has a surplus of $250 at the end of each month. He can use this surplus for savings, investing, or paying off debts.

Figure 17.4 shows the income statement for Northeast Art Supply. For a business, revenues *less* cost of goods sold *less* operating expenses equals net income.

Revenues

Revenues are the dollar amounts earned by a firm from selling goods, providing services, or performing business activities. Like most businesses, Northeast Art obtains its revenues solely from the sale of its products or services. The revenues section of its income statement begins with gross sales. **Gross sales** are the total dollar amount of all goods and services sold during the accounting period. Deductions made from this amount are

- *Sales returns*—merchandise returned to the firm by its customers
- *Sales allowances*—price reductions offered to customers who accept slightly damaged or soiled merchandise
- *Sales discounts*—price reductions offered to customers who pay their bills promptly

revenues the dollar amounts earned by a firm from selling goods, providing services, or performing business activities

gross sales the total dollar amount of all goods and services sold during the accounting period

Figure 17.4 Business Income Statement

An income statement summarizes a firm's revenues and expenses during a specified accounting period. For Northeast Art, net income after taxes is $30,175.

NORTHEAST ART SUPPLY, INC.

Income Statement
For the Year Ended
December 31, 20XX

Revenues			
Gross sales		$465,000	
Less sales returns and allowances	$ 9,500		
Less sales discounts	4,500	14,000	
Net sales			$451,000
Cost of goods sold			
Beginning inventory, January 1, 20XX		$ 40,000	
Purchases	$346,000		
Less purchase discounts	11,000		
Net purchases		335,000	
Cost of goods available for sale		$375,000	
Less ending inventory December 31, 20XX		41,000	
Cost of goods sold			334,000
Gross profit			$117,000
Operating expenses			
Selling expenses			
Sales salaries	$ 22,000		
Advertising	4,000		
Sales promotion	2,500		
Depreciation—store equipment	3,000		
Depreciation—delivery equipment	4,000		
Miscellaneous selling expenses	1,500		
Total selling expenses		$ 37,000	
General expenses			
Office salaries	$ 28,500		
Rent	8,500		
Depreciation—furniture	1,500		
Utilities expense	2,500		
Insurance expense	1,000		
Miscellaneous expense	500		
Total general expense		42,500	
Total operating expenses			79,500
Net income from operations			$ 37,500
Less interest expense			2,000
NET INCOME BEFORE TAXES			$ 35,500
Less federal income taxes			5,325
NET INCOME AFTER TAXES			$ 30,175

net sales the actual dollar amounts received by a firm for the goods and services it has sold after adjustment for returns, allowances, and discounts

cost of goods sold the dollar amount equal to beginning inventory *plus* net purchases *less* ending inventory

Inventory by the numbers. For most retailers, determining the level of available inventory in a store is a very important accounting function. In this photo, Chenille English-Boswell, an executive team leader at a Chicago-area Target Store, checks not only inventory levels but also prices to make sure merchandise is correctly priced.

The remainder is the firm's net sales. **Net sales** are the actual dollar amounts received by the firm for the goods and services it has sold after adjustment for returns, allowances, and discounts. For Northeast Art, net sales are $451,000.

Cost of Goods Sold

The standard method of determining the **cost of goods sold** by a retailing or a wholesaling firm can be summarized as follows:

Cost of goods sold = **beginning inventory + net purchases − ending inventory**

A manufacturer must include raw materials inventories, work in process, finished goods inventory, and direct manufacturing costs in this computation.

According to Figure 17.4, Northeast began its accounting period on January 1 with a merchandise inventory that

Ethical Challenges &

SUCCESSFUL SOLUTIONS

Trust and Accounting Fraud

Who's responsible for frauds committed against U.S. businesses? In the past, PricewaterhouseCoopers surveys have revealed an even split between insiders (such as employees and managers) and outsiders (such as customers and intermediaries). More recently, its surveys have found that insiders—mainly middle- and lower-level managers—are now responsible for the majority of frauds such as misappropriating funds and reporting phantom sales. Unfortunately, companies anticipate that such frauds will increase in the coming years.

As a result, companies face a delicate balancing act between showing employees that they're trusted and having internal controls in place to detect and prevent accounting fraud. This is a particular problem in small businesses where staff members must stretch to cover multiple job responsibilities. "Managers and small business owners have a tendency to trust their employees to a higher degree," says an official at the Association of Certified Fraud Examiners. "That level of trust is often betrayed."

Yet the entire workforce could be at risk if an employer falls victim to a scheme that sucks the financial life out of the business. This is why companies are working to strengthen their accounting oversight and hire outside experts to check on internal controls. To foster ethical accounting behavior, professional groups such as the American Institute of CPAs have developed codes of conduct to guide their members.

Sources: Elizabeth Wasserman, "How to Protect Your Business Against Fraud," *Inc.*, March 12, 2010, http://www.inc.com; Tammy Whitehouse, "IIA Offers Fraud Guidance for Internal Auditors," *Compliance Week*, March 2010, 30; Toby J. F. Bishop and Frank E. Hydoski, "Who's Allegedly 'Cooking the Books' and Where?" *Business Crimes Bulletin*, January 1, 2010, n.p.; American Institute of Certified Public Accountants, http://www.aicpa.org/Research/Standards/CodeofConduct/Pages/default.aspx; Emily Chasan, "Global Corporate Accounting Fraud Up Sharply: Survey," *Reuters*, November 19, 2009, http://www.reuters.com.

cost $40,000. During the next 12 months, the firm purchased merchandise valued at $346,000. After deducting *purchase discounts,* however, it paid only $335,000 for this merchandise. Thus, during the year, Northeast had total *goods available for sale* valued at $40,000 plus $335,000, for a total of $375,000.

Twelve months later, at the end of the accounting period on December 31, Northeast had sold all but $41,000 worth of the available goods. The cost of goods sold by Northeast was therefore $375,000 less ending inventory of $41,000, or $334,000. It is now possible to calculate gross profit. A firm's **gross profit** is its net sales *less* the cost of goods sold. For Northeast, gross profit was $117,000.

Operating Expenses

A firm's **operating expenses** are all business costs other than the cost of goods sold. Total operating expenses generally are divided into two categories: selling expenses or general expenses.

Selling expenses are costs related to the firm's marketing activities. For Northeast Art, selling expenses total $37,000. *General expenses* are costs incurred in managing a business. For Northeast Art, general expenses total $42,500. Now it is possible to total both selling and general expenses. As Figure 17.4 shows, total operating expenses for the accounting period are $79,500.

Net Income

When revenues exceed expenses, the difference is called **net income.** When expenses exceed revenues, the difference is called **net loss.** As Figure 17.4 shows, Northeast Art's *net income from operations* is computed as gross profit ($117,000) less total operating expenses ($79,500). For Northeast Art, net income from operations is $37,500. From this amount, *interest expense* of $2,000 is deducted to obtain a *net income before taxes* of $35,500. The interest expense is deducted in this section of the income statement because it is not an operating expense. Rather, it is an expense that results from financing the business.

gross profit a firm's net sales *less* the cost of goods sold

operating expenses all business costs other than the cost of goods sold

net income occurs when revenues exceed expenses

net loss occurs when expenses exceed revenues

One necessary business expense! Without jet airplanes, FedEx cannot provide overnight delivery services to its customers. Started in 1971 by entrepreneur Fred Smith in Memphis, Tennessee, Federal Express now employs 217,000 people and provides worldwide delivery services that generate annual revenues of $36 billion.

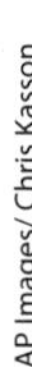

Northeast's *federal income taxes* are $5,325. Although these taxes may or may not be payable immediately, they are definitely an expense that must be deducted from income. This leaves Northeast Art with a *net income after taxes* of $30,175. This amount may be used to pay a dividend to stockholders, it may be retained or reinvested in the firm, it may be used to reduce the firm's debts, or all three.

6

Describe business activities that affect a firm's cash flow.

The Statement of Cash Flows

Cash is vital to any business. In 1987, the SEC and the FASB required all publicly traded companies to include a statement of cash flows, along with their balance sheet and income statement, in their annual report. The **statement of cash flows** illustrates how the company's operating, investing, and financing activities affect cash during an accounting period. Whereas a firm's balance sheet reports dollar values for assets, liabilities, and owners' equity and an income statement reports the firm's dollar amount of profit or loss, the statement of cash flow focuses on how much cash is on hand to pay the firm's bills. Executives and managers can also use the information on a firm's statement of cash flows to determine how much cash is available to pay dividends to stockholders. Finally, the information on the statement of cash flows can be used to evaluate decisions related to a firm's future investments and financing needs. Outside stakeholders including investors, lenders, and suppliers are also interested in a firm's statement of cash flows. Investors want to know if a firm can pay dividends in the future. Before extending credit to a firm, lenders and suppliers often use the information on the statement of cash flows to evaluate the firm's ability to repay its debts.

A statement of cash flows for Northeast Art Supply is illustrated in Figure 17.5. It provides information concerning the company's cash receipts and cash payments and is organized around three different activities: operating, investing, and financing.

statement of cash flows
a statement that illustrates how the company's operating, investing, and financing activities affect cash during an accounting period

- *Cash flows from operating activities.* This is the first section of a statement of cash flows. It addresses the firm's primary revenue source—providing goods

Figure 17.5 Statement of Cash Flows

A statement of cash flows summarizes how a firm's operating, investing, and financing activities affect its cash during a specified period—one month, three months, six months, or a year. For Northeast Art, the amount of cash at the end of the year reported on the statement of cash flows is $59,000—the same amount reported for the cash account on the firm's balance sheet.

NORTHEAST ART SUPPLY, INC.

Statement of Cash Flows
For the Year Ended
December 31, 20XX

Cash flows from operating activities		
Net Income		$30,175
Adjustments to reconcile net income to net cash flows		
Depreciation	$ 8,500	
Decrease in accounts receivable	1,000	
Increase in inventory	(5,000)	
Increase in accounts payable	6,000	
Increase in income taxes payable	3,000	13,500
Net cash provided by operating activities		$43,675
Cash flows from investing activities		
Purchase of equipment	$ (2,000)	
Purchase of investments	(10,000)	
Sale of investments	20,000	
Net cash provided by investing activities		8,000
Cash flows from financing activities		
Payments on debt	$(23,000)	
Payment of dividends	(5,000)	
Net cash provided by financing activities		(28,000)
NET INCREASE IN CASH		$23,675
Cash at beginning of year		35,325
CASH AT END OF YEAR		$59,000

and services. Typical adjustments include adding the amount of depreciation to a firm's net income. Other adjustments for increase or decrease in amounts for accounts receivable, inventory, accounts payable, and income taxes payable are also required to reflect a true picture of cash flows from operating activities.

- *Cash flows from investing activities.* The second section of the statement is concerned with cash flow from investments. This includes the purchase and sale of land, equipment, and other assets and investments.
- *Cash flows from financing activities.* The third and final section deals with the cash flow from all financing activities. It reports changes in debt obligation and owners' equity accounts. This includes loans and repayments, the sale and repurchase of the company's own stock, and cash dividends.

The totals of all three activities are added to the beginning cash balance to determine the ending cash balance. For Northeast Art Supply, the ending cash balance is $59,000. Note that this is the same amount reported for the cash account on the firm's balance sheet. Together, the statement of cash flows, balance sheet, and income statement illustrate the results of past business decisions and reflect the firm's ability to pay debts and dividends and to finance new growth.

Summarize how managers evaluate the financial health of a business.

Evaluating Financial Statements

All three financial statements—the balance sheet, the income statement, and the statement of cash flows—can provide answers to a variety of questions about a firm's ability to do business and stay in business, its profitability, and its value as an investment.

Using Accounting Information to Evaluate a Potential Investment

Many investors rely on accounting information to gauge the financial health of a business. Today, all three financial statements are included in a corporation's annual report. You can request a current annual report by contacting the corporation by mail or telephone. You can also obtain an annual report and additional accounting information by accessing the firm's Web site. Once at the corporate Web site, click on the button for "Investor Relations" or "Financial Information." Accounting information about a corporation is also available from many professional investment advisory services.

To help evaluate potential investments, investors often use a firm's three financial statements—the information on the balance sheet, income statement, and statement of cash flows. Although the numbers may be frightening, it helps to take a commonsense approach to evaluating accounting information. For example, consider the following questions:

1. Is an increase in sales revenues a healthy sign for a corporation? (Answer: yes)
2. Should a firm's net profit increase or decrease over time? (Answer: increase)
3. Should a corporation's retained earnings increase or decrease over time? (Answer: increase)

Although the answers to these questions are obvious, you will be surprised by how much you can learn from accounting information if you just spend some time with the numbers. In addition to a commonsense approach to evaluating a firm's accounting information, it helps to remember the following suggestions:

- All three financial statements should be audited by an outside source. The amounts reported on audited financial statements have been examined by an accountant(s) in order to determine if the firm used GAAPs.
- The balance sheet is a snapshot of the corporation's financial position at a single point in time. The dollar amounts for each asset, liability, and owners' equity account reported on a balance sheet will change over time. Therefore, be sure to use the most recent balance sheet available.
- The income statement reports sales revenues, expenses, and profit or loss for a specific period of time. Smart investors look for companies that are not only profitable, but also using new strategies to reduce operating expenses.
- The statement of cash flows indicates how much cash the business has and how it manages the cash that flows into and out of the business. This statement can help you determine if the firm can pay its debts and maintain its ability to borrow money in the future.
- Look at how the numbers relate to each other. For example, investors generally like to see that current assets are greater than current liabilities. This means the firm can pay its short-term liabilities quickly and maintain its ability to borrow additional money when needed.
- Learn how to calculate and interpret financial ratios. Some of the most important financial ratios are discussed in the last part of this chapter.

Sometimes additional information can be obtained by digging deeper into a firm's annual report. Be sure and read the letters from the chairman of the board and chief executive officer that describe the corporation's operations, prospects for the future, new products or services, financial strengths, and any potential problems. In addition, examine the footnotes closely, and look for red flags that may be

Figure 17.6 Comparisons of Present and Past Financial Statements for Microsoft Corporation

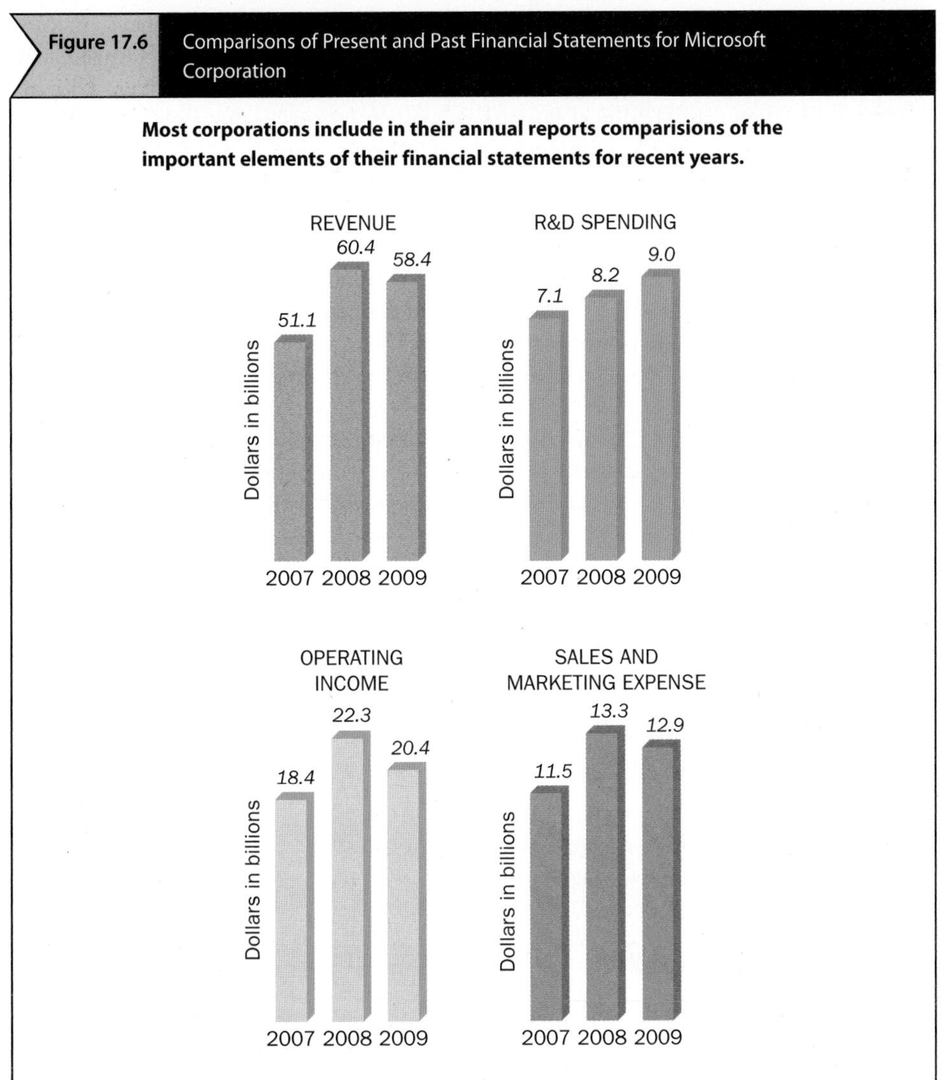

Source: Adapted from the Microsoft Corporation 2009 Annual Report, http://www.microsoft.com (accessed April 12, 2010).

in the fine print. Often, the footnotes contain (and sometimes hide) important information about the company and its finances. As one expert put it, "the footnotes are where they bury the bodies."

Finally, most corporations include in their annual reports comparisons of the important elements of their financial statements for recent years. Figure 17.6 shows such comparisons—of revenue, research and development (R&D), operating income, and sales and marketing expenses—for Microsoft Corporation, a world leader in the computer software industry. By examining these data, an operating manager can tell whether R&D expenditures have been increasing or decreasing over the past three years. The vice president of marketing can determine if the total amount of sales and marketing expenses is changing. Stockholders and potential investors, on the other hand, may be more concerned with increases or decreases in Microsoft's revenues and operating income over the same time period.

Comparing Data with Other Firms' Data

Many firms also compare their financial results with those of competing firms and with industry averages. Comparisons are possible as long as accountants follow GAAPs.

Except for minor differences in format and terms, the balance sheet, income statement, and statement of cash flows of Procter & Gamble, for example, will be similar to those of other large corporations, such as Alberto-Culver, Clorox, Colgate-Palmolive, and Unilever, in the consumer goods industry. Comparisons among firms give managers a general idea of a firm's relative effectiveness and its standing within the industry. Competitors' financial statements can be obtained from their annual reports—if they are public corporations. Industry averages are published by reporting services such as D&B (formerly Dun & Bradstreet) and Standard & Poor's, as well as by some industry trade associations.

Still another type of analysis of a firm's financial health involves computation of financial ratios. A **financial ratio** is a number that shows the relationship between two elements of a firm's financial statements. Among the most useful ratios are profitability ratios, short-term financial ratios, activity ratios, and the debt-to-owners'-equity ratio. Like the individual elements in financial statements, these ratios can be compared with the firm's past ratios, with those of competitors, and with industry averages. The information required to form these ratios is found in a firm's balance sheet, income statement, and statement of cash flows (in our examples for Northeast Art Supply, Figures 17.2, 17.4, and 17.5).

Profitability Ratios

A firm's net income after taxes indicates whether the firm is profitable. It does not, however, indicate how effectively the firm's resources are being used. For this latter purpose, three ratios can be computed.

Return on Sales **Return on sales (or profit margin)** is a financial ratio calculated by dividing net income after taxes by net sales. For Northeast Art Supply,

$$\text{Return on sales} = \frac{\text{net income after taxes}}{\text{net sales}} = \frac{\$30{,}175}{\$451{,}000}$$
$$= 0.067, \text{ or } 6.7 \text{ percent}$$

The return on sales indicates how effectively the firm is transforming sales into profits. A higher return on sales is better than a low one. Today, the average return on sales for all business firms is between 4 and 5 percent. With a return on sales of 6.7 percent, Northeast Art Supply is above average. A low return on sales can be increased by reducing expenses, increasing sales, or both.

Return on Owners' Equity **Return on owners' equity** is a financial ratio calculated by dividing net income after taxes by owners' equity. For Northeast Art Supply,

$$\text{Return on owners' equity} = \frac{\text{net income after taxes}}{\text{owners' equity}} = \frac{\$30{,}175}{\$230{,}000}$$
$$= 0.13, \text{ or } 13 \text{ percent}$$

Return on owners' equity indicates how much income is generated by each dollar of equity. Northeast is providing income of 13 cents per dollar invested in the business. The average for all businesses is between 12 and 15 cents. A higher return on owners' equity is better than a low one, and the only practical ways to increase return on owners' equity is to reduce expenses, increase sales, or both.

Earnings per Share From the point of view of stockholders, **earnings per share** is one of the best indicators of a corporation's success. It is calculated by dividing

financial ratio a number that shows the relationship between two elements of a firm's financial statements

return on sales (or profit margin) a financial ratio calculated by dividing net income after taxes by net sales

return on owners' equity a financial ratio calculated by dividing net income after taxes by owners' equity

earnings per share a financial ratio calculated by dividing net income after taxes by the number of shares of common stock outstanding

net income after taxes by the number of shares of common stock outstanding. For Northeast Art Supply,

$$\text{Earnings per share} = \frac{\text{net income after taxes}}{\text{common stock shares outstanding}} = \frac{\$30,175}{\$25,000}$$
$$= \$1.21 \text{ per share}$$

There is no meaningful average for this ratio mainly because the number of outstanding shares of a firm's stock is subject to change as a result of stock splits and stock dividends. In addition, some corporations choose to issue more stock than others. As a general rule, however, an increase in earnings per share is a healthy sign for any corporation.

Short-Term Financial Ratios

Two short-term financial ratios permit managers (and lenders) to evaluate a firm's ability to pay its current liabilities. Before we discuss these ratios, we should examine one other easily determined measure: working capital.

Working Capital **Working capital** is the difference between current assets and current liabilities. For Northeast Art,

Current assets	\$182,000
Less current liabilities	70,000
Equals working capital	\$112,000

Working capital indicates how much would remain if a firm paid off all current liabilities with cash and other current assets. The "proper" amount of working capital depends on the type of firm, its past experience, and its particular industry. A firm with too little working capital may have to borrow money to finance its operations.

working capital the difference between current assets and current liabilities

current ratio a financial ratio computed by dividing current assets by current liabilities

acid-test ratio a financial ratio calculated by adding cash, marketable securities, and receivables and dividing the total by current liabilities

Current Ratio A firm's **current ratio** is computed by dividing current assets by current liabilities. For Northeast Art Supply,

$$\text{Current ratio} = \frac{\text{current assets}}{\text{current liabilities}} = \frac{\$182,000}{\$70,000} = 2.6$$

This means that Northeast Art Supply has \$2.60 of current assets for every \$1 of current liabilities. The average current ratio for all industries is 2.0, but it varies greatly from industry to industry. A high current ratio indicates that a firm can pay its current liabilities. A low current ratio can be improved by repaying current liabilities, by reducing dividend payments to stockholders to increase the firm's cash balance, or by obtaining additional cash from investors.

Sometimes accountants dig deeper to get more facts. As part of the accounting process, a firm often calculates financial ratios to evaluate the information on its balance sheet, income statement, and statement of cash flows. Among the most useful are ratios that measure a firm's profitability, ability to pay its debts and borrow money, and inventory turnover.

Acid-Test Ratio This ratio, sometimes called the *quick ratio,* is a measure of the firm's ability to pay current liabilities *quickly*—with its cash, marketable securities, and receivables. The **acid-test ratio** is calculated by adding cash, marketable securities, and receivables and dividing the total by current liabilities. The value of inventory and other current assets is "removed" from current assets because these assets are not converted into cash as easily as cash, marketable securities, and receivables. For Northeast Art Supply,

$$\text{Acid-test ratio} = \frac{\text{cash} + \text{marketable securities} + \text{receivables}}{\text{current liabilities}} = \frac{\$139{,}000}{\$70{,}000}$$

$$= 1.99$$

For all businesses, the desired acid-test ratio is 1.0. Northeast Art Supply is above average with a ratio of 1.99, and the firm should be well-able to pay its current liabilities. To increase a low acid-test ratio, a firm would have to repay current liabilities, reduce dividend payments to stockholders to increase the firm's cash balance, or obtain additional cash from investors.

Activity Ratios

Two activity ratios permit managers to measure how many times each year a company collects its accounts receivables or sells its inventory.

Accounts Receivable Turnover A firm's **accounts receivable turnover** is the number of times the firm collects its accounts receivable in one year. This ratio can be calculated by dividing net sales by accounts receivable. For Northeast Art,

$$\text{Accounts receivable turnover} = \frac{\text{net sales}}{\text{accounts receivable}} = \frac{\$451{,}000}{\$38{,}000}$$

$$= 11.9 \text{ times per year}$$

Northeast Art Supply collects its accounts receivables 11.9 times each year, or about every 30 days. If a firm's credit terms require customers to pay in 25 days, a collection period of 30 days is considered acceptable. There is no meaningful average for this measure mainly because credit terms differ among companies. A high accounts receivable turnover is better than a low one. As a general rule, a low accounts receivable turnover ratio can be improved by pressing for payment of past-due accounts and by tightening requirements for prospective credit customers.

Inventory Turnover A firm's **inventory turnover** is the number of times the firm sells its merchandise inventory in one year. It is approximated by dividing the cost of goods sold in one year by the average value of the inventory.

The average value of the inventory can be found by adding the beginning inventory value and the ending inventory value (given on the income statement) and dividing the sum by 2. For Northeast Art Supply, average inventory is $40,500. Thus

$$\text{Inventory turnover} = \frac{\text{cost of goods sold}}{\text{average inventory}} = \frac{\$334{,}000}{\$40{,}500}$$

$$= 8.2 \text{ times per year}$$

Northeast Art Supply sells its merchandise inventory 8.2 times each year, or about once every 45 days. The average inventory turnover for all firms is about 9 times per year, but turnover rates vary widely from industry to industry. For example, supermarkets may have inventory turnover rates of 20 or higher, whereas inventory turnover rates for furniture stores are generally well below the national average. The quickest way to improve inventory turnover is to order merchandise in smaller quantities at more frequent intervals.

accounts receivable turnover a financial ratio calculated by dividing net sales by accounts receivable

inventory turnover a financial ratio calculated by dividing the cost of goods sold in one year by the average value of the inventory

Debt-to-Owners'-Equity Ratio

Our final category of financial ratios indicates the degree to which a firm's operations are financed through borrowing. Although other ratios can be calculated, the debt-to-owners'-equity ratio is used often to determine whether a firm has too much debt. The **debt-to-owners'-equity ratio** is calculated by dividing total liabilities by owners' equity. For Northeast Art Supply,

$$\text{Debt-to-owners'-equity ratio} = \frac{\text{total liabilities}}{\text{owners' equity}} = \frac{\$110{,}000}{\$230{,}000}$$
$$= 0.48, \text{ or } 48 \text{ percent}$$

A debt-to-owners'-equity ratio of 48 percent means that creditors have provided about 48 cents of financing for every dollar provided by the owners. The higher this ratio, the riskier the situation is for lenders. A high debt-to-owners'-equity ratio may make borrowing additional money from lenders difficult. It can be reduced by paying off debts or by increasing the owners' investment in the firm.

Northeast's Financial Ratios: A Summary

Table 17.2 compares the financial ratios of Northeast Art Supply with the average financial ratios for all businesses. It also lists the formulas we used to calculate

debt-to-owners'-equity ratio a financial ratio calculated by dividing total liabilities by owners' equity

Table 17.2 Financial Ratios of Northeast Art Supply Compared with Average Ratios for All Businesses

Ratio	Formula	Northeast Ratio	Average Business Ratio	Direction for Improvement
Profitability Ratios				
Return on sales	net income after taxes / net sales	6.7%	4%–5%	Higher
Return on owners' equity	net income after taxes / owners' equity	13%	12%–15%	Higher
Earnings per share	net income after taxes / common stock shares outstanding	$1.21 per share	—	Higher
Short-Term Financial Ratios				
Working capital	current assets − current liabilities	$112,000	—	Higher
Current ratio	current assets / current liabilities	2.6	2.0	Higher
Acid-test ratio	cash + marketable securities + receivables / current liabilities	1.99	1.0	Higher
Activity Ratios				
Accounts receivable turnover	net sales / accounts receivable	11.9	—	Higher
Inventory turnover	cost of goods sold / average inventory	8.2	9	Higher
Debt-to-owners'-equity ratio	total liabilities / owners' equity	48%	—	Lower

Northeast's ratios. Northeast seems to be in good financial shape. Its return on sales, current ratio, and acid-test ratio are all above average. Its other ratios are about average, although its inventory turnover and debt-to-equity ratio could be improved.

This chapter ends our discussion of accounting information. In Chapter 18, we begin our examination of business finances by discussing money, banking, and credit.

return to inside business

Deloitte

Deloitte has the expertise to dig deeply into the financial data of corporations in many industries, from aerospace and automotive products to retailing and real estate. It also offers accounting, auditing, and consulting services to state and local government agencies, helping officials improve productivity, deal with budget realities, and increase transparency.

Knowing that dedicated personnel are the heart of its business and the key to continued success, Deloitte works hard to be an outstanding and understanding employer. When managers conduct employee evaluations, they discuss life goals as well as work goals. The firm's Mass Career Customization program offers a variety of opportunities for balancing personal and professional commitments through telecommuting, flextime, shorter work weeks, time off, and other choices. This human touch has put Deloitte in the public eye and put it on many "best employer" lists, including *Fortune's* "100 Best Companies to Work For in America" and *BusinessWeek's* "Best Places to Intern."

Questions

1. When an accounting firm like Deloitte has been hired to sign off on a public corporation's annual report, should it limit its consulting work to avoid being influenced by financial ties to the client? Explain your answer.
2. Why would the Recording Academy hire Deloitte instead of having its own employees count votes for the Grammy awards?

CHAPTER REVIEW

SUMMARY

Summary

1 Explain why accurate accounting information and audited financial statements are important.

Accounting is the process of systematically collecting, analyzing, and reporting financial information. It can be used to answer questions about what has happened in the past; it also can be used to help make decisions about the future. In fact, the firm's accountants and its accounting system often translate goals, objectives, and plans into dollars and cents to help determine if a decision or plan of action makes "financial sense." Unfortunately, a large number of accounting scandals have caused people to doubt the financial information reported by a corporation. The purpose of an audit is to make sure that a firm's financial statements have been prepared in accordance with GAAPs. To help ensure that corporate financial information is accurate and in response to the accounting scandals that surfaced in the last part of the 1990s and the first part of the 21st century, the Sarbanes-Oxley Act was signed into law. This law contains a number of provisions designed to restore public confidence in the accounting industry.

2 Identify the people who use accounting information and possible careers in the accounting industry.

To be successful in the accounting industry, employees must be responsible, honest, and ethical; have a strong background in financial management; know how to use a computer and software to process data into accounting information; and be able to communicate with people who need accounting information. Primarily, management uses accounting information, but it is also demanded by lenders, suppliers, stockholders, potential investors, and government agencies. Although many people think that all accountants do the same tasks, there are special areas of expertise within the accounting industry. Typical areas of expertise include managerial, financial, cost, tax, government, and not-for-profit accounting. A private accountant is employed by a specific organization to operate its accounting system. A public accountant performs these functions for various individuals or firms on a fee basis. Most accounting firms include on their staffs at least one CPA. In addition to CPAs, there are also CMAs.

3 Discuss the accounting process.

The accounting process is based on the accounting equation: Assets = liabilities + owners' equity. Double-entry bookkeeping ensures that the balance shown by the accounting equation is maintained. The accounting process involves five steps: (1) source documents are analyzed, (2) each transaction is recorded in a journal, (3) each journal entry is posted in the appropriate general ledger accounts, (4) at the end of each accounting period, a trial balance is prepared to make sure that the accounting equation is in balance, and (5) financial statements are prepared from the trial balance. A firm's financial statements are included in its annual report. An annual report is a report distributed to stockholders and other interested parties that describes a firm's operating activities and its financial condition. Once statements are prepared, the books are closed. A new accounting cycle then is begun for the next accounting period.

4 Read and interpret a balance sheet.

A balance sheet (sometimes referred to as a statement of financial position) is a summary of a firm's assets, liabilities, and owners' equity accounts at the end of an accounting period. This statement must demonstrate that the accounting equation is in balance. On the balance sheet, assets are categorized as current, fixed, or intangible. Similarly, liabilities can be divided into current liabilities and long-term ones. For a sole proprietorship or partnership, owners' equity is shown as the difference between assets and liabilities. For corporations, the owners' equity section reports the values of stock and retained earnings.

5 Read and interpret an income statement.

An income statement is a summary of a firm's financial operations during the specified accounting period. On the income statement, the company's gross profit is computed by subtracting the cost of goods sold from net sales. Operating expenses and interest expense then are deducted to compute net income before taxes. Finally, income taxes are deducted to obtain the firm's net income after taxes.

6 Describe business activities that affect a firm's cash flow.

Since 1987, the Securities and Exchange Commission (SEC) and the FASB have required all publicly traded companies to include a statement of cash flows in their annual reports. This statement illustrates how the company's operating, investing, and financing activities affect cash during an accounting period. Together, the cash flow statement, balance sheet, and income statement illustrate the results of past decisions and the business's ability to pay debts and dividends as well as to finance new growth.

7 Summarize how managers evaluate the financial health of a business.

The firm's financial statements and its accounting information become more meaningful when compared with corresponding information for previous years, for competitors, and for the industry in which the firm operates. Such comparisons permit managers, employees, lenders, investors, and other interested people to pick out trends in growth, borrowing, income, and other business variables and to determine whether the firm is on the way to accomplishing its long-term goals. A number of financial ratios can be computed from the information in a firm's financial statements. These ratios provide a picture of the firm's profitability, its short-term financial position, its activity in the area of accounts receivable and inventory, and its debt financing. Like the information on the firm's financial statements, these ratios can and should be compared with those of past accounting periods, those of competitors, and those representing the average of the industry as a whole.

Key Terms

You should now be able to define and give an example relevant to each of the following terms:

accounting (499)
audit (500)
generally accepted accounting principles (GAAPs) (500)
managerial accounting (503)
financial accounting (503)
certified public accountant (CPA) (504)
certified management accountant (CMA) (504)
assets (505)
liabilities (505)
owners' equity (505)
accounting equation (505)
double-entry bookkeeping system (505)
trial balance (506)
annual report (506)
balance sheet (or statement of financial position) (507)
liquidity (508)
current assets (508)
fixed assets (508)
depreciation (508)

intangible assets (508)
current liabilities (510)
long-term liabilities (510)
retained earnings (510)
income statement (510)
revenues (511)
gross sales (511)
net sales (512)
cost of goods sold (512)
gross profit (513)
operating expenses (513)
net income (513)
net loss (513)
statement of cash flows (514)
financial ratio (518)
return on sales (or profit margin) (518)
return on owners' equity (518)
earnings per share (518)
working capital (519)
current ratio (519)
acid-test ratio (519)
accounts receivable turnover (520)
inventory turnover (520)
debt-to-owners'-equity ratio (521)

Review Questions

1. What purpose do audits and GAAPs serve in today's business world?
2. How do the major provisions of the Sarbanes-Oxley Act affect a public company's audit procedures?
3. List four groups that use accounting information, and briefly explain why each group has an interest in this information.
4. What is the difference between a private accountant and a public accountant? What are certified public accountants and certified management accountants?
5. State the accounting equation, and list two specific examples of each term in the equation.
6. How is double-entry bookkeeping related to the accounting equation?
7. Briefly describe the five steps of the accounting cycle in order.
8. What is the principal difference between a balance sheet and an income statement?
9. How are current assets distinguished from fixed assets? Why are fixed assets depreciated on a balance sheet?
10. Explain how a retailing firm would determine the cost of goods sold during an accounting period.
11. How does a firm determine its net income after taxes?
12. What is the purpose of a statement of cash flows?
13. For each of the accounts listed below, indicate if the account should be included on a firm's balance sheet, income statement, or statement of cash flows.

Type of Account	Statement Where Reported
Assets	____________
Income	____________
Expenses	____________
Operating activities	____________
Liabilities	____________
Investing activities	____________
Owners' equity	____________

14. How can accounting information help you evaluate a potential investment?
15. Explain the calculation procedure for and significance of each of the following:
    a. One of the profitability ratios
    b. A short-term financial ratio
    c. An activity ratio
    d. Debt-to-owners'-equity ratio

Discussion Questions

1. Why do you think there have been so many accounting scandals in recent years?
2. Bankers usually insist that prospective borrowers submit audited financial statements along with a loan application. Why should financial statements be audited by a CPA?
3. What can be said about a firm whose owners' equity is a negative amount? How could such a situation come about?
4. Do the balance sheet, income statement, and statement of cash flows contain all the information you might want as a potential lender or stockholder? What other information would you like to examine?
5. Why is it so important to compare a firm's current financial statements with those of previous years, those of competitors, and the average of all firms in the industry in which the firm operates?
6. Which do you think are the two or three most important financial ratios? Why?

Video Case 17.1

Accounting Information Helps Level the Playing Field for The Little Guys

As the "leading supplier of exclusive, high-end audio and video electronics for homes, businesses, educational institutions, and other organizations in greater Chicagoland," The Little Guys has built an enviable reputation since its founding in 1994. The Little Guys sells and installs top-brand home audio and theater equipment and does it well. The company prides itself on its highly knowledgeable salespeople and outstanding customer service, and these have helped it survive strong competition from both "big guys" like the Best Buy electronics chain, which has a store not far away, and economic downturns that have cut consumers' buying power. "We have the best employees," says the company's Web site, and "how we treat our customers makes us great."

David Wexler, the store's co-owner, describes how one of the firm's award-winning salespeople deals with his customers, for instance: "If a guy comes in to buy a $50 DVD player, Ed treats him the same as the guy who's spending $500,000 with us. I think that's what keeps people coming back over and over and over. He fights for them. Frankly, sometimes he fights too much for them. But he's their advocate, and they know it."

In response to recession-slowed sales, the company was recently forced to lay some people off and has reorganized departments from advertising to payroll (the latter is a major and complex expense for The Little Guys because its salespeople earn base pay plus a percentage of their sales). In another cost-cutting move, the company also recently moved to a new location not far from its original store, and it's keeping close track of its cash flows in and out. Salespeople are careful about customers' change orders, too, which often cost the company money.

"We're in survival mode as opposed to growth mode," says David Wexler of the downturn. "You can try to put cherries or chocolate sauce on it, but the fact is, it's... brutal out there right now.... But if there's a thin silver lining to the whole thing, it's that you are cleaning things up and eliminating waste and finding ways to do business better."

With the help of QuickBooks accounting software and a professional accountant who visits regularly, David Wexler and co-owner Evie Wexler have deepened their knowledge of accounting and finance as the business has grown. In the beginning, for instance, they checked sales figures every day, but David quickly realized that this practice created instant information overload. Now he looks at the numbers about every week or ten days, comparing each set with past results, and the accountant comes in at least once each quarter to help with more complex issues like depreciation of assets and equipment for tax purposes. Taxes are a big concern. As Evie Wexler points out, sometimes the firm has to make a special push to sell off inventory in order to generate extra cash flow when taxes are due, or when it wants to purchase new merchandise that customers are asking for and that will therefore sell faster. Keeping warehoused inventory low saves money, too.

One reason cash flow can be slow is that customers often negotiate prices at The Little Guys, so that an expensive system might not only be sold at a discount, but the customer may also be given extra time to pay. That certainly helps make customers happy, but if it means the company is paying its own suppliers on time while customers lag in their payments, cash can get tight. As David explains, that's partly why The Little Guys limits the number of brands it sells and works with only a few suppliers. Establishing good relationships with these suppliers, largely by ordering regularly and paying on time, allows the company to ask them for special discounts or improved payment terms—even when other retailers aren't getting them—and find yet another way to earn a little more profit on the same volume of sales.[8]

Questions

1. Do you think a fairly small company like The Little Guys still needs a professional accountant after its owners have had so much experience running a successful business? Why or why not?
2. Do you think The Little Guys is doing a good job of managing its cash flow? If so, why, and if not, how can the company improve this function?
3. What are some of the factors that contribute to The Little Guys' operating expenses?

Case 17.2

Making the Numbers or Faking the Numbers?

Will sales and profits meet the expectations of investors and Wall Street analysts? Managers at public corporations must answer this important question quarter after quarter, year after year. In an ideal world—one in which the economy never contracts, expenses never go up, and customers never buy competing products—the corporation's share price would soar, and investors would cheer as every financial report showed ever-higher sales revenues, profit margins, and earnings.

In the real world, however, many uncontrollable and unpredictable factors can affect a corporation's performance. Customers may buy fewer units or postpone purchases, competitors may introduce superior products, expenses may rise, interest rates may climb, and buying power may plummet. Faced with the prospect of releasing financial results that fall short of Wall Street's expectations, managers may feel intense pressure to "make the numbers" using a variety of accounting techniques.

For example, some executives at the telecom company WorldCom made earnings look better by booking billions of dollars in ordinary expenses as capital investments. The company was forced into bankruptcy a few weeks after the $11 billion accounting scam was exposed. As another example, top managers at the drug retailer Rite Aid posted transactions improperly to inflate corporate earnings. Later, when Rite Aid had to lower its earnings by $1.6 billion, investors fled and the share price fell.

Under the Sarbanes-Oxley Act, the CEO and CFO now must certify the corporation's financial reports. (For more information about Sarbanes-Oxley, visit http://www.aicpa.org, the Web site of the American Institute of Certified Public Accountants.) Immediately after this legislation became effective, hundreds of companies restated their earnings, a sign that stricter accounting controls were having the intended effect. "I don't mean to sugarcoat the figure on restatements," says Steve Odland, CEO of Office Depot, "but I think it is positive—it shows a healthy system." Yet not all earnings restatements are due to accounting irregularities. "The general impression of the public is that accounting rules are black and white," he adds. "They are often anything but that, and in many instances the changes in earnings came after new interpretations by the chief accountant of the SEC."

Now that stricter regulation has been in force for some time, fewer and fewer corporations are announcing restatements. In 2005, 1,400 companies restated earnings; in 2009, only 630 restated earnings. In fact, corporations and their accounting firms have learned to dig deeper and analyze the process used to produce the figures for financial statements, as well as checking the numbers themselves.

Because accounting rules are open to interpretation, managers sometimes find themselves facing ethical dilemmas when a corporation feels pressure to live up to Wall Street's expectations. Consider the hypothetical situation at Commodore Appliances, a fictional company that sells to Home Depot, Lowe's, and other major retail chains. Margaret, the vice president of sales, has told Rob, a district manager, that the company's sales are down 10 percent in the current quarter. She points out that sales in Rob's district are down 20 percent and states that higher-level managers want him to improve this month's figures using "book and hold," which means recording future sales transactions in the current period.

Rob hesitates, saying that the company is gaining market share and that he needs more time to get sales momentum going. He thinks "book and hold" is not a good business practice, even if it is legal. Margaret hints that Rob will lose his job if his sales figures don't look better and stresses that he will need the book-and-hold approach for one month only. Rob realizes that if he doesn't go along, he won't be working at Commodore for very much longer.

Meeting with Kevin, one of Commodore's auditors, Rob learns that book and hold meets GAAPs. Kevin emphasizes that customers must be willing to take title to the goods before they're delivered or billed. Any book-and-hold sales must be real, backed by documentation such as e-mails to and from buyers, and the transactions must be completed in the near future.

Rob is at a crossroads: His sales figures must be higher if Commodore is to achieve its performance targets, yet he doesn't know exactly when (or if) he actually would complete any book-and-hold sales he might report this month. He doesn't want to mislead anyone, but he also doesn't want to lose his job or put other people's jobs in jeopardy by refusing to do what he is being asked to do. Rob is confident that he can improve his district's sales over the long term. However, Commodore's executives are pressuring Rob to make the sales figures look better right now. What should he do?[9]

Questions

1. What are the ethical and legal implications of using accounting practices such as the book-and-hold technique to inflate corporate earnings?
2. Why would Commodore's auditor insist that Rob document any sales booked under the book-and-hold technique?
3. If you were in Rob's situation, would you agree to use the book-and-hold technique this month? Justify your decision.
4. Imagine that Commodore has taken out a multimillion-dollar loan that must be repaid next year. How might the lender react if it learned that Commodore was using the book-and-hold method to make revenues look higher than they really are?

Building Skills for Career Success

❶ JOURNALING FOR SUCCESS

More and more people are using computers and personal finance and accounting software to manage their finances. To complete this journal entry, use the Internet to research the Quicken software package or a software package offered by a local bank or financial institution. Then answer the following questions.

Assignment

1. Today, personal finance and accounting software packages are used by millions of people. Based on your initial research, would you prefer to purchase Quicken software or use a free software package available from a bank or financial institution? Why?

2. Why do you think these money-management software packages have become so popular? Do you think either type of software package could help you manage your finances?

c. What specific steps can you take to improve your financial condition?

3. Based on your findings, prepare a plan for improving your financial condition over the next six months.

❷ EXPLORING THE INTERNET

At the time of this text's publication, the U.S. economy was beginning to recover from an economic crisis. Still, obtaining business loans, home and automobile loans, and consumer credit was more difficult because of tightening of credit policies by major lenders. At the heart of the problem were two large home mortgage lenders—Fannie Mae and Freddie Mac—that provide funds to home mortgage lenders by either purchasing mortgage assets or issuing home mortgage loan guarantees that facilitate the flow of funds into the home mortgage market in the United States. Both firms have also been accused of doctoring earnings and questionable accounting practices.

Assignment

1. Using an Internet search engine such as Google or Yahoo!, locate two or three sites providing information about the recent accounting scandals at these two firms.
2. After examining these sites and reading journal articles, report information about the accounting scandals for each firm. What type of questionable accounting practices occurred in these firms?
3. Based on your assessment of the information you have read, what were the consequences of the questionable accounting practices that occurred?
4. In a two-page report, summarize the questionable accounting practices and what the consequences were for each firm and the executives involved in the scandal.

❸ DEVELOPING CRITICAL-THINKING SKILLS

According to the experts, you must evaluate your existing financial condition before establishing an investment plan. As pointed out in this chapter, a personal balance sheet provides a picture of your assets, liabilities, and net worth. A personal income statement will tell you whether you have a cash surplus or cash deficit at the end of a specific time period.

Assignment

1. Using your own financial information from last month, construct a personal balance sheet and personal income statement.
2. Based on the information contained in your personal financial statements, answer the following:
   a. What is your current net worth?
   b. Do you have a cash surplus or a cash deficit at the end of the month?

❹ BUILDING TEAM SKILLS

This has been a bad year for Miami-based Park Avenue Furniture. The firm increased sales revenues to $1,400,000, but total expenses ballooned to $1,750,000. Although management realized that some of the firm's expenses were out of control, including cost of goods sold ($700,000), salaries ($450,000), and advertising costs ($140,000), it could not contain expenses. As a result, the furniture retailer lost $350,000. To make matters worse, the retailer applied for a $350,000 loan at Fidelity National Bank and was turned down. The bank officer, Mike Nettles, said that the firm already had too much debt. At that time, liabilities totaled $420,000; owners' equity was $600,000.

Assignment

1. In groups of three or four, analyze the financial condition of Park Avenue Furniture.
2. Discuss why you think the bank officer turned down Park Avenue's loan request.
3. Prepare a detailed plan of action to improve the financial health of Park Avenue Furniture over the next 12 months.

❺ RESEARCHING DIFFERENT CAREERS

As pointed out in this chapter, job opportunities for accountants and auditors in the accounting area are expected to experience much faster-than-average employment growth between now and the year 2018. Employment opportunities range from entry-level positions for clerical workers and technicians to professional positions that require a college degree in accounting, management consulting, or computer technology. Typical job titles in the accounting field include bookkeeper, corporate accountant, public accountant, auditor, managerial accountant, and controller.

Assignment

1. Answer the following questions based on information obtained from interviews with people employed in accounting, from research in the library or by using the Internet, or from information gained from your college's career center.
   a. What types of activities would a person employed in one of the accounting positions listed above perform on a daily basis?
   b. Would you choose this career? Why or why not?
2. Summarize your findings in a report.

Graeter's Adds MIS to the Recipe

When a company begins to grow rapidly, it often discovers that it needs to adjust the way it does business to achieve new and more challenging goals. That's certainly been the case for Graeter's, the Cincinnati-based, family-owned maker of premium ice cream.

Husband and wife, Charlie and Regina Graeter, started the company in 1870, making ice cream and chocolates by hand in a small Cincinnati shop and living upstairs. While ice cream was already a novelty product because refrigeration by machine was still unknown, Graeter's ice cream was different from the beginning, relying on fresh seasonal ingredients and a painstaking small-batch production process to yield a deliciously creamy treat. The company was very successful, and for three generations management was content with few changes and slow expansion to a tiny handful of local stores.

GROWTH CALLS FOR NEW METHODS

Today, under the leadership of three of Charlie and Regina's great-grandsons, the insistence on quality, the freshest ingredients, and small-batch production remains. Graeter's ice-cream flavors are still hand-packed. But in almost every other respect, Graeter's is changing rapidly in its fourth generation. In a few months, it has expanded capacity from one factory to three, its staff has grown, it now operates a Web site and ships online orders around the country overnight, it nurtures customer relationships via Facebook and Twitter, it has expanded its retail operation to a few dozen stores in several nearby states, and it is now distributing its products to hundreds of chain supermarkets (such as Kroger) as far away as Denver, Dallas, and Houston. Graeter's even hopes someday to open stores in New York and California.

It would have been impossible for Graeter's to manage all this growth and expansion using only the simple information systems that served the company in its earlier years. "When you come into a small organization, an entrepreneurial organization," says Paul Porcino, a management consultant working with the firm, "there frequently is a very small amount of information, and ... it hasn't been pulled together in any meaningful way. So we have done a lot of work up front to define what performances we are going to develop, what are the sales measures, how do we understand the data and information that is out there in terms of helping us run the organization from a strategic perspective, where are we getting margins from? We need to understand that first, so we had to pull together a lot of information."

MIS WILL TRANSFORM DECISION MAKING

"Once this information has been gathered," Porcino says, "it will become input for a whole set of new management information systems, giving Graeter's management team some of the same powerful decision-making tools available to managers in much larger companies. We are going to be... bringing in probably a variety of different information systems, both point-of-sale in retail, so we fully have an understanding of what we are selling, as well as some other financial systems, and probably some human resources information systems.... There will be a fairly radical transformation... in terms of the software that we use.... We'll be in a very different place."

"Previously," says Porcino, "the stores did collect a certain amount of useful information, but it is not really enough to run the company of the future. With new MIS systems in place, we'll know in detail how many t-shirts we sell. We will know how many soda bottles we sell. We will know how many sundaes we sell. If we want, we will know how many ice-cream cones we sell.... Primarily, are we growing? Are we building our sales or reducing our sales?"

Graeter's has already experienced some of the benefits of having better information, particularly information about sales. When management noticed early on that bakery sales weren't up to par, for instance, "we had to adjust," says Porcino. The remedy was surprising: "We actually reduced the number of products we were selling in the store.... It wasn't very clear exactly how much we were selling, but at least [we had] the good-enough gut sense in terms of the ones that were *not* selling, and we... adjusted the total inventory line."

UPGRADING THE ACCOUNTING SYSTEMS

On the reporting side, Graeter's controller David Blink is responsible for preparing "all financial statements, all reports, payroll, [and] any ad hoc reports that any of the managers would need. I handle a lot of the reporting for the retail side as well as the manufacturing side," says Blink. Although an outside payroll company actually cuts the employees' checks, Blink's department is conducting its own information-gathering operation. "We are really tracking payroll right now. We are really working sales and payroll trying to get a real handle on that so I can produce reports for all the managers... biweekly, so it keeps them current and up to date." An outside accounting company also prepares the company's financial statements with information collected by Blink and his staff. "I will make sure everything lines up," he says. "I will add the... vacation time or sick time, and from there I will process the numbers and then forward them."[10]

Questions

1. From the information provided in the case, is Graeter's collecting data primarily from internal sources, external sources, or both? What cautions apply to the sources of its data?
2. Graeter's uses information to track cash, sales revenue, and expenses on a daily basis. How does this type of accounting system encourage effective decision-making and discourage store-level theft?
3. Which of the financial ratios might Graeter's, as a small privately owned business, want to track especially closely? Why?

To access the online *Interactive Business Plan,* go to www.cengagebrain.com.

Now that you have a marketing plan, the next big and important step is to prepare a financial plan. One of the biggest mistakes an entrepreneur makes when faced with a need for financing is not being prepared. Completing this section will show you that if you are prepared and you are credit-worthy, the task may be easier than you think. Remember, most lenders and investors insist that you submit current financial statements that have been prepared by an independent CPA. Chapter 17, "Using Accounting Information," should help you to answer the questions in this part of the business plan.

THE FINANCIAL PLAN COMPONENT

Your financial plan should answer at least the following questions about the investment needed, sales and cash-flow forecasts, breakeven analysis, and sources of funding.

6.1. What is the actual amount of money you need to open your business (start-up budget) and the amount needed to keep it open (operating budget)? Prepare a realistic budget.

6.2. How much money do you have, and how much money will you need to start your business and stay in business?

6.3. Prepare a projected income statement by month for the first year of operation and by quarter for the second and third years.

6.4. Prepare projected balance sheets for each of the first three years of operation.

6.5. Prepare a breakeven analysis. How many units of your products or service will have to be sold to cover your costs?

6.6. Reinforce your final projections by comparing them with industry averages for your chosen industry.

REVIEW OF BUSINESS PLAN ACTIVITIES

Throughout this project you have been investigating what it takes to open and run a business, and now you are finally at the bottom line: What is it going to cost to open your business, and how much money will you need to keep it running for a year? Before tackling the last part of the business plan, review your answers to the questions in each part to make sure that all your answers are consistent throughout the entire business plan. Then write a brief statement that summarizes all the information for this part of the business plan.

The information contained in this section will also assist you in completing the online *Interactive Business Plan.*

PART 7

Finance and Investment

← 22-51 WALL ST

In this part, we look at another business resource—money. First, we discuss the functions of money and the financial institutions that are part of our banking system. Then we examine the concept of financial management and investing for both firms and individuals.

18 Understanding Money, Banking, and Credit

Learning Objectives

What you will be able to do once you complete this chapter:

1. Identify the functions and characteristics of money.
2. Summarize how the Federal Reserve System regulates the money supply to maintain a healthy economy.
3. Describe the organizations involved in the banking industry.
4. Identify the services provided by financial institutions.
5. Understand how financial institutions are changing to meet the needs of domestic and international customers.
6. Explain how deposit insurance protects customers.
7. Discuss the importance of credit and credit management.

inside business

TD Bank Seeks to Wow Customers

Living up to its slogan, "America's most convenient bank," TD Bank works hard to wow its customers with convenient service from the northern tip of Maine to the southern coast of Florida. TD Bank is one of the 15 largest U.S. commercial banks, with 23,000 employees and 6.5 million customers in 13 states plus Washington, DC.

In all, TD Bank has more than 1,100 U.S. stores (its name for branches), while its Toronto parent, TD Bank Financial Group, has about 1,100 Canadian branches. With such a big network throughout North America, doing business with the bank is especially appealing for companies that reach across the border to sell to customers or buy from suppliers.

Like many other banks, TD Bank has been on both sides of the industry's merger and acquisitions activity. Until 2008, the bank was known as TD Banknorth, reflecting the names of its Canadian parent and the New England bank acquired by the parent for its U.S. expansion. Banknorth's history stretches back to 1852, when it was founded as Portland Savings Bank. Over the years, the Maine bank gobbled up smaller banks in a bid to widen its geographic scope and, in turn, was acquired by TD Bank Financial Group in 2007. Once TD Banknorth bought Commerce Bank in 2008 as part of its growth plans, it switched all stores to the TD Bank name.

As a commercial bank, TD Bank offers a full range of financial services for consumers and businesses of all sizes, including small-business loans backed by SBA guarantees and international banking services for large corporations. It did not get mixed up with the kinds of risky mortgage lending that have hurt so many banks in recent years, and it has kept its focus on service to build a solid customer base. TD Bank stores stay open much later than traditional bank branches and also offer convenient weekend hours for banking in person. In addition, the bank provides around-the-clock assistance by telephone, online, and via e-mail. TD Bank's personal touch is a competitive advantage. Not many banks post fan mail on their Web sites, but TD Bank does.[1]

FYI

Did You Know?

TD Bank is one of the 15 largest U.S. commercial banks, with 23,000 employees and 6.5 million customers in 13 states plus Washington, DC.

The Economic Crisis! These three words say a lot about the recent downturn in the nation's economy. These same three words do not tell the entire story, however, because the crisis caused a ripple effect through the entire economy—including the banking and financial industry. In reality, most Americans were frightened by a crisis that some experts described as the worst the nation had seen since the Great Depression. In fact, the economic crisis affected everyone in the United States in some way. For example,

- Many individuals lost their homes because they obtained loans they could not afford.
- Many individuals and business firms filed for bankruptcy because they could not repay money they had borrowed from financial institutions.
- Many individuals and businesses found that it was harder, or in some cases impossible, to borrow money from financial institutions.

Although some banks like TD Bank—the financial institution profiled in the Inside Business case for this chapter—continued to offer a full range of financial services for both consumers and businesses of all sizes, not all financial institutions were as well managed as TD Bank. Many of the nation's banks became known as "troubled" banks with too many nonperforming loans. Especially hard hit were large mortgage lenders that had financed home loans for customers who could no longer make their loan payments.

To help solve the problems, the Federal Reserve Bank became heavily involved in an effort to inject cash into the nation's banking system. The government also protected bank customers by merging troubled banks with financially stable banks. Finally, Congress passed two different rescue plans designed to restore confidence in the banking and financial industry. After all was said and done, two facts became obvious. First, it will take time for the U.S. economy to recover from what some experts describe as a financial meltdown. Second, healthy banks and financial institutions are necessary for both individuals and businesses to function in today's economic world.

Most people regard a bank, savings and loan association, credit union, or similar financial institution as a place to deposit or borrow money. When you deposit money, you *receive* interest. When you borrow money, you must *pay* interest. You may borrow to buy a home, a car, or some other high-cost item. In this case, the resource that will be transformed into money to repay the loan is the salary you receive for your labor.

Businesses also transform resources into money. A business firm (even a new one) may have a valuable asset in the form of an idea for a product or service. If the firm (or its founder) has a good credit history and the idea is a good one, a bank or other lender may lend it the money to develop, produce, and market the product or service. The loan—with interest—will be repaid out of future sales revenue. In this way, both the firm and the lender will earn a reasonable profit.

In each of these situations, the borrower needs the money now and will have the ability to repay it later. Although the decision to borrow money from a bank or other financial institution should always be made after careful deliberation, the fact is that responsible borrowing enables both individuals and business firms to meet specific needs.

In this chapter, we begin by outlining the functions and characteristics of money that make it an acceptable means of payment for products, services, and resources. Then we consider the role of the Federal Reserve System in maintaining a healthy economy. Next, we describe the banking industry—commercial banks, savings and loan associations, credit unions, and other institutions that offer banking services. Then we turn our attention to how banking practices meet the needs of customers. We also describe the safeguards established by the federal government to protect depositors against losses. In closing, we examine credit transactions, sources of credit information, and effective collection procedures.

1

Identify the functions and characteristics of money.

What Is Money?

The members of some societies still exchange goods and services through barter, without using money. A **barter system** is a system of exchange in which goods or services are traded directly for other goods or services. One family may raise vegetables and herbs, and another may weave cloth. To obtain food, the family of weavers trades cloth for vegetables, provided that the farming family is in need of cloth.

The trouble with the barter system is that the two parties in an exchange must need each other's products at the same time, and the two products must be roughly equal in value. Thus, even very isolated societies soon develop some sort of money to eliminate the inconvenience of trading by barter.

Money is anything a society uses to purchase products, services, or resources. Historically, different groups of people have used all sorts of objects as money—whales' teeth, stones, beads, copper crosses, clamshells, and gold and silver, for example. Today, the most commonly used objects are metal coins and paper bills, which together are called *currency*.

barter system a system of exchange in which goods or services are traded directly for other goods or services

money anything a society uses to purchase products, services, or resources

The Functions of Money

Money aids in the exchange of goods, services, and resources. However, this is a rather general (and somewhat theoretical) way of stating money's function. Let's look instead at three *specific* functions money serves in any society.

Two kinds of money. It's easy for U.S. citizens to think that their currency is the only currency in the world, but in reality there are many other currencies used throughout the world. In this photo, U.S. currency is on the left; the Chinese currency—the yuan—is on the right. Both currencies serve as a medium of exchange, a measure of value, and a store of value.

Money as a Medium of Exchange A **medium of exchange** is anything accepted as payment for products, services, and resources. This definition looks very much like the definition of money. It is meant to because the primary function of money is to serve as a medium of exchange. The key word here is *accepted*. As long as the owners of products, services, and resources *accept* money in an exchange, it is performing this function. For example, if you want to purchase a Hewlett-Packard Photosmart printer that is priced at $149 in a Best Buy store, you must give the store the correct amount of money. In return, the store gives you the product.

Money as a Measure of Value A **measure of value** is a single standard or "yardstick" used to assign values to, and compare the values of, products, services, and resources. Money serves as a measure of value because the prices of all products, services, and resources are stated in terms of money. It is thus the "common denominator" we use to compare products and decide which we will buy.

Money as a Store of Value Money received by an individual or firm need not be used immediately. It may be held and spent later. Hence, money serves as a **store of value**, or a means of retaining and accumulating wealth. This function of money comes into play whenever we hold onto money—in a pocket, a cookie jar, a savings account, or whatever.

Value that is stored as money is affected by *inflation*. Remember from Chapter 1 that *inflation* is a general rise in the level of prices. As prices go up in an inflationary period, money loses purchasing power. Suppose that you can buy a Bose home theater system for $1,000. Your $1,000 has a value equal to the value of that home theater system. However, suppose that you wait and do not buy the home theater system immediately. If the price goes up to $1,025 in the meantime because of inflation, you can no longer buy the home theater system with your $1,000. Your money has *lost* purchasing power because it is now worth less than the home theater system. To determine the effect of inflation on the purchasing power of a dollar, economists often refer to a consumer price index such as the one illustrated in Figure 18.1. The consumer price index measures the changes in prices of a fixed basket of goods purchased by a typical consumer, including food, transportation, housing, clothing, medical care, recreation, education, communication, and other goods and services. The base amount for the consumer price index is 100 and was established by averaging the cost of the items included in the consumer price index over a 36-month period from 1982 to 1984. In April 2010, it took approximately $218 to purchase the same goods that could have been purchased for $100 in the base period 1982 to 1984.

medium of exchange anything accepted as payment for products, services, and resources

measure of value a single standard or "yardstick" used to assign values to, and compare the values of, products, services, and resources

store of value a means of retaining and accumulating wealth

Figure 18.1 The Consumer Price Index and the Purchasing Power of the Consumer Dollar (Base Period 1982–1984 = 100)

Inflation causes a loss of money's stored value. As the consumer price index goes up, the purchasing power of the consumer's dollar goes down.

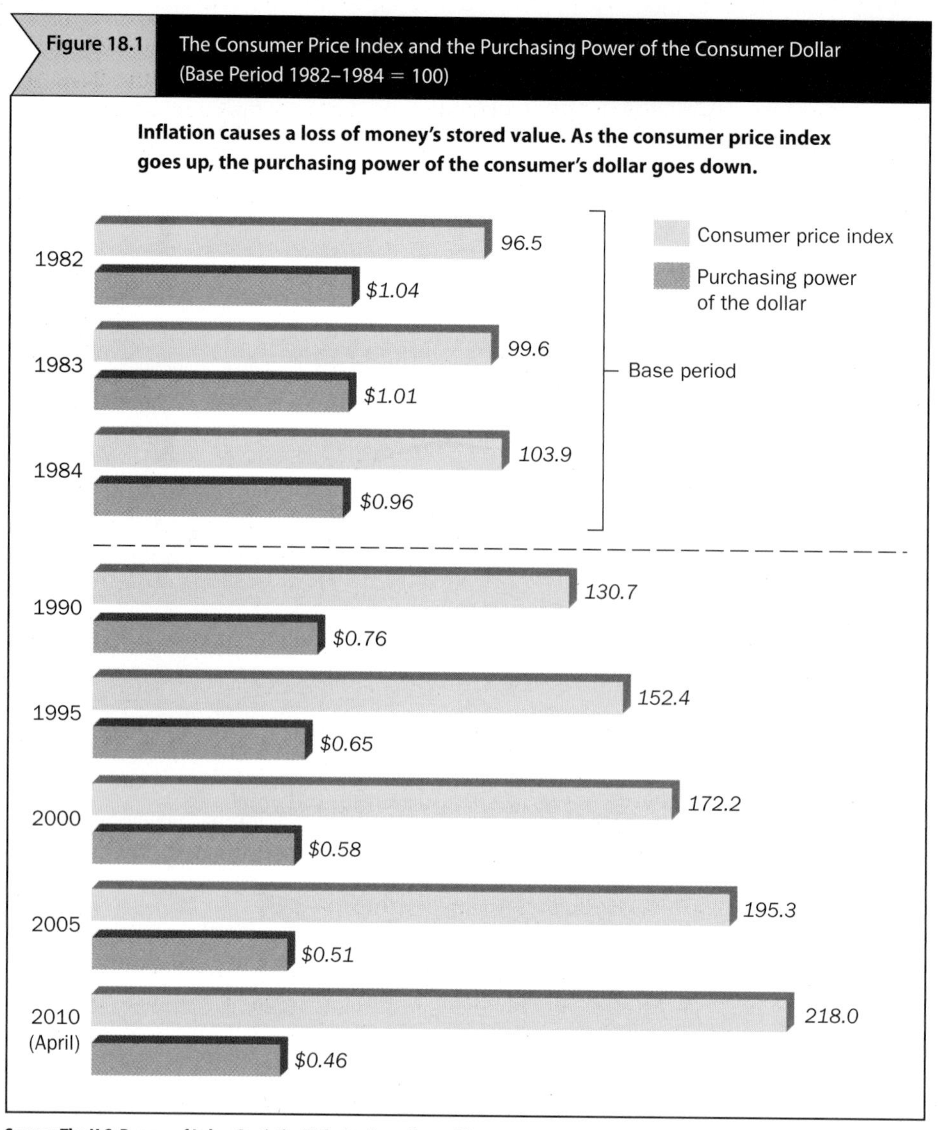

Source: The U.S. Bureau of Labor Statistics Web site, http://www.bls.gov (accessed June 16, 2010).

Important Characteristics of Money

Money must be easy to use, trusted, and capable of performing the three functions just mentioned. To meet these requirements, money must possess the following five characteristics.

Divisibility The standard unit of money must be divisible into smaller units to accommodate small purchases and large ones. In the United States, our standard is the dollar, and it is divided into pennies, nickels, dimes, quarters, and half-dollars.

Portability Money must be small enough and light enough to be carried easily. For this reason, paper currency is issued in larger denominations—5-, 10-, 20-, 50-, and 100-dollar bills.

Stability Money should retain its value over time. When it does not, people tend to lose faith in their money. When money becomes extremely unstable, people may turn to other means of storing value, such as gold and jewels, works of art, and real estate.

Durability The objects that serve as money should be strong enough to last through reasonable use. To increase the life expectancy of paper currency, most nations use special paper with a high fiber content.

Difficulty of Counterfeiting If a nation's currency were easy to counterfeit—that is, to imitate or fake—its citizens would be uneasy about accepting it as payment. In an attempt to make paper currency more difficult to counterfeit, the U.S. government periodically redesigns its paper currency and uses watermarks and intricate designs to discourage counterfeiting.

The Supply of Money: M_1 and M_2

How much money is there in the United States? Before we can answer this question, we need to define a couple of concepts. A **demand deposit** is an amount on deposit in a checking account. It is called a *demand* deposit because it can be claimed immediately—that is, on-demand—by presenting a properly made out check, withdrawing cash from an automated teller machine (ATM), or transferring money between accounts.

A **time deposit** is an amount on deposit in an interest-bearing savings account or certificate of deposit. Financial institutions generally permit immediate withdrawal of money from savings accounts. However, they can require advance written notice before withdrawal of certificates of deposit, and the customer may need to pay an early withdrawal penalty. The time between notice and withdrawal is what leads to the name *time* deposit. For this reason, they are called *near-monies*. Other near-monies include short-term government securities and money-market mutual fund accounts.

Now we can discuss the question of how much money there is in the United States. There are two main measures of the supply of money: M_1 and M_2.

The *M_1 supply of money* is a narrow definition and consists only of currency, demand and other checkable deposits, and traveler's checks. By law, currency must be accepted as payment for products, services, and resources. Checks (demand deposits) are accepted as payment because they are convenient, convertible to cash, and generally safe.

The *M_2 supply of money* consists of M_1 (currency and demand deposits) plus savings accounts, certain money-market securities, and small-denomination time deposits or certificates of deposit (CDs) of less than $100,000. The M_2 definition of money is based on the assumption that time deposits can be converted to cash for spending. Figure 18.2 shows the elements of the M_1 and M_2 supply of money.

Figure 18.2 The Supply of Money

Two measures of the money supply are M_1, which includes currency and demand deposits, and M_2, which includes M_1 plus certain securities and small-denomination time deposits.

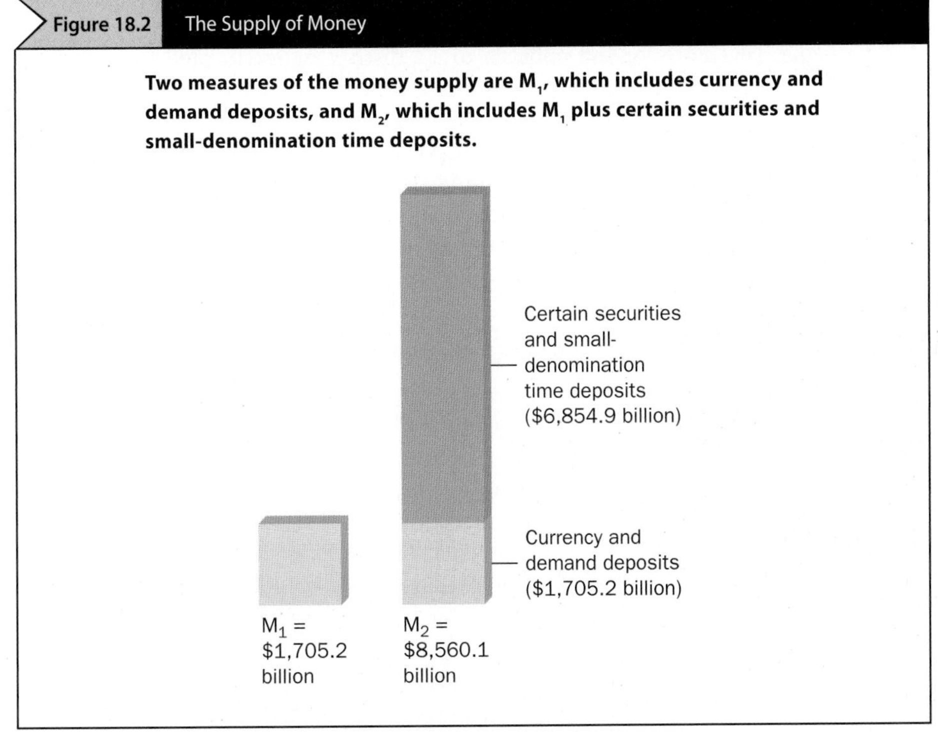

Source: The Federal Reserve Web site, http://www.federalreserve.gov (accessed June 15, 2010).

demand deposit an amount on deposit in a checking account

time deposit an amount on deposit in an interest-bearing savings account or certificate of deposit

We have, then, at least two measures of the supply of money. (Actually, there are other measures as well, which may be broader or narrower than M_1 and M_2.) Therefore, the answer to our original question is that the amount of money in the United States depends very much on how we measure it. Generally, economists, politicians, and bankers tend to focus on M_1 or some variation of M_1.

2

Summarize how the Federal Reserve System regulates the money supply to maintain a healthy economy.

The Federal Reserve System

How do Federal Reserve actions affect me? What is the Federal Reserve System? These are both good questions. The Federal Reserve Board, often referred to as the Fed, is responsible for not only regulating the nation's banking system, but also maintaining a healthy economy. Although many people became aware of the Federal Reserve's actions during the recent economic crisis, the Fed's lending programs have been used since the early 1900s to maintain a healthy economy. Here's how it works. The Fed lowers the interest rates that banks pay to borrow money from the Fed in an effort to shore up a sagging economy. When the Fed lowers rates, banks pay less to borrow money from the Fed. In turn, they often lower the interest rates they charge for business loans, home mortgages, car loans, and even credit cards. Lower rates often provide an incentive for both business firms and individuals to buy goods and services, which, in turn, helps to restore the economic health of the nation. On the other hand, rate increases are designed to sustain economic growth while controlling inflation. When the Fed raises rates, banks must pay more to borrow money from the Fed. And the banks, in turn, charge higher rates for both consumer and business loans.

Now let's answer the second question. The **Federal Reserve System** is the central bank of the United States and is responsible for regulating the banking industry. Created by Congress on December 23, 1913, its mission is to maintain an economically healthy and financially sound business environment in which banks can operate.

The Federal Reserve System is controlled by its seven-member board of governors, who meet in Washington, DC. Each governor is appointed by the president and confirmed by the Senate for a 14-year term. The president also selects the chairman and vice chairman of the board from among the board members for four-year terms.

Federal Reserve System the central bank of the United States responsible for regulating the banking industry

The Federal Reserve System consists of 12 district banks located in major cities throughout the United States, as well as 24 branch banks (see Figure 18.3). All national (federally chartered) banks must be members of the Fed. State banks may join if they choose to and if they meet membership requirements. For more information about the Federal Reserve System, visit its Web site at http://www.federalreserve.gov.

Two money men! U.S. Treasury Secretary Timothy Geithner (left) talks with Federal Reserve Chairman Ben Bernanke (right) while testifying before the U.S. House Financial Services Committee about the government's efforts to reduce the effects of the recent economic crisis.

Economic Crisis and the Fed's Response

Lately, it seems like the Federal Reserve Board has been in the news more than usual. The reason for all the news coverage is quite simple: The Fed was responsible for maintaining the health of the U.S. economy during the recent economic crisis. Although three of the obvious problems associated with the recent crisis were described in the first part of this chapter, there were many more problems that affected the entire economy. To maintain a healthy economy, the Federal Reserve Board took a number of specific steps to minimize the effects of the crisis for both business and individuals. Specifically, the Fed[2]

Figure 18.3 Federal Reserve System

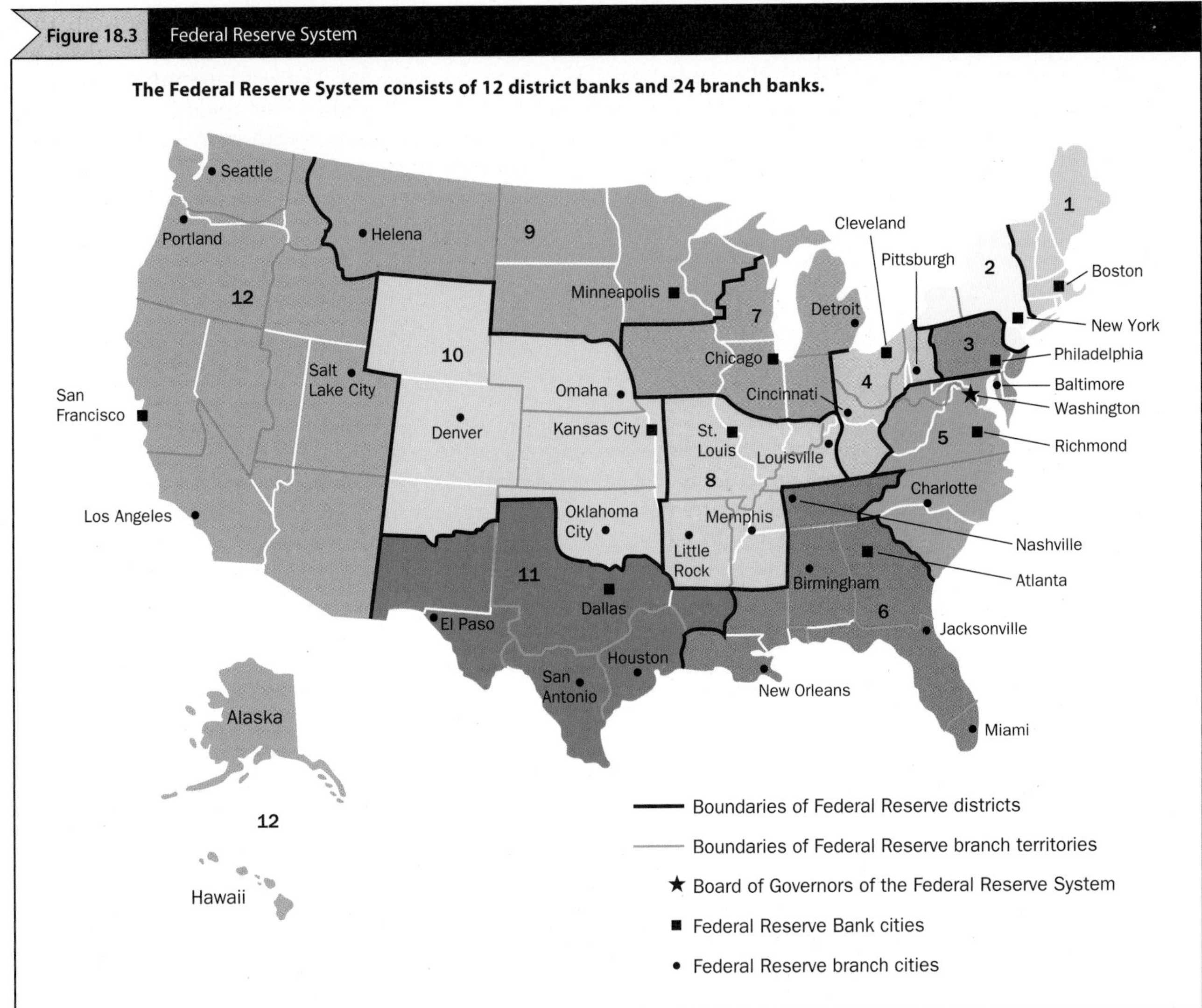

Source: "91st Annual Report, 2004," The Federal Reserve Board Web site, http://www.federalreserve.gov (accessed June 18, 2010).

- **Provided liquidity.** The Fed allowed banks in need of cash to borrow money from the Federal Reserve System. Without the ability to borrow needed funds from the Fed, some banks were in danger of failing. The Fed's lending activities also helped encourage other banks to continue loaning money to their customers. If they could not have borrowed money from the Fed, banks would have tightened lending requirements or stopped funding loans to both businesses and individuals.
- **Supported troubled financial markets.** For many businesses, short-term borrowing is essential to operate on a day-to-day basis. Often this much-needed financing is provided by individuals who buy shares in money-market mutual funds. The money-market funds, in turn, often purchase **commercial paper** issued by business firms that need short-term financing.

  During the first part of the crisis, investors feared that many commercial paper issues would become worthless and they stopped investing in money-market funds that held commercial paper. At the same time, many investors were withdrawing money from money-market funds. As a result, interest rates on commercial paper increased. In order to restore the commercial paper market and lower the cost of this type of short-term financing, the Federal Reserve provided secured loans to the financial institutions that sell this type of investment; as a result, the commercial paper market is now functioning well.

commercial paper a short-term promissory note issued by a large corporation

- **Supported important financial institutions.** The failure of investment bank Lehman Brothers and the commercial bank Washington Mutual fueled fears that other large financial institutions could fail. The resulting panic threatened to lead to a full-scale "run" on banks and lenders that could have caused the entire financial system to break down. To restore faith in the system, the Fed agreed to provide non-recourse loans to large banks. The ability to borrow money from the Fed and other government agencies helped to calm investors and avoid an even larger financial meltdown.
- **Conducted stress tests of major banks.** In the spring of 2009, the Federal Reserve, along with other federal agencies, conducted an unprecedented review of the financial condition of the 19 largest U.S. banks. This "stress" test measured how well these banks could weather the economic crisis. Banks that failed the test were required to obtain new capital by selling stock or bonds or accept federal government funds.

The Fed's actions did help to restore confidence in the financial system, to encourage continued lending, to stabilize an unstable economy, and to provide additional time to create a financial rescue plan to restore the nation's economy. At the time of publication, although the health of the banking and financial industry has improved, there are still concerns about the long-term effects of the Federal Reserve's actions, what future actions may be needed to ensure continued economic growth, and the cost of the financial rescue plan. According to Federal Reserve Chairman Ben Bernanke, "The federal budget appears to be on an unsustainable path," but that the "exceptional increase" in the deficit has been necessary to pull the country out of recession.[3]

The most important function of the Fed is to use monetary policy to regulate the nation's supply of money in such a way as to maintain a healthy economy. In Chapter 1, monetary policy was defined as the Federal Reserve's decisions that determine the size of the supply of money in the nation and the level of interest rates. The goals of monetary policy are continued economic growth, full employment, and stable prices. Three methods—controlling bank reserve requirements, regulating the discount rate, and running open-market operations—are used to implement the Fed's monetary policy.

Regulation of Reserve Requirements

When money is deposited in a bank, the bank must retain a portion of it to satisfy customers who may want to withdraw money from their accounts. The remainder is available to fund loans. By law, the Federal Reserve sets the reserve requirement for financial institutions, whether or not they are members of the Federal Reserve System. The **reserve requirement** is the percentage of its deposits a bank *must* retain, either in its own vault or on deposit with its Federal Reserve district bank. For example, if a bank has new deposits of $20 million and the reserve requirement is 10 percent, the bank must retain $2 million. The present reserve requirements range from 0 to 10 percent depending on such factors as the total amount individual banks have on deposit and the location of the particular member bank.[4]

Once reserve requirements are met, banks can use the remaining funds to create more money and make more loans through a process called *deposit expansion*. In the preceding example, the bank must retain $2 million in a reserve account. It can use the remaining $18 million to fund consumer and business loans. Assume that the bank lends all $18 million to different borrowers and also assume that before using any of the borrowed funds, all borrowers deposit the $18 million in their bank accounts at the lending institution. Now the bank's deposits have increased by an additional $18 million. Because these deposits are subject to the same reserve requirement described earlier, the bank must maintain $1.8 million in a reserve account, and the bank can lend the additional $16.2 million to other bank customers. Of course, the bank's lending potential becomes steadily smaller and smaller as it makes more loans. Moreover, we should point out that as bankers are usually

reserve requirement the percentage of its deposits a bank *must* retain, either in its own vault or on deposit with its Federal Reserve district bank

very conservative by nature, they will not use deposit expansion to maximize their lending activities; they will take a more middle-of-the-road approach.

The Fed's board of governors sets the reserve requirement. *When it increases the requirement, banks have less money available for lending.* Fewer loans are made, and the economy tends to slow. *On the other hand, by decreasing the reserve requirement, the Fed can make additional money available for lending to stimulate a slow economy.*

Because this means of controlling the money supply is so very potent and has such far-reaching effects on both consumers and financial institutions, the Fed seldom changes the reserve requirement.

Regulation of the Discount Rate

Member banks may borrow money from the Fed to satisfy the reserve requirement. The interest rate the Federal Reserve charges for loans to member banks, called the **discount rate**, is set by the board of directors of each Federal Reserve District bank. For the period from January 2003 to December 2007, the discount rate has been as low as 2 percent and as high as 6.25 percent.[5] In January 2008, in an attempt to stabilize the economy and encourage lending, the Federal Reserve began lowering the discount rate. By February 2010, the discount rate was 0.75 percent and remained low throughout the remainder of the year.[6]

When the Fed *lowers* the discount rate, it is easier and cheaper for banks to obtain money. Member banks feel free to make more loans and to charge lower interest rates. This action generally stimulates the nation's economy. When the Fed *raises* the discount rate, banks begin to restrict loans. They increase the interest rates they charge and tighten their own loan requirements. The overall effect is to slow the economy. Although the discount rate has decreased to 0.75 percent, you should remember that the Fed can increase rates in an effort to maintain a healthy economy.

discount rate the interest rate the Federal Reserve System charges for loans to member banks

open-market operations the buying and selling of U.S. government securities by the Federal Reserve System for the purpose of controlling the supply of money

Open-Market Operations

The federal government finances its activities partly by buying and selling government securities issued by the U.S. Treasury (Treasury bills, notes, and bonds) and federal agency securities. These securities, which pay interest, may be purchased by any individual, firm, or organization—including the Fed. **Open-market operations** are the buying and selling of U.S. government securities by the Federal Reserve System for the purpose of controlling the supply of money.

The Federal Open Market Committee (FOMC) is charged with carrying out the Federal Reserve's open-market operations by buying and selling U.S. Treasury securities through the trading desk of the Federal Reserve Bank of New York. To reduce the nation's money supply, the FOMC simply *sells* government securities. The money it receives from purchasers is taken out of circulation. Thus, less money is available for investment, purchases, or lending. To increase the money supply, the FOMC *buys* government securities. The money the FOMC pays for securities goes back into circulation, making more money available to individuals and firms.

Because the major purchasers of government securities are banking and financial institutions, open-market operations tend to have an immediate effect on lending and investment.

Of the three tools used to influence monetary policy, the use of open-market operations is the most important. When the Federal Reserve buys and sells securities, the goal is to change the federal funds rate. The

How are banking and the stock market related? As many Americans found out during the recent economic crisis, it takes a strong banking system and a healthy stock market for a nation to experience economic prosperity. In this photo, traders on the floor of the New York Stock Exchange (NYSE) are buying and selling stocks for their clients. Without a healthy economy, consumers don't usually borrow money from banks and investors don't buy stocks.

Table 18.1 Methods Used by the Federal Reserve System to Control the Money Supply and the Economy

Method Used	Immediate Result	End Result
Regulating Reserve Requirement		
1. Fed *increases* reserve requirement	Less money for banks to lend to customers—reduction in overall money supply	Economic slowdown
2. Fed *decreases* reserve requirement	More money for banks to lend to customers—increase in overall money supply	Increased economic activity
Regulating the Discount Rate		
1. Fed *increases* the discount rate	Less money for banks to lend to customers—reduction in overall money supply	Economic slowdown
2. Fed *decreases* the discount rate	More money for banks to lend to customers—increase in overall money supply	Increased economic activity
Open-Market Operations		
1. Fed *sells* government securities	Reduction in overall money supply	Economic slowdown
2. Fed *buys* government securities	Increase in overall money supply	Increased economic activity

federal funds rate is the interest rate at which a bank lends immediately available funds on deposit at the Fed to another bank overnight to meet the borrowing bank's reserve requirements. Because the Fed funds rate is what banks pay when they borrow, it affects the rates they charge when they lend. Although the FOMC sets a target for the federal funds rate, it does not actually set the rate because it is determined by the open market.[7] (*Note:* There is a difference between the federal funds rate and the discount rate discussed earlier in this section. The *federal funds rate* is the interest rate paid by a bank to borrow funds from other banks. The *discount rate* is the interest rate paid by a bank to borrow funds from the Federal Reserve.) Table 18.1 summarizes the effects of open-market operations and the other tools used by the Fed to regulate the money supply and control the economy.

Other Fed Responsibilities

In addition to its regulation of the money supply, the Fed is also responsible for serving as the government's bank, clearing checks and electronic transfers, inspecting currency, and applying selective credit controls.

Serving as Government Bank The Federal Reserve is the bank for the U.S. government. As the government's bank, it processes a variety of financial transactions involving trillions of dollars each year. For example, the Federal Reserve provides financial services for the U.S. Treasury, including accounts through which incoming tax deposits and outgoing government payments are handled.

Clearing Checks and Electronic Transfers Today, many people use checks to pay for nearly everything they buy. A check written by a customer of one bank and presented for payment to another bank in the same town may be processed through a local clearing-house. The procedure becomes more complicated, however, when the banks are not in the same town. This is where the Federal Reserve System comes in. The Fed is responsible for the prompt and accurate collection of 15 to 17 billion checks each year.[8] Banks that use the Fed to clear checks are charged a fee for this service. Through the use of electronic equipment, most checks can be cleared within two or three days.

federal funds rate the interest rate at which a bank lends immediately available funds on deposit at the Fed to another bank overnight to meet the borrowing bank's reserve requirements

Inspection of Currency As paper currency is handled, it becomes worn or dirty. The typical $1 bill has a life expectancy of less than two years. Most $50 and $100 bills usually last longer because they are handled less. When member banks deposit their surplus cash in a Federal Reserve Bank, the currency is inspected. Bills unfit for further use are separated and destroyed.

Selective Credit Controls The Federal Reserve System has the responsibility for enforcing the Truth-in-Lending Act, which Congress passed in 1968. This act requires lenders to state clearly the annual percentage rate and total finance charge for a consumer loan. The Federal Reserve System is also responsible for setting the margin requirements for securities transactions. The *margin* is the minimum amount (expressed as a percentage) of the purchase price that must be paid in cash or eligible securities. (The investor may borrow the remainder.) The current initial margin requirement is 50 percent. Thus, if an investor purchases $4,000 worth of stock, he or she must pay at least $2,000 in cash or its equivalent in securities. The remaining $2,000 may be borrowed from the brokerage firm. Although the minimum margin requirements are regulated by the Federal Reserve, margin requirements and the interest charged on the loans used to fund margin transactions may vary among brokerage firms and different security exchanges. For example, although an initial investment of at least $2,000 is required to open a margin account, some brokerage firms require more than $2,000.

The American Banking Industry

3

Describe the organizations involved in the banking industry.

Most bankers will tell you that the last few years have been frustrating for the American banking industry, to say the least. Furthermore, it's not just bankers who were affected. Almost everyone has been affected in one way or another by the nation's economic crisis.

Banks, savings and loan associations, credit unions, and other financial institutions were at the center of the nation's economic problems. Aggressive lending practices that led to record numbers of home foreclosures and nonperforming loans caused a financial meltdown. As the economic problems within the banking and financial industry became larger, the ability to borrow money became more difficult for both individuals and business firms—a very serious problem for both borrowers and lenders. In fact, the nation's economic problems (and the world's) became so severe that the government needed to take action. Both the Bush and the Obama administrations developed financial plans to rescue the economy. In addition, both the Federal Reserve Board and the U.S. Treasury took action. Eventually, the rescue plans did help relieve at least some of the financial problems associated with the economic crisis. Still, there was need for more changes in the way that banks and financial institutions operate.

Banking and Financial Reform: New Regulations

During the first part of 2010, the U.S. Congress tackled the issue of banking and financial reform. At the time of publication of this text, it is unclear what actions will be taken and how new regulations will affect individuals and businesses, banks and financial institutions, and Wall Street. Although there are many critics of increased regulation, it is apparent that something needs to be done to prevent the type of economic problems the nation has experienced over the past three years from happening again.

According to President Barack Obama, the goals of new government banking and financial regulations are more than justified in the wake of the crisis and include the following:[9]

- Protect American families from unfair and abusive financial and banking practices.
- Close the gaps in our financial system that allowed large banks and financial firms to avoid strong, comprehensive federal oversight.
- Curb the high-risk investment strategies that led to the financial problems at some major financial institutions and the nation's economic crisis.
- Require banks and financial firms to pay back bailout funds they received during the economic crisis.
- Provide a foundation for stable economic growth.

To accomplish these goals, a number of actions are currently being discussed by both the U.S. House of Representatives and the U.S. Senate. From an individual's standpoint, the most important action that may be included in new government regulations is the creation of a new consumer financial protection agency. Although there are currently seven federal agencies that divide responsibility for enforcing financial regulations, this new "super" agency will be responsible for setting clear rules for the entire industry and regulating the big financial service providers.[10] For individuals, specific areas of concern include home mortgages, credit card accounts, auto loans, overdraft fees, financial literacy, and alternative financial services.[11]

To provide this type of comprehensive consumer protection, it will be necessary to make sure banks and financial institutions are complying with the new regulations. In addition to increasing consumer protection, future regulations will subject banks and financial institutions to more in-depth evaluations to determine their financial health and provide an early warning system to spot signs of trouble before they affect individuals, the American economy, and the world economy.

For more information about existing regulations and proposed new regulations, go to the Federal Reserve Board's Web site at http://www.federalreserve.gov, the U.S. Treasury Web site at http://www.ustreas.gov., or use a search engine like Google or Yahoo! and enter "banking reform" or "financial reform."

In addition to the nation's economic problems, competition among banks, savings and loan associations, credit unions, and other business firms that want to perform banking activities has never been greater. Let's begin this section with some information about one of the major players in the banking industry—the commercial bank.

Commercial Banks

A **commercial bank** is a profit-making organization that accepts deposits, makes loans, and provides related services to its customers. Like other businesses, the bank's primary goal—its mission—is to meet its cutomers' needs while earning a profit.

Because they deal with money belonging to individuals and other business firms, banks must meet certain requirements before they receive a charter, or permission to operate, from either federal or state banking authorities. A **national bank** is a commercial bank chartered by the U.S. Comptroller of the Currency. There are approximately 1,700 national banks.[12] These banks must conform to federal banking regulations and are subject to unannounced inspections by federal auditors.

A **state bank** is a commercial bank chartered by the banking authorities in the state in which it operates. State banks outnumber national banks by about four to one, but they tend to be smaller than national banks. They are subject to unannounced inspections by both state and federal auditors.

Table 18.2 lists the seven largest banks in the United States. All are classified as national banks.

commercial bank a profit-making organization that accepts deposits, makes loans, and provides related services to its customers

national bank a commercial bank chartered by the U.S. Comptroller of the Currency

state bank a commercial bank chartered by the banking authorities in the state in which it operates

Table 18.2 The Seven Largest U.S. Banks, Ranked by Total Revenues

Rank	Company	Revenues ($ millions)	Profits ($ millions)	Employees
1	Bank of America Corp.	150,450.0	6,276.0	283,717
2	J.P. Morgan Chase & Co.	115,632.0	11,728.0	222,316
3	Citigroup	108,785.0	−1,606.0	267,150
4	Wells Fargo	98,636.0	12,275.0	267,300
5	Goldman Sachs Group	51,673.0	13,385.0	36,200
6	Morgan Stanley	31,515.0	1,346.0	61,388
7	American Express	26,730.0	2,130.0	58,300

Source: The Fortune Web site, http://www.fortune.com (accessed June 20, 2010).

Other Financial Institutions

In addition to commercial banks, at least eight other types of financial institutions perform either full or limited banking services for their customers.

Convenient banking! For both customers and employees, banking is different than it used to be. Bank customers, like the people in this photo, expect banks to provide ATM machines where customers can withdraw money and complete many banking activities. For employees, the name of the game is customer service whether the customer is standing at a bank teller's window or banking online.

Savings and Loan Associations A **savings and loan association (S&L)** is a financial institution that offers checking and savings accounts and CDs and that invests most of its assets in home mortgage loans and other consumer loans. Originally, S&Ls were permitted to offer their depositors *only* savings accounts. However, since Congress passed legislation regarding S&Ls in the 1980s, they have been able to offer other services to attract depositors.

Today, there are approximately 1,150 S&Ls in the United States insured by the Federal Deposit Insurance Corporation.[13] Federal associations are supervised by the Office of Thrift Supervision, a branch of the U.S. Treasury. State-chartered S&Ls are subjected to unannounced audits by state authorities.

Credit Unions The United States currently has an estimated 7,800 credit unions.[14] A **credit union** is a financial institution that accepts deposits from, and lends money to, only those people who are its members. Usually, the membership consists of employees of a particular firm, people in a particular profession, or those who live in a community served by a local credit union. Credit unions may pay higher interest on deposits than commercial banks and S&Ls, and they may provide loans at lower cost. The National Credit Union Administration regulates federally chartered credit unions and many state credit unions. State authorities also may regulate credit unions with state charters.

Organizations that Perform Banking Functions Six other types of financial institutions are involved in banking activities. Although not actually full-service banks, they offer customers some banking services.

- *Mutual savings banks* are financial institutions that are owned by their depositors and offer many of the same services offered by banks, S&Ls, and credit unions, including checking accounts, savings accounts, and CDs. Like other financial institutions, they also fund home mortgages, commercial loans, and consumer loans. Unlike other types of financial institutions, mutual savings banks are owned by their depositors. The profits of a mutual savings bank go to the depositors, usually in the form of dividends or slightly higher interest rates on savings. Today, most mutual savings banks are located in the Northeast.
- *Insurance companies* provide long-term financing for office buildings, shopping centers, and other commercial real estate projects throughout the United States. The funds used for this type of financing are obtained from policyholders' insurance premiums.
- *Pension funds* are established by employers to guarantee their employees a regular monthly income on retirement. Contributions to the fund may come from the employer, the employee, or both. Pension funds earn additional income through generally conservative investments in corporate stocks, corporate bonds, and government securities, as well as through financing real estate developments.
- *Brokerage firms* offer combination savings and checking accounts that pay higher-than-usual interest rates (so-called money-market rates). Many people have switched to these accounts because they are convenient and to get slightly higher rates.

savings and loan association (S&L) a financial institution that offers checking and savings accounts and CDs and that invests most of its assets in home mortgage loans and other consumer loans

credit union a financial institution that accepts deposits from, and lends money to, only the people who are its members

- *Finance companies* provide financing to individuals and business firms that may not be able to get financing from banks, S&Ls, or credit unions. Firms such as Ford Motor Credit, GE Capital, and General Motors Acceptance Corporation (now known as Ally Bank) provide loans to both individuals and business firms. Lenders such as Household Finance Corporation (HFC) and Ace Cash Express, Inc., provide short-term loans to individuals. The interest rates charged by these lenders may be higher than the interest rates charged by other financial institutions.
- *Investment banking firms* are organizations that assist corporations in raising funds, usually by helping sell new issues of stocks, bonds, or other financial securities. Although these firms do not accept deposits or make loans like traditional banking firms, they do help companies raise millions of dollars. More information about investment banking firms and the role they play in American business is provided in Chapters 19 and 20.

Careers in the Banking Industry

Take a second look at Table 18.2. The seven largest banks in the United States employ approximately 1,200,000 people. If you add to this amount the people employed by smaller banks not listed in Table 18.2 and those employed by S&Ls, credit unions, and other financial institutions, the number of employees grows dramatically. However, be warned: According to the *Career Guide to Industries*, published by the U.S. Department of Labor, banking employment is projected to grow more slowly than other jobs in the economy between now and the year 2018. Even though employment within the industry is expected to increase more slowly when compared with other industries, there will be job growth for office and administrative support workers because workers often leave these positions for other jobs that offer higher pay or greater responsibilities.[15]

To be successful in the banking industry, you need a number of different skills. For starters, employees for a bank, S&L, credit union, or other financial institution must possess the following traits:

1. *You must be honest.* Because you are handling other people's money, many financial institutions go to great lengths to discover dishonest employees.
2. *You must be able to interact with people.* A number of positions in the banking industry require that you possess the interpersonal skills needed to interact not only with other employees but also with customers.
3. *You need a strong background in accounting.* Many of the routine tasks performed by employees in the banking industry are basic accounting functions. For example, a teller must post deposits or withdrawals to a customer's account and then balance out at the end of the day to ensure accuracy.
4. *You need to appreciate the relationship between banking and finance.* Bank officers must interview loan applicants and determine if their request for money is based on sound financial principles. Above all, loan officers must be able to evaluate applicants and their loan requests to determine if the borrower will be able to repay a loan.
5. *You should possess basic computer skills.* Almost all employees in the banking industry use a computer for some aspect of their work on a daily basis.

How do you get a job in banking? To attract new employees, many banks send recruiters to college job fairs. In this photo, Wendy Weber of Charter One Bank interviews two potential employees. For banks and other financial institutions, honesty, the ability to interact with people, a strong background in accounting and finance, and basic computer skills are prerequisites for a career in banking.

Depending on qualifications, work experience, and education, starting salaries generally are between $18,000 and $30,000 a year, but it is not uncommon for college graduates to earn $35,000 a year or more.

If banking seems like an area you might be interested in, why not do more career exploration? You could take a banking course if your college or university offers one, or you could obtain a part-time job during the school year or a summer job in a bank, S&L, or credit union.

Traditional Services Provided by Financial Institutions

4

Identify the services provided by financial institutions.

To determine how important banking services are to you, ask yourself the following questions:

- How many checks did you write last month?
- Do you have a credit or debit card? If so, how often do you use it?
- Do you have a savings account or a CD?
- Have you ever financed the purchase of a new or used automobile?
- How many times did you visit an ATM last month?

If you are like most people and business firms, you would find it hard to live a normal life without the services provided by banks and other financial institutions. Typical services provided by a bank or other financial institution are illustrated in Figure 18.4.

The most important traditional banking services for both individuals and businesses are described in this section. Online banking, electronic transfer of funds, and other significant and future developments are discussed in the next section.

Checking Accounts

Imagine what it would be like living in today's world without a checking account. Firms and individuals deposit money in checking accounts (demand deposits) so that they can write checks to pay for purchases. A **check** is a written order for a bank or other financial institution to pay a stated dollar amount to the business or person indicated on the face of the check. To attract new customers, many financial institutions offer free checking; others charge activity fees (or service charges) for checking accounts. Fees and charges generally range between $5 to $20 per month for individuals. For businesses, monthly charges are based on the average daily balance in the checking account, the number of checks written, or both. Charges for business checking accounts are often higher than those for individual accounts.

Most financial institutions offer interest-paying checking accounts, often called *NOW (negotiable order of withdrawal) accounts*. A **NOW account** is an interest-bearing checking account. For these accounts, the usual interest rate is between 0.05 percent and 0.25 percent. Typically, online Internet banks pay slightly higher

Figure 18.4 Typical Services Provided by Banks and Other Financial Institutions

Banking services can be divided into three broad categories: traditional services, electronic services, and international services.

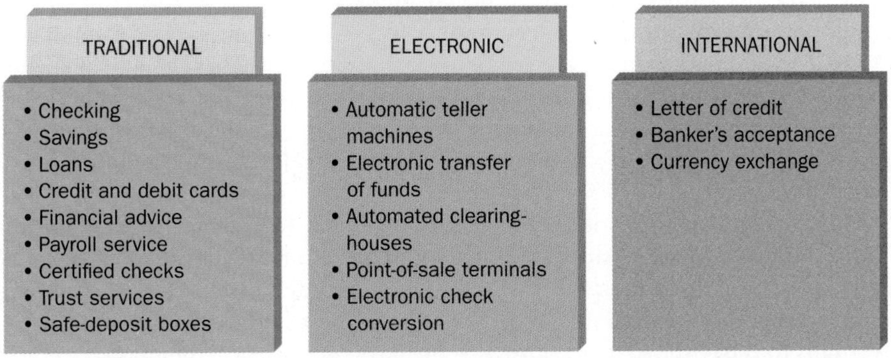

TRADITIONAL	ELECTRONIC	INTERNATIONAL
• Checking • Savings • Loans • Credit and debit cards • Financial advice • Payroll service • Certified checks • Trust services • Safe-deposit boxes	• Automatic teller machines • Electronic transfer of funds • Automated clearing-houses • Point-of-sale terminals • Electronic check conversion	• Letter of credit • Banker's acceptance • Currency exchange

check a written order for a bank or other financial institution to pay a stated dollar amount to the business or person indicated on the face of the check

NOW account an interest-bearing checking account; *NOW* stands for *negotiable order of withdrawal*

Sustaining the Planet

UN Capital Development Fund

The UN Capital Development Fund has made $200 million in small loans available to entrepreneurs in dozens of the world's least-developed countries, from Afghanistan to Zambia, to help strengthen local economies without compromising sustainability. Take a look: http://www.uncdf.org/english/index.php.

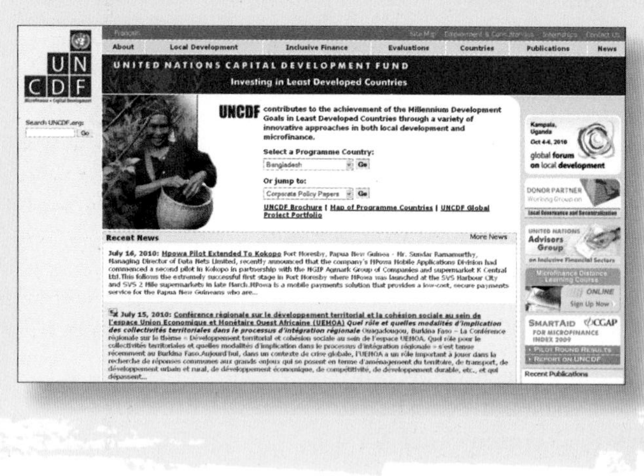

interest rates. However, individual banks may impose certain restrictions on their NOW accounts.

Although banks and other financial institutions may pay low interest rates on checking accounts, even small earnings are better than no earnings. In addition to interest rates, be sure to compare monthly fees before opening a checking account.

Savings Accounts

Savings accounts (time deposits) provide a safe place to store money and a very conservative means of investing. The usual *passbook savings account* earns between 0.25 percent and 0.80 percent in commercial banks and S&Ls and slightly more in credit unions or online Internet banks.

A depositor who is willing to leave money on deposit with a bank for a set period of time can earn a higher rate of interest. To do so, the depositor buys a certificate of deposit. A **certificate of deposit (CD)** is a document stating that the bank will pay the depositor a guaranteed interest rate on money left on deposit for a specified period of time. The interest rates paid on CDs change weekly; they once briefly exceeded 11 percent in 1980. Recently, interest rates have ranged from 0.50 to 3 percent. The rate always depends on how much is invested and for how long. Generally, the rule is: The longer the period of time until maturity, the higher is the rate. Depositors are penalized for early withdrawal of funds invested in CDs.

Short- and Long-Term Loans

Banks, S&Ls, credit unions, and other financial institutions provide short- and long-term loans to both individuals and businesses. *Short-term business loans* must be repaid within one year or less. Typical uses for the money obtained through short-term loans include solving cash-flow problems, purchasing inventory, financing promotional needs, and meeting unexpected emergencies.

To help ensure that short-term money will be available when needed, many firms establish a line of credit. A **line of credit** is a loan that is approved before the money is actually needed. Because all the necessary paperwork is already completed and the loan is pre-approved, the business can obtain the money later without delay, as soon as it is required. Even with a line of credit, a firm may not be able to borrow money if the bank does not have sufficient funds available. For this reason, some firms prefer a **revolving credit agreement**, which is a guaranteed line of credit.

Long-term business loans are repaid over a period of years. The average length of a long-term business loan is generally three to seven years but sometimes as long as 15 years. Long-term loans are used most often to finance the expansion of buildings and retail facilities, mergers and acquisitions, replacement of equipment, or product development.

Most lenders require some type of collateral for long-term loans. **Collateral** is real estate or property (stocks, bonds, equipment, or any other asset of value) pledged as security for a loan. For example, when an individual obtains a loan to pay for a new Chevrolet Malibu, the automobile is the collateral for the loan. If the borrower fails to repay the loan according to the terms specified in the loan agreement, the lender can repossess the car.

certificate of deposit (CD) a document stating that the bank will pay the depositor a guaranteed interest rate on money left on deposit for a specified period of time

line of credit a loan that is approved before the money is actually needed

revolving credit agreement a guaranteed line of credit

collateral real estate or property pledged as security for a loan

Repayment terms and interest rates for both short- and long-term loans are arranged between the lender and the borrower. For businesses, repayment terms may include monthly, quarterly, semiannual, or annual payments. Repayment terms (and interest rates) for personal loans vary depending on how the money will be used and what type of collateral, if any, is pledged. However, individuals typically make monthly payments to repay personal loans. Borrowers always should "shop" for a loan, comparing the repayment terms and interest rates offered by competing financial institutions.

How do you pay for everyday items like clothing? More and more people are using credit or debit cards to pay for purchases like clothing. For the customer, credit and debit cards are easy and convenient. For merchants, credit and debit card transactions can be quickly processed to improve a firm's cash flow.

Credit-Card and Debit-Card Transactions

By 2010, 181 million Americans will use credit cards to pay for everything from tickets on American Airlines to Zebco fishing gear.[16] Why have credit cards become so popular?

For a merchant, the answer is obvious. By depositing charge slips in a bank or other financial institution, the merchant can convert credit-card sales into cash. In return for processing the merchant's credit-card transactions, the financial institution charges a fee that generally ranges between 1.5 and 4 percent. Typically, small, independent businesses pay more than larger stores or chain stores. Let's assume that you use a Visa credit card to purchase a microwave oven for \$300 from Gold Star Appliance, a retailer in Richardson, Texas. At the end of the day, the retailer deposits your charge slip, along with other charge slips, checks, and currency collected during the day, at its bank. If the bank charges Gold Star Appliance 4 percent to process each credit-card transaction, the bank deducts a processing fee of \$12 (\$300 × 0.04 = \$12) for your credit-card transaction and immediately deposits the remainder (\$288) in Gold Star Appliance's account. The number of credit-card transactions, the total dollar amount of credit sales, and how well the merchant can negotiate the fees the bank charges determine actual fees.

Do not confuse debit cards with credit cards. Although they may look alike, there are important differences. A **debit card** electronically subtracts the amount of your purchase from your bank account at the moment the purchase is made. (By contrast, when you use your credit card, the credit-card company extends short-term financing, and you do not make payment until you receive your next statement.) Debit cards are used most commonly to obtain cash at ATMs and to purchase products and services from retailers.

Innovative Banking Services

5 Understand how financial institutions are changing to meet the needs of domestic and international customers.

Today, many individuals, financial managers, and business owners are finding it convenient to do their banking electronically. Let's begin by looking at how banking will change in the future.

Changes in the Banking Industry

While the experts may not be able to predict with 100 percent accuracy the changes that will affect banking, they all agree that banking *will* change. The most obvious changes the experts do agree on are as follows:

- More emphasis on evaluating the credit-worthiness of loan applicants as a result of the recent economic crisis
- An increase in government regulation of the banking industry
- A reduction in the number of banks, S&Ls, credit unions, and financial institutions because of consolidation and mergers
- Globalization of the banking industry as the economies of individual nations become more interrelated

debit card a card that electronically subtracts the amount of your purchase from your bank account at the moment the purchase is made

Going for SUCCESS

Mobile Banking Lets Customers Make the Call

© AP Images/Wells Fargo by Court Mast

Banking on-the-go? Let your cell phone make the call. Many banks now offer mobile banking via text message or apps (software applications) downloaded to cell phones. The goal is to let customers use their cell phones to check account balances, transfer money, and track deposits at any time, from anywhere. This is especially convenient for busy businesspeople who don't live or work next door to a bank branch and can't always get to a computer to use online banking.

Wells Fargo has found that its average mobile-banking customer sends 19 text messages per month to handle banking transactions. "There's a whole group of customers for whom text banking is very attractive, and there are customers whose lives don't revolve around a PC," says an official. And because no account numbers appear in these messages, personal details remain secure.

USAA Federal Savings Bank offers a slightly different twist on mobile banking. After registering their cell phone numbers, customers choose a four-digit code and download the bank's app. When they click on the app and enter the code to get into their accounts, the software automatically verifies their information before allowing access. The whole process is fast and easy, offering "much more secure access and definitely a better experience for the customer," notes a USAA executive. For extra convenience, customers can use cell phone cameras to photograph checks and make electronic deposits without visiting an ATM or a branch.

Sources: Daniel Wolfe, "For USAA, Less Is More with Security," *American Banker*, March 2, 2010, 1; Kathy Brister, "Making the Most of Mobile," *US Banker*, March 1, 2010, 17; Daniel Wolfe, "Channel Surfing," *Bank Technology News*, March 1, 2010, 1; Daniel Wolfe, "Banks' Eureka Moment on Mobile Services," *American Banker*, February 9, 2010, 1.

- The importance of customer service as a way to keep customers from switching to competitors
- Increased use of credit and debit cards and a decrease in the number of written checks
- Increased competition from nonbank competitors that provide many of the same services as banks, S&Ls, credit unions, and other financial institutions
- Continued growth in online banking

© Eric Carr/Alamy

More and more people are banking online. Because online banking is convenient, the number of people using their computers to bank online increases every year. In fact, almost any banking activity—checking your balance, reconciling your checking account, or applying for a loan—can be accomplished with the click of your computer's mouse.

Online Banking and International Banking

Online banking allows you to access your bank's computer system from home, the office, or even while you are traveling. For the customer, online banking offers a number of advantages, including the following:

- The ability to obtain current account balances
- The convenience of transferring funds from one account to another
- The ability to pay bills
- The convenience of seeing which checks have cleared
- Easy access to current interest rates
- Simplified loan application procedures

For people who bank online, the largest disadvantage is not being able to discuss financial matters with their "personal banker." To overcome this problem, many larger banks are investing huge amounts on electronic customer relationship management systems that will provide the type of service and financial advice that customers used to get when they walked through the doors of their financial institution.

Online banking provides a number of advantages for the financial institution. Probably the most important advantage is the lower cost of processing large numbers of transactions. As you learned in Chapter 17, lower costs often lead to larger profits. In addition to lower costs and increased profits, financial institutions believe that online banking offers increased security because fewer people handle fewer paper documents.

Electronic Funds Transfer (EFT) Although electronic funds transfer systems have been used for years, their use will increase dramatically as we continue through the 21st century. An **electronic funds transfer (EFT) system** is a means of performing financial transactions through a computer terminal or telephone hookup. The following four EFT applications are changing how banks do business:

1. *Automatic teller machines (ATMs).* An ATM is an electronic bank teller—a machine that provides almost any service a human teller can provide. Once the customer is properly identified, the machine dispenses cash from the customer's checking or savings account or makes a cash advance charged to a credit card. ATMs are located in bank parking lots, supermarkets, drugstores, and even gas stations. Customers have access to them at all times of the day or night. There may be a fee for each transaction.
2. *Automated clearing-houses (ACHs).* Designed to reduce the number of paper checks, automated clearing-houses process checks, recurring bill payments, Social Security benefits, and employee salaries. For example, large companies use ACHs to transfer wages and salaries directly into their employees' bank accounts, thus eliminating the need to make out individual paychecks.
3. *Point-of-sale (POS) terminals.* A POS terminal is a computerized cash register located in a retail store and connected to a bank's computer. At the cash register, you pull your credit or debit card through a magnetic card reader. A central processing center notifies a computer at your bank that you want to make a purchase. The bank's computer immediately adds the amount to your account for a credit-card transaction. In a similar process, the bank's computer deducts the amount of the purchase from your bank account if you use a debit card. Finally, the amount of your purchase is added to the store's account. The store then is notified that the transaction is complete, and the cash register prints out your receipt.
4. *Electronic check conversion (ECC).* Electronic check conversion is a process used to convert information from a paper check into an electronic payment for merchandise, services, or bills. When you give your completed check to a store cashier, the check is processed through an electronic system that captures your banking information and the dollar amount of the check. Once the check is processed, you are asked to sign a receipt, and you get a voided (canceled) check back for your records. Finally, the funds to pay for your transaction are transferred into the business firm's account. ECC also can be used for checks you mail to pay for a purchase or to pay on an account.

electronic funds transfer (EFT) system a means of performing financial transactions through a computer terminal or telephone hookup

Looks like a typical Citibank branch. Take another look. This branch is located in Chongqing, China. This branch—along with other Citibank locations in China—offers full-service banking for both individuals and businesses. Experts predict that Citibank, along with its major competitors, will continue to open branches in China and other countries around the globe.

Bankers and business owners generally are pleased with online banking and EFT systems. Both online banking and EFT are fast, and they eliminate the costly processing of checks. However, many customers are reluctant to use online banking or EFT systems. Some simply do not like "the technology," whereas others fear that the computer will garble their accounts. Early on, in 1978,

Congress responded to such fears by passing the Electronic Funds Transfer Act, which protects the customer in case the bank makes an error or the customer's account information is stolen.

International Banking Services For international businesses, banking services are extremely important. Depending on the needs of an international firm, a bank can help by providing a letter of credit or a banker's acceptance.

A **letter of credit** is a legal document issued by a bank or other financial institution guaranteeing to pay a seller a stated amount for a specified period of time—usually 30 to 60 days. (With a letter of credit, certain conditions, such as delivery of the merchandise, may be specified before payment is made.)

A **banker's acceptance** is a written order for a bank to pay a third party a stated amount of money on a specific date. (With a banker's acceptance, no conditions are specified. It is simply an order to pay guaranteed by a bank without any strings attached.)

Both a letter of credit and a banker's acceptance are popular methods of paying for import and export transactions. For example, imagine that you are a business owner in the United States who wants to purchase some leather products from a small business in Florence, Italy. You offer to pay for the merchandise with your company's check drawn on an American bank, but the Italian business owner is worried about payment. To solve the problem, your bank can issue either a letter of credit or a banker's acceptance to guarantee that payment will be made. In addition to a letter of credit and a banker's acceptance, banks also can use EFT technology to speed international banking transactions.

letter of credit a legal document issued by a bank or other financial institution guaranteeing to pay a seller a stated amount for a specified period of time

banker's acceptance a written order for a bank to pay a third party a stated amount of money on a specific date

One other international banking service should be noted. Banks and other financial institutions provide for currency exchange. If you place an order for merchandise valued at $50,000 from a company in Japan, how do you pay for the order? Do you use U.S. dollars or Japanese yen? To solve this problem, you can use a bank's currency-exchange service. To make payment, you can use either currency. If necessary, the bank will exchange one currency for the other to complete your transaction.

Explain how deposit insurance protects customers.

The FDIC and NCUA

During the Great Depression, which began in 1929, a number of banks failed, and their depositors lost all their savings. To make sure that such a disaster did not happen again and to restore public confidence in the banking industry, Congress enacted legislation that created the *Federal Deposit Insurance Corporation (FDIC)* in 1933. The primary purpose of the FDIC is to insure deposits against bank failures.

Today, the FDIC provides basic deposit insurance of $250,000 per depositor. Because of a recent change in government policy, the $250,000 limit is now permanent.[17] Deposits maintained in different categories of legal ownership are insured separately. Thus, you can have increased coverage for different categories of ownership in a single institution. The most common categories of ownership are single (or individual) ownership and joint ownership. A depositor also may obtain additional coverage by opening separate accounts in different financial institutions. To determine if your deposits are insured or if your bank or financial institution is insured, visit the FDIC Web site at http://www.fdic.gov.

To obtain coverage, banks and S&Ls must pay insurance premiums to the FDIC. In a similar manner,

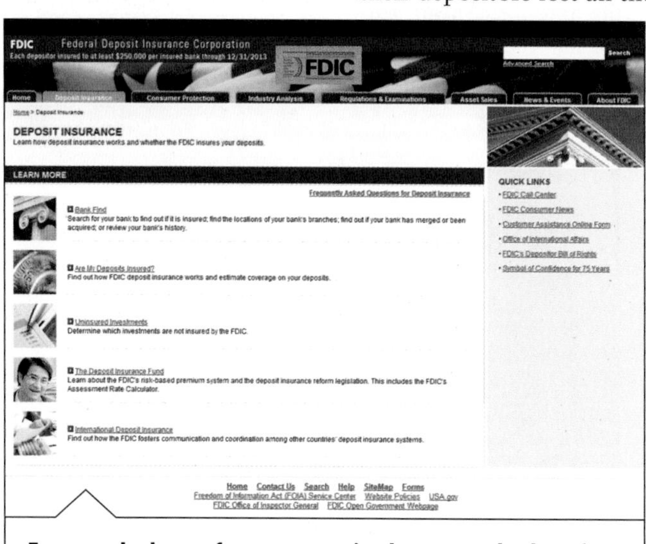

Ever wonder how safe your money is when you make deposits at a bank? It's easy to find out if your bank has FDIC insurance coverage. Just go to the FDIC Web site (http://www.fdic.gov) and take a look. While you're there, explore the Web site. There are many topics that explain more about insured deposits and what the FDIC is doing to regulate and improve banking in the United States.

Courtesy of the Federal Deposit Insurance Corporation (www.fdic.gov)

the National Credit Union Association (NCUA) insures deposits in member credit unions for up to $250,000 per depositor. Like FDIC coverage, increased coverage is provided for accounts with different categories of ownership.

The FDIC and NCUA have improved banking in the United States. When either of these organizations insures a financial institution's deposits, they reserve the right to examine that institution's operations periodically. If a bank, S&L, savings bank, or credit union is found to be poorly managed, it is reported to the proper banking authority.

Lending to individuals and firms is a vital function of banks. Making wise decisions regarding to whom it will extend credit is one of the most important activities of any financial institution or business. The material in the next section explains the different factors used to evaluate credit applicants.

SPoTLIGHT

Because of deposit insurance, you do not have to worry about losing money—you are protected up to $250,000 in an FDIC-insured bank or savings institution. Statistics are for insured institutions as of March 31, 2010.

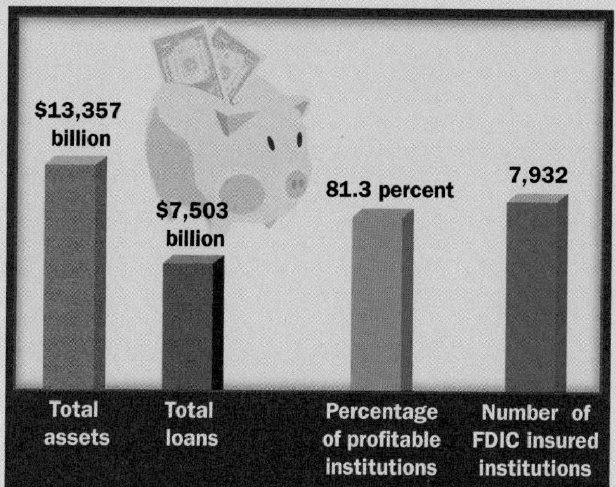

Source: The Federal Deposit Insurance Corporation Web site at http://www.fdic.gov (accessed June 21, 2010).

Effective Credit Management

7

Discuss the importance of credit and credit management.

credit immediate purchasing power that is exchanged for a promise to repay borrowed money, with or without interest, at a later date

Credit is immediate purchasing power that is exchanged for a promise to repay borrowed money, with or without interest, at a later date. A credit transaction is a two-sided business activity that involves both a borrower and a lender. The borrower is most often a person or business that wishes to make a purchase. The lender may be a bank, some other lending institution, or a business firm selling merchandise or services on credit.

For example, suppose that you obtain a bank loan to buy a $150,000 home. You, as the borrower, obtain immediate purchasing power. In return, you agree to certain terms imposed by the bank, S&L, or home mortgage company. The lender requires that you make a down payment, make monthly payments, pay interest, and purchase insurance to protect your home until the loan is paid in full.

Banks and other financial institutions lend money because they are in business for that purpose. The interest they charge is what provides their profit. Other businesses extend credit to their customers for at least three reasons. First, some customers simply cannot afford to pay the entire amount of their purchase immediately, but they *can* repay credit in a number of smaller payments stretched out over some period of time. Second, some firms are forced to sell goods or services on credit to compete effectively when other firms offer credit to their customers. Finally, firms can realize a profit from interest charges that a borrower pays on some credit arrangements.

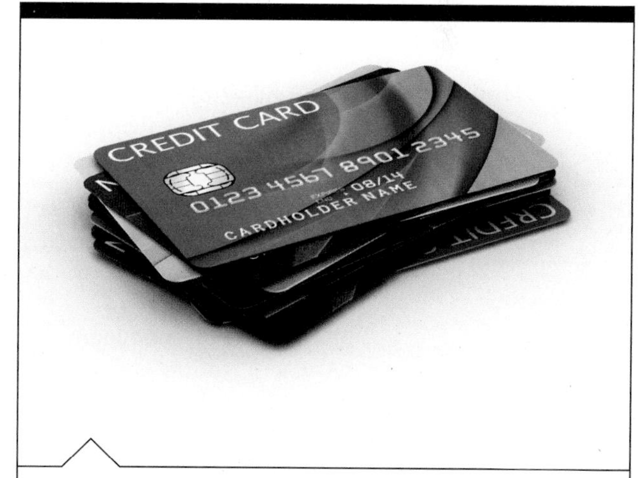

Too much of a good thing! Personal finance experts recommend that you have one or two credit cards and that you use them only for emergencies. Unfortunately, many Americans spend more than they make on a regular basis by paying with "plastics."

Ethical Challenges & SUCCESSFUL SOLUTIONS

Banks as Eco-Cops?

Should banks consider environmental and societal issues as well as credit-worthiness when loaning money to customers? If they adopt the Equator Principles, they do. The Equator Principles are voluntary standards that require banks to determine whether borrowers comply with environmentally and socially responsible policies and procedures. The idea is to avoid funding projects that carry significant ecological- or social-responsibility risk.

For example, London-based Standard Chartered Bank applies the Equator Principles to its commercial lending decisions. "Our financing decisions—who and what we finance—enable us to make our strongest contribution to sustainable development," says an executive. The bank will not approve loans for logging in ecologically sensitive forests, for example. Instead, it works with borrowers to ensure that projects meet independent environmental criteria before extending credit. In Argentina, Banco Galicia was guided by the Equator Principles when it made a $10 million loan to build an eco-resort in a nature preserve. The bank required the borrower to follow strict, internationally recognized standards for protecting both land and wildlife before providing funding.

In the United States, the multinational banking giants Citigroup, Bank of America, and JP Morgan Chase are three of many financial institutions that abide by the Equator Principles. Citigroup alone has loaned more than $100 billion for projects that meet with these standards. But should banks serve as eco-cops for projects they might finance anywhere in the world?

Sources: Yap Leng Kuen, "Banks' Role in Fostering Sustainable Practices," *The Star Online* (Malaysia), March 10, 2010, http://biz.thestar.com.my/news/story.asp?file=/2010/3/10/business/5826682&sec=business; Keren Fallwell, "Banking on the Environment," *TTJ The Timber Industry Magazine*, December 26, 2009, 26; Jane Monahan, "LatAm Banks Take CSR Plunge," *The Banker*, July 1, 2009, n.p.; http://www.equator-principles.com.

Getting Money from a Bank or Lender After a Credit Crisis

Many individuals and business owners are nervous when applying for a loan. They are not sure what information they need. They are also concerned about what happens if they are turned down. Let's begin with the basics. While lenders need interest from loans to help pay their business expenses and earn a profit, they also want to make sure that the loans they make will be repaid. Your job is to convince the lender that you are able and willing to repay the loan. That job is more difficult than it has ever been because of the recent economic crisis in the banking and financial industry. Today, bankers, lenders and suppliers, and credit-card companies are much more careful when evaluating credit applications. The reasons are simple: Many lenders already have a large number of "bad" or nonperforming loans and they want to make sure all borrowers are qualified and will be able to repay borrowed money.

For individuals, the following suggestions may be helpful when applying for a loan:

- Obtain a loan application and complete it at home. At home, you have the information needed to answer *all* the questions on the loan application.
- Be prepared to describe how you will use the money and how the loan will be repaid.
- For most loans, an interview with a loan officer is required. Here again, preparation is the key. Think about how you would respond to questions a loan officer might ask.
- If your loan request is rejected, try to analyze what went wrong. Ask the loan officer why you were rejected. If the rejection is based on incorrect information, supply the correct information and reapply.

Business owners in need of financing may find the following additional tips helpful:

- It is usually best to develop a relationship with your banker before you need financing. Help the banker understand what your business is and how you

may need future financing for expansion, cash-flow problems, or unexpected emergencies.
- Apply for a pre-approved line of credit or revolving credit agreement even if you do not need the money. View the application as another way to showcase your company and its products or services.
- In addition to the application, supply certified public accountant (CPA)-prepared financial statements and business tax returns for the last three years. If your business is small, you may want to supply your own personal financial statements and tax returns for the same period.
- Update your business plan in case the lender wants to review your plan. Be sure the sales estimates and other projections are realistic.
- Write a cover letter describing how much experience you have, whether you are operating in an expanding market, or any other information that would help convince the banker to provide financing.

From the lender's viewpoint, the major pitfall in granting credit is the possibility of nonpayment. However, if a lender follows the five C's of credit management, it can minimize this possibility.

The Five C's of Credit Management

When a business extends credit to its customers, it must face the fact that some customers will be unable or unwilling to pay for their credit purchases. With this in mind, lenders must establish policies for determining who will receive credit and who will not. Most lenders build their credit policies around the five C's of credit.

Character *Character* means the borrower's attitude toward credit obligations. Experienced lenders often see this as the most important factor in predicting whether a borrower will make regular payments and ultimately repay a credit obligation. Typical questions to consider in judging a borrower's character include the following:

1. Is the borrower prompt in paying bills?
2. Have other lenders had to send the borrower overdue notices before receiving payment?
3. Have lenders been forced to take the borrower to court to obtain payment?
4. Has the customer ever filed for bankruptcy? If so, did the customer make an attempt to repay debts voluntarily?

Although it is illegal to discriminate, personal factors such as drinking or gambling habits or other information may affect a lender's decision to loan money or extend credit to an individual or a business owner.

Capacity *Capacity* means the borrower's financial ability to meet credit obligations—that is, to make regular loan payments as scheduled in the credit or loan agreement. If the customer is a business, the lender looks at the firm's income statement. For individuals, the lender checks salary statements and other sources of income, such as dividends and interest. The borrower's other financial obligations and monthly expenses are also taken into consideration before credit is approved.

Capital The term *capital* as used here refers to the borrower's assets or net worth. In general, the greater the capital, the greater is the borrower's ability to repay a loan. The capital position of a business can be determined by examining its balance sheet. For individuals, information on net worth can be obtained by requiring that the borrower complete a credit application such as the one illustrated in Figure 18.5. The borrower also must authorize employers and financial institutions to release information to confirm the claims made in the credit application.

Figure 18.5 Credit Application Form

Lenders use the information on credit application forms to help determine which customers should be granted credit.

Apply today! Just complete this application or call 1-800-438-9222.

Citizens Bank Customer Credit Card Application

Branch # ________

This offer is for existing Citizens Bank Customers applying for a new credit card account

Existing Citizens Bank cardholders should call 1-800-438-9222 for special cardholder rate information.

Citizens Bank VISA® (Code: BVCFNU)

Please tell us about yourself

First Name Middle Initial Last Name

Address (street)

(City, state, zip)

Date of Birth Social Security Number

❑ Own ❑ Rent ❑ Live with Parents

Years/Months at Present Address

$ ( )

Monthly Housing Payment Home Telephone

Previous Address Years/Months There
(if less than 2 years at present address)

Mother's Maiden Name

Citizens Bank Account Information

❑ Checking ❑ Savings ❑ Loan ❑ Citizens Circle[SM] Checking

account # ________

Please tell us about your employment

Present Employer Position

( )

Years/Months Employed There Business Telephone

Previous Employer Years/Months There
(if less than 2 years at present employer)

$ $

Gross Monthly Household Income Other Monthly Income*

*Alimony, child support, or separate maintenance income need not be revealed if you do not wish it to be considered as a basis for repaying this obligation.

24-hour banking convenience

Your card(s) can be encoded with a four-digit personal identification number (PIN) to obtain cash advances at automated teller machines. This four-digit PIN will be known only to you. So that we may properly encode your card(s), please select the four digits of your choice and enter them in the spaces below:

____ ____ ____ ____

Please send a second card at no cost for

First Name Middle Initial Last Name

Please read and sign

Your Signature Date

All information on this application is true and complete, and Citizens Bank of Rhode Island, the card issuer, is authorized to obtain further credit and employment information from any source. I understand that you will retain this application whether or not it is approved. You may share with others, only for valid business reasons, any information relating to me, this application, and any of my banking relationships with you. I request issuance of a Citizens credit card and agree to be bound by the terms and conditions of the Agreement received with the card(s). I understand that Citizens Bank of Rhode Island will assign a credit line based on information provided and information obtained from any other source; and the issuance of a Gold card is subject to a minimum annual income of $35,000 and qualification for a minimum $5,000 credit line.

Transfer balances and save

Citizens will transfer your high interest rate balances to your new Citizens Bank VISA Card at no extra charge. Use the form below to indicate the amount(s) to be transferred in order of priority. (Citizens Bank will not transfer balances from existing Citizens Bank accounts.) (see reverse side for balance transfer disclosure)

Creditor Name	Account Number	$ Amount
Creditor Name	Account Number	$ Amount
Creditor Name	Account Number	$ Amount

Bank Use Only Bank Code: ❑ CBMA ❑ CBRI ❑ CBCT Sales ID# ________ Application code: 1122

Source: Courtesy of Citizens Financial Group, Inc., Providence, Rhode Island.

Collateral For large amounts of credit—and especially for long-term loans—the lender may require some type of collateral. As mentioned earlier, collateral is real estate or property (stocks, bonds, equipment, or any other asset of value) pledged as security for a loan. If the borrower fails to live up to the terms of the credit agreement, the lender can repossess the collateral and then sell it to satisfy the debt.

Conditions *Conditions* refers to the general economic conditions that can affect a borrower's ability to repay a loan or other credit obligation. How well a business firm can withstand an economic storm may depend on the particular industry the firm is in, its relative strength within that industry, the type of product or service it sells, its earnings history, and its earnings potential. For individuals, the basic question focuses on security—of both the applicant's job and the firm for which he or she works. For example, if the economy takes a downturn, some employees may lose their jobs. Even though these former employees lost their jobs, they still have mortgage payments, car payments, and credit-card payments that must be paid.

Checking Credit Information

The five C's of credit are concerned mainly with information supplied by the applicant. But how can a lender determine whether this information is accurate? This depends on whether the potential borrower is a business or an individual consumer.

Credit information concerning businesses can be obtained from the following four sources:

- *Global credit-reporting agencies.* D&B (formerly Dun & Bradstreet) is the most widely used credit-reporting agency in the world. Their reports present detailed credit information about specific companies. For more information on D&B services, visit the company's Web site at http://www.dnb.com.
- *Local credit-reporting agencies.* These agencies may require a monthly or yearly fee for providing information on a continual basis.
- *Industry associations.* These associations may charge a service fee.
- *Other firms.* This refers to other firms that have given the applicant credit.

Various credit bureaus provide credit information concerning individuals. The following are the three major consumer credit bureaus:

- Experian—at http://www.experian.com or toll-free at 888-397-3742
- TransUnion—at http://www.transunion.com or toll-free at 800-888-4213
- Equifax Credit Information Services—at http://www.equifax.com or toll-free at 800-685-1111

Note: With the recent rise in identity theft, experts recommend that you check your credit report at least once a year or more often if you suspect suspicious activity. For more information about protecting your identity, complete the Journaling for Success exercise on page 563.

Consumer credit bureaus are subject to the provisions of the Fair Credit Reporting Act. This act safeguards consumers' rights in two ways. First, every consumer has the right to know what information is contained in his or her credit bureau file. In addition to the provisions contained in the federal Fair Credit Reporting Act, the Fair and Accurate Credit Transaction Act requires each of the nationwide credit reporting companies—Equifax, Experian, and TransUnion—to provide you with a free copy of your credit report, at your request, once every 12 months. To obtain your free credit report, go to http://www.annualcreditreport.com. (*Note*: Beware of other sites that may look and sound similar to this site but may charge for information or require that you spend money on credit monitoring.[18]) In other situations, the consumer may obtain the information for a fee that is usually about $8 to $15 per request. It is also possible to obtain credit reports on a monthly or quarterly basis by subscribing to a credit-reporting service, which usually charges higher fees.

Second, a consumer who feels that some information in the file is inaccurate, misleading, or vague has the right to request that the credit bureau verify it. If the disputed information is found to be correct, the consumer can provide a brief explanation, giving his or her side of the dispute. This explanation must become part of the consumer's credit file. If the disputed information is found to be inaccurate, it must be deleted or corrected. Furthermore, you may request that any lender or prospective employer that has been supplied an inaccurate credit report in the last six months be sent a corrected credit report.

New Protection for Consumers: The Credit Card Act of 2009

The Credit Card Act of 2009, which was enacted on February 22, 2010, also provides additional protection for credit card customers. This new federal law is designed to level the playing field between credit card customers and financial institutions that issue credit cards. This act[19]

- Encourages disclosures written in plain language that include more information about due dates, late fees, and the amount of time required to pay off card balances if only minimum monthly payments are made
- Provides new protections against arbitrary rate increases and requires a 45-day notice before existing rates are changed
- Increases protections for students and young people under the age of 21
- Standardizes billing dates and eliminates some common deceptive practices including due dates that change each month, weekend due dates, and payment deadlines that fall in the middle of the day
- Requires that all fees be necessary, reasonable, and proportional in relation to a violation of the cardholder's credit agreement
- Provides new measures for accountability including posting credit card contract information on the Internet and review of contract agreements by the Federal Reserve Board
- Increases existing penalties for companies that violate the Truth-in-Lending Act for credit card customers

If you want more information about provisions in the Credit Card Act of 2009, contact the financial institution that issued your credit card, the Federal Reserve Board (http://www.federalreserve.gov), or use the Internet.

Sound Collection Procedures

The vast majority of borrowers follow the lender's repayment terms exactly. However, some accounts inevitably become overdue for a variety of reasons. Experience shows that such accounts should receive immediate attention.

Some firms handle their own delinquent accounts; others prefer to use a professional collection agency. (Charges for a collection agency's services are usually high—up to half the amount collected.) Both tend to use the following techniques, generally in the order in which they are listed:

1. Subtle reminders, such as duplicate statements marked "Past Due"
2. Telephone calls to urge prompt payment
3. Personal visits to business customers to stress the necessity of paying overdue amounts immediately
4. Legal action, although the time, expense, and uncertain outcome of a lawsuit make this action a last resort

Good collection procedures should be firm, but they also should allow for compromise. Harassment is both illegal and bad business. Ideally, the customer will be convinced to make up missed payments, and the firm will retain the customer's goodwill.

In the next chapter, you will see why firms need financing, how they obtain the money they need, and how they ensure that funds are used efficiently, in keeping with their organizational objectives.

return to inside business

TD Bank

Although the banking industry has been hard hit by problems with risky loans, TD Bank has grown and prospered through careful credit management, innovative services, and close attention to its customers' needs. At least five times a month, every store is visited by mystery shoppers who report back to headquarters about their customer service experiences. The bank also surveys more than 140,000 customers every year to find out what they think of its services.

TD Bank aims to be not only "America's most convenient bank" but also an outstanding corporate citizen. Its philanthropic contributions support financial literacy efforts, affordable housing initiatives, and non-profit groups that provide shelter and meals to people in need. And it's going green by investing in renewable energy, reducing its carbon footprint, stepping up recycling, and building new stores with solar panels and fixtures made of wood from sustainable sources. Investing in its communities is another way that TD Bank shows customers it cares about what they care about.

Questions

1. Why would TD Bank's customers care whether the bank was involved in risky lending practices?
2. Would you like to work for a commercial bank like TD Bank, which serves consumers, small businesses, and major corporations? Explain your answer.

SUMMARY

Summary

1 Identify the functions and characteristics of money.

Money is anything a society uses to purchase products, services, or resources. Money must serve as a medium of exchange, a measure of value, and a store of value. To perform its functions effectively, money must be divisible into units of convenient size, light and sturdy enough to be carried and used on a daily basis, stable in value, and difficult to counterfeit. The M_1 supply of money is made up of coins and bills (currency) and deposits in checking accounts (demand deposits). The M_2 supply includes M_1 plus savings accounts, certain money-market securities, and small-denomination time deposits.

2 Summarize how the Federal Reserve System regulates the money supply to maintain a healthy economy.

The Federal Reserve System is responsible for regulating the U.S. banking industry and maintaining a sound economic environment. Banks with federal charters (national banks) must be members of the Fed. State banks may join if they choose to and if they can meet the requirements for membership. Twelve district banks and 24 branch banks compose the Federal Reserve System, whose seven-member board of governors is headquartered in Washington, DC. During the recent economic crisis, it was necessary for the Federal Reserve to take specific actions to avoid the worst economic problems since the Great Depression. Specifically, the Fed provided liquidity to the banking and financial industry, supported troubled financial markets, supported troubled financial institutions, and conducted stress tests of major banks. These actions did help to restore confidence in the financial system.

To control the supply of money, the Federal Reserve System regulates the reserve requirement, or the percentage of deposits a bank must keep on hand. It also regulates the discount rate, or the interest rate the Fed charges member banks for loans from the Federal Reserve. It also engages in open-market operations, in which it buys and sells government securities. Of the three tools used to influence monetary policy, the use of open-market operations is the most important. When the Federal Reserve buys and sells securities, the goal is to increase or decrease the federal funds rate. The federal funds rate is the interest rate at which a bank lends immediately available funds on deposit at the Fed to another bank overnight in order to meet the borrowing bank's reserve requirements. The Fed serves as the government's bank and is also responsible for clearing checks and electronic transfers, inspecting currency, enforcing the Truth-in-Lending Act, and setting margin requirements for securities transactions.

3 Describe the organizations involved in the banking industry.

Most everyone has been affected in one way or another by the nation's economic problems. Now that the nation's economy shows signs of improvement, there is a movement in Washington to reform the banking and financial industry and increase government regulation. A commercial bank is a profit-making organization that accepts deposits, makes loans, and provides related services to customers. Commercial banks are chartered by the federal government or state governments. Savings and loan associations and credit unions offer the same basic services that commercial banks provide. Mutual savings banks, insurance companies, pension funds, brokerage firms, finance companies, and investment banking firms provide some limited banking services. A large number of people work in the banking industry because of the number of banks and other financial institutions. To be successful in the banking industry, you must be honest, be able to interact with people, have a strong background in accounting, appreciate the relationship between banking and finance, and possess basic computer skills.

4 Identify the services provided by financial institutions.

Banks and other financial institutions offer today's customers a tempting array of services. Among the most important and attractive banking services for both individuals and businesses are checking accounts, savings accounts, short- and long-term loans, and credit-card and debit-card transactions. Other traditional services include financial advice, payroll services, certified checks, trust services, and safe-deposit boxes.

5 Understand how financial institutions are changing to meet the needs of domestic and international customers.

Competition among banks, brokerage firms, insurance companies, and other financial institutions has increased. As we enter the 21st century, an increasing use of technology and the need for bankers to help American businesses compete in the global marketplace will change the way banks and other financial institutions do business. The use of technology will increase as financial institutions continue to offer online banking. Increased use of electronic funds transfer systems (automated teller machines, automated clearing-houses, point-of-sale terminals, and electronic check conversion) also will change the way people bank. For firms in the global marketplace, a bank can provide letters of credit and banker's acceptances that will reduce the risk of nonpayment for sellers. Banks and financial institutions also can provide currency exchange to reduce payment problems for import or export transactions.

6 Explain how deposit insurance protects customers.

The Federal Deposit Insurance Corporation (FDIC) and the National Credit Union Association (NCUA) insure accounts in member financial institutions for up $250,000. The $250,000 limit is now a permanent change in the amount of deposit insurance. Deposits maintained in different categories of legal ownership are insured separately. The most common ownership categories are single ownership and joint ownership. It is also possible to obtain additional coverage by opening separate accounts in different banks, S&Ls, or credit unions. The FDIC and NCUA have improved banking in the United States. When either of these organizations insures a financial institution's deposits, they reserve the right to examine that institution's operations periodically. If a bank, S&L, or credit union is found to be poorly managed, it is reported to the proper banking authority.

7 Discuss the importance of credit and credit management.

Credit is immediate purchasing power that is exchanged for a promise to repay borrowed money, with or without interest, at a later date. Banks lend money because they are in business for that purpose. Businesses sell goods and services on credit because some customers cannot afford to pay cash and because they must keep pace with competitors who offer credit. Businesses also may realize a profit from interest charges.

Decisions on whether to grant credit to businesses and individuals usually are based on the five C's of credit: character, capacity, capital, collateral, and conditions. Credit information can be obtained from various credit-reporting agencies, credit bureaus, industry associations, and other firms. The techniques used to collect past-due accounts should be firm enough to prompt payment but flexible enough to maintain the borrower's goodwill. A number of federal regulations protect consumers from harassment and illegal collection procedures.

Key Terms

You should now be able to define and give an example relevant to each of the following terms:

barter system (534)
money (534)
medium of exchange (535)
measure of value (535)
store of value (535)
demand deposit (537)
time deposit (537)
Federal Reserve System (538)
commercial paper (539)
reserve requirement (540)
discount rate (541)
open-market operations (541)
federal funds rate (542)
commercial bank (544)
national bank (544)
state bank (544)
savings and loan association (S&L) (545)
credit union (545)
check (547)
NOW account (547)
certificate of deposit (CD) (548)
line of credit (548)
revolving credit agreement (548)
collateral (548)
debit card (549)
electronic funds transfer (EFT) system (551)
letter of credit (552)
banker's acceptance (552)
credit (553)

Review Questions

1. How does the use of money solve the problems associated with a barter system of exchange?
2. What are three functions money must perform in a sound monetary system?
3. Explain why money must have each of the following characteristics:
   a. Divisibility
   b. Portability
   c. Stability
   d. Durability
   e. Difficulty of counterfeiting
4. What is included in the definition of the M_1 supply of money? Of the M_2 supply?
5. What is the Federal Reserve System? How is it organized?
6. Describe the actions the Federal Reserve took to maintain a healthy economy during the recent economic crisis. In your opinion, were the actions necessary? Were the Fed's actions effective?
7. Explain how the Federal Reserve System uses each of the following to control the money supply:
   a. Reserve requirements
   b. The discount rate
   c. Open-market operations
8. The Federal Reserve is responsible for enforcing the Truth-in-Lending Act. How does this act affect you?
9. What is the difference between a national bank and a state bank? What other financial institutions compete with national and state banks?
10. Describe the major banking services provided by financial institutions today.
11. For consumers, what are the major advantages of online banking? What is its major disadvantage?
12. How do automated teller machines, automated clearing-houses, point-of-sale terminals, and electronic check conversion affect how you bank?
13. How can a bank or other financial institution help American businesses to compete in the global marketplace?
14. What is the basic function of the FDIC and NCUA? How do they perform this function?
15. List and explain the five C's of credit management.
16. How would you check the information provided by an applicant for credit at a department store? By a business applicant at a heavy-equipment manufacturer's sales office?

Discussion Questions

1. Based on what you know at the time you are answering this question, how would you describe the financial health of the U.S. economy? Of the global economy?
2. It is said that financial institutions use a process called deposit expansion to "create" money when they make loans to firms and individuals. Explain what this means.
3. Why does the Fed use indirect means of controlling the money supply instead of simply printing more money or removing money from circulation when necessary?
4. Why would banks pay higher interest on money left on deposit for longer periods of time (e.g., on CDs)?
5. How could an individual get in financial trouble by using a credit card? If you were in trouble because of credit-card debt, what steps could you take to reduce your debts?

6. Lenders generally are reluctant to extend credit to individuals with no previous credit history (and no outstanding debts). Yet they willingly extend credit to individuals who are in the process of repaying debts. Is this reasonable? Is it fair? Explain your answer.
7. Assume that you want to borrow $10,000. What can you do to convince the loan officer that you are a good credit risk?

Video Case 18.1

Chase Bank Helps Small Business Owners

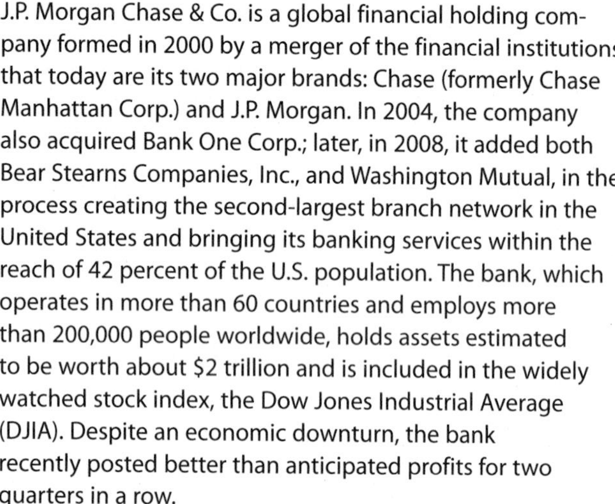

J.P. Morgan Chase & Co. is a global financial holding company formed in 2000 by a merger of the financial institutions that today are its two major brands: Chase (formerly Chase Manhattan Corp.) and J.P. Morgan. In 2004, the company also acquired Bank One Corp.; later, in 2008, it added both Bear Stearns Companies, Inc., and Washington Mutual, in the process creating the second-largest branch network in the United States and bringing its banking services within the reach of 42 percent of the U.S. population. The bank, which operates in more than 60 countries and employs more than 200,000 people worldwide, holds assets estimated to be worth about $2 trillion and is included in the widely watched stock index, the Dow Jones Industrial Average (DJIA). Despite an economic downturn, the bank recently posted better than anticipated profits for two quarters in a row.

Most people are probably more familiar with the functions performed on the Chase side of the operation. These operations include conducting everyday banking via branch offices, ATMs, telephone, and online; issuing consumer credit cards; serving small businesses with financing and banking services; offering home mortgages and home equity loans; helping customers with personal retirement and investment planning; and making auto and educational loans.

In its small-business banking operations, Chase exemplifies the words of J.P. Morgan, who told a Senate subcommittee in 1933 that "Another very important use of the banker is to serve as a channel whereby industry may be provided with capital to meet its needs for expansion and development." Providing capital to small businesses is one of the most important functions the bank fulfills for these business clients. Whether small companies need short-term loans to expand their operations or to bridge the time gap between manufacturing a product and collecting money for the sale, a line of credit to ease their cash flow during a tough period, or a commercial mortgage loan to buy a new factory or warehouse, Chase is ready to lend the necessary funds. The bank also offers several kinds of business credit cards, which small-business owners can use for everyday needs when cash is tight. These cards offer different incentives such as no annual fee, cash back for purchases, bonus points, or no interest on balances paid in full each month. Business debit cards are another option, backed by fraud monitoring and account alerts.

Chase is also there to help firms hang on to their money—not only by providing all those branch offices for making deposits but also by handling the safe collection of payments through its lock-box service (through which consumers send bill payments to a post-office box for collection). Chase makes it easier for its small-business customers to deposit checks, too. Now firms can scan paper checks right in their own offices, transforming them into electronic payments so they can take advantage of online banking's convenience, safety, and speed. Business checking accounts are available as well, with a wide range of specially tailored features and overdraft protection. Business savings accounts and CDs are offered, and business customers can link their accounts to Chase Business Packages to earn additional benefits, such as waived fees and reduced interest rates on borrowing. The bank even offers payroll processing.

Retail firms that accept credit cards like Visa, American Express, MasterCard, and Discover can rely on Chase for payment processing, and they can use the processed funds the very next day. Free technical support is available 24/7, and monthly statements and online reports help firms manage their credit card operations. Business owners can even pay bills, transfer funds, view account balances and transaction history, and send wire transfers by texting the bank from their mobile phones. Additionally, Chase makes it possible for small businesses to conduct transactions globally, whether that means buying goods abroad or accepting orders from international customers.[20]

Questions

1. If you were a small-business owner, would you take advantage of any of Chase's or another bank's small-business banking services? Why or why not?
2. Can you think of any additional financial or banking services that banks could offer small-business owners?
3. Chase prides itself on its ability to know many of its business customers personally and to keep up-to-date on the industries in which they operate. Why would this familiarity be an advantage for the bank?

Case 18.2 Are You Credit Savvy?

Never mind the national budget deficit: U.S. consumers are $2.5 trillion deep in consumer debt. Students are increasingly part of this credit tsunami. A little credit can be a good thing, but too much credit can be hazardous to your long-term financial health, especially when you're just starting on your career.

Studies show that more than 80 percent of all undergraduates carry a credit card; half of all undergrads have four or more credit cards. In addition the average credit-card debt of a new graduate is $4,100. "Students are using credit cards as a last resort to pick up the slack when they have difficulty getting loans or jobs to cover their expenses," explains a consumer finance analyst. "With fewer loans and jobs available, you have the makings of an increase in college student credit card debt on top of existing student loan debt." No wonder so many students feel overwhelmed as they try to keep up with credit repayments.

Of course, credit can come in handy when you need or want to make a large purchase but haven't got the cash. Payday may be a week away but that super-sale ends today or your gas tank is empty—so you plunk down your plastic. When the credit-card statement arrives, however, you have to pay in full or the interest-rate meter starts ticking. Suppose you only pay the minimum amount, planning to pay more next time. But if you don't pay more than the minimum month after month, the interest charges can mount up quickly. What happens if you have other debts or you suddenly lose your job?

That's what happened to Diane McLeod. She worked two jobs to pay two mortgages with escalating interest rates, a car loan, and high-interest credit cards. After the twin disasters of medical emergencies and lost employment, her home is being foreclosed and her credit rating is destroyed. McLeod admits creating some of her own problems by overspending and failing to read the fine print in credit agreements. But interest payments on her debts equal almost half her pretax income, and she owes thousands of dollars in fees alone.

How can you protect yourself from getting too deeply in debt? First, don't apply for or carry cards you don't need. Next, check your attitude about money. According to the National Association of Retail Collection Attorneys, more than 25 percent of students think it's okay to use cards to raise cash and are overoptimistic about paying back debt. Don't be fooled. With fees and interest rates, your outstanding balance can rise even if you stop using your card. A good rule of thumb is not to charge purchases unless you already have cash on hand to pay for them. Know what you can afford by creating a personal balance sheet and personal income statement—both topics covered in Chapter 17. Finally, use cash. It carries no interest charges or hidden fees, and any "rewards" you might earn with credit card purchases will be far from free when the bills come due.

If you want to apply for credit, shop around and know your rights. For example, under the Credit Card Act of 2009, interest rates can't be raised on a new credit account until after the first year. Be sure to check your credit report before you apply, so you'll know how credit-worthy you'll look to a lender.

If you must use a card, always pay on time, pay as much as you can, and certainly pay more than the minimum to avoid letting your balance climb. Consider substituting a debit card for a credit card to avoid debt. Don't take cash advances on your card (why pay 19 percent or even higher interest for money?), and avoid making impulse purchases. In the end, your credit health is up to you.[21]

Questions

1. If you have one or more credit cards, check your credit history for free at http://www.annualcreditreport.com. What does your history tell you about your spending and borrowing habits? What, if anything, do you need to change? Why should you check your credit reports on a regular basis?
2. What do you think is the real cost of "free" rewards offered on many credit cards? Who pays it? Do you think these rewards are worth the cost? Why or why not?
3. Imagine you've applied to a bank for a home mortgage, car loan, or tuition loan (or perhaps you already have such a loan or loans). Now put yourself in the bank's place. How do *you* rate on the five C's of credit management? Which of these criteria is most affected by your credit-card history?

Building Skills for Career Success

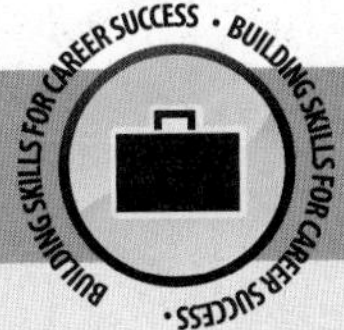

❶ JOURNALING FOR SUCCESS

You could be one in a million—the 1 million Americans who fall victim to the crime of identity theft every year. Crooks who steal your name, birth date, credit-card numbers, bank account numbers, and Social Security number can withdraw money from your bank accounts, charge merchandise in your name, or contract for cell-phone service.

Assignment

1. Use the Internet to obtain information about how to prevent identity theft. Then, according to the professionals, describe the steps someone should take to protect his or her identity.
2. Complete a "security audit" of your personal information and financial records. Based on your audit and the recommendations from professionals, what should you do now to protect your identity?
3. It always helps to have a plan in case your identity is stolen. Based on the information you obtained from your Internet research, what immediate steps should you take if your identity is stolen?

❷ EXPLORING THE INTERNET

Internet-based banking is no longer a new concept. For many Americans, technology has changed the way they conduct their banking transactions. For example, most people no longer carry their paychecks to the bank to be deposited; instead, the money is deposited directly into their accounts. In addition, an increasing number of individuals and businesses are using computers and the Internet to handle their finances, apply for loans, and pay their bills. Banking with the help of a home computer is continually being made easier, giving bank customers access to their accounts 24 hours a day and seven days a week. As a result, you have more control over your money.

Assignment

1. Examine the Web sites of several major banks with which you are familiar. Describe their online banking services. Are they worthwhile in your opinion?
2. In the past three years, how has technology changed the way you handle your money and conduct your banking transactions, such as depositing your paychecks, paying your monthly bills, obtaining cash, paying for purchases, and applying for loans?
3. In the next five to ten years, what will the banking industry be like? How will these changes affect you and the way you do your banking? The Internet and the library can help you to learn what is in the forefront of banking technology.
4. Prepare a report explaining your answers to these questions.

❸ DEVELOPING CRITICAL-THINKING SKILLS

Assumption: There are banks, savings and loan associations, credit unions, and other financial institutions that want your business. Therefore, it pays to shop around for the lowest interest rates for loans needed to purchase a home mortgage or an automobile. It's also easy to compare interest rates when investing in certificates of deposit (CDs) or savings accounts. A logical place to start is with the financial institution where you do your banking. You can also compare interest rates at other local banks and financial institutions located close to where you live or work. Finally, you can use the Internet and Web sites like http://www.bankrate.com or http://www.interest.com to determine interest rates for loans and CD investments.

Assignment

To answer each question below, contact at least three different financial institutions in your city or town or three different Internet Web sites. *Hint*: If you use the Internet, use a search engine like Google or Yahoo! and enter "interest rates" in the search window.

1. What is the lowest rate you found for a 30-year $150,000 home mortgage?
2. Based on your research, what is the difference between the lowest interest rate and the highest interest rate for a home mortgage? Assuming you pay back the loan in 30 years, how could the difference in interest rates affect the total amount you will pay for your home?
3. What is the highest interest rate you found for a one-year certificate of deposit?
4. Based on your research, what is the difference between the highest rate and the lowest rate for a one-year CD? How could this affect the amount of money you would earn for the 12-month period?
5. In a one- to two-page report, summarize what you have learned from this critical-thinking exercise.

❹ BUILDING TEAM SKILLS

Three years ago, Ron and Ginger were happy to learn that, upon graduation, Ron would be teaching history in a large high school, making $35,000 a year, and Ginger would be working in a public accounting firm, starting at $38,000. They married immediately after graduation and bought a new home for $110,000. Since Ron had no personal savings, Ginger used her savings for the down payment. They soon began furnishing their home, charging their purchases to three separate credit cards, and that is when their debt began to mount. When the three credit cards reached their $10,000 limits, Ron and Ginger signed up for one additional credit card with a $10,000 limit. Soon their monthly payments were more than their combined take-home pay. To make their monthly payments, Ron and Ginger began to obtain cash advances on their credit cards. When they reached the credit ceilings on their four credit cards, they could no longer get the cash advances they needed to cover their monthly bills. Stress began to mount as creditors called and demanded payment. Ron and Ginger began to argue over money and just about everything else. Finally, things got so bad they considered filing for personal bankruptcy; ironically, they could not afford the legal fees. What options are available to this couple?

Assignment

1. Working in teams of three or four, use your local library, the Internet, and personal interviews to investigate the following:
   a. Filing for personal bankruptcy.
      - What is involved in filing for personal bankruptcy?
      - How much does it cost?
      - How does bankruptcy affect individuals?
   b. Review Money Management International at http://www.cccsintl.org or How to Get Out of Debt at http://www.getoutofdebt.org
      - What services do these organizations provide?
      - How could they help Ron and Ginger?
      - What will it cost?
2. Prepare a specific plan for repaying Ron and Ginger's debt.
3. Outline the advantages and disadvantages of credit cards, and make the appropriate recommendations for Ron and Ginger concerning their future use of credit cards.
4. Summarize what you have learned about credit-card misuse.

5 RESEARCHING DIFFERENT CAREERS

It has long been known that maintaining a good credit record is essential to obtaining loans from financial institutions, but did you know that employers often check credit records before offering an applicant a position? This is especially true of firms that handle financial accounts for others. Information contained in your credit report can tell an employer a lot about how responsible you are with money and how well you manage it. Individuals have the right to know what is in their credit bureau files and to have the credit bureau verify any inaccurate, misleading, or vague information. Before you apply for a job or a loan, you should check with a credit bureau to learn what is in your file.

Assignment

1. Using information in this chapter, use the Internet or call a credit bureau and ask for a copy of your credit report. A small fee may be required depending on the bureau and circumstances.
2. Review the information.
3. Have the bureau verify any information that you feel is inaccurate, misleading, or vague.
4. If the verification shows that the information is correct, prepare a brief statement explaining your side of the dispute, and send it to the bureau.
5. Prepare a statement summarizing what the credit report says about you. Based on your credit report, would a firm hire you as its financial manager?

Mastering Financial Management

19

© iStockphoto.com /Damir Karan

Learning Objectives

What you will be able to do once you complete this chapter:

1. Explain the need for financial management in business.
2. Summarize the process of planning for financial management.
3. Describe the advantages and disadvantages of different methods of short-term debt financing.
4. Evaluate the advantages and disadvantages of equity financing.
5. Evaluate the advantages and disadvantages of long-term debt financing.

FYI

Did You Know?

Ford Motor Company, the only one of the Big Three U.S. automakers to avoid bankruptcy during the economic crisis, rings up more than $125 billion in annual revenue worldwide.

inside business

Ford's Financial Fuel

Question: Which one of the Big Three U.S. automakers did *not* file for bankruptcy during the recent economic crisis? Answer: Ford Motor Company. While General Motors and Chrysler both sought bankruptcy protection, Ford had the financial fuel to keep going, despite sagging sales and worldwide economic turmoil. How did Ford do it?

Months before the recession hit, Ford's financial executives recognized the early warning signs of business-cycle change. They also knew that Ford was unprofitable and losing market share to international competitors. In response, the executives drew up a financial plan to prepare for leaner times while implementing a turnaround. The purpose was to be sure that money was available for near-term expenses such as restructuring through layoffs and plant closings as well as for long-term projects such as researching environmentally friendly engines and creating the concept cars of tomorrow—activities that would pay off far in the future.

Ford found lenders offering attractive interest rates without overly burdensome loan requirements and borrowed $7 billion, using assets such as factories and trademarks as collateral to secure the loans. It also arranged for an $11.5 billion line of credit to be available if and when needed. In addition, Ford raised $4.5 billion by selling a special type of bond that can be converted to common stock. Although the company would be paying interest to bondholders every six months for 30 years, the deal helped strengthen its cash position.

As economic conditions deteriorated, sales of many consumer goods, including cars and trucks, plummeted. Ford began drawing on its credit to implement its plan for returning to profitability. Before bills came due, Ford parked the money in low-risk investments such as time deposits, yielding a low return but keeping the money safe.

Eventually, the economy finally perked up and Ford poured on the gas, launching a series of award-winning new cars and adding high-tech touches to woo buyers back. The company also issued 300 million new shares of common stock to raise more money. As cash flow improved month by month, Ford even began paying down debt. Can the carmaker use its financial strength to stay on course toward sustained profitability?[1]

Although most managers and employees have been affected by the economic crisis, the last few years have been especially difficult for financial managers. After all, they are the ones that must be able to raise the money needed to pay bills and expenses to keep a company's doors open. Executives at Ford—the company profiled in the Inside Business case for this chapter—used aggressive financial planning to anticipate the automaker's need for financing. To avoid the same fate as General Motors and Chrysler—bankruptcy—Ford's financial managers borrowed money in anticipation of a downturn in the company's sales and profits. Ford also sold both stocks and bonds to raise the money they needed to keep the company operating during the crisis and even build for the future. Did their financial plan work? The answer: A definite yes! Today, Ford is selling more cars, developing environmentally friendly engines, creating concept cars for the future, and has returned to profitability. Although there are many factors that account for Ford's success, most experts agree that the firm's financial planning enabled it to weather the economic storm and build for the future.

In reality, the crisis was a wake-up call for all corporate executives, managers, and business owners because one factor became obvious. The ability to borrow money (debt capital) or obtain money from the owners of a business (equity capital) is necessary for the efficient operation of a business firm *and* our economic system. In this chapter we focus on how firms find the financing required to meet two needs of all business organizations: the need for money to start a business and keep it going, and the need to manage that money effectively. We also look at how firms develop financial plans and evaluate financial performance. Then we compare various methods of obtaining short-term financing. We also examine sources of long-term financing.

What Is Financial Management?

1 Explain the need for financial management in business.

Financial management consists of all the activities concerned with obtaining money and using it effectively. Within a business organization, the financial manager not only must determine the best way (or ways) to raise money, but he or she also must ensure that projected uses are in keeping with the organization's goals.

The Need for Financing

Money is needed both to start a business and to keep it going. The original investment of the owners, along with money they may have borrowed, should be enough to open the doors. After that, ideally sales revenues should be used to pay the firm's expenses and provide a profit as well.

This is exactly what happens in a successful firm—over the long run. However, income and expenses may vary from month to month or from year to year. Temporary financing may be needed when expenses are high or sales are low. Then, too, situations such as the opportunity to purchase a new facility or expand an existing plant may require more money than is currently available within a firm.

Financial management often involves managing inventory. Retailers often invest large amounts of money in order to have just the right merchandise to sell to their customers. For retailers like Family Dollar, managing inventory can be a problem. To help families live within their budget, this retailer offers hundreds of toys for $5 or less, including Disney merchandise, Hot Wheels, and more.

© AP Images/PRNewsFoto/Family Dollar

Short-Term Financing **Short-term financing** is money that will be used for one year or less. As illustrated in Table 19.1, there are many short-term financing needs, but two deserve special attention. First, certain business practices may affect a firm's cash flow and create a need for short-term financing. **Cash flow** is the movement of money into and out of an organization. The ideal is to have sufficient money coming into the firm in any period to cover the firm's expenses during that period. This ideal, however, is not always achieved. For example, California-based Callaway Golf offers credit to retailers and wholesalers that carry the firm's golf clubs, balls, clothing, and golf accessories. Credit purchases made by Callaway's retailers generally are not paid until

Table 19.1 Comparison of Short- and Long-Term Financing

Whether a business seeks short- or long-term financing depends on what the money will be used for.

Corporate Cash Needs	
Short-Term Financing Needs	Long-Term Financing Needs
Cash-flow problems	Business start-up costs
Current inventory needs	Mergers and acquisitions
Speculative production	New product development
Monthly expenses	Long-term marketing activities
Short-term promotional needs	Replacement of equipment
Unexpected emergencies	Expansion of facilities

financial management all the activities concerned with obtaining money and using it effectively

short-term financing money that will be used for one year or less

cash flow the movement of money into and out of an organization

Figure 19.1 Cash Flow for a Manufacturing Business

Manufacturers such as Stanley (Stanley Black & Decker) often use short-term financing to pay expenses during the production process. Once goods are shipped to retailers and wholesalers and payment is received, sales revenues are used to repay short-term financing.

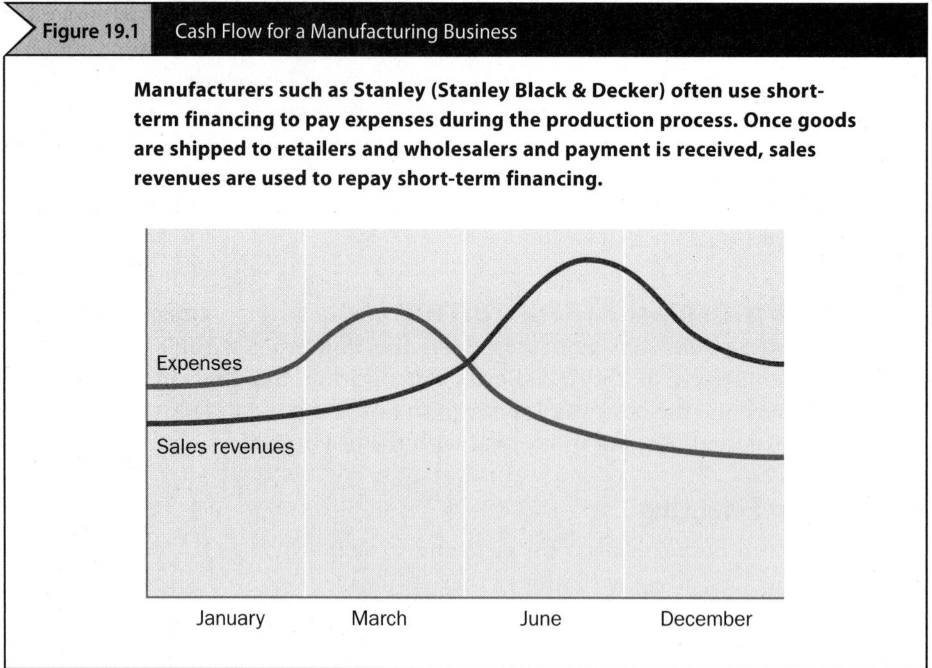

30 to 60 days (or more) after the transaction. Callaway therefore may need short-term financing to pay its bills until its customers have paid theirs.

A second major need for short-term financing is inventory. For most manufacturers, wholesalers, and retailers, inventory requires considerable investment. Moreover, most goods are manufactured four to nine months before they are actually sold to the ultimate customer. This type of manufacturing is often referred to as speculative production. **Speculative production** refers to the time lag between the actual production of goods and when the goods are sold. Consider what happens when a firm such as Stanley Black & Decker begins to manufacture electric tools and small appliances for sale during the Christmas season. Manufacturing begins in February, March, and April, and the firm negotiates short-term financing to buy materials and supplies, to pay wages and rent, and to cover inventory costs until its products eventually are sold to wholesalers and retailers later in the year. Take a look at Figure 19.1. Although Stanley Black & Decker manufactures and sells finished products all during the year, expenses peak during the first part of the year. During this same period, sales revenues are low. Once the firm's finished products are shipped to retailers and wholesalers and payment is received (usually within 30 to 60 days), sales revenues are used to repay short-term financing.

Retailers that range in size from Walmart to the neighborhood drugstore also need short-term financing to build up their inventories before peak selling periods. For example, Dallas-based Bruce Miller Nurseries must increase the number of shrubs, trees, and flowering plants that it makes available for sale during the spring and summer growing seasons. To obtain this merchandise inventory from growers or wholesalers, it uses short-term financing and repays the loans when the merchandise is sold.

speculative production the time lag between the actual production of goods and when the goods are sold

long-term financing money that will be used for longer than one year

Long-Term Financing

Long-term financing is money that will be used for longer than one year. Long-term financing obviously is needed to start a new business. As Table 19.1 shows, it is also needed for business mergers and acquisitions, new product development, long-term marketing activities, replacement of equipment that has become obsolete, and expansion of facilities.

The amounts of long-term financing needed by large firms can seem almost unreal. The 3M Company—a large multinational corporation known for research and development—has invested more than $6.9 billion over the last five years to develop new products designed to make people's lives easier and safer.[2]

The Need for Financial Management

To some extent, financial management can be viewed as a two-sided problem. On one side, the uses of funds often dictate the type or types of financing needed by a business. On the other side, the activities a business can undertake are determined by the types of financing available.

Financial Management During the Economic Crisis Financial managers must ensure that funds are available when needed, that they are obtained at the lowest possible cost, and that they are used as efficiently as possible. During the recent economic crisis, many companies found it was increasingly difficult to use many of the traditional sources of short- and long-term financing described later in this chapter. In some cases, banks stopped making loans even to companies that had always been able to borrow money. Even companies that had always been able to sell commercial paper had difficulty finding buyers. For example, both GE and AT&T—two premier names in corporate America—could not get the short-term financing they were looking for.[3] Furthermore, the number of corporations selling stock for the first time to the general public decreased because investors were afraid to invest in new companies. The worst case scenario: There was an increase in the number of businesses that filed for bankruptcy, as illustrated in Figure 19.2.

Although the number of business bankruptcies increased, fortunately there were many more business firms that were able to weather the economic storm and keep operating because of their ability to manage their finances. Proper financial management during both good and bad times must ensure the following:

- Financing priorities are established in line with organizational goals and objectives.
- Spending is planned and controlled.
- Sufficient financing is available when it is needed, both now and in the future.
- A firm's credit customers pay their bills on time, and the number of past due or delinquent accounts is reduced.
- Bills are paid promptly to protect the firm's credit rating and its ability to borrow money.
- The funds required for paying the firm's taxes are available when needed to meet tax deadlines.
- Excess cash is invested in certificates of deposit (CDs), government securities, or conservative, marketable securities.

Figure 19.2 Business Bankruptcies in the United States

The number of businesses that filed for bankruptcy increased during the economic crisis. (*Note*: At the time of publication, 2009 was the most recent year for which complete statistics were available.)

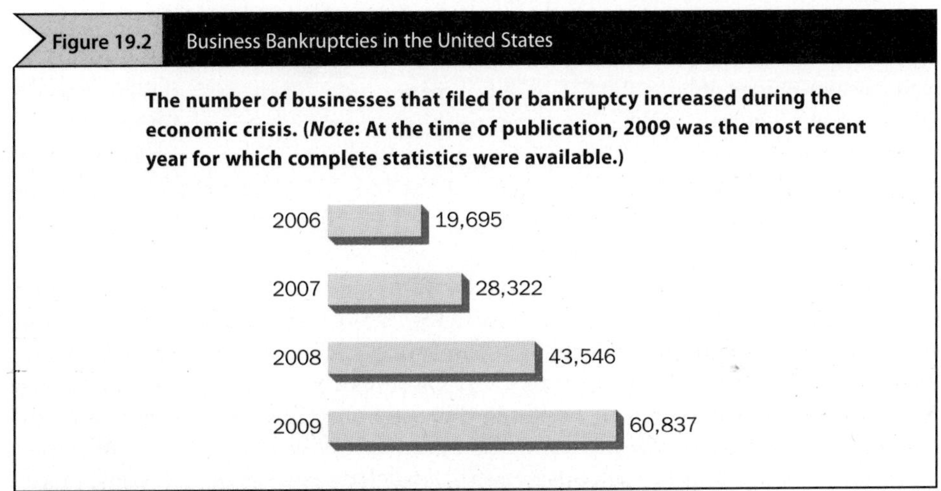

Source: The American Bankruptcy Institute Web site at http://www.abiworld.org (accessed June 24, 2010).

Entrepreneurial SUCCESS

Barter Gets a Boost

Barter—the exchange of goods or services—is becoming increasingly popular as small businesses look for creative ways to manage their money. Instead of spending cash or tapping credit, many are arranging informal barter deals with other companies or joining barter associations for access to a wider variety of possible trades. Field of Flowers, a florist in Florida, has traded flowers for public-relations services. Labongo Computer Systems, in Indianapolis, has bartered tech support for legal services.

As many as 175,000 small businesses belong to organized barter groups such as the International Reciprocal Trade Association and the Community Connect Trade Association. Members pay a monthly fee and a small commission on the value of each barter transaction. They list what they are willing to barter, including prices, and they can browse what other businesses are offering. Businesses earn barter credits when they provide goods or services to other members. In turn, they can "spend" these barter credits on anything listed by other members.

Because such deals do not put money in the bank, entrepreneurs should not go overboard with bartering. They should be sure that they can actually use what is being offered and consider the overall value before they strike a deal. Some businesses have found that barter stimulates cash sales as satisfied "customers" spread the word about goods and services they like.

Sources: Brian R. Hook, "Bartering 2.0: No Cash? No Problem," *E-Commerce Times*, April 23, 2010, http://www.ecommercetimes.com; Bridget Carey, "Bartering Helps Small Companies Survive When Cash Is Tight," *Miami Herald*, April 4, 2010, http://www.miamiherald.com/2010/04/04/v-fullstory/1562698/bartering-helps-small-companies.html#ixzz0kE3ljTSc; Minda Zetlin, "To Barter or Not to Barter? Some Swaps Can Be Deceptively Costly," *Inc.*, November 2009, 1021; Peter Schnitzler, "Bartering Booms: Trading of Goods and Services Spikes During Recession," *Indianapolis Business Journal*, September 28, 2009, 27A.

Financial Reform After the Economic Crisis At the time of publication of this text, it has been more than a year since the financial crisis peaked during 2009. As the economy began to improve, it became apparent that something needed to be done to stabilize the financial system and prevent future economic meltdowns. In the wake of the crisis that affected both business firms and individuals, a cry for more regulations and reforms became a high priority.

Although the U.S. House of Representatives and Senate debate proposed regulations, the goals are to hold Wall Street firms accountable for their actions, end taxpayer bailouts, tighten regulations for major financial firms, and increase government oversight. There has also been debate about limiting the amount of executive pay and bonuses, limiting the size of the largest financial firms, and curbing speculative investment techniques that were used by banks before the crisis. Because of the relationship between banking and finance, any new regulations will also provide more protection for consumers. As mentioned in Chapter 18, new regulations will protect American families from unfair, abusive financial and banking practices. For business firms, the impact of new regulations could increase the time and cost of obtaining both short- and long-term financing.

Although there are many critics of increased government regulation and the debate still continues, it is apparent that something needs to be done to prevent the type of economic problems the nation has experienced over the past three years. To date, no comprehensive bill has been sent to the president. For the latest information about financial reform, go to the Securities and Exchange Web site at http://www.sec.gov, the Federal Reserve Board Web site at http://www.federalreserve.gov, or use a search engine like Google or Yahoo! and enter "financial reform."

The Risk-Return Ratio According to financial experts, business firms will find it more difficult to raise capital in the future for two reasons. First, financial reform and increased regulations will lengthen the process required to obtain financing. Second, both lenders and investors are more cautious about who receives financing. As a result of these two factors, financial managers must develop a strong financial plan that describes how the money will be used and how it will be repaid. When developing a financial plan for a business, a financial manager must also consider the risk-return ratio when making decisions that affect the firm's finances.

The **risk-return ratio** is based on the principle that a high-risk decision should generate higher financial returns for a business. On the other hand, more conservative decisions (with less risk) often generate lesser returns. Although financial managers want higher returns, they often must strive for a balance between risk and return. For example, American Electric Power may consider investing millions of dollars to fund research into new solar technology that could enable the company to use the sun to generate electrical power. Yet, financial managers (along with other managers throughout the organization) must determine the potential return before committing to such a costly research project.

Executives in the hot seat! While everyone has an opinion about what caused the recent economic crisis, these protestors believe that Wall Street firms and their top executives should be held accountable for their actions. In reality, the protest would not have been necessary if some executives had remembered what it takes to be a successful financial manager.

Careers in Finance

When you hear the word *finance,* you may think of highly paid executives who determine what a corporation can afford to do and what it cannot. At the executive level, most large business firms have a **chief financial officer (CFO)** for financial management. A CFO is a high-level corporate executive who manages a firm's finances and reports directly to the company's chief executive officer or president. Some firms prefer to use the titles vice president of financial management, treasurer, or controller instead of the CFO title for executive-level positions in the finance area.

Although some executives in finance do make $300,000 a year or more, many entry-level and lower-level positions that pay quite a bit less are available. Banks, insurance companies, and investment firms obviously have a need for workers who can manage and analyze financial data. So do businesses involved in manufacturing, services, and marketing. Colleges and universities, not-for-profit organizations, and government entities at all levels also need finance workers.

People in finance must have certain traits and skills. One of the most important priorities for someone interested in a finance career is honesty. Be warned: Investors, lenders, and other corporate executives expect financial managers to be above reproach. Moreover, both federal and state government entities have enacted legislation to ensure that corporate financial statements reflect the "real" status of a firm's financial position. In addition to honesty, managers and employees in the finance area must:

1. Have a strong background in accounting or mathematics.
2. Know how to use a computer to analyze data.
3. Be an expert at both written and oral communication.

Typical job titles in finance include bank officer, consumer credit officer, financial analyst, financial planner, loan officer, insurance analyst, and investment account executive. Depending on qualifications, work experience, and education, starting salaries generally begin at $25,000 to $35,000 a year, but it is not uncommon for college graduates to earn higher salaries. In addition to salary, many employees have attractive benefits and other perks that make a career in financial management attractive.

risk-return ratio a ratio based on the principle that a high-risk decision should generate higher financial returns for a business and more conservative decisions often generate lower returns

chief financial officer (CFO) a high-level corporate executive who manages a firm's finances and reports directly to the company's chief executive officer or president

financial plan a plan for obtaining and using the money needed to implement an organization's goals

Planning—The Basis of Sound Financial Management

2 Summarize the process of planning for financial management.

In Chapter 6, we defined a *plan* as an outline of the actions by which an organization intends to accomplish its goals. A **financial plan**, then, is a plan for obtaining and using the money needed to implement an organization's goals.

Figure 19.3 The Three Steps of Financial Planning

After a financial plan has been developed, it must be monitored continually to ensure that it actually fulfills the firm's goals.

1. Establish organizational goals
2. Budget the money needed to accomplish the goals
3. Identify the sources of funds

Sales revenue	Equity capital	Debt capital	Sale of assets
• Revenue projections for this planning period	• Money from sole proprietor or partners • Common stock • Preferred stock	• Short-term borrowing • Long-term borrowing	• For profit • To raise cash

Monitor and evaluate

Developing the Financial Plan

Financial planning (like all planning) begins with establishing a set of valid goals. Financial managers must then determine how much money is needed to accomplish each goal. Finally, financial managers must identify available sources of financing and decide which to use. The three steps involved in financial planning are illustrated in Figure 19.3.

budget a financial statement that projects income, expenditures, or both over a specified future period

To be a successful retailer, it takes a financial plan. Many would-be business owners assume that if they have enough money, they will be successful. The truth is that effective financial planning involves more than just spending money. In fact, sound financial planning is built on the firm's goals and objectives, different types of budgets, and available sources of funds.

Establishing Organizational Goals As pointed out in Chapter 6, a *goal* is an end result that an organization expects to achieve over a one- to ten-year period. If goals are not specific and measurable, they cannot be translated into dollar costs, and financial planning cannot proceed. Goals also must be realistic. Otherwise, they may be impossible to finance or achieve. For large corporations, goals can be expensive. For example, ever wonder how much Geico's advertising program costs? Well, the clever advertisements featuring the green gecko are not cheap. In fact, Berkshire Hathaway, the parent company of Geico Insurance, spent over $600 million in 2009 to attract new customers and to increase Geico's market share in the very competitive insurance industry.[4]

Budgeting for Financial Needs Once planners know what the firm's goals are for a specific period—say, the next calendar year—they can budget the costs the firm will incur and the sales revenues it will receive. Specifically, a **budget** is a financial statement that projects income, expenditures, or both over a specified future period.

Usually, the budgeting process begins with the construction of budgets for sales and various types of expenses. (A typical sales budget—for Stars and Stripes Clothing, a California-based retailer—is shown in Figure 19.4.) Financial managers can easily combine each department's budget for sales and expenses into a company-wide cash budget. A **cash budget** estimates cash receipts and cash expenditures over a specified period. Notice in the cash budget for Stars and Stripes Clothing, shown in Figure 19.5, that cash sales and collections are listed at the top for each calendar quarter. Payments for purchases and routine expenses are listed in the middle section. Using this information, it is possible to calculate the anticipated cash gain or loss at the end of each quarter.

Why is Blockbuster closing this store? Closing a store is one of the hardest decisions that executives have to make. Recently, Blockbuster has closed a large number of stores because of lower sales revenue and increased competition from other movie rental firms, including Netflix and Redbox. While Blockbuster still has over 4,000 stores in the United States, it must control costs for each store in order to earn profits.

Most firms today use one of two approaches to budgeting. In the *traditional* approach, each new budget is based on the dollar amounts contained in the budget for the preceding year. These amounts are modified to reflect any revised goals, and managers are required to justify only new expenditures. The problem with this approach is that it leaves room for padding budget items to protect the (sometimes selfish) interests of the manager or his or her department. This problem is essentially eliminated through zero-base budgeting. **Zero-base budgeting** is a budgeting approach in which every expense in every budget must be justified.

To develop a plan for long-term financing needs, managers often construct a capital budget. A **capital budget** estimates a firm's expenditures for major assets, including new product development, expansion of facilities, replacement of obsolete equipment, and mergers and acquisitions. For example, Kraft Foods constructed a capital budget to determine the best way to finance the $19.5 billion acquisition of British candy maker Cadbury in 2010.[5]

cash budget a financial statement that estimates cash receipts and cash expenditures over a specified period

zero-base budgeting a budgeting approach in which every expense in every budget must be justified

capital budget a financial statement that estimates a firm's expenditures for major assets and its long-term financing needs

Identifying Sources of Funds The four primary sources of funds, listed in Figure 19.3, are sales revenue, equity capital, debt capital, and proceeds from the sale of assets. Future sales revenue generally provides the greatest part of a firm's financing. Figure 19.5 shows that for Stars and Stripes Clothing, sales for the year are expected to cover all expenses and to provide a cash gain of $106,000, or about 16 percent of sales. However, Stars and Stripes has a problem in the first quarter, when sales are expected to fall short of expenses by $7,000. In fact, one of the primary reasons for

Figure 19.4 Sales Budget for Stars and Stripes Clothing

Usually, the budgeting process begins with the construction of departmental budgets for sales.

STARS AND STRIPES CLOTHING
Sales Budget From January 1, 2010 to December 31, 2010

Department	First Quarter ($)	Second Quarter ($)	Third Quarter ($)	Fourth Quarter ($)	Total ($)
Infants'	50,000	55,000	60,000	70,000	235,000
Children's	45,000	45,000	40,000	40,000	170,000
Women's	35,000	40,000	35,000	50,000	160,000
Men's	20,000	20,000	15,000	25,000	80,000
Total	150,000	160,000	150,000	185,000	645,000

Figure 19.5 Cash Budget for Stars and Stripes Clothing

A company-wide cash budget projects sales, collections, purchases, and expenses over a specified period to anticipate cash surpluses and deficits.

STARS AND STRIPES CLOTHING
Cash Budget

From January 1, 2010 to December 31, 2010

	First Quarter ($)	Second Quarter ($)	Third Quarter ($)	Fourth Quarter ($)	Total ($)
Cash sales and collections	150,000	160,000	150,000	185,000	645,000
Less payments					
Purchases	110,000	80,000	90,000	60,000	340,000
Wages/salaries	25,000	20,000	25,000	30,000	100,000
Rent	10,000	10,000	12,000	12,000	44,000
Other expenses	4,000	4,000	5,000	6,000	19,000
Taxes	8,000	8,000	10,000	10,000	36,000
Total payments	157,000	122,000	142,000	118,000	539,000
Cash gain or (loss)	(7,000)	38,000	8,000	67,000	106,000

financial planning is to provide management with adequate lead time to solve this type of cash-flow problem.

A second type of funding is **equity capital**. For a sole proprietorship or partnership, equity capital is provided by the owner or owners of the business. For a corporation, equity capital is money obtained from the sale of shares of ownership in the business. Equity capital is used almost exclusively for long-term financing. Thus, it would not be considered for short-term financing needs, such as Stars and Stripes Clothing's first-quarter $7,000 shortfall.

A third type of funding is **debt capital**, which is borrowed money. Debt capital may be borrowed for either short- or long-term use—and a short-term loan seems made to order for Stars and Stripes Clothing's shortfall problem. The firm probably would borrow the needed $7,000 (or perhaps a bit more) at some point during the first quarter and repay it from second-quarter sales revenue.

Proceeds from the sale of assets are the fourth type of funding. Selling assets is a drastic step. However, it may be a reasonable last resort when sales revenues are declining and equity capital or debt capital cannot be found. Assets also may be sold when they are no longer needed or do not "fit" with the company's core business. In 2010, American International Group (AIG) sold its Alico life insurance unit to MetLife. The transaction generated more than $15.5 billion. Although companies often say they are selling assets to concentrate on their core business, to fund expansion, or to pay for new product development, these AIG assets were sold to raise money that could be used to repay government bailout funds it received during the economic crisis.[6]

Monitoring and Evaluating Financial Performance

It is important to ensure that financial plans are being implemented properly and to catch potential problems before they become major ones. Despite efforts to raise additional financing, reduce expenses, and increase sales to become profitable, both General Motors and Chrysler filed for bankruptcy protection in 2009. Eventually, both firms were reorganized and evolved as important U.S. automakers.

To prevent problems such as those just described, financial managers should establish a means of monitoring financial performance. Interim budgets (weekly, monthly, or quarterly) may be prepared for comparison purposes. These comparisons

equity capital money received from the owners or from the sale of shares of ownership in a business

debt capital borrowed money obtained through loans of various types

point up areas that require additional or revised planning—or at least areas calling for a more careful investigation. Budget comparisons can also be used to improve the firm's future budgets.

Sources of Short-Term Debt Financing

3

Describe the advantages and disadvantages of different methods of short-term debt financing.

Typically, short-term debt financing is money that will be repaid in one year or less. During the economic crisis, many business firms found that it was much more difficult to borrow money for short periods of time to purchase inventory, buy supplies, pay salaries, and meet everyday expenses. Today the amount of available short-term financing has increased. Nevertheless, a business must be able to repay borrowed funds before lenders and investors will provide this type of financing.

The decision to borrow money does not necessarily mean that a firm is in financial trouble. On the contrary, astute financial management often means regular, responsible borrowing of many different kinds to meet different needs. In this section, we examine the sources of *short-term debt financing* available to businesses. In the next two sections, we look at long-term financing options: equity capital and debt capital.

Sources of Unsecured Short-Term Financing

Short-term debt financing is usually easier to obtain than long-term debt financing for three reasons:

1. For the lender, the shorter repayment period means less risk of non-payment.
2. The dollar amounts of short-term loans are usually smaller than those of long-term loans.
3. A close working relationship normally exists between the short-term borrower and the lender.

Most lenders do not require collateral for short-term financing. If they do, it is usually because they are concerned about the size of a particular loan, the borrowing firm's poor credit rating, or the general prospects of repayment. Remember from Chapter 18 that *collateral* was defined as real estate or property pledged as security for a loan.

Unsecured financing is financing that is not backed by collateral. A company seeking unsecured short-term financing has several options.

unsecured financing financing that is not backed by collateral

trade credit a type of short-term financing extended by a seller who does not require immediate payment after delivery of merchandise

Trade Credit Manufacturers and wholesalers often provide financial aid to retailers by allowing them 30 to 60 days (or more) in which to pay for merchandise. This delayed payment, known as **trade credit**, is a type of short-term financing extended by a seller who does not require immediate payment after delivery of merchandise. It is the most popular form of short-term financing, because most manufacturers and wholesalers do not charge interest for trade credit. In fact, from 70 to 90 percent of all transactions between businesses involve some trade credit.

Let us assume that a Barnes & Noble bookstore receives a shipment of books from a publisher. Along with the merchandise, the publisher sends an invoice that states the terms of payment. Barnes & Noble now has two options for payment. First, the book retailer may pay the invoice promptly and take advantage of any cash discount the publisher offers. Cash-discount terms are specified on the invoice. For instance, "2/10, net 30" means that the customer—Barnes & Noble—may take a "2" percent discount if it pays the invoice within ten days

Short-term financing helped build these security cameras. Often firms like this Chinese manufacturer need trade credit and other types of short-term financing to pay employees and purchase the materials required to manufacture closed-circuit security cameras. When short-term financing is used, manufacturers don't have to pay suppliers and lenders for 30 to 60 days or more.

of the invoice date. Let us assume that the dollar amount of the invoice is $140,000. In this case, the cash discount is $2,800 ($140,000 × 0.02 = $2,800).

A second option is to wait until the end of the credit period before making payment. If payment is made between 11 and 30 days after the date of the invoice, the customer must pay the entire amount. As long as payment is made before the end of the credit period, the customer maintains the ability to purchase additional merchandise using the trade-credit arrangement.

Promissory Notes Issued to Suppliers A **promissory note** is a written pledge by a borrower to pay a certain sum of money to a creditor at a specified future date. Suppliers uneasy about extending trade credit may be less reluctant to offer credit to customers who sign promissory notes. Unlike trade credit, however, promissory notes usually require the borrower to pay interest. Although repayment periods may extend to one year, most short-term promissory notes are repaid in 60 to 180 days.

A promissory note offers two important advantages to the firm extending the credit.

1. A promissory note is legally binding and an enforceable contract.
2. A promissory note is a negotiable instrument.

Because a promissory note is negotiable, the supplier (or company extending credit) may be able to discount, or sell, the note to its own bank. If the note is discounted, the dollar amount the supplier receives is slightly less than the maturity value because the bank charges a fee for the service. The supplier recoups most of its money immediately, and the bank collects the maturity value when the note matures.

Unsecured Bank Loans Banks and other financial institutions offer unsecured short-term loans to businesses at interest rates that vary with each borrower's credit rating. The **prime interest rate**, sometimes called the *reference rate,* is the lowest rate charged by a bank for a short-term loan. Figure 19.6 traces the fluctuations in the average prime rate charged by U.S. banks from 1980 to May 2010. This lowest rate generally is reserved for large corporations with excellent credit ratings. Organizations with good to high credit ratings may pay the prime rate plus "2" percent. Firms with questionable credit ratings may have to pay the prime rate plus "4" percent. (The fact that a banker charges a higher interest rate for a higher-risk loan is a

Figure 19.6 Average Prime Interest Rate Paid by U.S. Businesses, 1980-May 2010

The prime rate is the interest rate charged by U.S. banks when businesses with the "best" credit ratings borrow money. All other businesses pay higher interest rates than the prime rate.

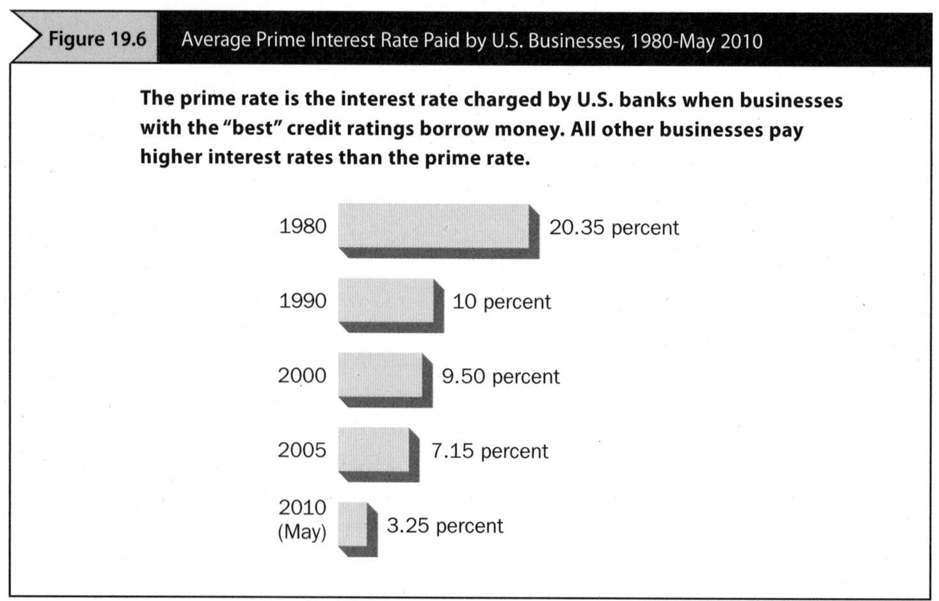

Source: Federal Reserve Bank Web site, http://www.federalreserve.gov (accessed June 23, 2010).

promissory note a written pledge by a borrower to pay a certain sum of money to a creditor at a specified future date

prime interest rate the lowest rate charged by a bank for a short-term loan

practical application of the risk-return ratio discussed earlier in this chapter.) Of course, if the banker believes that loan repayment may be a problem, the borrower's loan application may well be rejected.

Banks generally offer unsecured short-term loans through promissory notes, a line of credit, or a revolving credit agreement. A bank promissory note is similar to the promissory note issued to suppliers described in the preceding section. For both types of promissory notes, interest rates and repayment terms may be negotiated between the borrower and a bank or supplier. A bank that offers a promissory note or line of credit may require that a *compensating balance* be kept on deposit at the bank. Compensating balances, if required, are typically 10 to 20 percent of the borrowed funds. The bank may also require that every commercial borrower *clean up* (pay off completely) its short-term promissory note or line of credit at least once each year and not use it again for a period of 30 to 60 days.

Even with a line of credit, a firm may not be able to borrow on short notice if the bank does not have sufficient funds available. For this reason, some firms prefer a *revolving credit agreement,* which is a *guaranteed* line of credit. Under this type of agreement, the bank guarantees that the money will be available when the borrower needs it. In return for the guarantee, the bank charges a commitment fee ranging from 0.25 to 1.0 percent of the *unused* portion of the revolving credit agreement. The usual interest is charged for the portion that *is* borrowed.

Commercial Paper As defined in Chapter 18, commercial paper is a short-term promissory note issued by a large corporation. Commercial paper is secured only by the reputation of the issuing firm; no collateral is involved. It is usually issued in large denominations, ranging from $5,000 to $100,000. Corporations issuing commercial paper pay interest rates slightly below the interest rates charged by banks for short-term loans. Thus, issuing commercial paper is cheaper than getting short-term financing from a bank. The interest rate a corporation pays when it issues commercial paper is tied to its credit rating and its ability to repay the commercial paper. It is most often used to purchase inventory, pay salaries and other necessary expenses, and solve cash-flow problems.

Large firms with excellent credit reputations like Microsoft, Procter & Gamble, and Caterpillar can raise large sums of money quickly by issuing commercial paper. However, during the recent financial crisis, even companies that had always been able to sell commercial paper had difficulty finding buyers. To help provide additional short-term financing, the Federal Reserve Bank stepped in and began to purchase the commercial paper from firms in need of financing to pay for day-to-day business operations.[7]

Sources of Secured Short-Term Financing

If a business cannot obtain enough capital through unsecured financing, it must put up collateral to obtain additional short-term financing. Almost any asset can serve as collateral. However, *inventories* and *accounts receivable* are the assets most commonly pledged for short-term financing. Even when it is willing to pledge collateral to back up a loan, a firm that is financially weak may have difficulty obtaining short-term financing.

Loans Secured by Inventory Normally, manufacturers, wholesalers, and retailers have large amounts of money invested in finished goods. In addition, manufacturers carry raw materials and work-in-process inventories. All three types of inventory may be pledged as collateral for short-term loans. However, lenders prefer the much more salable finished merchandise to raw materials or work-in-process inventories.

A lender may insist that inventory used as collateral be stored in a public warehouse. In such a case, the receipt issued by the warehouse is retained by the lender. Without this receipt, the public warehouse will not release the merchandise. The lender releases the warehouse receipt—and the merchandise—to the borrower when the borrowed money is repaid. In addition to paying the interest on the loan, the borrower must pay for storage in the public warehouse. As a result, this type of loan is more expensive than an unsecured short-term loan.

Loans Secured by Receivables As defined in Chapter 17, *accounts receivable* are amounts owed to a firm by its customers. A firm can pledge its accounts receivable as collateral to obtain short-term financing. A lender may advance 70 to 80 percent of the dollar amount of the receivables. First, however, it conducts a thorough investigation to determine the *quality* of the receivables. (The quality of the receivables is the credit standing of the firm's customers, coupled with the customers' ability to repay their credit obligations when they are due.) If a favorable determination is made, the loan is approved. When the borrowing firm collects from a customer whose account has been pledged as collateral, generally it must turn the money over to the lender as partial repayment of the loan. An alternative approach is to notify the borrower's credit customers to make their payments directly to the lender.

Factoring Accounts Receivable

Accounts receivable may be used in one other way to help raise short-term financing: They can be sold to a factoring company (or factor). A **factor** is a firm that specializes in buying other firms' accounts receivable. The factor buys the accounts receivable for less than their face value; however, it collects the full dollar amount when each account is due. The factor's profit thus is the difference between the face value of the accounts receivable and the amount the factor has paid for them. Generally, the amount of profit the factor receives is based on the risk the factor assumes. Risk, in this case, is the probability that the accounts receivable will not be repaid when they mature.

Even though the firm selling its accounts receivable gets less than face value, it does receive needed cash immediately. Moreover, it has shifted both the task of collecting and the risk of non-payment to the factor, which now owns the accounts receivable. In many cases, the factor may purchase only selected accounts receivable—usually those with the highest potential of repayment. In other cases, the firm selling its accounts receivable must obtain approval from the factor *before* selling merchandise to a credit customer. Generally, customers whose accounts receivable have been factored are given instructions to make their payments directly to the factor.

Cost Comparisons

factor a firm that specializes in buying other firms' accounts receivable

Table 19.2 compares the various types of short-term financing. As you can see, trade credit is the least expensive. Factoring of accounts receivable is typically the highest-cost method shown.

Table 19.2 Comparison of Short-Term Financing Methods

Type of Financing	Cost	Repayment Period	Businesses that May Use It	Comments
Trade credit	Low, if any	30–60 days	All businesses with good credit	Usually no finance charge
Promissory note issued to suppliers	Moderate	One year or less	All businesses	Usually unsecured but requires legal document
Unsecured bank loan	Moderate	One year or less	All businesses	Promissory note, a line of credit, or revolving credit agreement generally required
Commercial paper	Moderate	One year or less	Large corporations with high credit ratings	Available only to large firms
Secured loan	High	One year or less	Firms with questionable credit ratings	Inventory or accounts receivable often used as collateral
Factoring	High	None	Firms that have large numbers of credit customers	Accounts receivable sold to a factor

For many purposes, short-term financing suits a firm's needs perfectly. At other times, however, long-term financing may be more appropriate. In this case, a business may try to raise equity capital or long-term debt capital.

Sources of Equity Financing

4

Evaluate the advantages and disadvantages of equity financing.

Sources of long-term financing vary with the size and type of business. As mentioned earlier, a sole proprietorship or partnership acquires equity capital (sometimes referred to as *owners' equity*) when the owner or owners invest money in the business. For corporations, equity-financing options include the sale of stock and the use of profits not distributed to owners. All three types of businesses can also obtain venture capital and use long-term debt capital (borrowed money) to meet their financial needs. Different types of debt capital are discussed in the next section. Regardless of the type of long-term financing chosen, most financial managers have found that financing is more expensive and harder to obtain since the recent financial crisis. Both investors and lenders are more cautious than they were before the crisis.

Selling Stock

Some equity capital is used to start every business—sole proprietorship, partnership, or corporation. In the case of corporations, stockholders who buy shares in the company provide equity capital.

Initial Public Offering and the Primary Market An **initial public offering (IPO)** occurs when a corporation sells common stock to the general public for the first time. To raise money, Financial Engines—an independent investment advisory firm that uses software and computer technology to help millions of Americans plan for retirement—used a 2010 IPO to raise $125 million that it could use to fund expansion and other business activities.[8] Established companies that plan to raise capital by selling subsidiaries to the public can also use IPOs. In 2010, Citigroup sold shares in its Primerica financial services and life insurance unit to raise more than $320 million.[9] The money that Citigroup received from the IPO was used to increase the amount of cash available to pay current expenses, solve cash-flow problems, and pay for other business activities. In addition to using an IPO to increase the cash balance for the parent company, corporations often sell shares in a subsidiary when shares can be sold at a profit or when the subsidiary no longer fits with its current business plan. Finally, some corporations will sell a subsidiary that is growing more slowly than the rest of the company's operating divisions.

initial public offering (IPO) occurs when a corporation sells common stock to the general public for the first time

primary market a market in which an investor purchases financial securities (via an investment bank) directly from the issuer of those securities

investment banking firm an organization that assists corporations in raising funds, usually by helping to sell new issues of stocks, bonds, or other financial securities

When a corporation uses an IPO to raise capital, the stock is sold in the primary market. The **primary market** is a market in which an investor purchases financial securities (via an investment bank) directly from the issuer of the securities. An **investment banking firm** is an organization that assists corporations in raising funds, usually by helping to sell new issues of stocks, bonds, or other financial securities. The investment banking firm generally charges a fee of 2 to 20 percent of the proceeds received by the corporation issuing the securities. The size of the commission depends on the financial health of the corporation issuing the new securities and the size of the new security issue.

Although a corporation can have only one IPO, it can sell additional stock after the IPO, assuming that there is a market for the company's stock. Even though the cost of selling stock (often referred to as *flotation costs*) is high, the *ongoing* costs associated with this

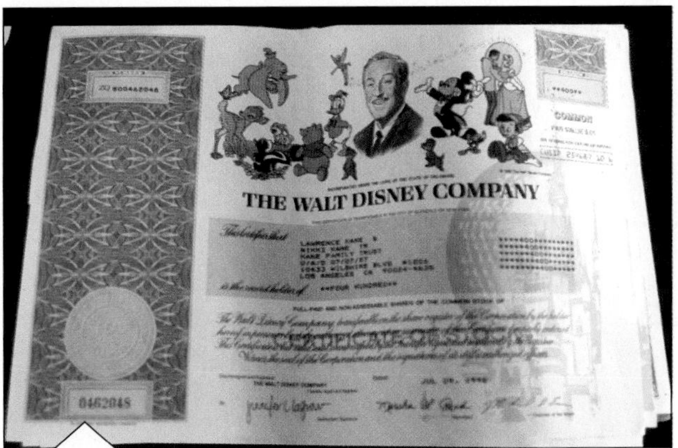

One way to raise capital. The Walt Disney Company, like many corporations, chose to sell stock to raise the money it needed to expand and become one of the largest entertainment companies in the world. On the other hand, investors purchase stock because they can profit from their investment if the price for a share of the corporation's stock increases and a corporation pays dividends.

Going for SUCCESS

What Makes a Good IPO?

What makes a good IPO? Dozens of U.S. corporations go public every year. Some, like MasterCard, go public after decades in business. Others, like Google, are ambitious young firms aiming for big things.

With so many stocks vying for investor attention, corporate decision-makers know they need more than an innovative product, a trendy brand name, or a short-term record of growth. To attract savvy investors who will stick with a new stock through Wall Street's ups and downs, a company must demonstrate long-term profit potential and sustainable competitive strength.

Google's IPO is a good example. The company went public in August 2004, with shares of stock priced at $85 each. At the end of the first trading day, the price had soared above $108. Although some investors thought the price was too high, others bought the stock because they saw Google's dominance of the online search industry as the path to solid future profits. Since its IPO, Google's revenue has grown, on average, more than 25 percent each year, and its stock price has been known to trade above $600. Google has made good use of its high share price: When it acquired YouTube, it paid in stock. Of course, not every IPO will be successful, but smart investors are always in the market for an investment with a promising future.

Sources: Scott S. Smith, "Robert Selander, Master of Credit Card Growth," *Investor's Business Daily*, March 19, 2010, A3; Peter Edmonston, "Google's I.P.O., Five Years Later," *New York Times*, August 19, 2009, http://dealbook.blogs.nytimes.com; Jim Goldman, "Google at Five: Happy IPO Birthday," *CNBC*, August 19, 2009, http://www.cnbc.com/id/32475159/Google_at_Five_Happy_IPO_Birthday; http://www.google.com.

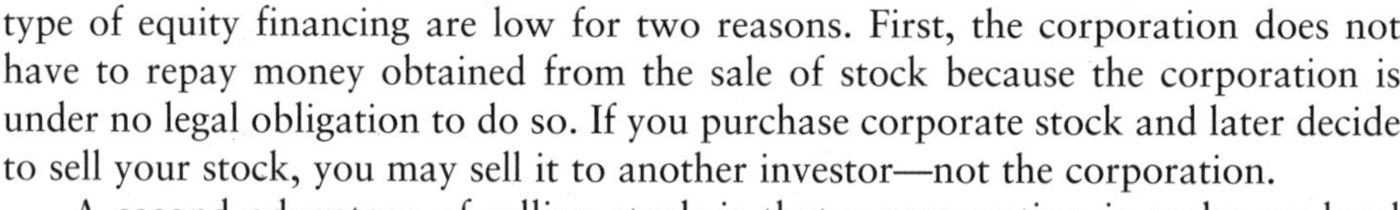

type of equity financing are low for two reasons. First, the corporation does not have to repay money obtained from the sale of stock because the corporation is under no legal obligation to do so. If you purchase corporate stock and later decide to sell your stock, you may sell it to another investor—not the corporation.

A second advantage of selling stock is that a corporation is under no legal obligation to pay dividends to stockholders. As noted in Chapter 4, a *dividend* is a distribution of earnings to the stockholders of a corporation. For any reason (e.g., if a company has a bad year), the board of directors can vote to omit dividend payments. Earnings then are retained for use in funding business operations. Of course, corporate management may hear from unhappy stockholders if expected dividends are omitted too frequently.

secondary market a market for existing financial securities that are traded between investors

A big thrill! For most corporate executives, ringing the bell on the New York Stock Exchange is one of the highlights of their career. In this photo, executives from Express, Inc. are celebrating "taking their company public" and raising over $165 million by selling stock for the first time—often referred to as an initial public offering.

The Secondary Market Although a share of corporate stock is only sold one time in the primary market, the stock can be sold again and again in the secondary market. The **secondary market** is a market for existing financial securities that are traded between investors. Although a corporation does not receive money each time its stock is bought or sold in the secondary market, the ability to obtain cash by selling stock investments is one reason why investors purchase corporate stock. Without the secondary market, investors would not purchase stock in the primary market because there would be no way to sell shares to other investors. Thus, both the primary and secondary markets are needed for a corporation to raise capital by selling stock. Usually, secondary-market transactions are completed through a securities exchange or the over-the-counter (OTC) market.

A **securities exchange** is a marketplace where member brokers meet to buy and sell securities. Generally, securities issued by larger corporations are traded at the New York Stock Exchange (NYSE) (now owned by the NYSE Euronext holding company), or at regional exchanges located in different parts of the country. The securities of very large corporations may be traded at more than one of these exchanges. Securities of firms also may be listed on foreign securities exchanges—in Tokyo or London, for example.

One of the largest and best-known securities exchanges in the world is the NYSE. This exchange, located in New York, along with other NYSE Euronext exchanges located in six different countries, lists more than 8,500 different issues.[10] Before a corporation's stock is approved for listing on the NYSE, the firm usually must meet specific criteria. The various regional exchanges also have listing requirements, but typically these are less stringent than the NYSE requirements. The stock of corporations that cannot meet the NYSE requirements, find it too expensive to be listed on the NYSE exchange, or choose not to be listed on the NYSE is often traded on one of the regional exchanges, or through the OTC market.

Stocks issued by several thousand companies are traded in the OTC market. The **over-the-counter (OTC) market** is a network of dealers who buy and sell the stocks of corporations that are not listed on a securities exchange. The term *over-the-counter* was coined more than 100 years ago when securities actually were sold "over the counter" in stores and banks. Most OTC securities today are traded through an *electronic* exchange called the NASDAQ (pronounced "nazzdack"). The NASDAQ quotation system provides price information on more than 3,600 different stocks.[11] Begun in 1971, the NASDAQ is now one of the largest securities markets in the world. Today, the NASDAQ is known for its forward-looking, innovative, growth companies. Although most companies are small, the stock of some large firms, including Intel, Microsoft, Cisco Systems, and Dell Computer, is traded through the NASDAQ.

There are two types of stock: common and preferred. Each type has advantages and drawbacks as a means of long-term financing.

Common Stock A share of **common stock** represents the most basic form of corporate ownership. In return for the financing provided by selling common stock, management must make certain concessions to stockholders that may restrict or change corporate policies. Every corporation must hold an annual meeting, at which the holders of common stock may vote for the board of directors and approve or disapprove major corporate actions. Among such actions are:

1. Amendments to the corporate charter or corporate by-laws
2. Sale of certain assets
3. Mergers and acquisitions
4. New issues of preferred stock or bonds
5. Changes in the amount of common stock issued

Few investors will buy common stock unless they believe that their investment will increase in value. Information on the reasons why investors purchase stocks and how to evaluate stock investments is provided in Chapter 20.

Preferred Stock As noted in Chapter 4, the owners of **preferred stock** must receive their dividends before holders of common stock receive theirs. When compared to common stockholders, preferred stockholders also have first claim (after creditors) on assets if the corporation is dissolved or declares bankruptcy. Even so, as with common stock, the board of directors must approve dividends on preferred stock, and this type of financing does not represent a debt that must be legally repaid. In return for preferential treatment, preferred stockholders generally give up the right to vote at a corporation's annual meeting.

The dividend on a share of preferred stock is stated on the stock certificate either as a percent of the par value of the stock or as a specified dollar amount.

securities exchange a marketplace where member brokers meet to buy and sell securities

over-the-counter (OTC) market a network of dealers who buy and sell the stocks of corporations that are not listed on a securities exchange

common stock stock whose owners may vote on corporate matters but whose claims on profits and assets are subordinate to the claims of others

preferred stock stock whose owners usually do not have voting rights but whose claims on dividends and assets are paid before those of common-stock owners

The **par value** of a stock is an assigned (and often arbitrary) dollar value printed on the stock certificate. For example, Pitney Bowes—a U.S. manufacturer of office and business equipment—issued 4 percent preferred stock with a par value of $50. The annual dividend amount is $2 per share ($50 par value × 0.04 = $2 annual dividend).

Although a corporation usually issues only one type of common stock, it may issue many types of preferred stock with varying dividends or dividend rates. For example, New York–based Consolidated Edison has one common-stock issue but three preferred-stock issues.

When a corporation believes that it can issue new preferred stock at a lower dividend rate (or common stock with no specified dividend), it may decide to "call in," or buy back, an earlier preferred stock issue. In this case, management has two options. First, it can buy shares in the market—just like any other investor. Second, it can exercise a call provision because practically all preferred stock is *callable*. When considering the two options, management will naturally purchase the preferred stock in the less costly way.

par value an assigned (and often arbitrary) dollar value printed on a stock certificate

retained earnings the portion of a corporation's profits not distributed to stockholders

Retained Earnings

Most large corporations distribute only a portion of their after-tax earnings to stockholders. The portion of a corporation's profits *not* distributed to stockholders is called **retained earnings**. Because they are undistributed profits, retained earnings are considered a form of equity financing.

The amount of retained earnings in any year is determined by corporate management and approved by the board of directors. Most small and growing corporations pay no cash dividend—or a very small dividend—to their stockholders. All or most earnings are reinvested in the business for research and development, expansion, or the funding of major projects. Reinvestment tends to increase the value of the firm's stock while it provides essentially cost-free financing for the business. More mature corporations may distribute 40 to 60 percent of their after-tax profits as dividends. Utility companies and other corporations with very stable earnings often pay out as much as 80 to 90 percent of what they earn. For a large corporation, retained earnings can amount to a hefty bit of financing. For example, in 2009, the total amount of retained earnings for General Electric was over $126 billion.[12]

Venture capitalists extraordinaire. No discussion about venture capital would be complete without mentioning Tom Perkins—a legend in the field. His experience as head of research at Hewlett Packard gave him the needed skills to identify companies that have the potential to be very successful. Over the years, he has had a hand in the success of numerous marketplace heavyweights, including Applied Materials, Compaq, Corning Glass, and Genentech.

Venture Capital and Private Placements

To establish a new business or expand an existing one, an entrepreneur may try to obtain venture capital. In Chapter 5, we defined *venture capital* as money invested in small (and sometimes struggling) firms that have the potential to become very successful. Most venture capital firms do not invest in the typical small business—a neighborhood convenience store or a local dry cleaner—but in firms that have the potential to become extremely profitable. Although venture capital firms are willing to take chances, they have also been more selective about where they invest their money after the recent economic crisis.

Generally, a venture capital firm consists of a pool of investors, a partnership established by a wealthy family, or a joint venture formed by corporations with money to invest. In return for financing, these investors generally receive an equity or ownership position in the business and share in its profits. Venture capital firms vary in size and scope of interest. Some offer financing for start-up businesses, whereas others finance only established businesses.

Another method of raising capital is through a private placement. A **private placement** occurs when stock and other corporate securities are sold directly to insurance companies, pension funds, or large institutional investors. When compared with selling stocks and other corporate securities to the public, there are often fewer government regulations and the cost is generally less when the securities are sold through a private placement. Typically, terms between the buyer and seller are negotiated when a private placement is used to raise capital.

5

Evaluate the advantages and disadvantages of long-term debt financing.

Sources of Long-Term Debt Financing

As pointed out earlier in this chapter, businesses borrow money on a short-term basis for many valid reasons other than desperation. There are equally valid reasons for long-term borrowing. In addition to using borrowed money to meet the long-term needs listed in Table 19.1, successful businesses often use the financial leverage it creates to improve their financial performance. **Financial leverage** is the use of borrowed funds to increase the return on owners' equity. The principle of financial leverage works as long as a firm's earnings are larger than the interest charged for the borrowed money.

To understand how financial leverage can increase a firm's return on owners' equity, study the information for Texas-based Cypress Springs Plastics presented in Table 19.3. Pete Johnston, the owner of the firm, is trying to decide how best to finance a $100,000 purchase of new high-tech manufacturing equipment. He could borrow the money and pay 7 percent annual interest. As a second option, Johnston could invest an additional $100,000 in the firm. Assuming that the firm earns $95,000 a year and that annual interest for this loan totals $7,000 ($100,000 × 0.07 = $7,000), the return on owners' equity for Cypress Springs Plastics would be higher if the firm borrowed the additional financing. Return on owners' equity—a topic covered in Chapter 17—is determined by dividing a firm's net income by the dollar amount of

The future of power. Often long-term loans are used to finance alternative energy development—even when nations are involved. In this photo, visitors look at a model of a solar power farm in Beijing, China. Preliminary estimates are that this project, along with other Chinese alternative energy projects, could require investments and loans totaling more than $3 trillion yuan—that's $440 billion in U.S. currency.

Table 19.3 Analysis of the Effect of Additional Capital from Debt or Equity for Cypress Springs Plastics, Inc.

Additional Debt		**Additional Equity**	
Owners' equity	$ 500,000	Owners' equity	$ 500,000
Additional equity	+ 0	Additional equity	+100,000
Total equity	$ 500,000	Total equity	$ 600,000
Loan (@ 9%)	+100,000	No loan	+ 0
Total capital	$ 600,000	Total capital	$ 600,000
Year-End Earnings			
Gross profit	$ 95,000	Gross profit	$ 95,000
Less loan interest	− 7,000	No interest	− 0
Operating profit	$ 88,000	Operating profit	$ 95,000
Return on owners' equity	17.6%	Return on owners' equity	15.8%
($88,000 ÷ $500,000 = 17.6%)		($95,000 ÷ $600,000 = 15.8%)	

private placement occurs when stock and other corporate securities are sold directly to insurance companies, pension funds, or large institutional investors

financial leverage the use of borrowed funds to increase the return on owners' equity

Green Energy Loans

Did you know that the U.S. Department of Energy offers loan guarantees to companies that further sustainability through high-potential alternative energy projects and innovative clean-power technologies? Take a look: http://www.lgprogram.energy.gov/.

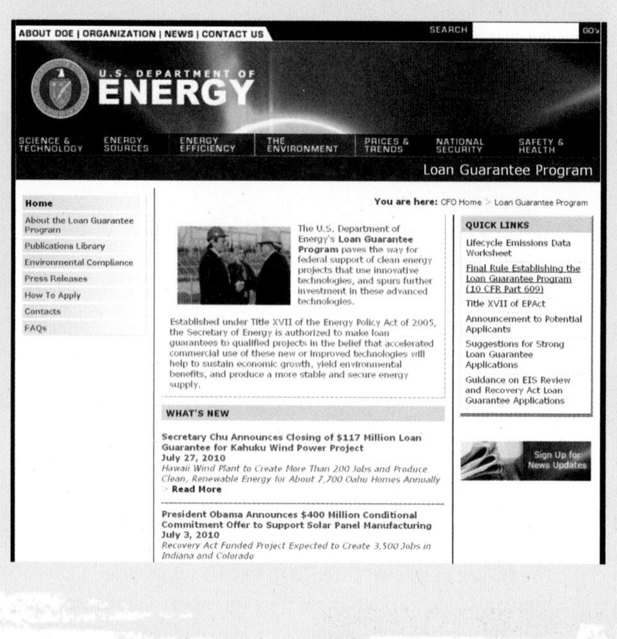

owners' equity. Based on the calculations illustrated in Table 19.3, Cypress Springs Plastics' return on owners' equity equals 17.6 percent if Johnston borrows the additional $100,000. The firm's return on owners' equity would decrease to 15.8 percent if Johnston invests an additional $100,000 in the business.

The most obvious danger when using financial leverage is that the firm's earnings may be less than expected. If this situation occurs, the fixed interest charge actually works to reduce or eliminate the return on owners' equity. Of course, borrowed money eventually must be repaid. Because lenders always have the option to turn down a loan request, many managers are reluctant to rely on borrowed money.

For a small business, long-term debt financing is generally limited to loans. Large corporations have the additional option of issuing corporate bonds.

Long-Term Loans

Many businesses satisfy their long-term financing needs, such as those listed in Table 19.1, with loans from commercial banks, insurance companies, pension funds, and other financial institutions. Manufacturers and suppliers of heavy machinery may also provide long-term debt financing by granting credit to their customers.

Term-Loan Agreements When the loan repayment period is longer than one year, the borrower must sign a term-loan agreement. A **term-loan agreement** is a promissory note that requires a borrower to repay a loan in monthly, quarterly, semiannual, or annual installments. Although repayment may be as long as 15 to 20 years, long-term business loans normally are repaid in 3 to 7 years.

Assume that Pete Johnston, the owner of Cypress Springs Plastics, decides to borrow $100,000 and take advantage of the principle of financial leverage illustrated in Table 19.3. Although the firm's return on owners' equity does increase, interest must be paid each year and, eventually, the loan must be repaid. To pay off a $100,000 loan over a three-year period with annual payments, Cypress Springs Plastics must pay $33,333 on the loan balance plus $7,000 annual interest, or a total of $40,333 the first year. Although the amount of interest decreases each year because of the previous year's payment on the loan balance, annual payments of this amount are still a large commitment for a small firm such as Cypress Springs Plastics.

The interest rate and repayment terms for term loans often are based on factors such as the reasons for borrowing, the borrowing firm's credit rating, and the value of collateral. Although long-term loans occasionally may be unsecured, the lender usually requires some type of collateral. Acceptable collateral includes real estate, machinery, and equipment. Lenders may also require that borrowers maintain a minimum amount of working capital. Finally, lenders may consider the environmental and social impact of the projects they are asked to finance before funding a loan request.

term-loan agreement a promissory note that requires a borrower to repay a loan in monthly, quarterly, semiannual, or annual installments

The Basics of Getting a Loan According to many financial experts, preparation is the key when applying for a long-term business loan. In reality, preparation begins before you ever apply for the loan. To begin the process, you should get to know potential lenders before requesting debt financing. Although there may be many potential lenders that can provide the money you need, the logical place to borrow money is where your business does its banking. This fact underscores the importance of maintaining adequate balances in the firm's bank accounts. Before applying for a loan, you may also want to check your firm's credit rating with a national credit bureau such as D&B (formerly known as Dun & Bradstreet).

Typically, business owners will be asked to fill out a loan application. In addition to the loan application, the lender will also want to see your current business plan. Be sure to explain what your business is, how much funding you require to accomplish your goals, and how the loan will be repaid. Next, have your certified public accountant (CPA) prepare financial statements. Most lenders insist that you submit current financial statements that have been prepared by an independent CPA. Then compile a list of references that includes your suppliers, other lenders, or the professionals with whom you are associated. You may also be asked to discuss the loan request with a loan officer. Hopefully, your loan request will be approved. If not, try to determine why your loan request was rejected. Think back over the loan process and determine what you could do to improve your chances of getting a loan the next time you apply.

Corporate Bonds

In addition to loans, large corporations may choose to issue bonds in denominations of $1,000 to $50,000. Although the usual face value for corporate bonds is $1,000, the total face value of all the bonds in an issue usually amounts to millions of dollars. In fact, one of the reasons why corporations sell bonds is that they can borrow a lot of money from a lot of different bondholders and raise larger amounts of money than could be borrowed from one lender. A **corporate bond** is a corporation's written pledge that it will repay a specified amount of money with interest. Figure 19.7 shows a corporate bond for PepsiCo, Inc.

Figure 19.7 A Corporate Bond

A corporate bond is a corporation's written pledge that it will repay on the date of maturity a specified amount of money with interest.

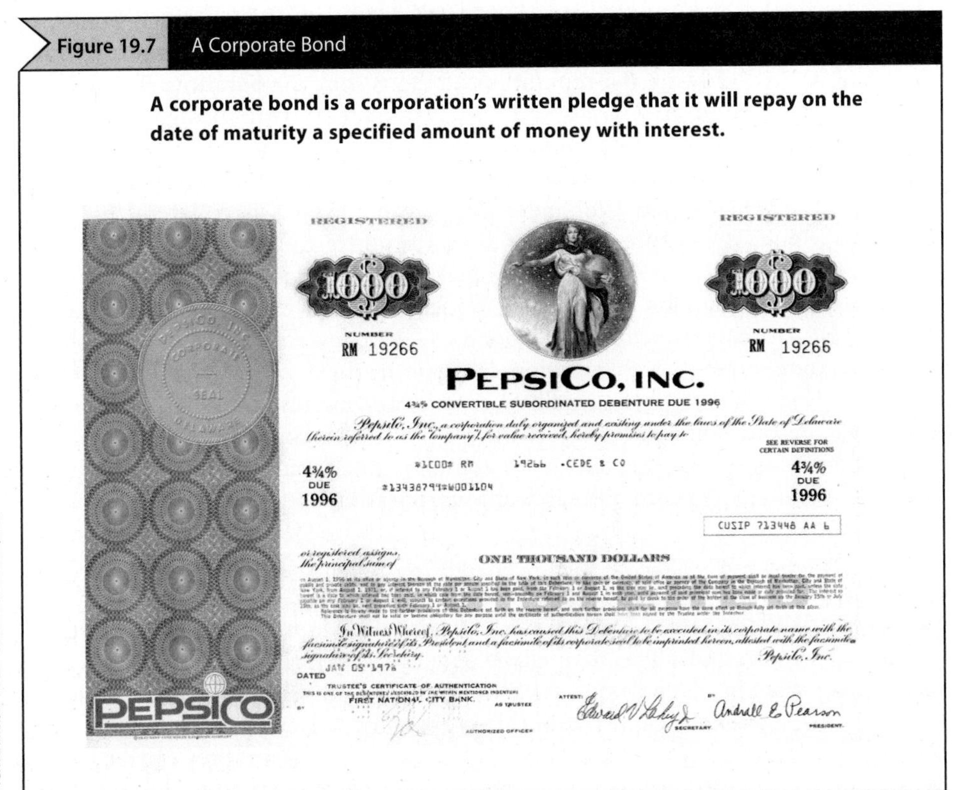

corporate bond a corporation's written pledge that it will repay a specified amount of money with interest

SPOTLIGHT

When financial managers sell new bond issues to raise capital, they are very aware of average yields on comparable bonds. Below are average bond yields for corporate bonds.

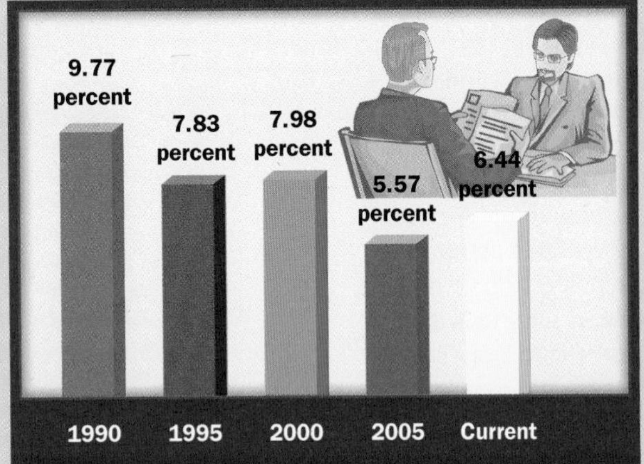

Source: Statistical Abstract of the United States 2010, U.S. Bureau of the Census Web site http:// www.census.gov (accessed June 30, 2010), Washington, DC: U.S. Government Printing Office, Table 1161.

The **maturity date** is the date on which the corporation is to repay the borrowed money. Today, many corporations do not issue actual bonds like the one illustrated in Figure 19.7. Instead, the bonds are recorded electronically, and the specific details regarding the bond issue, along with the current owner's name and address, are maintained by computer. Although some people like to have physical possession of their corporate bonds, computer entries are easier to transfer when a bond is sold. Computer entries are also safer because they cannot be stolen, misplaced, or destroyed—all concerns that you must worry about if you take physical possession of a corporate bond.

Until a bond's maturity, a corporation pays interest to the bond owner at the stated rate. For example, owners of the American & Foreign Power Company bonds that mature in 2030 receive 5 percent per year for each bond. Because interest for corporate bonds is usually paid semiannually, bond owners receive a payment every six months for each bond they own.

Types of Bonds Today, most corporate bonds are registered bonds. A **registered bond**—like the PepsiCo bond—is a bond registered in the owner's name by the issuing company. Until the maturity date, the registered owner receives periodic interest payments. On the maturity date, the registered owner receives cash equaling the face value.

Corporate bonds are generally classified as debentures, mortgage bonds, or convertible bonds. Most corporate bonds are debenture bonds. A **debenture bond** is a bond backed only by the reputation of the issuing corporation. To make its bonds more appealing to investors, a corporation may issue mortgage bonds. A **mortgage bond** is a corporate bond secured by various assets of the issuing firm. Typical corporate assets that are used as collateral for a mortgage bond include real estate, machinery, and equipment that is not pledged as collateral for other debt obligations. The corporation can also issue convertible bonds. A **convertible bond** can be exchanged, at the owner's option, for a specified number of shares of the corporation's common stock. An Advanced Micro Devices (AMD) bond that matures in 2015 is convertible: Each bond can be converted to 35.6125 shares of AMD common stock.[13] A corporation can gain in three ways by issuing convertible bonds. First, convertibles usually carry a lower interest rate than nonconvertible bonds. Second, the conversion feature attracts investors who are interested in the speculative gain that conversion to common stock may provide. Third, if the bondholder converts to common stock, the corporation no longer has to redeem the bond at maturity.

maturity date the date on which a corporation is to repay borrowed money

registered bond a bond registered in the owner's name by the issuing company

debenture bond a bond backed only by the reputation of the issuing corporation

mortgage bond a corporate bond secured by various assets of the issuing firm

convertible bond a bond that can be exchanged, at the owner's option, for a specified number of shares of the corporation's common stock

Repayment Provisions for Corporate Bonds Maturity dates for bonds generally range from 10 to 30 years after the date of issue. If the interest is not paid or the firm becomes insolvent, bond owners' claims on the assets of the corporation take precedence over the claims of both common and preferred stockholders. Some bonds are callable before the maturity date; that is, a corporation can buy back, or redeem, them. For these bonds, the corporation may pay the bond owner a call premium. The amount of the call premium is specified, along with other provisions, in the bond indenture. The **bond indenture** is a legal document that details all the conditions relating to a bond issue.

Before deciding if bonds are the best way to obtain corporate financing, managers must determine if the company can afford to pay the interest on the corporate bonds. It should be obvious that the larger the bond issue, the higher the dollar amount of interest. For example, assume that American Express issues bonds with a face value of $100 million. If the interest rate is 4.875 percent, the interest on this bond issue is $4,875,000 ($100 million × 0.04875 = $4,875,000) each year until the bonds are repaid. In addition, the American Express corporate bonds must all be redeemed for their face value ($100 million) at maturity. If the corporation defaults on (does not pay) either interest payments or repayment of the bond at maturity, owners of bonds can force the firm into bankruptcy.

A corporation may use one of three methods to ensure that it has sufficient funds available to redeem a bond issue. First, it can issue the bonds as **serial bonds**, which are bonds of a single issue that mature on different dates. For example, a company may use a 25-year $50 million bond issue to finance its expansion. None of the bonds mature during the first 15 years. Thereafter, 10 percent of the bonds mature each year until all the bonds are retired at the end of the 25th year. Second, the corporation can establish a sinking fund. A **sinking fund** is a sum of money to which deposits are made each year for the purpose of redeeming a bond issue. When Union Pacific Corporation sold a $275 million bond issue, the company agreed to contribute to a sinking fund until the bond's maturity in the year 2025.[14] Third, a corporation can pay off an old bond issue by selling new bonds. Although this may appear to perpetuate the corporation's long-term debt, a number of utility companies and railroads use this repayment method.

A corporation that issues bonds must also appoint a **trustee**, an individual or an independent firm that acts as the bond owner's representative. A trustee's duties are handled most often by a commercial bank or other large financial institution. The corporation must report to the trustee periodically regarding its ability to make

Table 19.4 Comparison of Long-Term Financing Methods

Type of Financing	Repayment	Repayment Period	Cost/Dividends Interest	Businesses that May Use It
Equity				
Common stock	No	None	High initial cost; low ongoing costs because dividends not required	All corporations that sell stock to investors
Preferred stock	No	None	Dividends not required but must be paid before common stockholders receive any dividends	Large corporations that have an established investor base of common stockholders
Debt				
Long-term loan	Yes	Usually 3–7 years	Interest rates between 3.25 and 12 percent depending on economic conditions and the financial stability of the company requesting the loan	All firms that can meet the lender's repayment and collateral requirements
Corporate bond	Yes	Usually 10–30 years	Interest rates between 3 and 9 percent depending on economic conditions and the financial stability of the company issuing the bonds	Large corporations that are financially healthy

bond indenture a legal document that details all the conditions relating to a bond issue

serial bonds bonds of a single issue that mature on different dates

sinking fund a sum of money to which deposits are made each year for the purpose of redeeming a bond issue

trustee an individual or an independent firm that acts as a bond owner's representative

interest payments and eventually redeem the bonds. In turn, the trustee transmits this information to the bond owners, along with its own evaluation of the corporation's ability to pay.

Cost Comparisons

Table 19.4 on page 589 compares some of the methods that can be used to obtain long-term equity *and* debt financing. Although the initial flotation cost of issuing stock is high, selling common stock is generally a popular option for most financial managers. Once the stock is sold and upfront costs are paid, the *ongoing* costs of using stock to finance a business are low. The type of long-term financing that generally has the highest *ongoing* costs is a long-term loan (debt).

To a great extent, firms are financed through the investments of individuals—money that people have deposited in banks or have used to purchase stocks, mutual funds, and bonds. In Chapter 20, we look at how securities markets help people invest their money in business.

return to inside business

Ford

Ford executives have used their financial management skills to execute a tricky U-turn away from heavy losses. With the global economy on the verge of a severe downturn, the company borrowed billions of dollars and issued convertible bonds to have cash on hand for immediate and future needs. Little by little, sales improved and the company was soon able to lighten its debt load by repaying a big chunk of the outstanding revolving credit balance. Before the recession ended, Ford had raised more money by selling 300 million new shares of common stock.

Although Ford is continuing its drive for long-term profitability, the road remains bumpy. "We recognize we have too much debt on our balance sheet," says the CFO, "but we think the best way to fix that is by rebuilding our business." To do that, he will "make sure we maintain positive cash flow and continue to invest strongly in new products and growth around the world."

Questions

1. Why would Ford rely on both debt and equity financing to fund its turnaround?
2. Ford suspended stock dividends in 2006 and did not resume them even when it had gained access to billions of dollars in credit. Do you agree with this decision? Why or why not?

Summary

1 Explain the need for financial management in business.

Financial management consists of all activities concerned with obtaining money and using it effectively. Short-term financing is money that will be used for one year or less. There are many short-term needs, but cash flow and inventory are two for which financing is often required. Long-term financing is money that will be used for more than one year. Such financing may be required for a business start-up, for a merger or an acquisition, for new product development, for long-term marketing activities, for replacement of equipment, or for expansion of facilities. Financial management can be viewed as a two-sided problem. On one side, the uses of funds often dictate the type or types of financing needed by a business. On the other side, the activities a business can undertake are determined by the types of financing available. Financial managers must also consider the risk-return ratio when making decisions. The risk-return ratio is based on the principle that a high-risk decision should generate higher financial returns for a business. On the other hand, more conservative decisions generate lesser returns. Financial managers must ensure that funds are available when needed, that they are obtained at the lowest possible cost, and that they are available for the repayment of debts. During the recent economic crisis, the number of business bankruptcies increased. Fortunately, there were many more business firms that were able to weather the economic storm and keep operating because of their ability to manage their finances.

2 Summarize the process of planning for financial management.

A financial plan begins with an organization's goals. Next, these goals are "translated" into departmental budgets that detail expected income and expenses. From these budgets, which may be combined into an overall cash budget, the financial manager determines what funding will be needed and where it may be obtained. Whereas departmental and cash budgets emphasize short-term financing needs, a capital budget can be used to estimate a firm's expenditures for major assets and its long-term financing needs. The four principal sources of financing are sales revenues, equity capital, debt capital, and proceeds from the sale of assets. Once the needed funds have been obtained, the financial manager is responsible for ensuring that they are used properly. This is accomplished through a system of monitoring and evaluating the firm's financial activities.

3 Describe the advantages and disadvantages of different methods of short-term debt financing.

Most short-term financing is unsecured; that is, no collateral is required. Sources of unsecured short-term financing include trade credit, promissory notes issued to suppliers, unsecured bank loans, and commercial paper. Sources of secured short-term financing include loans secured by inventory and accounts receivable. A firm may also sell its receivables to factors. Trade credit is the least-expensive source of short-term financing. The cost of financing through other sources generally depends on the source and on the credit rating of the firm that requires the financing. Factoring is generally the most expensive approach.

4 Evaluate the advantages and disadvantages of equity financing.

A corporation can raise equity capital by selling either common or preferred stock. The first time a corporation sells stock to the general public is referred to as an initial public offering (IPO). With an IPO, the stock is sold in the primary market. Once sold in the primary market, investors buy and sell stock in the secondary market. Usually, secondary market transactions are completed through a securities exchange or the over-the-counter market. Common stock is voting stock; holders of common stock elect the corporation's directors and must approve changes to the corporate charter. Holders of preferred stock must be paid dividends before holders of common stock are paid any dividends. Another source of equity funding is retained earnings, which is the portion of a business's profits not distributed to stockholders. Venture capital—money invested in small (and sometimes struggling) firms that have the potential to become very successful—is yet another source of equity funding. Generally, the venture capital is provided by investors, partnerships established by wealthy families, or a joint venture formed by corporations with money to invest. In return, they receive an equity position in the firm and share in the profits of the business. Finally, a private placement can be used to sell stocks and other corporate securities.

5 Evaluate the advantages and disadvantages of long-term debt financing.

For a small business, debt financing is generally limited to loans. Large corporations have the additional option of issuing corporate bonds. Regardless of whether the business is small or large, it can take advantage of financial leverage. Financial leverage is the use of borrowed funds to increase the return on owners' equity. The rate of interest for long-term loans usually depends on the financial status of the borrower, the reason for borrowing, and the kind of collateral pledged to back up the loan. Long-term business loans are normally repaid in 3 to 7 years but can be as long as 15 to 20 years. Money realized from the sale of corporate bonds must be repaid when the bonds mature. In addition, the corporation must pay interest on that money from the time the bonds are sold until maturity. Maturity dates for bonds generally range from 10 to 30 years after the date of issue. Three types of bonds—debentures, mortgage bonds, and convertible bonds—are sold to raise debt capital. When comparing the cost of equity and debt long-term financing, the ongoing costs of using stock (equity) to finance a business are low. The most expensive is a long-term loan (debt).

CHAPTER REVIEW

Key Terms

You should now be able to define and give an example relevant to each of the following terms:

financial management (569)
short-term financing (569)
cash flow (569)
speculative production (570)
long-term financing (570)
risk-return ratio (573)
chief financial officer (CFO) (573)
financial plan (573)
budget (574)
cash budget (575)
zero-base budgeting (575)
capital budget (575)
equity capital (576)
debt capital (576)
unsecured financing (577)
trade credit (577)
promissory note (578)
prime interest rate (578)
factor (580)
initial public offering (IPO) (581)
primary market (581)
investment banking firm (581)
secondary market (582)
securities exchange (583)
over-the-counter (OTC) market (583)
common stock (583)
preferred stock (583)
par value (584)
retained earnings (584)
private placement (585)
financial leverage (585)
term-loan agreement (586)
corporate bond (587)
maturity date (588)
registered bond (588)
debenture bond (588)
mortgage bond (588)
convertible bond (588)
bond indenture (589)
serial bonds (589)
sinking fund (589)
trustee (589)

Review Questions

1. How does short-term financing differ from long-term financing? Give two business uses for each type of financing.
2. For a business firm, what type of activities does financial management involve?
3. In your own words, describe the risk-return ratio.
4. What is the function of a cash budget? A capital budget?
5. What is zero-base budgeting? How does it differ from the traditional concept of budgeting?
6. What are four general sources of funds?
7. How does a financial manager monitor and evaluate a firm's financing?
8. How important is trade credit as a source of short-term financing?
9. Why would a supplier require a customer to sign a promissory note?
10. What is the prime rate? Who gets the prime rate?
11. Explain how factoring works. Of what benefit is factoring to a firm that sells its receivables?
12. How does an investment banking firm help a corporation sell stock in the primary market?
13. What are the advantages of financing through the sale of stock?
14. From a corporation's point of view, how does preferred stock differ from common stock?
15. Where do a corporation's retained earnings come from? What are the advantages of this type of financing?
16. Describe how financial leverage can increase return on owners' equity.
17. For a corporation, what are the advantages of corporate bonds over long-term loans?
18. Describe the three methods used to ensure that funds are available to redeem corporate bonds at maturity.

Discussion Questions

1. During the recent economic crisis, many financial managers and corporate officers have been criticized for (a) poor decisions, (b) lack of ethical behavior, (c) large salaries, (d) lucrative severance packages worth millions of dollars, and (e) extravagant lifestyles. Is this criticism justified? Justify your opinion.
2. What does a financial manager do? How can he or she monitor a firm's financial success?
3. If you were the financial manager of Stars and Stripes Clothing, what would you do with the excess cash that the firm expects in the second and fourth quarters? (See Figure 19.5.)
4. Develop a *personal* cash budget for the next six months. Explain what you would do if there are budget shortfalls or excess cash amounts at the end of any month during the six-month period.
5. Why would a lender offer unsecured loans when it could demand collateral?
6. How can a small-business owner or corporate manager use financial leverage to improve the firm's profits and return on owners' equity?
7. In what circumstances might a large corporation sell stock rather than bonds to obtain long-term financing? In what circumstances would it sell bonds rather than stock?

Video Case 19.1

Financial Planning Equals Profits for Nederlander Concerts

Nederlander Concerts is in the business of booking, promoting, and producing live music shows in the western United States. The company presents artists from James Taylor to Flogging Molly, Bruce Springsteen, Bonnie Raitt, and the Allman Brothers Band. But, says its CEO, "We're not trying to be necessarily a national player or an international player. We seek out opportunities that fit within and leverage our existing portfolio of small- to mid-size venues .... It's one of the few remaining family-run entertainment enterprises worldwide .... What this means for us on a day-to-day basis is that we can focus on running the business. We're not as guided by Wall Street, we don't have the same constraints, we don't have the same reporting responsibilities, and it allows us to focus on ... our business strategy for development."

Of course, being a privately owned company and not needing to respond to shareholders (Wall Street) doesn't mean that Nederlander has *no* reporting responsibilities. As the CEO explains, "We assess at the beginning of the year not only concert revenue and expenses but also special event revenue. When we rent the facilities to, for example, movie premieres here in Los Angeles, what kind of revenue are we going to see? What kind of expenses are attended to generating that revenue? What's our fixed overhead for the year? Who's on the payroll, whether full-time, or part-time, or seasonal, and how much does it cost us to run the business on a day-to-day basis in order to secure those revenues and pay those expenses? That's wrapped up into an annual budget at the beginning of every year, which is kind of a guideline for me to know how we achieve growth. It also allows me to communicate to our owners what our growth orientation is for that given year .... Every event has its own profit and loss statement ... which is a mini version of that annual plan."

In addition to daily, weekly, and quarterly event reports, Nederlander's financial team generates daily and weekly reports of ticket sales. Monthly reports on company-wide performance feed into quarterly and annual reports. Each annual report is compared to that year's budget. The finance department tallies hundreds of transactions in order to arrive at some of these annual numbers, which are reported to the company's owners to ensure that the company is running as profitably as it can be.

Nederlander's managers say growth in the concert industry must be measured in the long term because the business is cyclical and the cost of real estate is so high that short-term profit is hard to generate. Still, the company is in a strong financial position (it is part of a profitable global theater-owning company called the Nederlander Organization), so it can afford to fund its own growth and expansion, or it can borrow on favorable terms. "We're very fortunate to have an ownership that is very well capitalized with over 80 years in the business," says the CEO. "Our balance sheet is so strong that we have the ability to tap into debt financing if it makes the most sense .... or [use] the corporate treasury. ... If it makes more sense to borrow the money, we will, and we're typically able to do that on very favorable rates because of very long-term banking relationships."

It can be thrilling to meet some of the artists the company books. "But at the end of the day it's a business," the CEO points out. "If we're not successful in growing our revenue and managing our expense, ultimately we won't be profitable, and our ownership will not be happy with those results."[15]

Questions

1. Here's what Nederlander's chief operating officer has to say about its business model: "A show has a short lifetime. You go and sell two months out, and the tickets have no value on any day but the day of the show. So it's a very interesting model in that sense." How do you think the short life of the company's products affects its financial planning?
2. The company uses its own arenas and theaters about 90 percent of the time. What are some of the possible disadvantages of owning its own venues?
3. Why would Nederlander choose to sometimes borrow funds for expansion if it has capital of its own?

Case 19.2

Darden Restaurants Serve Up Long-Term Growth

Growth has been on the menu ever since Bill Darden opened his first Red Lobster restaurant in Florida in 1968. The combination of fresh seafood and casual dining caught on quickly—and quickly caught the eye of General Mills, which bought the fast-growing company in 1970. In 1995, General Mills renamed the company after its founder and spun it off in a public offering. Once it went public, Darden Restaurants used the proceeds to chart a new financial path to long-term growth.

Today, Darden employs 180,000 people and serves more than 400 million meals across North America in 1,800 casual, full-service restaurants. The company's six restaurant brands are: Red Lobster (seafood), Olive Garden (Italian menu), LongHorn Steakhouse (Western-theme steaks and more), The Capital Grille (premium steak house), Bahama Breeze (Caribbean-theme casual dining), and Seasons 52 (fresh-grilled foods). In all, Darden's yearly revenue tops $7 billion.

Healthy cash flow is definitely on the menu. The average Capital Grille unit rings up $6.8 million in annual sales, the average Olive Garden rings up $4.8 million in annual sales, the average Red Lobster rings up $3.8 million, and the average LongHorn Steakhouse rings up $2.8 million. With the cash generated from restaurant revenue, Darden has been reinvesting in its businesses by opening new units, remodeling existing units, and greening its restaurants with eco-friendly materials and energy-saving touches. Because of its size, it can take advantage of economies of scale in buying foods and beverages from global sources, which in turn helps keep costs under control and supports good profit margins.

Over the years, the company has fueled its continued expansion with a combination of debt and equity. The company can draw on a revolving credit agreement of more than $600 million, which helps smooth out the financial bumps of its seasonal business. Typically, Darden's revenue spikes in the spring and falls to a low point in the fall, although sales are definitely affected by weather conditions, economic circumstances, holidays, and other uncontrollable elements. Having revolving credit in place provides the flexibility to borrow if and when needed.

Darden has also raised money by issuing corporate bonds, some of which mature in 5 years, some in 10 years, and some in 20 years. Twice a year, the company pays interest to its bondholders. On the equity side, Darden's common stock trades on the New York Stock Exchange, and it pays dividends to its shareholders. Its cash flow has been so strong, in fact, that Darden increased its dividend not long ago and has focused on paying down debt even as it invests in business.

Looking ahead, Darden expects to continue its growth spurt, despite an unpredictable economy and intense competition from big names in fast food and casual dining. It avoided the heavy, broad-based discounting that some chains used to attract customers during the recession. Instead, it used occasional, selective price promotions to heighten its message of affordability. The company's financial stability means that it has money available for making acquisitions, building new restaurants, developing new menu items, training new staff members, and launching new advertising campaigns.

Within the past decade, Darden has used its financial strength to buy and expand the Capital Grill and LongHorn Steakhouse restaurant chains. It is also catering to increased consumer interest in healthy dining by opening more of its Seasons 52 restaurants, which feature only steamed, baked, or grilled dishes. As its name implies, Seasons 52 adds new menu items regularly, depending on what's in season. The ever-changing menu brings customers back again and again to try seasonal specialties and enjoy old favorites.

Sometimes Darden closes under-performing units or sells entire chains so it can put its money and management attention into other growth opportunities. A few years ago, Darden divested its Smokey Bones Barbecue & Grill chain after determining that this restaurant concept did not have the potential for nationwide expansion and profit potential that Darden required. What will Darden do next in its quest for profitable, long-term growth?[16]

Questions

1. Darden is spending heavily to upgrade the interior of many of its Red Lobster and LongHorn Steakhouse restaurants. How would you suggest that the company measure the financial results of this remodeling program?
2. Why would Darden issue corporate bonds that mature in 5, 10, and 20 years?
3. If Darden needs cash to remodel existing restaurants and open new restaurants, as well as to pay down debt, why would it increase its stock dividend?

Building Skills for Career Success

1 JOURNALING FOR SUCCESS

Because many people spend more than they make on a regular basis, they often use credit cards to make routine daily purchases. As a result, the amount they owe on credit cards increases each month and there is no money left to begin a savings or investment program. This exercise will help you to understand (1) how you manage your credit cards and (2) what steps you can take to improve your personal finances.

Assignment

1. How many credit cards do you have?
2. Based on the information on your monthly credit-card statements, what types of credit-card purchases do you make?
3. Do you pay your balance in full each month or make minimum payments on your credit cards?
4. Most experts recommend that you have one or two credit cards that you use only if you are in an emergency situation. The experts also recommend that you avoid using credit cards to make inexpensive purchases on a daily basis. Finally, the experts recommend that you pay your credit-card balance in full each month. Based on the preceding information, what steps can you take to better manage your personal finances?

2 EXPLORING THE INTERNET

Finding capital for new business start-ups is never an easy task. Besides a good business plan, those seeking investor funds must be convincing and clear about how their business activities will provide sufficient revenue to pay back investors who help to get them going in the first place. To find out what others have done, it is useful to read histories of successful start-ups as well as failures in journals that specialize in this area. Visit the text Web site for updates to this exercise.

Assignment

1. Examine articles that profile at least two successes or failures in the following publications and highlight the main points that led to either result.

   Business 2.0 (http://www.business2.com)
   Red Herring (http://www.redherring.com)
   Fast Company (http://www.fastcompany.com)

2. What are the shared similarities?
3. What advice would you give to a start-up venture after reading these stories?

3 DEVELOPING CRITICAL-THINKING SKILLS

Financial management involves preparing a plan for obtaining and using the money needed to accomplish a firm's goals. To accomplish your own goals, you should prepare a *personal* financial plan. You must determine what is important in your life and what you want to accomplish, budget the amount of money required to obtain your goals, and identify sources for acquiring the funds. You should monitor and evaluate the results regularly and make changes when necessary.

Assignment

1. Using the three steps shown in Figure 19.3, prepare a personal financial plan.
2. Prepare a three-column table to display it.
   a. In column 1, list at least two objectives under each of the following areas: Financial (savings, investments, retirement), Education (training, degrees, certificates), Career (position, industry, location), and Family (children, home, education, trips, entertainment).
   b. In column 2, list the amount of money it will take to accomplish your objectives.
   c. In column 3, identify the sources of funds for each objective.
3. Describe what you learned from doing this exercise in a comments section at the bottom of the table.

4 BUILDING TEAM SKILLS

Suppose that for the past three years you have been repairing lawn mowers in your garage. Your business has grown steadily, and you recently hired two part-time workers. Your garage is no longer adequate for your business; it is also in violation of the city code, and you have already been fined for noncompliance. You have decided that it is time to find another location for your shop and that it also would be a good time to expand your business. If the business continues to grow in the new location, you plan to hire a full-time employee to repair small appliances. You are concerned, however, about how you will get the money to move your shop and get it established in a new location.

Assignment

1. With all class members participating, use brainstorming to identify the following:
   a. The funds you will need to accomplish your business goals
   b. The sources of short-term financing available to you
   c. Problems that might prevent you from getting a short-term loan
   d. How you will repay the money if you get a loan
2. Have a classmate write the ideas on the board.
3. Discuss how you can overcome any problems that might hamper your current chances of getting a loan and how your business can improve its chances of securing short-term loans in the future.
4. Summarize what you learned from participating in this exercise.

❺ RESEARCHING DIFFERENT CAREERS

Financial managers are responsible for determining the best way to raise funds, for ensuring that the funds are used to accomplish their firm's goals and objectives, and for developing and implementing their firm's financial plan. Their decisions have a direct impact on the firm's level of success. When managers do not pay enough attention to finances, a firm is likely to fail.

Assignment

1. Investigate the job of financial manager by searching the library or Internet, by interviewing a financial manager, or both.
2. Find answers to the following questions:
   a. What skills do financial managers need?
   b. How much education is required?
   c. What is the starting salary? Top salary?
   d. What will the job of financial manager be like in the future?
   e. What opportunities are available?
   f. What types of firms are most likely to hire financial managers? What is the employment potential?
3. Prepare a report on your findings.

Understanding Personal Finances and Investments

20

© Patrizia Tilly/Shutterstock.com

Learning Objectives

What you will be able to do once you complete this chapter:

1. Explain why you should manage your personal finances and develop a personal investment program.
2. Describe how the factors of safety, risk, income, growth, and liquidity affect your investment program.
3. Understand how securities are bought and sold.
4. Recognize how you can reduce investment risk and increase investment returns.
5. Identify the advantages and disadvantages of savings accounts, bonds, stocks, mutual funds, and real estate investments.
6. Describe high-risk investment techniques.
7. Use financial information to evaluate investment alternatives.

FYI

Did You Know?

Raymond James, based in St. Petersburg, Florida, has 5,300 financial advisors working in 2,300 offices worldwide and rings up $2.6 billion in annual revenue.

inside business

Raymond James: Professional Investing with the Personal Touch

Expert financial advice, personalized service, and access to a wide range of investments—that's how Raymond James has built its reputation as a brokerage firm and investment bank. Since 1964, when Edward Raymond and Robert A. James merged their companies, Raymond James has been offering investment advice from its headquarters in St. Petersburg, Florida, as well as from its 2,300 offices worldwide.

Raymond James's 5,300 financial advisors help its two million customers choose just the right mix of investments to build a sizable nest egg for retirement, save for major outlays such as paying for a child's education, or put money aside for the next generation. Taking individual needs and concerns into consideration, an advisor examines each customer's assets, expenses, investments, and overall financial situation. Then he or she prepares a detailed financial plan for meeting the customer's short- and long-term investment goals, with the flexibility to make changes as requirements change and markets move up or down.

So that its advisors can make informed recommendations about buying and selling stocks, bonds, and other investments, Raymond James's economists monitor the global financial system and its securities analysts follow the fortunes of more than 1,000 public corporations. In addition, Raymond James works closely with companies to set up and manage retirement plans and provide a menu of investment choices for business owners, managers, and employees. On the investment banking side, it helps corporations obtain either debt or equity financing from sources such as an initial public offering, private placement, issuance of corporate bonds, and other sources.

Thanks to its reputation for providing professional, quality service with the personal touch, Raymond James is able to compete effectively against larger brokerage rivals such as Charles Schwab and Fidelity Investments. In fact, Raymond James now rings up $2.6 billion in annual revenue and has been attracting new customers and expanding its investment offerings for individual investors. The company is ready to help customers make the most of their investments and make sound financial decisions for today and tomorrow.[1]

As the saying goes, "I've been rich and I've been poor, but believe me, rich is better." Yet, just dreaming of being rich does not make it happen. Although being rich does not guarantee happiness, managing your personal finances and beginning an investment program are both worthy goals. Firms such as Raymond James—the company profiled in the Inside Business feature for this chapter—offer an array of services to help people manage their personal finances, research investments, and buy and sell stocks, bonds, mutual funds, and other securities. Nevertheless, you must be willing to invest the time and effort required to manage your personal finances and become a good investor. Furthermore, do not underestimate how important you are when it comes to managing your money. No one is going to make you manage your money. No one is going to make you save the money you need to fund an investment program. These are your decisions—important decisions that literally can change your life.

Many people ask the question: Why begin an investment program now? At the time of publication, this is a very important question given the recent economic crisis. Although it is true that many investors have lost a great deal of money as a result of the crisis, the experts agree that the best investment program is one that stresses long-term growth over a 20- to 40-year period. Although the dollar value of your investments may decrease over a short time period, historically the value of securities has always increased over a long time period. To illustrate this point, it may help to think of the financial markets as a roller coaster ride with ups (periods of increasing values) and downs (periods of declining values). The recent crisis is a very real example of how worldwide economic problems can cause the value of stocks, bonds, mutual funds, real estate, and other investments to decline. Faced with large dollar losses, many investors make a decision to sell their investments at the bottom of the roller coaster ride. The investors who decide to hold their investments will eventually see them recover and increase in value over time. In fact, many experts recommend buying quality stocks, mutual funds, and real estate during an economic downturn.

A second compelling reason to start an investment program is that the sooner you start an investment program, the more time your investments have to work for you. So why do people wait to begin investing? In most cases, there are two reasons. First, they do not have the money needed to fund an investment program. However, once you begin managing your personal finances and get your spending under control, you will be able to save the money needed to fund an investment program. The second reason people do not begin investing is because they do not know anything about investing. Again, this chapter provides the basics to get you started.

We begin this chapter by examining everyday money management activities and outlining the reasons for developing a personal investment plan. Next, we examine the process of buying and selling securities. Then we discuss both traditional and high-risk (or speculative) investments. Finally, we explain how to use information to evaluate potential investments. It is time! Take the first step, and begin managing your personal finances.

1

Explain why you should manage your personal finances and develop a personal investment program.

Managing Your Personal Finances

Although it would be nice if you could accumulate wealth magically, it is not magic. Most people begin by making sure that their "financial house" is in order. In this section, we examine several steps for effective money management that will help you to prepare for an investment program.

Step 1: Tracking Your Income, Expenses, Assets, and Liabilities

net worth the difference between the value of your total assets and your total liabilities

Many personal finance experts recommend that you begin the process of managing your money by determining your current financial condition. Often the first step is to construct a personal income statement and balance sheet. (*Note*: Both personal income statements and balance sheets were examined in more detail in Chapter 17.) A *personal income statement* lists your income and your expenses for a specific period of time—usually a month. By subtracting expenses from income, you can determine if you have a surplus or a deficit at the end of the time period. Surplus funds can be used for savings, investing, or for any purpose that you feel is important. Simply put: It is your choice how you spend the surplus. On the other hand, if you have a deficit, you must take actions to reduce spending and pay down any debts you may have that will keep you from starting an investment program.

To get another picture of your current financial condition, you should construct a personal balance sheet. A *personal balance sheet* lists your assets and liabilities on a specific date. By subtracting your total liabilities from your total assets, you can determine your net worth. For an individual, **net worth** is the difference between the value of your total assets and your total liabilities. Over time, the goal is to increase the value of your assets (items of value that you own) and decrease liabilities (your debts).

Based on the information contained in these two statements, you can determine your current financial

A good investment program can make a difference. The driving force behind your investment program should be the financial goals that are important to you. For some investors, having enough money to retire and sail around the world is a very important goal. For others, financial security and not having to worry about money is a more important goal.

condition and where you spend your money. You can also take the next step: Construct a personal budget.

Step 2: Developing a Budget that Works

A **personal budget** is a specific plan for spending your income. You begin by estimating your income for a specific period—for example, next month. For most people, their major source of income is their salary. The second step is to list expenses for the same time period. Typical expenses include savings and investments, housing, food, transportation, entertainment, and so on. For most people, this is the area where you can make choices and increase or decrease the amount spent on different items listed in your budget. For example, you may decide to reduce the dollar amount spent on entertainment to increase the amount for savings. Above all, it is important to balance your budget so that your income is equal to the money you spend, save, or invest each month.

After you have constructed your personal budget, you will need to compare the amounts included in your budget with your actual income and expenses. The goal is that estimated income and expenses are correct and that you have a surplus at the end of the budgeting period. If income is less than anticipated or expenses are more than budgeted, then you will need to take corrective actions to get your budget back on track. For example, you may need to review areas where spending has been more than expected.

Like most personal financial planning, it will be necessary to review your budget on a regular basis. Certain changes in income or expenses may trigger a budget revision. A salary increase, for example, will affect your personal budget. Often one change will affect other areas of your budget as well. An increase in your monthly rent payment, for instance, may mean that you have to reduce the amount spent on entertainment to balance your budget. *Caution*: Avoid the temptation to spend more than you make by using credit cards or borrowing money.

Step 3: Managing Credit Card Debt

Unfortunately, many individuals spend more than they make. They purchase items on credit and then make monthly payments and pay finance charges ranging from 10 to 21 percent or more. It makes no sense to start an investment program until payments for credit card and installment purchases, along with the accompanying finance charges, are reduced or eliminated.

Although all cardholders have reasons for using their credit cards, the important point to remember is that it is *very easy* to get in trouble by using your credit cards. Watch for the following five warning signs.

1. Don't fall behind on payments. One of the first warning signs is the inability to pay your entire balance each month. Experts suggest that you pay your balance in full each month if you use credit cards.
2. Do not use your credit cards to pay for many small purchases during the month. This can often lead to a "real surprise" when you open your credit card statement at the end of the month.
3. Do not use the cash advance provision that accompanies most credit cards. The reason is simple: The interest rate is usually higher for cash advances when compared to credit card purchases.
4. Think about the number of cards you really need. Most experts recommend that an individual have one or two cards and use these cards for emergencies.
5. Get help if you think you are in trouble. An organization like Consumer Credit Counseling Service (http://www.cccs.net) can often help you work out a plan to pay off credit card debt.

By reducing or eliminating credit purchases, eventually the amount of cash remaining after the bills are paid will increase and can be used to start a savings and investment program that will help you obtain your investment goals.

personal budget a specific plan for spending your income

Career SUCCESS

It Is Never Too Early to Think About Retirement

Whether you are interviewing for your first full-time job or have already started climbing the career ladder, it is never too early to think about retirement. Here are some questions to help you think through the possibilities:

Does your employer offer a defined benefit retirement plan? These pension plans provide a specific monthly amount after you retire. Your employer sets up the plan, makes contributions, and handles investment decisions. Check the fine print: Even if you change jobs, you may still be able to receive pension income after retiring.

Does your employer offer a 401(k) plan (or, in the case of non-profits and government agencies, a 403(b) plan)? These plans allow you, the employee, to contribute toward your retirement, subject to a yearly cap, with many employers matching some or all of an employee's contributions. You will make investment decisions from a menu of options provided by your employer, usually mutual funds.

© Stephen Coburn/Shutterstock.com

Are you eligible for a traditional IRA or Roth IRA account? If your employer has no retirement plan, and your income meets IRS guidelines, consider a traditional IRA or Roth IRA to start investing on your own. Contributions to traditional IRAs are tax-deductible and provide immediate tax benefits. With a traditional IRA, you pay tax on the money you withdraw when you retire. Contributions to Roth IRAs are not tax-deductible. However, you do not pay tax on money you withdraw after you retire.

Remember: The sooner you begin an investment program, through your employer or on your own, the better off you will be at retirement. It's never too early to start!

Sources: Veronica Dagher, "The Game Plan: He's Young—and a Saver," *The Wall Street Journal*, April 12, 2010, http://www.wsj.com; Walter Updegrave, "First Job? Start Your First 401(k)," *Money*, September 3, 2009, http://money.cnn.com/2009/09/03/pf/expert/starter_401k.moneymag/index.htm.

Investment Goals

Personal investment is the use of your personal funds to earn a financial return. Thus, in the most general sense, the goal of investing is to earn money with money. However, such a goal is completely useless for the individual because it is so vague and so easily attained.

In reality, an investment goal must be specific and measurable. It must be tailored to you so that it takes into account your particular financial needs. It must also be oriented toward the future because investing is usually a long-term undertaking. A long-term investment program has a number of advantages. By investing small amounts of money each year over a 20- to 40-year period, you can accumulate money for emergencies and retirement. In addition, if you choose quality investments, the value of your investments will grow over a long period of time. Despite the recent economic crisis, financial experts believe that long-term investors will not only see the value of their investment portfolio recover, but also increase over the next few years. Finally, an investment goal must be realistic in terms of current economic conditions and available investment opportunities.

Some financial planners suggest that investment goals should be stated in terms of money: "By January 1, 2020, I will have total assets of $80,000." Others believe that people are more motivated to work toward goals that are stated in terms of the particular things they desire: "By May 1, 2022, I will have accumulated enough money so that I can take a year off from work to travel around the world." Like the goals themselves, the way they are stated depends on you. The following questions can be helpful in establishing valid investment goals:

1. What financial goals do you want to achieve?
2. How much money will you need, and when?

personal investment the use of your personal funds to earn a financial return

3. What will you use the money for?
4. Is it reasonable to assume that you can obtain the amount of money you will need to meet your investment goals?
5. Do you expect your personal situation to change in a way that will affect your investment goals?
6. What economic conditions could alter your investment goals?
7. Are you willing to make the necessary sacrifices to ensure that your investment goals are met?

A Personal Investment Program

Once you have formulated specific goals and have some money to invest, investment planning is similar to planning for a business. It begins with the evaluation of different investment opportunities—including the potential return and risk involved in each. At the very least, this process requires some careful study and maybe some expert advice. Investors should beware of people who call themselves "financial planners" but who are in reality nothing more than salespersons for various financial investments, tax shelters, or insurance plans.

A true **financial planner** has had at least two years of training in investments, insurance, taxation, retirement planning, and estate planning and has passed a rigorous examination. As evidence of training and successful completion of the qualifying examination, the Certified Financial Planner (CFP) Board of Standards (http://www.cfp.net) in Washington, DC, allows individuals to use the designation CFP. Similarly, the American College (http://www.theamericancollege.edu) in Bryn Mawr, Pennsylvania, allows individuals who have completed the necessary requirements to use the designation Chartered Financial Consultant (ChFC). Most CFPs and ChFCs do not sell a particular investment product or receive commissions for their investment recommendations. Instead, they charge consulting fees that range from $100 to $250 an hour.

Many financial planners suggest that you accumulate an "emergency fund"—a certain amount of money that can be obtained quickly in case of immediate need—before beginning an investment program. The amount of money that should be salted away in a savings account varies from person to person. Most financial planners agree that an amount equal to at least three months' living expenses is reasonable. However, you may want to increase your emergency fund in anticipation of a crisis.

financial planner an individual who has had at least two years of training in investments, insurance, taxation, retirement planning, and estate planning and has passed a rigorous examination

After the emergency account is established, you may invest additional funds according to your investment program. Some additional funds may already be available, or money for further investing may be saved out of earnings. For suggestions to help you obtain the money needed to fund your investment program, see Table 20.1.

Table 20.1	Suggestions to Help You Accumulate the Money Needed to Fund an Investment Program
1.	*Pay yourself first.* Many financial experts recommend that you (1) pay your monthly bills, (2) save a reasonable amount of money, and (3) use whatever money is left over for personal expenses.
2.	*Take advantage of employer-sponsored retirement programs.* Many employers will match part or all of the contributions you make to a 401(k) or 403(b) retirement account.
3.	*Participate in an elective savings program.* Elect to have money withheld from your paycheck each payday and automatically deposited in a savings account.
4.	*Make a special savings effort one or two months each year.* By cutting back to the basics, you can obtain money for investment purposes.
5.	*Take advantage of gifts, inheritances, and windfalls.* During your lifetime, you likely will receive gifts, inheritances, salary increases, year-end bonuses, or federal income tax returns. Instead of spending these windfalls, invest these funds.

Source: Jack R. Kapoor, Les R. Dlabay, and Robert J. Hughes, *Focus on Personal Finance*, 3rd ed. Copyright © 2010 by The McGraw Hill Companies Inc. Reprinted with permission of The McGraw Hill Companies Inc., 353.

Once your program has been put into operation, you must monitor it and, if necessary, modify it. Your circumstances and economic conditions are both subject to change. Therefore, all investment programs should be re-evaluated regularly.

Important Factors in Personal Investment

2 Describe how the factors of safety, risk, income, growth, and liquidity affect your investment program.

How can you (or a financial planner) tell which investments are "right" for your investment program and which are not? One way to start is to match potential investments with your investment goals in terms of safety, risk, income, growth, and liquidity.

Safety and Risk

Safety and risk are two sides of the same coin. *Safety* in an investment means minimal risk of loss; *risk* in an investment means a measure of uncertainty about the outcome. If you want a steady increase in value over an extended period of time, choose safe investments, such as certificates of deposit (CDs), highly rated corporate and municipal bonds, and the stocks of highly regarded corporations—sometimes called *blue-chip stocks*. A **blue-chip stock** is a safe investment that generally attracts conservative investors. Blue-chip stocks are generally issued by corporations that are industry leaders and have provided their stockholders with stable earnings and dividends over a number of years. Selected mutual funds and real estate may also be very safe investments.

If you want higher dollar returns on investments, you must generally give up some safety. In general, *the potential return should be directly related to the assumed risk*. That is, the greater the risk assumed by the investor, the better the potential monetary reward. As you will see shortly, there are a number of risky—and potentially profitable—investments.

blue-chip stock a safe investment that generally attracts conservative investors

rate of return the total dollar amount of return you receive on an investment over a specific period of time divided by the amount invested

Often beginning investors are afraid of the risk associated with many investments. However, it helps to remember that without risk, it is impossible to obtain larger returns that really make an investment program grow. In fact, some investors often base their investment decision on projections for rate of return. You can also use the same calculation to determine how much you actually earn on an investment over a specific period of time. To calculate **rate of return**, the total dollar amount of return you receive on an investment over a specific period of time is divided by the amount invested. For example, assume that you invest $5,000 in Home Depot stock, you receive $95 in dividends, and the stock is worth $5,300 at the end of one year. Your rate of return is 7.9 percent, as illustrated here.

Step 1: Subtract the investment's initial value from the investment's value at the end of the year.

$$\$5,300 - \$5,000 = \$300$$

Step 2: Add the dividend amount to the amount calculated in step 1.

$$\$95 + \$300 = \$395$$

Step 3: Divide the total dollar amount of return calculated in step 2 by the original investment.

$$\$395 \div \$5,000 = 0.079 = 7.9 \text{ percent}$$

Note: If an investment decreases in value, the steps used to calculate the rate of return are the same, but the answer is a negative number. With this information, it is possible to compare the rate of return for different investment alternatives that offer more or less risk.

© Daniel Acker/Bloomberg via Getty Images

What better way to learn about a company and its products and services. Many corporations, like Berkshire Hathaway, use their annual stockholders' meeting to showcase their products and services. In this photo, stockholders are encouraged to visit the exhibit hall to see what the companies owned by Berkshire Hathaway actually sell to their customers. As an added bonus, stockholders can purchase the products and services they like—often at a discount.

Investment Income

Investors sometimes purchase certain investments because they want a predictable source of income. For example, CDs, corporate and government bonds, and certain stocks pay interest or dividends each year. Some mutual funds and real estate may also offer steady income potential. Such investments are generally used by conservative investors or retired individuals who need a predictable source of income.

When purchasing investments for income, most investors are concerned about the issuer's ability to continue making periodic interest or dividend payments. Investors in CDs and bonds know exactly how much income they will receive each year. The dividends paid to stockholders can and do vary, even for the largest and most stable corporations. As with dividends from stock, the income from mutual funds and real estate may also vary from one year to the next.

Investment Growth

To investors, *growth* means that their investments will increase in value. For example, growing corporations such as eBay, Adobe Systems, and the Apollo Group usually pay a small cash dividend or no dividend at all. Instead, profits are reinvested in the business (as retained earnings) to finance additional expansion. In this case, the value of their stock increases as the corporation expands.

Other investments that may offer growth potential include selected mutual funds and real estate. For example, many mutual funds are referred to as growth funds or aggressive growth funds because of the growth potential of the individual securities included in the fund.

Investment Liquidity

Liquidity is the ease with which an investment can be converted into cash. Investments range from cash or cash equivalents (such as investments in government securities or money-market accounts) to the other extreme of frozen investments, which you cannot convert easily into cash.

Although you may be able to sell stock, mutual-fund, and corporate-bond investments quickly, you may not regain the amount of money you originally invested because of market conditions, economic conditions, or many other reasons. It may also be difficult to find buyers for real estate. Furthermore, finding a buyer for investments in certain types of collectibles may also be difficult.

Managing Your Investments in an Economic Crisis

In fall 2007, the stock market, as measured by the Dow Jones Industrial Average, reached an all-time high at 14,000. By March 2009, the same average had declined to 6,600. What happened? The simple answer is that the United States (and most of the world) experienced an economic meltdown. This economic crisis had many causes including a banking and financial crisis, a downturn in home sales, lower consumer spending, and high unemployment rates. Although the economy shows signs of improving at the time of publication, it could happen again.

Although monitoring your investment program and re-evaluating your investment choices are always important, the recent economic crisis underscores the importance of managing your personal finances *and* your investment program. Because of the nation's economic problems, many people were caught off guard and had to scramble to find the money to pay their monthly bills. Many of these same individuals had to borrow money or use their credit cards to survive from one payday to the next. Moreover, some individuals were forced to sell some or all of their investments at depressed prices just to buy food for the family and pay for everyday necessities.

liquidity the ease with which an investment can be converted into cash

If you think the economy is about to take a nosedive, many experts recommend that you take action to make sure your financial affairs are in order. Eight steps you can take are:

1. *Establish a larger-than-usual emergency fund.* Although under normal circumstances, an emergency fund of three months' living expenses is considered adequate, you may want to increase your fund in anticipation of a crisis.
2. *Know what you owe.* It helps to make a list of all your debts and the amount of the required monthly payments. Then identify the debts that *must* be paid. Typically these include the mortgage or rent, medicine, utilities, food, and transportation costs.
3. *Reduce spending.* Cut back to the basics and reduce the amount of money spent on entertainment, dining at restaurants, and vacations. Although not pleasant, the money saved from reduced spending can be used to increase your emergency fund or pay for everyday necessities.
4. *Pay off credit cards.* Get in the habit of paying your credit-card bill in full each month. If you have credit-card balances, begin by paying off the balance on the credit card with the highest interest rate.
5. *Apply for a line of credit at your bank, credit union, or financial institution.* As defined in Chapter 18, a line of credit is a preapproved loan and will provide access to cash if needed for future emergencies.
6. *Notify credit-card companies and lenders if you are unable to make payments.* Although not all lenders are willing to help, many will work with you and lower your interest rate, reduce your monthly payment, or extend the time for repayment.
7. *Monitor the value of your investment accounts.* Tracking the value of your stock, mutual fund, and retirement accounts, for example, will help you decide which investments to sell if you need cash for emergencies. Continued evaluation of your investments can also help you reallocate your investments to reduce investment risk.
8. *Consider converting investments to cash to preserve value.* According to most personal finance experts, investors accumulate more money when they use a long-term approach when investing their money. Nevertheless, there may be times when you could sell some of your investments and place the cash in a savings account to weather an economic crisis. For this strategy to work, you must be able to sell when the economy is beginning a downturn and then repurchase quality investments before the economy begins to rebound.

Above all, do not panic. While financial problems are stressful, it helps to stay calm and consider all the options. Keep in mind that bankruptcy should be a last resort. The reason is simple: A bankruptcy will remain on your credit report for up to ten years.

How Securities Are Bought and Sold

3

Understand how securities are bought and sold.

To purchase a Geoffrey Beene sweater, you simply walk into a store that sells these sweaters, choose one, and pay for it. To purchase stocks, bonds, mutual funds, and many other investments, you often work through a brokerage firm. In turn, an employee of the brokerage firm buys or sells securities for you in either the primary or secondary market. The *primary market,* as discussed in Chapter 19, is a market in which an investor purchases financial securities (via an investment bank) directly from the issuer of these securities. The *secondary market* is a market for existing financial securities that are traded between investors. In the secondary market, securities are traded on a securities exchange or in the over-the-counter (OTC) market with the help of an account executive.

Brokerage Firms and Account Executives

An **account executive**—sometimes called a *stockbroker* or *registered representative*—is an individual who buys and sells securities for clients. Before choosing an account executive, you should have already determined your investment goals. Then you must be careful to communicate these goals to the account executive so that she or he can do a better job of advising you.

account executive an individual, sometimes called a *stockbroker* or *registered representative,* who buys and sells securities for clients

A system that works! Located in New York City's financial district, the New York Stock Exchange (NYSE) allows investors to buy and sell stocks and securities every business day. Organized under a buttonwood tree in 1792, today the NYSE is one of the largest and best-known security exchanges in the world.

Choosing an account executive can be difficult for at least three reasons. First, you must trust your account executive to make investment recommendations to enhance your wealth. At the same time, your account executive is interested in your investment trading as a means to swell commission. Unfortunately, some account executives are guilty of *churning*—a practice that generates commissions by excessive buying and selling of securities.

Second, account executives are generally not liable for client losses that result from their recommendations. In fact, most brokerage firms require new clients to sign a statement in which they promise to submit any complaints to an arbitration board. This arbitration clause generally prevents a client from suing an account executive or a brokerage firm.

Third, you must decide whether you need a *full-service* broker or a *discount* broker. A full-service broker usually charges higher commissions but gives you personal investment advice and provides detailed research information. A discount broker simply executes buy and sell orders, usually over the phone or online. Most discount brokers offer no or very little investment advice; you must make your own investment decisions.

Before deciding if you should use a full-service or a discount brokerage firm, you should consider how much help you need when making an investment decision. Many full-service brokerage firms argue that you need a professional to help you make important investment decisions. Although this may be true for some investors, most account executives employed by full-service brokerage firms are too busy to spend unlimited time with you on a one-on-one basis, especially if you are investing a small amount. On the other side, many discount brokerage firms argue that you alone are responsible for making your investment decisions. Furthermore, they argue that discount brokerage firms have both the personnel and research materials to help you to become a better investor.

The Mechanics of a Transaction Once investors have decided on a particular security, most simply telephone their account executive or use the Internet to place a market or limit order. A **market order** is a request that a security be purchased or sold at the current market price. Figure 20.1 illustrates one method of executing a market order to sell a stock listed on the New York Stock Exchange (NYSE) at its current market value. It is also possible for a brokerage firm to match a buy order for a security for one of its customers with a sell order for the same security from another of its customers. Matched orders are not completed through a security exchange or OTC. Regardless of how the security is bought or sold, payment for stocks and many other financial securities generally is required within three business days of the transaction.

A **limit order** is a request that a security be bought or sold at a price equal to or better than (lower for buying, higher for selling) some specified price. Suppose that you place a limit order to *sell* Coca-Cola common stock at $52 per share. Your broker's representative sells the stock only if the price is $52 per share or *more*. If you place a limit order to *buy* Coca Cola at $52, the representative buys it only if the price is $52 per share or *less*. Usually, a limit order is good for one day, one week, one month, or good until canceled.

market order a request that a security be purchased or sold at the current market price

limit order a request that a security be bought or sold at a price that is equal to or better than some specified price

Commissions Most brokerage firms have a minimum commission ranging from $7 to $35 for buying and selling stock. Additional commission charges are based on the number of shares and the value of stock bought and sold.

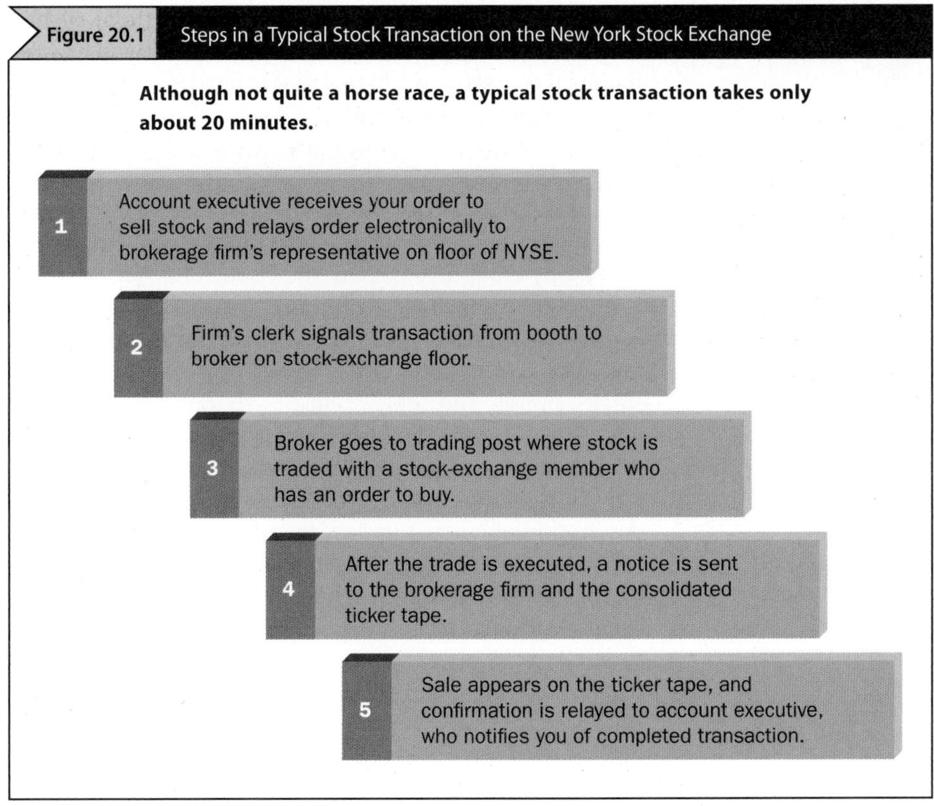

Figure 20.1 Steps in a Typical Stock Transaction on the New York Stock Exchange

Table 20.2 shows typical commission fees charged by online brokerage firms. Generally, online transactions are less expensive when compared with the costs of trading securities through a full-service brokerage firm. As a rule of thumb, full-service brokerage firms charge as much as 1 to 2 percent of the transaction amount. Commissions for trading bonds, commodities, and options are usually lower than those for trading stocks.

For example, the charge for buying or selling a $1,000 corporate bond typically is $5 to $25. With the exception of most mutual funds, the investor generally pays a commission when buying *and* selling securities. When purchasing mutual funds, you usually pay a commission to buy or sell shares. *Reminder*: For fund investments, you will also pay other fees that are usually assessed each year.

It should be apparent that vast sums of money are involved in securities trading. In an effort to protect investors from unfair treatment, both federal and state governments have acted to regulate securities trading.

Regulation of Securities Trading

Government regulation of securities was begun as a response to abusive and fraudulent practices in the sale of stocks, bonds, and other financial securities. Today, with

Table 20.2 Typical Commission Costs Charged by Online Brokerage Firms

	Internet ($)	Interactive Voice-Response Telephone System ($)	Broker-Assisted ($)
TD Ameritrade	9.99	34.99	44.99
E*Trade	12.99	12.99	57.99
Schwab	12.95	17.95	37.95
Scottrade	7.00	17.00	27.00

Source: The BestCashCow.com Web site at http://www.bestcashcow.com (accessed July 13, 2010).

A man in big trouble. While you may not recognize Daniel Bonventre, you can be sure that many investors know this man. Mr. Bonventre was director of operations for Bernard Madoff Investment Securities LLC. He was arrested in 2010 for helping to run an investment scheme that bilked millions of dollars from investors. To prevent this type of investment fraud, securities regulations are enforced by the Securities and Exchange Commission (SEC).

© Jin Lee/Bloomberg via Getty Images

so many news reports of banks with a portfolio of bad loans and of corporations that are in "hot water" over financial reporting problems that range from simple mistakes to out-and-out fraud, the concerns of both government officials and investors have grown.

Today, a regulatory pyramid consisting of four different levels exists to make sure that investors are protected. The U.S. Congress is at the top of the pyramid. Early on, Congress passed the Securities Act of 1933 (sometimes referred to as the Truth in Securities Act). This act provides for full disclosure. **Full disclosure** means that investors should have access to all important facts about stocks, bonds, and other securities so that they can make informed decisions. This act also requires that corporations issuing new securities file a registration statement and publish a prospectus. A **prospectus** is a detailed, written description of a new security, the issuing corporation, and the corporation's top management. Since 1933, Congress has passed additional legislation that includes creating the Securities Investor Protection Corporation to protect investors. Congress also has passed legislation to curb insider-trading abuses. **Insider trading** occurs when insiders—board members, corporate managers, and employees—buy and sell a corporation's stock. Although insiders can buy and sell a corporation's stock, they must disclose their trading activities to the public. More recently, Congress passed the Sarbanes-Oxley Act to improve corporate accountability and financial reporting (see Chapter 17).

On the next level of the regulatory pyramid is the Securities and Exchange Commission (SEC), created in 1934 by the Securities Exchange Act of 1934. The SEC is the agency that enforces federal securities regulations. The SEC also supervises all national exchanges, investment companies, the OTC market, brokerage firms, and just about every other organization involved in trading securities.

On the next level of the regulatory pyramid is individual states. Today, most states require that new security issues be registered with a state agency and that brokers and securities dealers operating within the state be licensed. Most state regulations also provide for the prosecution of individuals accused of the fraudulent sale of stocks, bonds, and other securities.

The foundation and most important level of the regulatory pyramid is self-regulation by securities exchanges and brokerage firms. According to the NYSE, self-regulation—the way the securities industry monitors itself to create a fair and orderly trading environment—begins here.[2] To provide guidelines of ethical behavior, the NYSE has published rules, policies, and standards of conduct. These standards are applied to every member in the NYSE's investment community. The NYSE also conducts a thorough examination of each member firm that does business with the public at least once a year.[3] In addition, there are more than 300 brokerage firms that buy and sell securities for their customers. These firms are responsible for ensuring that their employees are highly trained and meet rigorous ethical standards.

full disclosure requirement that investors should have access to all important facts about stocks, bonds, and other securities so that they can make informed decisions

prospectus a detailed, written description of a new security, the issuing corporation, and the corporation's top management

insider trading the practice of board members, corporate managers, and employees buying and selling a corporation's stock

4

Recognize how you can reduce investment risk and increase investment returns.

Factors that Can Improve Your Investment Decisions

We begin this section with an overview of how portfolio management can reduce investment risk. Then we describe how specific investments can help you to reach your investment goals. A number of the investments listed in Table 20.3 have been discussed. Others have only been mentioned and will be examined in more detail.

Portfolio Management

"How can I choose the right investment?" Good question! Unfortunately, there are no easy answers because your investment goals, age, tolerance for risk, and financial resources are different from those of the next person. To help you to decide what investment is right for you, consider the following: Since 1926, as measured by the Standard and Poor's 500 stock index, stocks have returned on average about 10 percent a year. During the same period, U.S. government bonds have returned about 6 percent.[4] Therefore, why not just invest all your money in stocks or mutual funds that invest in stocks? After all, they offer the largest potential return. In reality, stocks may have a place in every investment portfolio, but there is more to investing than just picking a bunch of stocks or stock mutual funds.

SPOTLIGHT

The More You Make, the More You Can Invest!

Even if you make more money, you still must control spending and manage debt in order to develop a successful investment program. Below are household income levels for U.S. families.

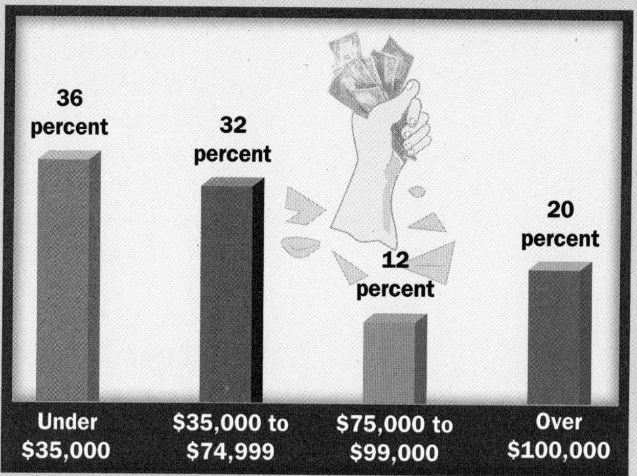

Source: The U.S. Bureau of the Census, *Statistical Abstract of the United States 2010* (Washington, DC: U.S. Government Printing Office), Table 676, http://www.census.gov.

Asset Allocation, the Time Factor, and Your Age

Asset allocation is the process of spreading your money among several different types of investments to lessen risk. Although the term *asset allocation* is a fancy way of saying it, simply put, it really means that you need to diversify and avoid the pitfall of putting all of your eggs in one basket—a common mistake made by investors. Asset allocation is often expressed in percentages. For example, what percentage of my assets do I want to put in stocks and mutual funds? What percentage do I want to put in more conservative investments such as CDs and government bonds? In reality, the answers to these questions are determined by:

- The time your investments have to work for you
- Your age
- Your investment objectives
- Your ability to tolerate risk
- How much you can save and invest each year
- The dollar value of your current investments
- The economic outlook for the economy
- Several other factors

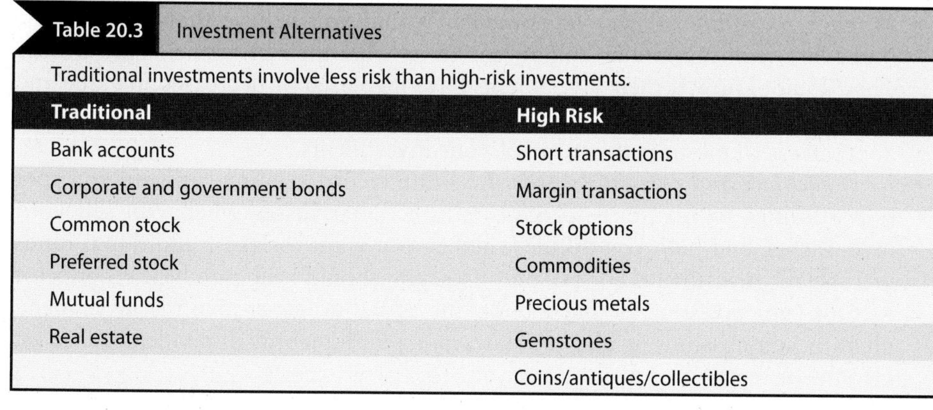

Table 20.3 Investment Alternatives

Traditional investments involve less risk than high-risk investments.

Traditional	High Risk
Bank accounts	Short transactions
Corporate and government bonds	Margin transactions
Common stock	Stock options
Preferred stock	Commodities
Mutual funds	Precious metals
Real estate	Gemstones
	Coins/antiques/collectibles

asset allocation the process of spreading your money among several different types of investments to lessen risk

Two factors—the time your investments have to work for you and your age—are so important they deserve special attention.

The Time Factor The amount of time you have before you need your investment money is crucial. If you can leave your investments alone and let them work for five to ten years or more, then you can invest in stocks, mutual funds, and real estate. On the other hand, if you need your investment money in two years, you probably should invest in short-term government bonds, highly rated corporate bonds, or CDs. By taking a more conservative approach for short-term investments, you reduce the possibility of having to sell your investments at a loss because of depressed market value or a staggering economy. For example, during the recent economic crisis, many retirees who were forced to sell stocks and mutual funds to pay for everyday living expenses lost money. On the other hand, many young investors with long-term investment goals could afford to hold their investments until the price of their securities recovered.

Your Age You also should consider your age when developing an investment program. Younger investors tend to invest a large percentage of their nest egg in growth-oriented investments. On the other hand, older investors tend to choose more conservative investments. As a result, a smaller percentage of their nest egg is placed in growth-oriented investments. How much of your portfolio should be in growth-oriented investments? Well-known personal financial expert Suze Orman suggests that you subtract your age from 110, and the difference is the percentage of your assets that should be invested in growth investments. For example, if you are 30 years old, subtract 30 from 110, which gives you 80. Therefore, 80 percent of your assets should be invested in growth-oriented investments, whereas the remaining 20 percent should be kept in safer conservative investments.[5]

Your Role in the Investment Process

Investors want large returns, yet they are often unwilling to invest the time required to become a good investor. They would not buy a car without a test drive or purchase a home without comparing different homes, but for some unknown reason they invest without doing their homework. The suggestions given here will help you choose investments that will increase in value.

- *Evaluate potential investments.* Keep in mind that successful investors evaluate their investments before making investment decisions. Often, it is useful to keep copies of the material you used to evaluate each investment. Then, when it is time to re-evaluate an existing investment, you will know where to begin your search for current information. Much of the information in the last section of this chapter will help you learn how to evaluate different investment opportunities.
- *Monitor the value of your investments.* Would you believe that some people invest large sums of money and do not know what their investments are worth? They do not know if their investments have increased or decreased in value and if they should sell their investments or continue to hold them. A much better approach is to monitor the value of your investments.
- *Keep accurate and current records.* Accurate record keeping can help you spot opportunities to maximize profits, reduce dollar losses when you sell your investments, and help you decide whether you want to invest additional funds in a specific investment. For tax purposes, you should keep purchase records for each of your investments that include the actual dollar cost of the investment, plus any commissions or fees you paid, along with records of dividends, interest income, or rental income you received.

Traditional Investment Alternatives

5

Identify the advantages and disadvantages of savings accounts, bonds, stocks, mutual funds, and real estate investments.

Bank Accounts

Bank accounts that pay interest—and therefore are investments—include passbook savings accounts, CDs, and interest-bearing accounts. These were discussed in Chapter 18. The interest paid on bank accounts can be withdrawn to serve as income, or it can be left on deposit and increase the value of the bank account and provide for growth. At the time of this publication, one-year CDs were paying between 1 and 2 percent. Although CDs and other bank accounts are risk-free for all practical purposes, many investors often choose other investments because of the potential for larger returns.

Corporate and Government Bonds

In Chapter 19, we discussed the issuing of bonds by corporations to obtain financing. The U.S. government and state and local governments also issue bonds for the same reason. Investors generally choose bonds because they provide a predictable source of income.

Corporate Bonds Because they are a form of long-term debt financing that must be repaid, investment-grade bonds are generally considered a more conservative investment than either stocks or mutual funds. One of the principal advantages of corporate bonds is that they are primarily long-term, income-producing investments. Between the time of purchase and the maturity date, the bondholder will receive interest payments—usually semiannually, or every six months. For example, assume that you purchase a $1,000 bond issued by the rail-based transportation giant CSX Corporation and that the interest rate for this bond is 6 percent. In this situation, you receive interest of $60 ($1,000 × 0.06 = $60) a year from the corporation. CSX pays the interest every six months in $30 installments.

Most beginning investors think that a $1,000 bond is always worth $1,000. In reality, the price of a bond may fluctuate until its maturity date. Changes in the overall interest rates in the economy are the primary cause of most bond price fluctuations. For example, when overall interest rates in the economy are rising, the market value of existing bonds with a fixed interest rate typically declines. Then they may be purchased for less than their face value. By holding such bonds until maturity or until overall interest rates decline (causing the bond's market value to increase), bond owners can sell their bonds for more than they paid for them. In this case, the difference between the purchase price and the selling price is profit and is in addition to annual interest income. However, remember that the price of a corporate bond can decrease and that interest payments and eventual repayment may be a problem for a corporation that encounters financial difficulty. To compare potential risk and return on corporate bond issues, many investors rely on the bond ratings provided by Moody's Investors Service, Inc., Fitch Ratings, and Standard & Poor's Corporation.

Convertible Bonds Some corporations prefer to issue convertible bonds because they carry a lower interest rate than nonconvertible bonds—by about 1 to 2 percent. In return for accepting a lower interest rate, owners of convertible bonds have the opportunity for increased investment growth. For example, assume that you purchase a Medtronic $1,000 corporate bond that is convertible to 18.0474 shares of the company's common stock. This means that you could convert the bond to common stock whenever the price of the company's stock is $55.41 ($1,000 ÷ 18.0474 = $55.41) or higher.[6] However, owners may opt not to convert their bonds to common stock even if the market value of the common stock does increase to $55.41 or more. The reason for not exercising the conversion feature is quite simple. As the market value of the common stock increases, the price of the convertible bond also increases. By not converting to common stock, bondholders enjoy interest income from the bond in addition to the increased bond value caused by the price movement of the common stock.

Government Bonds The federal government sells bonds and securities to finance both the national debt and the government's ongoing activities. Generally, investors choose from five different types of U.S. government bonds:

1. *Treasury bills.* Treasury bills, sometimes called *T-bills,* are sold in minimum units of $100, with additional increments of $100 above the minimum. Although the maturities may be as long as one year, the Treasury Department currently only sells T-bills with 4-, 13-, 26-, and 52-week maturities. T-bills are sold at a discount, and the actual purchase price is less than $100. When the T-bill matures, you receive the $100 maturity value.
2. *Treasury notes.* Treasury notes are issued in $100 units with a maturity of more than one year but not more than ten years. Typical maturities are two, three, five, seven, and ten years. Treasury notes pay interest every six months until maturity.
3. *Treasury inflation-protected securities (TIPS).* TIPS are sold in $100 units and are sold with 5-, 10-, or 30-year maturities. The principal of TIPS increases with inflation and decreases with deflation, as measured by the consumer price index. When TIPS mature, you are paid the adjusted principal or original principal, whichever is greater. TIPS also pay interest twice a year, at a fixed rate.
4. *Treasury bonds.* Treasury bonds are issued in minimum units of $100 and have a 30-year maturity. Like Treasury notes, Treasury bonds pay interest every six months until maturity.
5. *Savings bonds.* Series EE bonds are often called *U.S. savings bonds.* Paper bonds are purchased for one-half their maturity value. Thus, a $100 bond costs $50 when purchased. Electronically issued bonds purchased on the TreasuryDirect Web site (http://www.treasurydirect.gov) are sold at face value. (*Note:* If the interest derived from savings bonds is used to pay qualified college expenses, it may be exempt from federal taxation.)

municipal bond sometimes called a *muni,* a debt security issued by a state or local government

A conservative investment backed by the U.S. government. The securities issued by the U.S. Treasury Department are often referred to as the "safest" investments because they are backed by the full faith and credit of the U.S. government. In order to secure these safe investments, investors must accept smaller returns. In fact, the search for larger returns is why some investors choose stocks, mutual funds, real estate, and other investment alternatives.

© www.treasurydirect.gov

The main reason investors choose U.S. government bonds is that they consider them risk-free. The other side of the coin is that these bonds pay lower interest than most other investments. Interest paid on U.S. government securities is taxable for federal income tax purposes, but is exempt from state and local taxation.

Like the federal government, state and local governments sell bonds to obtain financing. A **municipal bond,** sometimes called a *muni,* is a debt security issued by a state or local government. One of the most important features of municipal bonds is that the interest on them may be exempt from federal taxes. Whether or not the interest on municipal bonds is tax-exempt often depends on how the funds obtained from their sale are used. *Caution: It is your responsibility, as an investor, to determine whether or not the interest paid by municipal* *bonds is taxable. It is also your responsibility to evaluate municipal bonds.* Although most municipal bonds are relatively safe, defaults have occurred in recent years.

Common Stock

As mentioned in Chapter 19, corporations issue common stock to finance their business start-up costs and help pay for expansion and their ongoing business activities. Before investing in stock, keep in mind that corporations do not have to repay the money a stockholder pays for stock. Usually, a stockholder may sell her or his stock to another individual.

How do you make money by buying common stock? Basically, there are three ways: through dividend payments, through an increase in the value of the stock, or through stock splits.

Dividend Payments One of the reasons why many stockholders invest in common stock is *dividend income*. Generally, dividends are paid on a quarterly basis. Although corporations are under no legal obligation to pay dividends, most corporate board members like to keep stockholders happy (and prosperous). A corporation may pay stock dividends in place of—or in addition to—cash dividends. A **stock dividend** is a dividend in the form of additional stock. It is paid to shareholders just as cash dividends are paid—in proportion to the number of shares owned.

stock dividend a dividend in the form of additional stock

capital gain the difference between a security's purchase price and its selling price

market value the price of one share of a stock at a particular time

stock split the division of each outstanding share of a corporation's stock into a greater number of shares

Increase in Dollar Value Another way to make money on stock investments is through capital gains. A **capital gain** is the difference between a security's purchase price and its selling price. To earn a capital gain, you must sell when the market value of the stock is higher than the original purchase price. The **market value** is the price of one share of a stock at a particular time. Let's assume that on June 8, 2007, you purchased 100 shares of General Mills at a cost of $59 a share and that you paid $35 in commission charges, for a total investment of $5,935. Let's also assume that you held your 100 shares until June 8, 2010, and then sold the General Mills stock for $75. Your total return on investment is shown in Table 20.4. You realized a profit of $1,781 because you received dividends totaling $2.61 a share during the three-year period and because the stock's market value increased by $16 a share. Of course, if the stock's market value had decreased, or if the firm's board of directors had voted to reduce or omit dividends, your return would have been less than the total dollar return illustrated in Table 20.4.

Stock Splits Directors of many corporations feel that there is an optimal price range within which their firm's stock is most attractive to investors. When the market value increases beyond that range, they may declare a *stock split* to bring the price down. A **stock split** is the division of each outstanding share of a corporation's stock into a greater number of shares.

The most common stock splits result in one, two, or three new shares for each original share. For example, in 2010, the board of directors of NetLogic, the semiconductor and technology company, approved a two-for-one stock split. After this split, a stockholder who originally owned 100 shares owned 200 shares. The value of an original share was proportionally reduced. In the case of NetLogic, the market value per share was reduced to half the stock's value before the two-for-one stock split. There is no evidence to support that a corporation's long-term performance is improved by a stock split; however, some

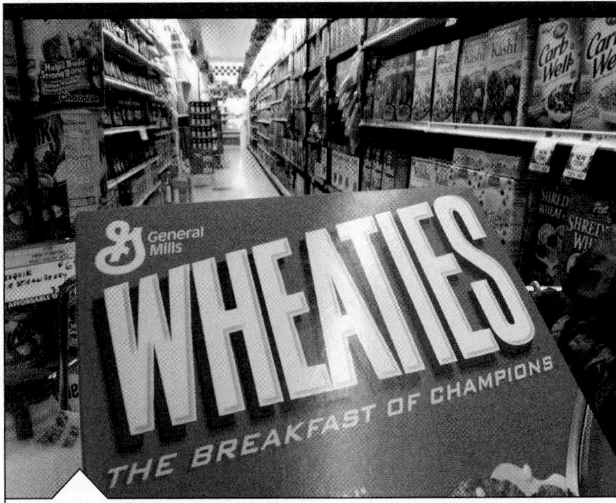

Is General Mills a good investment? To be a good investment, a corporation must increase sales revenues *and* profits. For most companies, the way to accomplish both financial goals is to produce products or services that customers need and want. During the 2007–2010 time period, General Mills, the corporation that manufactures Wheaties—the Breakfast of Champions—was a good (and profitable) investment. To see how much money you could have made by investing in General Mills, see Table 20.4.

Table 20.4	Sample Common-Stock Transaction for General Mills		
Assumptions: 100 shares of common stock purchased on June 8, 2007, for $59 a share; 100 shares sold on June 8, 2010, for $75 a share; dividends for three years total $2.61 a share.			
Cost when Purchased		**Return when Sold**	
100 shares @ $59	$5,900	100 shares @ $75	$7,500
Plus commission	+ 35	Minus commission	− 45
Total investment	$5,935	Total return	$7,455
Transaction Summary			
Total return	$7,455		
Minus total investment	−5,935		
Profit from stock sale	$1,520		
Plus total dividends (three years)	+ 261		
Total return for this transaction	$1,781		

Source: Price data and dividend amounts were taken from the Yahoo Finance Web site, http://finance.yahoo.com (accessed July 14, 2010).

investors do profit from stock splits on a short-term basis. *Be warned: There are no guarantees that the stock will increase in value after a split.* However, the stock may be more attractive to the investing public because of the potential for a rapid increase in dollar value. This attraction is based on the belief that most corporations split their stock only when their financial future is improving and on the upswing.

Merrill Lynch makes it easy to develop an investment program. Beginning investors often feel that the investment world is a jungle because of the different investment alternatives. At Merrill Lynch, professionals can help you choose the right stocks, mutual funds, bonds, and other securities to build an investment program that will achieve not only your investment goals, but also your dreams for the future.

Image courtesy of The Advertising Archives

Preferred Stock

As we noted in Chapter 19, a firm's preferred stockholders must receive their dividends before common stockholders are paid any dividend. Moreover, the preferred-stock dividend amount is specified on the stock certificate. In addition, the owners of preferred stock have first claim, after bond owners and general creditors, on corporate assets if the firm is dissolved or enters bankruptcy. These features make preferred stock a more conservative investment with an added degree of safety and a more predictable source of income when compared with common stock.

In addition, owners of preferred stock may gain through special features offered with certain preferred-stock issues. Owners of *cumulative* preferred stocks are assured that omitted dividends will be paid to them before common stockholders receive any dividends. Owners of *convertible* preferred stock may profit through growth as well as dividends. When the value of a firm's common stock increases, the market value of its *convertible* preferred stock also increases. Convertible preferred stock thus combines the lower risk of preferred stock with the possibility of greater speculative gain through conversion to common stock.

Mutual Funds and Exchange-Traded Funds

For many investors, mutual funds are the investment of choice. There are plenty of funds from which to choose. In 1970, there were only about 400 mutual funds. In January 2010, there were just over 12,000 funds.[7]

According to the Mutual Fund Education Alliance (http://www.mfea.com), a **mutual fund** pools the money of many investors—its shareholders—to invest in a variety of different securities.[8] The major advantages of a mutual fund are its professional management and its diversification, or investment in a wide variety of securities. Most investment companies do everything possible to convince you that they can do a better job of picking securities than you can. In reality, mutual funds are managed by professional fund managers who devote large amounts of time to picking just the "right" securities for their funds' portfolios. *Be warned:* Even the best portfolio managers make mistakes. So you, the investor, must be careful and evaluate different funds before investing. Diversification spells safety because an occasional loss incurred with one security is usually offset by gains from other investments.

Mutual-Fund Basics There are basically three types of mutual funds: (1) closed-end funds, (2) open-end funds, and (3) exchange-traded funds (ETFs). A *closed-end fund* sells shares in the fund to investors only when the fund is originally organized. Once all the shares are sold, an investor must purchase shares from some other investor who is willing to sell them. The mutual fund itself is under no obligation to buy back shares from investors. The investment company sponsoring an *open-end fund* issues and sells new shares to any investor who requests them. It also buys back shares from investors who wish to sell all or part of their holdings.

An **exchange-traded fund (ETF)** is a fund that generally invests in the stocks or other securities contained in a specific stock or securities index. Although most investors think of an ETF as investing in the stocks contained in the Standard & Poor's 500 Stock Index, there are many different types of ETFs available that attempt to track all kinds of indexes including stocks, bonds, and even commodities. Exchange-traded funds tend to mirror the performance of a specific index, moving up or down as the individual stocks or securities contained in the index move up or down.

Like a closed-end fund, shares of an exchange-traded fund are traded on a securities exchange or in the OTC market at any time during the business day. Although exchange-traded funds are similar to closed-end funds, there is an important difference. Most closed-end funds are actively managed, with portfolio managers making the selection of stocks and other securities contained in a closed-end fund. Almost all exchange-traded funds, on the other hand, normally invest in the stocks, bonds, or securities included in a specific index. Therefore, there is less need for a portfolio manager to make investment decisions. Because of passive management, fees associated with owning shares are generally less when compared to both closed-end and open-end funds. Although increasing in popularity, there are only about 775 exchange-traded funds.[9]

The share value for any mutual fund is determined by calculating its net asset value. **Net asset value (NAV)** per share is equal to the current market value of the mutual fund's portfolio minus the mutual fund's liabilities divided by the number of outstanding shares. For most mutual funds, NAV is calculated once a day and is reported in newspapers and financial publications and on the Internet.

Mutual-Fund Sales Charges and Fees With regard to costs, there are two types of mutual funds: load and no-load funds. An individual who invests in a *load fund* pays a sales charge every time he or she purchases shares. This charge may be as high as 8.5 percent. Although many exceptions exist, the average load charge for mutual funds is between 3 and 5 percent. Instead of charging investors a fee when they purchase shares in a mutual fund, some mutual funds charge a *contingent deferred sales fee*. Generally, this fee ranges from 1 to 5 percent of the amount withdrawn during the first five to seven years. Typically, the amount of the contingent deferred sales fee declines each year that you own the fund until there is no withdrawal fee. The purchaser of shares in a *no-load fund* pays no sales charges at all. Although some fund salespeople claim that load funds outperform no-load

mutual fund pools the money of many investors—its shareholders—to invest in a variety of different securities

exchange-traded fund (ETF) a fund that generally invests in the stocks or other securities contained in a specific stock or securities index

net asset value (NAV) current market value of a mutual fund's portfolio minus the mutual fund's liabilities divided by the number of outstanding shares

funds, there is no significant performance difference between funds that charge load charges (commissions) and those that do not.[10] Because no-load funds offer the same type of investment opportunities as load funds, you should investigate them further before deciding which type of mutual fund is best for you.

Mutual funds also collect a yearly management fee of about 0.25 to 1.5 percent of the total dollar amount of assets in the fund. Although fees vary considerably, the average management fee is between 0.50 and 1 percent of the fund's assets. Finally, some mutual funds charge a 12b-1 fee (sometimes referred to as a *distribution fee*) to defray the costs of advertising and marketing the mutual fund. Annual 12b-1 fees are calculated on the value of a fund's assets and cannot exceed 1 percent of the fund's assets. Unlike the onetime sales fees that some mutual funds charge to purchase *or* sell mutual-fund shares, the management fee and the 12b-1 fee are ongoing fees charged each year. Together, all the different management fees; 12b-1 fees, if any; and additional operating costs for a specific fund are referred to as an **expense ratio**. As a guideline, many financial planners recommend that you choose a mutual fund with an expense ratio of 1 percent or less.

Today, mutual funds can also be classified as A, B, or C shares. With A shares, investors pay commissions when they purchase shares in the mutual fund. With B shares, investors pay commissions when money is withdrawn or shares are sold during the first five to seven years. With C shares, investors pay no commissions to buy or sell shares but usually must pay higher ongoing management and 12b-1 fees.

Managed Funds Versus Indexed Funds Most mutual funds are managed funds. In other words, there is a professional fund manager (or team of managers) who chooses the securities that are contained in the fund. The fund manager also decides when to buy and sell securities in the fund.

Instead of investing in a managed fund, some investors choose to invest in an index fund. Why? The answer to this question is simple: Over many years, index funds have outperformed managed funds. The exact statistics vary depending on the year and the specific fund, but a common statistic is that the Standard & Poor's 500 stock index outperforms 80 percent of all mutual funds.[11] Simply put: It is hard to beat an index such as the Standard & Poor's 500. If the individual securities included in an index increase in value, the index goes up. Because an index mutual fund is a mirror image of a specific index, the dollar value of a share in an index fund also increases when the index increases. Unfortunately, the reverse is also true. A second reason why investors choose index funds is the lower fees charged by these passively managed funds. (*Note:* Various indexes are discussed later in this chapter.)

Types of Mutual-Fund Investments Based on the type of securities they invest in, mutual funds generally fall into three broad categories: stocks, bonds, and other. The majority of mutual funds are *stock funds* that invest in stocks issued by small, medium-size, and large corporations that provide investors with income, growth, or a combination of income and growth. *Bond funds* invest in corporate, government, or municipal bonds that provide investors with interest income. The third category includes funds that stress asset allocation and money-market investments or strive for a balance between stocks and bonds. In most cases, the name of the category gives a pretty good clue to the type of investments included in the fund. Typical fund names include:

- Aggressive growth stock funds
- Global stock funds
- Growth stock funds
- High-yield (junk) bond funds
- Income stock funds
- Index funds
- Lifecycle funds
- Long-term U.S. bond funds

expense ratio all the different management fees; 12b-1 fees, if any; and additional operating costs for a specific fund

Ethical Challenges & SUCCESSFUL SOLUTIONS

Balancing Returns with Social Responsibility

How far can "ethical" investing go in achieving social responsibility objectives as well as generating a solid return? Some investors with a social-responsibility agenda steer clear of stocks, bonds, and mutual funds that invest in controversial products such as tobacco, gambling, and guns. Others go even further, avoiding investments in corporations that do business with suppliers or countries that violate human rights. Finding the right balance of social responsibility and financial return is, well, a balancing act as the list of restrictions gets longer, which narrows the number of investment choices.

Even large investors that use investments to advance social responsibility may have difficulty with this balance. For example, the California Public Employees' Retirement System (CalPERS) handles retirement benefits for more than a million people and has billions of dollars to invest. Despite its long record of social responsibility, CalPERS had invested in some real estate deals where financial returns depended on raising rents above regulated levels or ending rent controls for tenants. After being criticized, CalPERS changed its policy to avoid such real-estate investments.

The good news is that more mutual fund companies are offering investments linked to specific social-responsibility goals. Choices include funds such as those holding securities issued by companies recognized for treating employees well, companies involved in alternative energy, and companies that have a low carbon footprint. The experts recommend that before you invest, you should understand your personal goals, study each investment carefully, and make an educated decision that is right for your situation.

Sources: Paul Sullivan, "With Impact Investing, a Focus on More Than Returns," *The New York Times*, April 23, 2010, http://www.nytimes.com; "CalPERS Changes Policy on Real Estate Investing," *Associated Press*, April 19, 2010, http://www.nytimes.com; Jamie Heller, "Calpers Rule Would Limit Evictions at Investments," *The Wall Street Journal*, April 15, 2010, http://www.wsj.com; Richard Marwood, "Industry Voice: Ethical Is Not a Dirty Word," *Investment Adviser*, November 23, 2009, n.p.; Sophia Grene, "The Long Road to Sustainable Investing," *Financial Times*, October 19, 2009, 14.

- Regional funds
- Sector stock funds
- Small-cap stock funds

To help investors obtain their investment objectives, most investment companies now allow shareholders to switch from one fund to another fund within the same family of funds. A **family of funds** exists when one investment company manages a group of mutual funds. For example, shareholders, at their option, can change from the Fidelity International Growth Fund to the Fidelity Growth and Income Fund. Generally, investors may give instructions to switch from one fund to another fund within the same family either in writing, over the telephone, or via the Internet. Charges for exchanges, if any, are small for each transaction.

Real Estate

Real estate ownership represents one of the best hedges against inflation, but like all investments it has its risks. A piece of property in a poor location, for example, can actually decrease in value. Table 20.5 lists some of the many factors you should consider before investing in real estate.

There are, of course, disadvantages to any investment, and real estate is no exception. If you want to sell your property, you must find an interested buyer with the ability to obtain enough money to complete the transaction. Finding such a buyer can be difficult if loan money is scarce, the real estate market is in a decline, or you overpaid for a piece of property. For example, many real estate investors were forced to hold some properties longer than they wanted because buyers could not obtain financing during the recent economic crisis. If you are forced to hold your investment longer than you originally planned, taxes, interest, and installment payments can be a heavy burden. As a rule, real estate increases in value and eventually sells at a profit, but there are no guarantees. The degree of your success depends on how well you evaluate different alternatives.

family of funds a group of mutual funds managed by one investment company

Table 20.5	Real Estate Checklist	
Although real estate offers one of the best hedges against inflation, not all property increases in value. Many factors should be considered before investing in real estate.		
Evaluation of Property	**Inspection of the Surrounding Neighborhood**	**Other Factors**
Is the property priced competitively with similar property?	What are the present zoning requirements?	Why are the present owners selling the property?
What type of financing, if any, is available?	Is the neighborhood's population increasing or decreasing?	How long will you have to hold the property before selling it to someone else?
How much are the taxes?	What is the average income of people in the area?	How much profit can you reasonably expect to obtain?
How much will it cost to repair or remodel a property?	What is the state of repair of surrounding property? Do most of the buildings and homes need repair?	Is there a chance that the property value will decrease?

high-risk investment an investment made in the uncertain hope of earning a relatively large profit in a short time

buying long buying stock with the expectation that it will increase in value and then can be sold at a profit

selling short the process of selling stock that an investor does not actually own but has borrowed from a brokerage firm and will repay at a later date

6

Describe high-risk investment techniques.

High-Risk Investment Techniques

A **high-risk investment** is one made in the uncertain hope of earning a relatively large profit in a short time. (See the high-risk investment category in Table 20.3.) Although all investments have some risk, some investments become high-risk because of the methods used by investors to earn a quick profit. These methods can lead to large losses as well as to impressive gains. They should not be used by anyone who does not fully understand the risks involved. We begin this section with a discussion of selling short. Then we examine margin transactions and other high-risk investments.

A high-risk investment that paid off. Vincent Zurzolo, chief operating officer of Metropolis Collectibles, holds a 1938 Action comic book that sold for $1 million in 2010. This comic book, which introduced Superman to the world, was a "super" investment. Because many high-risk investments like this collectible are too speculative for most people, most long-term investors choose the more traditional investments described in this chapter.

© AFP PHOTO / TIMOTHY A. CLARY/Newscom

Selling Short

Normally, you buy stocks expecting that they will increase in value and then can be sold at a profit. This procedure is referred to as **buying long**. However, many securities decrease in value for various reasons. Consider what happened to the values of many stocks during the economic crisis. Because of the nation's depressed economy, many corporations also experienced a financial downturn. Many of these same corporations experienced lower-than-expected sales revenues and profits. In some cases, corporations actually posted losses during this same time period. For the firms that were able to weather the economic storm, their stock values were quite a bit lower than they were before the economic downturn. When this type of situation occurs, you can use a procedure called *selling short* to make a profit when the price of an individual stock is falling. **Selling short** is the process of selling stock that an investor does not actually own but has borrowed from a brokerage firm and will repay at a later date. The idea is to sell at today's higher price and then buy later at a lower price. To make a profit from a short transaction, you must proceed as follows:

1. Arrange to borrow a certain number of shares of a particular stock from a brokerage firm.
2. Sell the borrowed stock immediately, assuming that the price of the stock will drop in a reasonably short time.
3. After the price drops, buy the same number of shares that were sold in step 2.
4. Give the newly purchased stock to the brokerage firm in return for the stock borrowed in step 1.

Your profit is the difference between the amount received when the stock is sold in step 2 and the amount paid for the stock in step 3. For example, assume that you think Barnes & Noble stock is overvalued at $20 a share. You also believe that the stock will decrease in value over the next three to four months. You call your broker and arrange to borrow 100 shares of Barnes & Noble stock (step 1). The broker then sells your borrowed stock for you at the current market price of $20 a share (step 2). In addition, suppose that three months later the Barnes & Noble stock has dropped to $13 a share. You instruct your broker to purchase 100 shares of Barnes & Noble stock at the current lower price (step 3). The newly purchased Barnes & Noble stock is given to the brokerage firm to repay the borrowed stock (step 4). In this example, you made $700 by selling short ($2,000 selling price − $1,300 purchase price = $700 profit).[12] Naturally, the $700 profit must be reduced by the commissions you paid to the broker for buying and selling the Barnes & Noble stock.

People often ask where the broker obtains the stock for a short transaction. The broker probably borrows the stock from other investors who have purchased Barnes & Noble stock and left stock certificates on deposit with the brokerage firm. As a result, the person who is selling short must pay any dividends declared on the borrowed stock. The most obvious danger when selling short, of course, is that a loss can result if the stock's value increases instead of decreases.

Buying Stock on Margin

An investor buys stock *on margin* by borrowing part of the purchase price, usually from a stock brokerage firm. The **margin requirement** is the portion of the price of a stock that cannot be borrowed. This requirement is set by the Federal Reserve Board.

Today, the current margin requirement is 50 percent, which means you can borrow up to 50 percent of the cost of a stock purchase. Some brokerage firms require that you deposit more cash, which reduces the percentage that can be borrowed. However, why would investors want to buy stock on margin? Simply because they can buy up to twice as much stock that way. Suppose that an investor expects the market price of a share of common stock of Duke Energy Corporation—a U.S. energy company—to increase in the next three to four months. Let us say that this investor has enough money to purchase 200 shares of the stock. However, if the investor buys on margin, he or she can purchase an additional 200 shares for a total of 400 shares. If the price of Duke Energy's stock increases by $8 per share, the investor's profit will be $1,600 ($8 × 200 = $1,600) if he or she pays cash. But it will be $3,200 ($8 × 400 = $3,200) if he or she buys the stock using margin. By buying more shares on margin, the investor will earn more profit (less the interest he or she pays on the borrowed money and customary commission charges).

Financial leverage—a topic covered in Chapter 19—is the use of borrowed funds to increase the return on an investment. When margin is used as leverage, the investor's profit is earned by both the borrowed money and the investor's own money. The investor retains all the profit and pays interest only for the temporary use of the borrowed funds. Note that the stock purchased on margin serves as collateral for the borrowed funds. Before you become a margin investor, you should consider two factors. First, if the market price of the purchased stock does not increase as quickly

margin requirement the portion of the price of a stock that cannot be borrowed

as expected, interest costs mount and eventually drain your profit. Second, if the price of the margined stock falls, the leverage works against you. That is, because you have purchased twice as much stock, you lose twice as much money.

If the value of a stock you bought on margin decreases to approximately 60 percent of its original price, you may receive a *margin call* from the brokerage firm. You then must provide additional cash or securities to serve as collateral for the borrowed money. If you cannot provide additional collateral, the stock is sold, and the proceeds are used to pay off the loan and commissions. Any funds remaining after the loan and commissions are paid off are returned to you.

Other High-Risk Investments

We have already discussed two high-risk investments—selling short and margin transactions. Other high-risk investments include the following:

- Stock options
- Derivatives
- Commodities
- Precious metals
- Gemstones
- Coins
- Antiques and collectibles

Without exception, investments of this kind are normally referred to as high-risk investments for one reason or another. For example, the gold market has many unscrupulous dealers who sell worthless gold-plated lead coins to unsuspecting, uninformed investors. It pays to be careful. *Although investments in this category can lead to large dollar gains, they should not be used by anyone who does not fully understand all the potential risks involved.*

Use financial information to evaluate investment alternatives.

Sources of Financial Information

A wealth of information is available to investors. Sources include the Internet, newspapers, professional advisory services, brokerage firm reports, business periodicals, corporate reports, and securities averages.

The Internet

By using the Internet, investors can access a wealth of information on most investment and personal finance topics. For example, you can obtain interest rates for CDs; current price information for stocks, bonds, and mutual funds; and experts' recommendations to buy, hold, or sell an investment. You can even trade securities online.

Because the Internet makes so much information available, you need to use it selectively. One of the Web search engines such as Yahoo! (http://www.yahoo.com) or Google (http://www.google.com) can help you locate the information you really need. These search engines allow you to do a word search for the personal finance or investment alternative you want to explore. Why not take a look? To access a search engine, enter the Web site address and then type in a key term such as *personal finance* or *financial planning* and see the results.

Corporations; brokerage firms; investment companies that sponsor mutual funds; real estate brokers and agents; and federal, state, and local governments also have Web sites where you can obtain valuable investment information. You may want to explore these Web sites for two reasons. First, they are easily accessible. All you have to do is type in the Web address or use a search engine to locate the site. Second, the information on these sites may be more up-to-date than printed material obtained from published sources.

In addition, you can access professional advisory services—a topic discussed later in this section—for information on stocks, bonds, mutual funds, and other investment alternatives. Although some of the information provided by these services is free, there is a charge for the more detailed information you may need to evaluate an investment.

Financial Coverage of Securities Transactions

Many local newspapers carry several pages of business news, including reports of securities transactions. *The Wall Street Journal* (published on weekdays) and *Barron's* (published once a week) are devoted almost entirely to financial and economic news. Both include coverage of transactions on major securities exchanges.

Because transactions involving stocks, bonds, and mutual funds are reported differently, we shall examine each type of report separately.

Common and Preferred Stocks Stock transactions are reported in tables that usually look like the top section of Figure 20.2. Stocks are listed alphabetically. Your first task is to move down the table to find the stock you are interested in. To read the *stock quotation,* you read across the table. The highlighted line in Figure 20.2 gives detailed information about common stock issued by Aflac—the insurance company with the talking duck.

Bonds Although some newspapers and financial publications provide limited information on certain corporate and government bond issues, it is usually easier to obtain more detailed information on a greater number of bond issues by accessing the Internet. Regardless of the source, bond prices are quoted as a percentage of the face value, which is usually $1,000. Thus, to find the current price, you must multiply the face value ($1,000) by the quotation. For example, a price quoted as 84 translates to a selling price of $840 ($1,000 × 0.84 = $840). Detailed information obtained from the Yahoo! Finance Web site for a $1,000 AT&T corporate bond, which pays 5.50 percent interest and matures in 2018, is provided in Figure 20.3.

Sustaining the Planet

GreenMoney Journal

The *GreenMoney Journal* has been reporting on the business side of sustainability since 1992, including coverage of eco-friendly stocks and mutual funds as well as industry analysis and commentary. Take a look: http://www.greenmoneyjournal.com.

GREENMONEY JOURNAL
FROM THE STOCKMARKET TO THE SUPERMARKET
investing in green since 1992

Summer 2010 issue
volume 18
issue 4
number 76

GREENMONEY JOURNAL E-News
Subscribe to FREE Quarterly E-News & Info from SR business colleagues

Investing in Socially Responsible Mutual Funds
SocialFunds.com

Home | Archives | Sponsors | Links | Contact Us | Advertising | SRI News

GREEN EVENTS CALENDAR

SocialFunds.com The Largest Personal Finance Site Devoted to Socially Responsible Investing

Click here and learn more about our Socially Responsible Deposit Fund!

GreenMoney Journal - publishing since 1992

Summer 2010 issue

Sustainable Business - Green Building & Design

Building on a Solid Foundation
by Cliff Feigenbaum and Ted Ketcham

It is finally summer and a great time to revisit the topics of Green Building and Renewable Energy as part of our ongoing Sustainable Business series. Happily, this all coincides with the recent completion of the ultra-green house built in Santa Fe called The Emerald Home. Beyond its emphasis on energy efficiency, the home sets the bar in five other categories, including water efficiency, indoor air quality, resource efficiency, site impact and homeowner education. Built by Faren Dancer, The Emerald Home also sets a standard for future custom home building and is projected to receive the prestigious LEED for Homes "Platinum" designation. I toured the home last year and saw how they incorporated and synthesized various approaches to build the most energy efficient home possible. For more information, visit http://www.theemeraldhomesantafe.com

It was 25 years ago when I came to really appreciate architecture and design. It began at an exhibition of visionary architect Frank Lloyd Wright's work and continued with books and calendars every year featuring his homes and designs. I eventually joined the Frank Lloyd Wright Society and visited many of his homes around the country. Then I began to see and read about the works of green architect and designer William McDonough and to hear corporate sustainability leader Ray Anderson's speeches. I encountered the brilliant Janine Benyus and her Biomimicry work at a Bioneers Conference. Her presentation and book took me to a new understanding of what designs in nature accomplish daily and how those designs can be adapted for positive human endeavors. And most recently I've been impressed by Ed Mazria's work developing the Architecture 2030 Challenge. To learn about his Blueprint for millions of green jobs and huge energy savings measures in the building sector go to http://www.architecture2030.org

Mutual Funds Purchases and sales of shares of mutual funds are reported in tables like the one shown in Figure 20.4. As in reading stock quotations, your first task is to move down the table to find the mutual fund you are interested in. Then, to find the mutual-fund price quotation, read across the table. Figure 20.4 gives information for the Vanguard 500 Index mutual fund.

Other Sources of Financial Information

In addition to the Internet and newspaper coverage, other sources, which include professional advisory services, brokerage firm reports, business periodicals, and corporate reports, offer detailed and varied information about investment alternatives.

Professional Advisory Services For a fee, various professional advisory services provide information about investments. Information from these services may also be available at university and public libraries.

As discussed earlier in this chapter, Moody's, Standard & Poor's, and Fitch Ratings provide information that can be used to determine the quality and risk

Figure 20.2 Reading Stock Quotations

Reproduced at the top of the figure is a portion of the stock quotations listed in *The Wall Street Journal*. At the bottom is an enlargement of the same information. The numbers above each of the enlarged columns correspond to the numbered entries in the list of explanations that appears in the middle of the figure.

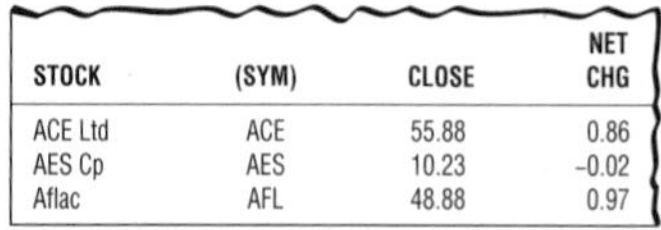

STOCK	(SYM)	CLOSE	NET CHG
ACE Ltd	ACE	55.88	0.86
AES Cp	AES	10.23	–0.02
Aflac	AFL	48.88	0.97

1. Name (often abbreviated) of the corporation: Aflac
2. Ticker symbol or letters that identify a stock for trading: AFL
3. Close is the price paid in the last transaction of the day: $48.88
4. Difference between the price paid for the last share sold today and the price paid for the last share sold on the previous day: 0.97 (in Wall Street terms, Aflac "closed up $0.97" on this day).

1	2	3	4
STOCK	(SYM)	CLOSE	NET CHG
ACE Ltd	ACE	55.88	0.86
AES Cp	AES	10.23	–0.02
Aflac	AFL	48.88	0.97

Source: *The Wall Street Journal*, July 14, 2010, C4.

Figure 20.3 Reading Bond Quotations

Reproduced at the top of the figure is bond information obtained from the Yahoo! Finance Web site. The numbers beside each line correspond to numbered entries in the list of explanations that appears at the bottom of the figure.

AT&T INC	
OVERVIEW	
1. Price	113.21
2. Coupon (%)	5.500
3. Maturity Date	1-Feb-2018
4. Yield to Maturity (%)	3.489
5. Current Yield (%)	4.858
6. Fitch Ratings	A
7. Coupon Payment Frequency	Semi-annual
8. First Coupon Date	1-Aug-2008
9. Type	Corporate
10. Callable	No

1. Price quoted as a percentage of the face value: $1,000 × 113.21% = $1,132.10
2. Coupon (%) is the rate of interest: 5.500 percent
3. Maturity Date is the date when bondholders will receive repayment: February 1, 2018
4. Yield to Maturity (%) takes into account the relationship among a bond's maturity value, the time to maturity, the current price, and the amount of interest: 3.489 percent
5. Current Yield (%) is determined by dividing the dollar amount of annual interest by the current price of the bond: ($55 ÷ $1,132.10 = 0.04858 = 4.858 percent)
6. Fitch Ratings is used to assess risk associated with this bond: A
7. Coupon Payment Frequency tells bondholders how often they will receive interest payments: Semi-annual
8. First Coupon Date: August 1, 2008
9. Type: Corporate
10. Callable: No

Source: The Yahoo! Finance bond Web site at http://bonds.yahoo.com (accessed July 18, 2010).

Figure 20.4 Reading Mutual-Fund Quotations

Reproduced at the top of the figure is a portion of the mutual-fund quotations as reported by *The Wall Street Journal*. At the bottom is an enlargement of the same information. The numbers above each of the enlarged columns correspond to numbered entries in the list of explanations that appears in the middle of the figure.

FUND	NAV	NET CHG	YTD %RET
Vanguard 500 Index	100.93	+1.54	-0.8
DevMktInst	8.86	+0.16	NS
EmerMktr	25.54	+0.20	-1.4
Europe	23.72	+0.58	-8.6

1. The name of the mutual fund: Vanguard 500 Index
2. The net asset value (NAV) is the value of one share of the Vanguard 500 Index Fund: $100.93
3. The difference between the net asset value today and the net asset value on the previous trading day: 1.54 (in Wall Street terms, the "Vanguard 500 Index fund closed up $1.54" on this day)
4. The YTD% RET gives the total return for the Vanguard 500 Index fund for the year to date: –0.8%

1	2	3	4
FUND	NAV	NET CHG	YTD %RET
Vanguard 500 Index	100.93	+1.54	–0.8
DevMktInst	8.86	+0.16	NS
EmerMktr	25.54	+0.20	–1.4
Europe	23.72	+0.58	-8.6

Source: ***The Wall Street Journal*, July 14, 2010, C13.**

associated with bond issues. Standard & Poor's, Mergent, Inc., and Value Line also rate the companies that issue common and preferred stock. Each investor service provides detailed financial reports. Take a look at the Mergent's research report for The Coca-Cola Company illustrated in Figure 20.5. Notice that there are six main sections that provide financial data, summary information about the company's business operations, recent developments, prospects, and other valuable information. Research reports published by Standard & Poor's and Value Line are like Mergent's report and provide similar information.

A number of professional advisory services provide detailed information on mutual funds. Morningstar, Inc., Standard & Poor's, Lipper Analytical Services, and Value Line are four widely tapped sources for such information. Although some information may be free, a fee is generally charged for more detailed research reports. In addition, various mutual-fund newsletters supply financial information to subscribers for a fee.

Brokerage Firm Analysts' Reports Brokerage firms employ financial analysts to prepare detailed reports on individual corporations and their securities. Such reports are based on the corporation's sales, profits or losses, management, and planning, plus other information on the company, its industry, demand for its products, its efforts to develop new products, and the current economic environment. The reports, which may include buy or sell recommendations, are usually provided free

Figure 20.5 Mergent's Research Report for The Coca-Cola Company

A research report from Mergent's is divided into six main parts that describe not only the financial condition of a company but also its history and outlook for the future.

COCA-COLA CO. (THE)

Exchange	Symbol	Price	52Wk Range	Yield	P/E	Div Acheiver
NYS	KO	$55.00 (3/31/2010)	59.11-42.24	3.20	18.77	47 Years

Interim Earnings (Per Share)

Qtr.	Mar	Jun	Sep	Dec
2005	0.42	0.72	0.54	0.37
2006	0.47	0.78	0.62	0.29
2007	0.54	0.80	0.71	0.52
2008	0.64	0.61	0.81	0.41
2009	0.58	0.88	0.81	0.66

Interim Dividends (Per Share)

Amt	Deci	Ex	Rec	Pay
0.41Q	04/23/2009	06/11/2009	06/15/2009	07/01/2009
0.41Q	07/23/2009	09/11/2009	09/15/2009	10/01/2009
0.41Q	10/22/2009	11/27/2009	12/01/2009	12/15/2009
0.41Q	02/18/2010	03/11/2010	03/15/2010	04/01/2010

Indicated Div: $1.76 (Div. Reinv. Plan)

Valuation Analysis		**Institutional Holding**
Forecast EPS	$3.42 (04/21/2010)	No of Institutions 1518
Market Cap	$126.7 Billion	Shares
Book Value	$24.8 Billion	1,720,219,648
Price/Book	5.11	% Held
Price/Sales	4.09	60.39

Business Summary: Beverages (MIC: 1.2.2 SIC: 2086 NAIC: 312111)

Coca-Cola is an owner and marketer of nonalcoholic beverage brands as well as a manufacturer, distributor and marketer of concentrates and syrups used to produce nonalcoholic beverages. Co. owns or licenses and markets over 500 nonalcoholic beverage brands, primarily sparkling beverages including Diet Coke. Fanta and Sprite as well as still beverages such as waters, enhanced waters, juices and juice drinks, ready-to-drink teas and coffees, and energy and sports drinks. Co. also manufactures, or authorizes bottling partners to manufacture, fountain syrups, which Co. sells to fountain retailers such as restaurants and convenience stores or to fountain wholesalers or bottlers.

Recent Developments: For the year ended Dec 31 2009, net income increased 17.6% to US$6.91 billion from US$5.87 billion in the prior year. Revenues were US$30.99 billion, down 3.0% from US$31.94 billion the year before. Operating income was US$8.23 billion versus US$8.45 billion in the prior year, a decrease of 2.5%. Direct operating expenses declined 2.5% to US$11.09 billion from US$11.37 billion in the comparable period the year before. Indirect operating expenses decreased 3.7% to US$11.67 billion from US$12.12 billion in the equivalent prior-year period.

Prospects: On Feb 25 2010, Co. signed an agreement with Coca-Cola Enterprises Inc. (CCE) to acquire CCE's North American operations for $3.40 billion and assumption of $8.90 billion of CCE debt. Simultaneously, Co. reached an agreement to sell its ownership interests in its Norway bottling operation Coca-Cola Drikker AS, and its Sweden bottling operation, Coca-Cola Drycker Sverige AB, to the new CCE entity for $822.0 million. Co. expects the transactions will close in the fourth quarter of 2010. Accordingly, Co. will generate immediate operational cost savings of $350.0 million over four years, and the transactions are expected to be accretive to earnings per share on a fully diluted basis by 2012.

Financial Data (US$ in Thousands)	12/31/2009	12/31/2008	12/312007	12/31/2006	12/31/2005	12/31/2004	12/31/2003	12/31/2002
Earnings Per Share	2.93	2.49	2.57	2.16	2.04	2.00	1.77	1.23
Cash Flow Per Share	3.54	3.26	3.09	2.54	2.69	2.45	2.22	1.91
Tang Book Value Per Share	5.20	3.45	4.11	5.08	5.29	5.02	4.14	3.34
Dividends Per Share	1.640	1.520	1.360	1.240	1.120	1.000	0.880	0.800
Dividend Payout %	55.97	61.04	52.92	57.41	54.90	50.00	49.72	65.04
Income Statement								
Total Revenue	30,990,000	31,944,000	28,857,000	24,088,000	23.104,000	21,962,000	21,044,00	19,564,000
EBITDA	9,294,000	9,430,000	8,404,000	7,266,000	6,767,000	6,355,000	5,758,000	5,719,000
Depn & Amortn	1,023,000	1,012,000	979,000	763,000	752,000	715,000	667,000	614,000
Income Before Taxes	8,165,000	8,313,000	7,205,000	6,476,000	6,010,000	5,601,000	5,089,000	5,115,000
Income Taxes	2,040,000	1,632,000	1,892,000	1,498,000	1,818,000	1,375,000	1,148,000	1,523,000
Net Income	6,824,000	5,807,000	5,981,000	5,080,000	4,872,000	4,847,000	4,347,000	3,050,000
Average Shares	2,329,000	2,336,000	2,331,000	2,350,000	2,393,000	2,429,000	2,462,000	2,483,000
Balance sheet								
Current Assets	17,551,000	12,176,000	12,105,000	8,441,000	10,250,000	12,094,000	8,396,000	7,352,000
Total Assets	48,671,000	40,519,000	43,269,000	29,963,000	29,427,000	31,327,000	27,342,000	24,501,000
Current Liabilities	13,721,000	12,988,000	13,225,000	8,890,000	9,836,000	10,971,000	7,886,000	7,341,000
Long-Term Obligations	5,059,000	2,781,000	3,277,000	1,314,000	1,154,000	1,157,000	2,517,000	2,701,000
Total Liabilities	23,872,000	20,047,000	21,525,000	13,043,000	13,072,00	15,392,000	13,252,000	12,701,000
Stockholders' Equity	24,799,000	20,472,000	21,744,000	16,920,000	16,355,000	15,935,000	14,090,000	11,800,000
Shares Outstanding	2,303,000	2,312,000	2,318,000	2,318,000	2,369,000	2,409,339	2,441,531	2,470,979
Statistical Record								
Return on Assets %	15.30	13.82	16.33	17.11	16.04	16.48	16.77	13.00
Return on Equity %	30.15	27.44	30.94	30.53	30.18	32.20	33.58	26.33
EBITDA Margin %	29.99	29.52	29.12	30.16	29.29	28.94	27.36	29.23
Net Margin %	22.02	18.18	20.73	21.09	21.09	22.07	20.66	15.59
Asset Turnover	0.69	0.76	0.79	0.81	0.76	0.75	0.81	0.83
Current Ratio	1.28	0.94	0.92	0.95	1.04	1.10	1.06	1.00
Debt to Equity	0.20	0.14	0.15	0.08	0.07	0.07	0.18	0.23
Price Range	59.11-37.85	65.56-41.01	64.09-45.89	49.00-40.09	45.25-40.31	53.00-38.65	50.75-37.07	57.64-43.47
P/E Ratio	20.17-12.92	26.33-16.47	24.94-17.86	22.69-18.56	22.18-19.76	26.50-19.32	28.67-20.94	46.86-35.34
Average Yield %	3.36	2.82	2.53	2.83	2.62	2.15	2.00	1.61

Address: One Coca-Cola Plaza, Atlanta, GA 30313
Telephone: 404-676-2121
Fax: 404-676-6792

Web Site: www.coca-cola.com
Officers: Ahmet Muhtar Kent - Chairman, President Chief Executive Officer Gary P. Fayard - Executive Vice President, Chief Financial Officer

Auditors: Ernst & Young LL.P
Investor Contact: 404-676-5766
Transfer Agents: ComputerShare Investor Services. Providence, RI

to the clients of full-service brokerage firms. Brokerage firm reports may also be available from discount brokerage firms, although they may charge a fee.

Business Periodicals Business magazines such as *Bloomberg BusinessWeek, Fortune,* and *Forbes* provide not only general economic news but also detailed financial information about individual corporations. Trade or industry publications such as *Advertising Age* include information about firms in a specific industry. News magazines such as *U.S. News & World Report, Time,* and *Newsweek* feature financial news regularly. *Money, Kiplinger's Personal Finance Magazine, Smart Money,* and similar magazines provide information and advice designed to improve your investment skills. These periodicals are available at libraries and are sold at newsstands and by subscription. Many of these same periodicals sponsor an online Web site that may contain all or selected articles that are contained in the print version. Why not check out the investing information available from *BusinessWeek Online* at http://www.businessweek.com or *Kiplinger's Personal Finance Magazine* at http://www.kiplinger.com.

Corporate Reports Publicly held corporations must publish annual reports which include a description of the company's performance, information about the firm's products or services, and detailed financial statements that readers can use to evaluate the firm's actual performance. There should also be a letter from the accounting firm that audited the corporation. As mentioned in Chapter 17, an audit does not guarantee that a company has not "cooked" the books, but it does imply that the company has followed generally accepted accounting principles to report revenues, profits, assets, liabilities, and other financial information.

In addition, a corporation issuing a new security must—by law—prepare a prospectus and ensure that copies are distributed to potential investors. A corporation's prospectus and its annual and quarterly reports are available to the general public.

Security Averages

Investors often gauge the stock market through the security averages reported in newspapers and on television news programs. A **security average** (or **security index**) is an average of the current market prices of selected securities. Over a period of time, these averages indicate price trends, but they do not predict the performance of individual investments. At best, they can give the investor a "feel" for what is happening to investment prices generally. Today, there are averages for stocks, mutual funds, bonds, mortgage rates, real estate, and most other investments.

Before they can start investing, most people have to decide on a career and obtain a job that will provide the money needed to finance an investment program. To help you find the right job (and the money needed to fund an investment program), read Appendix A where we provide information that can help you to explore different career options (see text Web site).

security average (or security index) an average of the current market prices of selected securities

return to inside business

Raymond James

Raymond James has nearly five decades of experience helping individual investors and small business owners achieve their financial goals as well as providing corporations with investment banking services of all kinds. The company itself went public in 1983 and today its stock is traded on the NYSE under the symbol RJF.

As a full-service brokerage firm, Raymond James specializes in personalized attention. Customers can choose to sit down with their advisors, call with questions, or go online to check their accounts. "Our business is people and their financial well-being" is the company's mission statement, and advisors live that mission every day by delivering service with integrity, educating customers about their investment options, striving for excellence in every detail, and giving back to their communities through philanthropy and volunteerism.

Questions

1. Would you choose a full-service brokerage firm such as Raymond James or a discount or deep-discount brokerage firm when investing for a long-term goal such as retirement? Explain your answer.
2. As an investor, what questions would you like to ask a Raymond James financial advisor? How do these questions relate to your financial goals?

SUMMARY

Summary

CHAPTER REVIEW

1 Explain why you should manage your personal finances and develop a personal investment program.

Many personal finance experts recommend that you begin the process of managing your money by determining your current financial condition. The first step often is to construct a personal balance sheet and a personal income statement. You can also construct a personal budget. Before you begin investing, you must manage your credit card debts. For most people, the next step is to formulate realistic investment goals. A personal investment program then is designed to implement these goals. Many financial planners also suggest that the investor should establish an emergency fund equivalent to at least three months' living expenses. Then additional funds may be invested according to the investment program. Finally, all investments should be monitored carefully, and if necessary, the investment program should be modified.

2 Describe how the factors of safety, risk, income, growth, and liquidity affect your investment program.

Depending on their particular investment goals, investors seek varying degrees of safety, risk, income, growth, and liquidity from their investments. Safety is, in essence, freedom from the risk of loss. Generally, the greater the risk, the greater should be the potential return on an investment. To determine how much risk you are willing to assume, many investors calculate the rate of return. It is also possible to compare the rate of return for different investments that offer more or less risk. Income is the periodic return from an investment. Growth is an increase in the value of the investment. Liquidity is the ease with which an asset can be converted to cash.

3 Understand how securities are bought and sold.

Securities may be purchased in either the primary or the secondary market. The secondary market involves transactions for existing securities that are currently traded between investors and are usually bought and sold through a securities exchange or the OTC market. If you invest in securities, chances are that you will use the services of an account executive who works for a brokerage firm. It is also possible to use a discount broker or trade securities online with a computer. Both a market order and a limit order can be used to purchase stocks on a securities exchange or in the OTC market. Full-service brokerage firms usually charge higher commissions than discount brokerage firms. With the exception of mutual funds, you generally pay a commission to buy *and* sell stocks, bonds, commodities, and options. Today, a regulatory pyramid consisting of four different levels exists to make sure that investors are protected. The U.S. Congress, the Securities and Exchange Commission (SEC), individual states, and securities exchanges and brokerage firms are all involved in regulating the securities industry.

 Recognize how you can reduce investment risk and increase investment returns.

Asset allocation is the process of spreading your money among several different types of investments to lessen risk. Two other factors—the time your investments have to work for you and your age—should also be considered before deciding where to invest your money. To reduce investment risk and increase the returns on your investments, you should evaluate potential investments before investing your money, monitor the value of your investments on a regular basis, and keep accurate and current records.

5 Identify the advantages and disadvantages of savings accounts, bonds, stocks, mutual funds, and real estate investments.

In this section, we examined traditional investments that include bank accounts, corporate bonds, government bonds, common stock, preferred stock, mutual funds, and real estate. Although bank accounts and bonds can provide investment growth, they are generally purchased by investors who seek a predictable source of income. Both corporate and government bonds are a form of debt financing. As a result, bonds are generally considered a more conservative investment than stocks or most mutual funds. With stock investments, investors can make money through dividend payments, an increase in the value of the stock, or stock splits. The major advantages of mutual-fund investments are professional management and diversification. Today, there are mutual funds to meet just about any conceivable investment objective. The success of real estate investments is often tied to how well each investment alternative is evaluated.

 Describe high-risk investment techniques.

High-risk investment techniques can provide greater returns, but they also entail greater risk of loss. You can make money by selling short when the market value of a financial security is decreasing. Selling short is the process of selling stock that an investor does not actually own but has borrowed from a brokerage firm and will repay at a later date. An investor can also buy stock on margin by borrowing part of the purchase price, usually from a stock brokerage firm. Because you can purchase up to twice as much stock by using margin, you can increase your return on investment as long as the stock's market value increases. Other high-risk investments include stock options, derivatives, commodities, precious metals, gemstones, coins, and antiques and collectibles.

 Use financial information to evaluate investment alternatives.

Today, there is a wealth of information on stocks, bonds, and other securities and the firms that issue them. There is also a wealth of investment information on other types of investments, including mutual funds, real estate, and high-risk investment alternatives. Two popular sources—the Internet and newspapers—report daily securities transactions. The Internet can also be used to obtain detailed research information about different investment alternatives. Often, the most detailed research information about securities—and the most expensive—is obtained from professional advisory services. In addition, brokerage firm reports, business periodicals, and corporate reports can also be used to evaluate different investment alternatives. Finally, there are a number of security indexes or averages that indicate price trends but reveal nothing about the performance of individual securities.

Key Terms

You should now be able to define and give an example relevant to each of the following terms:

net worth (599)
personal budget (600)
personal investment (601)
financial planner (602)
blue-chip stock (603)
rate of return (603)
liquidity (604)
account executive (605)
market order (606)
limit order (606)
full disclosure (608)
prospectus (608)
insider trading (608)
asset allocation (609)
municipal bond (612)
stock dividend (613)
capital gain (613)
market value (613)
stock split (613)
mutual fund (615)
exchange-traded fund (ETF) (615)
net asset value (NAV) (615)
expense ratio (616)
family of funds (617)
high-risk investment (618)
buying long (618)
selling short (618)
margin requirement (619)
security average (or security index) (625)

CHAPTER REVIEW

Review Questions

1. How could developing a personal budget help you obtain the money needed to fund your investment program?
2. What is an "emergency fund," and why is it recommended?
3. What is the trade-off between safety and risk? How do you calculate rate of return?
4. In general, what kinds of investments provide income? What kinds provide growth?
5. Would you use a full-service or a discount brokerage firm? Explain your answer.
6. What is the difference between a market order and a limit order?
7. Describe how the securities industry is regulated.
8. How do you think that asset allocation, the time your investments have to work for you, and your age affect the choice of investments for someone who is 25 years old? For someone who is 59 years old?
9. Characterize the purchase of corporate and government bonds as an investment in terms of safety, risk, income, growth, and liquidity.
10. Describe the three methods by which investors can make money with stock investments.
11. An individual may invest in stocks either directly or through a mutual fund. How are the two investment methods different?
12. When would a speculator sell short?
13. What are the risks and rewards of purchasing stocks on margin?
14. How could the Internet help you to research an investment?
15. In addition to the Internet, what other sources of financial information could help you to obtain your investment goals?

Discussion Questions

1. At the time of publication, many investors had lost money on stocks and mutual funds because of an economic crisis. At the same time, many experts argued that this was a "real investing opportunity" because of the depressed prices for many stocks and mutual funds. Based on current economic and investment information available at the time you answer this question, do you think that it is a good time to begin an investment program? Justify your answer.
2. What personal circumstances might lead investors to emphasize income rather than growth in their investment planning? What might lead them to emphasize growth rather than income?
3. In this chapter, it was apparent that stocks have outperformed other investment alternatives over a long period of time. With this fact in mind, why would investors choose to use asset allocation to diversify their investments?
4. What type of individual would invest in government bonds? In global mutual funds? In real estate?
5. Suppose that you have just inherited 500 shares of IBM common stock. What would you do with it, if anything?
6. What kinds of information would you like to have before you invest in a particular common stock or mutual fund? From what sources can you get that information?
7. Take another look at Figure 20.5 (Mergent's research report for The Coca-Cola Company). Based on the research provided by Mergent's, would you buy stock in Coca-Cola? Justify your decision by providing specific examples from Figure 20.5.

Video Case 20.1

For E*Trade Investors, Help Is Just a Click Away

E*Trade, the big online brokerage firm, offers products and services for investors at every level of experience and for almost every financial goal. Its free research and educational materials cater to the novice, the very experienced, and the investor in between by means of webinars, short videos, written articles, and other resources that users can access online at their own convenience. Users can make long-term investment plans, conduct quick trades for short-term gains, or track the performance of stocks and other securities they are thinking of buying or selling in the future.

"As I think about financial services," says one of the company's senior vice presidents, "you really separate it into two areas: there's long-term planning and then there's...single stock trading. You need to decide first which avenue you want to actually go down. The active traders have a completely different need than long-term investors. They're much more heavily reliant upon tools that can provide them with up-to-the-minute information about a company's financial performance." For long-term investors, E*Trade's Web site helps individuals determine why they are investing. What immediate goals do they want to achieve, for example, or what kind of lifestyle do they want to maintain in retirement. "Once we answer some of those questions...we can then give them a better idea of how to actually meet those particular goals. The first thing to understand is their risk tolerance."

E*Trade's automated Online Advisor tool asks a short series of questions to help investors gauge their own risk level for each investment while considering its purpose and its time horizon. One key question, for instance, is how soon the investor expects to start drawing money out of the investment program and for how many years. Another is the investor's age, and yet another is the investor's likely response to a sudden drop in the value of his or her investment. "Once you establish the type of risk [level] they have, then we can start developing a type of plan that's really comfortable for their risk level." Whether the investor wants to start college savings for a newborn, is ready to put money away for retirement, or has just come into an inheritance or other windfall and is looking for guidance about how to manage it, E*Trade can help.

Another way E*Trade helps customers invest at a comfortable risk level is through its Managed Investment Portfolios. For those investors with larger investment portfolios, the brokerage company offers a range of preselected portfolios, each with a different mix of securities offering different levels of risk and return, based on whether the investor's goals are aggressive (high risk and high return), moderate, or conservative (low risk and low return). So that one of the company's relationship managers can personally help customers choose the right portfolio, based on the investor's risk level and time horizon, this customized product is available at E*Trade's brick-and-mortar branches or by telephone. Ongoing monitoring of the portfolio, monthly statements, and quarterly performance reports are also provided, and portfolios can be periodically rebalanced to ensure that they continue to meet investors' goals.[13]

Questions

1. How would you determine whether investing in securities should be part of your personal financial plan at this time in your life? Would you prefer to manage your own investments or to invest in a managed portfolio like the one that E*Trade offers?
2. E*Trade focuses on two different types of investors, active and long term. What differentiates these investors in terms of their investing methods and goals and why?
3. Why does E*Trade offer its Managed Investment Portfolio only in person or on the phone?

Case 20.2 Investing in Your Financial Future

Nearly four in ten people in your age group (18 to 35) have already started investing for their future. What about you?

Although you may not think you have enough money to invest just now, you can start saving small amounts on a regular basis—weekly or monthly, or each time you get paid. Although it may feel like a stretch in the early months, once you get in the habit of "paying yourself first," soon you will have enough set aside to consider making some long-term investments.

Before you decide to put this step off, consider the cost of waiting. If you invest just $150 a month beginning at age 25, you can put away $1,800 a year. If the investments you choose earn a hefty 11 percent per year, for example, you'll have $1,047,294 by the time you're 65. If you wait a mere ten years, however, and begin at age 35, you will have only $358,236. That's almost $700,000 less you will have to live on when you tap your retirement account. To get a return of 11 percent, you will need to learn how to invest in stocks and mutual funds—investments that have the potential for larger returns and also carry more risk. Even if your investments earn just 5 percent per year, you will be thousands of dollars ahead if you start investing early.

Sure, the value of stocks and bonds can go down as well as up, especially during periods of financial crisis or economic uncertainty. That's why you have to take the long view when you commit your funds. You've probably heard the advice, "Buy low, sell high." During an economic slowdown, when stock prices hover near historic lows, think about starting or adding to your investment nest egg. Even when the market is soaring, there are good investments to be had.

Where should you put your investment? John C. Bogle, founder of the Vanguard Investment Company, is generally bullish about the stock market and mutual funds invested in it. Bogle advises choosing a conservative portfolio that's both balanced and diversified. Increase your investment regularly, he says, and ignore day-to-day market fluctuations. Remember, you are in this for the long term. Consider how much risk you can handle, and choose investments accordingly. Do not put all your dollars in one investment basket, and do your homework before you make your first move.

The late Sir John Templeton, whom *Money* magazine called "arguably the greatest stock picker of the century," founded a fund called Templeton Growth that grew an average of more than 15 percent each year for almost half a century. His maxims for successful investing agree with Bogle's focus on the long term. "Invest," Templeton advised. "Don't trade or speculate." Keep in mind that when you buy shares in companies that continue to grow, you are investing in their ability to keep earning money in good times and bad. Frantically buying and selling shares at the first sign of a decline is more like gambling than investing.

Of course, before you invest money you plan to park for the next 20 years or so, make sure you've eliminated as much of your current debts as possible, such as credit cards or student loans. Allow yourself enough financial flexibility to start (or continue) contributing to a separate retirement fund, especially if your employer matches your contributions. Set aside cash for emergencies, as well as for near-term purchases like a home, a car down payment, or graduate school tuition if these are in your five-year plan.

Finally, remember Bogle's observation: "If you were to put your money away and not look at it for many years, until you were ready for retirement, when you finally looked at it, you would probably faint with amazement at how much money is in there." Start investing now, and you will thank yourself in 30 years.[14]

For online quizzes and calculators to get you started, see http://www.finra.org/Investors/ToolsCalculators/index.htm.

Questions

1. Assume you can invest only half the amount suggested here, or about $75 a month. Use an online investment calculator to determine how much you can earn at 4 percent interest by age 65, if you start at age 25. Recalculate to see how much you would earn if you start at 35. What does the difference between the two results suggest about the value of long-term investing?
2. Why do you think experts advise buying low and selling high? Read the financial pages of a major newspaper for a few days or check the newspaper's Web site, paying particular attention to the behavior of buyers and sellers of securities. Do you think they consistently follow this advice? Why or why not? What other ways can investors profit from buying stock shares?
3. Make a list of your financial liabilities. How much debt do you need to pay down before you can begin setting aside money for long-term investing? Do not forget to allow for other kinds of saving, such as for retirement and emergencies.

Building Skills for Career Success

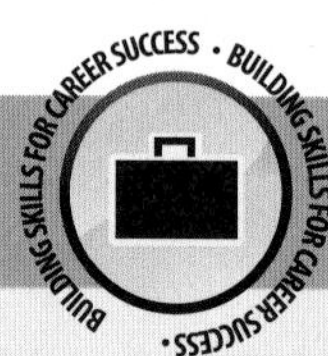

1 JOURNALING FOR SUCCESS

According to many financial experts, the logical place to begin the search for a quality investment is to examine the products and services you use on a regular basis—products and services that provide a high level of consumer satisfaction.

The preceding statement is based on the assumption that if you like the product or service and you feel that you got excellent value for your money, other consumers will too. And while it may be obvious, a satisfied, growing customer base can mean increased sales revenues, profits, and ultimately higher stock values for the company that manufactured the product or provided the service.

Assignment

1. To begin this journal exercise, think about purchases you made over the last month. Describe one product or service that you feel "was worth the money."
2. For the product or service you chose, describe the attributes or features that impressed you.
3. Determine if the company that made the product or provided the service is a public company that has issued stock.* Then use the Internet or go to the library to research the investment potential for this company. Finally, describe why you feel this would be a good or bad investment at this time.

*If the company that manufactured the product or service you chose is not a public company, choose another product or service.

2 EXPLORING THE INTERNET

For investors seeking information about individual companies and the industry to which they belong, the Internet is an excellent source. If you find the right Web site, it provides information about sales and revenue, graphs of recent trading activity, and discussions of anticipated changes within a firm or an industry. You can also look at Internet business reports of stock and bond market activity. Among the many companies that issue these reports are Mergent, Morningstar, Standard & Poor's, Moody's, and Value Line—all firms that provide research services. Visit the text Web site for updates to this exercise.

Assignment

1. Suppose that you are interested in investing within a particular industry, such as the semiconductor or computer industry. Explore some of the Web sites listed below, gathering information about the industry and a few related stocks that are of interest to the "experts."

   Bloomberg BusinessWeek: http://www.businessweek.com
   Fortune: http://www.fortune.com

Mergent: http://www.mergent.com
Standard & Poor's: http://www.standardandpoors.com
Morningstar: http://www.morningstar.com
The Wall Street Journal: http://www.wsj.com

2. List the stocks the experts recommend and their current trading value. In addition, list several stocks the experts do not like and their current selling prices. You can use one of the Web search engines such as Yahoo! Finance (http://finance.yahoo.com) to check the price. Then list your own choices of "good" and "bad" stocks.
3. Explain why you and the experts believe that these stocks are good or poor buys today. (You might want to monitor the value of all stocks over the next six months to see how well your stocks are performing.)

❸ DEVELOPING CRITICAL-THINKING SKILLS

One way to achieve financial security is to invest a stated amount of money on a systematic basis. This investment strategy is called *dollar-cost averaging*. When the cost is lower, your investment buys more shares. When the cost is higher, your investment buys fewer shares. A good way to begin investing is to select a mutual fund that meets your financial objectives and to invest the same amount each month or each year.

Assignment

1. Select several mutual funds from the financial pages of *The Wall Street Journal* or a personal finance periodical such as *Money, Kiplinger's Personal Finance*, or *SmartMoney* that provides information about mutual funds. Call the toll-free number for each fund and ask about its objectives. Furthermore, request that the company send you a prospectus and an annual report.
2. Select one fund that meets your financial objectives.
3. Prepare a table that includes the following data:
   a. An initial investment of $2,000 in the mutual fund you have selected
   b. The net asset value (NAV)
   c. The number of shares purchased
4. Record the investment information on a weekly basis. Look in *The Wall Street Journal* or on the Internet to find the NAV for each week.
5. Determine the value of your investment until the end of the semester.
6. Write a report describing the results. Include a summary of what you learned about investments. Be sure to indicate if you think that dollar-cost averaging (investing another $2,000 next year) would be a good idea.

❹ BUILDING TEAM SKILLS

Investing in stocks can be a way to beat inflation and accumulate money. Traditionally, stocks have returned about 10 percent per year since 1926. Bonds and certificates of deposit, on the other hand, often earn little more than the inflation rate, making it very difficult to accumulate enough money for retirement.

Assignment

1. Form teams of three people. The teams will compete against each other, striving for the largest gain in investments.
2. Assume that you are buying stock in three companies; some should be listed on the NYSE, and some should be traded in the NASDAQ OTC market.
   a. Research different investments, and narrow your choices to three different stocks.
   b. Divide your total investment of $25,000 into three amounts.
   c. Determine the number of shares of stock you can purchase in each company by dividing the budgeted amount by the price of the stock. Allow enough money to pay for the commission. To find the cost of the stock, multiply the number of shares you are going to purchase by the closing price of the stock.
   d. Assume that the commission is 1 percent. Calculate it by multiplying the cost of the stock by 0.01. Add the dollar amount of commission to the cost of the stock to determine the total purchase price.
3. Set up a table to reflect the following information:
   a. Name of the company
   b. Closing price per share
   c. Number of shares purchased
   d. Amount of the commission
   e. Cost of the stock
4. Record the closing price of the stock on a weekly basis. Prepare a chart to use for this step.
5. Before the end of the semester, assume that you sell the stock.
   a. Take the closing price on the day you sell your stocks and multiply it by the number of shares; then calculate the commission at 1 percent.
   b. Deduct the amount of commission from the selling price of the stock. This is the total return on your investment.
6. Calculate your profit or loss. Subtract the total purchase price of the stock from the total return. If the total return is less than the total purchase price, you have a loss.
7. Prepare a report summarizing the results of the project. Include the table and individual stock charts, as well as a statement describing what you learned about investing in stocks.

❺ RESEARCHING DIFFERENT CAREERS

Today many people choose a personal financial planner or financial advisor to help develop an investment program that will help them achieve their financial goals. Not only is this career choice an opportunity to help others, it is also one of the fastest growing career fields in the United States. According to the 2010-2011 *Occupational Outlook Handbook*, the job opportunities for personal financial planners and financial advisors are expected to increase by 30 percent between now and the year 2018. For help completing this exercise, use the *Occupational Outlook Handbook* in your college's library or career center or go to http://www.bls.gov.

Assignment

1. Answer the following questions based on information obtained in the *Occupational Outlook Handbook*.
   a. What is the nature of the work performed by personal financial planners and financial advisors?
   b. What type of training or qualifications is required for a career in financial planning?
   c. Where are the job opportunities for personal financial planners and advisors?
   d. What are typical annual wages for a personal financial planner or financial advisor?
2. Summarize your findings in a report. Be sure to include if you would choose this career and why.

Running a Business PART 7

Graeter's

Graeter's Plans for Financing Growth

So few family-owned companies are still in business after one generation that you might think a successful *fourth*-generation firm would be content to maintain the status quo, serving its current customers with a tried-and-true product and staying close to home.

That's not the strategic plan being followed by the premium ice-cream maker Graeter's, however. This 140-year-old family business, headquartered in Cincinnati where it was founded, has big ideas. Its current management team includes three great-grandsons of the original founders; one of them, Richard Graeter II, serves as CEO. In five years, "I'd like to see us basically from coast to coast in the United States," he says of the company's mid-range outlook. Thanks to Graeter's ambitious expansion plans, that vision could well come true.

FROM ONE FACTORY TO TWO

Graeter's, worth about $20 million in annual sales, currently operates a few dozen company-owned retail stores in Ohio, Missouri, Kentucky, and neighboring states. It makes and sells a particularly rich and creamy product derived from a simple old family recipe. Graeter's uses only the freshest natural ingredients and a unique manufacturing process yielding only about two gallons of ice cream every 20 minutes for each machine on one of its assembly lines. Flavor selections vary depending on which fresh fruits are in season. Graeter's stores also offer a selection of chocolate candies, bakery items, and frozen desserts. Its ice cream, available in quart containers that are still hand-packed in its factories, is also available in hundreds of supermarkets, most notably those in the Kroger chain, in states as far away as Colorado and Texas. It can also be purchased online for overnight UPS delivery anywhere in the continental United States.

For many years one factory met all of Graeter's production needs. However, a few years ago, in anticipation of its first major expansion, the company undertook the construction of a second plant, an $11 million, 28,000-square-foot facility in the Bond Hill neighborhood of Cincinnati. The city of Cincinnati contributed $3.3 million in financial incentives, some in the form of loans, to help pay for the land and the new building (Graeter's sought outside financing for the rest). In addition to adding at least 50 new jobs to the local economy, with the promise of more in the future as growth continues, Graeter's also committed to "stay and grow" in Cincinnati for at least 20 years.

"As a Cincinnati-based, family-run company, we are proud of our association with this wonderful city and look forward to new generations of success," said Richard Graeter. "We are incredibly grateful [for the City's assistance], because not only will their support help us expand nationally but it is also helping us create jobs locally."

FROM TWO FACTORIES TO THREE

A few months before the new plant was due to open. However, Graeter's found itself facing an unexpected opportunity. Its remaining franchisee, who operated several stores and a factory, decided to put the business up for sale and offered to sell it back to the company. Suddenly, Graeter's had the option to operate not one, not two, but three production facilities. The timing was almost perfect for its growth plans, but how would the company pay for this unanticipated acquisition?

"My role as CEO would be to evaluate those opportunities as they come along and really see how they can fit into our long-term strategic vision," says Richard Graeter. "In the case of buying the franchisee, we had to come up with several millions of dollars in additional financing over and above what we had borrowed to build our new plant. So that means working with the bankers and lawyers and accountants to model how the business would look after the acquisition to determine if it makes financial sense, and then going out and raising the investment that you need to make the acquisition."

Graeter's would like to make its premium-quality products available in supermarkets across the country, and to continue opening retail stores in new states—perhaps even California (already the most popular shipping destination on the company Web site) and New York. Based on those goals, it was clear why the firm would want to buy back the franchise and its factory. Quality control was an issue as well. While the firm has had no complaints about any of the three franchisees with which it has worked in the past, all its stores are now company-owned, and the management team is happy to keep it that way. "There is something about the personal touch on a product that you just can't replace," says a management consultant who works with the firm. "Franchising really is a financial game," Richard Graeter agrees, "and it's all about growth. You can quickly lose control of the product and the brand, and after dipping our toe in the waters of franchising we decided not to get any deeper. . . . We've never really been in it just to make the most money or to be everywhere. We've really been all about the quality of the product and our connection to the product, which tends to be pretty hands-on."[15]

Questions

1. At one point, Graeter's considered expanding solely through franchising. Why do you think the company decided to retain control of its production and sales operations instead, even though this strategy, unlike franchising, requires it to take on debt?
2. Graeter's needed to raise several millions of dollars to buy out its franchisee after borrowing to build its new plant. One of the strategies it did not use to raise the needed funds was going public, that is, issuing shares through an initial public offering to sell ownership shares in the firm. What are the advantages and disadvantages of issuing stock to obtain the money needed to expand a business?
3. As an investor, would you be willing to buy shares in Graeter's if it were to raise money through an IPO? Explain why the company's stock would or would not be a good investment for you.

Building a Business Plan PART 7

To access the online *Interactive Business Plan*, go to www.cengagebrain.com.

In this last section, provide some information about your exit strategy, and discuss any potential trends, problems, or risks that you may encounter. These risks and assumptions could relate to your industry, markets, company, or personnel. Make sure to incorporate important information not included in other parts of the business plan in an appendix. Now is also the time to go back and prepare the executive summary, which should be placed at the beginning of the business plan.

THE EXIT STRATEGY COMPONENT

Your exit strategy component should at least include answers to the following questions:

7.1. How do you intend to get yourself (and your money) out of the business?
7.2. Will your children take over the business, or do you intend to sell it later?
7.3. Do you intend to grow the business to the point of an IPO?
7.4. How will investors get their money back?

THE CRITICAL RISKS AND ASSUMPTIONS COMPONENT

Your critical risks and assumptions component should answer at least the following questions:

7.5. What will you do if your market does not develop as quickly as you predicted? What if your market develops too quickly?
7.6. What will you do if your competitors underprice or make your product obsolete?
7.7. What will you do if there is an unfavorable industry-wide trend?
7.8. What will happen if trained workers are not available as predicted?
7.9. What will you do if there is an erratic supply of products or raw materials?

THE APPENDIX COMPONENT

Supplemental information and documents are often included in an appendix. Here are a few examples of some documents that can be included:

- Résumés of owners and principal managers
- Advertising samples and brochures
- An organization chart
- Floor plans of a retail facility or factory

REVIEW OF BUSINESS PLAN ACTIVITIES

As you have discovered, writing a business plan involves a long series of interrelated steps. As with any project involving a number of complex steps and calculations, your business plan should be reviewed carefully and revised before you present it to potential investors or lenders.

Remember, there is one more component you need to prepare after your business plan is completed: The executive summary should be written last, but because of its importance, it appears after the introduction.

THE EXECUTIVE SUMMARY COMPONENT

In the executive summary, give a one- to two-page overview of your entire business plan. This is the most important part of the business plan and is of special interest to busy bankers, investors, and other interested parties. Remember, this section is a summary; more detailed information is provided in the remainder of your business plan.

Make sure that the executive summary captures the reader's attention instantly in the first sentence by using a key selling point or benefit of the business.

Your executive summary should include answers to at least the following:

7.10. *Company information.* What product or service do you provide? What is your competitive advantage? When will the company be formed? What are your company objectives? What is the background of you and your management team?

7.11. *Market opportunity.* What is the expected size and growth rate of your market, your expected market share, and any relevant market trends?

Once again, review your answers to all the questions in the preceding parts to make sure that they are all consistent throughout the entire business plan.

Although many would-be entrepreneurs are excited about the prospects of opening their own business, remember that it takes a lot of hard work, time, and in most cases a substantial amount of money. Though the business plan provides an enormous amount of information about your business, it is only the first step. Once it is completed, it is now your responsibility to implement the plan. Good luck in your business venture.

The information contained in "Building a Business Plan" will also assist you in completing the online *Interactive Business Plan.*

Glossary

A

absolute advantage the ability to produce a specific product more efficiently than any other nation (73)

accessory equipment standardized equipment used in a firm's production or office activities (364)

account executive an individual, sometimes called a *stockbroker* or *registered representative,* who buys and sells securities for clients (605)

accountability the obligation of a worker to accomplish an assigned job or task (198)

accounting the process of systematically collecting, analyzing, and reporting financial information (499)

accounting equation the basis for the accounting process: *assets = liabilities + owners' equity (505)*

accounts receivable turnover a financial ratio calculated by dividing net sales by accounts receivable (520)

acid-test ratio a financial ratio calculated by adding cash, marketable securities, and receivables and dividing the total by current liabilities (519)

ad hoc committee a committee created for a specific short-term purpose (207)

administrative manager a manager who is not associated with any specific functional area but who provides overall administrative guidance and leadership (177)

advertising a paid nonpersonal message communicated to a select audience through a mass medium (432)

advertising agency an independent firm that plans, produces, and places advertising for its clients (441)

advertising media the various forms of communication through which advertising reaches its audience (435)

affirmative action program a plan designed to increase the number of minority employees at all levels within an organization (58)

agency shop a workplace in which employees can choose not to join the union but must pay dues to the union anyway (322)

agent a middleman that expedites exchanges, represents a buyer or a seller, and often is hired permanently on a commission basis (408)

alien corporation a corporation chartered by a foreign government and conducting business in the United States (118)

analytic skills the ability to identify problems correctly, generate reasonable alternatives, and select the "best" alternatives to solve problems (177)

analytical process a process in operations management in which raw materials are broken into different component parts (218)

annual report a report distributed to stockholders and other interested parties that describes a firm's operating activities and its financial condition (506)

arbitration the step in a grievance procedure in which a neutral third party hears the two sides of a dispute and renders a binding decision (323)

asset allocation the process of spreading your money among several different types of investments to lessen risk (609)

assets the resources that a business owns (505)

audit an examination of a company's financial statements and the accounting practices that produced them (500)

authority the power, within an organization, to accomplish an assigned job or task (198)

autocratic leadership task-oriented leadership style in which workers are told what to do and how to accomplish it; workers have no say in the decision-making process (179)

automatic vending the use of machines to dispense products (415)

automation the total or near-total use of machines to do work (236)

B

balance of payments the total flow of money into a country minus the total flow of money out of that country over some period of time (76)

balance of trade the total value of a nation's exports minus the total value of its imports over some period of time (75)

balance sheet (or statement of financial position) a summary of the dollar amounts of a firm's assets, liabilities, and owners' equity accounts at the end of a specific accounting period (507)

banker's acceptance a written order for a bank to pay a third party a stated amount of money on a specific date (552)

bargaining unit the specific group of employees represented by a union (318)

barter a system of exchange in which goods or services are traded directly for other goods or services without using money (25)

barter system a system of exchange in which goods or services are traded directly for other goods or services (534)

behavior modification a systematic program of reinforcement to encourage desirable behavior (292)

benchmarking a process used to evaluate the products, processes, or management practices of another organization that is superior in some way in order to improve quality (184)

bill of lading document issued by a transport carrier to an exporter to prove that merchandise has been shipped (89)

blue-chip stock a safe investment that generally attracts conservative investors (603)

board of directors the top governing body of a corporation, the members of which are elected by the stockholders (119)

bond indenture a legal document that details all the conditions relating to a bond issue (589)

boycott a refusal to do business with a particular firm (324)

brand a name, term, symbol, design, or any combination of these that identifies a seller's products as distinct from those of other sellers (373)

brand equity marketing and financial value associated with a brand's strength in a market (374)

brand extension using an existing brand to brand a new product in a different product category (377)

brand loyalty extent to which a customer is favorable toward buying a specific brand (374)

brand mark the part of a brand that is a symbol or distinctive design (373)

brand name the part of a brand that can be spoken (373)

breakeven quantity the number of units that must be sold for the total revenue (from all units sold) to equal the total cost (of all units sold) (383)

broadband technology a general term referring to higher speed Internet connections that deliver data, voice, and video material (477)

broker a middleman that specializes in a particular commodity, represents either a buyer or a seller, and is likely to be hired on a temporary basis (408)

budget a financial statement that projects income, expenditures, or both over a specified future period (574)

bundle pricing packaging together two or more complementary products and selling them for a single price (387)

business the organized effort of individuals to produce and sell, for a profit, the products and services that satisfy society's needs (10)

business buying behavior the purchasing of products by producers, resellers, governmental units, and institutions (352)

business cycle the recurrence of periods of growth and recession in a nation's economic activity (20)

business ethics the application of moral standards to business situations (39)

business model represents a group of common characteristics and methods of doing business to generate sales revenues and reduce expenses (483)

business plan a carefully constructed guide for the person starting a business (146)

business product a product bought for resale, for making other products, or for use in a firm's operations (363)

business service an intangible product that an organization uses in its operations (364)

business-to-business (or B2B) model a model used by firms that conduct business with other businesses (484)

business-to-consumer (or B2C) model a model used by firms that focus on conducting business with individual consumers (484)

buying allowance a temporary price reduction to resellers for purchasing specified quantities of a product (447)

buying behavior the decisions and actions of people involved in buying and using products (352)

buying long buying stock with the expectation that it will increase in value and then can be sold at a profit (618)

C

capacity the amount of products or services that an organization can produce in a given time (225)

capital budget a financial statement that estimates a firm's expenditures for major assets and its long-term financing needs (575)

capital gain the difference between a security's purchase price and its selling price (613)

capital-intensive technology a process in which machines and equipment do most of the work (225)

capitalism an economic system in which individuals own and operate the majority of businesses that provide goods and services (13)

captioned photograph a picture accompanied by a brief explanation (448)

captive pricing pricing the basic product in a product line low, but pricing related items at a higher level (388)

carrier a firm that offers transportation services (420)

cash budget a financial statement that estimates cash receipts and cash expenditures over a specified period (575)

cash flow the movement of money into and out of an organization (569)

catalog marketing a type of marketing in which an organization provides a catalog from which customers make selections and place orders by mail, telephone, or the Internet (414)

catalog showroom a retail outlet that displays well-known brands and sells them at discount prices through catalogs within the store (410)

category killer a very large specialty store that concentrates on a single product line and competes on the basis of low prices and product availability (412)

caveat emptor a Latin phrase meaning "let the buyer beware" (51)

centralized organization an organization that systematically works to concentrate authority at the upper levels of the organization (198)

certificate of deposit (CD) a document stating that the bank will pay the depositor a guaranteed interest rate on money left on deposit for a specified period of time (548)

certified management accountant (CMA) an accountant who has met the requirements for education and experience, passed a rigorous exam, and is certified by the Institute of Management Accountants (504)

certified public accountant (CPA) an individual who has met state requirements for accounting education and experience and has passed a rigorous accounting examination prepared by the AICPA (504)

chain of command the line of authority that extends from the highest to the lowest levels of an organization (193)

chain retailer a company that operates more than one retail outlet (409)

channel of distribution (or marketing channel) a sequence of marketing organizations that directs a product from the producer to the ultimate user (401)

check a written order for a bank or other financial institution to pay a stated dollar amount to the business or person indicated on the face of the check (547)

chief financial officer (CFO) a high-level corporate executive who manages a firm's finances and reports directly to the company's chief executive officer or president (573)

closed corporation a corporation whose stock is owned by relatively few people and is not sold to the general public (117)

closed shop a workplace in which workers must join the union before they are hired; outlawed by the Taft–Hartley Act (321)

cloud computing a type of computer usage in which services stored on the Internet are provided to users on a temporary basis (488)

code of ethics a guide to acceptable and ethical behavior as defined by the organization (44)

collaborative learning system a work environment that allows problem solving participation by all team members (473)

collateral real estate or property pledged as security for a loan (548)

collective bargaining the process of negotiating a labor contract with management (318)

command economy an economic system in which the government decides what goods and services will be produced, how they will be produced, for whom available goods and services will be produced, and who owns and controls the major factors of production (16)

commercial bank a profit-making organization that accepts deposits, makes loans, and provides related services to its customers (544)

commercial paper a short-term promissory note issued by a large corporation (539)

commission a payment that is a percentage of sales revenue (262)

commission merchant a middleman that carries merchandise and negotiates sales for manufacturers (408)

common stock stock owned by individuals or firms who may vote on corporate matters but whose claims on profits and assets are subordinate to the claims of others (118, 583)

communication skills the ability to speak, listen, and write effectively (179)

community shopping center a planned shopping center that includes one or two department stores and some specialty stores, along with convenience stores (416)

comparable worth a concept that seeks equal compensation for jobs requiring about the same level of education, training, and skills (261)

comparative advantage the ability to produce a specific product more efficiently than any other product (73)

comparison discounting setting a price at a specific level and comparing it with a higher price (390)

compensation the payment employees receive in return for their labor (260)

compensation system the policies and strategies that determine employee compensation (260)

competition rivalry among businesses for sales to potential customers (21)

component part an item that becomes part of a physical product and is either a finished item ready for assembly or a product that needs little processing before assembly (364)

computer backup a process of storing data, information, and computer systems on secondary computer systems that can be accessed if a firm's main computer system fails (476)

computer network a group of two or more computers linked together that allows users to share data and information (477)

computer virus a software code designed to disrupt normal computer operations (487)

computer-aided design (CAD) the use of computers to aid in the development of products (237)

computer-aided manufacturing (CAM) the use of computers to plan and control manufacturing processes (237)

computer-integrated manufacturing (CIM) a computer system that not only helps to design products but also controls the machinery needed to produce the finished product (237)

conceptual skills the ability to think in abstract terms (177)

consumer buying behavior the purchasing of products for personal or household use, not for business purposes (352)

consumer price index (CPI) a monthly index that measures the changes in prices of a fixed basket of goods purchased by a typical consumer in an urban area (19)

consumer products goods and services purchased by individuals for personal consumption; a product purchased to satisfy personal and family needs (15, 363)

consumer sales promotion method a sales promotion method designed to attract consumers to particular retail stores and to motivate them to purchase certain new or established products (445)

consumerism all activities undertaken to protect the rights of consumers (54)

contingency plan a plan that outlines alternative courses of action that may be taken if an organization's other plans are disrupted or become ineffective (173)

continuous process a manufacturing process in which a firm produces the same product(s) over a long period of time (237)

controlling the process of evaluating and regulating ongoing activities to ensure that goals are achieved (174)

convenience product a relatively inexpensive, frequently purchased item for which buyers want to exert only minimal effort (363)

convenience store a small food store that sells a limited variety of products but remains open well beyond normal business hours (410)

convertible bond a bond that can be exchanged, at the owner's option, for a specified number of shares of the corporation's common stock (588)

cookie a small piece of software sent by a Web site that tracks an individual's Internet use (486)

cooperative an association of individuals or firms whose purpose is to perform some business function for its members (124)

cooperative advertising an arrangement whereby a manufacturer agrees to pay a certain amount of a retailer's media cost for advertising the manufacturer's product (447)

core competencies approaches and processes that a company performs well and may give it an advantage over its competitors (170)

corporate bond a corporation's written pledge that it will repay a specified amount of money with interest (587)

corporate culture the inner rites, rituals, heroes, and values of a firm (205)

corporate officers the chairman of the board, president, executive vice presidents, corporate secretary, treasurer, and any other top executive appointed by the board of directors (119)

corporation an artificial person created by law with most of the legal rights of a real person, including the rights to start and operate a business, to buy or sell property, to borrow money, to sue or be sued, and to enter into binding contracts (116)

cost of goods sold the dollar amount equal to beginning inventory *plus* net purchases *less* ending inventory (512)

countertrade an international barter transaction (91)

coupon an offer that reduces the retail price of a particular item by a stated amount at the time of purchase (446)

craft union an organization of skilled workers in a single craft or trade (309)

creative selling selling products to new customers and increasing sales to present customers (442)

credit immediate purchasing power that is exchanged for a promise to repay borrowed money, with or without interest, at a later date (553)

credit union a financial institution that accepts deposits from, and lends money to, only the people who are its members (545)

cross-functional team a team of individuals with varying specialties, expertise, and skills that are brought together to achieve a common task (203, 297)

cultural (or workplace) diversity differences among people in a workforce owing to race, ethnicity, and gender (6)

cultural (workplace) diversity differences among people in a workforce owing to race, ethnicity, and gender (253)

currency devaluation the reduction of the value of a nation's currency relative to the currencies of other countries (77)

current assets assets that can be converted quickly into cash or that will be used in one year or less (508)

current liabilities debts that will be repaid in one year or less (510)

current ratio a financial ratio computed by dividing current assets by current liabilities (519)

customary pricing pricing on the basis of tradition (388)

customer lifetime value a measure of a customer's worth (sales minus costs) to a business over one's lifetime (337)

customer relationship management (CRM) using information about customers to create marketing strategies that develop and sustain desirable customer relationships (337)

D

data numerical or verbal descriptions that usually result from some sort of measurement (465)

data mining the practice of searching through data records looking for useful information (487)

data processing the transformation of data into a form that is useful for a specific purpose (470)

database a single collection of data and information stored in one place that can be used by people throughout an organization to make decisions (466)

debenture bond a bond backed only by the reputation of the issuing corporation (588)

debit card a card that electronically subtracts the amount of your purchase from your bank account at the moment the purchase is made (549)

debt capital borrowed money obtained through loans of various types (576)

debt-to-owners'-equity ratio a financial ratio calculated by dividing total liabilities by owners' equity (521)

decentralized organization an organization in which management consciously attempts to spread authority widely in the lower levels of the organization (198)

decision making the act of choosing one alternative from a set of alternatives (181)

decision-support system (DSS) a type of computer program that provides relevant data and information to help a firm's employees make decisions (472)

deflation a general decrease in the level of prices (18)

delegation assigning part of a manager's work and power to other workers (197)

demand the quantity of a product that buyers are willing to purchase at each of various prices (22, 380)

demand deposit an amount on deposit in a checking account (537)

department store a retail store that (1) employs 25 or more persons and (2) sells at least home furnishings, appliances, family apparel, and household linens and dry goods, each in a different part of the store (409)

departmentalization the process of grouping jobs into manageable units (196)

departmentalization by customer grouping activities according to the needs of various customer populations (197)

departmentalization by function grouping jobs that relate to the same organizational activity (196)

departmentalization by location grouping activities according to the defined geographic area in which they are performed (196)

departmentalization by product grouping activities related to a particular product or service (196)

depreciation the process of apportioning the cost of a fixed asset over the period during which it will be used (508)

depression a severe recession that lasts longer than a typical recession (20)

design planning the development of a plan for converting an idea into an actual product or service (224)

direct marketing the use of the telephone, Internet, and nonpersonal media to introduce products to customers, who can then purchase them via mail, telephone, or the Internet (413)

direct selling the marketing of products to customers through face-to-face sales presentations at home or in the workplace (413)

directing the combined processes of leading and motivating (173)

direct-mail advertising promotional material mailed directly to individuals (435)

direct-response marketing a type of marketing in which a seller advertises a product and makes it available, usually for a short time period, through mail, telephone, or online orders (414)

discount a deduction from the price of an item (391)

discount rate the interest rate the Federal Reserve System charges for loans to member banks (541)

discount store a self-service general-merchandise outlet that sells products at lower-than-usual prices (409)

discretionary income disposable income *less* savings and expenditures on food, clothing, and housing (353)

disposable income personal income *less* all additional personal taxes (353)

dividend a distribution of earnings to the stockholders of a corporation (118)

domestic corporation a corporation in the state in which it is incorporated (118)

domestic system a method of manufacturing in which an entrepreneur distributes raw materials to various homes, where families process them into finished goods to be offered for sale by the merchant entrepreneur (25)

double-entry bookkeeping system a system in which each financial transaction is recorded as two separate accounting entries to maintain the balance shown in the accounting equation (505)

draft issued by the exporter's bank, ordering the importer's bank to pay for the merchandise, thus guaranteeing payment once accepted by the importer's bank (89)

dumping exportation of large quantities of a product at a price lower than that of the same product in the home market (77)

E

earnings per share a financial ratio calculated by dividing net income after taxes by the number of shares of common stock outstanding (518)

e-business (electronic business) the organized effort of individuals to produce and sell, for a profit, the products and services that satisfy society's needs through the facilities available on the Internet (26, 479)

economic community an organization of nations formed to promote the free movement of resources and products among its members and to create common economic policies (84)

economic model of social responsibility the view that society will benefit most when business is left alone to produce and market profitable products that society needs (52)

economics the study of how wealth is created and distributed (12)

economy the way in which people deal with the creation and distribution of wealth (12)

electronic funds transfer (EFT) system a means of performing financial transactions through a computer terminal or telephone hookup (551)

embargo a complete halt to trading with a particular nation or in a particular product (77)

employee benefit a reward in addition to regular compensation that is provided indirectly to employees (262)

employee ownership a situation in which employees own the company they work for by virtue of being stockholders (295)

employee training the process of teaching operations and technical employees how to do their present jobs more effectively and efficiently (264)

empowerment making employees more involved in their jobs by increasing their participation in decision making (295)

entrepreneur a person who risks time, effort, and money to start and operate a business (13)

entrepreneurial leadership personality-based leadership style in which the manager seeks to inspire workers with a vision of what can be accomplished to benefit all stakeholders (180)

Equal Employment Opportunity Commission (EEOC) a government agency with the power to investigate complaints of employment discrimination and the power to sue firms that practice it (59)

equity capital money received from the owners or from the sale of shares of ownership in a business (576)

equity theory a theory of motivation based on the premise that people are motivated to obtain and preserve equitable treatment for themselves (287)

esteem needs our need for respect, recognition, and a sense of our own accomplishment and worth (282)

ethics the study of right and wrong and of the morality of the choices individuals make (39)

everyday low prices (EDLPs) setting a low price for products on a consistent basis (388)

exchange-traded fund (ETF) a fund that generally invests in the stocks or other securities contained in a specific stock or securities index (615)

exclusive distribution the use of only a single retail outlet for a product in a large geographic area (404)

executive information system (EIS) a computer-based system that facilitates and supports the decision-making needs of top managers and senior executives by providing easy access to both internal and external information (472)

expectancy theory a model of motivation based on the assumption that motivation depends on how much we want something and on how likely we think we are to get it (287)

expense ratio all the different management fees; 12b-1 fees, if any; and additional operating costs for a specific fund (616)

expert system a type of computer program that uses artificial intelligence to imitate a human's ability to think (472)

Export-Import Bank of the United States an independent agency of the U.S. government whose function is to assist in financing the exports of American firms (94)

exporting selling and shipping raw materials or products to other nations (74)

express warranty a written explanation of the producer's responsibilities in the event that a product is found to be defective or otherwise unsatisfactory (379)

external recruiting the attempt to attract job applicants from outside an organization (255)

F

factor a firm that specializes in buying other firms' accounts receivable (580)

factors of production resources used to produce goods and services (12)

factory system a system of manufacturing in which all the materials, machinery, and workers required to manufacture a product are assembled in one place (26)

family branding the strategy in which a firm uses the same brand for all or most of its products (377)

family of funds a group of mutual funds managed by one investment company (617)

feature article a piece (of up to 3,000 words) prepared by an organization for inclusion in a particular publication (448)

federal deficit a shortfall created when the federal government spends more in a fiscal year than it receives (21)

federal funds rate the interest rate at which a bank lends immediately available funds on deposit at the Fed to another bank overnight to meet the borrowing bank's reserve requirements (542)

Federal Reserve System the central bank of the United States responsible for regulating the banking industry (538)

financial accounting generates financial statements and reports for interested people outside an organization (503)

financial leverage the use of borrowed funds to increase the return on owners' equity (585)

financial management all the activities concerned with obtaining money and using it effectively (569)

financial manager a manager who is primarily responsible for an organization's financial resources (176)

financial plan a plan for obtaining and using the money needed to implement an organization's goals (573)

financial planner an individual who has had at least two years of training in investments, insurance, taxation, retirement planning, and estate planning and has passed a rigorous examination (602)

financial ratio a number that shows the relationship between two elements of a firm's financial statements (518)

first-line manager a manager who coordinates and supervises the activities of operating employees (176)

fiscal policy government influence on the amount of savings and expenditures; accomplished by altering the tax structure and by changing the levels of government spending (21)

fixed assets assets that will be held or used for a period longer than one year (508)

fixed cost a cost incurred no matter how many units of a product are produced or sold (383)

flexible benefit plan compensation plan whereby an employee receives a predetermined amount of benefit dollars to spend on a package of benefits he or she has selected to meet individual needs (263)

flexible manufacturing system (FMS) a single production system that combines electronic machines and computer-integrated manufacturing (237)

flextime a system in which employees set their own work hours within employer-determined limits (293)

foreign corporation a corporation in any state in which it does business except the one in which it is incorporated (118)

foreign-exchange control a restriction on the amount of a particular foreign currency that can be purchased or sold (77)

form utility utility created by people converting raw materials, finances, and information into finished products (219, 337)

franchise a license to operate an individually owned business as though it were part of a chain of outlets or stores (153)

franchisee a person or organization purchasing a franchise (153)

franchising the actual granting of a franchise (153)

franchisor an individual or organization granting a franchise (153)

free enterprise the system of business in which individuals are free to decide what to produce, how to produce it, and at what price to sell it (4)

frequent-user incentive a program developed to reward customers who engage in repeat (frequent) purchases (447)

full disclosure requirement that investors should have access to all important facts about stocks, bonds, and other securities so that they can make informed decisions (608)

full-service wholesaler a middleman that performs the entire range of wholesaler functions (407)

functional middleman a middleman that helps in the transfer of ownership of products but does not take title to the products (401)

G

Gantt chart a graphic scheduling device that displays the tasks to be performed on the vertical axis and the time required for each task on the horizontal axis (231)

General Agreement on Tariffs and Trade (GATT) an international organization of 153 nations dedicated to reducing or eliminating tariffs and other barriers to world trade (82)

general partner a person who assumes full or shared responsibility for operating a business (112)

generally accepted accounting principles (GAAPs) an accepted set of guidelines and practices for companies reporting financial information and for the accounting profession (500)

general-merchandise wholesaler a middleman that deals in a wide variety of products (408)

generic product (or brand) a product with no brand at all (374)

goal an end result that an organization is expected to achieve over a one- to ten-year period (170)

goal-setting theory a theory of motivation suggesting that employees are motivated to achieve goals that they and their managers establish together (288)

grapevine the informal communications network within an organization (207)

green IT a term used to describe all of a firm's activities to support a healthy environment and sustain the planet (488)

grievance procedure a formally established course of action for resolving employee complaints against management (322)

gross domestic product (GDP) the total dollar value of all goods and services produced by all people within the boundaries of a country during a one-year period (18)

gross profit a firm's net sales *less* the cost of goods sold (513)

gross sales the total dollar amount of all goods and services sold during the accounting period (511)

groupware one of the latest types of software that facilitates the management of large projects among geographically dispersed employees as well as such group activities as problem solving and brainstorming (473)

H

hard-core unemployed workers with little education or vocational training and a long history of unemployment (59)

high-risk investment an investment made in the uncertain hope of earning a relatively large profit in a short time (618)

hostile takeover a situation in which the management and board of directors of a firm targeted for acquisition disapprove of the merger (126)

hourly wage a specific amount of money paid for each hour of work (262)

human resources management (HRM) all the activities involved in acquiring, maintaining, and developing an organization's human resources (250)

human resources manager a person charged with managing an organization's human resources programs (177)

human resources planning the development of strategies to meet a firm's future human resources needs (251)

hygiene factors job factors that reduce dissatisfaction when present to an acceptable degree but that do not necessarily result in high levels of motivation (284)

I

import duty (tariff) a tax levied on a particular foreign product entering a country (76)

import quota a limit on the amount of a particular good that may be imported into a country during a given period of time (77)

importing purchasing raw materials or products in other nations and bringing them into one's own country (75)

incentive payment a payment in addition to wages, salary, or commissions (262)

income statement a summary of a firm's revenues and expenses during a specified accounting period (510)

independent retailer a firm that operates only one retail outlet (409)

individual branding the strategy in which a firm uses a different brand for each of its products (376)

industrial union an organization of both skilled and unskilled workers in a single industry (311)

inflation a general rise in the level of prices (18)

infomercial a program-length televised commercial message resembling an entertainment or consumer affairs program (437)

informal group a group created by the members themselves to accomplish goals that may or may not be relevant to an organization (207)

informal organization the pattern of behavior and interaction that stems from personal rather than official relationships (207)

information data presented in a form that is useful for a specific purpose (465)

information society a society in which large groups of employees generate or depend on information to perform their jobs (476)

information technology (IT) officer a manager at the executive level who is responsible for ensuring that a firm has the equipment necessary to provide the information the firm's employees and managers need to make effective decisions (466)

initial public offering (IPO) occurs when a corporation sells common stock to the general public for the first time (581)

injunction a court order requiring a person or group either to perform some act or to refrain from performing some act (315)

insider trading the practice of board members, corporate managers, and employees buying and selling a corporation's stock (608)

inspection the examination of the quality of work-in-process (233)

institutional advertising advertising designed to enhance a firm's image or reputation (434)

intangible assets assets that do not exist physically but that have a value based on the rights or privileges they confer on a firm (508)

integrated marketing communications coordination of promotion efforts to ensure maximal informational and persuasive impact on customers (431)

intensive distribution the use of all available outlets for a product (403)

intermittent process a manufacturing process in which a firm's manufacturing machines and equipment are changed to produce different products (237)

internal recruiting considering present employees as applicants for available positions (256)

international business all business activities that involve exchanges across national boundaries (73)

International Monetary Fund (IMF) an international bank with 186 member nations that makes short-term loans to developing countries experiencing balance-of-payment deficits (95)

International Organization for Standardization (ISO) a network of national standards institutes and similar organizations from 161 different countries that is charged with developing standards for quality products and services that are traded throughout the globe (234)

Internet a worldwide network of computers linked through telecommunications (477)

interpersonal skills the ability to deal effectively with other people (178)

intranet a smaller version of the Internet for use within a firm's computer network (477)

inventory control the process of managing inventories in such a way as to minimize inventory costs, including both holding costs and potential stock-out costs (230)

inventory management the process of managing inventories in such a way as to minimize inventory costs, including both holding costs and potential stock-out costs (418)

inventory turnover a financial ratio calculated by dividing the cost of goods sold in one year by the average value of the inventory (520)

investment banking firm an organization that assists corporations in raising funds, usually by helping to sell new issues of stocks, bonds, or other financial securities (581)

invisible hand a term created by Adam Smith to describe how an individual's personal gain benefits others and a nation's economy (14)

J

job analysis a systematic procedure for studying jobs to determine their various elements and requirements (254)

job description a list of the elements that make up a particular job (254)

job enlargement expanding a worker's assignments to include additional but similar tasks (291)

job enrichment a motivation technique that provides employees with more variety and responsibility in their jobs (290)

job evaluation the process of determining the relative worth of the various jobs within a firm (261)

job redesign a type of job enrichment in which work is restructured to cultivate the worker–job match (292)

job rotation the systematic shifting of employees from one job to another (196)

job security protection against the loss of employment (321)

job sharing an arrangement whereby two people share one full-time position (294)

job specialization the separation of all organizational activities into distinct tasks and the assignment of different tasks to different people (194)

job specification a list of the qualifications required to perform a particular job (254)

joint venture an agreement between two or more groups to form a business entity in order to achieve a specific goal or to operate for a specific period of time (125)

jurisdiction the right of a particular union to organize particular groups of workers (318)

just-in-time inventory system a system designed to ensure that materials or supplies arrive at a facility just when they are needed so that storage and holding costs are minimized (230)

K

knowledge management (KM) a firm's procedures for generating, using, and sharing the data and information (466)

L

labeling the presentation of information on a product or its package (379)

labor union an organization of workers acting together to negotiate their wages and working conditions with employers (308)

labor-intensive technology a process in which people must do most of the work (225)

leadership the ability to influence others (179)

leading the process of influencing people to work toward a common goal (173)

letter of credit issued by a bank on request of an importer stating that the bank will pay an amount of money to a stated beneficiary; a legal document issued by a bank or other financial institution guaranteeing to pay a seller a stated amount for a specified period of time (88, 552)

liabilities a firm's debts and obligations (505)

licensing a contractual agreement in which one firm permits another to produce and market its product and use its brand name in return for a royalty or other compensation (87)

lifestyle shopping center an open-air-environment shopping center with upscale chain specialty stores (416)

limit order a request that a security be bought or sold at a price that is equal to or better than some specified price (606)

limited liability a feature of corporate ownership that limits each owner's financial liability to the amount of money that he or she has paid for the corporation's stock (120)

limited partner a person who contributes capital to a business but has no management responsibility or liability for losses beyond the amount he or she invested in the partnership (112)

limited-liability company (LLC) a form of business ownership that combines the benefits of a corporation and a partnership while avoiding some of the restrictions and disadvantages of those forms of ownership (122)

limited-line wholesaler a middleman that stocks only a few product lines but carries numerous product items within each line (408)

limited-service wholesaler a middleman that assumes responsibility for a few wholesale services only (408)

line extension development of a new product that is closely related to one or more products in the existing product line but designed specifically to meet somewhat different customer needs (369)

line manager a position in which a person makes decisions and gives orders to subordinates to achieve the organization's goals (201)

line of credit a loan that is approved before the money is actually needed (548)

line structure an organizational structure in which the chain of command goes directly from person to person throughout the organization (201)

line-and-staff structure an organizational structure that utilizes the chain of command from a line structure in combination with the assistance of staff managers (202)

liquidity the ease with which an asset or investment can be converted into cash (508, 604)

local-area network (LAN) a network that connects computers that are in close proximity to each other, such as an office building or a college campus (477)

lockout a firm's refusal to allow employees to enter the workplace (324)

log-file records files that store a record of the Web sites visited (486)

long-term financing money that will be used for longer than one year (570)

long-term liabilities debts that need not be repaid for at least one year (510)

lump-sum salary increase an entire pay raise taken in one lump sum (262)

M

macroeconomics the study of the national economy and the global economy (12)

maintenance shop a workplace in which an employee who joins the union must remain a union member as long as he or she is employed by the firm (322)

major equipment large tools and machines used for production purposes (364)

Malcolm Baldrige National Quality Award an award given by the U.S. president to organizations that apply and are judged to be outstanding in specific managerial tasks that lead to improved quality for both products and services (232)

malware a general term that describes software designed to infiltrate a computer system without the user's consent (487)

management the process of coordinating people and other resources to achieve the goals of an organization (168)

management by objectives (MBO) a motivation technique in which managers and employees collaborate in setting goals (290)

management development the process of preparing managers and other professionals to assume increased responsibility in both present and future positions (264)

management information system (MIS) a system that provides managers and employees with the information they need to perform their jobs as effectively as possible (466)

managerial accounting provides managers and employees with the information needed to make decisions about a firm's financing, investing, marketing, and operating activities (503)

manufacturer (or producer) brand a brand that is owned by a manufacturer (373)

manufacturer's sales branch essentially a merchant wholesaler that is owned by a manufacturer (408)

manufacturer's sales office essentially a sales agent owned by a manufacturer (408)

margin requirement the portion of the price of a stock that cannot be borrowed (619)

market a group of individuals or organizations, or both, that need products in a given category and that have the ability, willingness, and authority to purchase such products (340)

market economy an economic system in which businesses and individuals decide what to produce and buy, and the market determines quantities sold and prices (14)

market order a request that a security be purchased or sold at the current market price (606)

market price the price at which the quantity demanded is exactly equal to the quantity supplied (22)

market segment a group of individuals or organizations within a market that share one or more common characteristics (343)

market segmentation the process of dividing a market into segments and directing a marketing mix at a particular segment or segments rather than at the total market (343)

market value the price of one share of a stock at a particular time (613)

marketing the activity, set of institutions, and processes for creating, communicating, delivering, and exchanging offerings that have value for customers, clients, partners, and society at large (335)

marketing concept a business philosophy that a firm should provide goods and services that satisfy customers' needs through a coordinated set of activities that allow the firm to achieve its objectives (338)

marketing information system a system for managing marketing information that is gathered continually from internal and external sources (348)

marketing manager a manager who is responsible for facilitating the exchange of products between an organization and its customers or clients (177)

marketing mix a combination of product, price, distribution, and promotion developed to satisfy a particular target market (341)

marketing plan a written document that specifies an organization's resources, objectives, strategy, and implementation and control efforts to be used in marketing a specific product or product group (346)

marketing research the process of systematically gathering, recording, and analyzing data concerning a particular marketing problem (349)

marketing strategy a plan that will enable an organization to make the best use of its resources and advantages to meet its objectives (341)

markup the amount a seller adds to the cost of a product to determine its basic selling price (383)

Maslow's hierarchy of needs a sequence of human needs in the order of their importance (281)

mass production a manufacturing process that lowers the cost required to produce a large number of identical or similar products over a long period of time (218)

master limited partnership (MLP) a business partnership that is owned and managed like a corporation but often taxed like a partnership (112)

materials handling the actual physical handling of goods, in warehouses as well as during transportation (420)

materials requirements planning (MRP) a computerized system that integrates production planning and inventory control (230)

matrix structure an organizational structure that combines vertical and horizontal lines of authority, usually by superimposing product departmentalization on a functionally departmentalized organization (203)

maturity date the date on which a corporation is to repay borrowed money (588)

measure of value a single standard or "yardstick" used to assign values to, and compare the values of, products, services, and resources (535)

mediation the use of a neutral third party to assist management and the union during their negotiations (325)

medium of exchange anything accepted as payment for products, services, and resources (535)

merchant middleman a middleman that actually takes title to products by buying them (401)

merchant wholesaler a middleman that purchases goods in large quantities and then sells them to other wholesalers or retailers and to institutional, farm, government, professional, or industrial users (407)

merger the purchase of one corporation by another (126)

microeconomics the study of the decisions made by individuals and businesses (12)

middle manager a manager who implements the strategy and major policies developed by top management (176)

middleman (or marketing intermediary) a marketing organization that links a producer and user within a marketing channel (401)

minority a racial, religious, political, national, or other group regarded as different from the larger group of which it is a part and that is often singled out for unfavorable treatment (56)

mission a statement of the basic purpose that makes an organization different from others (169)

missionary salesperson a salesperson—generally employed by a manufacturer—who visits retailers to persuade them to buy the manufacturer's products (442)

mixed economy an economy that exhibits elements of both capitalism and socialism (15)

monetary policies Federal Reserve decisions that determine the size of the supply of money in the nation and the level of interest rates (21)

money anything a society uses to purchase products, services, or resources (534)

monopolistic competition a market situation in which there are many buyers along with a relatively large number of sellers who differentiate their products from the products of competitors (23)

monopoly a market (or industry) with only one seller, and there are barriers to keep other firms from entering the industry (24)

morale an employee's feelings about his or her job and superiors and about the firm itself (279)

mortgage bond a corporate bond secured by various assets of the issuing firm (588)

motivating the process of providing reasons for people to work in the best interests of an organization (173)

motivation the individual internal process that energizes, directs, and sustains behavior; the personal "force" that causes you or me to behave in a particular way (278)

motivation factors job factors that increase motivation although their absence does not necessarily result in dissatisfaction (284)

motivation–hygiene theory the idea that satisfaction and dissatisfaction are separate and distinct dimensions (283)

multilateral development bank (MDB) an internationally supported bank that provides loans to developing countries to help them grow (94)

multinational enterprise a firm that operates on a worldwide scale without ties to any specific nation or region (91)

multiple-unit pricing the strategy of setting a single price for two or more units (387)

municipal bond sometimes called a *muni,* a debt security issued by a state or local government (612)

mutual fund pools the money of many investors—its shareholders—to invest in a variety of different securities (615)

N

National Alliance of Business (NAB) a joint business–government program to train the hard-core unemployed (59)

national bank a commercial bank chartered by the U.S. Comptroller of the Currency (544)

national debt the total of all federal deficits (21)

National Labor Relations Board (NLRB) the federal agency that enforces the provisions of the Wagner Act (314)

natural monopoly an industry requiring huge investments in capital and within which any duplication of facilities would be wasteful and thus not in the public interest (24)

need a personal requirement (281)

negotiated pricing establishing a final price through bargaining (386)

neighborhood shopping center a planned shopping center consisting of several small convenience and specialty stores (416)

net asset value (NAV) current market value of a mutual fund's portfolio minus the mutual fund's liabilities divided by the number of outstanding shares (615)

net income occurs when revenues exceed expenses (513)

net loss occurs when expenses exceed revenues (513)

net sales the actual dollar amounts received by a firm for the goods and services it has sold after adjustment for returns, allowances, and discounts (512)

net worth the difference between the value of your total assets and your total liabilities (599)

network structure an organizational structure in which administration is the primary function, and most other functions are contracted out to other firms (205)

news release a typed page of about 300 words provided by an organization to the media as a form of publicity (448)

non-price competition competition based on factors other than price (381)

nonstore retailing a type of retailing whereby consumers purchase products without visiting a store (413)

nontariff barrier a nontax measure imposed by a government to favor domestic over foreign suppliers (77)

not-for-profit corporation a corporation organized to provide a social, educational, religious, or other service rather than to earn a profit (123)

NOW account an interest-bearing checking account; *NOW* stands for *negotiable order of withdrawal (547)*

O

objective a specific statement detailing what an organization intends to accomplish over a shorter period of time (170)

odd-number pricing the strategy of setting prices using odd numbers that are slightly below whole-dollar amounts (387)

off-price retailer a store that buys manufacturers' seconds, overruns, returns, and off-season merchandise for resale to consumers at deep discounts (412)

oligopoly a market (or industry) in which there are few sellers (23)

online retailing retailing that makes products available to buyers through computer connections (415)

open corporation a corporation whose stock can be bought and sold by any individual (117)

open-market operations the buying and selling of U.S. government securities by the Federal Reserve System for the purpose of controlling the supply of money (541)

operating expenses all business costs other than the cost of goods sold (513)

operational plan a type of plan designed to implement tactical plans (172)

operations management all activities managers engage in to produce goods and services (217)

operations manager a manager who manages the systems that convert resources into goods and services (176)

order-getter a salesperson who is responsible for selling a firm's products to new customers and increasing sales to present customers (442)

order processing activities involved in receiving and filling customers' purchase orders (419)

order-taker a salesperson who handles repeat sales in ways that maintain positive relationships with customers (442)

organization a group of two or more people working together to achieve a common set of goals (193)

organization chart a diagram that represents the positions and relationships within an organization (193)

organizational height the number of layers, or levels, of management in a firm (200)

organizing the grouping of resources and activities to accomplish some end result in an efficient and effective manner (173)

orientation the process of acquainting new employees with an organization (260)

out-of-home advertising short promotional messages on billboards, posters, signs, and transportation vehicles (436)

outsourcing the process of finding outside vendors and suppliers that provide professional help, parts, or materials at a lower cost (480)

over-the-counter (OTC) market a network of dealers who buy and sell the stocks of corporations that are not listed on a securities exchange (583)

overtime time worked in excess of 40 hours in one week (under some union contracts, time worked in excess of eight hours in a single day) (320)

owners' equity the difference between a firm's assets and its liabilities (505)

P

packaging all the activities involved in developing and providing a container with graphics for a product (377)

par value an assigned (and often arbitrary) dollar value printed on a stock certificate (584)

participative leadership leadership style in which all members of a team are involved in identifying essential goals and developing strategies to reach those goals (180)

partnership a voluntary association of two or more persons to act as co-owners of a business for profit (111)

part-time work permanent employment in which individuals work less than a standard work week (293)

penetration pricing the strategy of setting a low price for a new product (386)

perfect (or pure) competition the market situation in which there are many buyers and sellers of a product, and no single buyer or seller is powerful enough to affect the price of that product (22)

performance appraisal the evaluation of employees' current and potential levels of performance to allow managers to make objective human resources decisions (265)

periodic discounting temporary reduction of prices on a patterned or systematic basis (386)

personal budget a specific plan for spending your income (600)

personal income the income an individual receives from all sources *less* the Social Security taxes the individual must pay (353)

personal investment the use of your personal funds to earn a financial return (601)

personal selling personal communication aimed at informing customers and persuading them to buy a firm's products (432)

PERT (Program Evaluation and Review Technique) a scheduling technique that identifies the major activities necessary to complete a project and sequences them based on the time required to perform each one (231)

physical distribution all the activities concerned with the efficient movement of products from the producer to the ultimate user (417)

physiological needs the things we require for survival (282)

picketing marching back and forth in front of a place of employment with signs informing the public that a strike is in progress (323)

piece-rate system a compensation system under which employees are paid a certain amount for each unit of output they produce (280)

place utility utility created by making a product available at a location where customers wish to purchase it (337)

plan an outline of the actions by which an organization intends to accomplish its goals and objectives (171)

planning establishing organizational goals and deciding how to accomplish them (169)

planning horizon the period during which an operational plan will be in effect (227)

plant layout the arrangement of machinery, equipment, and personnel within a production facility (226)

point-of-purchase display promotional material placed within a retail store (447)

pollution the contamination of water, air, or land through the actions of people in an industrialized society (60)

positioning the development of a product image in buyers' minds relative to the images they have of competing products (450)

possession utility utility created by transferring title (or ownership) of a product to a buyer (337)

preferred stock stock owned by individuals or firms who usually do not have voting rights but whose claims on dividends and assets are paid before those of common-stock owners (118, 583)

premium a gift that a producer offers a customer in return for buying its product (446)

premium pricing pricing the highest-quality or most-versatile products higher than other models in the product line (388)

press conference a meeting at which invited media personnel hear important news announcements and receive supplementary textual materials and photographs (448)

price the amount of money a seller is willing to accept in exchange for a product at a given time and under given circumstances (379)

price competition an emphasis on setting a price equal to or lower than competitors' prices to gain sales or market share (381)

price leaders products priced below the usual markup, near cost, or below cost (389)

price lining the strategy of selling goods only at certain predetermined prices that reflect definite price breaks (389)

price skimming the strategy of charging the highest possible price for a product during the introduction stage of its life-cycle (386)

primary market a market in which an investor purchases financial securities (via an investment bank) directly from the issuer of those securities (581)

primary-demand advertising advertising aimed at increasing the demand for all brands of a product within a specific industry (433)

prime interest rate the lowest rate charged by a bank for a short-term loan (578)

private placement occurs when stock and other corporate securities are sold directly to insurance companies, pension funds, or large institutional investors (585)

problem the discrepancy between an actual condition and a desired condition (181)

problem-solving team a team of knowledgeable employees brought together to tackle a specific problem (296)

process material a material that is used directly in the production of another product but is not readily identifiable in the finished product (364)

producer price index (PPI) an index that measures prices that producers receive for their finished goods (19)

product everything one receives in an exchange, including all tangible and intangible attributes and expected benefits; it may be a good, a service, or an idea (362)

product deletion the elimination of one or more products from a product line (369)

product design the process of creating a set of specifications from which a product can be produced (225)

product differentiation the process of developing and promoting differences between one's products and all similar products (23, 381)

product life-cycle a series of stages in which a product's sales revenue and profit increase, reach a peak, and then decline (364)

product line a group of similar products that differ only in relatively minor characteristics (224, 367)

product mix all the products a firm offers for sale (367)

product modification the process of changing one or more of a product's characteristics (368)

productivity the average level of output per worker per hour (17, 235)

profit what remains after all business expenses have been deducted from sales revenue (11)

profit-sharing the distribution of a percentage of a firm's profit among its employees (262)

promissory note a written pledge by a borrower to pay a certain sum of money to a creditor at a specified future date (578)

promotion communication about an organization and its products that is intended to inform, persuade, or remind target-market members (430)

promotion mix the particular combination of promotion methods a firm uses to reach a target market (430)

promotional campaign a plan for combining and using the four promotional methods—advertising, personal selling, sales promotion, and publicity—in a particular promotion mix to achieve one or more marketing goals (449)

prospectus a detailed, written description of a new security, the issuing corporation, and the corporation's top management (608)

proxy a legal form listing issues to be decided at a stockholders' meeting and enabling stockholders to transfer their voting rights to some other individual or individuals (118)

proxy fight a technique used to gather enough stockholder votes to control a targeted company (126)

public relations communication activities used to create and maintain favorable relations between an organization and various public groups, both internal and external (433)

publicity communication in news-story form about an organization, its products, or both (448)

purchasing all the activities involved in obtaining required materials, supplies, components, and parts from other firms (229)

Q

quality circle a team of employees who meet on company time to solve problems of product quality (233)

quality control the process of ensuring that goods and services are produced in accordance with design specifications (233)

R

random discounting temporary reduction of prices on an unsystematic basis (387)

rate of return the total dollar amount of return you receive on an investment over a specific period of time divided by the amount invested (603)

ratification approval of a labor contract by a vote of the union membership (319)

raw material a basic material that actually becomes part of a physical product; usually comes from mines, forests, oceans, or recycled solid wastes (364)

rebate a return of part of the product's purchase price (445)

recession two or more consecutive three-month periods of decline in a country's GDP (20)

recruiting the process of attracting qualified job applicants (255)

reference pricing pricing a product at a moderate level and positioning it next to a more expensive model or brand (387)

regional shopping center a planned shopping center containing large department stores, numerous specialty stores, restaurants, movie theaters, and sometimes even hotels (417)

registered bond a bond registered in the owner's name by the issuing company (588)

reinforcement theory a theory of motivation based on the premise that rewarded behavior is likely to be repeated, whereas punished behavior is less likely to recur (286)

relationship marketing establishing long-term, mutually satisfying buyer–seller relationships (337)

replacement chart a list of key personnel and their possible replacements within a firm (251)

research and development (R&D) a set of activities intended to identify new ideas that have the potential to result in new goods and services (222)

reserve requirement the percentage of its deposits a bank *must* retain, either in its own vault or on deposit with its Federal Reserve district bank (540)

responsibility the duty to do a job or perform a task (198)

retailer a middleman that buys from producers or other middlemen and sells to consumers (402)

retained earnings the portion of a corporation's profits not distributed to stockholders (510, 584)

return on owners' equity a financial ratio calculated by dividing net income after taxes by owners' equity (518)

return on sales (or profit margin) a financial ratio calculated by dividing net income after taxes by net sales (518)

revenue stream a source of revenue flowing into a firm (481)

revenues the dollar amounts earned by a firm from selling goods, providing services, or performing business activities (511)

revolving credit agreement a guaranteed line of credit (548)

risk-return ratio a ratio based on the principle that a high-risk decision should generate higher financial returns for a business and more conservative decisions often generate lower returns (573)

robotics the use of programmable machines to perform a variety of tasks by manipulating materials and tools (236)

S

safety needs the things we require for physical and emotional security (282)

salary a specific amount of money paid for an employee's work during a set calendar period, regardless of the actual number of hours worked (262)

sales forecast an estimate of the amount of a product that an organization expects to sell during a certain period of time based on a specified level of marketing effort (347)

sales promotion the use of activities or materials as direct inducements to customers or salespersons (433)

sales support personnel employees who aid in selling but are more involved in locating prospects, educating customers, building goodwill for the firm, and providing follow-up service (442)

sample a free product given to customers to encourage trial and purchase (446)

Sarbanes-Oxley Act of 2002 provides sweeping new legal protection for employees who report corporate misconduct (43)

savings and loan association (S&L) a financial institution that offers checking and savings accounts and CDs and that invests most of its assets in home mortgage loans and other consumer loans (545)

scheduling the process of ensuring that materials and other resources are at the right place at the right time (230)

scientific management the application of scientific principles to management of work and workers (279)

S-corporation a corporation that is taxed as though it were a partnership (122)

secondary market a market for existing financial securities that are traded between investors (582)

secondary-market pricing setting one price for the primary target market and a different price for another market (386)

securities exchange a marketplace where member brokers meet to buy and sell securities (583)

security average (or security index) an average of the current market prices of selected securities (625)

selection the process of gathering information about applicants for a position and then using that information to choose the most appropriate applicant (257)

selective distribution the use of only a portion of the available outlets for a product in each geographic area (403)

selective-demand (or brand) advertising advertising that is used to sell a particular brand of product (434)

self-actualization needs the need to grow and develop and to become all that we are capable of being (282)

self-managed teams groups of employees with the authority and skills to manage themselves (296)

selling short the process of selling stock that an investor does not actually own but has borrowed from a brokerage firm and will repay at a later date (618)

seniority the length of time an employee has worked for an organization (320)

serial bonds bonds of a single issue that mature on different dates (589)

Service Corps of Retired Executives (SCORE) a group of businesspeople who volunteer their services to small businesses through the SBA (149)

service economy an economy in which more effort is devoted to the production of services than to the production of goods (27, 221)

shop steward an employee elected by union members to serve as their representative (322)

shopping product an item for which buyers are willing to expend considerable effort on planning and making the purchase (363)

short-term financing money that will be used for one year or less (569)

sinking fund a sum of money to which deposits are made each year for the purpose of redeeming a bond issue (589)

Six Sigma a disciplined approach that relies on statistical data and improved methods to eliminate defects for a firm's products and services (234)

skills inventory a computerized data bank containing information on the skills and experience of all present employees (252)

slowdown a technique whereby workers report to their jobs but work at a slower pace than normal (324)

small business one that is independently owned and operated for profit and is not dominant in its field (137)

Small Business Administration (SBA) a governmental agency that assists, counsels, and protects the interests of small businesses in the United States (148)

small-business development centers (SBDCs) university-based groups that provide individual counseling and practical training to owners of small businesses (151)

small-business institutes (SBIs) groups of senior and graduate students in business administration who provide management counseling to small businesses (151)

small-business investment companies (SBICs) privately owned firms that provide venture capital to small enterprises that meet their investment standards (152)

social audit a comprehensive report of what an organization has done and is doing with regard to social issues that affect it (65)

social needs the human requirements for love and affection and a sense of belonging (282)

social network site a Web site (often called a social site) that functions like an online community of Internet users where you can share your profile, messages, and photographs with family and friends (486)

social responsibility the recognition that business activities have an impact on society and the consideration of that impact in business decision making (47)

socioeconomic model of social responsibility the concept that business should emphasize not only profits but also the impact of its decisions on society (52)

sole proprietorship a business that is owned (and usually operated) by one person (108)

spamming the sending of massive amounts of unsolicited e-mails (486)

span of management (or span of control) the number of workers who report directly to one manager (199)

special-event pricing advertised sales or price cutting linked to a holiday, season, or event (389)

specialization the separation of a manufacturing process into distinct tasks and the assignment of the different tasks to different individuals (26)

specialty product an item that possesses one or more unique characteristics for which a significant group of buyers is willing to expend considerable purchasing effort (363)

specialty-line wholesaler a middleman that carries a select group of products within a single line (408)

speculative production the time lag between the actual production of goods and when the goods are sold (570)

staff manager a position created to provide support, advice, and expertise within an organization (202)

stakeholders all the different people or groups of people who are affected by the policies and decisions made by an organization (11)

standard of living a loose, subjective measure of how well off an individual or a society is, mainly in terms of want satisfaction through goods and services (24)

standing committee a relatively permanent committee charged with performing some recurring task (207)

state bank a commercial bank chartered by the banking authorities in the state in which it operates (544)

statement of cash flows a statement that illustrates how the company's operating, investing, and financing activities affect cash during an accounting period (514)

statistic a measure that summarizes a particular characteristic of an entire group of numbers (470)

statistical process control (SPC) a system that uses sampling to obtain data that are plotted on control charts and graphs to see if the production process is operating as it should and to pinpoint problem areas (233)

statistical quality control (SQC) a set of specific statistical techniques used to monitor all aspects of the production process to ensure that both work-in-process and finished products meet the firm's quality standards (233)

stock the shares of ownership of a corporation (116)

stock dividend a dividend in the form of additional stock (613)

stock split the division of each outstanding share of a corporation's stock into a greater number of shares (613)

stockholder a person who owns a corporation's stock (116)

store (or private) brand a brand that is owned by an individual wholesaler or retailer (373)

store of value a means of retaining and accumulating wealth (535)

strategic alliance a partnership formed to create competitive advantage on a worldwide basis (90)

strategic plan an organization's broadest plan, developed as a guide for major policy setting and decision making (171)

strategic planning process the establishment of an organization's major goals and objectives and the allocation of resources to achieve them (170)

strike a temporary work stoppage by employees, calculated to add force to their demands (310)

strikebreaker a non-union employee who performs the job of a striking union member (325)

supermarket a large self-service store that sells primarily food and household products (410)

superstore a large retail store that carries not only food and nonfood products ordinarily found in supermarkets but also additional product lines (410)

supply the quantity of a product that producers are willing to sell at each of various prices; an item that facilitates production and operations but does not become part of a finished product (22, 364, 380)

supply-chain management long-term partnership among channel members working together to create a distribution system that reduces inefficiencies, costs, and redundancies while creating a competitive advantage and satisfying customers (404)

sustainability meeting the needs of the present without compromising the ability of future generations to meet their own needs (28)

SWOT analysis the identification and evaluation of a firm's strengths, weaknesses, opportunities, and threats (170)

syndicate a temporary association of individuals or firms organized to perform a specific task that requires a large amount of capital (125)

synthetic process a process in operations management in which raw materials or components are combined to create a finished product (218)

T

tactical plan a smaller scale plan developed to implement a strategy (172)

target market a group of individuals or organizations, or both, for which a firm develops and maintains a marketing mix suitable for the specific needs and preferences of that group (341)

task force a committee established to investigate a major problem or pending decision (207)

team two or more workers operating as a coordinated unit to accomplish a specific task or goal (296)

technical salesperson a salesperson who assists a company's current customers in technical matters (442)

technical skills specific skills needed to accomplish a specialized activity (178)

telecommuting working at home all the time or for a portion of the work week (294)

telemarketing the performance of marketing-related activities by telephone (414)

television home shopping a form of selling in which products are presented to television viewers, who can buy them by calling a toll-free number and paying with a credit card (415)

tender offer an offer to purchase the stock of a firm targeted for acquisition at a price just high enough to tempt stockholders to sell their shares (126)

term-loan agreement a promissory note that requires a borrower to repay a loan in monthly, quarterly, semiannual, or annual installments (586)

Theory X a concept of employee motivation generally consistent with Taylor's scientific management; assumes that employees dislike work and will function only in a highly controlled work environment (284)

Theory Y a concept of employee motivation generally consistent with the ideas of the human relations movement; assumes that employees accept responsibility and work toward organizational goals, and by doing so they also achieve personal rewards (284)

Theory Z the belief that some middle ground between type A and type J practices is best for American business (285)

time deposit an amount on deposit in an interest-bearing savings account or certificate of deposit (537)

time utility utility created by making a product available when customers wish to purchase it (337)

top manager an upper-level executive who guides and controls the overall fortunes of an organization (175)

total cost the sum of the fixed costs and the variable costs attributed to a product (383)

total quality management (TQM) the coordination of efforts directed at improving customer satisfaction, increasing employee participation, strengthening supplier partnerships, and facilitating an organizational atmosphere of continuous quality improvement (184)

total revenue the total amount received from sales of a product (383)

trade credit a type of short-term financing extended by a seller who does not require immediate payment after delivery of merchandise (577)

trade deficit a negative balance of trade (75)

trade name the complete and legal name of an organization (373)

trade sales promotion method a sales promotion method designed to encourage wholesalers and retailers to stock and actively promote a manufacturer's product (445)

trade salesperson a salesperson—generally employed by a food producer or processor—who assists customers in promoting products, especially in retail stores (442)

trade show an industry-wide exhibit at which many sellers display their products (447)

trademark a brand name or brand mark that is registered with the U.S. Patent and Trademark Office and thus is legally protected from use by anyone except its owner (373)

trading company provides a link between buyers and sellers in different countries (90)

traditional specialty store a store that carries a narrow product mix with deep product lines (411)

transfer pricing prices charged in sales between an organization's units (390)

transportation the shipment of products to customers (420)

trial balance a summary of the balances of all general ledger accounts at the end of the accounting period (506)

trustee an individual or an independent firm that acts as a bond owner's representative (589)

U

undifferentiated approach directing a single marketing mix at the entire market for a particular product (341)

unemployment rate the percentage of a nation's labor force unemployed at any time (18)

union security protection of the union's position as the employees' bargaining agent (321)

union shop a workplace in which new employees must join the union after a specified probationary period (322)

union–management (labor) relations the dealings between labor unions and business management both in the bargaining process and beyond it (308)

unlimited liability a legal concept that holds a business owner personally responsible for all the debts of the business (110)

unsecured financing financing that is not backed by collateral (577)

utility the ability of a good or service to satisfy a human need (219, 337)

V

variable cost a cost that depends on the number of units produced (383)

venture capital money that is invested in small (and sometimes struggling) firms that have the potential to become very successful (152)

vertical channel integration the combining of two or more stages of a distribution channel under a single firm's management (404)

vertical marketing system (VMS) a centrally managed distribution channel resulting from vertical channel integration (404)

virtual office allows employees to work at any place where they have access to computers, software, and other technology that enables them to perform their normal work activities (475)

virtual team a team consisting of members who are geographically dispersed but communicate electronically (297)

virtuoso team a team of exceptionally highly skilled and talented individuals brought together to produce significant change (296)

W

wage survey a collection of data on prevailing wage rates within an industry or a geographic area (261)

warehouse club a large-scale members-only establishment that combines features of cash-and-carry wholesaling with discount retailing (411)

warehouse showroom a retail facility in a large, low-cost building with a large on-premises inventory and minimal service (410)

warehousing the set of activities involved in receiving and storing goods and preparing them for reshipment (419)

whistle-blowing informing the press or government officials about unethical practices within one's organization (44)

wholesaler a middleman that sells products to other firms (402)

wide-area network (WAN) a network that connects computers over a large geographic area, such as a city, a state, or even the world (477)

wildcat strike a strike not approved by the strikers' union (324)

working capital the difference between current assets and current liabilities (519)

World Trade Organization (WTO) powerful successor to GATT that incorporates trade in goods, services, and ideas (84)

World Wide Web (the Web) the Internet's multimedia environment of audio, visual, and text data (477)

Y

Yellow Pages advertising simple listings or display advertisements presented under specific product categories appearing in print and online telephone directories (435)

Z

zero-base budgeting a budgeting approach in which every expense in every budget must be justified (575)

Notes

Chapter 1

1. "Power Players: Jeff Bezos," *Advertising Age,* November 2, 2009, 32; Nancy Gohring, "Some Sony E-readers May Not Arrive for the Holidays," *PC World,* November 18, 2009, http://www.pcworld.com/article/182544/some_sony_ereaders_may_not_arrive_for_the_holidays.html; Franklin Paul, "Amazon's Jeff Bezos Talks About Kindle 2," *Reuters,* February 10, 2009, http://bx.businessweek.com/electronic-readers—writers/view?url=http%3A%2F%2Fis.gd%2FkzHy; Stephen H. Wildstrom, "Kindle 2: The Delight Is in the Details," *BusinessWeek,* March 2, 2009, 73.
2. The Horatio Alger Web site at http://www.horatioalger.org (accessed March 26, 2010).
3. Ibid.
4. The Dallas Mavericks Web site at http://www.nba.com/mavericks/news/cuban_bio000329.html (accessed March 28, 2010).
5. Idy Fernandez, "Julie Stav," *Hispanic,* June–July 2005, 204.
6. The Walmart stores Web site at http://www.walmartstores.com (accessed March 28, 2010).
7. The General Mills Web site at http://www.generalmills.com (accessed March 26, 2010).
8. The Bureau of Economic Analysis Web site at http://www.bea.gov (accessed March 29, 2010).
9. Bill Weir, "Made in China: Your Job, Your Future, Your Fortune," ABC News Web site at http://www.abcnews.com (accessed September 20, 2005).
10. The Bureau of Economic Analysis Web site at http://www.bea.gov (accessed March 30, 2010).
11. The Bureau of Labor Statistics Web site at http://www.bls.gov (accessed March 30, 2010).
12. The Bureau of Economic Analysis Web site at http://www.bea.gov (accessed March 30, 2010).
13. The Bureau of Labor Statistics Web site at http://www.bls.gov (accessed March 30, 2010).
14. The Treasury Direct Web site at http://www.treasurydirect.gov (accessed March 31, 2010) and the U.S. Census Bureau Web site at http://www.census.gov (accessed March 31, 2010).
15. The Investopedia Web site at http://www.investopedia.com (accessed March 31, 2010).
16. The Bureau of Labor Statistics Web site at http://www.bls.gov (accessed April 3, 2010).
17. Bill Weir, "Made in China: Your Job, Your Future, Your Fortune," ABC News Web site at http://www.abcnews.com (accessed September 20, 2005).
18. The Environmental Protection Agency Web site at http://www.epa.gov (accessed April 3, 2010).
19. Company Web site http://www.nederlanderconcerts.com (accessed August 20, 2010); "Nederlander Organization company overview," *BusinessWeek,* August 20, 2010, http://www.businessweek.com; Hannah Heineman, "Moving Forward on Capital Improvement Projects," *Santa Monica Mirror,* July 28, 2010, http://www.smmirror.com; Steve Knopper, "Tour Biz Strong in Weak Economy," *Rolling Stone,* October 2, 2008, 11–12; Ray Waddell, "Nederlander/Viejas Deal Offers Touring Opportunities," *Billboard,* January 10, 2008, http://www.billboard.com; interviews with Nederlander employees and the video "For Nederlander Concerts, Entertainment Is a Profitable Business."
20. Based on information from John Pletz, "Factories Start to Hire Again," *Crain's Chicago Business,* March 22, 2010, 1; Corinna Petry, "Caterpillar Eyeing New Factory in U.S.," *American Metal Market,* March 15, 2010, 5; Ivy Chang, "Demolition Equipment: Taller and Smaller," *Construction Bulletin,* March 15, 2010, 5; http://www.caterpillar.com.

Chapter 2

1. Leonie Nimmo and Dan Welch, "Chocolate Revolution From the World's Favourite Treat," *The Guardian (UK),* October 14, 2009, http://www.guardian.co.uk/environment/blog/oct/14/chocolate-week-fairtrade-ethical-living; Kiri Blakeley, "Entrepreneurs: Saving the World, One Chocolate Bar at a Time," *Forbes.com,* May 15, 2009, http://www.forbes.com/2009/05/14/small-business-ceo-forbes-woman-entrepreneurs-food.html; http://www.divinechocolate.com; http://www.divinechocolateusa.com.
2. The Wikipedia Web site at http://en.wikipedia.org/wiki/John_Rigas (accessed April 5, 2010).
3. The Wikipedia Web site at http://en.wikipedia.org/wiki/TAP_Pharmaceuticals (accessed April 5, 2010).
4. The United States Department of Justice Web site at http://www.usdoj.gov (accessed April 15, 2010).
5. Frontlines (Washington, DC: U.S. Agency for International Development, September 2005), 16.
6. Deere & Company Corporate Governance—Code of Ethics Web site at http://www.deere.com/en_US/globalcitizenship/values/ethics.html (accessed April 18, 2010).
7. U.S. Securities and Exchange Commission Web site at http://www.sec.gov/litigation/litreleases/2009/lr211129.htm (accessed April 5, 2010).
8. The Politico Web site at http://www.politico.com/news/stories/0310/3410/34105.html (accessed April 17, 2010).
9. The General Mills Web site at http://www.generalmills.com/corporate/commitment/foundation.aspx (accessed April 5, 2010).
10. The Michael and Susan Dell Foundation Web site at http://www.msdf.org/Programs/Urban_Education/default.aspx (accessed April 5, 2010).
11. IBM 2009 Corporate Responsibility Report, 21, http://www.ibm.com (accessed April 10, 2010).
12. GE 2008 Citizenship Report, 176, http://www.ge.com/citizenship/news_features/news.jsp (accessed April 5, 2010).
13. The Charles Schwab Foundation Web site at http://www.schwab.com (accessed April 21, 2010).
14. ExxonMobil 2008 Worldwide Giving Report, http://www.exxonmobil.com/corporate/community_contributions.aspx (accessed April 6, 2010).
15. AT&T News Release, http://www.att.com/gen/press-room?pid=4800&cdvn=news&newsarticleid=26457 (accessed April 27, 2009).
16. Wall Street Reform and Consumer Protection Act of 2009, http://www.govtrack.us/congress/bill.xpd?bill=h111-4173 (accessed April 5, 2010).
17. http://www.sholfieldhonda.com (accessed May 13, 2010); Adam Knapp, "Scholfield Honda Trying to Turn Green Movement into Good Business," *Wichita Business Journal,* http://wichita.bizjournals.com, March 7, 2008, and information provided through interviews with Scholfield Honda personnel and in the video "Scholfield Honda."
18. Based on information from "News: Belu Scrapes into Profit," Caterer & Hotelkeeper, January 22, 2010, n.p.; Jane Bainbridge, "Making a Smaller Splash," Marketing, December 2, 2009, 32; Danny Fortson, "Bottle vs Tap Grudge Match Hots Up," *Sunday Times (London),* June 7, 2009, 8; Belu Web site, http://www.belu.org; Schwab Foundation for Social Entrepreneurship, "Reed Paget," http://schwabfound.weforum.org/sf/SocialEntrepreneurs/Profiles/index.htm?sname=0&sorganization=73206&sarea=0&ssector=0&stype=0; "Case Study: Belu Water," London Evening Standard, http://www.thisislondon.co.uk/itsyourbusiness/article-23383046-details/Case+study:+Belu+Water/article.do.

Chapter 3

1. Based on information in Jung-Ah Lee, "Samsung Handset Sales on Track to Exceed 2009 Target," *Wall Street Journal,* November 30, 2009, http://www.wsj.com; Evan Ramstad, "Samsung's Swelling Size Brings New Challenges," *Wall Street Journal,* November 11, 2009, http://www.wsj.com; http://www.samsung.com.
2. The White House, Office of the Press Secretary, Press Release, August 6, 2002.
3. U.S. Bureau of Economic Analysis, U.S. Bureau of Commerce, *News Release,* March 18, 2010, http://www.bea.gov/newsreleases/rels.htm (accessed April 22, 2010).

4. This section draws heavily from the *World Economic Outlook Update*, January 26, 2010, International Monetary Fund Web site at http://www.imf.org/external/pubs/ft/weo/2010/update/01/index.htm (accessed April 19, 2010).
5. Micheal Chriszt and Elena Whisler, "China's Economic Emergence," *Econ South*, First Reserve Bank of Atlanta, Second Quarter 2005, 4–7.
6. World Trade Organization Web site at http://www.wto.org/english/news_e/press10_e/pr598_e.htm (accessed April 19, 2010).
7. Office of the United States Trade Representative, *NAFTA FACTS*, March 2008, 1, http://www.USTR.gov (accessed May 20, 2010).
8. U.S. CAFTA-DR Free Trade Agreement: How U.S. Companies Can Benefit, Export.Gov Web site at http://www.export.gov/FTA/cafta-dr/index.asp (accessed April 19, 2010).
9. ASEANSTATS Web site at http://www.aseansec.org/about_ASEAN.html (accessed April 19, 2010).
10. William M. Pride and O. C. Ferrell, *Marketing*, 2008 Edition (Boston, MA: Houghton Mifflin, 2008), 194.
11. The World Bank Web site at http://www.worldbank.org/ (accessed July 25, 2010).
12. http://www.evogear.com (accessed May 13, 2010), and information provided through interviews with Evo personnel and in the video "Evo: The Global Environment."
13. Based on information from "Jamie Oliver Praises McDonald's," *The Telegraph (UK)*, April 25, 2010, http://www.telegraph.co.uk; Bob O'Brien, "McDonald's Is Where the Beef Is," *Barron's*, April 21, 2010, http://online.barrons.com; Melanie Lindner, "McDonald's Hits the Spot," *Forbes*, March 8, 2010, http://www.forbes.com; http://www.mcdonalds.com; http://www.aboutmcdonalds.com.
14. Bob Driehaus, "A Cincinnati Ice Cream Maker Aims Big," *The New York Times*, September 12, 2010, N29; company Web site http://www.graeters.com (accessed September 2, 2010); Alexander Coolridge, "Winburn: Where Is Cincinnati Jobs Retention Plan?" Cincinnati.com, August 18, 2010, http://news.cincinnati.com; Lucy May, "Graeter's Northern Kentucky Franchisee Puts Stores on the Block," *Business Courier*, August 6, 2010, http://cincinnati.bizjournals.com; Ken Hoffman, "Graeter's Ice Cream Is Worthy Diet Buster," *The Houston Chronicle*, April 15, 2009, http://www.chron.com; Melissa Davis Haller, "The Big Chill," *Cincinnati Magazine*, February 2009, http://www.cincinnatimagazine.com; and interviews with company staff and the video, "Let's Go Get a Graeter's!"

Chapter 4

1. Farhad Manjoo, "To Sell or Not to Sell?" *Fast Company*, December 2009, 49–50; Kermit Pattison, "A 20-Something Makes a Mint (and Sells It to Intuit)," *New York Times*, December 3, 2009, http://www.nytimes.com/2009/12/03/business/smallbusiness/03mint.html?_r=1&pagewanted=all; Lauren Young, "Big Banks Take a Hint from Mint.com," *BusinessWeek*, October 12, 2009, 62; Spencer E. Ante, "Mint.com: Nurtured by Super-Angel VCs," *BusinessWeek Online*, September 16, 2009, http://www.businessweek.com/technology/content/sep2009/tc20090915_065038.htm; http://www.mint.com.
2. The Mint.com Web site at http://www.mint.com (accessed March 15, 2010).
3. Ibid.
4. The IVY Planning Group Web site at http://www.ivygroupllc.com (accessed March 15, 2010).
5. The National Association of Publicly Traded Partnerships Web site at http://www.naptp.com (accessed March 12, 2010).
6. The Procter & Gamble Web site at http://www.pg.com (accessed March 16, 2010).
7. Ibid.
8. The All Business Web site at http://www.allbusiness.com (accessed March 16, 2010).
9. The Hispanic PR Wire Web site at http://www.hispanicprwire.com (accessed March 10, 2010).
10. The Internal Revenue Service Web site at http://www.irs.gov (accessed March 20, 2010).
11. The Ocean Spray Cranberries, Inc. Web site at http://www.oceanspray.com (accessed March 20, 2010).
12. The Walmart Corporate Web site at http://www.walmartstores.com (accessed March 20, 2010).
13. "Buffett's Symetra Prices at Low End as 2010 U.S. IPOs Begin," *BusinessWeek*, Web site at http://www.businessweek.com (accessed March 20, 2010).
14. The Walmart Corporate Web site at http://www.walmartstores.com (accessed March 21, 2010).
15. The Oracle Web site at http://www.oracle.com (accessed March 21, 2010).
16. The IBM Web site at http://www.ibm.com (accessed March 22, 2010).
17. David Cho, "Weekend Merger Stuck with Bank of America," *The Washington Post* Web site at http://www.washingtonpost.com (accessed September 14, 2008).
18. http://www.annies.com (accessed May 18, 2010); Lauren McKay, "From Organic Goods to Sustainable Ones," *Customer Relationship Management*, April 2010, 14; Tara Siegel Bernard, "Winning a Place on Grocery Store Shelves Annie's Homegrown Finds Some Room as Market for Organic Food Grows," *Wall Street Journal*, March 29, 2005, http://www.w5j.com; "Leading Us All Into Temptation-In a Healthy Way," *Organic Style*, May 2005, and information provided through interviews with company personnel and in the video "Annie's Homegrown."
19. Based on information from Becky Quick, "Who Says the Economy Is Rebounding?" *Fortune*, May 3, 2010, http://www.fortune.com; Angela Greiling Keane and Ed Dufner, "CSX's Ward Calls Buffett's Rail Purchase 'Brilliant,'" *BusinessWeek*, April 14, 2010, http://www.businessweek.com; Alice Schroeder, *The Snowball: Warren Buffett and the Business of Life* (New York: Bantam Dell, 2008), Chapters 22 and 44, http://www.BerkshireHathaway.com.

Chapter 5

1. Michael Steinberger, "The Drawing Power of a US Burger Chain," *Financial Times*, November 21, 2009, http://www.ft.com/cms/s/2/e973cd44-d567-11de-81ee-00144feabdc0.html; Emily Bryson York, "Five Guys: An America's Hottest Brands Case Study," *Advertising Age*, November 16, 2009, http://www.adage.com; Elizabeth Licata, "Five Guys: Specialized Burger Concept Aims to Fulfill Customers' Cravings," *Nation's Restaurant News*, May 18, 2009, 58; http://www.fiveguys.com (accessed July 26, 2010).
2. U.S. Small Business Administration Web sites at http://www.sba.gov/contractingopportunities/officials/size/summaryofssi/index.html; http://web.sba.gov/faqs/faqindex.cfm?areaID=15 (accessed May 26, 2010).
3. U.S. Small Business Administration, Office of Advocacy, *Frequently Asked Questions*, September 2009, http://www.sba.gov/advo (accessed June 13, 2010).
4. Ibid.
5. U.S. Small Business Administration, Office of Advocacy, *Quarterly Indicators*, Second Quarter, http://www.sba.gov/advo (accessed October 3, 2008).
6. Thomas A. Garrett, "Entrepreneurs Thrive in America," *Bridges*, Federal Reserve Bank of St. Louis, Spring 2005, 2.
7. U.S. Small Business Administration, Office of Advocacy, *Small Business Research Summary*, Number 341, February 2009; U.S. Small Business Administration, SBA Press Office, *News Release*, September 10, 2008; and 2008 *The Small Business Economy*, a Report to the President, U.S. Business Administration (Washington, DC, December 2008), 61–63, 99.
8. U.S. Small Business Administration, *News Release*, Number 05–53, September 13, 2005, http://www.sba.gov/teens/brian_hendricks.html (accessed May 26, 2010).
9. U.S. Small Business Administration, Office of Advocacy, *Frequently Asked Questions*, September 2009, http://www.sba.gov/advo (accessed June 13, 2010).
10. SBA Press Release, "Computer Simulation Company from Florida Is National Small Business of the Year," May 25, 2010, http://www.sba.gov/news (accessed June 7, 2010).
11. U.S. Small Business Administration, Office of Advocacy, *Frequently Asked Questions*, September 2009, http://www.sba.gov/advo (accessed June 13, 2010).
12. U.S. Small Business Administration, Office of Advocacy, *News Release*, Number 10-03 ADVO, March 3, 2010, http://www.sba.gov/advo/press/10-03.html (accessed June 13, 2010).
13. Timothy S. Hatten, *Small Business Management: Entrepreneurship and Beyond*, 4th ed., Copyright © 2009 by Houghton Mifflin Company, 238. Reprinted with permission.
14. SCORE Web site at http://www.score.org/media_fact_sheet.html (accessed May 26, 2010).
15. Ibid.
16. SBA Press Release, *Fact Sheet*, September 11, 2008, 2.
17. U.S. Small Business Administration, *News Release*, Release Number 10–33, May 26, 2010, http://www.sba.gov/news (accessed June 13, 2010).
18. U.S. Small Business Administration, *News Release*, Release Number 10–33, May 26, 2010, http://www.sba.gov/news (accessed June 13, 2010).
19. SBA Press Release, "President Obama Proclaims National Small Business Week," May 21, 2010, http://www.sba.gov/news (accessed June 7, 2010).
20. SBA Press Release Number 10–414, *News Release*, May 14, 2010, http://www.sba.gov/news (accessed June 7, 2010).
21. Cindy Elmore, "Putting the Power into the Hands of Small Business Owners," *Marketwise*, Federal Reserve Bank of Richmond, Issue II, 2005, 13.
22. U.S. Small Business Administration, http://www.sba.gov/managing/marketing/intlsales.html (accessed October 4, 2008).
23. U.S. Commercial Service Web site at http://www.trade.gov/cs/ (accessed June 13, 2010).

24. SBA Press Release, "SBA 2010 Small Business Exporter of the Year," http://www.sba.gov/news (accessed June 6, 2010).
25. Based on information from company Web site http://www.murrayscheese.com (accessed April 23, 2010); http://www.murrayscheese.com/images_global/murrays_kroger_press_release.pdf (accessed April 23, 2010); Kelsey Blackwell, "Liz Thorpe," *Natural Foods Merchandiser*, March 2010; Kim Severson, "Murray's Cheese Will Open 50 Locations in Kroger Markets," *The New York Times*, November 24, 2009, http://dinersjournal.blogs.nytimes.com/tag/murrays-cheese/; Rosalind Resnick, "Market with Meaning," *Entrepreneur*, November 6, 2009, http://www.entrepreneur.com/marketing/marketingideas/article203938.html#.
26. Based on information from "Very Little House on the Prairie," *The Economist*, February 21, 2009, 45; http://www.tumbleweedhouses.com; Steven Kurutz, "The Next Little Thing?" *The New York Times*, September 11, 2008, F1, F8; Carol Lloyd, "Small Houses Challenge Our Notions of Need as Well as Minimum-Size Standards," *SFGate.com*, April 27, 2007, http://www.sfgate.com; Bethany Little, "Think Small," *The New York Times*, February 16, 2007, http://travel.nytimes.com; Hannah Bloch, "Downsizing, Seriously," *The New York Times*, September 10, 2006, http://www.nytimes.com.
27. Bob Driehaus, "A Cincinnati Ice Cream Maker Aims Big," *The New York Times*, September 12, 2010, N29; company Web site http://www.graeters.com (accessed September 2, 2010); Alexander Coolridge, "Winburn: Where Is Cincinnati Jobs Retention Plan?" *Cincinnati.com*, August 18, 2010, http://news.cincinnati.com; Lucy May, "Graeter's Northern Kentucky Franchisee Puts Stores on the Block," *Business Courier*, August 6, 2010, http://cincinnati.bizjournals.com; Ken Hoffman, "Graeter's Ice Cream Is Worthy Diet Buster," *The Houston Chronicle*, April 15, 2009, http://www.chron.com; Melissa Davis Haller, "The Big Chill," *Cincinnati Magazine*, February 2009, http://www.cincinnatimagazine.com; and interviews with company staff and the video, "Graeter's."

Chapter 6

1. Jack Neff, "P&G CEO Bob McDonald on Why Size Doesn't Matter," *Advertising Age*, January 18, 2010, 1ff; Ellen Byron, "Olay Highlights P&G's Push to Extend Brands," *Advertising Age*, January 7, 2010, http://www.adage.com; Jennifer Reingold, "The $79 Billion Handoff," *Fortune*, December 7, 2009, 80ff; http://www.pg.com.
2. "Eli Lilly Made China Pharma Market a Top Priority," *Transmedia.com*, January 1, 2010, http://www.transmedia-china.com/default.aspx?portalid=442&tabid=0&mid=5606&ctl=news&iid=3561.
3. Starbucks, http://www.starbucks.com/about-us/company-information/mission-statement (accessed February 4, 2010); Facebook, http://www.facebook.com/facebook#!/facebook?v=info (accessed August 27, 2010).
4. Starbucks, http://www.starbucks.com/SHAREDPLANET/ourGoals.aspx (accessed January 28, 2010).
5. "Walmart Makes Organizational Moves to Raise Efficiency," *Reuters*, January 29, 2010.
6. Han Tianyang and Xiao Gong, "Volkswagen Planning New Guangzhou Assembly Plant," *China Daily*, February 1, 2010, http://www.chinadaily.com.cn/bizchina/2010-02/01/content_9406566.htm.
7. http://www.bizjournals.com (accessed January 4, 2010).
8. http://www.fastcompany.com; http://www.ge.com/company/leadership/ceo.html (accessed May 8, 2010).
9. http://www.quantcast.com/monster.com (accessed January 8, 2010).
10. http://kwikiblog.blogspot.com/2008/03/Korean-management-practices-at-hyundai.html (accessed February 10, 2010).
11. http://www.flatworldknowledge.com/node/28982 (accessed February 4, 2010).
12. Andrew J. Dubrin, *Leadership: Research Findings, Practice and Skills*, 6th ed. (Mason, OH: South-Western/Cengage Learning, 2010).
13. http://www.1000ventures.com/business_guide/crosscuttings/leadership_entrepreneurial.html (accessed February 24, 2010).
14. Ricky Griffin, *Management*, 9th ed. (Boston, MA: Houghton Mifflin, 2008), 234.
15. Claire Cain Miller, "Tailoring Its Approach, Starbucks Rebounds," *New York Times*, January 20, 2010.
16. Micheline Maynard and Hiroku Tabuchi, "Rapid Growth Has Its Perils, Toyota Learns," *New York Times*, January 27, 2010.
17. http://www.foundation.phccweb.org/Library/Articles/TQM.pdf (accessed February 4, 2010).
18. Based on information on the company Web site http://www.llbean.com (accessed July 20, 2010); company news release, "L.L. Bean Installs a Solar Hot Water System to Its Flagship Store in Freeport," http://www.llbean.com, June 15, 2010; interviews with L.L. Bean employees, and the video, "L.L. Bean Relies on Its Core Values and Effective Leadership."
19. "DocuSign Board Appoints Keith Krach and Chairman and Steve King as President and CEO," *Wireless News*, February 4, 2010, n.p.; Cindy Waxer, "Sign on the Virtual Line," *FSB*, November 2009, 37; company Web site http://www.docusign.com; Douglas MacMillan, "The Issue: Workers as Crisis Consultants," *BusinessWeek*, April 9, 2008, http://www.businessweek.com.

Chapter 7

1. David Pinto, "Unilever Sets Goals," *MMR*, January 11, 2010, 85ff; Susan E. Reed, "Opinion: On the Death of the Cubicle," *GlobalPost*, December 24, 2009, http://www.globalpost.com/dispatch/worldview/091223/cubicles-office-culture-unilever; Nick Hughes, "Activism on Ice?" *Grocer*, December 12, 2009, 40ff; http://www.unilever.com.
2. Geoff Colvin, "How Top Companies Breed Stars," *Fortune*, September 20, 2007, http://money.cnn.com/magazines/fortune/fortune_archive/2007/10/01/100351829/index.htm.
3. "Avon Expects Savings and Benefits Approaching $900 Million From Original Restructuring, Product Line Simplification and Strategic Sourcing Programs—Higher Than Anticipated," *Avon, news release*, February 19, 2009, http://www.avoncompany.com/investor/businessnews/index.html.
4. "Company Overview," Martha Stewart Living Omnimedia, Inc., http://phx.corporate-ir.net/phoenix.zhtml?c=96022&p=irol-homeprofile (accessed May 1, 2010).
5. Rob Goffee and Gareth Jones, "The Character of a Corporation: How Your Company's Culture Can Make or Break Your Business," *Jones Harper Business*, December 2003, 182.
6. Based on information from http://www.numitea.com (accessed May 26, 2010), and information provided through interviews with Numi personnel and in the video "Turbulent Times: Numi's New Manager."
7. Based on information from Kathleen Kingsbury, "HP vs. Everybody," *Time*, April 26, 2010, GB4; "HP Agrees to Buy Palm for $1.2 Billion," *PC Magazine Online*, April 28, 2010, http://www.pcmag.com; "HP Closes 3Com Deal Takes Aim at Cisco," *EWeek*, April 12, 2010, http://www.eweek.com; Patrick Thibodeau, "Outsourcing Deal Gives P&G Clout with HP Execs," *Computerworld*, March 22, 2010, 12; "HP to Acquire 3Com in $2.7 Billion Deal," *InformationWeek*, November 11, 2009, http://www.informationweek.com; http://www.hp.com.

Chapter 8

1. Martin Mittelstaedt, "Eat the Chips, Compost the Bag," *Globe & Mail (Toronto)*, February 4, 2010, A9; Sandrine Rastello and Yi Tian, "Nestlé to Provide Cocoa Trees to Ivory Coast Farmers," *Bloomberg.com*, January 28, 2010, http://www.bloomberg.com/apps/news?pid=20601116&sid=a0LODCPwkNF0; Bob Sperber, "For 2009 Food Processing Processor of the Year, Nestlé USA, It's All About Creating Long-Term Value for the Bigger Picture and Serving Customer and Consumer Needs," *FoodProcessing.com*, November 30, 2009, http://www.bloomberg.com/apps/news?pid=20601116&sid=a0LODCPwkNF0; Katy Humphries, "UK: Nestlé Upgrades Kit Kat Plant," *Just-Food.com*, January 4, 2010, http://www.just-food.com; http://www.nestle.com.
2. The Bureau of Labor Statistics Web site at http://www.bls.gov (accessed May 1, 2010).
3. Ibid.
4. John Engler, "Forging a Second American Century," *Forbes*, May 28, 2009, Web site at http://www.forbes.com.
5. Thomas D. Kuczmarski, "Remanufacturing America's Factory Sector," *BusinessWeek*, September 9, 2009, Web site at http://www.businessweek.com.
6. The Bureau of Labor Statistics Web site at http://www.bls.gov (accessed May 1, 2010).
7. Robert Kreitner, *Management*, 11th ed. (Boston, MA: Houghton Mifflin, 2009), 474.
8. The 3M Corporation Web site at http://www.3m.com (accessed May 2, 2010).
9. The Berry Plastics Corporation Web site at http://www.berryplastics.com (accessed May 2, 2010).
10. The AT&T Supplier Web site at http://www.attsuppliers.com (accessed May 2, 2010).
11. The National Institute for Standards and Technology Web site at http://www.nist.gov (accessed May 3, 2010).
12. The iSixSigma Web site at http://www.isixsigma.com (accessed April 30, 2010).
13. The International Organization of Standardization (ISO) Web site at http://www.iso.org (accessed May 2, 2010).
14. The Bureau of Labor Statistics Web site at http://www.bls.gov (accessed May 3, 2010).
15. Ibid.
16. Ibid.
17. The Illumina, Inc., Web site at http://www.illumina.com (accessed May 3, 2010).
18. The Dell Computer Corporation Web site at http://www.dell.com (accessed May 4, 2010).
19. Company Web site http://www.burton.com (accessed June 30, 2010); Mike Lewis, "Jake Burton on Taking the Helm," *Transworld Business*, May 4, 2010, http://business.transworld.net; "Laurent Potdevin Resigns as Burton CEO," *ESPN.com*, May 3, 2010, http://sports.espn.go.com (accessed June 21, 2010); Bruce Edwards, "Burton Moving Factory to Austria," *Rutland Herland*, March

17, 2010, http://www.rutlandherald.com; interviews with company staff and the video "Burton Snowboards' High Quality Standards."

20. Based on Richard Tedlow, "Toyota Was in Denial. How About You?" *BusinessWeek*, April 19, 2010, 76; Kate Linebaugh, "Consumer Reports Calls Lexus GX 460 Unsafe," *Wall Street Journal*, April 13, 2010, http://www.wsj.com; Micheline Maynard, "Toyota Delayed a U.S. Recall, Documents Show," *New York Times*, April 11, 2010, http://www.nytimes.com; Alan Ohnsman, Jeff Green, and Kae Inoue, "The Humbling of Toyota," *BusinessWeek*, March 22, 2010, 33–36; "Getting the Cow Out of the Ditch," *The Economist*, February 13, 2010, 69; Micheline Maynard, "Quality Is Major Concern of Toyota's Visiting Chief," *The New York Times*, January 15, 2008, http://www.nytimes.com; Micheline Maynard, "The Dings and Dents of Toyota," *The New York Times*, November 3, 2007, http://www.nytimes.com; Martin Fackler, "The 'Toyota Way' Is Translated for a New Generation of Foreign Managers," *New York Times*, February 13, 2007, http://www.nytimes.com.
21. Bob Driehaus, "A Cincinnati Ice Cream Maker Aims Big," *The New York Times*, September 12, 2010, N29; company Web site http://www.graeters.com (accessed September 2, 2010); Alexander Coolridge, "Winburn: Where Is Cincinnati Jobs Retention Plan?" *Cincinnati.com*, August 18, 2010, http://news.cincinnati.com; Lucy May, "Graeter's Northern Kentucky Franchisee Puts Stores on the Block," *Business Courier*, August 6, 2010, http://cincinnati.bizjournals.com; Ken Hoffman, "Graeter's Ice Cream Is Worthy Diet Buster," *The Houston Chronicle*, April 15, 2009, http://www.chron.com; Melissa Davis Haller, "The Big Chill," *Cincinnati Magazine*, February 2009, http://www.cincinnatimagazine.com; and interviews with company staff and the video, "Graeter's Leadership and Management Efforts Enhance the Firm's Performance."

Chapter 9

1. "Now Hiring! Lynn Franklyn, HR Manager, Wegmans Food Markets," *Fortune*, February 8, 2010, 84; Martha Woodall, "Collegeville Wegmans Opening Just Grand," *Philadelphia Inquirer*, October 12, 2009, http://www.philly.com/inquirer/local/pa/20091012_Collegeville_Wegmans_opening_just_grand.html; Donna Owens, "Treating Employees Like Customers," *HR Magazine*, October 2009, 28ff; http://www.wegmans.com.
2. Nick Bunkley, "Ford Profit Comes as Toyota Hits a Bump," *New York Times*, January 28, 2010.
3. U.S. Department of Labor, Bureau of Labor Statistics, http://www.bls.gov (accessed February 24, 2010).
4. Barbara Frankel, "The DiversityInc Top 10 Global Diversity Companies List," *DiversityInc Magazine*, May 18, 2009.
5. http://hr.blr.com/about/about.aspx (accessed February 24, 2010).
6. Procter & Gamble, http://www.pg.com (accessed January 25, 2010).
7. Nanette Byrnes, "Start Search," *BusinessWeek*, October 10, 2005, 74–76.
8. U.S. Department of Labor, Bureau of Labor Statistics, *News Release*, December 9, 2009, http://www.bls.gov.
9. Milton Moskowitz, Robert Levering, and Christopher Tkaczyk, "100 Top Companies to Work For," *Fortune*, February 8, 2010 issue, http://money.cnn.com/magazines/fortune/bestcompanies/2010/.
10. Cynthia D. Fisher, Lyle F. Schoenfeldt, and James B. Shaw, *Human Resource Management* (Boston, MA: Houghton Mifflin, 2006), 464.
11. Ibid., 465.
12. http://www.whirlpool.com (accessed May 26, 2010); information provided through interviews with Whirlpool personnel and in the video "Meeting the Challenge of Diversity: Whirlpool."
13. Dina Berta, "Domino's Franchisee Pens Management Guidebook," *Nation's Restaurant News*, August 3, 2009, 12; Domino's Web site, http://www.dominosbiz.com; Louise Kramer, "For a Franchise, Success Is in the Hiring," *The New York Times*, January 6, 2008, http://www.nytimes.com; Mark A. DeSorbo, "65 Percent of Fast Food Restaurants Report Increased Employment in Q4," *QSR Magazine*, November 2007, http://www.qsrmagazine.com.

Chapter 10

1. Diane Brady, "Can GE Still Manage?" *BusinessWeek*, April 15, 2010, http://www.businessweek.com; Vikram Johri, "'Leaders Today Have to Be Comfortable With Ambiguity'—Q&A: Susan P. Peters," *Business Standard (India)*, March 9, 2010, http://www.business-standard.com; http://www.ge.com.
2. Milton Moskowitz, Robert Levering, and Christopher Tkaczyk, "100 Top Companies to Work For," *Fortune*, February 8, 2010 issue, http://money.cnn.com/magazines/fortune/bestcompanies/2010/.
3. Gary M. Stern, "Companies Switch Their Tack on Corporate Retreats," *Investor's Business Daily*, March 12, 2010, http://www.investors.com/NewsAndAnalysis/Article.aspx?id=527154&p=2.
4. Douglas McGregor, *The Human Side of Enterprise* (New York: McGraw-Hill, 1960).
5. William Ouchi, *Theory Z* (Reading, MA: Addison-Wesley, 1981).
6. Ricky W. Griffin, *Fundamentals of Management*, 3rd ed. (Boston, MA: Houghton Mifflin, 2008), 300.
7. Milton Moskowitz, Robert Levering, and Christopher Tkaczyk.
8. Apple, http://store.apple.com/us_smb_78313/browse/home/campaigns/corporate_gifting (accessed May 11, 2010).
9. S. C. Johnson & Son, Press Release, September 22, 2009.
10. "Companies Find Benefits in Flex-Time," *American Public Media*, May 21, 2008, http://marketplace.publicradio.org/display/web/2008/05/21/flex_time/.
11. "In Hard Times, Re-Commit to Flex Time," Sylvia Ann Hewlett, *Harvard Business Review*, October 12, 2009.
12. Starbucks, http://www.starbucks.com/career-center (accessed May 11, 2010).
13. Victoria Stagg Elliott, "Job-sharing Can Boost Work-Life Balance, Cut Practice Expenses," *American Medical News*, February 8, 2010, http://www.ama-assn.org/amednews/2010/02/08/bica0208.htm.
14. http://money.cnn.com/magazines/fortune/bestcompanies/2010/benefits/telecommuting.html, February 8, 2010 issue.
15. Arif Mohamed, "Bosses Split Over Productivity of Teleworkers," *Computer Weekly*, March 29, 2005, 55.
16. http://money.cnn.com/magazines/fortune/bestcompanies/2010/benefits/telecommuting.html; Cisco, http://www.cisco.com/en/US/products/index.html (accessed May 3, 2010); "Cisco Study Finds Telecommuting Significantly Increases Employee Productivity, Work-Life Flexibility and Job Satisfaction," *Cisco, News Release*, June 25, 2009, http://newsroom.cisco.com/dlls/2009/prod_062609.html.
17. Careers, W. L. Gore & Associates, http://www.gore.com (accessed May 3, 2010).
18. "A Brief Overview of Employee Ownership in the U.S.," http://www.nceo.org, January 2009.
19. Ricky W. Griffin, *Fundamentals of Management* (Boston, MA: Houghton Mifflin, 2008), 385–404.
20. Richard L. Doft, *Management* (Mason, OH: South-Western/Cengage Learning, 2010), 504.
21. Christine Tierney, "Quality Panel to Review Toyota," *The Detroit News*, April 30, 2010, http://www.detroitnews.com/article/20100430/AUTO01/4300359/1148/Quality-panel-to-review-Toyota.
22. Bill Fischer and Andy Boynton, "Virtuoso Teams," *Harvard Business Review*, July–August 2005, 116–123.
23. "Dow Wins Four 2010 Responsible Care® Energy Efficiency Awards," *Dow, Press Release*, May 5, 2010, http://news.dow.com/dow_news/corporate/2010/20100505c.htm.
24. Linda Webb, "Microsoft's New Ergonomic Keyboard More Comfortable," *Cleveland Plain Dealer*, November 7, 2005, E4.
25. Mozilla, http://www.mozilla.org/about/governance.html (accessed May 8, 2010).
26. Company Web site http://www.llbean.com (accessed July 20, 2010); Tom Tobin, "L.L. Bean Set for Splashy First Day," *Democrat and Chronicle.com*, June 27, 2010, http://www.democratandchronicle.com; Michael Arndt, "Customer Service Champs: L.L. Bean Follows Its Shoppers to the Web," *Bloomberg BusinessWeek*, February 18, 2010, http://www.businessweek.com; interviews with L.L. Bean employees and the video, "At L.L. Bean, Everyone Is Family."
27. Milton Moskowitz, Robert Levering, and Christopher Tkaczyk, "100 Best Companies to Work For," *Fortune*, February 8, 2010, 75–77; "'Don't Touch My Perks': Companies that Eliminate Them Risk Employee Backlash," *Knowledge@Wharton* (July 23, 2008), http://knowledge.wharton.upenn.edu; Joe Nocera, "On Day Care, Google Makes a Rare Fumble," *The New York Times*, July 5, 2008, http://www.nytimes.com; John Cook, "Perks Make Google Office Hardly Feel Like Work," *Seattle Post-Intelligencer*, January 16, 2008, http://seattlepi.nwsource.com; Elinor Mills, "Newsmaker: Meet Google's Culture Czar," *CNet News*, April 27, 2007, http://news.cnet.com; http://www.google.com.

Chapter 11

1. Terry Maxon, "Southwest Airlines Pilots Approve New Contract," *Dallas Morning News*, November 3, 2009, http://www.dallasnews.com; Scott Nishimura, "Southwest Airlines Pilots Ratify New Contract," *Fort Worth Star-Telegram*, November 2, 2009, http://www.star-telegram.com; Loren Steffy, "The Winds of Change Are Buffeting Southwest," *Houston Chronicle*, June 5, 2009, http://www.chron.com; Ann Schrader, "Southwest Pilots Reject Proposed Contract," *Denver Post*, June 4, 2009, http://www.denverpost.com; http://www.swapa.org; http://www.southwest.com.
2. U.S. Department of Labor, Bureau of Labor Statistics, "Union Members Summary," *News Release*, January 22, 2010, http://www.bls.gov/news.release/union2.nr0.htm.
3. U.S. Department of Labor, Bureau of Labor Statistics, "Employee Benefits in Private Industry," *Economic News Release*, July 28, 2009, http://www.bls.gov/news.release/ebs2.toc.htm, table 4.

4. Michael Gould-Wartofsky, "NYU Grad Students File for Union Recognition, Hope to Overturn Bush Era Ruling," *The Huffington Post,* May 3, 2010, http://www.huffingtonpost.com/michael-gouldwartofsky/nyu-grad-students-file-fo_b_561439.html.
5. U.S. Department of Labor, Bureau of Labor Statistics, "Work Stoppages Summary," *Economic News Release*, February 10, 2010, http://www.bls.gov/news.release/wkstp.nr0.htm.
6. Maynard Micheline, "Boeing Negotiations 'at a Standstill,'" *New York Times*, September 26, 2008, C4.
7. "Philadelphia Transit Workers Go on Strike," *CNN News*, November 4, 2009, http://www.cnn.com/2009/US/11/03/philly.transit.strike/index.html; "Philadelphia's Transit Strike Ends," *Associated Press*, November 9, 2009, http://www.washingtontimes.com/news/2009/nov/09/philadelphias-transit-strike-ends/.
8. "Players, Coaches Speak Out Against Law," *Associated Press*, May 1, 2010, http://sports.espn.go.com/mlb/news/story?id=5152397.
9. Chris Frank, "Hawker Beechcraft, Machinist Reach Tentative Deal," *KAKE*, August 25, 2008, http://www.fmcs.gov.
10. "2009 Annual Report," Federal Mediation & Conciliation Service, http://www.fmcs.gov/internet/itemDetail.asp?categoryID=228&itemID=17315 (accessed May 4, 2010).
11. Based on information from the organization Web site http://www.wgaeast.com (accessed July 14, 2010); Michael Rechtshaffen, "Writers Guild Members Claim Age Discrimination," *Toronto Sun*, May 9, 2010, http://www.torontosun.com; Michael Cieply, "Hollywood Directors Union Agrees to Early Contract Talks," *The New York Times*, April 28, 2010, http://mediadecoder.blogs.nytimes.com; Andy Plesser, "Writers Guild Explores Rules for Uncharted Online Video World," *The Huffington Post*, April 23, 2010, http://www.huffingtonpost.com; Richard Verrier, "Writers Guild Sings Same Tune as Composers and Lyricists," *Los Angeles Times*, http://latimesblogs.latimes.com; information provided by Guild employees, and in the video "The Writers Guild."
12. Based on information from Tony Dokoupil, "When Nurses Strike in New York," *Newsweek,* May 3, 2010, 8; Jane M. Von Bergen, "Temple and Nurses Settle Strike," *Philadelphia Inquirer,* April 28, 2010, http://www.philly.com; Stacey Burling, "A Study Shows Nursing Strikes Erode Patient Care," *Philadelphia Inquirer,* April 12, 2010, http://www.philly.com; Vince Lattanzio, "Tentative Agreement Reached in Temple Nurse Strike," *NBC Philadelphia,* April 28, 2010, http://www.nbcphiladelphia.com; Rob Carson, "Tacoma General Nurses Picket," *The News Tribune (Tacoma, WA),* January 20, 2010, http://www.thenewstribune.com; John Stucke, "Sacred Heart Nurses Picket Over Breaks, Benefits," *Spokesman-Review (Spokane, WA),* February 2, 2010, http://www.spokesman.com; Lori Rotenberk, "Nurse Super-Union Sets Agenda, Aims to Get Staff Ratio Laws Passed," *Hospitals & Health Networks,* December 2009, 12; Joe Goldeen, "St. Joseph's Nurses Won't Walk Out," *Records (Stockton, CA),* October 30, 2009, http://www.recordnet.com; Kris Maher, "Nurses' Union Plans to Strike. One-Day Event at 39 California, Nevada Hospitals Is Focused on Swine-Flu Precautions," *Wall Street Journal,* October 20, 2009, http://www.wsj.com.
13. Bob Driehaus, "A Cincinnati Ice Cream Maker Aims Big," *The New York Times,* September 12, 2010, N29; company Web site http://www.graeters.com (accessed September 2, 2010); Alexander Coolridge, "Winburn: Where Is Cincinnati Jobs Retention Plan?" *Cincinnati.com,* August 18, 2010, http://news.cincinnati.com; Lucy May, "Graeter's Northern Kentucky Franchisee Puts Stores on the Block," *Business Courier,* August 6, 2010, http://cincinnati.bizjournals.com; Ken Hoffman, "Graeter's Ice Cream Is Worthy Diet Buster," *The Houston Chronicle,* April 15, 2009, http://www.chron.com; Melissa Davis Haller, "The Big Chill," *Cincinnati Magazine,* February 2009, http://www.cincinnatimagazine.com; and interviews with company staff and the video, "Graeter's: Where Tenure Is a Proud Number."

Chapter 12

1. Marco Tabini, "iTunes Store," *MacWorld,* May 2010, 63; Paul McDougall, "iPad Goes International," *InformationWeek,* May 7, 2010, http://www.informationweek.com; Nathan Becker, "Apple Says iPad Sales Top 1 Million," *Wall Street Journal,* May 3, 2010, http://www.wsj.com; http://www.apple.com.
2. Marketing Power (American Marketing Association), http://www.marketingpower.com/AboutAMA/Pages/DefinitionofMarketing.aspx (accessed May 4, 2010).
3. Sears, http://www.shopyourwayrewards.com (accessed May 4, 2010).
4. V. Kumar, *Customer Lifetime Value* (Hanover, MA: now Publishers, 2008), 5.
5. Rajkumar Venkatesan and V. Kumar, "A Customer Lifetime Value Framework for Customer Selection and Resource Selection and Resource Allocation Strategy," *Journal of Marketing 68* (October 2004), 106–125.
6. Sears, press release, January 19, 2010, http://www.searsmedia.com/tools/press/content.jsp?id=2010-01-19-0005167078; Elaine Wong, "Why Sears Is Rebranding Kenmore," *Brandweek*, February 24, 2010, http://www.brandweek.com/bw/content_display/esearch/e3ie17592c1aa7a468849873c7d6a2fdc82.
7. "Nissan Announces U.S. Pricing on 2010 Cube," *PR Newswire*, January 28, 2010.
8. Paula Andruss, "New OfficeMax Catalog Courts Women Consumers," *Deliver Magazine*, June 29, 2009.
9. "Nissan Announces Nissan LEAF Purchase Process; Gives First Glimpse at Marketing Campaign," Nissan, news release, February 11, 2010, http://www.nissannews.com.
10. Brooks Barnes, "Movie Studios See a Threat in Growth of Redbox," *The New York Times*, September 6, 2009.
11. Michael Liedtke, "Newspaper Circulation May Be Worse Than It Looks," *The Seattle Times*, November 22, 2009.
12. Kevin Kelleher, "66,207,986 Bottles of Beer on the Wall," *Business 2.0 via CNN*, February 25, 2004, http://www.cnn.com.
13. Ellen Byron, "New Penney: Chain Goes for 'Missing Middle,'" *Wall Street Journal*, February 14, 2005, http://online.wsj.com/.
14. Catherine Arnold, "Self-examination: Researchers Reveal State of MR in Survey," *Marketing News*, February 1, 2005, 55, 56.
15. William M. Pride and O. C. Ferrell, *Foundations of Marketing* (Mason, OH: South-Western/Cengage Learning, 2011), 128.
16. Company Web site http://www.etrade.com (accessed August 3, 2010); Whitney Kisling, "E*Trade Gains Most Since December on Return to Profit," *Bloomberg BusinessWeek,* July 23, 2010, http://www.businessweek.com; Matt Ackerman, "E*Trade to Target Long-Term Investors," *American Banker,* January 29, 2010, http://www.americanbanker.com; interviews with company employees and the video "E*Trade Tries to Build Long-Term Customer Relationships."
17. Based on information from Betsy McKay, "PepsiCo Develops 'Designer Salt' to Chip Away at Sodium Intake," *Wall Street Journal,* March 22, 2010, http://www.wsj.com; Natalie Zmuda and Emily Bryson York, "Cause Effect: Brands Rush to Save World One Deed at a Time," *Advertising Age,* March 1, 2010, 1; Natalie Zmuda, "Pass or Fail, Pepsi's Refresh Will Be Case for Marketing Textbooks," *Advertising Age,* February 8, 2010, http://www.adage.com; Sarah Theodore and Elizabeth Fuhrman, "The Best Packages of 2009," *Beverage Industry,* December 2009, 40+; http://www.pepsico.com.

Chapter 13

1. Micah Maidenberg, "Threadless Eyes West Loop," *Chicago Journal,* May 5, 2010, http://www.chicagojournal.com; Julie Shaffer, "Social Climbing," *American Printer,* January 1, 2010, http://americanprinter.com; Laurie Burkitt, "Need to Build a Community? Learn from Threadless," *Forbes,* January 7, 2010, http://www.forbes.com; Alicia Wallace, "5 Questions for Jake Nickell, Founder and Chief Strategy Officer of Threadless," *Daily Camera (Boulder, CO),* May 18, 2009, http://www.dailycamera.com/; Max Chafkin, "The Customer Is the Company," *Inc.,* June 1, 2008, http://www.inc.com; http://www.threadless.com; Joshua Topolsky, "Apple iPad Review," *Engadget,* April 3, 2010, http://www.engadget.com/2010/04/03/apple-ipad-review/; Vladislav Savov, "Apple Sells 1,000,000 iPads in Revolution's First Month," *Engadget,* May 3, 2010, http://www.engadget.com/2010/05/03/apple-sells-1-000-000-ipads-in-revolutions-first-month?icid=sphere_blogsmith_inpage_engadget.
2. Joshua Topolsky, "Apple iPad Review," *Engadget*, April 3, 2010, http://www.engadget.com/2010/04/03/apple-ipad-review/; Vladislav Savov, "Apple Sells 1,000,000 iPads in Revolution's First Month," *Engadget*, May 3, 2010, http://www.engadget.com/2010/05/03/apple-sells-1-000-000-ipads-in-revolutions-first-month?icid=sphere_blogsmith_inpage_engadget/.
3. Apple, http://www.apple.com (accessed May 5, 2010).
4. "GM Ending Hummer: Controversial Brand to Be Discontinued," *Huffington Post*, April 26, 2010, http://www.huffingtonpost.com/2010/02/24/gm-ending-hummer-controve_n_475464.html.
5. Procter & Gamble, http://www.pg.com/en_US/brands/all_brands.shtml (accessed May 5, 2010).
6. http://www.virtualvender.coca-cola.com/ft/index.jsp; http://www.pepsico.com/Company/Our-Brands.html (accessed May 5, 2010).
7. Ben Rooney, "8 Names You Know, R.I.P.," *CNN Money*, December 20, 2009, http://money.cnn.com/galleries/2009/news/0912/gallery.brands_we_lost/8.html.
8. Nadira A. Hira, "Fahrenheit 212—The Innovator's Paradise," December 16, 2009, *Fortune*, http://money.cnn.com/2009/12/15/news/companies/fahrenheit_212.fortune/index.htm; http://www.fahrenheit-212.com (accessed May 20, 2010).
9. Joseph Peña, "Aptera Secures Financing, Introduces New 2e Electric Car," *San Diego News Network*, April 14, 2010, http://www.sdnn.com/sandiego/2010-04-14/business-real-estate/aptera-secures-financing-introduces-new-2e-electric-car.
10. "Market Update," http://www.plma.com (accessed May 5, 2010).
11. Nick Bunkley, "Toyota's Sales Fall as GM and Ford Gain," *The New York Times*, February 2, 2010, http://www.nytimes.com/2010/02/03/business/03auto.html.
12. "Coca-Cola Buys Glaceau, Maker of Vitaminwater, for $4.1 Billion," *The Star*, May 28, 2007, http://thestar.com.my/news/story.asp?file=/2007/5/28/apworld/20070528105438&sec=apworld.

13. http://www.amazon.com (accessed May 20, 2010).
14. Kenneth Hein, "BK Boxers Leads Pack of Worst Line Extensions," *BrandWeek*, December 15, 2008, http://www.brandweek.com/bw/content_display/esearch/e3ie36ce5eb50d8af30f302e69db2d0b6b.
15. Bruce Horovitz, "Earthbound Farm, Naked Juice to Use 100% Recycled Plastic," *USA Today*, July 9, 2009, http://www.usatoday.com/money/industries/environment/2009-07-08-recycled-plastic-food-packaging_N.htm?loc=interstitialskip.
16. Steve Everly, "Regulators Target Ink Cartridges," *Tennessean.com*, January 17, 2010, http://www.tennessean.com/article/20100117/BUSINESS01/1170352/Regulators-target-in-cartridges.
17. Janet Adamy, "Corporate News: Starbucks—Coffee Empire Seeks to Seem Less Expensive in Recession," *The Wall Street Journal*, February 9, 2009, B3.
18. Jim Zemlin, "Linux Can Compete with the iPad on Price, But Where's the Magic?" *The Linux Foundation*, January 28, 2010, http://www.linux-foundation.org/weblogs/jzemlin/2010/01/28/linux-can-compete-with-the-ipad-on-price-but-where%E2%80%99s-the-magic/.
19. Dominic Haber, "Abercrombie & Fitch Plans Further Price Cuts After 1Q Loss," *TopNews.com*, May 17, 2009, http://topnews.us/content/25241-abercrombie-fitch-plans-further-price-cuts-after-1q-loss.
20. The Verizon Web site at http://www.verizon.com (accessed May 20, 2010).
21. Based on information in http://www.bludot.com (accessed June 16, 2010); "Stuff," http://www.bludot.com (accessed April 21, 2010) and originally published in *Minnesota Monthly;* Carl Alviani, "Taking the Middle Ground: Massive Design for the Masses?" *Core 77*, http://www.core77.com (accessed April 21, 2010); Todd Wasserman, "Guerilla Marketing: The Technology Revolution," *Ad Week*, January 11, 2010, http://www.adweek.com; interviews with company personnel and the film, "Blu Dot."
22. Based on information in Yukari Iwatani Kane and Roger Cheng, "Surge in iPhone Powers Apple," *The Wall Street Journal*, April 21, 2010, http://www.wsj.com; Alice Z. Cuneo, "iPhone: Steve Jobs," *Advertising Age*, November 12, 2007, S13; Katie Hafner and Brad Stone, "iPhone Owners Crying Foul Over Price Cut," *The New York Times*, September 7, 2007, C1, C7; Yukari Iwatani Kane and Nick Wingfield, "For Apple iPhone, Japan Could Be the Next Big Test," *The Wall Street Journal*, December 19, 2007, B1; Brad Kenney, "Apple's iPhone: IW's IT Product of the Year," *Industry Week*, December 2007, 47+; Josh Krist, "The Painful Cost of First-on-the-Block Bragging Rights," *PC World*, December 2007, 53+; Alex Markels, "Apple's Mac Sales Are Surging," *U.S. News & World Report*, September 26, 2007, n.p.; Jon Swartz, "iPhone Helps Apple Earn Juicy Profit," *USA Today*, October 23, 2007, 1B.

Chapter 14

1. Victor Godinez, "Movie, Book, Game Companies Fight to Survive Plunge into Internet Age," *Dallas Morning News*, April 5, 2010, http://www.dallasnews.com; "GameStop Launches Its First Online Video Game," *Internet Retailer*, March 31, 2010, http://www.internetretailer.com; Andrew Bary, "GameStop Builds a Business Selling Used Games to Teens," *Barron's Insight*, March 28, 2010, http://www.wsj.com; http://www.gamestop.com.
2. "eBay Fined in LVMH Perfume Sales Row," *BBC News*, November 30, 2009, http://news.bbc.co.uk/2/hi/business/8386390.stm.
3. "About Pepsi Beverages Company," PepsiCo, http://www.pepsico.com/Company/The-PepsiCo-Family/Pepsi-Beverages-Company.html (accessed April 17, 2010).
4. "Gasoline Stations (NAICS 447)," U.S. Bureau of the Census, http://www.census.gov/econ/census/snapshots/SNAP44.HTM.
5. Sam's Club Fact Sheet, Costco Wholesale Corporation Fact Sheet, Hoover's Online, http://www.hoovers.com (accessed April 19, 2010).
6. "The Year Walmart Stole Christmas," *Gile Toys Blog*, December 19, 2008, http://blog.giletoys.com/2008/12/19/the-year-the-walmart-stole-christmas/.
7. http://www.dsa.org (accessed May 17, 2010).
8. Maris Halkias, "J.C. Penney's Big Catalog Soon to Be But a Memory," *TheSeattleTimes.com*, November 27, 2009, http://seattletimes.newsource.com/html/businesstechnology/2010365217_jcpenneycatalog27.html.
9. Jack Neff, "Snuggie: An America's Hottest Brands Case Study," *AdAge.com*, November 16, 2009, http://adage.com/article?article_id=140485.
10. http://www.ftc.gov/os/2010/01/100104dncadditionalreport.pdf; http://www.donotcall.gov (accessed April 19, 2010).
11. http://www.netflix.com (accessed May 17, 2010).
12. Jeff Clabaugh, "Black Friday Online Sales Up 11%," *South Florida Business Journal*, November 30, 2009, http://www.bizjournals.com/southflorida/stories/2009/11/30/daily4.html.
13. "Redbox's Vending Machines Are Giving Netflix Competition," *NYTimes.com*, June 21, 2009, http://www.nytimes.com/2009/06/22/business/media/22redbox.html.
14. Zoom Systems, http://www.zoomsystems.com/ (accessed May 20, 2010).
15. Sandra O'Loughlin, "Out with the Old: Malls versus Centers," *Brandweek*, May 9, 2005, 30.
16. Lauren B. Cooper, "Bayer Properties to Manage S.C. Shopping Center," *BizJourals.com*, May 14, 2009, http://www.bizjournals.com/birmingham/stories/2009/05/11/daily34.html; http://www.mtpleasanttownecentre.com/go/dirListing.cfm?FL=all (accessed March 4, 2010).
17. Company Web site http://www.tazachocolate.com (accessed August 30, 2010); Courtney Holland, "Sweet Batches of Local Flavor," *The Boston Globe*, August 18, 2010, http://www.boston.com; Kerry J. Byrne, "Festival of Food Trucks," *The Boston Herald*, August 6, 2010, http://www.bostonherald.com; interviews with company staff and the video "Taza Cultivates Channel Relationships With Chocolate."
18. Based on information in Alaric DeArment, "No Sign of Recession as Chain Expands," *Drug Store News*, April 19, 2010, 50; "The Costco Way," *BusinessWeek*, April 12, 2004, http://www.businessweek.com/magazine/content/04_15/b3878084_mz021.htm; Doug Desjardins, "Costco Comps Up 7%, Despite 4Q Lag," *DSN Retailing Today*, October 27, 2003, 8; John Helyar, "The Only Company Wal-Mart Fears," *Fortune*, November 24, 2003, 158; Kris Hudson, "Warehouses Go Luxe," *The Wall Street Journal*, November 11, 2005, B1, http://online.wsj.com/public/us; "Investor Relations: Company Profile," Costco, http://phx.corporate-ir.net/phoenix.zhtml?c_83830&p_irol-homeprofile.

Chapter 15

1. Claudia Deutsch, "Panera's Ronald Shaich," *Institutional Investor*, April 2010, n.p.; Kavita Kumar, "While Competitors Fall Flat, Panera's Fortune Rises," *St. Louis Post-Dispatch* (St. Louis, MO), April 11, 2010, http://www.stltoday.com/; Christine LaFave Grace, "Ron Shaich, Panera Bread Co.," *Restaurants & Institutions*, January 1, 2010, 12; Emily Bryson York, "Panera: An America's Hottest Brands Case Study," *Advertising Age*, November 16, 2009, http://www.adage.com; http://www.panerabread.com.
2. Sarah Rabil, "U.S. Advertising to Rise 3.5% in 2010, Barclays Says," January 28, 2010, *Bloomberg*, http://www.bloomberg.com/apps/news?pid=newsarchive&sid=aSXCF1nwQHrg.
3. "2010 U.S. National Edition Rates," *Time*, http://www.timemediakit.com/us/timemagazine/rates/national/index.html (accessed June 3, 2010).
4. Wayne Friedman, "TV Product Placement Delivers For '24,'" *Media Daily News*, January 19, 2010.
5. "Super Bowl XLIV Ad Cost Up Slightly Over Last Year," MoonDogSports.com, December 17, 2009, http://moondogsports.com/2009/12/17/super-bowl-xliv-ad-cost-up-slightly-over-last-year/.
6. "Don Shula for NutriSystem Silver Age-Based Men's Program," *FabulousSavings.com*, http://www.fabuloussavings.com/online/us/nutrisystemads/1/don_shula_for_nutrisystem_silver_age_based_mens_program/ (accessed Mach 26, 2010).
7. Elena Malykhina, "Miller Lite's Macho Maneuvers," *Brandweek*, April 29, 2010, http://www.adweek.com/aw/content_display/creative/new-campaigns/e3i72c63ee9c311def0c9a7ad6cd3b43fc7.
8. Jim Turner, "Fla. Pulls Ad Campaign Saying State Not Affected by Oil Spill; State Senate President Compares Sheen to 'Rainbow Effect' in Driveways," *TC Palm (Palm Beach, Florida)*, June 3, 2010, http://www.tcpalm.com/news/2010/jun/03/state-senate-president-kicking-off-ad-campaign/.
9. Courtney Rubin, "Coupon Use Hits Record High," *Inc.*, February 8, 2010, http://www.inc.com/news/articles/2010/02/coupon-use-hits-record-high.html; http://www.cellfire.com/whatiscf.php; http://sites.target.com/site/en/spot/page.jsp?title=text_alerts (accessed June 3, 2010).
10. http://www.inmar.com/promotion-services/news-events/press-releases/consumers-use-over$3.5-billion-in-coupons.htm (accessed May 18, 2010).
11. Mya Frazier, James Tenser, and Tricia Despres, "Retail Lesson: Small Programs Best," *Advertising Age*, February 7, 2005, 8.
12. http://bigapplebbq.org/ (accessed June 3, 2010).
13. http://www.facebook.com/MercedesBenz; http://www.youtube.com/user/mercedesbenztv?blend=2&ob=4 (accessed June 3, 2010).
14. Jason D. O'Grady, "Verizon Droid Ad Attacks iPhone on Features," *ZDNet*, October 19, 2009, http://blogs.zdnet.com/Apple/?p=5055.
15. Company Web site http://www.llbean.com (accessed July 20, 2010); "Photobrand 25 Ranks ESPN, GE, and Dunkin' Donuts as New England's Most Powerful Brands for 2010," *PR Newswire*, June 1, 2010, http://www.prnewswire.com; Michael Arndt, "Customer Service Champs: L.L. Bean Follows Its Shoppers to the Web," *Bloomberg BusinessWeek*, February 18, 2010, http://www.businessweek.com; interviews with L.L. Bean employees and the video, "L.L. Bean Employs a Variety of Promotion Methods to Communicate with Customers."
16. Based on information in Kirby Lee Davis, "Speech in Tulsa University of Tulsa: CEO of Columbia Says Company Charts Success with Innovation, Markets," *Journal Record* (Oklahoma City), May 2, 2010, http://journalrecord.com; Erica Iacono, "Corporate Case Study—Columbia Sportswear Speaks to Many with One Voice," *PR Week*, January 16, 2006; George Anders, "Drama's Profitable

at Sportswear Maker—Columbia Run by Mother and Son," *The Seattle Times*, October 12, 2005; http://www.columbia.com.

17. Bob Driehaus, "A Cincinnati Ice Cream Maker Aims Big," *The New York Times*, September 12, 2010, N29; company Web site http://www.graeters.com (accessed September 2, 2010); Alexander Coolridge, "Winburn: Where Is Cincinnati Jobs Retention Plan?" *Cincinnati.com*, August 18, 2010, http://news.cincinnati.com; Lucy May, "Graeter's Northern Kentucky Franchisee Puts Stores on the Block," *Business Courier*, August 6, 2010, http://cincinnati.bizjournals.com; Ken Hoffman, "Graeter's Ice Cream Is Worthy Diet Buster," *The Houston Chronicle*, April 15, 2009, http://www.chron.com; Melissa Davis Haller, "The Big Chill," *Cincinnati Magazine*, February 2009, http://www.cincinnatimagazine.com; and interviews with company staff and the video, "Graeter's Is Synonymous with Ice Cream."

Chapter 16

1. "Profile: Net-a-Porter's Natalie Massenet," *Sunday Times (London)*, April 4, 2010, http://women.timesonline.co.uk; Alexandra Topping, "Natalie Massenet Sells Net-a-Porter Stake to Richemont for £50m," *Guardian (UK)*, April 1, 2010, http://www.guardian.co.uk; Jim Armitage, "Net-A-Porter Founder Turns Glad Rags to Riches and Sells for £350m," *London Evening Standard*, April 6, 2010, http://www.thisislondon.co.uk; Kate Walsh, "Net-a-Porter Delivers a Dozen Millionaires," *Times Online (London)*, April 4, 2010, http://business.timesonline.co.uk; Tom Mulier, "Richemont Buys Net-a-Porter, Online Fashion Retailer," *BusinessWeek*, April 1, 2010, http://www.businessweek.com.
2. The Symantec Web site at http://www.symantec.com (accessed May 28, 2010).
3. Ibid.
4. Bradley Mitchell, "What Is (Wireless/Computer) Networking?," the About.com Web site at http://www.about.com (accessed May 28, 2010).
5. "Bradley Mitchell, LAN—Local Area Network," the About.com Web site at http://www.about.com (accessed May 28, 2010).
6. Charlene Li, Julie M. Katz, and Christina Lee, "U.S. Interactive Marketing Forecast, 2007 to 2012," the Forrester Web site at http://www.forrester.com (accessed May 29, 2010).
7. The Internet World Stats Web site at http://www.internetworldstats.com (accessed May 30, 2010).
8. The Clickz Web site at http://www.clickz.com (accessed May 30, 2010).
9. Ibid.
10. Ibid.
11. The Javelin Strategy and Research Web site at http://www.idsafety.net (accessed June 1, 2010).
12. Ibid.
13. Company Web site http://www.etrade.com (accessed August 3, 2010); Whitney Kisling, "E*Trade Gains Most Since December on Return to Profit," *Bloomberg BusinessWeek*, July 23, 2010, http://www.businessweek.com; Matt Ackerman, "E*Trade to Target Long-Term Investors," *American Banker*, January 29, 2010, http://www.americanbanker.com; interviews with company employees and the video "E*Trade Uses e-Business to Meet Customer Needs."
14. Based on information in Meghan Keane, "Q&A: eBags' Peter Cobb on Online versus Traditional Retail," *Econsultancy*, March 5, 2010, http://econsultancy.com/blog/5523-q-a-peter-cobb-of-ebags; "Customer Interaction Is in the Bag at eBags," *Internet Retailer*, October 8, 2008, http://www.internetretailer.com; Katie Deatsch, "Corralling Content," *Internet Retailer*, September 2008, http://www.internetretailer.com; "eBags Broadens Its Horizons as Tech Provider to Retailers," *Internet Retailer*, http://www.internetretailer.com, March 18, 2008; Janet Forgieve, "Refusing to Pack It In," *Rocky Mountain News*, September 6, 2006, http://www.rockymountainnews.com; http://www.ebags.com.

Chapter 17

1. Based on information from Roger O. Crockett, "Deloitte's Diversity Push," *BusinessWeek Online*, October 5, 2009, http://www.businessweek.com; Laura Fitzpatrick, "We're Getting Off the Ladder," *Time*, May 25, 2009, 45; "Deloitte Announces Historical Milestone, Tops 1,000 Women Partners, Principals, and Directors," *Women's Health Weekly*, June 25, 2009, 335; http://www.deloitte.com.
2. The Deloitte Web site at http://www.deloitte.com (accessed April 7, 2010).
3. John Smith, "Financial Reporting in a Changing World," The International Accounting Standards Board Web site at http://www.iasb.org (accessed April 7, 2010).
4. Joseph Nocera, et.al. "System Failure Corporate America Has Lost Its Way," *Fortune*, June 24, 2002, 64.
5. "Summary of the Provisions of the Sarbanes-Oxley Act of 2002," the AICPA Web site at http://www.aicpa.org (accessed April 8, 2010).
6. *Occupational Outlook Handbook*, The U.S. Bureau of Labor Statistics Web site at http://www.bls.gov/oco/ocos001.htm (accessed April 8, 2010).
7. The American Institute of Certified Public Accountants Web site at http://www.aicpa.org (accessed April 8, 2010).
8. Based on information found at http://www.thelittleguys.com/home.asp; Alan Wolf, "The Little Guys Get New Home, Amended Name," *TWICE*, April 19, 2010, 6, 22; Audrey Gray, "Perfecting a Soft Sell," *Dealerscope*, March 2009, 82; and information from interviews with company staff and the video, "The Little Guys."
9. Based on information from Matt Krantz, "Companies Are Making Fewer Accounting Mistakes," *USA Today*, March 1, 2010, http://www.usatoday.com; Jane Sasseen, "White-Collar Crime: Who Does Time?" *BusinessWeek*, February 6, 2006, http://www.businessweek.com; Stephen Labaton, "Four Years Later, Enron's Shadow Lingers as Change Comes Slowly," *New York Times*, January 5, 2006, C1; *Making the Numbers at Commodore Appliance* (Cengage video).
10. Bob Driehaus, "A Cincinnati Ice Cream Maker Aims Big," *The New York Times*, September 12, 2010, N29; company Web site http://www.graeters.com (accessed September 2, 2010); Alexander Coolridge, "Winburn: Where Is Cincinnati Jobs Retention Plan?" *Cincinnati.com*, August 18, 2010, http://news.cincinnati.com; Lucy May, "Graeter's Northern Kentucky Franchisee Puts Stores on the Block," *Business Courier*, August 6, 2010, http://cincinnati.bizjournals.com; Ken Hoffman, "Graeter's Ice Cream Is Worthy Diet Buster," *The Houston Chronicle*, April 15, 2009, http://www.chron.com; Melissa Davis Haller, "The Big Chill," *Cincinnati Magazine*, February 2009, http://www.cincinnatimagazine.com; and interviews with company staff and the video, "Graeter's Adds MIS to the Recipe."

Chapter 18

1. Sean B. Pasternak, "TD Bank to Add Branches, Mortgage Staff in Quebec, Dorval Says," *BusinessWeek Online*, March 24, 2010, http://www.businessweek.com; "TD Bank Unveils New Green Prototype Design," *Contract*, February 25, 2010, n.p.; Bonnie McGeer, "The 25 Most Powerful Women in Banking: #21, Colleen Johnston," *US Banker*, October 1, 2009, 37; http://www.tdbank.com.
2. "The Economy: Crisis & Response," The Federal Reserve Board of San Francisco Web site at http://www.frsb.org (accessed June 17, 2010).
3. Jeff Brown, "When It's OK to Carry Debt," the Yahoo! Finance Web site at http://finance.yahoo.com (accessed June 14, 2010).
4. The Federal Reserve Board Web site at http://www.federalreserve.gov (accessed June 19, 2010).
5. The Federal Reserve Bank of New York Web site at http://www.newyorkfed.org (accessed June 19, 2010).
6. The Federal Reserve Board Web site at http://www.federalreserve.gov (accessed June 19, 2010).
7. The Investopedia.com Web site at http://www.investopedia.com (accessed June 20, 2010).
8. The Federal Reserve Board at http://www.federalreserve.gov (accessed June 20, 2010).
9. "Wall Street Reform," the White House Web site at http://www.whitehouse.gov (accessed June 20, 2010).
10. Ibid.
11. Ibid.
12. The Office of the Comptroller of the Currency Web site at http://www.occ.gov (accessed June 20, 2010).
13. The Federal Deposit Insurance Corporation Web site at http://www.fdic.gov (accessed June 20, 2010).
14. U.S. Census Bureau, *Statistical Abstract of the United States, 2010* (Washington, DC: U.S. Government Printing Office), table 1146.
15. "Career Guide to Industries," the Bureau of Labor Statistics Web site at http://www.bls.gov (accessed June 21, 2010).
16. U.S. Census Bureau, *Statistical Abstract of the United States, 2010* (Washington, DC: U.S. Government Printing Office), table 1151.
17. The Federal Deposit Insurance Corporation Web site at http://www.fdic.gov (accessed June 20, 2010).
18. The Federal Trade Commission Web site at http://www.ftc.gov (accessed June 17, 2010).
19. The United States Senate Committee on Banking, Housing, and Urban Affairs Web site at http://banking.senate.gov (accessed June 15, 2010).
20. Company Web sites http://www.chase.com and http://www.jpmorganchase.com (accessed July 19, 2010); "J.P. Morgan Chase Discloses Results," *American Banking and Market News*, July 15, 2010, http://www.americanbankingnews.com; Eric Dash, "JP Morgan Chase Easily Exceeds Estimates," *The New York Times*, July 15, 2010, http://www.nytimes.com; and the video, "Chase Bank Helps Small Business Owners."
21. Based on information in "Family Finance: Credit Cards Part of College Plans," *Associated Press*, March 19, 2010, http://www.nytimes.com; Jennifer Tescher, "Take Financial Education Beyond 101 (BankThink)," *American Banker*, February 25, 2010, 8; Ron Lieber, "One Thing You Can Control: Your Credit Score," *The New York Times*, October 11, 2008, http://www.nytimes

.com; "Kaulkin Ginsberg Report Says Increased College Student Credit Card Debt Causing Financial Straits for Graduating Students," *Business Wire,* September 12, 2008, http://www.reuters.com; Gretchen Morgenson, "Given a Shovel, Americans Dig Deeper into Debt," *The New York Times,* July 20, 2008, http://www.nytimes.com; Charles De La Fuente, "Pushing Colleges to Limit Credit Offers to Students," *The New York Times,* October 17, 2007, http://www.nytimes.com; Rob Walker, "A For-Credit Course," *The New York Times,* September 30, 2007, http://www.nytimes.com.

Chapter 19

1. Paul Hochman, "Ford's Big Reveal," *Fast Company,* April 2010, 90ff; Matt Andrejczak, "Ford Lightens Debt Load as It Eyes Improving Conditions," *MarketWatch,* March 29, 2010, http://www.marketwatch.com; Joe Light, "How Ford Is Taking on Toyota," *Money,* March 25, 2010, http://money.cnn.com; Mark Crumpton, "Lewis Booth, CFO, Ford Motor Company," *Bloomberg.com,* March 24, 2010, http://www.pddnet.com; Richard Gamble, "Treasury Keeps Ford from Running on Empty," *Treasury & Risk,* June 2009, 34ff; Mark Pittman and Elizabeth Hester, "Ford Boosts Convertible Bond Sale to $4.5 Billion," *Bloomberg,* December 6, 2006, http://www.bloomberg.com; http://www.ford.com.
2. The 3M Corporation Web site at http://www.3m.com (accessed May 2, 2010).
3. Maria Bartiromo, "BlackRock's Peter Fisher on When the Pan Will End," the *BusinessWeek* Web site (accessed October 8, 2008).
4. The Advertising Age Web site at http://www.adage.com (accessed June 24, 2010).
5. Guy Beaudin, "Kraft-Cadbury: Making Acquisitions Work," the *BusinessWeek* Web site (accessed February 9, 2010).
6. The Alico Corporate Web site at http://www.alico.com (accessed June 25, 2010).
7. Matthew Boyle, "The Fed's Commercial Paper Chase," the *BusinessWeek* Web site at http://www.businessweek.com (accessed October 7, 2008).
8. The IPO Scoop Web site at http://www.iposcoop.com (accessed June 29, 2010).
9. Ibid.
10. The New York Stock Exchange Web site at http://www.nyse.com (accessed June 29, 2010).
11. The NASDAQ corporate Web site at http://www.nasdaqomx.com (accessed June 29, 2010).
12. The General Electric Web site at http://www.ge.com (accessed June 30, 2010).
13. The Advanced Micro Devices corporate Web site at http://www.amd.com (accessed June 10, 2010).
14. *Mergent Transportation Manual* (New York: Mergent, Inc., 2009), 64.
15. Company Web site http://www.nederlanderconcerts.com (accessed August 20, 2010); Nederlander Organization company overview, *BusinessWeek,* http://www.businessweek.com (accessed August 20, 2010); Hannah Heineman, "Moving Forward on Capital Improvement Projects," *Santa Monica Mirror,* July 28, 2010, http://www.smmirror.com; Steve Knopper, "Tour Biz Strong in Weak Economy," *Rolling Stone,* October 2, 2008, 11–12; Ray Waddell, "Nederlander/Viejas Deal Offers Touring Opportunities," *Billboard,* January 10, 2008, http://www.billboard.com; interviews with Nederlander employees and the video "Financial Planning and Budgets Equal Profits for Nederlander Concerts."
16. Based on information from Jason Daley, "The 500 Calorie Smack Down," *Entrepreneur,* May 2010, 85ff; Jim Johnson, "Darden Plans Eco Eateries," *Waste & Recycling News,* March 29, 2010, 6; Ron Ruggless, "Darden Says No to Discounting," *Nation's Restaurant News,* March 25, 2010, http://www.nrn.com; Jonathan Birchall, "Darden Claws Back Custom of US Diners," *Financial Times,* March 25, 2010, 18; "Darden 3Q Profit Rises 25 Percent," *BusinessWeek,* March 23, 2010, http://www.businessweek.com; Michael Sanson, "Darden Restaurants," *Restaurant Hospitality,* August 2009, 28; http://www.darden.com.

Chapter 20

1. Joe Rauch, "Raymond James Fees, Assets Lag Growth in Advisers," *Reuters,* March 25, 2010, http://www.reuters.com; Roya Wolverson, "Ranking the Full-Service Brokers: 1. Raymond James," *Smart Money,* May 29, 2009, http://www.smartmoney.com; http://www.raymondjames.com.
2. "The Regulatory Pyramid," The New York Stock Exchange Web site (accessed July 13, 2010).
3. Ibid.
4. "Money 101 Lesson 4: Basics of Investing," the CNN/Money Web site at http://www.money.cnn.com (accessed July 13, 2010).
5. Suze Orman, *The Road to Wealth* (New York: Riverbend Books, 2001), 371.
6. The 2009 Medtronic Annual Report, the Medtronic Web site at http://www.metronic.com (accessed July 14, 2010).
7. The Investment Company Institute Web site at http://www.ici.org (accessed July 16, 2010).
8. The Mutual Fund Education Alliance Web site at http://www.mfea.com (accessed July 16, 2010).
9. The Investment Company Institute Web site at http://www.ici.org (accessed July 16, 2010).
10. Bill Barker, "Loads," The Motley Fool Web site at http://www.fool.com (accessed July 16, 2010).
11. "The Low Down on Index Funds," The Investopedia Web site at http://www.investopedia.com (accessed July 16, 2010).
12. The Yahoo! Finance Web site at http://finance.yahoo.com (accessed July 16, 2010).
13. Company Web site http://www.etrade.com (accessed August 3, 2010); Whitney Kisling, "E*Trade Gains Most Since December on Return to Profit," *Bloomberg BusinessWeek,* July 23, 2010, http://www.businessweek.com; Matt Ackerman, "E*Trade to Target Long-Term Investors," *American Banker,* January 29, 2010, http://www.americanbanker.com; interviews with company employees and the video "For E*Trade Investors, Help Is Just a Click Away."
14. Based on information in Selena Maranjian, "Advice for Young Investors," *Motley Fool,* January 14, 2010, http://www.fool.com; Ben Steverman, "Advice for Young Investors," *BusinessWeek,* April 13, 2009, http://www.businessweek.com; Jim Mueller, "3 Lessons from an Investing Master," The Motley Fool.com, http://www.fool.com, October 31, 2008; Elizabeth Ody, "Start Investing in 3 Simple Steps," *The Washington Post,* October 30, 2008, http://www.washingtonpost.com; David Leonhardt, "Are Stocks the Bargain You Think?" *New York Times,* October 29, 2008, http://www.nytimes.com; Jeff Sommer, "Extolling the Value of the Long View," *The New York Times,* October 26, 2008, http://www.nytimes.com.
15. Randy A. Simes, "Bond Hill to Celebrate Dedication of $11M Graeter's Production Facility," *UrbanCincy.com,* September 28, 2010, http://www.urbancincy.com; Bob Driehaus, "A Cincinnati Ice Cream Maker Aims Big," *The New York Times,* September 12, 2010, N29; company Web site http://www.graeters.com (accessed September 2, 2010); Alexander Coolridge, "Winburn: Where Is Cincinnati Jobs Retention Plan?" *Cincinnati.com,* August 18, 2010, http://news.cincinnati.com; Lucy May, "Graeter's Northern Kentucky Franchisee Puts Stores on the Block," *Business Courier,* August 6, 2010, http://cincinnati.bizjournals.com; Ken Hoffman, "Graeter's Ice Cream Is Worthy Diet Buster," *The Houston Chronicle,* April 15, 2009, http://www.chron.com; Melissa Davis Haller, "The Big Chill," *Cincinnati Magazine,* February 2009, http://www.cincinnatimagazine.com; and interviews with company staff and the video, "Graeter's Plans for Financing Growth."

Name Index

U

V

W

X

Y

Z

Subject Index

C

D

E

F

J

K

L

M

N

O

P

U

V

W

Y

Z